… Year of 5773 be filled with
good health, happiness, joy and
inspirational learning.
A gift to you presented through the
generosity of an Anonymous Donor.
Rabbi Ellen S. Wolintz-Fields

The Observant Life

The Wisdom of Conservative Judaism for Contemporary Jews

מוקדש לזכר המורים בחסד עליון הורינו יעקב יוסף וחנה למשפחת קקסט ז"ל

With Contributions By

Kassel Abelson • Carl N. Astor • Jacob Blumenthal
Nina Beth Cardin • Martin S. Cohen • Eliezer Diamond
Elliot N. Dorff • Paul S. Drazen • Arnold M. Eisen • David J. Fine
Edward M. Friedman • Michael Graetz • David M. Greenstein
Jeremy Kalmanofsky • Jane Kanarek • Michael Katz
Benjamin J. Kramer • Vernon H. Kurtz • Barry J. Leff
David H. Lincoln • Alan B. Lucas • Daniel S. Nevins • Cheryl Peretz
Avram Israel Reisner • Karen G Reiss Medwed • Tracee L. Rosen
Craig T. Scheff • Julie Schonfeld • Gershon Schwartz ז"ל
Laurence A. Sebert • Gerald C. Skolnik • Abigail N. Sosland
Lawrence Troster • Gordon Tucker

MARTIN S. COHEN
senior editor

MICHAEL KATZ
associate editor

The Observant Life

The Wisdom of Conservative Judaism for Contemporary Jews

with a Foreword by
ARNOLD M. EISEN
Chancellor, The Jewish Theological Seminary

and a Prolegomenon by
JULIE SCHONFELD
Executive Vice President, The Rabbinical Assembly

The Rabbinical Assembly
NEW YORK

Library of Congress Cataloging-in-Publication Data

The observant life : the wisdom of Conservative Judaism for contemporary Jews / Martin S. Cohen, senior editor ; Michael Katz, associate editor ; with a foreword by Arnold M. Eisen and a prolegomenon by Julie Schonfeld.
p. cm.
Includes bibliographical references and index.
ISBN 978-0-916219-49-9 (alk. paper)
1. Spiritual life—Judaism. 2. Jewish way of life. 3. God (Judaism)—Worship and love. 4. Jewish ethics. I. Cohen, Martin Samuel, 1953–. II. Katz, Michael, 1952–.
BM723.O25 2011
296.7—dc23

2011051808

Published by the Rabbinical Assembly
3080 Broadway, New York, NY 10027
www.rabbinicalassembly.org

Cover design by Rebecca Neimark

Printed in the United States of America by

G&H Soho, Inc.
www.ghsoho.com

The ornaments used in this volume come from the edition of the Zohar published in Jerusalem in 1844 by Israel Bak, who restored Hebrew printing to the Land of Israel two and a half centuries after the first Hebrew-language books were published there in the late sixteenth century.

Table of Contents

Hatznei·a Lekhet Im Elohekha
Walking Humbly with God

Prayer   Karen G Reiss Medwed   5

The Goals and Functions of Prayer • Prayer as Petition and Praise • Prayer as an
Expression of Anger • Prayer as an Expression of Historical Awareness •
Theological Issues Regarding Prayer • Keva and Kavvanah • Liturgical Change •
Does God Answer Prayer? • The Experience of Prayer • Communal Prayer •
Physical Prayer • Jerusalem • Sacred Space • The Times for Prayer •
Prayer Leaders • The Language of Prayer • The Prayerbook •

Holy Days and Holidays ALAN B. LUCAS 137

The Jewish Calendar • Working and Cooking on Holy Days • Eiruv Tavshilin • Counting the Years • Elul • S'liḥot • The Jewish New Year • Erev Rosh Hashanah • Rosh Hashanah at Home • The Evening and Morning Services on Rosh Hashanah • The Shofar • The Musaf Service on Rosh Hashanah • Tashlikh • The Ten Days of Repentance • The Day of Atonement • The Work of Yom Kippur • Erev Yom Kippur • Kol Nidrei • The Evening Service on Yom Kippur • The Morning Service and Torah Service on Yom Kippur • Yizkor • The Musaf Service on Yom Kippur • The Afternoon Service on Yom Kippur • Ne'ilah • The Festival of Sukkot • The Rituals of Sukkot • The Sukkah • The Arba·ah Minim • Sukkot at Home • Sukkot in the Synagogue • The Intermediate Days of Sukkot • Hoshana Rabbah • Sh'mini Atzeret • Simḥat Torah • Ḥeshvan • Ḥanukkah • Tu Bi-sh'vat • Two Special Shabbatot • Purim • Three More Special Shabbatot • Nisan • The Passover Festival • Passover as History and Destiny • The Fast of the Firstborn • Ḥameitz • Kashrut on Passover • When Erev Pesaḥ Falls on Shabbat • Passover at Home • The Seder • Passover in the Synagogue • The Intermediate Days of Passover • The Concluding Days of Passover • Counting the Omer • Lag Ba-omer and Pesaḥ Sheini • Yom Ha-sho·ah, Yom Ha-zikkaron, Yom Ha-atzma·ut, and Yom Y'rushalayim • Shavuot • Fast Days • Tishah Be'av • Tu Be'av • Rosh Ḥodesh • Kiddush L'vanah • Birkat Ha-ḥamah

The Jewish Life Cycle CARL N. ASTOR 239

Procreation and Birth • The First Mitzvah • Circumcision • The Birth of a Daughter • Choosing a Jewish Name • Redemption of the Firstborn • Bar Mitzvah and Bat Mitzvah • Conversion • Getting Married • Marriage as Mitzvah • Prohibited Marriages • T'nayim • The Time and Place of Marriage • Before the Wedding • Weddings • Yiḥud • The Wedding Feast • The Laws of Family Purity • Divorce • Dealing with Illness • Visiting the Sick • Confronting Death • When Death Is Imminent • Autopsies and Organ Donation • Suicide • Aninut • The Funeral • Kohanim and Funerals • Cremation and Disinterment • The Shivah Period • Comforting the Bereaved • Sh'loshim • Mourning for Parents • Yahrtzeit • Unveilings • Yizkor

The Dietary Laws PAUL S. DRAZEN 305

Why Keep Kosher? • Kosher and Non-Kosher Animals • Land Animals • Fish • Birds and Fowl • Insects • Preparing Kosher Meat • Blood • Kosher Slaughter • Inspection • Restricted Portions • Soaking and Salting Meat • Meat and Dairy • Pareve Foods • Kosher Supervision • Food Additives • Wines and Liquors •

Asot Mishpat
Acting Justly

Ahavat Ḥesed
Deeds of Lovingkindness

Foreword

ARNOLD M. EISEN

"Law and tradition" has long been the watchword of "Positive-Historical" or Conservative Judaism. That was so particularly in early decades when the movement's major thinkers in Germany and America struggled to explain what was unique about their approach to Judaism—or rather what made that approach the most authentic and compelling continuation of the rabbinic path that had guided Jewish life for centuries. Zacharias Frankel and his allies in the mid-nineteenth century could not conceive of a serious Judaism *not* rooted in the authority of law and enriched by the daily routines, private and public, that law prescribed. Solomon Schechter repeatedly put the case at the start of the twentieth century for a kind of Judaism that *conserves* tradition in part by *changing* it when change is required. He wrote provocatively in 1894, for example, that—contrary to popular opinion—"it is not the mere revealed Bible that is of first importance to the Jew, but the Bible as it repeats itself in history, in other words, as it is interpreted by tradition." From the Talmud onward, Schechter explained, "the interpretation of Scripture is mainly a product of changing historical influences." Torah was kept vital in this fashion, and only in this fashion; a community of learned and committed interpreters was required to know at every point what changes were needed—and what changes needed to be resisted—in order for Torah to speak loudly and clearly to each new generation.

Schechter and Frankel would have welcomed *The Observant Life,* I believe; I certainly do. It's a pleasure to hear the many voices gathered in this community of learned and committed interpreters sorting through a wide range of issues that Jews confront in the contemporary world. It is both helpful and inspiring to receive the intelligent, frank, and clear-headed guidance that Conservative rabbis have derived from major sources of the Jewish legal tradition. There are times when the territory covered overlaps almost completely with what might have been written a century ago, or centuries before that. At other moments, one sees tradition pushed gently forward, whether through the adaptation of existing *halakhah* to somewhat new conditions or by the reconceptualization of existing categories to suit new social or economic arrangements.

In still other cases, however, we are forcibly reminded of just how much has changed, in our world and in ourselves. We desperately want tradition to guide us nonetheless, craving both the framework of law and its constraint. These are the points at which I found the volume especially welcome. Ethical questions that have never before been confronted in the way we face them now require answers in an equally new key. The voice of *mitzvah* that has been sounding among Jews since Sinai cannot but sound somewhat differently today. We struggle to hear what once seemed loud or clear.

I was especially grateful to my generation's rabbis in the chapters that directly address new perplexities, from the ever-vexed and ever-important area of sexuality to the field of interfaith relations in a diverse society that aspires to cultural and religious pluralism. The underlying principles that guide Jewish behavior in both areas have not changed much over the centuries. Application of those principles, however, has changed significantly.

The breadth of the volume is itself a mark of change. Readers of *The Observant Life* are offered guidance on issues that arise when "sitting in your home" (family relations, dietary laws) and when "walking on the way" (the workplace, taxation and contracts, interfaith relations). The assumption throughout this volume is that Jews want full engagement with Jewish tradition—and so with law and a life of observance guided by law—as well as full engagement with contemporary culture and society. The tensions caused by that dual focus are without apology and on full view: another mark of just how far Conservative Judaism (like the community as a whole) has evolved since Schechter's day.

A comment by Louis Finkelstein in his classic address from 1937, "Tradition in the Making," captures well the significance and achievement of the book before you: "Conservative Jews," he wrote, "regard Judaism not as an ossified museum piece, but as a living and vital tradition. The Code of Hammurabi can rest unchanged in the Louvre. The Torah endures in human life and must partake of the vitality, the adaptability, and fluidity of all living organisms."

The Observant Life lives and breathes this commitment from cover to cover—which is cause for celebration at the vitality of the tradition that the volume presents and carries forward. It gives me great pleasure as chancellor of the Jewish Theological Seminary to congratulate the authors and editors on their achievement. It is an honor to welcome readers to the experiences of meaning, community, and life in the presence of God that have for centuries been vouchsafed to Jews by the observance and interpretation of the commandments.

Prolegomenon

JULIE SCHONFELD

Every Jewish community in every generation invents itself anew. Conservative Judaism is one such brilliant reinvention, one which now finds *itself* in a phase of dynamic reinvention. With roots in European Jewish Emancipation of the nineteenth century, Conservative Judaism provides an approach to Jewish thinking and practice that allows us to engage with the broader world and live our lives fully as Jews in that world. As a result, Conservative Judaism nurtures the optimistic faith that an ancient tradition can be successfully carried forward by people wholly invested in the success of an open society . . . *if* they use methods of inquiry that are intellectually honest, and also developed in the framework of a caring spiritual community. Conservative Jewish Torah thus becomes the "grid" on which the religious and spiritual framework of modern Jewish life and thought can be built by those committed to engaging with the world—intellectually, emotionally, socially, and spiritually. And so the Conservative approach has evolved. Generations of knowledgeable practicing Jews have brought the Jewish passion for justice, community, and Torah into every sphere of life. The movement has helped build and support the State of Israel; Conservative Jewish scholars and knowledgeable Jewish professionals lead institutions of all types around the world; and Conservative Jewish communities have taken root in every major city, providing opportunities for Jews throughout the world to live lives guided by the tenets of the Torah, as interpreted for modern times through the lens of Conservative Jewish ideology and belief.

The essays in this book are a product of modern times, speaking to the realities of Jewish life in the twenty-first century. The wisdom and learning of the rabbis who authored them remains emblematic of Conservative Judaism's primary vision and mission: to bring the moral mandates of the Torah to life in every Jewish community and to teach a Judaism of love and respect that opens the hearts of Jews to Jewish tradition. Observance of *mitzvot* is therefore not to be limited to the synagogue, but to be extended to all walks of life—from the home to the workplace, from the family to the broader community—in the way we seek guidance from Torah. Contemporary Rabbinical Assembly responsa thus mirror ancient texts on the same topics, yet without supplanting them, as we strive to bring challenging present-day questions to the table.

In recent years Conservative Judaism's message of pursuit of a life of Torah within the framework of a diverse community has become more urgent as Jews have chosen to live in societies where externally defined boundaries have become increasingly permeable. In the past, society played a much larger role in determining identity. In open societies, however, identity is largely a construction of the self. As a consequence, a distinctive Jewish identity—not only culturally speaking, but most especially religiously—is increasingly harder to promulgate, just as engagement in Jewish community and Jewish religious practice itself has become a distinctly harder sell than it once was. Our rabbis and teachers are the easiest to hear when they lead by emphasizing the joy and the meaning in Jewish life, rather than its challenges. As a result, Jewish tradition has come to be seen, at least by many, as circumscribed to specific moments of our lives. Nevertheless, the need to make difficult decisions and to confront our own moral limitations must be part and parcel of a serious Jewish life and study. Judaism promulgates a profound religious worldview that seeks to place us in direct and honest confrontation with the tension that naturally exists between the routines of our daily lives and aspiration to infuse all aspects of our being with a sense of holiness.

Some of Judaism's most foundational organizing principles, and its most central rituals, are not subject to logical analysis. Moreover, some occasionally run quite counter to other deeply held values of secular society. In a perfect world, it might well be possible to make Judaism completely harmonious with all the finest contemporary values. Indeed, even in an imperfect world, many propose that we do just that! But this does not mirror reality. And, that being the case, we must always acknowledge that what we are asking of people may be hard for them to do. If Conservative Judaism promotes an approach requiring commitment, honesty, integrity, and a willingness to confront the inevitable conflicts that trying to keep faith with a tradition dating back thousands of years will eventually present, will some Jews inevitably seek other, less demanding paths . . . and will our movement's numbers consequently decrease? That may indeed happen. By the measure of a market-driven society—in other words, if the sole point is to keep our numbers high—we need really go no further in examining the issue.

But we hope that, when history records our contributions, we will be remembered not for the size of our constituencies but rather by the quality of the lives we have lived, and the mark we have left on those around us. Indeed, the actions we take today that can best deliver a vibrant and viable Jewish framework to future generations are not necessarily the ones that will speak directly to our immediate needs. But we Jews are good at taking the long view. Judaism is a sacred framework built around the ongoing epic of our people's evolution: it is the path of values and of faith.

This concept is illustrated by a passage in *Midrash T'hillim* (22:13) that offers an engaging comparison between the predictable, incremental unfolding of daybreak and the inscrutable nature of sacred history (and the concomitant revelation of holy purpose), as outlined toward a triumphant outcome for the Jewish people in the book of Esther.

> "Who is she that shines through like the dawn" (Song of Songs 6:10)? Rabbi Ḥiyya bar Abba and Rabbi Simon ben Ḥalafta were walking in the Arbael valley at dawn and saw the first rays of daybreak rising above the horizon. Rabbi Ḥiyya said, "Similar is the redemption of Israel." Rabbi Simon said: "Indeed! For it is written, 'Though I sit in the dark, the Eternal is my light' (Micah 7:8): at first it shines forth little by little, then it breaks through in stronger measure, then it becomes ever greater and more powerful, and only then, after all that, does it fully shine forth. [And this incremental process is mirrored in the story of Queen Esther's visit to King Ahasuerus.] At first, 'And Mordecai sat at the gate of the king' (Esther 2:21). Then, 'When the king saw Esther the queen' (Esther 5:2). Then, 'And Haman took the royal clothing and the horse' (Esther 6:11). Then, 'And they hanged Haman' (Esther 7:10). After that, 'And they wrote regarding the Jews' (Esther 8:8). After that, 'And Mordecai went out before the king wearing royal garments' (Esther 8:15). And only then, after all [those prior incremental stages]: And the Jews had light' (Esther 8:16)."

The lesson here is more subtle than it might at first seem. Whereas one might predict with reasonable certainty that after the first light of dawn, the day will continue to brighten incrementally, this is not necessarily the case in other arenas of human endeavor. The actions, for example, that we take to deepen our own Judaism—and, moreover, to strengthen the Jewish people as a whole—offer no such satisfying predictability. That Esther will be successful in her attempt to ensure safety for herself and deliverance for her people is, after all, not at all clear at the beginning of the Book of Esther—and so the analogy with the first light of dawn as it grows incrementally stronger until it illuminates the entire sky appears not to apply. But that is just the point of the comparison: Esther's actions were guided by faith and courage, and specifically *not* by what appeared most expedient in the short term. She had no guarantee of success; she was specifically *not* mirroring a natural phenomenon that had no "choice" but to unfold in the same predictable way it already had over countless millennia. Yet her path led directly to her people's deliverance. And such has been the case throughout Jewish history: while our tradition has been eminently adaptable to numerous cultures and influences, its durability and strength have been the result of the actions of countless Jews willing to break with the norms of their own cultural milieus in order to give expression to a Judaism whose vibrancy and enduring merit can only be sought on its own terms. There are no guarantees. Rabbi Ḥiyya bar Abba and Rabbi Simon ben Ḥalafta looked into the past and saw the future. We who have been blessed to live in one of the most open periods in all of Jewish history may ask no less of ourselves.

As the Conservative movement moves from the first to the second decade of the twenty-first century, we are reaching a turning-point in our *approach*, one which will be determinative for setting out the path that will inspire future generations. That turning point is characterized by several important themes. Two of them bear noting here:

1. We share our love of performing *mitzvot*, as well as our love of studying Torah. This book is called *The Observant Life* because we remain steadfast in belief that *observing* Judaism—that is, practicing *mitzvot*—is the pathway to uncovering the full richness of Judaism in our lives.
2. We focus on Conservative Judaism as a religious *movement* shaped by the Jewish journeys we undertake, rather than as a denomination defined by the support of institutions. In doing so, we take up our mantle as champions of Jews and Judaism, a religious movement unequivocally committed to allowing thoughtful change in order to promote eternal values.

The Conservative movement opens its doors wherever people are embarking on the path outlined above and, even as we acknowledge growth to date, we challenge all Jews continually to seek further growth. Hebrew language, Torah study, and commitment to Israel are challenges we lay squarely before our community. We embrace the realization that, if we are "commanded" or obligated to perform the *mitzvot*, that commitment applies to the ethical precepts as well as the ritual ones. Performance of *mitzvot* is the sacred vehicle by which we carry our vision of justice and lovingkindness to the next generation. Articulating the ethical framework of Judaism is key, but *merely* articulating it is insufficient. We cannot pass a torch forward just by talking about torches (or by talking about passing them forward). To pass a torch to future generations, we must light the torch in question, then proudly hold it aloft as we carry it forward ourselves into the future with the intention of handing it off to those we hope to inspire to take it from our hands and carry it further into the future than we ourselves ever could. We are all presented with the choice to be part of this great effort to convey the past into the future, thus to make the message of Judaism as eternal as the Jewish people itself. If we consent, we will confront ourselves and embrace our communities, but we will also encounter God, just as Scripture suggests by a simple progression of ideas: first, "build for Me a sanctuary" (Exodus 25:8); then, "and there shall I dwell" (ibid.), and finally, "and there shall I meet you and speak with you" (Exodus 25:22).

Preface

MARTIN S. COHEN

The Torah provides a framework for the infusion of spiritual and religious values into every aspect of daily life, yet the word *halakhah*—used both in classical sources and by Jews today to denote Jewish law in the fullness of its detail and complexity—conjures up for many only the rules that govern the ritual lives of observant Jews. As a result, the question "What is the *halakhah* regarding . . ." usually ends with a reference to some aspect of ritual law, and dramatically less often to a question of ethics that the questioner wishes to resolve in a way consonant with Jewish principles and standards. Yet one could argue that the *halakhah* is actually at its most creative when it is dealing with issues of moral concern, and that it is precisely this context in which the values of Scripture become the most vibrant and inspiring. These are the values that the ancient sages wished to project into the world through the prism of their interpretive tradition into the lives of ordinary Jews.

Yet most modern books of *halakhah,* including the ones that have become latter-day classics, focus almost exclusively on areas of ritual law. It is true that many books have been written about specific ethical topics within the *halakhah,* especially in recent years in the area of business ethics, but major works dealing with a broad spectrum of halakhic issues outside the sphere of ritual behavior have been very few and far between—and this is especially true when one considers particularly works written from the vantage point of non-Orthodox Judaism in its various denominational permutations.

Within the Conservative movement, for example, Isaac Klein's classic book, *A Guide to Jewish Religious Practice,* is devoted almost entirely to matters of ritual behavior. And, indeed, a full third of the present work is addressed more or less exactly to the issues covered in Rabbi Klein's book. The other two thirds, however, are devoted almost exclusively to topics left untreated there: family matters and workplace issues, questions resulting from living in the world, others related to matters of economics and finance, and still others related to our status as citizens of the countries in which we reside.

The *halakhah,* therefore, lives in two different realms.

One is the idealized realm of ritual behavior in which people construct their own invisible temples and then serve God (or attempt to serve God) in those places with all the fervor and attention to detail they can muster. This is the realm of *kashrut* and Shabbat observance, the realm of marriage and divorce law, the realm of family purity and formal mourning practices—in short, the collective realm of the slightly artificial institutions designed to help us feel the presence of God profoundly and palpably by imposing highly effective contexts in which to do so upon the hours of their days and the years of their lives.

The other realm is the arena of human society, where the *halakhah* flourishes as people devoted to serving God wholly attempt to find holiness in even the most banal aspects of daily life as it is actually lived. This is the realm of how we dress and how we speak, how we relate to our employers and to our employees, how we conduct our social lives and our sexual lives. It is the realm of thoughtful advertising executives wondering what kind of impact the laws that forbid lying should have on their craft, of spiritually sensitive journalists speculating about the degree to which they can report the news without contravening the scriptural prohibition of talebearing, and of ethical, humane physicians attempting to practice a kind of medicine infused with the values of faith. It is the realm of lawyers wondering how exactly the *halakhah* crosses paths with the techniques of modern jurisprudence, and whether Judaism formally discourages—or perhaps even actually forbids—them to engage in any of those practices. It is the realm of real people living in the real world and trying not to *invent* space for God in the world, but rather to *find* God in the nooks and crannies of their actual lives as they are already living them.

By its very nature, there is something just a bit gritty about a volume such as this. Treating, as it does, the real world of real people, this book provides insight into the way an observant Jewish individual might respond to all sorts of distressing, unexpected—and unexpectedly complicated—aspects of living in that world. True, the *halakhah* provides a way to infuse spiritual values into the more banal and ordinary aspects of daily life, but, more often than not, the world presented and discussed in the pages of this book is a world filled with unsavory, upsetting things. It is a world in which people do not always behave well, and in which poor behavior inevitably requires some sort of response from people in contiguous spheres of existence. It is a world in which even the most pious, ethical human being cannot avoid coming into contact with vulgarity, obscenity, impropriety, and boorish behavior. And it is a world that, though it may profess allegiance to the bedrock morality presumed to underlie society at its best, rarely pauses long enough to inspect that foundation and actually to address itself to the fissures and cracks that develop *inevitably,* given a long enough period of time, in even the sturdiest concrete.

For all that, this is neither a book of philosophical essays about moral and ritual issues nor a guide to the history of Jewish thinking about such matters *per se,* but a book of *halakhah* designed to bring the strictures, attitudes, and insights of the Jewish legal tradition to bear on the stuff of daily life. For example, the chapters about modern legal practice and the *halakhah* are not essays about the relationship of Western law and Jewish law. Instead, they are about the precise ways people caught up in the judicial system—as lawyers, plaintiffs, defendants, judges, or jurors—might behave without violating their principles or their allegiance to God and the Torah. Similarly, our chapter about the *halakhah* of being single does not address the question of whether or not people should marry, but rather the halakhic dimension of being unmarried in a mostly-married world, and the specific issues that face unmarried adults as they try to live a life in conformity with the values and ethical strictures of Judaism. In short, this is not a book about Jewish law *per se* as much as it is a book about people trying to live halakhic lives. As such, the authors of its chapters have not come together to preach or to admonish, but to demonstrate the reasonableness of seeking to live lives suffused with values of faith in the context of allegiance to divine law.

It may come as a surprise to some readers that the *halakhah* has anything at all to say about some of the arenas of daily life addressed in this book, areas usually considered too secular to warrant consideration from a spiritual point of view: the bank and the stock exchange, the theater and the law court, the tax accountant's office and the old age home and the emergency room. Yet it is the unyielding principle of all halakhic thought that, just as no place on earth is devoid of the divine spirit, so must there also be no aspect of life deemed *a priori* impervious to the infusion of religious and spiritual values by people whose sense of *tikkun olam*—the noble effort to mend the torn fabric of our world—brings them to attempt to infuse the patch of ground they occupy with the spirit of godliness and with holiness. The great goal of this book is to make that point even more clear than it might otherwise have been and, more specifically, to make precise suggestions about how one might go about undertaking to live such a life. Nothing more, but also nothing else.

In a famous talmudic passage, four of Israel's greatest prophets are imagined as competing with each other to reduce the Torah to its most essential elements. Each effort has something unique to recommend it, but none of the passages cited is as famous as the one from the sixth chapter of the Book of Micah in which the prophet teaches (or at least is imagined to be teaching) that all the commandments of the Torah branch out in one way or another from the three central obligations to behave kindly, to act justly, and to conduct oneself modestly and humbly. Taking the talmudic understanding of the prophet's lesson seriously, we have organized the chapters of *The Observant Life* into three categories named for the prophet's three overarching rubrics: *Hatznei·a Lekhet Im Elohekha*: Walking Humbly with God, *Asot Mishpat*: Acting Justly, and *Ahavat Ḥesed:* Deeds of Lovingkindness. And, indeed, it turns out that the prophet was right: the commandments of the Torah do indeed fall almost naturally, all of them, into one of the three categories mentioned.

Astute readers will notice that there is no section of this book in which are listed articles of faith that are declared incumbent upon every Jewish soul to accept. In the past, some of the classical compendia of Jewish law attempted to legislate regarding dogma, while others chose not to do so. In this volume, we have chosen to create a book regarding practice and the philosophy of practice rather than about dogmatic belief *per se*. Perhaps a future volume will address the thorny issue of what Jews in the modern world must attempt to believe in order to remain faithful to the covenant without that effort necessarily entailing the sacrifice of their intellectual or spiritual integrity. That undertaking, however, lies in the future.

The authors of these chapters are a varied group of rabbis who represent a wide spectrum of experience and personal philosophy. They are men and women, Americans and non-Americans, seasoned authors and new writers. They have different areas of expertise and serve a surprisingly diverse array of Jewish institutions, but all bring to this volume their deeply held conviction that the *halakhah* is a valid framework for the infusion of holiness into daily life, and that the notion that spiritual seekers must flee the world to better seek God is a fantasy that will appeal chiefly to those looking for an excuse to avoid the journey. The essays in this volume have been edited to provide them with a more unified style than they might otherwise have had, but the voices you will read in this book are the voices of their authors. Occasionally, the authors represented in this volume are not in agreement about specific points of *halakhah*. That is as it should be: the elaboration of the *halakhah* is a living, dynamic art form that cannot be handled precisely the same way by any two who approach it sincerely and with full spirits and full hearts. As a result, no attempt has been made to enforce a uniform approach to *halakhah* throughout the pages of this volume. Still, most authors agree on most points and readers will not sense that they are stepping into an acrimonious debate as much as they will feel that they are entering a universe of sustained, sacred, and passionate discourse. It also bears emphasizing that this is a book of essays about *halakhah,* not a book of ultimate legal decisions that reflect more than the views of their authors. Readers concerned with adapting the information contained in this volume to the specifics of their own situations, therefore, should seek counsel from a rabbi well-versed in that specific area of halakhic inquiry. Although the authors of all the chapters in this book are members of the Rabbinical Assembly, the international organization of Conservative and Masorti rabbis, the fact that an opinion is presented in this volume should not necessarily be taken to imply that the Committee on Jewish Law and Standards of the Rabbinical Assembly, the highest halakhic authority within the Conservative movement, has debated the point and come to the conclusion herein presented.

In a book such as this, the specific way to render into English the various ways God is referenced in Hebrew, and particularly in biblical texts, presents a special challenge. For the sake of simplicity, we have opted to use the English word "God" to translate all the words used in classical Hebrew to denote the Deity other than the four-letter name of ineffable sanctity used in Scripture as a kind of personal name for the God of Israel. That name, however, appears in two different guises in this book: in benedictions it appears as "Adonai" (the Hebrew word for "my Lord" that is how even Hebrew speakers give voice to it in the liturgical context), while elsewhere it appears translated as "the Eternal" or "the Eternal One." Readers who can control the original Hebrew are encouraged to consult the sources to see how any specific text cited reads in the original. Most of the biblical citations in this volume appear either in the authors' own translations or else in the version of the Bible in English published in 1985 by the Jewish Publication Society. The citations from that translation that appear in *The Observant Life* are used here with the very kind assent of the publisher, which permission I am pleased to acknowledge formally and with gratitude.

I would also like to say a brief word about the style of transliteration used in this volume, which is the system for presenting Hebrew and Aramaic in English letters that is in general use in the liturgical publications of the Rabbinical Assembly. The Hebrew letters *ḥet* and *kof* are represented by *ḥ* and *k* respectively. *Kaf* appears here, depending on context, either as the letter *k* or as the letter combination *kh*. *Tzadi* appears as the combination *tz*. The letter *heh* is represented by an English *h* even when it is silent. The letters *alef* and *ayin* are not represented in transliteration other than as English vowels. The *shva na* vowel is generally represented by an apostrophe. Hyphens are used in this volume to separate prefixes from the words to which they are attached. When consecutive vowels are correctly to be pronounced in two syllables, a raised dot has been used to separate those syllables. Generally speaking, the scholarly convention of doubling the English consonant to denote the presence in Hebrew of a pointed letter has been followed. The Hebrew vowel *tzeirei* is represented in transliteration by the vowel combination *ei*, but exceptions were made for words that are so widely used in English-language books that it would only be confusing not to follow what has become their standard spelling.

I have personally written three chapters for this book, as well as this preface, the introductions to each section, and the book's afterword, but I could never have produced this work on my own and so must I offer my most sincere and humble thanks to the men and women who have contributed to this volume, and especially to Rabbi Michael Katz with whom I worked on this project from the very beginning until the very end. Indeed, it is only stating the obvious to say that this book could not have come about without the participation of the wide and varied cast of characters who responded to the invitation to participate in its creation. In accordance with the rabbinic tradition preserved in the *Pirkei Avot* (6:3) to the effect that we must show reverence to anyone from whom we have learned even a single *halakhah,* they all have my deepest respect and admiration. An old rabbinic *midrash,* the *Sifrei D'varim* (Eikev §48), teaches that one of the three ways to fulfill the biblical injunction to keep the commandments in all their vast fullness (Deuteronomy 6:17) is to study *halakhah* (the others are to study *midrash* and *aggadah*—respectively, the exegetical and literary traditions of the ancient rabbis). For this reason as well I am grateful to my co-authors. To them all, I offer this heartfelt prayer: may you all be privileged to begin and finish many other books and literary projects, and may you all go from strength to strength in the study of *halakhah*.

Finally, I would like formally to express my personal gratitude to the donors whose gifts made possible the publication of this volume and in particular to Gershon Kekst, without whose generosity this book would probably not be seeing the light of day. (All those who have contributed to the publication of this volume are listed in the Acknowledgments section following Michael Katz's introduction.) I know I speak for all those who have labored so intensely on *The Observant Life* over these many years when I say that we are grateful from the bottom of our hearts for the support of donors possessed of the wherewithal and the desire to underwrite projects such as this one. To them all, we offer our most sincere gratitude.

MSC
Roslyn, New York
2002–2012

Introduction

MICHAEL KATZ

What is the "stuff" of Judaism properly called? In Hebrew school, our teachers spoke (sometimes just a bit too dispassionately) about "customs and ceremonies." When we became a bar or bat mitzvah, our rabbis congratulated us on our new obligation to observe the "commandments." At Passover seders, our grandparents showed us the power and the beauty of "tradition." In college, our professors lectured to us about how every culture develops its own "folkways." And as we marry, give birth to children, and bury parents, we turn to "rituals" to bring order and meaning into our lives.

There is another term that Judaism applies to all the religious acts we do at various moments in our lives, however: *halakhah,* from the Hebrew root meaning "to walk or to go." In one sense, *halakhah* is the Jewish roadmap that shows how to navigate through life with a sense of holiness. But, in another, *halakhah* is the road itself, and *k'dushah*—holiness—is the sacred destination to which that road leads over a lifetime characterized by fidelity to divine law.

Conservative Judaism teaches that *halakhah* is a code of Jewish living that represents the revealed will of God as codified by our rabbis and ultimately adopted and shaped by the Jewish people over the course of their four-thousand-year-long history. The *halakhah* is more, therefore, than an endless list of rules. And, for all that the many authoritative works of *halakhah* composed over the generations contain much good advice, the *halakhah* itself does not merely offer sage counsel to the faithful. Rather, *halakhah* is what committed Jews do. It is how they live their real-world lives imbued with a sense of divine favor and infused with optimism born of faith. It is a promise offered by the Torah that adherence to divine law offers the possibility of communion with God, the highest goal of all human striving.

Among the core tenets of Conservative Judaism is the belief that *halakhah* evolves and develops over the course of time. Furthermore, just as every generation faces new issues and challenges, so must the *halakhah* be deemed capable of responding and adapting to new circumstances. The ultimate source of *halakhah* is the Torah itself. But later works superseded Scripture as the basis for halakhic discourse. The Mishnah and the Talmud were the ancient rabbis' attempt to apply Jewish law to real life during centuries of crisis and upheaval. During the Middle Ages, the two most significant compilations of *halakhah* were the *Mishneh Torah* of the Rambam (Moses Maimonides, 1135–1204), usually cited by its initials in this book simply as *MT* and the *Shulḥan Arukh* of Rabbi Joseph Karo (1488–1575) with the glosses and comments of Rabbi Moses Isserles (1525–1572), known as the Rema, cited in bibliographical references in this book simply as *SA*. The process of reviewing and renewing Jewish law continues into modern times.

In 1979, the Jewish Theological Seminary published the first code of *halakhah* composed within the spirit and approach of Conservative Judaism. *A Guide to Jewish Religious Practice,* by Rabbi Isaac Klein (1905–1979), quickly became a classic and remains even today the standard sourcebook for Conservative Jews in matters of *halakhah*. Now, more than a quarter of a century later, there are several reasons for us to take a new step forward. First, there have been many advances in technology and science, especially medical science, in the last thirty years. Also, the spirit of egalitarianism has created a set of issues to be considered that were largely left unpondered in previous generations. In turn, the Committee on Jewish Law and Standards of the Rabbinical Assembly has discussed and debated many of these questions and has issued numerous responsa on matters of Jewish life and law. There was a need to update Rabbi Klein's book to incorporate many of these changes.

It also bears saying that Klein's masterwork, which was based on his lectures to rabbinical students at the Jewish Theological Seminary, was originally meant for those whom the author hoped would eventually become experts in *halakhah*. (His chapters on *kashrut,* for example, go into the kind of detail about the anatomy of kosher animals that lay readers will hardly ever wish to know.) This book, however, is intended specifically for laypeople.

Finally, there was an entire area of halakhic discourse omitted from *A Guide to Jewish Religious Practice:* the realm of ethics and ethical behavior.

That omission is formally addressed in this work. As is too the strong sense that *halakhah* encompasses the so-called *mitzvot bein adam la-makom* (commandments that concern the relationship between human beings and God) AND the *mitzvot bein adam la-ḥaveiro* (commandments that concern relations between human beings). And so this book is divided into three major sections. The first, *Hatznei·a Lekhet Im Elohekha:* Walking Humbly with God, concerns matters of Jewish ritual. The second section, *Asot Mishpat:* Acting Justly, deals with the challenges that face committed Jews who are engaged with the modern secular world. The third, *Ahavat Ḥesed:* Deeds of Lovingkindness, considers our relationships with others. While the first section touches on familiar territory, the rest of the book is revolutionary in that it is a first comprehensive attempt to address seriously (if not always ultimately to resolve) ethical issues from the standpoint of Conservative Jewish *halakhah*.

In matters of Jewish law, there is no central authority. Jews turn to their *mara de'atra,* usually the rabbi of an individual's community (the term means, literally, "teacher of one's place") for guidance and for answers. Jewish law is vast, yet it is very often *not* monolithic. Indeed, it is often the case that there are many different traditions about some specific matter of law, all of them considered legitimate.

The reader may find some unfamiliar ground covered here, or some teachings that feel different from the norm. (The Talmud teaches us, however, that it is perfectly possible for two mutually exclusive opinions both to be considered the words of the living God.) When in doubt, one should always turn to the local *mara de'atra.* At times of uncertainty, his or her decision on matters of *halakhah* is always considered authoritative in the Conservative Jewish world.

For many decades, Conservative Jews have engaged in serious soul-searching about their own sincerity and integrity when it came to Jewish observance. Yet although observance levels vary, sometimes dramatically, from individual to individual, or even from community to community, Conservative Judaism has always taught that being Jewish is like traveling along a sacred path: the goal is not to be where you are, but to know where you are going. Rabbis are often asked if there is not something hypocritical about observing some rituals while at the same time being unable, or unwilling, to observe others. Our approach has always been to aim higher, and never to consider even minimal observance as meaningless or pointless. Our goal, at any given moment, is to climb higher and higher—*le'eilla le'eilla,* as the Maḥzor says—toward the great goal of full, sustained observance. It doesn't matter where we are today; the key is where we will try to be tomorrow.

Doing a little is better than doing nothing. But we should never be satisfied to remain where we are, for there is nothing as inimical to living a full Jewish life as complacency. The more a Jew does, the better off he or she will be. And the rewards of Jewish observance, both in this world and in the World to Come, are immense.

The authors of this book are rabbis. Most grew up in Conservative Jewish homes and were educated and ordained at the Jewish Theological Seminary or other Conservative schools. All serve now or have served the institutions of the movement: Conservative synagogues, Camp Ramah, the United Synagogue Youth movement, the Solomon Schechter schools, the American Jewish University in Los Angeles, and the different arms of the United Synagogue of Conservative Judaism. This book is an expression of their devotion to Judaism and to the Jewish people, but it is also their prayer that readers come to learn about the beauty and richness of Jewish life from its pages, and that that learning prompt its readers to adopt a better informed and more profound level of halakhic observance.

A few words about God. There is no chapter in this book on theology or belief. Yet in a real way, God is to be found on every single page. God is at the center of all religion, and that is most true of Judaism, which introduced monotheism to the world. As Conservative Jews, we recognize that all people must come to their own understanding of God. A famous teaching asks why the word "God" is repeated in the opening sentence of the Amidah: "God of Abraham, God of Isaac, God of Jacob." The answer offered is that the God of Abraham was different than the God of Isaac, and his God was in some ways different than the God of Jacob. Each of us receives the traditions and beliefs of those who came before us, but we all must search for our own understanding of, and relationship with, God. Two of the greatest Jewish philosophers of the twentieth century—Mordecai Kaplan and Abraham Joshua Heschel—were both associated with the Jewish Theological Seminary. Yet their notions of God were as different as night and day. Kaplan (especially in his masterwork *Judaism as a Civilization*) rejected the notion of a supernatural God, and instead defined God as "the power that makes for salvation." Heschel (especially in his classic book *God in Search of Man*) brings a traditional view of God that is steeped in the teaching of the hasidic rebbes. Conservative Jews will find in Kaplan or in Heschel (or in numerous other teachers) spiritual guides whose writings help us in our struggle to find God on our own.

Many people make the mistake of thinking that the differences between Orthodox, Conservative, and Reform Judaism are a matter of quantity: Orthodox do the most, Reform the least, while Conservative is somewhere in the middle. This is not accurate. The real differences that distinguish the movements from one another are about theology—that is, what we believe. It is what we believe about God that leads us to do what we do. Jews searching for God must address the three great themes of Jewish theology and the questions that they pose: Creation (Did God play a role in the genesis of the universe? How did creation unfold? After the world began, does God continue to play a role in its day to day running?); Revelation (Is God the Author of the Torah? May laws in the Torah be changed over time? In what ways—if any—does God continue to communicate with human beings?); and Redemption (Does God reward and punish us for our deeds? Why do good people suffer? Is there a heaven, a hell, and a resurrection of the dead?). It is our beliefs about these issues and our answers to these questions that define us as Orthodox, Conservative, or Reform, or as Reconstructionist or Renewal.

The prophet Micah (eighth century B.C.E.) asked the question that is at the heart of the Jewish religion: "What does the Eternal require of you?" (6:8). Sometimes, it is pretty clear what God wants: honor your father and mother, remember the Sabbath day and keep it holy, do not steal. But more often than not, the infinite complexities of life are not covered by the finite commands in the Torah. For two thousand years, in each generation and in every Jewish community, rabbis and serious Jews have struggled to determine exactly what it is that God wants of us. This book is a contemporary Conservative Jewish response to that question.

While it takes parents nine months to create a child, it took more than nine years to bring this volume into the world. More than anyone else, it was our editor, Rabbi Martin S. Cohen, who labored over its every chapter, page, and sentence. He deserves our admiration, our thanks, and a *mazal tov*. We rejoice at the birth of this book, and we pray that it live a long and meaningful life.

MK
Westbury, New York
2002–2012

Acknowledgments

MARTIN S. COHEN & MICHAEL KATZ

This project has evolved over a long period of time and has involved many people who have assisted us in various aspects of the production of this work. We are grateful to them all, but wish to pause here formally to acknowledge among them Amy Gottlieb, Rabbi Jan C. Kaufman, Rabbi Joel Meyers, and Rabbi Julie Schonfeld of the Rabbinical Assembly staff; Rabbi Kassel Abelson, Rabbi Wayne Franklin, the late Kenneth Goldrich, Rabbi Michael Graetz, Rabbi Ron Isaacs, Rabbi Chaim Listfield, Rabbi Mayer Rabinowitz, Rabbi Joel Roth, Rabbi Ira F. Stone, and Rabbi Gordon Tucker for their support, their encouragement, their intelligent criticism, and their thoughtful counsel; Rabbi Benjamin J. Kramer, who checked the biblical, talmudic, and later rabbinic references for the entire volume and who created the book's index; Rabbis Cecelia Beyer, Joel Seltzer, and Michael D. Stanger, who served as proofreaders; Lisa Feld and Eric Schramm, both of whom copyedited the entire manuscript; Michelle Kwitkin-Close, who expertly reviewed and improved each chapter of *The Observant Life* and who brought order and consistency to its every page; James K. Harris of G&H Soho, who freely shared with us his great knowledge and his consummate professional expertise in every aspect of the production of this volume, and his colleagues Kathie Kounouklos, who turned our raw files into publishable chapters with great skill and even greater patience, and Mary Jo Rhodes, who reviewed the manuscript for consistency of style; Rabbis Robert Fine, Vernon Kurtz, and Loel Weiss, who served as the liaisons between the editors and the Committee on

Jewish Law and Standards of the Rabbinical Assembly; Rosalind Judd and Rabbis Joshua Z. Heller and Loel Weiss, who proofread the final version of the manuscript of this book on behalf of the CJLS; and Gabriel N. Seed, who cheerfully and skillfully provided bibliographical data that might otherwise have been lacking or incorrectly given.

In their own category, we wish to acknowledge Gershon and Carol Kekst, whose munificent gift made possible the publication of this volume. Through their great generosity, and also through the trust they placed in us personally and in our ability to bring as complicated a project as this one to fruition, the Keksts have made even more secure their place as truly great benefactors of Jewish book publishing. We are very grateful! And we hope that this volume amply justifies their decision to step forward and personally to guarantee the publication of *The Observant Life*.

We also wish to acknowledge generous gifts from Joel and Lillian Cohen, Bernard Goldberg, Gershon and Carol Kekst, Dr. Michael Kogan, Jeffrey Loria, and Paul and Joan Schreiber, all of whom are members of the Park Avenue Synagogue in New York and all of whose gifts were intended as a tribute to Rabbi David H. Lincoln on the occasion of his retirement after many years of loyal and learned service to the congregation. And we wish as well to acknowledge gifts from the Keren Leah Devorah charity fund and the Rabbi's Discretionary Fund of Temple Beth Torah in Westbury, New York. King Kohelet was surely right to note that there is no end to the making of books, but it is also true that there would be no beginning to their publication without the support of donors such as these. We deeply appreciate their confidence in us and their support for this project.

Finally, we would also like formally to acknowledge the leadership, membership, and office staffs of our synagogues over the many years we have worked toward the publication of *The Observant Life*. (In the latter category, we would especially like to acknowledge the assistance of Barbara Liss and Barbara Mazzei.) The presidents of the Shelter Rock Jewish Center in Roslyn, New York, during the years we devoted to this volume were Harold Rabinowitz, Dr. Stephen Teitelbaum, Gary T. Zelman, Debra Hoffman, and Ellis Rudman. The presidents of Temple Beth Torah in Westbury, New York, during those years were Howard Kaufman, Harry Newman, Steve Dershowitz, Fred Hauser, and Rich Rothstein. Their generous understanding of what it means to be a rabbi, and what it means specifically for *us* to be rabbis, made it possible for us to undertake and complete work on this book in the course of the years we have served as the spiritual leaders of their communities. We are grateful to them all.

MSC & MK
JANUARY 31, 2012

Abbreviations, Acronyms, and Other References

AT The *Arba·ah Turim* of Rabbi Jacob ben Asher

BT Babylonian Talmud

CJ *Conservative Judaism* (the quarterly journal)

CJLS Committee on Jewish Law and Standards

CJLS Responsa 1980–1990 The Committee on Jewish Law and Standards of the Conservative Movement, *Responsa 1980–1990,* ed. David J. Fine (New York: The Rabbinical Assembly, 2005)

CJLS Responsa 1991–2000 The Committee on Jewish Law and Standards of the Conservative Movement, *Responsa 1991–2000,* eds. Kassel Abelson and David J. Fine (New York: The Rabbinical Assembly, 2002)

Dorff, *Matters of Life and Death* Elliot Dorff, *Matters of Life and Death: A Jewish Approach to Modern Medical Ethics* (Philadelphia: The Jewish Publication Society, 1998)

Encyclopedia Judaica *Encyclopedia Judaica,* 16 vols., eds. Cecil Roth and Geoffrey Wigoder (Jerusalem: Keter and New York: Macmillan, 1971–1972)

Encyclopedia Talmudit *Entziklopeidiah Talmudit Le'inyanei Halakhah,* 24 vols., eds. Meir Bar-Ilan, Shlomo Yosef Zevin, Zalman Nehemiah Goldberg *et al.* (Jerusalem: Yad Ha-rav Herzog, 1947–)

Etz Hayim *Etz Hayim: Torah and Commentary* (New York: The Rabbinical Assembly and The United Synagogue of Conservative Judaism, 2001)

IDF Israel Defense Forces

JTS The Jewish Theological Seminary

Klein Isaac Klein, *A Guide to Jewish Religious Practice* (New York: The Jewish Theological Seminary of America, 1979)

Klein, *Responsa and Halakhic Studies* Isaac Klein, *Responsa and Halakhic Studies,* 2nd edition, eds. David Golinkin and Monique Susskind Goldberg (Jerusalem: Schechter Institute of Jewish Studies, 2005)

M Mishnah

MT Maimonides' *Mishneh Torah*

NJPS *TANAKH: A New Translation of the Holy Scriptures According to the Traditional Hebrew Text* (Philadelphia: The Jewish Publication Society, 1985)

Proceedings of the CJLS 1927–1970 *Proceedings of the Committee on Jewish Law and Standards 1927–1970,* ed. David Golinkin (Jerusalem: The Rabbinical Assembly and The Institute of Applied Halakhah, 1997)

Rambam Rabbi Moses ben Maimon (1135–1204), called Maimonides

Rashbam Rabbi Samuel ben Meir (c. 1085–c. 1158)

Rashi Rabbi Solomon ben Yitzḥak (1040–1105)

Ravad Rabbi Abraham ben David of Posquières (c. 1120–1198)

Rema Rabbi Moses Isserles (1520–1572)

Responsa of the Va·ad Halakhah, vol. 1 *The Rabbinical Assembly of Israel Law Committee Responsa 5746* (Jerusalem: The Rabbinical Assembly of Israel and The Movement of Masorti Judaism in Israel, 1986)

Responsa of the Va·ad Halakhah, vol. 2 *The Rabbinical Assembly of Israel Law Committee Responsa 5747* (Jerusalem: The Rabbinical Assembly of Israel and The Movement of Masorti Judaism in Israel, 1987)

Responsa of the Va·ad Halakhah, vol. 3 *Responsa of the Va·ad Halakhah of the Rabbinical Assembly of Israel, Vol. 3, 5748–5749*

(Jerusalem: The Rabbinical Assembly of Israel and The Masorti Movement, 1989)

Responsa of the Va·ad Halakhah, vol. 4 *Responsa of the Va·ad Halakhah of the Rabbinical Assembly of Israel, Vol. 4, 5750–5752*, ed. David Golinkin (Jerusalem: The Rabbinical Assembly and The Masorti Movement, 1992)

Responsa of the Va·ad Halakhah, vol. 5 *Responsa of the Va·ad Halakhah of the Rabbinical Assembly of Israel, Vol. 5, 5752–5754*, ed. David Golinkin (Jerusalem: The Rabbinical Assembly and The Masorti Movement, 1994)

Responsa of the Va·ad Halakhah, vol. 6 *Responsa of the Va·ad Halakhah of the Rabbinical Assembly of Israel, Vol. 6, 5755–5758*, ed. David Golinkin (Jerusalem: The Institute of Applied Halakhah at The Schechter Institute of Jewish Studies, The Rabbinical Assembly of Israel, and The Masorti Movement, 1998)

SA *Shulḥan Arukh*

Sim Shalom I *Siddur Sim Shalom*, first edition (New York: The Rabbinical Assembly and The United Synagogue of Conservative Judaism, 1985)

Sim Shalom II *Siddur Sim Shalom*, second edition (vol. 1, ed. Lawrence Cahan [New York: The Rabbinical Assembly and The United Synagogue of Conservative Judaism, 1998]; vol. 2, ed. Avram I. Reisner [New York: The Rabbinical Assembly and The United Synagogue of Conservative Judaism, 2003])

T Tosefta

Y The Palestinian Talmud, called the Yerushalmi

The Observant Life

The Wisdom of Conservative Judaism for Contemporary Jews

Hatznei·a Lekhet Im Elohekha

Walking Humbly with God

. . . what does the Eternal require of you if not to love mercy,
to do justice, and to walk humbly with your God?

(Micah 6:8)

When the ancient prophet Micah declared that what God wants of Israel is that Jewish people walk humbly with God, that they ever strive to behave toward each other justly and with equity and fairness, and that they devote themselves passionately to the propagation of deeds of mercy and kindness in the world, he did not continue on to say exactly which commandments of the Torah he had in mind for which category. Nevertheless, and taking the prophet at his (implied) word that all the commandments of the Torah will somehow fall into one of his three categories, this book is presented to the reading public in three parts, each named for one of the prophet's rubrics.

Under the category of walking humbly with God, the first section of this book presents the chapters that treat of the specific obligations the Torah teaches that Jewish people bear toward God, as well as those that consider the ways that faith itself will impact upon the lifestyles of the faithful. Included, of course, are the laws that govern the famous avenues of ritual expression known to all as hallmarks of Jewish life such as keeping the Sabbath and the dietary laws, the celebration of festivals, and the maintenance of an ongoing prayer life. But also included are chapters that may at first seem less clearly related to the relationship between a people and its God, but all of which, each in its own way, constitute the foundation stones upon which the edifice of traditional Jewish observance rests. Included here, for example, are the laws that govern Torah study, understood in this context not merely as an instructive exercise but actually as a form of communion with the Divine through the medium of the ruminative contemplation of sacred texts, as well as chapters discussing the *halakhah* as it applies to matters of personal integrity and to personal appearance and behavior, both of which categories have as their underlying principle the notion that the way we appear to others and the way we behave must always reflect the belief that we, like all humanity, are created in God's sacred image. And here too will readers find the laws that govern charitable giving and repentance, the two areas of traditional endeavor that, along with prayer, are said in the liturgy to be the most effective ways for individuals to seek God's favor for themselves or for their families. In its own category is the chapter on Israel, presented in this section not only because so much of modern Jewish life is reflective in one way or another of the ceremonial of the great Temple that stood in ancient Jerusalem and because *aliyah* is considered by many authorities to be a commandment in its own right, but also because devotion to the commandments that have to do with the Holy Land or with the Holy City has traditionally been taken to constitute a reliable way of deepening the bond between the Holy One of Israel and the nation called in Scripture both a kingdom of priests and a holy people. Taken as a unit, then, the chapters in this section coalesce as discussions of the various rituals, practices, and customs that have at their core the establishment of a relationship of intimacy and succor between members of the House of Israel and their God.

Prayer

KAREN G REISS MEDWED

The obligation to engage in daily prayer is one of Scripture's less well-defined commandments. In its rabbinic guise, however, it became a *mitzvah* to pray, using pre-selected texts, three times a day most days of the year and even more on certain special days. But prayer is not just focused talking. Indeed, the Talmud, at *BT* Ta·anit 2a, describes prayer as the "service of the heart," not merely because it is an example of exalted speech, but because tradition understands prayer to be as introspective an act as it is a communicative one.

T'fillah, Jewish prayer, is more than the sum of its parts and encompasses far more than just the obligation to recite certain specific prayers three or more times a day. Jewish prayer incorporates *b'rakhot,* benedictions, designed to sanctify, thus to grant a deep spiritual dimension, to experiences as diverse as eating a peach, smelling a rose, hearing a clap of thunder, and seeing a head of state. But *t'fillah* also incorporates spontaneous prayer, words we say when we find ourselves in moments of ill ease or worrisome need, or in moments of sublime gratitude. We pray as Jews to feel connected to our common history, to feel attached to Jews throughout the world, and to solidify our sense of belonging to our own communities. We pray as a people eager to communicate with God in the context of an ongoing covenantal relationship, but we also pray as individuals intent on establishing an intimate and wholly personal relationship with God.

The Goals and Functions of Prayer

T'fillah, the Hebrew word for prayer, comes from a three-letter root that expands in other contexts to yield a range of words mostly related to the concept of judgment. From this, we learn that, when we pray, we stand before God and before ourselves in judgment. *T'fillah*, however, is not a final verdict, but far more of a stopping-off point on the long journey toward deciding who we are and how we are living our lives, and how the answers to those questions correlate with our sense of God's will in both matters. *T'fillah* is a God-given moment to measure the lives we are living today and, if that measure comes up short, to use the inspiration that comes from feeling ourselves to be in the presence of God to envisage the lives we wish to be living tomorrow. *T'fillah* is our "time out," an opportunity that comes three times a day to breathe, to take stock, to pause, and to evaluate who and where we are. As we anchor our awareness of these moments in life itself, we develop a greater capacity to recognize the extraordinary within our ordinary lives, and we gain the concomitant ability to sanctify those lives as well.

Prayer as Petition and Praise

One of the ways that humans express need is through prayer. In our formal prayers, we have many different opportunities to petition God for things wanting or lacking from our personal lives or the lives of our communities. (Even though we recite our prayers as individuals, the prayers themselves are communal, their texts ordained by tradition and presented in a common prayerbook all worshipers use.) But prayer is not only petition. It also serves as a vehicle to assist worshipers in coming to recognize God's presence in their midst. In this sense, prayer is both the path to faith and a response to faith, both the spur to the great spiritual achievement of recognizing God's presence in the world and also a response to it. Through prayer, we come to believe in the cogency of faith, and, in turn, that belief helps us develop a humble appreciation of our place within creation.

When we stand in awe of God, we stand looking up to a powerful Being. There are, however, other times in our prayer lives during which we stand beside, not before, God, imbued with a sense of God as divine Friend and possessed of the conviction that God is not only governance and judgment, but also love. Indeed, among the special gifts of communal prayer is the insight that comes to those who participate in it regularly that the power of our love for God is inextricably bound up with our sense of ourselves as members of the people of God. This love, of course, is not unrequited, and the prayer service makes that point clearly, if subtly, to the worshiper every morning of the year: the blessing before the Sh'ma, the daily proclamation of divine unity, refers openly to God's deep love for Israel, but the paragraph that follows refers just as clearly to Israel's love for God. This mutual relationship of love goes far beyond awe or praise to encompass the deepest aspects of our covenantal relationship with God: reciprocity, mutuality, and a commonality of commitment within the context of abiding love and the deepest sense of shared destiny.

Prayer as an Expression of Anger

There are times in our lives when we feel God has let us down. And there are times when we are uncertain about the degree to which we trust in God or believe in God's essential beneficence. These are not instances of blasphemous outrage, but important admissions of how things occasionally are. And, indeed, one important function of prayer is precisely to allow the worshiper to speak to God openly about feelings of anger, disbelief, fear, and potentially crippling doubt. We can do this by "praying through" our own uncertainty, by continuing to recite familiar words precisely when the dissonance is so jarring as almost to be painful. Indeed, this is one of the reasons that the Torah presents prayer, at least partially, as obligation and commandment: one need not feel absurd reciting the Hallel, the liturgy of praise and celebration recited on holidays, merely because one is feeling blue or unable to perceive the beneficent hand of God in one's daily life at that particular moment. We may never walk away from prayer, but we may change the rhythm, the accent, or the punctuation marks we use while praying. And, indeed, the experience of raising one's voice slightly at the end of a requisite prayer as though nodding slightly to an unseen question mark—or pausing briefly to acknowledge an unprinted exclamation point—has its validity and meaning. Of course, we can also recite those psalms that are formally expressions of anger, distress, and disappointment. Praying is not numbly reciting other people's poems, but engaging in an intense spiritual exercise designed precisely to carry us just as safely through the difficult times in our lives as through the joyous moments.

Prayer as an Expression of Historical Awareness

Jewish prayer is also the context in which Jewish individuals are best able to reflect on the religious nature of their community. Indeed, the prayerbook, for all it is *about* the relationship of the worshiper and God, is also *about* the history of Israel. Worship is thus also an opportunity to step into the flowing stream of Jewish history and to take our places in the pageant of events stretching from hoariest antiquity to the present, and from the present into the distant future. Thus prayer is also a kind of reenactment of history and a rededication to its lessons. We recite the Song of the Sea from Exodus 15 during our early morning prayers, therefore, not out of some delusional fantasy that we are those people for whom the waters parted, but as a way of accepting our place in an ongoing sequence of historical events in which that instance of miraculous deliverance plays such a prominent role. Similarly, when we begin our Amidah prayer by acknowledging God not solely as our personal Redeemer, but specifically also as the Redeemer of the greatest heroes of biblical antiquity, we affirm our belief in the concept of a shared history and destiny with those figures from ancient times.

Theological Issues Regarding Prayer

By endorsing the use of set prayers in our service, are we *ipso facto* guaranteeing that some worshipers will be obliged to recite words they do not consider true or meaningful? This issue has troubled Jewish scholars for generations, but, in the end, it became the general consensus among scholars and authorities that the good that derives from fostering communal prayer far outweighs the problems it entails. And that must be our approach as well.

T'fillah is a difficult craft. It requires openness to change, sensitivity, creativity, and the ability to keep a well-established routine from becoming stale and stultifying. While Jewish prayer reflects our relationship with God, it is also about the world of relationships among humans and about the struggles of the spirit within one's self. In order to engage in Jewish prayer, therefore, it will sometimes be necessary to transcend one's assumptions about the literal meaning of a given text, and sometimes even to suspend our own theological assumptions and presuppositions. This may require searching for an alternate understanding of a text, altering the punctuation of a text slightly to transform its implied meaning, or, at times, simply sitting with a text and "praying through it" to allow its literal meaning to move through us and speak to us directly rather than through the filter of the critical intellect. Individuals at prayer with *siddurim*—prayerbooks—in their hands can think of themselves as actors working through a script as they strive to get "inside the head" of the person who authored the text, and to see the world from that person's perspective. There are times these attempts will bring us to a deeper understanding of the text, thus helping us come to believe in its core ideas. There are other times when the basic presuppositions of a text will be so unacceptable that the community itself will insist that the text be rewritten.

These issues are also part of the larger set of reasons that our tradition so valorizes prayer in the communal setting: so that sacred and ancient texts can be analyzed and evaluated, and then either be found reinterpretable or in need of casual or radical reediting.

Keva and Kavvanah

In *Pirkei Avot,* we read this lesson of Rabbi Shimon: "When you pray, do not make your prayers a set routine (Hebrew: *keva*), but offer them instead as pleas for mercy and grace before God" (*M* Avot 2:13). Because prayer is viewed as central to Jewish religious life, it cannot be dependent upon uncertainties of mood and spirit. As a result, Jewish ritual has established statutory prayers and a detailed schedule of times, seasons, and occasions when one should recite them. Within this formalized context, however, Jews are expected to pray with the highest level of *kavvanah,* that is to say, with the most powerfully focused spiritual intentionality. This intentionality is the personal touch brought to each prayer. It is the new meaning or the alternative emotional response to the ancient text that makes each prayer a private, idiosyncratic plea for God's mercy and love.

It is often the case that *keva* and *kavvanah* are thought of as polar opposites, such that achieving one almost by definition negates the ability to achieve the other. But the reality is quite different and our prayers are almost always a mixture of both *keva* and *kavvanah.* The goal, therefore, cannot be to embrace the one and eschew the other. Instead, the goal has to be to blend the two in each instance of heartfelt *t'fillah* in such a way that we utilize the familiarity of the oft-recited text as a spur to finding ever deeper layers of meaning in it. This heightened awareness of old and new intertwined in the ancient prayers of a modern worshiper is the great goal. It may not always be achieved, but it will always be worthy of the effort invested.

Nevertheless, it will always be more comfortable to recite one's prayers in a routine fashion, especially after one has memorized the words and can recite the prayers by rote. Obviously, this routine can be an essentially negative experience and it would be optimal to approach the text afresh with every single reading. That, of course, can only be the case once, so the next best thing is to exploit the routine of *t'fillah* so that the familiarity itself becomes a means of helping each individual move to a deeper level of spiritual life. The routine of *t'fillah* can and should serve to make the language and movement of the service familiar, and, in turn, this familiarity can allow the willing worshiper to access a better and ever deeper understanding of the concept of prayer itself.

Liturgical Change

Changes in liturgy are born out of changes in the theological and historical life of a people. These changes take place not in the personal liturgical life of the individual, but on the communal level as evolving theological ideas, ritual practices, or historical realities insinuate themselves into the consciousness of a people at prayer.

Although there have been changes over the years that have gained almost universal acceptance in every Jewish community, there are also instances of liturgical development that reflect the evolving theology of the Conservative movement specifically. Among the early morning benedictions, for example, there are blessings in which worshipers praise God, among many other things, for their freedom, their Jewishness, and their specific gender. Traditionally, the first two of these were formulated in the negative and thus God was thanked for not making the worshiper a heathen or a slave. The third had two formulations: a negative one for men, in which the male worshiper thanked God for not making him a woman, and a positive one for women, in which the female worshiper thanked God (if that is the right word in this context) for creating her "according to divine will." The history of these blessings is long and complex, but the prayerbooks of the Conservative movement have almost universally tried, at least somehow, to make these blessings sound less haughty and arrogant. In particular, the blessing in which male worshipers thank God for not making them women rankled and was simply omitted in some prayerbooks. In the *Sabbath and Festival Prayer Book,* edited by Rabbi Morris Silverman and published by the Rabbinical Assembly and the United Synagogue in 1946, the three blessings are presented in a positive guise and God is thanked by worshipers for making them free people, for making them Jews, and for making them in the divine image. This is an example of communal liturgical development at its most normative: a text is found wanting or even slightly offensive, a way is found to preserve the acceptable element without maintaining the unacceptable formulation, and the changed text is printed in a movement-wide prayerbook that then becomes the standard against which other texts are judged. Other liturgical changes that characterize Conservative movement prayerbooks have followed this pattern, at least for the most part.

It is also possible to see liturgical change in progress. Over the decades, it has become popular in some congregations to add references to the ancient matriarchs of Israel into the opening paragraph of the Amidah alongside the names of the patriarchs. Other congregations have rejected this innovation as faddish and unnecessary, however, and the published prayerbooks of the movement reflect this state of liturgical flux: the original edition of *Siddur Sim Shalom* (1985) had no reference to the matriarchs, but the second edition

(1998) included the option of including them (without, however, supplanting the original text that features only the names of Abraham, Isaac, and Jacob). Published by the Rabbinical Assembly in 2010, *Maḥzor Lev Shalem* was even more assertive in this regard. As the Conservative movement itself struggles with issues of gender identity in covenantal language, our liturgical publications reflect the different sides of the issue.

Does God Answer Prayer?

Louis Finkelstein used to say, "When I pray, I speak to God; when I study, God speaks to me." We hear from God through our participation in liturgical prayer, and also through the study of religious texts that constitute an integral part of Jewish liturgy. That is not to say that human beings cannot ask God specific questions and hope for equally specific answers. Still, our all-knowing God rarely deigns to share the outcome of the World Series with the faithful in advance! What seems more practical, then, is to look to God to answer our prayers by strengthening our faith, by granting us insight into the workings of the world, and by helping us find the resolve and the courage to live lives infused with the finest human values. And there will never be anything base about praying for guidance or patience, for wisdom or for strength. Abraham Joshua Heschel taught that prayer helps us to engage in what he called "radical amazement," that is, to reach out to the mysteries of life and, in so doing, to rediscover God in those mysteries.

In the end, *t'fillah* functions on the personal level as an affirmation of the private relationship of the pray-er with God, and on the national level as a daily reminder of the covenant between God and the Jewish people. Through our prayers we continually assert the reality of both aspects of any individual's relationship with God, the personal and the communal, and affirm and confirm the centrality of that multivalent relationship in our spiritual and ritual lives.

The Experience of Prayer

Public prayer is called *t'fillah b'tzibbur* in Hebrew. The rabbis of classical times clearly preferred public to private prayer, and, accordingly, they praised it very highly. They urged that a person should always seek to pray together with a congregation, but communal prayer can be a difficult mandate to fulfill. It requires being able to get to a prayer quorum at the appointed time, as well as having the time available to pause in one's daily routine for prayer. For moderns torn between work and home, adding the obligation to attend a prayer service at a given location and at a specific time can be very difficult.

It is for this reason that some Conservative synagogues find themselves unable to hold a daily *minyan* both mornings and evenings. This should not be seen as an exemption from the *mitzvah* of daily prayer. Rather, it should be viewed as a challenge to the community to rededicate itself to the values of daily *t'fillah b'tzibbur* with a *minyan*, and so to pursue prayer in the setting that the ancient sages considered by far the most optimal and potentially effective.

Communal Prayer

Although individuals surely may open their hearts to God in prayer according to the thrice-daily halakhic regimen, the ideal in Jewish tradition is to pray with a *minyan*, a quorum of ten Jewish adults. There are no specific requirements with respect to where this quorum may or may not convene. Traditionally, *minyanim* gather in synagogues to recite their prayers, but it is permitted to convene a *minyan* outside the sanctuaries of synagogues in any dignified setting as well. (Maimonides delineates the specific requirements with respect to the cleanliness of a prayer site at *MT* Hilkhot T'fillah U-n'si·at Kappayim 4:8–9.)

Historically, a *minyan* consisted of ten Jewish males aged thirteen or older. In 1973, however, the Committee on Jewish Law and Standards of the Rabbinical Assembly ruled that Jewish women could be counted in a *minyan*, and the decision to do so was left to individual congregations. In practice, although most congregations within the Conservative movement have adopted the policy of counting all adult Jews in the *minyan*, there are also those that have not.

Some congregations fall back on different customs to create some kind of a *minyan* even in the absence of ten adults. Thus, there are congregations that will count one child among the worshipers (if that child is holding a sacred book, usually a printed edition of the Torah, popularly called a *ḥumash*) to consider the quorum duly constituted and others that will open the Ark and count a Torah scroll, so to speak, among the worshipers. This practice is deemed acceptable by some communities in constrained situations (cf. the gloss of the Rema to *SA* Oraḥ Ḥayyim 55:4).

In more recent times, the concept of video or audio conferencing over the Internet or telephone lines has presented itself for halakhic consideration. The response of halakhic authorities has been a bit equivocal. For instance, the CJLS has ruled that an individual may participate in communal prayer over a two-way audio or video hook-up (for the purpose, for example, of that individual fulfilling his or her obligation to recite the Mourner's Kaddish), but that an individual connected to the rest of the worshipers solely by electronic means cannot be counted as part of the basic quorum. As our communities evolve into the future, questions of the precise relationship between prayer and technology will continue to be addressed.

A *minyan* is about more than joining together ten individual Jewish adults in prayer—it is about creating sacred space by creating sacred community. Thus, there are particular prayers, called collectively the *d'varim she-bi-k'dushah* (that is, "prayers of special sanctity") that can only be recited in the presence of a *minyan.* Among these are the Kaddish (whether being recited as part of the service or by mourners), the Bar'khu call to prayer, and the K'dushah (but only the version inserted into the repetition of the Amidah). Also, the Torah is only read in public from the Torah scroll in the presence of a *minyan.*

Requiring a *minyan* for those parts of our service that cannot be recited by individuals reinforces the notion that the Jew at prayer is bound to history, to Jews across the world, and to tradition itself. Prayers can be said alone, but we raise our own level of potential sanctification when we join a community. This is why Jewish prayers are written predominantly in the plural, even when it was necessary to alter the biblical verse from which a given turn of phrase originated.

What of the pray-er filled with the creative urge to address God in idiosyncratic, wholly personal prayer? For most, the very concept of liturgy connotes a set text with standardized language and prescribed movements. But there is always room, even within formal worship, for spontaneous prayer. Spontaneous prayer is usually spoken as a reaction to, or in anticipation of, a specific event and allows an individual to address his or her particular spiritual needs in the context of prayer. It is a noble, well-trod avenue of self-expression and spontaneous, creative prayer is thus neither forbidden nor restricted by tradition.

Finally, the public prayer service also provides opportunities for Torah study. The early part of the weekday Morning Service, for example, calls upon worshipers to recite the blessing for study of Torah, and then to follow it with the recitation of three passages (one each from the Bible, the Mishnah, and the Talmud) that are deemed emblematic of the larger enterprise of Torah study. Also, a weekly portion of the Torah is read aloud on Shabbat morning in synagogue, and part of the next weekly Torah portion to be read in its entirety is read aloud following the Amidah on Saturday afternoon and then again on Monday and Thursday morning, and this too, obviously, should be considered an opportunity for Torah study.

Physical Prayer

One aspect of prayer that tends to mystify the uninitiated has to do with the physical nature of public prayer in the synagogue. Swaying, standing, sitting, pointing, turning to the right or to the left (or turning around entirely), walking down stairs backwards, stepping forward and stepping backwards—all of these are parts of the way prayer is orchestrated in traditional Jewish settings. However, since these instructions rarely appear written out in prayerbooks to guide worshipers in knowing what to do and when to do it, these gestures generally end up as the province solely of the priorly initiated. Here, I discuss some of the most prominent of these gestures for the edification of the uninitiated worshiper.

The most characteristic way to move during prayer is to sway gently back and forth. Generally referred to by English-speaking Jews as *shuckling* (an anglicized version of the Yiddish word with the same meaning), this movement is a physical way of putting ourselves "in the moment." Putting the whole body to work in prayer helps us attain a greater level of focused intention during our *t'fillah*. Indeed, by involving our entire bodies and not just our mouths in prayer, we respond to the psalmist's ancient injunction that all one's bones together should praise God, not merely one's vocal cords (Psalm 35:10).

The swaying also has another purpose: it puts us in touch with the ebb and flow of the liturgy itself. The rhythm and the motion might feel strange at first to the neophyte, but one of the secrets of learning how to pray involves finding one's personal pace at prayer, and the gentle swaying of the body allows us to find that rhythm as we measure the ease of our involvement in the larger enterprise by noting the degree to which our bodies are tense or relaxed during prayer.

Another hallmark of the prayer service is the practice of standing during certain prayers. During our weekday prayers we stand for the morning blessings, for the opening prayer in the P'sukei D'zimra section of the liturgy, from just before introductory passages leading into the Song of the Sea through the Bar'khu call to prayer that formally begins the Morning Service, from the Tzur Yisra·el blessing that leads directly into the Amidah through the end of the silent recitation of that prayer, for the K'dushah insertion in the prayer leader's repetition of the Amidah, when the Ark is opened to take the Torah out and then again to return it, and at the end of the service for Aleinu. When Hallel is recited, we also rise for that litany of praise. I shall return below to the quite varied customs related to standing up for Kaddish below.

It is also customary to bow from the waist at certain moments during the service. We bow, for example, at the beginning and end of the first and penultimate benedictions of the Amidah and during Aleinu. The rule of thumb is that, whenever we have bowed down out of reverence for God, we always stand erect upon the subsequent recitation of God's name.

Prayer is movement as well as language in Judaism and certain specific gestures and movements are ordained for the individual at prayer.

As noted, there are four places during the recitation of the Amidah when worshipers must bow from the waist: at the beginning and end of the opening blessing, called Avot, and at the beginning and end of the penultimate blessing, called Hoda·ah. One should bend the knee at the word *barukh,* bow down while saying *attah,* and return to the upright position before uttering the name of God (*SA* Oraḥ Ḥayyim 113:7). However, at the word *modim* one simply bows at the waist without bending the knee. The image suggested by this choreography is that of a sovereign being approached by a respectful subject. Although the concept of God as an absolute monarch will inevitably strike moderns used to republican forms of government as archaic, the model is more antique than obsolete: although there are indeed contexts in which tradition urges us to think of ourselves as partners of the Almighty, we are bidden to approach God in prayer precisely as would the subjects of an all-powerful monarch, and that is the imagery invoked by the obligation to bow during the Amidah.

As another nod to the concept of God as divine Sovereign, worshipers prepare to recite the Amidah by taking three steps backwards, then three steps forward, while reciting the six Hebrew words of Psalm 51:17 ("Adonai, open my lips that I may proclaim the praises due You"). The imagery here is rooted in an amalgam of related notions. We step back in worried awe as we contemplate the prospect of standing in prayer before the divine throne. However, Adonai is not only Sovereign God, but Friend God as well, and so, encouraged by the gently attentive nature of God's listening presence, we step forward again and only then begin to pray.

Throughout the Amidah, one should stand with one's feet together and one's eyes cast downward (*MT* Hilkhot T'fillah U-n'si·at Kappayim 5:4).

The Amidah concludes with a closing prayer originally composed in ancient times by Mar, son of Ravina (*BT* B'rakhot 17a). When reciting the last words of this prayer, *oseh shalom bi-m'romav hu ya·aseh shalom aleinu ve'al kol yisra·el ve'imru amein,* worshipers take three steps backwards, then bow to the left, to the right, and forward, and then return to their original position by taking three steps forward. This allows worshipers to conclude their prayers in the same manner in which they entered into them, and the parallel rhythm adds a dimension of order to the prayers.

Jewish worship is not solely language, but rather a kind of mixed theatric of spoken language, symbolic body language, and concentrated thought. Some other orchestrated moves during the Amidah are as follows:

- During the K'dushah, when the prayer leader intones the words *zeh el zeh* to make reference to the angels turning "this way and that" as they recite the heavenly liturgy on high, it is customary to bow to the left, then to the right in imitation of the heavenly minions at prayer.

- During the K'dushah, when Isaiah 6:3 is cited, it is customary to rise up on the balls of one's feet three times, once on each recitation of the word *kadosh*. With this theatrical gesture, we indicate our wish to attain the sanctity of the angels at prayer as we recite our earthly liturgy.
- During the repetition of the Amidah, when the prayer leader reaches the penultimate benediction, Hoda·ah, worshipers all bow slightly while still seated, and only then proceed to recite the text of the so-called "Rabbis' Modim" prayer, which is recited by worshipers quietly as the prayer leader repeats the full text of the Hoda·ah benediction.
- Finally, when the prayer leader repeating the Amidah reaches the three-part priestly benediction (which is inserted into the Amidah between the penultimate and final blessings when the Amidah is repeated aloud during the Shaḥarit and Musaf Services, as well as during the Afternoon Service on fast days), the leader bows to the left at the first line, to the right at the second line, and toward the front at the third.

Jerusalem

It is required that we face toward Jerusalem, and specifically toward the site of the ancient Temple there, when we say our prayers. According to Maimonides (*MT* Hilkhot T'fillah U-n'si·at Kappayim 5:3), there is a very specific order we follow in this regard: Jews outside of Israel face toward the Holy Land when they pray, Jews in Israel face toward Jerusalem, and Jews actually in Jerusalem face toward the Temple Mount. In a situation in which it is not possible to determine which direction is which, it is sufficient to imagine ourselves turning toward the Holy City and, in so doing, mentally and emotionally to come into the domain of God's holy presence on earth.

The veneration of Israel as the Holy Land is a central tenet of the Jewish religious experience; facing toward Israel in prayer is thus a way of physically demonstrating our commitment to the Land of Israel.

Sacred Space

It is possible to pray at any time and in any dignified place. And, indeed, both theology and logic tell us that it makes no sense to imagine that God only dwells within grand sanctuaries filled with expensive furnishings. Nonetheless, the *halakhah* demands that we invoke God's name in prayer only in settings that, though they may be simple and plain, are worthy that the sacred enterprise of public or private prayer take place there. And, indeed, there should be a degree of decorum as well in any space where liturgical language is invoked, not solely out of respect for God, but also as an assertion of the respect we feel for ourselves and our lives as servants and worshipers of God. Therefore, one should not pray in the vicinity of garbage, nor should one's place of prayer be in close proximity to a privy or even to an unoccupied toilet. According to the *Shulḥan Arukh,* "One should not pray in a place that will destroy concentration" (*SA* Oraḥ Ḥayyim 98:2). Maimonides even goes so far as to ordain that one should not even conduct business in a place generally used for prayer, lest profane transactions hinder worshipers' ability truly to think of that locale as sacred space (*MT* Hilkhot T'fillah U-n'si·at Kappayim 11:6–7).

Although we have the right to pray anywhere and at any time, as religious individuals we also desire to create aesthetically pleasing spaces for prayer. Therefore, inappropriate ostentation is often eschewed in favor of a simple dignity regarding architecture and adornments.

The physical structure of a synagogue is just one aspect of its service as sacred space. A synagogue with a sanctuary brings with it the presence of a congregation, the presence of community, and as such the opportunity to recite communal prayers that one may not say when praying alone. Furthermore, prayer is enhanced when praying with a congregation.

What makes a synagogue sacred is more than the elaborate design or the number of Torah scrolls in its Holy Ark. A synagogue is sacred space when it is full of a congregation of loving and compassionate Jews who live their lives with devotion to the ideals of the Torah. They create a space where communal prayer is devotional and spiritual, where one can experience God amidst the people.

The Times for Prayer

As noted, there are three prescribed times of day for Jewish prayer: morning, afternoon, and evening. One *midrash* preserved in the Talmud (at *BT* B'rakhot 26b) explains that the obligation to pray three times a day was instituted in honor of our three patriarchs, each of whom inaugurated his own prayer service: Abraham was moved to pray to God while gazing out at the ruins of Sodom in the morning, Isaac prayed out in the field upon noticing Rebecca's approach in the afternoon light, and Jacob prayed at nightfall when he lay down to sleep on the ground at the place later to be called Bethel. So, too, when we say our prayers, we hope that we can achieve the deep intentional focus attained by our ancestors during their different moments of needful supplication.

When do these specific prayer periods fall? The talmudic system supposes that the time between dawn and dusk is to be divided into twelve seasonal "hours." (Unlike fixed, sixty-minute hours, these seasonal "hours" vary in length throughout the year depending on how much time there actually is between sunrise and sunset.) According to this system, the period during which the morning Sh'ma may be recited begins at sunrise and continues to the end of the third hour—that is to say, the first quarter of the day. The morning Amidah, however, may be recited until the end of the fourth hour—that is, the first third of the day. The afternoon Amidah may be recited after the onset of the first half of the seventh hour of the day. Opinions differ on how late in the day one may recite this afternoon Amidah, but the prevalent custom in Conservative synagogues is to recite it until sundown. The Evening Amidah may be recited throughout the night, beginning at sundown. If it is unlikely that a *minyan* will gather after nightfall, however, the Evening Amidah may be recited even earlier than sundown, as long as the Sh'ma is repeated later in the night.

The *halakhah* requires that a Jew pray three times a day, every day. However, it is inevitable that there will be times in every person's life when it will simply be impossible to fulfill this obligation. It is for that reason that the *halakhah,* not begrudgingly but realistically, sets some minimal standards for daily prayer. (These are not intended to provide a less arduous alternative to fulfilling the *mitzvah* in its fullest detail, merely to nod to the exigencies of daily life.) For example, it is permissible to scale the Morning Service back to its barest minimum by reciting the morning blessings, the Barukh She-amar prayer that introduces the P'sukei D'zimra section of the liturgy, Ashrei, Psalms 148 and 150, the Yishtabbaḥ prayer that closes P'sukei D'zimra, and then proceeding with the Sh'ma and its opening and closing benedictions, the Amidah, and the Aleinu hymn. (This abridgement is based on *SA* Oraḥ Ḥayyim 52.)

For those mornings when time is so limited as practically to preclude the possibility of reciting the full Amidah, there is also a shortened version of the Amidah, called Havineinu, that can be recited. This version incorporates the first three blessings of the standard Amidah, an abbreviated version of the intermediary thirteen blessings, and the full version of the three concluding blessings. It is not permitted, however, to recite Havineinu during the months of the rainy season in Israel, when Jews worldwide include a prayer for rain in the Amidah, nor may one use the Havineinu option during the Evening Service following Shabbat or festivals (*SA* Oraḥ Ḥayyim 110:1).

The Afternoon and Evening Services, being so brief, may only be abbreviated by reciting the shorter version of the Amidah instead of the longer one. The restrictions mentioned above still apply, however.

The halakhic sources also consider the issue of one who simply arrives in synagogue late in the service and is unsure what to omit in order to catch up to the rest of the community.

During the Morning or Afternoon Service, the rules are similar. If one comes in and finds the community at prayer, one must estimate whether or not one will be able to begin and end the Amidah before the prayer leader is ready to recite the K'dushah. If one can, then one should immediately begin the Amidah. If not, one should wait until the prayer leader begins to repeat the Amidah, and then recite the prayer quietly, word for word, until the K'dushah. After joining in the K'dushah, one should finish one's prayers quietly. In the morning, one then recites the Sh'ma. If one errs in one's estimation and, after beginning to recite the Amidah, then realizes the prayer leader will come to the K'dushah while one is still in the middle of one's prayers, one should not participate in the K'dushah but should rather continue with one's private recitation of the Amidah. One should also not interrupt one's prayers to respond to the prayer leader during Kaddish (*MT* Hilkhot T'fillah U-n'si·at Kappayim 10:16; cf. *SA* Oraḥ Ḥayyim 109:1–2).

Upon entering the synagogue to recite the Evening Service and finding that the congregation has already recited the Sh'ma, one should join the congregation in the Amidah and then recite the Sh'ma with its blessings afterward (*SA* Oraḥ Ḥayyim 236:3).

The basic rule of thumb is that when one arrives at synagogue at a point when one can join the communal prayer in a section that cannot be recited by an individual, one participates in the communal prayer first, and then returns to catch up on those prayers that an individual can recite without a *minyan*. This emphasizes the centrality of community in Jewish prayer without depriving the individual of the opportunity to recite his or her prayers fully.

Prayer Leaders

In the Jewish liturgical setting, an individual is designated to lead the prayer service. If this individual is a trained musical professional, the term "cantor" (*ḥazzan* in Hebrew) is used. If the individual in question is qualified to lead the service but lacks formal cantorial education and investiture, the terms *ba·al t'fillah* (prayer leader) or *sh'li·aḥ tzibbur* (representative of the congregation) are used. (The acronym *shatz* [pronounced "shots"] is also used, derived from the initial letters of the words *sh'li·aḥ tzibbur*.) The feminine forms are *ba·alat t'fillah* and *sh'liḥat tzibbur*.

Generally speaking, the title "cantor" in the Conservative movement is reserved for individuals affiliated with a professional cantorial organization, either the movement's own Cantors Assembly or another. Although a cantor always retains a certain degree of personal and professional autonomy, affiliation with a professional organization implies that the clergy in question must maintain the standards of observance and policies required by that organization. Members of the Cantors Assembly, for example, are free to counsel and to reach out to interfaith couples. They are, however, formally forbidden from officiating at interfaith wedding ceremonies, just as are members of the Rabbinical Assembly.

The individual honored to lead the congregation in prayer, whether professional cantor or lay *shatz,* must be skilled in singing and well-versed in Torah learning. That individual must also have fine moral character and exemplify the highest standards of ethical behavior.

These attributes, prescribed in the Talmud at *BT* Ta·anit 16a, can and ought to serve us well in assigning the role of *shatz* in our communities. In Solomon Schechter schools and at Ramah camps, for example, the process of defining the standards of moral character and ethical behavior requisite to lead the community in prayer should be pursued as an important educational imperative in its own right.

Any discussion of the role of cantor or *shatz* must also include some reference to the issue of *nusaḥ*. Music and chanting have always been part of the Jewish liturgical tradition. Indeed, the psalms were early songs of prayer to God. The Torah itself has always been chanted according to a special and precise cantillation system, not merely declaimed aloud. And the prayer service too is characterized by special melodies and musical modes deemed appropriate for specific parts of the service. The term *nusaḥ* refers to musical modes that may change according to the hour of the day, the time of the year, and the specific part of the service being chanted. Trained cantors help educate a community in the use of proper *nusaḥ* for different liturgical settings and moments. They also enhance the service by knowing when and how to introduce congregational melodies or cantorial set pieces that are well suited to the particular *nusaḥ* of a given service. Existing at the confluence of law and custom, *nusaḥ* sets the tone for traditional worship and should be considered an indispensable part of the service.

The Language of Prayer

Jews are permitted to pray in any language, but the *halakhah* requires the same precision and concern to be used when praying in any language as would be requisite in Hebrew (see, e.g., Maimonides' comments at *MT* Hilkhot K'ri·at Sh'ma 2:10 and Hilkhot B'rakhot 1:6). Nonetheless, Conservative movement prayerbooks, rooted in the belief that the Hebrew language captures particular religious and cultural values and meanings that cannot adequately be transmitted in translation, contain the entire service in Hebrew. For example, the Hebrew word *tz'dakah* is not truly captured by the English "charity," nor is *t'shuvah* exactly the same as "repentance." With the emergence of the State of Israel and the revival of the Hebrew language, there is an added importance to communal *t'fillah* in Hebrew. The language of our liturgy is thus also a link to Jews in Israel and around the world.

The Prayerbook

The Hebrew word for prayerbook, *siddur,* derives from the same Hebrew root that, in other contexts, generates words related to order and organization. The *siddur* is thus best understood not as a formal literary work composed at a specific moment in history, but rather as the organization of our formalized and codified liturgy as it has evolved to our own era. It is a good name for another reason as well: this book that organizes our liturgy also organizes our day.

The codified liturgy varies from community to community. Still, it is remarkable how similar a service from one tradition is to another—to *all* others—and so much so that it is usually easy to recognize the same core elements in any Jewish prayer service regardless of one's particular background.

The current *siddur* used by most Conservative synagogues, and recognized by the umbrella organizations of the Conservative movement, is the second edition of *Siddur Sim Shalom.* This *siddur* contains in it the liturgical changes that reflect the theological underpinnings of Conservative Judaism. There are other *siddurim,* as well, each created and edited for some specific Conservative synagogue or educational setting (such as Camp Ramah and the Solomon Schechter schools). The text used in these *siddurim* and the commentaries included are the key elements that allow these books to stake their claim to a place within the liturgical tradition of the Conservative movement.

Appropriate Dress for Prayer

In the *Mishneh Torah,* Maimonides (at *MT* Hilkhot T'fillah U-n'si·at Kappayim 5:5) presents a detailed exposition of the way individuals should dress when preparing to stand before God in prayer. There, Maimonides suggests that the appropriateness of specific items of clothing depends on the customs that prevail in a given societal setting—he notes, for example, that one may not recite one's prayers while wearing short pants in a place in which adult men do not normally appear in public other than wearing long pants—and that is the rule we follow today as well. Although the norm is to define appropriate clothing in terms of taste and issues of modesty, the issue will always turn on the customs of a particular culture.

What that means practically is that the matter must always be viewed in context. Shabbat attire should differ from weekday attire. The right way to dress in an urban setting will not be the same as at summer camp. There are also, however, invariable standards not deemed dependent on context: one must always take care to be dressed cleanly and neatly, one may never wear clothing that could conceivably offend other worshipers, and the body should not be exposed during prayer in a lascivious or suggestive way.

The Kippah

Although, strictly speaking, not halakhically required, the general practice among Jews for many centuries has been for men to keep their heads covered during prayer, at mealtime, and during study out of a sense of reverence for God. There have also always been Jews who have kept their heads covered at all times. Within the Conservative Jewish world, there are those who wear a hat, usually a skullcap (popularly called a *kippah* or a *yarmulke*), at all times, and there are those who limit their wearing of a *kippah* to spiritually charged moments like prayer or study. Although married women have traditionally kept their hair covered out of a sense of modesty and unmarried women did not cover their hair at all, the modern practice among Conservative Jews is not to distinguish between married and unmarried women. There is, however, a wide range of specific customs related to the issue of covering the head, among which the central and most widely observed ones are the practice of covering the head when in the sanctuary of a synagogue, when engaged in prayer or Jewish study, when performing a *mitzvah,* and when eating. There are also those who cover their heads when entering a synagogue building for any reason at all.

Wearing a *kippah* is a tradition sanctified by long generations of practice, not an actual *mitzvah* of the Torah. Therefore, there is no blessing to recite when donning a *kippah* analogous to the one recited when donning the *tallit.* Nonetheless, many Jews today feel that the tradition of wearing a *kippah* has acquired quasi-legal status and should therefore be treated as an unofficial *mitzvah.* Within the Conservative movement, the Solomon Schechter schools, Camp Ramah, and the United Synagogue Youth movement all mandate the wearing of a *kippah* during ritual activity, including prayer, because doing so instills reverence for God and strengthens one's sense of connectedness to the Jewish people. The question of covering one's head is discussed elsewhere in this volume by Rabbi Gordon Tucker in his chapter on public appearance and behavior.

The Tallit

The Torah commands the faithful to put fringes on the corners of their garments in the Book of Numbers: "They shall put tassels on the corners of their garments in every generation" (Numbers 15:38). These tassels, collectively called by the name *tzitziyyot* in Hebrew, are explicitly intended to serve as a reminder of God's commandments. (The singular version of the word, *tzitzit,* is in much more common use, however.)

Since ancient times, Jews have tried to explain their symbolism. Rashi, for example, in his comment to Numbers 15:41 (*s.v. p'til t'kheilet*), says that the eight strands of the *tzitzit* correspond to the eight days that elapsed between the day that the Israelites offered up the paschal sacrifice that set the stage for their journey out from Egypt and the day they crossed the Sea of Reeds. The five knots, corresponding to the Five Books of Moses, serve to remind us to fulfill the commandments of the Torah. Together, then, the *tzitzit* serve to remind us that God is the Redeemer of Israel, and that, just as God redeemed our ancestors from Egypt and at the Sea of Reeds, so too will God continue to protect and redeem the Jewish people in every generation.

In ancient times, garments with four corners that were worn during the day had *tzitzit* attached to their four corners, but today the faithful at prayer don a special four-cornered garment called a *tallit* that requires that *tzitzit* fringes be attached to it. Wearing a *tallit* during morning prayers thus provides us with an opportunity to reflect on God's commandments in a tactile manner. There are also those who feel that the *tallit* is a Jewish prayer uniform of sorts, and that, as such, it provides worshipers with an opportunity to connect with members of the Jewish community across history and geography, thus providing a sense of universal Judaism within one's personal prayer space.

The laws that govern the use of the *tallit* are relatively straightforward. Before beginning morning prayers, one should put on the *tallit* and then don *t'fillin.* When putting on the *tallit,* one should hold it with both hands, then recite this blessing: *barukh attah adonai, eloheinu, melekh ha-olam, asher kidd'shanu b'mitzvotav v'tzivvanu l'hitatteif ba-tzitzit* ("Praised are You, Adonai, our God, Sovereign of the universe, who, sanctifying us with divine commandments, has commanded us to wrap ourselves in these *tzitzit*"). Then one should place the *tallit* around one's shoulders like a shawl. There are also those who put the *tallit* over their head first, and only then wrap it around the shoulders.

When wrapping oneself in a *tallit,* many reflect on the image in the Hashkiveinu prayer from the Evening Service in which we pray that God might spread over us a "*sukkah* of peace." When wrapping ourselves in the *tallit,* we can imagine God's wide embrace as we surrender to God's enveloping presence. This is an additional way to prepare for prayer.

The *tallit* is usually made of wool, silk, or cotton. The *tzitzit* on it must be made of the same material. However, it is possible to use woolen *tzitzit* on every *tallit,* regardless of its material (*MT* Hilkhot Tzitzit 3:5; gloss of the Rema to *SA* Oraḥ Ḥayyim 9:2).

In recent years, the *tallit* has become a personalized feature of American Jewish life. Many boys and girls create their own *tallitot* as a way of preparing for their bar or bat mitzvah. In other communities, families purchase a special *tallit* for each child at birth to be used at their naming ceremony and then again at their bar or bat mitzvah. Many *tallitot* are designed to reflect our integration of American and Jewish values, and are thus emblematic of the modern interest in personalizing symbols and rituals. One should be careful, however, that the design of a *tallit* respects the fact that its use constitutes the fulfillment of one of the sacred commandments of our faith and that it is not, therefore, designed or treated in a casual, vulgar, or disrespectful manner.

When making one's own *tallit,* one way to attach and tie the *tzitzit* is as follows. At each corner of the *tallit,* there should be a hole an inch or two from the edge. Four strands, three of equal length and a longer one, are brought through the hole and folded over in such a way so as to yield eight strands, of which one, dubbed the *shammash* (servant) is longer than the other seven. The two sets of four strands are now knotted together with a double knot, whereupon the *shammash* is wound seven times around the other seven threads. Another double knot is made, then the *shammash* is wound around the other strands eight times. Another double knot is made, and then the *shammash* is wound around the others eleven times. Another double knot is made, and then the *shammash* is wound around the others thirteen times. Lastly, a final double knot is made.

The number of knots tied for all four *tzitzit* specifically stand for the commandment "and you shall see them and remember all God's commandments" (Numbers 15:39). But how exactly do they accomplish that? The answer has to do with *g'matriyyah,* the art of midrashic commentary based on the numerical value of Hebrew letters. Using this system, the word *tzitzit* is deemed to have a numerical value of six hundred, which, together with the eight strands and five knots, yields a total of 613, the number of *mitzvot* in the Torah. Thus, one can, at least theoretically, look at the *tzitzit* and be reminded of the 613 commandments.

Although there are statements here and there in rabbinic literature that wonder about the appropriateness of women wearing *tallitot,* historically it was only male Jews who wore the *tallit* during prayer. As Conservative Judaism attempts to integrate modern values with Jewish practice, however, egalitarian ritual practices have been adopted and those that were not customary but not formally forbidden were the first and simplest to gain acceptance. Today, Jewish women regularly wear *tallitot* in Conservative synagogues, and female clergy generally wear a *tallit* as part of daily morning worship. Although it is the custom in many communities for men to begin wearing a large *tallit* during prayer only after marriage, this is rarely the practice in Conservative congregations. Instead, in most Conservative synagogues children of the age of bat/bar mitzvah begin to wear a *tallit.*

Except on the eve of Yom Kippur and during the Afternoon Service on the Ninth of Av, the *tallit* is generally donned only during morning prayers by regular worshipers. (The prayer leader, however, may wear a *tallit* at other times as well.) Some Jews wear a *tallit katan* (small *tallit*), also known as *arba kanfot* (four corners), under (or even, sometimes, over) their garments. This enables such individuals to see, thus to be conscious of, their *tzitzit* all day long, and so to be constantly reminded of the *mitzvot.*

T'fillin

T'fillin, occasionally called "phylacteries" in older English prose, consist of two black boxes provided with leather straps to hold them in place. Each of these boxes contains pieces of parchment on which are written out the passages of the Torah in which the *mitzvah* of donning *t'fillin* is mentioned: Exodus 13:1–10 and 13:11–16, and Deuteronomy 6:4–9 and 11:13–21. The singular form of the word *t'fillin* is *t'fillah.* Thus, the box bound to the arm is called the *t'fillah shel yad* (the *t'fillah* for the arm) and the other is called the *t'fillah shel rosh* (the *t'fillah* for the head). The *t'fillah shel yad* (sometimes called simply the *shel yad*) has one single piece of rolled parchment containing all four passages on it inside, but the *t'fillah shel rosh* (sometimes called simply the *shel rosh*) has four separate folded pieces of parchment in four separate compartments inside. The divisions between these compartments are visible from the outside of the box as well, thus offering a simple way to tell the *shel yad* from the *shel rosh,* especially if the straps are not present.

By placing the *t'fillin* on the arm and around the head, we are effectively binding our hearts and our minds to God as we pray. This act of physically binding God's word to our heads and arms is meant to suggest several deep truths: that worship cannot be done solely intellectually, that the mere will to serve God is not the equivalent of actually serving God, and that even the saintly individual needs a physical daily reminder to walk in God's ways and not to fall prey to base inclinations to sin. Also, the passages inside the *t'fillin* direct our thoughts toward the concept of God in history, reminding us that it was the Almighty who redeemed our ancestors from slavery in Egypt and who chose to give us the Torah and the commandments. *T'fillin* thus also serve as a powerful physical/tactile reminder of the freedom each of us enjoys as a child of God, and also of the choice we make to affirm the covenantal relationship with God which our ancestors established at Sinai when they declared their personal willingness to obey the laws of the Torah as their part of the covenantal bargain.

During morning prayers, the *t'fillin* should be put on immediately after the *tallit* is donned (*SA* Oraḥ Ḥayyim 25:1, and cf. the gloss of the Rema *ad loc.*). The *shel yad* is put on the weaker of the two arms. For most people, this means that the *shel yad* should be placed on the left arm, but those who are wholly left-handed should place the *shel yad* on the right arm. Ambidextrous individuals, or individuals who only favor their left arms under certain specific circumstances, should put the *shel yad* on their left arms. If a person suffers from a long-term injury to the arm that is usually favored, then that person would change the arm on which the *shel yad* is placed as well. In cases of uncertainty, a rabbi's opinion should be sought.

The *shel yad* is donned first by placing the box over the bicep on the upper arm with the knot facing in toward the heart. Before tightening the strap one should recite the blessing: *barukh attah adonai, eloheinu, melekh ha-olam, asher kidd'shanu b'mitzvotav v'tzivvanu l'hani·aḥ t'fillin* ("Praised are You, Adonai, our God, Sovereign of the universe, who, sanctifying us with divine commandments, has commanded us to put on *t'fillin*"). Then one should tighten the strap and wrap it around the arm seven times between the elbow and the wrist. While this is done, the familiar verse "You open Your hand and Your favor sustains all the living" (Psalm 145:16) may be recited to help count the seven turns of the strap without actually numbering them aloud, a practice traditionally deemed dangerous. (The verse has exactly seven words only in Hebrew, however.) Others recite the names of the patriarchs and matriarchs of ancient Israel: Abraham, Sarah, Isaac, Rebecca, Jacob, Rachel, and Leah. There are different customs regarding the direction, clockwise or counterclockwise, in which the straps are wrapped. Worshipers donning *t'fillin* for the first time who have no specific family tradition on which to rely should consult a rabbi regarding the custom that prevails in their congregation.

Following this, the *shel rosh* is placed over the head, so that the knot rests on the base of the skull and the box is just on the hairline. When this is being accomplished, but before the *shel rosh* is actually set in its correct spot, the worshiper recites this blessing: *barukh attah adonai, eloheinu, melekh ha-olam, asher kidd'shanu b'mitzvotav v'tzivvanu al mitzvat t'fillin* ("Praised are You, Adonai, our God, Sovereign of the universe, who, sanctifying us with divine commandments, has commanded us regarding the commandment of *t'fillin*"). The blessing is then followed by the familiar declaration of divine sovereignty: *barukh sheim k'vod malkhuto le'olam va·ed* ("May the name of the glorious sovereignty of God forever be blessed").

After placing the *shel rosh* on the head, the worshiper returns to the *shel yad* to wrap its leather strap around the fingers as well. There are different methods of doing this, but the most prevalent in Conservative congregations is the one according to which the strap is wound around the middle finger, twice on the lower joint closest to the hand and once on the middle joint. While this is done, the verses are recited: "I will betroth you to Me forever. I will betroth you with righteousness, with justice, with love, and with compassion. I will betroth you to Me with faithfulness, and you shall love the Eternal" (Hosea 2:21–22). The remainder of the strap is then wrapped around the palm, forming the Hebrew letter *shin* on the back of the hand. This *shin* is generally understood as a reference to the divine name Shaddai, regularly translated as "the Almighty" in modern texts.

For many worshipers, reciting a verse that describes the relationship between God and Israel using the language of betrothal while wrapping the strap of the *shel yad* around one's hand reflects the loving and binding nature of the relationship between the Jewish people and God. According to this interpretation, the straps wrapped around the fingers suggest an elongated wedding band, and the seven wraps on the arm are deemed reminiscent of the seven blessings recited under the wedding canopy.

After worship, the *t'fillin* are removed in the reverse order from the way in which they were put on. One should stand while putting on and taking off *t'fillin*. This requirement may be set aside for handicapped individuals, however.

Should women don *t'fillin*? There is a talmudic reference (at *BT* Eiruvin 96a) to King Saul's daughter, Michal, wearing *t'fillin* and the sages of her day not objecting, and there is a widespread but unsubstantiated story about the daughters of Rashi wearing *t'fillin* that is often cited in the context of this issue. Nevertheless, it is certainly the case that historically only Jewish men wore *t'fillin*. In the Conservative movement today, however, rabbis, male and female, don *t'fillin* as part of their personal ritual observance, as do many lay women. And this is a development with ample halakhic precedent: although there were prominent naysayers, the dominant position among the classical halakhists, including such luminaries as the Rashba (Rabbi Solomon ben Aderet, 1235–1310), Rabbeinu Tam (1100–1171), and Rabbi Zeraḥiah Halevi (1125–1186), is that the law exempting women from wearing *t'fillin* neither bans them from doing so if they wish nor implies that women who do perform this *mitzvah* should not recite the appropriate blessings.

Weekday Prayers and Prayer Services

Perhaps the most daunting difficulty facing any newcomer to the world of formal worship is the service itself. Indeed, just being able to isolate the elements in each service, understand how they fit together, and remember which elements go with which service is beyond the capabilities of most casual worshipers who open a prayerbook and find themselves facing only an endless sea of words and repetitive paragraphs. This book being neither a prayerbook nor a prayer manual, I describe here only the largest building blocks that constitute the greater part of most services.

Before I turn to those building blocks themselves, it might be helpful to organize them in terms of the services in which they appear.

The Morning Service, called Shaḥarit, begins with a complex series of opening prayers and passages for devotional study that include, among many other things, the special blessings recited every morning as a series of set introductory benedictions. These blessings, called Birkhot Ha-shaḥar, are generally chanted aloud by the prayer leader. The introductory portion of the Morning Service concludes with the recitation of the thirtieth psalm and its attendant Mourner's Kaddish, then the service continues with a long series of psalms and other biblical texts collectively called P'sukei D'zimra (literally "Verses of Song"), after which the congregation is formally called to worship. The Kaddish itself is discussed in more detail below.

After this call to prayer, popularly known as the Bar'khu, the congregation recites the large-scale version of the Sh'ma, including its two long opening blessings, the three paragraphs of the Sh'ma itself, and a long closing benediction. The congregation then rises to recite the Amidah prayer, which is generally repeated aloud by the cantor or the individual leading the service. In the course of this repetition, the third blessing is expanded to include the K'dushah prayer, a litany of special sanctity that may only be recited in the presence of a prayer quorum. (In many congregations, the Amidah is sung aloud until the congregation is led in the K'dushah, after which worshipers conclude their prayers silently. The issues surrounding the choice between these versions of reciting the Amidah are discussed in more detail below.) This is then followed directly by private penitential prayers collectively called Taḥanun. Taḥanun, however, is recited on most days of the year, but not on days deemed even slightly joyous. A full list of the days of the year on which Taḥanun is not recited appears later in this chapter in a special section devoted to the Taḥanun section of the liturgy.

On Monday and Thursday mornings, the service continues with the formal chanting of the beginning of next full Torah portion to be read aloud as part of the regular calendar of readings. The service, including on days the Torah is not read, then concludes with Ashrei (the liturgical setting of Psalm 145), the twentieth psalm, a long miscellany of verses and other material called U-va L'tziyyon Go·eil, the Full Kaddish, the Aleinu hymn, the Mourner's Kaddish, and the so-called psalm of the day followed by another recitation of the Mourner's Kaddish.

The Afternoon Service, called Minḥah, is much shorter than the Morning Service and has no components that are not part of the Morning Service. The service consists, in fact, solely of five elements: Ashrei, a slightly different version of the Amidah than the one recited in the morning, a short version of Taḥanun, the closing Aleinu hymn, and the Mourner's Kaddish. In many congregations, the Amidah is repeated in full after it is recited silently. In others, only the opening blessings are recited aloud so that the congregation may be led in the K'dushah, after which worshipers continue reciting their prayers silently. It is not customary to wear a *tallit* or to don *t'fillin* during Minḥah.

The Evening Service, called Ma·ariv or Arvit, is slightly longer than the Afternoon Service. It begins with the Bar'khu call to prayer, then features the full Sh'ma with two introductory blessings, the three-paragraph Sh'ma and two concluding blessings, then features the third daily recitation of the Amidah, the Full Kaddish, the Aleinu hymn, and the Mourner's Kaddish. The Amidah is never repeated during the Evening Service.

Every day of the year, the Morning, Afternoon, and Evening Services follow some variation of the order of prayers outlined above. Thus, it is always possible for any Jew from any community to walk into a service in any other synagogue that maintains a traditional prayer service and be able to follow along and to participate fully.

What follows concerns principally the various weekday prayer services. The prayer services for Shabbat and festivals are discussed elsewhere in this volume.

The Morning Service

Modeh/Modah Ani

The first thing a person should do upon awakening in the morning is to recite the Modeh Ani prayer. The words *modeh ani* mean "I am grateful" or "I acknowledge" and the prayer goes on to specify that the waking individual both acknowledges and is grateful to God for the restoration of the soul following the dormancy of sleep. This statement of faith reasserts God's daily presence and compassion in our lives. (Women use the feminine form of the opening verb and say *modah ani.*)

The Modeh Ani was constructed specifically without mention of any of the names of God that one should not pronounce before washing one's hands. It is therefore a wholly appropriate prayer to recite upon waking as a way of creating a symmetry of faithful utterance on either side of sleep: the last words uttered at night and the first words uttered in the morning are thus words of praise to God. (The practice of reciting the Sh'ma at bedtime is discussed below.)

Birkhot Ha-shaḥar

The early morning benedictions, called Birkhot Ha-shaḥar in Hebrew, are a series of blessings that refer serially to those of God's gifts we acknowledge as we rise in the morning and prepare to begin the day. Once, it was customary to recite a benediction for each part of one's morning routine as each deed was accomplished: when washing one's hands, upon dressing for the day, upon putting on one's shoes, and so on. Maimonides (*MT* Hilkhot T'fillah U-n'si·at Kappayim 7:1–8) followed the lead of the Talmud and ordained that just such a procedure be followed and that the blessings be pronounced as they naturally devolve upon an individual. We follow the later codes, however, and include all the benedictions at the beginning of the Morning Service (*SA* Oraḥ Ḥayyim 46:1–2).

It is also customary to include a section of Torah study in the early part of the Morning Service and to follow it with the recitation of the Kaddish D'rabbanan, the Kaddish for teachers and students. Incorporating the study of Torah into the daily liturgy provides an opportunity to fulfill the commandment of daily study even when time is limited. This introductory section of the morning liturgy concludes with the thirtieth psalm, after which the Mourner's Kaddish is recited.

P'sukei D'zimra

Rabbi Simlai is quoted in the Talmud at *BT* B'rakhot 32a as saying that we should always recount the praises due God before we actually recite our prayers. This idea developed eventually into the practice of reciting a series of psalms, now called P'sukei D'zimra ("Verses of Song"), before the formal beginning of the service. This section of the service begins and ends with a blessing and comprises only miscellanies of biblical verses and full chapters of several psalms, including Psalms 100 and 145–150.

P'sukei D'zimra also includes a full liturgical rendition of the Song of the Sea (Exodus 15:1–18), presumably intended to serve as a reminder of the Exodus and as an acknowledgment of the miracle of ancient Israel's liberation from bondage.

The Song of the Sea celebrates the drowning of the Egyptians, but the point of its recitation is not to revel in the downfall of others, even oppressive others, but rather to recognize the role of the miraculous in the history of Israel and to glorify God's supreme rule over all nations.

The Sh'ma

The Sh'ma is not, strictly speaking, a prayer; it is the declaration of God's uniqueness and unity that the Torah commands us to declaim twice daily. Although Deuteronomy 6:4 is called the Sh'ma in our sources (as in *M* B'rakhot 1:1), the fuller rabbinic version comprises three distinct passages, all taken from the Bible: Deuteronomy 6:4–9, Deuteronomy 11:13–21, and Numbers 15:37–41. Together, these are called K'ri·at Sh'ma (the recitation of the Sh'ma) and it is in that full liturgical setting that the Sh'ma is read aloud as part of the synagogue service.

The recitation of the Sh'ma is preceded and followed by benedictions: two before and one after in the morning, and two before and two after in the evening.

The benedictions that surround the Sh'ma contain key theological ideas intended to supplement the ideas presented in K'ri·at Sh'ma. The first of the preceding blessings, for example, focuses on creation, the second on revelation, and the blessing that follows (which is the first of the blessings that follow the Sh'ma in the Evening Service) on redemption. This central confession of faith is thus presented aloud in the synagogue surrounded by the core beliefs of the Jewish people about their origins, their destiny, and their God.

When reaching the word *va-havi·einu* in the blessing before the Sh'ma, it is customary to gather the four *tzitzit* from the *tallit* in one's left hand. Then, as we begin to recite the final paragraph of the Sh'ma, which concerns the ritual donning of *tzitzit*, we switch the fringes to the right hand and, at the three mentions of the word *tzitzit*, kiss the *tzitzit* gathered together. We also kiss the *tzitzit* at the end of this paragraph, and then again when we say the words *la·ad kayyamet* in the paragraph following the Sh'ma, at which point we let go of the gathered *tzitzit*. Although this custom is not a universal one and there are halakhic authorities who object to it, it is very widespread and considered acceptable in almost all Conservative synagogues. Also, when the *t'fillin* are mentioned at the end of the first paragraph of the Sh'ma, it is customary to touch the boxes of the *t'fillin* with the right hand. This is done again in the second paragraph as well. We kiss the *tzitzit* and touch the *t'fillin* as a tactile reminder of our obligations to remain faithful to the *mitzvot* in our daily lives, and also as a sign of our love for the commandments.

After reciting the primary verse of the Sh'ma aloud, every individual recites the words *barukh sheim k'vod malkhuto le'olam va·ed* in a subdued voice or in an undertone. There are different explanations of this practice. In his work on the High Holy Day liturgy, *Justice and Mercy* (New York: Holt, Rinehart & Winston, 1963, pp. 72f.), Max Arzt suggested the simple explanation that the verse is recited in an undertone merely to underscore that it is a non-biblical passage interpolated into a section of biblical verses. Whatever its ultimate origin, however, this personal affirmation of faith in God's enduring sovereignty over the earth is an opportunity for the worshiper to personalize the proclamation of God's unity by speaking almost in the same breath in wholly human words not taken from Holy Writ.

When reciting one's prayers without a *minyan,* the Sh'ma is preceded by the three words *eil melekh ne·eman.* When reciting the Sh'ma as part of a formally led prayer service, these three words are left out (see the gloss of the Rema to *SA* Oraḥ Ḥayyim 61:3). The point is to keep the number of words in the greater Sh'ma constant at 248—the number of positive commandments and the number of separate limbs and organs the ancients counted in the human body—by compensating for the words the prayer leader chants aloud during public worship with a *minyan,* and also for the "amen" omitted when the prayer leaders does not recite aloud the blessing before the Sh'ma; the added phrase's initial letters in fact spell out the Hebrew word for "amen." Thus, this passage provides an individual the opportunity to affirm her or his own belief in the unity of God by introducing the Sh'ma with a special, subtle kind of amen.

There should not be any interruptions in the service from the start of the Bar'khu through the end of the Amidah, except in the context of communal singing and the response of "amen" to a benediction. Included in this category of forbidden interruption is any casual speech at all; other than in an extreme circumstance, worshipers should feel obliged to focus wholly on their prayers during the recitation, private or public, of the service. There is some slight halakhic leeway to utter a word of greeting to someone of stature or particular personal worth between the paragraphs of the Sh'ma, however (*SA* Oraḥ Ḥayyim 66:1).

At the end of the third paragraph of the Sh'ma, the prayer leader includes the word *emet* from the next paragraph. The Hebrew word *emet* means "truth" and so, by having the leader finish with that single word, we affirm our sense that the unity of God is utterly true, not merely theologically, metaphorically, or symbolically so. The paragraphs of the Sh'ma illustrate God's vast role in our lives. By concluding the Sh'ma with the word for "truth," we publicly commit ourselves to doing the best we can to uncover the slivers of truth that glimmer through the obfuscating details of daily life and that emerge nonetheless from the focused, completely engaged effort to proclaim daily our belief in the unity and uniqueness of God.

In the mornings, the Sh'ma is followed by a single benediction that ends with a formula praising God as the Redeemer of Israel. It is universally agreed by the sources (e.g., *BT* B'rakhot 4b, 9b, and 30a; *MT* Hilkhot T'fillah U-n'si·at Kappayim 7:17; *SA* Oraḥ Ḥayyim 66:8) that one must proceed directly from this blessing to the recitation of the Amidah, a liturgical procedure called "adjoining [the blessing of] redemption to [the recitation of] prayer." To eliminate the requirement even to respond "amen" to the prayer leader's blessing, there grew up a very widespread custom for the prayer leader to recite the final words of the blessing, *ga·al yisra·el,* in an undertone (or even almost silently) so that those present would be freed from the normal obligation of responding to it and thus be able to go from their own recitation of the blessing directly into the Amidah. In approving a 2003 responsum by Rabbi Robert Harris, the CJLS agreed that this custom may be regarded as optional and that if the prayer leader does recite the end of the blessing aloud, the congregation may respond "amen" in the normal way.

The Amidah

The Amidah is considered the central part of daily Jewish prayer. Indeed, when ancient sources mention the *t'fillah,* "prayer," with no further qualification, it is invariably the Amidah to which they refer. This prayer is actually a series of blessings, some shorter and some longer, the original weekday number of which gave this prayer its alternate name, the Sh'moneh Esreih, that is "The Eighteen [Blessings]." Even though a nineteenth blessing was added millennia ago, the name remains as it originally was, and it is this name that remains current in some segments of the Jewish world.

The Amidah is the central prayer text in the Morning, Afternoon, and Evening Services. Although it is the "set liturgy" *par excellence,* the Amidah designates particular places for personal petitions and devotions as well.

The prayers are divided into three sections devoted serially to praise, petition, and thanksgiving. The first three benedictions are more or less the same at every service throughout the year. The intermediate blessing or blessings, those between the first three and the last three, are different, however, and reflect the mood of the day on which that particular version of the prayer is being recited. The final three blessings are given over to different expressions of thanksgiving and, although slightly less invariable than the opening blessings, remain mostly constant throughout the year.

Our classical sources designate a name for each benediction based on its content.

1. Avot (Ancestors): an acknowledgment of God as the Author of history and destiny.
2. G'vurot (Divine Might): an acknowledgment of God as Redeemer and Author of life.
3. K'dushat Ha-sheim (Divine Holiness): an acknowledgment of God as the source of holiness in the world.
4. Binah (Understanding): a prayer for insight and wisdom.
5. T'shuvah (Repentance): a prayer for the strength to repent us of our sins and to return wholeheartedly to the service of God.
6. S'liḥah (Forgiveness): a prayer for forgiveness for sin.
7. Ge'ullah (Redemption): a prayer for the redemption of Israel.
8. R'fu·ah (Healing): a prayer for healing from illness.
9. Birkat Ha-shanim (Blessing for the Years): a prayer for good weather, for ample rainfall, and for divine beneficence in general.
10. Kibbutz Galuyyot (Ingathering of the Exiles): a prayer for the end of the exile.
11. Mishpat (Justice): a prayer for an effective, efficient, and fair justice system, and for the wellbeing of those who administer it.
12. Birkat Ha-minim (Against Apostates): an imprecation directed against those who pervert the message of Judaism by subverting it to their own ends, and against the wicked of this world in general.
13. Tzaddikim (The Righteous): a prayer for the righteous.
14. Y'rushalayim (Jerusalem): a prayer that God always show divine favor to the Holy City.
15. David (King David): a prayer that the messiah come speedily and within our time.
16. T'fillah (A Prayer for Prayer): a prayer that our prayers be acceptable and accepted.
17. Avodah (The Temple Service): a prayer that our worship be considered the

latter-day equivalent of the worship that took place in the Holy Temple in Jerusalem in ancient times.

18. Hoda·ah (Thanksgiving): an acknowledgment of the degree to which we must feel beholden to God for all that we are and for all that we possess.
19. Shalom (Peace): a prayer for peace.

A special liturgy of sanctification, called the K'dushah, is inserted into the third benediction of the Amidah in the Morning and Afternoon Services when the prayer leader repeats the Amidah aloud, but not when worshipers recite the prayer silently. There are, however, different methods of reciting the K'dushah and these vary from congregation to congregation based on local custom and the specific pace of the service.

The practice of repeating the Amidah aloud after worshipers have recited it silently was originally instituted because, without printed prayerbooks, many people did not know the text of the Amidah and the order of its blessings. (Even before the age of printing, there were handwritten manuscripts of the prayerbook, of course. But these were too expensive for synagogues to provide to individual worshipers and, as a result, most worshipers could only recite their prayers silently and privately if they had memorized them. Repeating the Amidah therefore allowed worshipers who did not know the liturgy by heart to fulfill their obligation to recite the Amidah by responding "amen" after each of the prayer leader's blessings.) Because the whole point of repeating the Amidah is somewhat obviated in modern congregations that can easily afford to provide printed *siddurim* for all worshipers, there are many synagogues in which the current practice is for worshipers to recite the Amidah aloud together until the end of the K'dushah and then to continue silently to the end of the prayer. In other congregations, however, this is only done when time is an issue. The Amidah is never repeated at the Evening Service.

When the congregation is led by the prayer leader in the K'dushah, the practice is for each line to be read aloud by the congregation, then for the prayer leader to repeat that passage and lead the worshipers into the next communal response. The feel is therefore one of interlocking responses: the congregation chants, the prayer leader repeats what was chanted and goes further, whereupon the congregation responds, the prayer leader repeats the response and then moves to the next section.

If the Amidah is not being repeated fully and the congregation is merely reciting the opening blessings together and then joining in the K'dushah, worshipers should recite the third blessing to themselves while the prayer leader recites the passage beginning *l'dor va-dor*. They should then recite the blessing formula ending with the words *ha-eil ha-kadosh* with the prayer leader, and then move on to the rest of the prayer.

The text of the Amidah is fluid in that there are certain minor variations in the way the prayer is recited that depend on the time of day one is praying, the specific day of the year, and even the season.

For example, the final blessing, the prayer for peace, has two versions: Sim Shalom, which is recited in the Morning Service, and Shalom Rav, which is recited during the Afternoon and Evening Services. On fast days, however, Sim Shalom is recited during the Afternoon Service as well (gloss of the Rema to *SA* Oraḥ Ḥayyim 127:2). Except on fast days, the priestly blessing is not recited by the prayer leader at the Afternoon Service, nor is it ever included in the silent prayer of individuals.

Some liturgical variations are meant to foster a sense of involved relationship between the worshiper and nature and, specifically, the natural phenomena of the Land of Israel. Between the first and second sentences of the G'vurot blessing, for example, worshipers add a phrase acknowledging God as the divine source of wind and rain (the Hebrew words are *mashiv ha-ru·aḥ u-morid ha-geshem* or *ha-gashem*) during the winter months, beginning with the Amidah recited during the Musaf Service on Sh'mini Atzeret and concluding with the Amidah recited during the Musaf Service of the first day of Passover. During the rest of the year, Sephardic Jews and Israelis add a reference to God as the divine source of dew (the Hebrew is *morid ha-tal*). Most Conservative synagogues generally follow the Ashkenazic tradition and do not include *morid ha-tal* as part of the Amidah.

From the beginning of Passover until the fourth of December, a phrase beseeching God to grant the blessing of fecundity and good weather in general (the Hebrew is *v'tein b'rakhah*) is recited in Birkat Ha-shanim. During the rest of the year, a phrase specifically asking God for generous rainfall (the Hebrew is *v'tein tal u-matar li-v'rakhah*) is recited instead. The switch generally takes place at the Evening Service on December 4. If, however, the number of the Hebrew year is divisible by four, then the switch takes place at the Evening Service on December 5. In both cases, it is recited until the first day of Passover. (The unusual phenomenon of the *halakhah* pegging Jewish liturgical practice to the solar calendar has to do with an ancient method of calculating the latest possible "normal" onset of the rainy season in Israel based on number of days deemed to have passed since the autumnal equinox.)

At the conclusion of Shabbat and festivals, a special paragraph acknowledging God as the Author of the distinction between Shabbat and weekday, as well as other profound distinctions in the world (e.g., between light and darkness, between sacred and profane, and between Israel and the nations), is inserted into the fourth blessing of the Amidah.

On Rosh Ḥodesh and on the three pilgrimage festivals, including their intermediate days, a special prayer called Ya·aleh V'yavo is added into the Avodah blessing of the Amidah.

On public fast days, a special benediction called Aneinu is added, but it is not inserted in the same place during the silent recitation of the Amidah and during its repetition. During the Morning Service, the private worshiper does not say it at all, but the prayer leader inserts it in the repetition between the seventh and eighth blessings (that is, between Ge'ullah and R'fu·ah). In the Afternoon Service, the prayer leader inserts the prayer in the same place when the Amidah is recited aloud, but the private worshiper adds it in between the sixteenth and seventeenth blessings, between T'fillah and Avodah. The Aneinu blessing is not recited during the Evening Service at all.

On Ḥanukkah and Purim—and in many congregations also on Yom Ha-aztma·ut (Israel Independence Day)—a special prayer called Al Ha-nissim is inserted into the eighteenth blessing, the Hoda·ah. (A different version is used for each occasion so that specific mention of the details of the historical event in question can be made explicit.)

Between Rosh Hashanah and Yom Kippur, the following additions and changes are made: a prayer that God remember us for good (called Zokhreinu) is added between the first and second paragraphs of Avot, a line acknowledging the uniqueness of God (called after its opening words, Mi Khamokha) is added in between the first and second paragraphs of G'vurot, the last words in the third benediction are changed to *ha-melekh ha-kadosh* (so as specifically to acknowledge the holy sovereignty of God at a time of year when that notion comes to the fore), the last words in the eleventh blessing (Mishpat) are changed to *ha-melekh ha-mishpat* (this too is to stress the concept of divine sovereignty), the words *u-kh'tov l'ḥayyim tovim kol b'nei v'ritekha* ("and write up for good all to whom You are bound in covenant") are added before the final paragraph of Hoda·ah, and a prayer that the worshiper be inscribed for good in the divine Book of Life (called B'seifer Ḥayyim, after its opening words) is included at the end of the final blessing, Shalom, which is also provided with an alternate closing benediction acknowledging God as the Maker of Peace. These changes are all intended to assist worshipers in acknowledging the unique nature of the Days of Awe by proposing an image of God as a just Ruler whose sovereignty is absolute.

A special version of the Y'rushalayim blessing, called Naḥeim, is recited in the Amidah during the Afternoon Service on the Ninth of Av.

On fast days and during the days between Rosh Hashanah and Yom Kippur, the Avinu Malkeinu prayer is recited after the prayer leader concludes the Amidah during the Morning and Afternoon Services.

A book detailing the day-to-day changes in the daily liturgy, now edited by Rabbi Miles B. Cohen and Leslie Rubin, is published annually by the United Synagogue of Conservative Judaism and the Rabbinical Assembly under the name *Lu·aḥ Ha-shanah*.

Taḥanun and Concluding Prayers

Taḥanun ("Supplication") is the name for a series of penitential prayers that follow the Amidah during the Morning and Afternoon Services. The original intent of this portion of the service was to create space for personal prayer, but over the centuries these prayers too became formalized and they now appear as set prayers alongside the rest of the liturgy of the prayerbook.

There are two versions of Taḥanun, a long version recited on Monday and Thursday mornings and a short version recited on the other weekday mornings and during the Afternoon Service. Taḥanun is followed by the Half Kaddish.

It is customary for worshipers physically to demonstrate their penitential mood by resting their foreheads on the forearms when reciting the words *va-yomeir david* ("and David said"), and then by remaining in that position until the end of the sixth psalm. When resting the forehead on the arm, worshipers use their right arm when *t'fillin* are worn on the left arm, and the left arm during the Afternoon Service. Individuals wearing *t'fillin* on their right arms during the Morning Service rest their foreheads on their left arms in the morning as well. This act of prostration, called *n'filat appayim* in Hebrew, is done while seated, but only in the presence of a Holy Ark with a Torah scroll in it.

Taḥanun is not recited on days of great joy or, paradoxically, great sorrow. We omit Taḥanun, therefore, on the following weekdays: Rosh Ḥodesh, the entire month of Nisan, Pesaḥ Sheini (14 Iyyar), Lag Ba-omer, all the days between Rosh Ḥodesh Sivan until the day after Shavuot, Tishah Be'av, the fifteenth of Av, Erev Rosh Hashanah, from Erev Yom Kippur until the second of Ḥeshvan, the entire week of Ḥanukkah, Tu Bi-sh'vat, the fourteenth and fifteenth of Adar (and, in leap years, of Adar Sheini as well), Yom Ha-atzma·ut, Yom Y'rushalayim, Yom Ha-zikkaron, and Yom Ha-sho·ah. (There are also congregations that omit Taḥanun following Shavuot until the fourteenth day of Sivan.) Taḥanun is also omitted in a house of mourning during the *shivah* week; on a wedding day if either the bride or the groom is present during the service; on the day of a circumcision if the *sandek*, the *moheil*, or either parent is present; and during a service in the course of which a bar or bat mitzvah will be celebrated. Some also omit Taḥanun on certain secular holidays such as Thanksgiving and Independence Day in the United States.

On Mondays and Thursdays, the Torah is read aloud at this point in the service. The Torah Service is discussed below.

The conclusion of the Morning Service begins with Ashrei, the liturgical setting of Psalm 145 with two introductory verses, Psalm 84:5 and Psalm 144:15. The Talmud suggests that Ashrei is a kind of catechism of basic beliefs and therefore should be recited three times a day (*BT* B'rakhot 4b). What is striking about Ashrei is the manner in which it moves from singular to plural language. Within the context of words of prayer most often spoken in the plural, Ashrei provides an opportunity for a personal pledge of faith and for a private examination of belief in God.

Ashrei is followed by Psalm 20 and a long miscellany of verses called U-va L'tziyyon Go·eil. Because it speaks of "the day of trouble," Psalm 20 is omitted on Rosh Ḥodesh; Ḥanukkah; Ḥol Ha-mo·eid; Purim and Purim Katan (the date of Purim in the first Adar of a thirteen-month year); the days before and after Passover, Shavuot, and Sukkot; the day before Rosh Hashanah; the day before Yom Kippur; Yom Ha-atzma·ut; Yom Y'rushalayim; Tishah Be'av; and in a house of mourning.

All services conclude with the Aleinu hymn. (Originally, this hymn was said only on Rosh Hashanah, but it has been a feature of all services since at least medieval times.) Aleinu should be said while standing. At the words *va-anaḥnu korim,* one should bend the knee and bow at the waist. Aleinu is then followed by the Mourner's Kaddish.

The prayerbooks of the Conservative movement have continued to eliminate one line from the Aleinu that was originally removed by censors during the Middle Ages. This line, undoubtedly original, evaluates the supreme worth of Jewish faith in comparison with the faiths of others and declares those other faiths to be empty and meaningless. In that moderns tend to esteem the kind of positive self-evaluation that does not involve the concomitant denigration of others, this line has been kept out of the modern version of the hymn.

In many congregations, Aleinu is followed by the daily psalm and then by a final Mourner's Kaddish. The psalm of the day is a vestige of Temple days, when a psalm was assigned to each day of the week and then sung aloud on that day by the Levites. The Talmud (*BT* Rosh Ha-shanah 31a) gives a specific reason why each psalm is connected to its day of the week.

There are also special psalms for specific days and seasons of the year. Thus, Psalm 104 is read on Rosh Ḥodesh and Psalm 27 is read throughout the entire High Holiday season, beginning with the first of Elul and ending only on Hoshana Rabbah, the day the ancients imagined the final verdicts for all humankind to be sealed.

The Afternoon Service

The Afternoon Service, called Minḥah, is associated with the daily sacrifice that was offered in the afternoon in Temple times. The name itself is associated with the prophet Elijah, who personally called the afternoon offering by that name (cf. 1 Kings 18:29 and 36).

It is difficult for many to imagine pausing in the middle of a busy workday to gather a *minyan* of fellow Jews and spend fifteen minutes in reflective prayer. But prayer allows us to breathe deeply and to consider who we are and what matters most to us in our lives. And, precisely because it is so inconvenient to find the time to worship when we are so busy doing things that feel as though they really matter, the Afternoon Service has the potential to have an unexpectedly profound effect on the way we live our lives in general.

The order of the Afternoon Service is as follows. The service begins with Ashrei, followed by Half Kaddish. The congregation then rises in silent prayer to recite the Amidah, which is then repeated by the prayer leader and the K'dushah is included in the repetition. If the Minḥah Service is begun close to nightfall, it is usually best to follow the practice of reciting the Minḥah Amidah without repetition. (In such a case, the reader recites the first two benedictions of the Amidah aloud and the congregation responds at the K'dushah. The reader then says the third blessing aloud and completes the rest silently. The congregation then returns to the start of the Amidah and recites it silently. On fast days, the special Aneinu prayer is added to the T'fillah blessing in the silent Amidah, but as a separate benediction in the repetition of the Amidah. The service then concludes with the short version of Taḥanun followed by the complete Kaddish, Aleinu, and the Mourner's Kaddish.

It is customary in many communities to recite Minḥah close to nightfall, followed immediately by Ma·ariv, thus solving the problem of convening a separate afternoon *minyan* (*SA* Oraḥ Ḥayyim 233:1). A *t'shuvah* of the CJLS from 1994 stipulates, however, that it is forbidden to begin Minḥah after sundown (*CJLS Responsa 1991–2000,* pp. 50–52).

Taḥanun is not said at Minḥah when it was omitted in the morning or is to be omitted the following morning.

On fast days and during the Ten Days of Repentance, the Avinu Malkeinu prayer is recited after the reader has repeated the Amidah.

On Shabbat, and on all fast days (including Yom Kippur), the Torah is read at Minḥah before the Amidah. On Yom Kippur and other fast days, a *haftarah* is chanted after the Torah reading as well. The Torah Service is discussed in more detail below.

The prayer leader dons a *tallit* to lead the Afternoon Service, but without reciting the blessing.

The Evening Service

The Evening Service, called Ma·ariv or Arvit, is structured in a parallel way to the Morning Service in that it has at its core the Sh'ma (with its accompanying benedictions) and the Amidah. It does not, however, have the extensive preliminary and concluding prayers of the Morning Service.

Ma·ariv is the opportunity to provide spiritual closure for the day that has passed and prepare the worshiper for the night that lies ahead. Recited at a time of day when people naturally feel more vulnerable, Ma·ariv is a daily liturgical opportunity to make peace with the world before going to sleep. It serves, or can serve, as a daily cleansing of soul and mind. And while it might not always be possible to recite Ma·ariv with a *minyan,* the inclusion of a nightly ritual of prayer in our lives not only allows us to fulfill the *mitzvah* of daily prayer, but it can also create a ritual of daily spiritual cleansing that can be deeply satisfying.

The *tallit* is generally not worn at night, not even by the prayer leader.

As in the morning, the service begins with a call to prayer prefaced by two verses, Psalm 78:38 and Psalm 20:10, after which the congregation responds. Also, just as in the morning, the Sh'ma is preceded by two benedictions. Unlike the morning Sh'ma, however, the evening recitation of the Sh'ma is followed by two different benedictions. The themes of the evening blessings are similar to the morning ones, however.

The prayer Barukh Adonai Le'olam is recited just before the Amidah. This prayer was originally inserted in the service to accommodate latecomers who could use the time it took for the congregation to recite this long prayer to catch up and join the rest of the congregation in the recitation of the Amidah. The original concept had to do with the dangers of walking alone in the country at night, but once it became customary for synagogues to be built within towns (and the original need to lengthen the service thus no longer existed), the custom of reciting this prayer nevertheless continued.

The Amidah is then recited silently by the prayer leader and the members of the congregation at the same time. There is no repetition of the prayer, and the K'dushah is not recited.

The service ends with Aleinu, followed by the Mourner's Kaddish.

The time prescribed for the recitation of the Evening Service is a function of the earliest time one may recite the evening Sh'ma—that is, when three stars appear in the sky (*SA* Oraḥ Ḥayyim 235:1). Under certain circumstances, one may recite the Evening Service as early as the time officially known as *p'lag haminḥah,* a quarter-hour before the end of the eleventh hour of the day, as calculated according to the system of flexible hours in which each one represents one-twelfth of the time between sunrise and sunset (*SA* Oraḥ Ḥayyim 233:1, with the gloss of the Rema). In such a case, however, one must recite the Sh'ma again once the stars come out. According to a 1994 responsum of the CJLS, however, the Evening Service should not be recited before *p'lag ha-minḥah* under any circumstances (*CJLS Responsa 1991–2000,* pp. 50–52).

Torah Reading

The public reading of the Torah takes place as part of an elaborate ceremonial that weaves prayer and movement together in a highly choreographed, deeply symbolic fashion. It is a central part of the Morning Service on Shabbat, holidays, and, in a less dramatic way, on Monday and Thursday mornings and Saturday afternoons as well. The Torah is also read aloud on Rosh Ḥodesh and on fast days.

The congregation rises as Numbers 10:35 and Isaiah 2:3 are chanted aloud. (Additional verses are recited on Shabbat.) The Torah is removed from the Holy Ark, which is then closed as the prayer leader calls on the congregation to praise God using the language of Psalm 34:4. The congregation responds by chanting a hymn about the greatness and glory of God while a processional leaves the *bimah* and proceeds to walk amidst the people. The act of leaving the *bimah* with the Torah is intended to be reminiscent of Moses's bringing the Torah down from atop the mountain to the people. The custom of kissing the scroll as it passes by is meant to affirm the worshiper's wish to be part of that ongoing pageant of divine revelation and popular acceptance.

When leaving the *bimah,* the individual holding the Torah should hold it on the right side of his or her body (gloss of the Rema to *SA* Oraḥ Ḥayyim 134:1). The procedure for reading the Torah is explained below in the section called "The Aliyah."

After the Torah reading is completed, the Torah is lifted and displayed to the congregation. This is called *hagbahah* (lifting). When the Torah is being held aloft, the congregation chants a line acknowledging God as the ultimate source of Torah. It is customary to point at the Torah when singing out this line, which begins with the words *v'zot ha-torah,* partially to affirm our certainty that the Torah in which we believe is not some elusive teaching vouchsafed only to the lucky few, but the actual scroll being held aloft from which we continually read in public. (The pointing also serves to prevent misunderstanding that could conceivably arise due to the fact that the line in question is an amplification of Deuteronomy 4:44, which verse refers in its original context only to the Book of Deuteronomy, not to the entire Torah.) In some congregations, an effort is made to make this act of pointing unique and unusual by using the pinky finger to point instead of the index finger.

The Torah is then rolled, tied with a tie, usually a velvet one, and dressed in its mantle by the person who has the honor of *g'lilah* (rolling).

The Torah is then carried again around the sanctuary. While this happens, the prayer leader chants biblical verses that affirm the covenantal relationship between God and the people through the medium of the Torah. In some congregations, this procession follows the opposite direction from the earlier one.

After the Torah is placed in the Ark, Numbers 10:36, followed by Psalm 132:8–10 and Proverbs 4:2, are recited. The Ark is then closed and, finally, three verses beginning with *eitz ḥayyim hi* (Proverbs 3:18) are sung aloud. The third of these verses is Lamentations 5:21 and so the Torah Service concludes with a plea for the future, described as a time when a penitent and regenerated people will be restored to its former glory, ringing in the ears of the congregation. This hymn is a reminder that Jewish living is not done in isolation, that it is a real partnership between God and the Jewish people. The Torah is thus appropriately described as a living entity that adapts to its surroundings while staying true to its core values, and we, as a people, can access faith in God through holding tight to this living Torah. This idea of a living Torah means a life of dynamic change. It does not imply that each and every individual must immediately embrace all that there is to living a life of Torah. Instead, it is the never-ending plea that each day bring a renewed commitment to this life, toward this kind of spiritual fulfillment, toward this sacred journey.

Many Jews have heard of a custom that requires someone who drops a Torah scroll, or even who is present when someone drops a scroll, to fast as an act of vicarious atonement for the disrespect to Scripture inherent even in an accident that involves a Torah falling to the ground (see the comments of Rabbi Abraham Abele Gombiner (c. 1635–1682), called the Magein Avraham, in his comment to *SA* Oraḥ Ḥayyim 44, section 6, who mentions the custom without exactly endorsing it). Given that this is a relatively modern custom that is not mentioned in the Talmud at all, we would do better to respond to such a mishap, aside from immediately repairing any damage to the scroll or to any of its accouterments, by performing acts of atonement relating to what happened, by giving gifts of *tz'dakah,* and by studying the laws that govern the care due to Torah scrolls (responsum of Rabbi David Golinkin, in *Responsa of the Va·ad Halakhah,* vol. 6, pp. xi and 23–32.

The Annual and Triennial Cycles

The Torah is divided into fifty-four portions, one (or, occasionally, two) of which is read each Shabbat of the year except on those that coincide with holidays. (When festival days fall on Shabbat, there are special readings taken from outside the ongoing cycle of readings that have to do with the festivals themselves.) Torah portions are doubled up on six or seven Sabbaths in non-leap years.

The Talmud mentions that it was the custom in ancient Palestine to complete the reading of the Torah in three years rather than one (*BT* M'gillah 29b), a custom that has been recently revived. In accordance with a 1987 responsum of the CJLS, this is deemed acceptable and, indeed, a specific triennial cycle of Torah readings was subsequently adopted and endorsed by the CJLS (*CJLS Responsa 1980–1990,* pp. 74–76 and 77–128). Many modern synagogues have adopted this system in order to shorten the service or to allow for more time for discussion and study; however, there are also many congregations that remain faithful to the concept of an annual cycle of Torah readings.

On Shabbat afternoons, the reader reads the beginning of the Torah portion that follows the portion just read that morning. (Unless a holiday intervenes, this is generally the portion that is read in full the following Shabbat.) The same passage is then read on the upcoming Monday and Thursday. (For the rabbis of ancient times, Torah was as vital to the survival of the Israelites as the water that sustained them in the desert. Just as one cannot endure more than three days without water, it was felt that three days should never be allowed to pass without a Torah reading. For this reason, it became customary to read the Torah not only on Shabbat, but also on Mondays and Thursdays.)

During the Morning and Afternoon Services on fast days other than Yom Kippur, we read a noncontiguous passage consisting of Exodus 32:11–14 and 34:1–10. Three people are called up, and, in the afternoon, the third chants Isaiah 55:6–56:8 afterward, the special *haftarah* for fast days. The only exception to this rule is during the Morning Service on the Ninth of Av, when the Torah reading is Deuteronomy 4:25–40 and the *haftarah,* also chanted by the person called for the third *aliyah,* is Jeremiah 8:13–9:23.

The Torah is read on the morning of every festival and on every Rosh Ḥodesh, and also during the Evening Service on Simḥat Torah. Through these holiday and Rosh Ḥodesh readings, worshipers come to appreciate the biblical roots of the festivals of the Jewish year.

When the last lines of one of the books of the Torah is read aloud, the congregation rises. And then, when the final verse is read, all respond by chanting *ḥazak, ḥazak, v'nit·ḥazzeik* (be strong, be strong, and let us all make each other strong), which is then repeated by the Torah reader. Even in congregations that have adopted a triennial cycle of Torah readings, a 2000 responsum of the CJLS permits the recitation of these words when the final verse of a book is read aloud (*CJLS Responsa 1991–2000,* pp. 43–49).

The Aliyah

After the Torah is placed on the *bimah* and opened to the proper place, and its wraps removed and set aside, the first person to be called forward approaches the scroll and recites the opening blessing. Although it was once the norm for individuals honored with *aliyot* to read from the scroll themselves, today most congregations have readers designated in advance since most members of the congregation are not prepared or trained to read the Torah from the scroll.

When it is time for an individual's *aliyah,* the individual charged with calling people to the Torah, called the *gabbai,* invites that person forward using the full version of his or her Hebrew name. Historically, only the father's name was used in the full version of an individual's name that takes the form of X, son/daughter of Y. Today, the mother's name is regularly used as well, in which case the name takes the form X, son/daughter of Y and Z.

The person called for an *aliyah* during the Morning Service should wear a *tallit.* In some congregations, women who do not regularly wear a *tallit* during prayer are not required to wear one when accepting an *aliyah.* However, a communication of the CJLS from 1993 indicates that egalitarian communities should encourage women who come forward for *aliyot* to don a *tallit* for the occasion even if they do not normally wear one. It is not customary to don a *tallit* when called to the Torah for an *aliyah* during an Afternoon Service featuring Torah reading.

When the congregant honored with an *aliyah* comes up to the *bimah,* the reader should indicate the place in the scroll where the reading will begin. The congregant then touches the place with the *tzitzit* and kisses the part that touched the Torah. Then, taking hold of the scroll's two wooden rollers, the congregant recites the blessing before the Torah reading (*SA* Oraḥ Ḥayyim 139:11). There are varying customs regarding whether or not the scroll should be rolled closed while the blessing is recited. The more prevalent custom is for it to be closed and then reopened for the reading. The individual called to the Torah, if able, should read along quietly with the person reading aloud. If unable, then the individual called for an *aliyah* should at least follow the reading as closely as possible. At the end of the reading, that person then again uses the *tzitzit* to kiss the Torah, closes the scroll, and recites the second blessing while holding the wooden rollers. Out of respect to the Torah, the individual honored with an *aliyah* remains on the *bimah* until the person honored with the next *aliyah* has completed the second blessing (*SA* Oraḥ Ḥayyim 141:7 in light of the comment of the *Magein Avraham* commentary of Rabbi Abraham Gombiner, to which may be compared the gloss *ad loc.* of the Rema).

If possible, one who is given an *aliyah* should always approach the Torah by the shorter way and leave by the longer one to indicate eagerness to reach the Torah and reluctance to leave it. Otherwise, we ascend to the right and descend to the left (*SA* Oraḥ Ḥayyim 141:7).

Between two *aliyot,* or when there is a pause for a commentary or for a prayer to be said for the individual honored with the *aliyah,* the scroll is kept rolled together and covered with a mantle or other covering (*SA* Oraḥ Ḥayyim 139:5, in light of the gloss *ad loc.* of the Rema).

In addition to the reader and the person honored with the *aliyah,* there must be two *gabba·im* at the table as well. The role of these individuals is twofold. The head *gabbai* calls up each individual for an *aliyah,* but both *gabba·im* follow the Torah reading along in a printed text to check for any mistakes in the reading and to correct the reader. Only mistakes that affect the meaning of the Hebrew text should be corrected aloud, however. Therefore, it is considered optimal to have *gabba·im* who can distinguish between those errors that should be corrected and those that can safely be ignored.

Except at the Afternoon Service on Shabbat and on fast days, the Half Kaddish is recited when the Torah reading is completed (*SA* Oraḥ Ḥayyim 282:4). At the Afternoon Service on Shabbat, however, the Half Kaddish is delayed until just prior to the Amidah.

Immediately after the Torah reading and the recitation of the Kaddish, two people are called up, one for the honor of *hagbahah,* the act of lifting the Torah aloft for the congregation to see its text, and the other for the honor of *g'lilah,* the act of rolling the Torah back together, binding it, and covering it with its mantle. The person called for *hagbahah* raises the Torah with the scroll open and shows the writing to the congregation. Three columns of the Torah should be unrolled for the congregation to see.

The individual honored with *g'lilah* is called the *goleil* or the *golelet* (the masculine and feminine forms, respectively). He or she wraps the Torah in the same order it was unwrapped, taking special care to use a *tallit* or some other fabric as a kind of barrier so as not to touch the actual parchment inside the scroll with a bare hand. After the Torah is wrapped, the silver pointer that was used during the reading is draped over the right side and the silver ornamentation is replaced. The Torah is now ready to be returned to the Ark.

Receiving an *aliyah* is considered a great honor. It bespeaks honor to the Torah as well as to the individual. Indeed, in the past, great emphasis was placed on which individuals received these honors. In many communities, in fact, *aliyot* were sold to the highest bidder in a kind of auction that raised money for the synagogue. Because this kind of bidding eventually came to be considered indecorous, the custom has mostly fallen away in Conservative congregations. Still, the idea that the honor is something to strive for and be willing, even, to pay for is a worthy one. When one comes forward for an *aliyah,* it is an awe-inspiring moment. Standing before a scroll that contains the ancient text of the Torah, feeling the presence of one's ancestors, and following along with the reader—it is as if one is personally standing before God at Sinai and receiving the Torah.

In the Jewish world, there are those who maintain a family tradition that they are descended either from the priests of ancient times or from the Levites. Those who recall their ancestry from the priesthood are called *kohanim* (singular: *kohein*) and it has been customary since ancient times to call a *kohein* for the first *aliyah,* a Levite for the second *aliyah,* and "regular" Israelites for the third and subsequent *aliyot* (*SA* Oraḥ Ḥayyim 135:3). In accordance with a 1989 responsum accepted by the Committee on Jewish Law and Standards, it is possible to call daughters of *kohanim* for the first *aliyah* and daughters of Levites for the second (*CJLS Responsa 1980–1990,* pp. 49–64). A responsum from 1990, however, also permits setting this system aside entirely, so that any individual may be called up for either of the first two *aliyot* (*CJLS Responsa 1980–1990,* pp. 67–73). In the end, there is some theological ambivalence in the Conservative movement about the place of *kohanim* in ritual life. For some Conservative Jews, retaining the priestly class of Jews is an important educational aspect of Judaism precisely because it fosters a sense of connection to a glorious past, and also because fidelity to tradition is understood as a worthy goal in its own right. For other Conservative Jews, however, the retention of a caste system in Judaism runs contrary to their beliefs in a Judaism that treats all equally and fairly.

A 1993 responsum of the CJLS penned by Rabbi Kassel Abelson permits calling up two individuals jointly to the Torah for an *aliyah* (*CJLS Responsa 1991–2000,* pp. 36–42). This responsum also permits group *aliyot,* although solely on a case-by-case basis and not as a matter of course. If several individuals are called up together, they should recite the benedictions together, "as one voice." There is an alternate view, however, espoused in a different responsum (*CJLS Responsa 1991–2000,* pp. 21–35). According to this view, only one individual should recite each of the blessings, even if others are called forward at the same time.

Only three individuals are called to the Torah on Mondays and Thursdays, because these are workdays and, as such, days on which we should not lengthen the service unnecessarily (*SA* Oraḥ Ḥayyim 135:1). There are also only three *aliyot* on Saturday afternoons because it is close to the conclusion of Shabbat and we do not wish to detain the congregation unduly.

On fast days, on Purim, and on all days of Ḥanukkah (except the one or two Sabbaths that fall during the holiday and the day or days of Rosh Ḥodesh Teivet), three individuals are called to the Torah as well. On days other than festivals when there is a Musaf Service, such as Rosh Ḥodesh or the intermediate days of Passover and Sukkot, there are four *aliyot.* On the three pilgrimage festivals—Passover, Shavuot, and Sukkot—and also on Rosh Hashanah, there are five *aliyot.* On Yom Kippur, there are six *aliyot* in the morning and three in the afternoon (*MT* Hilkhot T'fillah U-n'si·at Kappayim 12:16).

On Shabbat, there are seven *aliyot.* In addition, the concluding portion of the final *aliyah* is read a second time so that the individual honored with the recitation of the *haftarah* can have an *aliyah* as well. This *aliyah,* popularly called the *maftir* (because the individual who reads the *haftarah* is called the *maftir* or the *maftirah*), follows the recitation of Half Kaddish and is independent of the rules governing *aliyot* mentioned above. Therefore, a *kohein* or a Levite may be called for the this *aliyah,* even in congregations that are faithful to the traditional allocation system of *aliyot.* There is also a *maftir* on holidays, though in these cases (as well as on special Sabbaths, as detailed below) a new section of the Torah pertaining to the day in question is read from a second scroll rather than a repetition of the final portion of the concluding *aliyah.* I will return to the question of *haftarot* below in a separate subsection of this chapter.

The number of *aliyot* is fixed on all occasions, except for Shabbat, when the number may be increased to accommodate special occasions and/or numerous guests (*SA* Oraḥ Ḥayyim 282:1).

On days when there are only three *aliyot,* a minimum of ten verses must be read (*SA* Oraḥ Ḥayyim 137:1). These must be divided, however, in such a way that at least three verses are read for each *aliyah.* On Purim, however, only nine verses are read because the reading comprises a story that is complete in that many verses and it would be strange to add an extraneous verse to the reading as it is actually presented in Scripture.

How did the ancients arrive at these specific numbers for *aliyot?* One interpretation is that the three weekday *aliyot,* the five festival *aliyot,* and the seven *aliyot* on Shabbat were intended to correspond to the number of words in each line of the priestly benediction. (For another explanation, see *BT* M'gillah 22b.) Whether this is accurate historically or not, it encapsulates a deep truth: that the experience of hearing the Torah read aloud in public is itself a profound blessing, one that brings peace, love, and the light of God to all who listen attentively and take the words they hear to heart.

Although the individual who reads from the Torah will generally be an adult Jew, a 1980 responsum of the CJLS specifically permits children as young as ten or eleven years of age (i.e., before bar or bat mitzvah age) to read from the Torah (*CJLS Responsa 1980–1990,* pp. 187–191). Even in a community with many competent adult readers, it should be viewed as a special *mitzvah* to encourage young people to participate in the public reading of the Torah.

If there is no one present who can read the Torah with the proper pronunciation and cantillation, a congregant may read quietly from a printed pentateuch and thereby prompt a reader who then reads the passage aloud from the scroll (gloss of the Rema to *SA* Oraḥ Ḥayyim 143:2).

If there is no Torah scroll available, the portion may be read aloud from a printed pentateuch so that the institution of the reading of the Torah will not be neglected. In such a case, no benedictions are recited, the reading is not divided into sections, and no one is called up formally for an *aliyah* (gloss of the Rema to *SA* Oraḥ Ḥayyim 143:2).

If an error is discovered in a Torah scroll, that scroll should not be read from in public (*SA* Oraḥ Ḥayyim 143:4). In this context, an error is defined as a missing word, an extra word, or a misspelling that changes the meaning of the word (*SA* Oraḥ Ḥayyim 143:4). If, however, a vowel letter such as a *vav* or a *yod* is missing or written when not necessary, this does not disqualify the Torah. A letter that has partially worn away should be repaired, but does not in and of itself disqualify the scroll from use if the letter remains legible to the average reader.

If a disqualifying error is discovered as the Torah in question is actually being read, another Torah must be taken from the Ark and used to complete the prescribed reading. In such a case, if the error is discovered when at least three verses have already been read, *and* there are at least three more verses left before the end of the section, the person with the *aliyah* recites the second benediction before the first scroll is put away. The first benediction is then recited again before the reading is started in the replacement scroll and the number of *aliyot* is then completed in the normal way. Otherwise, we recite the second benediction only after the section is completed in the second scroll (*SA* Oraḥ Ḥayyim 143:4, with the gloss of the Rema).

The public reading of the weekly Torah portion affords every Jew the opportunity to fulfill the commandment of Torah study. But there is another reason that the reading was integrated into the worship service: to encourage reflection on the narratives that serve as the spiritual, legal, and mythic foundation of our lives as Jewish people and to facilitate familiarity with the laws that govern Jewish life.

Birkat Ha-gomeil

The Talmud (at *BT* B'rakhot 54b) ordains that all who have come through times of special difficulty—a long sea journey, an arduous overland trip, a life-threatening illness, or a period of incarceration in prison—should recite a special blessing of thanksgiving called Birkat Ha-gomeil. Although this blessing is normally recited after the closing Torah benediction, one does not have to receive an *aliyah* to recite the benediction. In our day, all those whose lives have been seriously endangered are encouraged to accept an *aliyah* to the Torah and recite this blessing. Those who have undergone surgery, even if not to cure illness (e.g., a woman who has given birth via cesarean section), are encouraged to recite Birkat Ha-gomeil as a way of expressing their thanks to God for having come through the procedure, as are all who have recovered from serious illness.

After the blessing that follows the Torah reading, the person wishing to recite Birkat Ha-gomeil recites the words of the blessing: *barukh attah adonai, eloheinu, melekh ha-olam, ha-gomeil la-ḥayyavim tovot, she-g'malani kol tov* ("Praised are You, Adonai, our God, Sovereign of the universe, who bestows kindness to the undeserving, who has bestowed every goodness upon me"). Upon the conclusion of the blessing, the congregation responds with the customary "amen," then recites its own response, which in the Hebrew differentiates for the gender of the person making the blessing: "May the God who treated you on this occasion with such beneficence always treat you similarly."

Haftarot

On Shabbat and holiday mornings and during the Afternoon Service on fast days, and also on the morning of Tishah Be'av and in some communities on the morning of Israel Independence Day (Yom Ha-atzma·ut), a special lesson from one of the books of the prophets is chanted following the reading of the Torah. This is called the *haftarah* (completion), because it is usually a passage the ancient sages considered an elucidation or illumination of the Torah portion in some way. (For the ten weeks before Rosh Hashanah, however, the *haftarot* are unrelated to the Torah portion. Instead, they are related to the fast of the Ninth of Av. The three that precede it are dour, menacing passages intended to create a sober, thoughtful mood in the attentive worshiper. The seven that follow the fast are texts of consolation and spiritual encouragement deemed appropriate for a people recalling the devastation of Jerusalem and the destruction of the Temple.) The person who is to read the *haftarah* is called up to the Torah for the *maftir aliyah,* after which the *haftarah* is chanted from a printed book. (There are, however, *haftarah* scrolls that are increasing in popularity in Conservative congregations). Before and after the *haftarah,* the reader recites the special blessings that serve as the liturgical setting for the *haftarah.*

Blessings

What constitutes a blessing?

A *b'rakhah,* or a blessing, is a tool for sanctifying moments in our lives. There are *b'rakhot* that are incorporated into our daily prayers, and others that are recited before a sacred action, or a profane one, or following it. The *b'rakhah* is a way of bringing God's presence into moments of life outside of those specifically designated for prayer. While it is always appropriate to express gratitude to God for all that one enjoys of this world, one may not fulfill one's halakhic obligation to acknowledge God in such a role other than by reciting the *b'rakhah* according to the particular formula endorsed by our sages and codified by the ancient and medieval halakhists.

In the Talmud (*BT* M'naḥot 43b), we read that a person should recite one hundred blessings every day. Imagine what our day might be like if we were to spend an entire day invoking God's presence to attain our requisite hundred blessings! But even when we fall short of the full hundred, there are still plenty of opportunities to create a sense of the sacred within the mundane, and a sense of the extraordinary within the commonplace, through the recitation of the blessings ordained by our sages and endorsed by generations of Jewish observance.

There are two formulations for blessings: the short one and the long one, and there are two subcategories of long blessings as well. The short blessings always begin with the words *barukh attah* and those words do not repeat. The long formula either begins with other material and ends with the *barukh attah* formula or else, more uncommonly, begins *and* ends with the *barukh attah* formula.

The liturgical blessing is pointedly not in the singular: it is not about "my God," but rather about "our God." Even in the most personal moments, the liturgy helps worshipers transcend their individual needs and desires by leading them to express their affiliation with the larger community of Israel.

Because the standard formula for benedictions includes God's name, it is considered inappropriate to recite a blessing that is not incumbent upon oneself to recite. Such a pointless prayer is called a *b'rakhah l'vatalah* ("a blessing for no reason") and should be avoided. It is generally not considered inappropriate to utter blessings, including with the use of the divine name, in the educational context, however, and this is so regardless of whether the students involved are children or adults.

Mitzvah Blessings

Rabbi Abraham Joshua Heschel taught that when we recite a *b'rakhah,* we are sanctifying a particular moment in time by evoking our appreciation of God's relationship with us in this world at that specific moment. This is especially so when we recite one of the many blessings that precede the performance of a specific *mitzvah.* Yet not all the commandments have attendant liturgical blessings attached to them. Generally speaking, there are no blessings for negative commandments, since they are observed passively rather than by doing some specific thing. Also, there are no blessings for *mitzvot* that one is never done performing. Therefore, there is no blessing for giving charity to the poor, because the obligation is ongoing: one may not turn away from someone in need by explaining that one has already helped some different needy person. Nor is there a blessing for showing honor and respect to one's parents or for rising before the elderly or rebuking a friend who is behaving poorly and would likely respond positively to one's input. But for ritual commandments that need only be done once on a specific day—for shaking a *lulav* or for blowing the *shofar,* for eating *matzah* or bitter herbs on the night of Passover, or upon affixing a *m'zuzah* to the doorpost of a home—for all these there *are* specific blessings to be recited as a way of sanctifying the action and—perhaps especially *because* they are not ongoing obligations—making oneself even more aware of the innate holiness of the deed in question. (The blessings connected with eating are in a different category and are discussed below.)

Blessings of Delight

The largest category of independent blessings consists of the *birkhot hanehenin,* the blessings for those things we enjoy on various occasions. Many of these blessings can be subdivided into different categories according to the senses we use to enjoy specific sources of pleasure: taste, smell, sight, and hearing. There are also blessings of gratitude in this category. All may be found in any standard edition of the prayerbook.

The blessings over things possessed of delightful odors are not numerous, but we must recall that we are not blessing the things in this world that smell good (fragrant spices, trees, fruits, or oils); rather, we are blessing God for granting us the ability to enjoy the good smells that we experience in this world.

Similarly, when we recite blessings over things we have seen that bring us pleasure or inspire us, we are not venerating things in this world that are awe-inspiring to behold (such as the sea, a rainbow, or people who are beautiful, unusual, wise, or important). We are honoring God for creating them and for giving us the ability to perceive them.

There are blessings upon hearing things as well: upon hearing good news or bad, and upon hearing thunder.

There are also blessings related to emotional pleasure. Of these, the most familiar is surely the She-heḥeyyanu blessing, recited as an expression of gratitude to God for having "granted that we live, that we survive, and that we attain" some specific peak moment in our lives. Traditionally, the She-heḥeyyanu is recited whenever we experience something new, when we embark on the celebration of a holiday, or when there is a milestone of significance in the family. There are times this blessing is recited alone (i.e., without any accompanying liturgical text), such as when wearing new clothes or using something new for the first time, but there are other times when the She-heḥeyyanu accompanies another blessing. (At the onset of holidays, for example, it is recited along with the blessing over lighting the festival candles or as part of Kiddush.) These blessings provide us with a liturgical framework within which to express our appreciation for the many gifts we receive from God in this world and our understanding that the *mitzvot* themselves are all acts of worship, not mere folkways or superstitious customs.

Eating and Drinking

The *halakhah* stipulates that blessings are to be recited before eating any food or drinking any beverage. At a meal, however, the blessing over bread, popularly called the Ha-motzi blessing (or sometimes just the Motzi), is deemed sufficient for all the food and beverages that will be served in the course of that meal, and this is so even if one is a guest in someone else's home, or at a banquet, and does not know specifically what food is about to be served (*SA* Oraḥ Ḥayyim 177:1). The only exception to this general rule has to do with wine, which requires its own blessing if served in the course of a meal. Also, whenever a meal is preceded by the blessing over bread, it should be concluded with the recitation of the Grace after Meals, called Birkat Ha-mazon. In this way, by framing the physical act of eating with blessings, eating becomes a religious act that brings physical craving for nourishment into the realm of the spiritual. By acknowledging God in a moment of physical need, we transcend those needs and, ideally, develop a sense of control over the desires and cravings that motivate so much of human activity.

All blessings begin with the same formula: *barukh attah adonai, eloheinu, melekh ha-olam.* There is a huge literature discussing what, precisely, these words mean: whether *barukh* means "blessed," "praised," or "worthy of worship"; whether *melekh ha-olam* means "Sovereign of the Universe," "King of the World," or "Source of Universal Governance," and what the specific point of the unexpected, slightly unnatural, shift from the second person to the third in the larger benediction formulary is intended to convey to the worshiper reciting these words. The usual understanding of the opening formula, though, is something like "Praised be Adonai, our God, Sovereign of the world," but there are many variations on that theme that could be justified just as easily. In the end, however, those six words are the defining feature of the Jewish liturgical blessing. No formula of acknowledgment, thanksgiving, or praise that omits them can be considered a blessing in the liturgical sense, nor can one fulfill one's obligation to praise God through the medium of blessing without uttering them.

For fruit that grows on a tree, one recites the blessing that begins with the standard formulary and ends with the words *borei p'ri ha-eitz* ("who creates the fruit of trees"). Dried fruit has the same status as fresh fruit.

Bananas and pineapples are in a different category, however. Since they are not, at least technically speaking, the fruit of a real tree, the correct blessing is the one that applies to foodstuffs that grow from the ground, beginning with the standard formula and ending with the words *borei p'ri ha-adamah* ("who creates the fruit of the soil"). This category includes vegetables, beans, and other products of the earth.

For foods that are made from wheat, oats, barley, spelt, or rye, one ends the blessing with the words *borei minei m'zonot* ("who creates the various varieties of grain"). This category also includes baked goods that are not breads, such as cookies, cakes, pastries, and other flour-based dishes. There is a longstanding debate regarding the correct blessing to recite over bagels, a kind of bread product that is boiled and then baked. The most common custom is to recite the Ha-motzi blessing over bagels.

For foods that are not the products of soil at all, such as meat, dairy products, eggs, and fish, one concludes one's blessing with the words *she-ha-kol nih'yeh bi-d'varo* ("by whose word all that exists came into being"). This is also the blessing for all beverages other than wine or grape juice. Over wine or grape juice, one recites a blessing composed of the standard opening formula and then the words *borei p'ri ha-gafen* ("who creates the fruit of the vine"). However, it is *borei p'ri ha-eitz* rather than this blessing that is recited over actual grapes.

The point of reciting these blessings is to prevent ourselves from engaging in mindless eating; instead, we are led along liturgically to be mindful of every bite that we take and, in so doing, to become that much more aware of the degree to which we are beholden, or should be beholden, to God for the nourishment we take from the earth that God created.

Once a blessing has been recited aloud, one should not talk or pause before eating the foodstuff for which it was recited. In this way, the blessing remains connected to the action.

The Grace after Meals is recited when a meal is preceded by the Ha-motzi blessing. This long liturgical formula, called Birkat Ha-mazon in Hebrew, is not only expressive of the gratitude people ought to feel for the food they eat, but also echoes other themes as well: the hope for the unity of Israel, a sense of beholdenness to God for favors granted in the past to the Jewish people, and the deeply expressed hope for a future in which Jerusalem will be rebuilt and restored to its ancient glory.

The Talmud (at *BT* B'rakhot 48b) designates the four principal benedictions in the Grace after Meals by name: Birkat Ha-zan, in which God is acknowledged as the great Provider of food for all; Birkat Ha-aretz, in which God is acknowledged as the source of fertility and fecundity in the world; Birkat Boneh Y'rushalayim, in which God is acclaimed as the Restorer and Rebuilder of Jerusalem; and Birkat Ha-tov V'ha-meitiv, in which God is acclaimed as beneficent, endlessly generous, and kind. Over the years, other material has been added to the Grace after Meals as well: special references to specific occasions, specific prayers for messianic redemption, and a miscellany of biblical verses devoted to the subject of divine sustenance of the righteous of this world.

When three or more adults Jews have eaten together, a special introductory formula known as the *zimmun* ("invitation") is added to Birkat Ha-mazon. (This quorum is sometimes colloquially referred to as a *m'zumman.*) The leader invites those present to join in praising God, beginning with the words *ḥaveirai n'vareikh* ("Friends, let us praise!") or with some variant of that invitation. The *zimmun* formula is slightly different if a *minyan* is present. Additional variations are used at the meals following weddings and circumcisions, and in houses of mourning.

Birkat Ha-mazon is quite long, and so a number of abbreviated versions exist as well. The basic idea underlying all legitimate abridgements is that some form of all four basic benedictions must appear in the shortened version.

Washing the Hands

Whenever bread is eaten, the *halakhah* ordains that one's hands be washed first (*SA* Oraḥ Ḥayyim 158:1). This is done in a way that relieves the hands of their implicit impurity, however, and not in a truly efficacious way to clean them. Therefore, if one's hands are dirty, they should be washed in the normal way (i.e., with soap) first, and then washed ritually. This ritual is called *n'tilat yadayim,* literally "the lifting of the hands." To do *n'tilat yadayim,* one fills a vessel that is neither chipped nor damaged with water, then holds it in one hand and pours the water over the other, then does the same with the second hand pouring the water over the first. (Traditionally, right-handed individuals begin by pouring the water over the right hand and left-handed individuals begin with the left.) After both hands are washed at least twice, we recite the blessing: *barukh attah adonai, eloheinu, melekh ha-olam, asher kidd'shanu b'mitzvotav v'tzivvanu al n'tilat yadayim* ("Praised are You, Adonai, our God, Sovereign of the universe, who, sanctifying us with divine commandments, has commanded us concerning the ritual washing of our hands"). It is necessary to remove all rings before doing *n'tilat yadayim* (*SA* Oraḥ Ḥayyim 161:3).

Between the washing of hands and the recitation of the blessing over the bread, it is required to remain focused on the deeds at hand. Therefore, it is customary to not talk at the table between the two blessings, except about matters directly related to the rituals being performed.

B'rakhah Aḥaronah

After eating foods individually, or in a meal that did not include bread (and which, therefore, did not begin with the Ha-motzi blessing), one recites an alternate closing prayer called B'rakhah Aḥaronah. There are actually several forms of this blessing.

The first (and shortest) is *barukh attah adonai, eloheinu, melekh ha-olam, borei n'fashot rabbot v'ḥesronan al kol mah she-barata l'haḥayyot ba-hem nefesh kol ḥai, barukh ḥei ha-olamim* ("Praised are you, Adonai, our God, Creator of all life and its needs, for all things You have created to sustain every living being. Praised are You, Life of the universe"). This blessing is recited over all food except for grapes, figs, pomegranates, olives, dates, food made from the five species of grain mentioned above (i.e., those over which one recites the blessing that ends in *borei minei m'zonot*), wine, or grape juice. After eating these foods, we recite a longer B'rakhah Aḥaronah, which has more the feel of a short version of the Grace after Meals. The different versions of the prayer may be found in any edition of the prayerbook.

When we eat a combination of foods for which several versions of B'rakhah Aḥaronah are ordained, we recite a version of the blessing that contains references to all the foods ingested. As with Birkat Ha-mazon, there are special inclusions for Shabbat, Rosh Ḥodesh, and the various holidays.

Other Prayers and Practices

The M'zuzah

It is a commandment of the Torah to affix a *m'zuzah,* a small box containing an even smaller piece of parchment on which the first two paragraphs of the Sh'ma have been written, to the doorways of one's home, including the front door (*SA* Yoreh Dei·ah 285:1). The parchment is rolled and inserted into a case that is affixed to the right side of the doorway. (Right and left in this context may be a bit confusing, but the general rule is that we imagine someone coming through the front door of one's home and walking toward the back. The sides of the various archways and doorways such a person would regard as being on his or her right are the sides to which the *m'zuzah* should be affixed.) It is attached about one-third of the way down (at about eye level for most adults) and should be attached diagonally, with the upper end tilted inward. Nor are children's bedrooms exempt from the *mitzvah.* Indeed, the *Shulḥan Arukh* specifically notes (at *SA* Yoreh Dei·ah 291:3) that children should be trained to put up the *m'zuzot* on their own doors.

The *m'zuzah* serves as a reminder that the rooms of our homes are potentially sacred space in which God may be encountered. The *m'zuzah* reminds us to remain open to the potential encounters with the sacred as we enter our homes and move through its rooms.

The *m'zuzah* should be affixed to every doorway of the house except for bathrooms. (If two rooms flow into each other without there actually being an archway or doorway, there is no need for a second *m'zuzah.*) Before affixing the *m'zuzah,* a blessing is recited: *barukh attah adonai, eloheinu, melekh haolam, asher kidd'shanu b'mitzvotav v'tzivvanu likbo·a m'zuzah* ("Praised are You, Adonai, our God, Sovereign of the universe, who, sanctifying us with divine commandments, has commanded us to affix the *m'zuzah*").

If one is affixing more than one *m'zuzah* at the same time, it is sufficient to recite the benediction once. Aside from the fact that doing so constitutes the fulfillment of one of the most prominent *mitzvot* of the Torah, the presence of the *m'zuzah* at the entrance to a Jewish home also serves as a symbol of pride in Jewish identity and an affirmation of Jewish unity.

The Traveler's Prayer

In the Talmud (*BT* B'rakhot 29b), there is a reference to travelers reciting a prayer for a safe journey. Today, we recite this prayer, known as T'fillat Ha-derekh, to ask for God's protection on our journey and for a safe return home.

Reciting this prayer allows the traveler formally to allay some of the anxieties that are associated with travel, especially journeys destined to last a long time or that will take the traveler especially far from home. Furthermore, it can serve as a reminder to view even journeys undertaken for business or for pleasure as opportunities for spiritual growth.

The Bedtime Sh'ma

There is a special version of the Sh'ma that is recited at night before bed. The recitation of this specific Sh'ma at night can be a very special home ritual, particularly between parents and children. The act of reciting the Sh'ma as we prepare to retire for the night acknowledges the vulnerability we experience with the onset of darkness and sleep.

The bedtime Sh'ma is introduced with a unique blessing called Birkat Hamapil, after the phrase *ha-mappil ḥevlei sheinah,* in which God is acclaimed as the ultimate source of the tranquility that leads to sleep. This blessing, also unique in that it is written almost entirely in the first person singular, acknowledges the great importance of sleep to our wellbeing and can serve as a reminder that sleep, like all other human functions, should not be taken for granted; it too is a gift from God.

The Sh'ma (followed by the Ve'ahavta paragraph, as in the Morning and Evening Services) is followed at bedtime by Psalms 91, 3, and 128, and then with the words of Adon Olam, which concludes with these highly appropriate lines: "Into God's hand, I commend my spirit / both while asleep and when awake / And with my spirit, I so commend my body as well / for God is with me; I have no fear."

If one has not recited the three paragraphs of the Sh'ma during the Evening Service, then all three paragraphs should be included during the bedtime recitation of the Sh'ma.

The Kaddish

Most people outside the Jewish world would surely name the Kaddish if challenged to name a Jewish prayer of which they had heard. And almost all would think of Kaddish as a prayer for the dead. Even among Jews, "saying Kaddish" denotes the act of acclaiming God's sovereignty in the face of grievous loss. Yet the Kaddish does not mention death. Instead, it is a prayer that acknowledges God's greatness and sovereignty, glorifies God's name, and expresses a deep hope for everlasting peace. It is indeed a prayer recited during the mourner's period of bereavement, but it fills many other functions in the liturgy of the Jewish people as well.

There are actually six different forms of the Kaddish. All have some common material, but are sufficiently different to be easily distinguished.

Kaddish D'rabbanan (the Rabbinical Kaddish) is recited after Torah study when a *minyan* of adults is present and is, in the opinion of some scholars, the original version of the Kaddish. The Full Kaddish is the "complete" Kaddish that is recited to mark the end of a service or a major part of the service. The Half Kaddish is the version of Kaddish that serves to separate smaller parts of the service in a less dramatic way than would the Full Kaddish. Kaddish Yatom (the Orphan's Kaddish, usually called the Mourner's Kaddish) is the prayer recited by mourners at certain points in the service for thirty days or eleven months, depending on the relation of the deceased person to the individual in mourning, and also on the anniversary of the death of such a loved one. Kaddish De'it·ḥad'ta (the Renewal Kaddish) is an expanded form of the Mourner's Kaddish that is exclusively recited at the cemetery after a burial. Finally, there is a special version of Kaddish D'rabbanan that is specifically recited at the conclusion of the study of a full tractate of Talmud.

There are different customs regarding the propriety or necessity of standing during the recitation of Kaddish. Many follow the rule that worshipers should stand when Kaddish marks the completion of a specific section of prayers, but that they otherwise should remain seated. Others rise for every Kaddish. There are also congregations where no one rises for any Kaddish at all, other than mourners for the Mourner's Kaddish. The custom of many Reform congregations is for everyone to rise for the Mourner's Kaddish and actually to join together in its recitation. This is not done in Conservative congregations, however, because it denies, or at least dilutes, the opportunity for mourners publicly to affirm their personal faith in the wake of their personal loss. In any event, worshipers should follow the custom of the congregation in which they are worshiping.

Prayer holds a special place in Jewish observance because it affords us two very important opportunities: both to speak with God in a shared language and also to bring sacredness to the everyday moments of our lives by injecting our behavior with prayer language, with blessings. Many acts in our lives that might otherwise strike us as mundane, or which we might not notice at all, are thus brought to our attention by the simple obligation to recite the blessing or prayer attached to them by tradition. Reciting the words of past generations allows us to transform everyday moments into sanctified ones, and ordinary experiences into unique opportunities for spiritual growth. In turn, this transformative nature of prayer guides us forward in all other areas of Jewish observance as well. This chapter deals mostly with the nature of formal prayer and with the language of liturgy. And, indeed, almost every chapter in this book that describes the details of observant Jewish life also contains detailed instructions regarding the liturgical language that tradition ordains accompany and sanctify the specific prescribed rituals and behaviors under consideration.

One final thought and reminder: despite the importance of well-crafted written liturgical language shared across the ages and used during the sanctified liturgical times of the day, it is no less crucial for Jews to learn to speak with God at any time through the medium of freely conceived thoughts and words. Spontaneous prayer, heartfelt and private, is an important part of the personal spiritual relationship each and every person—from young children to adult men and women, and onwards through life into old age—can cultivate and maintain with God. The spiritual journey that each of us undertakes throughout our lifetime is thus one of balancing the *keva* of the fixed liturgy with the *kavvanah* of discovering and cultivating our spontaneous and personal prayer relationships with God.

Synagogue Life

CRAIG T. SCHEFF

In the ideal world, the *halakhah* as it applies to the life of a synagogue would operate simply as an extension of its application to the life of the individual Jew. The synagogue community, however, is an exceedingly complex institution and, as a result, the issues it faces are rarely simply the individual's issues writ large. For example, the synagogue is surely a place of prayer, learning, and spiritual assembly, but it is also a business institution, driven largely by the energy and the financial support of volunteer laypeople who come from highly diverse backgrounds of Jewish commitment and observance. And, for all that the synagogue is expected in theory to be guided by the values and laws of the Torah both in planning its day-to-day affairs and in seeking to attain its long-term goals, it is also the case that the non-Orthodox synagogue today is supported by a membership that often does not appreciate the centrality of *halakhah* to Jewish observance. Although each major Jewish denomination faces a dramatically different set of issues in this particular regard, I will speak primarily of my own denomination, Conservative Judaism, in this chapter. In any event and even within a single denomination, the normative *halakhah* of synagogue life will vary dramatically from one community to the next. Indeed, as matters of halakhic importance come to the foreground, the role of the rabbi as *mara de'atra* (the halakhic authority for the community) becomes all the more important. The *mara de'atra,* ideally with the support of the lay leadership, will define the *halakhah* of the synagogue by balancing the law with a community's customs, values, and vision.

The following examples of how *halakhah* operates in synagogue life are characterized by competing ethics and ideals. And, indeed, the diversity of opinions with respect to any given topic will almost always reflect the different weight that different rabbis place on competing values. Considerations such as *k'vod ha-b'riyyot* (showing dignity to every person), *darkhei shalom* (preserving a peaceful ambience in the community), and *keiruv* (bringing people near to observance by drawing them into the synagogue) are all important factors in the derivation of *halakhah* for a synagogue community, but these values will be weighted differently from one community to another. Similarly, any halakhic considerations must recognize the need for the synagogue itself to model the highest standard of observance for its membership, both in order to impress on the congregation the expectations of a committed life, and also to inspire synagogue members personally to reach ever higher on the ladder of observance. Ultimately, the determination of the *halakhah* of synagogue life must be achieved with integrity and with faith in the enduring strength of the halakhic process.

The Role of the Rabbi

The rabbi is considered the teacher of Jewish law for the individual community, as well as the authority for the religious practices and halakhic decisions of a congregation. The rabbi receives this authority in the eyes of Conservative Judaism by virtue of his or her ordination from an institution recognized by the Rabbinical Assembly, the international organization of Conservative rabbis. And the rabbi's authority is *ipso facto* accepted by the congregation by virtue of its choice to hire that individual as its spiritual leader. But how much power, exactly, should a rabbi wield in terms of governing a synagogue community according to the norms and standards of the *halakhah* as he or she interprets it in any given situation?

A rabbi in the Conservative movement is guided, and sometimes bound, by the decisions of the Rabbinical Assembly's Committee on Jewish Law and Standards, often referred to as the Law Committee or the CJLS. The Committee is a body consisting of twenty-five voting members, all rabbis, and six non-voting members, one of whom is a cantor representing the Cantors Assembly and five of whom are lay members representing the United Synagogue of Conservative Judaism. The CJLS debates and responds both to questions that have not previously been discussed by the Committee or other halakhic sources and those that have. After debate and discussion, a written responsum, a *t'shuvah,* is voted upon. A *t'shuvah* that receives at least six votes by CJLS members is considered an official position of the Law Committee, and thus a valid halakhic position for any individual rabbi to hold in the Conservative rabbinate. As a result, there are times when mutually exclusive opinions regarding a specific principle or matter of law may both gain recognition as equally valid positions of the CJLS.

The decisions of the Committee on Jewish Law and Standards do not answer every question or respond to every conceivable special circumstance that a rabbi may face within an individual community. As *mara de'atra* of the synagogue, therefore, the rabbi will regularly have to base halakhic decisions on his or her personal interpretation of the halakhic sources, and might even occasionally find him or herself in disagreement with a decision of the CJLS. The Conservative rabbi is free to follow his or her personal halakhic decisions, but all Conservative rabbis are bound by several rabbinic standards of practice approved by the CJLS and ratified by the Rabbinical Assembly. These standards of practice include the prohibition of performing a marriage for a divorced man or woman who has not obtained a *get* or *hafka·at kiddushin* (a formal Jewish divorce or an annulment of any previous marriage), the prohibition of officiating or even being physically present at the marriage of a Jew to a non-Jew, the prohibition of officiating at a purely civil marriage ceremony, the prohibition of determining Jewish status based on anything other than matrilineal descent or conversion, and the prohibition of supervising any conversion that omits *t'vilah* (immersion in a *mikveh*) in the case of a female or *t'vilah* and *b'rit milah* (ritual circumcision) in the case of a male (*CJLS Responsa 1991–2000,* pp. x–xi).

Beyond being bound by these standards of practice, the rabbi of the synagogue bears the deep, personal responsibility of interpreting the *halakhah* based on the guidance of the CJLS, the rabbi's personal reading of the halakhic sources, and the rabbi's consideration of the unique circumstances within the individual synagogue community.

Membership in the Synagogue

While individual synagogues are free to ratify the by-laws that govern those institutions and to define the rights and privileges of individual members, these rights and privileges of membership in a synagogue may be extended only to individuals who are considered Jewish by Conservative halakhic standards. Thus, the Jewish individual seeking membership must either have been born to a Jewish mother or else must have undergone a process of conversion under the conditions outlined above. While synagogues should be devoted to drawing people closer to our traditions and to establishing good relations between Jews and non-Jews, these principles should not override the basic requirement that synagogue members be halakhically Jewish. This principle also extends to individuals who are in the process of converting to Judaism. Such a non-Jew's attendance at services and classes and his or her participation in programs should be welcomed and encouraged, but granting membership to individuals prior to conversion would misrepresent the status of the individual to the community.

The issue of a non-Jewish individual seeking membership in a synagogue usually arises in the context of an interfaith couple seeking joint or family membership. In March 1982, the Committee on Jewish Law and Standards adopted as "deliberations of the Committee" five different statements on the *mitzvah* of *keiruv*. This unusual step was taken specifically to provide Conservative rabbis with a relatively wide spectrum of views on intermarriage and how to deal with intermarried Jewish individuals and their non-Jewish spouses effectively and kindly, but also with halakhic integrity.

Our synagogues should be as open and welcoming as possible without blurring the line between Jewish and non-Jewish individuals. In their statement on the topic of *keiruv*, for example, in light of the "urgency of the status quo in many communities," Rabbis Joel Roth and Daniel Gordis recognized the necessity for "undeniable and significant compromise of [those] traditional halakhic standards which consider conversions solely for the sake of marriage as undesirable" (*CJLS Responsa 1980–1990*, p. 667). And, indeed, by departing from tradition just far enough to include the non-Jewish spouses of Jews in the class of those eligible for consideration as potential converts (with the ultimate goal being to convert the non-Jewish spouse), policies and programs may be created for bringing non-Jewish spouses closer to Judaism.

While membership in the synagogue may be restricted to the Jewish spouse, therefore, the non-Jewish spouse should be encouraged to attend services, to participate in educational activities, and to participate in the social events of the synagogue, including programs of the synagogue's affiliate organizations. Indeed, it is only in the best interest of all concerned for the non-Jewish spouses (and children) of synagogue members to be welcomed warmly and made to feel like part of the larger synagogue community.

Children of interfaith marriages fall into two categories in this discussion. Regarding the children of non-Jewish fathers and Jewish mothers, and children who have formally been converted to Judaism, no halakhic issue exists regarding participation in a synagogue's religious school or youth group. The children of non-Jewish mothers who have not been converted to Judaism and who are not preparing to convert are unambiguously not Jewish and cannot be treated as Jews within the synagogue community. In the case of non-Jewish children whose parents have made a commitment to convert them but have not yet done so, Rabbis Kassel Abelson, Seymour Siegel, and Harry Sky, in separate statements, recommend a different approach. In their opinion, such children should be regarded as potential converts and thus be admitted into a religious school or youth group. Even though the parents' procrastination (if such it is) may cast doubt upon their intention to follow through, insofar as conversion of children is a relatively easy process, nevertheless we should be willing to help strengthen their commitment to Judaism by encouraging the children's participation in synagogue youth activities such as enrollment in the synagogue's religious school.

Conservative rabbis have also debated the matter of participation in religious schools and youth groups by non-Jewish children whose parents have made *no* commitment to convert them. Rabbis Roth and Gordis hold that non-Jewish children whose parents have not made a commitment to convert them should not be permitted to participate in the religious school or in youth group activities, on the grounds that doing so would permit "socializing with peers whom we would ultimately not permit them to marry, and it might contribute to the weakening of the clear distinctions we seek to draw between Jews and non-Jews in ritual and religious affairs." Rabbis Abelson, Siegel, and Sky have written opinions in support of permitting attendance at religious school and participation in youth groups, arguing that the children of intermarried Jewish men should be treated as potential converts based precisely on their parents' willingness to enroll them in Jewish schools or to permit their participation in Jewish youth groups.

Ultimately, the decision of which course any synagogue follows lies in the hands of the rabbi who, acting as *mara de'atra,* defines the synagogue's halakhic policies. While a rabbi may consider the principle of *keiruv* almost sacred and thus maintain the hope that the non-Jewish children in the community will come to embrace Judaism through formal conversion, the rabbi must balance these goals against the potential problems such situations create in the religious school environment, as well as the effect the presence of such children will almost inevitably have on the teachers and the other children. On the one hand, an eventual change in Jewish status will usually come about as a direct result of an individual's developing sense of Jewish identity. But the rabbi may also want to consider the mixed message being sent to the individual non-Jewish child, who may well perceive him or herself as being tacitly told simply to pass as Jewish. Jewish communities should always seek the best for all children, Jewish and non-Jewish, but synagogue policy should always be organized around the principle of acting in the best interests of the Jewish children in its midst with an eye toward helping them mature into committed Jewish adults. Muddying the waters with respect to the halakhic status of the children of intermarried individuals will rarely, if ever, be a kindness in the long run.

Gender Issues

The role of women in society has undergone enormous changes in the last half-century and so has the role women play in synagogue life, both in its administration and in its ritual, undergone immense transformation over those same fifty years. Whereas it was once normal for women not to be voting members of the congregations with which their families were affiliated, it is now universally accepted, at least in the non-Orthodox world, that when a couple acquires a family membership in a synagogue it is both of them who become members in good standing and thus also both of whom who may participate in congregational elections by voting and by running for office.

In the area of synagogue ritual life, women's roles have similarly evolved, but there is a divide in Conservative rabbinic opinion as to how exactly the concept of "equality" should be defined under Jewish law. More specifically, while some rabbis advocate for what is in essence an "equal rights amendment" under Jewish law that would obliterate gender-based distinctions in ritual behavior, other rabbis choose to address these issues within the context of obligation in the performance of *mitzvot*. This second approach follows the line of reasoning that, because the ritual enfranchisement of men over women followed from the different way the *halakhah* understood their ritual obligations, women who wish to be similarly enfranchised need to accept obligations similar to those the *halakhah* has traditionally assigned to men. And there are also rabbis within the Conservative movement who prefer to maintain traditional attitudes toward the participation of women in ritual and synagogue life.

Conservative rabbis have also reexamined the traditional sources with an eye toward differentiating between those instances in which women were prohibited from participation and those instances where women were only exempted. Finally, some women's issues have been addressed by distinguishing between *minhag* and *halakhah* (i.e., between custom and law), and then showing greater willingness to ignore gender-based distinctions rooted in mere custom and greater reluctance to tamper with the traditional norms and strictures of gender-based distinctions rooted in actual law.

Some issues, once considered monumental, have lost all their contentiousness within the Conservative movement. The question of men and women sitting together in the sanctuary, for example, faded into the background more than half a century ago when the CJLS determined that there was no specific prohibition against mixed seating (*Proceedings of the CJLS 1927–1970,* pp. 1060–1084). The ordination of women as rabbis has also become a widely accepted feature of Jewish life in Conservative communities since the first women were admitted to the Rabbinical School of the Jewish Theological Seminary in 1983. Nor is there any ongoing debate about whether bat mitzvah celebrations may be held in the course of Shabbat morning services. (This was once a controversial issue; cf. Rabbi Ben Zion Bokser's responsum, "Shabbat Morning Bat Mitzvah," in *CJLS Responsa 1980–1990,* pp. 195–196.)

Questions surrounding the participation of women in synagogue ritual have also faded from prominence as the egalitarian principle has taken root, at least to some extent, within virtually all Conservative congregations. The large majority of Conservative congregations, for example, both call women forward to the Torah for *aliyot* and permit them to read aloud from the Torah scroll. (See in this regard Rabbi Sanders Tofield's responsum in *Proceedings of the CJLS 1927–1970,* pp. 1100–1108, and Rabbi Aaron Blumenthal's, published in that same volume on pp. 1086–1099).

Slightly less universally resolved is the issue of counting women in the *minyan* or permitting women to serve as leaders during all or part of the prayer service. Ultimately, it is the task of the *mara de'atra* to guide individual synagogue communities to embrace one or another of the endorsed halakhic options. (See the discussion of this topic by Rabbi Joel Roth in *The Ordination of Women as Rabbis: Studies and Responsa,* ed. Simon Greenberg [New York: The Jewish Theological Seminary, 1988], pp. 127–187, as well as by Rabbi Mayer Rabinowitz in that same volume, pp. 107–123.)

One set of issues that remains largely unresolved regarding the participation of women in synagogue life has to do with the specific question of the place of the descendants of the priests and Levites of antiquity, called *kohanim* and *l'viyyim,* in congregational worship. Not all synagogues maintain the traditional custom of honoring *kohanim* and *l'viyyim* with the first two *aliyot* when the Torah is read aloud in public. For synagogues that maintain these distinctions and that also grant women *aliyot,* the question arises as to how the daughters of *kohanim* or *l'viyyim* are to be called to the Torah. In a 1989 *t'shuvah,* Rabbi Joel Roth argues that the exemption of boys born to women who are the daughters of *kohanim* or *l'viyyim* from the ritual of *pidyon ha-bein,* the redemption of the firstborn, offers sufficient "indication of lineal sanctity for the daughters of *kohanim,* even if married" to warrant considering their status "real" enough to count in the matter of *aliyot* ("The Status of Daughters of Kohanim and Levites for Aliyot," *CJLS Responsa 1980–1990,* p. 59). Rabbi Roth holds, therefore, that daughters of *kohanim* and *l'viyyim,* even if married to husbands of a different lineage, should be accorded the same status with respect to *aliyot* as male *kohanim* and *l'viyyim.* Nevertheless, there are many Conservative synagogues that offer women *aliyot,* but which reserve the first two for male *kohanim* and *l'viyyim.*

Another issue related to the question of the place of *kohanim* in the congregation has to do with the question of who may come forward to pronounce the priestly benediction. Rabbi Mayer Rabinowitz, in a 1994 *t'shuvah,* relies upon the arguments of lineal sanctity, the role women play in Jewish tradition as conduits of divine blessing, and the historical development of the ritual itself to conclude that women should be permitted to participate in the service of *n'si·at kappayim* ("Women Raise Your Hands," *CJLS Responsa 1991–2000,* pp. 9–12). The opposing position was taken by Rabbis Stanley Bramnick and Judah Kogen, who concluded that, as the ceremony was specifically retained in the first place for the sake of recalling the ritual of the ancient Temple in Jerusalem, *n'si·at kappayim* should only be performed by those who would have been eligible to do so in the Temple in ancient days ("Should *Nesi'at Kappayim* Include *Benot Kohanim?*" *CJLS Responsa 1991–2000,* pp. 13–15). Both practices are found in Conservative synagogues today.

A final issue relating to women in the congregational setting has to do with the question of attire. In Conservative synagogues, the requirement of head coverings for women, whether married or single, whether receiving an honor on the *bimah* or simply being present in the sanctuary, is purely one of custom. Each synagogue, therefore, is free to follow its own tradition in conjunction with its rabbi's wishes, prevailing custom, and accepted standards of behavior. It is the practice of some synagogues, however, to ask all worshipers, or at least all adult worshipers, to cover their heads out of respect while in the sanctuary. It seems reasonable that egalitarian congregations would seek a uniform policy with respect to covering the head in the sanctuary that would apply similarly to males and females, and both to children and to adults.

There is no prohibition in the *halakhah* against women wearing *tallitot.* Nor is there any specific requirement that one who receives an *aliyah* to the Torah wear a *tallit* when coming forward. In egalitarian congregations, the prevailing custom is for women to use the *tallit* the way men do. Customs vary, however, from synagogue to synagogue.

The Place of the Interfaith Family in Synagogue Life

Aside from issues that specifically have to do with membership in synagogues for intermarried couples and their children (which I have discussed above in some detail), halakhic issues also arise with respect to the extent to which the Jewish members of such families should be permitted to participate in synagogue life. The following sections consider the areas of synagogue leadership and ritual.

Intermarried Individuals and Synagogue Leadership

In a 1963 paper adopted by the Committee on Jewish Law and Standards entitled "The Jew Who Has Intermarried," Rabbi Max Routtenberg argues that the Jew who has intermarried, while admissible for membership in the congregation, "shall not be entitled to hold any office or to serve as chairman of any committee, nor shall he be singled out for any special honors" (*Proceedings of the Rabbinical Assembly* 28 [1964], p. 247). Twenty years later, Rabbi Joel Roth affirmed that position, arguing that permitting an intermarried Jew to hold synagogue office sends a message that the intermarriage is irrelevant to the community ("Synagogue Honors for the Intermarried Jew," *CJLS Responsa 1980–1990,* pp. 682–684). Dissenting views, however, also began to be heard. For example, eight rabbis of the CJLS, while affirming Rabbi Routtenberg's position in principle, nonetheless asserted that individual rabbis must have "the maximum possible latitude in formulating strategies for preventing and treating intermarriage," and that Rabbi Routtenberg's position must be "subject to interpretation at the local level" ("Synagogue Honors for the Intermarried Jew: A Dissenting Opinion," ibid., p. 685). Today, most synagogues value above all other concerns the need and wish to draw all Jews to synagogue life without subjecting an individual's desire to serve the community to harsh or exclusionary standards.

The Participation of Intermarried Individuals in Synagogue Ritual

Rabbi Routtenberg's position, as cited above, is that intermarried Jews should not be singled out for any special honors, but he does not specify what kind of honors are meant. Rabbi Joel Roth, for example, understands the rule to apply to making such an individual an honoree at a dinner or to appointing an intermarried Jew to a communal organization as the representative of the synagogue, but he also extends the definition of special honors to include *aliyot* to the Torah (*CJLS Responsa 1980–1990,* pp. 682–684). There is no clear movement-wide standard of behavior in this regard; individual rabbis are free to define Rabbi Routtenberg's position according to the circumstances of their individual synagogues, and thus, if they wish, to approve the granting of *aliyot* and other ritual honors to intermarried Jews. The key, always, is to draw in and make welcome all Jewish people who wish to participate in synagogue life, but without appearing to condone behavior considered inimical to the best interests of the synagogue community or the Jewish people. No one's interests are ever served by distancing Jews from Judaism.

The Participation of Non-Jewish Spouses in Synagogue Life

Conservative rabbinic opinion on the issue of permitting the non-Jewish spouses of Jewish congregants to participate in life-cycle rituals such as *b'rit milah,* naming ceremonies, and bar or bat mitzvahs is varied and ranges from absolute permission of such involvement to absolute prohibition. There are also rabbis who permit that a symbolic role in the ceremony be granted to a non-Jewish individual, especially a parent or grandparent.

Rabbis Joel Roth and Daniel Gordis argue that we should prohibit all participation by non-Jewish parents in any life-cycle ritual ("*Keiruv* and the Status of Intermarried Families," *CJLS Responsa 1980–1990,* p. 670). At the other end of the halakhic spectrum, we find rabbis arguing that we must do all we can to include a non-Jewish parent, both because it is polite to do so and also to honor that individual's commitment to raising his or her child or children Jewishly. This inclusiveness is extended to life-cycle rituals as well. Rabbi Kassel Abelson, for example, argues that it is possible to justify giving a non-Jewish spouse a role to play merely by differentiating that role from the role that a Jewish parent may play. While the principle of inclusiveness may not be applied to any honors associated with the Torah, Rabbi Abelson does advocate permitting a non-Jewish parent to recite the She-heḥeyyanu as part of a group, permitting such a parent to present a *tallit* to a bar or bat mitzvah child, or permitting a non-Jewish parent to stand beneath the *ḥuppah* at a wedding ("The Non-Jewish Spouse and Children of a Mixed Marriage," ibid., pp. 646–659).

Acknowledging Intermarriage or the Birth of Non-Jewish Children

The public acknowledgment in a synagogue bulletin or any synagogue announcement of an intermarriage or of the birth of a non-Jewish child (where the parents have yet to make a commitment to convert the child) grants legitimacy and approval to such events. In a responsum adapted by the CJLS in 1989 and published in *CJLS Responsa 1980–1990*, pp. 689–698, Rabbi Jerome Epstein held that intermarriages should not be publicly acknowledged in any official synagogue forum, but that congratulations may be offered when a child is born to a Jewish mother or where the parents have committed themselves to converting the child to Judaism. Practices in this regard vary from synagogue to synagogue, but the general principle is always the same: to avoid alienating Jews from synagogue life and to create an inclusive atmosphere that will draw the non-Jewish spouses, children, and grandchildren of synagogue members to Judaism and Jewish life.

The Synagogue as Halakhic Exemplar

To what extent should the synagogue itself model the halakhic behavior it wishes to instill in its members? Should it mirror the general pattern of observance displayed by its own congregants, or should it set a higher standard for itself—even to a level that few, if any, members of the congregation personally meet? Or should the rabbi be the model of observance that the synagogue adopts? I consider specific issues of this sort in the following sections.

Shabbat in the Synagogue

The question of the permissibility of various forms of audio or video recording on Shabbat turns on the question of whether recording should be considered a form of writing or not. Because still photography involves an intentional act on Shabbat to create a meaningful and enduring record either through chemical, magnetic, or digital means, it is prohibited on Shabbat as a violation of the law and spirit of the day. (See in this regard Rabbi Joel Roth in Klein, p. 530.) In 1982, the Committee on Jewish Law and Standards unanimously adopted a motion to disallow videotaping on Shabbat, based on papers submitted by Rabbis David Lincoln and Mayer Rabinowitz. Rabbi Lincoln concluded that the practice should be prohibited since it does not enhance the ambience of Shabbat, and also because the recording introduces a disruptive element in the synagogue. He also pointed to the temptation to adjust the taping device as another reason for its being disallowed. Basing himself on a technological understanding of the recording process, however, he does not consider such recording to be a form of writing (Rabbi David Lincoln, "Videotaping on Shabbat," *CJLS Responsa 1980–1990*, pp. 212–214). While agreeing with Rabbi Lincoln's conclusions, Rabbi Rabinowitz holds that recording should indeed be prohibited as *k'tivah* (writing) on Shabbat because the purpose of recording is to make a permanent record. Rabbi Rabinowitz also argues that the use of an automatic device for recording should be prohibited as well, because the recording of sound is initiated by the speaker who, merely by speaking, causes a magnetic field to come into being ("An Addendum to 'Videotaping on Shabbat,'" *CJLS Responsa 1980–1990,* pp. 215–217). Subsequent *t'shuvot* and opinions have permitted recording on Shabbat with the use of an automated device, even where the recording is considered to create a kind of writing.

In a 1989 responsum, Rabbi Gordon Tucker determined that the use of closed circuit television on Shabbat is permissible, albeit not desirable, as long as certain conditions are met: that no recording is taking place, that the equipment is set up and turned on before Shabbat, that no Jew becomes involved in adjusting the equipment, and that there is no noticeable distortion in the visual or sound components of the system (*CJLS Responsa 1980–1990,* pp. 222–228). (Distortion could lead an individual to attempt to adjust or repair the system, but could also prevent a participant from fulfilling certain *mitzvot,* such as hearing the sound of the *shofar.*)

The Committee on Jewish Law and Standards has validated more than one opinion regarding the question of food preparation on Shabbat. Rabbi Kassel Abelson's responsum, adopted by the CJLS in 1981 as the majority opinion, was written with an eye toward encouraging families to celebrate their *se'udot mitzvah* (celebratory meals following life-cycle events) in the synagogue ("Preparing and Serving Food on Shabbat," *CJLS Responsa 1980–1990,* pp. 197–199). Rabbi Abelson holds, however, that all cooking for a meal to be served on Shabbat must be completed before Shabbat begins, but that cooked solid foods, including frozen foods, may be warmed up on Shabbat, that liquid foods (including coffee and water) that have been prepared or boiled before Shabbat may be reheated but not boiled, and that non-Jewish employees may be told before Shabbat (as part of their overall job responsibilities) to clean up, sweep up, and set tables in preparation for a Saturday night meal. Most synagogues permit the preparation of tables and cold food on Shabbat.

In a minority opinion, also adopted by the CJLS, Rabbi Mayer Rabinowitz recognizes the importance of a maximalist halakhic approach for synagogue observance ("Preparation and Serving of Food on Shabbat in the Synagogue," ibid., pp. 200–204). Among the principles that Rabbi Rabinowitz suggests as guidelines for the synagogue to follow is the general prohibition of any preparation *on* Shabbat for a function that will begin *after* Shabbat. This prohibition includes the warming of food to be eaten after

Shabbat, the setting of tables and the like for a Saturday evening affair, and the arrival of caterers or their employees in the synagogue before Shabbat is over. Rabbi Rabinowitz also holds that, if we are to have standards rooted both in the letter and the spirit of the law, we must not permit the assigning of non-Jews to perform acts prohibited to Jews on Shabbat. "Even though a non-Jew can be assigned specific duties on Shabbat as part of his responsibilities, we should prohibit any and all [such] duties that are either done publicly or are obviously done for the sake of Jews" (p. 203).

Kashrut in the Synagogue

The synagogue must adopt a standard of food preparation that is clearly defined and which, by its nature, will instill confidence among the synagogue's congregants that all food served in the synagogue meets a rational standard of *kashrut.* Preserving this model standard of *kashrut* necessitates prohibiting individual congregants, who will invariably maintain differing standards of *kashrut,* from bringing food into the synagogue that they have prepared in their own homes (responsum of Rabbi George Pollak, *CJLS Responsa 1980–1990,* pp. 290–294). Furthermore, all foods purchased and brought into the synagogue, regardless of whether they are brought into the synagogue's kitchen, should meet the synagogue's *kashrut* standards. While some rabbis permit non-Jewish employees to bring their own food into the synagogue for their personal consumption, great care should be taken to ensure that these foods do not come into contact with the synagogue's kitchen facilities or food utensils.

Rabbi Paul Drazen has prepared a manual entitled "*Kashrut* Supervision in the Synagogue," which provides a list of areas in which decisions must be made by the *mara de'atra* with respect to Shabbat and festival observance and preparations, *t'shuvot* of the CJLS relating to *kashrut* issues in the Conservative movement, and a collection of training materials for synagogue supervision. Rabbi Drazen's manual is available on the website of the Rabbinical Assembly.

The Synagogue G'nizah and the Disposal of Sheimot

The synagogue has the unique opportunity to teach the sanctity and centrality of God's name in our tradition through the way in which it disposes of *sheimot,* books or pages that bear the name of God. The synagogue will often have a container or storeroom, called a *g'nizah,* in which these items can be deposited, along with other ritual articles whose sanctity merits respectful treatment at the end of their usefulness. When the depository is full, or when an appropriate occasion arises, the contents can be solemnly collected and buried on the synagogue grounds as part of a communal ceremony. While there is no set liturgical text for the burial ceremony for *sheimot,* the occasion presents an opportunity for the creation of a communal liturgy that can include prayers, texts, poetry, and song.

In all printed materials created by synagogues, including materials mailed to congregants' homes and materials distributed in the synagogue building, it is judicious to avoid printing God's Hebrew name wherever possible so as to prevent inadvertent disposal of pages bearing the divine name by people not familiar with the issue.

The Synagogue as a Business Entity

Just as the synagogue must strive to be a model of observance for its congregation in ritual matters, so must the synagogue be cognizant of its status as a role model and representative of the Jewish community in its business dealings. General issues relating to the *halakhah* of commerce are covered elsewhere in this volume in the chapters by Rabbis Jacob Blumenthal, Jane Kanarek, Barry Leff, and Cheryl Peretz. In this section, therefore, I shall discuss issues specifically related to the concept of the synagogue as a business.

Accepting Advertisements from Non-Kosher Establishments

While the synagogue must maintain high standards of observance with respect to *kashrut,* the Conservative movement's various positions on individual observance—especially with respect to the permissibility of eating in non-kosher establishments—give rise to an equal number of opinions on the topic of advertising non-kosher establishments in a synagogue bulletin or journal. If, as in the case of intermarriages, recognition gives an aura of authenticity or approval, the synagogue must be concerned with how an advertisement of a non-kosher establishment in a bulletin or journal will be perceived. Some authorities believe that carrying such an advertisement suggests endorsement. Conversely, it is argued that a synagogue is also a business entity and must raise a certain amount of money annually in order to ensure its survival. (In many communities, advertisements in the synagogue bulletin constitute a significant source of income.) At the very least, if advertisements for non-kosher facilities are to be carried, they should be accompanied by a disclaimer stating that the synagogue does not certify the *kashrut* of the establishments that advertise in its publications. Furthermore, if a non-kosher establishment's advertisement is carried in a synagogue journal, the advertisement should appear as a personal one placed by the owner rather than as an institutional one. The Committee on Jewish Law and Standards has not adopted any official position on this matter.

Synagogues confront a similar set of issues when considering the sale or raffling of vouchers or gift certificates for non-kosher restaurants or non-kosher food, or prize packages involving stays at lodgings where neither kosher nor dairy or vegetarian meals are available. Again, the issue of synagogue endorsement presents itself, and is compounded by the idea that the synagogue is actually profiting by the whole procedure that leads congregants to frequent these establishments or to use these products. It has been suggested, therefore, that such a practice should be prohibited. While a synagogue may choose to sell an advertising coupon booklet that includes discounts for non-kosher establishments, among other services, it is recommended that the synagogue include a cover letter stating that it does not certify the *kashrut* of any of the restaurants in the booklet.

Employing Intermarried Jews in the Synagogue Setting

The same issues involved in the question of intermarried Jews holding synagogue offices apply to the hiring of certain employees as well. Indeed, just as rabbis and cantors serve as role models for their communities, so do teachers and administrators. "Anyone who represents the congregation—on any level, coming into contact in a regular and significant fashion with a member—will inevitably impact on that individual. . . . It is natural to assume that those who represent the congregation may be perceived as synonymous with the congregation" (Rabbi Jerome Epstein, "Issues Regarding Employment of an Intermarried Jew by a Synagogue or Solomon Schechter Day School," *Responsa 1991–2000,* p. 608). The Committee on Jewish Law and Standards has adopted Rabbi Epstein's prohibition against the synagogue hiring any rabbi, cantor, educator, teacher, youth worker, or executive director—all considered Jewish role models—who has intermarried.

Renting Space to Church Groups

There can be little doubt that a synagogue should not open its space for use by a group hostile to Judaism or Israel, or seeking to practice missionary activities, but it is good practice to reach out to members of other faiths and especially to those in need or in times of crisis. In a 1990 responsum, Rabbi Elliot Dorff determined that it is therefore permissible to rent or loan space in the synagogue to a church group (*CJLS Responsa, 1980–1990,* pp. 165–184). Where possible, it is best to lend a room other than the sanctuary or a space generally used for prayer or study and the Ark, if present, should be covered by a partition or curtain. In addition, signs should be posted alerting people to the fact that a non-Jewish worship service is taking place, yet these signs should be worded in such a way so as to make the synagogue's guests feel welcome and to avoid giving the impression that the synagogue's hospitality is being offered in a begrudging way. These precautions should serve to minimize confusion, while at the same time making members of the congregation feel proud that their synagogue is generous and tolerant. Because the facility in question is a synagogue, non-Jewish groups should be expected not to bring non-kosher food into the facility even for their own consumption.

Similarly, a congregation is permitted to hold its services in a church facility in time of need. Non-Jewish symbols should be covered in such cases, and the congregation should ask their hosts to post signs alerting their own people to the fact that a synagogue service is taking place on their premises.

Gambling

The synagogue is the physical space that is meant to house the spiritual, ethical, and ritual aspirations of the individual Jew. The sanctity of that space is safeguarded by the types of activities we conduct there, and also by the way we try to conduct ourselves while in that space. We would not wish to pursue any course of conduct that would ultimately serve to detract from the sanctity of the synagogue or from the high moral and spiritual goals it represents.

In 1981, Rabbi Henry Sosland issued a paper, adopted by the Committee on Jewish Law and Standards, strongly urging rabbis to guard against the evils of gambling both among individuals within the synagogue and also as part of synagogue fiscal management ("A Statement on Gambling," *CJLS Responsa, 1980–1990,* pp. 794–797). While games like bingo are not technically prohibited halakhically, they do not represent the moral standards and sanctity of the synagogue at its finest. The specific issue of synagogues sponsoring gambling events as a way of raising funds is discussed elsewhere in this volume by Rabbi Elliot Dorff in his chapter on the halakhic dimension of charitable giving.

Interdenominational Participation

The Conservative synagogue should always seek to be a place that is guided both by the desire to be inclusive and welcoming, and also by the need to maintain normative boundaries with respect to Jewish tradition and law. While the tension created between these two values often comes to the fore with respect to the treatment of non-Jews or intermarried couples within a synagogue community, it can also inform relationships the synagogue and its members have with other Jewish denominations.

The sad reality is that all too often those within Orthodox circles do not regard the practices of Conservative communities as falling within the normative practice of traditional Judaism. When members of Conservative congregations invite Orthodox family members or friends to join them for celebrations, for example, the Orthodox guest will sometimes refuse the invitation so as to avoid being seen within the walls of the Conservative congregation. Many Orthodox rabbis hold that an individual guest's presence in the Conservative synagogue could create an assumption in the minds of others that the guest condones the practices taking place around them. Alternatively, an Orthodox guest may come to the Conservative synagogue but overtly avoid participating in the service. In either event, the members of the Conservative community are often left feeling judged or even insulted.

At the other end of the denominational spectrum, Reform Jews visiting the Conservative synagogue are often uncomfortable with the more traditional structure of the service or with the expectations that guests should cover their heads or wear *tallitot*. Moreover, Reform acceptance of patrilineal descent is viewed by the Conservative community to be outside the bounds of normative Jewish practice. As a result, it will sometimes occur that an involved, engaged member of a Reform temple will be denied an honor at a bar or bat mitzvah in a Conservative congregation and feel that what is being implied is that he or she is not "really" Jewish. This reality can leave the Reform Jew in the Conservative congregation feeling similarly judged and marginalized.

The best policy in both regards is to attempt always to be welcoming and respectful, but without abandoning any core beliefs in doing so. Orthodox guests in a Conservative setting should be encouraged to participate, then left to accept or reject the invitation as they see fit. Guests from Reform congregations should be similarly welcomed, but not in such a way that involves violating the standards of the congregation. A willingness to compromise reasonably should inform all such decisions.

Conservative Jews who choose to attend Reform temples or Orthodox synagogues to pray should also be aware of the implications of their presence in those places. We are guided by the values of *k'lal yisra·el* (Jewish peoplehood) and *darkhei shalom* (peaceful cooperation with our neighbors), both of which policies dictate that we should avoid offending anyone whose beliefs or practices differ, even sharply, from our own. However, our Conservative understanding of *halakhah* must also dictate how we fulfill our own obligation to pray, to observe, and to teach in the presence of those whose practices differ from our own. The guiding principle should therefore be to maintain our standards and our practices to the greatest extent possible without giving offense or appearing to treat our hosts with disdain or condescension. It can certainly never be considered sound policy to behave boorishly in someone else's spiritual home or to disparage the local custom or the spiritual leader of another Jewish community. In situations in which one feels that one absolutely cannot maintain one's integrity in a place to which one has been invited as a guest, the most reasonable policy is simply not to attend at all, rather than to attend but be perceived as behaving ungraciously or rudely.

Messianic Jews in Synagogue Life

A more recent phenomenon confronting Conservative congregations is the presence of individuals who claim to embrace Judaism as their faith but who *also* espouse belief in Jesus of Nazareth as the messiah. These so-called Messianic Jews (also known as Jews for Jesus, Hebrew Christians, or Jewish Christians) often observe Jewish rituals strictly or reasonably strictly. While the first Messianic Jews were converts from Judaism to Christianity who simply held on to their Jewish rituals, Messianic Jewish congregations have grown into communities of their own over the last few decades, often seeking to bring Jews into their fold.

Our sages teach that Jews remains Jews even though they may sin (*BT* Sanhedrin 44a). Nevertheless, Messianic Jews—regardless of whether they were born Jewish and subsequently embraced Jesus or are Christians who subsequently came to embrace Jewish ritual—are not Jewish. (This is the formal policy of the State of Israel too. In the 1962 "Brother Daniel" case, the Israeli Supreme Court affirmed that Jews who adopt Christianity are to be considered Christian under Israeli law regardless of whether they worship in Hebrew or observe Shabbat.) For purposes of membership, Conservative congregations must regard Messianic Jews as having crossed a theological boundary that may never be traversed. There are some Lubavitch Jews who cling to the idea that the late Rabbi Menachem Mendel Schneerson (who died in 1994) was the messiah sent to redeem Israel. They do not advocate that he was divine, however, nor do their prayers that he intercede on their behalf constitute anything approaching worship of him as a divine figure. When Messianic Jews embrace Jesus as part of the trinity, on the other hand, they are in effect elevating the man they consider to be the messiah to the level of divinity, a belief so absolutely incompatible with traditional Jewish belief that it firmly places those who hold it outside the House of Israel. As is the case with respect to all Jews who abandon Judaism, however, the gates of repentance remain forever open.

Funerals in the Synagogue

While we seek to associate the synagogue with life and celebration, there is no specific prohibition against using the synagogue for funeral services. It is not something to encourage as a general practice or as a source of additional income, but the funeral service in the synagogue does give the rabbi greater control over the rituals undertaken in connection with the service, and this is to be regarded positively (Rabbi Ben Zion Bokser, "Statement on Funerals in the Synagogue," *CJLS Responsa 1980–1990,* pp. 617–618). While traditionally funerals have been held in funeral chapels, "an exception was always made in the case of an important individual in Jewish communal life to whom special honors were shown by having the funeral service in the synagogue" (ibid., p. 618). Today, it is more difficult than it perhaps once was to decide who should qualify as an "important individual," and the practice has been extended to include situations where a Jewish funeral chapel is unavailable or impractical. While Rabbi Bokser holds that it is preferable to leave the casket outside the sanctuary when the sanctuary is being used for a funeral service, even he acknowledges that there is nothing specifically wrong or halakhically "offensive" about bringing the casket into the sanctuary.

While the Committee on Jewish Law and Standards has not adopted any official position with respect to memorial services in the synagogue for deceased individuals who have been cremated, such a practice would undermine the basic assumptions upon which Rabbi Bokser based his opinion. Allowing such a service would lend an aura of authenticity to a practice forbidden by *halakhah* and should therefore not be permitted.

The issues addressed above are only a sampling of the many complex halakhic issues the Conservative synagogue faces. The challenge of setting and meeting certain halakhic standards in Conservative Jewish communities is compounded by the synagogue's desire to meet the diverse needs of today's

Conservative congregation. Confronted by constantly changing realities, the synagogue community should always seek to be guided by its rabbi, whom it should regard as its ultimate arbiter of matters of Jewish law and practice. The rabbi and synagogue community may thus wander the path of *halakhah* together. They should look back to view the customs of the community in earlier times and seek to understand the halakhic precedents that were set in place by their forebears. They should observe the present situation and together consider carefully the implications of following a particular halakhic path. They should then strategize and educate for the future, forging and following a vision for the synagogue that keeps it true to the highest ideals, in letter and spirit, of halakhic observance.

Torah Study

ELIEZER DIAMOND

Without question, life-long devotion to *talmud torah* (Torah study) has been the hallmark of the Jewish people. Of the five books of the Pentateuch, Deuteronomy in particular stresses the importance of studying and reviewing the commandments. In the passages that we recite as the first paragraph of the Sh'ma, we are told to "recite [God's teachings] when at home and when away, when lying down and when rising up" (Deuteronomy 6:7). The monarch of Israel is obligated to have God's teachings (called here simply *torah*) written for him on a scroll, which is "to remain with him [so that he may] read it all the days of his life" (Deuteronomy 17:19). At the end of his life, Moses wrote down the divine teachings and gave the scroll to the priests—or, according to another tradition, the Levites—and commanded them to place it beside the Ark of the Covenant (Deuteronomy 31:24–26). Moreover, this scroll is not to remain a mere relic. Every seven years during Sukkot, the scroll is to be read in the presence of the men, women, and children of Israel and the strangers in their midst (Deuteronomy 31:10–13). While this reading may have been ceremonial rather than pedagogical, it implies that all Israelites, and those who have chosen to join them, have an obligation to familiarize themselves with God's teachings.

Torah Study through the Ages

The scholarly consensus is that the period in which the various strands of tradition were woven together to create the Pentateuch—the moment at which the various *torot* became Torah—was sometime after the return to Judea from the Babylonian exile, probably around the time of Ezra (who came to Judea c. 458 B.C.E.). Indeed, some scholars have suggested that Ezra himself was responsible for the final editing of the Torah. The Book of Nehemiah describes a ceremony in which Ezra, who was both priest and scribe, and the Levites read "from the scroll of the Teaching of God, translating it and giving the sense, so they understood the reading" (Nehemiah 8:8). Moreover, this was done in public, in the presence of the people. From that moment on, the Torah became a sacred book that embodied God's word and will; from then on Jews were enjoined to study and observe its commandments.

Two important changes occurred during the Second Temple period. Although initially, as was the case during the period of the First Temple, the Torah was studied and taught mainly by the priests—see, for example, Malachi 2:7—the circle of scholars began to widen to include sages who were not of priestly descent. Additionally, during this period the public reading of the Torah became a regular practice among many Jews. The first-century Jewish historian Josephus boasts that the Jews actually read their sacred book, the Torah, in public every Sabbath, in contrast to other peoples who reserved their sacred texts only for their priesthoods (Josephus, *Against Apion* 2.175). In fact, the scholarly consensus is that, at least in the Land of Israel, synagogues were used for public reading of the Torah even before they were used for communal prayer.

There was also a second, equally important shift. Once the Five Books of Moses had been widely accepted as the unalterable word of God, study generally took the form of commenting upon these books. During most of the Second Temple period, this commentary generally took the form of what Bible scholar James Kugel calls "rewritten Bible." Rather than commenting on the Torah directly, authors wrote alternate versions of the biblical narratives in which they freely recast the story line of the Torah's narrative and sometimes even the content of its legislation. Thus, for example, the author of the Book of Jubilees, who probably wrote in the second century B.C.E., explains the origin of Yom Kippur as commemorating the day on which Joseph was sold into slavery, an idea that apparently appeared nowhere in Scripture as the author found it (Jubilees 34:18).

The importance of Torah study only increased as Judaism developed under the influence of the sages of the rabbinic era, scholars who many believe were the successors to the Pharisees. After the destruction of the Second Temple in 70 C.E., in fact, a group of sages arose who argued that Torah study had replaced sacrifice as the central sustaining act of Jewish life. For these sages, the biblical text was canonical and unalterable; their commentaries, known as *midrashim,* were clearly distinguishable from the Bible itself. The Mishnah, believed to be the earliest extant work composed by these sages, contains an assertion that the study of Torah is by itself equal in importance to all the other *mitzvot* combined (*M* Pei·ah 1:1). Later, the sages of the talmudic era saw themselves as living in a time when God's will could no longer be known through prophecy. In their view, prophecy had ended with the deaths of Haggai, Zechariah, and Malachi at the beginning of the Second Temple period (the early fifth century B.C.E.) and so the will of God, therefore, could now be known only through the study of Scripture. The rabbis saw themselves as the inheritors of the prophets' mandate to bring God's word to the world. Indeed, when the rabbis asserted that "a sage is greater than a prophet," they clearly meant it as a pointed comment about the worth of their own work. (This remark is preserved in the Talmud at *BT* Bava Batra 12a.)

Eventually this ideal was accepted by the larger Jewish community and the Torah scholar became a revered and influential figure. The ideal of study and the valuing of knowledge are characteristic of the Jewish people to this very day, although for many Jews this ideal has taken on a more secular character.

At this moment, there are more Jews enrolled in schools of Jewish learning than at any other time in Jewish history. The Conservative movement, like the Orthodox and—to a lesser degree—the Reform movements, sponsors numerous Jewish day schools and high schools as well as a wide variety of college-level and post-college programs intended to provide intensive Jewish education for both men and women. Furthermore, synagogues everywhere have afternoon Hebrew schools and a variety of adult education programs that feature weekly study of the Torah portion, lectures in Jewish history, and book discussion groups. Clearly these developments help Jewish life flourish worldwide. The purpose of this essay is both to delineate the *mitzvah* of *talmud torah* as it has been understood traditionally and to outline the challenges and opportunities facing contemporary Jews in their engagement with this crucial aspect of Jewish life.

An important proviso must be stated at the outset. Within the Conservative movement, all the key terms that I use here—foremost among them God, *mitzvah,* Torah, and revelation—have a multiplicity of meanings. It is impossible, or at least unwieldy, to offer alternative formulations of *talmud torah* in accordance with each of the theologies that are current in our movement. Consequently, readers must transpose the statements below to make them meaningful according to their own beliefs. At the same time, I put the views of tradition into fruitful conversation with the foundational beliefs of Conservative Judaism and the sociological realities of the Conservative community. That is to say, we ought to hear clearly the voice of tradition and be challenged by its assertions at the same time that we challenge that tradition creatively, reverentially, and productively.

The Ideal of Torah Li-sh'mah and Its Interpretations

Any discussion of *talmud torah* needs to begin with a consideration of why *talmud torah* has been, and continues to be, a foundation of Jewish life, an issue encapsulated by a phrase used a number of times in rabbinic literature, *torah li-sh'mah.* These words are often translated as "Torah for its own sake." However, as Rabbi Norman Lamm points out in his book *Torah Lishmah: Torah for Torah's Sake in the Works of Rabbi Ḥayyim of Volozhin and His Contemporaries* (New York: KTAV, 1989), the concept has been interpreted in at least three different ways.

One, which Lamm designates as instrumental, sees the ultimate value of Torah study in its relationship to the larger concept of observance in general. This notion is expressed in the Talmud itself, which records a debate among the rabbis regarding the question of whether study or action is the greater value. They conclude there that "study is greater, for it brings one to action" (*BT* Kiddushin 40b). This is true in several senses. Most obviously, knowledge of the particulars of the law makes possible the meticulous observance of the *mitzvot.* There is also a psychological aspect to studying the details of the *mitzvot.* Having such knowledge gives one greater confidence in performing the *mitzvot,* which in turn increases one's sense of ownership of one's own observance. Moreover, knowledge of Torah can increase our sense of obligation to attend to the voice of Torah. In this vein Rabbi Israel Salanter asserts that intensive study of any of the *mitzvot* and their details will lead to a greater commitment to a life of Torah and *mitzvot.*

Related to this first view is that of Maimonides, who places a special emphasis on the importance of seeking to understand the reasons behind the *mitzvot* through study and reflection. (As will be explained further, this emphasis is largely driven by Rambam's theological and philosophical outlook.) Study of these reasons, called *ta·amei ha-mitzvot* in the literature, has the potential to strengthen our sense of observance as the reasoned adoption of a cogent code of behavior rather than blind acceptance of arbitrary decrees. Through this process we affirm God's wisdom in prescribing the *mitzvot* and fulfill part of what Rambam considers our ongoing obligation to understand that wisdom within the limits of human capacity.

A second understanding of the ideal of *li-sh'mah* is that the great goal of *talmud torah* is to achieve intimacy with the Divine. This aspect of *talmud torah* is stressed in particular in kabbalistic and hasidic literature. In this view, through Torah study we uncover the deep secrets of the cosmos and clear a path to connecting with the Divine that is present everywhere in God's creation. Whereas the Talmud and *halakhah* primarily address our actions, Kabbalah speaks to our inner spiritual being. Hasidic literature adds a psycho-spiritual element, focusing on the degree to which despair, fear, self-deception, greed, and other emotions and psychological states block the way to a joyous engagement in *avodat ha-sheim,* the service of God.

Interestingly, although the rationalist ideals of Rambam would seem to be the antithesis of kabbalistic mysticism, in a sense he shares some of their ideals in his understanding of the value of *talmud torah.* While Rambam asserts that God's essence and being are beyond human grasp, he nonetheless views the major purpose of *talmud torah* as knowing God to the extent that it is humanly possible to do so. This is true in at least two ways. First, by studying the Bible (and particularly its legal passages) and the traditional rabbinic sources, we learn to act in a godly fashion; for Rambam the only aspect of God that can be comprehended clearly by human beings is the aggregate of God's actions. Indeed, Rambam cites this as one of the prime reasons for performing the *mitzvot.* As he states in his *Guide for the Perplexed* (I 54), the most important virtue of the human being is to become like God to the greatest extent possible; which means that our actions should emulate God's. Second, by studying the traditional corpus of Torah, as well as the natural sciences and philosophy, we understand the greatness of God and come to love and feel reverence for the Almighty (cf. Rambam's *MT* Hilkhot Y'sodei Ha-torah 2:2 and his *Sefer Ha-mitzvot,* positive commandment 3).

The third and final ideal that Lamm delineates is intellectual. Though this ideal is as old as the wisdom literature of the biblical period, it is given a unique meaning by Rabbi Ḥayyim of Volozhin, a nineteenth-century Lithuanian scholar who was a student of Rabbi Elijah Kramer, called the Vilna Gaon. For Rabbi Ḥayyim any meaningful knowledge of God is impossible, and in any case is not the task that the Torah has assigned us. Rather, we are meant to delight in the intellectual pleasure of studying and analyzing the Torah itself, apart from any connection such study may ultimately have to observance, religious character formation, and communion with God. This is not to say that these latter goals are not of concern. Rather, Rabbi Ḥayyim argues that Torah should not become merely a means to achieve these ends, but should instead serve as a source of intellectual delight for those who toil to understand it. Moreover, the processes of reasoning and analyzing, and of raising questions and providing answers, are as much the point of study as the effort to reach definitive conclusions. This understanding of Torah study is particularly helpful to those Jews whose connection to Judaism is primarily intellectual. It also brackets questions of belief, inviting Jews to study Torah regardless of their beliefs and level of observance.

It should be obvious that Jews focus their study on different Torah texts depending on what they understand as being the central goal of *talmud torah*. Beyond this, however, there is the specific definition of the word "Torah" to consider. We now turn to this question.

What Is Torah?

Until Jewish mysticism began to spread in Spain and Provence in the thirteenth century, "Torah" meant, for the vast majority of Jews, biblical literature (including the Bible itself and its traditional Jewish commentaries) and rabbinic literature (including the Mishnah, the Talmud, and codes of *halakhah*). By the sixteenth century, however, most Jewish communities had added the Zohar and other kabbalistic literature to the canon. The eighteenth century saw the rise of the hasidic movement; the Hasidim added their own particular version of biblical commentary and considered stories about the Baal Shem Tov and his successors to be Torah as well. Rabbi Naḥman of Bratslav even composed and taught his followers stories that were, in effect, judaized folktales. The nineteenth century saw the development of the Musar movement among some Lithuanian Jews. The works produced by this movement emphasize thoroughgoing self-assessment as the path to righteousness.

Each of the later additions to the canon—kabbalistic literature, the writings of the Hasidim, and works of Musar—was the subject of controversy when it first came into being. There are still Jews who do not consider some or all of these writings as Torah. For the most part, however, Jews regard all these texts as Torah, though some might yet see them as not worthy of serious study.

There are two other areas of study whose status as Torah has been controversial, and the debate concerning these studies is of particular importance to contemporary Jews. The first is philosophy; the second is the critical study of biblical and rabbinic texts.

Jews who lived under Muslim rule were influenced considerably by Muslim culture. Beginning in the ninth century Muslims began studying Greek philosophical texts that had been translated into Arabic, and Jews also took up the study of philosophy. The first major Jewish work that addressed philosophical issues was Saadiah Gaon's *Book of Beliefs and Opinions*, written in the early tenth century in Baghdad. However, intensive study of philosophy by Jews took place mainly in Al-Andalus, the southern part of the Iberian peninsula that was under Muslim rule to varying degrees from 711 to 1492. The greatest of the Jewish philosophers of Al-Andalus was Maimonides himself (1138–1204), almost universally called Rambam in Jewish circles, although by the time he wrote his famous *Guide for the Perplexed* he had been living in Egypt for many years. The twentieth-century scholar Isadore Twersky has shown that Rambam, in his magisterial code of Jewish law, the *Mishneh Torah,* equates the study of the natural sciences and philosophy with the genre of Torah called *talmud* by the talmudic sages; this genre is supposed to occupy most of one's Torah study time. Could we then say that, in Rambam's view, by studying biology, chemistry, or Kant we are studying Torah?

There are several reasons to answer in the negative. Regarding the study of the sciences, it is worth noting that, in his *Sefer Ha-mitzvot,* Rambam himself takes issue with his predecessors and excludes engaging in astronomical calculation from the enumeration of the 613 commandments (*Sefer Ha-mitzvot,* principle 2), although he does list the obligation "to sanctify each month and to calculate the months and years" (ibid., positive commandment 153), activities that obviously involve detailed astronomical knowledge. This may indicate that Rambam considers study of the sciences to be a *hekhsheir mitzvah,* an important prerequisite for the fulfillment of a *mitzvah,* rather than a *mitzvah* in and of itself. The study of the sciences is crucial for the proper fulfillment of certain *mitzvot.* Consider, for example, the degree of expertise in food science necessary today to supervise the *kashrut* of commercially produced foods. Similarly, many passages in biblical and rabbinic literature cannot be understood fully without knowledge of biology, physics, anatomy, mathematics, ancient Near Eastern languages, Greek, Syriac (as the Aramaic dialect spoken by some ancient Christians was called), ancient and medieval history, and many other disciplines. The Vilna Gaon, certainly no advocate of immersion in non-Jewish culture, is reported by Rabbi Barukh of Shklov to have said, "For every deficiency of knowledge that one has in the sciences [*ḥokhmah*], one will have ten deficiencies of knowledge in the study of the Torah." The Gaon himself authored works on mathematics, geometry, and astronomy and encouraged Rabbi Barukh—again, according to Rabbi Barukh himself—to translate seminal scientific and mathematical treatises into Hebrew.

The distinction between *mitzvah* and *hekhsheir mitzvah* may seem to be without real importance, but it is actually quite significant. Although a *mitzvah,* including the *mitzvah* of Torah study, can be performed in a manner contrary to the spirit of the Torah (this issue is discussed at length by

Naḥmanides in his commentary to Leviticus 19:1), an act that is a *mitzvah* is deemed by Jewish tradition to be inherently good. On the other hand, whether a *hekhsheir mitzvah* is good has to do with the purpose for which it is performed. In *MT* Hilkhot Y'sodei Ha-torah (Laws of the Foundation of the Torah), Rambam advocates for the study of science because through this study one can come to understand the greatness of creation, and thus come to love and fear God even more strongly. Surely such study would qualify as *hekhsheir mitzvah.* If, on the other hand, one studies biology for intellectual stimulation or out of a desire to understand the workings of nature without any theological underpinnings, one is engaging in the study of *ḥokhmah,* wisdom, but not necessarily Torah.

As for philosophy, Leo Strauss argues in his introduction to Shlomo Pines' edition of Rambam's philosophical magnum opus, his *Guide of the Perplexed,* that the work is "not a philosophic book—a book written by a philosopher for philosophers—but a Jewish book written by a Jew for Jews" (Maimonides, *The Guide of the Perplexed,* ed. and trans. Shlomo Pines [University of Chicago Press, 1963], p. xiv). By this Strauss means that the major goal of the *Guide* is to enable rationally- and philosophically-inclined Jews to reconcile their intellectual convictions with the teachings of the Torah. Much of the *Guide* is given over to interpreting biblical and rabbinic narrative and terminology in accordance with Aristotelian philosophy. In addition, much of Book III of the *Guide* is an attempt to put all the commandments on a rational footing and, in so doing, to make them palatable to the philosophically inclined. It would seem, then, that the study of philosophy purely for its own sake without reference to understanding God, God's creation, and God's commandments—in other words, philosophical study other than metaphysics, a branch of philosophy rendered moot by Kant—is not an act of *talmud torah* in Rambam's view.

However, there is more to say. Note that Rambam's *Guide,* for all that the author's contemporaries found radical about it, is actually quite traditional in at least one respect: it takes the form of a commentary on the central texts of Torah. This would seem to be a central characteristic of *talmud torah;* any study to be included under the rubric of Torah must seek in some way to derive its wisdom from, or at least relate itself to, the classical canon of Torah.

What of the critical-historical study of biblical and rabbinic texts? (I refer here not to the work of professional scholars, but of those who wish to engage in *talmud torah* by using the tools of scholarship or by focusing on scholarship itself.) It is noteworthy that, beginning with the nineteenth-century founders of the *Wissenschaft des Judentums* movement devoted to the so-called scientific study of Judaism and continuing to our own day, this kind of scholarship has generally been denoted by its practitioners as *ḥokhmah*, by which term they intended to distinguish it from Torah. The founders and practitioners of *Wissenschaft* saw scholarship as a useful tool for properly understanding the meaning and significance of the texts that constitute Torah, but not as Torah in and of itself—in essence, as *hekhsheir mitzvah*.

However, we cannot leave the matter there. Critical scholarship begins from a position of skepticism toward the claims of tradition, and indeed often serves to undermine the claims of traditional Judaism. In a sense critical scholarship can even be seen as a sort of anti-Torah. How can scholarship be a preparation for the study of the teachings of Torah when it questions their accuracy and thus their authority?

This problem was addressed by a number of early *Wissenschaft* scholars. Many of them viewed critical scholarship as saving Judaism rather than undermining it, despite the fact that—or perhaps because—it questioned traditional assumptions and beliefs. The early nineteenth-century Jewish historian and thinker Naḥman Krochmal argued that it was precisely through historical study that Judaism could be made relevant and compelling for modern Jews. A dogmatic insistence on the truth of traditional claims that had been disproven or at least brought into question, Krochmal argued, would only alienate intellectually sophisticated Jews from Jewish life. Using the tools of scholarship to produce a more nuanced and historically accurate view of Judaism would, he believed, allow Jews to engage in traditional Jewish life without having to abandon their critical view of religion and tradition. To describe this approach, the nineteenth-century rabbinic scholar Zacharias Frankel, often called the spiritual father of Conservative Judaism, coined the term "Positive-Historical Judaism." By this he meant an understanding of Judaism that was historically oriented but which had the goal of preserving and strengthening Jewish life rather than transforming Judaism into a lifeless relic, an accusation leveled against the *Wissenschaft* school by neo-Orthodox leaders like Samson Raphael Hirsch on the one hand and secular Zionists like Gershom Scholem—himself a scholar of international repute—on the other.

The point made by Krochmal and Frankel is particularly relevant to Conservative Judaism, which embraces a broad range of beliefs concerning God, revelation, and a host of other theological issues, as well as halakhic pluralism. To insist that all teaching or study of Torah be premised on the beliefs and assumptions of traditional Judaism (or of a particular wing of Conservative Judaism) is to risk undermining the entire enterprise of *talmud torah* for many Conservative Jews. Moreover, it is often by taking a vigorously critical view of Torah while not rejecting it out of hand that we embrace the Torah most fully. According to rabbinic *midrash*, Jeremiah and Daniel intentionally omitted certain praises of God from their prayers as acts of protest against God's apparent absence. When the Talmud expresses amazement at their temerity, the sage Rabbi Eleazar responds, "They knew that the blessed Holy One is a God of truth and therefore they did not dissemble in God's presence" (*BT* Yoma 69b).

This last point will be particularly—but not exclusively—relevant for people sensitive to women's issues who undertake the study of the traditional texts of Torah. The study of many biblical and rabbinic texts is difficult for such people, in part because these texts were written by men on whose agenda feminist issues did not loom large and in part because the view of women expressed in these texts is often a source of pain and anger. In response to these difficulties we must first acknowledge that, as Rachel Adler puts it, "God heals the broken-hearted, but it is our teachers who break those hearts" ("The Virgin in the Brothel," *Tikkun* 3:6 [1988], p. 28). The biblical authors and the rabbis, like all those from whom we seek wisdom, are limited in their vision and understanding by gender and cultural context. Having accepted this truism, and having acknowledged that it applies to us no less than to our ancestors, women can respond to traditional texts that are problematic by offering their own commentary. Such commentary can, and should, include critiques of biblical and rabbinic teachings and narratives, in part by illuminating the ramifications of these teachings from a female and/or feminist perspective. The alternate option, wholesale rejection of the corpus of biblical and rabbinic writings as irredeemably misogynous, is an oversimplification that cuts women off from the transgenerational conversation that has been created and sustained for thousands of years. I would argue that for women, and indeed for contemporary Jews in general, the *mitzvah* of *talmud torah* includes a version of the *mitzvah* of *pidyon sh'vuyim*, the traditional name for the commandment to redeem those held in captivity against their will. Indeed, by redeeming those passages and teachings of the Torah that are held captive by narrowness of vision, and by understanding that narrowness to be a function of the time and place in which those teachings were formulated—and also through the dual process of deconstruction through historical and philosophical critique and reconstruction through midrashic reinterpretation—we can breathe new life into texts that may seem dead to us.

A final caveat regarding the relationship between Torah and scholarship is in order. By nature of its critical and questioning stance, what the philosopher Paul Ricoeur calls "the hermeneutics of suspicion," scholarship is often a demythologizing force. It attempts to uncover the messy reality behind the master narratives of religions and cultures. Moreover, because scholarship brackets questions of ultimate truth such as the existence of God and the possibility of the miraculous, it treats all truth claims that are not empirically based as the product of human societies, each bounded by its own cultural assumptions and prejudices. In a word, the working assumption of scholarship is that all truths are relative. This characteristic of scholarship has the potential to generate radical relativism, or even cynicism, as a response to any truth claims made by traditional religion. Central to *talmud torah* is the conviction that there are timeless truths to be found in the words of Torah. Therefore, for the Bible, the Talmud, and other Jewish writings to be Torah for us, we must be able to transcend the diminishing and relativizing power of critical inquiry and engage in Ricoeur's "hermeneutics of revival." This means that through our determination to give the words of Torah meaning for our own time and place—to engage, in essence, in *midrash*—we recover a sense of purpose, meaning, and direction as the Torah calls us to take Abraham Joshua Heschel's "leap of action." The same texts that have been dissected, analyzed, and historicized thus become living Torah.

Finally, it should be said that perhaps what designates study as *talmud torah* more than any other factor is that it is devotional rather than simply intellectual. In effect, study of Torah texts and ideas becomes the *mitzvah* of *talmud torah* by virtue of our treating it as such. While this claim may seem to be a tautology, its true meaning is that ultimately the most important determinant of whether we are engaged in *talmud torah* is not only what we study but how we study it.

The *halakhah* in fact provides a means of designating an act as a *mitzvah:* by reciting a benediction prior to that act. The Talmud (at *BT* B'rakhot 11b) prescribes that two (or three; this is a subject of debate) benedictions be recited before studying Torah. Our practice is to recite these blessings once at the beginning of the day. The first begins, "Praised are You, Adonai, our God, Sovereign of the universe . . . who has commanded us to engage (*la·asok*) in the [study of the] words of Torah." *La·asok* has the sense of intensive labor; we are called upon to give our full attention and energy to Torah study. The text continues with a prayer: "Make the words of the Torah sweet in our mouths and in the mouths of all of Your people Israel [and may it be] that we all know Your name and study the Torah for its own sake (*li-sh'mah*). Praised are You, Adonai, who teaches Torah to God's people, to Israel." With these words we ask that we experience Torah study as pleasurable rather than the discharge of an unpleasant duty and, simultaneously, that we study not just for the sake of pleasure but also for the sake of the transcendent ideal or ideals represented by the term *li-sh'mah*. We also recognize that God is not merely the Giver of Torah but, through the divinely granted blessing of intelligence, our Mentor in the study of Torah.

There is one final blessing to be recited before we engage in *talmud torah*, the benediction that we also recite upon being called to the Torah: "Praised are You . . . who has chosen us from among all the nations and given us God's Torah. Praised are You, Adonai, Giver of the Torah." In this blessing, we acknowledge the privilege granted us to receive God's Torah. By implication, we also acknowledge that whatever is unique about us as a people is linked to the Torah and our acceptance and fulfillment of its words. Finally, this blessing serves as a counterpoint to the first one. On the one hand we are active partners in discovering and giving meaning to Torah. At the same time, we must receive with love and attention the Torah that we receive from God through our ancestors and teachers. It is our role not only to speak to and about the Torah, but also to hear its age-old voice.

How Much Torah Study?

The key to making *talmud torah* part of our lives is to treat it as a "set" or "fixed" obligation of the kind known in the literature as *keva* (see *M* Avot 1:15 and *BT* Shabbat 31a). To make Torah *keva* means to give it regularity and centrality in our lives. Of course, the two are connected; by establishing a set time every day to study Torah we demonstrate that it is a fundamental part of our lives by making it so. Making specific times for *talmud torah* also ensures that we will actually study. We can all testify to the fact that tasks that we do not schedule into our day often do not get done. "Hillel says . . . do not say, 'When I have leisure I will study'; perhaps you will never have leisure" (*M* Avot 2:5). One of the best ways to ensure that one will study regularly is to arrange for a study partner (*ḥevruta*) or to participate in a class given at a synagogue, school, or JCC.

Both the Bible and the rabbis speak of constant study of Torah as the ideal. Still, the rabbis also state that, for those who have little or no time to study, reciting the Sh'ma in the morning and in the evening will suffice as the barest minimum of daily study (*BT* M'naḥot 99b). Given that none of us engages in constant study, what is the relevance of this ideal to us? It can serve as encouragement to look to the Torah throughout our day, measuring our thoughts and actions against the ideals that Torah embodies. Ideally, through constant and assiduous study we make Torah a part of us, becoming what Heschel calls "text people." Torah is then no longer simply a set of books or ideas but a force within us that helps shape our lives.

The Parental and Communal Obligations to Teach and Transmit Torah

Rambam begins his Hilkhot Talmud Torah (Laws of Torah Study) not with the obligation to study Torah, but with the obligation to teach it to our children. In doing so he reminds us that, although each of us is personally obligated to study, our parents are charged with giving us the ability and the inclination to do so. We are reminded as well that the obligation of *talmud torah* encompasses both studying Torah and teaching it to others, especially to the next generation. Of course one can begin to study Torah at any age. Indeed, rabbinic tradition relates that Rabbi Akiva, one of the most revered of the talmudic sages, only began to study Torah at age forty and that he, an illiterate, initially had to sit with young schoolchildren in order to learn the alphabet (*Avot D'rabbi Natan,* Text A, chap. 6).

In theory, all of us should personally teach Torah to our own children; in reality, most of us do not have the time, knowledge, or skill to do so. Consequently, we can discharge our obligation by employing others. Our responsibility does not end at the schoolhouse door, however. The primary obligation remains ours; our children's teachers are merely the agents we authorize to discharge our duty. This means that we must play an active role to make sure that our children are being educated properly.

We can do this in a number of ways. The first is by choosing our child's school carefully. Inevitably location and cost play a part in this decision; we must also do our best to select a school whose Jewish and educational philosophies are similar to our own. That being said, our children will inevitably hear ideas and viewpoints with which we disagree. This places a dual responsibility upon us. On the one hand, we need to engage our children in dialogue about what they have learned and express our own view, respectfully but clearly, when it diverges from what they have been taught. (Of course, initiating such discussions is also a way of showing our children that we value what they are learning.) On the other hand, we need to acknowledge that what our children are hearing in school is a legitimate interpretation of Judaism as well. Above all, we should keep in mind that Torah is meant to be a guide for life, not simply a body of theoretical knowledge. It is neither realistic nor consonant with the ideal of *talmud torah* to view our children's Jewish education as consisting only of learning "about" Judaism; we should expect and even welcome the opportunities that Jewish education provides for our children and, through them, for us to reconsider what it means to commit oneself to a life of Torah.

The two types of Jewish educational institutions most commonly available are Jewish day schools and synagogue schools. Choosing between the two is often a complex process, determined by considerations of cost, availability, and ideology. Day school education indisputably offers the important advantage of significantly more time devoted to Torah study. Time is particularly significant for the acquisition of language skills. Facility with Hebrew (and, to approach much of later rabbinic literature, Aramaic) contributes mightily toward one's Jewish literacy by making possible direct knowledge of the classical texts of Torah rather than requiring that they be read through the filter of translation. The amount of time necessary to obtain these skills is, at least in theory, available in a day school but not in most synagogues schools, particularly if they meet only once or twice a week.

Yet the matter is not so simple. The *mitzvah* of *talmud torah* is about inspiration and identification as much as it is about edification, particularly for Jews living as a minority in an open society. A school offering fewer hours may have a more dynamic faculty; one's child may feel more at home at a synagogue school because of the presence of friends. Some parents are concerned that the day school experience may segregate their children to their own detriment by cutting them off from meaningful interaction with the larger society. What is important, no matter what choice is made, is to recognize that without positive Jewish experiences in addition to schooling, our children will not experience Judaism as a joyful and vibrant way of life. It is our responsibility, not the school's, to provide these experiences through regular synagogue attendance and a rich Jewish home life. Above all, we cannot expect our children to view the study of Torah as an important component of their Jewish identity if it is not an integral part of our own lives.

As we all know, Jewish education comes with a hefty price tag and our obligation to teach our children Torah includes responsibility for their tuition. (It is worth noting that when parents are financially unable to provide their children with a Jewish education, the *halakhah* places that responsibility on the child's grandparents; see the comment of *Siftei Kohein* commentary of Rabbi Shabbetai Kohein [1621–1662], known as the Shakh, in his first note to *SA* Yoreh Dei·ah 245.) In the case of Jewish day schools, this is a particularly onerous burden that has generated an ongoing crisis in the American Jewish community. While there are no easy solutions to the problem, two observations are in order. The first is that if we truly consider Jewish education to constitute a fundamental necessity, we must be ready to forgo luxuries if necessary. Second, we should remember that the obligation to provide Jewish education is communal as well as parental. The Talmud attributes an ordinance to Joshua ben Gamla, one of the last High Priests of the Second

Temple period, requiring each community to provide for the religious education of all its male children from the age of six or seven (*BT* Bava Batra 21a). Jewish communities throughout the ages have shouldered the responsibility of providing Jewish education to their youth. Consequently, federations and other communal institutions should make it their top priority to increase the availability and affordability of Jewish education for all Jewish children regardless of gender. After all, it is Jewish education that is the most important guarantor of Jewish continuity; more crucially, it is only through education that we can create a Jewish community worth perpetuating.

How Do We Study Torah?

Torah texts, especially rabbinic ones, have traditionally been studied aloud in pairs or study groups called *ḥevrutot.* There are historical, pedagogical, and religious reasons for this tradition. Rabbinic teachings were studied and transmitted orally. In fact, the style of the rabbinic work studied most often, the Babylonian Talmud, is largely dialectical and dialogical; it reads as an ongoing give-and-take about a myriad of topics. It is not surprising, therefore, that paired or group study has long been the preferred method of Talmud study. Reading texts aloud to one another also gives all students a chance to experience the text aurally as well as visually, thereby imprinting it more deeply in their consciousness. Finally, the Talmud is traditionally not only read but actually chanted aloud. In the Talmud (at *BT* M'gillah 32a), we read the lesson that Rabbi Shefatiya transmitted in the name of Rabbi Yoḥanan: "One who does not chant Scripture or recite rabbinic traditions melodiously—of such a one it is said, 'Moreover I gave them statutes that were not good' [Ezekiel 20:25]." The chanting of the text also lends a liturgical quality to the study experience, and it allows engagement with the text emotionally and aesthetically as well as intellectually.

Not everyone will be comfortable chanting, nor will all people find it, or paired study, helpful. Nonetheless, having a *ḥevruta* embodies values that are central to *talmud torah* and that should be part of everyone's Torah study. The first value is that of humility, which should express itself in part by a willingness to learn from others. An underlying assumption of the *ḥevruta* system is that we will understand what we study better if we are open to seeing it through the eyes of a fellow student. We may not always agree with the interpretation being offered or the point of view being expressed, but the very act of having to defend and thereby sharpen our own position makes a valuable contribution to our comprehension of Torah. Moreover, the words of a *ḥevruta* often help us see that our own grasp of the matter under discussion is, if not incorrect, at least incomplete. Study with others is a complementary effort from which larger truths and understandings emerge. In a striking passage the Talmud states that when a father and son or a master and pupil study together they become each other's adversary, yet they do not move from that place before becoming each other's friend (*BT* Kiddushin 30a). Moderns can certainly assume the same applies to parents and children of both genders!

One effect of reading the text aloud or chanting it, especially in tandem with a study partner, is to increase our sense of the text as something real outside of ourselves. This attitude is important in shaping our relationship to Torah, helping us to see and respect it as a source of transcendent truth rather than simply a book worthy of intellectual scrutiny. Whether we study in a group, with a friend, or alone, we ought to see Torah as a source of illumination in whose light we should reflect on our own understanding of life and self.

Entering the World of Torah Study

The talmudic sages were well aware of how daunting a task the study of Torah appears to the beginner. The sheer volume of Torah, not to mention its complexity, can lead one to yield to the counsel of despair; however, say the rabbis, this is actually the counsel of foolishness. "The fool says, 'Who could possibly study the entire Torah? Tractate N'zikin contains thirty chapters! Tractate Keilim contains thirty chapters!'" The solution, the rabbis continue, is to commit oneself to the gradual and incremental study of the Torah on a daily basis: "The wise one says, 'Behold, I will study two *halakhot* today and two *halakhot* tomorrow until I have studied the entire Torah'" (*Va-yikra Rabbah* 19:2). This program of study requires establishing a set time each day for study and a realistic goal for each study session. To expect too much of oneself is to court despair, and the Talmud specifically warns against this approach: "When you grasp too much, you grasp nothing at all" (*BT* Yoma 80a).

How much time should we devote to the study of Hebrew and Aramaic, in order to understand the classical texts of Judaism in their original languages? For most adult learners with limited study opportunities, language acquisition is not a profitable use of time. Nonetheless, there is value in learning some of the basic terms and concepts of Jewish thought and law in the original, in part because their meaning is often altered in translation. A famous example of this is the word *tz'dakah*. While the usual translation is "charity," *tz'dakah* has a connotation of justice that "charity" lacks. We give *tz'dakah* not simply out of generosity, but because justice dictates that those with financial resources have an obligation to help those in need.

Finally, while in-depth study can be intellectually satisfying, breadth of knowledge is an important part of bringing us into the world of Torah. There is great value in achieving familiarity with basic Jewish concepts through works such as Joseph Telushkin's *Jewish Literacy* (1991; revised ed., New York: William Morrow, 2008), and one can receive guidance in how to begin studying the classic texts of Judaism from books like *Back to the Sources: Reading Classic Jewish Texts,* edited by Barry Holtz (New York: Summit Books, 1984). There have also been many useful books and pamphlets published by the various arms of the Conservative movement, including the Jewish Theological Seminary, the Rabbinical Assembly, the United Synagogue of Conservative Judaism, and the United Synagogue Youth.

Always More to Learn

When the High Priest finished reading from the Torah scroll on Yom Kippur he would declare, "There is more written here than what I have read to you" (*M* Yoma 7:1). This statement can serve as a useful metaphor both for this essay and for the process of Torah study. Any essay delineating the parameters of a halakhic topic will inevitably fail to touch on every aspect of the subject. Much more can be said about the *mitzvah* of *talmud torah;* to those interested in further information I recommend that one begin by reading the section of Maimonides' *Mishneh Torah* devoted to Torah study, called Hilkhot Talmud Torah, which is available to readers of English in a number of translations.

The statement of the High Priest also serves to remind us that *talmud torah* is meant to be a lifelong vocation. To those who have begun this journey, I wish continued growth, enlightenment, and pleasure through your engagement with the teachings of the Torah. To those at the beginning of the path, know that the Torah waits for you with open arms. "Sift through it again and again, for it contains everything; contemplate it, grow old with it, and do not move away from it, for you can receive no greater measure" (*M* Avot 5:22).

Shabbat

MICHAEL KATZ & GERSHON SCHWARTZ ז"ל

Preparing for Shabbat

The school of Shammai said: "From the first day of the week, prepare for Shabbat" (*BT* Beitzah 16a), and, as observant moderns know all too well, their lesson is well taken. Shabbat doesn't happen spontaneously as the sun sets on Friday, or as we light Shabbat candles. Abraham Joshua Heschel referred to Shabbat as "a palace in time." That can hardly be denied, but what he left unsaid was just how much work it takes to design, build, and furnish that palace.

There are three major categories of Shabbat preparation that must be attended to: physical setting, food preparation, and personal grooming.

To the best of our ability, and given the limits of time, we prepare for Shabbat by cleaning our homes, or the houses (or motel rooms or campsites) in which we are planning to spend Shabbat. The reason for this is self-evident: it is difficult to enjoy Shabbat if we are surrounded by a physical mess. In addition, the very act of cleaning helps us to prepare ourselves for Shabbat spiritually as we transform ordinary space into an arena for sacred activity.

We take care of those things that we cannot, may not, or choose not to deal with on Shabbat: setting timers (called "Shabbos clocks" in some circles) so that we do not have to turn electric lights on or off, setting up electric urns to keep water warm for tea or coffee, and turning off cellular phones. The level of preparation will, of course, mirror the level of observance in a given home: in homes in which the normal use of solid soap is considered sufficiently transformational to be forbidden on Shabbat, preparing for Shabbat will include filling liquid soap dispensers; similarly, preparing pre-cut toilet tissue and paper toweling will be undertaken in homes in which the prohibition of tearing something even as inconsequential as a square of tissue is considered a forbidden activity.

Some of the Shabbat restrictions listed above are not features of Shabbat in most Conservatives homes—it is the rare Conservative Jew who pre-cuts squares of toilet tissue—yet we mention practices like that in the same breath as more widely observed aspects of observance specifically to make a point that all readers should take to heart: the common effort behind all Shabbat observance, from its most stringent guise to its most lenient, should always be the same: to seek to know God the Creator through allegiance to the laws of Shabbat, however interpreted.

Regarding Shabbat—and every other realm of Jewish observance—there will be multiple, sometimes even conflicting, interpretations and approaches. (A more lenient ruling is often referred to as a *kulla;* a more stringent one as a *ḥumra*). There are some Jews who believe that stricter is always the more authentic approach, and a sure sign of one's seriousness and piety. Other Jews will search for the least restrictive rulings, holding that easier is always better. Conservative Judaism teaches that there are times when it is appropriate to be lenient, and times when it prudent to be strict. Tradition should always be regarded seriously, yet at the same time we do not want it to be seen as onerous and burdensome. As we say when we place the Torah in the Ark, "All its ways are pleasantness" (Proverbs 3:17).

It is also customary to decorate the home and the table with fresh flowers on the eve of Shabbat. In so doing, we are reminded that Shabbat is not just a day for the spirit and the intellect—it is a day of sensory pleasure as well.

A good deal of Shabbat preparation involves shopping. We must make sure we have enough candles. We must purchase wine and *ḥallah*, as well as special Shabbat treats, such as cakes, desserts, and snacks.

Inviting guests into our home is a major part of making Shabbat special and this too, obviously, must be undertaken in advance. Similarly, menus for the Shabbat meals need to be planned out in advance and the shopping and food preparation must be completed before the Shabbat candles are kindled—that is, no later than eighteen minutes before sunset. (Foods that Ashkenazic Jews most often associate with Shabbat, like gefilte fish, chicken soup, and *cholent,* often have cultural, socioeconomic, or halakhic significance. Sometimes foods became staples because they were plentiful and affordable to the poor, but other foods were expensive delicacies that people scrimped and saved all week to be able to purchase. Other times, foods were chosen for the way they could be prepared and kept warm when ordinary cooking was prohibited.)

All cooking must be completed prior to the onset of Shabbat, and a way must be found to keep already cooked foods warm (*SA* Oraḥ Ḥayyim 250). Some leave the oven on throughout Shabbat, but others use an electric warming drawer or tray, or else a *blech* (a piece of metal that covers the stovetop so that the burners can be kept on low, thereby creating a kind of simple warming tray). A *kumkum* (an urn, usually electric, sometimes called a "Shabbos pot") is filled and turned on and allowed to heat up before the onset of Shabbat. In very observant homes, packages and bottles are opened before Shabbat to avoid the inevitable ripping and tearing of modern packaging.

In terms of personal preparation, it is not merely our homes that we must make ready for Shabbat, but our bodies as well: bathing and personal grooming, setting aside and ironing appropriate clothes, going for a pre-Shabbos haircut, or even a pre-Shabbat trip to the gym to work off the tension of a long week of work before returning home to begin Shabbat—all of these are ways of preparing for Shabbat and, although not all will occur every week, the basic idea behind all of them is the same: the Shabbat faithful must ready themselves in the anteroom before entering the palace.

Clothing is especially important. If clothes make the man (or the woman), then how we dress contributes mightily to our effort to make Shabbat a delight. Wearing weekday clothing puts us in a weekday frame of mind. Having special clothes for Shabbat and laundering or ironing those clothes in preparation for Shabbat are ancient customs that assist us in approaching the onset of Shabbat in a positive, pleasant way (*SA* Oraḥ Ḥayyim 262:2–3).

On Shabbat, we are not only what we eat and what we wear; we are also what we handle or even touch. Before the onset of Shabbat, we put aside our wallets and our purses, our money, our pens, our electronic devices, and all other articles that are deemed *muktzeh* and that we are therefore not permitted to handle. (The term *muktzeh* refers to things that, because they have no licit use on Shabbat, may not be moved or even touched throughout the day. Thus, although there are forbidden activities one could undertake with a kitchen knife, it is not considered *muktzeh* because there are many licit uses to which such an implement may be put. Coins, on the other hand, which have no licit purpose on Shabbat, are considered *muktzeh* and should not be handled even casually.) The concept is discussed below in its own sub-section of this chapter.

In addition to physical preparations, we must make spiritual preparations as well. In some circles, it is common for men to go to the *mikveh* every week on the eve of Shabbat. Others put aside money for *tz'dakah* (charity). And many people review the weekly Torah portion on Friday afternoon as a way of preparing for the onset of Shabbat intellectually and spiritually.

Shabbat Candles

We usher in Shabbat with the lighting of candles (*SA* Oraḥ Ḥayyim 261, 263–265). In ancient times, this was a part of making the home physically ready, as the flames from the lamps or candles were an essential source of light in the house. In our day, homes are generally lit by electric lights, but the Shabbat candles retain their importance because they are deemed powerfully symbolic of the spiritual light that Shabbat can bring into our lives.

Shabbat technically should begin at sunset. However, because it is prohibited to kindle a flame once Shabbat begins, the *halakhah* sets a barrier in time between the last moment to light the Shabbat candles and the actual onset of Shabbat, thereby guaranteeing that no errors will be made. Therefore, we light Shabbat candles no later than eighteen minutes prior to sunset. This is an example of "making a fence around the Torah" mentioned in *Pirkei Avot* (*M* Avot 1:1). For similar reasons, we delay the ceremony that concludes Shabbat on Saturday evening, and this makes Shabbat last twenty-five, not twenty-four hours, each week. Jewish calendars list candle-lighting times for every Friday evening of the year.

The candles should be lit in the room in which we intend to eat Shabbat dinner so that we can see the candles and enjoy their light during dinner.

At Exodus 20:8, the Torah commands Israel to remember the Shabbat day, while at Deuteronomy 5:12, the commandment is specifically to observe Shabbat, not merely to remember it. In a nod to these two versions of the fourth commandment, it is customary to light a minimum of two Shabbat candles (*SA* Oraḥ Ḥayyim 263:1). Some, however, light one candle for each member of the family, or seven candles, one for each day of the week. There are also those who kindle ten candles, corresponding to the Ten Commandments.

Traditionally, women light the Shabbat candles. If, however, no woman is present, then a man must light his own Shabbat candles. Similarly, it is more traditional for a man to recite Kiddush, although the obligation to recite Kiddush falls on women as well (*SA* Oraḥ Ḥayyim 271:2). For those who take a more egalitarian approach to ritual, however, we stress that both these *mitzvot* may be performed by either men or women, even in the presence of members of the opposite sex. Still, the tradition (as recorded, e.g., at *M* Shabbat 2:6) is very clear that women need to be especially scrupulous in lighting Shabbat candles, as well as taking a special pinch of dough while baking bread and burning it (in recollection of the ancient practice of giving gifts to the *kohanim* when baking bread in large enough quantities, as described elsewhere in this volume by Rabbi Martin S. Cohen in his chapter on Israel), and observing of the laws of family purity.

First, the candles are lit. If a woman is lighting the candles, she closes her eyes and draws her hands to her face in a circular motion three times. (The gesture itself is purely optional. Women may simply cover their eyes with their hands if they wish, but the more traditional procedure represents the woman's wish to invite Shabbat into her home and her family's life.) With her hands covering her eyes, she then recites the traditional blessing, *barukh attah adonai, eloheinu, melekh ha-olam, asher kidd'shanu b'mitzvotav v'tzivvanu l'hadlik neir shel shabbat* ("Praised are You, Adonai, our God, Sovereign of the universe, who, sanctifying us with divine commandments, has commanded us to kindle the Shabbat lamp"). The reason for this ritual is complicated. The basic concept is that blessings are generally recited before performing the acts that they sanctify. However, since the blessing over the candles, when recited by a woman, is deemed to inaugurate Shabbat, the woman would then be forbidden to light the candles subsequent to her own blessing because kindling a flame is prohibited on Shabbat. Consequently, she lights the candles first, then covers her eyes so that she can recite the blessing before enjoying and benefiting from the light of the candles.

It is also customary to recite a personal meditation at this moment. An example, by Navah Harlow, is as follows:

> As I light these Shabbat candles, I feel the frenzied momentum of the week slowly draining from my body. I thank You, Creator, for the peace and relaxation of Shabbat, for moments to redirect my energies toward those treasures in my life which I hold most dear. Had You not in Your infinite wisdom created the Shabbat day, I may not have stopped in time. May the peace of Shabbat fill our hearts, fill our home, fill the world. Amen. (*Siddur Sim Shalom I*, p. 720)

Friday Evening Services

Traditionally, Shabbat services on Friday were held around sunset, whatever time that happened to be. Dinner then followed, and the family remained at home for the rest of the evening.

By the middle of the twentieth century, however, it became apparent that many people were unable to make it home on Fridays in time for a traditional

Shabbat service at sundown, especially during the fall and winter months when Shabbat can sometimes begin very early. In response, synagogues began offering late Friday evening services that usually began at 8:00 or 8:30 P.M. year-round. This enabled people to attend a Friday night Shabbat service at synagogue (though it also meant that the Friday night meal at home had to end in time to enable the family to get there).

For decades, late Friday night worship was the more attended Shabbat service in many Conservative synagogues. In recent years, another trend has developed as large numbers of congregations have gone back to the practice of having Friday evening services at sundown. This return to tradition may stem from several factors, foremost among them the influence of Camp Ramah, the realization that the home (not the synagogue) should be the primary focus of Jewish observance, the disappearance of Friday night bat mitzvah ceremonies in Conservative synagogues, and the preference of many clergy and laity for more authentic modes of Shabbat observance. Most of all, however, the shift back to a more traditional framework has been prompted by the sense that there is something inimical to the spirit of Shabbat about having to go out again after a traditional Friday night dinner at home in the company of one's family and one's guests.

In preparation for the formal worship service on Friday evenings, some have the custom of reading the Song of Songs, and this worthy custom should be encouraged. Though ostensibly a series of secular love poems, the rabbis of classical antiquity understood the Song of Songs to be an allegory about God's love for the Jewish people. The poet refers to his beloved as his bride, the very term used to describe Shabbat. Reciting the Song of Songs, or parts of it, helps us to view Shabbat as a day devoted to the celebration of God's love for Israel, as well as Israel's love for God and for Shabbat itself. It is also appropriate as a subtle reminder to married couples that Friday night is the traditional time for marital intimacy.

Another custom is to sing the hymn Y'did Nefesh, composed in sixteenth-century Safed by Rabbi Eleazar Azikri, whose theme is also the Jew's longing for communion with the Divine.

Formally speaking, there are two major parts to the Friday evening service: Kabbalat Shabbat and Ma·ariv. Kabbalat Shabbat (literally, "Welcoming Shabbat") was created by the mystics of Safed among whom Rabbi Azikri lived, who believed that Shabbat functions as a foretaste of the ultimate redemption even more than it serves as a day of rest from labor.

The concept of Kabbalat Shabbat itself was based on a talmudic teaching (preserved at *BT* Shabbat 119a): "Rabbi Ḥanina would wrap himself in a robe on the eve of Shabbat and say: 'Come, let us go out to greet Queen

Shabbat.' Rabbi Yannai would get dressed on the eve of Shabbat and say: 'Come, O bride! Come, O bride!'"

Why did Rabbi Ḥanina and Rabbi Yannai conceive of Shabbat as a female figure, a bride or a queen? Perhaps they saw the other days of the week, devoted all to hard work, as corresponding to the role of men in their world, while Shabbat was about the home, the family, and peace, which they considered the domain of the feminine. Their specific approaches are not exactly the same, however. Rabbi Ḥanina, imagining someone regal and powerful who commands respect and obedience, speaks of a queen. On the other hand, Rabbi Yannai, conjuring up the image of a beautiful and tender woman who primarily symbolizes love, talks of a bride. The two combine to draw a picture of Shabbat as a set of complex laws that must be obeyed, yet that somehow also create the context in which Jewish individuals can come to know and love God with ever greater levels of intimacy.

Kabbalat Shabbat begins with the recitation of Psalms 95, 96, 97, 98, 99, and 29, which are considered representative of the six days of the week. All six psalms refer to God as *melekh* (king), and speak of God as Creator and Ruler of the world. Thus, in the context of the Kabbalat Shabbat liturgy, the Jew at prayer is attending the mystic wedding of King God and Queen Shabbat.

The six psalms lead into L'khah Dodi, a long liturgical poem written in 1529 by Rabbi Shlomo Halevi Alkabetz (whose name is spelled out by the initial letters of the first eight stanzas). The chorus, based on the talmudic passage cited just above, is "Come, my beloved, to greet the bride / let us welcome Shabbat." Several of the verses refer to the city of Jerusalem, to its desolation and destruction in past times, and to its renewal in the context of the future redemption of humanity. Jerusalem, in this context, is understood as a symbol of the Jewish people. As Jerusalem will be revived, the poet says, so will the Jews. In L'khah Dodi, therefore, people, place, and time all come together in the complex concept of salvation through God.

During the final stanza of L'khah Dodi, the congregation rises and turns around symbolically to greet Shabbat. As the final line of the hymn is sung, the congregation bows twice, once to the left and once to the right. This act of subservience can be interpreted both according to the opinion of Rabbi Ḥanina and that of Rabbi Yannai. By bowing to Queen Shabbat, the congregation at once pledges its allegiance and demonstrates its subservience to its laws and precepts. If, however, it is to Bride Shabbat that the congregation bows, then it is to show its devotion and love for Shabbat in its guise as the welcome harbinger of redemption.

It is also at this moment in the service, at the conclusion of L'khah Dodi, that mourners still in their first week of mourning (the *shivah* week) enter the synagogue. The congregation, which has just risen to welcome Queen Shabbat and Bride Shabbat, remains standing to greet the mourners with the traditional words of consolation: *ha-makom y'naḥeim etkhem b'tokh she·ar aveilei tziyyon virushalayim* ("May God comfort you together with the other mourners of Zion and Jerusalem"). By singing L'khah Dodi, the congregation has just proclaimed that the destruction of Jerusalem will be followed ultimately by its redemption. As the mourners enter, the worshipers pray that, though the mourners have recently experienced personal devastation, they too will find comfort and redemption. For Jews, the national and the personal always are intertwined.

L'khah Dodi is followed by Psalms 92 and 93. Psalm 92, the only poem in the Psalter connected to a specific day of the week, was imagined by the ancients to have been uttered originally by Adam as an ode of thanksgiving on the very first Shabbat. Also, the Mishnah (at *M* Tamid 7:4) teaches that the Levites used to sing this psalm every Shabbat in the Temple and that it will be the hymn of choice in the messianic era as well. Psalm 93 also hints at the messianic theme, looking forward to a time when God, "crowned in splendor," will rule directly over the world.

Kabbalat Shabbat concludes with the Mourner's Kaddish.

It is the custom of some to recite the second chapter of the mishnaic tractate Shabbat between Kabbalat Shabbat and the Evening Service (*SA* Oraḥ Ḥayyim 270:2). These seven *mishnayyot* are an example of the use of the study of traditional texts as a kind of intense spiritual preparation. The practice also had a very practical aspect: it delayed the beginning of the Evening Service so that latecomers would not be forced to make their way home alone in the dark after finishing their prayers after the departure of the other worshipers.

The liturgy of contemporary Conservative Judaism preserves this tradition, while changing some of the texts. The traditional chapter from tractate Shabbat (often called *Ba-meh Madlikin,* after its first words) focuses on the technical question of which materials may be used for lighting oil lamps on Shabbat, an issue rendered irrelevant by the almost universal use of wax candles in modern times. Conservative prayerbooks, therefore, often offer other *mishnayyot* and rabbinic texts thought to be both instructive and inspirational. Any of these texts should be followed by Kaddish D'rabbanan.

The Ma·ariv service for Friday night is similar to the weekday service, but with a few changes. The opening line that precedes the Bar'khu call to prayer, for example, is eliminated because its subjects (sin and punishment) are not considered to be in the spirit of Shabbat. Also, an additional line and a slightly expanded benediction are added to the end of the Hashkiveinu prayer, the second blessing that follows the Sh'ma. In this version of the blessing, the worshiper speaks of God spreading a *sukkah* of peace over all Israel and over Jerusalem. As in the L'khah Dodi hymn, people, place, and time all come together in a dream-like vision of future redemption.

A special passage referring specifically to Shabbat, Exodus 31:16–17 (often called V'sham'ru after its first word), is added just after Hashkiveinu. In the Hashkiveinu prayer, the worshiper asks God to guard and watch over Israel, and this passage from Exodus uses similar language to describe Israel's observance of Shabbat—suggesting that, just as the Jewish people guard and watch over Shabbat, so does God care for and watch over the Jewish people.

There are also some major omissions from the weekday service, such as the long miscellany of verses recited on weekdays just before the Kaddish that leads into the Amidah. Also, the entire middle portion of the Amidah, which consists on weekdays of thirteen different petitionary prayers, is replaced by a single paragraph referring to Shabbat itself. (The petitions in the middle section of the weekday Amidah are eliminated because it is considered inappropriate to express concern for material needs on Shabbat.)

The Amidah on Friday evening, therefore, has only seven blessings, as do the morning and afternoon versions of the Amidah on Shabbat. The specific theme of this central section changes for each of the three services of the day, however. On Friday night, the central passage cites Genesis 2:1–3 and is primarily about Shabbat today as a memorial to the first Shabbat, the one that followed the week of creation. On Saturday morning, the central prayer speaks more about revelation, and depicts Shabbat as a central pillar of the commandments revealed to Israel at Mount Sinai. On Saturday afternoon, the central paragraph focuses on redemption and points to Shabbat as kind of weekly herald of the kind of peaceful world that all will enjoy when the world finally is redeemed. Creation, revelation, and redemption are the three great themes of Jewish theology and each has its moment in the liturgy of Shabbat.

Following the Amidah, the congregation remains standing to recite Genesis 2:1–3, popularly called Va-y'khullu. This is followed by a special, highly abbreviated version of the Amidah called the "Blessing Reminiscent of the Seven [Blessings of the Amidah]," the *b'rakhah mei-ein sheva*. This in turn is followed by the Magein Avot prayer, and then by the prayer leader's repetition of a key passage from the Amidah. All these additions were intended simply to delay the service sufficiently for latecomers to catch up so that they would not be forced to walk home alone.

There is also a very old custom of reciting Kiddush, the prayer of sanctification over the wine normally recited at dinner, in the synagogue as well (*SA* Oraḥ Ḥayyim 269). This custom goes back to a time when Jewish travelers lodged in the synagogue and had their meals there, and it thus created an opportunity for the regular worshipers to join with the community's guests before parting company. Today, it is rare for worshipers to dine in the synagogue after the service, but the custom remains as a pleasant reminder of ancient times when a community's hospitality could be measured easily in terms of how it treated strangers, travelers, and the indigent on Shabbat by providing for their needs in a gracious and friendly way. The service then concludes with Aleinu and the Mourner's Kaddish, followed in most congregations by the Yigdal hymn.

Friday Night at Home

Shabbat meals are about much more than just food. Prayers, rituals, songs, and words of Torah combine to create a unique experience rich in symbolism and meaning. Although far less structured than, say, a Passover *seder,* the three Shabbat meals—Friday night dinner, Saturday lunch, and the third meal (called either *se'udah sh'lishit* or, far more colloquially, *shalashudis* or *shalshudis*)—have their own programmatic order.

On Friday evenings, we begin with the blessing of children. Traditionally, the parent places his or her hands on the child's head, then proceeds with a different opening prayer for boys and girls, then with a common prayer for all children.

For boys, the parent begins with the prayer that God make the boy "like Ephraim and Manasseh." This was Jacob's blessing for his grandsons, Joseph's two boys, as recorded at Genesis 48:20. Even though Ephraim and Manasseh are not well-known biblical figures, we refer to them as the model sons we hope our boys grow up to be because of Jacob's specific remark in their regard, "By you [i.e., by using your names] shall Israel invoke God's blessing, saying, '[May] God make you as Ephraim and as Manasseh.'" One commentary explains the significance of Ephraim and Manasseh as role models for us by noting that, though they grew up as members of a tiny minority in a much larger culture, they managed nevertheless to remain faithful to their family's religious traditions. So may we, we pray, by invoking their names, and so may our sons.

For girls, the parent begins, "May God make you like Sarah, Rebecca, Rachel, and Leah." These four women, the matriarchs of the Jewish people, raised the first generations of the Jewish people. Although this blessing does not correspond to a specific scriptural injunction like the blessing for boys does, it has its own roots in the Bible, as at Ruth 4:11, where Ruth herself is blessed that she be like Rachel and Leah, who together "built up the House of Israel."

For both boys and girls, parents continue with the priestly benediction found at Numbers 6:24–26: "May the Eternal bless you and protect you! May the Eternal deal kindly and graciously with you! May the Eternal grant divine favor upon you and thus grant you peace!"

Although the Bible presents these words as a special blessing transmitted by the priests of old to the people, it is customary for others to recite it in certain contexts. By using these words to bless their sons and daughters, parents acknowledge that they are the agents, not the source, of God's blessing in their children's lives, just the *kohanim* in Temple times were the transmitters, not the originators, of the blessings they offered the people.

Many use this opportunity to add personal prayers or meditations for their children. The following, taken from the second edition of *Siddur Sim Shalom,* are worthy examples. For boys, one could say: "May you be blessed by God as were Ephraim and Manasseh, who understood that wherever they lived, their Jewishness was the essence of their lives; who loved and honored their elders and teachers; and who cherished one another without pettiness or envy, accepting in humility the blessings that were theirs." For girls, the following would be highly appropriate: "May God bless you with the strength and vision of Sarah, with the wisdom and foresight of Rebecca, with the courage and compassion of Rachel, with the gentleness and graciousness of Leah, and their faith in the promise of our people's heritage."

As the diners take their places around the table, the hymn Shalom Aleikhem is sung aloud. Based on a teaching preserved in the Talmud at *BT* Shabbat 119b, the song supposes that two ministering angels accompany worshipers home from the synagogue each Friday night. "If they find candles lit and the Shabbat table set," the text in the Talmud reads, "the good angel says: 'May it be God's will that there be another Shabbat like this one,' and the wicked angel is forced against his will to say 'Amen.'" The inverse, however, is also true: if there are no signs of a traditional Shabbat in the home, the wicked angel prays that it ever be thus and the good angel is obliged to respond with an a begrudging amen. It is to these angels that diners seated at the Shabbat table sing the hymn Shalom Aleikhem.

After Shalom Aleikhem, husbands traditionally sing or recite the Eishet Ḥayil passage (taken directly from Proverbs 31:10–31) to their wives. It is a way of acknowledging and praising the women who work so hard to prepare Shabbat, to run the household, and to raise their children. Popularly translated as "A Woman of Valor," some take the Eishet Ḥayil as an allegory about Shabbat and the nurturing role "she" plays in a traditional Jewish home even though the simpler way to understand the text is as a husband's ode to his wife's virtues. In the spirit of egalitarianism, the second edition of *Siddur*

Sim Shalom suggests Psalm 112:1–9 as a parallel passage women might wish to recite to their husbands.

Shabbat dinner begins formally with the recitation of the Kiddush over a full cup of wine. Popularly called "making Kiddush," the act of sanctifying Shabbat by blessing God as the Creator of "the fruit of the vine" is rooted in the biblical conception of wine as an agent of joy. The psalmist (at Psalm 104:15) wrote that "wine . . . cheers the human heart" and so a cup filled to the brim with sweet wine has come to suggest the abundance of God's blessings in a family's life. The text may be found in any edition of the prayerbook.

One may recite Kiddush over grape juice instead of wine. In the absence of either, however, one makes Kiddush over the *ḥallot* instead (*SA* Oraḥ Ḥayyim 289). If doing so, however, the blessing over bread should be used to begin the prayer instead of the blessing over wine.

As noted above, in traditional homes women light the candles and men recite the Kiddush. Since, as noted above, the *mitzvah* of sanctifying the onset of Shabbat with wine devolves upon both men and women, women may recite the Kiddush for others at the table. Some people stand for Kiddush, but others sit as it is recited. Either is considered an acceptable practice (gloss of the Rema to *SA* Oraḥ Ḥayyim 271:10).

At home, Kiddush begins with an introductory paragraph, Genesis 2:1–3. There is, however, a widespread custom to begin not with the opening words of that first verse, but with the last words of the previous chapter of Genesis. By doing so, the worshiper begins with four words, the initial letters of which spell out the four-letter name of God. In this subtle way, God's blessings on a Jewish home are invoked.

Prior to reciting the blessing for bread, we perform the ritual washing of the hands known as *n'tilat yadayim.* Rings are removed so that the water comes in contact with all parts of the hands, then a vessel is filled with water. The water is poured over the right hand and then over the left hand at least twice, although some follow the custom of pouring water three times over each hand. The following blessing is recited: *barukh attah adonai, eloheinu, melekh ha-olam, asher kidd'shanu b'mitzvotav v'tzivvanu al n'tilat yadayim* ("Praised are You, Adonai, our God, Sovereign of the universe, who, sanctifying us with divine commandments, has commanded us concerning the washing of the hands"). The hands are then dried.

The purpose of washing our hands in this peculiar way is not specifically hygienic. (Indeed, people should certainly wash their hands with soap and water before *n'tilat yadayim* if their hands are dirty.) After the destruction of the Temple, the Jewish house took the place of the ancient sanctuary and, in many ways, the Shabbat and festival table became latter-day substitutes for the altar. We wash our hands before eating bread today just as the priests washed their hands and feet before commencing the sacrificial service in ancient times.

On Shabbat, two loaves, or two rolls, are placed on the table. Traditionally, a rich egg bread known popularly as *ḥallah* is used, but any kind of kosher bread may be used in its stead. The two loaves represent the double portion of manna the Israelites gathered each Friday during their forty years of wandering in the desert, as related at Exodus 16:22.

The loaves are covered by a cloth during the recitation of Kiddush (*SA* Oraḥ Ḥayyim 271:9). One explanation for this is that the tablecloth and the *ḥallah* cover symbolize the two layers of dew that protected the manna from the desert sand. Another reason we cover the *ḥallah* is to prevent it from being "jealous" that the rituals for the wine come prior to those for the bread. This may sound just a bit far-fetched, but it masks a profound lesson: if we are bidden to be sensitive to the "feelings" of inanimate objects, then how much the more so must we be sensitive to the feelings of human beings!

From the time of the washing of the hands until the blessing over the bread, we remain silent unless the words we speak are directly relevant to the situation. Some people use these moments to hum a melody, thus focusing the attention of those present on the rituals at hand.

The cloth is then removed, the two loaves are raised, and the blessing over bread is recited (*SA* Oraḥ Ḥayyim 274:1). (This blessing may be found in any standard edition of the prayerbook.) The loaves are cut, sprinkled with salt, and distributed to those assembled. What is the point of the salt? Salt was added to each offering in the Temple, as noted at Leviticus 2:13. We sprinkle salt on our bread to remind us that we are gathered in holy space, that our tables today are the equivalent of the altar of ancient times, and that a Shabbat meal is an occasion for worshiping God. There are some variant customs in widespread use. Some pour salt onto the bread board and then dip the bread into the salt. Others use the knife to make an impression on the bread, and then tear it by hand.

In addition to the special foods on the menu, it is traditional to sing special table songs, popularly called *z'mirot,* during the course of the meal. The meal, relaxed and convivial, is thus a time for family members to enjoy each other's company.

The Grace after Meals is recited in its customary place. On Shabbat, there are significant variations and additions to the standard weekday version. For example, the recitation begins with Psalm 126, and a special prayer for Shabbat is added in the third section of the Grace just prior to the blessing for the restoration of Jerusalem. Then, toward the end of the Grace, a special prayer, beginning with the word *ha-raḥaman* ("The Merciful One"), is added to the other lines that begin with that same word as a tribute to Shabbat and the role it plays in Jewish life. Finally, following the last *ha-raḥaman,* the usual word *magdil* is changed to its biblical variant, *migdol.* This verse comes from one of those rare chapters of Scripture that appears twice in our edition of the Hebrew Bible, once as the eighteenth psalm and once as the twenty-second chapter of the Second Book of Samuel. On weekdays, we use the version that appears in the psalm, but on Shabbat and festivals we use the version that appears in Second Samuel. Instead of choosing one source over the other, both versions were incorporated into the liturgy. This act of accommodation and inclusion is a typically Jewish approach to textual variation.

The Saturday Morning Service

There are a number of significant additions that set the Shabbat Morning Service apart from its weekday counterpart. The 100th psalm is omitted from the opening P'sukei D'zimra section and nine additional psalms (Psalms 19, 34, 90, 91, 135, 136, 33, 92, and 93) are added in its place. Although only one of the added psalms has any specific connection to Shabbat—Psalm 92 is specifically labeled "a psalm-song for the Shabbat day"—all give voice to the dream-like mixture of recollection of the past and hope in the future that Shabbat itself inspires in the hearts of the faithful. Because the Sabbath itself is a sign of the covenant, *t'fillin* are not worn on Shabbat.

A long section beginning with the words *nishmat kol ḥai t'vareikh et shimkha* ("May the soul of every living creature bless Your name") is added before the Yishtabbaḥ blessing that closes the P'sukei D'zimra section of the service. The word *nishmat* may possibly be an allusion to the *n'shamah y'teirah,* "the additional soul" that, according to the Talmud (*BT* Beitzah 16a), enters every Jew at the onset of every Shabbat. It is during this interpolated *nishmat kol ḥai* section that the cantor or prayer leader begins the formal chanting of the Morning Service.

Following the Bar'khu call to prayer, three extra paragraphs are added to the first of the two blessings that precede the Sh'ma. The three paragraphs are poetic statements—one is actually cast as a singable hymn—regarding the majesty and mystery of divine creation, a central theme of the Shabbat liturgy in general.

The Amidah for Shabbat consists of seven blessings: the standard opening and closing benedictions, and a middle one dealing with the special nature of the day which ends with a blessing praising God as *m'kaddeish ha-shabbat,* the divine source of the sanctity of Shabbat. This intermediate paragraph, which differs from Amidah to Amidah in the course of the Shabbat liturgy, here emphasizes the fact that Shabbat observance is a commandment of the Torah revealed by God to Moses at Mount Sinai. This has an appropriate feel to it, since the congregation recites these words shortly before taking the Torah from the Ark and reading from it.

As is always the case when the prayer leader recites the Amidah aloud, a responsive reading called the K'dushah is inserted into the third blessing. The K'dushah in the Shaḥarit Amidah speaks of the restoration of God's rule over Jerusalem, and of the ultimate redemption of the Jewish people. The repetition of the Amidah is followed by Kaddish.

The service for taking the Torah from the Ark is also enhanced on Shabbat morning. We begin with a stirring liturgical introduction that starts with the words *ein kamokha* ("there is none like You") and then add a long prayer taken from the Zohar, called B'rikh Sh'meih after its opening words, once the Ark is opened. Also, before the Torah is taken around the room in solemn procession, the Sh'ma and an extra line proclaiming the uniqueness and unity of God are chanted aloud.

In the Conservative movement, a bar or bat mitzvah can be celebrated anytime the Torah is taken out to be read, and the young person coming of age can be called up for an *aliyah*. More often than not, these celebrations take place at the Morning Service on a Shabbat. Saturday morning provides more opportunities for participation by the bar or bat mitzvah (reading the Torah, chanting the *haftarah,* leading parts of the service, delivering a *d'var torah*), and more *aliyot* and honors for the assembled congregation. It is the optimum time for a Jewish community to welcome another Jew into its midst, and to celebrate this milestone with the family.

On Shabbat, seven people are called up to the Torah. (It is permissible to call up more, but not fewer, than seven.) The number seven is significant in this context. Not only does it recall the seven days of the week, but it is also a subtle halakhic comment on the supreme place of Shabbat in the hierarchy of holy days, since there are six *aliyot* on Yom Kippur, five on all other festival days, four on Rosh Ḥodesh and the intermediary days of festivals, and three on ordinary weekdays when the Torah is read. After the last regular *aliyah* is concluded, the Half Kaddish is recited and an extra *aliyah,* popularly called the *maftir,* is given to the person who will chant the *haftarah.*

For about four-fifths of the year, the *haftarot* are chapters from one or another of the books of the prophets chosen to elucidate the Torah portion for that specific Shabbat in some obvious or obscure way. During the ten weeks preceding the High Holidays, however, a different approach is followed: for the three weeks before the fast of the Ninth of Av, three gloomy *haftarot* actually called "the *haftarot* of doom" are read aloud. For the seven weeks that follow the fast, which commemorates the destruction of Jerusalem in ancient times, seven special *haftarot* called "the *haftarot* of consolation" are read aloud. (There are also special *haftarot* for all the festivals and even for the Sabbaths that fall during those festivals, as well as for other special Sabbaths that fall during the year, each geared to the specific holiday or special Shabbat being observed rather than specifically to the Torah reading for that day, whatever it might be. These are discussed elsewhere in this volume by Rabbi Alan Lucas.)

In the course of the Torah service, many congregations add in prayers for the sick or special prayers (collectively called Mi She-beirakh prayers after their opening words) for different members of the congregation, either to honor special occasions in their lives or simply to honor an individual's *aliyah* to the Torah. There are special versions of the prayer for those soon to be wed and for naming newborn baby girls. (Newborn boys are generally named at their *b'rit milah* ceremonies.) After the reading of the *haftarah*, the Torah service also contains several additional prayers: one for sages of Israel, another for the congregation, one for the country in which the congregation is situated and for its leaders, and one for the State of Israel. On the Shabbat before Rosh Ḥodesh, a prayer for the upcoming Jewish month is recited. Different congregations follow different customs regarding these prayers; some add in prayers for world peace or for the repose of the souls of the martyrs of Israel as well. After all these prayers are concluded, a liturgical setting of Psalm 145 (popularly called Ashrei or "the" Ashrei after its first word) is recited for a second time. (It was also included in the P'sukei D'zimra section of the service before the formal beginning of the Morning Service.)

Following Ashrei, the Torah is returned to the Ark in procession as the congregation sings the twenty-ninth psalm. In many congregations, the rabbi delivers a sermon after the Ark is closed. In some congregations, the sermon is replaced with some other form of Torah study. In others, however, the congregation proceeds directly to the Musaf Service.

An extra Amidah prayer is recited on Shabbat and festivals. This extra prayer, colloquially called the Musaf Amidah (*musaf* means "addition" in Hebrew) is included to remind worshipers that in ancient times extra sacrifices were offered in the Temple on Shabbat and on other festive days. As with the other services, the Musaf Amidah consists of the standard opening and closing blessings, with a middle paragraph devoted to the occasion at hand. At Musaf on Shabbat, this section focuses on the additional offerings that were brought to the Temple on Shabbat, as described at Numbers 28:9–10. Opening with a reverse acrostic, the middle section traditionally continues with requests for the return of the Jewish people to their land, for the rebuilding of the Temple, and for the restoration of the sacrifices, specifically including those for Shabbat.

In the middle decades of the twentieth century, many Conservative ideologues began to question the idea of praying for the reinstitution of animal sacrifices in a future Temple to be built in Jerusalem. This led to a near universal change in the text of the Musaf Amidah in Conservative movement prayerbooks, so that the prayer henceforth merely nodded to the practices of the past without actually asking the worshipers to pray that such practices be restored. Since it seemed peculiar to recite a prayer in which the worshiper was not actually praying for any specific thing, however, the Musaf Amidah prayer itself was reinterpreted as a way for moderns to look forward to a messianic era, to the ingathering of the exiles, and to the rebuilding of the Temple in Jerusalem as a house of prayer, not animal sacrifice. This continues to be the norm in Conservative congregations, although it is not a universal practice.

There is also a special version of the K'dushah that is recited in the third benediction of the Musaf Amidah on Shabbat when it is chanted aloud by the prayer leader.

The Ein Keloheinu hymn is added to the service on Shabbat after the Full Kaddish that follows the Musaf Amidah. This is traditionally followed by a selection from the Talmud (taken from *BT* K'ritot 6a) recounting the ingredients of the incense offering in the Temple. Many Conservative prayerbooks have eliminated this passage, inserting instead one from the talmudic tractate called B'rakhot that speaks about the possibility of bringing peace to the world through Torah study. Often this is followed by Kaddish D'rabbanan, and then the service concludes with Aleinu, the Mourner's Kaddish, and the Adon Olam hymn.

Strictly speaking, Kiddush on Saturday morning takes place at Shabbat lunch. It has become the custom in many synagogues to recite Kiddush over a cup of wine as services end. This is done because, in many cases, a luncheon is served in the synagogue. It may also be a way for those who will not have a traditional Shabbat meal at home to participate in this ritual.

Shabbat Lunch

Although taking a light meal before prayers in the morning is permissible, the second of the three formal Shabbat meals follows the Shaḥarit and Musaf Services. As on Friday evening, the meal begins with the Kiddush over wine. The Saturday blessing is referred to as Kiddusha Rabba ("the great Kiddush"), but this term is just a bit ironic since the Saturday Kiddush is much shorter than its Friday night counterpart. (Some explain the grand title not as mere irony, but rather as a way of stressing its importance.) There is another important difference between Kiddusha Rabba and the Friday evening Kiddush: in the absence of wine or grape juice, it is considered acceptable to recite this Kiddush (using the correct blessing, of course) over liquor, beer, or even fruit juice (*SA* Oraḥ Ḥayyim 289:2). The full text varies widely in different communities. Minimally, a verse from the Ten Commandments (Exodus 20:11) is recited, followed by the appropriate blessing for the substance over which Kiddush is recited. Other versions include Isaiah 58:13–14, Exodus 31:16–17, and/or Exodus 20:8–11.

The second meal then proceeds with the formal washing of the hands, called *n'tilat yadayim,* and the blessing over the bread. It is customary to conclude the meal with Shabbat table songs (called *z'mirot*) and then, finally, with the Grace after Meals.

The Afternoon Service

The Minḥah Service on Saturday afternoon contains a number of significant additions to the regular weekday Afternoon Service. First, the prayer U-va L'tziyyon Go·eil ("A Redeemer Shall Come to Zion") is added after the opening Ashrei psalm. This is a prayer that speaks about messianic hopes, a theme that is at the forefront of our thoughts as Shabbat draws to a close.

Second, the Torah is read publicly. We call three people to the Torah and read aloud the first section of the next Torah portion, which, almost always, will be read in synagogue on the following Shabbat. According to tradition, it was the biblical personality Ezra who instituted the practice of reading the Torah on Saturday afternoons as a way to accommodate people unable to come during the week to hear the Torah read on Monday and Thursday mornings. The feeling, however, is anticipatory rather than compensatory: as one Shabbat winds down, we are already looking forward to the next.

Third, the central benediction of the Amidah changes to a unique passage based on the notion that God, Israel, and Shabbat testify to each other's rare qualities. This paragraph also mentions the word *m'nuḥah* (rest) seven times, stressing that Shabbat rest is not merely a cessation of strenuous activity or relaxation, but actual worship. Shabbat, we are reminded, is not a "day off" from our daily tasks as much as it is a day on which we, like our ancestors, are called upon to reconnect with God, with our people, and with our inmost selves.

Finally, many recite three verses, Psalm 119:142, Psalm 71:19, and Psalm 36:7, after the Amidah. These melancholy verses reflect a sense that Shabbat is ending, and that another week of work and struggle will soon be upon us.

There is a custom that calls upon worshipers to recite Psalms 104 and 120–134 beginning from Shabbat B'reishit, the Shabbat on which the first portion of the Book of Genesis is read aloud, through Shabbat Ha-gadol, the Shabbat that precedes Passover. Psalm 104 speaks of God's creation of the world, thus connecting it to Shabbat B'reishit. The fifteen other psalms, popularly called the Songs of Ascent because of their common superscription, are envisaged as the songs pilgrims sang on their way up to Jerusalem. According to the Talmud (at *BT* Sukkah 53a), these were written by David when he prepared the foundation of the Temple. Reciting them now is a way to connect Shabbat with Jerusalem as the day comes to an end, just as L'khah Dodi connects Shabbat and Jerusalem as Shabbat begins. It is a way for worshipers to imagine themselves as pilgrims on their way to a rebuilt and reunited Jerusalem on the eve of the messianic era.

Also, in the weeks between Passover and Shavuot, it customary to study *Pirkei Avot* (sometimes called "The Ethics of the Fathers"), a collection of rabbinic maxims and ethical teachings preserved as a tractate of the Mishnah. Traditionally, one chapter is reviewed each week. The sixth chapter, an ancient addition to the collection, is known as Perek Kinyan Torah ("The Chapter on Acquiring Torah") because it speaks of the greatness of Torah and the qualities necessary for its successful study. This chapter is thus read the week before Shavuot, the festival that commemorates the experience of receiving the Torah at Mount Sinai. Another widespread custom is to continue learning *Pirkei Avot* throughout the summer months and only to conclude at Sukkot. That brings the worshiper full circle back to Shabbat B'reishit, when the cycle of additional liturgical passages begins anew.

The Third Meal

It was the practice of many in pre-modern times to eat only two full meals a day, but, to make Shabbat special, the rabbis of ancient times ordained that there be three meals on Shabbat (*SA* Oraḥ Ḥayyim 291:1). Of these, the third should ideally be consumed in the afternoon between the Afternoon and the Evening Services. A biblical justification for this third meal was found in the account of the Israelites' wandering in the desert. A double portion of manna fell on Fridays, so the Israelites would not have to go out and collect it on Shabbat. Speaking of the manna, Moses said, "Eat it today, for today is a Shabbat of the Eternal and you will not find it today on the plain" (Exodus 16:25). The three times the word "today" appears in the verse were taken as subtle references to the three Shabbat meals.

This "third meal" is called *se'udah sh'lishit* in Hebrew, but Jews of Ashkenazic origin often refer to it as *shalashudis* or *shalshudis,* both corruptions of the Hebrew words *shalosh se'udot,* meaning "three meals." Generally speaking, because lunch has only ended a few hours earlier, this is a light meal. For those who attend the Minḥah Service in synagogue, *se'udah sh'lishit* is often served at the synagogue so the worshipers need not return home before the Evening Service. (Herring or gefilte fish are dishes typically served.) Kiddush is not recited, but the Ha-motzi blessing is said over bread (*SA* Oraḥ Ḥayyim 291:4).

The ancient teacher Bar Kappara taught that those who fulfilled the requirement of three Shabbat meals are spared three aspects of earthly suffering: those that will precede the coming of the messiah, those that await the wicked in Gehenna (that is, in Hell), and those that will come as part of the War of Gog and Magog, the great apocalyptic war that will end this era of human existence (*BT* Shabbat 118a). Moderns, especially those who are careful about eating three meals on Shabbat, can certainly hope Bar Kappara was correct, but the third meal on Shabbat will for most be more about spiritual sustenance than physical need. Participation in this final meal is invested with profound meaning in kabbalistic circles, but moderns can simply find it a quiet moment to break bread with members of the community one final time before the maelstrom of the workaday week begins, and to feel nourished and sustained by each other's company.

One of the best-known table songs for the third Shabbat meal is Y'did Nefesh, composed (as mentioned above) in sixteenth-century Safed by Rabbi Eleazar Azikri. Y'did Nefesh speaks of the Jews' deep longing for God and the first letters of the four paragraphs spell out the four-letter name of God. In congregations that begin Kabbalat Shabbat with the chanting of this same hymn, the resultant image is of a people that begins and ends its day of rest with a formal statement of longing for communion with God, and for redemption.

The Saturday Evening Service

We often say that a Jewish day begins at sundown, yet Shabbat does not end precisely at sundown on Saturday. There are two reasons for this. First, it feels unseemly to end Shabbat at the first possible moment—as though it were a burden to be abandoned as soon as possible. Second, the *halakhah* wants to guarantee that no one ever ends Shabbat early due to a miscalculation of the correct time.

The *halakhah* sets the time for the end of Shabbat at the appearance of three medium-sized stars in the sky. (The *Shulḥan Arukh,* at *SA* Oraḥ Ḥayyim 293:2, requires that they be close together, not spread out across the night sky.) Since it is often difficult, especially in urban settings, to see such stars, it was eventually determined that Shabbat ends forty-two minutes after the time that

Shabbat candles were lit the night before. (Others wait seventy-two minutes after candle-lighting time. Many Jewish calendars will list both these times.)

Once it is late enough, the Evening Service for the conclusion of Shabbat is recited. Some people precede the service with the recitation of Psalms 144, 29, and 67, which are considered appropriate prayers for the transitional moment between the day of rest and a week of days given over to the struggle for sustenance and survival.

Except for a special addition to the fourth blessing of the Amidah, the Evening Service through the end of the Amidah is the same as on any weekday. This paragraph, beginning with the words *attah ḥonantanu,* serves as a *havdalah,* a "separation," between Shabbat and the new week, and speaks of how God distinguishes between sacred and ordinary, between light and darkness, between Israel and the other peoples of the world, and between Shabbat and the other days of the week. Why is this paragraph inserted into this specific blessing? The fourth benediction of the weekday Amidah asks God to grant us "knowledge, discernment, and wisdom." Just as we imagine God using knowledge and wisdom to discern between all the aforementioned pairs of things, so too we ask God to give us those same qualities so that we become able to distinguish clearly between the workaday week and Shabbat.

Following the Amidah, we recite Psalm 91 (preceded by the final verse in Psalm 90) and a special version of the K'dushah called the K'dushah D'sidra that omits its opening passage, two lines that refer to the arrival of the messiah. (This reflects the ancient tradition that the messiah will not come to redeem the world at night. The K'dushah D'sidra is also sometimes called U-va L'tziyyon after its opening words.)

Some congregations and individuals have the custom of adding an anthology of blessings found in the Bible to the service at this point. This section, if it is recited, ends with Psalm 128.

Before reciting Aleinu, we recite the Havdalah prayer. In many synagogues, its first paragraph, reserved for home use, is omitted.

Havdalah

The rabbinic understanding of the Torah's injunction to remember the Shabbat day and keep it holy is that one should not merely recall that it is Shabbat, but actually inaugurate the day formally with Kiddush and mark its end just as formally with the Havdalah ceremony (*BT* P'saḥim 106a; cf. *MT* Hilkhot Shabbat 29:1). There are actually two forms of Havdalah: the paragraph added to the fourth blessing in the Saturday evening Amidah, marking the formal end of Shabbat, and the home ritual involving wine, spices, and candle. Traditionally, the recitation of the Havdalah paragraph in the Amidah was the way that men ended Shabbat, as only men were obliged to recite the Amidah three times daily. The home ritual, on the other hand, was originally designed to conclude Shabbat for women and children. This version of Havdalah consists, essentially, of blessings over wine, spices, and fire, and concludes with a prayer acknowledging God's plan to make manifest the presence of the Divine in the world by clearly distinguishing between the sacred and the profane. In our world, the distinction between the two ceremonies is more a function of location than gender: in synagogue, we end Shabbat by inserting the Havdalah paragraph into the Amidah and by performing the synagogue version of the home ritual, and at home we end Shabbat with the home version of Havdalah. In some synagogues, as noted, the opening paragraph is omitted and Havdalah begins with the blessing over wine. Of course, any who choose to recite their prayers at home also include the Havdalah paragraph in the Amidah.

An interesting feature of the Havdalah ceremony is that it engages all five senses. Havdalah thus serves as a kind of sensory antidote to the melancholy that many experience on Saturday afternoon at twilight. As the day grows quiet and Shabbat nears its end, there is a feeling of subdued sadness in the air. But when nightfall comes, Havdalah calls out to the five senses and reminds us that there is pleasure in this world that comes from work, not only from rest.

There are some interesting parallels between the onset and the departure of Shabbat. At sunset on Friday night, for example, at least two separate candles are lit. On Saturday night, on the other hand, we light one braided candle with (at least) two wicks. On Friday nights, Kiddush is recited over wine at the dinner table to begin the Shabbat meal; on Saturday night, Havdalah is recited over wine (or, in a pinch, over some other popular beverage), often at the same table, to end Shabbat. Even the use of spices on Saturday night is reminiscent of the pleasant aromas that permeate a traditional home on Friday night.

Havdalah is introduced by seven biblical selections: Isaiah 12:2–3, Psalm 3:9, Psalm 46:12, Psalm 84:13, Psalm 20:10, Esther 8:16, and Psalm 116:13. The seven selections remind us of the seven days of the week, but they also have the common theme that God will bring ultimate deliverance to Israel. Shabbat, the liturgy suggests, is a refuge from the difficulties of life. But, as Shabbat ends, the same liturgy reminds us that we can also pray and hope for permanent redemption.

Havdalah is recited over a full cup of wine, a symbol of our hope for God's blessings in the coming week. (As noted above, any beverage except water will suffice in the absence of wine, in which case the correct blessing is recited.) In addition, Havdalah requires a special multi-wicked candle and a container of spices. (Cinnamon or cloves are most commonly used, although any fragrant spice will do. Sephardic Jews often use fragrant myrtle branches.)

The ritual is conducted in the following way. (The order of blessings is fixed: wine, spices, candle, and the Havdalah blessing itself. The order is easy to remember if one knows the Hebrew terms for the four items—*yayin, b'samim, neir, havdalah*—because they spell out the name Yavneh.) First, the lights are dimmed, as it is customary to perform the Havdalah ritual in the dark. Then, the cup of wine is lifted up using the right hand. At the recitation of the words, "I shall lift the cup of deliverance," it is customary to raise the cup a little higher. We do not, however, drink the wine immediately after reciting the blessing. Instead, the wine is sipped after the final benediction is pronounced. After the blessing over the wine is intoned, the spice box is then taken in the right hand and the appropriate blessing is recited. (The use of spices is rooted in an old Jewish belief preserved in the Talmud at *BT* Beitzah 16a and Ta·anit 27b in the name of the great teacher, Reish Lakish, according to which each Jew receives an additional soul, a *n'shamah y'teirah,* for the duration of Shabbat. On Saturday evening, this additional soul departs, thus leaving the individual from whom it departs spiritually diminished and physically spent. The spices are thus imagined to revive the person who has so recently suffered the loss of this second soul.)

Next, the blessing over the multi-wicked Havdalah candle is recited. One must make immediate use of the light in some way upon hearing the blessing, and this is traditionally accomplished by bending the tips of one's fingers in toward one's wrists and by looking at one's fingernails in the candlelight. Kindling a fire is one of the basic acts of work forbidden during Shabbat. By lighting the flame, we thus demonstrate that Shabbat is over and ordinary weekday activities may resume. We are also reminded that, according to the Book of Genesis, God began the work of creation by making light on the first day of the week, the very day that begins with the end of Shabbat. By starting our new week by imitating God, we are reminded that human beings are God's partners in the ongoing creation of the world. The torch—literally—has been passed to us.

We now lift the cup of wine again and recite the final paragraph of Havdalah before drinking the wine. It is customary to extinguish the candle by dipping it into a dish or cup into which some of the wine over which the blessing was pronounced has been poured. Some follow the custom of placing a drop of Havdalah wine onto their eyelids to evoke the verse from Psalm 19:9: "The commandment of God is pure, illuminating the eyes." Others dip a finger into the wine and then place it in their pocket as a symbolic prayer for material prosperity.

Following Havdalah, a number of liturgical poems may be traditionally sung or recited. These include the Yiddish-language *Gott fun Avrohom* and the Hebrew hymns *Ha-mavdil Bein Kodesh L'ḥol* and *Eliyahu Ha-navi.*

A chorus of *Eliyahu Ha-navi* is also sung by some as an introduction to the Havdalah ceremony itself. It speaks about the prophet Elijah, who, according to Malachi 3:23, will be sent by God to herald the coming of the Messiah. Shabbat is a day of peace in the midst of a week of strife. As Shabbat draws to a close, it is natural to look forward to our ultimate redemption, and thus we sing and pray for the coming of Elijah. Jewish tradition refers to Shabbat as "a foretaste of the world to come." And, in turn, the idealized world to come is often spoken of as an age in which every day will be like Shabbat.

The traditional greeting following Havdalah is *shavu·a tov* ("a good week"). In many synagogues, the Yiddish equivalent, *a gute voch,* is heard as well.

When Shabbat is immediately followed by a holiday, a form of the regular Havdalah ritual is included in the recitation of the festival Kiddush by reciting a special paragraph that concludes by acclaiming God as the One who "distinguishes one domain of sacred time from another." The blessing over fire is still recited (albeit over the flames of the festival candles), but the spices are omitted.

At the conclusion of festivals that are followed by a weekday, the final Havdalah paragraph alone is recited over a cup of wine, but without the use of the candle or the spices (*SA* Oraḥ Ḥayyim 491:1). (The Havdalah recited at the end of Yom Kippur is the sole exception to this rule, because both the candle and the wine are used even though Yom Kippur is invariably followed by a weekday and never by Shabbat.) When a festival day is immediately followed by Shabbat (i.e., when the days of the festival are Thursday and Friday), Havdalah is deferred until Saturday evening.

For traditional Jews, Havdalah is the final ritual in a twenty-five hour day packed with rituals. For Jews who are new to the tradition or who are not ready to incorporate all of Shabbat into their lives, Havdalah can still serve as a dramatic reminder of the beauty and emotional power of Judaism.

The M'lavveh Malkah

Although it is rarely observed within Conservative congregations, the term M'lavveh Malkah (literally "The Queen's Escort") refers to the custom of holding an especially festive meal on Saturday evening to honor the end of Shabbat. The concept of Shabbat as Queen Shabbat is key: just as we go out to greet the queen with the Kabbalat Shabbat service as she arrives on Friday evening, so too did the custom evolve of honoring the queen by escorting her as she takes her leave.

There is another side to this tradition as well, one rooted in the custom of calling the M'lavveh Malkah "the Feast of David." According to a legend preserved in the Talmud at *BT* Shabbat 30a, King David once asked God when he would die. While not giving an exact date, God informed him it would be on Shabbat. Thus, as each Shabbat ended, David celebrated one more week of life. For contemporary Jews, then, celebrating David's sense of gratitude each Saturday evening became a way of strengthening belief in the reality of the messianic era, in which David's descendant will come to Israel as its redeemer.

A small amount of food is all that is required for a minimal M'lavveh Malkah. (The Talmud, at *BT* Shabbat 119b, speaks of preparing hot water and fresh warm bread as a way of fulfilling the teaching of Rabbi Ḥidka preserved at *BT* Shabbat 117b that there be *four* meals over the course of a Shabbat.) A M'lavveh Malkah is also a time to sing special *z'mirot,* especially those which speak of King David or Elijah the Prophet, the messianic herald.

Creating the Ambience of Shabbat

Many and complicated are the labors prohibited by the *halakhah* on Shabbat. Not only are there the famous thirty-nine specific labors forbidden by Scripture, but most of them have derivatives, called *toladot,* that the rabbis coaxed from them to widen the scope of their applicability. (These are discussed and enumerated below.) On top of those original and derivative prohibitions, there are also activities prohibited under the category called *sh'vut* in Hebrew, which includes activities not formally forbidden under any other rubric, but nonetheless deemed incompatible with the spirit of Shabbat observance.

Among Ashkenazic Jews, even those who do not speak Yiddish, the term *shabbosdik* is often used to describe activities appropriate for Shabbat, but defining what activities do or do not qualify can be difficult. One often hears the argument stated, sometimes forcefully, that certain forbidden activities—activities like sewing or writing a letter or going for a drive in the country—are relaxing and pleasant and should therefore be considered entirely consonant with the spirit of Shabbat. While they may be very enjoyable, this approach overlooks the crucial detail that Shabbat is not merely a day of pleasant activities, but also a profound and spiritually charged context for worshiping God, which may never take place in the contravention of divine law. But it is also true that merely being permitted is not reason enough to describe a specific activity as *shabbosdik*—and it is also so that a Shabbat day lived in sync with the *halakhah,* but which ends up being boring, stultifying, or even oppressive, is almost by definition not an act of worship. In a sense, it is the way we spend our leisure hours on Shabbat that is key: praying, eating, and sleeping are already programmed as part of the day; the challenge rests in how we choose to spend our time beyond those activities.

For almost all, Shabbat observance includes Torah study. For people who work hard at their jobs and at serving their families, there is often very little quality time during the week to study Torah, or even casually to discuss topics of Jewish interest. Shabbat, on the other hand, provides the perfect opportunity for Jewish learning. In some communities, the rabbi leads classes in the synagogue on Shabbat. In others, there are *ḥavurah* fellowships that bring friends together to study Torah on Shabbat. Learning may also take place in private homes, where families spend time together studying the weekly Torah portion or other texts of Jewish interest. Moreover, countless individuals dedicate a portion of each Shabbat to personal study, delving into Jewish texts on their own in a way they have no time to do during the week.

The most obvious starting place for Shabbat learning is that week's Torah portion. The Torah is divided into fifty-four weekly sections, popularly called *parashot* or *parashiyyot* (singular for both forms: *parashah*) or *sidrot* (singular: *sidrah,* often pronounced *sedrah*), one of which (or at least part of one of which) is read on every Shabbat of the year except the ones that fall during Sukkot and Passover. (There are also occasional weeks when two *parashot* are read together.) There are countless translations and commentaries on the Torah for study. The beginner will do best to start off with the classic commentaries of Rashi (Rabbi Shlomo Yitzḥaki, 1040–1105) which exists in a complete, annotated English translation. But there are also more modern commentaries rooted in contemporary biblical scholarship that will provide an interesting counterpoint to the more traditional sources, of which a fine example is the *Etz Hayim ḥumash* published in 2001 by the Rabbinical Assembly and the United Synagogue of Conservative Judaism. (The Hebrew word *ḥumash* is used to refer to editions of the Torah printed as books rather than written out on scrolls.) The key is to move from commentary to commentary, always seeking new ways to understand the spiritual lessons of the Torah and to allow those lessons to deepen one's understanding of what it means to be an observant Jew. The very book that the reader now holds in his or her hands could be another source of Shabbat reading and study.

As we visit with each other, eat together, and take Shabbat walks together, a lot of time on Shabbat is spent talking. Yet the Talmud (at *BT* Shabbat 113b) teaches that "your Shabbat talk should not be like your weekday talk." Rashi's simple comment is that one should avoid talking about business and money matters, but most moderns will want to take an even broader approach and try to limit conversation on Shabbat to matters of the spirit. Talk on Shabbat should be elevating and inspirational. Conversation at the Shabbat table, especially, should be of sacred matters and should center on questions of values, ethics, and morality. There should be no place in Shabbat discourse for vulgar or profane talk. Of course, one should avoid gossip and talebearing as assiduously on Shabbat as on weekdays, or even perhaps even more so. And one should avoid any sort of conversation on Shabbat that could lead to argument, tension, or friction. Indeed, there is a stirring *midrash* on Exodus 35:3, the scriptural passage prohibiting the kindling of a flame on Shabbat, that interprets the fire mentioned therein as symbolic of angry, contentious disagreement.

May one use the telephone on Shabbat to talk to distant friends or family? Since the 1950s, the Committee on Jewish Law and Standards has permitted the use of electricity on Shabbat when such use will enhance the enjoyment of Shabbat, reduce personal discomfort, or help in the performance of a *mitzvah* (*Proceedings of the CJLS 1927–1970,* pp. 1162–1168). According to this view, the use of the telephone to bring families and friends into closer contact is allowed as long as the content of the conversation is in the spirit of Shabbat. Still, many rabbis counsel not using the phone at all on Shabbat except in case of emergency. Bringing a cell phone to Shabbat services is especially inappropriate because it disrupts the sanctity of the service.

For many families, singing is a very traditional way to establish bonds of closeness and intimacy at the Shabbat table. Special table songs called *z'mirot* are assigned to each of the Shabbat meals, although few observe these assignments carefully and most sing *z'mirot* as the spirit moves them without reference to the specific meal for which they were originally composed. Usually sung at the end of the meal, *z'mirot* can also be sung between courses to help slow down the meal, thus prolonging it so it can be savored all the more fully.

There are many compilations of these table songs, including laminated editions intended for use during meals. The best known of the Friday evening *z'mirot* are M'nuḥah V'simḥah, Mah Y'didut, Yah Ribbon, and Tzur Mishello. The most popular songs formally designated for Shabbat lunch are Yom Zeh M'khubbad, Yom Shabbaton, and D'ror Yikra. The songs traditionally sung at Saturday supper, the third of the Shabbat meals, are Y'did Nefesh and the twenty-third psalm. There is no specific need to limit singing to the traditional *z'mirot,* however, and many people sing other Jewish songs on Shabbat as well. The sole criterion should be that the song itself, and especially its lyrics, be consonant with the values of Shabbat.

May musical instruments be used to enhance the singing of *z'mirot?* The large majority of halakhic authorities view the use of musical instruments on Shabbat as forbidden. Some justify this with reference to the fact that something new—the musical sound itself—is being created. Others understand the prohibition as a kind of precautionary decree that prevents us in advance, so to speak, from being tempted to fix an instrument that malfunctions or replace a string that breaks. While some Conservative authorities have allowed the use of musical instruments, such as an organ, at Shabbat services, the majority opinion of the Committee on Jewish Law and Standards follows the responsum penned by Rabbi Eli Bohnen in 1962, which prohibited music even at social functions held in the synagogue. Before deciding whether or not to use musical instruments at home on Shabbat, one should seek a rabbi's opinion. Some avoid the radio and CD and mp3 players on Shabbat because the news, the commercials, and the choice of music can destroy the sacred spirit that Shabbat tries to instill. Others will selectively play music electronically if it serves to enhance Shabbat.

For many, having uninterrupted time to read is one of the great pleasures of Shabbat. However, the same rules that apply to Shabbat conversation should apply here as well. Ideally, reading on Shabbat should be spiritually elevating and Jewishly relevant. We should always try to choose reading material that reflects the atmosphere and ambience of Shabbat. Rabbi David Booth, writing in the winter 2010 issue of *CJ: Voices of Conservative/Masorti Judaism,* notes the halakhic problems in using a Kindle or other e-readers on Shabbat: even if it were to be turned on before Shabbat, it would still not permitted to adjust it by pushing a button to turn the page during Shabbat. (In addition, turning the page in a sense erases the words from the previous page, which would also constitute a forbidden activity on Shabbat.) A deeper question is how these "weekday devices" draw us away from the special atmosphere we try to create on Shabbat.

For others, a Shabbat walk is a regular part of the day, but here, too, tradition dictates that even something as ordinary as walking can be done in a way that reflects the sanctity of the day. The Talmud (*BT* Shabbat 113a) teaches us that our mode of walking on Shabbat should differ from that of weekdays. (This is usually interpreted to mean we should take smaller steps, and not rush around at breakneck speeds.) One should also take care not to violate the prohibitions against carrying things from one domain to another on Shabbat unless one is in space bounded by an *eiruv*. An *eiruv* is an artificial combination of all the homes and streets in a given area into a single domain through the use of poles and wires that act as the newly created domain's symbolic boundaries. The laws that govern setting up an *eiruv* are exceedingly complex and rest far beyond the purview of this volume. Setting up an *eiruv* is a job for a trained, competent rabbi.

In addition to being a sacred day, Shabbat can also be a day of fun. Indeed, especially if children are present, it is important to find a way to incorporate pleasurable, fun activities into the course of the day. Nevertheless, these activities must be consonant with the spirit of Shabbat and with the laws that govern forbidden activity. Playing cards or board games, for example, raises a few issues that the observant will have to address in advance. Keeping score has to be done without writing. Gambling is *not* an appropriate Shabbat activity, nor are games that use money. In addition, combatative games (as opposed to merely competitive ones) violate the spirit of Shabbat and should be avoided. Of course, games that utilize electricity will be acceptable only to those who follow the view that electricity may be used on Shabbat.

Active games raise other concerns. Carrying balls or other equipment from inside the house to the outside is prohibited, unless there is an *eiruv*. Also, games that lead to bruised knees or bruised egos, or which leave the players grimy and dirty, do not foster a spirit of Shabbat and should be avoided.

While Shabbat is supposed to be a day of spiritual renewal, it is also a day of physical rest. That being the case, the Shabbat nap is a distinguished and widely observed feature of Shabbat observance in every corner of the Jewish world. In fact, one clever sage saw in the Hebrew letters of the word Shabbat a hidden message: *sheinah b'-shabbat ta·anug*, sleep on Shabbat is a joy! The traditional table song, Mah Y'didut, says this explicitly: "And sleep is praiseworthy as a means of reviving the soul."

The Shabbat Prohibitions

Shabbat is governed by two sets of commandments, positive ones and negative ones. The positive ones, ordaining that we do specific things, give Shabbat its unique character. The negative ones, the ones specifying things that must not be done, are prohibitions that prevent Shabbat from becoming an ordinary day like any other. The uninitiated might view the restrictions as infringements on their freedom to conduct their affairs as they wish, but insiders will see these prohibitions as a very effective means to ensure their freedom from the ordinary, mundane, burdensome demands of the everyday world. As with all aspects of Jewish ritual, what at first seems different and even difficult soon becomes more familiar, more natural, and more comfortable.

The ancient rabbis took the term *m'lakhah* ("work") in the Ten Commandments as a technical term, not as a general reference to labor. From the perspective of the *halakhah*, therefore, the text would read: "Remember the Shabbat day to keep it holy. Six days shall you labor and do all forms of *m'lakhah*, but the seventh day is a Shabbat of the Eternal, your God: [on it]

you shall not do any *m'lakhah*" (Exodus 20:8–10). We might best define *m'lakhah* as referring specifically to "creative endeavor," especially given that this very same Hebrew root is used to refer to God's efforts in creating the world: "On the seventh day," the Bible teaches at Genesis 2:2, "God finished the *m'lakhah* of making the world." From this, it is clear that God's *m'lakhah* is creation.

The rabbis of the Talmud, noting the juxtaposition of Shabbat prohibitions at Exodus 31:12–17 and the laws of the Tabernacle at Exodus 31:1–10, reasoned that those activities necessary to constructing the Tabernacle were the very ones prohibited on Shabbat. Thus, they spoke of thirty-nine *avot m'lakhah* (that is, thirty-nine broad, archetypal categories of labor) prohibited on Shabbat. The Mishnah lists them at *M* Shabbat 7:2 as follows: sowing, plowing, reaping, binding (of sheaves), threshing, winnowing, separating fit from unfit crops, grinding, sifting, kneading, baking, shearing wool, washing it, beating it, dyeing it, spinning it, weaving it, making two loops, weaving two threads, separating two threads, tying, untying, sewing two stitches, tearing in order to sew two stitches, trapping a deer, slaughtering it, flaying its skin, salting its flesh, curing its hide, scraping its hide, cutting it up, writing two letters, erasing two letters in order to write two letters, building, tearing down, extinguishing a flame, kindling a flame, beating with a hammer, and moving from one domain to another.

To these *avot m'lakhah,* the rabbis added a long list of *toladot* (literally, "offspring") that they perceived to issue, like descendants, from the broader categories. For example, planting is an *av m'lakhah,* while watering that same plant is a *toladah* of planting. Kindling a fire is an *av m'lakhah,* whereas adding oil to a preexisting fire is a *toladah* of kindling. While the Tabernacle no longer exists, the numerous categories of work forbidden on Shabbat derived from the Tabernacle narrative still do.

For moderns, the concept of *m'lakhah* can also be interpreted in a broader sense that enhances the ancient rubrics without replacing them. Rabbi Samuel Dresner, for example, writing in *The Sabbath* (New York: United Synagogue of America, 1970, p. 81), taught that the larger category of "work" should include earning one's livelihood, engaging in business or commercial transactions, shopping, performing strenuous physical exertion, changing the physical world by kindling or extinguishing a flame, repairing, improving, constructing, destroying, planting, cooking, sewing, writing, tearing, traveling from one community or neighborhood to another, making preparations during Shabbat for events that will take place after Shabbat ends, engaging in any activity that constitutes drudgery, allowing oneself to be preoccupied, distracted, or anxious about any of the above, or to be angry, hateful, grieved, or despairing about anything at all, and defiling, profaning, or cheapening the precious holiness of Shabbat by deed, word, or thought. Thus, according to this wider concept, the prohibition of doing *m'lakhah* on Shabbat would include going to work, doing one's household chores, and even doing homework.

Businesses on Shabbat

The Jew who owns a business faces a particularly difficult issue with respect to Shabbat observance. (While moderns tend to consider this to be a uniquely modern phenomenon, it is actually an ancient problem.) There are two halakhic ways to deal with this matter. The first is for the Jewish owner of a business to lease the business to a non-Jew before Shabbat. Thus, a non-Jew technically owns the business from some time before Shabbat until after Shabbat ends. (This is similar to the widely accepted custom of selling one's leavened food products to a non-Jew before Passover, during which it would be forbidden to own them.) The second is a function of the concept of corporate ownership, according to which the business becomes a closed corporation of which the Jewish party owns shares in proportion to the permitted days of the week. A non-Jew is sold shares equivalent to the proportion of holy days (including Shabbat and holidays on which work is forbidden) in the year. It should be made clear that these approaches are solely for the purpose of Jewish law and do not supersede civil law in matters of partnership or incorporation.

Work Done by Gentiles

In general, the *halakhah* prohibits Jews from asking non-Jews to do anything that they themselves may not do on Shabbat. However, there are exceptions to this general principle. In an emergency situation or in the case of illness, for example, it is permitted to ask a non-Jew to light a fire to relieve the cold or to do something otherwise forbidden to relieve an animal's pain (Klein, p. 90). Also, when some normally forbidden action is undertaken by a non-Jew for his or her own benefit, Jews may also benefit from it (*BT* Shabbat 122b). The laws governing the use of gentile labor on Shabbat are very complicated and one should always inquire of a rabbi well-versed in the laws of Shabbat on how to proceed.

In some circles, for example, it is considered acceptable to pay a gentile in advance to undertake some forbidden labors for a Jew in the course of the Shabbat. This is different from the general situation of a non-Jew who works for a Jewish employer on Shabbat. The *halakhah* here too is complicated, but the basic rule is that if the non-Jew is working independently, is paid for the entire job in advance (or at least not on Shabbat), and is not *specifically* told to do forbidden work on Shabbat, then he or she may do the work on Shabbat and Jews may benefit from it. For example, Jews may bring shirts to the cleaners one week and pick them up the next week without attempting to ascertain if the non-Jewish launderer is going to wash them on Shabbat. When work is done publicly and specifically for a Jew, however the situation is different (*SA* Oraḥ Ḥayyim 244). Thus, a non-Jewish contractor that is building an addition to the synagogue should not work there on Shabbat, even though he may obviously work on Shabbat for other clients. Note, however, that the concept of "work" under discussion here has to do with the concept of *m'lakhah* on Shabbat. A gentile employee who is merely working for a Jewish employer and *not* being asked to undertake any forbidden labors may go to work and perform his or her normal tasks. Thus, there is no reason that a non-Jewish custodian employed by a synagogue should not come to work on Saturday to unlock the building, straighten up the chairs in the sanctuary, set the table, or put out the food for a Kiddush luncheon.

Carrying on Shabbat

One of the rabbinic categories of *m'lakhah* is carrying objects from one domain to another. The rabbis of the Talmud understood the verse "Let no one leave one's place on the seventh day" (Exodus 16:29) to refer to the act of taking an object and moving it from one "domain" to another. The four "domains" the rabbis perceived to exist are the public domain (defined as an open area frequented by the public, at least twenty-eight feet wide), the private domain (a space not less than fifteen inches square enclosed by walls), the *karm'lit* (defined by the rabbis as a space like the public domain, only smaller), and an area the rabbis called the "free place" (an enclosed space less than fifteen inches square within a public domain; *SA* Oraḥ Ḥayyim 345).

Observant Jews do not carry anything from one domain or area to another on Shabbat. For example, one may not carry a book from inside one's house to a nearby park.

Not carrying any burden at all from one area to another can actually be quite burdensome on Shabbat. A parent, for instance, may find it far less burdensome to push a child in a stroller than to walk very slowly with that same child the half mile between home and synagogue. The rabbis acknowledged this difficulty and created a means of carrying from one place to another through the creation of an *eiruv*, a symbolic mixing of domains or areas. As noted above, the precise method of creating this "mixed domain" in which one can carry freely on Shabbat is extremely complicated and should not be undertaken by someone unversed in the technicalities of the relevant *halakhot*. When done properly, however, an *eiruv* can be a huge boon to a community of Shabbat observers. The Ramah summer camps, for example, set up an *eiruv* so that the entire camp becomes one large domain, and things may be carried freely from one place to another within the boundaries of the marked *eiruv*.

Strictly observant Jews do not carry anything on Shabbat at all unless they are within an area bounded by an *eiruv*. Even without an *eiruv*, however, there are some ways around the general prohibition of carrying things from one domain to another. While one may not carry one's *tallit* to synagogue, for example, one could always wear it there. (Others might prefer simply to leave the *tallit* in the synagogue over Shabbat.) When an object like a house key becomes a kind of jewelry like a tie clip, then it is not being carried but worn, and this too is a way around the general prohibition. In Conservative congregations, a very wide range of practices prevail in communities without an *eiruv*. There are some who simply empty their pockets entirely and carry nothing at all. Others carry some small things in their pockets, but not in their hands. Still others only carry objects that have a religious purpose. People who avail themselves of the CJLS decision permitting driving to synagogue for those who have no other way to get there may wish to carry only what is absolutely necessary, like a driver's license, but not money or credit cards.

On a symbolic level, the rabbinic concept that nothing be moved from one domain to another on Shabbat can make an important statement to us today. We are used to constant motion. People move around all the time. Many people even move from one community to another with some regularity. Isaac Newton is famous for having noticed that objects at rest tend to stay at rest. If Newton were a rabbi, he might have said instead that objects that remain at rest one day a week allow us to cease our constant motion and observe a day of quiet, rest, and peace. One day a week, we need to stop moving the objects around us, so that those objects at rest, in turn, will allow us too to rest.

Muktzeh

Feeling that Shabbat had to be not only observed but also honored, the classical rabbis extended the official prohibitions of Shabbat to other activities that might impinge on the sanctity of the day. Thus, they developed a concept called *muktzeh,* meaning "set aside" or "excluded." They found their inspiration in a verse from Isaiah: "If you refrain from trampling Shabbat [and] from pursuing your affairs on My holy day, if you call Shabbat 'delight,' and [you call] the Eternal One's day 'honored' *and* if you honor it and go not your ways, nor look to your affairs, nor strike bargains, then shall you delight in the Eternal and I will cause you to ride upon the high places of the earth and nourish you with the heritage of your ancestor Jacob; for the mouth of the Eternal has spoken" (Isaiah 58:13–14).

The laws governing *muktzeh* prohibit handling objects that are not intended for use on Shabbat. Of these, the most common are those objects that are always *muktzeh* because they have no licit use on Shabbat at all, like money and writing implements. Certain religious objects also fall into this category. *T'fillin,* for example, are worn only on weekdays. Thus, handling them on Shabbat is not allowed because they are deemed *muktzeh,* "set aside," and thus untouchable on Shabbat.

Today, we might add pagers, cell phones, and computers to the list of *muktzeh* items. Whether or not they have some licit use on Shabbat, they are by their very nature weekday items whose presence in our personal space on Shabbat will only impair our ability fully to enjoy the day.

Personal Hygiene, Health, and Safety on Shabbat

Halakhic authorities list three main problems with taking a hot shower or bath on Shabbat: heating the water, using a bar of soap (and changing its state from a solid to a liquid), and wringing out a towel (also a forbidden activity). Added to that, of course, would be the use of an electric hair dryer. Observant Jews should wash up with cold water and with liquid soap. It is forbidden to shave, cut one's hair, or trim one's nails on Shabbat. These things should be done on Friday afternoon as part of our preparation for Shabbat.

In cases of illness, the situation is far more liberal and all measures deemed capable, even just plausibly, of saving of a human life supersede the laws of Shabbat. Indeed, in a medical emergency, even the most strictly observant are obligated to do whatever it takes to save another's life. In cases of doubt, the law expressly requires acting forcefully if there is any chance at all that a person's life might be at risk. In less severe cases, however, the question is always whether medical attention can wait until Shabbat is over. Here, common sense is clearly an important component of the halakhic process. If there is no apparent danger involved in waiting until after Shabbat to seek medical attention—for example, if one were to sprain one's ankle—then the correct thing to do would be to wait until Havdalah and then to seek treatment. In dealing with toothaches or ear infections, some Sabbath observers will make do with home remedies until Shabbat is over. But there are lenient opinions that allow anyone in severe pain to go to an emergency room or to a doctor even on Shabbat.

Traveling on Shabbat

Traditionally, travel beyond certain delineated areas—like the limits of the city—on Shabbat was prohibited. Boat journeys, however, were allowed if the boat departed before Shabbat, or at least if one was on board before Shabbat commenced.

How different travel is today! City limits are no longer so well defined in an age of sprawling suburbs, and travel no longer involves matters like hitching wagons to animals or saddling those animals for the journey. Still, the primary concerns of the rabbis remain and, indeed, changing one's location even today involves at least some inevitable violations of the Shabbat laws. The changes in American life in the postwar period forced the Conservative movement to confront the question of travel on Shabbat in a way that had never previously seemed that urgent.

The issue was discussed for many years until two responsa were finally presented to the Committee on Jewish Law and Standards for consideration and voted upon in 1950. A majority opinion allowed for driving to the synagogue on Shabbat when walking would be unreasonably difficult (*Proceedings of the CJLS 1927–1970,* pp. 1109–1134). This ruling was a concession not only to the realities of life in the suburbs, where Jews lived at great distances from their synagogues, but also to the fact that many synagogues remained in downtown areas that were suddenly very far from their constituencies. A minority opinion prohibited all driving on Shabbat (*Proceedings of the CJLS 1927–1970,* pp. 1153–1160). In 1960, the same Committee on Jewish Law and Standards acknowledged that it had "voted on a previous occasion to exempt riding to the synagogue from the usual prohibition of travel on the Sabbath" (*Proceedings of the CJLS 1927–1970,* p. 1188). The Committee admitted that it was still divided on whether there was a general permission for riding to the synagogue on Shabbat, or if riding to the synagogue should be allowed only in emergency situations.

This ruling created quite a controversy. Some criticized Conservative Judaism for being too accommodating and for allowing the general public to dictate the limits of the law. Some complained that permitting driving on Shabbat, while strengthening communal worship, actually weakened the community by allowing people to move farther from the synagogue, thus not actually to live within the community they were supposedly building. Throughout this discussion, however, it was always clear to the CJLS that the ideal practice was to walk to synagogue on Shabbat. We would like to reaffirm that ideal as ours as well. However, we do not live in an ideal world. At times, there is a conflict between two values of great worth—for example, between the ideal of not using a car on Shabbat and the ideal of participating in communal prayer—and one value must take precedence over the other.

For those who determine that participation in communal prayer trumps observing the laws that forbid driving on Shabbat, we offer the following guidelines. Those who can walk to the synagogue should do so. Every attempt should be made to spend Shabbat within walking distance of a synagogue. It is never acceptable to choose to drive on Shabbat when one can avoid doing so. Where this is not possible, travel should be limited to trips to and from the synagogue.

While the desire to do other *mitzvot* on Shabbat (such as visiting the sick in a distant hospital) is praiseworthy, driving to do such *mitzvot* is not permitted on Shabbat.

Rabbi David Golinkin, in *Responsa of the Va·ad Halakhah,* vol. 4, p. 25, writes that most halakhic authorities do not permit riding a bicycle on Shabbat, mentioning several arguments that support that stance: one might travel beyond the allowed area on Shabbat (two thousand cubits past the last building), one might have to fix the bicycle, and riding is not an activity in the spirit of Shabbat. Furthermore, in the absence of an *eiruv,* riding a bicycle falls under the category of "carrying" the bicycle itself from place to place.

The Use of Fire and Electricity on Shabbat

At Exodus 35:3, the Torah tells us, "You shall kindle no fire throughout your settlements on the Sabbath day." The long history of the interpretation of this verse is very interesting, at least in terms of what it reveals about Jewish sects, but the classical halakhic authorities have always understood that verse to mean just what it says and no more: that one may not light a fire on Shabbat, but that a flame lit before Shabbat could be kept burning into, or throughout, Shabbat. In fact, the rabbis not only allowed for this: they actually mandated it, creating a special benediction to be recited when kindling the Shabbat lamps or candles just before Shabbat begins (*SA* Oraḥ Ḥayyim 263:5). Nor was this deemed a mere concession to the natural desire not to sit in the dark. Indeed, lighting the Shabbat lights has always been deemed a worthy and spiritually meaningful act capable of transforming something as mundane as the simple need for light on Friday night into an especially opportune moment to experience the presence of God.

Just as we may benefit from Shabbat lights kindled before the onset of Shabbat, we may also take advantage of appliances that run throughout Shabbat, including those that do not shut themselves off at all and those that turn themselves off at a particular moment through the use of a timing device. In both cases, the principle is the same: if the machinery is set in motion before Shabbat, one may derive benefit from *m'lakhah* that would ordinarily be forbidden. Thus, for example, we may program an oven to keep food warm until it is served and then turn itself off, even though the meal may take place long after candle lighting. Of course, one may also leave the oven on throughout Shabbat.

Some observant Jews avoid using elevators on Shabbat entirely; others only use a pre-programmed "Shabbos elevator" or only take the elevator if a non-Jew has already entered it and pushed one of the floor buttons. Similarly, some people staying at hotels over Shabbat ask for traditional keys instead of using the electronic door swipes.

There has been much discussion of the use of electricity on Shabbat. Electricity, of course, is not fire. However, some authorities hold that electricity has enough of the qualities of fire to warrant its prohibition anyway. More liberal authorities assert that electricity is not enough like fire to warrant that kind of sanction against its use for the simple reason that fire produces heat and leaves ash, while electricity produces heat without creating ash; one, therefore, is a transformative process, while the other is not. In the opinion of these authorities, then, fire and electricity are similar enough to make the discussion reasonable, but not identical enough to warrant the actual prohibition of the latter based on the law as it relates to the former.

Some Conservative authorities permit the use of electricity on Shabbat for simple, non-mechanical purposes like the switching on or off of lights. But it is also important to live not solely according to the letter of the law, but also according to its spirit. In his 1950 responsum on the use of electricity, Rabbi Arthur Neulander wrote as follows: "It must be clearly understood that whatever use of electric apparatus we permit on the Sabbath, we allow only on condition that use is in consonance with the spirit of the Sabbath. Thus the telephone may be used for conversation to strengthen family ties, to foster friendship and neighborliness, to convey a message of cheer to the sick or for a similar *d'var mitzvah* (that is, some activity that involves the performance of one of the commandments). But the telephone should not be used for shopping purposes, for making a business appointment, much less a business transaction. The first group is in keeping with the holiness of the Sabbath. The second group violates the *m'nuḥah sh'leimah* (i.e., the complete sense of rest) of the Sabbath" (*Proceedings of the CJLS 1927–1970*, p. 1168).

In light of Rabbi Neulander's strictures, using an electric light to read a sacred book on Shabbat seems reasonable, even perhaps worth encouraging, but not using that same light to review last year's tax return.

The issue of using electricity on Shabbat has been a controversial one for sixty years at least and continues to be debated. (A new responsum regarding electricity and Shabbat, written by Rabbi Daniel Nevins, is currently before the Committee on Jewish Law and Standards of the Rabbinical Assembly.)

Cooking and Preparing Food

Jewish law prohibits cooking on Shabbat. Therefore, Shabbat meals must be planned and prepared in advance.

The concept of cooking was interpreted, even in ancient times, in a fairly liberal way to mean making raw foodstuffs at least minimally edible. (See, e.g., the statement in the name of Rabbi Ḥanina at *BT* Shabbat 20a and the comment of the Tosafot to *BT* Shabbat 36b, *s.v. ḥamin v'tavshil.*) Thus, cooking could start before Shabbat and continue into Shabbat, so long as the food was deemed at least formally ingestible before the start of Shabbat. For example, a slow-cooked pot of ingredients, called *cholent* by Ashkenazic Jews and *ḥamin* by Sephardic and Oriental Jews, is a traditional Shabbat food. The dish is not really at its best as the sun sets on Friday, but it is deemed sufficient that the food be minimally edible before the start of Shabbat (*SA* Oraḥ Ḥayyim 254). Once this is the case, the dish may continue to cook throughout the hours of Shabbat as long as it is in the oven or on the stove before Shabbat begins. In modern times, the use of slow cookers makes the preparation of this dish even simpler, but the concept remains the same: the food must be cooked to the point of edibility before Shabbat and then may continue cooking after that for as long as desired.

One may not turn ovens and stoves on or off during Shabbat, or even adjust their temperature, nor may water be boiled. It is, however, permitted to use an automatic urn that has been filled, plugged in, and turned on before Shabbat to provide hot water.

It is permitted to use the refrigerator on Shabbat, even though the possibility exists that opening the door will activate the motor. Since this is not one's specific intention, and since it may not happen—the motor, generally speaking, will only go on if the temperature drops below the trigger temperature during the time the door is opened—it is permitted to open the door of the refrigerator, and this is the general practice even of people who do not use electrical devices on Shabbat. Individuals, however, who do not wish to use electricity at all on Shabbat, even casually, should loosen the light bulb inside the refrigerator before the onset of Shabbat so that it does not go on when the door is opened.

It is permitted to open cans with a manual can opener, and other packages on Shabbat, as long as the food in them will be consumed during Shabbat. Whenever possible, however, all food preparation should be done in advance.

Similarly, one may wash dishes by hand if they will be used again during Shabbat. Dishwashers should not be used, and, as with showering, many avoid using hot water from the tap.

The issues involved in warming food on Shabbat are very complex, but the general principle is that warming is allowed as long as the warming does not lead to cooking, and also as long as it does not tempt the individual doing the warming to adjust a flame on Shabbat. Solid cooked foods may be warmed to make them more appealing or tasty, but liquids may be warmed only if they are not entirely cold, or if they *are* cold but are warmed in way that guarantees that they will not come to a boil (*SA* Oraḥ Ḥayyim 318:15 and cf. the gloss of the Rema *ad loc.;* Klein, p. 88).

In the Talmud (at *BT* Avodah Zarah 3a), the rabbis of ancient times imagined God personally commenting that only those "who prepare on the eve of Shabbat will eat on Shabbat." The rabbis' comment can be interpreted on many different levels, but its most basic meaning is simply the literal one: to enjoy Shabbat requires advance planning. We often speak of Shabbat preparation as "making Shabbos." It is such a familiar expression, however, that we sometimes forget that it encapsulates a profound truth: Shabbat does not just happen. Our day of enjoyment and rest requires advance effort and planning. When we have prepared adequately beforehand, we will truly find Shabbat a delight.

Holy Days and Holidays

ALAN B. LUCAS

We all complain endlessly about time. We protest our inability to slow down its passage. As we grow older, birthdays are less and less occasions for honest celebration. Time feels more and more like a thief that surreptitiously steals our lives from us, day by day, year by year. The truth, however, is quite different. Time is neither friend nor foe, but neutral—a wholly human construct, an invention of human consciousness. Time can be neither retrieved nor stopped. It can be anticipated, of course, but that is surely not the same as halting it in its tracks. Frustrated, then, we behave like unruly children, resentful of not getting our way. We kill time. We waste time. Occasionally, we invest time—but rarely all that cleverly.

The one thing we do know about time is that it does not, cannot, and will not stand still. Like manna, it cannot be hoarded. As a result, we can only experience one day at a time. As we mature and come to terms with how things are, we come to accept that yesterday is always gone and tomorrow is always just beyond our reach. But even today itself cannot be halted in mid-flight, although there are surely times we wish the case were otherwise. Sometimes we come to a moment so exquisite that we don't want it to end. We look into the faces of our children, we share a moment of unrestrained laughter with truly dear friends, we are wholly possessed by the love of a soulmate, and we wish the moment we are in could last forever. But wishing is all we can do. Moments can only be enjoyed in the present for as long as they last. Later, we draw upon the storehouses of recollective memories as a way of savoring them again and again, but it is never quite the same. We settle for whatever pleasure memory provides and we hope with all our hearts that God will provide more moments to savor and enjoy tomorrow.

For Jews, time is a gift to be accepted in gratitude and sanctified through human endeavor. Writing in one of his most famous books, *The Sabbath* (New York: Farrar, Straus & Giroux, 1952, p. 8), Abraham Joshua Heschel taught us: "Judaism is a religion of time, aiming at the sanctification of time." We Jews have no sacred relics, no holy water. Our rituals feature sacred appurtenances, of course, but even the Torah itself is treated with consummate respect more because of the words it contains than because of its physical form. We show our respect to sacred objects, of course, but far more profoundly to sacred moments. And the Jewish calendar is the framework through which Jews endeavor to make time holy. When we sit down with family and friends at a Passover *seder,* we know that others are having dinner as usual. When we sit in the synagogue on Rosh Hashanah, we understand that others are at home watching television. We choose to make these moments sacred when we join with other Jews in sanctifying them. Time is sanctified when we join in observances commanded by God and sanctified by Jews for thousands of years. While it is surely true that every day can be made holy and every moment sacred, it is through our observance of the Jewish holidays that our year takes on character, profundity, and meaning. The psalmist addressed this prayer to God: "Teach us, O God, to measure our days so that we may attain a heart of wisdom" (Psalm 90:12). The Jewish calendar is the sacred guide that teaches us how to measure our days so that we may indeed achieve the gift of wisdom, for truly the beginning of all wisdom is the reverence shown to God.

The Jewish Calendar

The Jewish calendar is essentially a lunar calendar based on the moon's revolutions around the earth. Twelve lunar months total about 354 days, about eleven fewer than a solar year. Many cultures that use solely lunar calendars live with the unavoidable result of that eleven-day shortfall and tolerate that specific dates move backward through the seasons in a cycle that takes decades to complete. But, because the Torah specifically ties the festivals to specific seasons (specifying, for example, that Passover is to be a springtime festival), this will not do in Judaism and so it was necessary to develop a way around the shortfall. As early as the third century C.E., this was accomplished by adding a "leap month" roughly every three years. (In turn, this explains why Jewish holidays tend to "slip" back and forth slightly from year to year in relation to the secular calendar.) Eventually, however, the calendar was set in place and the practice of adding seven extra months every nineteen years was set into place. (The extra month is a second month of Adar, added in before—not after—the regular Adar.) And the result is quite satisfactory: there are, roughly speaking, 210 more days in nineteen solar years than there are in nineteen lunar years, and the seven added (intercalated) months make up just that many days.

The Jewish calendar needs to be appreciated on its own merits, however, and not solely in terms of the degree to which it manages to conform to the secular one. Our ancestors measured time by the holidays and, in turn, the holidays gave their lives texture and created recognizable signposts to chart a family's journey through the year. Moderns will do well, then, not to focus overly on whether Rosh Hashanah is in September or October in a given year, but rather to notice the beginning of Elul, the month that precedes Rosh Hashanah, and, in so doing, to begin to sense the arrival of a New Year. The cycle and the rhythms of Jewish life and Jewish living are embedded in the Jewish calendar. Each holiday has its own message and its own mood, and each one guides us on our journey through life.

Working and Cooking on Holy Days

As discussed in detail elsewhere in this volume by Rabbi Michael Katz and the late Rabbi Gershon Schwartz in their chapter about Sabbath observance, one of the most common assumptions about Jewish life is that it is forbidden to work on Shabbat and holy days. This is somewhat misleading, however, because most people use the term "work" to mean whatever they do to earn a living, even though many of the specific activities involved in most people's livelihoods are not prohibited on Shabbat or holy days. Similarly, many things that we are forbidden from doing are not especially arduous or strenuous, and may in fact be associated more in most people's minds with leisure activities. A better conceptual approach would be to understand these laws not as prohibiting "work" *per se,* but promoting a policy of "reasonable non-interference with the world" that can and should apply to activity on Shabbat and on the holy days. Erich Fromm (in *You Shall Be As Gods* [New York: Henry Holt, 1966], pp. 154ff.) suggests that what we should try to achieve is more a question of perspective than of leisure. Six days a week we are God-appointed masters of the universe and are allowed, for better or worse, to direct and manipulate the world. On Shabbat and on the holy days, we relinquish our role as creators and recognize that we too are creatures who serve at the will of the one true Creator of the universe. In this view, keeping the holy days becomes an exercise in conceptualization and perspective. Yet the laws that pertain to Shabbat and the holy days recognize that total non-interference in the world is simply not practical, and so the goal becomes reasonable non-interference. Thus, the *halakhah* permits such compromises as carrying within private domains but not in public ones, and cutting up food but not paper decorations.

"Work," according to this definition, is prohibited on the biblical holidays of Rosh Hashanah, Yom Kippur, Sukkot, Passover, and Shavuot. Work, of course, is also prohibited on Shabbat, but there is an interesting distinction between the Shabbat laws and those that pertain on these other holy days. (Note that for purposes of this discussion, Yom Kippur is considered to be a kind of a Shabbat rather than a festival day like the others of Jewish year.) Based on a close reading of the pertinent texts (especially Leviticus 23:3, which concerns Shabbat, and Leviticus 23:4, which concerns the other holidays), the ancient rabbis concluded that there were certain leniencies, mostly regarding issues related to food preparation, that were appropriate for these holidays but not for Shabbat.

Therefore, although most Shabbat prohibitions also apply to these holidays, certain activities connected with the preparation of food, transferring fire, and carrying were permitted on these days (*SA* Oraḥ Ḥayyim 495:1). Maimonides explains this difference as motivated by the desire to make the holidays more joyous (*MT* Hilkhot Sh'vitat Yom Tov 1:4–6). These prohibitions remain in effect on Yom Kippur, which, as mentioned, is considered a kind of Shabbat, or whenever a festival day falls on Shabbat.

There is also a distinction made between transferring fire from a preexistent flame and kindling a new fire where none existed before. The former is permitted on these holidays, but the latter is not. (Neither, of course, is permitted on Shabbat or Yom Kippur.) Using gas and electric ovens for the purposes of cooking, therefore, is permitted on these holidays (Klein, p. 98, based on the text at *SA* Oraḥ Ḥayyim 514:1 and the *Mishp'tei Uzzi·el* commentary to *SA* Oraḥ Ḥayyim 19, ed. Tel Aviv, 1935, p. 66b). To take an already lit flame from the pilot light and transfer it to one of the burners would constitute an acceptable use of fire, while kindling a new flame would not. Many authorities consider the use of an electric burner, or even gas stoves that have electric ignition, to be a form of transferring fire as well, and thus licit on festival days.

This same issue becomes relevant when lighting candles to usher in the second night of a holiday (or the first night, when it immediately follows Shabbat). On Friday eve or the first night of a holy day there is no problem lighting a match to kindle the candles, as the kindling takes place *before* the holiday has begun. On the second night of a holiday (or the first night, if it follows Shabbat), transferring a flame would be permitted, but not kindling one, as the kindling is taking place on the holy day itself. So it has become customary to light a twenty-four-hour candle at the same time the candles are lit on the first night, so that on the second night (or the first night that is immediately preceded by Shabbat) the candles can be lit from the flame of the twenty-four-hour candle, which is taken to be the mere transferring of a flame.

Even though grinding grain is not permitted on festivals (because this could easily be done before the onset of the festival), grinding coffee beans manually is nevertheless permitted because the freshness of the coffee would be lost if the beans were ground far in advance of use (Klein, p. 98).

Although food preparation for use on holidays other than Shabbat may be done on the holy day itself, the spirit of the day would suggest that doing as much as possible prior to the festival (rather than on the holy day itself) is certainly praiseworthy (see the gloss of the Rema to *SA* Oraḥ Ḥayyim 495:1).

Purchasing food is not permitted on festival days (*SA* Oraḥ Ḥayyim 500:1). Even though one could argue that such purchases enhance the enjoyment of the holiday, they are still prohibited because the purchases easily could have been made prior to the holiday.

Smoking presents an interesting halakhic situation. Traditionally, most halakhic authorities permitted habitual smokers to smoke on the festivals as long as the cigarette was lit from an existing source (as suggested by the first section of the *Ba·eir Heiteiv* commentary to *SA* Oraḥ Ḥayyim 514:1, to which may be compared the comment of the *Magein Avraham,* to the same passage, section 4). Of course, these evaluations of the halakhic propriety of smoking on festival days were all undertaken in the days before there was overwhelming medical evidence about the dangers of smoking. Given the fact that the Torah specifically forbids willfully causing damage to one's own body, many authorities today feel that smoking should be prohibited at all times. The question of smoking is discussed in more detail below by Avram Israel Reisner in his chapter on Jewish medical ethics and was the subject of a responsum by Rabbi Seymour Siegel approved by the CJLS in 1986 and published in *CJLS Responsa 1980–1990,* pp. 833–837, and also of a Hebrew-language responsum by Rabbi David Golinkin published in *Responsa of the Va·ad Halakhah,* vol. 4, pp. 37–52.

The *halakhah* also takes into account violations of the spirit of the law, not merely its letter. If something is technically permitted by the laws that govern festivals, but clearly violates the spirit of the holy day, it should not be done (*MT* Hilkhot Sh'vitat Yom Tov 1:5, and cf. the *Turei Zahav* commentary to *SA* Oraḥ Ḥayyim 495:2). Moving heavy furniture across the room, therefore, may be technically permitted according to the laws regarding carrying, but is clearly contrary to the spirit of the day. If one must undertake one of these technically permitted activities that run counter to the spirit of the festival, one should do so in a way that acknowledges that the boundaries of the permissible are being stretched. For example, the *Shulḥan Arukh* suggests that if one were to grind pepper or other spices, one should use a different grinder than the one normally employed (*SA* Oraḥ Ḥayyim 504:1). If one must carry an unusually heavy object, one should do it in an unusual way (*SA* Oraḥ Ḥayyim 510:8).

Eiruv Tavshilin

If Rosh Hashanah or any of the other festivals falls on a Thursday and Friday, when may one cook for Shabbat? Under normal circumstances, one is only permitted to cook on festival days to make food for the holiday itself, not for any day beyond that. We make an exception to this rule when the next day is Shabbat, however, by creating a legal fiction called *eiruv tavshilin:* we "begin" cooking for Shabbat before the onset of the festival and then merely "continue" with our already-begun Shabbat preparations during the course of the ensuing festival. While this may seem peculiar, it is actually a wonderful way both to maintain the integrity of the system while at the same time allowing for the kind of reasonable flexibility that will only enhance the joy of celebrating these special days.

To make an *eiruv tavshilin,* one must place two cooked items (for example, a roll or a slice of bread [or, on Passover, a sheet of *matzah*] and a cooked or roasted dish, like a piece of meat or fish) on a plate and then recite a blessing. This blessing, found in any standard prayerbook and in the Haggadah, is the regular blessing for the performance of commandments and ends with the words *al mitzvat eiruv* (by commanding us regarding the *eiruv*). One must then recite an additional declaration: "By means of this *eiruv,* we are permitted to bake, cook, warm, kindle lights, and make all the necessary preparations during the festival for Shabbat, we and all who live in this place." Ideally, this food should be consumed on Shabbat to demonstrate that it was prepared specifically for Shabbat.

Counting the Years

Most Jews would guess that the year begins with Rosh Hashanah, and in some ways they would be right. But the Mishnah at *M* Rosh Hashanah 1:1 informs us that there are actually four New Years, each with its own purpose, each emphasizing the simple, stirring truth that life is a constant process of new beginnings. The counting of the years begins with Rosh Hashanah, making it a reasonable starting point. But the counting of the months starts with Nisan, the month of Passover—so we could just as logically start there as well. (This is why the Torah gives the dates of Rosh Hashanah [at Numbers 29:1] as "the first day of the seventh month," but also commands at Exodus 12:1 that Nisan, the month of Passover, be "the first of the year's months for you.") The former celebrates the birth of the world and the latter celebrates the birth of the Jewish people, but there are other New Years as well: the first of Elul, which tradition made the New Year for the purpose of tithing cattle, and the fifteenth of the month of Sh'vat (or, according to an alternate vision, the first of Sh'vat), acclaimed as the New Year for the laws that govern planting trees and eating their fruit. So where should a survey of the Jewish year begin? In a circle, one beginning is as good as another, so let's begin with the High Holidays. The Hebrew name for these holy days is *yamim nora·im* (days of awe), but this name is less old than one might think. Isaac Klein, writing in *A Guide to Jewish Religious Practice* (p. 176), attributes the term to Rabbi Jacob ben Moses Moelin, known as the Maharil (1365–1427), and infers from this that the solemn mood we associate with Rosh Hashanah is the result of a long and complicated development that occurred over a period of hundreds of years.

Elul

Every great experience requires preparation, and the High Holidays are no exception. Indeed, the preparations for the *yamim nora·im* begin a full month in advance with the onset of the month of Elul. In a certain sense, the High Holiday period could be said to begin as early as the first day of Elul and only to end with Yom Kippur. This creates a period of approximately forty days during which the dominant theme is repentance. (Some, however, even understand the High Holiday period to extend until Hoshana Rabbah, the seventh day of Sukkot and the final of its intermediate days.)

The number forty resonates in Jewish tradition on many levels: it is the number of years the Israelites wandered in the wilderness before reaching the Promised Land and also the number of days that Moses dwelt in the presence of God while receiving the Torah on Mount Sinai. Similarly, Elul initiates a very special period of introspection and self-analysis when every Jew is challenged to reenact the journey from exile to redemption on a personal level and to strive to experience the presence of God in a way that echoes Moses's communion with God during his time atop the mountain.

The *shofar* is sounded at the end of every weekday Morning Service beginning with the first day of Elul and ending the morning before Erev Rosh Hashanah (glosses of the Rema to *SA* Oraḥ Ḥayyim 581:1 and 581:3). The *shofar* is not sounded on the day before Rosh Hashanah, in order to differentiate between the blasts heard during Elul, which are merely a custom, and the blasts of the *shofar* sounded on Rosh Hashanah itself, which are ordained by Scripture (gloss of the Rema to *SA* Oraḥ Ḥayyim 581:3, and see the comment of the *Mishnah B'rurah ad loc.,* note 24). Hearing the *shofar* alerts attentive worshipers to the approach of the Days of Awe and challenges even the hesitant among them to get busy with the work of *t'shuvah,* repentance. The concept of *t'shuvah* is discussed in more detail by Rabbi David Lincoln elsewhere in this volume in a chapter specifically devoted to that subject.

It is also the custom to recite Psalm 27 at the conclusion of the Morning Service just after the *shofar* is sounded, and also at the end of the Evening Service, throughout the entire High Holiday period from the first of Elul to Hoshana Rabbah. (Some end the recitation of this psalm at Yom Kippur.) Psalm 27 suggests the themes of the season, as evidenced by an ancient *midrash* on its opening line preserved at *Midrash T'hillim* 27:4: "God is my light—on Rosh Hashanah—and my salvation—on Yom Kippur. Whom then shall I fear—on Hoshana Rabbah?"

We also prepare for the coming of the High Holidays at home. Just as with Shabbat, there is an increase in the tempo of the household routine as everything is cleaned, polished, and made ready for the holidays. Friends and relations begin to arrive, sometimes from great distances. Indeed, no matter how far a sibling, child, or cousin may have wandered during the course of the year, Rosh Hashanah is a time for all Jewish people to come home to their families, their people, and their God.

There is also the touching custom of visiting the graves of loved ones in anticipation of the New Year. Some do this the day before Rosh Hashanah (cf. the gloss of the Rema to *SA* Oraḥ Ḥayyim 581:4), but many go at any convenient time throughout this period from Elul through Yom Kippur. Many synagogues hold communal memorial services at their congregational cemetery during this time of the year. At these services, there is usually an opportunity for shared communal prayers as well as private time for individuals to visit their family members' graves. Visiting the graves of one's parents and grandparents helps establish a sense of continuity between the sacred past and the unborn future and fosters a sense of oneself as the vital link between the two. Tradition also imagines our late relations, and especially our parents, as intercessors capable of pleading our case and cause before God. It is therefore appropriate that we not take them for granted, and this custom of visiting their graves reflects that hope.

Many have adopted the custom of sending New Year's cards to family and friends wishing them well as the new year is about to begin. While it is tempting to dismiss this as an example of crass commercial opportunism on the part of the greeting card industry, the truth is that this practice is well grounded in Jewish custom (see, e.g., the gloss of the Rema to *SA* Oraḥ Ḥayyim 582:9). Originally, the concept was simply to wish others that they be inscribed in the Book of Life for the year to come, but sending out cards has become less theologically charged over the years and is now hardly more than an effort to reconnect with loved ones near and far. Even so, sending out Rosh Hashanah cards as a way to strengthen the bonds we share with our friends and family is a commendable endeavor.

Another commendable and widespread custom is the practice of making charitable contributions in anticipation of the High Holidays (gloss of the Rema to *SA* Oraḥ Ḥayyim 581:4). Giving charity is a *mitzvah* all year round, but there is something especially beautiful about making a special effort around the High Holidays to help others. As we strive to be our best selves, the giving of charity emphasizes that self-inspection and thoughtful introspection must lead to outward improvement. A person wrapped up in him or herself makes for a small package. Participation in synagogue charity appeals, on the other hand, constitutes a tangible expression of one's determination to translate good intentions into the kind of good deeds that can transform and improve the world.

S'liḥot

S'liḥot are special prayers that are recited in anticipation of the High Holidays. These beautiful prayers composed by the greatest ancient and medieval poets introduce us to the themes of the upcoming High Holidays and intensify our avid anticipation of their arrival. According to Sephardic custom, these special penitential prayers are recited every morning during the month of Elul. In traditional Ashkenazic synagogues, and in some Conservative synagogues, the custom is to recite these prayers beginning on the Sunday before Rosh Hashanah, unless there will be fewer than four days between Sunday and the onset of the festival. Since there should be a minimum of four days of S'liḥot, the recitation of S'liḥot begins on the Sunday of the previous week in years in which Rosh Hashanah begins on Monday or Tuesday.

A contemporary American custom is the midnight S'liḥot service held late Saturday night before the first Sunday when S'liḥot are to be recited. (For many congregations, this is the sole vestige of S'liḥot recitation.) This late night service highlights the beautiful liturgical pieces of the High Holidays and, for many, truly initiates the High Holiday season.

The Jewish New Year

Erev Rosh Hashanah

On the Shabbat before any new month, a special prayer called Birkat Ha-ḥodesh is recited in the synagogue to announce the name of the new month and the day on which it is to begin. This is not done in anticipation of Rosh Hashanah, however (*Mishnah B'rurah* to *SA* Oraḥ Ḥayyim 417, note 1). The most logical reason for this omission is that Rosh Hashanah is deemed the beginning of all beginnings, thus the benchmark by which all the other festivals will be measured, and as such is not in need of any sort of formal introduction. Popular folklore, however, has suggested an alternative explanation. There is a traditional conception that we are all judged during the so-called Ten Days of Repentance that fall between Rosh Hashanah and Yom Kippur. In this drama, God plays the role of judge and we are the defendants whose very lives are on the line. Satan, playing the role of prosecuting attorney, anxiously awaits the arrival of Rosh Hashanah every year so the trial can begin and he can present all the most damning evidence he can gather against each defendant. Accordingly, we do not announce the coming of Rosh Hashanah in public in the hope that omitting the prayer will somehow confuse Satan, thus causing him to miss the trial entirely and leaving God to judge us mercifully. This same explanation is given as to why we do not blow the *shofar* on the morning before Rosh Hashanah, although the far more likely explanation is the one given above: that we omit it to distinguish between the blowing of the *shofar* during Elul, which is a custom, and the blowing of the *shofar* on Rosh Hashanah, which is a *mitzvah*.

Other customs for Erev Rosh Hashanah include the recitation of longer than normal S'liḥot prayers and the omission of Taḥanun in the Morning and Afternoon Services (*SA* Oraḥ Ḥayyim 581:3).

In addition, most synagogues change the Torah mantles and the *parokhet,* the curtain that hangs before the Ark, to white ones in honor of the High Holidays. Similarly, it is customary to wear a white robe, often called a *kittel,* during services on the High Holidays and especially on Yom Kippur. White symbolizes purity and thus exemplifies the worshiper's desire to achieve atonement and forgiveness.

There is a custom of immersing oneself in the *mikveh* before Rosh Hashanah (*BT* Rosh Ha-shanah 16b), although some suggest it should be done just before Yom Kippur. As in the case of immersion in a *mikveh* before a wedding, or as part of a couple's intimate life together after marriage, the *mikveh* is a means of personal purification and therefore perfectly suited to the spirit of spiritual purification and internal preparation before the High

Holidays. Some have suggested that immersion in the *mikveh* is a model of personal rebirth: just as one emerges from the watery environment of the womb into a new world, so too does one emerge from the purifying waters of the *mikveh* into the world reborn. The use of the *mikveh* teaches us that life constantly gives us chances to begin anew. That is certainly the optimistic message of the High Holidays, and a visit to the *mikveh* at this time of the year merely reinforces that message.

Rosh Hashanah at Home

The only biblically ordained ritual connected with the day we now know as Rosh Hashanah will strike moderns as a rather simple one: in addition to the requisite animal sacrifices ordained for the day, the entire people is to gather together and stand in silence while listening to the sounding of the *shofar*. Apparently, the medium was enough of a message for the ancients to have required no further interpretation of the *shofar* blasts. The challenge for moderns, therefore, is to learn how to listen. When we walk into a synagogue on Rosh Hashanah today, the experience the ancients had when they heard the blasts of the *shofar* is available to us no less than it was once to them. While worship in ancient times was entirely different from and, apparently, dramatically shorter than in today's synagogues, the richness of the experience is no less available to us than it was in ancient times, and the subtle shadings added by generations of Jews can surely result in a religious experience of no less profound beauty and meaning "even today, if My people would only learn to listen" (Psalm 95:7).

Like every other day in the Jewish calendar, Rosh Hashanah begins at sunset. As explained in more detail above in Rabbi Katz and Rabbi Schwartz's chapter on Shabbat, however, candle lighting on both Shabbat and festivals is moved back to a minimum of eighteen minutes before sundown. (On the second night of a holiday, however, the candles should not be lit until after the conclusion of the first day—or at least one hour after the candle lighting of the first night.) The point of the eighteen minutes is merely to create a margin of time between the cessation of labor and the actual setting of the sun, and thus to guarantee that no one accidentally profanes the festival or Shabbat. (It is also so that dusk, the brief period of time when the sun is not precisely gone from the sky but has already begun its descent to below the horizon, is considered in some sense part of the festival, just as it is considered part of the Shabbat.)

Candles should be lit in a prominent place where they will be seen. In pre-modern times, when the lamps that illuminated people's homes could not be lit on Shabbat or on festival days, those lamps served the very practical purpose of providing illumination during the evening hours. Today, those same lamps or candles are symbolic reminders of the beauty and meaning of the holiday.

Traditionally, candle lighting was a women's *mitzvah*. Should moderns eager to eradicate irrational gender bias drop all ritual distinctions between the genders as archaic and ultimately destructive to the creation of a truly just society? Or should they accept such gender-specific enfranchisement as a quaint and harmless throwback to a day when women were deemed responsible for their families' homes in a way that men simply were not? Must equality mean equivalence? In a ritual world that so regularly barred women from full participation, is it noble or perverse to propose *dis*enfranchising women in one of the few ritual contexts in which their participation is traditionally preferred to men's? There are no simple answers to any of these questions, but one of the most exciting aspects of contemporary Judaism is the vital and vibrant debate over the issue of gender roles and the relationship of those roles to traditional practice. By becoming a part of a Jewish community, one joins in the ongoing conversation of what God wants from us today. There is no question, however, that the obligation to light candles applies to men as well as to women. There is no need for every individual to light the candles, however; only one family member needs to light for the entire household. As stated, this is traditionally the role of the woman of the house. But a man who is single, or who finds himself alone or solely in the company of other men for the Shabbat or for the observance of a festival, is obliged to kindle the festival or Shabbat candles on his own and to recite the blessing as he does so (*MT* Hilkhot Shabbat 5:1).

The laws for lighting candles on Rosh Hashanah (and for all the festival days on which candles are lit) are the same as on Shabbat (except for the custom of the waving one's hands over the flames and covering the eyes while the blessing is recited, which is not done as on Shabbat because a flame can be transferred on Rosh Hashanah, Sukkot, Pesaḥ and Shavuot and there is no need to have lit the candles before reciting the blessing.) The blessing is: *barukh attah adonai, eloheinu, melekh ha-olam, asher kidd'shanu b'mitzvotav v'tzivvanu l'hadlik neir shel yom tov* ("Praised are You, Adonai, our God, Sovereign of the universe, who, sanctifying us with divine commandments, has commanded us to kindle the festival lamp"). This is followed by the She-heḥeyyanu blessing, which is recited on both nights. The She-heḥeyyanu for the second night of Rosh Hashanah functions differently than the one recited on the second night of other festivals, however. On Sukkot, Pesaḥ, and Shavuot, we observe two days of the festival because of a doubt as to which was the actual festival day. Not so with Rosh Hashanah, which is considered a *yoma arikhta* (one long day). Therefore, there is a question as to whether a She-heḥeyyanu is appropriate on the second night of Rosh Hashanah. The problem is resolved by saying it, but also wearing a new garment or eating a fruit one has not eaten for a long time—both of which are occasions for a She-heḥeyyanu in their own right.

When Shabbat and Rosh Hashanah coincide, the blessing concludes *l'hadlik neir shel shabbat v'shel yom tov,* "to light the Shabbat and festival lamp." Why is Shabbat mentioned first? The talmudic maxim *tadir v'she-eino tadir, tadir kodeim* (meaning that when two rituals devolve upon us simultaneously and one is more frequently performed than the other, the more frequently performed takes precedence) teaches us to value the fidelity and trustworthy friendship of the more regular visitor. In this case, Shabbat is the friend who arrives every week of our lives—and Judaism encourages us to value it for its sacred constancy and to signal that we do not take it for granted by granting it primacy of liturgical place.

The customary greeting for Rosh Hashanah is *l'shanah tovah tikkateivu* (may you be inscribed for a good year). Often, this is shortened to *shanah tovah or l'shanah tovah.*

After reciting the Evening Service, families gather for a festive Rosh Hashanah meal. The special Kiddush for Rosh Hashanah is recited, concluding with the She-heḥeyyanu blessing, thanking God for "granting us life, sustaining us, and enabling us to reach this day." On Shabbat, of course, we add the Shabbat insertions to the Rosh Hashanah Kiddush.

There are a wide variety of customs that apply to dinner on Rosh Hashanah. One popular custom is to eat apples and honey. Right after reciting the Ha-motzi blessing and eating some bread, we dip a slice of apple into honey and then, before eating it say: *Y'hi ratzon mi-l'fanekha adonai eloheinu veilohei avoteinu [v'immoteinu] she-t'ḥaddeish aleinu shanah tovah u-m'tukah* ("May it be Your will, Adonai our God and God of our ancestors, to grant us a good and sweet new year"). Some have the custom of eating the apple dipped in honey first and then reciting the declaration. Many Jews have a more elaborate ritual that involves eating a large number of symbolic foods, each one intended to symbolize a specific hope for the coming year. For example, some eat a pomegranate as a way of expressing the hope that its numerous seeds will come to represent the many *mitzvot* to be performed in the year to come.

Instead of sprinkling salt over the bread after saying the blessing, some use honey. This too is meant to symbolize the hope for a sweet new year.

The Evening and Morning Services on Rosh Hashanah

In the minds of most people, Rosh Hashanah means spending a lot of time in synagogue. This is not an unreasonable assessment: the prayers for the New Year that have developed over the generations are long and complex—beautiful, to be sure, but also elaborate. (Even the prayerbook in use on Rosh Hashanah and Yom Kippur is popularly referenced as *the maḥzor,* even though the word *maḥzor* itself, a generic word for prayerbook, has no specific connection to the High Holidays and could theoretically be used to denote the traditional prayerbook in use on any festival.) Still, even worshipers who do not understand all the Hebrew prayers can have a profound experience worshiping with the larger community on Rosh Hashanah if they let themselves be moved by the experience of reciting their prayers in the midst of so many fellow worshipers gathered in their own synagogue and in synagogues like theirs around the world. There is also an almost uncanny temporal aspect to that sense of solidarity as well: it is possible to feel connected not only to the Jews of other places, but also to the Jews of other times, to those who recited these same prayers in ghettos, in the *shtetlach* of Eastern Europe, in the Jewish quarters of the medieval and modern worlds, east and west, even in the death camps—and thus to feel connected not only to the Jews of our own day, but to all Jews of all times.

The main parts of the Evening Service and the first parts of the Morning Service are similar to other holy days and Shabbat. But even those parts of the worship service that are not changed in word are almost wholly transformed by the use of a set of hauntingly beautiful musical motifs and flourishes—popularly called by the general term *nusaḥ*—that are unique for the High Holidays. Also unique to Rosh Hashanah is the frequent repetition of Psalm 81:4–5 ("blow the horn on the new moon, on the full moon for our feast day. . ."), the first phrase of which is taken as a reference to the *shofar.*

In the Kaddish prayer (and in all forms of Kaddish that are recited between Rosh Hashanah and Yom Kippur) the word *le'eilla* ("exalted") is doubled as a subtle means of expressing our sense of God's unutterable majesty and sovereignty during the holiday period. (As a nod to the ancients who attributed importance to maintaining precisely the same number of words in different versions of the same prayer, the words *min kol* ["from all"] are replaced with a one-word contraction, *mi-kol.*)

The Amidah prayer for Rosh Hashanah is unique. Although the structure is not entirely dissimilar from the versions of the Amidah recited on Shabbat and on other festivals, the differences between the prayer as recited on Rosh Hashanah and other festival prayers are quite marked nonetheless. For example, almost every blessing is provided with an interpolated passage that changes its feel and even its basic meaning. In the first and second blessings of the Amidah, for example, we add single sentences. (These may be found in any edition of the High Holiday prayerbook, including the recently published *Maḥzor Lev Shalem.*) In the third blessing, however, a whole series of prayers beginning with the word *u-v'khein* ("and thus") is added in and the blessing itself is altered to refer to God as *ha-melekh ha-kadosh,* our holy Sovereign, instead of the regular ending, *ha-eil ha-kadosh,* referencing the Almighty as our holy God. There are also interpolations into the closing blessings: a prayer that all Israel be inscribed in the Book of Life in the penultimate blessing and, in the final benediction, a prayer of graceful brevity and power: "May we and the entire House of Israel be remembered and recorded in the Book of Life, blessing, sustenance, and peace." To those on less than intimate terms with the daily and Shabbat liturgy, these changes will seem minor, even unimportant. But for the Jew who is accustomed to the daily or weekly repetition of these prayers, the changes highlight the unique nature of Rosh Hashanah and underscore its uplifting and inspiring message. Psalm 27 is added to the service as well, just as it is throughout the High Holiday season.

The meaning of the day is brought to the fore, however, in the middle blessing of the Amidah for Rosh Hashanah, which is an elaborate, poetic confession of the sovereignty of God, and of Israel's role in bringing that aspect of divine reality to the attention of the nations. Indeed, the passage at the very center of the Amidah on Rosh Hashanah, "Our God and God of our ancestors, cause Your sovereignty to be acknowledged throughout the world," could reasonably be taken as the foundational idea of which the rest of the prayer is a poetic elaboration.

If Rosh Hashanah falls on Shabbat, we insert the appropriate additions for Shabbat into the Amidah and into Kiddush.

One of the subtle distinctions between worship services that the uninitiated might easily miss has to do with the specific moment at which the individual leading the preliminary part of the service cedes to the cantor or the prayer leader who will guide the congregation through Shaḥarit, the formal Morning Service. Generally speaking, the first words the cantor or prayer leader chants at any Shabbat or festival service are intended to point to the themes of the day. On Rosh Hashanah and Yom Kippur, therefore, the first word intoned aloud is *ha-melekh* (the Sovereign), which brings the theme of God's ineffable majesty subtly, but unmistakably, to the fore. Although the symbolism is a bit archaic —and although no modern worshipers will live in countries governed by absolute monarchs—the idea that God rules the world as an all-powerful sovereign is not an idea moderns should casually dismiss. To affirm God as Sovereign of the universe is to affirm that the world is neither an accident nor the result of purely mechanical happenstance. Indeed, images that portray God as the Sovereign of the world, to the extent that they allow worshipers to imagine themselves as the subjects of God's kingdom, can and should be no less inspiring today than they were when they were first developed.

The High Holiday liturgy also features a series of beautiful but occasionally quite challenging poems called *piyyutim* (singular: *piyyut,* from the same Greek root that gives us the words "poem" and "poet"), written by rabbis and scholars in many different lands over thousands of years. It is customary to open the Ark when reciting many of these *piyyutim.* Do these ancient poems, many couched in arcane language that even fluent Hebrew speakers have trouble understanding, add to the High Holiday worship experience or detract from it? Conservative editions of the High Holiday prayerbook, including *Maḥzor Lev Shalem,* attempt judiciously to choose *piyyutim* that will enhance the quality and feel of the service without overwhelming it with burdensome, uninspiring obscurity.

Other than when Rosh Hashanah falls on Shabbat, the Avinu Malkeinu prayer is recited at the end of the Morning Service.

The Torah reading for the first day of Rosh Hashanah is the twenty-first chapter of Genesis; the twenty-second chapter is read on the second day. Five people are called to the Torah for *aliyot.* (If the first day of Rosh Hashanah coincides with Shabbat, the Torah reading remains the same but is divided into seven *aliyot.*) The number of *aliyot* on Rosh Hashanah clearly establishes its place in the sacred pecking order of the days on which the Torah is read: three on weekdays and on Shabbat afternoons, four on Rosh Ḥodesh and *Ḥol Ha-mo·eid,* five on Rosh Hashanah and the other festivals, six on Yom Kippur, and seven on Shabbat. It is not permitted to add extra *aliyot* on Rosh Hashanah, unless the holiday falls on Shabbat.

The Torah portion for the first day of Rosh Hashanah tells the story of the announcement to Abraham and Sarah that Sarah is to give birth to a child despite her advanced years. The reading for the second day is the story of the Binding of Isaac. There has been considerable discussion as to why these particular portions were chosen for these special days. Both readings combine two themes wholly appropriate for Rosh Hashanah: divine beneficence, as demonstrated by God's kindness to the aged Abraham and Sarah (and by God's intervention to save Isaac's life), and *z'khut avot,* the notion that personal merit may outlive people's earthly lives and remain an intercessory force for good in the lives of their descendants.

The *maftir* reading for both days of Rosh Hashanah is Numbers 29:1–6, which prescribes the sacrifices that were to be offered up on Rosh Hashanah. The *haftarah* for the first day is 1 Samuel 1:1–2:10, which tells of the birth of the prophet Samuel in terms clearly meant to echo the story in the Torah reading about the birth of Isaac. The point of reading this story aloud in the synagogue on Rosh Hashanah suggests itself easily. The image of a God who keeps promises is a comforting one for worshipers as they recite their prayers that God ever maintain the covenant with Israel. And the recollection of God's concern for the barren mothers Hannah and Sarah is also comforting as worshipers formally encapsulate in prayer their personal hope that God will be sensitive to their needs and concerns.

The *haftarah* for the second day is Jeremiah 31:2–20, which also reinforces some of the major themes of Rosh Hashanah, specifically God's enduring recollection of the covenant and the ongoing reality of divine mercy. When considered together, the *haftarot* seem to be widening the frame of reference as the festival wears on: the *haftarah* for the first day is about the travails of a Jewish family, while the *haftarah* for the second day is about the destiny of the Jewish people itself.

The Shofar

In some ways, the sounding of the *shofar* is the most characteristic *mitzvah* of Rosh Hashanah. Indeed, one of the scriptural names of this holiday (found at Numbers 29:1) is *yom t'ru·ah,* the Day of Sounding the Shofar. The *mitzvah,* however, need not be fulfilled personally by blowing the *shofar* oneself, but simply by hearing it blown. It is an art and a great privilege, however, to be the *ba·al t'ki·ah* or the *ba·alat t'ki·ah,* that is, the individual chosen to sound the *shofar* for the larger community. Before the notes are sounded, a special blessing acknowledging God as the Author of the commandment to sound the *shofar* is recited, followed by the She-heḥeyyanu blessing.

A *shofar* is the natural horn of a kosher animal and, with the exception of a cow or an ox, any kosher animal's horn may be used (*SA* Oraḥ Ḥayyim 586:1). Customarily, however, a ram's horn is used in order to connect the sounding of the *shofar* with the story of the Binding of Isaac and specifically with its climactic detail: when Abraham's hand is stayed, his attention is drawn to a ram caught in the thicket and he offers this animal as a sacrifice instead. By using the horn of a kosher animal, we may fulfill the *mitzvah* of blowing the *shofar*. But by using a ram's horn, we subtly remind God of the supreme merit of our forefather Abraham. The Talmud also explains that the *shofar* should be curved, not straight. This is intended to symbolize the spirit of humility appropriate for the season of national repentance (*BT* Rosh Ha-shanah 26b).

Although the sound of the *shofar* is meant to pierce the heart and ought not require any elaborate explanation, this has not stopped generations of rabbis and scholars from speculating about the reason the ritual is so effective. The most famous of these is probably Maimonides' comment (*MT* Hilkhot T'shuvah 3:4) cited in *Maḥzor Lev Shalem* (p. 118) to the effect that the *shofar* calls to each of us and says: "Awake, you sleepers from your sleep. Arouse you slumberers from your slumber and ponder your deeds; remember your Creator and return to God in repentance. Do not be like those who miss the truth in pursuit of shadows and waste their years seeking vanity. Look well to your souls and consider your deeds; turn away from your wrong ways and improper thoughts."

Generations of the Jewish people have found the sounding of the *shofar* to be one of the peak moments of the entire Jewish year. As such, it resonates with generations' worth of associations, bringing contemporary worshipers back to the wilderness in which the Israelites wandered and to the foot of Mount Sinai where they received God's Torah as the sound of the *shofar* was heard from on high (Exodus 19:19). Its sound does not solely pierce through the generations, however. It also pierces the layers of indifference that separate even the most willing supplicant from embracing wholehearted, unfettered faith in God. To respond to the sound of the *shofar* requires neither formal training nor any knowledge of complex Hebrew texts, only the most basic of any supplicant's tools: an open heart and a willing spirit.

Tradition dictates that there are to be one hundred separate blasts of the *shofar* on each day of Rosh Hashanah (cf. the comment of the Tosafot to *BT* Rosh Ha-shanah 33b, *s.v. shei·ur t'ru·ah*). The notes are divided into three types: the *t'ki·ah* (a long, strong blast), the *sh'varim* (a series of three short broken blasts), and the *t'ru·ah* (nine short staccato notes). The *t'ki·ah,* the three-part *sh'varim,* and the nine-part *t'ru·ah* should each be of similar length. These are the only three notes, but they are combined in various ways to result in the one hundred requisite blasts. Different communities, however, have different customs as to how and when the notes are sounded to arrive at the desired total. The first time the *shofar* is sounded is right after the Torah service at the conclusion of the *haftarah* and its blessings. The *shofar* is also sounded during each of the three parts of the repetition of the Amidah during the Musaf Service. Some congregations sound a final set of blasts in the Full Kaddish at the end of the service to arrive at the total of one hundred. An alternate custom included as an option in some Conservative prayerbooks for the High Holidays is to blow the *shofar* during each of the three sections of the silent recitation of the Musaf Amidah and then again during the repetition.

The *shofar* is such an important *mitzvah* that those who are ill or incapacitated and cannot come to synagogue to hear the blasts should still arrange to have someone sound the *shofar* for them at home or in the hospital. Most synagogues are glad to assist in arranging volunteers to help fulfill this important *mitzvah*.

The *shofar* is not sounded when Rosh Hashanah coincides with Shabbat (*BT* Rosh Ha-shanah 29b). Since Rosh Hashanah is always a two-day holiday, however, the *mitzvah* will never be completely eliminated in any given year.

If the *shofar* is such an important *mitzvah*, one might ask why it does not supersede the laws that govern Shabbat rest. And this is even more pointed a question when we note that the sounding of the *shofar* would not actually involve any direct violation of the laws of Shabbat, but was forbidden only out of the fear that it might lead indirectly to such a violation. Indeed, it was precisely because the *mitzvah* was so important and so beloved that the rabbis feared that a community without a *shofar* might arrange for someone to retrieve one from some distant place, thus carrying and possibly traveling on Shabbat. (Dispensing with the sounding of the *shofar* when the festival coincided with Shabbat eliminated even the possibility of such an eventuality.) And thus the ancients taught a valuable and profound lesson: that Shabbat takes precedence even over something as important as sounding the *shofar* on Rosh Hashanah. As a result, congregations that faithfully omit the *shofar* service when Rosh Hashanah falls on Shabbat experience a renewed awareness of the ineffable sanctity of Shabbat and the unreasonableness of risking its even inadvertent neglect.

The Musaf Service on Rosh Hashanah

The Musaf Service for Rosh Hashanah contains the familiar opening and closing blessings of the Amidah with the usual High Holiday interpolations. The central part of the Amidah, however, is organized around three main sections, each with its own particular theme: the Malkhuyot section, which emphasizes God's divine sovereignty; the Zikhronot section, which emphasizes the theme of divine and human memory; and the Shofarot section, which emphasizes the redemptive meaning of the sounding of the *shofar*.

Each of these three sections has the same structure and consists of a poetic introduction, a middle part made up of ten biblical verses on the theme of that section, and a conclusion that includes the formal blessing. The middle section that contains the biblical verses also follows a set format: the first three are from the Torah, the second three from the Writings, and the third section from the Prophets. Then, a concluding passage from the Torah makes ten verses. Since the Prophets come before the Writings in the Bible, why is the order reversed in the service? The answer is simply that the verses from the Writings are all taken from the Psalms, attributed to King David, who lived before any of the other prophets quoted (Tosafot to *BT* Rosh Ha-shanah 32a, *s.v. matḥil ba-torah u-m'sayyeim b'navi*).

After the concluding prayer of each of these sections, the *shofar* is sounded and the prayers Ha-yom Harat Olam and Areshet S'fateinu are recited.

The Musaf Amidah on Rosh Hashanah also includes the hymn regularly known as Aleinu. While this prayer is now the familiar concluding hymn of every service during the year, it was once recited only as part of the Musaf Amidah on Rosh Hashanah. Its theme fits in with that section too, with its celebration and recognition of God's sovereignty and the wish that the entire world will one day be united in the worship of God. Normally when we recite the Aleinu we bend the knee and bow from the waist at the words: "And we bend the knee and bow." During the repetition of the Amidah on Rosh Hashanah, however, worshipers may actually fall to the floor and prostrate themselves in a fuller expression of submission before God. While there are many congregations in which only very few prostrate themselves totally in this manner, the practice can still be a powerful reminder that Jews bow to no human being, yet bow completely in submission to God's will.

Tashlikh

One of the beautiful customs associated with Rosh Hashanah is Tashlikh, a brief service that takes place by a body of water. Tashlikh is held on the afternoon of the first day of Rosh Hashanah unless the first day is Shabbat, in which case it is then deferred to the second day. The ritual for this custom is very simple and involves the casting of bread crumbs onto the water and the recitation of some biblical verses, of which the main ones are from the Book of Micah: "You will hurl all their sins into the depths of the sea, thus keeping faith with Jacob and showing loyalty to Abraham just as You promised to our ancestors in days gone by" (Micah 7:19b–20). Tashlikh is not an ancient custom and, indeed, it does not appear in Jewish sources until Rabbi Jacob Moelin, who died in 1427, mentions it in his *Sefer Maharil.* It has, however, become a compelling contemporary tradition expressive of the desire to cast off sin and to be purified and spiritually renewed. Even the preference for flowing water inhabited by fish may be interpreted symbolically as an expression of the precariousness and fragility of human life. If for some reason Tashlikh is not performed at this time, it can actually be done any time during the High Holiday season, even up until Hoshana Rabbah.

The Ten Days of Repentance

The days between Rosh Hashanah and Yom Kippur are known as the *Aseret Y'mei T'shuvah,* the Ten Days of Repentance. Although there are no specific rituals that pertain to these days of introspection and quiet self-analysis, the special High Holiday interpolations in the daily Amidah are maintained. The Shabbat between Rosh Hashanah and Yom Kippur is known as Shabbat Shuvah, and it takes its name from the special *haftarah* from the Book of Hosea that begins "Return (*shuvah*), O Israel, to God" (Hosea 14:2), which focuses wholly on the intertwined holiday themes of regret, repentance, and return.

The day after Rosh Hashanah is the Fast of Gedaliah, a minor fast day. (If that day falls on Shabbat, the fast is postponed to Sunday.) Gedaliah ben Aḥikam was a Jewish governor appointed by the Babylonians in the days following the destruction of Jerusalem in the sixth century B.C.E. who was subsequently assassinated by his own people and whose death held dramatic implications for the Jews living under Babylonian rule. (His story is told in some detail in the Bible in Jeremiah 40 and 41.) Although it might strike some observers as excessive for Jews to continue so formally to regret a political assassination that happened millennia ago, the assassination of Yitzḥak Rabin on November 4, 1995, granted new relevance to the day. The prime minister was murdered by a Jewish citizen of Israel who opposed Rabin's willingness to compromise and his readiness and eagerness to negotiate for the sake of peace, much as was Gedaliah ben Aḥikam all those years ago. By fasting on this day, Jews everywhere renew their dedication to the peaceful solution of conflict and their commitment to reject violence as a way of dealing with political opponents. The Torah reading and the specific changes in the prayer service are described below in the section on fasts at the end of this chapter.

The Day of Atonement

The Work of Yom Kippur

The themes and mood of Yom Kippur are subtly different from those of Rosh Hashanah. The atmosphere in synagogue is more serious and more solemn, as the effort to renounce sin and return unto God in heartfelt repentance intensifies. There is a certain spirit of homey good will on Rosh Hashanah that finds expression in family feasts, in the custom of eating apples dipped in honey, and even in the practice of gathering together for Tashlikh. Yom Kippur, on the other hand, is a day spent entirely, or almost entirely, in the synagogue as worshipers engage in the kind of intense soul searching that comes from an earnest desire to wipe clean the slate of life and begin anew. Yom Kippur calls on each of us to review our lives, to reconsider our ways, and to reimagine our hopes and our dreams. Yom Kippur challenges us to confront honestly the people we have become, to dare to envision the persons we wish we were (and know we could actually become), and *then* to begin the hard work of moving ourselves from where we are to where we wish to be. Yom Kippur is a long, exhausting, and difficult day not because of the fasting, but because of the emotional and spiritual concentration required. At the end of this twenty-five-hour journey to the center of the human heart, worshipers emerge exhausted and emotionally spent, yet also refreshed, renewed, and energized to face a new year.

All the prohibitions that pertain to Yom Kippur accentuate the seriousness and solemnity of this special day. One is not permitted to eat, drink, bathe, anoint oneself with perfumes or scented oil, wear leather shoes, or engage in marital relations (*M* Yoma 8:1, *SA* Oraḥ Ḥayyim 611:1). These restrictions are the halakhic elaboration of the biblical command found at Leviticus 23:27 to afflict oneself on this day, and the point is very well taken: it is precisely acquisitiveness, gluttony, and indecency that led to the large majority of the sins for which we seek forgiveness on Yom Kippur. But these prohibitions also serve another function by effectively eliminating the distractions of everyday life that would naturally impede concentration on the matters of the moment. Abstinence on Yom Kippur from food and drink, as well as from different kinds of sensual pleasure, demonstrates not only the control people can exercise over their lives and their appetites, but also the possibility of gaining purposeful, meaningful perspective on life through introspection and ruthless self-analysis.

In the minds of most, fasting is the central *mitzvah* of Yom Kippur. A young person is obliged to begin fasting on Yom Kippur upon becoming a bar or bat mitzvah, but children should be introduced to the concept of fasting at a much earlier age. Indeed, if properly inspired, young children may even wish to fast before they are fully obliged to do so and, within reason, this can be a positive feature of a child's development. Younger children, for example, can begin by giving up favorite foods for the entire day. Then, as they approach bar and bat mitzvah age, they may want to limit their eating by skipping one meal or two, gradually increasing their ability to fast so that the transition to the full adult obligation is a subtle one. This will not only make the full fast easier for them when they become adults, but it will also help them to think of themselves as a part of a spiritual community even from a very young age.

If fasting presents a possible health issue, a physician must be consulted. If the physician says that fasting is likely to cause an individual significant harm, then the patient should observe Yom Kippur without fasting. There is a tendency for people to be overly pious and to insist that they know themselves better than any physician ever could, especially one who forbids them to fast on Yom Kippur. Such behavior is in violation of Jewish law (Klein, p. 210; *SA* Oraḥ Ḥayyim 618:1). In fact, the *halakhah* is just to the contrary: a physician who forbids fasting must be obeyed, but patients who truly feel unable to fast should listen to their own instincts over the advice of a physician who believes they will be able to fast. In other words, the benefit of the doubt always falls on the side of health and safety. Pregnant women and nursing mothers instructed by their doctors not to fast are permitted to eat on Yom Kippur. For all these people, eating on Yom Kippur becomes permitted. However, they should nevertheless only consume as much food as they feel is necessary. Since such eating is licit, it should be preceded by the appropriate blessing and, if bread is consumed, followed by the Grace after Meals. The latter should include the typical holy day insertions.

The prohibition against bathing or washing is also considered a fulfillment of the biblical injunction to "afflict oneself" on Yom Kippur. However, those who are ill are released from this prohibition as well. Washing one's hands for hygienic purposes, for example after visiting the washroom or before preparing food for children to eat, is permitted (Klein, p. 210; *SA* Oraḥ Ḥayyim 613:1).

Leather shoes are not worn on Yom Kippur because they were considered a sign of luxury and material excess inconsonant with the spirit of the day. Some authorities also connected this prohibition with the ancient custom of removing one's shoes when approaching a holy place (see, e.g., Exodus 3:5) or to symbolize the depth of one's sense of God's presence (see, e.g., Isaiah 20:3). Today we permit wearing of non-leather shoes made of cloth or synthetic materials. Some people mistakenly believe that the requirement is to wear athletic shoes. These were once all made with cloth and became popular for that reason, but today many are made with leather and are therefore inappropriate on Yom Kippur.

While fasting is perceived to be the central observance of the day, in fact it and most of the above mentioned customs serve only to highlight what is truly the central occupation of this remarkable day: *viddui,* confession. In some religions, confession requires a human intercessor; in Judaism, it does not. The possibility exists for each Jew to turn to God and personally request forgiveness for his or her own sins. This process actually takes place every day, three times a day, as prayers about repentance and forgiveness are part of every weekday Amidah prayer. (The Amidah on Shabbat and festivals is reserved for expressions of gratitude rather than for prayers petitioning God for forgiveness.) Yom Kippur is a day that is wholly given over to this enterprise. It is as if the entire year is telescoped into this twenty-five-hour *viddui* experience. Immersing ourselves in prayer and soul-searching for one whole day we achieve so much more than when we are distracted by our everyday concerns. Everything about this day calls on us to get things right with God. *Viddui,* confession, is the means and *s'liḥah,* forgiveness, is the goal. We fast, we pray, we isolate ourselves from all other normal distractions in the hope that we will emerge cleansed and renewed. It is one of the most spiritually powerful experiences in Judaism—and as the shofar sounds at the end of Ne'ilah we feel both physically exhausted and spiritually energized by the assurance that one who goes through this day wholeheartedly is guaranteed forgiveness from God.

Erev Yom Kippur

The preparations for this awe-inspiring day are intrinsic to its observance. Just as one is required to fast on Yom Kippur, so one is required to eat on the day before Yom Kippur (Klein, p. 207; *BT* Yoma 81b; *SA* Oraḥ Ḥayyim 604:1). There is a mood of optimism and confidence in the air—for all that Yom Kippur is a day of judgment to be taken seriously, perhaps even feared, the hours before and after the fast are given over to a sense of confidence in God's ultimate mercy and compassion. We are confident that our God is above all a God of forgiveness and we feel certain that, if we do our *t'shuvah* seriously and honestly, our loving and generous God will look favorably on our work.

One of the ways we demonstrate the seriousness of our repentance is through charitable gifts. There was an old practice, now mostly abandoned except in certain extremely conservative communities, of swinging a chicken around one's head on the eve of Yom Kippur as a symbolic way of divesting oneself of one's sins by transferring them to the bird. The chicken was then slaughtered or sold, and the meat or the sale price was donated to the poor. While no harder to accept as symbolically meaningful than Tashlikh, this custom has fared less well and there have been rabbis from the very early times who opposed it as essentially counterproductive to the work of Yom Kippur. As noted, it finds few proponents in contemporary times, yet the idea of preparing for our day of prayer and soul-searching by performing positive deeds of kindness and by helping the poor through tangible gifts and donations is surely itself commendable. Some synagogues have collection centers where people bring food for the poor as they arrive for Kol Nidrei; others have charity boxes that are filled during the year and brought to the synagogue before Kol Nidrei. Many congregations hold a Kol Nidrei appeal to raise money for communal needs. The objections that these enterprises might interfere with the more spiritual nature of the day and intrude on the introspection and soul-searching of the hour miss the point that, in the Jewish conception, spiritual growth can never be achieved in the absence of good deeds and that, indeed, the most efficient, effective way to create better people is to involve them in the creation of a better world. A version of this ritual can be found in *Maḥzor Lev Shalem.*

The meal eaten on Erev Yom Kippur is unique. It is not a regular festival meal such as one might eat on Rosh Hashanah or other holidays. There is no special Kiddush prayer recited, for example. Indeed, the meal is called the *se'udah mafseket* ("the meal of demarcation") precisely because it separates the normal day from the upcoming fast day. The Minḥah Service preceding the meal is expanded to include special prayers of repentance and sets the mood for the meal itself. It is also customary for parents to bless their children at this meal as on every Friday night, but also to add wishes for a good and healthy year and any other appropriate wishes for the year to come. The meal must obviously conclude before candle-lighting time.

Following the meal, candles are lit just as they are on Friday night. The blessing, found in any edition of the High Holiday prayerbook is *barukh attah adonai, eloheinu, melekh ha-olam, asher kidd'shanu b'mitzvotav v'tzivvanu l'hadlik neir shel yom ha-kippurim* ("Praised are You, Adonai, our God, Sovereign of the universe, who, sanctifying us with divine commandments, has commanded us to light the Yom Kippur lamp"). If Yom Kippur coincides with Shabbat, the blessing concludes *l'hadlik neir shel shabbat v'shel yom ha-kippurim* ("has commanded us to kindle the Shabbat and Yom Kippur lamp"). In either event, it is followed by the She-heḥeyyanu blessing.

In addition, a special Yizkor candle is lit just prior to the formal Yom Kippur candles by those who will be reciting the Yizkor Service on Yom Kippur. There is no blessing recited on the kindling of this candle, although many prayerbooks include appropriate devotional material to recite just before lighting the memorial candle.

Kol Nidrei

Yom Kippur begins with one of the most dramatic moments in the entire Jewish calendar: the Kol Nidrei service. This service actually must be completed before Yom Kippur begins and is therefore held before sunset. The reason for this is not that widely understood, but is straightforward enough: since the technical purpose of the service is the annulment of vows, and since one may not attend to legal matters on a holy day of rest, the service is held just prior to the beginning of the sacred day. It is ironic that this incredibly emotional and moving service is based on something as banal as the technical procedure for undoing rash oaths, but history and custom somehow come together to infuse the liturgy with a sense of holiness and spirituality that is almost without parallel. As the traditional melody of Kol Nidrei is chanted by the cantor, worshipers feel the ghostly presence of countless generations of Jews in the synagogue, people who were moved by these words, this melody, and this moment in their day. There is no other moment like this in the entire year. To accentuate the holiness of the moment, a *tallit* is worn and the blessing is duly recited. This is the sole time a *tallit* is worn for evening prayers.

At the very beginning of the service, the Ark is opened and, depending on the custom of the community, either two scrolls or all the Torah scrolls are removed. Taking the scrolls from the Ark and holding them during Kol Nidrei is considered a great honor and is customarily given to very distinguished and respected members of the community. The Kol Nidrei prayer is then chanted three times to emphasize the importance of the ceremony.

Isaac Klein (p. 213) explains that there is some controversy as to the historical origin of the Kol Nidrei prayer. Since the prayer is essentially about the nullification of vows, most historians look back to some point in Jewish history when Jews were forced by non-Jewish authorities to make promises against their will publicly. Kol Nidrei would then have originated in their wish to apologize to God, and in the presence of God, for what they were forced to do. Some look to the reign of Reccared I (586–601), a king of Visigothic Spain who was known to have persecuted Jews. Unfortunately there have been similar persecutions throughout Jewish history, so it is hard to know where the truth lies. Whatever its origins, however, Kol Nidrei became so popular because, time and time again, Jews were forced by others to do and say things they did not believe. Kol Nidrei served as the religious antidote to these oppressive obligations.

It is essential to note—and this is emphasized in all reputable High Holiday prayerbooks—that the only vows that Kol Nidrei has the power to annul are those between an individual and God. Kol Nidrei does not, nor did it ever, refer to vows, promises, or commitments made to other people. These binding commitments can only be nullified by a mutual agreement between the parties themselves.

One of the most fascinating parts of the Kol Nidrei service is the section at the beginning, before the actual Kol Nidrei prayer is chanted, when the congregation grants itself permission to worship with sinners. Some have explained this strange declaration with reference to people who were forced to take blasphemous vows: as these "sinners" sought absolution from their sinful oaths on Yom Kippur, the community expressed its understanding of their plight and affirmed their right to pray together with the other members of the community. Today these lines resonate with additional meaning. The synagogue is called a "sacred community"—a *k'hillah k'doshah*. As a result, people sometimes do not understand why congregations are not more particular about whom they allow to join. Why should someone who has been convicted of embezzlement, or who is known to have been unfaithful to his or her spouse, be accepted into a community that claims to be striving for holiness? Indeed, why do people who do not follow the laws of *kashrut* strictly or who do not strictly embrace the laws of Shabbat have a place in the sanctuary, and why should such people be given honors and even called to the Torah? The answer can be found in the humble declaration that it is permitted, indeed expected, to pray with "sinners." Perfection is not a prerequisite of joining a holy community. We are all imperfect, and the synagogue, therefore, is at best a collection of people who are "works in progress." What unites the faithful is not what they have accomplished, but what they are striving to accomplish. We join together on Yom Kippur in recognition of the fact that we want to be better, that we need to be better, and that we understand that, in accepting imperfections in others, we can hope that they will in turn accept and forgive our own imperfections.

The Evening Service on Yom Kippur

The Evening Service, called Ma·ariv, is similar to the regular service in that it begins with the Bar'khu call to worship and continues with the Sh'ma and its blessings, then with the Amidah, and then ends with the usual concluding prayers. What is unusual is the vocal recitation of the second line of the Sh'ma, *barukh sheim k'vod malkhuto le'olam va·ed* (Praised be God's glorious sovereignty throughout all time), which is recited in an undertone every other day of the year. (It is also chanted aloud at the other Yom Kippur services.) Since this line hearkens back to the worship service of the High Priest in the ancient Temple (see, e.g., *M* Yoma 3:8, 4:1–2, or 6:2), it is deemed appropriate for us today to highlight these words as a way of honoring the High Priest's central role in the Yom Kippur service in ancient times.

There are two confessional prayers: the shorter Ashamnu confessional and the much longer Al Ḥeit, which are repeated over and over throughout the services on Yom Kippur. It is customary to "beat one's breast" (tapping the right hand, either folded into a loose fist or else using only the fingertips, lightly over the heart) when reciting these prayers as a sign that we are taking these words to heart. Rabbi Mana said: "Why do people beat their hearts? Because the heart is the source of sin" (*Kohelet Rabbah* 7:9).

Following the Amidah, there is a series of liturgical poems that focus on the theme of confession. Then, except on Shabbat, Avinu Malkeinu is recited. When leaving the synagogue after Kol Nidrei and Ma·ariv, worshipers strive to behave in a way that befits a day of solemnity and judgment. The usual post-worship banter is replaced by a more serious and solemn conversation as we demonstrate even in our casual speech patterns the degree to which we are preoccupied with the matters of a very serious day. The traditional greeting for the day is thus not *ḥag samei·aḥ* ("have a happy holiday"), but *g'mar tov or g'mar ḥatimah tovah,* both of which convey a wish that the person being addressed be judged for good on the coming Day of Judgment.

The Morning Service and Torah Service on Yom Kippur

The Morning Service is roughly the same as on Rosh Hashanah, with the exception of the Amidah itself and a few added lines and hymns that are unique to Yom Kippur, and is then followed by the Torah Service. As on Rosh Hashanah, two scrolls are removed from the Ark. First, six people are called forward for *aliyot* as Leviticus 16, which contains a description of the ancient sacrificial service for Yom Kippur, is read from the first scroll. (When Yom Kippur falls on a Shabbat, seven are called up.) Then Numbers 29:7–11, which also speaks of the ancient sacrifices offered on Yom Kippur, is read as the *maftir* portion. The *haftarah* is Isaiah 57:14–58:14, a very stirring passage that deals with the use of ritual to achieve spiritual ends. The prophet challenges us to remember that ritual is, at best, a means to an end and is never to be confused with magic. The chanting of the Ashrei and the formal ceremony putting the Torah scrolls back into the Ark are delayed until after the Yizkor Service.

Yizkor

The Memorial Service, called Yizkor, is recited four times during the course of the year: on Yom Kippur and, in diaspora communities, on Sh'mini Atzeret, on the eighth day of Passover, and on the second day of Shavuot. For such a well-known service, however, Yizkor is a relatively late liturgical development, and was possibly composed in reaction to the Crusades and the terrible loss of Jewish life in that dark chapter of history. But whatever its origins, Yizkor is certainly in keeping with the serious mood of Yom Kippur and it is wholly appropriate to remember those departed individuals who have shaped and influenced our lives for good on the very day we seek to reconnect with our truest selves.

The Yizkor Service itself is a bit fluid, but generally consists of a collection of readings and recitations revolving around two central prayers: the individual Yizkor prayers, in which worshipers invoke God's continued protection of the souls of loved ones who have passed on, and the El Malei Raḥamim, the traditional memorial prayer that poetically expresses the hope that the dead rest in peace under God's divine protection.

It is customary in many communities for individuals whose parents are still living to leave the sanctuary during Yizkor. Partially the result of a superstitious fear that remaining in the sanctuary would be to tempt fate and partially rooted in the feeling that those who have suffered terrible loss in their lives deserve some privacy in which to mourn publicly for their lost parents, spouses, siblings, or children, the unfortunate outcome in many congregations is a kind of mass exodus from the sanctuary right before Yizkor. In the end, there is no halakhic or rational reason not to remain in the sanctuary during Yizkor. Even those whose parents are still alive will surely have lost friends or other relatives who are deserving of being remembered at this time. And it is fully appropriate that every member of every Jewish community pause to remember those who perished in the Shoah, as well as Jewish martyrs of every age, during the Yizkor Service.

It is customary to give gifts of charity in memory of those remembered during Yizkor. Individuals who recite versions of the Yizkor service in which they formally pledge to give charity in honor of the specific people they are remembering should consider such gifts requisite.

The Musaf Service on Yom Kippur

The Musaf Service for Yom Kippur contains two lengthy interpolated passages, the Avodah Service and the Martyrology Service.

The Avodah is an elaborate retelling of the original sacrificial service that took place on Yom Kippur when the Temple stood in Jerusalem and sacrifices were the primary mode of worship. These sacrifices were offered by the priests in the outer courtyard of the Temple, but the highlight of the Yom Kippur ceremonial involved the annual visits of the High Priest to the Holy of Holies, and it is this experience that is re-created in the Avodah on Yom Kippur. On Yom Kippur, the High Priest entered the Holy of Holies three times: the first time, to pray for himself and his family and to ask forgiveness for all of their sins; the second time, to do so on behalf of all the priests and those who served in the Temple with him; and a final time, to supplicate on behalf of all Israel. Each time the High Priest disappeared from sight to enter the Holy of Holies, the thousands of worshipers outside waited breathlessly to see if he would emerge. If he emerged safely, this was taken as a signal that God had accepted his efforts. Each time the people standing outside heard the High Priest declare the ineffable name of God that was used on this occasion, and on this occasion only, the people would fall prostrate on the ground out of relief and exaltation and cry out: *barukh sheim k'vod malkhuto le'olam va·ed* ("Praised be God's glorious sovereignty throughout all time"). When it was clear that the service of the High Priest had been successful, it was an incredible moment of exultation for the entire people, and we today seek to re-create the drama, holiness, and majesty of this ancient service through our recitation of the Avodah Service on Yom Kippur. It is one of the most dramatic moments of the entire High Holiday liturgy and clearly constitutes one of the spiritual climaxes of the day.

Another special addition to the Musaf Service is the Martyrology, also called the Eilleh Ezk'rah after its opening words. If the Avodah represents a peak of spiritual emotion, the Eilleh Ezk'rah represents a deep valley. Yom Kippur is a day filled with dramatic and varied emotions. The Martyrology Service recalls the moments in Jewish history when Jews were subjected to persecution. The original Eilleh Ezk'rah poem is a long, dramatic lament that describes the torture and execution of ten rabbis who insisted on teaching Torah in defiance of the Roman ban against doing so. Most contemporary High Holiday prayerbooks, including *Maḥzor Lev Shalem,* have expanded on this original poem by adding readings that allude to other instances of Jewish martyrdom, including the Shoah. We include these terrible reminiscences as part of our Yom Kippur liturgy because it seems fitting that, on the very day when we attempt to reconnect with our finer selves, we also seek to reconnect with those who gave their lives for their Jewishness throughout history. Reciting the Eilleh Ezk'rah is a way to ask God to remember those of our ancestors who died as martyrs for the sanctification of God's name. Perhaps if we do not merit forgiveness for our own sake, we may still merit being forgiven for theirs.

The Musaf Service ends simply with the Full Kaddish. There are no closing hymns, as is traditional on other festival days.

The Afternoon Service on Yom Kippur

The Afternoon Service begins with the Torah Service. (Ashrei, which usually begins the Minḥah Service, is deferred to the Ne'ilah Service.) The Torah reading is Leviticus 18, which delineates the different varieties of forbidden sexual relationships. There are a number of explanations for this unusual choice of text. The first is prosaic: the reading picks up from almost exactly where the morning reading left off and so may have been chosen because the scroll was already rolled to that spot. (This ignores the question, however, of why the reading isn't the previous chapter, Leviticus 17, which follows the morning reading even more directly.) Another explanation has to do with the lesson preserved in the Mishnah at *M* Ta·anit 4:8 to the effect that Yom Kippur afternoon was a time set aside for courtship and flirtatious behavior. Given this custom, the reading could be imagined as the perfect counterpart to such activities, as a timely reminder of which relations were permitted and which forbidden. This suggestion too comes up short, however, in that the custom, even if once widely observed, has not been a feature of Jewish life for millennia and is not formally observed at all today. In the end, the most cogent explanation for the choice of reading for Yom Kippur afternoon is also the least fanciful. Sexuality is one of the arenas in which people sin the most avidly, and the self-control necessary to remain faithful to the laws of the Torah that govern intimate relationships is especially difficult to attain, even for otherwise obedient, God-fearing people. According to this view, the reading is meant to remind those prone to rationalize their own sexual transgressions as private matters (and, as such, as transgressions for which they need not seek formal atonement) that they have made a grave error in thinking along these lines, but that there is still time to correct their error and to pray for forgiveness for those sins as well. Some have suggested that the focus of the reading should be on broader issues of holiness. To that end, many contemporary *maḥzorim* (including *Maḥzor Lev Shalem*) include a substitute reading of the very next passage in the Torah, Leviticus 19.

Three people are called to the Torah during the Afternoon Service on Yom Kippur. Of them, the third is the *maftir* honored with the recitation of the *haftarah*. The *haftarah* for Yom Kippur afternoon is the entire Book of Jonah (with three verses from the Book of Micah appended to the end). While most people associate the Book of Jonah with the story of the prophet being swallowed alive by the great fish, the story is no fish tale and its use on Yom Kippur afternoon is not to entertain, but to chasten. On one level, the book is about the impossibility of fleeing from God, a lesson well taken on Yom Kippur. But there is another aspect of the story of Jonah that is just as germane. The book hints, at least obliquely, that Jonah actually wanted the people of Nineveh to be punished for their sins. He knew that if he warned them of their fate, they would probably repent, God would forgive them, and life would go on. In the end, this is exactly what does happen, but Jonah apparently does not think this is fair. The book's lesson for us, then, is the same as God's lesson for Jonah. God does not seek the punishment of sinners, but rather that they change their ways and live justly and righteously. God seeks not our destruction, but our repentance, our *t'shuvah*. If we change our ways, we too will be worthy of God's compassion and we too will be forgiven. And *t'shuvah* is the means by which flawed and imperfect people can live in God's world. These are the lessons of the Book of Jonah on which we should focus when the book is read aloud on Yom Kippur afternoon.

The service concludes with the private, then public, recitation of the Amidah, including the usual interpolated passages for Yom Kippur, and (except on Shabbat) Avinu Malkeinu.

Ne'ilah

Ne'ilah is an additional service recited today only at the conclusion of Yom Kippur. It means "locking up" and is based on imagery taken from the time of the ancient Temple in Jerusalem. The Temple was enclosed by a large wall and entrance was possible only through designated gates. These gates were closed at nightfall. As long as the gates remained open, worshipers could bring their sacrifices and their offerings, but once the gates were closed, they had to wait until the next day to enter.

This image heightens the drama and increases the sense of urgency as the most sacred day of the year draws to its inexorable close. For more than twenty-four hours, the community has been occupied with the work of repentance and is now feeling exhausted and emotionally drained as worshipers imagine the heavenly gates of repentance swinging shut. Ne'ilah, therefore, is one last chance, one final appeal, one final opportunity to cast off sin and return to God.

There are a number of customs that emphasize the unique mood of the Ne'ilah Service. There is a custom that the Ark remains open throughout the service. Many congregations have instituted an opportunity for worshipers to spend a few moments standing before the open Ark as they share their final urgent appeals. And it is a touching sight indeed to see the long line of young and old, all of them coming with their personal prayers: this one is getting married in a few months, that one is expecting a baby, a third prays for a seriously ill loved one. Normally, when the Ark is opened, the congregation remains standing. To do this at the end of a long and difficult day of fasting and prayer highlights the drama of the moment. If someone is physically unable to remain standing, it is not considered at all disrespectful to be seated at this time even if the Ark is open. The sight of a weary but determined community standing before an open Ark is part of the unique charm of this final service of Yom Kippur. Avinu Malkeinu is recited at the end of Ne'ilah (uniquely, even if it is Shabbat), but there is one way in which our recitation of this prayer at Ne'ilah differs from the version recited earlier in the day: at Ne'ilah the word *kotveinu* ("inscribe us") is replaced with *ḥotmeinu* ("seal us") in the Book of Life—yet another sign of the urgency of this final appeal. (This liturgical shift occurs as well in the Amidah as it is recited at Ne'ilah.)

The magnificent melody used during this special service suggests the urgency of the moment as well. The image of the "closing gate" challenges us to recognize that life and time are not limitless resources. Our days are numbered. Our time on earth is limited. Ne'ilah challenges us to make the most of the blessings we have been granted for as long as we have them. As Ne'ilah provides a final surge of energy, strength, and excitement, the congregation feels energized as the day comes to its triumphant conclusion with the final sounding of the *shofar,* one last long triumphant *t'ki·ah* blast of hope and confidence. This long and difficult day ends, literally, on a positive note as the community declares its faith in the ultimate redemption promised by God.

The Havdalah which concludes Yom Kippur is also unique, as it is the only time the blessings are said on the wine and the candle but not the spices.

There is a custom that one goes home from Ne'ilah and drives the first nail into the building of the *sukkah* to create a sense of continuity and move from this very cerebral holiday to the very physical holiday of Sukkot.

The Festival of Sukkot

The Rituals of Sukkot

Five days after Yom Kippur, we celebrate Sukkot, one of the *shalosh r'galim,* the three so-called pilgrimage festivals. While each of these holidays has a specific historical framework, a unique spiritual theme, and an individual agricultural aspect, they all celebrate the bounty of the land. Sukkot, however, is the quintessential harvest festival. Furthermore, its annual commemoration of the wandering of the Jewish people in the wilderness on their way to the Promised Land leads worshipers to a profound and inspiring spiritual lesson: that one of the most effective paths an individual can follow to faith in God is the one along which the fragility and ephemeral nature of life are taken truly to heart and allowed to energize and inspire the human spirit.

American readers will also enjoy thinking of Sukkot as the original Thanksgiving and as the historical model that inspired the Pilgrims.

There are two specific *mitzvot* observed solely during Sukkot that serve as its most potent symbols: the *sukkah* (a booth or hut) and the *arba·ah minim,* the "four species" or "four kinds," more popularly known as the *lulav* and *etrog* (the former of which is combined with two other "species," as described below).

Sukkot begins on the fifteenth of Tishrei and continues for seven days. In Israel, only the first day of Sukkot is a full festival day and the remaining days are *Ḥol Ha-mo·eid,* additional days that are awarded a kind of semi-holiday status. This accords with the simple meaning of the biblical text at Leviticus

23:35, "The first day shall be a sacred occasion." In the Diaspora, however, the second day is considered a festival day as well and is called: *yom tov sheini shel galuyot,* "the second festival day of the Diaspora."

This much-maligned practice of an extra festival day deserves an explanation. In ancient times, the holy days were not set by a fixed calendar, but were rather determined based on careful observation of the lunar cycle. In an elaborate system of notification honed over the generations, witnesses would come before a religious court and testify that the new moon had been sighted and then, through a system of messengers and bonfires, the word was spread near and far (*M* Rosh Ha-shanah 2:2–5). This system was obviously predicated on the assumption that the entire Jewish population of the world could be reached efficiently by messengers traveling on foot or carried forward by animals, but this stopped being the case early in Jewish history. To make absolutely sure, then, that the "correct" day was never missed, the rabbis of the Diaspora established a two-day festival. Surely one of the days would be the right one! With the establishment of the calendar we now use, however, it became possible to fix the date of each holiday exactly, thereby rendering the doubling of the festivals theoretically unnecessary. Yet, when the issue came before the rabbis even in talmudic times, they refused to cancel what had already been put in place, saying, either regretfully or proudly—there's no clear way to know—*minhag avoteinu b'yadeinu,* the custom of our ancestors is inviolate and cannot be set aside by changing circumstance (*BT* Beitzah 4b). Of course, that is not invariably how things are. Some ancient customs rooted in realities that have long since ceased to exist have indeed been allowed to fall into desuetude, and there is a responsum of the CJLS permitting communities who so desire to observe only one day of the pilgrimage festivals (*Proceedings of the CJLS 1927–1970,* pp. 1247–1258). This innovative leniency has not gained much popularity in Conservative congregations, however, and, while some congregations observe only one day, most communities continue to observe the two days of each festival outside of Israel as a way of preserving one of the most traditional distinctions between life in the Holy Land and life in the Diaspora. With respect to ritual and liturgy, the laws and customs for the second day are the same as those that govern the first, including the recitation of She-ḥeḥeyyanu on the second night when lighting the candles and when saying Kiddush.

The laws for lighting candles on Sukkot are the same as on Shabbat (except that the custom of the waving of one's hands over the flames and covering the eyes while the blessing is recited is not done as on Shabbat because a flame can be transferred on Sukkot as on the other festivals and there is no need to have lit the candles before reciting the blessing.) The blessing is *barukh attah adonai, eloheinu, melekh ha-olam, asher kidd'shanu b'mitzvotav v'tzivvanu l'hadlik neir shel yom tov* ("Praised are You, Adonai, our God, Sovereign of the universe, who, sanctifying us with divine commandments, has commanded us to kindle the festival lamp"). If it is Shabbat as well, the blessing concludes: *l'hadlik neir shel shabbat v'shel yom tov* ("to kindle the Shabbat and festival lamp"). This is followed by the She-heḥeyyanu blessing, which (as mentioned above) is recited on both nights.

Sukkot ends with a festival that is both part of it yet also distinct. Its name, Sh'mini Atzeret ("The Eighth Day of Assembly"), points to its connection with Sukkot. Yet the *halakhah* treats it as a separate and distinct festival in many contexts, including, for example, the laws that govern mourning. In the Diaspora, Sh'mini Atzeret is observed for two days, but the second day has its own name: Simḥat Torah. Also, each of these days has its own rituals and liturgy. (In Israel, the rituals and liturgical flourishes connected with both Sh'mini Atzeret and Simḥat Torah are observed on the same day.)

The historical aspect of Sukkot is emphasized by the Bible itself: "You shall live in *sukkot* (booths) for seven days. Indeed, all citizens of Israel shall live in *sukkot,* in order that future generations may know that I caused the Israelite people to live in *sukkot* when I brought them out of the land of Egypt" (Leviticus 23:42–43). But the Bible also speaks of the holiday in agricultural terms, as at Leviticus 23:39: "On the fifteenth day of the seventh month when you have gathered in the yield of your land, you shall observe the festival of the Eternal for seven days." The symbols of the festival are rooted mostly in one of these two conceptions. The *sukkah,* the temporary hut we erect to remind ourselves of the way our ancestors lived and traveled during their years in the wilderness, adds a historical aspect to the holiday, while the *mitzvah* of taking up the *arba·ah minim* emphasizes the agricultural dimension of the festival. It is not surprising, therefore, that this multi-dimensional holiday has several different names, each focusing on a different aspect of its observance or background. The name *ḥag ha-sukkot,* the most familiar, means literally "the holiday of the *sukkot* [booths]." The name *ḥag ha-asif* ("the harvest festival") refers to the agricultural aspect of the holiday. And, as the rabbis considered Sukkot to be the quintessential festival, they referred to it simply as the *he-ḥag* ("*the* festival"), with no further qualification.

Sukkot is thus a very happy holiday (also known as *z'man simḥateinu,* the time of our rejoicing), and its contrast with the preceding High Holidays could not be more dramatic. The High Holidays are spent mostly indoors and are devoted to prayer and deep, introspective contemplation. Sukkot, on the other hand, is spent mostly outdoors and is devoted to different kinds of celebration and rejoicing. Rosh Hashanah and Yom Kippur are very cerebral festival days, but Sukkot has a far more physical feel to it. The High Holidays engage the mind, but Sukkot engages the body as well, as we build our *sukkot,* climb up ladders to put the special roofs in place, and wave and shake our *lulavim* during the synagogue service. As mentioned above, one tradition (cf. the gloss of the Rema to *SA* Oraḥ Ḥayyim 625:1) teaches that the building of the *sukkah* should begin right after Yom Kippur, and some go so far as to suggest that the first nails should be hammered into the *sukkah* immediately after the end of the fast! Clearly tradition understands the two festivals, Yom Kippur and Sukkot, as ends of a single continuum and, in turn, this is intended to remind the faithful that Yom Kippur could not exist without Sukkot: the world of intellectual and spiritual pursuits cannot be separated from the world of physical and bodily endeavor and, at least in the end, one without the other can never feel totally right or lead to spiritual wholeness.

The Sukkah

The *sukkah* has some very basic requirements, but beyond these rules its construction is left to one's imagination and creativity. It must be built under the open sky, rather than under a tree or in a larger room. It usually consists of four walls that may be made of any material (*SA* Oraḥ Ḥayyim 630:1), but it will also suffice if there are at least two complete walls and part of a third. The *sukkah* should be made sturdy enough to survive normal weather conditions in whatever climate the *sukkah* is built (*SA* Oraḥ Ḥayyim 630:10).

At best, *sukkot* are fragile things. In many diaspora communities, it is not uncommon to experience severe autumn weather during the holiday. Some readers may remember when Hurricane Gloria made her way up the east coast of North America just before Sukkot in 1985. In the community I served at the time, everyone came to synagogue unhappy and depressed that first morning because the wind had decimated the *sukkot* in our costal community. They were greeted by their rabbi, who happily informed them that any *sukkah* still standing after a hurricane was probably not too kosher a *sukkah* in the first place! (The second chapter of *M* Sukkot teaches that a *sukkah* that falls may be rebuilt on the intermediate days of the festival in order to fulfill the biblical requirement at Deuteronomy 16:13 that for "seven days you shall observe the festival of Sukkot.")

One of the oldest rules concerning the *sukkah* is that it may not be more than thirty feet tall (*M* Sukkot 1:1), nor should it be less than about three feet high. However, it should be at least big enough to fit one person inside, although most of our *sukkot* are significantly larger than that (*MT* Hilkhot Shofar V'sukkah V'lulav 4:1). It cannot be shaped like a teepee or a lean-to because it is considered indispensable that the *sukkah* have a roof.

In fact, most of the requirements for a *sukkah* revolve around the roof and its materials.

The *s'khakh,* or roof covering, must be material that grew from the ground but which is not still attached to the ground. (Among other reasons, this is why a *sukkah* may not be built under a tree.) Additionally, the material used for *s'khakh* must not be deemed susceptible to contamination with ritual impurity. Materials like metal or cloth can become ritually impure and therefore cannot be used as a roof covering. Hides cannot be used because they do not grow from the ground. Vines or leafy trees cannot be used because they are still attached to the ground. It should also be pointed out that, although grass and leaves meet all the technical requirements for kosher *s'khakh,* they should not be used because they dry out so quickly and become unattractive. The most commonly used materials for *s'khakh* today are some mixture of pine or other evergreen coniferous tree branches and/or bamboo poles or bamboo mats. If the *s'khakh* becomes dried out over the holidays, it is important to replenish it so that it is dense enough and remains attractive.

The density of the covering is also an important consideration. The general rule is that it should not be so dense that one cannot see the sky during the day or the stars at night, but neither should it be so loosely layered over the frame that the amount of light that shines through to the ground exceeds the amount of shadow cast by the *s'khakh.* Additionally, there should be no gaps in the *s'khakh* longer or wider than a single foot (Klein, p. 161; *SA* Oraḥ Ḥayyim 631:1). Obviously, this calls for a lot of subjective judgment as to whether there is too much *s'khakh* or too little, but people generally tend to put too little *s'khakh* atop their *sukkot* rather than too much. Therefore, one should be especially careful in making sure the *s'khakh* is dense enough. It is also customary to decorate *sukkot* with posters, drawings, and colorful paper, and also with fruit and vegetable hangings. Many synagogues today even have "*sukkah* hops" during which the participants visit various *sukkot* in the community and admire their creativity and beauty. While not technically required, all this extra adornment falls under the general category of *hiddur mitzvah,* the rabbinic injunction not merely to perform the *mitzvot* correctly, but in as aesthetically pleasing a way as possible.

It is not actually a *mitzvah* to build a *sukkah,* merely to "dwell" in one—which requirement, in the opinion of most authorities, is satisfied by eating there. Although one could theoretically eat solely in other people's or a synagogue's *sukkah,* the *mitzvah* should be pursued personally by all Jews with the space and opportunity to build one themselves. Today there are prefabricated *sukkah* kits that put this *mitzvah* within the reach of almost everyone. Some synagogue communities even organize volunteers to help less able congregants put up their own *sukkot*. Apartment dwellers and others who cannot build their own *sukkot*, however, should not feel exempt from the *mitzvah*, nor should they imagine that they can fulfill the commandment by belonging to a community that builds a communal *sukkah* without actually frequenting it during the festival.

Because it is a *mitzvah* to use the *sukkah* but not technically to build one, there is no blessing recited upon the construction of a *sukkah*. However, there is a benediction recited as part of the pre-meal ritual when dining in a *sukkah: barukh attah adonai, eloheinu, melekh ha-olam, asher kidd'shanu b'mitzvotav v'tzivvanu leisheiv ba-sukkah* ("Praised are You, Adonai, our God, Sovereign of the universe, who, sanctifying us with divine commandments, has commanded us to dwell in the *sukkah*"). During the intermediary days of the festival, the blessing is recited whenever one takes a formal meal in the *sukkah* immediately after breaking bread, regardless of whether one is dining in one's own *sukkah*, in someone else's, or in a communal *sukkah* (*MT* Hilkhot Shofar V'sukkah V'lulav 6:12; cf. the gloss of the Rema to *SA* Oraḥ Ḥayyim 643:3). On the actual festival days of Sukkot, however, the blessing is recited after Kiddush, but before the She-heḥeyyanu benediction. (There is also a widely observed custom to reverse the final two blessings, the blessing over the *sukkah* and the She-heḥeyyanu, on the second night of Sukkot.) One should formally sit down after reciting the blessing *leisheiv ba-sukkah*, even in communities in which it is customary to remain standing for Kiddush (*SA* Oraḥ Ḥayyim 643:2). A common misconception arises from an overly literal translation of *leisheiv ba-sukkah* as meaning "to sit in the *sukkah*." A more accurate translation is "to dwell in the *sukkah*." In fact one may say this blessing while standing in a *sukkah* if eating a meal while standing, and one should not say it while sitting in a *sukkah* if a meal is not being eaten. Eating in the *sukkah* is, according to the rabbis, how we fulfill the obligation of "dwelling." A house becomes a home when we eat together in it, and similarly, eating together in a *sukkah* is when we fulfill the mitzvah of *leisheiv ba-sukkah* regardless of whether we are actually sitting or standing.

"Dwelling" in the *sukkah* was further understood to mean living there as much as possible during the week of Sukkot. As a result we are encouraged to also sleep in the *sukkah*. This was much more reasonable an expectation in Israel rather than in North America or Europe where many Jews currently find themselves. The weather in Israel at Sukkot time is very conducive to outdoor living, but this will not necessarily be so in the Diaspora. Sleeping in the *sukkah* has taken on an air of adventure in many parts of the world and as an adventure should be encouraged. The concept, however, needs to be balanced by issues of comfort and good judgment when the weather is less than accommodating.

Weather is a major consideration in the fulfillment of many aspects of our Sukkot observance. The observance of the *mitzvot* of Sukkot are supposed to bring us joy and it is not very joyful to sit in a *sukkah* with rain drenching us. The rabbis commented that we are supposed to dwell in the *sukkah* as we dwell in our homes—just as we would not remain in our homes if there was a leaky roof and we were getting wet, so we need not remain in our *sukkah* in inclement weather. There is some discussion as to whether the first two nights of the holiday have a higher degree of importance attached to them with respect to actually eating and saying Kiddush in the *sukkah*. As a result, all effort should be made to eat in the *sukkah* and say Kiddush and the Ha-motzi blessing there on the first two nights, even if it means delaying the start of dinner. Second best would be to find an opportunity to say Kiddush and the Ha-motzi and then finish the meal indoors. And, finally, if the weather really is unforgiving, we may rely on the exemption that certainly applies to all the rest of the nights of Sukkot, which releases us from dwelling in the *sukkah* in bad weather.

But when the weather is nice, we should spend time in our *sukkot* and enjoy their beauty, and we should use every opportunity to do so. Having coffee with friends? Do it in the *sukkah*. Reading or studying? Do it in the *sukkah*. Playing board games with the kids? Do it in the *sukkah*. Not only will you be truly fulfilling the mitzvah *leisheiv ba-sukkah,* but you will be creating wonderful memories of time well spent with family and quality time with God.

The Arba·ah Minim

The other significant *mitzvah* of Sukkot is the taking up of the *arba·ah minim,* literally "the four species," better known as the *lulav* and *etrog* after the two most prominent of the four: the palm branch and the citron. The other two species are attached to the sides of the palm branch: the myrtle branches, called *hadasim,* and the willow branches, called *aravot.* The biblical source for this observance is Leviticus 23:40: "On the first day, you shall take the product of *hadar* trees, branches of palm trees, boughs of leafy trees, and willows of the brook, and you shall rejoice before the Eternal, your God, for seven days." (The rabbis took the reference to the fruit of the *hadar* to be the *etrog* and the boughs of leafy trees to refer to the myrtle.)

There are many wonderful explanations as to why these specific species were chosen for use on Sukkot. One has it that the "four species" represent the different parts of the human body: the tall palm represents the spine, the ovoid myrtle leaf represents the eyes, the willow represents the lips, and the *etrog* represents the heart. By bringing them together, the worshiper indicates his or her intention to unite all the parts of the body in the worship of God. Alternately, the four species are likened to different kinds of Jews. The *etrog,* which has both taste and fragrance, represents the pious, learned Jew who combines learning with good deeds. The *lulav,* which has a pleasant taste but no fragrance, represents the kind of Jew who pursues sacred learning, but who fails to perform many positive deeds. The myrtle, which has a delightful fragrance but no taste, represents the kind of Jew who actively does good deeds, yet who never takes the time to study Torah seriously. Finally, the willow, which possesses neither fragrance nor taste, is representative of the kind of Jew who combines a lack of interest in Torah study with a lack of interest in performing good deeds. Yet the symbolism of the *lulav* and *etrog* suggests they can still all come together in the worship of God. The Jewish world is not complete without all types of people. All have their personal places in God's plan for the world, and each has something personal and irreplaceable to contribute to its fulfillment (*Va-yikra Rabbah* 30:12).

A *lulav* and *etrog* set can be purchased through most synagogues, and should include one palm frond, two willow branches, three myrtle branches, and one *etrog.* When they are attached to the palm, the myrtle is placed on the right of the palm branch, the willow on the left, and the spine of the palm should be facing the holder.

The palm frond should not be too small and certainly not less than about sixteen inches long (Klein, p. 162). Similarly, the myrtle and willow branches should be at least twelve inches long. In any event, the palm frond should be at least four inches longer than the myrtle and the willow (Klein, p. 162; *SA* Oraḥ Ḥayyim 650:1). For its part, the *etrog* should be as least as large as a chicken's egg (Klein, p. 162; *SA* Oraḥ Ḥayyim 648:22).

Because so much of this *mitzvah* centers around the beauty and enjoyment of the *arba·ah minim,* effort should be made to make sure that the various components are kept as attractive and fragrant as possible throughout the festival and to prevent them from drying out. One popular method, for example, is to take the *aravot* out of the holder, wrap them in damp paper toweling, and leave them refrigerated until it is time to use them again the following day.

The *lulav* and *etrog* are used as part of the holiday worship. The general practice is to take the *lulav* and *etrog* in hand just prior to the recitation of the Hallel Service, thus immediately following the Morning Service and before the Torah Service. If for some reason the *mitzvah* is not performed just before Hallel, it may be performed at any time during the day.

The blessing upon taking the *lulav* and *etrog* is: *barukh attah adonai, eloheinu, melekh ha-olam, asher kidd'shanu b'mitzvotav v'tzivvanu al n'tilat lulav* ("Praised are You, Adonai, our God, Sovereign of the universe, who, sanctifying us with divine commandments, has commanded us regarding the taking up of the *lulav*"). The first time each year that one uses the *lulav* and *etrog,* the She-heḥeyyanu blessing is also recited. It is customary to begin by holding the *etrog* upside down, with its tip, called the *pitom,* facing down and the stem facing up. After the two blessings are recited, the *etrog* is turned into the proper position and the *lulav* and *etrog* are held together.

The waving of the *lulav* and *etrog* is done holding the *lulav* with the spine in the right hand and the *etrog* in the left hand. (In some Ashkenazic communities there is a custom that people who are left-handed hold the *lulav* in the left hand and the *etrog* in the right. Uncertain worshipers should consult their rabbis to determine the practice in their communities.) They are then brought together and waved in six directions: to the front, to the right, to the back, to the left, upward, and downward. This same waving procedure is followed each time the *lulav* and *etrog* are waved: first after the original blessings are recited before the Hallel service, and then also during the recitation of the Hallel service when the first two verses of Psalm 118 are recited, then again when the first half of Psalm 118:25 is repeated twice later in the Hallel service, and then yet again when Psalm 118:29 is recited. The waving of the *lulav* corresponds to the verses themselves. Psalm 118:1, for example, has exactly seven words, God's name and six others. The six other words correspond to each of the six directions of the waving mentioned above, but no movement occurs when God's name is recited. Similarly, the beginning phrase of Psalm 118:25 is made up of four words, God's name plus three others. Those three other words, however, have a total of six syllables, and these correspond to the six directions in which the *lulav* is waved. And Psalm 118:29 consists of six words as well. (Readers may consult in this regard Klein, p. 164; *M* Sukkot 3:9; and *BT* Sukkot 37b).

In some ways, the *mitzvah* of the *lulav* and *etrog* presents a bit of a challenge to moderns accustomed to rituals that are transparent in their meaning and easily decipherable. Still, one of the dangers in contemporary Judaism is precisely that we have become overly cerebral in our approach to religion. After the intense High Holiday period of prayer and introspective thought, Sukkot appeals to our senses. We build the *sukkah* with our hands, and we smell the four species and shake them back and forth as a sign of our exuberant sense of thanksgiving to God for all that we have in this world. Judaism makes demands both on the intellect and the spirit, both on the brain and on the heart, and Sukkot is a vibrant reminder of this lesson.

The *lulav* and *etrog* are not used on Shabbat for the same reason the *shofar* is not sounded when Rosh Hashanah falls on Shabbat: to prevent the desecration of the Shabbat by those who might feel compelled to carry the ritual accouterments of the festival to a synagogue. Anticipating this potential problem, the rabbis established that these items not be used at all on Shabbat. We strive to keep the willow and myrtle fresh to make the *mitzvah* pleasant. If the *pitom* of the *etrog* (that is, the tip on opposite side from the green stem) breaks off, it is invalid for use and a blessing should not be recited until a suitable replacement is found.

Sukkot at Home

Sukkot begins, as was explained above, with the lighting of the candles. As on Shabbat, the candles should be lit no later than eighteen minutes before sunset on the first night and they should be lit an hour later on the second night. Some have the custom of lighting the festival candles in the *sukkah* on Sukkot, but this should not be done if it seems likely that the wind will blow them out. Others light the candles in the house and then go into the *sukkah* to recite Kiddush.

If Sukkot falls on a Thursday and/or Friday, the problem of cooking for Shabbat necessitates an *eiruv tavshilin* as explained above for Rosh Hashanah. To make an *eiruv tavshilin,* one must place two cooked items (a roll, a slice of bread and a cooked or roasted dish, like a piece of meat or fish) on a plate and then recite a blessing. This blessing, found in any standard prayerbook, is the regular blessing for the performance of commandments and ends with the words *al mitzvat eiruv* (by commanding us regarding the *eiruv*). One must then recite an additional declaration: "By means of this *eiruv,* we are permitted to bake, cook, warm, kindle lights, and make all the necessary preparations during the festival for Shabbat, we and all who live in this place." Ideally, this food should be consumed on Shabbat to demonstrate that it was prepared for Shabbat.

The Evening Service follows the standard festival format. Kiddush is not said in its usual place toward the end of the service, however, but is deferred and then recited in the *sukkah* after the end of the service. The regular festival Kiddush is recited with the proper references to Sukkot. On the first night, the Kiddush is followed first by the blessing regarding the *mitzvah* of "dwelling" in the *sukkah* and then by the She-heḥeyyanu (which applies both to the recitation of Kiddush and the act of "dwelling" in the *sukkah.*) This is followed by *n'tilat yadayim* and then the Ha-motzi blessing. On the second night it is customary to recite the She-heḥeyyanu after the Kiddush but before the blessing regarding the *mitzvah* of "dwelling" in the *sukkah,* which is then followed by the Ha-motzi blessing (as there remains doubt regarding which of the two days is the first day of the festival but no doubt that this will not be the first time you dwell in the *sukkah*).

There is also a wonderful custom developed by the mystics of welcoming certain specific honored guests into the *sukkah* each night. These spectral visitors, called the *ushpizin* ("guests"), are traditionally identified as Abraham, Isaac, Jacob, Joseph, Moses, Aaron, and David. In addition to these guests, some also welcome the matriarchs and female leaders of ancient Israel: Sarah, Rebecca, Leah, Rachel, Miriam, Deborah, and Ruth. This modern custom follows the logic that, if we include women in our *minyanim,* then we should also include them as honored guests in our *sukkah.*

Sukkot in the Synagogue

On the mornings of Sukkot, the Morning Service and the Musaf Service follow the standard festival format. After the end of the Morning Service, we recite the blessing over the *lulav* and *etrog,* then Hallel. Two Torah scrolls are then taken from the Ark. From the first we read Leviticus 22:26–23:44, which describes the festivals of Israel in some detail. This reading is divided into five *aliyot* unless it coincides with Shabbat, in which case it is divided into seven *aliyot* instead. From the second Torah, we read the *maftir* portion. This reading, Numbers 29:12–16, describes the sacrifices that were offered in the Temple on Sukkot. The *haftarah* for the first day of Sukkot is the fourteenth chapter of the book of the prophet Zechariah, a vision about the coming of the messiah, which tradition teaches us to expect on Sukkot. On the second day of Sukkot, the same Torah portions are read, but the *haftarah* is 1 Kings 8:2–21, which tells how King Solomon dedicated the Temple on Sukkot.

After the Musaf Service, we recite special prayers called Hoshanot. The Ark is opened, a Torah scroll is removed, and a procession of individuals carrying the *lulav* and *etrog* walks around the sanctuary. There are different Hoshanot prayers for each day of Sukkot, each named for its opening words. On Shabbat, a special version of the Hoshanot is recited. The Ark is opened, but a scroll is not removed and there is no procession around the sanctuary. (The *lulav* and *etrog* are not used on Shabbat either, of course.)

The Hoshanot ceremony has its origins in the Temple. According to the Mishnah at *M* Sukkot 4:5, there was a similar procession with the *lulav* and *etrog* in Temple times, but it was led by the priests around the altar in the Temple courtyard. In his *Or Ḥadash: A Commentary on Siddur Sim Shalom for Shabbat and Festivals* (New York: The Rabbinical Assembly, 2003, p. 200), Rabbi Reuven Hammer suggests that it is possible that even in Temple times the people joined in this procession. At the very least, they joined in the singing that accompanied it, quite possibly singing the very same Hoshanot prayers that we recite today. Today, the Hoshanot procession is one of the highlights of Sukkot in every synagogue.

The Intermediate Days of Sukkot

The intermediate days of Sukkot and Passover are called *ḥol ha-mo·eid,* literally, "the 'weekday' [part] of the festival." And they have an unusual character to go with their unusual name, combining some features of festival days with others associated with normal weekdays to create a kind of day that is wholly unique. On these intermediate days of Sukkot, we continue to eat in the *sukkah,* to wave the *lulav* and *etrog* every morning at services, and to recite the complete Hallel. The Torah is also read each of these days, as four individuals are called forward for *aliyot.* (This number makes perfect sense in this context as well: one more than a regular weekday and one less than a full festival day.) A special Torah reading is also designated for the Shabbat of *ḥol ha-mo·eid* Sukkot, Exodus 33:12–34:36. The *maftir* portion on that intermediary Shabbat describes the sacrifices that were offered in the Temple on that particular day. The *haftarah* is Ezekiel 38:18–39:16, a passage that deals with the End of Days and forecasts that a dramatic victory for justice and peace will take place on Sukkot. It is also customary to read the Book of Ecclesiastes (popularly called by its Hebrew name, Kohelet) on the Shabbat that falls during Sukkot or, if none does, then on Sh'mini Atzeret.

The dual nature of *ḥol ha-mo·eid,* half-holiday and half-weekday, is reflected in the ongoing debate about whether or not one should don *t'fillin* for part of the Morning Service or not at all (*SA* Oraḥ Ḥayyim 31:2, cf. the comment of the Rema *ad loc.*). In general, *t'fillin* are not worn on Shabbat or on holidays because the days themselves are considered signs of the covenant, which is also the function of *t'fillin.* If *ḥol ha-mo·eid* were to be considered more of a festival day, we would not don *t'fillin.* If it were to be considered more of a weekday, we would. But, since the days of *ḥol ha-mo·eid* are in some ways in both categories, we are left with a dilemma. Not surprisingly, custom varies regarding the issue of putting on *t'fillin* on *ḥol ha-mo·eid.* Some Jews do and some do not. But even those Jews who don their *t'fillin* on *ḥol ha-mo·eid* remove them before Hallel as a nod toward the special nature of the day. Individuals should follow their family's custom in the matter of *t'fillin* on *ḥol ha-mo·eid.* If one has no such family tradition, one should follow the custom of one's synagogue community. In cases of uncertainty, a rabbi should be consulted and his or her counsel followed. Generally speaking, if one dons one's *t'fillin* during *ḥol ha-mo·eid,* one should recite the normal blessings. There are those, however, who do not recite the blessings and yet others who recite them inaudibly.

There are also special rules concerning funerals on *ḥol ha-mo·eid.* Under normal circumstances, we do not permit funerals on holidays. On *ḥol ha-mo·eid,* the general practice is to permit burial, but to defer formal *shivah* observance until after the festival is finally over. It is customary, however, not to include long eulogies at funerals that take place during the intermediate days of festivals.

Musaf is appended to the morning services on each day of *ḥol ha-mo·eid.* In addition, a paragraph beginning with the words *ya·aleh v'yavo* is added during every recitation of the Amidah and the Grace after Meals during this period. It is customary to greet one another by saying: *mo·adim l'simḥah* ("May the holiday be joyous") or *a guten moyed* ("Have a good holiday").

Hoshana Rabbah

Although the fifth intermediate day of Sukkot is known as Hoshana Rabbah, it is technically just the last day of *ḥol ha-mo·eid.* To understand the unusual aspects of Hoshana Rabbah, it is important to understand that Hoshana Rabbah is considered the conclusion of the long High Holiday season. There are, in fact, a number of connections between Hoshana Rabbah and the High Holidays. The period of *t'shuvah* that began on the first day of Elul is extended until, and concluded on, Hoshana Rabbah. Thus, Hoshana Rabbah is understood as the final opportunity during this season of heightened spiritual awareness to do *t'shuvah,* hence a final appeal for God's mercy and forgiveness. The custom of striking the willow branches described below is connected to this theme of repentance. It teaches us that just as it is extremely difficult to separate the willow leaves from the willow branch, so too is it difficult for us to separate ourselves from our bad habits and evil ways. In addition, the twenty-seventh psalm, which congregations begin reciting on the first day of Elul, is recited for the final time on Hoshana Rabbah. (Some congregations end their recitation of this psalm on Yom Kippur, however.) The concept of Hoshana Rabbah being the very end of the penitential season is also reflected in the traditional wish of *a guten kvitel* extended by many Ashkenazic Jews to others on this day. Literally meaning "a good record," the greeting refers to the final verdict on our lives said to be written up during the period of judgment and finally entered into the record on Hoshana Rabbah.

Thus, because of its status as the very last day of the penitential season, Hoshana Rabbah has some of the ambience of festival days as well. This is seen in the ways the Morning Service is expanded to be more like a festival than a weekday morning. In the P'sukei D'zimra section of the service, for example, additional psalms are added to make it feel almost (but not entirely) like a festival day or like Shabbat—and similar additions are found throughout the Morning Service. By far, however, the most significant change is during the Hoshanot. At the end of every other day of *ḥol ha-mo·eid,* a Torah scroll is taken from the Ark and a procession with the *lulav* and *etrog* is conducted around the sanctuary. On Hoshana Rabbah, however, it is customary to remove all the Torah scrolls from the Ark and to hold seven distinct processions around the sanctuary. After these processions are completed, the *lulav* and *etrog* are set aside and a bunch of five fresh willow branches called *hoshanot* are taken in hand and struck against the floor or against a seat hard enough to separate at least some leaves from the branch. It is an unfamiliar ritual to many, but any who attend the Hoshana Rabbah service will be struck by the dramatic finale this unobtrusive, under-recognized semi-holiday provides for the entire High Holiday season. In the end, the simple act of beating the *hoshanot* says it all. No one can return to God merely by wishing to do so. And it is precisely the wrenching, difficult, painful act of separating oneself from sin that beating the *hoshanot* symbolizes.

Sh'mini Atzeret

The final two days of Sukkot are, at least formally, a totally separate holiday. The Torah itself makes this clear and unclear at the same time, defining Sh'mini Atzeret as the eighth day of Sukkot at the same time that it grants it independent existence in the festival calendar: "Seven days you shall bring gifts to God," the Torah states, "and then, on the eighth day, you shall observe a sacred festival and bring a gift to God; it is to be a solemn gathering" (Hebrew: *atzeret;* Leviticus 23:36).

Unfortunately, the Torah does not offer any additional details regarding the nature of this eighth day of assembly. Some suggest that since the pilgrims of ancient times had traveled long distances to be in Jerusalem for Sukkot, it was a merely a kindness for Scripture to add one additional day of enforced leisure and worship to the festival. Others imagined that it was, so to speak, God whom the Torah was treating kindly, almost as though God could be imagined to wish for one final day to enjoy the pilgrims' presence in the Holy City (Rashi on Leviticus 23:36). Still others suggest that it demonstrates a reluctance on the pilgrims' own part to leave God's holy presence. But whatever the real reason for Sh'mini Atzeret, the holiday season finally concludes at the end of Sukkot. After celebrating all these demanding yet endlessly satisfying holy days, it is now time to return to a more normal routine.

If it is not clear exactly what Scripture means Sh'mini Atzeret to be, it is clear what it is not. It is not, for example, Sukkot. As a result, we do not continue the observances that are most notably connected to that holiday: the *lulav* and the *etrog* are not used during the service and dwelling in the *sukkah* is not required. There are actually a variety of customs with respect to eating in the *sukkah* on Sh'mini Atzeret. Some people do not use the *sukkah* at all, but others continue to eat in it and even to say Kiddush in it. No one, however, recites the blessing over "dwelling" in the *sukkah* on Sh'mini Atzeret, however, because doing so is not, formally speaking, the fulfillment of a commandment.

The laws for lighting candles on Sh'mini Atzeret are the same as on Shabbat (except that the custom of the waving of one's hands over the flames and covering the eyes while the blessing is recited is not done as on Shabbat, because a flame can be transferred on Sh'mini Atzeret as on the other festivals and there is no need to have lit the candles before reciting the blessing). The blessing is *barukh attah adonai, eloheinu, melekh ha-olam, asher kidd'shanu b'mitzvotav v'tzivvanu l'hadlik neir shel yom tov* ("Praised are You, Adonai, our God, Sovereign of the universe, who, sanctifying us with divine commandments, has commanded us to kindle the festival lamp"). This is followed by the She-heḥeyyanu blessing, which as mentioned above is recited on Sh'mini Atzeret and Simḥat Torah. In addition a special Yizkor candle is lit just prior to the formal Sh'mini Atzeret candles by those who will be reciting the Yizkor Service on Sh'mini Atzeret. There is no blessing recited on the kindling of this candle, although many prayerbooks include appropriate devotional material to recite just before lighting the memorial candle.

The liturgy of Sh'mini Atzeret is very much like the liturgy of other festival days. Where the worshiper is called upon to name the festival, however, the phrase *yom ha-sh'mini ḥag ha-atzeret ha-zeh* ("this eighth day of festival observance") is inserted into the text of the prayers. The Torah reading for Sh'mini Atzeret is Deuteronomy 14:22–16:17, which describes the festival calendar of ancient Israel. The reading is divided into five *aliyot* when the festival falls on a weekday, and into seven *aliyot* when it falls on Shabbat. The *maftir* portion read from the second Torah is Numbers 29:35–30:1. The *haftarah* is 1 Kings 8:54–66, an appropriate selection because it cites the blessing that begins with the words *ba-yom ha-sh'mini* (on the eighth day) declaimed by King Solomon on the eighth day of the celebration dedicating the Temple in Jerusalem.

Two notable liturgical additions for Sh'mini Atzeret are the recitation of the Yizkor Service (described in detail above in my section about Yom Kippur) and the prayer for rain that is added into the second blessing of the Amidah during the Musaf Service when the cantor or prayer leader repeats the prayer aloud. (The text of this prayer may be found in any traditional prayerbook.) It is customary for the cantor or the prayer leader to don a white robe, colloquially called a *kittel* by Ashkenazic Jews, for the recitation of this prayer and to use a special melody, reminiscent of certain tunes sung during the High Holidays, in chanting the prayer. The prayer concludes with a declaration that it is God who causes the wind to blow and the rain to fall. From this moment forward, these words—the Hebrew is *mashiv ha-ru·aḥ u-morid ha-gashem*—are interpolated into the second blessing of the Amidah and remain in place until the prayer for dew is recited on the first day of Passover. It is the custom in some synagogues for worshipers to include these words in the Amidah when it is recited silently, even before the cantor or prayer leader has changed them aloud in the repetition of the Amidah (comment of the Rema to *SA* Oraḥ Ḥayyim 114:2). Other congregations wait until after the cantor or prayer leader chants the prayer before instructing worshipers to include it in their personal prayers. In such synagogues, therefore, the first time worshipers include the words *mashiv ha-ru·aḥ u-morid ha-gashem* in the silent Amidah would be during the Afternoon Service on Sh'mini Atzeret.

We begin including this prayer for rain at the end of Sukkot and stop reciting it just before Passover because pilgrims to Jerusalem in ancient times did not wish for rain during either pilgrimage holiday.

The prayer for rain recited on Sh'mini Atzeret and its companion prayer for dew recited on the first day of Passover are intimately connected to the cycle of seasons in the Land of Israel. The ancients needed little reminder of the importance of regular rainfall (or of life-sustaining dew during the dry season), but it sometimes takes a hurricane or an earthquake to remind moderns to what extent we remain at the mercy of natural forces far beyond human control. This is one of the reasons we retain these prayers, even outside the Land of Israel where they are the most relevant in terms of the actual climate. Reciting them is also a dramatic affirmation of the connection Jewish worshipers the world over maintain to the Land of Israel.

Simḥat Torah

Simḥat Torah literally means "the joy of Torah" and is the special name given to what would otherwise be the second day of Sh'mini Atzeret in the Diaspora, the day on which the annual cycle of Torah readings begins and ends. There is no biblical reference to this holiday because it came into existence after the close of the canon, and it is not even mentioned in the Talmud. Since Simḥat Torah was a relatively late addition to the calendar, most liturgical texts continue to refer to the day in exactly the same terms as Sh'mini Atzeret, as *yom ha-sh'mini ḥag ha-atzeret ha-zeh* ("this eighth day of festival observance"). It also explains why in Israel, where there is only one day of each scriptural holiday other than

Rosh Hashanah, the celebration connected in the Diaspora with Simḥat Torah and the Yizkor Service both take place on the one day of Sh'mini Atzeret.

The celebration of Simḥat Torah begins in the evening.

The laws for lighting candles on Simḥat Torah are the same as on Shabbat (except that the custom of the waving of one's hands over the flames and covering the eyes while the blessing is recited is not done as on Shabbat because a flame can be transferred on Simḥat Torah as on the other festivals and there is no need to have lit the candles before reciting the blessing). The blessing is *barukh attah adonai, eloheinu, melekh ha-olam, asher kidd'shanu b'mitzvotav v'tzivvanu l'hadlik neir shel yom tov* ("Praised are You, Adonai, our God, Sovereign of the universe, who, sanctifying us with divine commandments, has commanded us to kindle the festival lamp"). This is followed by the Sheheḥeyyanu blessing, which as mentioned above is recited on both nights.

The Evening Service in the synagogue follows the usual format for festival evenings. After the Full Kaddish is recited at the end of the service, however, worshipers remove the Torah scrolls from the Ark and make a series of circuits, called *hakkafot,* around the sanctuary. These circuits are joyous in nature and many express their joy at the completion of yet another cycle of Torah readings by singing and dancing around the sanctuary with the Torah. There are seven *hakkafot* so as to give as many people as possible a chance to carry and rejoice with the Torah scrolls. A different prayer of introduction is chanted at the outset of each of the seven *hakkafot,* but it is customary before the scrolls are even taken from the Ark to recite a special hymn called Attah Horeita La-da·at, a collection of biblical verses. In most congregations, each verse of the hymn is recited aloud by the cantor or prayer leader and then repeated by the congregation. In others, different members of the congregation take turns reciting the verses aloud, and they are then repeated by the congregation. The atmosphere in the sanctuary is upbeat and lively in a way that is truly unique as the congregation openly expresses its love for the Torah and for Jewish tradition.

After the *hakkafot,* all but one of the scrolls are returned to the Ark and a brief passage from the last *parashah* of the Torah, divided into three *aliyot,* is read from that scroll. This is the only time during the year when the Torah is read formally in the evening as part of the synagogue service.

The celebration continues the next morning. Until the Torah is taken from the Ark, the service follows the format of the usual festival Morning Service. (In congregations in which the *kohanim* ascend to the *bimah* to recite the Priestly Blessing, however, they do so during the Morning Service on Simḥat Torah rather than during the Musaf Service.) Once again the Attah Horeita La-da·at hymn is recited. Once again, all the scrolls are removed from the Ark and another seven *hakkafot* are made around the sanctuary, just as on the evening before. This time, however, when most of the scrolls are returned to the Ark, three are kept out. The end of Deuteronomy is read from the first scroll, the beginning of Genesis from the second, and the *maftir* reading from the Book of Numbers from the third.

It is customary for everyone, or almost everybody, present to have an *aliyah* to the Torah on Simḥat Torah (comment of the Rema to *SA* Oraḥ Ḥayyim 669:1). In some synagogues, this is done by having several simultaneous Torah readings in order to make time for everyone to have a personal *aliyah*. In other synagogues, there is one central reading of the Torah and large groups of people are called forward for each *aliyah*. While the practice of calling up many people at once for an *aliyah* is not without its detractors (see Rabbi Avram Reisner's responsum on joint *aliyot* in *CJLS Responsa 1991–2000,* pp. 21–35, it also has its supporters and it appears to have become the dominant practice in many contemporary congregations.

It is also customary to call all the children forward for an *aliyah* to the Torah. Since they are not yet old enough to have an *aliyah* of their own, it is customary for one adult, sometimes the rabbi, to lead them in reciting the blessings. A large *tallit* is held over the children's heads and, after the final Torah blessings are recited, the blessing that Jacob gave his grandchildren (as found at Genesis 48:15–16) is recited as well to expresses the congregation's prayers for its children. Some congregations have beautifully embellished this custom by designing a special covering to hold over the children for this *aliyah*.

The last *aliyot* to the Torah are special honors and are given to people whom the community wishes especially to honor. The first is called the Bridegroom of the Torah or the Bride of the Torah (the *ḥatan torah* or *kallat torah*) and is the individual honored with the final *aliyah* of the entire Torah reading cycle. The second is called the Bridegroom of Genesis or the Bride of Genesis (the *ḥatan b'reishit* or *kallat b'reishit*) and is the individual honored with the first *aliyah* of the new Torah reading cycle.

There is a special, very elaborate formula that is recited to call these honorees forward. These honors are often further embellished by calling the honorees forward with great fanfare, by allowing them to be accompanied by their families, or even by escorting them to the *bimah* under an actual wedding canopy or a large prayer shawl.

It is customary for the Torah reader to pause before chanting the final verse of the entire Torah, as is done when chanting the final verse of each of the five books of the Torah, to give the congregation the opportunity to rise and chant the final words out loud, thus ensuring that no one miss the climactic last few words of the annual cycle of Torah readings. The reader then repeats the final words and the entire congregation joins in the recitation of *ḥazak, ḥazak, v'nit·ḥazzeik* ("May we be strong, may we be strong, and may we strengthen one another").

It is also customary when reciting the opening verses of the Torah, from its beginning through Genesis 2:3, to have the congregation participate by pausing at the end of each of the days of creation so that the congregation may recite the concluding words out loud first. These words are then repeated by the reader.

The balance of the liturgy follows the normal format for festivals.

The warm ambience that prevails in the synagogue on Simḥat Torah reflects the spirit of a close and loving community that has made the journey together through the long holiday season and that, as a result of that journey, has come closer to God and to each other.

The series of penitential prayers called *Taḥanun* is omitted from the daily service through the end of the month of Tishrei.

Ḥeshvan

Following Tishrei, with all its holidays, the next month in the Hebrew calendar is Ḥeshvan, also known as Marḥeshvan. It is one of the only two months in the Jewish calendar that does not contain a single Jewish holiday, major or minor. As a result, folk etymology suggests that its alternate name is a compound formed of the Hebrew *mar* (bitter) and the name of the month, although this is apparently neither etymologically nor historically correct.

Ḥanukkah

Although both Ḥanukkah and Purim are considered minor festivals to which the laws regarding the prohibition of labor on festivals do not apply, both are significant in their own right and both have won a special place in the hearts of the Jewish people.

Some might find it strange to refer to Ḥanukkah as a "minor" festival, given that it is probably one of the best-known of all the Jewish holidays. But the fact is that Ḥanukkah has fared well in contemporary times for reasons unrelated to its traditional place in the pecking order of Jewish festivals. For Jews in the Diaspora, Ḥanukkah has benefited from its proximity to Christmas. In Israel, Ḥanukkah has benefited (far more reasonably) from the resonance its themes of national pride and identity have with the core values of the modern State of Israel.

The historical narrative that forms the background for Ḥanukkah is found in the First and Second Books of Maccabees, works preserved as part of the extra-canonical library known as the Apocrypha, as well as in some other ancient works, including the final sections of the Book of Daniel. Modern scholars debate the actual sequence of events that led to the Maccabean revolt, the success of which led to the institution of Ḥanukkah as a festival. However, the basic picture is clear enough. After the death of Alexander the Great, the Jewish homeland passed back and forth between the Seleucid Empire (based in Syria) and the Ptolemaic Empire (based in Egypt) until the land was firmly part of the Syrian empire named for Seleucus I (c. 358–281 B.C.E.), its first emperor. Some suggest that the Greeks grew impatient with Jewish resistance to Hellenization, and also with the slow spread of Greek culture, ideas, and spiritual/religious values in the wake of Alexander's death and the dismemberment of his empire among his generals. Seeking to speed up the process, then, Antiochus IV Epiphanes, the Seleucid king, decreed that the Temple should incorporate sacrifices to Greek gods and that the law of Moses be rescinded as the law of the land. This development appealed to some assimilationist segments of the Jewish population, but dramatically less to the traditionalists among them, who rose up in a revolt led by one Matityahu (sometimes called Mattathias in English) and his sons, foremost among them the one history would eventually call Judah the Maccabee. (The names are a bit obscure. "Maccabee" is sometimes derived from the Hebrew word for "hammer," thus making Judah the ancient Jewish equivalent of Charles Martel. The term "Hasmonean," also of obscure meaning and etymology, is used to describe his family as well.) In the first war ever fought for religious freedom, Judah, his brothers, and their followers drove the Hellenizers from the Temple, if not entirely from Jerusalem, and then managed to reestablish Jewish sovereignty. Other scholars, utilizing the same historical data, describe the revolt against the Seleucids as far more of a civil war between Jews enamored of the Hellenistic ideal and the so-called "community of the pious," whose members were more zealous for the preservation and maintenance of Jewish law. When these two sides could not reconcile, Antiochus intervened on the side of the Hellenizers. The exact details of the conflict may never be known with certainty, but all scholars agree that, once the fuse was lit, an armed struggle ensued and the eventual result was the reestablishment of Jewish sovereignty over the Temple and throughout the Land of Israel. Among the first acts of the newly victorious traditionalists was the rededication of the Temple. When this was accomplished, a festival was proclaimed to commemorate the event.

The First Book of Maccabees (4:52–59) describes the inauguration of the festival in these terms: "Now on the twenty-fifth day of the ninth month, which is called the month of Kisleiv . . . they rose up in the morning and offered sacrifice according to the law upon the new altar of burnt offerings, which they had made. At the very season and on the very day that the gentiles had profaned it, it was now rededicated with song. . . . And so they celebrated the dedication of the altar for eight days. . . . Moreover, Judah and his brothers, with the whole congregation of Israel, ordained that the days of the dedication of the altar should be observed with mirth and gladness in that same season from year to year for eight days, starting on the twenty-fifth day of the month of Kisleiv."

In the talmudic era, the rabbis understood this event not so much as the historical victory of the Hasmoneans over the Seleucids, but as a miraculous triumph of God's might in defense of the Jewish people. The talmudic discussion of these events (at *BT* Shabbat 21b) describes the Maccabees and their followers entering the Temple that had been defiled by the supporters of the Seleucids. Finding only enough consecrated oil to relight the Temple candelabrum, the *m'norah,* for one day and knowing that it would take a full week to produce new supplies of oil, they kindled the lights of the *m'norah* anyway, despite the obvious futility of such an act. However, a miracle occurred, similar to the one that Scripture describes in the story of the destitute prophet's widow told in 2 Kings 4, and oil continued to flow out of the lone jug they had found for eight days, thus buying the faithful enough time to prepare new supplies and keep the *m'norah* burning.

As mentioned briefly above, Ḥanukkah is a holiday that has been embraced in modern times by many different kinds of Jews for many different reasons. Modern Israel has embraced the *m'norah* as its national symbol, and Ḥanukkah has come to be seen as a festival of Jewish rebirth in defiance of overwhelming odds. Modern diaspora Jews identify Ḥanukkah with their own ongoing struggle against assimilation and, indeed, the *m'norah* shines brightly in many nonreligious Jewish homes as a badge of honor and identity. The real challenge for Jews of all types, secular and religious, inside and outside Israel, is to identify with and affirm Ḥanukkah's authentic message of optimism and faith. As is stated in the *haftarah* read in synagogue on the Shabbat of Ḥanukkah: "Not by might, nor by power, but by My spirit, says the Eternal One of Hosts!" (Zechariah 4:6).

Ḥanukkah begins on the evening of the twenty-fifth day of Kisleiv and lasts for eight days and eight nights. The central *mitzvah* of the holiday is the lighting of the *m'norah* at home and in the synagogue. (Some, noting that the Ḥanukkah candelabrum has nine branches and wishing to distinguish it from the seven-branched *m'norah* that stood in the Temple, refer to the former as a *ḥanukkiyyah* instead. In Israel, Hebrew speakers use both terms interchangeably, but the term used in English is almost invariably *m'norah.*) Care should be taken to make sure that every home has at least one kosher *m'norah*. Some prefer to light one *m'norah* for the entire family, while others prefer having each member of the family light a separate *m'norah*. A *m'norah* can use either oil or candles. An electric *m'norah* may be used only for decoration, but not for the actual performance of the *mitzvah* (Klein, p. 229). All the candle holders in a kosher *m'norah* must either be in a straight line or, at least, on the same plane. (This rule does not apply to the *shammash*, the "helper" candle used to light the others, which is usually elevated and set apart from the rest.) When viewing a fully lit *m'norah*, the flame of one candle should not visually merge with, or be directly in front of, the flame of another. Each flame should be viewed as independent and separate, thus marking and celebrating its separate day effectively and clearly (gloss of the Rema to *SA* Oraḥ Ḥayyim 671:2).

The *m'norah* may be lit anytime after sundown, except on Friday evening when the *m'norah* should be lit just prior to the Shabbat candles. Special effort should be made on Friday night to make sure that the Ḥanukkah candles lit prior to sundown are long or thick enough to last well into the evening. Other than on Shabbat, the candles may be lit into the evening for as long as there are people out and about in the street to see them burning (*SA* Oraḥ Ḥayyim 672:1).

The *shammash* is lit first and it is used to light the rest of the candles. On the first night of Ḥanukkah, the *shammash* is used to light one candle. On the second night, it is used to light two, and so on, until all eight candles are lit on the eighth night of the holiday. The candles are placed in the *m'norah* from right to left as one faces the *m'norah*, but are lit from left to right so that the first candle lit first is the one being kindled for the first time that evening (*SA* Oraḥ Ḥayyim 676:5).

After the *shammash* is lit, but before the rest of the candles are lit, three blessings are recited the first night, and two on each remaining night. These and the following prayers can be found in any standard prayerbook. The first blessing is *barukh attah adonai, eloheinu, melekh ha-olam, asher kidd'shanu b'mitzvotav v'tzivvanu l'hadlik neir shel ḥanukkah* ("Praised are You, Adonai, our God, Sovereign of the universe, who, sanctifying us with divine commandments, has commanded us to kindle the Ḥanukkah lamp"). The second is a blessing recited in only two contexts in the course of the year, when we read the Book of Esther at Purim and on this occasion of lighting the Ḥanukkah candles: *barukh attah adonai, eloheinu, melekh ha-olam, she-asah nissim la-avoteinu ba-yamim ha-heim ba-z'man ha-zeh* ("Praised are You, Adonai, our God Sovereign of the universe, who wrought miracles for our ancestors at this time in ancient days"). On the first night of Ḥanukkah, the She-heḥeyyanu blessing is also recited. The candles are then lit. After lighting the candles, it is customary to recite the paragraph Ha-neirot Hallalu, which makes explicit the purpose of our lighting the *m'norah* and the prohibition of making practical use of the light it casts. (That is why we use the *shammash* in the first place, to guarantee that the light of the *m'norah* is always mixed with other light, thus at least ensuring that it is never used all by itself for practical purposes.) This is followed by the singing of Ma·oz Tzur (Rock of Ages), the most famous of all Ḥanukkah songs.

If the *m'norah* has been lit elsewhere, it should then be placed in a window, a doorway, or any place where it will visible from the street (*SA* Oraḥ Ḥayyim 671:5). This is done because the express purpose of this *mitzvah* is to publicize the miracle that happened so long ago, an aspect of the *mitzvah* usually referenced with the Aramaic expression *pirsuma d'nissa* (literally, "the promulgation of the miracle.") To share the light of our *m'norah* with all who pass by is the fulfillment of this *mitzvah*. Given that the newest candle should be the one the furthest left *and* that the point of the *mitzvah* is to publicize the miracle, the general custom is to light the *m'norah* in the correct way for those looking at it from inside the house, then to turn it around to facilitate proper viewing from the street when it is on display.

The *shammash* should be allowed to burn with the rest of the candles and not be extinguished after use, because its presence also guarantees that the light of the "real" Ḥanukkah candles are not used for any other purpose without the admixture, at least, of some "permitted" light (*SA* Oraḥ Ḥayyim 673:1).

It has become customary to celebrate Ḥanukkah by eating potato pancakes, commonly called by their Yiddish name, *latkes,* by Ashkenazic Jews. In Israel, jelly doughnuts, called *sufganiyyot* in Hebrew, are the more common holiday delicacy. What they have in common is that both are cooked in oil and so are able to evoke the miracle of the oil. Other Jewish communities also have special fried foods associated with Ḥanukkah for the same reason.

Another custom associated with Ḥanukkah is the four-sided spinning top called *s'vivon* in Hebrew, but more commonly referred to by its Yiddish name, *dreidl.* Each side displays a Hebrew letter that corresponds to the first letter of the words: *neis gadol hayah sham* (a great miracle happened there). In Israel, the final letter is the first letter of the word *poh* (here) instead. The sentence is just a made-up phrase, however; the real meaning of the letters has to do with the rules of the popular gambling game played with the *dreidel,* in which, depending on the letter one spins, one may win all or half the pot, or have to give some coins into it. (Although some rabbis have suggested the *dreidel* dates back to Ḥanukkah's origins and was used as a ploy to distract the Greeks while the Jews studied Torah, Rabbi David Golinkin argues that the *dreidel* is based on a sixteenth-century game popular in England around Christmastime called *totum.* Our *dreidel* games are very similar to a German version of this game.) The giving of gifts in the days and weeks around the winter solstice, when daylight is minimal and the weather is cold and unpleasant, is part of many cultures, especially those indigenous to temperate climates where the distinction between the seasons is the most pronounced. The point is clear. Giving gifts is a sign of confidence in the future and in the eventual arrival of spring: one can afford to be generous with one's stores since one clearly believes that they will soon be replenished. Thus, gift-giving is connected in different cultures with winter festivals—with Ḥanukkah among Jews, but also with Saturnalia among the ancient Romans, Christmas among Christians, and Diwali among Hindus. Traditionally, Jews gave children coins. (Among Ashkenazic Jews, these coins were called by the Yiddish name of Ḥanukkah *gelt.*) In North America and Western Europe, this has mostly developed into more elaborate gift-giving, especially to children. While there is nothing wrong with making Ḥanukkah into a holiday that children associate with presents and thus anticipate all the more keenly, care should be taken not to allow that specific aspect of the holiday to overwhelm its spiritual character or to make its historical background seem to be of lesser importance.

In some circles, and especially in North America, the Christian festival of Christmas exercises a distinctly counterproductive influence on Ḥanukkah. Indeed, when Jewish parents make the holiday into a parallel orgy of materialistic acquisitiveness, imagining just a bit pathetically that they are merely helping Ḥanukkah to "compete" successfully with Christmas for their children's attention, they are merely bowdlerizing the meaning of the holiday, subverting its significance, and ruining its spiritual potential. Sensitive Jewish parents will always try to resist unfair comparisons to the festivals of other religions, for no good can ever come from fostering the impression that Judaism is merely the Jewish version of Christianity (or any other faith, for that matter). Ḥanukkah is not the Jewish Christmas any more than Passover is the Jewish Easter, and suggesting even obliquely to children that this is the case will at best confuse them. Moreover, doing so will set up a kind of competitive evaluative process that will inevitably denigrate the worth of both festivals and both faiths.

During Ḥanukkah, a special prayer, called Al Ha-nissim (after its first words), is interpolated into both the penultimate blessing of the Amidah and the Grace after Meals. Also, the complete Hallel Service is recited every morning just after the repetition of the Amidah. Except on Shabbat and on the day or days of Rosh Ḥodesh, there is no Musaf Service on Ḥanukkah. It is customary to light the *m'norah* in synagogue just before the Evening Service and to recite the appropriate blessings. It is also customary to light the *m'norah* in synagogue before the Morning Service, but without saying the blessings. This is not intended as the performance of the specific *mitzvah* to kindle lights at Ḥanukkah (which must be done in the evening), but merely to publicize the festival and to proclaim a community's faith in the miracle story that rests at its center.

The Torah is read each day of Ḥanukkah. Three individuals are called forward for *aliyot;* the reading, taken from the seventh chapter of the Book of Numbers, details the gifts the princes of Israel donated to the Tabernacle when it was inaugurated for use. The reading for each day follows the Torah's description of the twelve days of the Tabernacle's dedication (with the passage detailing the last five of the twelve days, ending at Numbers 8:4, read on the eighth day of the holiday).

The sixth day of Ḥanukkah is always Rosh Ḥodesh, the beginning of the new month of Teivet, and so two scrolls are always removed from the Ark. Three people are called forward for *aliyot* as a passage about Rosh Ḥodesh is read from the first scroll, then a fourth individual is called up for an *aliyah* as a passage about Ḥanukkah is read from the second scroll. In some years, however, Rosh Ḥodesh is observed for two days and so the sixth and seventh days of Ḥanukkah are both days of Rosh Ḥodesh. In years in which the seventh day of Ḥanukkah is the second day of Rosh Ḥodesh, the Torah reading procedure (with the exception of the specific passage read as the fourth *aliyah*) is the same for both days.

Depending on the year, one or two Shabbatot will fall during Ḥanukkah. On such days, two scrolls are taken from the Ark. The portion for the week is read from the first and the *maftir* reading, in honor of Ḥanukkah, is read from the second. The *haftarah* is Zechariah 2:14–4:7, which contains not only a reference to the *m'norah* but also the verse: "Not by might, nor by power, but by My spirit, says the Eternal One of Hosts," which can serve as an appropriate motto for the entire holiday. In years in which there are two Shabbatot during Ḥanukkah, the *haftarah* for the second Shabbat is 1 Kings 7:40–50, which also deals with the Temple. If Rosh Ḥodesh and Shabbat fall on the same day of Ḥanukkah, then three scrolls of the Torah are removed from the Ark. (This happens only rarely.) In such a case, the weekly portion is divided into six *aliyot,* which are read from from the first scroll, the Rosh Ḥodesh portion is read from the second scroll as the seventh *aliyah,* and then the Ḥanukkah portion is read from the third as the *maftir.* The *haftarah* on such a Shabbat is Zechariah 2:14–4:7.

Tu Bi-sh'vat

While most Jews associate the beginning of a new year with Rosh Hashanah, as discussed above, the Mishnah informs us at *M* Rosh Ha-shanah 1:1 that there are actually four New Years, each with its own purpose, its own accounting, and its own role in demonstrating that life, as exemplified by the calendar, is a constant parade of new beginnings. The fifteenth of the month of Sh'vat (called Tu Bi-sh'vat in Hebrew) was, at least according to the view of the school of Hillel, the New Year for agricultural purposes, and specifically for paying the annual tithes due on fruit. (The Talmud, at *BT* Rosh Ha-shanah 14a, explains that, as the majority of the winter season's rainfall has already fallen by this date, fruit trees that only blossom later on are considered part of the following year's crop.) Also, the law that prohibits eating the fruit of trees for the first three years they produce fruit requires a specific date after which the fruit may be eaten in the fourth year, and that too was the fifteenth of Sh'vat (Leviticus 19:23–25; cf. *MT* Hilkhot T'rumot 5:11 and Hilkhot Ma·aseir Sheini V'neta Reva·i 9:9–10).

Later, when the original meaning of Tu Bi-sh'vat became less important to Jews in the Diaspora, it became customary to enjoy fruit from the Land of Israel on Tu Bi-sh'vat, as a way of strengthening the bond between a people scattered around the globe and the Holy Land. One of the most popular of these fruits was (and is) the fruit of the carob tree, called *bokser* in Yiddish and also occasionally referred to in English as St. John's bread. In the sixteenth century, the mystics of Safed found especially profound meaning in Tu Bi-sh'vat and created an elaborate liturgy for this day modeled on the Passover *seder*. With the founding of the modern State of Israel, there has been a revival of interest in Tu Bi-sh'vat. In Israel, for example, it is customary for schoolchildren to go out on that day to plant saplings, thus transforming the day into a kind of Jewish Arbor Day. Many contemporary synagogues have revived the Tu Bi-sh'vat *seder* as well, as a means both of deepening the spiritual connection between the Jews of the Diaspora and the Land of Israel. Also, Tu Bi-sh'vat has been given an environmental spin in some circles in recent years. When viewed in this light, Tu Bi-sh'vat can serve to remind us that the world is God's sacred gift to humanity, a precious legacy entrusted to our care.

Two Special Shabbatot

A series of special Sabbaths precede Purim and Passover. Before discussing Purim, the next holiday on the calendar, I will mention briefly the two special Shabbatot that occur before Purim.

In ancient times, all Jews were expected to help subvent the operating and maintenance budgets for the Holy Temple in Jerusalem by paying an annual assessment of one-half *shekel*. (This tax was only levied on men over the age of twenty.) This assessment had to be paid by the beginning of the month of Nisan, and a reminder to pay was instituted in the form of Shabbat

Sh'kalim, which the sages of ancient times ordained to be observed every year on the Shabbat immediately preceding the beginning of Adar, the month before Nisan. (If, however, the first day of Adar falls on Shabbat, that day is Shabbat Sh'kalim, not the preceding Shabbat.) Today, the single aspect of formal observance has to do with the reading of a special *maftir,* Exodus 30:11–16, and a special *haftarah,* 2 Kings 12:1–17, which deals with the repair of the Temple in the days of King Jehoash.

Since it is possible that Shabbat Sh'kalim might coincide with Rosh Ḥodesh Adar, Shabbat Sh'kalim has the potential to be one of the rare times that three Torah scrolls are taken from the Ark: one for the regular weekly portion, one for the Rosh Ḥodesh reading, and one for the special *maftir* reading associated with Shabbat Sh'kalim. If Rosh Ḥodesh and Shabbat Sh'kalim coincide, the *haftarah* for Shabbat Sh'kalim takes precedence over the regular *haftarah* for Rosh Ḥodesh.

The Shabbat that precedes Purim is called Shabbat Zakhor, literally the Shabbat of Remembrance, which name derives from the first word of the special *maftir* portion that is read on that Shabbat, Deuteronomy 25:17–19. This *maftir* retells the story of the battle the ancient Israelites fought against Amalek when they left Egypt and were traveling toward Mount Sinai. Since Haman, the villain of the Purim story, was imagined by tradition to be a descendant of the Amalekites, this was deemed an appropriate way to inaugurate the Purim festivities. And there is also a special *haftarah* for Shabbat Zakhor, one recounting the story of the war between Israel and Amalek in the days of King Saul as told in 1 Samuel 15.

Purim

Technically a minor holiday, Purim is nevertheless one of the high points of the festival cycle for Jews all over the world. While it is formally based on events discussed in the biblical Book of Esther, the real appeal of the holiday is its ongoing relevance to the nature of Jewish life in the Diaspora, and to the ongoing saga of the Jewish presence in history in general. Purim is about the struggle to maintain identity in a world that mostly values assimilation, to value tolerance in a world that tolerates persecution, and to live proudly as Jews in the midst of an ocean of non-Jews. Countless generations of Jews embraced the story of Purim not only as a means of retelling something that once happened, but as their own story, as a version of the story they themselves were living. And embedded in the affection Jewish people have for the story of Purim is the deep and abiding hope that its happy ending would be their happy ending as well.

The Purim story is also unusual for another reason. The Book of Esther, unlike other biblical works, describes salvation as coming not from a God acting above and beyond the natural order, but from a God who appears to work through and within history. In the Book of Esther, the day is won through the clever machinations of Esther and Mordecai, representatives of a politically astute and well-connected Jewish community wholly integrated into the political and social life of their time and place. And the fact that God's name does not appear even once in the entire Book of Esther subtly underlines the point that God, at least in our day, governs the world by acting through history, not by circumventing it. All of these things, together with the fact that the Purim story is a joyous tale about snatching victory from the jaws of defeat, make Purim one of the most beloved of all the Jewish holidays and the occasion of unabashedly joyous celebrations in synagogues the world over.

Purim is preceded by the Fast of Esther, a minor fast that lasts from sunrise until the stars come out that evening. Some suggest the fast should not end prior to the reading of the *m'gillah*. (The Book of Esther is commonly and popularly called the *m'gillah*, literally "the scroll," i.e., of Esther.) Others permit eating a modest amount of food if there is sufficient time after sunset but prior to the reading. The Fast of Esther (Ta·anit Esteir in Hebrew) is based on the fast Esther herself observed and that the people observed along with her in sympathy with her plight and in anticipation of her willingness to put her life at risk when presenting herself before the king unannounced (Esther 4:16). (Fast days in general, including the Fast of Esther, are discussed below in a separate section of this chapter.)

Purim is celebrated on the fourteenth day of the month of Adar. When a leap year occurs and an additional month of Adar is inserted in the calendar, Purim is celebrated in the second Adar. In such a year, the fourteenth day of the first month of Adar is referred to as Purim Katan (minor Purim). On that day, Taḥanun is not recited, but there is otherwise no specific ritual observance of the fact that, had it not been a leap year, that day would have been Purim.

Purim itself begins with the recitation of the regular Evening Service. As on Ḥanukkah, a version of the Al Ha-nissim prayer is added in the penultimate blessing of the Amidah and in the Grace after Meals. The morning Torah reading (Exodus 17:8–16, divided into three *aliyot*) describes the attack of Amalek.

Surprisingly, Hallel is not recited on Purim. The Talmud (at *BT* M'gillah 14a) suggests that the salvation that came to the Jews on Purim is of a more limited nature than the salvation of Passover, where the Jews were not only saved from imminent destruction but also delivered out of Egypt and out of the hands of Pharaoh. Such is also the case on Ḥanukkah: the Jews were not only saved from imminent destruction but also delivered from the tyranny of Antiochus. In the Purim story, on the other hand, while the Jews were delivered from imminent danger, they were specifically *not* delivered from Ahasuerus's dominion, nor were they freed from any future threats he might yet have posed to their well-being. As a result, Hallel is not recited. It is also worth noting Maimonides' opinion, codified in the *Mishneh Torah,* that there actually *is* an obligation to recite Hallel on Purim (presumably because the Jewish people of Persia were indeed saved from destruction), but that the reading of the *m'gillah* serves as Purim's version of Hallel (*MT* Hilkhot M'gillah Va-ḥanukkah 3:6).

The main *mitzvah* of Purim is the reading of the *m'gillah,* the parchment scroll that contains the Book of Esther. The *m'gillah* is read aloud in the synagogue both in the evening and on the morning of Purim. The reading must be from a kosher scroll, not from a printed book, and custom dictates that the scroll be folded in such a manner as to look like one of the "letters of decree" referred to in the Purim story (at Esther 9:26 and 29; cf. *MT* Hilkhot M'gillah Va-ḥanukkah 2:12). There is a special method of cantillation for the *m'gillah,* a musical variation on the normal Torah reading trope.

The reading is preceded by three blessings and followed by another. The first blessing is *barukh attah adonai, eloheinu, melekh ha-olam, asher kidd'shanu b'mitzvotav v'tzivvanu al mikra m'gillah* ("Praised are You, Adonai, our God, Sovereign of the universe, who, sanctifying us with divine commandments, has commanded us regarding the reading of the *m'gillah*"). The second blessing is the same one recited over the Ḥanukkah candles: *barukh atah adonai, eloheinu, melekh ha-olam she-asah nissim la-avoteinu ba-yamim ha-heim ba-z'man ha-zeh* ("Praised are You, Adonai, our God, Sovereign of the universe, who accomplished miracles for our ancestors at this time in ancient days"). The third blessing, which is also recited in the morning, is the Sheheḥeyyanu. These three blessings are recited even in the absence of a *minyan,* but the blessing following the reading is only recited in the presence of a quorum. The text of the blessing that follows the reading of the *m'gillah* can be found in any standard edition of the prayerbook.

During the reading of the *m'gillah,* there are several customs that require the participation of the congregation. There are four verses, Esther 2:5, 8:15, 8:16, and 10:3, called *p'sukei ge'ullah* (verses of redemption), which are first declaimed by the congregation and only then repeated by the reader. Since these verses all refer to Mordecai, it has become the practice of many egalitarian synagogues to pause and allow the congregation to recite the following verses of redemption that refer to Esther as well, notably Esther 2:7, 4:16, and 9:32. There are also certain key verses that contain phrases that the reader should chant in a raised voice for emphasis: *li-h'yot kol ish* at Esther 1:22, *v'ha-na·arah asher titav be'einei ha-melekh* at Esther 2:4, *va-ye·ehav ha-melekh et esteir* at Esther 2:17, *revaḥ v'hatzalah ya·amod la-y'hudim* at Esther 4:14, *yavo ha-melekh v'haman* at Esther 5:4, and especially *ba-lailah ha-hu nad'dah sh'nat ha-melekh* at Esther 6:1, which verse is considered the turning point of the drama (Klein, p. 235). It is also customary to chant the following verses or parts of verses in Eikhah trope which is intended to lend them an air of sadness: *v'kheilim mi-keilim shonim* at 1:7, all of 2:6, *v'ha·ir shushan navokhah* at 3:15, all of 4:1 and 4:3, *v'kha·asheir avad'ti avad'ti* at 4:16, and 8:6. It is also customary to read Esther 9:7–10, which recounts the hanging of Haman's ten sons, in one breath. The Talmud (at *BT* M'gillah 16b) explains that, since they all died together, their names should be recited together. Others have added a moral dimension to the custom, noting that reciting their names slowly and dramatically might be perceived as an act of gloating over their demise. Others take a less charitable view and imagine that we read their names in one breath so as not to waste *more* than one breath on this evil bunch.

The most popular and best-known custom associated with the reading of the *m'gillah* is the practice of making noise whenever Haman's name is read in an attempt to drown it out. Special noisemakers, called *ra·ashanim* in Hebrew or, more commonly, *groggers* in Yiddish, are often distributed to children in the synagogue specifically for this purpose. The use of noisemakers during the reading of the *m'gillah* is an old and worthy custom, but care must be taken that the noise does not drown out the actual reading of the scroll. Since most children are quite vigilant in the observance of this custom, synagogues must find a way to guarantee that the adult worshipers will hear every word of the *m'gillah* without ruining the children's fun.

While the *m'gillah* is normally read in the synagogue in the presence of a *minyan* and with the appropriate cantillation, the scroll (unlike the Torah) may also be read without a *minyan* if one is not available. It may also be read without the proper cantillation if qualified readers are not available. And it is even considered preferable to read it in the vernacular than not to read it at all (*MT* Hilkhot M'gillah Va-ḥanukkah 2:4)!

Another popular custom is dressing up in costumes on Purim. Many congregations have Purim parades preceding or following the reading of the *m'gillah* encouraging all the little Queen Esthers and Mordecais to parade in front of the entire congregation. Costumes need not be limited to the little ones or just to the Purim characters—creativity and festivity are the order of the day.

Tradition dictates that Purim be observed on the fourteenth day of Adar. However, in any city that was surrounded by walls in the days of Joshua, the festival is observed a day later on the fifteenth of Adar (Esther 9:17–18, as interpreted in *M* M'gillah 1:1). Outside of Israel there are no cities with Jewish communities that meet this requirement. But Jerusalem, even today, is deemed to be in that category and therefore Purim is observed there on the fifteenth of Adar, called Shushan Purim. Some other cities are of ambiguous status, and thus many communities in Lod, Tiberias, and Safed read the *m'gillah* on both the fourteenth and the fifteenth. While the calendar is arranged so that Purim can never fall on Shabbat, it is possible for Shushan Purim to fall on Shabbat—which creates a three-day commemoration, Friday being Purim, and Shabbat being Shushan Purim with respect to some prayers but not with respect to the reading of the *m'gillah,* which is deferred to Sunday.

Hearing the *m'gillah* read aloud is considered of such paramount importance that it is customary even for mourners in the middle of the *shivah* week to come to synagogue to hear the reading (Rema to *SA* Oraḥ Ḥayyim 696:4). If, however, it seems possible to arrange for the *m'gillah* to be read in the house of mourning itself, that would be optimal (ibid.).

The reading of the *m'gillah* is not the only *mitzvah* connected with Purim, however. There are a number of others, each of which has its origins in Esther 9:20–22: "Mordecai recorded these events and sent dispatches to all the Jews . . . charging them to observe the fourteenth and fifteenth days of Adar, every year . . . as days of feasting and merrymaking, and as an occasion for sending gifts to one another and gifts for the poor."

The "feasting and merrymaking" which Mordecai commanded the Jews to observe developed into the *mitzvah* of holding a feast on the afternoon of Purim, a meal commonly called the Purim *se'udah.* This meal is one of the rare occasions in Judaism when *almost* anything goes. Funny skits, humorous stories, and even making fun of rabbis and teachers are all part of the spirit of merrymaking that prevails at this unique time. The Talmud goes so far as to suggest that one should carry on with one's merrymaking until one can no longer distinguish between the words "blessed be Mordecai" and "cursed be Haman" (*BT* M'gillah 7b). How exactly one accomplishes this is left to later interpretation, however. In Israel, there are national *adloyada* parades (after that same lesson in the Talmud that one should go on with one's fun until "one does not know" Mordecai from Haman) with costumes, floats, and even marching bands. When Purim falls on a Friday, the custom is to have the Purim feast following the *m'gillah* reading in the morning (gloss of the Rema to *SA* Oraḥ Ḥayyim 695:2).

Traditionally, the consumption of alcohol was considered the simplest and best way to arrive at the state of no longer being able to distinguish between "blessed be Mordecai" and "cursed be Haman." In recent years, especially on college campuses, this time-honored custom has led to excess and many rabbis now discourage the consumption of alcohol, especially by young people, as part of Purim observance. How central drinking is to the celebration of Purim remains an issue that contemporary scholars continue to debate.

In the above-cited verse, Mordecai also charges that Purim be "an occasion of sending gifts (*mishlo·aḥ manot*) one to another." The rabbis of ancient times, all of them scholars who studied each word of Scripture with the greatest care, noticed that the word for gifts, *manot,* was in the plural but the words in the phrase "one to another" were in the singular. They therefore determined that the minimum way to fulfill this requirement is to send at least two separate foods to at least one person. Anything qualifies as food as long as it is ready to eat—so fruit, packaged candy, cakes, and cookies are all appropriate. Today, the custom is to take gifts of food to friends as an expression of the sense of communal warmth and friendship that prevails on Purim (*SA* Oraḥ Ḥayyim 695:4). Many synagogue communities today facilitate the performance of the *mitzvah* of *mishlo·aḥ manot* by taking "orders" for such gifts and then delivering them on Purim or just before the holiday.

The *m'gillah* also speaks of sending "presents to the poor" (*mattanot la-evyonim;* Esther 9:22). Because the word for poor people is in the plural here, the rabbis of ancient times decreed that the minimum requirement is to send gifts to at least two people (*SA* Oraḥ Ḥayyim 694:1). Many synagogues aid in the fulfillment of this *mitzvah* by creating opportunities on Purim for congregants to make donations to the poor and to various organizations that aid the poor. Sometimes as one enters the synagogue on Purim, one will notice two plates with a sign that reads *mattanot la-evyonim.* By putting a donation in each of these plates, congregants fulfill their obligation to aid the needy on Purim with gifts that ideally are actually delivered on Purim. Taken together, the *mitzvot* of Purim create a holiday that is more about giving than getting, and more about being concerned for the less fortunate than about spending money on oneself.

The food that everyone associates with Purim are three-cornered pastries filled with jam, poppy seeds, or even chocolate that, according to some, are intended to recall the three-cornered hat that Haman is said to have worn. In Hebrew they are called *oznei haman* (Haman's ears), but they are more commonly called *hamentaschen* (Yiddish for "Haman's pockets") by Jews of Ashkenazic origin. Whatever their origin, they are a holiday favorite of generations of Jewish children.

To refer to Purim as a minor holiday is to focus more on its halakhic status than on its overall importance. The people who celebrated it with joy, year after year, understood its importance, as did the ancient rabbis who proclaimed that "all the other holidays will cease in the days of the messiah, but Purim will never end" (*Midrash Mishlei* 9:2; Klein, p. 240). What could these rabbis have meant when they insisted that Purim would survive longer than Yom Kippur or Passover? Maybe they understood that, of all the holidays, Purim speaks to the hearts and minds of a people scattered across the face of the earth, a people obliged to survive in fragile accommodation with a dominant society that has only occasionally treated them with generosity and tolerance. The spirit of optimism and faith in God's ultimate deliverance inherent in Purim rendered it the most relevant of holidays for the ancients and, in some sense, so has it remained.

Three More Special Shabbatot

The third of the special Sabbaths that lead up to Passover is called Shabbat Parah ("the Sabbath of the Heifer"). A special, unusually long *maftir* portion (Numbers 19:1–22) is read from a second Torah concerning the ritual of the red heifer. In ancient times, a Jew who had become ritually contaminated through direct or even indirect contact with a corpse could not participate in the Passover offering. The procedure to return to a state of ritual purity involved being sprinkled with water mixed with the ashes of a red heifer that had been slaughtered and immolated for this specific purpose. Since this rite obviously did not survive the destruction of the Temple, reading of it today merely serves to recall the ancient practice. The *haftarah* for this Shabbat, Ezekiel 36:16–38, also focuses on the theme of purification.

The fourth of the special Sabbaths is Shabbat Ha-ḥodesh, the Sabbath of the New Moon. This Shabbat celebrates the arrival of the month of Nisan, the first month of the Jewish year and the month of Passover. Shabbat Ha-ḥodesh is either the Shabbat immediately preceding Rosh Ḥodesh Nisan or, if the first day of Nisan falls on Shabbat, it *is* Rosh Ḥodesh Nisan. A special *maftir,* Exodus 12:1–20, is chanted from a second Torah scroll. When Shabbat Ha-ḥodesh coincides with Rosh Ḥodesh Nisan, three scrolls are used: one for the weekly Torah portion, one for the Rosh Ḥodesh reading, and one for the *maftir* reading for Shabbat Ha-ḥodesh. The special *haftarah,* Ezekiel 45:16–46:18, presents the prophet's vision for Passover observance in the rebuilt Temple. When Shabbat Ha-ḥodesh coincides with Rosh Ḥodesh Nisan, some have the tradition of appending verses from the standard *haftarah* for Rosh Ḥodesh to the reading from Ezekiel.

The Shabbat before Passover is called Shabbat Ha-gadol, the Great Sabbath. Although technically not one of the "special Shabbatot," it is considered that way by most regular synagogue attendees. Shabbat Ha-gadol has no special *maftir* reading, but there is a special *haftarah,* Malachi 3:4–24. The name itself is slightly obscure; some take it to mean "the Sabbath of the Great Sage" and suppose its name to be a reference to the ancient rabbinic custom of delivering a major sermon on this Shabbat. Others suppose it to derive from the use of the word *ha-gadol* in the day's *haftarah* (at Malachi 3:23) to qualify the great day on which Elijah will come to herald the arrival of the messiah. In either event, Shabbat Ha-gadol is the harbinger of the most complicated of all Jewish festivals to observe correctly.

Nisan

With the commencement of the month of Nisan, preparations for Passover begin in earnest. Tradition nods to the coming celebration by requiring that Taḥanun, at best a lugubrious addition to the worship service, be omitted during morning prayers and that long eulogies be omitted at funerals (*SA* Oraḥ Ḥayyim 429:2). Also, certain prayers deemed too mournful or distressing are omitted from the funeral liturgy. The idea is that the approaching communal celebration should take precedence over the personal mourning of individuals.

The Passover Festival

Passover as History and Destiny

Passover, widely known by its Hebrew name, Pesaḥ, commemorates the exodus from Egypt. On a spiritual level, the festival confronts us with the notion of redemption. In terms of the calendar, it occurs in the spring. All three of these concepts—freedom, redemption, and springtime—come together in different aspects of Passover observance.

Historically, the exodus from Egypt that Passover commemorates was (along with the events at Mount Sinai) one of the defining moments in Jewish history, but Passover, more than any other festival, also looks to the future toward God's redemption. Indeed, Passover provides the context for traveling from the ancient past into the glorious future: just as God brought Israel out of Egypt, and just as the Jewish people continues to observe Passover in every generation, so too will God deliver Israel from the suffering of this world, bringing us from a world of poverty, pain, and loss to a world of wholeness, peace, and contentment.

It has been a long journey. Still, at its core Judaism is an optimistic faith and Passover is the holiday of hope that enables us to continue the journey from year to year and from generation to generation. Passover is also called the Springtime Festival (*ḥag ha-aviv*) at Deuteronomy 16:1.

On Passover, we open the doors to our homes and declare, "Let all who are hungry come and eat!" Rather than wait until the very last minute to look after the needy, however, it is an ancient custom to collect money prior to Passover to provide for the less fortunate. Many rabbis today conduct Passover appeals, often referred to as *ma·ot ḥittim* (money for wheat) campaigns, for this purpose.

The Fast of the Firstborn

The last of the ten plagues, the "slaying of the firstborn sons of Egypt" was the dramatic culmination of the events that led up to the exodus from Egypt. To formalize the unwillingness of the formerly oppressed to celebrate the suffering of the innocent that led to their liberation from slavery, and to nurture the deep humility that ought to accompany such unwillingness, the custom arose for the firstborn sons in every Jewish family to fast on the eve of Passover. When Passover begins on Saturday night, however, the fast is moved up to the preceding Thursday. (Other than when Yom Kippur falls on Shabbat, it is considered inappropriate to fast on Shabbat or Erev Shabbat, though the Tenth of Teivet can sometimes fall on a Friday.)

Most congregations hold a *siyyum* to circumvent this fast, preferring to avoid any public expression of regret for what was, in effect, a divine miracle of salvation. Since the fast of the firstborn is not biblically mandated, participation in a joyous feast, like one marking the completion of a tractate of Talmud, overrides the fast.

Traditionally, the fast of the firstborn was undertaken by men, not women, because it was understood to reflect the biblical plague brought by God against the firstborn sons of Egypt, not its firstborn daughters. There is, however, no reason for women who wish to acknowledge the suffering of the innocent children of Egypt not to fast on the eve of Passover as well, if they wish, or to participate in a *siyyum* feast to relieve themselves of the need to complete a fast that they have personally accepted upon themselves.

Ḥameitz

There are few aspects of Jewish observance as complicated as preparing for Passover. The Torah, at Exodus 12:15–20, prohibits the eating of leavened food, popularly called *ḥameitz,* during the entire festival. But the situation is even more stringent than that, for the *halakhah* forbids not only eating *ḥameitz,* but even deriving any benefit from it or permitting the presence in our homes of any *ḥameitz* that belongs to us during the entire festival period. It is this last requirement that results in the kind of intense labor most of us associate with preparing for Passover.

The forbidden substance, *ḥameitz,* is defined as any food made of any of the five species of grain—wheat, barley, oats, spelt, and rye—that has been made wet with water, then left unbaked for more than eighteen minutes. Baking halts the leavening process, so if water is added to any of the above grains but baked within the eighteen-minute period, it is deemed to be unleavened. This is why *matzah* is called "unleavened bread," as it is supervised to give assurance that no more than eighteen minutes ever elapse between the time the water is added and the time it finishes baking. To the five original grains, Ashkenazic custom adds rice, corn, millet, and certain kinds of legumes, generally called *kitniyyot,* for reasons that are explained below.

Since the possession of any amount of *ḥameitz* at all is considered a violation of the law, great effort must be made to remove all food substances that contain *ḥameitz* from the home before Passover. After intense cleaning and the removal of all visible *ḥameitz,* a search—popularly called *b'dikat ḥameitz*—is undertaken the night before Passover after sundown. (This search takes place on Thursday evening when the first night of Passover falls on Saturday night.) Since, by now, almost all *ḥameitz* should have been removed from the house, it is customary to leave a few crumbs of bread or cake (or any leavened substance) around the house so that something can be found and the search will not feel as though it were carried out in vain. A candle is lit and used to search out the *ḥameitz* hidden in even the darkest recesses of the house. The blessing recited before the search can be found at the beginning of the Passover Haggadah. Then, after the search concludes, a special prayer is recited that declares any unlocated *ḥameitz* to be null and void, "as if it did not exist," and affirms that a good-faith effort was made to find and remove all *ḥameitz* in one's possession. The text of this declaration too can be found in the front of any Passover Haggadah. One who is away from home on the night before Pesaḥ can perform the *b'dikah* earlier (Magein Avraham to *SA* Oraḥ Ḥayyim 432:6; *Mishnah B'rurah ad loc.,* note 10). Those who will be away for the entire holiday can sell their *ḥameitz* early and not be obligated for *b'dikah* (*Mishnah B'rurah* to *SA* Oraḥ Ḥayyim 436:32).

The next morning we participate in a ceremonial burning of the small amount of *ḥameitz* that was found during the search the night before. This ceremonial burning is called *bi·ur ḥameitz* ("destruction of *ḥameitz*"). This can be done at home, but some communities sponsor communal bonfires where the public brings *ḥameitz* for burning. A declaration similar to the one made after the search for leaven the previous evening is recited following the burning of the *ḥameitz*. The remaining crumbs of *ḥameitz* must be destroyed long before noon on the day before Passover. (Most synagogues announce the precise time by which the *ḥameitz* must be destroyed so as not to require individuals to calculate the precise time on their own.) The deadline for actually eating *ḥameitz*, however, is even earlier than that. Nor, however, may *matzah* be eaten on the eve of Passover until the *seder* meal itself (*SA* Oraḥ Ḥayyim 471:2). And some suggest that one should not eat *matzah* from Rosh Ḥodesh Nisan on in order to increase one's appetite for the *mitzvah* of *matzah* on the first night of Passover (*Mishnah B'rurah* to *SA* Oraḥ Ḥayyim 471:2, note 11).

Finally, there is the custom of selling *ḥameitz*. The original intention of tradition was completely to rid one's house of all traces of *ḥameitz*. As time went on and households grew in size, this became more difficult, more costly, and more wasteful. In turn, this led to the creation of a legal mechanism known as *m'khirat ḥameitz*, the selling of leavened foods. The procedure is as follows. All remaining *ḥameitz* is put out of sight for the entire length of the festival. It is then formally sold to a non-Jew. Even though it remains in the house, it is no longer deemed technically to be in one's legal possession and thus, equally technically, not to contravene the requirement to rid one's home of *ḥameitz*. This *ḥameitz* may be purchased back after the conclusion of the holiday. Most often, this sale is a service arranged by synagogues with the rabbi acting as the community's agent. Through a formal procedure, interested parties give the rabbi the authority to sell their remaining *ḥameitz*, which is accomplished through a formal transaction with a non-Jew some time before the deadline for possessing *ḥameitz* in a Jewish home. The sale involves certain requirements on the part of the purchaser, however, and, when the non-Jewish purchaser does not complete the requirements of the sale at the end of the holiday, the *ḥameitz* reverts back to its original owners. Some rabbis actually repurchase the *ḥameitz* formally to restore it to its original owners after the festival ends. In any event, it is not sufficient merely to store away *ḥameitz* in a Jewish home over Passover and not sell it formally because of the concept of *ḥameitz she-avar alav ha-pesaḥ*, *ḥameitz* after the holiday ends that somehow remained in the possession of a Jew *during* Passover. Any such *ḥameitz* may not be eaten after Passover, as a kind of punishment for ignoring this stricture against owning *ḥameitz* during the festival. So it is important to either get rid of or sell *ḥameitz* before Passover.

Kashrut on Passover

All the normal laws of *kashrut* apply on Passover with one additional requirement: the prohibition of *ḥameitz* in a Jewish home.

As mentioned above, any foodstuff made of any of the five grains is considered leavened if it comes into contact with water for more than eighteen minutes. Once any amount of any of these grains has been in contact with water for eighteen minutes or more, the result is *ḥameitz*. (This is so even if the grain does not appear to the naked eye to have become leavened, because the mere presence of water for a long enough period of time is presumed to have set off the process of fermentation that results in *ḥameitz*.) Therefore, any product that contains any of these five grains requires rabbinic supervision and certification to guarantee that leavening did not take place. It is for this reason that *matzah* has to be baked so quickly: to be kosher for Passover use, it must be baked completely before eighteen minutes pass from the moment it is kneaded with water. Once baking has been completed, however, fermentation can no longer occur. There is a hasidic custom known as *gebrokts,* which literally means "broken," that is concerned that some unbaked flour may remain in the *matzah*. Those following this tradition maintain that *matzah* should never be broken and mixed with water or other liquids, as for example in making *matzah brei,* a traditional dish involving *matzah* crumbled, then mixed with eggs and fried. We believe this to be an unnecessary stringency.

Traditionally, Ashkenazic authorities considered rice, millet, corn, soy, and legumes of various sorts to be forbidden on Passover because these items could be made into flour that could, in turn, be baked into bread. Some authorities permit corn oil because it could never be confused with a forbidden substance. Although many rabbinic authorities have prohibited the use of peanuts and peanut oil, the Committee on Jewish Law and Standards has permitted their use and consumption on Passover, provided that these items have proper kosher certification and do not contain any *ḥameitz* ingredients. (A responsum by Rabbi Ben Zion Bergman to that effect was adapted by CJLS in 1986 and appears in *CJLS Responsa 1980–1990,* pp. 263–266.) Beans, too, could be made into flour; hence they were prohibited. String beans are a vegetable, however, and could never be confused with a prohibited substance; therefore they are permitted (Klein, p. 116). Sephardic tradition never imposed these additional prohibitions, and so Sephardic authorities permit the eating of rice, corn, beans, millet, soy, and legumes. Some have suggested that for the sake of Jewish unity all Jews should adopt the Sephardic tradition, but this has not yet become the standard practice and readers should consult their rabbis for further guidance in this matter. Quinoa is neither *ḥameitz* nor a legume and most Conservative authorities therefore permit its use on Passover as long as it was not processed with *ḥameitz.*

Whiskey produced from one of the five grains is considered *ḥameitz.* However, even whiskeys made from other substances should not be used during Passover unless they were produced under rabbinic supervision.

There is an important halakhic difference between food items purchased before Passover and those purchased on Passover. This is based on the fact that there is one standard of tolerance for the presence of small amounts of *ḥameitz* that might be inadvertently found in food mixtures for food items purchased before the holiday and another, far more stringent, standard for food items purchased during the holiday itself. As a result, there are foods that require a "kosher for Passover" label when purchased during Passover that do not require one when purchased before the holiday.

The standards that prevail within the Conservative movement, as endorsed by the Committee on Jewish Law and Standards, are as follows:

- These products require a kosher for Passover label no matter when they are purchased: all baked products (*matzah* or any product containing *matzah,* cakes, *farfel,* etc.), decaffeinated coffee and tea, wine, vinegar, liquor, oils, dried fruits, candy, chocolate-flavored milk, ice cream, yogurt, cheeses, butter, soda, canned tuna, all kinds of processed foods, frozen uncooked vegetables, and fruit juice. (Tuna in water may contain hydrolyzed protein or vegetable broth that may be *ḥameitz.* And many canned and bottled juices are clarified or stabilized with legume-based products, however, which are not listed on the ingredients.) For Sephardic Jews, the presence of *kitniyyot* in some of these products does not present a problem as long as there is no actual *ḥameitz* present. Any processed food bought during Passover must be formally certified as kosher for consumption during the festival.
- The following are permitted without a kosher for Passover label if purchased before the festival, but require rabbinic certification if purchased during Passover: pure white sugar with no additives, non-iodized salt, pepper, natural spices, frozen fruit, milk, filleted fish, olive oil (extra virgin only), and quinoa (with no additional ingredients).
- The following are permitted without a kosher for Passover label when purchased at any time, during as well as before Passover: fresh fruits and vegetables, eggs, fresh whole fish, and fresh or frozen kosher poultry and meat (other than chopped meat), whole (i.e., unground) spices and nuts (including whole or half pecans), pure black, green, or white unprocessed tea leaves or tea bags, baking soda, and unflavored coffee.

The Committee on Jewish Law and Standards has ruled that baking powder is prohibited because of the corn starch in it (*CJLS Responsa 1980–1990*, pp. 267–269). Baking soda and bicarbonate of soda, on the other hand, may be used provided it comes from a new, unused box. Brown sugar, if pure cane sugar, can be used on Passover. If sugar is granulated, the situation depends on what has been added to it. If nothing that is *ḥameitz* has been added, one can buy it before Passover and use it. Corn syrup is prohibited by some authorities and permitted by others.

Any detergents, cleaners, etc. which are not edible and which are therefore never eaten, may be used for Passover and do not require rabbinic supervision. These items include: isopropyl alcohol, aluminum products, ammonia, coffee filters, baby oil, powder and ointment, bleach, charcoal, contact paper, plastic wrap, polish, sanitizers, scouring pads, and stain remover. Bottled water with no additives may also be used throughout the holiday without formal certification as kosher for Passover.

Prescription medicines are permitted. Non-prescription pills and capsules are generally permitted; for liquids, a rabbi should be consulted.

Some Conservative rabbis have recommended that vegetarians, even if they are Ashkenazic Jews, need not feel obliged to abstain from rice, corn, millet, soy, and legumes on Passover.

Since there are many differences in practices regarding these issues, it is always important to consult one's rabbi. It is almost never possible to determine if a product is kosher for Passover merely by reading the list of ingredients and, since production standards change from year to year, it is always a good idea to check the Rabbinical Assembly website for its annual Passover updates or to consult a local rabbi.

Because utensils, pots, and dishes are deemed capable of absorbing *ḥameitz* during the course of the year, it is customary to remove all utensils from the kitchen and replace them with special ones for Passover use. Some utensils, however, can be made acceptable for Passover use, if necessary, by putting them through a process that removes the *ḥameitz*. This process is popularly called *kashering* the utensils. The following explanation contains general guidelines, but for more details one should seek a rabbi's counsel.

Metal cooking utensils used for boiling food can be *kashered* by boiling them. First, the utensils must be thoroughly cleaned. After a period of twenty-four hours passes, they must be immersed in a container of water heated to a rolling boil. (This process is formally called *hagalah.*) The utensils are then cleaned again and ready for use on Passover (*CJLS Responsa 1980–1990*, pp. 259–262). For pots and pans, the handles must be cleaned thoroughly. If the handle can be removed, one must remove it for a more thorough cleaning. To effect *hagalah*, the item must be completely exposed to the boiling water. Pots and pans are either immersed in a larger pot of boiling water (for large items this may be done one section at a time), or filled with water brought to a rolling boil, after which a heated stone is dropped into the pot, causing the water to flow over the sides of the pot. In the case of silverware, every part of each piece must be exposed to the boiling water. Following this *hagalah* process, each utensil is rinsed in cold water. Heavy-duty plastic items, including dishes, cutlery or serving pieces, provided they can withstand very hot water and do not permanently stain, may be *kashered* by *hagalah*. If there is some doubt as to whether a particular item can be *kashered,* a rabbi should be consulted.

Purely metal utensils used in fire must be first thoroughly scrubbed and cleaned and then subject to direct fire (*libbun*). To accomplish this, place the item in a self-cleaning oven and run it through the self-cleaning cycle, or use a blowtorch. The use of a blowtorch is a complicated and potentially dangerous procedure and may result in discoloration or warping of the metal item being purged. Caution should be exercised when performing *libbun.* Metal baking pans and sheets cannot be *kashered* because the requisite direct fire will cause warping.

Utensils that are used only for cold food and never come into contact with heated foods or fire can be *kashered* by being washed thoroughly.

Earthenware (china, pottery, ceramic dishes, mugs, or other kinds of pots or jugs) used for hot food during the year cannot be *kashered.* However, fine china that had been used for *ḥameitz* but that has not been used for over a year may be used for Passover if thoroughly scoured and cleansed in hot water (*CJLS Responsa 1980–1990,* pp. 259–262). This china is considered *pareve* and may be designated for meat or dairy use.

Glass is deemed non-absorbent and therefore does not require *kashering* beyond careful cleaning and rinsing. However, some authorities believe that glassware should be *kashered* through a process of immersion in boiling water (*CJLS Responsa 1980–1990,* pp. 259–262). Others recommend a more extensive process of soaking whereby the glassware is placed in a larger container, then soaked for seventy-two hours and the water changed every twenty-four hours.

Ovens are *kashered* in the following way. First, every part of the oven that comes into contact with food must be thoroughly scrubbed and cleaned. The oven should be then made as hot as possible for an hour. (If there is a broil setting, it should be used.) Self-cleaning ovens should be scrubbed and cleaned, then put through the self-cleaning cycle. Continuous cleaning ovens must be *kashered* in the same manner as regular ovens (*CJLS Responsa 1980–1990,* pp. 259–262). If the oven was very dirty to begin with, two cycles may be needed to assure a thorough cleaning. Stovetops should be thoroughly cleaned and scrubbed, then turned on and left on until red-hot. Convection ovens are *kashered* like regular ovens. When cleaning, one must be sure to clean thoroughly around the fan.

Smooth glass-top electric ranges require *kashering* by *libbun* and *irui* (pouring boiling water over the surface of the range top). First, one must clean the top of the range thoroughly; then one must turn the coils on maximum heat until they are red-hot. Then boiling water must be poured on the surface area and around the burners. The range top may now be used for cooking.

Microwave ovens that have no convection option should be scoured thoroughly. One should then place an eight-ounce cup of water inside the oven and microwave until the water almost disappears. (At least six of the eight ounces need to evaporate.) There is no need to heat until the water is completely evaporated, as this may damage the oven. A microwave that has a browning element cannot be *kashered* (*CJLS Responsa 1980–1990,* pp. 248–249).

As mentioned above, glass dishes used for eating and serving hot food may be *kashered* by cleaning and then immersing in boiling water (*hagalah*). Glass cookware is *kashered* in the same method used for a metal pot (see above). The issues regarding glass bakeware such as CorningWare®, Corelle®, and Pyrex®, are complex. Some authorities allow glass bakeware to be *kashered,* while others do not. A rabbi should be consulted for guidance.

Pressure cookers can be *kashered.* The separate parts of the machine should each be *kashered* separately.

Most authorities do not permit Teflon®-coated cookware to be *kashered* especially if there are scratches in the Teflon® surface. Those that do, however, permit it only if it is carefully cleaned and then immersed in boiling water. Such items should only be *kashered* after twenty-four hours of non-use. Teflon®-coated baking pans may not be *kashered.*

A metal sink can be *kashered* first by cleaning it thoroughly and then pouring boiling water over it. A porcelain sink should be cleaned and a sink rack used. If dishes are to be soaked in a porcelain sink, a dish basin must be used.

Tables, closets, refrigerators, and countertops should be thoroughly cleaned and covered. Suitable coverings include: contact paper, regular paper, foil, or cloth that does not contain *ḥameitz.* Many countertop surfaces can be *kashered* simply by a thorough cleaning, a twenty-four-hour wait, and *irui* (pouring boiling water over the surfaces). For *irui* to be effective for *kashering,* the surface must have no hairline cracks, nicks, or scratches that can be seen with the naked eye. Plastic laminates, limestone, soapstone, granite, marble, glass, Corian®, Staron®, Ceaserstone®, Swanstone®, Surell®, and Avonite® surfaces can be *kashered* by *irui.* A wood surface that does not contain scratches may be *kashered* by *irui.* The potential effectiveness of *irui* depends on the material of which the counter is made. If a counter cannot be *kashered,* it should simply be cleaned and covered.

A dishwasher needs to be cleaned as thoroughly as possible, including the inside area around the drainage and filters. Then a full cycle with detergent (with racks inserted) should be run while the machine is empty. After twenty-four hours of not being used, the dishwasher should again be run empty (with its racks inserted), and set on the highest heat for the purpose of *kashering*. If the sides of the dishwasher are made of enamel or porcelain, the dishwasher cannot be *kashered* for Passover (*CJLS Responsa 1980–1990,* p. 262).

Electrical appliances can be *kashered* if the parts that come into contact with *ḥameitz* themselves are removable. If the parts are not removable, or if they are removable but not *kasher*-able, the appliance cannot be *kashered* (*CJLS Responsa 1980–1990,* p. 262). All non-Passover utensils should be stored with any *ḥameitz* that has been sold and locked away to prevent accidental use. It is recommended that one purchase small appliances to be designated strictly for Passover use, thus avoiding the difficulty of *kashering* these appliances.

Non-Passover dishes, pots, utensils, and *ḥameitz* foods that have been sold should be separated, covered, or locked away to prevent accidental use.

All the above standards are in keeping with the annually published Passover Guide of The Rabbinical Assembly and its Kashrut Subcommittee. Because production standards in the food industry are constantly changing, it is always wise to bring specific issues directly to a rabbi.

Passover presents a unique challenge to pet owners. The laws of *kashrut* are only incumbent on Jews and even though Fido or Fluffy may seem like members of the family they are not expected to follow the laws of *kashrut.* But Passover still presents a challenge because Jews are prohibited from not only eating *ḥameitz* but also from benefiting from it—and using it to feed our pets is generally considered to be a benefit to their Jewish owners and therefore not permissible. The food we feed our pets on Passover does not need to be kosher but it should not contain *ḥameitz*. If it contains any of the secondarily restricted *kitniyyot* products, that is not a problem. It is possible to find pet food that bears a kosher for Passover certification and it is also possible to find pet food that does not contain *ḥameitz*. If changing over to a different food for your pet for Passover, you should begin the gradual changeover in advance so as to avoid any problems on the holiday.

When Erev Pesaḥ Falls on Shabbat

When the first night of Passover falls on a Saturday night, there are a number of changes in the normal procedures. The search for *ḥameitz* takes place Thursday evening, but instead of leaving just enough *ḥameitz* to burn the following morning, enough must be left over for the Shabbat meals as well.

The formal burning of the *ḥameitz* takes place on Friday morning. In general, Friday should be treated as an ordinary eve of Passover with respect to burning the *ḥameitz* and *kashering* the kitchen, including the stove. The *kol ḥamira* formula recited for nullifying unseen *ḥameitz* should not, however, be recited at this time so that the *ḥameitz* set aside for Shabbat is not included.

To facilitate the lighting of candles for the first day of the festival on Saturday night, it is the usual custom to light a twenty-four-hour candle before Shabbat, usually in the form of a *yahrtzeit* or any similar twenty-four-hour candle. That way, the candles may be lit from a preexistent flame.

Food for Shabbat, and also for the first *seder,* should be prepared on Friday in Passover utensils. One *ḥameitz* plate should be set aside for the *ḥallot* to be served Friday evening. (Using a disposable plate is even simpler.) Extreme care should be taken to prevent any crumbs from coming in contact with the Passover utensils, however. The use of disposable paper or plastic dishes and plastic cutlery at the Friday evening and Shabbat morning meals is extremely desirable and solves any number of problems.

Ḥameitz may not be eaten on Shabbat, as usual on the eve of Passover, after the first third of daylight hours. Some synagogues begin services very early that Shabbat morning to allow people time to get home afterward to have their final *ḥameitz* meal. After the last meal, the remaining *ḥameitz* must be disposed of in some way other than burning it, since that would constitute forbidden activity on Shabbat. (It can be flushed down the toilet or put in a public trash receptacle, for example, but it cannot be put in garbage cans or other receptacles on one's own property.) The tablecloth should be shaken out outside and then stored with the other *ḥameitz* utensils. The *kol ḥamira* formula that nullifies any overlooked *ḥameitz* should be recited at this time. Subsequent Shabbat meals should include neither *ḥallah* nor *matzah*. Indeed, it is formally forbidden to eat *matzah* at all on Erev Pesaḥ, even if it falls on Shabbat. If there is difficulty in following these instructions, it is permitted to use a special product called "rich" *matzah* for Friday night and Saturday lunch. (The product, called *matzah ashirah* in Hebrew, is sometimes misleadingly called egg *matzah,* although it has no eggs in it.) The use of *matzah ashirah* is seen as an attractive alternative by many because it is neither *ḥameitz* nor, at least technically, *matzah*. The Committee on Jewish Law and Standards has ruled that the use of *matzah ashirah* is actually preferable when the eve of Passover coincides with Shabbat. There is less of a chance of making any mistakes and this, in turn, provides for a more relaxing and less stressful Shabbat.

Passover at Home

No later than eighteen minutes before sundown on Erev Pesaḥ, candles are lit. Two blessings are recited: the standard blessing over festival candles, *barukh attah adonai, eloheinu, melekh ha-olam, asher kidd'shanu b'mitzvotav v'tzivvanu l'hadlik neir shel yom tov* ("Praised are You, Adonai, our God, Sovereign of the universe, who, sanctifying us with divine commandments, has commanded us to kindle the festival lamp") and the She-heḥeyyanu. On Shabbat, the first blessing is *barukh attah adonai, eloheinu, melekh ha-olam, asher kidd'shanu b'mitzvotav v'tzivvanu l'hadlik neir shel shabbat v'shel yom tov* ("Praised are You, Adonai, our God, Sovereign of the universe, who, sanctifying us with divine commandments, has commanded us to kindle the Sabbath and festival lamp"). On the second night of Passover or the first night if it follows Shabbat, the candles should be lit one hour later. The kindling of a flame, however, is not permitted, as the candles are not being lit prior to the holiday but on it. While fire cannot be kindled on the holiday, however it may nonetheless be transferred and so it has become customary to light a twenty-four-hour candle at the same time the candles are lit on the first night. In that way, on the second night (or the first night that is immediately preceded by Shabbat), the candles can be lit from the flame of the twenty-four-hour candle merely by transferring the flame.

The Seder

The Passover *seder* is, for many Jews, the most important ritual feast of the year. Indeed, recent studies indicate that more Jews observe the Passover *seder* than almost any other aspect of Jewish ritual life. There is something about this tradition that Jews find compelling above all others, and this appears to be the case no matter how far they may have traveled from mainstream Jewish observance in other ways. Perhaps it is the fact that it is a home-based *mitzvah* that by its very nature brings far-flung families together, or perhaps it is simply nostalgia or the appeal of the message of freedom from tyranny. In any event, the importance of the Passover *seder* (plural: *s'darim*) in the life of Jews everywhere is hard to deny. Correctly, the Hebrew word should be written *seider* in English letters to reflect the way it is pronounced. The spelling *seder,* however, is so prevalent among English-speaking Jews that we have retained it in this volume nonetheless.

Contemporary *s'darim* are as varied as the Jews who gather to observe them. They can be long or short, traditional or creative, but all revolve around the central biblical imperative expressed in Exodus 13:8: "And you shall explain to your child on that day, saying that [all] this is because of what the Eternal did for me when I came forth from Egypt," which tradition understands as a requirement that the story of the exodus from Egypt be told to Jewish children in every generation. The Passover *seder* is the cumulative result of untold generations of Jews telling the same story. The Haggadah, the book that guides participants through the *seder* meal and serves as its libretto, is a composite text developed over the centuries as a fulfillment of that same mandate.

One of the most crucial factors in determining the quality of a *seder* has to do with the choice of the right edition of the Haggadah. There are many from which to choose. In fact, the Haggadah has been published in more editions than any other Jewish book since the dawn of printing, more than three thousand of them. *The Feast of Freedom,* for example, an edition of the Haggadah published by the Conservative movement, is a fine example of the kind of Haggadah that brings together a modern translation, attractive artwork, contemporary additional readings, and many elucidating explanations of how exactly to perform the rituals correctly. Some families like all participants to have the same edition of the Haggadah in front of them so that everyone can literally be on the same page. Other families distribute different editions of the Haggadah to different participants so as to be able to ask each to share insights from his or her own Haggadah, thus adding to the variety of comments at the table. Either approach works, but the key detail is that time must be taken in advance to determine which edition or editions of the Haggadah will be best for the kind of *seder* one is hoping to create in one's home.

It will often be the case that many different people of different ages and different approaches to Judaism will all end up sitting around the same *seder* table. Rather than seeing this as a problem to be solved, it is more productive to view such a situation as an opportunity to make the *seder* interesting and lively. The Haggadah can be seen as a fixed script to be read out loud, or as a jumping-off point for lively discussion and debate. A *seder* discussion that veers off from "we were slaves to Pharaoh in Egypt" to a debate regarding the various things that still enslave people today is not a bad thing: it is the main thing.

It is not necessary to recite every word of the Haggadah out loud, but every effort should be made to cover each of the fourteen traditional parts of the *seder* that are listed at the beginning of every traditional Haggadah:

- *Kaddeish* (the recitation of Kiddush),
- *U-r'ḥatz* (the first washing of the hands, done without the recitation of the traditional blessing),

- *Karpas* (the eating usually of a green vegetable like parsley, or any vegetable that grows in the ground),
- *Yaḥatz* (the breaking of the middle *matzah,* which will subsequently be used as the *afikomen* dessert at the end of the meal),
- *Maggid* (the actual retelling of the story of the exodus from Egypt, including the asking of the famous Four Questions, the recitation of the Ten Plagues, the singing of Dayyeinu, and the drinking of the second cup of wine),
- *Roḥtzah* (the formal washing of the hands a second time, this time with the blessing),
- *Motzi Matzah* (eating the *matzah,* with its two introductory blessings),
- *Maror* (eating the bitter herbs, with its blessing),
- *Koreikh* (combining the *matzah,* the bitter herbs, and the *ḥaroset* into a kind of a sandwich in accordance with the lesson of Hillel included in the Haggadah),
- *Shulḥan Oreikh* (eating dinner),
- *Tzafun* (eating the *matzah* that had earlier been set aside as the *afikomen* dessert),
- *Bareikh* (reciting the Grace after Meals, including the third cup of wine and the ritual opening of the door to Elijah, the harbinger of messianic tidings),
- *Hallel* (singing most of Hallel aloud, concluding with the fourth cup of wine), and
- *Nirtzah* (a closing hymn stressing the redemptive hopes embedded in all Passover celebration and concluding with the famous words, "Next Year in Jerusalem!"), followed by a series of well-known closing table songs.

Each of these fourteen stages of the *seder* should be seen as an opportunity for creative, interesting discussion. Participants should be open to the insights and input of the unique personalities seated around the table. There are many ways to innovate while remaining faithful to the specific halakhic requirements of the *seder,* but the bottom line is always the same: not to be slaves to the Haggadah.

The *seder* plate must be prepared in advance and should have the following items on it: the *z'ro·a* (a roasted shank bone), the *beitzah* (an egg), the *maror* (some bitter herbs or horseradish), the *ḥaroset* (a chutney made, in the Ashkenazic tradition, of apples, wine, and nuts), and the *karpas* (a green vegetable, usually parsley, although potatoes could also be used as, in fact, may any vegetable over which the *borei p'ri ha-adamah* blessing is recited). Some *seder* plates contain a spot for *ḥazeret* (a bitter vegetable, often romaine lettuce). This stems from a controversy over the commandment in Numbers 9:11 that requires that we are to eat the paschal lamb "with unleavened bread and bitter herbs." (Some authorities interpret this reference to bitter herbs in the plural as requiring a second form of bitter herb to be consumed in addition to the *maror*. Most, however, do not feel this is necessary.) A plate should also be prepared with three *matzot,* two in place of the regular two loaves that adorn any festival or Shabbat table, and the third for the *afikomen.*

The Passover *seder* is patterned after an ancient Greco-Roman meal of luxury. Pillows are often provided for the diners to facilitate their obligation to recline while eating. This is not so much an opportunity merely to list to one side as it is a way to express gratitude for the freedom granted the Israelite slaves by dining in a way that was, by rabbinic times, the preferred dining position of the free and the wealthy.

There should be enough wine to fulfill the requirement of the four cups for each diner. More wine than that may be consumed during the actual meal. Kosher grape juice should be provided for children and for those who must refrain from alcohol.

The eating of *matzah* is a *mitzvah* at the *seder*. Eating *matzah* is optional during the rest of Passover, however, although, of course, eating *ḥameitz* is strictly forbidden for the duration of the festival. Some very pious Jews purchase and eat only a special kind of *matzah* called *matzah sh'murah* (or, more popularly, *sh'murah matzah*). This *matzah* is special in that extra care was taken to guarantee that the grain from which it was made did not come into contact with water even before it was made into flour. This far exceeds the legal requirement for *matzah,* however, and is, generally speaking, not a feature of *s'darim* in most Conservative homes.

There are many ancient and modern traditions associated with the Passover *seder*. A special cup called the Cup of Elijah is set on the table because tradition expects the prophet Elijah to announce our ultimate redemption and the coming of the messiah. (Some fill this cup at the onset of the *seder,* but others wait to pour the wine until the moment at which the door is opened formally to welcome Elijah to the *seder*. Still others pass the cup around the table with all participants adding a little of their own wine as a way of symbolizing that redemption today requires that each and every one of us pitch in and offer our help.) Many families today also feature a Cup of Miriam on their the *seder* tables. Unlike the Cup of Elijah, this one is filled with water as a way symbolically of recalling that Miriam is remembered by tradition as having been instrumental in the Israelites' successful effort to find water during their years spent wandering in the desert. Also, this cup enables *seder* participants to pay tribute to the heroines of Jewish history, past and present.

There is another custom connected with the wine served at the *seder*. As we count off the ten plagues in the Magid section of the Haggadah, there is a custom of removing ten drops of wine from our cups by dipping a finger in the wine and transferring the wine onto a dinner plate. Some explain this use of our hands recalls that the plagues were the work of God's hand (cf. Exodus 8:15) and not merely a series of conveniently timed natural catastrophes. Others say that the custom is intended to remind us that all humanity is created in God's image and that the death of any human being, therefore, diminishes God's presence in the world.

Many families begin the *seder* meal by eating a hard-boiled egg dipped in salt water. Many reasons are offered for this custom, but the mostly likely is that the egg is a symbol of spring and of rebirth, and thus a fitting first course at the feast of freedom.

In the Diaspora, a second *seder* is conducted on the second night of Passover. This *seder* follows the same format as the first night, although there are some slight liturgical changes.

Passover in the Synagogue

The Evening Service follows the standard format for festival evenings, with the omission of Kiddush. On Shabbat, the three paragraphs that normally follow the chanting of Genesis 2:1–3 (the Va-y'khullu prayer) are also omitted. The service is recited quickly, although in a dignified manner befitting the festival, so that worshipers may adjourn with reasonable haste to their *seder* tables. The Morning and Musaf Services also follow the standard outline. The full version of Hallel is recited on the first two days of the festival (*SA* Oraḥ Ḥayyim 488:1).

On both the first two days of Passover, two Torah scrolls are taken from the Ark. On the first day, Exodus 12:21–51, which focuses on the observance of the first Passover when the Israelites were still in Egypt, is read from the first scroll. This reading is divided into five *aliyot* unless it coincides with Shabbat, in which case it is divided into seven *aliyot*. The *maftir* portion, Numbers 28:16–25, which describes the sacrifices that were offered in the Temple on Passover, is read from the second scroll. The *haftarah*, Joshua 5:2–6:1, describes the way Passover was observed when the Israelites arrived in the Land of Israel. On the second day of Passover, Leviticus 22:26–23:44 is read from the first scroll and the same *maftir* reading as on the first day is read from the second Torah scroll. The *haftarah*, 2 Kings 23:1–9 and 21–25, describes how Passover was observed in the days of King Josiah.

On the first day of Passover, a special Prayer for Dew is chanted as part of the opening benediction in the repetition of the Amidah in the Musaf Service, and thereafter the congregation stops inserting the phrase *mashiv ha-ru·aḥ u-morid ha-gashem* ("who causes the wind to blow and the rain to fall") in the Amidah until the fall. (There are congregations, however, in which the phrase is omitted even in the silent recitation of the Amidah that precedes its public repetition.) In Israel, these words are henceforth replaced with the words *morid ha-tal,* referring to God as the source of dew in the world.

The Intermediate Days of Passover

The intermediate days of Passover, like the middle days of Sukkot, are called *ḥol ha-mo·eid.* All of the laws that govern eating during Passover remain in effect. During the Morning Service, the abbreviated version of Hallel is recited (*SA* Oraḥ Ḥayyim 490:4). The Torah is also read on each of these days, each day's reading divided down into four *aliyot.* Three *aliyot* are read from the first scroll—the readings for the four intermediate days are, respectively, Exodus 13:1–16, Exodus 22:24–23:19, Exodus 34:1–26, and Numbers 9:1–14—but the reading from the second scroll, Numbers 28:19–25, is the same for all four days. If one of the days of *ḥol ha-mo·eid* coincides with Shabbat, the reading that day is Exodus 33:12–34:26, divided into seven *aliyot.* If that Shabbat is the first day of *ḥol ha-mo·eid,* then the portions cited above for the first and second days of *ḥol ha-mo·eid* are instead read on the second and third days, respectively. The reading for the fourth day remains the same, however.

There is also a custom to read the Song of Songs, with its description of spring, on the Shabbat that falls during Passover. When it is read, it is done so without reciting any introductory blessings. Another custom is to begin the study of *Pirkei Avot,* the tractate of the Mishnah popularly called The Ethics of the Fathers, on this Shabbat. One chapter is then studied each Shabbat between Passover and Shavuot.

As mentioned above in the section about Sukkot, there is some ongoing controversy regarding the wearing of *t'fillin* during *ḥol ha-mo·eid.* Among Conservative Jews, the most prevalent custom is to don *t'fillin* at the beginning of the service and to remove them before Hallel. Others do not don *t'fillin* at all during *ḥol ha-mo·eid* and some put them on without reciting the blessings, but all who do put them on remove them before Hallel.

There are also special rules concerning funerals on *ḥol ha-mo·eid.* Burial is permitted, but the onset of the mourning week is delayed until after the festival. Also, the liturgy for funerals conducted during *ḥol ha-mo·eid* is somewhat different from the normal funeral liturgy and long eulogies are not given.

The Concluding Days of Passover

The seventh and eighth days of Passover are full festival days. (In Israel, there is no eighth day at all and the festival concludes at the end of the seventh day.) The liturgy for these days follows the same format as the first two days, except that the shortened version of Hallel is said and the She-heḥeyyanu blessing is neither recited when the festival candles are kindled nor included as part of Kiddush.

No later than eighteen minutes before sundown candles are lit for the seventh day of Passover. (They are kindled one hour later on the eighth day.) The standard blessing over festival candles, *barukh attah adonai, eloheinu, melekh ha-olam, asher kidd'shanu b'mitzvotav v'tzivvanu l'hadlik neir shel yom tov* ("Praised are You, Adonai, our God, Sovereign of the universe, who, sanctifying us with divine commandments, has commanded us to kindle the festival lamp") is recited. On Shabbat, the blessing is *barukh attah adonai, eloheinu, melekh ha-olam, asher kidd'shanu b'mitzvotav v'tzivvanu l'hadlik neir shel shabbat v'shel yom tov* ("Praised are You, Adonai, our God, Sovereign of the universe, who, sanctifying us with divine commandments, has commanded us to kindle the Sabbath and festival lamp"). On the eighth night of Passover the kindling of a flame would not be permitted, as the candles are not being lit prior to the holiday but on it. But while fire cannot be kindled on the holiday it may be transferred, so it has become customary to light a twenty-four-hour candle at the same time the candles are lit on the seventh night so that on the eighth night the candles can be lit merely by transferring the flame. In addition, a special Yizkor candle is lit just prior to the formal holiday candles for the eighth day by those who will be reciting the Yizkor Service the following morning. There is no blessing recited when kindling this memorial candle, although many prayerbooks include appropriate devotional material to recite just before doing so.

The use of the shortened version of Hallel on the last two days of Passover is an anomaly, as these are the only festival days of the year on which the full Hallel is not recited. The explanation for this is based on a noble tradition that forbids any sort of response to deliverance that could be misinterpreted as gloating over the downfall of the enemy. An old *midrash* depicts the Israelites singing with joy at their deliverance at the Sea of Reeds and the angels in heaven joining in. God, the legend goes, was not pleased and rebuked these angels with the words: "My creatures are drowning and you sing songs of praise?" (*BT* M'gillah 10b). As a result, the custom grew up to abbreviate the Hallel as a way of nodding to the fact that salvation came to Israel through the suffering of others. Alternative theories explain that the last days of Passover have a different feel to them than the last days of Sukkot. On Sukkot, since each day has a value of its own (as symbolized by the unique set of sacrifices that were brought on each of its days), each day deserves its full Hallel. The final days of Passover, however, are merely a continuation and conclusion of the first days and, as such, do not.

Two scrolls are taken out of the Ark on the seventh day of Passover. From the first scroll, we read Exodus 13:17–15:26, which focuses on the events at the Sea of Reeds. The *maftir* is then read from the second scroll, but it is the same reading as on all the intermediary days of Passover.

The *haftarah* is 2 Samuel 22:1–51, which echoes the themes of the Torah reading.

Two scrolls are also taken from the Ark on the eighth day. The reading on the eighth day is Deuteronomy 15:19–16:17. If, however, the eighth day of the festival falls on Shabbat, the reading begins with Deuteronomy 14:22 and the number of *aliyot* is increased from five to seven. The *maftir* is the same as the other days and the *haftarah* is Isaiah 10:32–12:6, which relates a vision of the ultimate redemption of mankind.

Yizkor is also recited on the eighth day of Passover after the conclusion of the *haftarah*.

Counting the Omer

Counting the *omer* highlights the agricultural dimension of the festivals of Passover and Shavuot. In ancient times, a measure of the first barley to be harvested (called an *omer*) was brought to the Temple as an offering of thanksgiving and gratitude. This is actually a *mitzvah* of the Torah, as codified at Leviticus 23:10: "When you enter the Land that I am giving to you and you reap its harvest, you shall bring the first sheaf (*omer*) of your harvest to the priest." This is only the first part of the requirement, however, and Scripture specifically goes on in that same chapter to require that the faithful count off fifty days and then, on the fiftieth day, offer a different set of sacrifices to God on the festival of Shavuot (Leviticus 23:15–16 and Deuteronomy 16:9–10, and cf. the elaboration of these verses by Maimonides in the *Mishneh Torah* in the seventh chapter of Hilkhot T'midin U-musafin). This forty-nine-day period is called colloquially the *s'firah*, "the counting."

Every evening, starting with the second night of Passover, we count the *omer* just before the Aleinu hymn. Some introduce the actual act of counting the day aloud with a meditative opening prayer, but this prayer is optional. The blessing before counting the *omer* is *barukh attah adonai, eloheinu, melekh ha-olam, asher kidd'shanu b'mitzvotav v'tzivvanu al s'firat ha-omer* ("Praised are You, Adonai, our God, Sovereign of the universe, who, sanctifying us with divine commandments, has commanded us regarding the counting of the *omer*"). Then, each evening for forty-nine days, the counting itself ensues. The counting should take place after the Evening Service is recited. The *omer* may not be counted before nightfall. Therefore, if the Evening Service in the synagogue is being held before sundown, the last day that was counted is announced to indicate the correct number to be counted later that evening. It is required not only to count the days, but also to note how many full weeks and how many extra days of the *omer* have passed as well (*SA* Oraḥ Ḥayyim 489:1).

If one forgets to count one night of the *omer,* one may do so all night long and one may say the blessing as well. If the entire night is missed, one can count during the day, but without the blessing. One may then resume the counting with a blessing the next night. If an entire night and day is missed, one is obliged to count the remaining nights of the *omer* anyway, but one may no longer say the blessing, since the possibility of performing the entire *mitzvah* no longer exists (*SA* Oraḥ Ḥayyim 489:8).

In an agricultural society, where existence was wholly dependent on the produce of the land, an expression of gratitude for the fecundity of the soil needed little further explanation. As with other such gifts required by biblical law, counting the days of the *omer* was intended to express humility and to give voice to one's understanding that prosperity on the land is inevitably a combination of human effort and divine blessing.

Since the destruction of the Temple, the custom of counting the *omer* mostly serves to draw a direct line between Passover and Shavuot, a line that can be taken to connect the concept of growth from *mere* freedom from slavery to the point at which one understands that *ultimate* freedom comes to human beings through obedience to divine law.

Traditionally, the *s'firah* period is a time of semi-mourning. The Talmud describes a tragedy that occurred in the time of Rabbi Akiva, when thousands of his students died in this period between Passover and Shavuot (*BT* Y'vamot 62b). The exact circumstances of this tragedy are unclear, but the Talmud looks inward and blames the debacle on the lack of respect that these students showed toward one another. Scholars also note that this was the period of the Hadrianic persecutions in the beginning of the second century C.E. and that Rabbi Akiva was one of the principal players in the Bar Kokhba revolt just a short time after that. Regardless of the ultimate cause, however, the impact of the tragedy was undeniable. Over the generations, other sorrows and tragedies were added to the list of disasters that befell the Jewish people during this particular period, and it became a kind of magnet in time for sadness and grief. As a result, even in modern times we pass through these weeks in a spirit of semi-mourning (*SA* Oraḥ Ḥayyim 493:1–4).

There are actually many different patterns of observance that prevail during all or part of the *s'firah* period, all suggestive of mourning rituals. For example, some men do not shave during the *s'firah,* even in otherwise licit ways. (The laws governing shaving in general are discussed elsewhere in this volume by Rabbi Gordon Tucker.) And it is also customary not to cut one's hair.

Traditionally, weddings were not scheduled during the *s'firah* period. The Committee on Jewish Law and Standards has ruled, however, that although weddings and other festive parties should not be held from Passover through Yom Ha-sho·ah (Holocaust Memorial Day, which falls on the twenty-seventh day of Nisan), the days of *s'firah* from then on may be treated as any other time of the year with respect to parties and weddings (Klein, p. 143). Some are more stringent, however, maintaining the ban on parties until Lag Ba-omer (the eighteenth day of Iyyar, the thirty-third day of the *omer*) and then permitting them after that date (Klein, p. 144). Still others avoid celebrations during this entire period with the exception of Lag Ba-omer, Yom Ha-atzma·ut (Israel Independence Day), and Rosh Ḥodesh. Individuals anxious to plan weddings or parties during *s'firah* should consult the rabbi of their community to determine what custom prevails.

Lag Ba-omer and Pesaḥ Sheini

One day of special interest that occurs during *s'firah* is Pesaḥ Sheini, the Second Passover, which falls on the fourteenth day of the month of Iyyar. Coming a month after Passover, it was an opportunity in Temple times for those who had been in a state of ritual impurity during Pesaḥ to offer a delayed version of the paschal sacrifice. Today, the day is marked solely by the omission of Taḥanun in the Morning and Afternoon Services.

And just a few days later on the eighteenth of Iyyar falls Lag Ba-omer ("the thirty-third day of the *omer*"). Believed to be the day on which the plague that afflicted Rabbi Akiva's students ceased, Lag Ba-omer is a day of respite from the sadness of *s'firah*. Taḥanun is not said, weddings are permitted, and haircuts and shaving are allowed even for those who refrain from both during the *s'firah* weeks. Kabbalists also observe this special day as the Yahrtzeit of Rabbi Shimon bar Yoḥai, and to this day many in Israel make pilgrimages to his grave in Meiron. To mark the fact that Lag Ba-omer is also said to be the anniversary of the revolt against Rome led by the students of Rabbi Akiva, the day is also observed in many Jewish schools as a field day.

Yom Ha-sho·ah, Yom Ha-zikkaron, Yom Ha-atzma·ut, and Yom Y'rushalayim

By a decree of the Israeli Knesset, the twenty-seventh day of the Hebrew month of Nisan is observed annually as Holocaust Memorial Day, called Yom Ha-sho·ah in Hebrew, in memory of the victims of the Nazis and in honor of those who resisted their efforts at genocide. The original date, the fourteenth of Nisan, was chosen to pay tribute to the Warsaw Ghetto uprising which took place on that date. Later, however, Yom Ha-sho·ah was moved to the twenty-seventh of Nisan so that it could be observed after Passover. When the twenty-seventh of Nisan falls on Saturday night and Sunday, however, Yom Ha-sho·ah is observed on Sunday night and Monday so as to avoid any conflict with Shabbat. While there is no universally accepted liturgy for this commemoration, it is a time to pause and reflect on the horrors of the Holocaust. To this end, many synagogues and communities hold special services on the evening of Yom Ha-sho·ah that incorporate speakers, prayers, and poetry appropriate to the day. Many synagogues invite survivors, or their children or grandchildren, to participate in a ceremonial lighting of a six-branched *m'norah* intended to recall the six million martyrs. *Megillat Hasho·ah: The Shoah Scroll* is a text produced jointly by the Schechter Institute of Jewish Studies in Jerusalem and the Rabbinical Assembly to give structure to the observance of Yom Ha-sho·ah. Many prayerbooks also have special readings that are appropriate for this solemn day of remembrance.

The State of Israel was proclaimed on the fifth of Iyyar, 5708, corresponding to May 14, 1948, and this day is celebrated as Israel Independence Day, also popularly known by its Hebrew name, Yom Ha-atzma·ut. In Israel, the day is celebrated with parades and great celebration. For Jews everywhere, the fact of Israeli independence is considered not merely in terms of its political implications, but also in terms of its religious significance. Nevertheless, a specific formal liturgy for its commemoration has not yet been established. Some prayerbooks, including *Siddur Sim Shalom,* incorporate a new Al Ha-nissim prayer modeled on the versions recited at Ḥanukkah and on Purim into the Amidah and the Grace after Meals. Some congregations also recite the full version of Hallel. Further, some synagogues call three people to the Torah to read a special passage about God's protection of Israel in the Promised Land, Deuteronomy 7:12–8:18. In such synagogues, the third *aliyah* is considered the *maftir* reading and is then followed by a *haftarah,* Isaiah 10:32–12:6 (the same as for the eighth day of Passover), which deals with God's promises of national redemption. It is also customary to recite the Prayer for the Welfare of the State of Israel that appears in most prayerbooks.

Although Yom Ha-atzma·ut falls during *s'firah,* the celebration of Israel Independence Day is usually, and reasonably, deemed to take precedence over the restrictions on joyous behavior normally associated with the weeks between Passover and Shavuot.

The day before Yom Ha-atzma·ut is called Yom Ha-zikkaron, Memorial Day, and is dedicated to the memory of all those who have died in defense of the State of Israel since 1948 and of the Jewish *yishuv* in pre-State days. As on Yom Ha-sho·ah, there is no special liturgy for this day. It is appropriate to add special prayers to the service and to recite the El Malei Raḥamim memorial prayer in memory of those who have died in defense of Israel. Many congregations recite Kaddish in memory of the fallen. A memorial candle may also be lit at home or in the synagogue, or in both places. In Israel, an air raid siren is sounded early in the morning of Yom Ha-zikkaron as the entire country pauses to observe a national moment of mourning. Observing a similar moment of silence in sympathy with the citizens of Israel is also an appropriate gesture for Jews in the Diaspora.

When the fifth of Iyyar falls on Friday or Saturday, Yom Ha-atzma·ut is observed on the previous Thursday. When it falls on a Monday, it is observed on the following Tuesday. This is done so that the festivities do not fall just before, on, or just after Shabbat. And a Monday Yom Ha-atzma·ut would make Yom Ha-zikkaron fall just after Shabbat.

On the twenty-eighth day of Iyyar in 1967, the IDF entered the Old City of Jerusalem, which Jordan had occupied since the War of Independence in 1948. Among other things, this meant that the Western Wall (the *kotel*), the last surviving remnant of the Temple, was again in Jewish hands, as were many other sites of incomparable historical and cultural significance. It has become customary to observe the twenty-eighth of Iyyar as Yom Y'rushalayim (Jerusalem Day). There is no fixed liturgy for this day, nor are there any specific home or communal rituals that have evolved. It is merely an opportunity to reflect on the sanctity of Jerusalem and to honor the men and women of the Israel Defense Forces who participated in its liberation. It is also appropriate to remember those who fell in the battle for the city, both in 1948 and then again in 1967.

Shavuot

Shavuot falls on the sixth and seventh days of the Hebrew month of Sivan. (The festival is observed only on the sixth of Sivan in Israel.) Like Sukkot and Passover, it is a multi-dimensional holiday, embracing profound historical, spiritual, and agricultural aspects.

From the agricultural perspective, Shavuot marks the end of the counting of the *omer* that began on Passover, but it is also referred to in the Torah at Numbers 28:26 as *yom ha-bikkurim* (the day of first fruits) and at Exodus 23:16 as *ḥag ha-katzir,* the harvest festival. In Israel, especially on the agricultural kibbutzim, much has been made of this aspect of the festival, and elaborate ceremonies involving the first fruits of the harvest season have been developed. Outside of Israel, many synagogues attempt to incorporate this theme by adorning their sanctuaries with flowers or other symbols of the fertile earth.

The historical dimension of the festival has to do with the receiving of the Torah at Mount Sinai, which, according to tradition, took place on the sixth day of Sivan. This theme is especially prominent liturgically, as Shavuot is repeatedly called *z'man mattan torateinu* (the time of the giving of our Torah).

Spiritually speaking, Shavuot is the festival of revelation. *Emet Ve-Emunah: Statement of Principles of Conservative Judaism* (New York: The Jewish Theological Seminary of America and The Rabbinical Assembly, 1988), opens with the words, "We believe in God. Indeed, Judaism cannot be detached from belief in God. Conservative Judaism affirms its belief in revelation, the uncovering of an external source of truth emanating from God." It goes on to explain that

> the single greatest event in the history of God's revelation took place at Sinai, but was not limited to it. . . . Some of us conceive of revelation as the personal encounter between God and human beings. Among them there are those who believe that this personal encounter has propositional content—that God communicated with us in actual words. For them, revelation's content is immediately normative, as defined by rabbinic interpretation. The commandments of the Torah themselves issue directly from God. Others, however, believe that revelation consists of an ineffable human encounter with God. The experience of revelation inspires the verbal formulation by human beings of norms and ideas, thus continuing the historical influence of this revelational encounter. Others among us conceive of revelation as the continuing discovery, through nature and history, of truths about God and the world. These truths, although always culturally conditioned, are nevertheless seen as God's ultimate purpose for creation. Proponents of this view tend to see revelation as an ongoing process rather than as a specific event.

These inspirational words should show the way for contemporary Jews attempting to relate to Shavuot. However revelation is defined, Shavuot celebrates the "single greatest event" in Jewish history. Shavuot is the holiday that reminds us that faith in the truth of revelation is at the heart of all legitimate varieties of Judaism and Jewish identity.

The custom of not reciting Taḥanun on the days before Shavuot is interesting to consider in its own right. On the first of Sivan, Taḥanun is omitted because it is Rosh Ḥodesh. On the second day of Sivan, formally called Yom Ha-m'yuḥas, it is omitted as a kind of nod to the fact that it was on that day that God specified the destiny of Israel to become "a kingdom of priests and a holy nation" (Exodus 19:6). Then, on the following three days, called Sh'loshet Y'mei Hagbalah ("The Three Days of Demarcation"), Taḥanun is omitted because these were the days regarding which God command the Israelites at the foot of Mount Sinai to be careful neither to "go up the mountain or [even] to touch the border of it . . ." (Exodus 19:12). These are thus days of the most sacred anticipation and it would be counterproductive to include especially somber prayers such a Taḥanun on such days.

The standard laws that relate to rest on the festivals apply to both days of Shavuot. No later than eighteen minutes before sundown on the eve of Shavuot, candles are lit. Two blessings are recited: the standard blessing over festival candles, *barukh attah adonai, eloheinu, melekh ha-olam, asher kidd'shanu b'mitzvotav v'tzivvanu l'hadlik neir shel yom tov* ("Praised are You, Adonai, our God, Sovereign of the universe, who, sanctifying us with divine commandments, has commanded us to kindle the festival lamp") and the She-heḥeyyanu. On Shabbat, the first blessing ends: *l'hadlik neir shel shabbat v'shel yom tov* ("to kindle the Sabbath and festival lamp"). On the second night of Shavuot (or the first night if it follows Shabbat), the kindling of a flame would not be permitted, as the candles are not being lit prior to the holiday but on it. But while fire cannot be kindled on the holiday it may be transferred, and so it has become customary to light a candle at the same time the candles are lit on the first night so that on the second night, or the first night that is immediately preceded by Shabbat, the candles can be lit merely by transferring a flame. In addition, a special Yizkor candle is lit just prior to the formal holiday candles for the second day of Shavuot by those who will be reciting the Yizkor Service the following day. There is no blessing recited on the kindling of this candle, although many prayerbooks include appropriate devotional material to recite just before lighting the memorial candle.

There is a custom that services should not begin early on Shavuot as they may on the other holidays so as to make sure that the full *s'firah* counting-period is completed before the holiday begins. On both days of the festival, Hallel is read and two scrolls of the Torah are removed from the Ark. On the first day, we read from the first scroll the nineteenth and twentieth chapters of Exodus, which describe the giving of the Ten Commandments at Mount Sinai. It is customary for the congregation to stand while the Ten Commandments are read aloud, and to remain standing until the individual honored with that *aliyah* concludes the final blessing. The *maftir* portion, Numbers 28:26–31, which describes the sacrificial requirements for Shavuot, is then read from the second scroll. The *haftarah* is Ezekiel 1:1–28, 3:12, which describes the prophet's experience of God's revelatory presence, a kind of personal version of the national revelation that took place at Sinai.

On the second day, the reading from the first scroll is Deuteronomy 15:19–16:17, which describes the observance of the festivals in ancient times. On Shabbat, however, the reading begins at Deuteronomy 14:22 and the number of *aliyot* is increased to seven. The *haftarah* is taken from the second and third chapters of the Book of Habakkuk.

A long, complex, and very beautiful hymn known as Akdamut is read in many synagogues as part of the Shavuot liturgy. It is customarily chanted before the Torah reading on the first day. It is also customary to read the Book of Ruth on the second day of Shavuot. When it is read in synagogue, Ruth is generally read from a printed book, not from a scroll. Even in congregations in which Ruth is read from a scroll, however, there is neither an introductory nor a concluding blessing. Why is Ruth associated with this holiday? The simplest answer is merely that the Book of Ruth describes events that took place in the season of Shavuot. Another, more satisfying explanation is that Ruth herself is understood as a model of Jewish piety: just as she accepted Judaism wholeheartedly and refused to return to her parents' home in Moab after the death of her husband, so did the Jewish people accept the revelation of God's Torah at Sinai without hesitation or uncertainty.

The Yizkor Service, discussed in more detail above and elsewhere in this volume by Rabbi Carl Astor, is recited on the second day of Shavuot, just as on Yom Kippur, Sh'mini Atzeret, and the eighth day of Passover.

One of the most interesting (and unexpected) revivals of a custom long fallen into almost universal disuse has to do with the reintroduction of the Tikkun Leil Shavuot in recent years. Originally a custom developed by medieval mystics, the Tikkun is an event during which people remain awake throughout the first night of Shavuot studying Torah and then recite the Morning Service at sunrise. What could be more appropriate than immersion in Torah study as part of one's observance of the holiday which celebrates the receiving of the Torah? Rabbi Isaac Klein relates an alternate explanation of staying awake all night: that this custom arose because the Israelites camped at Sinai were sleeping far too soundly and the thunder that accompanied the giving of the Torah was sent along to wake them up! Today, we demonstrate our eagerness to accept the Torah by staying up all night, lest we too be caught sleeping when we should be ready to receive the Torah (Klein, p. 149). Many synagogues organize Torah study sessions that continue through the night.

Some synagogues conduct confirmation ceremonies on the first day of Shavuot for young people who have completed a certain stage of their Jewish educations. This ceremony was originally introduced in Reform temples to replace the bar and bat mitzvah ceremony at age thirteen with confirmation at age sixteen. Even Reform congregations no longer use it in place of bar or bat mitzvah, but some modern congregations have nevertheless retained it as a way of encouraging teenagers to pursue their Jewish studies.

Although there are those who see a halakhic obligation to serve meat at all festivals meals, "for there can be no truly joyful feasting except when meat is served" (*BT* P'saḥim 109a), it is nevertheless widely customary to serve only dairy meals on Shavuot (see, however, the gloss of the Rema to *SA* Oraḥ Ḥayyim 494:3, who only seems to know the custom of eating dairy foods on the first day of the festival and who recommends that meat be served after the dairy). The background reason for this tradition is not at all clear. Klein offers the explanation that it might be derived from an interpretation of the verse "honey and milk shall be under your tongue" (Song of Songs 4:11), as a reference to the Torah, whose words are as dear to our hearts as milk and honey are to our lips. Others connect it to the sacrifices that were offered on this day (see the Rema's comments referenced above). Still others suggest a more practical explanation: after the Torah was revealed at Sinai, the Israelites could no longer eat the non-kosher meat they had prepared for their journey and so, at least until new provisions could be made, they had no choice but to eat only dairy foods. Klein (p. 151) also suggests one symbolic explanation according to which dairy is the food of restraint, but meat is the food of indulgence. Since the Torah exists, among other things, to inculcate restraint and self-control in its adherents, tradition endorses as appropriate the idea of celebrating its revelation with dairy foods. It has become a popular custom to eat cheesecake or crepes filled with cheese, often called by the Yiddish name *blintzes,* on Shavuot.

Fast Days

Fasting as a spiritual exercise reflects two very different aspects of human nature: the desire to afflict the soul for spiritual gain and the desire to limit the practice of asceticism to certain communal, predetermined rituals that will prevent the kind of excessive self-denial that might conceivably be misconstrued as a rejection of God's gifts to humankind. Both of these concepts have a place in Judaism. On the one hand, the Torah recognizes the positive place of self-denial in sensitizing people to the degree to which they must be thankful to God for the good things in their lives. On the other hand, by setting aside predetermined fast days, Judaism simultaneously gives license and limit to this tendency.

There are three different kinds of fasts within Jewish spiritual and legal tradition: statutory public fasts, occasional public fasts (i.e., those decreed on an *ad hoc* basis), and private fasts undertaken by individuals for their own private reasons. The second and third of these kinds of fasts are rare today, but many statutory public fasts are well-known and widely observed. The best known in this category, of course, is Yom Kippur, the sole statutory fast decreed by the Torah itself. The other statutory fasts are the Fast of Gedaliah, the Tenth of Teivet, the Fast of Esther, the Seventeenth of Tammuz, and the Ninth of Av. On fast days other than Yom Kippur and the Ninth of Av, the only prohibitions in effect are those that forbid eating and drinking. Yom Kippur is discussed above; Tishah Be'av (the Ninth of Av) is discussed below.

There are a number of changes and additions to the fast day's services. A special prayer, called Aneinu, is added in the reader's repetition of the Amidah during the Morning Service. Following the Amidah, Avinu Malkeinu is recited. Three people are called forward to the Torah and a standard reading for fast days (Exodus 32:11–14 and 34:1–10) is read with the interesting added feature that the Torah reader pauses three times to allow the congregation vocally to participate in the reading by declaiming aloud three specific phrases (the last seven words in Exodus 32:12, the last ten words of Exodus 34:6 and the first eight words of Exodus 34:7, and the last four words in Exodus 34:9), before the reader repeats them as part of the formal reading. During the Afternoon Service, the same Torah portion is read again. The third person is designated the *maftir* and subsequently chants the special *haftarah* for fast days, Isaiah 55:6–56:8. In the silent Amidah, those who are fasting add the Aneinu paragraph in the T'fillah blessing, but the cantor or prayer leader repeating the Amidah aloud adds it in as a separate blessing, a rare twentieth benediction, right after the Ge'ullah blessing, and also adds the Priestly Benediction to the repetition of the Amidah. The Sim Shalom version of the final blessing, the prayer for peace, is recited instead of the usual afternoon version, Shalom Rav. Avinu Malkeinu is also added to the Afternoon Service.

The Fast of Gedaliah has already been mentioned above in the section of this chapter about the High Holidays. As noted, it falls on the third day of the month of Tishrei, the day following Rosh Hashanah, and hearkens back to the days of Gedaliah ben Aḥikam, who was a Jewish official appointed by the Babylonians after the destruction of the First Temple (Jeremiah 40:7, 2 Kings 25:22, and cf. *BT* Rosh Ha-shanah 18b; Klein, p. 251). This minor fast commemorates his assassination and the end of hopes that a reasonable accommodation with the Babylonians could be achieved. The fast begins at sunrise and ends at nightfall.

The Tenth of Teivet marks the beginning of the siege of Jerusalem that would continue with the breach of the walls of Jerusalem on the Seventeenth of Tammuz and culminate with the destruction of Jerusalem on the Ninth of Av.

If the Fast of Gedaliah, the Tenth of Teivet, the Seventeenth of Tammuz, or the Ninth of Av should fall on Shabbat, their observance is postponed until Sunday. (The Fast of Esther can never fall on Shabbat.)

The Fast of Esther was mentioned above. While a fast is mentioned in the Bible at Esther 4:16, it is not at all explicit there that an analogous fast was meant to be observed by successive generations; its ongoing observance was an addition of the rabbis of ancient times. In the Book of Esther, the heroine proclaims a three-day fast so the people can pray for her before she dares present herself before King Ahasuerus. We commemorate this three-day fast with a one-day version on the day preceding Purim. This fast is observed from sunrise until nightfall. If Purim falls on Sunday, the fast is observed the previous Thursday. This is the least strict of all the statutory fasts. Even if one's eyes are merely aching as a result of not eating, one may break the fast (gloss of the Rema to *SA* Oraḥ Ḥayyim 686:2)—the essential element is not to ruin the enjoyment of Purim itself by taking an overly fastidious approach to the fast that precedes it.

The Seventeenth of Tammuz is also a sunrise-to-nightfall fast day. Coming just three weeks before the Ninth of Av, this fast commemorates the breach of the walls of Jerusalem by the Romans after many months of siege in 70 C.E. (The fast also commemorates the breach of the walls during the Babylonian siege of the city in the sixth century B.C.E., although historically this occurred a week earlier in the month, as noted at Jeremiah 39:7.) Three weeks later, the great fast of the Ninth of Av recalls the destruction of Jerusalem during both sieges. (At Jeremiah 52:12, the prophet gives the precise date for the destruction of the city as the tenth of Av, but this is not taken into account in our liturgical calendar.)

The Seventeenth of Tammuz inaugurates a mournful period that culminates three weeks later on the Ninth of Av. This period, popularly called the Three Weeks, is observed as a time of communal sadness and mourning. Weddings and other joyous occasions are not scheduled during this period (*SA* Oraḥ Ḥayyim 551:2).

The days between Rosh Ḥodesh Av and the Ninth of Av are called the Nine Days and are characterized by the rabbinic dictum: "When Av begins, our joy is diminished" (*M* Ta·anit 4:6). Except on Shabbat, it is customary to refrain from eating meat and drinking wine during this nine-day period (*SA* Oraḥ Ḥayyim 551:9, where several variants of this custom are listed). The reason for both prohibitions is simply that meat and wine are commonly associated in our tradition with joy and celebration. Others observe still other restrictions of public celebration during these final days leading up to the Ninth of Av.

On the Sabbaths that fall during the Three Weeks, special *haftarot* that emphasize the sad themes of the season are read. The *haftarah* for the first Shabbat is Jeremiah 1:1–2:3; for the second, Jeremiah 2:4–28, 3:4, and 4:1–2; and for the third, Isaiah 1:1–27. The last Shabbat is called Shabbat Ḥazon, a name derived from the opening words of that week's *haftarah*. There are numerous customs regarding the use of the melody used to chant the Book of Lamentations on the Ninth of Av during this introductory period. Much of the *haftarah* on Shabbat Ḥazon is chanted to this special trope, for example. Similarly, some sing parts of L'khah Dodi to the tune of Eili Tziyyon, one of the most popular dirges sung on the Ninth of Av, during the Kabbalat Shabbat service leading into Shabbat Ḥazon.

Tishah Be'av

Aside from Yom Kippur, the only other full-day fast on the annual calendar is the fast of the Ninth of Av, popularly called by its Hebrew name, Tishah Be'av. By common consensus, Tishah Be'av is the saddest day of the Jewish year. According to tradition, it was on this very day that the First Temple was destroyed by the Babylonians in 586 B.C.E. and that the Second Temple was destroyed by the Romans in the year 70 C.E. Subsequently, many other tragedies have befallen the Jewish people on this date, including the expulsion of the Jews from Spain in 1492.

The observance of Tishah Be'av itself begins at sundown. A simple meal, commonly called the *se'udah mafseket* ("the meal of demarcation") precedes the fast. Many customs are associated with services on Tishah Be'av. In some synagogues, the curtain that hangs before the Ark is replaced with a black one reminiscent of the pall that covers a casket on its last journey to the grave. Many synagogues also dim the lights, or even illuminate the sanctuary solely with candles so as to induce a mood of solemnity. It is also customary to read the Book of Lamentations while sitting on the floor or on low stools or cushions, another sign of mourning. The other practices associated with Yom Kippur also apply to Tishah Be'av. In addition to fasting, these include not wearing leather shoes (which were taken as a sign of luxury), refraining from sexual intimacy, refraining from washing for pleasure (as opposed to for hygienic purposes), and not wearing perfumes or using scented oils (*SA* Oraḥ Ḥayyim 554:1).

The Evening Service is recited in a special way, either by omitting any singing altogether or by chanting the service in a mournful undertone.

After the Amidah is recited, the Book of Lamentations, called *Eikhah* or *M'gillat Eikhah* in Hebrew, is chanted with a special, mournful trope. There are five chapters in the book, but the third chapter has a unique melody of its own that reflects both its unusual meter and its pivotal place in the book. The penultimate verse of the book is repeated after the final verse so as to finish the reading on a slightly positive note. This verse is chanted first by the congregation and then sung out by the reader. It is also customary to recite liturgical dirges popularly called *kinot* that have been written over the generations, all of which expand and expound on the theme of suffering and loss. One of the most famous of these is Eili Tziyyon, mentioned above as the source of the mournful melody for L'khah Dodi on Shabbat Ḥazon. A full selection of traditional and innovative liturgical selections for Tishah Be'av edited by Rabbi Jeffrey Hoffman, including the prayer services for the day and a translation of *Eikhah*, was published in 2003 by the Rabbinical Assembly under the title *Siddur Tishah Be'av*.

During the Morning Service, it is customary not to put on *tallit* or *t'fillin* as usual, but rather to defer both until later in the day (*SA* Oraḥ Ḥayyim 555:1). For the knowledgeable, the absence of these important daily rituals is a very visible sign of mourning and is clearly reminiscent of the exemption of mourners from these *mitzvot* in the days between the death of a close relative and his or her burial. During the repetition of the Amidah, the special Aneinu paragraph is interpolated between the seventh and eighth blessings. One Torah scroll is taken from the Ark, and three people are called forward to participate in the reading of Deuteronomy 4:25–40. A *haftarah*, Jeremiah

8:13–9:23, is also chanted. The normal *haftarah* trope is not used, however, in favor of that of Lamentations. After the Torah is returned to the Ark, it is customary to repeat the recitation of Lamentations and to recite *kinot*. The daily psalm is deferred until the Afternoon Service. Some congregations do not repeat Lamentations in the morning, however.

It is customary to hold a special early Afternoon Service on Tishah Be'av so that, having omitted the donning of *tallit* and *t'fillin* during the Morning Service, worshipers need not delay unduly in the performance of these *mitzvot*. The Torah is read at the Afternoon Service and the reading is the normal one for a fast day. The third individual called to the Torah also chants the *haftarah*. The sense that the mournful nature of the day is waning is accentuated in synagogue: not only are *tallit* and *t'fillin* donned, but the Torah and *haftarah* are chanted in their usual modes. A special version of the blessing for Jerusalem beginning with the word Naḥeim ("Grant comfort!") is substituted for the regular text. As on all fast days other than Yom Kippur, worshipers add the Aneinu paragraph to the T'fillah blessing. The prayer leader, however, recites Aneinu as a separate paragraph immediately following the Ge'ullah benediction.

While there are no formal restrictions against work on Tishah Be'av, effort should be made to conduct oneself in the spirit of the day. The study of Torah should be avoided as well, except for texts related to appropriately sad themes, because the pleasure associated with such intellectual endeavor is deemed inappropriate for such a doleful day (*SA* Oraḥ Ḥayyim 554:1–2).

If the Ninth of Av falls on Shabbat, the fast is deferred until Sunday. (This creates the peculiar situation of the Ninth of Av being observed on the tenth of Av.) By deferring the fast rather than moving it back to Thursday, we demonstrate our reluctance to embrace this very sad day.

Just as the three weeks that lead into Tishah Be'av have their own name and some special customs, so too do the seven weeks following Tishah Be'av. The Shabbat immediately following the Ninth of Av is called Shabbat Naḥamu, which name derives from the opening words of the *haftarah* chanted on that day, *naḥamu, naḥamu, ammi* ("Be comforted, be comforted, My people"), from Isaiah 40:1. There are six subsequent special *haftarot* for the Sabbaths that fall during these weeks, each featuring its own message of comfort and consolation. The seven Sabbaths on which these seven *haftarot* are read lead directly into Rosh Hashanah, thus bringing the liturgical year to a close with an extended message of comfort and optimism.

It is interesting to note that it takes three special Shabbatot to prepare for Tishah Be'av, but seven to recover from it. This simply reflects the nature of loss and recovery: bonds that bind us to those we love can be severed in the blink of an eye, but recovery takes time and patience. That this is true on the national level no less so than it is on the level of the individual is one of the enduring lessons of Jewish history.

Some wonder how to relate the events of the Shoah to the observance of Tishah Be'av. The rituals of Tishah Be'av seem, after all, to presuppose that the sins of Israel brought on the destruction of Jerusalem and that the Babylonians or the Romans were merely instruments of divine punishment. Can anyone speak of the Shoah in such terms? Those who find it inconceivable to describe the Holocaust as reflective of God's will to punish Israel make a special effort to avoid any mention of the Shoah in their observance of Tishah Be'av. Such people consider the Shoah to represent human evil and cannot tolerate any sort of theological justification. Others find a kind of solace in connecting the events of the Shoah to the long pageant of Jewish suffering and martyrdom and do not avoid mention of the Shoah and its martyrs during Tishah Be'av. Indeed, some special dirges have been written about those who died during the Shoah, and some synagogues make a point of including them among the more traditional *kinot*.

The existence of the modern State of Israel presents a different challenge to the traditional observance of Tishah Be'av. Some claim not to see an issue and insist that the existence of Israel should have no impact on Tishah Be'av because, whatever Israel represents, it does not present any sort of cogent reason not to regret the disasters of the past. Others find it peculiar, even slightly grotesque, to mourn for Jerusalem as though it were in ruins, thus also to ignore the fact that the city today is the thriving, dynamic capital of a Jewish state. Some have even advocated abandoning the observance of Tishah Be'av entirely. Most Conservative Jews find themselves somewhere between these two extremes. Not yet ready to dispense with Tishah Be'av and its sad and difficult message, they find it hard to deny that something very fundamental has changed with the establishment of the State of Israel. No clear avenue of resolution has presented itself in this debate, but the large majority of Conservative synagogues maintain the traditional set of observances and customs on Tishah Be'av, perhaps nodding to the dilemma by talking about the great success of the Zionist endeavor while still chanting *kinot* in recollection of the long centuries of unfulfilled yearning for Zion that preceded the founding of the State. Some have suggested ending our fast after reciting the Afternoon Service as an acknowledgement of the miracle of the modern State of Israel.

With regard to fasts in general, it is worth noting that the difficulty many modern Jews have in dealing with this particular aspect of our tradition mirrors the degree to which modern culture is obsessed with food. It is no wonder that occasions which demand that we refrain from eating are such a challenge to so many! For our ancestors, fast days were a much more normal part of life. In addition to public fasts, many people regularly made fasting a part of their personal spiritual lives as well. David fasted when his child was sick (2 Samuel 12:16). Nehemiah fasted over the bad news he received about Jerusalem (Nehemiah 1:4). Ezra fasted when he heard reports about the challenges of the new community in Israel (Ezra 8:23). Even wicked King Ahab fasted when he received bad news (1 Kings 21:27)! For them, it was a natural way to express their concerns and emotions. For us, on the other hand, nothing could be *less* natural. In a world of eating disorders, rampant obesity, and binge dieting, the traditions regarding fasting can serve as a helpful framework for reevaluating our relationship to food. One thing seems clear: the ancients had a far healthier control of their diet than do moderns. They consumed food, but food did not consume them—and in that, they exercised precisely the kind of control over their lives that moderns find so elusive and so desirable. That should give us all food for thought!

Tu Be'av

Tu Be'av, the fifteenth of the month of Av, is a minor holiday. According to the Talmud it was celebrated as a day of rejoicing in the times of the Temple. It was almost like a Jewish Sadie Hawkins day where in ancient times the unmarried Jewish girls of Jerusalem would dress in white and go out dancing in the streets and vineyards. According to the Talmud, there were no happier times in the Jewish year than the successful completion of Yom Kippur and Tu Be'av (*BT* Ta·anit 30b). In modern Israel it is called *ḥag ha-ahavah,* the holiday of love.

Rosh Ḥodesh

Although it is clear that Rosh Ḥodesh, the first day of every lunar month, was once embraced with fervor and enthusiasm, today Rosh Ḥodesh is mostly observed through some additions to the prayer service, a special Torah reading, and, on the preceding Shabbat, a special announcement and prayer.

Traditionally, Rosh Ḥodesh was a special holiday for women, a monthly day on which they were freed from work (cf. *SA* Oraḥ Ḥayyim 417:1). This serendipity came to women as a reward for their refusal to offer their jewelry for the making of the Golden Calf and today many synagogues have instituted all-female prayer *minyanim,* study sessions, and discussion groups in honor of Rosh Ḥodesh.

The Shabbat before a new moon is called Shabbat M'var'khim because a special prayer called Birkat Ha-ḥodesh is recited publicly. (The Hebrew word *m'varkhim* means "we bless," so the name of the Shabbat is specifically related to the practice of reciting the blessing.) This blessing contains an announcement of when the new month will begin and a prayer that the coming month will be one of blessing and prosperity. Birkat Ha-ḥodesh is not recited in the month of Elul in anticipation of the arrival of Tishrei, the first two days of which are Rosh Hashanah, since that occasion is deemed momentous enough that no additional announcement is needed.

As mentioned, there are some changes to the liturgy on Rosh Ḥodesh. Taḥanun is omitted. A paragraph beginning with the words *ya·aleh v'yavo* is added into the first of the final three blessings of the Amidah. The short version of Hallel is recited. Four individuals are called forward to the Torah and Numbers 28:1–15 is read aloud. (Anomalously, the third verse is read twice, as both the final verse in the first *aliyah* and as the opening verse in the second. This enables the entire fourth *aliyah* to be about Rosh Ḥodesh without requiring that any of the rules that govern the public reading of the Torah be broken.) There is a special version of the Amidah that is recited as part of the Musaf Service on Rosh Ḥodesh. *T'fillin* are removed before the recitation of the Musaf Service to emphasize the semi-festive nature of the day.

If Rosh Ḥodesh coincides with Shabbat, two scrolls are taken from the Ark. Seven individuals are called forward for *aliyot* read from the first scroll (the week's regular Torah portion), and the *maftir,* read from the second scroll, is Numbers 28:9–15, a passage devoted to the topic of Rosh Ḥodesh. There is also a special *haftarah,* Isaiah 66:1–24, that refers explicitly to the observance of Rosh Ḥodesh. An alternate version of the Amidah is recited at the Musaf Service.

When Rosh Ḥodesh falls on a Sunday, there is also a special *haftarah* read on the previous Shabbat, 1 Samuel 20:18–42, which contains the words *maḥar ḥodesh* ("tomorrow is the new moon").

Rosh Ḥodesh is sometimes observed for one day and sometimes for two. This is due to the fact that a complete revolution of the moon around the earth takes more than twenty-nine days but less than thirty. Since a calendar cannot effectively deal with fractions of days, it compensates by adding this portion of a day to some months and subtracting it from others. The practical result of this calculation is that some Hebrew months are twenty-nine days long and others thirty. (The technical term for a twenty-nine-day month is *ḥaseir,* "lacking," while thirty-day months are called *malei,* "full.") Therefore, when a month is twenty-nine days long, the Rosh Ḥodesh celebration for the following month lasts one day and that one day is the first of the new month. When a month is thirty days long, the Rosh Ḥodesh of the following month is celebrated for two days, of which the first is the final day of the previous month and the second is the first day of the ensuing month. (For an explanation of which months are twenty-nine days and which thirty, and why it is that two of the months vary in length from year to year, see Klein, pp. 257ff.)

Kiddush L'vanah

In keeping with the sense that the appearance of the new moon in the nighttime sky is an event suggestive specifically of divine beneficence toward a people whose calendar depends on its sighting, the ancients developed the custom of leaving the synagogue after evening prayers once a month formally to acknowledge God as the source of astronomical precision in the heavens. This act, called the Blessing of the Moon in traditional sources but popularly called Kiddush L'vanah ("the Sanctification of the Moon"), is generally recited on a Saturday night when people are still dressed in their Shabbat finery (*SA* Oraḥ Ḥayyim 426:1), but may actually be recited any night before the fifteenth day of the lunar month (*SA* Oraḥ Ḥayyim 426:3–4). Ideally, the prayer, which is printed in most complete editions of the traditional prayerbook, should be recited outdoors, but may also be recited by an open window or door. The prayer should also be recited while standing (*MT* Hilkhot B'rakhot 10:17, and cf. the gloss of the Rema to *SA* Oraḥ Ḥayyim 426:2) because its recitation is deemed to be in some sense equivalent to receiving the Sh'khinah, the divine presence, into one's personal ambit (*MT* Hilkhot B'rakhot 10:17, citing Rabbi Yoḥanan's dictum as preserved at *BT* Sanhedrin 42a). In the month of Av, the blessing is not recited before Tishah Be'av nor should it be recited before Yom Kippur in the month of Tishrei (Rema to *SA* Oraḥ Ḥayyim 426:2).

Birkat Ha-ḥamah

The ancients possessed remarkable astronomical acumen, which modern Jews do well to honor even when it seems not precisely to correspond to physical reality as understood by modern scientists. An excellent example has to do with the theory, put forward by the ancient talmudic master Abaye, that the sun (and with it the heavens in their fullness) returns every twenty-eight years to the specific spot it occupied when it was first created by God "when the [vernal] equinox falls in Saturn on Tuesday evening going into Wednesday"

(*BT* B'rakhot 59b). How exactly Abaye came to that conclusion is not recorded, nor is it obvious how the ancients themselves understood the talmudic text cited, which refers specifically to the sun returning to its "turning point," the moon attaining its fullest "power," and the constellations displaying the fullest orderliness of their progress across the nighttime sky. Nonetheless, modern Jews continue to recite a blessing specifically acknowledging God as Creator every twenty-eight years on the Wednesday morning following the onset of a new twenty-eight year cycle (*MT* Hilkhot B'rakhot 10:18, *SA* Oraḥ Ḥayyim 429:2). In the twenty-first century C.E., the blessing (called Birkat Ha-ḥamah) was recited last on April 8, 2009, and will be recited again on April 8, 2037; April 8, 2065; and April 8, 2093.

The Jewish Life Cycle

CARL N. ASTOR

One of the most wonderful features of the Jewish religion is the way in which it adds meaning and holiness to life literally from birth to death. Each detail in its own way helps to concretize the values of Judaism in the most helpful and practical fashion. This chapter, although not exhaustive, outlines the basic observances of the Jewish life cycle, beginning with birth itself.

Procreation and Birth

The First Mitzvah

The very first *mitzvah* in the Torah, recorded at Genesis 1:28 and then repeated at Genesis 9:1 and 9:7, is the commandment to procreate and, indeed, tradition has always regarded this as one of the most important of *mitzvot.* The author of *Sefer Ha-ḥinnukh,* for example, lists procreation as first in order and importance: "The purpose of this commandment is that the world be populated; and the *mitzvah* to procreate is [also] a great commandment, because through it all the other commandments—which were given to humanity and not to angels—may be fulfilled" (*Sefer Ha-ḥinnukh,* commandment no. 1). (The *Sefer Ha-ḥinnukh,* a thirteenth-century book listing and discussing all of the commandments of the Torah, is usually attributed to Rabbi Aaron Halevi of Barcelona.) Although the traditional sources understand the *mitzvah* as applying solely to men, not to women (cf., e.g., *MT* Hilkhot Ishut 15:2), the nature of human reproduction suggests that women, no less than men, should feel called upon by the Torah to participate in the production of the next generation of Jews who, like themselves, will eventually be called upon to procreate and thus create a subsequent generation.

In light of the decimation of Jews in the dark days of the Holocaust, but also in light of dwindling population numbers caused by Jewish assimilation into secular culture in unprecedented numbers, this *mitzvah* has taken on added significance. The reality is that Jews are an endangered species. Therefore, the much discussed goal of achieving a kind of universal Zero Population Growth in the world is simply not an option if Jews hope to survive as a people. Interested readers may profitably consult the responsum by Rabbis Kassel Abelson and Elliot Dorff entitled "Mitzvah Children," which was approved by the CJLS in 2007 and which is available on the website of the Rabbinical Assembly.

Nothing is as simple as it seems, however, and the very powerful and positive value placed on having children also presents a set of dilemmas, some painful even to contemplate, for individuals who, for whatever reason, cannot produce children. The questions are complicated and sensitive. May one (or must one) use fertility drugs or other medical procedures if one is unable to have children naturally? If yes, then which procedures are permitted and which are not? Is it possible to fulfill the obligation to be fruitful and multiply by adopting a child or children? Is there an obligation to divorce one's spouse if one is fully capable of producing children, but one's spouse proves incapable? How many children exactly does it take to fulfill the Torah's commandment to procreate? Is one permitted to use birth control to delay procreation and, if so, which methods are permissible? Are unmarried persons or gay people free of the obligation to procreate? If they are not, then how does tradition imagine them actually proceeding to fulfill that obligation?

For all these are thorny and complex issues, however, there are also certain basic principles that are universally, or almost universally, agreed upon.

As stated above and as discussed elsewhere in this volume by Rabbi David J. Fine in his chapter on the *halakhah* of marriage, it is a positive *mitzvah* of the Torah to have children. According to the school of Shammai, one fulfills this *mitzvah* by producing at least two male children, but the school of Hillel requires at least one male and one female child and the law follows the school of Hillel (*M* Y'vamot 7:6; cf. *MT* Hilkhot Ishut 15:4). The phrase "at least" is key here, as it suggests the desirability of having more than two children in order to replenish and to add to the small population of Jewish people in the world. Environmental issues related to overpopulation are real concerns, but the bottom line has to be that Jews represent only a very small minority of the world's citizens and cannot survive unless they compensate, through procreation and conversion, for losses due to intermarriage and assimilation.

Up to a third of all couples have some difficulty in producing offspring, but many techniques have been developed to assist such couples. These procedures are not without risk, however, and many raise specific halakhic concerns, some of which have been dealt with by the Committee on Jewish Law and Standards of the Rabbinical Assembly. All these matters are discussed at length by Rabbi Avram I. Reisner in his chapter elsewhere in this volume on medical ethics. The basic principle, however, is that all treatments to enhance fertility are permitted as long as they are neither harmful nor dangerous, and as long as they do not entail any activity on the part of either putative parent that contravenes Torah law or rabbinic norms of behavior. Still, each case will invariably be different, and couples grappling with these issues should always consult their rabbi before determining the halakhic permissibility of a specific therapeutic response to infertility. The specific situations of single persons and gay people with respect to the commandment to procreate are discussed by Rabbi Jeremy Kalmanofsky and Rabbi Elliot N. Dorff respectively elsewhere in this volume.

Circumcision

The ritual most closely associated with Jewish identity, at least for boys, is *b'rit milah,* which term, often colloquially pronounced *bris* after the Yiddish by Ashkenazic Jews, denotes the covenant of circumcision. (The phrase is used colloquially both to denote the ritual act itself and the festive occasion surrounding a baby boy's circumcision.) Yet *b'rit milah,* although it is indeed a requirement for men who wish to convert to Judaism, is not itself a requirement for Jewishness nor is the Jewish status of the uncircumcised sons of Jewish mothers considered in doubt. Put differently, circumcision is a *mitzvah* of the Torah, but dereliction in its regard does not deprive the uncircumcised individual of his Jewishness any more than would dereliction with respect to any other commandment.

The origin of *b'rit milah* is in the biblical story of Abraham in Genesis 17:9–12, where the text reads as follows: "And God said to Abraham, 'Keep My covenant throughout the generations, both you and your descendants. And this is [to be the evidence of] the covenant that is to exist between Me and you, and your descendants after you: [that you] circumcise every male among you. Indeed, you must remove your foreskins and [that procedure] shall be the sign of the covenant between Me and you. Every eight-day-old boy among you shall be circumcised throughout every generation.'" The commandment is then repeated at Leviticus 12:2–3 in even clearer language: "When a woman gives birth to a boy . . . his foreskin shall be removed on the eighth day [of his life]."

Are there specific health benefits connected to circumcision? Medical opinion has flip-flopped through the years about the relative advantages and disadvantages of circumcision, but the issue remains a religious one for Jews, not a medical one, and needs to be evaluated solely on its own terms. (It is worth noting, however, that no research has ever concluded that there is something inherently unhealthy about the procedure.) The purpose of *b'rit milah* is to mark the eternal covenant between God and the Jewish people. By its very nature, then, circumcision represents both an obligation on the part of the Jewish people to fulfill the *mitzvot,* and God's concomitant promise to protect and watch over Israel. Indeed, it is precisely because it is deemed symbolic of all the *mitzvot* that *b'rit milah* is designated "an everlasting pact" by Scripture at Genesis 17:13.

Why does the Torah choose to represent the covenant with a sign that will so rarely be seen by anyone other than the circumcised individual himself? Throughout the generations, there have been many attempts to answer this question, but the simplest and the most compelling is simply that the penis is the organ of generation—the Torah reflects an understanding of the human reproductive process that was current in antiquity—and the covenant, for it to be historically and spiritually meaningful, must be passed on from generation to generation. Therefore, the organ of generation is the ideal place to bear its sign. Nor is this a specifically male concept in which women have no role or place: while the sign of the covenant is carved into the flesh of men, *all* Jewish children with Jewish fathers, both boys and girls, are conceived beneath that sign, thus bearing its spiritual imprint from the moment of conception and for the rest of their lives.

The *halakhah* specifically requires every Jewish father to circumcise his son on the eighth day, or to designate someone to perform the circumcision (*MT* Hilkhot Milah 1:1, *SA* Yoreh Dei·ah 260:1). If a child is born to a Jewish mother and a non-Jewish father, or if the father is derelict in his responsibility to circumcise his son, the *mitzvah* is traditionally imagined to devolve upon the community itself or, once the boy attains his majority, on the uncircumcised adult man (*MT loc. cit., SA* Yoreh Dei·ah 261:1). In modern times, most Conservative rabbis stress the fact that the *mitzvah* belongs, if not technically, than at least emotionally and practically, to both parents. Therefore, the mothers of Jewish boys should feel equally obliged to look after their son's circumcision. If, for instance, the Jewish father does not wish to be involved in the *b'rit milah,* the mother should step in and see that the *b'rit* takes place in a timely manner, even filling in for the father ceremonially if necessary. In the event that a Jewish boy is not circumcised as an infant or a child, the responsibility passes to the young man himself upon attaining the age of bar mitzvah (*MT* Hilkhot Milah 1:2).

Although circumcision is primarily a parent's responsibility, it is the rare father or mother who is capable or willing to circumcise his or her own son. For that reason, circumcision is generally carried out by a trained professional called a *moheil.* (Most *mohalim* are men, but there are some female *mohalot* and this is explicitly permitted in the sources, e.g., at *SA* Yoreh Dei·ah 264:1, cf. *MT* Hilkhot Milah 2:1). In many communities, observant Jewish doctors train to become *mohalim,* but in others there are non-medically trained individuals who successfully learn how to carry out circumcisions and, at least in larger Jewish population centers, who make their livings doing so. Other than medical and ritual training (and certification), the sole requirement for being a *moheil* or a *mohelet* are that the individual in question be an observant Jew. Some communities are without *mohalim* and, in such cases, a Jewish physician may be used if a rabbi is also present. The Rabbinical Assembly, in conjunction with the Jewish Theological Seminary, has a program called B'rit Kodesh in which observant physicians are trained to become *mohalim* and encouraged to serve in this capacity especially where no other *mohalim* are available.

The *b'rit milah* must be performed on the eighth day of the child's life during the daylight hours, even on Shabbat or a holiday (*SA* Yoreh Dei·ah 262:1 and 266:2). The eighth day is reckoned from the first day of the child's life, however, so that the *b'rit milah* of a baby born on a Sunday before sundown will be on the following Sunday. (In other words, the time from a child's birth until sundown is counted as the first day.) If the baby is born after sundown on Sunday, the *b'rit milah* is performed a week later, on Monday, during daylight hours. It is traditional to plan the *b'rit* as early in the day as possible to demonstrate one's eagerness to perform the *mitzvah.*

The only exception to this rule is in the case of a child who is medically unfit to be circumcised on the eighth day. In such a case, parents must wait until a doctor determines that there will be no danger to the child (*SA* Yoreh Dei·ah 262:2). If the *milah* is not to be performed on the eighth day of life, it may not be scheduled on Shabbat or on a festival day (*SA* Yoreh Dei·ah 266:2).

The obligation to circumcise a boy on the eighth day of his life overrides the general laws of Shabbat, but only with respect to those aspects of the circumcision ceremony that cannot be readied in advance (*MT* Hilkhot Milah 1:9 and *SA* Yoreh Dei·ah 266:2). If the eighth day of a boy's life falls on a Shabbat or on a festival and one cannot arrange for a *moheil* to be there on that day, the first preference would be to have a qualified Jewish doctor perform the circumcision under the supervision of a rabbi on the appropriate day. A less desirable solution would be to postpone the *b'rit* until the next day, although this is an acceptable alternative.

Why does the Torah specify the boy's eighth day as the earliest time that circumcision may be carried out? Several authorities have suggested that the concept is that child must pass one Shabbat, also called a sign of the covenant at Exodus 31:17, before being granted the more indelible of its signs. (Circumcision is specifically called a sign of the covenant at Genesis 17:11. At Deuteronomy 6:8, *t'fillin* too are described as a sign of the covenant.) Others say that it is because the clotting factor of the blood spikes during the seventh, eighth, and ninth days of a child's life, but there is also a theological implication behind the concept of the eighth day, one related to the notion that the world was created in six days. It thus follows that, after the seventh day, Shabbat, human beings became God's partners in perfecting the work of creation, and it is this partnership with God that is symbolized by circumcision on the eighth day, for circumcision is referred to in classical texts as the perfection of the male body (see, e.g., Rashi's comment to Genesis 17:1, *s.v. ve-h'yeih tamim*). Whatever the actual reason, however, it is having the *b'rit* on the eighth day after birth that, above all else, distinguishes it from a medical circumcision.

If the circumcision is performed before the eighth day, therefore, it is not ritually valid. Since it obviously cannot be redone, the circumcision must be validated by drawing a drop of blood from the shaft of the penis just behind the corona (Klein, p. 425). This ritual, called *hattafat dam b'rit,* is done by a *moheil,* an observant Jewish physician, or a qualified rabbi. Men who become aware later in life that they were circumcised in a nonreligious way are obliged, regardless of their age, to undergo the ceremony of *hattafat dam b'rit.* This is not an act of conversion, however, because the Jewishness of the individual in question does not depend on being circumcised; it is merely the performance of a *mitzvah.*

The *b'rit* may be performed anywhere. If the baby has not yet been brought home, it can be performed in the hospital. (In earlier times, when new mothers routinely spent a week or more in the hospital, holding a *b'rit milah* at home was the exception rather than the rule.) Some families, especially when a large crowd of guests is expected, prefer to hold the *b'rit* in the synagogue. Most families, however, choose to have the *b'rit milah* performed in their homes. This adds to the familial aspect and the warmth of the ceremony.

It is not necessary to have a *minyan* for the *b'rit milah,* nor should a *b'rit milah* ever be delayed past the eighth day of life merely so that more people, even important family members, be able to attend. Even if only the parents, the baby, and the *moheil* are present, the *b'rit* is deemed kosher.

There are several honors regularly given out at a *b'rit*. Typically, there are the *kvatter* and the *kvatterin* (a couple, usually a married couple, that brings the baby into the room where he will be circumcised), the *sandek* (who holds the baby during the *b'rit*), and the individual who either holds the baby while he receives his name or actually recites the prayer used to name the baby. There is no standard rule as to whom these honors should be offered, other than that they should always be given to Jews.

When the child is brought into the room, the guests greet him with the words *barukh ha-ba* ("welcome"). A chair is designated as "the chair of Elijah" and the child is placed there, usually by the *kvatter*, and a prayer is read. The chair should be special in some way and the ritual should be explained as being symbolic of the old belief that the prophet Elijah comes to every *b'rit milah*. The belief reflects an incident related in the First Book of Kings that takes place just after Elijah's confrontation with the prophets of Baal on Mount Carmel. In this part of the story, Elijah questions the loyalty of the Israelites, saying to God: "I am consumed with zeal for the Eternal, the God of Hosts, for the Israelites have abandoned Your covenant, destroyed Your altars, and put Your prophets to the sword, so that I alone am left" (1 Kings 19:10). As a result of this, tradition imagines that Elijah was subsequently destined to attend every *b'rit milah* in order to witness that he had spoken harshly and mistakenly about the people of Israel. Also, Elijah was understood to be the protector of the Jewish people and the eventual herald whom God would send to earth to proclaim news of the coming of the messiah. Placing the baby on the seat of Elijah is, therefore, a kind of prayer that he live to witness the advent of messianic peace and harmony on earth.

Since, technically speaking, it is the father's obligation to have his son circumcised, he must formally designate the *moheil* as his agent to perform the *b'rit*. Some parents, however, remembering how Abraham was commanded to circumcise his own son, wish to participate in the circumcision, and this can be done with the cooperation of the *moheil* who sets up a shield that is clamped shut so that only the foreskin is visible above it. The father may then cut along the face of the shield, secure that no harm can possibly come to the baby.

The blessing recited just before the circumcision is pronounced by the person who is making the cut. It follows the formal blessing formula: *barukh attah adonai, eloheinu, melekh ha-olam, asher kidd'shanu b'mitzvotav v'tzivvanu al ha-milah* ("Praised are You, Adonai, our God, Sovereign of the universe, who, sanctifying us with divine commandments, has commanded regarding circumcision").

There are three steps in the circumcision procedure: *milah* (the actual cutting of the foreskin), *p'ri·ah* (the tearing of the membrane covering the head of the penis to expose the glans), and *m'tzitzah* (the drawing of blood from the site of the circumcision, traditionally done by sucking it out either directly with the mouth or else through a glass tube). There are some modern variations relating to the second and third steps. For example, the second part of the procedure, *p'ri·ah,* is obviated when a clamp is used because the foreskin and the membrane are clamped together and the membrane is cut along with the foreskin. Also, many *mohalim* perform *m'tzitzah* today by daubing the penis with a gauze pad, thus drawing out some blood. This is considered by far the more hygienic way to draw the blood forth and is to be preferred.

Traditionally, sweet wine was the only "anesthetic" administered to the child during the procedure. Today many doctors recommend a topical anesthetic cream, usually EMLA® or lydocaine, that can be applied one hour before the *b'rit milah.* It is unknown whether this alleviates the pain or not, and it should therefore be the parents' decision whether or not to use it.

Immediately after *m'tzitzah,* the father recites this blessing: *barukh attah adonai, eloheinu, melekh ha-olam, asher kidd'shanu b'mitzvotav v'tzivvanu l'hakhniso bi-v'rito shel avraham avinu* ("Praised are You, Adonai, our God, Sovereign of the universe, who, sanctifying us with divine commandments, has commanded us to bring this child into the covenant of Abraham, our forefather").

After the father has recited the blessing, the assembled say *k'sheim she-nikhnas la-b'rit, kein yikkaneis la-torah, la-ḥuppah, u-l'ma·asim tovim* ("As the child has entered the covenant, so may he become learned in the Torah, may he marry, and may he perform many good deeds").

After the *b'rit,* the baby is named. A designated person holds the baby and a prayer that includes the bestowal of a Jewish name is recited over a goblet of wine. Customarily the child is given a drop of wine on a fingertip or a piece of wine-soaked gauze at the recitation of the phrase "and I said to you, in your blood, live!" (Ezekiel 16:6). The issues involved in choosing a Jewish name for a child are discussed below. It is customary not to use a boy's name in public until after he has been named at his *b'rit milah.*

It is traditional to invite guests to a celebratory meal following the ceremony. There is also a special version of the Grace after Meals recited after the meal, which can be found in any standard prayerbook.

The Birth of a Daughter

It is customary to name a daughter in the synagogue at the first opportunity after birth. The father, the mother, or both parents together are called forward for an *aliyah,* after which a special version of the standard Mi She-beirakh prayer is recited in which the girl is given her Jewish name. Sometimes this naming may be delayed until the mother is able to attend the service, but this delay should not be a long one. There is also a special prayer that is recited for the health of the mother after the delivery.

Many families wish to have more elaborate naming ceremonies for their daughters. Consequently, creative and participatory services have been developed for welcoming baby girls into the covenant of Israel. These are known by the names Simḥat Bat ("Rejoicing in a Daughter"), Zeved Ha-bat ("Celebrating the Gift of a Daughter"), or occasionally B'rit Banot ("The Daughters' Covenant"). Even when a Simḥat Bat is planned for a later date at home, it should not replace the traditional naming that takes place at the synagogue before the open scroll of the Torah. Just as with boys, it is customary not to use a girl's name publicly until after she has been named formally.

There are several ceremonies in use within the context of the above-named celebrations for the naming of a newborn girl in the synagogue or in the home. The B'rit Torah ceremony centers around the Torah, the symbol of Jewish learning. Sometimes the baby is brought close to the Torah and may even be permitted to touch the silver that traditionally adorns the scroll. The parents thus express the hope that their daughter will grow up in the ways of the Torah, and that the Torah will always be central in her life. The Tallit Ceremony calls for wrapping the child in a *tallit* and reading verses about the beauty, the warmth, and the security of Jewish tradition, and a prayer that the girl ever be a proud member of the Jewish community who feels herself always to be sheltered beneath the protective wings of God's presence. The B'rit Ha-neirot Ceremony is probably the ritual most suited for the home. Various members of the family light candles, accompanied by readings involving the themes of light and life. Each of these ceremonies may be followed by a special Mi She-beirakh prayer, similar to the one used in synagogue, in which the name of the child is announced and she is welcomed into the Jewish community. A celebratory meal akin to the meal that follows a traditional *b'rit milah* then follows any of these ceremonies

Choosing a Jewish Name

Names have always had a great importance in the Jewish world. Therefore, when choosing a child's Jewish name, it is important not simply to pick a name that is popular or that sounds nice. A child's name should be suffused with family meaning and Jewish significance.

Somewhat surprisingly, there are no actual *halakhot* that govern the choice of children's names. Most often, family custom and tradition will be the most important factors. Among Ashkenazic Jews, the most common practice is to name children for deceased relatives, often their grandparents or great-grandparents, while Sephardic Jews often choose to give their children the names of living relatives or names associated with significant events. Absent family tradition, children may be named for heroic figures, ancient or modern, or for individuals deemed to possess the specific qualities parents hope their children come to embody. Originally, of course, Jewish children received only traditional Jewish names. In the wake of large-scale immigration to Western Europe and North and South America, it became customary to give children two names: a secular one for use in the outside world and a Jewish one for use at home. There was some precedent for that development—even Queen Esther had a different "Jewish" name, Hadassah—but the custom of giving children two names has evolved over the generations and it is now far more common for children to be called by their secular names even at home and for their Jewish names to be reserved for use solely in highly charged spiritual contexts, such as when being called to the Torah. Times, however, continue to change. Many ethnic groups have now reverted to the practice of giving their children a single name reflective of their family's cultural background, and many Jews also consider that option seriously. In a world free of overt cultural or religious discrimination, the whole concept of "inside" and "outside" names feels grounded in the kind of cultural nervousness unbecoming of the proud citizens of multicultural democracies.

Traditionally, a Jewish name includes the patronymic, i.e., the word *ben* ("son of") or *bat* ("daughter of") and the individual's father's name, plus the word *ha-kohein* or *ha-leivi* if the father is of priestly or levitical stock. Today, many Jews have begun to refer to themselves using their mothers' names in addition to their fathers'. Regardless, however, children should be taught to cherish their Jewish names and to use them as often as possible. Individuals who never received a Jewish name can still choose one at any time, but the assistance of a rabbi should be sought so as to infuse the occasion with religious significance. There is also an ancient Jewish custom of adding a new name to the existing name of a person who is very sick. This is done in a brief ceremony that contains a prayer for healing. A name signifying life (like Ḥayyim or Ḥayyah) or good health (Raphael or Raphaela) is most often chosen. When a baby is seriously ill, there is a touching custom among Ashkenazic Jews of adding the Yiddish name Alter ("Elder") to a child's name as a way of expressing the hope that the child survive into old age.

Redemption of the Firstborn

The ceremony of redeeming a firstborn son, called *pidyon ha-bein,* is one of the least understood rites of passage in Judaism, yet it can nevertheless be used creatively to strengthen the family ties and the emotional bond to Jewish tradition of those who participate in it. (The name of the ceremony is usually pronounced as *pidyon ha-ben* by English-speaking Jews.)

The ceremony has its roots in the ancient custom of dedicating the male firstborn of an Israelite family to priestly service. Later, however, the tribe of Levi was singled out for this honor instead, perhaps as a reward for their singular faithfulness during the incident of the Golden Calf. The language of Scripture makes this explicit: "For I now take the tribe of Levi to My service in place of the firstborn of Israel" (Numbers 3:41). None pre-selected for divine service may be so simply decommissioned, however, and the commandment of Scripture speaks directly to this point by requiring that every firstborn son be formally redeemed from divine service. This too is made explicit: "You must surely redeem every firstborn son" (Numbers 18:15).

It is specifically the obligation of fathers to redeem their firstborn sons from a *kohein.* This, however, only applies if the child is the firstborn of his mother, and neither parent is the child of a *kohein* or a Levite (*SA* Yoreh Dei·ah 305:18).

At Numbers 18:15, Scripture refers to a woman's firstborn son as the child who "opens her womb" when he is born, and this was taken as a reference specifically to vaginal birth. If a child is delivered through Caesarean section, therefore, there is no need for that child to be redeemed. In such a case, children born in subsequent vaginal births are exempt from the obligation to be redeemed as well (*SA* Yoreh Dei·ah 305:24).

If a woman's first pregnancy ends in miscarriage within forty days of conception, or even if she miscarries before the fetus develops a recognizable human form and then subsequently gives birth to a son, that child needs to be redeemed because he is considered her firstborn son. If a woman suffers a miscarriage after forty days, there is no *pidyon ha-bein* for a subsequently born son, however, because he is not considered the first issue of her womb. In doubtful cases, a rabbi should be consulted for a precise ruling.

Since the ritual is about redeeming firstborn sons from priestly service, there is no need for a member of a priestly or levitical family to be redeemed, and this is the case regardless of whether it is the child's mother or father who is the child of a *kohein* or a Levite (*SA* Yoreh Dei·ah 305:18).

The child must be at least thirty days old to be redeemed. Therefore, because it is deemed unseemly to delay in the performance of the commandments, the *pidyon ha-bein* ceremony should be held on the thirty-first day after the baby is born or as close to that time as possible. It may not be held on a Shabbat or on a festival, during which money may not be handled, however, since the ceremony involves an exchange of coins. It may take place on any of the intermediate days of Passover or Sukkot. If the ceremony is inadvertently performed before a boy is thirty-one days old, it is deemed invalid and must be performed again (*SA* Yoreh Dei·ah 305:11 and 13). If it is performed after, even long after, the thirty-first day, however, it is still deemed wholly valid.

It is customary to perform the ceremony in the daytime. However, in urgent cases, the ritual may be performed on the evening going into the thirty-first day of the child's life.

Until a boy reaches the age of thirteen, it remains his father's obligation to redeem him. After age thirteen, however, the obligation devolves onto the firstborn himself and can be looked after at any age (*SA* Yoreh Dei·ah 305:15).

It is necessary to have a *kohein* present to perform the ritual. A rabbi may act as host or master of ceremonies, but no one but a *kohein* can undertake to redeem the child.

In preparation for the ceremony, one should have the symbolic equivalent of five *sh'kalim*. Special coins have been minted over the years for this purpose, but it is very usual in the United States and Canada for silver dollars to be used.

Often, the *kohein* will return these special coins to the family after the ceremony and request that they make a contribution to a charity of their choice in honor of their son's redemption. In this way, the emphasis is placed on *tz'dakah* and the coins themselves can remain as a meaningful keepsake for the family.

The *pidyon ha-bein* ceremony traditionally takes place in the course of a meal. Usually, the blessing over the bread is said and then, before the actual meal is served, the *pidyon ha-bein* ceremony takes place. The meal is then served. If the thirty-first day of a boy's life falls on a fast day, the *pidyon ha-bein* should not be deferred and should take place without the meal.

There is no redemption ceremony for a firstborn daughter. The question has been asked whether the concept of redemption should be widened to include girls. In that the ceremony is specifically rooted in the concept of undoing an ancient obligation that affected boys only, most Conservative rabbis have followed Rabbi Gerald Skolnik, who wrote as follows in a 1993 responsum for the Committee on Jewish Law and Standards: "The biblically mandated practice of *pidyon ha-bein* is restricted to male firstborn children only, and should not be expanded to include firstborn female children. However, all gatherings which serve the purpose of enhancing the sense of blessing and specialness associated with the birth of firstborn female children are to be encouraged" (*CJLS Responsa 1991–2000,* pp. 163–165).

Bar Mitzvah and Bat Mitzvah

Perhaps the most significant rite of passage for a Jewish young person is the moment he or she becomes legally responsible for the performance of the commandments, popularly referred to as the day he or she becomes a bar mitzvah or bat mitzvah. For many centuries, it has been customary to celebrate this milestone with honors in the synagogue and with a celebratory party. Over the centuries, these too have come to be called a bar mitzvah or a bat mitzvah, and so people speak loosely of attending a child's bar mitzvah when they are actually attending the ceremonies surrounding the child in question *becoming* a bar or bat mitzvah, usually by being present in the synagogue when the child is called forward to the Torah for the first time. (Sometimes people conflate the bar or bat mitzvah with a party celebrating the child coming of age, though there is little or no religious significance to the party itself; as such, no equivalence between the synagogue service and a party should be imputed since the latter lacks the religious significance of the former.)

The key point is that the bar or bat mitzvah is not by its nature a transformational experience: boys become responsible to perform the *mitzvot* when they turn thirteen and girls when they turn twelve whether they are formally called to the Torah to mark the transition to adult responsibility or not, and regardless of whether their parents make a huge party to celebrate that fact. The ages themselves, thirteen for boys and twelve for girls, were chosen as approximations. Ideally, the transition should take place at puberty, but the ancient rabbis were savvy enough to know what a very poor idea it would have been to try to make such a public determination for children at the onset of adolescence, and so were content to fix an age that seemed reasonably accurate and to leave it at that. Thus the words of Judah ben Tema in *Pirkei Avot* (at M Avot 5:21), "At age thirteen comes responsibility for the *mitzvot,*" have traditionally been understood to constitute permission to fix the attainment of majority in terms of a child's physical age, and the concept of thirteen and twelve as the ages of majority became codified as the halakhic standard, although the relationship to puberty was not entirely erased (see, e.g., Maimonides' comments in *MT* Hilkhot Ishut 2:9–10). In our day, the actual question of whether a child has attained puberty is considered irrelevant and the age of majority is deemed fixed at the above-mentioned ages regardless of whatever milestones a child may or may not have reached in his or her physical development.

The concept of making a formal celebration for a child who becomes a bar mitzvah is first mentioned by the thirteenth-century German rabbi Mordecai ben Hillel (c. 1240–1298). The early version of the ceremony consisted simply of a boy receiving his first *aliyah* to the Torah or, on Shabbat, being called up as the *maftir* and thus invited to chant the *haftarah* in public for the first time. After the service there would be a celebratory feast in the course of which the boy would deliver some remarks based on that week's Torah portion. On weekdays, the boy would put on his *t'fillin* and recite the blessings as a bar mitzvah.

The concept of celebrating when a girl attains her majority is a much later development and, for many years, consisted mostly of the girl delivering some remarks in front of the congregation either on a weekday or a Friday evening, followed by a celebratory meal. The first formal bat mitzvah ceremony is said to have taken place in New York in 1922, when the daughter of Mordecai Kaplan, Judith Kaplan, was called forward to read from the Torah at the Society for the Advancement of Judaism, her father's congregation, when she was twelve years old. Now every Conservative congregation features a bat mitzvah ceremony in which girls are welcomed into the congregation as adults. To facilitate the education of children by having them prepare for their bar and bat mitzvah services together, it has become exceedingly common for girls to have their bat mitzvah celebrations at age thirteen as well. Since there is no obligation to call anyone to the Torah at all at a given age for the first time, much less to make a party in celebration of that fact, there is no reason for parents to insist on having a daughter's bat mitzvah celebration at age twelve and they may instead rely on local custom. An interesting question arises in communities in which the bat mitzvah ceremony is routinely deferred until age thirteen: may a girl over age twelve who has not formally marked her bat mitzvah nevertheless be counted in the *minyan* and considered an adult in other ways? The answer varies from community to community, but the simplest answer is that the ages of majority are, at least in terms of halakhic importance, independent of any celebratory ceremonies. Therefore, a girl over age twelve should be considered to have attained her majority even if the celebration of that fact will only take place when she turns thirteen. There is, of course, no reason for a community *not* to wait to call twelve-year-old girls to the Torah until after the bat mitzvah ceremony if that is the custom of the congregation.

Traditionally, the parents of a bar mitzvah or a bat mitzvah come forward publicly to thank God for releasing them from the burden of responsibility for their child's subsequent actions. (The traditional formulation, in fact, was *barukh she-p'tarani mei-onsho she-la-zeh,* "Blessed [be God] who has released me from having to bear any punishment for this child's actions." The formulation for a daughter would end with the phrase *mei-onshah she-la-zo.*) Although this declaration was merely intended as a parent's public acknowledgment of a child's maturity, the use of this sentence—which sounds as though parents who say it consider themselves quit of any further responsibility for their children's actions—has fallen into disuse in many congregations. In modern society, parents are anything but quit of those responsibilities when a child has barely entered middle school, and proclamations to the contrary will therefore have a peculiar, even perhaps an inappropriate, ring to them. Generally speaking, no reformulation is substituted and the declaration is simply omitted.

The modern bar or bat mitzvah takes place, ideally, as soon as possible after a child's twelfth or thirteenth birthday according to the Jewish calendar. So that the child can be called forward to the Torah, it is normative to schedule a child's bar or bat mitzvah when the Torah is read aloud in public, for example on Saturday morning or afternoon. But Monday or Thursday mornings, or Rosh Ḥodesh or any Jewish holiday on which the Torah is read aloud as part of the synagogue service, are also appropriate times to schedule a bar or bat mitzvah.

In recent decades, the concept of the adult bar or bat mitzvah has been introduced in many congregations. Most of the time, the adults involved are women who grew up in congregations that did not permit or endorse bat mitzvah celebrations for girls and who now wish to affirm their commitment to Judaism publicly. Other adult participants might be men or women whose families were sufficiently estranged from Jewish ritual when they were children so as not to have had a formal bar mitzvah or a bat mitzvah ceremony. Still others will be converts to Judaism who were not Jewish at age twelve or thirteen. These adult bar and bat mitzvah celebrations can be extremely meaningful and generally come at the culmination of a course of study that includes instruction in the skills necessary for meaningful participation in the synagogue service.

Although it is regular to celebrate a child's coming of age with a celebratory party, every effort should be made to underscore the fact that the party is a celebration of a child's first *aliyah* to the Torah, not to suggest that the *aliyah* is the prelude to the party. For a celebration in honor of a child's acceptance of the yoke of the commandments to have real meaning, the party itself must conform to those commandments. Parties in honor of child's acceptance of the commandments that involve public desecration of Shabbat or at which non-kosher food is served are, to say the least, wholly inappropriate. Nor is there any rationale to the argument that a family that is not strictly observant at home is somehow behaving hypocritically by hosting a party that conforms to the accepted communal standards of Jewish ritual and law. Just the opposite is the more rational stance, in fact: for a family that is not strict in its level of observance to make a party that conforms to the standards of their synagogue signals the seriousness with which they take the entire bar or bat mitzvah celebration. In so doing, they demonstrate for their children that they place greater emphasis on the true meaning of this rite of passage than on a party undertaken solely for its own sake.

The party in honor of a child becoming a bar or bat mitzvah should have the feel of a celebration of profound religious importance. It is, therefore, highly inappropriate for such affairs to feature unsuitable or vulgar entertainment. In the past, in fact, Jewish communities often restricted the amount of money families, even wealthy ones, could spend on a celebration by passing binding regulations called sumptuary laws. In our day, bar and bat mitzvah parties are often exercises in tasteless extravagance far beyond anything the communities that passed those sumptuary laws could have imagined. Different communities will invariably have different standards, but the basic rule should always be that anything that detracts from the party as a *se'udat mitzvah,* a celebratory feast of deeply religious significance, should be avoided. To underscore the spiritual significance of bar or bat mitzvah, many congregations developed the concept of a "*mitzvah* project" that boys and girls must fulfill as a requirement for becoming a bar or bat mitzvah in that synagogue. Although this is a modern innovation unrelated to the child actually coming of age, it is a worthy way to emphasize the religious dimension of the whole enterprise and, as such, should be encouraged. At any rate, the bar or bat mitzvah party should feature the ritual ambience of a traditional Jewish meal by beginning with the formal Ha-motzi blessing over bread and concluding with the recitation of the Grace after Meals.

There is also a relatively modern tradition for older men to celebrate a "second" bar mitzvah at the age of eighty-three. (Although very few women in their eighties, if any, will have had bat mitzvahs as girls, there is no reason why an analogous ceremony of recommitment to Jewish values should not also be developed for female members of the congregation.) The origin of this custom rests in the biblical conviction that the normal life span is seventy years (cf. Psalm 90:10) and that, as a result, each subsequent year is a special gift. Ceremonies like this, although lacking much history or any particular halakhic significance, can nevertheless be wonderful opportunities to celebrate an individual's long, rich, and blessed life with family and friends.

Conversion

All Jewish individuals are either people born to Jewish mothers or converts to Judaism. (In recent years, some Reform Jewish communities have begun to accept the children of Jewish fathers as Jews even in the absence of formal conversion. This innovation has not been adopted by the more traditional denominations, however. And a "standard of rabbinic practice" written by Rabbis Joel Roth and Akiba Lubow, approved by the CJLS in 1985 and then formally adopted by the Rabbinical Assembly at its 1986 convention, forbids Conservative rabbis from applying the patrilineal principle in the ascription of Jewishness. The text of the standard is published in *CJLS Responsa 1980–1990,* pp. 379–380.) The actual process that leads to conversion varies from community to community. However, conversion in all cases is viewed as a serious undertaking meant to indicate a life-transforming decision about religious beliefs and affiliation.

To convert to Judaism requires a commitment to both the Jewish religion and to the Jewish people. This commitment is summed up in the words of Ruth, the prototypical righteous convert—the Hebrew term for such a man or woman is *geir tzedek* or *giyyoret tzedek*—who declared to her mother-in-law, Naomi: "Your people shall be my people and your God, my God" (Ruth 1:16). In other words, Ruth adopted both her mother-in-law's faith and her sense of membership in the House of Israel. Converts today must do exactly the same thing and cannot be content merely to feel part of the Jewish people without accepting a concomitant obligation to observe the commandments of the Torah.

When a person converts to Judaism, that individual becomes fully Jewish and should be treated as a Jew in all respects. Indeed, showing respect and affection for converts is a specific *mitzvah* of the Torah, as it is written, "And you shall love the proselyte" (Deuteronomy 10:19), and this concept was formally codified and accepted as *halakhah* for all generations (*MT* Hilkhot Dei·ot 6:4).

While it is true that Jews have traditionally not sought out converts or encouraged conversion, the Conservative movement does endorse the concept of outreach to non-Jewish individuals who are married to Jews to encourage the conversion of those individuals to Judaism. Indeed, non-Jewish spouses should be encouraged to participate in synagogue life to the greatest extent possible within halakhic parameters and to learn more about Judaism. It is, at any rate, considered a solemn obligation for Jews never to cast doubts about the validity of the Jewishness of a convert or to bring up potentially embarrassing details of his or her past (*SA* Ḥoshen Mishpat 420:37).

In order to convert to Judaism, an individual must participate in a program of learning under the supervision of a rabbi. The period of study is determined by the rabbi or by the rabbinic organization that offers the program. The learning, however, should not be specifically for the purpose of conversion nor should there be any prior agreement about the ultimate goal of the study. A simple and reasonable pattern has developed over the years: people potentially interested in Judaism study the Torah and decide if this is the path they wish to adopt as their own. If they do, then they proceed with the rest of the requirements. If not, then they do not—but no commitments can be undertaken before the individual in question knows what it means to be a Jew.

There are numerous courses of study recommended for potential converts. The standard curriculum will include instruction in the basics of Jewish history, the customs and ceremonies of Jewish life, a survey of the Hebrew Bible, an introduction to Jewish liturgy, and lessons in reading Hebrew. At the end of the learning period, if both the supervising rabbi and the potential convert agree, the conversion may be scheduled.

The conversion procedure itself is slightly different for women and men. An appearance before a *beit din* (a rabbinic court of at least three) is required for both, as is a supervised visit to the ritual bath, or *mikveh*. In addition, uncircumcised men must be circumcised, and men who have already been circumcised must undergo the ritual known as *hattafat dam b'rit* (mentioned above in the section on circumcision and in more detail below). Both of these procedures usually precede immersion in the *mikveh* (*SA* Yoreh Dei·ah 268:2).

The *beit din* consists of three rabbis who are responsible for overseeing the conversion process. (Under some circumstances, two observant Jewish individuals may help form the *beit din* under the guidance of a supervising rabbi. It is preferable, however, for all the members of the *beit din* to be rabbis.) It is their responsibility to question potential converts to determine the sincerity of their commitment, the level of their knowledge, and their overall suitability for conversion. A commitment to *halakhah* is required of every convert. The *beit din* may question the potential convert concerning many aspects of Jewish life or only a few, but it is only after determining that the individual being questioned is ready for conversion that the conversion process may continue.

As noted, male converts must undergo circumcision. Generally speaking, this is done before the immersion. If a potential male convert is already circumcised, the procedure of *hattafat dam b'rit* ("the drawing of a drop of blood") is performed. A drop of blood is drawn from behind the corona of the penis in order to "complete" the circumcision a doctor performed many years, usually decades, earlier. An adult male requiring circumcision is generally circumcised by a urologist in a hospital under local or general anesthesia. If the patient is awake, the physician is Jewish, and a rabbi can be present to instruct regarding the blessing to be recited before the moment of incision, then the circumcision is deemed ritually valid and no further action need be taken. If there is no Jewish urologist available, the usual procedure is for the circumcision to take place with no ritual at all, and then, once the skin has healed, for a rabbi to perform *hattafat dam b'rit.*

There are differing opinions as to whether the *hattafat dam* is to be accompanied by a blessing. The supervising rabbi should make that determination. If, however, a blessing is to be recited, it would be the standard blessing for the performance of a commandment ending with the words *v'tzivvanu la-mul et ha-geirim* ("and who commanded us concerning the circumcision of converts").

In the case of Jewish parents adopting a newborn boy, the conversion begins with the *b'rit milah* ceremony. (This need not be done on the eighth day of life, however.) The blessings are those for conversion and at a later date, after the circumcision has fully healed, the boy is brought to a *mikveh* to complete the conversion. The procedure at the *mikveh* is then the same for adopted children of both genders.

As stated above, immersion in a kosher *mikveh* is required of all converts, adults and juveniles. A kosher *mikveh* may be a formal ritual bath facility maintained by a synagogue or by the larger community, or it may be a body of water suitable for use in this way. An ocean, a river, or a natural (i.e., not man-made) pond can serve as a suitable *mikveh,* especially when a more formal *mikveh* is not accessible. The purpose of the *mikveh* is to symbolize a new beginning in one's life. When one converts to Judaism, one is said spiritually to be reborn into the Jewish faith. The *mikveh* is the symbol of this rebirth.

At the *mikveh,* male and female potential converts must remove all clothing, makeup, jewelry, eyeglasses, contact lenses, hairpins, bandages, and anything else that could serve even as a small barrier between the waters of the *mikveh* and the body of the individual. Once undressed, the potential convert then enters the water and completely immerses three times. If the convert is a female and any of the rabbis is male, a female attendant supervises her immersion and the men remain outside a closed door. Similarly, female rabbis do not personally witness the immersion of male candidates.

Before the final act of immersion, the convert recites two blessings: *barukh attah adonai, eloheinu, melekh ha-olam, asher kidd'shanu b'mitzvotav v'tzivvanu al ha-t'vilah* ("Praised are You, Adonai, our God, Sovereign of the universe, who, sanctifying us with divine commandments, has commanded us concerning immersion") and the She-heḥeyyanu blessing.

The procedure is not invariable, however, and varies from rabbi to rabbi or with respect to local custom. Some instruct potential converts to immerse themselves three times and then to recite the blessings, while other rabbis instruct would-be converts to immerse themselves once, then to say the first blessing, then to immerse a second time, then to say the second blessing, and only then to immerse themselves a third time. Both systems have the same concept guiding them, however: that the potential convert who has not yet immersed in the *mikveh* at all is not yet Jewish and cannot, therefore, meaningfully say the words "who has sanctified *us* with divine commandments."

The convert is then welcomed into the Jewish people as a righteous proselyte, and a ceremony including the reading of the conversion documents, a declaration of faith, and the assigning of a Jewish name follows.

A Jewish name may be suggested by the rabbi or chosen by the convert. The name should be carefully chosen, however, because it will be associated with the individual receiving it for the rest of his or her life and, indeed, longer than that: it will eventually be chiseled onto the individual's gravestone.

A full Jewish name traditionally includes the names of one's father, but many moderns also include their mothers' names. Converts, of course, do not have Jewish parents and are, at least formally, considered to be newly born into the Jewish faith. Traditionally, therefore, they are considered the spiritual children of Abraham and Sarah. The name of a male convert, therefore, consists of his chosen first name followed by the words *ben avraham avinu* or *ben avraham avinu v'sarah immeinu*. The name of female converts is similar: the chosen name followed by *bat avraham avinu* or *bat avraham avinu v'sarah immeinu*. (This practice is the subject of a responsum by Rabbi Barry Leff approved by the CJLS in 2010 and available on the website of the Rabbinical Assembly.) It is also permissible to use the names *Avraham* and *Sarah* without *avinu* ("our father") or *immeinu* ("our mother"). Since there are many people in the Jewish community named Abraham and Sarah, this protects the convert's privacy.

The same rules of conversion apply to adopted infants or older children. The only difference would be that in such instances a formal period of study would not be necessary since the child would be educated in the normal manner in a religious school or day school setting. According to Jewish law, the child retains the option of rejecting the conversion upon reaching adulthood if he or she so chooses. In the case of adoption, it is permissible for the child to be called by the name of his or her adoptive father or parents. This becomes slightly complicated when the adoptive father is a *kohein* or a *leivi*. In such cases, the priestly status does not pass on to an adopted child and this should be explained clearly to the family. It is, however, permissible to use the word *ha-kohein* or *ha-leivi* following the father's name, since the sobriquet is understood to apply to the father's name and not the child's.

As per the CJLS decision of 1998 by Rabbi Joel Rembaum, converts to Judaism may observe all mourning rituals for their non-Jewish relatives, both during the *shivah* week and during the *sh'loshim* month or year-long secondary mourning periods that follow. This includes the right to say Kaddish for a non-Jewish parent. Conservative Judaism rejects outright the notion of some Orthodox rabbis that converts must consider their ties of affection and allegiance to their non-Jewish parents extinguished. To the contrary: showing respect for the memory of a devoted parent is a *mitzvah* of the Torah, and the fact that the parent in question was not Jewish is considered an irrelevant point.

The Conservative movement adheres to a policy of conversion in accordance with Jewish law. This means that study, the interview before the *beit din,* the visit to the *mikveh,* and circumcision for males are all required. The Reform movement does not consider immersion in a *mikveh* mandatory for all converts, nor do Reform rabbis universally require circumcision. Furthermore, many Reform rabbis consider children born of mixed marriages to be Jewish, regardless of which parent is Jewish, as long as the children in question are being brought up to think of themselves as Jewish. In contrast, Conservative Judaism does not accept patrilineality as a decisive factor in the determination of Jewish status. Therefore, the only Jews recognized by the Conservative movement are converts to Judaism and the children of Jewish mothers.

When an individual who was converted under Reform auspices wishes to join a Conservative synagogue or attend a Conservative school or camp, the matter can become quite sensitive. Different rabbis proceed in slightly different ways at this juncture, but the basic procedure is for the individual whose conversion process did not include all the required rituals listed above to be guided gently through them. This may involve immersion in a *mikveh* or, for men, circumcision or *hattafat dam b'rit.* It also may involve an appearance before a *beit din,* although this is less often required.

Many Orthodox rabbis do not accept Conservative conversions as valid. This has become a difficult issue particularly in Israel, where converted Jews have the same theoretical right to citizenship under the Law of Return as individuals who are Jewish because of the circumstances of their birth. Currently, all converts from the Conservative movement are accepted as Jews under the Law of Return as long as the conversion takes place outside of Israel. This issue remains politically explosive and no one can predict how it will eventually be resolved.

When a couple wishes to be married in Israel, however, an officiating Orthodox rabbi may not accept a Conservative conversion as valid. The unsatisfying and slightly demeaning solution to this problem is for the couple to have a civil wedding outside of Israel which the State will recognize as valid, and only then to come to Israel where a Masorti/Conservative rabbi may then conduct the religious ceremony.

In the case of a non-Jewish spouse converting to Judaism after marriage, it is recommended that a formal Jewish wedding take place after the conversion. This can be a small, private ceremony at home or in the rabbi's study, or it can be in a larger setting. It provides an affirmation of the transformative power of conversion. This is the case even if a "Jewish-style" wedding was performed before the non-Jew converted.

Persons considering conversion may profitably consult the late Rabbi Simchah Kling's book, *Embracing Judaism,* now available in a revised edition prepared by Rabbi Carl M. Perkins (New York: The Rabbinical Assembly, 1999), or Rabbi Ronald Isaac's book, *Becoming Jewish: A Handbook for Conversion* (New York: The Rabbinical Assembly, 1993). Also of interest to many will be Rabbi Jonathan Lubliner's *At the Entrance of the Tent: A Rabbinic Guide to Conversion,* published by the Rabbinical Assembly in 2011.

Getting Married

Marriage as Mitzvah

The Torah teaches us that marriage between men and women is the ideal toward which single individuals should strive. Indeed, the biblical account of the creation of woman makes it clear that the whole concept of there even *being* two genders is for each to provide the other with helpful, supportive companionship. Jewish tradition, therefore, has never considered celibacy or prolonged single living desirable or natural. Quite the contrary: the rabbis of ancient times found the prospect of spiritual accomplishment for the unmarried unlikely at best, explaining with just a touch of hyperbole that husbands and wives need each other to flourish fully as men and women, in the same way that men and women both require a relationship with God to reach the fullest flower of their humanity (*B'reishit Rabbah* 8:9). For his part, and although there was considerable debate regarding his stance, Maimonides says clearly that the act of getting married is the fulfillment of a positive commandment of the Torah (*MT* Hilkhot Ishut 1:2) The question of same-sex marriage is discussed below by Rabbi Elliot Dorff in his chapter on the *halakhah* of same-sex relationships.

In the eyes of Jewish law and tradition, marriage encompasses the practical, emotional, and spiritual elements of life. On a practical level, marriage helps to create the kind of stable family unit that functions as the bedrock foundation of a healthy, productive society. It also creates the framework within which procreation, the key to the continued existence of any people, can take place in a dignified, efficient, and wholesome manner. Emotionally, marriage provides the companionship, love, and sexual gratification that make life rich and pleasurable. But it is on the spiritual level that marriage reaches its fullest potential to bring good to the world by inducing a state of holiness in the men and women who accept its sacred bonds. For this reason, the most popular Hebrew term for marriage is *kiddushin,* literally "sanctification." Indeed, the parallels the prophets drew with such tender passion between the relationship of husband and wife and the relationship between God and Israel will seem exaggerated or daring only to outsiders. To those on the inside of Jewish marriages characterized by fidelity, trust, and love, however, the analogy will seem almost self-evident. Elsewhere in this volume, Rabbi David J. Fine discusses the marriage bond between husband and wife in great detail.

Scripture pays much attention to the choice of a proper mate. In the biblical story of how Abraham's servant chose a wife for Isaac (Genesis 24), for example, it is clear that the primary considerations were kindness and hospitality. Subsequent Jewish tradition identified numerous other qualities deemed essential for a long and a happy marriage such as a love of learning, compatibility, family, generosity, and industriousness.

Although polygyny, the marriage of a man to more than one woman, was certainly permitted in biblical times, it was not widely practiced at any time in Jewish history. It is also worth noting that the biblical precedent is rarely depicted in Scripture as smooth or peaceful. In the end, the practice was finally banned by Rabbeinu Gershom of Mainz, called the Light of the Exile, who lived at the end of the tenth and the beginning of the eleventh centuries C.E. Rabbeinu Gershom's ban only applied to Ashkenazic Jews, however, and there remained some Sephardic communities in which polygyny was practiced until 1950, when the chief rabbinate of Israel finally banned the practice categorically. However, even in communities that maintained the possibility of polygyny in theory, it was only permitted under very particular conditions. With the rarest exception to the rule, monogyny has been the standard in Jewish family life since ancient times.

There is a Torah statute (at Deuteronomy 25:7–10) to the effect that the brother of a married man who dies childless is called upon to take his brother's widow as a wife in order to keep her as part of her late husband's family. And, indeed, the living brother steps into his late brother's shoes financially as well as connubially in that the *halakhah* specifies that he himself becomes his brother's heir, not their father (who, should he still be alive, would normally inherit a childless son's estate) and not any children later born of that union. (The specifics are set forth by Maimonides at *MT* Hilkhot Naḥalot 3:7.) This kind of marriage is called *yibbum* in Hebrew, but because the Latin word for such a brother-in-law is *levir* one sometimes hears it referenced as "levirate marriage" in English. Scripture also provides a remedy for those who did not wish to marry under such circumstances in a complex ceremony called *ḥalitzah,* which releases the bereaved brother from the obligation to wed his widowed sister-in-law. Generally speaking, *ḥalitzah* is always performed today. These laws and procedures are discussed in detail by Rabbi David M. Greenstein in his chapter on sibling relationships later in this volume.

Prohibited Marriages

There are a number of conceivable marriage relationships that are forbidden under Jewish law due to issues of consanguinity, marital or religious status, and/or physical condition. However, these marriages are not all forbidden to the same degree. Some, for example, are prohibited to the extent that they have no legal standing even if attempted. No formal divorce is required to dissolve such marriages and the children from them are considered illegitimate. Included in this list are many kinds of marriages—for example, unions between parents and their own children or between grandparents and grandchildren—that scarcely exist in real life. Other prohibited marriages in this category are more in the realm of possibility, such as those between full- and half-siblings, between stepparents and stepchildren, between a man and his brother's former wife (except in the case of levirate marriage), between men and the sisters of their divorced wives, between aunts and nephews (although not between uncles and their nieces; cf. *BT* Y'vamot 62b), and adulterous unions between men and married women, including women who may have received civil divorces from their former husbands but not a formal Jewish bill of divorce called a *get.*

Marriages that are forbidden to a lesser degree are considered valid if they do take place and must therefore be dissolved formally by divorce. Also, children born of such marriages are considered to be legitimate. In this category, the Torah forbids a man to marry his own ex-wife if she has been married to another man in the interim, and this is the case regardless of whether her second marriage ended in divorce or if she was widowed (Deuteronomy 24:1–4; cf. *SA* Even Ha-eizer 10:1 and Klein, p. 385). In addition, *kohanim* are barred by traditional *halakhah* from marrying divorced women and women who have converted to Judaism. Modern Conservative practice, however, permits such marriages on the grounds that the priestly status of *kohanim* today has no real halakhic validity and the epidemic levels of intermarriage make it intensely counterproductive to discourage Jewish endogamy based on matters of questionable status. As a result, such marriages may now take place, although the *kohein* is expected to forego the priestly privileges of taking the first *aliyah,* coming forward to pronounce the priestly blessing from the *bimah,* and passing these privileges and responsibilities along to his children. There are those, however, who feel that there should be no negative consequences to participating in legally sanctioned unions merely because they were once forbidden. Rabbi Arnold Goodman authored a responsum in 1996, for example, in which he wrote that a *kohein* who marries a divorced woman or a convert "is no longer disqualified to serve as a *kohein* in our services or rituals," and that this inclusive policy should extend to the sons of such men as well (*CJLS Responsa 1991–2000,* pp. 593–598).

Conservative rabbis are absolutely forbidden from officiating at or participating in intermarriages. (The rabbinic standard authored by Rabbis Joel Roth and Akiba Lubow and referenced above with respect to the question of patrilineal descent also bars members of the Rabbinical Assembly from being associated in either of these ways with intermarriages; cf. *CJLS Responsa 1980–1990*, pp. 379–380.) Such a marriage is not a Jewish marriage and a rabbi's authority to perform weddings is by definition limited to weddings that solemnize Jewish marriages. Furthermore, even a rabbi's casual participation in such a marriage would send a strong message of the rabbi's approval. However, the movement's attitude toward intermarried couples themselves is more inclusive, and synagogues are encouraged to reach out to such couples and to welcome them into the congregation. Indeed, by doing so, we hope to encourage the non-Jewish spouse to consider conversion to Judaism so that he or she will become part of a fully Jewish family.

T'nayim

The practice of signing a formal agreement, called *t'nayim* (conditions), shortly after a couple decides to get married goes back to the Middle Ages. The two families would get together and sign a document stipulating all the financial and logistical arrangements connected with the wedding ceremony and reception. After the document was read and signed by the parties to it, a piece of crockery, usually a plate, was traditionally smashed to seal the deal.

The broken plate is explained in different ways. Some maintain that it was meant to symbolize the destruction of the Temple, but others claim that it was intended as a warning that, just as a broken plate cannot be repaired, so too is there no remedy for a broken engagement.

The *t'nayim* ceremony is not halakhically required. It may be done, however, if the couple chooses to do so. Today some couples create their own document of commitment and understanding prior to the wedding, then gather family and friends together for a formal reading and celebration of this document some time before the actual wedding ceremony. More usual, however, if *t'nayim* are to be signed at all, is for the document to be signed at the wedding before the ceremony.

The Time and Place of Marriage

There are certain days and periods of time during the year that marriages may not take place, and, conversely, there are days that are deemed especially propitious for weddings. Even though there are varying opinions concerning several of these periods, there are other dates on which weddings are almost universally prohibited. Weddings may never be performed on Shabbat or on festival days because one may not enter into contractual agreements at these times. In addition, weddings are not held on the intermediate days of Passover and Sukkot because of the mixing of joyous occasions is considered to lead to a diminishing of the separate joys of each (*MT* Hilkhot Ishut 10:18).

The weeks between Passover and Shavuot are considered a time of national mourning for the Jewish people. Therefore, weddings are not held during much of this period, because the joyous nature of such events is deemed inconsonant with the general spirit of the season (*SA* Oraḥ Ḥayyim 493:1). There are many different customs regarding the specific parts of this period during which weddings may take place, however. Universally agreed upon is that weddings may take place on Lag Ba-omer (the thirty-third day of the *omer,* as this period of time is called), Rosh Ḥodesh Iyyar, and Rosh Ḥodesh Sivan. Some also include Yom Ha-atzma·ut (Israel Independence Day) as a day on which weddings may be celebrated. More liberal congregations permit weddings during part of these seven weeks, either ending the prohibited time with Lag Ba-omer or, even earlier, on Yom Ha-sho·ah. Still others only begin the prohibited time with the day after Rosh Ḥodesh Iyyar. (This matter is discussed in more detail in Rabbi Alan Lucas's chapter on the festivals of the Jewish year.)

Also, the three weeks between the fasts of the Seventeenth of Tammuz and the Ninth of Av are considered a time of national mourning in memory of the siege of Jerusalem and the destruction of the two Temples. The Committee on Jewish Law and Standards has permitted weddings to take place from the day after the Seventeenth of Tammuz until the end of that month, however. There is even an opinion that weddings may take place between the first of Av and Tishah Be'av, but that these must be small private ceremonies that take place in the rabbi's study (*Proceedings of the CJLS 1927–1970,* pp. 1291–1295).

Mourners may not get married during the first thirty days of their bereavement (*SA* Yoreh Dei·ah 392:1). There are exceptions to this rule, however, especially in a case where the wedding had been planned before the death occurred or if there are other compelling reasons why the marriage should not be delayed. In such cases a rabbi should be consulted. If the wedding is to proceed under such circumstances, however, it is considered inappropriate to have an elaborate wedding with music and dancing.

In addition, it is customary not to have weddings take place between Rosh Hashanah and Yom Kippur due to the great solemnity and introspective nature of those days. However, this is more of a custom than an actual law.

Traditionally, Tuesdays were considered especially propitious days on which to schedule weddings because the biblical story of creation includes the phrase "that it was good" twice in its description of God's creative activity associated with that day.

Before the Wedding

Traditionally, a groom is called up to the Torah for an *aliyah* on the Shabbat before his wedding. This is popularly called an *aufruf* by Ashkenazic Jews. In congregations that give *aliyot* to women, the bride and the groom both receive Torah honors and are blessed by the community. There is a custom of tossing candies at the couple to symbolize the wish of the congregation for sweetness in the life of the soon-to-be newlyweds. An *aufruf* need not be on the Shabbat immediately preceding the wedding, but can take place on any Shabbat prior to the wedding or, for that matter, any other day on which the Torah is read.

The bride customarily immerses herself in a *mikveh* prior to the wedding. This custom has a dual purpose: it puts the bride in a state of ritual purity on the wedding day so that the couple may consummate their marriage, and it also symbolizes a new beginning for the married couple. Many grooms also visit the *mikveh* as a sign of beginning a new stage of life.

Immersion in the *mikveh* follows a specific procedure and is governed by the law and traditions discussed in detail below in the section of this chapter on the laws of family purity. Men and women who visit the *mikveh* in preparation for marriage may wish to recite the following prayer, which underscores the special nature of prenuptial immersion: "As I prepare to enter this *mikveh* to purify myself before my wedding, may its waters purify my heart so that I begin my married life as pure and wholehearted as a newborn. May our love be true and untainted, and our commitment to a Jewish life together, firm and unyielding. As the waters of the *mikveh* surround me completely, so may we be always surrounded and protected by God's sheltering presence."

There is a custom for a bride or groom to visit the grave of a deceased parent just prior to the wedding, and to have the El Maleh Raḥamim prayer recited just prior to the wedding ceremony in that parent's memory. (Some people actually have this prayer chanted under the ḥuppah, hoping that the solace that comes from feeling a late parent's presence at one's wedding outweighs the melancholy hearing the prayer will undoubtedly engender.) These customs are ways for the bride and groom to feel that all parents, living and dead, are included in this most important day of their lives.

And it is also customary for brides and grooms to fast on their wedding day from sunrise until the ceremony (gloss of the Rema to *SA* Even Ha-eizer 61:1). This custom ensures the solemnity of the wedding and is rooted in the sense that marriage, like Yom Kippur itself, is a chance for both new spouses to begin a new life together free of the sins, indiscretions, and improprieties of their previous lives as single people. This practice, however, is not observed on days on which fasting is traditionally forbidden, i.e., Rosh Ḥodesh, Ḥanukkah, Purim, Tu Be'av, Tu Bi-sh'vat, and Shabbat.

Weddings

Although it is not technically a *mitzvah* to watch another person get married, one of the most important *mitzvot* is the commandment to rejoice with a bride and bridegroom before, during, and after their marriage. Indeed, when the rabbis of ancient times listed the commandments that "yield immediate reward and continue to yield reward in the future" (*BT* Shabbat 127a), they included *hakhnasat kallah,* "escorting the bride to her wedding canopy," among them. Therefore, no one should feel that it is beneath him or her to honor the bride and groom, nor should anything be considered to be too important to interrupt in order to greet a bridegroom and bride.

Prior to the wedding, the groom is required to formally accept the terms of the Jewish marriage contract, called the *k'tubbah*. This is usually done through the procedure of *kinyan sudar,* wherein the groom tugs on a cloth handkerchief held by the rabbi performing the wedding to indicate his willingness to accept upon himself the obligations of a Jewish bridegroom as referenced in the *k'tubbah*. This document, traditionally written in Aramaic, enumerates the husband's material, conjugal, and moral obligations to his wife and protects her financially should she be divorced. It also commits the husband and wife to love and honor each other in their marriage. Creative and original English translations of the *k'tubbah* are acceptable as long as the traditional language remains intact. It is a legal document establishing the material and ethical obligations of the husband to support and to care for his wife in accordance with Jewish law and tradition. The *Rabbi's Manual* published by the Rabbinical Assembly in 1998 contains a Hebrew-language version of the traditional text of the *k'tubbah* as well as the original Aramaic.

Two witnesses must sign the *k'tubbah* after having witnessed the transaction. (Some *k'tubbot* provide spaces for the rabbi, the groom, and the bride to sign the document as well. There is no objection to including their signatures, but these have no halakhic significance.) Traditionally, the witnesses have to be Jewish, male, and unrelated to each other or to the bride or the groom. (This includes relations by marriage, as well as by blood.) It is considered crucial that the witnesses sign their names in legible Hebrew letters. The Committee on Jewish Law and Standards has determined that women may act as witnesses and, therefore, that they may sign the *k'tubbah,* but the traditional requirements for witnesses are otherwise maintained. (Responsa by Rabbis Myron Geller and Susan Grossman favoring the eligibility of women to act as witnesses were approved by the CJLS in 2001 and are available on the website of the Rabbinical Assembly.)

The groom is expected personally to lower the veil over his bride's face prior to the wedding ceremony. This ceremony is popularly called by the Yiddish name *badeken.* The origin of this custom is the story of the first meeting of Rebecca and Isaac described in Genesis 24, where it is specified that, upon seeing Isaac approaching, Rebecca "took her veil and covered herself" (Genesis 24:65). The veil thus became a sign of modesty and virtue. There is also a connection with the story of how Jacob was tricked into marrying Leah, when he had wished to marry her sister Rachel. Thus, grooms ever since check to make sure that they are marrying the right person before the wedding. In this context, the veil serves as a sign of sincerity and trust. Although there is no legal requirement to wear a veil, it has become such a time-honored tradition that most rabbis require that it be worn.

After the veil is lowered, the bride is blessed with these words, usually recited in Hebrew and then in English translation: "Our sister, may you be the mother of thousands of myriads! May God make you like Sarah, Rebecca, Rachel, and Leah. May God bless you and keep you. May God's face shine upon you and may God be gracious to you. May God's face be lifted up unto you and may God grant you peace." The first sentence is from Genesis 24:60, there directed to Rebecca before her marriage to Isaac; the second, the traditional blessing for girls based on Genesis 48:20; and the others constitute the priestly blessing from Numbers 6:24–26.

It is also traditional for the bride, especially for her first wedding, to wear white as a sign of purity and forgiveness on the wedding day. Some grooms also wear a white *kittel* or robe over their clothes for the wedding ceremony for similar reasons. The *kittel* is also a reminder of our mortality, since it is similar to one of the shrouds in which Jewish people are buried.

An authorized person, called the *m'saddeir kiddushin,* must perform the ceremony. (The feminine form of the term is *m'sadderet kiddushin.*) Although, theoretically, a couple can be married under Jewish law just by performing any of the acts that solemnize a marriage in the presence of proper witnesses, this is not the way marriages are conducted today. Especially in jurisdictions where rabbis are permitted to register the marriages they solemnize with the secular government, thus obviating the need for a separate civil ceremony, it is essential that the ceremony be performed by a licensed clergyperson. Generally speaking, it is forbidden by civil law for a rabbi to marry two individuals in a religious ceremony without registering their union with the civil authorities. Nor may any rabbi make exceptions that contravene civil law in this regard. In the case of a couple that has actually had a civil ceremony previously, of course, this requirement does not apply.

Officially, the wedding ceremony is divided into two distinct parts, which in ancient times were often separated by as much as a year. The first part is called *eirusin* (betrothal) or *kiddushin* (sanctification). While somewhat akin to the concept of engagement, *kiddushin* is a much more formal union. For example, a couple that has been united in *kiddushin* must divorce if they decide subsequently not to live together as man and wife. And, although a couple in ancient times did not live together after *kiddushin* before moving on to *nissu·in* ("marriage"), the second stage of commitment, they were considered bound to each other in a way that most moderns would describe as a kind of marriage. By contrast, *nissu·in* is the ceremony that formalizes the physical union of the couple and that makes them fully and truly married. Because the obligations imposed upon a couple entering into the state of *kiddushin* are so serious, and so similar to what Westerners think of as marriage, it has been customary for a millennium to perform both ceremonies, *kiddushin* and *nissu·in,* at the same time and to separate them merely by some public remarks and by the reading aloud of the *k'tubbah*. Legally, however, each retains its separate identity and a blessing over a separate cup of wine is recited for each.

During the wedding ceremony, the bride and groom stand under a canopy, either hand-held or freestanding, known as a *ḥuppah,* which is set up wherever the wedding is being held. There are no specific requirements as to its size, material, or style. In lieu of a more formal *ḥuppah,* a *tallit* may be held aloft over the heads of the bride and groom. The *ḥuppah* represents the couple's new home, but it is obvious that the bride and groom will have to work together to build a more complete and lasting home of their own.

In some very traditional circles, it is customary to hold the *ḥuppah* under the open sky as a sign of hope that the couple will have as many offspring as there are stars in the sky (cf. the gloss of the Rema to *SA* Even Ha-eizer 61:1).

It is a well-known custom for the bride to circle the groom seven times as they stand under the *ḥuppah*. Some see this as a kind of symbolic ring the bride gives the groom, as a parallel to the real ring he gives her as the instrument of betrothal. (Indeed, some biblical support for this custom is found at Jeremiah 31:22, where the prophet predicts that "a woman shall encircle a man.") The number seven may also be connected to the number of times the phrase "when a man marries a woman" appears in the Bible. There is even a connection with the practice in Temple times of circling the altar seven times on Hoshana Rabbah. Most moderns, however, will prefer to think of the custom as a kind of folk response to the androcentric nature of the wedding ceremony. Circumambulation is a famous method of drawing an object into one's own domain, as symbolized classically by God's instruction to Abraham that he walk throughout the Land of Israel and thus come to possess it formally (Genesis 13:17). The custom, therefore, not only does not denigrate women, but, just to the contrary, establishes the bride as an active player in the proceedings and suggests that just as the groom draws her legally into his sphere, she is no less powerfully drawing him into hers. There is also a custom of the bride circling the groom only three times, and some couples in recent times have tried to develop an egalitarian version of the custom by having the groom circle the bride as well.

The wedding ceremony begins with a welcome to the assembled congregation, which is altered slightly when the ceremony takes place in a synagogue to make reference to the setting as a "House of God." (The latter version is used by some rabbis regardless of venue, however.) A short acrostic poem of welcome then follows, intoned either by the cantor or by the officiating rabbi.

The *kiddushin* ceremony then ensues. A cup of wine is lifted and the blessing over wine is recited, followed by a second blessing, this one an elaborate version of the regular blessing before the performance of a *mitzvah* (*MT* Hilkhot Ishut 3:23–24). This blessing is called *birkat eirusin,* using the alternate name for *kiddushin,* and praises God as the Author of sexual morality and the divine source of those laws that declare some unions licit and others illicit. This blessing is always pronounced by the officiating rabbi acting as *m'saddeir* or *m'sadderet kiddushin.* After it is recited aloud, the bride and groom share the first cup of wine. The bride's veil is lifted to permit her to drink easily, then lowered again.

The groom then gives the bride a ring. This ring must form a continuous circle and may not be studded with any stones, including even the most precious gemstones. The reason for this rule is practical: only experts are deemed able to distinguish true gems from ordinary stones or pieces of glass, and the validity of the wedding depends on the bride accepting the ring and correctly estimating its value (cf. *SA* Even Ha-eizer 31:2). By using only precious metal, the ring can be evaluated merely by inspecting it and weighing it, and the bride is deemed fully capable of doing this if she wishes. The requirement that the ring be a continuous circle reflects the belief that true love is endless, unconditional, and permanent.

Sometimes, a couple will wish to use a ring that has sentimental value for the ceremony. As long as the ring conforms to the halakhic requirements, this is an acceptable practice. However, it is essential that the groom own the ring so that he can legally give it as a gift to the bride. Before the ceremony, therefore, the groom should acquire possession of the ring by paying a nominal amount to the owner of the ring. The previous owner of the ring then affirms that the ring has been sold to the groom, who then gives it to the bride. If she chooses, in turn, to return it to its original owner after the ceremony, that is her right.

The groom places the wedding ring on the forefinger of the bride's right hand and pronounces the words that constitute the declaration of *kiddushin:*

harei at m'kuddeshet li b'tabba·at zo k'dat mosheh v'yisra·el ("With this ring, you are consecrated unto me in accordance with the laws of Moses and Israel"). Although it is traditional for the groom to make this declaration in Hebrew, its validity depends on the bride understanding what he is saying and accepting the ring as a token of her willingness to enter into the state of *kiddushin* with the groom (*SA* Even Ha-eizer 27:1). Therefore, if the bride does not understand what is being said in Hebrew, it is essential that it be repeated in a language the bride can understand. There are several reasons given for the use of the right forefinger. First of all, it is considered the most prominent of the fingers, and one purpose of the ceremony is publicly to announce to the community that the bride is about to become a married woman. More to the point, however, is the fact that the forefinger is *not* the ring finger and, anxious for the act of *kiddushin* not to resemble the mere act of gift-giving, the *halakhah* specifies that the ring *not* be given in the way a man would normally offer a woman the gift of a ring, i.e., by putting it on her ring finger. Having accepted the ring, however, the bride may then place it on whichever finger she wishes of the hand on which she plans to wear it.

Most modern couples favor a double-ring ceremony so as to create a sense of reciprocity and equality between bride and groom. In giving the groom his ring, the bride will often make a declaration of some sort, often one based on verses taken from the Song of Songs, e.g., "I am my beloved's and my beloved is mine" (6:3) or "Let me be a seal upon your heart, like the seal upon your arm" (8:6). Some couples prefer using the same language that was used with the bride's ring, only in the feminine form. Whether or not this is permitted is a decision to be made by the officiating rabbi.

Although the *halakhah* does not technically require that contracts be read aloud in the presence of the parties to them, the *k'tubbah* is read aloud after the exchange of rings in order to make a clear separation between the *kiddushin* and *nissu·in* ceremonies. Some *k'tubbot* are elaborately decorated documents written out by talented calligraphers and adorned with beautiful artwork, but others are merely printed documents with little or no ornamentation. Both are valid; unlike divorce documents, *k'tubbot* may be printed in advance and then just filled in with the names of the bride and groom and signed by the witnesses. Although the specific economic terms delineated in the *k'tubbah* are now antiquated, the value of maintaining the traditional text of the *k'tubbah* is still real. There are *k'tubbot* on the market that have non-traditional texts or translations, sometimes even to the exclusion of the traditional text entirely, but most Conservative rabbis require the use of the traditional text so as to create a link with the past and to discourage the efforts of any who might attempt to disparage the validity of the marriage by pointing to an idiosyncratic, non-traditional *k'tubbah* text. However, a special version of the text that includes a clause committing both husband and wife to seek a traditional Jewish divorce in addition to a civil one, in the event the marriage fails, is regularly used. This addition is known as the Lieberman Clause after its author, Rabbi Professor Saul Lieberman, and has been inserted into most Conservative *k'tubbot* since the 1950s. According to this clause, in the case that the husband refuses to grant a *get* to his wife, both agree to come before a rabbinic court recognized by the Jewish Theological Seminary and abide by their directives. This clause could theoretically be enforced in the civil courts. Far more important, however, is its intent to be morally binding, as it is designed to avoid the possibility of a woman becoming an *agunah,* a woman who cannot be Jewishly remarried because she lacks a *get* regardless of whether she is or is not divorced civilly. (The related issue of a separate pre-nuptial "Letter of Intent" is discussed below by Rabbi Vernon Kurtz in his chapter on civic morality.)

The *k'tubbah* becomes the property of the wife, as it specifically delineates her rights as a wife under Jewish law. If the *k'tubbah* should be lost in the course of the marriage, it should be replaced as quickly as possible (*SA* Even Ha-eizer 66:3).

After the *k'tubbah* is read aloud, the seven blessings (or *sheva b'rakhot*) that seal the nuptials are chanted, after which the bride and groom share a second cup of wine. Normally the cantor chants these blessings aloud, but they may also be recited by the rabbi or by guests called forward serially to be so honored. The *sheva b'rakhot* refer to marriage only in the final two blessings. The first blessing is the blessing over the wine, marking the separate nature of the *nissu·in* ceremony. The other blessings establish a context for Jewish marriage by invoking the harmony and perfection of creation and the idea of perfecting the world that is so strongly associated with marriage in Jewish tradition, and also by linking the love of bride and groom with the love Jewish people have for the Land of Israel. The final blessings specifically mention the joy and delight of the bride and the bridegroom.

At the close of the ceremony, the officiating rabbi often blesses the couple with the words of the priestly blessing, Numbers 6:24–26. This practice is not limited to rabbis who are *kohanim,* but some couples do ask to have this blessing recited specifically by a *kohein* or by a respected elder. There is a Sephardic tradition occasionally seen in Conservative synagogues to wrap the bride and groom in a large *tallit* for this final blessing.

As the ceremony ends, the groom breaks a glass by stamping his foot down on it. There are numerous interpretations of this custom. The most traditional is that breaking the glass serves as a reminder of the destruction of the First and Second Temples, and thus reminds those present that, even during the happiest moments in life, Jews may not forget the destruction of Jerusalem (gloss of the Rema to *SA* Oraḥ Ḥayyim 560:2). Others feel that the shattered pieces of glass should be taken paradoxically to represent the years of joy that friends and family wish for the new couple in accordance with the psalmist's injunction (at Psalm 90:15) to "match days of sorrow with days of joy."

Yiḥud

After the ceremony concludes, the bride and groom are expected to seclude themselves together for a brief period of time (cf. *SA* Even Ha-eizer 61:1 and the gloss of the Rema). This seclusion, called *yiḥud* in Hebrew, is intended symbolically to represent the consummation of the marriage, a crucial detail subsequently left to the bride and groom to look after on their own time. Couples who have been fasting on their wedding day generally break their fast in the *yiḥud* room. This brief period of seclusion also offers the newlyweds, who may be pulled in many directions in the course of a day of very public celebration, a chance to catch their breaths and reconnect with each other.

The Wedding Feast

As with the other life-cycle occasions, the wedding is generally followed by a celebratory meal. Following this feast, there is a special version of the Grace after Meals that concludes with the seven blessings that were chanted under the *ḥuppah,* although in a slightly different order. Often, special guests are honored by being chosen to recite these blessings.

Traditionally, two wine cups are filled before the Grace after Meals is recited (*SA* Even Ha-eizer 62:9). After the end of the seventh of the seven blessings (in this version, the seventh being the blessing over wine), the wine from the two cups is poured into a third cup, then shared by the bride and the groom.

Traditionally, the *sheva b'rakhot* are recited after a meal each day for the first week after the wedding. Usually the couple is joined on these days by friends who participate in the joyous week-long celebration of the marriage. At least one new guest (one who did not attend the wedding and did not hear the blessings there) is sought each day (*SA* Even Ha-eizer 62:7). In the absence of such a new guest, the celebratory meal is still held, but the seven benedictions are not recited as part of the Grace after Meals. Also, the seven blessings are not recited in the absence of a *minyan.*

The Laws of Family Purity

The laws of family purity are based on the biblical injunction at Leviticus 18:19 that married couples may not engage in intercourse during the wife's menstrual period. Different explanations of this law have been offered throughout the ages, but common to all of them is the basic assumption that human beings can attain a state of holiness through spiritual, emotional, and physical discipline undertaken in the context of obedience to divine law. Popularly, the laws that govern this specific aspect of the marital relationship are known under the general rubric of *tohorat ha-mishpaḥah* ("the purity of the family") laws and need to be understood in the larger context of married life, as explained elsewhere in this volume by Rabbi David J. Fine in his chapter on the *halakhah* of marriage.

A menstruating woman is known as a *niddah,* a name derived directly from Leviticus 18:19 (cf. Ezekiel 18:6). A woman becomes a *niddah* when she first notices her menstrual flow (*MT* Hilkhot Issurei Bi·ah 6:2). The menstrual period is deemed to last minimally for seven days (as specifically noted at Leviticus 15:19), counting the first day as the one on which she first noticed bleeding.

Once the flow of blood has ceased, the woman counts an additional seven days during which there is no bleeding or spotting. Although the Torah itself does not actually speak about these seven extra days, during which sexual contact continues to be prohibited, these additional days are considered requisite in the traditional sources (*SA* Yoreh Dei·ah 190:1). Today, there are couples who find great meaning and significance in the laws of family purity but, finding the stringency of the additional seven days too restrictive, prefer to follow the biblical prescription more literally. A responsum by Rabbi Avram I. Reisner entitled "Observing Niddah in Our Day" and proposing that the additional seven days of abstention be considered optional was approved by the Committee on Jewish Law and Standards in 2006 and is available on the website of the Rabbinical Assembly. Responsa on the same and related topics by Rabbis Miriam Berkowitz and Susan Grossman were also accepted by the CJLS in 2006 and are similarly available on the Rabbinical Assembly website, as is a joint statement by all three rabbis entitled, "Mikveh and the Sanctity of Family Relations."

During the *niddah* period, the general principle is that a couple may not have sexual relations. Some couples observe additional restrictions, however, including not sleeping in the same bed and not touching each other (*SA* Yoreh Dei·ah 195:6).

At the end of the days of impurity, the wife goes to the *mikveh* in the evening. Only if there is no alternative should she go to the *mikveh* during the daytime.

At the *mikveh,* she removes all items that could potentially separate her from the water, including clothing, jewelry, make-up, bandages, nail polish, and contact lenses. She then thoroughly cleanses herself. In a place where complete privacy is impossible (for example, in a town where there is no *mikveh* and a natural body of water must be used in its place), a woman may wear a loose-fitting garment that will not impede the contact of the water with all parts of her body.

Under the supervision of a female attendant, she fully immerses herself in the water and recites the blessing: *barukh attah adonai, eloheinu, melekh ha-olam, asher kidd'shanu b'mitzvotav v'tzivvanu al ha-t'vilah* ("Praised are You, Adonai, our God, Sovereign of the universe, who, sanctifying us with divine commandments, has commanded us regarding immersion").

Following the blessing, the woman immerses a second time. Thereafter, sexual relations may be resumed.

Because the Torah presumes a woman's virginity before marriage, her first visit to a *mikveh* is normally supposed to occur just prior to her wedding. (The question of whether sexually active single women should also visit the *mikveh* is discussed below by Rabbi Jeremy Kalmanofsky in his chapter on the *halakhah* of being a single person.) The procedure for brides is intuitive: she waits until her last pre-wedding menstrual period has ended, then waits for seven "clean" days and goes to the *mikveh*. It is permissible to wait more than seven days, however, if the bride wishes to visit the *mikveh* directly before the wedding date. In simpler times, the date of a marriage was, at least in part, based on the likelihood that a woman would be able to go to the *mikveh* just prior to the ceremony and then consummate her marriage once the ceremony takes place. Today, given that many weddings are planned well over a year in advance, it is very difficult to guess where a woman will be in terms of her monthly cycle that far into the future. If a woman cannot visit the *mikveh* before her wedding (either because of logistics or because she is actually menstruating at the time of the wedding) and she and her husband wish to be faithful to the laws of family purity, then they may not consummate their marriage until a post-nuptial visit to the *mikveh* can be arranged. If there is vaginal bleeding following the consummation of a marriage, the bride is considered to be in a state of *niddah* thereafter (comment of the Rema to *SA* Yoreh Dei·ah 193:1). She must abstain from additional relations for four days, then wait another seven "clean" days before resuming relations (*SA* Yoreh Dei·ah 190:1 and cf. 192:2 and the comment of the Rema *ad loc.*). The question of the seven additional days of abstinence was the topic of recent responsa by Rabbis Susan Grossman and Avram Reisner, as discussed in more detail below by Rabbi Jeremy Kalmanofsky in his chapter on the *halakhah* of being single.

Pregnant women and nursing mothers who have not resumed their menstrual periods may conduct their intimate lives without reference to any *niddah*-based restrictions. However, women who become pregnant are obliged to check themselves on the day of the month they would normally expect to menstruate for the first three months, just as nursing mothers must for as long as twenty-four months (or until they begin to menstruate regularly; *SA* Yoreh Dei·ah 189:33). As long as menstruation has not recommenced, the *niddah* laws do not apply.

A woman also becomes a *niddah* after giving birth to a child. After the cessation of bleeding, she counts seven "clean" days, after which she goes to the *mikveh* and then may resume relations with her husband. The only proviso in the case of a new mother is that, no matter how soon after the birth of a daughter she stops bleeding, she cannot go to the *mikveh* until a minimum of fourteen days have passed (*SA* Yoreh Dei·ah 194:1). This distinction between giving birth to a son and giving birth to a daughter reflects the purity laws of the Torah as given at Leviticus 12:1–8.

The bleeding that accompanies miscarriage, if it occurs fewer than forty days into the pregnancy, is considered the same as any other menstrual bleeding (*SA* Yoreh Dei·ah 194:2). If, however, a woman suffers a miscarriage more than forty days into her pregnancy, the *niddah* laws that apply to a woman who has given birth apply as described just above. If the gender of the fetus cannot be determined, the requirement that she wait at least fourteen days before going to the *mikveh* applies (*SA* Yoreh Dei·ah 194:2).

When women enter menopause and cease to menstruate, the laws of *niddah* no longer apply (*SA* Yoreh Dei·ah 189:28).

The issue of contraception is discussed at length elsewhere in this volume by Rabbi Avram I. Reisner in his chapter on medical ethics.

Divorce

Just as Jewish law has established a formal procedure for the creation of marriage, so has it also established a formal procedure for dissolving a marriage. In modern times, citizens are subject to the jurisdiction of the civil courts of the countries in which they live with respect to divorce, but Jews also follow their own religious tradition in these matters. In Jewish law, a marriage may be formally concluded with the transfer of a bill of divorce, called a *get,* from husband to wife before either party may lawfully remarry. (In the event of recalcitrance on the part of one spouse in participating in the *get* ceremony, however, the resultant situations for men and women is not precisely the same. Partially, this is due to the fact that, while polyandry—that is, marriage to more than one husband at a time—is forbidden by scriptural law, polygyny, the marriage of one man to several women, is only forbidden by rabbinic decree. Other sociological and halakhic factors also come into play. Individuals facing such a problem should seek the counsel of a rabbi well-versed in these matters before determining how best to deal with the situation.)

The *get* has a fixed text that specifies for whom it was written and for what purpose. When it is handed to the wife by her husband (or by an agent of the husband) in the presence of witnesses, a marriage is deemed terminated. After the *get* procedure is completed, each party eventually receives a certificate of release, called a *p'tor,* stating that a *get* has been effected and that both parties are henceforth free to remarry if they wish.

The *get* does not indicate any grounds for the divorce, nor does the ritual surrounding its transmission call upon either party to divulge the specific reasons the marriage failed.

Jews who are undergoing, or who have already completed, a civil action for divorce, annulment, or the dissolution of their marriage should seek a *get* as well. Even if the marriage ceremony was civil or nontraditional, a *get* should nevertheless be arranged so that both spouses can feel wholly quit of their responsibilities to each other and thus free to move forward with their lives. There is also the likelihood that the union, although civil, became halakhically valid after the fact since the consummation of a marriage may be considered an *ex post facto* indicator of a couple's desire to effectuate the kind of legally binding betrothal that leads to marriage (Isaac Klein, *Responsa and Halakhic Studies,* pp. 1–16).

Generally, a *get* is arranged after the civil decree is final. However, if the parties wish to arrange for the *get* before the civil decree, they may do so. In such a case, though, the *p'tor* will usually not be issued until the civil decree becomes final. It is also possible in certain jurisdictions for a spouse to ask the judge issuing the divorce to order the other spouse to remove any impediments, including religious ones, to the remarriage of either party. Where this is possible, it is certainly desirable for the civil decree to include participation in a *get* ceremony as part of each spouse's closing set of obligations to the other.

There are several ways in which the *get* may be effected. Both husband and wife may appear before a rabbi specially trained in matters of Jewish divorce, a scribe, and at least two witnesses. Such a specially trained rabbi is called a *m'saddeir gittin* and may also function as the scribe. (The feminine form is *m'sadderet gittin,* but I will use the masculine form in the following paragraphs.) The husband instructs the scribe (or the *m'saddeir gittin*) to write the *get* in the presence of witnesses while husband and wife wait. The husband then formally delivers the *get* to his wife in the presence of the witnesses. The individuals who witness the delivery of the *get* do not have to be the same individuals who saw it being written (*SA* Even Ha-eizer 133:1).

Alternately, the husband may appear briefly before the *m'saddeir gittin* to fill out a document and then, in the presence of witnesses, order the scribe to write the *get.* The husband then charges the scribe with looking after its delivery either personally or through the appointment of an agent. In such a case, the scribe may then write the *get* at a later time and then appoint the *m'saddeir gittin* to deliver the *get* to the wife. When the *m'saddeir gittin* does so in the presence of witnesses, the divorce is deemed executed (*SA* Even Haeizer 140:1).

The wife too may appoint an agent to receive the *get* on her behalf. This too is done in the presence of witnesses and is valid, although current practice is to avoid scenarios in which both spouses appoint agents to act on their behalf.

In each case, "delivery" means handing the *get* to the wife before witnesses, normally in the office of the *m'saddeir gittin*. Special difficulties will arise if either spouse is uncooperative or unresponsive, or if the whereabouts of one spouse are unknown, or if either spouse is institutionalized because of severe mental illness. A rabbi well-versed in the laws of Jewish divorce should be consulted on how to proceed in such situations. Almost always, however, there is a remedy that can be sought and applied to end a marriage in a dignified and halakhically acceptable manner. If all else fails, the Joint Bet Din of the Conservative movement can be approached to have a marriage formally annulled through a ceremony known as *hafka·at kiddushin*.

The *get,* as noted above, is a formal document with a fixed Aramaic text. An English translation follows:

> On the _______ day of the week, the _______ day of the month of _______, in the year _______ since the creation of the world, according to the calculation to which we are accustomed here, in the city of _______ (which is known also as _______) that is located on the river _______ (and on the river _______ *or* situated near sources of water), I, _______ (also known as _______), son of _______ (also known as _______), who today am present in the city _______ (also known as _______), that is located on the river _______ (and on the river _______ *or* situated near sources of water), do willingly consent, being under no restraint, to release, set free, and put aside you, my wife, _______ (also known as _______), daughter of _______ (also known as _______), who today is present in the city _______ (also known as _______), that is located on the river _______ (and on the river _______ *or* situated near sources of water), who has been my wife from time past until now. I do hereby set free, release, and put you aside, in order that you may have permission and the authority over yourself to go and marry any man you may desire. No person may hinder you from this day onward, and you are permitted to be married to any man. This shall be for you, from me, a written bill of dismissal and a legal document granting you your freedom in accordance with the laws of Moses and the people of Israel.

A woman whose marriage has effectively ended, but who, for some reason, is not free to remarry is called an *agunah,* literally a woman "anchored" to her unhappy situation. This situation might obtain in the case of a husband who disappears and who is presumed dead, but whose death is never actually confirmed by even a single witness. The more common *agunah,* however, is the woman whose marriage ends in civil divorce, but whose husband refuses, or is unable, to participate in the ceremony granting her a *get.*

Because both situations were seen as intolerable, certain leniencies were granted to alleviate them. For example, the laws concerning evidence and witnesses were relaxed to allow the *beit din* to accept testimony concerning the disappearance of a married man that would ordinarily not be permitted (*SA* Even Ha-eizer 17:3).

In the case of the woman whose husband refuses, or is unable, to participate in a formal Jewish divorce, however, the situation is even more complicated. In the case of recalcitrance after a civil divorce has been granted, every effort should be made to secure the husband's cooperation. If such cooperation cannot be obtained, the only remedy, as mentioned above, is to petition the Joint Bet Din of the Conservative movement (the highest legal authority within the Conservative movement) retroactively to nullify the marriage and thus to allow for a woman's subsequent remarriage. A rabbi should be consulted to make all of these arrangements. The nullification procedure, called *hafka·at kiddushin,* is discussed below by Rabbi David J. Fine in his chapter regarding the *halakhah* of marriage.

If a wife becomes mentally incompetent, and as such is unable meaningfully to accept a *get* from her husband, the *beit din* can prepare a document that addresses the issue and seeks to resolve it by allowing the husband to prepare a *get* and deposit it with the *beit din,* then to marry again even though his first wife remains technically married to him until she becomes able to accept her *get.* The document, called *hetteir mei·ah rabbanim* ("the permission from one hundred rabbis"), describes the wife's condition (as confirmed by appropriate doctors) and lays out both the husband's difficulty living with her as well as his urgent need to remarry. This is then signed by one hundred rabbis, who reside in at least three different countries or states (gloss of the Rema to *SA* Even Ha-eizer 1:10 and Klein, p. 499–500).

When a couple has been granted a civil divorce, but the wife unjustifiably refuses to accept a *get* (which, given that she has divorced her husband civilly and clearly does not wish to be married to him, is understood to work to her advantage by freeing her from an unwanted union and in no way to her detriment), a *get al y'dei zikkui* ("a bill of divorce accepted by a third party") may be issued. The procedure follows the norm in that the husband has a *get* written for his wife, but it is then presented to a *beit din,* which accepts it on her behalf until such time that she decides to retrieve it (Klein, pp. 496–499).

Some of the ethical issues surrounding divorce are discussed elsewhere in this volume by Rabbi David J. Fine in his chapter on the *halakhah* of marriage.

Dealing with Illness

The Jewish approach to illness and death is very much akin to its approach to birth and life. Life is a gift and a blessing. We give thanks to God every day for the gift of life, but recognize that we are mortal and that our time in this world is limited. We believe that, while death is the end of our earthly life, it is not the end of our existence, and so the following words are found in our daily prayers: "My God, the soul You have given me is pure. You created it. You fashioned it. You breathed it into me and You keep it alive within me just as surely as it is You who will take it from me on the day of my death, only to return it to me in the distant future. For the moment, however, and as long as my soul is within me, I give thanks to You, Adonai, my God and the God of my ancestors, Sovereign of all existence, Ruler over all souls. Praised are You, Adonai, who is capable of restoring the souls to bodies long dead and gone from the world."

The laws and rituals relating to illness and death reflect these beliefs, as well as the real human needs that arise from these situations. Together, they guide the individual carefully through the difficult and painful processes of loss and grief. In the end, each individual must find his or her own way of dealing with illness and death. However, the wisdom of our tradition as expressed in Jewish law can serve the bereaved as a source of strength and deep healing.

Judaism endorses a preventative approach to healing. Indeed, one must do whatever is necessary to restore one's health, even if it means violating the Shabbat, a holiday, or almost all other Jewish laws. The justification for this rule is the verse from Leviticus 18:5: "These are My law and My statutes that an individual should observe and live by doing them; I am the Eternal," which the rabbis (at *BT* Yoma 85b) interpret as meaning that one should live by doing them and not die by remaining steadfast to them. And the Talmud also says (at *BT* Shabbat 151b and Yoma 85b) that it is permitted to desecrate one Shabbat so that one might live to fulfill many others.

The Torah views life as being so precious that it is strictly forbidden deliberately to shorten one's life or the life of another individual. In our day, when it is possible to extend life almost indefinitely through the use of mechanical respiratory devices and other technological advances in medicine, questions surrounding the removal of artificial life support have become extremely complicated. The Conservative movement has attempted to distinguish between active and passive euthanasia. The former, actively hastening one's own death or the death of another individual, is strictly forbidden in the strongest possible terms. The latter, however, which generally means allowing the terminally ill patient to die at his or her own pace in a dignified and kind way by *not* hooking such an individual up to machinery that will merely prolong the process of dying, is looked upon far more kindly. The consensus of opinion is that terminally ill patients have the right to die naturally, either by declining artificial life support or by disconnecting machinery that is merely preventing death from occurring naturally. All of these issues are discussed in detail elsewhere in the essay in this volume by Rabbi Avram I. Reisner in his chapter on medical ethics.

Jewish physicians and health care workers are permitted to do whatever is necessary on Shabbat in order to save lives. However, they should attempt to arrange their schedules and coverage so that they will not have to practice on Shabbat on a regular basis.

There is no requirement to injure one's health for the sake of performing any positive commandments. Therefore, it is considered forbidden to fast on fast days if doing so could be injurious to one's health (*SA* Oraḥ Ḥayyim 618:1). Vital medications should be taken on fast days, even with food, if that is the proper way to ingest the medicine. However, one should not eat more than is necessary to maintain one's health. If an individual feels that fasting will be harmful, then that individual is permitted to eat on a fast day even if a physician determines that fasting will not cause real damage to that person's health (*SA* Oraḥ Ḥayyim 618:1). On the other hand, if a physician determines that an individual should not fast on one of the fast days, then that opinion should be followed even if the individual in question feels quite capable of fasting (ibid.). The bottom line is that one's health always comes first: when eating is necessary to a person's continued good health, it becomes a requirement for that person to eat.

The question of radical or experimental therapies is also related to this general willingness to do whatever it takes to restore good health. If one is gravely ill, for example, one may elect to participate in treatments that are only experimental in nature even if the realistic chances of recovery they offer are slim. Conversely, one who is gravely ill and who has little or no chance of recovery may choose not to use treatments known to have unbearable side effects.

One may request that a DNR ("Do Not Resuscitate") order be activated if there is no realistic chance for long-term survival. This is not considered tantamount to suicide, nor are doctors, nurses, or other healthcare providers who comply with such an order considered parties to the murder of the individual in question.

In the case of patients who have entered a persistent vegetative state, family members or a designated healthcare proxy may decide to withhold all treatment, including nutrition, hydration, and all other artificial means of keeping the patient alive. This issue in particular is discussed in detail below by Rabbi Reisner.

It is permitted to sign a so-called "living will" in which one specifies one's wishes concerning treatment in the event of terminal illness should it not be possible for an individual to make his or her own wishes clear at that time. The Committee on Jewish Law and Standards has developed a version of the "living will" that meets all necessary halakhic criteria. This will is available on the website of the Rabbinical Assembly or from any Conservative rabbi. Interested readers may further consult the document entitled, "Jewish Medical Directives for Health Care," written by Rabbi Aaron Mackler and based on responsa by Rabbis Elliot Dorff and Avram Reisner, as published in *CJLS Responsa, 1980–1990,* pp. 589–605.

Visiting the Sick

At *BT* Shabbat 127a, the Talmud notes that visiting the sick is counted as one of the *mitzvot* that is rewarded both in this world and also in the World to Come. Indeed, the conviction that visiting the sick, *bikkur ḥolim,* could bring actual therapeutic benefit—the Talmud (at *BT* N'darim 39b) cites Rabbi Abba bar Ḥanina's rather fanciful theory that visitors take one-sixtieth of the patient's illness away when they leave after a visit—caused *bikkur ḥolim* to be heralded as one of the principal *mitzvot* that pertain to relations among people. The laws pertaining to the obligation to visit the sick are discussed and analyzed elsewhere in this volume by Rabbi Elliot N. Dorff.

One should be considerate of the needs of the sick when visiting. The visit should not take place when the individual is so uncomfortable that he or she cannot appreciate it. Indeed, except in cases of very grave illness, one should only visit after three days have elapsed so as to grant the patient some initial privacy (*SA* Yoreh Dei·ah 335:1). Also, any visit should be cut short if one sees that the sick person is uncomfortable or in need of rest.

It is traditional to recite a prayer of healing on behalf of the ill. Normally, this is done in synagogue in the course of the Torah reading when a Mi Shebeirakh prayer for individual sick people or for the sick in general is recited. Since a large part of the effectiveness of such a prayer derives specifically from the patient knowing that he or she is in the thoughts and prayers of the community, visitors should let the sick individual know that these prayers are being offered on his or her behalf.

When the Mi She-beirakh prayer is recited, an unusual form of the patient's name is used, one that combines his or her first name and the name of the patient's mother (rather than the more usual use of his or her father's name). The most commonly cited reason for this is that it was the mother who traditionally cared for her sick children. If one does not know the name of a patient's mother, one may use his or her father's name instead. Indeed, some consciously choose to mention the father's name as well. In such a case, however, the mother's name should precede the father's.

Does prayer really help the sick individual? In this matter too, there are different opinions. Some believe that there is a direct benefit to be had from invoking God's healing powers on the part of a specific individual. Others reject this thinking because it appears to imply that God might not intervene on behalf of someone for whom no prayers are recited, and the Bible teaches us at Psalm 145:9 that God's mercy extends to all creation. But even for those who reject the notion that one can curry divine favor with prayer, praying for the sick can help by showing that the community cares about their fate and that their situation is weighing heavily on the minds of their friends and relations. Also, public prayer on the behalf of a sick individual makes people more likely to call on them, or to do other helpful things to ease their plight.

Confronting Death

When Death Is Imminent

If at all possible, the dying person should try to recite the Sh'ma with his or her dying breath. If that is impossible, either because of the progression of the illness or because the individual is unconscious, a rabbi or any family member can recite the prayer instead.

There is a longer prayer, usually called the Viddui (confession), that can be recited at a patient's deathbed, but which can also be recited in advance of the patient's last moments and, if possible, which should be said while the patient is still aware of his or her surroundings and able to respond, even slightly, to the words of the prayer. When death becomes imminent, however, the recital of this prayer is appropriate by anybody at all on behalf of the dying individual. One should always explain that reciting the Viddui is part of the traditional response to grave illness and is not necessarily an indication of imminent demise. This explanation should be directed toward the patient even if that individual appears to be indifferent or unable to respond in any visible way.

There are several different versions of the Viddui prayer. A short form of this prayer is as follows: "My God and God of my ancestors, accept my prayer. Do not turn away. Forgive me for all the times I may have disappointed You, for I am aware of the wrongs I have committed. May my pain and suffering serve as atonement. Forgive my shortcomings, for against You have I sinned. May it be Your will, Eternal God, my God and God of my ancestors, that I endure my illness with a clear conscience and in accordance with Your will. Send a *r'fu·ah sh'leimah,* a complete healing, to me and to all who suffer. My life and death are in Your hands, O Eternal God, my God. May it be Your will to heal me. Guardian of the bereaved, protect my beloved family, for our souls are bound together. In Your hands lies my spirit. Hear, O Israel: the Eternal is our God, the Eternal is one."

Whenever possible, a dying person should not be left alone. Illness is often not only a painful, but also a frightening and lonely experience. Many friends sever contact with a dying person, either because they are uncomfortable around illness and are uncertain what to say or because of some deeply rooted traumatic experience with death, or simply because it reminds them of their own mortality. Whatever the reason anyone feels tempted to flee the presence of the dying, tradition demands that we attempt to overcome our anxiety or ill ease and not to leave a dying person alone. Even a non-responsive patient at the very last moments of life is to be treated with loving attention and dignity. Judaism does not recognize any gray area between life and death. As long as someone is living, he or she is to be treated as a cherished friend or relation, and as someone not to be abandoned simply to spare the living the pain of witnessing their own loss. There often is very little else that non-physicians can do for the dying, but merely staying with the dying individual can be the greatest of all kindnesses and should not be trivialized.

When family and friends cannot be with the dying individual around the clock for days at a time, it is a worthy gesture to arrange for a nurse or companion to be present at all hours the patient would otherwise be alone.

Autopsies and Organ Donation

The *halakhah* does not generally permit autopsies, understanding these to be an affront to the honor due the dead and the integrity of the corpse. There are, however, two exceptions. If state authorities require an autopsy (when, for example, there is suspicion of foul play, or in a public health emergency), then Jewish law also permits it. And when an autopsy could conceivably help to save another person's life (for example, in a case where a puzzling disease continues to threaten living members of the family of the decedent), the procedure is also allowed (CJLS responsum of 1958 authored by Rabbi Isaac Klein and now published in the author's *Responsa and Halakhic Studies,* pp. 42–52, cf. also my *A Time to Be Born, A Time to Die* [New York: The United Synagogue of Conservative Judaism, 1976], p. 23, and Klein, pp. 274–275).

Similarly, because organ transplants save lives, it is considered meritorious to donate one's organs posthumously. This procedure and its halakhic and moral implications are discussed elsewhere in this volume by Rabbi Avram I. Reisner in his chapter on Jewish medical ethics and by Rabbi David M. Greenstein with special reference to the ethics of sibling-to-sibling organ donation. A brochure featuring a form for future organ donors to fill out is available on the website of the Rabbinical Assembly.

Suicide

Suicide is strictly and categorically forbidden by Jewish law (*SA* Yoreh Dei·ah 345:1). Therefore, suicides have traditionally been denied burial rights in a Jewish cemetery. However, as rabbis have come to better understand what it means for an individual to take his or her own life, leniency in this regard has become far more normal than undue stringency. In order to be a confirmed suicide, there must be at least two witnesses to the act. More to the point, the deceased must have alerted them in advance that suicide was being planned and would occur. Also, the act itself must be seen as a formal, intentional repudiation of God's gift of life and not an act of despair, depression, or despondency. Today, most rabbis tend to see the willingness to take one's own life as a form of mental illness and realize that denying burial in a Jewish cemetery would only bring further pain to the survivors. The flexibility of the law, then, upholds the strict repudition of suicide in theory, while in practice responding with understanding and compassion when people do take their own lives.

Aninut

The period from the time of death until burial is known as *aninut,* a term for which there is no exact English translation, and the mourners—or rather, those who will become mourners after the burial, i.e., the parents, siblings, spouse, and children of the decedent—during this initial stage of bereavement are called *on'nim* (singular: *onein* or *onenet*). Because these close relatives of the deceased are generally supposed to be charged with arranging the funeral and subsequent burial of the deceased, the *halakhah* exempts them from the performance of all positive *mitzvot,* perhaps finding it in poor taste for people who have suffered the loss of such a close family member to be overly concerned with their own spiritual needs. Many people turn to the synagogue for solace during this period, but it is considered inappropriate to recite the Mourner's Kaddish until after the burial takes place. In addition, *on'nim* should refrain from eating meat, drinking wine, or enjoying other obvious physical pleasures.

When death occurs, the immediate relations of the deceased are required to tear a garment. The act of tearing a garment, called *k'ri·ah* in Hebrew, is an ancient expression of grief that appears repeatedly in the biblical narrative, where it appears to symbolize how one's heart can be torn by the loss of such a close relative. (Cf., for example, the stories regarding Jacob at Genesis 37:34, Joshua at Joshua 7:6, and King David at 2 Samuel 1:11 or 2 Samuel 13:31.) Once a spontaneous response to grief, today this is often done at the funeral chapel just before the funeral begins. Many people now prefer to rip small black ribbons instead of actual garments and then to wear those ribbons throughout the week of mourning. (Any rent garments must be worn throughout the *shivah* week.) While this practice is technically acceptable, it lacks the immediacy of tearing an actual garment and can rarely provide the cathartic, physical release that comes from tearing one's clothing.

One is required to perform *k'ri·ah* for one's parents, children, spouse, and siblings (*SA* Yoreh Dei·ah 340:1).

The mourner should be standing when *k'ri·ah* is performed and the tear should be made on one's right side unless one has suffered the loss of a parent. In that case, the tear is made, or the torn ribbon is worn, on the left side, directly over the heart (Klein, p. 279).

One should make the tear oneself. Even if it is started by someone else, it should be completed by the mourner as a personal expression of grief.

Before *k'ri·ah,* a blessing is recited in which God is acknowledged as the just and true Judge of the world. After *k'ri·ah,* some recite Job 1:21:

adonai natan vadonai lakaḥ / y'hi sheim adonai m'vorakh ("The Eternal has given and the Eternal has taken away; praised be the name of the Eternal One").

Except on Shabbat, the torn clothing or ribbon is worn for the entire week of mourning. After the secondary mourning period of thirty days for a sibling, spouse, or child, the clothing may be mended and worn again if so desired. The tear made after a parent's death, however, may not be mended (*SA* Yoreh Dei·ah 340:15).

Though there is a tradition posthumously to circumcise a baby boy who dies before his eighth day of life (*SA* Yoreh Dei·ah 263:5), Isaac Klein, observing that Maimonides fails even to mention this custom in passing, recommends that we not do so and this would surely be the approach of most Conservative rabbis today (Klein, p. 426).

The Funeral

An essential element of reverence for the dead is the rite of ritual purification. This act is the most important part of readying the body for burial and should be undertaken as soon as possible after death. The washing and purifying of the body is done by members of a *ḥevra kaddisha,* a Jewish burial society. Since the procedure involves undressing, cleaning, and re-dressing the body, it is considered inappropriate for men to prepare a woman's body for burial or *vice versa.*

The actual ritual of cleansing the body is called *tohorah,* purification. (The more common pronunciation is *taharah.*) The entire body is washed with the prescribed quantity of water while certain appropriate prayers are recited. The body is treated with extreme dignity and respect and, indeed, among the most essential elements in the training of a *ḥevra kaddisha* is instruction in the best way to preserve the dignity due the deceased.

The *tohorah* procedure need not be done at a Jewish funeral home. Many non-denominational homes have the proper facilities for the performance of the ritual. It should, however, only be undertaken by Jewish men or women trained to serve as members of a *ḥevra kaddisha.*

If the body is very badly mutilated—for example, if someone dies in a traumatic accident—the deceased individual should be placed in the casket in his or her bloodstained clothing without a full *tohorah.* A rabbi or an expert should be consulted in such matters. Individuals who die during surgery, however, may be cleansed with a full *tohorah.* In such a case, bloodstained sheets or drapes are interred with the deceased if there is any possibility that the bleeding was posthumous (*SA* Yoreh Dei·ah 364:4, cf. Klein, p. 277).

It is a universal custom for the deceased to be buried in shrouds rather than regular clothing. These shrouds, called *takhrikhim,* are simple white garments without pockets. The shroud has great symbolic meaning. All Jews are buried in similar shrouds because in death all are equal. The shroud has no pockets, because we take nothing with us when we die. The white color indicates purity and innocence, and reflects the rabbinic belief that death itself may be perceived as the great *kapparah* that atones for the sins and indiscretions of a lifetime (cf. *SA* Yoreh Dei·ah 338:2).

Traditionally, a man is buried in his *tallit.* If the family wishes, however, a substitute *tallit* may be used. In either case, one fringe is cut from the corner of the *tallit* as a symbolic statement that the deceased is no longer obligated to observe the *mitzvot.* Women who wore a *tallit* while alive may also wish to be buried wearing a *tallit.*

Where a casket is used for interment, it must be a so-called kosher casket—that is, one made entirely of wood. The purpose of a using a casket made entirely of wood is to allow the process of decomposition to occur as quickly and naturally as possible. In some countries, including Israel, the norm is for the dead to be buried wrapped only in a winding sheet. If cemetery rules require the use of a vault, the top of the casket should be covered with earth before the vault is put into place. The above-ground disposition of the bodies of deceased individuals is wholly inconsonant with Jewish tradition as it is not a form of burial at all.

Embalming is prohibited except in cases where it is required by law, such as when the body is transported long distances or across state or international boundaries. In such cases, the minimum amount of embalming that is possible should be done, and nothing should be done that would damage or disfigure the body.

Another way of showing respect to the dead is not leaving the body unattended from the time of death until the funeral. This is accomplished either by family members and friends taking turns attending the body or by engaging a guard, called a *shomeir* or *shomeret* (plural: *shom'rim*), to remain with the body until the funeral begins. It is traditional for the *shom'rim* to recite psalms. In modern times, when far more people die in a hospital than at home (and when even those who die at home are routinely taken to a hospital and pronounced dead there), it is often impractical for *shom'rim* to attend the body of a deceased individual when it is brought to the hospital morgue. Most rabbis agree that it is not an offense to the dignity of the dead for a body to be stored in a guarded morgue until it is retrieved for the funeral. In the event of a hospital death, the body should not be left alone, even briefly, until it is taken to the morgue. From the moment the body arrives in the funeral chapel, however, *shom'rim* should be present so that the body is not left unattended between that time and burial.

While in many jurisdictions members of the immediate family are required to identify the body of a deceased individual before the funeral may begin, this should be a private moment to which no attention is drawn. It is never appropriate to leave a casket open for a public viewing of the dead.

The Jewish funeral is generally a brief and dignified ceremony. It includes the recitation of appropriate psalms, a eulogy, and chanting of the El Malei Raḥamim, a memorial prayer in which the name of the deceased is specifically mentioned. Even though it is desirable that the funeral occur as soon as possible after death (even, where possible, on the same day that death occurs), it may also be delayed for a few days to allow time for family members to arrive from distant locations.

Traditionally, the officiating rabbi delivers the eulogy at a funeral. There is a growing trend, however, to invite friends or family members to deliver their own eulogies as well. Although there is no formal reason to forbid this practice, there are several reasons for which it should be discouraged. At times, it places an unwanted burden on the shoulders of mourners who do not feel capable or willing to speak in public. At others, it creates the possibility of remarks being delivered that at least some in attendance may find inappropriate, no matter how sincerely they are meant as praise. Finally, a eulogy is not an opportunity to evaluate a deceased individual with brutal frankness, but rather a time to speak honestly, but also positively and sympathetically, about an individual's life and work. A rabbi will know how to speak well of the dead without resorting to false praise or the kind of hyperbole that may ring sarcastic or even belittling to the dead, but untrained others may not. Of course, those close relatives or friends who wish to speak at a funeral and who can do so in a dignified and respectful manner should be allowed to do so.

Different congregations have different customs about whether the synagogue may be used for funerals. Traditionally, only the most highly respected members were afforded this honor, and the use of the synagogue for funerals was frowned upon as a general practice. Many synagogues that allow their sanctuaries to be used for funerals limit that honor to clergy, to officers of the congregation, and to former presidents. There are also congregations that extend the privilege of sanctuary funerals to all members in good standing.

As noted above, funerals should take place as soon as possible after death, but no funeral may occur on Shabbat. While it is theoretically permissible for funerals to be held on Jewish festivals in order not to delay burial, this practice is strongly discouraged because it will most likely lead to many violations of the festival laws. If, however, the funeral does take place on the first day of the festival, all the work that is forbidden on the festival must be done by non-Jews (*SA* Oraḥ Ḥayyim 526:1). On the second day, Jews may perform work that is connected to the funeral (*SA* Oraḥ Ḥayyim 526:4). Most Conservative rabbis will not perform funerals on either day of a two-day festival.

It is permissible to delay a funeral slightly if the deceased wished to be buried in Israel and special transportation arrangements have to be made. If there is a legal issue involved, such as a criminal investigation, the funeral may also have to be delayed. In such a case, the bereaved continue in their state of *aninut* until the funeral actually occurs.

It is not traditionally the custom for flowers to be used in Jewish funerals in the United States, Canada, or most Western countries. In Israel, however, the use of flowers is considered acceptable. Both in Israel and the Diaspora, however, it is more appropriate to donate the money that would have been spent on flowers to a charitable cause that might benefit the living and do honor to the dead.

Traditionally, no eulogy is delivered on days when the Taḥanun prayers are omitted in the synagogue service, as well as on the eve of Shabbat or a holiday (*SA* Oraḥ Ḥayyim 697:1).Words of a general nature to comfort the mourners are permitted in such situations, however, including brief remarks about the fine attributes of the deceased. Many rabbis today blur the distinction between these two kinds of public discourse about the dead, feeling that the needs of the bereaved and the dignity due the dead are best served by delivering speeches virtually indistinguishable from eulogies on such occasions. The El Malei Raḥamim prayer is omitted on days when Taḥanun is omitted, but substitute prayers with similar themes may be recited in its place.

In ancient times, the dead were carried to their graves directly from the funeral either in a casket or on a bier. Today, it is far more regular to have the funeral and the burial in locations at some distance from each other. In such cases, the traditional funeral procession bearing the casket from the hearse to the grave is led by the mourners, who walk either in front of or behind the casket, as soon as possible after the hearse arrives in the cemetery.

The casket is generally carried or accompanied by pallbearers. Traditionally, these pallbearers are Jewish, and may include family members, including the mourners themselves. However, some traditions discourage or even forbid mourners from being pallbearers, and this has become the standard practice in modern times.

When possible, it is traditional for the funeral procession to stop seven times on the way to the grave as Psalm 91 is read aloud. However, no stops are made nor is Psalm 91 read aloud on days on which Taḥanun is not recited. The seven stops are derived from the seven times the word "vanity" is mentioned in the Book of Kohelet, also called Ecclesiastes. These stops are sacred moments for the bereaved to consider the fragility of life and the profound meaning of death as they participate in the burial of a loved one.

When the procession arrives at the grave, the casket is placed in the grave with the deceased face up and his or her feet toward the entrance of the cemetery or toward the road leading to the entrance. The family and others then cover the casket with earth. The tradition is to use the shovel in the inverted position for the first two or three scoops and only then to use it in its normal manner, intending that this unnatural and inefficient procedure serve as a sign of reluctance to part from the deceased. Actually shoveling earth into the grave of a beloved family member is very difficult. Nevertheless, the mourners, even the children of the deceased, should be encouraged to do so. There is a profound psychological value in hearing the sound of the clods of earth on the casket, and this leads in a healthy way toward confronting the reality of one's loss. However, if the decedent has left behind young children, it is normal not to ask them to participate actively in the burial. The shovel should not be passed from person to person, but should rather be returned to the mound of earth after each person uses it. Each individual who participates in the burial, therefore, does so wholly as a function of his or her own desire to participate in this final act of caring for a beloved relative or friend, which act has traditionally been called the *ḥesed shel emet,* the most selfless of all acts of charity.

Except on days when Taḥanun is not recited, a special prayer called Tzidduk Ha-din, in which God's judgment is formally acknowledged and accepted, is intoned. The El Malei Raḥamim prayer is sometimes repeated at the cemetery as well. Except on days on which Taḥanun is not recited, the service is concluded with a long, unusual version of the Kaddish called either the Burial Kaddish or the Kaddish De'it·ḥad'ta, which adds to the body of the Kaddish references to the Jewish belief in eternal life and a messianic time when idolatry and strife will be eliminated from the world. The name Kaddish De'it·ḥad'ta derives from the first important word in the prayer that deviates from the normal Kaddish formula. On days on which Taḥanun is not recited, the standard Mourner's Kaddish is recited at the end of the burial service instead.

When the mourners leave the cemetery, the assembled form two parallel lines so that the mourners may walk between them as they leave the gravesite and hear some first words of comfort. Usually, the traditional formula *ha-makom y'naḥeim etkhem b'tokh she·ar aveilei tziyyon virushalayim* ("May God comfort you among the other mourners for Zion and Jerusalem") is recited, but other expressions of comfort may be substituted by well-wishers uncomfortable with the Hebrew or with the traditional formulation. These words are also said to mourners when visiting during the mourning week.

One of the more mysterious Jewish customs is the practice of placing one or more stones on the gravestone or on the grave before leaving the cemetery. This custom has been interpreted in several ways, but the most likely is also the simplest: in harsher times, when graves that appeared to be abandoned and unvisited were reused by civil authorities, family and friends were anxious to leave some physical sign of their visit for cemetery officials to notice. Today, we place a little stone on the big stone as a way of expressing our hope that the grave remain intact and that God, known in the liturgy as the Rock of Israel, continue to watch over it when those who now visit the grave are themselves gone from the earth.

Either when leaving the cemetery or else when arriving at the house of mourning, all the participants should wash their hands, symbolically removing the impurity of death from them. A pitcher of water should be placed outside of the cemetery or at the front door of the house of mourning for this purpose. There is no real halakhic importance to this act. Indeed, the ritual the Torah ordains for purification after contact with the dead is far more elaborate than merely washing one's hands and cannot be carried out today in the absence of a Temple in Jerusalem. Therefore, we content ourselves with this simple gesture instead. Because the washing is symbolic, there is no blessing recited. One simply pours water over both hands and then sets down the pitcher for the next person. As with the passing of the shovel, it should not be handed from one to the next. The questions of where and under what circumstances to bury the non-Jewish spouse and/or children of a Jewish individual are discussed in detail in a responsum jointly written by Rabbis Kassel Abelson and Loel Weiss that was approved by the CJLS in 2010 and which is available for readers' perusal on the website of the Rabbinical Assembly.

Kohanim and Funerals

Generally speaking, our tradition considers it a *mitzvah* unto itself for the living to accompany the deceased to their graves. Indeed, rabbinic tradition defines the prophetic injunction to walk humbly with God, the title of this section of this book, as being fulfilled specifically by accompanying brides to their wedding canopies and deceased persons to their graves (*BT* Sukkah 49b and Makkot 24a). Nevertheless, the Torah makes it clear that *kohanim,* the priests of ancient Israel, were forbidden to come into even casual contact with the bodies of dead persons other than those of their closest of relatives or even to share the same indoor space with them (Leviticus 21:1–4 and Numbers 19:14). And rabbinic tradition endorsed this prohibition, adding to it an exception which allowed a *kohein* personally to look after the disposition of an unattended corpse (*MT* Hilkhot Eivel 3:1 and 3:8). How should moderns relate to these ancient laws?

Building on a responsum by Rabbi Louis Epstein that was approved by the CJLS (then called the Committee on Jewish Law) in 1929 and which is now published in the *Proceedings of the CJLS 1927–1970,* pp. 1433–1446, most Conservative rabbis counsel that we consider the observance of these prohibitions today as acts of homage to ancient tradition rather than as obedience to actual laws still in effect. Given that the "*kohanim*" of today's Jewish communities lack any genealogical evidence to back their claim—and so are precisely what Maimonides himself called "*kohanim* by self-definition," as discussed elsewhere in this volume by Rabbi Martin S. Cohen in his chapter on Israel—there can be no real certainty regarding their obligation in the first place. (In this regard, interested readers may consult the comments of Rabbi Abraham Abele Gombiner [c. 1635–1682], the Magein Avraham, to *SA* Oraḥ Ḥayyim 201:4.) Moreover, the laws regarding the obligation of *kohanim* to avoid contamination with impurity clearly presupposes a means of restoring such an impure individual to a state of ritual purity, which means has not existed since the destruction of the Temple. Finally, there is ample halakhic justification for considering the impure individual exempt from the law forbidding contamination with impurity because, by virtue already of being in a state of impurity, such (re-)contamination cannot actually take place. This was the view of Rabbi Abraham ben David (c. 1120–1198), called Ravad, as made clear in his response to Maimonides' law codified at *MT* Hilkhot N'zirut 5:15, cf. his comment to *MT* Hilkhot Eivel 3:7, as well as the opinion of Rabbi Isaac bar Sheshet Perfet [1326–1408], called Rivash, as set forth in his 124th responsum [ed. Jerusalem, 1975, pp. 50–51] and it forms a sound basis for counseling today's *kohanim* to avoid casual contact with the dead out of respect for the laws that governed the priests of antiquity, but not to feel themselves bound by law never to attend a funeral, visit a grave, enter a hospital, attend medical or dental school, or visit sites of profound spiritual significance such as Rachel's Tomb in Bethlehem or the Tomb of the Patriarchs in Hebron. Nevertheless, the decision of any *kohein* today to avoid attending funerals and entering cemeteries should be taken as an act of piety and allegiance to tradition, and respected as such.

Cremation and Disinterment

Judaism regards the human body as a sacred trust from God that none has the right to desecrate or destroy, and this has been the view of Judaism since ancient times. Therefore, cremation, considered the ultimate expression of disrespect to the dead, is absolutely forbidden in all instances. In the light of the Shoah, in the course of which millions of Jews were murdered and their bodies burnt to ash, the practice has taken on a new air of repulsiveness. Normally, cremated remains (occasionally called cremains) are not buried in a Jewish cemetery. There are, however, certain exceptions to this rule. For instance, in the cases of families who brought the cremated remains of beloved family members with them when they left the former Soviet Union, most rabbis, noting the complete repression of Jewish tradition under the Communists and the lack of alternative to cremation, have agreed that those remains be buried in dignified Jewish graves. More delicate is the situation that ensues when Jewish individuals leave specific instructions to their heirs that they wish to be cremated, often noting explicitly that they are aware of the fact that this is forbidden and they wish their bodies to be cremated nevertheless. The family of such individuals should be informed that they are not duty-bound to obey the wishes of their parents in this matter since cremation is explicitly forbidden under Jewish law and that Jewish tradition is completely clear that parents do not have the authority to instruct their children to violate *halakhah*. In this way, every effort should be made to discourage cremation. If the heirs feel, however, that they cannot go against the specific instructions of an otherwise lucid, now deceased, parent, such cremated remains may be buried in a Jewish cemetery. This validates the ancient principle that the wishes of the dead are to be considered a sacred trust by the living (cf. the tradition ascribed to Rabbi Meir preserved in the Talmud at *BT* Ta·anit 21a and other places), but in such a way that precludes any possibility of the Jewish community appearing to condone a decision that tradition considers abhorrent and which the Shoah renders incomprehensible. A responsum by Rabbi Morris Shapiro permitting wide rabbinic discretion in dealing with issues relating to cremation and the disposition of cremated remains was adopted by the CJLS in 1986 and is published in *CJLS Responsa 1980–1990,* pp. 608–616.

Because the human body must in all instances be treated with respect and dignity, exhumation and reburial are forbidden under almost all circumstances (*SA* Yoreh Dei·ah 363:1). The Committee on Jewish Law and Standards has ruled, however, that under certain specific conditions, it may be permissible to disinter and rebury a body elsewhere (*CJLS Responsa 1991–2000,* pp. 413–417). If a deceased individual is buried in the wrong grave, for example, the body may be exhumed and reburied in the proper place. (This is especially so if the grave in which the individual was buried actually belongs to someone else.) The immediate family members should regard the day of reburial as akin to the original day of burial by re-rending their garments and then by observing all the laws of mourning until evening. Similarly, if there is a family plot in which the deceased was meant to be buried, the body may be moved to that plot if it was accidentally interred elsewhere.

If there is a danger that the grave might be desecrated or vandalized, the body may be moved to a more secure location. Also, if a Jew was inadvertently buried in a non-Jewish cemetery, the body may be moved to a Jewish cemetery. Deceased individuals buried in the lands of the Diaspora who expressed a formal wish while still alive that they be buried in the Land of Israel may be disinterred and removed to Israel for burial if that wish went unheeded or was unknown to those who arranged the burial.

In all cases of reburial, the body must be handled with great respect and a one-day period of mourning should be observed (cf. *SA* Yoreh Dei·ah 403:1).

The Shivah Period

The word *shivah* means "seven" in Hebrew and refers, at least in the context of the laws of mourning, to the seven days of mourning that follow the burial of a parent, child, sibling, or spouse. (The observance of this week of formal mourning is known colloquially as "sitting *shivah.*") Only the so-called seven relations listed above (mother, father, sister, brother, son, daughter, and spouse) are required to observe the laws of *shivah,* but, at least within the Conservative movement, it is generally accepted that adopted children too should sit *shivah* for their adoptive parents. The same would apply to step-parents, half-siblings and step-siblings.

The case of converts to Judaism who lose siblings or parents who are not Jewish themselves was discussed above. Traditionally, conversion to Judaism presumed that the convert's ties to his or her non-Jewish family were severed, but this is rarely the case today. The norm today is for such an individual to arrange a funeral for a deceased non-Jewish parent that adheres to the religious traditions the decedent maintained in his or her lifetime and then, after burial, to observe the normal practices of *shivah* as one normally would for a Jewish parent. The advice of a rabbi should be sought in determining how precisely to participate in a dignified and meaningful way in a non-Jewish funeral without contravening the halakhic standards that forbid active participation in the religious rituals of other religions.

The general principle in counting the days of *shivah* is that a part of a day counts as the whole day. Thus, one counts the remainder of the day of burial as the first day and it is normal only to observe the laws of *shivah* briefly on the seventh day. The decision on the part of some moderns to return to work after only three days of *shivah* should be countenanced only in cases of extreme financial hardship, and even then the work permitted should be done as privately and modestly as possible (*SA* Yoreh Dei·ah 380:2). Otherwise, ignoring the end of the *shivah* week can neither be sanctioned by *halakhah* nor considered at all advisable from the perspective of the healing process that must follow loss.

The *shivah* period begins immediately after the interment. If a festival falls during the *shivah* period, *shivah* is terminated before the holiday and not resumed afterward (*SA* Yoreh Dei·ah 399:1). It is customary to light a seven-day candle and to let it burn throughout the *shivah* week. In the case of a *shivah* week cut short by a festival, the candle should be allowed to burn for the full seven days.

If the death occurs on one of the days of Rosh Hashanah, Passover, Shavuot, or Sukkot, or on Yom Kippur or one of the intermediary days of Passover or Sukkot, *shivah* is not begun until after the festival ends even if the burial itself has already taken place (*SA* Yoreh Dei·ah 399:2). Therefore, even if the burial takes place during one of the intermediary days of Sukkot or Passover, or on the second day of a festival—or even, in extreme circumstances, on the first day—the week of bereavement only begins after the festival.

Shivah should be observed in the home of the deceased or the home of the mourner. Although there is value to sitting together as a family, *shivah* may also be observed in separate homes. During the *shivah* week, mourners remain at home and should not leave the house except for emergencies or to attend religious services. In many communities, daily services are held in the house of mourning precisely so that the mourners do not have to leave. If a *minyan* cannot be arranged for the house of mourning, the mourner may then go to the synagogue to say Kaddish, but must then immediately return to the house of mourning.

The week of mourning is a time for quiet reflection, for remembering, and for beginning to work through grief. None of this can take place if the mourner is preoccupied with worldly affairs. As mentioned above, mourners should not go to work during *shivah* unless severe economic loss will result. If one must go to work, one should resume sitting *shivah* upon returning home. Individuals who work at home may not pursue their normal activities during the *shivah* week either.

Although the custom lacks a real halakhic basis, there is a widespread practice to cover up the mirrors in a house of mourning. The reasons given for this are basically threefold: to free the mourner from inappropriate fretting about his or her own appearance, to encourage the mourner to focus on the deceased, and, as one is not supposed to pray in front of a mirror, to aid those who come to participate in services in the house of mourning.

As mentioned earlier, it is widely customary to light a seven-day candle in the house of mourning. This candle should be allowed to burn itself out, even if that means that it continues to burn after the formal observance of *shivah* concludes. If there is more than one house of mourning, a candle should be lit in each house. If one does not have a seven-day candle, individual *yahrtzeit* candles may be lit daily during the mourning week. No blessing is recited when the *shivah* candle is lit.

Upon return from the cemetery, a meal called a *se'udat havra·ah* ("a meal of healing") should be served in the house of mourning by friends and relatives who are not mourners themselves. It is customary to serve hard-boiled eggs as part of the menu since the eggs are deemed symbolic of the cycle of life. (Another reason often given is that since eggs are the only food that becomes harder, not softer, when cooked, they are deemed symbolic of the way in which human beings can become stronger, not weaker, by encountering adversity, sadness, and loss.) Other traditional foods served in some houses of mourning are lentils and wine. The drinking of wine at the house of mourning is probably based on Proverbs 31:6, "Give strong drink to the hapless, and wine to the embittered." In the Talmud at *BT* Eiruvin 65a, Rabbi Ḥanin goes even further and says that "wine was created only for the purpose of comforting mourners."

The mourners should sit on low benches or boxes during the *shivah* period as a sign of mourning. Also, they should not wear leather shoes during the *shivah* period, nor are married couples permitted to engage in intimate relations during the week of bereavement (*SA* Yoreh Dei·ah 383:1).

Mourners should not cut their hair during *shivah,* nor may male mourners shave (*SA* Yoreh Dei·ah 390:1).

A somber atmosphere should prevail in the house of mourning. Mourners should not watch television or listen to music. In times of national or public emergency, however, one may watch or listen to news broadcasts.

All public displays of mourning other than the public recitation of Kaddish are suspended on Shabbat, and this includes wearing the torn garment or the mourner's ribbon. However, the rules that govern private mourning, such as the prohibition of intimacy between husband and wife, remain in effect (*SA* Yoreh Dei·ah 400:1). Traditionally, mourners do not enter the Friday evening service until just after L'khah Dodi, at which time they are welcomed into the synagogue with the traditional words of comfort cited above.

If the parent of a bride or groom should pass away immediately before the wedding, the wedding may continue even immediately following burial. If such a wedding takes place during what would normally be the *shivah* week, the bride and groom may consummate their marriage, but they must then separate until the end of the *shivah* week (*SA* Yoreh Dei·ah 383:2).

Traditionally, there are no mourning rituals at all for potential parents when a woman suffers a miscarriage. Although this law was no doubt meant as a kindness in a world in which miscarriage was commonplace, today many people yearn for ritual framework to deal with the loss.

Rabbi Debra Reed Blank, in a responsum concerning miscarriage approved by the CJLS in 1991, wrote that although the *halakhah* does not sanction responding to such a loss with the traditional rituals of mourning, we should instead consider the grieving couple to be stricken and respond much in the same way tradition ordains that we respond to sick individuals. Rabbi Amy Eilberg, in a dissenting response, rejected the notion that a couple that has suffered a miscarriage should be treated as though they were ill and instead suggested that the rituals of mourning be modified and applied to help them through their grief, and she included among those rituals the tearing of a garment, the serving of a formal meal of consolation, the observance of a day of sitting *shivah,* and the recitation of Kaddish for 30 days. Rabbi Stephanie Dickstein, in a 1996 responsum also approved by the CJLS, recommended in the case of a stillbirth that a funeral service be held, followed by a one-day observance of *shivah.*

Comforting the Bereaved

As noted above, it is traditional to comfort mourners with the hope that they find solace among all Jews who have suffered loss and who have subsequently known recovery. Beyond this, however, what is said is often far less important than the simple presence of others. For visitors to a house of mourning to express their condolences and sympathy in their own words is perfectly adequate. Something as simple as "I'm so sorry" will often be more moving, and provide more comfort, than an elaborate speech. Also, there is no need to offer deep wisdom or complicated advice to mourners during the *shivah* week. Listening is far more important than talking. And what conversation there is in the *shivah* house should be about the deceased, not about the mourners and even less appropriately about those who have come to visit.

Visitors should not attempt to keep the mourner's mind off his or her loss, as focusing on the mourner's loss is precisely the point of observing a week of intense mourning in the first place. Jokes, gossip, business talk, and idle chatter do not belong in a *shivah* house.

The best thing visitors can do in a house of mourning is to share their own memories of the deceased with the mourners, or to listen to the mourners' recollections. Sometimes, sitting in silence with someone is all that is needed to provide solace.

Certain common-sense rules should apply when visiting a house of mourning. Visitors should not come at meal time. Visitors should neither stay late nor too long. Above all, visitors must be sensitive to the physical and emotional exhaustion of the mourners.

It is traditional to bring gifts of food to a house of mourning so that the mourners do not have to look after the preparation of their own meals. Visitors themselves, however, should make a point of not eating or drinking in the *shivah* home. Gifts of substantial food will often be far more appreciated than cakes and cookies. It is also considered appropriate to give gifts of charity to the poor or to worthy organizations in memory of the deceased.

Mourners continue the rituals of mourning only for an hour or so on the final day of *shivah.* It is then customary to end the mourning week by walking together in the street or around the block. By exiting the home, mourners formally re-enter the world in which they must now live without the individual who has passed away.

If news of the death of a relative for whom one would normally mourn only comes more than thirty days after that person's death, then the custom is to observe a kind of abbreviated *shivah* that lasts for an hour and features only the obligation not to wear leather shoes. Nor, unless the sad tidings regard the death of a parent, is the mourner obligated to rend his or her garment. If, however, the news of a relative's death comes within the thirty day period, the regular week of mourning commences with the arrival of the sad news, as does *sh'loshim* (*SA* Yoreh Dei·ah 402:1–2).

Sh'loshim

The first thirty days after the interment are collectively called *sh'loshim,* the Hebrew word for "thirty." The part of these thirty days that follows the week of *shivah* is considered a period of reduced mourning. Many of the restrictions of *shivah* are lifted and mourners are permitted to begin reintegrating themselves into society and to resume their daily work.

The calculation of *sh'loshim* begins with the burial and ends on the morning of the thirtieth day. Unlike *shivah,* the days of *sh'loshim* are not ended by festivals. They are, however, shortened. Each festival day (or, in the Diaspora, each two-day festival) is counted as a full week of *sh'loshim* (*SA* Yoreh Dei·ah 399:1). The end of Passover is not considered a full festival in this regard, but Sh'mini Atzeret is. Therefore, if someone were buried on the eve of Passover, *shivah* itself would be cancelled by the festival and there would be only fifteen days of *sh'loshim* observance after the end of the festival (because the festival counts for seven, which number is added to the eight days of the actual holiday for a total of fifteen. There would, therefore, be fifteen other days remaining). If someone were buried on Erev Sukkot, *shivah* would be canceled, and there would only be seven days of *sh'loshim* left after the festival—the nine days of the festival itself plus two seven-day subtractions for Sukkot and Sh'mini Atzeret yield a total of twenty-three days, which then leaves a single week of *sh'loshim* to be observed (*MT* Hilkhot Eivel 10:3). There are, however, a number of other rules that apply. The rules just cited apply when a festival cancels *shivah* observance. If one has finished *shivah,* however, then the festival cancels the rest of *sh'loshim* no matter how much of it has or has not been observed (*SA* Yoreh Dei·ah 399:2). And if someone dies and is buried less than a week before Rosh

Hashanah, then Rosh Hashanah ends the *shivah* and Yom Kippur ends the observance of *sh'loshim* (*SA* Yoreh Dei·ah 399:6).

While mourners may resume work and other activities during *sh'loshim,* the restrictions on entertainment continue. Mourners during this secondary mourning period should not attend parties featuring live music or other similar social events. Haircuts and shaving too are not permitted until after *sheloshim* (Klein, pp. 290–291). Marital intimacy, however, may recommence after *shivah*.

Single people should not plan to get married during *sh'loshim*. However, if a couple has already made the arrangements before the death and canceling them would entail great financial loss, they may go ahead with the wedding. In such a case, the wedding may involve music and dancing. If a wedding takes place, the seven days of festivity after the wedding should also be observed and are counted as part of the *sh'loshim* (*SA* Yoreh Dei·ah 342:1).

One may likewise attend the wedding ceremony of a relative or close friend during *sh'loshim* if it is felt that one's presence will enhance the joy of the bride and groom. However, one should not attend the festivities after the ceremony.

In synagogue, the mourner should not lead the congregation in prayer on Shabbat, festivals, or intermediary festival days. Nor should mourners lead the Morning Service on any days that Hallel is recited unless no one else present is qualified to do so.

The period of *sh'loshim* is the extent of formal mourning for all relatives other than for one's parents.

Mourning for Parents

The period of mourning for one's parents is a full twelve months, counted from the day of interment. Unlike *shivah* and *sh'loshim,* however, part of a day does not count as the full day for the termination of the twelve months. The rules are similar to the ones that pertain to *sh'loshim* observance for siblings, children, and spouses. The restrictions for haircuts and shaving are lifted after *sh'loshim* as soon as one is chided by another for looking unkempt (*SA* Yoreh Dei·ah 390:4).

Attending parties with music and dancing, social events with music, concerts, movies, or plays is not permitted. However, one may get married during the mourning year for a parent if there are compelling reasons not to defer the ceremony.

Alone among the customs that pertain to the year of mourning, the Mourner's Kaddish is only recited by people mourning their parents for eleven months. The custom of reciting Kaddish for only eleven months pertains even in a leap year which has thirteen months, as do the twelve-month restrictions. In such a year, then, there will be a month between the end of Kaddish and the end of the twelve months of mourning, then another month between the end of those restrictions and the first anniversary of death. The point of stopping the recitation of Kaddish a month early has to do with the popular understanding of Kaddish as a kind of intercessory prayer for the deceased. Since it was deemed vaguely insulting to the memory of one's parents to assume that they would require every last prayer possible to be recited on their behalf, the custom was to recite Kaddish for only eleven of the twelve months. A responsum by Rabbi Richard Plavin and Mayer Rabinowitz recommending the original custom of reciting Kaddish for twelve months after the death of a parent was approved by the CJLS in 2008 and is available to the public on the website of the Rabbinical Assembly.

Stepchildren and adopted children may recite Kaddish for their step- or adoptive parents.

If a deceased individual leaves behind no children, or if it is impossible for children to recite the Kaddish for their late parent or if they are unwilling to do so, the question sometimes arises if it is appropriate for another to take on the obligation of reciting the Kaddish. The answer is that, although it is permitted to recite Kaddish for someone other than a close relative, this custom should not be encouraged. In the end, saying Kaddish serves a deeply therapeutic function for the mourner. Knowing that a good friend, either of the mourner or of the decedent, is saying Kaddish can serve that function only slightly. Paying a stranger to say Kaddish for a parent cannot serve that function at all. Whenever possible, the mourner himself or herself should go to the synagogue to say Kaddish.

Yahrtzeit

The gradual lessening of intensity of mourning continues after the initial periods of mourning with the annual observance of the anniversary of a loved one's death. That day, popularly known among Ashkenazic Jews as the individual's *yahrtzeit,* should be a day given over to remembering and honoring a deceased individual for whom one once sat *shivah* and with whose loss one is learning to live. Giving gifts of charity, doing good deeds, or studying selections of Mishnah in memory of a loved one are appropriate ways of observing the *yahrtzeit.*

The *yahrtzeit* of an individual falls exactly one year after the date of his or her death according to the Jewish calendar. This is different from the calculation of *shivah* and *sh'loshim,* which are calculated from the time of burial (gloss of the Rema to *SA* Yoreh Dei·ah 402:12, cf. *SA* Oraḥ Ḥayyim 568:8).

If death occurs during the month of Adar in a non-leap year (in a year in which there is only one Adar), there are different opinions about whether the *yahrtzeit* should be observed in the first Adar or both the first and second Adar; the prevalent custom is for the *yahrtzeit* to observed during the first month of Adar in a leap year. If, however, death occurs during one of the months of Adar in a leap year, then the *yahrtzeit* is observed in the same Adar in which the death occurred in leap years. In a non-leap year, of course, all Adar *yahrtzeits* are observed in the single month of Adar.

There are two Jewish months, Kisleiv and Teivet, in which Rosh Ḥodesh is sometimes observed for one day and sometimes for two. (When it is observed for two days, the first day is actually the thirtieth day of the preceding month.) The custom is to fix the *yahrtzeit* in terms of the situation that pertains in the first year following death. If death occurs on the first day of Rosh Ḥodesh in a year when the Rosh Ḥodesh of either month has two days (i.e., on the thirtieth day of the previous month), and then the first anniversary of the death falls in a year in which that day does not exist (because the preceding month only has twenty-nine days, and Rosh Ḥodesh, therefore, is only observed for one day, the first day of the subsequent month), then the *yahrtzeit* is fixed on the twenty-ninth day of the previous month. (This way, the *yahrtzeit* at least falls in the same month as the death occurred, if not precisely on the same day.) If, however, the first year after death has a Rosh Ḥodesh that is observed for two days (and so the actual day the decedent died exists in the first year following death), then *yahrtzeit* is fixed on Rosh Ḥodesh, either on the only day in years when there is only one single day of observance, or on the first of the two days if there are two days (Klein, p. 295).

If one forgets to observe a *yahrtzeit,* it should be observed as soon as one remembers it in the same fashion one would have observed it on the correct date. If one does not know the date of a relative's death, one should choose a date that is close to the probable date of death, and the *yahrtzeit* should be observed on that date every year. If even an approximate date cannot be reasonably chosen, then any day at all may be selected, either at random or because it has some family significance, and that day should be permanently observed as that person's *yahrtzeit.*

The El Malei Raḥamim prayer is recited on a Torah-reading day before or on the *yahrtzeit.*

It is customary to light a twenty-four-hour candle on the evening of the *yahrtzeit* and to let it burn for the entire day. There is no special prayer or blessing to be recited upon lighting the *yahrtzeit* candle. Where lighted candles are not permitted, as in a hospital or nursing home, an electric memorial lamp may be used in place of the candle.

One should try to attend all three daily services on the day of the *yahrtzeit* and recite the Kaddish at these services.

Those observing a *yahrtzeit* are traditionally given precedence to lead the prayer service if they are capable of doing so.

Unveilings

Marking a grave clearly is a religious obligation (*MT* Hilkhot Tumat Meit 8:9), and this has traditionally been done with a stone marker of some sort. Also, setting a tombstone up on the grave of a loved one is another way of memorializing the name of the deceased and his or her Hebrew name and dates. Often, the outstanding characteristics of the deceased are noted briefly on the tombstone as well.

A tombstone should be inscribed and erected within the first year, but it can be done any time after *shivah* concludes. In Israel, the custom is to erect the monument at the end of the *sh'loshim* period.

While there are no firm halakhic guidelines regarding the text, the inscription on a tombstone should include the full Hebrew name of the deceased. The name of the deceased individual's father is also mentioned, and more recently some have chosen to memorialize the name of his or her mother as well. The inscription should note the Hebrew date of death, i.e., the individual's *yahrtzeit.*

On the top of the stone, it is traditional to inscribe the letters *pei-nun* which stand for *poh nitman* or *poh nitm'nah* ("here lies interred") or *poh nikbar* or *poh nikb'rah* ("here is buried"). On the bottom, the Hebrew words for "May the soul of the deceased be bound up in the bond of life everlasting" are usually represented by their initial letters only: *tav-nun-tzadi-bet-hei.*

It has become customary to dedicate the tombstone formally, usually somewhere around the date of the first *yahrtzeit.* The most usual procedure is for a cloth of some sort to be draped over the stone so that it may formally be unveiled, at which time psalms are read, the El Malei Raḥamim memorial prayer is chanted, and, if a *minyan* is present, the Kaddish is recited.

Yizkor

Four times each year, on Yom Kippur, Sh'mini Atzeret, the last day of Passover, and the second day of Shavuot, a special memorial service, popularly known as Yizkor (after the first word in its most prominent prayer), is recited. Special twenty-four-hour candles are lit at home on the eve of the occasion, and the memorial boards in synagogues are illuminated as well.

It is widely believed that it is inappropriate to participate in the Yizkor Service during the first year following a relative's death. However, most traditional authorities urge mourners to say the memorial prayers for family members even during the first year following their deaths. Either custom is acceptable, but most mourners will derive comfort from reciting Yizkor even shortly after losing a parent or other close relative.

It is also customary in many congregations for individuals whose parents are still living to leave the sanctuary just before Yizkor. Most rabbis today feel that this practice, rooted in the superstitious belief that being present for Yizkor will somehow tempt fate into bringing about one's parents' untimely demise, should be discouraged. Most synagogues today, therefore, encourage all members of the congregation to remain in the sanctuary for Yizkor. After all, these prayers are said for all relatives, not just for parents, as well as for the martyrs of Israel throughout history and, in many congregations, especially for those who died during the Shoah or in defense of the State of Israel. Many other congregations make special note of the victims of terrorism, both at home and abroad, in their memorial prayers. To absent oneself from such a moving and deeply meaningful prayer service for purely superstitious reasons does not seem like worthy behavior and should be discouraged. Individuals whose parents formally instruct them not to remain in the sanctuary for Yizkor, however, should obey those instructions without mocking their parents' fears or beliefs.

The Dietary Laws

PAUL S. DRAZEN

The Hebrew word *kasheir,* of which "kosher" is merely the anglicized version, means simply "fit" or "proper" for use. In classical Jewish sources, the term is used for all sorts of things, but primarily for foodstuffs deemed edible according to biblical stricture and for ritual items, such as a Torah scroll or a *lulav* and *etrog,* that meet prescribed halakhic requirements. Colloquially, however, the term is even applied to people if they are qualified or permitted to perform certain religious or legal functions (such as serving as witnesses) or if they act in an exemplary moral way. Still, when English-speaking Jews use the word "kosher" or speak about *kashrut,* the reference, more often than not, is to the dietary laws and traditions that have been an integral part of the Jewish people's way of life for millennia.

Why Keep Kosher?

Given the importance of *kashrut* in Jewish life, it is unfortunate that so much about it is so widely misunderstood. Some people, for example, assume that *kashrut* is only about cleanliness and hygiene, and therefore believe it is no longer necessary in the modern world. Others believe that "kosher" is merely a word for Jewish ethnic food. Still others assume that food that is misleadingly marketed as "kosher-style" is virtually identical to kosher food.

None of these assumptions is correct. *Kashrut* is among the most important institutions of the Jewish religion, and constitutes nothing less than an attempt to turn the act of eating—surely among the most banal and ordinary of life's daily tasks—into a holy opportunity to acknowledge God as the Source and Sustainer of all life.

Perhaps I should begin by mentioning the classic argument *against* keeping kosher: that the primary purpose for keeping kosher in bygone days was to promote and maintain good physical health. "All food is safe now," the argument goes, and "the laws of *kashrut* are obsolete because we now have government oversight of food preparation." Beyond a doubt, the systems for growing, preparing, and distributing food have improved vastly over the millennia, but there is no evidence that physical health was ever the basic reason Jews kept kosher. Nor does the fact that there are healthy aspects to maintaining a kosher diet constitute convincing proof that health considerations were the original context in which these laws were developed. (It is worth noting that one can obey the laws of *kashrut* carefully and still eat unhealthily.) Indeed, in the opinion of most authorities, if there is a relationship between *kashrut* and the health of the individual, it is his or her *spiritual* health that is in question—specifically, the question of how best to bring a spiritual dimension to even the most bestial of human needs, the need to nourish oneself and to sate one's hunger.

While all living creatures must consume nourishment, we human beings are different because we have the ability to add new dimensions to even the most mundane aspects of life by making them holy. That opportunity, that chance, to add a level of sanctity to the everyday act of eating is the essential element of keeping kosher. Keeping kosher forces us to stop and think about what we eat, when we eat, even about the plates on which we eat and the pots and pans in which we cook. In turn, this effort to ensure that we are following the rules appropriately forces us to focus on God's structure for living and eating and, in so doing, to allow a spark of holiness to illumine our everyday lives.

It also bears mentioning that the reverence for life engendered by the dietary laws has contributed over the generations to the development of a tradition that demands humane treatment of all living creatures. Even as we depend on animals for food, we are directed to ensure that we do not become callous toward animal life.

Keeping kosher also facilitates and strengthens Jewish identification. Faithfully observing the laws of *kashrut* helps maintain the connection between our own generation and past generations of Jews. Taking care with our eating also creates a link among Jews today by establishing an overarching bond with them that transcends the details of ethnic cuisine or dining customs. Keeping kosher is an active, vital way to identify as a Jew.

Finally, many people have long felt that there is a disconnect between scrupling mightily regarding the observance of the law while demonstrating an apparent disregard for the health, safety, and dignity of food industry workers. Responding to the dissonance, the Rabbinical Assembly and the United Synagogue of Conservative Judaism began in 2006 to work together to create Magen Tzedek, a system intended to certify adherence to ethical standards with respect to the treatment of workers in the food industry in a variety of diverse areas such as the payment of decent wages and the provision of appropriate safety training, as well as proper treatment of the animals to be slaughtered. The project has helped to move the discussion of ethics in *kashrut* to the mainstream *kashrut* supervision agencies and has thus made consumers of all stripes sensitive to the meta-issues involved in *kashrut* observance. The process of establishing reasonable yet enforceable standards continues and, as of this writing, initial inspection and supervision of kosher food providers has already begun to determine which will receive a certification mark known as the "Magen Tzedek."

For readers approaching the laws of *kashrut* for the first time, a very accessible introduction is the late Rabbi Samuel Dresner's *The Jewish Dietary Laws,* now published with a practical guide to the laws of *kashrut* by Rabbi Seymour Siegel and David M. Pollock as *Keeping Kosher: A Diet for the Soul* (New York: The United Synagogue of Conservative Judaism and The Rabbinical Assembly, 2000).

Kosher and Non-Kosher Animals

The most basic rules of *kashrut* are presented in the Torah, primarily in the eleventh chapter of Leviticus and the fourteenth chapter of Deuteronomy. Simply put, the Torah declares that certain animals may be eaten (after they have been slaughtered, inspected, and prepared appropriately) and others not.

Land Animals

The rule for land animals is a simple one: kosher animals must both chew their cud and have split hooves (Leviticus 11:3 and Deuteronomy 14:6). Therefore, the animal species that can be kosher include cows, oxen, goats, sheep, buffalo, and deer. The concept of chewing the cud may be unfamiliar to urban moderns, but it is really a simple matter. Certain animals, called ruminants, have a series of stomach chambers instead of the single stomach human beings have. Once food is eaten, only some of it is immediately digested, while another part, the cud, is then regurgitated and rechewed until it is reswallowed and then digested. Why such land animals were considered acceptable as food but not others is never explained in the Torah. (It will simply have to remain a topic for moderns to chew over!) As a result, land animals that present split hooves but do not chew their cud can never be kosher, no matter how they are slaughtered. The best known example of this is surely the pig, which has split hooves but does not chew its cud. Both signs are required in order to be kosher—there is no category of "partially kosher" animals.

Fish

A fish can be kosher if it has both scales and fins (Leviticus 11:9 and Deuteronomy 14:9). Sharks, whales, and dolphins are thus all excluded, as are octopuses, squid, and similar sea animals. Catfish, because they lack scales, may not be eaten. Also excluded are sea creatures referred to under the general rubric of "seafood," such as crab, lobster, shrimp, oyster, and eel. The most common fish species that are not kosher are blowfish, catfish, dogfish, eel, eelpout, ocean pout, puffer, and shark.

There are, of course, many varieties of fish having scales and fins which may be eaten, so there is always a plentiful selection available. Popular kosher fish include albacore, anchovies, carp, cod, flounder, haddock, halibut, herring, mackerel, muskellunge (muskie), perch, pike, pollock, red snapper, salmon, sardine, sea bass, smelt, sole, striped bass, tilapia, trout, tuna, and whitefish. (The lists here are not to be considered exhaustive; in cases of uncertainty, a competent rabbi should be consulted.) Caviar, like any kind of roe, is kosher only when the fish from which it comes is kosher.

One of the areas in which Conservative and Orthodox authorities differ has to do with the *kashrut* of swordfish and sturgeon. After researching the detail of rabbinic law and working with ichthyologists, Conservative scholars determined that swordfish and sturgeon may be considered kosher (Klein, p. 305).

It is precisely because of the great variety of both kosher and non-kosher fish that consumers must be careful when purchasing fish. The names of many fish varieties, kosher and non-kosher, are often similar. Mahi-mahi, for example, often marketed as "dolphin fish," is kosher, but real dolphins are not, and similar situations can cause confusion. Therefore, when choosing fish for meals, it is important to be careful to purchase only kosher species.

Aside from the issue of confusing names and unknown varieties, there are two related factors that make it especially important to exercise great care when purchasing filleted fish. When set out on a fishmonger's table, the skinned fillet of a kosher fish and that of a non-kosher fish are more or less impossible to tell apart, even for an expert. Therefore, buying fish prepared under kosher supervision is by far the best way to be sure the fish purchased is truly kosher. The second issue has to do with the equipment on which the fish is prepared. Under normal circumstances, consumers should always assume there is only one set of knives, cutting boards, and other utensils used for preparing the fish offered for sale. As such, it is reasonable to assume that the same knives used to fillet non-kosher fish or seafood are going to be used to prepare the kosher fish as well. Although washing and sharpening the knife between non-kosher and kosher fish may be sufficient to permit the use of the fish (*SA* Yoreh Dei·ah 121:7), the preference remains to purchase fish from a kosher supervised source.

There is an ancient custom dating back as far as the days of the Talmud not to eat meat and fish on the same plate. This notion is based on some putative danger involved in eating them together, however, not on any actual concern related to *kashrut* (see, e.g., how the *SA* refers to the matter at Yoreh Dei·ah 116:2). In 1998, the Committee on Jewish Law and Standards determined that meat and fish may be eaten together (*CJLS Responsa 1991–2000,* pp. 112–114). In the précis of the decision, the following explanation is offered: "The prohibition of fish and meat is based on a specific danger to the consumer. Historically when the danger ceased to exist, the rabbis had the power to end the prohibition. Today we know that there is no danger caused by eating fish and meat together. Therefore, we would permit not only putting fish and meat on the same plate, but would allow them to be consumed together."

Birds and Fowl

Unlike the specific descriptions Scripture offers regarding the traits of kosher mammals and fish, the Torah offers no specific traits by means of which to determine the *kashrut* of birds. Instead, the Torah contents itself simply to present lists of prohibited birds at Leviticus 11:13–19 and Deuteronomy 14:11–18. Nevertheless, over the years, rabbinic authorities have established certain rules of thumb to aid the consumer in determining whether a bird is likely kosher or not.

Generally speaking, a careful inspection of the lists yields the principle that birds of prey are not kosher, while birds that live off grains and grasses usually are. This principle notwithstanding, it is the lists of birds in the Torah which are considered authoritative, not the latter principle. Therefore, birds of prey *not* on the Torah's list are not necessarily deemed unkosher. Since, however, the rules of kosher slaughter (discussed below) do apply to fowl, the only rational way to be sure that fowl is kosher is to purchase it from a shop under reliable *kashrut* supervision.

One of the great dilemmas of *kashrut* legislation has traditionally rested in determining which birds are the ones mentioned in the Torah. (Many of the names are unique to these lists and have never been identified with any real certainty.) There are also some families that have maintained unique, entirely idiosyncratic traditions about specific modern-day birds, identifying them with birds on the Torah's list of forbidden fowl. (One such tradition, for example, considers turkey to be unacceptable, identifying it as the biblical bird *dukhifat* mentioned at Leviticus 11:19 and Deuteronomy 14:18.) Generally speaking, individuals should maintain the customs of their own ancestors, but there is no need for others to do so. All halakhic authorities today, for example, consider turkey to be a kosher bird.

Insects

Although the Torah says clearly at Leviticus 11:22 that some insects are kosher, it is today generally considered impossible to identify these insects correctly. As a result, therefore, today the practice is to consider all insects to be forbidden. If the food into which an insect falls is uncooked—if, for example, a beetle falls into a bag of flour or sugar—the beetle can simply be removed and the food used. (Whether this is a good idea from a hygienic point of view is another issue.) Although the general rule in cases of the inadvertent mixture of prohibited and kosher foods is that the mixture itself is permitted if the kosher foodstuff is more than sixty times greater in volume than the non-kosher item (according to the rule known as *bateil b'shishim*), that rule does not apply in the case of an entire creature like the beetle mentioned above. Therefore, if a whole insect falls from a bag of noodles into a pot of soup and is cooked with the noodles, the insect is not considered annulled regardless of the volume of the soup. The soup cannot be used in such a case and the pot must be *kashered* by boiling. (The term *kashering* is widely used to denote the process of making non-kosher kitchenware of various sorts kosher. The variant *koshering* is also in use.)

Of course, the prohibition of eating insects requires diligence when washing vegetables so as to assure that any minuscule insects present are rinsed away. Once vegetables appear clean to the naked eye, they are permitted (*Arukh Ha-shulḥan*, Yoreh Dei·ah 84:36).

Questions about insects or small crustaceans found in water have been raised in many communities over the past few years. The rule noted above, that *kashrut* concerns end with what can be seen by the naked eye, applies here as well. One need be concerned about the *kashrut* of the water (not to mention health issues and aesthetics) only if insects or other minute organisms can actually be seen swimming or floating around in a glass of tap water (*SA* Yoreh Dei·ah 84:1). If we were to avoid all potentially prohibited microscopic organisms, we would not be able to eat, drink, or even breathe.

Preparing Kosher Meat

Because the Torah also requires specific methods of slaughter, inspection, and preparation before acceptable animals may be eaten, determining the *kashrut* status of a specific species is only the first step in preparing meat for consumption.

Blood

Primary among the requirements is that blood not be consumed (Genesis 9:4, Leviticus 17:11–12, and Deuteronomy 12:23). Professor Edward L. Greenstein set forth the rationale of these laws in the following way: "The ban on eating blood is the most basic eating rule in the Torah, a notion expressed in diverse ways. First, an animal that dies naturally (*n'veilah*) or at the hands of another beast (*t'reifah*) may not be eaten, for its blood cannot be properly removed. Second, the blood of sacrificed animals must be either collected for purification rites or drained beside the altar. Third, the blood of an animal that is slaughtered for eating must be returned to God. Killing an animal is taking a life and may be done only in a way that nods to the severity of the act by insisting that it conform to divine law. Leviticus (17:6) has the blood dashed on the altar or, in the case of an animal killed in the hunt, poured onto the ground (17:13). Deuteronomy (12:16) would have the blood of all animals killed for food poured onto the ground" (*Etz Hayim*, p. 1461). The process of kosher slaughter, as well as soaking and salting meats (discussed below), are designed to remove as much of the animal's blood as possible.

One other place we still watch carefully for blood is in the yolks of eggs. Even though there is an ongoing halakhic debate over whether such blood spots must be avoided, it is a widespread tradition to break eggs individually into a cup or bowl to inspect for blood. If there is a blood spot visible, the egg is to be discarded and the cup or bowl rinsed with water before reuse. However, the so-called "rule of the majority" that pertains in matters of doubt concerning non-liquids applies to eggs: since the majority of eggs do not have blood spots, any specific egg is more likely than not to be acceptable in that regard. Therefore, even strictly observant Jews may and do eat hard-boiled eggs that have not been inspected in this careful way on an egg-by-egg basis.

Kosher Slaughter

In order to ensure that as much blood as possible is drained from the animal, a very specific manner of slaughter, known as *sh'ḥitah,* was instituted. The method was established to promote both the greatest possible loss of blood while reducing the level of pain the animal experiences to an absolute minimum. Mammals and fowl must be slaughtered according to the laws of kosher *sh'ḥitah,* but not fish (*SA* Yoreh Dei·ah 21:1–2).

To maximize the flow of blood in *sh'ḥitah,* the animal's neck must be slit with a very sharp knife. In the case of mammals, both the trachea and esophagus must be cut; for birds, at least one of the two must be cut (*SA* Yoreh Dei·ah 21:1–2). This method of slaughter causes very little pain, as the animal quickly loses consciousness from the swift loss of blood. Death then occurs after a few minutes, sometimes even sooner.

The professional slaughterer, called a *shoḥeit* or a *shoḥetet* (plural: *shoḥ'tim*), is required to be a religious and caring individual. Indeed, one of the fundamentals of the whole system of *kashrut* is the unyielding requirement that the people who have accepted the responsibility of taking the lives of animals themselves be acutely aware of the preciousness—and the sanctity—of God's gift of life. Although eating meat outside the sacrificial context is formally allowed by the Torah at Deuteronomy 12:15 (which was apparently intended to clear up the ambiguity of Leviticus 17), there is little question that the Torah posits the ideal menu to be the vegetarian one offered to Adam and Eve in the Garden of Eden. Therefore the slaughterer's role is, by definition, an ethically difficult one because the act of taking an animal's life so that people can eat meat is, at best, a compromise. With that in mind, the *halakhah* mandates that the slaughterer of God's creatures must be scrupulous in terms of devotion to even the slightest detail of the law. To take life, even animal life, requires that the slaughterer be wholly attuned to the serious nature of the activity and never callous or uncaring.

In light of the serious religious nature of this task, it is required that a blessing be recited before the animal is killed. The blessing itself is *barukh attah adonai, eloheinu, melekh ha-olam, asher kidd'shanu b'mitzvotav v'tziv-*

vanu al ha-sh'ḥitah ("Praised are You, Adonai, our God, Sovereign of the universe, who, sanctifying us with divine commandments, has commanded us regarding slaughter"). Praising God, the Source of life, at the moment of taking a life forces the slaughterer to work in a state of constant awareness that the serious task at hand, for all that it is sacred work, is also a concession to human weakness and to the voraciousness of human appetite.

The slaughterer's tools include a set of knives that must be sharpened to the highest possible level. Even so, the knife must be inspected anew for the slightest nick just before each use, lest such an imperfection in the blade cause a tear in the animal's flesh when its neck is slit. After the animal has been slaughtered, the knife must be inspected again to ensure that nothing has interfered with the actual cutting. All this is intended to spare the animal the realization that its life is ending until it loses consciousness just prior to actually dying.

Some countries have banned *sh'ḥitah,* ostensibly out of concern for the well-being of animals. Whatever the real motivation behind such legislation, however, the *halakhah* itself has the means to deal with issues of animal cruelty as they arise. For example, large industrial abattoirs need a system to keep animals still and in place while the *shoḥ'tim* work. There are two methods in use to accomplish this. The more modern method is to have the animal restrained comfortably in a special pen with a device holding the animal's head in place while exposing the neck to the slaughterer's blade. The older method requires that the animal be shackled by a back leg, then hoisted up so that it is suspended upside down, and only then conveyed by machine to the *shoḥeit.* While this method does not seem technically to contravene the laws that govern *sh'ḥitah,* it is widely understood today that this method of restraining animals in the abattoir is actually quite cruel. In 2000, therefore, the Committee on Jewish Law and Standards forbade this practice as inconsonant with the highest values of halakhically mandated kindness to animals even at the very end of their lives. "Now that kosher, humane slaughter using upright pens is both possible and widespread," the CJLS paper declares, "we find shackling and hoisting to be a violation of Jewish laws forbidding cruelty to animals" (*CJLS Responsa 1991–2000,* pp. 93–97). The issue of shackling and hoisting is discussed from the vantage point of the laws prohibiting cruelty to animals later in this volume by Rabbi Edward M. Friedman.

Slaughtering animals for kosher consumption is a very precise, extremely technical procedure requiring expertise in many areas. As such, the slaughter of animals for consumption may be done only by trained *shoḥ'tim.*

Special *kashrut* issues relating to the way veal calves are raised for slaughter are discussed in a detailed responsum by Rabbi Pamela Barmash approved by the CJLS in 2007 and available to interested readers on the website of the Rabbinical Assembly.

Inspection

Animals other than fish that are not slaughtered according to the laws of *sh'ḥiteh* may not be eaten—whether the animal died on its own due to illness, was hunted, was slaughtered in a non-kosher facility, or died in some other manner. However, even if an animal is killed appropriately by a qualified slaughterer, it is still possible for its meat to be considered non-kosher if it is posthumously determined that the animal was ill or maimed internally in a significant way. Therefore, after an animal has been killed, its carcass must be carefully inspected for any number of internal defects, as well as for evidence of disease. The term *t'reifah,* often used as a synonym for "non-kosher," actually refers to animals that have the kind of physical defects that make their flesh unkosher regardless of the care with which they were slaughtered.

There are a number of different parts of mammals which must be inspected, but the focus of the inspection today is mostly on the lungs. There are some lung imperfections, such as certain kinds of adhesions or the presence of scar tissue, that are permitted in kosher meat. If, however, the inspected lung is found to be smooth to the touch, the animal's flesh is often described not simply as being kosher, but as being *glatt* kosher. (The word *glatt* is the Yiddish word for "smooth." In non-Yiddish-speaking venues and in Israel, the Hebrew word *ḥalak,* with the same meaning, is sometimes used.) The designation "*glatt* kosher" is properly applied only to meat from mammals and refers specifically to this quality of having unscarred lungs free of all abrasions. In the vernacular, however, *glatt* kosher has come to indicate a level of *kashrut* supervision above the basic requirements. Consumption of any kosher meat is acceptable, however, and there is no requirement to eat only *glatt* kosher except as an act of extreme piety. Businesses that prey on the naïve by suggesting that people who are serious about *kashrut* would only eat *glatt* kosher meat are, therefore, behaving unscrupulously.

Restricted Portions

Even in ancient days, not all the meat of animals offered up as sacrifices in the Temple could be eaten. Certain parts—for example, the fat around the kidneys—were set aside for burning, to be consumed neither by the person bringing the sacrifice nor by the priests officiating at the sacrifice. Today, there are still restrictions on eating certain portions of the animal. The sciatic nerve, for example, as well as certain veins and forbidden fats, must be removed from the meat and not consumed. The process is called *nikkur* (*treiberin* in Yiddish) and must be done only by those who have been trained to do so.

The Torah prohibits eating of the sciatic nerve, known in Hebrew as *gid ha-nasheh,* at Genesis 32:33, but does not forbid the consumption of the meat surrounding it. Therefore, in theory, once the prohibited fats, veins, and sciatic nerve itself have all been removed, the entire slaughtered animal may be eaten. Yet the proper removal of these parts is so difficult, time-consuming, and costly that it is rarely financially worthwhile to do so. As a result, it is rare for the hindquarters of a slaughtered animal, where the forbidden sinew is located, to be marketed as kosher meat. Instead, the rear sections of the animal are usually sold as non-kosher, even though they could be prepared for kosher consumption. It is not unheard of but merely very unusual for commercial butchers in North America to offer this service. Before purchasing such meat, however, thoughtful kosher consumers should assure themselves about both the skill of the butcher and the level of *kashrut* supervision in the establishment in question.

Soaking and Salting Meat

After an animal has been butchered by a kosher slaughterer according to the norms and strictures of the *halakhah,* the meat inspected, and the forbidden parts removed, the meat may still not be eaten until it undergoes a final procedure intended to remove as much blood as possible. To accomplish this, the meat is rinsed in cold water, then salted with coarse-cut salt (which should be called *kashering* salt or *koshering* salt, but has come to be known as kosher salt—a misleading term that suggests that there could be salt that is not kosher). As noted above, this procedure is known as *kashering* the meat. Butchered meat that has not been *kashered* must be washed down at least every seventy-two hours to ensure that any remaining blood does not dry into the meat. When meat is transported before being *kashered*, washing stops are made on the road. All meat must be *kashered* before it is ground or chopped up into hamburger, and it is deemed highly desirable that meats be *kashered* before being frozen. If meat is frozen before being *kashered*, soaking and salting should take place immediately upon defrosting (cf. Klein, p. 353). In such cases, because the meat is not yet considered kosher, it may not be defrosted in a microwave oven. Instead, it should be defrosted in a refrigerator on pans or plates reserved for that purpose.

Most meat producers *kasher* the meat at the slaughtering plant, thereby eliminating the subsequent concerns relating to the transporting and freezing of the meat. As a result, one would be hard pressed to find meat not fully *kashered* and ready for use in most kosher meat markets today. However, there are some butcher shops that do sell kosher-slaughtered meat that has not been soaked or salted. Therefore, unless it is clearly labeled, it is important to ask specifically if meat one is about to purchase in a kosher facility has been *kashered*. To *kasher* meat one needs the following items: a dedicated tub (or other vessel) large enough to place the meat fully inside it, a dedicated surface on which to salt the meat (usually a board with a grooved surface which allows the blood to flow away from the meat), and a sufficient quantity of so-called "kosher" salt.

The meat is soaked in cold water for thirty minutes, then rinsed fully with cold water. The salt is then spread liberally over the entire surface of the meat. For poultry, the salt must fully cover both the inside cavity and the outside of the bird. The salt is left on the meat for an hour, and then the meat is thoroughly rinsed in cold water three times to remove all the salt. (Coarse salt is specifically used because it is easy to remove by rinsing the meat. If done properly, the meat should not end up with a salty taste and the procedure should not impact individuals on low-sodium diets.)

Liver presents a special issue for *kashrut* observers because the soaking and salting procedure is not deemed sufficient to remove the blood. One may, however, *kasher* liver by broiling it over a direct flame or on the broiler in an electric or gas oven. However, the grids or broiling pans must have holes large enough to allow the blood to drip out freely (*Arukh Ha-shulḥan,* Yoreh Dei·ah 73:19, cf. Klein, p. 354). Those who do not wish to rely on the rinsing procedure to remove all the salt may *kasher* other whole pieces of meat by broiling them as well. (It is customary to wash the meat in cold water and to salt it with kosher salt before broiling, but that is not required.) After the meat has been broiled, it should be rinsed to remove any blood globules still clinging to the surface. The utensils used for cooking such meat should be used only for that purpose, however.

Buying kosher meat is easier today than ever before. (Even in communities where fresh kosher meat is not available, frozen kosher meat can generally be procured without difficulty. And, in places where not even frozen meat is available, the possibility of ordering kosher meat by telephone or over the Internet certainly exists.) With the exception of raw liver, commercially frozen meat is almost invariably *kashered* before being frozen and therefore needs no further treatment before use. Nevertheless, it is always best to check each package of meat to be sure that the meat has been appropriately soaked and salted. When buying frozen meat, it is especially important to look for evidence that the meat was *kashered* before being frozen and packaged.

Clearly one must exercise great care when choosing a kosher butcher. In addition to the natural integrity of an honest businessperson, a kosher butcher bears great responsibility toward the public and, as such, must display the finest moral qualities. When looking for a butcher, one should be able to see evidence of *kashrut* certification clearly displayed, usually in the form of a letter. (Documents solely in Hebrew are rarely displayed in butcher shops outside of Israel. Consumers not fluent in Hebrew should be wary of signs they cannot read and not just assume that it "must" be the store's certification document.) One should certainly expect that a kosher butcher will be closed on Shabbat and major Jewish holidays. All commercially prepared prepackaged meat should have proof of being kosher, and of having been duly soaked and salted, inside the plastic in which the meat is wrapped.

Meat and Dairy

Three times, at Exodus 23:19, Exodus 34:26, and Deuteronomy 14:21, Scripture ordains that one may not eat the flesh of a kid that has been cooked in its own mother's milk. The oral tradition connected with these verses vastly expands the concept to include three major areas of prohibition: dairy and meat products may be neither eaten nor cooked together, nor may one derive even ancillary benefit from such a forbidden mixture (*MT* Hilkhot Ma·akhalot Asurot 9:1). Although there is no specific source in the Bible or the Talmud that clearly states the reason for this supremely stringent policy of separation, many ideas have been suggested throughout the ages.

Maimonides, for example, writing in the *Guide for the Perplexed* (III 98), took a historical approach, writing that he imagined these laws to be a kind of reaction to the pagan custom of boiling a kid in its mother's milk, which practice he imagined tied to pagan fertility rites. More recently, however, Professor Edward L. Greenstein of Bar-Ilan University has taken a more anthropological approach, writing that the prohibition has symbolic meaning: "Milk, which is meant to sustain life, may not be turned into a means of preparing an animal for eating. A clear distinction must be made between life, which is godly, and death. The post-biblical Jewish tradition underscores the distinction by broadening it: not only milk, but all dairy products and the utensils used for serving them must be kept apart from meat products and utensils" (*Etz Hayim*, p. 1461). Whatever its rationale, however, the rabbis understood the law to apply to situations far beyond the literal meaning of the biblical verses.

The flesh of mammals and birds are both considered meat. Furthermore, even foods made with meat additives or meat by-products are considered meat in this context, even if there are no actual pieces of meat present. Although, strictly speaking, clear consommés are in a different halakhic category than real meat, it is more or less universally the custom to consider clear soups made with meat bases to be meat with respect to these laws (see the gloss of the Rema to *SA* Yoreh Dei·ah 89:3). The flesh of fish, however, even "meaty fish," is not considered meat. Among many Jews of Ashkenazic descent, the Yiddish terms *fleishig* or *fleishidik* denote foods made of or with meat.

Foods made with milk or milk products are considered dairy. Milk, cream, cheeses, and butter are easily identifiable as being dairy. Among Jews of Ashkenazic descent, the Yiddish terms *milchig, milchidik,* or *milichdik* denote dairy foods.

Of course, there are also many edible items or ingredients used in commercial food products that have their beginning in either meat or dairy foods, but which might not be obviously meat or dairy by the time they are brought to market. In matters of doubt, a competent rabbi should be asked to determine the *kashrut* status of food additives of various sorts.

The *halakhah* specifically forbids eating meat and milk products together. But what exactly does this mean? The basic prohibition has to do with putting both substances in the mouth at the same time and ingesting them simultaneously, but because meat leaves a residual taste in the mouth—and also as an extra step to ensure the separation of meat and dairy—the rabbis imposed a waiting period after eating meat before eating dairy. How long exactly must one wait? Customs vary and there is no one specific answer, but the most common customs are to wait between one hour and six hours (Klein, p. 360). The norm for most Conservative Jews is to wait three hours after eating meat before eating any dairy foods, this being a typical amount of time between meals in our society.

It is also necessary to wait an equal length of time after eating hard cheeses before eating meat products. (Hard cheeses are cheeses aged at least six months that cannot be sliced without falling apart or crumbling; parmesan is the best known of such cheeses.) No such delay is required after eating other dairy products, such as cottage cheese, butter, ice cream, or soft cheeses, however (gloss of the Rema to *SA* Yoreh Dei·ah 89:2). One should, however, wash out one's mouth after eating dairy foods before ingesting meat or meat products. And though there is no technical reason forbidding it, it is customary not to serve dairy products as hors d'oeuvres before a meat meal.

Pareve Foods

Some foods, neither meat nor dairy in origin, are known as *pareve* (popularly pronounced PAR-veh or PAH-rev, a term clearly taken from the Yiddish but of uncertain etymological origin). Vegetables and fruits in their natural state, for example, are *pareve.* Eggs are *pareve.* Fish is *pareve.* Many other food products are *pareve,* but there are also many kinds of margarine and milk substitutes which blur the lines between what appears to be dairy and what can and cannot be eaten with meat. It is important to remember that government standards for what may be called "non-dairy" differ from country to country and almost always fail to conform precisely to the rabbinic definition of *pareve* foodstuffs. Therefore, many products, such as certain coffee whiteners or imitation cheeses, may be labeled "non-dairy" under U.S. law because they may be innocuous for the lactose intolerant, but are still considered dairy foods within the system of *kashrut* because an ingredient is, strictly speaking, a dairy product. Similarly, there are many meat-substitute products available today, but not all of these are *pareve* either—and some artificial meat may actually be considered dairy from the vantage point of *kashrut.* Nor does a label referring to a product as "vegetarian" constitute reliable assurance that the product is *pareve.*

The kosher consumer who reads the list of ingredients on a product needs to know that some common ingredients such as whey, sodium caseinate, lactose, and casein are considered dairy. On the other hand, there are some additives with dairy-sounding names that are considered *pareve,* including cream of tartar, lactic acid, and oleic acid. Other ingredients may not be kosher at all, but few consumers are well enough versed in food science to make sense of every term on the product label. To make life easier, there are *kashrut* supervision agencies throughout the world whose job is to endorse food products as kosher.

Kosher Supervision

Generally speaking, one should only consume processed foods prepared under the supervision of a rabbi or an accepted *kashrut* supervision agency. Special symbols (called *hekhsheirim;* singular: *hekhsheir,* usually pronounced by English-speakers as *hekhsher* with the accent on the first syllable) unique to each agency appear on the labels of food products. There are hundreds of such markings, some national, some local, some trusted by nearly all kosher consumers and others not. Consumers encountering unfamiliar *hekhsheir* symbols should check with a rabbi for advice as to the reliability of the symbol in question. Many of these symbols and the names and addresses of the agencies and institutions that use them are listed conveniently on the website maintained by Arlene J. Mathes-Scharf at www.kashrut.com/agencies.

Some products are marked with just the letter K by itself. Unlike the *hekhsheir* marks of supervising agencies, which are copyrighted and so may be used only with permission, the letter K (which cannot be copyrighted) generally indicates only the manufacturer's own assertion of the *kashrut* of the product. Sometimes, however, the K is used on a product that actually has been produced under rabbinic supervision, but which is sold without the *hekhsheir* because of a corporate policy. Manufacturers will usually respond with the name of their supervising rabbi or organization if asked, but consumers should check with a rabbi for advice about the use of products marked with only a K. The question of the use of the letter K as a *kashrut* symbol is discussed by Rabbi Kassel Abelson in a responsum approved by the CJLS in 1993 and published in *CJLS Responsa 1991–2000,* pp. 91–92.

There are a number of good reasons why kosher foods require formal rabbinic supervision during production. These include many foods that might not, at first glance, seem to need it. One reason has to do with the equipment in which the product was prepared. Often, the same cauldrons, pots, and baking equipment are used for producing something non-kosher (such as pork and beans) and then used for another product that might appear to be kosher (such as vegetarian beans). When the product is marked with a *hekhsheir,* however, the consumer can be certain that the ingredients and the equipment have been inspected and that the product is fully certifiable as kosher. Merely perusing a list of ingredients can never provide the same level of certainty.

A second reason for needing a *hekhsheir* has to do with governmental food and drug labeling laws. The laws and standards of government entities are based on civil laws guided by many different concerns, but not by Jewish law. A product reasonably considered non-dairy by the U.S. Food and Drug Administration, as noted, may in fact be considered dairy by the standards of normative *kashrut* observance. A reference to "natural flavor" may sound innocuous, but the product may still be made from animal sources. The willingness to go beyond the information on the label is a key part of keeping kosher.

In addition to their standard *hekhsheir* symbol, many *kashrut* supervision agencies affix the letter D or the word "Dairy" to make explicit the non-*pareve* status of the product. The letter P usually designates "Passover"; agencies typically add "*pareve*" after their *hekhsheir* when appropriate. Occasionally "Meat" or "Fish" will appear after the *hekhsheir* as well. In the latter case, as on products such as Worcestershire sauce, this is because there has been a custom not to eat fish with meat, as noted, even though fish is considered *pareve*. However, since we do not enforce this custom, based as it is on the supposition that there was some physical danger inherent in eating fish and meat together, there is no reason not to use a substance that contains fish products, like Worcestershire sauce, together with meat.

Some products marked as *pareve* might carry an additional designation such as "DE" or (less commonly) "ME." This indicates that the product itself is *pareve*, but was made on either dairy or meat equipment that had been cleaned, but not restored to a pristine (non-meat, non-dairy) state through halakhic procedures. Products with these designations are considered *pareve* and may be served after any meal on either pareve plates or on dishes appropriate for the meal being served. There is a caveat regarding DE products, however: although they may be served at a meat meal, they should not be served at the same time as meat itself (*SA* Yoreh Dei·ah 95:2). Similarly, ME products should not be served at the same time as dairy products. For example, chocolate chip cookies marked as DE may be served after a meat meal, but not together with the meat itself. To understand the rationale behind this concept, it is necessary to understand the distinction the *halakhah* draws between products considered able to impart flavor directly from the flavor's source (called *notein ta·am*) and those in which the flavor imparted is deemed to come from a flavored item, not from the original source of the flavor (*notein ta·am bar notein ta·am*). Foods cooked in a pot, for example, are deemed to leave a taste of some sort in the pot, and the *halakhah* holds that this taste can be passed along to the next item cooked in the pot. A third generation of taste no longer needs to be taken into account, however. Products marked DE can therefore be considered *pareve* because the level of dairy absorbable by the final product, if any, is in the category of *notein ta·am bar notein ta·am*.

Natural unprocessed foods, such as fruits and vegetables, may be purchased without any formal *kashrut* designation. They should, however, be thoroughly washed before use. Items such as sugar and flour also do not require a *hekhsheir*. A good rule of thumb is this: if a food product has been through cooking or extensive processing, it should not be used unless it has a *hekhsheir*. As always, questions about which products require a *hekhsheir* or that can be used without a *hekhsheir* should be addressed to a rabbi. Suffice it to say, the changes in food manufacturing processes and in labeling laws have brought about two major results: a growing number of *kashrut* supervising agencies and an inability to rely simply on a casual perusal of a product's label. Fortunately, the amount and variety of foods produced under rabbinic supervision continue to grow.

Food Additives

The Conservative and Orthodox movements also differ with regard to the *kashrut* of certain food additives. Because of the chemical changes that take place during processing, the CJLS has determined that many additives are so totally reconstituted that they may be considered a totally new food (*davar ḥadash*) and that their origins are therefore no longer of concern (*CJLS Responsa 1980–1990,* pp. 286–289). Among the chemical additives considered kosher and *pareve* by the Rabbinical Assembly are: dextrose, mono- and diglycerides, lactate, lactic acid, lecithin, pepsin, polysorbate 80, propylene glycol, sodium stearoyl-2-lactylate, and sorbitol. Should one find an additive of unknown origin in a product without a *hekhsheir,* it is best to consult a rabbi for advice.

One specific food impacted by the kashrut of additives is cheese, specifically focusing on rennet, an additive which helps the cheese to curdle. The Committee on Jewish Law and Standards of the Rabbinical Assembly has determined that commercially made cheeses, unless they are mixed with non-kosher ingredients, can be considered kosher even without a *hekhsheir* because the rennet or microbial rennin are a totally new food, as noted above (Klein, p. 306). This is one area of difference between the Conservative and Orthodox movements.

Yet another difference between many Conservative and Orthodox rabbis in the area of *kashrut* involves gelatin. Gelatin is made from dried hide, bones, horns, and hoofs, which are not edible in an unprocessed state. Because the process that reduces them to gelatin essentially creates a new entity, many Conservative rabbis permit the use of gelatin, even without a specific *hekhsheir,* in food products (Isaac Klein, "The Kashrut of Gelatin," in *Responsa and Halakhic Studies,* pp. 71–88).

Wines and Liquors

There are many issues involved in decisions about what kind of wines to use in a kosher home. Through the generations, use of wine that was not kosher-certified (called *s'tam yeinam,* "plain wines") was banned largely to reduce the possibility of extended social intercourse between Jews and non-Jews. Various responsa of the Rabbinical Assembly have allowed the use of non-certified wines, but recommended the exclusive use of kosher-certified wines for ritual purposes (*CJLS Responsa 1980–1990,* pp. 295–318). This is another area of difference between the Conservative and Orthodox movements. The preference, however, remains for use of kosher-certified wines and wines from Israel when possible.

Part of the process of manufacturing wine is "fining," or clarifying, the wine. This particular aspect of wine making can also be problematic in terms of the laws of *kashrut*. The CJLS, however, has concluded that wine fined with unkosher or dairy substances is not unkosher or dairy (*CJLS Responsa 1980–1990*, pp. 203–226).

Some beers and alcoholic beverages are made under *kashrut* supervision, but many are not. Because many liqueurs are based on wine or brandy or might have a small amount of wine or brandy added to them, some products that are acceptable to consumers who freely drink *s'tam yeinam* may not have a *hekhsheir* for that reason. Beer and grain-based liquors do not require formal *kashrut* supervision during the manufacturing process, nor do fruit-based liquors. Among the authorities who disallow *s'tam yeinam,* some also prohibit alcohol that has been aged in wine casks, including some kinds of Scotch or Irish whiskey. Bourbon, which must be aged in new casks, is not impacted by that issue. Many of these issues are discussed elsewhere in this volume by Rabbi Jeremy Kalmanofsky in his chapter on interfaith relations.

Food Cooked by Non-Jews

Some authorities maintain that staple foods, such as bread, must be cooked or baked solely by Jews, and that this rule applies without respect to the question of the *kashrut* of the ingredients involved. The resulting ban on foods cooked by non-Jews was a way to reduce social contact between the communities. Today, most Conservative rabbis feel it is counterproductive to create extra-halakhic rules merely to minimize intercourse between Jews and non-Jews and do not, therefore, require that all foods deemed kosher be cooked by Jews. In the world of *kashrut* symbols and abbreviations, the words *pat yisra·el* (sometimes pronounced *pas yisroel*) are generally used when a Jew has been directly involved in preparing the food (even in a minimal way, such as simply lighting the oven). This issue too is discussed by Rabbi Jeremy Kalmanofsky in his chapter on interfaith relations.

When milk has been under rabbinic supervision from "cow to carton," it is called *ḥalav yisra·el.* The concern about drinking milk other than *ḥalav yisra·el* is based on the fear that a non-Jew might add forbidden milk (i.e., the milk of non-kosher animals) to kosher milk, but the classical sources (e.g., *SA* Yoreh Dei·ah 115:1) already lay the groundwork for setting this worry aside if the Jewish consumer can be certain that such adulteration of the merchandise simply cannot happen. Given the mechanized, modern dairy farms of today and USDA supervision, Conservative rabbis do not require the purchase solely of *ḥalav yisra·el* by their congregants or synagogues.

The Kosher Kitchen

To maintain the separation of meat and dairy during cooking, the kosher kitchen must have at least two sets of utensils, one for meat and another for dairy foods. This requirement includes dishes, flatware, pots, pans, and all other utensils used in the preparation, serving, or eating of food. Many homes will have at least some additional utensils for preparing *pareve* foods, especially baked goods. Using only *pareve* utensils for preparation and storage makes it easier to assure the continued neutral nature of the *pareve* foods.

The requirement to have two sets of utensils has to do with the materials from which the items are made. Although many of the materials from which these utensils are made will seem impermeable to most observers, the rabbis of ancient times felt sure that minuscule amounts of food could become absorbed into dishes or utensils made of even marginally porous materials. As a result, it became part of standard *kashrut* observance to maintain two separate sets of dishes, utensils, and pots and pans for cooking and serving.

To help keep things organized, it is imperative to choose patterns for flatware, dishes, and cookware different enough from one another to be easily distinguished. While correcting mistakes is almost always possible, choosing patterns that do not look alike helps avoid confusion. It is best to choose pots and pans made by different manufacturers for meat and dairy use, thereby dramatically increasing the visible difference between the sets.

In order to maintain the proper level of separation, utensils should also be stored separately. Having separate and distinct cabinets and drawers is the best way to ensure that items are not used for the wrong food. In the case of items that by their nature will be hard to distinguish from one another, such as cookie sheets or cutting boards, it is best to mark items clearly as being either dairy, meat, or *pareve*. Marking with paint, etching, or using colored adhesive tags are all commonly accepted ways of marking utensils.

There is no need to have two sets of drinking glasses, however. Because of its nature, glass is not deemed capable of absorbing even minuscule amounts of food and so cannot become either meat or dairy (*SA* Oraḥ Ḥayyim 451:26). Therefore, one may, technically speaking, use a single set of glass plates in a kosher home. The predominant custom, however, is to have two sets of dishes, even if glass, in order to maintain the look and feel of a kosher home and reduce confusion involving the use of other utensils.

The CJLS has ruled that Corelle® is considered to be glass (*CJLS Responsa 1980–1990*, pp. 250–254). However, glass used for baking (including

Corningware® and Pyrex®) or for stovetop cooking (such as Visions®) is not to be used for both dairy and meat foodstuffs.

Plastic containers or utensils should be designated for meat, dairy, or *pareve* use and may not be used interchangeably. Soft or non-dishwasher safe plastics (such as Tupperware®) or disposable multi-use plasticware (such as GladWare® or Ziploc® storage items) should be marked upon use to ensure that they are reused with only the same type of food as originally stored in them.

There is no requirement for a kosher home to have separate stoves, ovens, refrigerators, freezers, or dishwashers. However, care must be taken to prevent the mixing of meat and dairy when using appliances.

For example, if cooking meat, dairy, or *pareve* items at the same time on a stove, one must take care that food does not splash from one pot to another. The simplest advice is to cook only one kind of food at a time. Similarly, only one kind of food should be cooked in an oven at any given time. Before switching from one kind of food to another, any spills should be wiped out of the oven. If it is absolutely necessary, one may bake meat and dairy foods at the same time, as long as both pans are tightly covered. A self-cleaning oven may be *kashered* by running a complete cleaning cycle. The same rules that apply to regular ovens should be observed when cooking in microwave ovens. (A microwave oven can be *kashered* by microwaving a cup of water on high, as discussed in detail below.) With regard to refrigerators and freezers, as long as food is wrapped carefully and marked clearly, meat, dairy, and *pareve* foods may be stored on the same shelves.

Dishwashers present a special dilemma. It would be simplest to have two, but this will rarely be feasible in most homes. In such cases, only meat or dairy dishes should be washed at a time. In order to use a dishwasher for meat and dairy sequentially, it is recommended to run an empty cycle with detergent between full cycles. The same dish racks may then be used for meat and dairy.

Sinks should be treated similarly. Only one kind of dish should be washed at a single time. All surfaces must be cleaned thoroughly between food types. The use of separate sink racks is highly recommended.

Freshly washed dish towels may be used with any type of dish. Rather than constantly changing towels after a single use, however, many people have different color towels for meat and dairy use. The same is true of potholders.

A special law governs knives used to cut foods called *davar ḥarif*—sharp-tasting foods such as onions or garlic. These special rules apply because an item considered *davar ḥarif* is deemed capable of absorbing other foodstuffs, even in minuscule quantities (cf. *SA* Yoreh Dei·ah 96:1–2 and Klein, p. 363). Therefore, it is a good idea to use *pareve* knives to cut onions or to chop garlic, because using a meat or dairy knife would, depending on which knife was used, give the cut onion itself the status of a meat or dairy foodstuff. Questions about the status of other foodstuffs with respect to its status as a *davar ḥarif* should be addressed to a rabbi.

Kashering a Kitchen

It is a daunting task to transform a non-kosher kitchen into a kosher one. Yet, while the process is labor intensive, each individual step is actually rather straightforward. The goal is simply to remove all non-kosher food and food residue. The information given below covers both the process of making a kitchen kosher and also how to proceed when mistakes occur.

Dishes, utensils, pots, pans, and other items must be cleaned thoroughly and then left unused for at least twenty-four hours before *kashering*.

One well-known custom is to bury flatware which needs to be *kashered* in the ground for a period of at least twenty-four hours. This practice has its source in the requirement for thorough cleansing before *kashering*. (As campers know, the gritty nature of dirt makes for a useful scouring agent.) But although putting flatware into the ground or into a flowerpot is an acceptable method of preparing the utensil for being made kosher, it is *not* itself a valid method of *kashering*. (See below for more about the *kashering* of flatware.)

There is a custom in some communities of taking new pots, pans, dishes and other utensils to be immersed in a *mikveh,* ritual bath, before use. The Committee on Jewish Law and Standards has ruled that this is not necessary. Should one choose to do such immersion, a blessing is not required. (The responsum, written by Rabbis Mayer Rabinowitz and Avram Reisner and relating to *SA* Yoreh Dei·ah 120:4, is available on the Rabbinical Assembly website.)

Dishes

Corelle® and other glass dishes can be *kashered* by running them through a full cycle in a dishwasher and then heat-drying them. Earthenware, stoneware, and non-translucent china cannot be *kashered*. Hard, heat-resistant plastic, such as melamine, may be *kashered* after thorough cleansing by boiling. This may be accomplished either by dipping the dish in boiling water or by pouring boiling water on the dish.

Pots and Pans

Pots used for stovetop cooking may be *kashered* by being thoroughly scrubbed, then degreased and cleaned. If the utensil has a removable handle, it must be removed, cleaned, and *kashered* separately. The pot should then be immersed completely in boiling water. Pots too large to be immersed may be filled to the top with water, which is then brought to a boil. A heated stone or a heated piece of metal is then dropped into the pot so that the boiling water flows over the edge of the pot.

Flatware

One-piece flatware may be *kashered* by being thoroughly scrubbed, degreased, and cleaned, then completely immersed in boiling water. (A mesh net, such as a lingerie bag, may be used for immersing the utensils.) Two-piece flatware with non-porous handles (i.e., handles made of metal or plastic) may be *kashered* by cleaning all crevices with a wire brush, and then by proceeding according to the rules above. For knives with wooden handles the process is more complex. If the handles can be detached, however, they should be removed, cleaned, and *kashered* by boiling. If the handle cannot be detached but is joined tightly enough that no particles can penetrate, the knife may be *kashered* (*SA* Oraḥ Ḥayyim 451:3, cf. comment no. 5 of the *Turei Zahav* commentary of Rabbi David Halevi Segal [c. 1586–1667]).

Glassware

Glassware may be *kashered* by being cleaned thoroughly (*SA* Oraḥ Ḥayyim 451:26). Special care must be taken, however, to brush-clean the inside of any designs engraved in the glass. The glassware must then be run through the dishwasher on the regular cycle and then heat-dried. An alternative to this method is to soak the glassware in a tub for seventy-two hours, changing the water after twenty-four and forty-eight hours.

Cabinets, Drawers, and Storage Areas

A kosher home must have appropriate storage spaces. To prepare the cupboards and drawers of a non-kosher kitchen for use, all non-kosher foods must be removed and all opened packages of food must be taken away. Cabinets may be wiped clean with normal cleaning solutions. Shelf paper and other kinds of liners must be replaced. To be practical and functional, the kosher kitchen should have enough cabinet space to store meat, dairy, and *pareve* dishes, cutlery, and utensils in separate areas.

Sinks, Countertops, and Tabletops

Sinks are a special challenge in a kosher home. Most sinks, unless they are made of metal, cannot be *kashered.* Therefore, rubber or plastic sink liners or basins should always be used when dishes are washed or placed in the sink. An in-sink garbage disposal unit will often make it practical to consider the sink non-kosher space, thus allowing the use of the disposal unit for meat and dairy food alike. If a sink is metal, however, it may be *kashered* by being cleaned thoroughly with appropriate cleansers, including the lip around the edge of the sink where food tends to accumulate and in the seam areas around the drain. Boiling water is then poured over all surfaces and directly into the garbage disposal and drain.

Formica (and similar kinds of countertops) may be *kashered* by being scoured with appropriate cleansers, paying careful attention to seams. The counter must then be left unused for at least twenty-four hours, whereupon boiling water must be poured over the surfaces. Raw wood or butcher block surfaces must be sanded to be made usable in a kosher kitchen. Then, after twenty-four hours have passed, boiling water must be poured over the surface. Tabletops made of fine-finish woods must be cleaned with appropriate wood cleaners and then washed.

It is important to note, however, that the water poured onto the sink or countertop must come directly from the kettle or pot in which the water was boiled. This procedure is called *irui mi-k'li rishon,* "pouring [hot water] from the 'first' vessel," the vessel in which the water was first boiled.

Appliances

REFRIGERATORS AND FREEZERS

To ready a refrigerator for use in a kosher kitchen, it should be emptied, then washed inside thoroughly with soapy water and rinsed. Wire or glass shelves should be cleaned and rinsed.

Freezers should be defrosted fully and washed thoroughly. Special care must be taken to clean the ice storage bins in automatic ice makers and to clean out the crumbs from seams and corners.

DISHWASHERS

Dishwashers may be *kashered* by cleaning them as thoroughly as possible, taking special care to scour the inside area around the drain and the filters. One should then run the machine through a full cycle with detergent, leaving the racks in place but empty of dishes. After twenty-four hours of not being used, the dishwasher should then again be run (again with nothing but the racks inside), and then dried at the highest heat available.

OVENS AND STOVES

To ready a self-cleaning oven for use in a kosher home, the inside must first be wiped free of all visible food particles and drippings. The self-cleaning cycle is then run with the racks still in the oven. If one follows the manufacturer's recommendation that racks not be in the oven during the cleaning cycle, one must purchase new racks or use a blowtorch as described below.

To ready a non-self-cleaning oven for use, the inside must first be wiped free of all visible food particles and drippings. An oven cleaner may then be used to clean the oven and the racks. After being cleaned, the oven must be heated to the highest temperature possible and then left on for thirty minutes. The broiler must be run at full heat with the door closed and the racks in place minimally for fifteen minutes. Alternately, one may use a blowtorch to heat all surfaces of the oven and racks until they are hot enough to ignite a piece of tissue on contact. Care must be taken, however, not to singe the gaskets around the door.

To prepare a gas stovetop for use in a kosher home, the underburner bowls must first be scoured thoroughly or replaced. The area under the cooktop must then be cleaned thoroughly. Finally, each burner must be left burning on its highest setting until the pot grids glow red.

To *kasher* an electric stove with heating coils, the underburner bowls and drip pans must first be thoroughly scoured or replaced. The area under the cooktop must then be cleaned thoroughly, and each burner must be scoured and then turned on at its highest setting for at least ten minutes.

To *kasher* an electric stove with a glass top, the top must first be cleaned according to the manufacturer's directions. Each burner must then be left on its highest setting until the coils are red-hot. Boiling water must then be poured over the surface area.

To *kasher* a microwave oven, the interior must first be cleaned thoroughly with standard cleaners. After that, an eight-ounce cup of water must be placed in the oven, which is then run on high until the entire cavity fills with steam. The exact time for this will vary from oven to oven because of differences of size and power, but the usual amount of time needed is roughly three minutes after the water has first come to a boil.

TOASTERS AND TOASTER OVENS

It is possible to *kasher* a toaster, but it will usually make more sense simply to buy a new one. To *kasher* a toaster, it must first be fully cleaned of all crumbs and drippings, including on the crumb tray, then run empty for two cycles at its darkest toast setting. A toaster oven with a broiler, including its racks and crumb tray, may be *kashered* by being fully cleaned of all crumbs and drippings and scoured with steel wool. The toaster oven should then be run at the broil setting for ten minutes with its rack in place.

A toaster oven without a broiler may be *kashered* by being cleaned fully of all crumbs and drippings, including those in the crumb tray, its sides, and its door or doors. The racks must then be cleaned with steel wool, then two empty cycles run at the darkest toast setting followed by fifteen minutes at the highest baking heat with the rack or racks in place.

MIXERS, BLENDERS, FOOD PROCESSORS, AND JUICERS

As with toasters, it will often be more reasonable to replace the entire mixer. However, it is possible to *kasher* appliances like mixers and blenders, which is often undertaken precisely because so many mixer bowls and attachments are needed in a kosher home: one set each for *pareve* and dairy, and perhaps even a third set for meat. Multiple sets of accessories for the same brand or model of mixer must be marked clearly. The motor unit of a mixer may be *kashered* by thoroughly cleaning the body and stand thoroughly, as well as the seams and joints.

As far as bowls, beaters, and whisks go, the easiest alternative is always to purchase new ones. It is possible to *kasher* them, however. Glass mixing bowls need to be cleaned thoroughly, ideally in a dishwasher with a heated drying cycle. Metal bowls, including the seam beneath the lip, need to be cleaned thoroughly and then covered with boiling water, either by having the water poured over the bowl or by dipping the bowl in boiling water. The beaters and whips must be cleaned thoroughly, especially in the seams, then submerged in a pot of boiling water.

Rubber parts must be replaced. Blades and wholly heat-resistant, knick-free plastic parts may be *kashered* by being submerged in boiling water. Glass containers must be washed carefully, then run through a dishwasher.

COFFEE MAKERS, CAN OPENERS, SLOW COOKERS, AND KNIFE RACKS

Coffee makers may be *kashered* relatively simply by cleaning the body of the coffee maker thoroughly, then by submerging all washable parts in boiling water either by pouring the water over the parts or by immersing them in a pot of boiling water.

It is easiest to replace can openers. If one chooses not to do so, a can opener may be *kashered* by cleaning the cutting head thoroughly—an exceedingly difficult task—and then immersing it in boiling water. Considering the low price, it is best to have separate can openers for dairy, meat, and *pareve*.

Because they are so useful for Shabbat cooking, slow cookers are very popular in observant Jewish homes. One-piece units must be replaced. Two-part units, however, can be *kashered*. New inserts must be purchased. The heating unit itself must be cleaned fully with approved cleaners and may then be used, with different inserts, for different kinds of food. The inserts must be marked as to type.

Because they can generally not be opened, the kind of knife racks into which the knives are inserted cannot be *kashered*. A new one should be procured, and its slots marked for meat, dairy, or *pareve* knives, then used exclusively for that specific kind of knife. The kind of magnetized rack from which the knives are suspended may be *kashered* by being cleaned thoroughly, after which its slots must be marked for meat, dairy, or *pareve* knives.

BROILING PANS AND SKEWERS

Broiling pans and skewers that come into direct contact with fire during use may be *kashered* either by exposing them to the same heat source or by heating them with a blowtorch until the item glows red or until a tissue flames when touched to the surface.

Errors in the Kosher Kitchen

No matter how careful one might be, mistakes will happen. Most, fortunately, are easily corrected, and even those that cannot be dealt with simply can be corrected with a little more effort. We should note that these corrective actions are after-the-fact remedies, in Hebrew *b'di-avad* (often pronounced *b'di-eved*). One should take care to avoid such situations, but can rest assured that, when accidents do happen, the majority can be dealt with easily.

Of course, setting up the kitchen with storage areas clearly marked and working with only one kind of food at a time are the most effective ways to avoid mistakes. What follows is a description of some typical mistakes and their corrective actions. In other cases, the best course of action will be to contact a rabbi for advice.

If you have put clean dishes or utensils in the wrong cabinet or drawer, simply put them back in the right place.

In terms of foodstuffs being mixed together inadvertently, the law distinguishes between mixtures of like and like, and mixtures of like and unlike. A mixture of like substances, such as kosher and non-kosher beef, is called *min b'mino*. Identifying the single non-kosher piece of stew meat in of a package of kosher stew meat would be impossible. For such a mixture to be considered usable, therefore, the meat must be reasonably dry and the majority of the meat mixed must be kosher. A mixture of unlike substances, such as non-kosher meat that has fallen into a pot of vegetables, is called *min b'sheeino mino* and is significantly easier to deal with, as the offending item is far more easily removed and measured (*SA* Yoreh Dei·ah 98). The following rules presuppose these distinctions.

If dairy and meat foods were inadvertently mixed together, the laws are more complex. If meat and dairy foods that were cold and dry come into contact, both remain kosher and usable. If the products were cold, but moist to the touch, then the point of contact must be rinsed. After doing so, however, both remain kosher and usable. If bread comes in contact with a moist food, the bread may be used only with the same kind of food, be it meat or dairy (*SA* Yoreh Dei·ah 91).

If a piece of meat should fall into a pot of milk, things become still more complicated. If both the meat and the liquid in the pot are cold, then the meat must be immediately removed and rinsed, but both remain kosher and usable. If, however, both substances are hot, neither can be used and the pot itself must be *kashered* by boiling (as outlined above). If only one of the two substances is hot, the principle of *tata·a g'var*—according to which food that falls on or is placed on top of another foodstuff acquires the temperature status of the lower food—applies as follows. If the top one of the two was the hot substance (e.g., if a piece of hot meat were to fall into a bowl of cold milk), the meat must be removed, rinsed and its top layer pared off, whereupon it may be used. If the bottom of the two was hot (e.g., if cold meat were to fall into a bowl of warm milk), neither can be used and the pot must be *kashered* by boiling. However, if the volume of the milk was at least sixty times the volume of the meat, the procedure outlined above may be used even if the milk was hot and the meat cold (*SA* Yoreh Dei·ah 91).

If a drop of milk were to fall onto a piece of meat cooking in a pot, the rules are as follows. If the piece of meat was on the surface and the pot had *not* been stirred since the accident, then the meat is permitted if the volume of the piece of meat was sixty times greater than the volume of the milk which fell on it. If the meat was on the surface and the pot had been stirred since the accident, then the contents of the pot are kosher only if the volume of the contents of the pot is at least sixty times the volume of the piece of meat on which the milk fell. If the volume of the pot is less than sixty times the volume of the meat, the contents may not be used and the pot itself must be *kashered* by boiling. If the piece of meat on which the milk fell was partially or fully submerged, the rule of *bateil b'shishim* (i.e., the annulment of a forbidden or unwanted substance by a licit or desired substance sixty times its volume) applies in such a way that the volume of the entire contents of the pot is measured against the milk (*SA* Yoreh Dei·ah 92).

If one inadvertently uses a utensil for the wrong type of food, the following rules apply. Even if the contents of the pot are hot and the utensil itself had been used within the previous twenty-four hours, the food may still be used if the volume of the pot is sixty times the volume of the surface area of the immersed utensil. If the volume of the contents of the pot is less than sixty times the volume of the area of the utensil immersed, the contents may not be used and the utensil itself, if made of metal, must be *kashered* by boiling. If the utensil is made of wood, it cannot be *kashered* and may not be used. Utensils that have not been used for twenty-four hours or more may be *kashered* by boiling. If the utensil is made of heat-resistant plastic, extra care must be taken to scrub it perfectly clean before boiling.

If one inadvertently uses the wrong dishes or pot for cooking, the law is as follows. If the pot had been used within the previous twenty-four hours, then the food is prohibited and the pot itself must be *kashered*. If, however, the pot had not been used within the previous twenty-four hours, the food is permitted, but the pot still requires *kashering* (*SA* Yoreh Dei·ah 93:1).

If one inadvertently used a dairy knife to cut hot meat, then the law is as follows. If the knife had been used within twenty-four hours, it must be *kashered*. If the volume of the meat is at least sixty times the volume of the portion of the knife which touched the meat, then the meat may be used. If less than sixty times the volume, however, it is prohibited. If the knife had not been used within the previous twenty-four hours, the knife must still be *kashered*, but the meat may be used after paring off the layer of meat the knife touched (*SA* Yoreh Dei·ah 94:7).

The law considers pickling with vinegar-based marinades to be akin to cooking. Therefore, if one inadvertently soaks or pickles kosher and non-kosher foods together, the volume of the kosher food must be more than sixty times that of the prohibited food for the resultant mixture to be permitted for consumption once the non-kosher foodstuffs have been removed (*SA* Yoreh Dei·ah 105:1). If the volume is less than sixty times, then the entire mixture is not kosher and must be discarded. (The principle that the prolonged soaking of a food in liquid is considered akin to cooking is called *kavush ki-m'vushal.* In any event, care must be taken to marinate only meats that have been soaked and salted and to use meat utensils.)

There is one important caveat to all the rules mentioned above: one is not permitted to create a prohibited mixture on purpose, even if the proportion of non-kosher to kosher foods will be less, even far less, than the crucial 1:60 ratio. An accidental mixture can be corrected, but a deliberate manipulation of the 1:60 annulment rule to circumvent prohibitions cannot be corrected. Also, any portion or piece of food cooked and ready to serve (called *ḥatikhah ha-re'uyah l'hitkabbeid*) cannot be annulled by the 1:60 rule (*SA* Yoreh Dei·ah 101).

The concept of *n'tinat ta·am li-f'gam* (literally "imparting a bad taste") is relevant here. If a bad-tasting forbidden substance (something rancid, for example) falls into permitted food, the food remains permitted regardless of the ratio of the forbidden substance to the permitted (*SA* Yoreh Dei·ah 103:1).

Even if the food that fell is not bad-tasting by itself, but is so in combination with the food into which it has fallen, the combination also remains permitted (*SA* Yoreh Dei·ah 103:1). A utensil left unused for twenty-four hours is considered to impart a bad taste no matter what. The most practical application of the principle of imparting a bad taste is the accidental washing of dirty meat and dairy dishes together in a sink filled with soapy water. In this case, the dishes remain kosher after a thorough rinse.

Finally, the principle of *ta·am ke'ikkar* (meaning "the flavor is the same as the substance") must also be mentioned. If a piece of forbidden food falls onto permitted food or into a pot of permitted food, and still imparts a recognizable flavor even though subsequently removed, it is considered as if the forbidden food itself were still present (*BT* Ḥullin 108a, and cf. Rashi's comment *ad loc., s.v. amar abbayei ta·amo v'lo mamasho be'alma de'oraita*). Therefore, if a piece of highly seasoned sausage fell on cold pizza, the flavor imparted by it on the pizza would render the pizza non-kosher.

Feeding Pets in a Kosher Home

Since most pet foods are made with non-kosher meats, meat by-products, or flavorings, it is important to keep pet food away from kosher utensils and dishes. It is not, however, forbidden for Jewish individuals to feed their pets non-kosher food; the laws of *kashrut* specifically apply to human beings, not to the animals they own. For practical reasons, however, one should maintain a special set of utensils for opening, scooping, and serving pet foods. The situation on Passover is different. Concerned pet owners should consult with their rabbis about the use of pet foods on Passover, as many are made with ingredients that may not be permitted in Jewish homes on Passover regardless of whether they are ingested only by pets. The issues involved in feeding pets on Passover are discussed elsewhere in this volume by Rabbi Alan Lucas in his chapter on the festivals of the Jewish year.

Embracing a Kosher Lifestyle

As they move up the ladder of observance, some people choose to observe *kashrut* at home long before they are ready to adopt *kashrut* observance at all times. This is not a bad thing, because incremental growth often leads to long-term life changes. As *kashrut* becomes part of our lives, it feels less like a burden and more like something we wish to observe not just at home, but in all venues. It is not necessary to take an all-or-nothing approach. Indeed, there are incremental steps one can take toward *kashrut* that, even before deciding to eat only in strictly kosher establishments, can serve as meaningful steppingstones for the individual seeking to move toward a more fully observant life.

Small beginnings can be very meaningful. One could, for instance, begin by refraining from eating foods clearly forbidden by the Torah, such as shellfish or pork. The next step would be to avoid prohibited foods not clearly stipulated in the Torah, but forbidden by unambiguous Jewish tradition (like, for example, cheeseburgers). While those steps are small ones, they begin the process of thinking about the nature of the food being eaten, even in non-kosher restaurants, and that can only be a good thing in the development of Jewish religious consciousness.

Many people were brought up with, or have adopted, the practice of observing *kashrut* at home while eating non-kosher food elsewhere. Is such a choice totally consistent with observing *kashrut?* No, but consistency need not be the primary goal when first moving toward an increasingly kosher lifestyle. Striving to move forward is more important than attempting to be fully consistent at any one station on the journey. Adopting an observant Jewish lifestyle is indeed a journey, but it can also be conceptualized as a ladder: no matter what step an individual might be on, he or she should always strive to climb just a little bit higher.

Eating in Non-Kosher Restaurants

The question of eating in non-kosher restaurants is very complex and was first addressed directly in a CJLS responsum that dates back to the 1950s. Since that time, one of the hallmarks of Conservative Jewish practice has been the basic understanding that it is possible to eat in unsupervised restaurants responsibly.

There are, however, a number of issues related only tangentially to the question of the actual ingredients but that can nonetheless impact the *kashrut* of foods in a non-supervised restaurant. Plates and flatware, cooking utensils, and grills and griddles used for food preparation must be considered in terms of their putative effect on the *kashrut* of the food served. Is washing dishes in commercial machines considered the same as *kashering?* What about utensils, knives, and cutting surfaces? These are thorny, vexing questions even for experts to ponder, let alone for newcomers to *kashrut* observance.

To be completely compliant with the system of *kashrut,* the only way to be certain that one will never inadvertently eat non-kosher food when dining out is not to eat in non-kosher restaurants at all. However, this option will not always appeal to people still traveling up the ladder to the halakhic ideal. Unforeseen circumstances may also arise. What about traveling? What of long business meetings that include some food service? Is there an alternative between certified kosher food and no food at all? A number of accommodations have been developed over the years. None is perfect, but all are acceptable approaches for people who are trying to incorporate the principles of *kashrut* into their lives, but are not quite ready simply to abandon all food in all unsupervised venues.

A first choice can be to search out vegan or vegetarian restaurants. In these establishments, many of the problematic issues are solved almost *ipso facto.* When there are no meat products or meat by-products of any kind in the restaurant, one can feel relatively confident that the food is acceptable, even if the establishment is not kosher-certified or supervised.

The next best choice would be to eat only minimally processed foods when eating in unsupervised establishments. Breakfast, for instance, can be relatively simple. Many outlets serve some foods prepared under certification, such as pastry, bagels, cold cereal, and yogurts. These foods can be consumed with confidence, as can coffee, tea, juices, and other beverages. For other meals, the choices become a bit more limited, but eating only minimally processed cold foods is always a reasonable option. Salad bars can provide many possibilities, although it is always best to ask what ingredients pre-prepared salads (and salad dressings) actually contain, and also to pay special attention to mysterious items one cannot identify easily. One should always assume that ersatz meat products like bacon bits are at least partially made from meat products.

Less preferable than cold food is strictly vegetarian hot food. Many restaurants expect some clients to be vegans or vegetarians, and are eager to accommodate them and to make them feel welcome. An excellent source of information on which restaurant chains offer vegetarian food options is the Vegetarian Resource Group (located on-line at www.vrg.org), which seeks out vegetarian restaurants and vegetarian options in chain restaurants. This organization also helps make vegetarian customers aware of hidden areas of concern in restaurant food, and that information can be valuable to the kosher diner in a non-kosher restaurant.

Eating hot and cooked foods in restaurants is a complex decision for the kosher consumer. Grilled and fried foods, for example, are usually made with utensils and on cooking surfaces that are rarely fully cleaned before cooking. And although waffle irons are rarely used for anything but waffles, pancakes are more than likely made on the same griddles as various meat products. Similarly, boiled eggs present fewer issues to resolve than fried or scrambled eggs. Cooked foods must be truly vegetarian if even a minimal standard of *kashrut* is being maintained.

Most restaurants are happy to accommodate patrons who make special requests. Potatoes or fish can sometimes be baked wrapped in foil. Pasta can be served sprinkled with only olive oil and spices, thereby affording the kosher diner the opportunity to avoid sauces made with unknown ingredients. With advance notice, most event caterers can and will provide vegetarian or vegan meals for meetings without much difficulty.

When asking about the foods in a restaurant, it is important to know what questions need to be answered. It is, for example, essential to inquire what type of shortening was used for baking and treating pans. And the kosher diner will also have to establish clearly whether beef or chicken broth or stock has been added to soups or sauces, or whether such products were used as flavorings in foods such as pilafs or mashed potatoes. It is also commonplace for beef or chicken stock or fat to be added to cream soups, cheese soups, or tomato sauce. Other questions are more basic. Are separate pans used for different foods? Are products cooked together on the grill? Is a separate grill used for cooking fish, or is fish prepared on the same grill as meat? Are fish, chicken, and potatoes fried in separate fryers? If a server cannot answer these questions clearly or find out the answers in the kitchen, then the responsible kosher consumer has to assume that the foods in question are likely problematic from the perspective of *kashrut*.

Eating in Non-Kosher Homes

Obviously, in communities where there are many decent kosher restaurants, the question of how to observe the laws of *kashrut* outside the home is much less complex. But even in cities with large observant Jewish populations, there will still be vexing questions for *kashrut* observers to answer. What should be done if relatives who do not keep kosher invite their more observant relations to join them for meals at their homes? What should be the policy of the observant Jew who is invited over to dine at the home of non-Jewish friends or to attend a non-Jewish wedding or celebration? Does it make a difference if the friends in question actually are Jewish, but are indifferent to the laws of *kashrut*? And how should the newly observant individual relate to non-kosher parents or siblings? Does the *mitzvah* of showing honor to one's parents override the *mitzvah* of only eating kosher food? What if the non-kosher home in question belongs to one's adult children? Is it ever right to decline an invitation to be present in one's child's home? Each situation presents new, different, and complex issues to consider and should be discussed with a competent, sympathetic rabbi before any attempt is made conclusively to resolve it.

Many of the same issues that arise in non-kosher restaurants will apply as well when dining in non-kosher homes. The difference, however, is that most people who have invited guests to their home try to accommodate special needs when those needs are enunciated clearly and politely in advance. Depending on the occasion, it can be very easy to eat in non-kosher homes without compromising one's commitment to *kashrut*. If there are kosher takeout or frozen meals available, the kosher guest can always suggest that course as among the simplest ways to join together for a meal.

The kosher guest can, and should, also offer to help the host plan the menu. Dairy meals, especially cold ones, are rather easy to assemble. Bagels, lox, cheeses, and bakery sweets can easily be the core of an easy kosher-in-any-home meal. If the host wants to serve hot food, suggest fish made in foil pans and baked potatoes. For an informal meal, suggest microwaving kosher hot dogs wrapped in paper towels. Generally, the more open communication there is in advance, the smoother the whole experience will be. One should never arrive at a host's home with an unexpected list of dietary requirements!

If the non-kosher home belongs to one's parent(s), the question of *kashrut* observance will almost certainly be colored by personal issues. Offering to bring a portion of the meal will often go a long way to defusing tension by making the whole meal into more of a joint effort. In the end, the Jewish adult child must remember that the *mitzvah* of honoring one's parents, given pride of place in the Ten Commandments, applies to all children of living parents, not only to young boys and girls. Although the *halakhah* is entirely clear that one may not break the laws of the Torah merely because a parent wishes or orders one to do so, honoring one's parents is a *mitzvah* and accommodation must always be sought. In the end, it is important to be as accommodating as possible for the sake of *sh'lom bayit*—peace in the home—and, with kindness and a willing, generous spirit, such accommodation can almost always be found.

Israel

MARTIN S. COHEN

The special place of the Land of Israel in the rabbinic worldview hardly needs to be demonstrated. Not only did the classical rabbis believe that the Land of Israel was the holiest of all lands (as the Mishnah specifically notes at *M* Keilim 1:6), but they appear almost to have vied with each other to find ever more dramatic ways to make manifest their feelings. Rabbi Abba, for example, sought to demonstrate his deep love for the Land of Israel by kissing its cliffs (*BT* K'tubbot 112a). Rabbi Ḥiyya ben Gamda, not to be outdone, would roll around in the dust of Israel in order to embody the poet's declaration at Psalm 102:15 that the truly pious take pleasure not only in the stones of Israel, but also in her dust (*BT* K'tubbot 112b). Other rabbis sought to express their esteem for the Land by teaching openly about the wondrous effect it has on those who live or even visit there. Rabbi Eleazar, for example, taught that all who dwell in the Land of Israel are considered to live unsullied by sin (*BT* K'tubbot 111a). Recorded on the same page of the Talmud is Rabbi Yoḥanan's opinion that any who walk even just four cubits in the Land of Israel are guaranteed a portion in the World to Come. And Rabbi Zeira said that even the air of Israel has the miraculous ability to make wise the simple (*BT* Bava Batra 158b).

How are Jews, especially those living in the Diaspora, to relate in their theology, prayers, and rituals to this level of venerative behavior and rhetoric regarding the Land of Israel? Is it possible to yearn for the Land without actually living there? Is it appropriate to recite dirges lamenting the destruction of the Holy City, when that very city is now the capital of a vibrant Jewish state? Are the ancient pilgrimage requirements still in effect all these many centuries after the destruction of the Temple which was once the pilgrims' holy destination? And if they are indeed still in effect, do they apply differently to those who live in Israel and to those who live in the Diaspora? And what of the other laws that presuppose the existence of a Temple in Jerusalem—should any of them, or all of them, be allowed to fall into desuetude now that there is no Temple standing? And, perhaps most crucial of all for diaspora Jews to confront: what should be the precise impact of the modern State of Israel on the *halakhah* as it relates to the Land of Israel? That is, however, a question far more simply posed than answered with compelling cogency and consistency.

Over the centuries (and especially in the years since the State of Israel has come into existence), the *halakhah* has struggled to answer these and many related questions. This chapter considers the most important issues facing Jews both inside and outside of Israel with regard to the relationship between a people and its ancient homeland.

The Mitzvot of Aliyah and Yishuv Ha-aretz

First among the issues to be considered must be the question of *aliyah* itself. (*Aliyah,* literally "ascent," is the word Jews use to denote the act of immigration to the Land of Israel.) Should Jews see *aliyah* as a *mitzvah,* drawing them to live in Israel? Or is living in the Diaspora an equally valid option for Jews in the modern age?

At first blush, the sources sound unequivocal. "One should ever strive to live in the Land of Israel, even in a city in which most of the inhabitants are idolaters," an early talmudic source declares, "and one should prefer that over living outside the Land, even in a city mostly inhabited by Jews. For one who lives in the Land of Israel is like a person who has a God, while those who live outside the Land are like those who live without God" (*BT* K'tubbot 110b). Furthermore, for those who already live there, leaving the Land of Israel is characterized as the ultimate in self-destructive behavior: "Even when people have the merit of their ancestors supporting them," the Talmud notes, "this merit does not stand by them once they leave the Land" (*BT* Bava Batra

91a). And dozens of other sources suggest the same thing, that there is no greater error of spiritual judgment than choosing to dwell outside the Land of Israel and no greater misfortune than to have to leave the Land once one already has settled there.

But do these aggadic statements, as passionately put and as forcefully stated as they are, carry the force of law? That, it turns out, is an entirely different question.

Maimonides, for example, dances strange circles around the issue. Any number of laws that appear in the *Mishneh Torah,* for example, are clearly based on the assumption that living in the Land of Israel is one of the greatest endeavors Jews can take upon themselves. Rather anomalously he even quotes several aggadic passages like those cited above to make his point clearer and more forceful than it might otherwise have been. And yet nowhere in the code does Maimonides actually declare unequivocally that it is a scriptural or rabbinic commandment to move to the Land of Israel or to live there. And, indeed, when Maimonides offers his list of the 613 commandments in the *Sefer Ha-mitzvot, aliyah* is not listed as one of the divine precepts every Jew must strive to fulfill.

At *MT* Hilkhot M'lakhim U-milḥ'moteihem 5:9, however, we learn that, except in times of severe famine, it is forbidden to leave the Land of Israel to settle elsewhere permanently. (Although one may leave temporarily to conduct business in other lands, to find a spouse, to study Torah in a diaspora academy, or to save a Jew in the Diaspora from mortal danger, these are clearly short-lived exceptions to the general rule that could never be invoked to justify leaving the Land permanently.) Even laws of the greatest seriousness are rendered unexpectedly flexible by the overriding importance of settling in Israel: a Jew attempting to purchase a home in the Land of Israel from a gentile, Maimonides notes at *MT* Hilkhot Shabbat 6:11 (basing himself on *BT* Bava Kamma 80b and Gittin 8b), may ask the gentile to write up the deed of sale on Shabbat because, even though it is generally forbidden on the Sabbath to ask gentiles to do work forbidden to Jews on their day of rest, that rabbinic enactment was not applied to an action that would encourage the strengthening of the Jewish community in the Land of Israel. Elsewhere in the *Mishneh Torah*, Maimonides declares that it is ample grounds for divorce if one spouse wishes to move to the Land of Israel and the other does not (*MT* Hilkhot Ishut 13:20, based on *M* K'tubbot 13:11). Yet Maimonides himself, after fleeing danger in Morocco and spending a few months in Israel in 1165 and 1166, did not remain but moved on instead to Egypt and remained there, first in Alexandria and then in Fustat, until his death in the late autumn of 1204.

On the other hand, Naḥmanides, Maimonides' younger contemporary, was convinced that *aliyah* to Israel was a *mitzvah* of the Torah and that it was therefore incumbent upon every Jew to attempt to live in the Land. Indeed, when commenting on the passage in the Torah that reads, "You shall take possession of the Land and settle in it" (Number 33:53), Naḥmanides writes simply, "I consider this to be a positive commandment of the Torah." In his comments on Maimonides' *Sefer Ha-mitzvot,* he writes exactly the same thing: that *aliyah* to the Land of Israel is the fulfillment of a scriptural commandment. And, indeed, after a life in the Diaspora, Naḥmanides fled Catalonia for the Land of Israel in 1267 and remained there until his death three years later, living at first in Jerusalem and then in Acre.

Later authorities equivocated between these two views, with most believing *aliyah* to be a worthwhile ideal but not considering it an actual commandment. Some based this apparent leniency on the difficult economic straits the Jews of the Land of Israel were obliged to endure in their day, while others wrote of the gravely dangerous conditions that faced those who attempted to settle there. Still others felt that there was no point legislating laws that only a small minority of people would fulfill; this approach has talmudic precedent in the principle that legislation may never be enacted if it is obvious that most people will be unable to obey the law as promulgated (*BT* Bava Batra 60b and elsewhere).

In our day, and especially in the wake of the establishment of the State of Israel in 1948, the rise of political and religious Zionism has sharpened the debate considerably. Volumes have been written debating the halakhic issues surrounding the topic of *aliyah,* but a clear consensus has yet to emerge. Just as there are deeply religious Jews who have moved to Israel out of a profound sense of halakhic obligation, there are also many deeply committed Jews who have elected to remain in the Diaspora. And there are also Jews in Israel who consider *aliyah* to be merely preferable, but ultimately optional, for Jews who live elsewhere.

There are divergent opinions among rabbis who have written on the topic. Among Conservative rabbis, the most authoritative opinion put forward to date belongs to Rabbi David Golinkin, who authored a responsum on the topic originally published in *Moment* magazine and now reprinted in the author's *Responsa in a Moment* (Jerusalem: Schechter Institute of Jewish Studies, 2002, pp. 79–83) in which he delineated five different approaches to the issue of *aliyah* as commandment, all of which he considered acceptable approaches with roots in valid halakhic sources. In the end, however, he concluded that it would be a misreading of all the relevant biblical and talmudic passages not to acknowledge that one of the foundational ideas of Judaism is that all Jews are supposed to live in the Land of Israel. "That," he wrote, "is what God repeatedly promised our ancestors, that is why God redeemed us from Egypt, and that is where a large percentage of the *mitzvot* need to be observed. . . . In conclusion, one should make *aliyah* because living in Israel is a *mitzvah* in and of itself as well as a preparatory act which enables one to observe all of the *mitzvot* and to live a full Jewish life by living in a Jewish state."

Pilgrimages

The scriptural injunction to make three annual pilgrimages to Jerusalem provides an interesting counterpoint to the preceding question of *aliyah,* and also provides the background for the concept of visiting Israel as a tourist in the framework of religious obligation.

The obligation to visit Jerusalem three times a year, technically referenced in halakhic literature as the *mitzvah* of *aliyah la-regel,* is stated three times in the Torah, twice in Exodus (at 23:17 and 34:23) and once in Deuteronomy (at 16:16). These texts seem to present a blanket requirement that all Jewish males visit Jerusalem to offer sacrifices in the Temple thrice yearly, yet a perusal of early rabbinic texts yields a long list of people exempted from the obligation for one reason or another: blind people (*M* Ḥagigah 1:1, and cf. *T* Ḥagigah 1:2 and *BT* Ḥagigah 2a), deaf people (ibid.), people who cannot speak (cf. *BT* Ḥagigah 2b), individuals of indeterminate gender or hermaphrodites (ibid.), mentally deficient individuals (ibid.), children (ibid.; cf. *T* Ḥagigah 1:3), lame people (ibid.), amputees (*BT* Ḥagigah 3a), elderly people (*M* Ḥagigah 1:1), infirm people (ibid.), leather and copper workers (*BT* Ḥagigah 4a), slaves (*M* Ḥagigah 1:1), uncircumcised men (*BT* Ḥagigah 4b), and people in a state of ritual impurity (*T* Ḥagigah 1:1, cf. *BT* Ḥagigah 4b). There are interesting things to say about all of these categories, but the most interesting for an evaluation of the *halakhah* as it applies in our own day is the final one because moderns, lacking any means of purification from the kind of impurity that derives from contact with (or even presence under the same roof as) a corpse, must all consider themselves to be in a state of permanent ritual impurity. Thus, in addition to there being no Temple in Jerusalem in which the pilgrims' requisite sacrifices may be offered, this exemption of the impure means that moderns may reasonably consider themselves exempt from the obligation to undertake a pilgrimage three times annually to Jerusalem as well.

Most traditional halakhic sources follow this line of thinking and suppose that the absence of the Temple implies that the obligation to visit Jerusalem as a pilgrim is no longer in force. The thirteenth-century author of the *Sefer Ha-*

ḥinnukh, for example, notes succinctly that "this *mitzvah* applies only to Temple times" (*Sefer Ha-ḥinnukh,* commandment no. 71. Other acclaimed latter-day halakhists sharing this opinion include Rabbi Ezekiel Landau (1713–1793, in *Noda Bihudah,* second ed.: Oraḥ Ḥayyim 94, ed. New York, 1960, pp. 60–61), and Rabbi Moses Sofer (1762–1839, in the *Responsa of the Ḥatam Sofeir,* vol. 2, responsum 234, ed. Bratislava, 1851, pp. 94b–95b). Nonetheless, there are traces of evidence in the Talmud that suggest that people continued to make these pilgrimages to Jerusalem even after the Temple was destroyed. For example, at *BT* N'darim 23a, a tannaitic source presents a couple quarreling decades after the destruction of Jerusalem about whether or not the wife was justified in disregarding her husband's vow that she not make the pilgrimage and seeking adjudication of their dispute from a rabbi. Indeed, Rabbi Jacob Emden (1679–1776, in his collection of responsa *She'eilat Ya·avetz* part 1, responsum 87, ed. Lvov, 1884, pp. 54 a–b), effectively demonstrated that rabbinic authorities both in the age of the Mishnah and the Talmud continued to consider the holiness of Jerusalem wholly intact.

This practice appears to have continued beyond the talmudic period as well. *Sefer Ḥasidim* (ed. Wistinetzki [Frankfurt, 1924], §630), for instance, recalls that Rav Hai Gaon, one of the great luminaries of Babylonian Jewry in the geonic period, used to make an annual pilgrimage to Jerusalem on Sukkot, and the Ḥatam Sofeir (at vol. 2, responsum 233, the responsum just preceding the one cited above, ed. cit., pp. 93b–94b) wrote that this was the practice of many in the geonic period. Rabbi Nissim ben Reuben Gerondi (1315–1375) wrote that a certain edict was in effect "even after the destruction of the Temple, because Jewish people continued to come from their own countries to Jerusalem on the three pilgrimage festivals, just as they continue to do today" (see his comments to *BT* Ta·anit 10a, in the *Sefer Ha-halakhot* of the Rif, Rabbi Isaac Alfasi (1013–1103), page 2a, *s.v. ve'ikka*). Slightly later, Rabbi Simon ben Tzemaḥ Duran (1361–1444) even went so far as to say that some of the miracles that attended the pilgrims in ancient times survived into his own day and could be observed by those who traveled to Jerusalem to observe the obligatory pilgrimage at the appointed times each year (*Sefer Tashbetz* 3:201, ed. Lvov, 1891, pp. 32a–b).

In the wake of the rise of modern Zionism, a new approach to the issue has emerged. Rabbi Meshulam Rath (1875–1963), for example, in his volume of responsa entitled *Kol M'vasseir,* wrote that the notion of *aliyah la-regel* is "surely an important thing [even] in our day" (vol. 2, responsum 10, ed. Jerusalem, 1962, pp. 19–20), and he relies on two *midrashim* preserved in *Shir Ha-shirim Rabbah.* The first says that just as mother doves do not abandon their dovecotes even after their chicks have been taken away, so too does

Israel continue to observe the three pilgrimage festivals even though the Temple has been destroyed (1:64). The other declares that "although the Temple had been destroyed, yet Israel did not cease from their thrice-annual pilgrimages" (8:13).

Similarly, Rabbi Eliezer Waldenberg, in a responsum published in the *Tzitz Eliezer,* wrote that although the halakhic obligation may itself be suspended, countless Jews continue to visit the Western Wall, the site of the ancient Temple, "especially during the festival seasons." This can only be explained, he says, as a function of the fact that the Temple Mount, the site of the ancient pilgrimage, is "the ultimate root and conscious and subconscious source of the holiness of the Jewish people in general and of every single Jewish individual in particular" (vol. 10, responsum 1, sect. 93 [ed. Jerusalem, 1970, p. 37]).

Finally, Rabbi Ovadiah Yosef composed a responsum (published in his collection of responsa entitled *Y'ḥavveh Da·at* vol. 1, responsum 25, ed. Jerusalem, 1977, pp. 71–73) specifically devoted to the issue of *aliyah la-regel* in our day. He begins by reviewing previous halakhic opinions on the matter and concludes that the ancient *mitzvah* of *aliyah la-regel* is inoperative today. However, because of the great and ongoing sanctity of Jerusalem itself, it is nevertheless "a *mitzvah* to visit Jerusalem even in our own day, to feel the presence of the living God, to visit the city's synagogues and study halls . . . and, especially, to visit the Western Wall, from which the Sh'khinah, God's perceptible presence on earth, has never departed." (He does however consider it completely forbidden to visit the Temple Mount itself today; this issue is discussed in more detail below.)

For contemporary Jews, the implication of all this halakhic theorizing should be clear. Although, technically speaking, the Torah commandment to visit Jerusalem three times a year on the festivals of Sukkot, Passover, and Shavuot is no longer in effect, visiting Israel, and especially visiting Jerusalem, should still be considered a laudatory practice of the most sacred order. Almost all the authors cited above quote the words of Rabbi Aḥa (preserved at *Sh'mot Rabbah* 2:2, *Midrash T'hillim* 11:3, and elsewhere) to the effect that the Sh'khinah will never depart from the Western Wall, the sole surviving remnant of the Temple. Surely, visiting this holy place as often as possible must be one of the ways that we can fulfill our obligation to show reverence to God. Following Maimonides' unequivocal pronouncement that the holiness of Jerusalem is eternal and incontestable (*MT* Hilkhot Beit Ha-b'ḥirah 6:14–15, discussed in detail below), Jews who long for the succor of God's holy presence in their lives can do no better than to seek the Holy One in the Holy Land and, specifically, in the Holy City that contains the site of the Holy Temple.

Visiting the Temple Mount

The question of visiting the Temple Mount is related to the nature of the sanctity of Jerusalem: is it permanent or temporal? At first blush, this issue too seems relatively clear-cut. Scripture forbids people contaminated by impurity to remain in the Israelite camp (Numbers 5:2 and Deuteronomy 23:11). The laws pertaining to the wilderness camp were applied by the rabbis to the Temple district, which was seen as the "camp" with the latter-day Tabernacle (that is, the Temple itself) in its center. Thus, those contaminated by impurity would likewise be excluded from the Temple environs. (The precise correlation between the sections of the ancient desert camp and the districts of latter-day Jerusalem is given by Maimonides at *MT* Hilkhot Beit Ha-b'ḥirah 7:11.)

The crux of the matter for latter-day halakhists, however, lies in a dispute between Maimonides and Rabbi Abraham ben David of Posquières (known as the Ravad, c. 1120–1198). In *MT* Hilkhot Beit Ha-b'ḥirah 6:14–15, Maimonides turns to the question of the sanctity of Jerusalem in the post-Temple period and writes unambiguously that the ritual sanctification performed by King Solomon (as described in detail in 1 Kings 8) made the city holy for all time; the city thus retains its sanctity even in the absence of a Temple. "Therefore," he writes, "one may offer up sacrifices even though there is no Temple building standing, and one may eat sacrificial meat of the most sacred variety anywhere within the Temple courtyards [as the law permits] even though they be in ruins and not surrounded by any sort of barrier [as they were in ancient times]. Furthermore, one may eat sacrificial meats of lesser sanctity and second-tithe produce anywhere in Jerusalem [as the law permits], even should the city have no walls around it, because the original sanctity granted the city [in the days of King Solomon] was effective for its own day and retains its efficacy permanently."

The implications of this line of reasoning are profound. Although people impure due to contact with a corpse may enter any other part of Jerusalem, including the outer sectors of the Temple Mount (cf. Maimonides, *MT* Hilkhot Bi·at Ha-mikdash 3:4), they may not enter the actual area on which the enclosed parts of the Temple precincts once stood. Since it is impossible to ascertain exactly where the specific parts of the Temple actually stood in ancient times, Maimonides would thus consider it forbidden for an observant Jew to visit any part of the Temple Mount today. (It is clear, incidentally, that the modern-day Temple Mount—upon which the Dome of the Rock and the Al-Aksa mosque sit today—is much larger than its ancient counterpart. So there may well be parts of the Temple Mount today that were not even part of the Temple Mount in antiquity, let alone the part where the Temple stood.) Still, Maimonides' statement clearly implies that any part of the Temple Mount should be considered off-limits to Jewish persons of impure status. By common consent, this includes all Jewish people living today.

In response to Maimonides' statement about the permanent holiness of Jerusalem, the Ravad opined that the former had merely written "his own opinion [that the sanctity of Jerusalem is permanent] and I have no idea whence it came to him." He goes on to say that Maimonides is incorrect, and the punishment of excision (*kareit,* to be inflicted on any who enter the Temple in a state of impurity; cf. Maimonides, *MT* Hilkhot Bi·at Ha-mikdash 3:12) does not apply in our day, since the sanctity of Jerusalem was temporal and did not outlast the Temple itself.

Among Conservative authorities, Rabbi David Golinkin and Rabbi Reuven Hammer have both written responsa dealing with the issue of entering the Temple Mount in our day (*Responsa of the Va·ad Halakhah,* vol. 1, pp. 3–10 and 11–14). After noting that many authorities follow Maimonides in this matter, Rabbi Golinkin suggests that even those who accept that position could still consider it permissible to enter at least part of the Temple Mount today: specifically, the southern area near the Al-Aksa mosque and the part north of the elevated area of the Dome of the Rock. Rabbi Hammer's view on the matter, even more lenient than Rabbi Golinkin's, is based on *M* Keilim 1:6: "The Land of Israel is more holy than any other land. And whence derives its holiness? That from its produce come the first sheaf offering [*omer*], the first fruits [brought as offerings on Shavuot], and the two loaves of bread [brought as special Shavuot offerings], which is not the case for any other land." Rabbi Hammer writes that "it is clear that the concept of sanctity spoken about in this *mishnah* is related to the cult . . . [and that] this sanctity is not eternal and does not exist today, since the Temple was destroyed." He concludes that we may follow the Ravad in this matter and suppose that there is no prohibition whatsoever against entering any part of the Temple Mount in our day. Nonetheless, he also notes that a Jew should not actually enter the Dome of the Rock, presumed to be the site of the Holy of Holies in ancient times to which only the High Priest was allowed entry.

Both Rabbi Golinkin and Rabbi Hammer refer to a passage in the Talmud (*BT* Y'vamot 6a–b) in which the scriptural injunction to revere God's sanctuary (Leviticus 19:30) is applied to specific ways of respecting the sanctity of the Temple Mount. They conclude that whether one feels permitted to enter all parts of it or only certain areas, a Jew is obligated to treat the site with the greatest reverence and respect.

It would therefore be acceptable in our day either to enter all parts of the Temple Mount except for the Dome of the Rock or else to avoid the central portion of the Mount entirely. Of course, it would also be acceptable to adopt a stricter position and follow Maimonides by avoiding the entire Temple Mount. This was also the view of Abraham Abele Gombiner (c. 1635–1682), the author of the *Magein Avraham* commentary on the *Shulḥan Arukh* (see his comment to *SA* Oraḥ Ḥayyim 561:2), and it is the view of many other halakhic authorities as well. Jews considering a visit to the Temple Mount will obviously also have to take political considerations into account in making a final decision how or whether to proceed.

T'rumot and Tithes

The Torah dictates that a certain amount of produce be given every year to the priests and Levites to compensate them for the fact that they were not given any property when the Land of Israel was divided up among the tribes of Israel in the days of the conquest. The precise way the system eventually evolved, based on relevant scriptural passages like Numbers 18:21–29 and Deuteronomy 12:17–19, 14:28–29, and 26:12–15, is a complex example of rabbinic exegesis well beyond the scope of this chapter, but the basic picture that emerged comprised an annual tax of unspecified amount (fixed in *M* T'rumot 4:3 at somewhere between one-thirtieth and one-sixtieth of the whole, depending on the generosity of the donor) called *t'rumah* for the priests and an annual tithe constituting ten percent of the remainder for the Levites. An additional second tithe (constituting one-tenth of the remainder, once the other taxes were paid) was also due annually, but this amount was taken to Jerusalem in the first, second, fourth, and fifth years of the sabbatical year cycle, to be consumed there as a way of supporting the economy of the Holy City, and given to the poor in the third and sixth years. (In the seventh year, no cultivation of land was permitted and therefore no taxes were owed.) Also, Levites were required to pay a secondary *t'rumah* tax on the tithed produce they took in as well.

Are these taxes still in effect today? Even in antiquity, they were imposed only on individuals who lived in the Land of Israel. The Mishnah, in fact, declares simply that "commandments which Scripture institutes with respect to the Land of Israel do not apply outside the Land" (*M* Kiddushin 1:9), and that this blanket exemption applies to all agricultural commandments with the exception of *orlah* (the prohibition of eating the fruit of trees less than four years old), *kilayim* (the prohibition of sowing a field with two different kinds of produce), and, at least according to Rabbi Eliezer, *ḥadash* (the prohibition of eating from the new crop of grain before the *omer* was offered on the second day of Passover).

Do the obligations regarding *t'rumah* and tithes exist today with respect to produce grown in Israel? In a *midrash* preserved in *Sifrei B'midbar* (at Koraḥ §1), Rabbi Tarfon explains to Rabban Gamliel that in the post-Temple era, the phrase *avodat mattanah* (literally, "worship by gift") at Numbers

18:7 means that we must maintain the custom of giving out the appropriate foodstuffs to the priests and Levites, as a latter-day equivalent of the (now defunct) Temple worship. That sounds clear enough, but, as is almost always the case, the law is not that simple.

Maimonides describes the situation in these terms: "The *mitzvah* of *t'rumah* in our day . . . is not a Torah-derived obligation but rather a rabbinic one, because the Torah-derived obligation only applies to the original Land of Israel when the entire Jewish people is in residence there . . . and this, it seems to me, is the status of tithes in our day as well" (*MT* Hilkhot T'rumot 1:26; cf. ibid. 13:14; based largely on the talmudic discussions at *BT* Y'vamot 82a–b, K'tubbot 25a, and Niddah 46b–47a). Furthermore, Maimonides writes (based on *T* Ma·aseir Sheini 3:13–14) that it is actually forbidden to consume second-tithe produce in Jerusalem in our day, or even to redeem it there. (Maimonides' opinions can be found in the edition of his responsa edited by Joshua Blau in responsa 129 and 336 [Jerusalem: Mekitzei Nirdamim, 1957–1961, vol. 1, pp. 235–242 and vol. 2, pp. 608–609, respectively].) Generally speaking, however, the distinction between Torah-based and rabbinically ordained commandments is of theoretical importance only and has no practical import for ritual observance. And that seems to be the case for the *mitzvot* of *t'rumah* and tithes in our day, as well.

The more interesting question has to do with the so-called "great *t'rumah*" that is initially taken from the whole lot of produce. There are those, including Maimonides (at *MT* Hilkhot Issurei Bi·ah 20:3), who teach that this *t'rumah* may be given to a priest in our day—that is, to a Jew possessed of the family tradition that he is a *kohein*. (Since this is not the fulfillment of the original Torah-based commandment, it is reasonable that we may include in this even priests who lack the genealogical certification that would have been required in antiquity of any priest who wished to benefit from his sacerdotal status.) These Maimonides calls "priests by self-definition," and it is his opinion that they may eat the *t'rumah* food if they wish. His approach is not accepted by other authorities, however, most notably not by Ravad, whose comment to that passage insists that *t'rumah* set aside in the Land of Israel cannot be consumed by priests of doubtful lineage because, even if they did have unimpeachable genealogical certification, they would still lack the requisite state of purity.

Taking all this into account, the simplest procedure for Israeli farmers to follow today is to separate a small amount of produce and set it aside as *t'rumah*. (Maimonides notes that even a single stalk of wheat is enough to serve as *t'rumah* for an entire lot of grain; see *MT* Hilkhot T'rumot 3:1, based on *BT* Avodah Zarah 73b and Ḥullin 137b; cf. also Shabbat 17b.) Since no priest may eat *t'rumah* in our day, this portion should either simply be left either to rot or else it should be buried or burned. Alternatively, those hoping to preserve a greater sense of the traditions as they were observed in antiquity may wish symbolically to give this small amount of produce to a self-proclaimed *kohein*—thus retaining the form, if not quite the content, of the ancient practice.

The situation regarding tithes is the least complicated to unravel in our day, because ritual purity is not required for their consumption. Furthermore, once the *t'rumah* is taken from the tithe (the so-called "lesser *t'rumah*"), the tithe itself may be consumed by anyone at all. (Levites are no longer deemed of sufficient sanctity to warrant the gift of the tithe in our day; cf. Maimonides' explanation at *MT* Hilkhot T'rumot 1:11 and *SA* Yoreh Dei·ah 331:4). Therefore, the procedure is simple: a tenth part of a given amount of produce that has been reaped and prepared either for consumption or sale is designated as tithe-produce. A small portion of it—the usual figure given is one percent—is designated the tithe's *t'rumah* and is set aside and buried, burned, or left to rot. The rest of the tithe may then be eaten by anyone at all.

The law, as mentioned above, also required the separation of a second tithe that was consumed in Jerusalem four out of every seven years, given to the poor in two other years, and not collected at all in the sabbatical year. In our day, the procedure for dealing with second tithe follows a similar pattern. In the first, second, fourth, and fifth years of the cycle, one-tenth of what remains after the greater *t'rumah* and the first tithe have been removed should be estimated at about a quarter over market value, then exchanged for a single coin which, possessed of the sanctity of second-tithe money, may then be given to charity. (Maimonides' exposition of this concept of redeeming a large sum of money for a single coin appears in *MT* Hilkhot Ma·aseir Sheini V'neta Reva·i 2:2.) In the third and sixth years, the second tithe is designated as *ma·asseir ani,* that is, as the tithe for the poor. Although it is acceptable to most authorities for this tithe merely to be designated as such, after which it may be consumed by anyone, moderns seeking to imbue their agricultural efforts with even greater sanctity may wish to consider donating a tenth of the value of their marketable produce to charity. This would serve as a sign of their understanding that the ancient obligation to donate a tenth of one's produce twice in every seven-year period was designed to inspire generosity toward the poor, surely a worthy attitude for moderns to cultivate. Thus, although doing so would be the fulfillment of neither a scriptural nor a rabbinic obligation, it could still serve as an opportunity to act kindly toward the poor and would surely capture the essence of the ancient *mitzvah*.

Interested readers may wish further to consult chapters 2–4 of the second volume of Dayan Dr. I. Grunfeld's *The Jewish Dietary Laws* (New York: Soncino, 1972).

The Sabbatical and Jubilee Years

The Torah ordains that once the Israelites were established in their land, the land was to be allowed to lie fallow every seventh year. During this sabbatical year, debts were to be forgiven and Jews who had become the indentured servants of other Jews were to be released from their servitude. (See principally Exodus 23:10–11, Leviticus 25:1–7 and 19–22, and Deuteronomy 15:1–11.) Furthermore, every fiftieth year (following every seventh seven-year period) was called the jubilee year and was to be a kind of super-sabbatical year. During the jubilee, land sales were cancelled and all properties (except those specifically excluded by Scripture) returned to their original owners. (See Leviticus 25:8–17, 23–55; cf. also Numbers 36:5–10.) The English word "jubilee" is merely the anglicized version of the Hebrew *yoveil,* used a bit obscurely in Leviticus 25 to denote the fiftieth year in the cycle. Do these laws apply in modern times?

Even in ancient times, the *halakhah* maintained that the remission of debts in the sabbatical year was only operative when the laws regarding non-cultivation of the Land in the sabbatical year were observed (*BT* Mo·eid Katan 2b; cf. Gittin 36a). Furthermore, the laws connected with letting the Land lie fallow in the seventh year are themselves in our day only a rabbinic obligation, since their Torah-based observance depends on also observing the jubilee, which practice ceased once the tribal allocations of land and the tribal affiliation of individual Jewish persons were no longer known. (See the opinion of Rabbi Judah the Patriarch at *Y* Sh'vi·it 10:3, 39c, and cf. also the comments of Maimonides in his commentary to *M* Sh'vi·it 10:3.)

Since the State of Israel came into being in 1948, there have been nine sabbatical years: 5712 (1951–1952), 5719 (1958–1959), 5726 (1965–1966), 5733 (1972–1973), 5740 (1979–1980), 5747 (1986–1987), 5754 (1993–1994), 5761 (2000–2001), and 5768 (2007–2008). How should Jews cultivating land in Israel observe future sabbatical years? Maimonides (in his comments to *M* Sh'vi·it referenced above; cf. *MT* Hilkhot Sh'mittah V'yoveil 9:1) is emphatic in his remarks that the remission of debts every seven years—debts not barred from remission by the various halakhic techniques developed by rabbis in ancient, medieval, and modern times—remains in effect "as a rabbinic commandment in every place and in every era." Is the same true for the obligation to let the land lie fallow every seven years? Most contemporary rabbinic authorities hold that the obligation, though now rabbinic (rather than Torah-based) in nature, is indeed still in effect. Maimonides states that the obligation to observe the sabbatical year, although it only applies to the Land of Israel, does not depend on the existence of a Temple; indeed, he writes, of all the

Torah-based commandments we have mentioned here, including the jubilee year, the only ones that remain in effect are the rabbinic commandments that ordain the observance of a sabbatical year in Israel and the remission of debts in every place (*MT* Hilkhot Sh'mittah V'yoveil 4:25, 10:9). This is, more or less, the opinion of most authorities, e.g., the thirteenth-century author of the *Sefer Ha-ḥinnukh,* commandments 326 and 333–339, and Rabbi Yom Tov ben Abraham Ishbili (known as the Ritba, c. 1250–1330) in his novellae to *BT* Gittin 36a.

Among Conservative authorities, a formal statement about the sabbatical year appears as a responsum written by Rabbi David Golinkin and published in *Responsa of the Va·ad Halakhah,* vol. 1, pp. 37–45. In that responsum, Rabbi Golinkin proposes that moderns rely neither on the view that the observance of the sabbatical year in our time is a Torah-based commandment nor on those many earlier authorities who considered it to be rabbinically required. Instead, he suggests that we follow those early authorities like Rabbi Zeraḥiah Halevi (c. 1125–c. 1186) and the Ravad, who considered the law to be inoperative in the modern era so that those who choose to follow it must be understood to be doing so as an act of special piety (*li-f'nim mi-shurat ha-din*). This approach encourages those who wish to observe the laws of *sh'mittah* to do so, but without placing an unbearable strain on the efforts of struggling Israeli farmers to run profitable businesses if letting the land lay fallow were to prove ill-advised economically. Nevertheless, Rabbi Golinkin proposes that even those who opt not to observe a formal sabbatical year should nevertheless adopt certain practices designed to foster the spirit of these *mitzvot.* They could, for example, attempt to sow their winter crop early, planting grass and trees before Rosh Hashanah in any designated sabbatical year. (Technically, the sabbatical year begins on the first of Tishrei.) Furthermore, they should avoid (or minimize) any biblically forbidden labors such as sowing, pruning, harvesting, and plowing as best they can. (If this proves impossible, however, they should attempt to carry out these labors in a way different from their normal practice, thus suggesting by the difference that they are aware of the Torah's law.) Also, they should avoid planting or tending gardens that are not specifically required to prevent erosion during the rainy season, and they should do their best to plan the agricultural cycle to fit in between two sabbatical years. In addition, they should leave one field fallow as a token of their allegiance to the ancient laws. Finally, they should devote themselves during the sabbatical year to the study of the laws pertaining to these *mitzvot* and they should also donate special funds to charity, in keeping with the spirit of the Torah's explanation that the sabbatical year exists "so that the poor of your people may eat" (Exodus 23:11).

The Mitzvot of the Land of Israel

The laws pertaining to agriculture in the Torah fall easily into two categories: those tied specifically to the Land of Israel and those in effect anywhere that Jews cultivate land. Those in the former category are called *mitzvot ha-t'luyot ba-aretz,* commandments that by their nature can only be fulfilled in the Land of Israel.

The Torah ordains that we are not to eat from the new crop of one of the traditional five grains of the Land of Israel (wheat, oats, spelt, barley, and rye) until after the first sheaf of barley, called the *omer,* was formally harvested and its flour offered up (and a lamb sacrificed) on the second day of Passover (Leviticus 23:9–14). Although differing points of view are presented in the Talmud (at *BT* Kiddushin 37a and M'naḥot 68b), the prevailing view is that the *mitzvah* applies both within the boundaries of the Land of Israel and in the Diaspora. This is also the viewpoint of Maimonides (at *MT* Hilkhot Ma·akhalot Asurot 10:2), where he notes that observance of this *mitzvah* is not dependent on the existence of a Temple in which the *omer* could be formally offered; he also states that, as a rabbinic "hedge," new grain is prohibited in our day until the evening of the sixteenth of Nisan in Israel and in the Diaspora until the evening of the seventeenth, the day after the day on which the *omer* was offered up in ancient times. This opinion is shared by Rabbi Jacob ben Asher in the *Arba·ah Turim* at *AT* Yoreh Dei·ah 293, and Rabbi Joseph Karo in the *SA* Yoreh Dei·ah 293.

The next two *mitzvot* to consider go together. Based on Leviticus 19:23–25, the law is that one may not eat the fruit produced during a tree's first four fruit-bearing years. Whereas the fruit of the first three years, called *orlah,* must be discarded, the fruit of the fourth year, called *neta r'va·i,* is sacred and must either be consumed in Jerusalem or redeemed for money that is then spent there. (The precise way the three years were calculated is a bit complex, but the basic principle is that any tree planted before the sixteenth of Av is considered to have concluded its first year with the Rosh Hashanah that follows six weeks later.) The fruit of the fifth and subsequent years may simply be eaten with no ritual prelude at all. At *MT* Hilkhot Ma·akhalot Asurot 10:15, Maimonides teaches that only a truncated version of the law applies in the Diaspora (one waits for the requisite three years and then simply eats the fruit of the fourth year), but that the full version applies in the Land of Israel in every era. Rabbi Asher ben Yeḥiel (known as Rabbeinu Asher, c. 1250–1327), on the other hand, was of the opinion that the full law applies both in the Diaspora and in the Land of Israel (as quoted by his son, Rabbi Jacob ben Asher at *AT* Yoreh Dei·ah 294), and this was the opinion of Rabbi Joseph Karo as well (*SA* Yoreh Dei·ah 294:7). The normal custom today follows the view of the Rema (in his gloss to the section of the *Shulḥan Arukh* referenced just above) to the effect that the law of *orlah* and *neta r'va·i* applies to all the produce of the Land of Israel and in the Diaspora only to the cultivation of grapes.

Kilayim, the general name for the prohibition of mixed species and mixed fields of various sorts, derives primarily from Leviticus 19:19 and Deuteronomy 22:9–11. We discuss here only the two agricultural varieties of *kilayim: kilei z'ra·im* (admixtures as they apply to the sown field) and *kilei ha-kerem* (admixtures as they apply to the vineyard). The former category refers to sowing a field with different kinds of crops or grafting two different kinds of trees together; the latter applies the same concept to the vineyard. (The laws that govern the specific kinds of forbidden grafts and mixtures are complex and form the bulk of the material in the tractate of the Mishnah called Kilayim.) There are differing opinions presented in the Talmud at *BT* Kiddushin 39a regarding the issue, but Rabbi Jacob ben Asher writes in the *Arba·ah Turim* (at *AT* Yoreh Dei·ah 295) that while *kilei z'ra·im* are only forbidden in the Land of Israel, the prohibition against grafting different kinds of trees together is in effect in the Diaspora as well. (Maimonides, writing at *MT* Hilkhot M'lakhim U-milḥ'moteihem 10:6 and basing himself on *BT* Sanhedrin 56b and 60a, notes that grafting of trees to each other is forbidden by the Torah even to non-Jews under the so-called Noahide statutes.) *Kilei ha-kerem,* on the other hand, are forbidden both in Israel and in the Diaspora—in Israel by biblical decree and in the Diaspora by rabbinic edict.

Ḥallah, which term has passed into both modern Hebrew and many Western languages as the name of a special bread eaten on the Shabbat and at festival meals, is used in Scripture at Numbers 15:17–21 to denote a special portion of the dough that is set aside and given to a priest when dough is being prepared for baking. (At Ezekiel 44:30, it is specifically noted that the performance of this commandment will bring God's blessing to one's home.) Because the relevant passage in Scripture begins with the words "When you enter the land to which I am bringing you," the Talmud determines (at *BT* K'tubbot 25a–b) that the Torah-derived commandment only applies within the Land of Israel, and only when all Israel is resident in the Land. (This is the law given by Maimonides at *MT* Hilkhot Bikkurim 5:5 as well.) In our day, the observance of the commandment in Israel is understood to be rabbinically ordained. In the Diaspora, on the other hand, the practice is not even, strictly speaking, a commandment, but merely a rabbinic requirement "so that the law of *ḥallah* not be forgotten entirely by the Jewish people" (*MT* Hilkhot Bikkurim 5:7, based on *BT* B'khorot 27a). The law, at any rate, only applies to dough made of one or several of the five traditional grains: oats, rye, barley, spelt, and wheat. Furthermore, the obligation only applies if the amount of dough being baked is of sufficient quantity to sustain an individual for an entire day. This amount was fixed by the ancient sages as an *omer* of dough, defined by Maimonides as equivalent to the bulk of 43.2 eggs (at *MT* Hilkhot Bikkurim 6:15) and generally presumed to constitute about five pounds' worth of dough.

The name *bikkurim* applies to the first fruits of the spring harvest as set forth at Exodus 23:19 and 34:26 and at Deuteronomy 26:1–12. It is universally understood that this obligation applies only within the Land of Israel and only when there is a Temple standing to which the first fruits may be brought, as stated by Maimonides at *MT* Hilkhot Bikkurim 2:1. Furthermore, the law applies only to the seven most famous products of the Land of Israel: figs, pomegranates, olives, dates, wheat, barley, and grapes (cf. *MT* Hilkhot Bikkurim 2:2). After being placed on the altar, the declaration found in Deuteronomy 26 was made, after which the fruit could be eaten by a priest within the city limits of Jerusalem (*MT* Hilkhot Bikkurim 3:1).

The Torah (at Leviticus 19:9–10 and 23:22 and at Deuteronomy 24:19–22) ordains three special gifts that farmers must make to the poor. *Leket* ("gleaning," called *peret* by Scripture when applied to the vineyard) refers to the practice of leaving behind produce that falls to the ground during the harvesting process for the poor to take after the harvest is done. *Shikh'ḥah* ("the forgotten sheaf") refers to one or two sheaves of grain forgotten in the field which may not be retrieved when their absence is noted but which must instead be left for the poor to collect. *Pei·ah* ("corner") refers to the corners of every field that must be left unharvested (and, by rabbinic extension, to the trees of an orchard that must not be totally denuded of fruit during the harvesting process; cf. Maimonides, *MT* Hilkhot Matt'not Aniyyim 1:2), so that the poor may come and help themselves to the produce there. Together, these three gifts are called *matt'not aniyyim* ("gifts to the poor").

The language of Scripture implies that the concept of *matt'not aniyyim* applies only to the Land of Israel, but the sages (cf., e.g., *BT* Ḥullin 137b) extended the law of *pei·ah* to apply to the lands of the Diaspora as well. Maimonides cites that opinion (at *MT* Hilkhot Matt'not Aniyyim 1:14) and says that he feels certain that the same applies to *leket* and *shikh'ḥah* as well. Nonetheless, Maimonides also rules that these gifts are only to be given to actual poor people; when no poor people are available to receive them, anybody (including the owner of the field) may claim them, for the produce involved (unlike *t'rumah*-produce), has no inherent sanctity (ibid., 1:10). In subsequent generations, the practice of leaving these gifts for the poor fell into desuetude. Rabbi Jacob ben Asher, for example, writes in the *Arba·ah Turim* that it was no longer the practice in his day to bother with these gifts at all (*AT* Yoreh Dei·ah 332), and this sentiment is echoed by the Rema (commenting *ad loc.* to the parallel passage in the *Shulḥan Arukh*), who echoes Maimonides and the *Arba·ah Turim* of Rabbi Jacob ben Asher almost verbatim. The *Shulḥan Arukh* itself, however, rules at *SA* Yoreh Dei·ah 332 that the obligation to offer these gifts to the poor remains in effect where there are Jewish poor people to accept them.

In our day, these laws are left unobserved by all (or surely by most)—even in Israel, where the presence of a Jewish majority would appear to make them binding as Torah-based legislation. Although it would surely be appropriate to encourage the observance of these commandments, the more practical approach for Jews living in Israel today would be to devote special effort during the harvest season to raise funds for the poor and especially to distribute food and produce to them. While these commandments are not binding on Jews living in the Diaspora, it would be appropriate to act in accordance with their spirit by using the harvest season as a special time of the year devoted especially to collecting charity earmarked for the hungry and the poor.

Serving in the Israel Defense Forces

Many of the halakhic questions concerning military service, including those specifically pertinent to service in the Israel Defense Forces, are discussed by Rabbi Michael Graetz elsewhere in this volume. Furthermore, detailed responsa dealing with the contentious issues of military service for Israeli women and for Orthodox yeshivah students were published by the Va·ad Halakhah of the Rabbinical Assembly of Israel in its second volume of responsa published in Jerusalem in 1987. (The responsa were written by Rabbi Robert Harris and Rabbi Reuven Hammer, respectively, and support obligatory military service for both groups). In this section, therefore, I will discuss only the question of service in the IDF for Jews residing in the Diaspora.

At first, the question would appear to be a non-issue: people either live in countries where military service is obligatory or where it is optional, but no one in the modern world is considered obliged to serve in the armed forces of a country of which he or she is not a citizen. Still, the Torah clearly considers the relationship of Jewish individuals to the Land of Israel to be a function of Jewishness rather than Israeli citizenship, and so it is not at all unreasonable to ask what obligations the *halakhah* places on Jews who are not Israeli citizens with respect to the defense of the Land of Israel.

The evidence of Scripture is equivocal. On the one hand, in the single direct parallel to the issue when the tribes of Gad and Reuben (and eventually half of the tribe of Manasseh) express their desire to settle outside the borders of the Land of Israel, Moses grants their request on the condition that they agree still to fight alongside their brethren (Numbers 32:20–24). On the other hand, the laws of war set down in Scripture (e.g., at Deuteronomy 20:1–9, 21:10–14, and 23:10–15) seem to be addressed only to residents of the Land of Israel, and nowhere do we find any intimation that Jews residing outside the Land must travel there so as to come to its defense.

In the rabbinic view, there were basically two kinds of wars: the "discretionary" war (*milḥemet r'shut*) and the obligatory war (*milḥemet mitzvah*). The distinction between the two has to do with halakhic responsibility to participate: there can be different kinds of exemptions from service in the case of discretionary wars, but when a war is deemed obligatory "even a bridegroom must leave his nuptial chamber or a bride her *ḥuppah*" to participate in the fighting (*M* Sotah 8:7). (The Mishnah's terminology may seem confusing to casual readers, but the law is unequivocal; see Rabbi Michael Graetz's essay "War and Peace" in the *Etz Hayim*, p. 1387.)

Maimonides defines each variety of war at *MT* Hilkhot M'lakhim U-milḥ'moteihem 5:1. In his view, an obligatory war is one fought against one of the seven indigenous peoples of Canaan to establish the Jewish people in the land God gave them as their homeland, a war fought in accordance with scriptural command (at Exodus 17:16) against the fiendish nation of Amalek, or—and this is crucial for our discussion—a war undertaken to defend Jewish people against aggression wherever it may find them and, one must assume, no less so in the Land of Israel than in any other place. An optional war, on the other hand, is one undertaken to add territory to the Jewish state or to win glory or respect for its military prowess. Since the biblical laws presume that a king will lead the people of a Jewish kingdom forth into battle—and since the Jewish people in Maimonides' day had neither a king nor a country nor an army—the laws were not updated to reflect situations that even a man of Maimonides' vision would have considered almost unimaginable. And yet, we, like the dreamers mentioned in the first verse of Psalm 126, have witnessed in our own day the establishment of a Jewish state in the Land of Israel with an array of enemies dedicated to its destruction—and a powerful army of its own which specifically exists to defend the State and its citizens against outside aggression perpetrated against it and them by those enemies.

That the very existence of the State of Israel depends on the might of its armed forces seems obvious. Yet the halakhic literature delineating the obligations of diaspora Jewry, in light of Maimonides' injunction that all Jews must participate in an obligatory war defending the Jewish people against aggression, is extremely slim. In part this is because the existence of a Jewish army anyone can join is a relatively new development. But it is also partially because the issue is politically contentious: large sections of the ultra-religious community whose members might be considered the most likely to want to fulfill their halakhic obligations are not only unwilling to make IDF service obligatory for Jews outside Israel, but are unwilling even to consider it obligatory for religious Jews living in Israel. There would also be a certain amount of embarrassment in the Diaspora if Jewish citizens who generally do not volunteer in impressive numbers to serve in the armed forces of their own countries of residence were to suggest that they feel religiously obligated to serve in the armed forces of another country. And, of course, it also bears mentioning that the army Maimonides has in mind is one led into battle by a king of the House of David ruling over the kind of theocratic monarchy presented in Scripture as the ideal form of Jewish government, not a Western-style democracy ruled over by its citizens' elected representatives.

How should modern Jews deal with this set of issues? For most, the issue will turn on the question of whether the war Israel has been fighting since 1948 is truly a *milḥemet mitzvah*. (It is also worth noting in this regard the strongly worded talmudic opinion at *BT* Sotah 44b that an aggressive war against enemies of Israel "to keep them from marching against the [Jewish] people" is also called a *milḥemet mitzvah*—and that it would not be too far off the mark to qualify the day-to-day work of the IDF as falling clearly into that category of endeavor.) Most thoughtful moderns will reject the ultra-Orthodox opinion that none of this applies in the absence of a Davidic king and functioning Sanhedrin. Instead, they would do better to adopt the position that, because a decisive loss in an all-out war between Israel and its enemies would constitute a disaster of incalculable magnitude for Jews everywhere, the Torah clearly commands all Jews to consider how best they may best assist in the ongoing work of defending Israel against its enemies and then to act decisively to do so either by volunteering to serve or to be of service, or through the giving of charitable gifts to one or several of the many organizations that exist to serve the soldiers of the Israel Defense Forces.

Leaving Israel

May a Jew residing in Israel leave the country and settle elsewhere? Basing himself on a tannaitic teaching preserved at *BT* Bava Batra 91a and on several other passages from the Talmud, Maimonides writes unequivocally at *MT* Hilkhot M'lakhim U-milḥ'moteihem 5:9 that "it is forbidden [for a resident] to leave the Land of Israel for the Diaspora permanently, unless it is specifically to study Torah or to marry or to save a fellow Jew from idolaters, after which activities one must then return to the Land. Similarly, one may travel to conduct business, but to settle permanently abroad is forbidden except in time [of severe famine or financial need]. Still, even though it is permitted to leave under such circumstances, it is nevertheless not the way of the pious to do so."

The simplest way to understand Maimonides' ruling is to take it as a halakhic expression of the extreme love for the Land of Israel he presumed to exist in every Jewish breast. And, indeed, he continues in his code immediately with a series of statements, each more extravagant than the next, describing the love the ancients felt for the Land of Israel and clearly implying that these sentiments ought to be shared by all Jews, in all times and places.

In our day, it is clearly a *mitzvah* for all Jews living in the Diaspora to cultivate a sense of inner passion for Israel and to allow that passion to affect their lives in certain specific ways: by inspiring them to travel there, by making them feel wistful when they must leave, by challenging them to ask why it is that they are content to live outside its borders (especially in an age when there is a Jewish state for them to inhabit in the Land of Israel), and by goading them into honestly examining how they can bear watching others devote their lives and their resources to building up the Land of Israel while they themselves sit on the sidelines and look on from afar. These will be serious, stress-inducing questions for Jews of the Diaspora to confront. But it will be through just such reflective soul-searching that diaspora Jews will develop a reasonable response to the reality of a modern Jewish state in the Land of Israel. In countless passages, the Torah challenges Jewish people everywhere constantly to evaluate and re-evaluate their feelings for the Land of Israel. And such evaluative rumination should not start and end as mere philosophizing, but should rather lead directly to the resolve to live one's life in a way fully consonant with the inexpressible love for the Land of Israel that Scripture expects to fill every Jewish heart and to animate every Jewish soul. For, as Rabbi Ismar Schorsch, the sixth chancellor of the Jewish Theological Seminary, wrote in *The Sacred Cluster* (New York: The Jewish Theological Seminary, 1995), "Israel is not only the birthplace of the Jewish people, but also its final destiny."

Personal Integrity

KASSEL ABELSON

The eternal light that hangs above the ark in the Beth El Synagogue in Minneapolis is a large illuminated globe representing the world resting upon the Hebrew words *emet* (truth), *din* (justice), and *shalom* (peace). It is thus a symbolic representation of the teaching of Rabbi Shimon ben Gamliel that the world rests on these three basic principles (*M* Avot 1:18). But what exactly is the relationship of these three principles to each other? And, if they come into conflict, which one is the most important?

Rabbi David Aronson, an outstanding rabbi and the author of *The Jewish Way of Life* (New York: The United Synagogue of America, 1965), would often say, "If there is no truth, there cannot be justice, and without justice there will not be peace." From this we learn that truth is primary, for in its absence neither justice nor peace can prevail. And, indeed, the importance of truth-telling is so basic to the biblical worldview that it is included in the Ten Commandments: "You shall not bear false witness against your neighbor" (Exodus 20:13 and Deuteronomy 5:17, which differ slightly in wording in the Hebrew original). With these words, the Torah formally forbids testifying falsely in court under any circumstances. (In this context, the word "neighbor" does not delimit the application of the law to friends or people in close proximity, but denotes any other person at all.) This absolute dedication to truth-telling is also a rabbinic value. Indeed, when Rabbi Ḥanina said that the Hebrew word for truth, *emet,* is the personal seal of God, he was merely expressing the same idea in a more poetic way. (Rabbi Ḥanina's comment is preserved in the Talmud at *BT* Shabbat 55a.)

In the Western legal system, truthful testimony is deemed so essential to the effort to mete out justice fairly that witnesses are asked to swear in God's name that they will speak only the whole truth. And although invoking God's name will surely help to elicit truthful testimony, the legal system also tries to assure honest testimony from all by condemning perjury as a severely punishable crime. The *halakhah,* therefore, in addition to dealing with the concept of Jewish citizens taking oaths in God's name, must deal with a host of questions that originate outside its own system. Is a Jewish citizen's obligation to participate in the secular justice system absolute, or are there instances in which religious scruples may or should override the requirements of civil law? Can lying ever be justified with reference to a noble, just end?

One very relevant question concerns the issue of a Jew dissembling in court for the sake of bringing about a verdict that accords with scriptural principles. Imagine, for example, that a Jew is the sole witness to a murder. If he or she testifies honestly in an American court of law, the accused individual might receive the death penalty. It is unambiguously the case, however, that biblical law (at Deuteronomy 17:6) requires minimally two witnesses to convict in a capital case, and the *halakhah* upholds this requirement absolutely (see, e.g., Maimonides' comment at *MT* Hilkhot Eidut 4:1). Should the Jewish witness testify truthfully, knowing that his testimony might conceivably result in a conviction contrary to Jewish law and to the death of an individual as a result of that conviction? Would a Jewish witness who speaks the truth in such a case be fulfilling his or her civic responsibility by participating in the justice system, or would doing so effectively mean becoming party to the murder of a halakhically unconvictable individual? In the third century C.E., a Jewish legal principle was formulated by the Babylonian sage Samuel which addressed the issue of the relationship of Jews to the laws of the state in which they live. He summed his view up in just three words: *dina d'malkhuta dina,* "the law of the land is the law" (*BT* N'darim 28a, Gittin 10b, Bava Kamma 113a–b, and Bava Batra 55a). This principle, discussed in several other chapters of this book, was understood to mean that the laws of the state must be obeyed in both civil and criminal matters. However, in matters of religion, even Samuel maintained the supremacy of Jewish law. Hence, in a criminal case such as the one mentioned above, the witness not only may, but *must,* testify truthfully in accordance with American law, and this is so even if doing so increases the likelihood that the defendant will subsequently be convicted on the testimony of one single witness.

Within the Jewish legal system, the *halakhah* puts great emphasis on the need to be truthful. To associate God's name with a lie was considered such a serious offense that some Jews would even drop valid legal claims so as to avoid the necessity of taking an oath using God's name for fear that they might become involved inadvertently in telling an untruth. After all, when asked to repeat a conversation one had overheard, one might easily forget some small details—and the retelling might then contain some untruth. Similarly, it is difficult to remember everything that one has witnessed and to describe it in court with complete accuracy.

When Jews were required to testify in court, they were enjoined: "Let your 'yes' be yes and let your 'no' be no" (*BT* Bava M'tzi·a 49a). This simple statement masks a profound truth: although it may not always be possible to know the whole truth, the court is concerned only with truthfulness itself—that is to say, with the issue of whether the witness is telling the truth as he or she knows it or whether he or she is intentionally manipulating the facts with the intention of misleading the court. Manipulating testimony is considered to be lying, and subject to the penalty meted out for perjury. Forgetting a detail is considered a natural feature of the way human beings recount events they have experienced. The philosopher Sissela Bok, for example, defined a lie as simply "an intentionally deceptive message in the form of a statement" (*Lying* [New York: Vintage, 1999], p. 15). This definition should be deemed acceptable in the halakhic context as well, and applies to all aspects of daily life and not solely to courtroom testimony.

Honesty in Business Negotiations

The great injunction to "let your 'yes' be yes and your 'no' be no" cited above is also applied to matters of commerce. Merchants who make verbal commitments in business deals are expected to abide by them, even if they are tempted to renege on them at a later time. Maimonides devotes several chapters of his *Mishneh Torah* to the high standards of business ethics set by the Torah for buyers and sellers, using examples drawn from the mercantile world in his Hilkhot M'khirah (especially chapters 7, 9, 11, 21, 22, and 29).

Maimonides, of course, was basing himself on ancient tradition. A verse in the Book of Psalms, for example, lists among the qualifications for pilgrims hoping to be worthy of entering the holy Temple that they speak the truth in their hearts (Psalm 15:2). This verse is interpreted to mean that even if one makes a promise in one's heart without expressing it verbally, one should nonetheless keep the promise. The talmudic story of Rav Safra illustrates this principle. Rav Safra was a merchant. A customer came to him and offered a price for an object he was selling. The price was acceptable to Rav Safra, but he could not tell the customer that he agreed to it because he was reciting the Sh'ma at the time and did not want to be interrupted. The customer, under the impression that the rabbi had rejected the price, raised his offer and then continued to raise it again and again. When Rav Safra finally finished his prayers, he insisted on selling it for the original price, because that was the one to which he had "consented to in his heart." (Allusion to the story of Rav Safra is made in the Talmud at *BT* Makkot 24a, but the story itself is not told there and is cited here in the version that appears in the thirty-sixth chapter of one of the first post-talmudic works of *halakhah,* the *She'iltot.* Rav Jacob Blumenthal comments upon this story in his chapter elsewhere in this volume on the *halakhah* of commerce, and cf. Rashi's retelling of the story in his commentary to the page in *BT* Makkot just mentioned, *s.v. rav safra.*)

One could say, perhaps, that Rav Safra was a saint and that this standard of behavior could hardly have been intended to serve as the model for ordinary individuals pursuing their daily affairs. The story could well be taken that way, but Judaism nevertheless sets a very high standard for commercial transactions conducted by every Jew and not only by the saintly. "Shopkeepers must wipe their measures clean twice a week, their weights once a week, and their scales after each use," the Mishnah declares simply at *M* Bava Batra 5:10. Furthermore, the *halakhah* forbids a seller to overcharge, or a buyer to offer less than the object is worth. It is wrong to tell a potential buyer the merits of an object while intentionally concealing its defects, and this becomes the law, as we read in the Mishnah: "Vendors may not combine different grades of produce in one bin. . . . Vendors whose wine has become diluted with water may not sell it unless they make full disclosure to the customer, and, in any event, they may not sell it to another retailer, even if they do make disclosure, for fear that the second retailer will deceive his or her customers" (*M* Bava M'tzi·a 4:11). And honesty is not solely a matter of business dealings. "As there is wronging in buying and selling," the Mishnah declares, "there is wronging with words. One must not ask 'How much is this thing?' if one has no intention of buying it" (*M* Bava M'tzi·a 4:10, and cf. the discussion of this *mishnah* by Rabbi Jacob Blumenthal elsewhere in this volume).

In business, the *halakhah* requires that an individual observe the highest standards of honesty and good faith. A person must not set self-interest above truth. The Jew must deal with integrity in business and in relationships with others. Does this mean that there is no room to negotiate in business deals?

Hardly. Just as one would not want to take advantage of another person, one need not put oneself at a financial disadvantage. Where it is a common practice to begin negotiations at a higher figure than one would expect to end with, it is not deceiving the other person to start with a figure that, after negotiation, would decline to a mutually acceptable figure. Being honest does not mean being simple, nor does profit indicate unscrupulousness. The *halakhah* does not intend for people to behave foolishly or naïvely, only for them not to behave dishonestly or deceptively.

Truth in Personal Relationships

The Torah commands: "You shall not steal; you shall not deal deceitfully or falsely with one another" (Leviticus 19:11). This may sound simple, but the idea of *g'neivat da·at* (literally "stealing the mind") must be understand in order to see how Judaism translates this concept into the fabric of daily relationships. The Talmud tells us, again in the name of Samuel, that "it is forbidden to steal the mind of other people, even of non-Jews" (*BT* Ḥullin 94a). But how can one person steal another's mind? One "steals the mind" by misleading another person, by goading that person into believing to be true what one knows oneself not to be true. Thus, it is forbidden to pretend that one has performed a service for others so as to win their gratitude, even without demanding payment for work not actually undertaken or accomplished. Nor should one invite a neighbor over to enjoy one's hospitality, knowing that the neighbor is busy at that time and will refuse. Similarly, it is forbidden to offer gifts to another person knowing in advance that they will be refused. (For more examples, see the *Encyclopedia Talmudit,* volume 6, pp. 225ff.)

None of these actions, when viewed in a vacuum, seems to be of major import. Yet they all intend to mislead others into giving undeserved credit to someone who has not earned it—thereby distorting the relationship between those two parties and possibly opening the way for harm to be done to the one who has been deceived. These, and other deceptive actions like them, are forbidden not because they cause grievous harm, but because they chip away at the honesty that Judaism demands must underlie all relationships, be they between or among neighbors, friends, or family members.

The Evil Tongue

Despite the importance placed on being truthful, there are times when the stark truth can cause harm to another person. Judaism uses the term *l'shon ha-ra,* literally "evil tongue" or "evil language," to denote the act of passing on harmful information about another person. And the Torah strictly forbids *l'shon ha-ra,* saying "Do not go about as a talebearer among your people" (Leviticus 19:16). The rabbis were deeply concerned about the power of *l'shon ha-ra* and quoted Proverbs 18:21 ("Death and life are in the power of the tongue") to show its potential as a lethal weapon capable of destroying a person. Not only is the target of the gossip harmed, but also the person who tells the gossip and the person who listens to it (*BT* Arakhin 15b), for the consequences of *l'shon ha-ra* are unpredictable and can undermine the stability of a community, causing all kinds of collateral damage. The topic of *l'shon ha-ra* is discussed in several other chapters of this book, including in a chapter specifically devoted to the topic by Rabbi Benjamin Kramer, but here, in a chapter about personal integrity, I focus on a specific aspect of the larger topic that is particularly germane: not the question of whether it is forbidden to say hateful lies about others, but rather whether one may utter embarrassing truths about others that one knows perfectly well to be accurate.

L'shon ha-ra is gossip, but the English term does not translate this halakhic concept exactly. To qualify as an example of *l'shon ha-ra,* a statement may be either true or false. If it is false, it is forbidden anyway under the general injunction not to lie. But even a statement that is perfectly true but denigrates another individual in the eyes of others is *l'shon ha-ra* just as surely as injurious speech that is not factually correct or accurate. *L'shon ha-ra* even includes praising an individual to a third party with the intent of evoking a critical response. The fact that something is true does not mean that it is not *l'shon ha-ra* or that it is everyone's business. The notion that one will always do well to speak the truth is not even remotely a halakhic teaching.

On the other hand, what should one do if the only way to prevent harm to another person is to speak ill of a third party? To ask the question differently: is *l'shon ha-ra* ever permitted? Or, to pose the question in still different words: under what circumstances might speaking about another person, perhaps even saying things that could be seen as hurtful, be considered worthy behavior? For example, suppose a person is thinking of going into business with an individual who has a reputation for being dishonest. Knowing the putative partner's business history would seem important here, as it may influence the decision. Should someone who knows the whole story step forward to warn the person considering this new business venture? Or consider the case of a young woman engaged to a man who has a medical history of mental illness of which she knows nothing. Should she be told? And, if so, by whom? What if one suspects not merely that she is ignorant of the situation, but that she has actually been lied to? Would that change the matter?

Rabbi Israel Meir Hakohen (known popularly as the Ḥafeitz Ḥayyim, after the name of his most famous book) points to the conclusion of the following passage in the Torah: "Do not go about as a talebearer among your people, nor shall you stand idly by the blood of your neighbor" (Leviticus 19:16). He argues that one has the responsibility not only to avoid talebearing but also to prevent harm, and that it is incumbent upon as to balance these obligations. Therefore, in cases like those mentioned above, the innocent party should be informed while there is still time to avert a potential catastrophe (Hilkhot Issurei R'khilut 1:1, ed. Jerusalem, 1975, p. 183).

Lying and Pikku·aḥ Nefesh

A Nazi patrol in occupied Poland knocks on the door of a peasant's home and asks if there are any Jews in the area. The peasant knows that several Jews are hiding in a nearby barn. Should the peasant lie and say he does not know where any Jews are hiding? Or should he tell the truth and cause the death of several people? And would the answer change if it were one's own life one hoped to spare by lying, or the lives of one's children?

The choices are clear and the stakes are high. There seems to be no way to prevent the murders without lying. The question, therefore, is which sacred value—the value of life or the value of truth—is paramount when one must choose between them. Some early Christian teachers taught that it is wrong to lie to save a life. For example, Saint Augustine, in the fourth century, said, "Since eternal life is lost by lying, a lie may never be told for the preservation of the temporal life of another" (Augustine, "On Lying," in his *Treatises on Various Subjects,* as cited by Sissela Bok in *Lying,* pp. 250–255). Through the years, Christian philosophers have grappled with the consequences of such an absolute prohibition of lying under any circumstances. Although some authorities have modified Augustine's absolute stance about lying, others have maintained it. John Wesley, for example, once said in a sermon that "there is no absurdity, however strange it may sound, in that saying of the ancient Father 'I would not tell a willful lie to save the souls of the whole world'" (cited in Bok, p. 32).

Judaism's approach to lying is very different. In the first chapter of the Book of Exodus, Pharaoh orders two midwives, Shifrah and Puah, to drown all the newborn males of the Israelites in the Nile. The midwives, instead of drowning the babies, save them. Pharaoh summons the midwives and demands to know why they have not carried out his command, whereupon the two midwives tell Pharaoh a lie. "The Hebrew women are not like the Egyptian women," they explain only semi-plausibly, "they are vigorous. Before the midwife can come to them, they have already given birth" (Exodus 1:19).

The Torah tells this story without even a hint of disapproval. Quite to the contrary, we are told: "And God dealt beneficently with the midwives" (Exodus 1:20). Clearly, Scripture is saying that saving lives comes before telling the truth. And could the same not be said of Rahab, the harlot of Jericho, whom tradition valorizes (and whom Joshua himself richly rewarded) specifically for lying to the king of her city about the whereabouts of the Israelites sent to scout out the city in advance of the Israelite attack?

Indeed, Judaism puts a supreme value on human life, and the *halakhah* rules that *pikku·aḥ nefesh,* the obligation to save one's own life or the life of another, takes precedence over all of the commandments except three: murder, immoral sexual acts, and idolatry (*BT* Sanhedrin 74a). Lying would thus be justified in all cases to save a life, whether the life at stake is that of a friend, a stranger, or one's own.

Lying to the Dying

Few would argue with the thesis that a lie may be told to save a life, but might a lie be used to resolve ethical dilemmas as well? For instance, may a doctor lie to a patient who has been diagnosed with a fatal illness if the doctor believes that the lie would be in the best interests of the patient because knowing the full truth could end up being so upsetting to the patient that it would cause him or her significant emotional distress and actually be deleterious to his or her overall condition?

Some people would argue that the physician should always be open and frank with a patient because patients are entitled to know what is wrong with them. Others would say that the job of a doctor is to help a patient and so the doctor must judge whether a truthful diagnosis would be more helpful than obscuring the truth. (This specific question is discussed elsewhere in this volume by Rabbi Avram I. Reisner in his chapter on halakhic medical ethics.)

The *halakhah* teaches us, as already noted, that life and health take precedence over all the *mitzvot* (except, as noted above, for the prohibitions of murder, sexual immorality, and idolatry). We are also instructed not to inform dangerously ill people of the death of close family members, lest they become upset and their conditions worsen as a result (*SA* Yoreh Dei·ah 337:1). Indeed, tradition endorses the idea that the dying need to be spoken to as comfortingly as possible. When the time comes for the mortally ill to recite the Viddui, the final confession, they are told that "many have recited the final confession, and have continued to live" (ibid., 338:1). This, of course, is not exactly an untruth, but it suggests a palliative approach to truth-telling rather than a more brutal (if more accurate) one: while some may have recited the Viddui and continued to live, the patient is reciting the prayer precisely because most of those who have recited it went on to die. It is evident that Judaism deems it important to keep hope alive even in the most dire of situations. A physician, therefore, need not feel obligated to tell the patient the whole truth.

On the other hand, the physician must take into consideration the implications of withholding the full truth about a patient's condition. Are there possible treatments that the patient may opt for that could alleviate pain or prolong life? Does the patient have business affairs, of which the doctor would almost certainly have no knowledge, that he or she would very much want to settle before facing death? Could there be personal matters that the patient would wish to deal with before it is too late, affairs of which the doctor knows nothing? Will the patient stop trusting a physician whom he or she suspects is not telling the whole truth? Or is just the opposite the case: will the patient lose confidence in a doctor who sounds dour and who appears to expect the worst? Does the patient really want to know the truth and have time to prepare for death? Or would most prefer not to face up to the fact of impending death at all? All these questions are equivocal issues that will have different answers in different contexts. The physician is not merely a healer of the body but also a healer of patients' souls. Finding the courage to ask these questions and answer them honestly will help the caring physician to know when to speak the truth and when to elect to hold back all or part of it.

The physician who elects to withhold the full truth from the patient is, nonetheless, responsible for consulting with the next of kin and informing them of the situation. Certainly the quandary for both the doctor and the family would be alleviated if patients made out living wills and said explicitly whether or not they wanted to be informed about their condition. In the event that such a living will exists, of course, the physician has no right to override its terms merely because they seem contrary to the physician's own beliefs.

Lying to Preserve the Peace

There is a category of statements called half-truths made up of remarks that, while they are not formally untrue, nevertheless do not tell the whole truth.

The Torah, for example, describes how God modified the truth to avoid causing a conflict between Abraham and Sarah. In Genesis we read how three angels came to tell Abraham at ninety-nine years of age that his eighty-nine-year-old wife Sarah, who had obviously long since gone through menopause, would nevertheless bear a child in a year. Sarah overheard the message and the Torah reports: "And Sarah laughed to herself, saying, 'Now that I am withered, am I to have enjoyment with my husband so old?' Then God said to Abraham, 'Why did Sarah laugh, saying, Shall I, in truth, bear a child, old as I am?'" (Genesis 18:12–13). The *Etz Hayim,* basing itself on the *midrash* preserved at *B'reishit Rabbah* 48:18, comments on Genesis 18:13 as follows: "God rephrases Sarah's comment to refer to her own advanced age rather than to Abraham's lest he be offended." Similarly, the Talmud states that "one is not obligated to tell the whole truth if it will hurt someone's feelings" (*BT* K'tubbot 16b–17a). The great goal of maintaining peace between spouses, and among people generally, trumps the need to be fully and brutally accurate.

In this vein, the Talmud tells of a debate between the school of Hillel and the school of Shammai regarding the correct way to fulfill the *mitzvah* of dancing before the bride at a wedding. The school of Shammai says that each bride should be described as she truly is, but the school of Hillel teaches that the dancers should chant the same words to each bride, to wit: "What a beautiful and graceful bride is she!" The school of Shammai said to the school of Hillel, "If she is lame or blind, are you going to say that she is beautiful and graceful? The Torah commands us to 'stay away from falsehood' (Exodus 23:7)." The school of Hillel responded with an analogy: if a person spends a lot of money purchasing a non-returnable item then and asks a friend's opinion of the object, what should the friend say (even if the friend thinks the object to be ugly)? The school of Shammai admitted that the friend should say that the object is nice, so as not to make the buyer unhappy. From this we learn that a person should always be sensitive to the feelings of others (*BT* K'tubbot 16b–17a).

The position of the school of Hillel seems to be that a well-meant lie is better than the stark, painful truth—at least some of the time. This teaching of the school of Hillel is accepted as the *halakhah.* From this it would seem that it is permitted to deviate from the truth when unvarnished honesty will hurt another person or destroy his or her self-respect. There are, however, several important points that should be noted. In the analogy of the school of Hillel, it was assumed that since there was no alternative to keeping the object, there was no sense in making the purchaser unhappy by criticizing it. If there had been an alternative action, presumably it would have been more helpful to tell the truth and encourage the friend to return the purchase. In the case of the bride, it would be hurtful both to the bride and the groom to tell the truth. In the case of the bride, as well, there is some element of truth in the statement that the bride is beautiful, for surely every bride is beautiful in the eyes of her groom!

Remarking on the beauty of a bride on her wedding day seems like a simple and kind gesture. But does this principle apply in other contexts as well? In other words, if telling the truth (we are not speaking, of course, of witnesses speaking in court) will harm a peaceful relationship between individuals, may one tell a falsehood? The Talmud says that "one may even stretch the truth for the sake of peace" (*BT* Y'vamot 65b).

Aaron, the brother of Moses and Israel's first High Priest, is described in the Mishnah as "a lover of peace and a pursuer of peace" (*M* Avot 1:12). A midrashic text, in fact, teaches that Aaron would even use gentle untruthfulness to reconcile people who had quarreled. He would go to one party and say how sorry that person's adversary was about the dispute and how eager to make up. Then he would go to the other party and say the same thing. When the two adversaries would meet, they would embrace and kiss each other. (This text is found in *Avot D'rabbi Natan* text A, ch. 12.) The lesson should be clear: if there is a conflict between truth and peace when individuals quarrel, peace comes first—as long as the lie that brings peace does not harm either party . . . or anybody else. A word of caution needs to be added, however. A peace that is based on a lie is destined to be a fragile, unstable peace. One of the antagonists could say to the other, "I'm glad that you admitted that you were wrong," and start the quarrel all over again!

White Lies

The most common types of lies are trivial untruths that are not meant to harm anybody. They are called white lies and are common and widely accepted. Such harmless lies are often meant to protect privacy without hurting other people by telling them to mind their own business.

Rabbi Judah in the name of Samuel tells us that a learned scholar is permitted, if he is not speaking in court under oath, to lie in three areas: in matters of tractate, bed, and hospitality (*BT* Bava M'tzi·a 23b–24a).

The reference to "matters of tractate" is simply a mandate to speak modestly, even if it involves saying something not wholly true. There is a story about the architect Frank Lloyd Wright, who, while testifying as a witness in a court, referred to himself as "the world's greatest living architect." When his wife chided him for speaking so immodestly, he replied, "I had no choice—I was under oath." (This story is retold by Rabbi Joseph Telushkin in his *The Book of Jewish Values* [New York: Harmony, 2000], p. 104.) But he did have a choice, and that is what Rabbi Judah is teaching us in the name of Samuel: when a scholar is asked if he is familiar with a tractate of the Talmud, he may answer untruthfully that he is ignorant of it. This would be done out of modesty and so as not to show off his learning. A small lie is permitted to ensure modesty of speech.

The reference to "matters of bed" will be simpler for moderns to relate to: if asked prying questions about their sex life, spouses are permitted to lie to prying outsiders to protect their privacy. (Of course, this does not apply when the health or well-being of the other party is at stake—for example, if one party's sexual history may put another at risk.)

Finally, matters relating to hospitality have to do with the importance of not abusing a host's kindness. A scholar who has enjoyed gracious hospitality and is asked about it, is permitted to minimize the degree to which the hosts involved behaved solicitously and generously if it seems that an accurate report will lead others to attempt to exploit the host's generosity.

Note well, however, that Samuel was speaking specifically of scholars—that is, people of the finest character who would be expected to be honest in everything and whose word, therefore, will always be taken without question as true (see *SA* Ḥoshen Mishpat 262:21 in this regard as well). Such a scholar may respond with a white lie for the sake of modesty to protect one's private life from gossip or to prevent harm to others. In determining whether Samuel's permission to tell the occasional white lie should extend to non-scholars as well, one must consider the weight one's words carry in the world. In other words, if one feels that one's personal probity is so widely considered to be absolute that one's words, even one's offhand comments, could cause damage to others, then one might attempt to emulate the scholars about whom Samuel was speaking. Otherwise, one should say nothing at all and simply decline to answer questions that are potentially embarrassing or exploitative, or which are simply vulgar and inappropriate.

The expression of polite sentiments in the context of normal day-to-day social intercourse between friends may be considered simply a social amenity devoid of moral import, for these words are not intended to deceive anyone. When an invitation is refused on the grounds of a non-existent prior engagement, when one really could go but simply does not wish to, the white lie is being told merely to protect the other person's feelings. Hurting the feelings of others may never be considered mere collateral damage that comes from speaking honestly. Nor may one lie freely simply to avoid difficult or delicate situations. From the creative tension between those two concepts will come a halakhically justifiable principle of speaking the truth—when the greater good would not be served by telling an unimportant white lie.

"Keep Lies from My Lips"

Telling the truth within Judaism is a complicated affair, requiring a thoughtful individual to weigh values that are often in conflict. The scholar who was permitted to lie in the three situations described above was permitted to do so because scholars have a reputation for integrity and can therefore be trusted to know the difference between self-aggrandizing distortions of the truth and helpful ones. Not being truthful, even for the best of reasons, requires maturity, life experience, and integrity. This is the lesson that the talmudic sage Rav taught his son in the following talmudic anecdote:

> Rav had a very difficult relationship with his wife. If Rav would ask his wife to cook lentil soup, she would cook pea soup. If he requested pea soup, she would cook lentil soup. Ḥiyya, Rav's son, had seen this go on for many years. One day he told his mother that his father wanted lentil soup when he knew that his father wanted pea soup so that she would prepare the kind of soup that his father really wanted. When Ḥiyya brought Rav the kind of soup he wanted, his father was surprised. Rav told his son that he thought his wife was changing for the better. Ḥiyya then told his father that he had lied to his mother, changing the message so that she would prepare the kind of soup that Rav wanted. Rav thanked his son and then told him not to do it again, because it was more important that he not lie (*BT* Y'vamot 63a).

This story about Rav explores several important implications of telling half-truths and lies. Rav teaches his son (and us) that one should not accept and enjoy a benefit that one gained by telling a lie. And he is also teaching us that it is dangerous for a child to learn to lie, even for a good reason—for a child who learns to lie, even to achieve worthwhile ends, will quickly discover that it is easy to lie and will be tempted to lie for selfish reasons as well.

An adult might better understand the circumstances in which modifying the truth and telling well-intentioned lies can sometimes help achieve good ends. Even then, those who are mature and blessed with good judgment must be cautious in resorting to half-truths or, even worse, to outright lies. There is a very human tendency to rationalize selfish gains and transform them into worthwhile purposes. This is why it is important that each of us recite the words of Mar, son of Ravina, three times a day at the conclusion of the Amidah prayer: "My God, keep my tongue from evil and my lips from speaking lies" (*BT* B'rakhot 17a).

Public Appearance and Behavior

GORDON TUCKER

The third chapter of the Book of Genesis contains an etiological tale that accounts for the fact that human society tends to shun public nudity, and this sums up much of the Jewish attitude toward *tz'ni·ut*—that is, "modesty"—in attire. According to this story, the first bit of practical knowledge acquired by Adam and Eve was that their nudity was undignified and inappropriate, and that clothes would be required to make their appearance acceptable. Among the details that are the most striking about this story, however, is the fact that it takes place at a time when there were no other human beings in the world, when Adam and Eve constituted all of human society. Nor is this a mere detail: the lesson it teaches is precisely that, even solely in one another's presence—and also, of course, in the presence of God—they could no longer expose their bodies indiscriminately. The first human beings thus learned almost immediately that they could not allow their bodies to be exposed and available for the sexual arousal of the others who would eventually join them as part of humanity, for they were humans endowed with intrinsic value that was not to be cheapened by tawdriness or vulgarity. In a sense, the story already contains within it a foreshadowing of Immanuel Kant's famous imperative that people must never be treated as means, but always as ends in themselves.

Tz'ni·ut

Rabbi Chaim Weiner, writing for the Va·ad Halakhah of the Rabbinical Assembly of Israel in 1990, put it this way: "*Tz'ni·ut* is among the fundamental values of Judaism. . . . The human body must be respected in life and in death, because of the image of God that is in it. The body must not be treated as an instrument for sexual arousal, and one must dress in such a way that the body will not play such a role. One must not demean the human being's nobility by the exposure of nakedness in public" (*Responsa of the Va·ad Halakhah,* vol. 4, p. 53).

There is little if any argument in Jewish sources about this fundamental idea. And it is especially relevant in contemporary society, which has seen a transformation in standards of public modesty with the so-called sexual revolution of the 1960s. But if there is little disagreement in Jewish sources over the general principle underlying *tz'ni·ut,* that of maintaining and preserving human dignity, the question of how specifically and practically to develop this value into law has created a wide spectrum of approaches that have, in turn, spawned a widely divergent set of behavior patterns in different segments of Jewish society.

The Talmud (at *BT* B'rakhot 24a) discusses what constitutes nakedness in women; the context is a legal discussion of whether men may say the Sh'ma in their presence. (Addressed primarily to men, the Talmud and other classical works tend to focus on what is sexually provocative in women, and to warn male readers about them.) As such, a handbreadth of exposed skin (that would normally be covered up), a bare calf, the hair on a married woman's head, and even a woman's singing voice are said to be examples of "nakedness." Taking this as an absolute list, many very traditional women today wear no clothing that exposes these areas of the body and they do not sing in the presence of men. And it is this approach to *tz'ni·ut* that gives rise to the signature female apparel of ultra-Orthodox communities: long skirts, long sleeves, high necklines, hats or wigs as head coverings for married women, a general avoidance of flashy colors, and a general ban on tight-fitting clothes. (Unmarried women are not enjoined to cover their hair, which may be to enable them to attract men for the purpose of marriage. See the comments of Rabbi Ovadiah Yosef in his *Yabbi·a Omer,* vol. 6, Oraḥ Ḥayyim 15, ed. Jerusalem, 1986, pp. 47–56). The men in these communities, while not answering to the same kind of talmudic exigencies as the women, nevertheless tend to dress according to similar principles: long, loose-fitting clothes in black and white, head coverings indoors and outdoors, and virtually no exposed skin, even on the hottest summer days.

These are highly effective measures, which indeed ensure that members of those communities, both male and female, are far less likely to be judged on the basis of their appearance, the monetary value of their clothes, or their body types. But these practices have several important disadvantages. One obviously has to do with comfort, particularly in the warm months of the year. A second disadvantage is fraught with irony, especially in the case of women: the insistent hiding of even the slightest part of the female body can send the message that the most salient thing about a woman is precisely her sexuality! Surely there ought to be a way to be faithful to the fundamental principle of *tz'ni·ut* that Judaism preaches without creating unnecessary inconvenience or discomfort, and without an obsessive focus on the very sexuality that ought to be downplayed in public.

There is a third disadvantage to the ultra-Orthodox approach, and that has to do with the ways in which their customs of dress and appearance tend to segregate their members from the larger society and restrict—or even make impossible—participation in some of the normal practices of the culture in which we live. It goes without saying that the very traditional do not consider this a disadvantage; it is precisely their intent to segregate themselves from secular culture that is considered essential in such communities—lest contact with those influences tempt them to stray from the norms of Jewish behavior.

How should modern, non-ultra-Orthodox Jews relate to these traditions regarding modesty? On the one hand, these traditions emphasize that the worth of people, and of women in particular, should never be gauged solely in terms of their sexual attractiveness. On the other hand, surely it must be possible to attain that noble goal without requiring total, or almost total, segregation from secular society. And it is also worth noting that these traditions are based on talmudic assumptions regarding a world in which women were rarely expected to appear in the public domain. But more modern Jewish communities do not view the ambient culture of North America (even with all its negative aspects) with the same kind of alarm. Engaging more fully with society is considered by moderns to be an opportunity for cultural enrichment, for economic advancement, and even for spiritual growth. How can such Jews affirm the values that lie at the heart of the *tz'ni·ut* laws without disengaging totally from the world around them?

Rabbi Weiner makes this point at the outset of the responsum cited earlier. (He refers, because of the particular question he is answering, only to traditional restrictions on women—but his argument may be easily extrapolated to address modesty issues for both sexes.) Rabbi Weiner writes:

> Defining norms for dressing is a complicated matter, which needs to take into account the cultural and social context, as well as the intent of the actors and the sensitivities of those in the environs. One should not fix universal rules that apply to all places and all situations. We shall see in this responsum that the multitude of approaches and principles found among Jewish legal authorities reflects an effort to make the value of *tz'ni·ut* correspond to changing circumstances and contexts. There is an effort to integrate the need to preserve *tz'ni·ut* with the need to allow for a normal social life. In our community it is certainly not possible or desirable to sequester women behind closed doors, and it is thus necessary to counsel ways to honor the principle of *tz'ni·ut* while not impairing the integration of modern women into society.

Circumstances and contexts surely differ from one society to another. In a society in which it is customary for men and women to wear short pants to ballgames and swimsuits at the beach, and to uncover their hair in public, and in which decent women of unchallengeable moral bearing expose their arms and wear dresses or blouses with lower than necessary necklines and skirts that end at or above the knee, doing so cannot be reasonably understood to be inappropriately sexually provocative or demeaning to the wearer. It may depend on context and intent, as even very stringently Orthodox authorities have acknowledged when asked about the unavoidable instances of bodily contact that occur on crowded rush-hour subway trains (see Rabbi Moshe Feinstein, *Igg'rot Mosheh,* Even Ha-eizer 2:14, ed. New York, 1964, pp. 326–328). This does not vitiate the principle of *tz'ni·ut.* On the contrary, it requires modern Jews to consider the issue even more deeply. While the constantly shifting context of the larger society's mores allows for no universal guidelines of dress and behavior, automatic conformity to a single standard must yield to a more mature understanding of the goals of *tz'ni·ut,* and how to apply this value rationally and effectively in the society in which we live. We may accept that it is reasonable to go to the beach, for example, but that does not mean that even the scantiest swimsuits—those that are designed clearly (and, in some cases, solely) to attract attention to the body of the individual wearing it—are appropriate or should be considered licit attire. The same is true of pants that are so tight that, as the old joke goes, they announce the male wearer's religion. Or the blouse with a radically plunging neckline, whose only purpose is to draw attention to a woman's cleavage. It is possible, without unnecessarily restricting the fashion options available to moderns, to condemn certain kinds of outfits as inconsonant with the dignity of human beings whom we hold to be created in the divine image. To be sure, doing so requires subjective judgment of intent, of context, and of sensitivities. But making such judgments is at the heart of what it means to observe and truly uphold the principle of *tz'ni·ut*.

Regarding the propriety of public expressions of affection, one must make similar judgments. Holding hands, dancing, hugging, and casual kissing are well accepted expressions of affection in the public sphere today, and the fact that they are carried out in public does not automatically make them inappropriate or forbidden. More intense expressions of affection, however—and especially those that suggest imminent sexual activity—clearly violate the human dignity of the individuals involved by making public something that, by its very nature, deserves to be a private matter. Sexual activity is highly esteemed in Jewish tradition for several reasons, but none of them justifies putting physical intimacy on display in a context wholly redolent of exhibitionism. How and where will the line between acceptable and lewd be defined? Imprecisely, to be sure. But the existence of gray areas does not mean that there aren't black and white ones, and the values set forth above may surely serve as useful guidelines.

What has been said thus far applies to the street, to the marketplace, to the workplace, and to the home. When it comes to especially sacred settings, however, more stringent standards of dress and displays of affection may reasonably be applied. It is commonplace, for example, for visitors to encounter restrictions on what they may wear when entering the houses of worship of virtually all religions. That should not be surprising—it was, after all, from God's presence that Adam and Eve felt obliged to hide in the story that underlies all these laws. In particular, Deuteronomy 23:10–15 codifies as law the implication of the narrative in Genesis: unseemly appearance or behavior in a place especially associated with God's presence can have the effect of distancing God's presence from that place and from the people there. (While the passage in Deuteronomy specifically discusses God's presence within a military camp, the same reasoning should certainly apply to synagogues and other places of worship.) Nor is this merely a theoretical or metaphorical argument. Anyone who has ever tried to concentrate on God's word when someone "dressed to kill" has just opened the Ark during a synagogue service will understand the enduring import of the law set forth in Deuteronomy.

Thoughtful reflection on the sanctity of the synagogue, then, should lead directly to higher standards of modesty for men and women in that place. Moreover, sloppiness (e.g., torn or dirty clothes) should be judged unseemly in the synagogue, along with nearly all inscriptions on clothing. (Such inscriptions inevitably distract attention from the atmosphere of worship and study, and this will be the case even if such inscriptions are not obscene.) Also, appropriate dress is not merely the kind of costuming that does not detract from the holy ambience of the sanctuary, but also the kind that actively adds to it. And this is even more acutely the case at certain times of the week, month, or year. There is, for example, a long-standing and highly valuable tradition of Shabbat clothing, attire that by its nature matches the heightened aura of sanctity that comes with the onset of the Shabbat or any of the festivals of the Jewish year (*SA* Oraḥ Ḥayyim 262:2–3). Particularly in the synagogue, dressing to a higher standard of neatness and elegance on holy days contributes to the atmosphere of sanctity. Again, all this needs to be adjudicated in terms of local mores; there are no universal rules. What the presence of God evokes, for example, will always be very much dependent on the images of God that we have before us. But the common inscription over many synagogue Arks—"Know before whom you stand"—can serve each individual and community as the yardstick against which tentative judgments of propriety may be measured.

Covering and Uncovering the Head in Synagogue, at Home, and in the Street

There are few practices that immediately signal a Jewish religious setting as readily as the covering of the head with a *kippah* (a skullcap, also commonly called by its Yiddish name, *yarmulke*). This practice is universal in Conservative synagogues among men, and is also increasingly common among women. Indeed, the universality of the rule for men is one of the ways by which Conservative synagogues may be distinguished from nearly all Reform congregations, in which many (but certainly not all) men wear *kippot.*

While the practice of covering the head during worship is long-standing, the basis of that practice in Jewish law will strike most as unexpectedly weak indeed. Rabbi Ovadiah Yosef, in the responsum cited earlier (*Yabbi·a Omer,* part 6, Oraḥ Ḥayyim 15) that addresses the propriety of single women praying and studying Torah with uncovered heads (since they do not normally cover their heads at all), had to acknowledge the tenuousness of the legal basis for covering the head in the first place. Among the authorities that he quotes is Rabbi Elijah Kramer of Vilna (1720–1797), called the Vilna Gaon, who wrote in his commentary to *SA* Oraḥ Ḥayyim 8:2 that there are very strong reasons to conclude that the covering of the head either by men or women, even during the recitation of prayers including God's name, is a custom of the especially pious and, as such, has good moral value without entailing any actual obligation: "According to the law, one may enter the synagogue and pray without covering the head . . . and as for that which is stated in Tractate Sof'rim [one of the so-called "minor tractates" from the post-talmudic era], that some say it is forbidden to say God's name [i.e., "Adonai"] with an uncovered head, that too is a trait of piety. . . . In other words, there is no prohibition on the uncovered head at all. It is just that in the presence of great sages, or during prayer, it is proper to do so as a good moral practice."

Thus, the wearing of a *kippah* in synagogue (or when praying elsewhere) is a custom, not a law. On the other hand, the practice is so well entrenched as to be virtually definitive of both Orthodox and Conservative synagogues. For that reason, it can be considered a rule of Jewish practice that all must observe in those settings; it is not to be deemed optional.

All this applies to men. As for women covering their heads in the synagogue, the custom is far less established. In Orthodox synagogues, as noted in the previous section, it is the general practice for married women to cover their hair (as they generally do outside the synagogue as well) and for unmarried women not to. (In his responsum cited above, Ovadiah Yosef accepts the latter state of affairs somewhat reluctantly.) In Conservative synagogues, however, the practice is much more mixed. Married women, who generally do not cover their hair in public, may or may not choose to cover their heads in the synagogue. Those who do, however, usually do so out of a sense of piety in a sacred place, or else out of a desire to promote equality of practice with men. And since there is little difference in Conservative circles between married and unmarried women regarding head covering, such options are equally available to unmarried women. Given the absence of a legal obligation and taking into account what has already been said on the subject of *tz'ni·ut,* all these practices may be considered legitimate. There may be some value in equalizing the practices of men and women, but since the *kippah* is still seen by many women as male attire, such equalization, if it is to come, will require an extended period of transition.

What has been said of the synagogue applies equally to the home. When reciting one's prayers or saying a blessing at home, one's synagogue practices regarding head covering should prevail. Moreover, since eating a meal requires the recitation of blessings before and after, it is convenient—and regular in our day—to keep the head covered throughout the meal. (The alternative—uncovering the head after the initial blessings, then covering it again for the Grace after Meals—was common once, but has fallen almost entirely into desuetude.) Doing so also tends to remind the wearer that the nourishment of food is a gift from God, and that a certain reverence for the Creator is appropriate when enjoying that gift even outside the context of liturgical expression. For similar reasons, it is also appropriate to cover the head when studying sacred literature, such as the Bible, the Talmud, or works of *halakhah*.

As for covering the head throughout the day generally, it is acknowledged by even the strictest of legal authorities that there is no identifiable halakhic obligation to do so. Indeed, if there is no absolute obligation to cover the head during prayer, how could there be a requirement to do so at other times? One searches in vain in biblical and talmudic literature for even offhand references to Jews making a point of covering their heads, or being chastised for not doing so. The most one finds is a cultural expectation that people of high social or scholarly standing should wear a distinctive head covering; occasionally this expectation is extended to include those standing in their presence. But it is quite clear that going through daily routines of work, play, secular study, exercise, and so on with the head uncovered violates no Jewish norm whatsoever. One important point should be noted, however: if in the course of one's day one finds oneself obligated to recite a liturgical blessing or a prayer and no head covering is available, the obligation to say the blessing or prayer is not in any way cancelled. One should recite the blessing or prayer in any case, since it is now well established that it is halakhically permissible to pray without wearing a *kippah*.

Finally, the wearing of a *kippah* has, at least in many settings, another significant function as well, and that is to establish and underscore the religious identity of the wearer. This is obviously true in the Diaspora, where the *kippah* serves to make wearers acutely aware of their Jewish identity, but it is also true in Israel, where the *kippah* marks one as a member of the religious, rather than secular, sector of society. This presents another issue connected with the *kippah* for Conservative Jews to consider. Identifying as a Jew, and being reminded of that identity, is of great value in the modern world, and this is especially so for those who live in cultures that seek to homogenize the differences among groups. On the other hand, integration into modern society, and avoiding separations that are not mandated by *halakhah,* is considered by most to be a worthy and desirable goal as well. There will thus be a range of practice within the Conservative community, based on the degree to which these competing values are rated against each other. Informed Conservative Jews must grapple with the competing pulls of identity and integration and come to a conclusion that is reflective of their own well considered and halakhically responsive personal philosophy.

Shaving

Although there is no recorded prohibition of shaving the hair off most parts of the body, Leviticus 19:27 forbids Israelite men to "destroy the side-growth" of their beards. Maimonides and others believed that this law was intended as a way of separating Israelites from pagan worship: "It was the practice of pagan priests to destroy their beards, and thus the Torah forbade destroying the beard" (*MT* Hilkhot Avodat Kokhavim 12:7). It seems reasonable to assume that creating a different appearance for Israelites would prevent them from too easily integrating into the pagan population around them and from adopting their forbidden pagan practices. And, indeed, growing a beard serves precisely that function in cultures in which beards are generally cut or shaven off. (Decrees in recent years by Muslim fundamentalists in Afghanistan and elsewhere bear this out.)

Just what "destroying the side-growth" of the beard actually forbids, however, has never been clearly established. Most likely, it refers simply to some primitive method of shaving. By rabbinic times, however, both the technology of shaving and its cultural mores had changed dramatically. Shaving, or at least trimming the beard closely, was considered to be a socially acceptable option for personal grooming, and was apparently no longer associated with idolatry. The Talmud (at *BT* Mo·eid Katan 13b–14a) assumes that shaving prior to the onset of a festival is a good thing, and thus that forbidding it during the intermediate days of Passover or Sukkot would be an added inducement to attend to one's personal grooming before the holiday actually begins (see commentary of Rashi to *BT* Mo·eid Katan 14a, *s.v. hakhi garsinan*). By the same token, mourners were forbidden to shave during the thirty-day mourning period called *sh'loshim,* and that prohibition clearly reflects the cultural assessment that a substantial beard, or at least an untrimmed one, symbolizes an aberrational state. Indeed, the *halakhah* incorporates this assumption of aberration when it prescribes that, following the death of a parent, the prohibition on shaving should proceed even beyond the *sh'loshim* period, but not longer than the point at which "one's friends scold him" for continuing to appear in public looking disheveled and unkempt (*SA* Yoreh Dei·ah 390:4).

But the Torah's prohibition of destroying the side-growth had to be taken into account as well. "Destroying" was understood to refer specifically to shaving down to the skin with a knife blade. "Side-growth" was understood to refer specifically to five distinct points on the face, although the exact location of these was a subject of some dispute (see Maimonides' text cited above). While removing the hair from other parts of the face (and by other methods) was permitted, this almost certainly did not result in a clean-shaven look. Thus, for reasons different from those that motivated the prohibition in Leviticus, "clean-shaven" took on a negative connotation in traditional Jewish circles because it implied that an individual had violated the biblical restriction on shaving with a blade.

Modern society displays a great deal of tolerance with respect to personal grooming practices. To be sure, there are certain settings, most notably the armed forces of most Western countries, in which beards are forbidden. But, generally speaking, neither growing a beard nor shaving it off is considered a profound statement of identity, and certainly neither suggests a personal association with any specific kind of worship, pagan or otherwise. And since there are very good methods today of getting a clean shave without the use of a blade, there is no reason not to appear in public as one wishes, either clean-shaven or barbate.

Cross-Dressing

Deuteronomy 22:5 decrees that "a woman must not put on man's apparel, nor shall a man wear woman's clothing; for whoever does these things is abhorrent to the Eternal your God." Once again, we are not given a clear explanation of why this practice is so inherently abhorrent. One opinion, expressed in the Talmud at *BT* Nazir 59a, suggests that the reason is simple: cross-dressers might be able to join gatherings of the opposite sex, thus creating opportunities for inappropriate behavior. According to this view, then, it is specifically the resultant forbidden behavior that is abhorrent, not the act of cross-dressing itself. There are, however, other views. One, stated in that same passage in the Talmud, understands transvestitism to be inherently forbidden even if the cross-dresser remains easily identifiable as a member of his or her own gender. Thus, it is not fully clear from the earliest sources whether the prohibition of cross-dressing is a scriptural attempt to avoid situations in which individuals will mix and experience inappropriate intimacy with members of the opposite sex, or whether it is forbidden because cross-dressing, regardless of circumstance, constitutes perverse behavior on its own. The latter view was accepted by both Maimonides and Joseph Karo (respectively, in the *Mishneh Torah* at *MT* Hilkhot Avodat Kokhavim 12:10 and in the *Shulḥan Arukh* at *SA* Yoreh Dei·ah 182:5).

Whatever the reason for the prohibition, however, the codifiers make it clear that the definition of gender-specific apparel is relative to the society in which one lives. Clearly, a man wearing a skirt is a very different act in traditional parts of Scotland from what it would be in Westchester County, New

York! Moreover, the Talmud itself (at *BT* N'darim 49b) recognizes that there are such things as "unisex" garments, for it describes how Rabbi Judah's wife made a woolen garment that served them both: she wore it to the marketplace and he wore it to the synagogue. Thus it is clear that, to the extent that it is common and accepted for women to wear pants or for men to carry handbags, there can be no objection raised by the Torah's decree, and this is the case regardless of whether the apparel or accessory in question is or is not clearly made (i.e., in style or in color) for the gender of the person using it, or if the item of apparel or the accessory in question is truly "unisex" in nature.

Again, as strict a decisor as Ovadiah Yosef not only reports this argument, but accepts it as *halakhah* (*Yabbi·a Omer,* part 6, Yoreh Dei·ah 14, ed. Jerusalem, 1986, pp. 189–194). And he also rules there that no violation occurs even when a garment associated with the opposite sex is worn, as long as it is being worn specifically for the purpose of greater comfort—for example, to cope with extremely warm or cold temperatures.)

Deuteronomy thus ought to be understood to prohibit cross-dressing specifically in the case of one who chooses to wear garments that are explicitly understood by society as "belonging" to the opposite sex. When that happens, cross-dressing blurs the lines of sexual distinction that both general society and Judaism endorse as reasonable and morally useful. The anthropological approach to biblical distinctions and taboos popularized by Mary Douglas would suggest that this "erasing" of fundamental distinctions was perhaps what triggered the Torah's prohibition in the first place. As in the case of *tz'ni·ut,* however, the issue should be understood by modern Jews as one of preserving the dignity of the human being by noting that, among all the other things that make us unique, we are also created with distinct sexual identities.

There are also people who cross-dress not specifically as a fashion statement or as a means of facilitating entry into the domain of the opposite sex, but out of an obsessive need to do so. This kind of obsessive-compulsive cross-dressing should be viewed as a disorder rather than as a sin and should be treated by mental health professionals.

Piercing the Ear and Other Body Parts

Halakhic objections to having one's ears pierced can come from one of two directions: one could either maintain that it is forbidden to injure the human body (even one's own body, an injunction that appears in the Mishnah at *M* Bava Kamma 8:6), or one could argue that it is forbidden to alter the body in a way that is not medically required. (That we do not own our bodies is clearly implied in *M* Bava Kamma 8:7. Alteration of the body for medical purposes is understood to be explicitly authorized by Exodus 21:19.) There is, of course, ample evidence in the biblical narrative that women pierced their ears and noses for the purpose of wearing rings in them. (God is metaphorically said to have put both nose rings and earrings on the personified Israel at Ezekiel 16:12.) But since narrative does not in and of itself establish legal precedent, it was still deemed necessary to speak to both avenues of potential halakhic protest.

Two responsa on the subject are of particular significance. One is, again, by Rabbi Ovadiah Yosef (*Yabbi·a Omer,* part 8, Ḥoshen Mishpat 12, ed. Jerusalem, 1995, pp. 494–496) and the other by Rabbi Moshe Feinstein (*Igg'rot Mosheh,* Ḥoshen Mishpat 2:66, ed. New York, 1985, pp. 289–292). Both these responsa address the more serious issue of whether a woman (even a married woman, who is thus not concerned with marriageability) may undergo plastic surgery, and its attendant anesthesia, in order to improve her appearance. Both these authorities note that injury requires both malice and an intent to hurt or humiliate another individual and so determine that surgery undertaken to improve one's appearance, even if it is not medically necessary, is halakhically permitted. At the end of his responsum on the subject, Rabbi Ovadiah Yosef adds the following words: "Moreover, go see what our people do, for they are accustomed to pierce women's earlobes so that they may adorn themselves with earrings and no one worries about a prohibition on injuring oneself or another, since it is for their good and for their good looks." In other words, piercing the ears of another is not to be considered tantamount to injuring that person. Furthermore, improving one's looks is considered a legitimate extension of the medical exception that allows us to alter our bodies for rational reasons.

Thus, both narrative and law are in agreement that the piercing of the earlobe in order to conform to the normal dictates of fashion or simply to make oneself attractive is permitted. Given the general permission to undergo plastic surgery for reasons that are not medically indicated, it seems reasonable also to maintain that piercing other body parts would also not be prohibited, as long as such piercings conform to generally accepted standards of what constitutes attractive appearance and is done specifically for that purpose.

In today's milieu (and especially in the social settings in which Conservative Jews tend to live and congregate), the piercing of ears for both men and women would thus be permitted, as would piercing a range of other body parts, such as the nose and the navel. Convention enters directly into the equation yet again. But two important qualifications should be noted:

1. Social conventions sometimes change rather quickly, and while the aesthetic of ear piercing has been around for a long time, other piercing practices

have not. Given the centrality of the Jewish principle that our bodies are held in trust, and that altering our bodies is permitted only for pressing medical or rational cosmetic purposes, a decision to pierce the body in a way that is not easily reversible should not be made on a whim or for faddish reasons. To the contrary: the individual considering piercing any visible body part other than his or her ear should feel totally secure beforehand that doing so will clearly add to his or her attractiveness and that it is already considered a normal social convention.

2. Piercing the sexual organs, or other body parts normally concealed from public display, should not be permitted. Since the permission to pierce is predicated on increasing a person's physical attractiveness, it must by definition be restricted to those body parts that will legitimately be seen in public. Especially in the case of the sexual organs, this is a violation of the principle of *tz'ni·ut* and suggests a desire to call attention to and/or publicly or privately to display those parts in a lewd way that is contrary to the standards of decency discussed above.

Tattooing

Although the Torah states a simple prohibition with respect to tattooing the body ("You shall not . . . incise any marks on yourselves," Leviticus 19:28), there was speculation as early as in talmudic times about what the contextual meaning of the prohibition actually was. The second-century sage Rabbi Shimon bar Yoḥai, for example, believed that the Torah meant only to prohibit incising the name of a pagan deity on one's body (*M* Makkot 3:6). And Maimonides, writing a millennium later, seems to have held a similar view of the context of the biblical prohibition (*MT* Hilkhot Avodat Kokhavim 12:11). All the more significant, then, is the fact that there has been unanimity in all subsequent legal codes (including that of Maimonides himself) that the prohibition on tattooing is general and independent of context. When such things occur in the legal literature, it is not possible to critique the rulings in question on the grounds that they are based on mistaken views of original contexts. And so, despite the fact that tattooing has become quite fashionable in recent years (including among Jews, and especially, and perhaps surprisingly, in secular Israeli society), it cannot be reconciled with a commitment to live according to traditional Jewish norms. Independent of its original context, though, how could the mandate of those traditional norms be understood today? Perhaps it can best be understood in our time as a commitment to be as careful as possible to preserve the integrity of the body with which each of us is gifted by

God (except when that integrity is breached for medical reasons, or for minimal or non-permanent cosmetic alterations, such as ear piercings). This will be, for many, sufficient reason for maintaining the age-old prohibition of tattooing, and for finding other avenues for self-expression. It should be noted, however, that having tattoos on one's body does not entail any enduring loss of standing in the Jewish community (despite a mysteriously persistent, though completely mistaken, notion that it somehow precludes burial in a Jewish cemetery).

The halakhic issues attached to tattooing and body piercing are discussed in detail in a responsum by Rabbi Alan Lucas and published by the Rabbinical Assembly in *CJLS Responsa 1991–2000,* pp. 115–120.

Profane and Vulgar Language

Words and language in general are highly esteemed in Jewish tradition. It was with words, after all, that God created the world. The Mishnah at *M* Avot 5:1 underscores this in pointing out that the entire world was created with ten distinct divine fiats. The message of the Mishnah is clear: words create worlds. And it follows that the kind of words that we use determines the kind of world that we create for ourselves and for those around us.

Jewish worship begins each morning in a curious but significant way. The first of the early morning blessings begins with the word *barukh* ("blessed" or "praised"), and inaugurates a series of fifteen blessings that begin the same way. The second part of the service, P'sukei D'zimra, begins with the same word, *barukh,* repeated another eleven times in quick succession. The Sh'ma section begins with *bar'khu* ("bless"), and the Amidah begins with *barukh,* as does the benedictory formula that concludes all nineteen of its blessings. The message is unmistakable. We are being conditioned to have blessings, and not curses, on our tongues as we begin each day. Pronouncing words of blessing will more likely create a world of blessing, whereas pronouncing curses will create an accursed milieu.

There are a handful of prohibitions on speech that are found in the Torah. We may not blaspheme (Exodus 22:27). We may not invoke the name of God in a false oath (Exodus 20:7 and Deuteronomy 5:11). We are not permitted to lie (Exodus 23:7). We may neither slander others nor gossip about them (Leviticus 19:16). The Talmud expands on all these in great detail, but amazingly we find no explicit prohibition of vulgar or obscene speech. Or perhaps it should not be that surprising that the Talmud does not go into detail about what constitutes vulgar speech, for what counts as obscene is mostly dependent on context and social custom.

A further complication arises from the fact that there are times when vulgarity may be temporarily necessary. The lesson of Rabbi Aibu preserved at *B'reishit Rabbah* 70:18 charmingly informs us that Jacob's rather vulgar way of expressing his desire to marry Rachel recorded at Genesis 29:21 was a function of his concern that he be sexually potent in order to have children quickly. And the Talmud (at *BT* M'gillah 25b) catalogues for us a number of places in the Bible where vulgar and even obscene language is used to make a point forcefully. Tellingly, however, the text also rules that those words must be written in the text, but are to be replaced by euphemistic substitutes when read aloud in public, because—especially in the synagogue—it would be unseemly to hear them spoken aloud.

All this being the case, we can say simply that a Jew should be expected to avoid obscene language, called *nibbul peh* in the sources (e.g., at *Va-yikra Rabbah* 24:7), as much as possible, because it befouls the God-given gift of speech and increases vulgarity in the world. As is the case with matters of *tz'ni·ut* in general, mature and insightful consideration must be brought to bear to locate the dividing line between vivid and vulgar, and between forceful and foul.

Pornography

Regarding the use of pornographic materials—texts, photographs, material art forms, videos, etc. that are sexually stimulating but are without any artistic or other substantial purpose—the matter raised in our context is very different from the same matter raised in, say, the American legal context. In the latter, the focus is primarily, and properly, on the question of whether the secular state has a legitimate interest in, and therefore a just cause for, restricting the production and consumption of verbal and graphic materials that offend many individuals (and perhaps the general public taste as well), but that are essentially victimless forms of expression entitled to protection. Those who see the First Amendment as the determinative factor deny that the state has any such just cause in general (though most make exceptions in the case of pornography involving, or aimed at, children). But in the context of the living of a Jewish life, First Amendment issues recede into the background, and other considerations come to the fore. Catharine MacKinnon, and others as well, have famously argued that women (and sometimes other vulnerable groups) are categorically harmed by pornography, which is thus not victimless and is more act-like than speech-like.

These arguments have naturally been controversial and, to many, are fatally suspect in the secular constitutional context. But the concerns behind them are potentially relevant in a Jewish values calculus, since the very possibility that a certain form of expression objectifies a whole class of people as instruments for sexual gratification may run afoul of some central principles of Jewish ethics. Could it be acceptable for a person to enjoy whatever pleasurable fantasies and stimulations are produced by pornography against the backdrop of the possibility that contributing to the marketing of such materials might harm innocent victims? We are charged by the Torah with refraining from "standing idly by the blood of another" (Leviticus 19:16), and that has always been understood as a general injunction against complacent acquiescence in (and certainly against pleasurable gain at the expense of) another person's oppression. And even if one were to argue (as some in the field do) that the "MacKinnon concerns" about promoting violence against women are not supported by the preponderance of the evidence, there are other Jewish considerations as well. In the case of a married person using pornography for sexual fantasizing, there may well be deep disappointment and hurt on the part of the spouse when he or she discovers the behavior. How would one justify this mode of pleasurable stimulation in the presence of the talmudic injunction recorded at *BT* Y'vamot 62b to "love a spouse as one loves one's own body and to honor a spouse more than one honors one's own body"?

Finally, "refinement" is another core principle of Jewish ethical living. "The *mitzvot* were given in order to refine human beings," teaches an oft-quoted text at *B'reishit Rabbah* 44:1. And while defining "refinement" is clearly a highly subjective task, few would seriously maintain that the depictions of human bodies and of sexual acts typical of pornography fit into any such definition. Two of the towering figures of medieval Jewish thought, Maimonides and Moses Naḥmanides, each in separate ways, made their thoughts known on this. Maimonides, following an Aristotelian path, insisted that ethical living was not first and foremost about the acts that one does or refrains from, but is rather about the character traits and tendencies that one cultivates. In other words, patterns of thought may be impossible to police, and quite dangerous for others to try to control, but they are nonetheless centrally relevant to a virtuous life, and thus to be worked on by each individual. And Naḥmanides, in his oft-quoted commentary on Leviticus 19:2, virtually refers to our subject here when he states that although certain forms of sexual expression may violate no rules of behavior, they may be so unrefined as to contradict the Torah's oft-repeated exhortation to sanctify ourselves.

This is not to say that exceptions to this approach cannot exist (apart from the already implied "artistic value" exceptions, discussed below—which, in any event, are not really cases of pornography principally for sexual stimulation). One comment about Jacob's apparent use (in Genesis 29:21) of vulgar sexual language when anticipating consummating his marriage, for example, has it that he was engaged in the legitimate attempt to stimulate his sexual drive for the laudable purpose of producing children. This would have a clear parallel today in approving of the use of pornographic materials to stimulate a sexual emission when pursuing a course of artificial insemination in order to create a family. Nonetheless, as a general principle and for all of these reasons, and also despite the fact that it would be unwise to demand or seek the outlawing of pornography in secular society, the use of pornography by people seeking to live ethical Jewish lives is thoroughly inappropriate.

Profanity, Nudity, and Violence in the Artistic Setting

Art forms present special complications and possible exceptions to many of the guidelines that have been set forth above.

As noted in the previous section, there are times when obscenities may be necessary in order to portray a state of affairs accurately, whether it is a quote in a documentary or a storyline in a novel. To take an extreme example, the horrors of the Shoah could never be conveyed adequately in either books or museums without violating some of the normal canons of dignified expression. To learn about the realities of the world, we must be exposed to them—and that is precisely the function art plays in the cultural life of the individual and of society itself. Indeed, certain stories that derive directly from the Bible are omitted in religious schools because they are not deemed suitable for young eyes and ears. But those omitted things—stories of rape, murder, seduction, and betrayal—possess what American law calls "redeeming social value" and also possess overriding, and wholly redeeming, religious value for adults engaged in Jewish study. To omit them because they concern vulgar or obscene behavior would be to miss the point entirely.

Just as often, however, vulgarity in art has little or no educational justification. The profanity and/or violence depicted may then strike one as gratuitous. Americans generally understand that the law in a pluralistic society, except in the most egregious of cases, cannot take it upon itself to make such distinctions and that gray areas are to be given the benefit of the doubt. But in crafting guidelines for the observant Jew who lives in the modern world, we are not bound by First Amendment issues. Rather, we once again must fall back on the need to make a reasoned judgment as to whether the nudity, vulgarity, or violence portrayed on the stage, on the screen, in the pages of a novel, or on the artist's canvas—and the attendant indignity done to God's image by such depictions—are reasonably outweighed by the educational and moral value of the presentation. The murders in Hamlet, for example, are an easy case. The explicit sexual activity in exploitative pornographic films is also easy to judge. But there will always be a large middle ground that cannot be ruled in or out *a priori,* but must be weighed according to the principles that have been developed throughout this chapter. And there would seem to be no essential difference between answering that question for those viewing the performance or for those performing in it. Art is not reality, but it can color our view of reality and even change reality. Whether a specific act of artistic expression will glorify and encourage illegal and immoral acts or depict them in ways that will prompt a reasonable person to ponder the nature of the society is the pivotal question in evaluating the worth of such artistry.

Charitable Giving

ELLIOT N. DORFF

Civilized societies have confronted poverty for millennia, but in very different ways. Some have seen the poor as criminals worthy of imprisonment in "debtors' prisons"once they fail to pay their debts; others have maintained that the poor are merely lazy and therefore deserving of no special treatment by others. Jews, in contrast, have developed an ideology and a code of law and ethics affirming that it is an obligation of both the individual and the community to care for the poor and, if possible, to help them earn a living. Nor does the tradition view the poor themselves as mere passive recipients of others' largesse: they too have duties incumbent upon them. Additionally, Jewish law requires that Jews provide for communal needs by building and maintaining synagogues, schools, and healthcare institutions of various sorts.

Tz'dakah

One concept fundamental to the matrix of laws and traditions relating to *tz'dakah* concerns the nature of the relationship between the community and the individual. Americans, and the citizens of Western republics in general, are used to voluntary communities that people can join or leave at will. Thus one can decide to join a club or synagogue, and one can just as easily decide to leave it. Americans who have not committed a felony can even give up their American citizenship at will. That is because the United States, like most Western countries, is based on Enlightenment philosophy, which sees each person, as the Declaration of Independence asserts, as an individual possessed of certain inalienable civil rights.

In contrast, although Judaism affirms that we are all unique individuals created in the image of God, it also asserts that we are fundamentally and inextricably part of a community. Furthermore, when we Jews stood at Sinai as a community, we did not receive rights at all, but rather 613 obligations. In fact, Jews who convert to another religion become apostates (*m'shummadim*), thus losing many of the privileges of being Jewish. (For example, apostates are excommunicated, such that it is forbidden even to talk to them, let alone do business with them [*MT* Hilkhot Avodat Kokhavim 2:5 and 9:17–18]; they are not eligible for receiving charity from the Jewish community [*SA* Yoreh Dei·ah 251:1–2] or serving as witnesses [*MT* Hilkhot Eidut 11:10]; they are not buried as Jews in a Jewish cemetery [*M* Sanhedrin 6:5 and *SA* Yoreh Dei·ah 345:5]; they cannot immediately become Israeli citizens as Jews under the Law of Return [cf. the Brother Daniel case, High Court Case 72/62, *Piskei Din* 16:2428–55].) Yet they are still burdened with all the responsibilities of Jewish law! That is an important expression of the organic nature of the Jewish community: just as your foot cannot decide to leave your body, so too individual Jews do not have the ability to abandon their identity as Jews, for "a Jew, even if he or she sins, is still a Jew" (*BT* Sanhedrin 44a; see also Naḥmanides' commentary on Deuteronomy 29:14). This Jewish understanding of community, in which our membership and our obligations to each other are both inescapable, is thus a much thicker sense of community than Americans and other Westerners are used to.

One corollary of this thick view of community is that Jewish tradition does not see contributions to its welfare as mere charity (that English word derives from the Latin for "love") or philanthropy (which derives from the Greek for "love of humanity"), but rather as *tz'dakah,* literally "acts of justice." That is, donating to the poor and to other social needs is not a supererogatory act of especially generous people, but rather an expected act of each and every Jew and of every Jewish community. Maimonides went so far as to say, "We have never seen nor heard of an Israelite community that does not have a charity fund" (*MT* Hilkhot Matt'not Aniyyim 9:3).

Furthermore, *tz'dakah* is demanded of us not only because we are all part of a thick community that can legitimately make demands on its members, but also because all our assets ultimately belong to God (Leviticus 25:23;

Deuteronomy 10:14; *M* Avot 3:8; *BT* K'tubbot 67b). Indeed, the ancient rabbis saw refusal to assist the poor as outright idolatry precisely because such behavior demonstrates that the person does not recognize God's sovereignty and ownership of the world (*T* Pei·ah 4:20).

In addition to these two general concepts that serve as the foundation for all acts of *tz'dakah,* support of the poor is also motivated by a series of other Jewish concepts and values, which I have described in detail in two books: *To Do the Right and the Good: A Jewish Approach to Modern Social Ethics* (Philadelphia: The Jewish Publication Society, 2002; ch. 6) and *The Way Into Tikkun Olam (Fixing the World)* (Woodstock, VT: Jewish Lights Publishing, 2005; chaps. 2 and 5). Among these are the concept of *pikku·aḥ nefesh* (saving or guarding human life), compassion, God's commandment to donate to the poor, the dignity of human beings created in God's image, membership in God's covenanted people, and our aspirations for holiness.

The Duty to Give

The Torah, presuming a primarily agricultural economy, specifies a number of gifts to the poor that a landowner must provide: leaving for the poor the corners of the fields (*pei·ah,* as described at Leviticus 19:9 and 23:22), sheaves or fruit forgotten while harvesting (*shikh'ḥah,* as described at Deuteronomy 24:19), the stalks that by chance fall aside from the edge of the farmer's sickle (*leket,* as described at Leviticus 19:9 and 23:22 and illustrated in the Book of Ruth), grapes separated from their clusters (*peret,* as described at Leviticus 19:10), and defective clusters of grapes or olives (*ol'lot,* as described at Deuteronomy 24:21–22). During the sabbatical year, when fields were to lie fallow, the poor had first rights to the sabbatical produce (Exodus 23:11, but see Leviticus 25:6–7, where it is the owners of land together with their slaves and hired workers who are entitled to it). In addition, during the third and sixth years of the sabbatical cycle, a tithe of all of one's crops was to be designated for the poor (*ma·aseir ani,* the tithe of the poor, as mentioned at Deuteronomy 14:28–29 and 26:12–13). The first tithe (*ma·aseir rishon*), given yearly to the Levites, was also a form of aid to the poor, for the Levites had no other income. Finally, the Torah provides that every fifty years, during the jubilee year, all land reverts to its original owners; this was intended to prevent permanent impoverishment (Leviticus 25:8ff.). These laws are discussed in more detail elsewhere in this volume by Rabbi Martin S. Cohen in his chapter on Israel.

In addition to these agricultural gifts, several other provisions of biblical law helped to prevent poverty. Specifically, workers were to be paid promptly

(Leviticus 19:13 and Deuteronomy 24:14–15), and those who had money were expected, indeed commanded, to extend loans to their fellow Israelites in need without interest (Exodus 22:24, Leviticus 25:36–37, and Deuteronomy 23:20). During the sabbatical year, debts were to be cancelled altogether, but Israelites were nevertheless forbidden to "harbor the base thought" of refusing to loan money to needy Israelites merely because the onset of the sabbatical year was near (Deuteronomy 15:1–2, 7–11). If clothing had been taken as a pledge for a loan, it was to be returned for use by the poor person at night (Exodus 22:25–26). Furthermore, when collecting such a pledge, the creditor had to stand outside the poor person's home (to avoid invading his or her space), thus reinforcing the abiding dignity of the poor person despite his or her poverty (Deuteronomy 24:10–15). Also, it was the duty of the judge to protect the rights of the downtrodden (Exodus 23:6–9; see also Deuteronomy 16:18–20 and 23:17–18, and Psalm 82:3). The poor, though, were not to be preferred in their legal cases before the court just because they were poor any more than the rich were to be given special consideration; rather, fairness to all litigants was to be the rule (Leviticus 19:15 and Deuteronomy 1:17).

It is surprising that there is any provision for the poor at all, much less to the extent that the Torah requires. No other ancient law code makes ongoing provisions for the poor based on each year's crops, as the Torah does. The closest we have to anything like that is in the Egyptian work called "The Instruction of Amen-em-Opet," a letter from sometime between the tenth and the sixth centuries B.C.E., which advises that widows should be permitted to glean unhindered and that gifts of oil should be given to the poor. This is described positively as conduct approved by the gods, but it is clearly not required by them—and certainly not by human governing authorities. (See *Ancient Near Eastern Texts Relating to the Old Testament,* ed. James B. Pritchard [Princeton: Princeton University Press, 1955], p. 424.)

In most law codes prior to modern times, in fact, it was assumed that poor people were not just unfortunate, but that their poverty was caused by some moral fault and therefore they did not deserve to be helped. On the contrary, they were to be punished. In England and the United States, for example, debtors' prisons were common until the nineteenth century, and even though they were theoretically abandoned at that time, imprisonment on other charges, such as concealment of assets, continued to propagate the idea that debtors should be imprisoned for their wrongdoing. (For a brief account, see "Debt" in *The New Illustrated Columbia Encyclopedia* [Garden City, NY: Rockville House Publishers, 1979], vol. 6, p. 1850.) These biblical laws, then, which proclaim that the poor are not to be blamed but to be helped, were truly unprecedented and innovative, and they can only be explained on the basis of the Israelites' theological convictions described in the previous section.

Building on biblical precedent, classical Jewish law legally required members of a community to contribute to its needs—the functional equivalent of a tax in modern society. The amounts varied with the wealth of the individual, but there was no escaping this obligation, as Maimonides noted (*MT* Hilkhot Matt'not Aniyyim 7:10): "The court may even seize property in its owner's presence and take from that person what it is proper for that person to give. It may pawn such possessions for purposes of charity, even on the eve of the Sabbath." (Maimonides is drawing on sources at *BT* Gittin 7b, where it is noted that the poor too must give charity. In this regard, see also *BT* Bava Batra 8b and *BT* K'tubbot 49b, where the point is made that compulsion may be applied to effect compliance. The Tosafot disagree; see also the *SA* Yoreh Dei·ah 248:1–2.) Furthermore, the degree to which a person was obligated to contribute to the poor became the mark of membership in a community (*MT* Hilkhot Matt'not Aniyyim 9:12, drawing on rabbinic sources found at *T* Pei·ah 4:9, *Y* Bava Batra 1:4, 12d, and *BT* Bava Batra 8a). Thus, one who settles in a community for thirty days becomes obligated to contribute to the charity fund together with the other members of the community. One who settles there for three months becomes obligated to contribute to the soup kitchen. One who settles there for six months becomes obligated to contribute clothing for the poor. One who settles there for nine months becomes obligated to contribute to the burial fund for burying the community's poor people. The thick sense of community underlying Jewish law thus means that Jews do not have the luxury of saying that the poor should just take care of themselves or go elsewhere to seek the aid of some other community; the members of a Jewish community are responsible for each other, whether they like it or not.

In rabbinic law, there are three primary forms of granting relief to the poor: feeding them in soup kitchens, arranging for low-cost or cost-free medical attention, and supplying them outright with monies drawn from charity funds.

The Mishnah establishes soup kitchens for the daily dietary needs of the poor. It also prescribes that a traveling poor person be given no less than a loaf of bread at such a kitchen, called a *tamḥui* in the traditional literature; if he or she stays overnight, the townspeople must supply enough food for a night's lodging. If the stay includes a Shabbat, however, the locals must give the traveler three meals (*M* Pei·ah 8:7; and see *T* Pei·ah 4:8, 10; *Y* Eiruvin 3:1, 20d; *BT* Shabbat 118a, Bava M'tzi·a 8b–9a, and Sanhedrin 17b). In the medieval period, synagogues were the site of daily food distribution to the local and traveling poor. As demonstrated by Israel Abrahams (in *Jewish Life in the Middle Ages* [1896; reprint, Philadelphia: The Jewish Publication Society, 1993], p. 311), this system was gradually superseded by three other forms of aid that included dietary assistance: reception of poor travelers in the homes of the rich, provision for vagrants in communal hostelries or inns, and aid offered by benevolent societies for strangers and the resident poor.

Although there was no formal institution akin to the *tamḥui* to give medical care to the poor, physicians gave of their services freely. The Talmud (at *BT* Ta·anit 21b) approvingly notes the example of Abba the Bleeder, who placed a box outside his office where his fees were to be deposited. (Taking blood from a sick person was a common medical therapy in ancient times.) Whoever had money put it in, but those who had none could come in and take advantage of his services without feeling embarrassed. When he saw people who were in no position to pay, he would offer them some money, saying, "Go, strengthen yourself [with food after the bleeding operation]."

S. D. Goitein (in *A Mediterranean Society* [Berkeley: University of California Press, 1971], vol. 2, p. 133) offers similar examples among medieval Jewish physicians, and the ethic must have been quite powerful because it was not until the nineteenth century that a rabbi needed to rule that the communal court should force physicians to give free services to the poor if they do not do so voluntarily (Rabbi Eleazar Fleckeles, *T'shuvah Mei-ahavah,* to *SA* Yoreh Dei·ah 336 [ed. Prague, 1815, vol. 3, p. 69b]). Moreover, the obligation to heal the poor devolves upon the community as well as the physician. The sick, in fact, enjoy priority over other indigent persons in their claim to private or public assistance, and they may not refuse medical aid out of pride or a sense of communal responsibility (*SA* Yoreh Dei·ah 249:16 and 255:2).

The most substantial form of assistance to the poor was the charity fund. Eligibility for its beneficence was generally limited to the resident poor rather than to passers-through, however (*T* Pei·ah 4:9). The charity fund provided clothing as well as food, although food for the starving took precedence over clothing for the naked (*BT* Bava Batra 9a, *SA* Yoreh Dei·ah 251:7). Community authorities also arranged for shelter, usually through a compulsory hospitality rotation wherein the townspeople were required to take turns providing lodging for guests (gloss of the Rema to *SA* Ḥoshen Mishpat 163:1; see also *Arukh Ha-shulḥan,* Ḥoshen Mishpat 163:1).

Moreover, our sources tell us: "Even a poor person who lives entirely on charity must give charity to another poor person" (*BT* Bava Kamma 119a, *BT* Gittin 7b, *MT* Hilkhot Matt'not Aniyyim 7:5, and *SA* Yoreh Dei·ah

248:1 and 251:12). This requirement is rooted not only in the thick sense of community that includes the poor as well as the rich, but also in the tradition's pervasive concern with preserving the dignity of the poor (Deuteronomy 24:10–11, *M* K'tubbot 13:3, *BT* K'tubbot 43a, *SA* Yoreh Dei·ah 251:8 and Even Ha-eizer 112:11, 16, and 93:4). In fact, the Talmud describes poverty as a paradigmatic example of degradation to which other forms can be instructively compared (*BT* Bava Kamma 86a). Thus, even if this provision of the law meant that one poor person would give something to another poor person who, in turn, would return it to the first, each person had to have the dignity of being a contributor to the community's welfare.

Limits on the Duty to Give

The rabbis of classical times were worried that some people would not give enough, but also that others would give too much, thus risking pushing themselves into poverty. To avoid both, the rabbis defined this duty's upper and lower limits. Specifically, each person had to give a minimum of a third of a *shekel* (*BT* Bava Batra 9a), but normally one was expected to give ten percent of one's income—for when the economy switched from an agricultural base to a monetary one, the rabbis applied the laws demanding a tithe of one's crops for the poor codified at Deuteronomy 14:28–29 to money (*Sifrei D'varim* §52 on Deuteronomy 14:22). At most, however, people may give away no more than one-fifth of their assets (*BT* K'tubbot 50a, *MT* Hilkhot Matt'not Aniyyim 7:5), and having done so once, they may give only from their income in succeeding years (*SA* Yoreh Dei·ah 249:1). They may, however, specify in their will their desire to distribute any amount of their assets to charity as a gift (*SA* Ḥoshen Mishpat 241–249, especially 241:5 [where it is noted that one may specify the use to which a gift one offers will later be put]), and there are even leniencies in the procedure for specifying such disbursements if the person is seriously ill (*SA* Ḥoshen Mishpat 250–258). In modern times this would include permission for Jews to establish in their lifetime foundations or charitable remainder trusts that will distribute any amount of their assets to charities of their choosing after their death. (For more about the specific methods available to the observant Jew who wishes to give gifts posthumously to charitable institutions, see the chapter on inheritance law by Rabbi Martin S. Cohen elsewhere in this volume.)

In addition to contributing to communal efforts to help the needy, individuals were also held responsible for responding directly to a beggar's request (*MT* Hilkhot Matt'not Aniyyim 7:7, where Maimonides extends the rule given in *BT* Bava Batra 9a to apply not only to communal collectors but to each individual in need), although one may give a minimal amount in such circumstances. One must remember that "God stands together with the poor person at the door, and one should therefore consider before whom one is [actually] standing" (*Va-yikra Rabbah* 34:9).

The Duty to Give in Our Time

Today, governments at various levels shoulder some of the responsibility to care for the poor and to provide all segments of the population with cultural resources and public education, which is now provided free of charge to everyone through high school. Thus, the respective obligations of the individual, the Jewish community, and the government to aid the poor in various ways and to provide for other communal needs must be reevaluated and adjusted. Do our taxes, or a portion of them, fulfill part of our religious obligations to provide for these services?

In some ways, the answer would have to be that they do. Some of the poverty provisions in the Torah's laws were, after all, simply taxes on a person's income. It is therefore legitimate to argue that at least part of the Jewish duty to care for the poor is fulfilled through paying taxes to the secular government that provides basic necessities for the poor. At the same time, however, American social policy specifically presumes that the safety net for the poor and the funding for educational and cultural resources will not be borne by government alone, but that private charity will also play a significant role in this endeavor. Tax provisions permitting deductions for charity make that intention explicit. Jews therefore can fulfill only a part of their obligations to the poor through their taxes; they must, in addition, contribute some of their income to the charities of their choice. Because, at least in the United States, Jewish educational facilities and synagogues receive no government funding, the duty to support Jewish religious and educational institutions continues to rest completely on the Jewish community, thus creating a special claim on American Jews to support these institutions. Talmudic tradition (as presented at *BT* Gittin 61a) and our full citizenship in contemporary Western countries also obligate us to contribute to general causes as well as Jewish ones.

Because Jewish courts no longer have authority to force Jews to give an amount commensurate with their income and the community's needs, modern fundraisers for Jewish causes must now depend on convincing people to donate by honoring those who do so and by reminding people of their religious duty.

Duties of the Recipient of Charitable Gifts

Donors and distributors of *tz'dakah* funds have certain specific halakhic obligations, as discussed above, but so do the poor. Based on God's words to Adam, "By the sweat of your brow shall you eat bread" (Genesis 3:19), the rabbis assert that people have a moral right to eat only if they earn it by their own effort (*BT* Bava Batra 110a; *B'reishit Rabbah* 14:10). The poor do not have to sell their homes or tools nor do they have to sell their fields at a substantial loss, but they are required to work and to sell off any luxurious possessions in a good-faith effort to become independent of public assistance (*M* Pei·ah 8:8, *BT* K'tubbot 68a, *MT* Hilkhot Matt'not Aniyyim 9:14–17).

Jewish law could assume that the poor would strive to make themselves self-sustaining in part because respect for labor runs deep within the Jewish tradition. In sharp contrast to many in the ancient world, including some of the greatest Greek philosophers, Jews are to disdain neither the working classes nor labor itself but are commanded, rather, to "love work and hate lordship" (*M* Avot 1:10; see also Rav's "pearl" in respect of the physical laborer at *BT* B'rakhot 17a). Furthermore, Jews are not permitted to wage war or engage in robbery or piracy to earn a living, as many other peoples did. It is also forbidden simply to rely on God to provide: "A person should not say, 'I will eat and drink and see prosperity without troubling myself since heaven will have compassion upon me,' for Scripture says, 'You have blessed the work of his hands' (Job 1:10), demonstrating that people should toil with both their hands, for only then will the blessed Holy One grant divine blessing" (*Midrash Tanḥuma,* Va-yeitzei §13).

Moreover, the rabbis of ancient times were sensitive to the extremely positive psychological effects of work, citing two of its greatest teachers, Rabbi Judah and Rabbi Shimon, as declaring, "Great is work, for it honors the worker" (*BT* N'darim 49b). Because of this ethic, and because poor Jewish communities could not provide much in the way of doles to the poor anyway, Jewish sources do not express the worry, as American legislators regularly do, that offering too much assistance to the poor will serve as a disincentive to them to become self-sustaining.

The poor who need aid until they can earn a living are encouraged to apply to the community fund and are discouraged from door-to-door begging, because that would diminish their own dignity (*BT* Bava Batra 9a, *SA* Yoreh Dei·ah 250:3–4). Moreover, in classical Jewish sources, Jewish poor people who could not sustain themselves through the provisions of the Jewish community alone were discouraged from taking charity from non-Jews in public, for that would bring shame on the Jewish community that obviously did not fulfill its duty to provide for the poor. This could even be considered a kind of *ḥillul ha-sheim,* a profanation of the divine name, because such behavior lowers the status of the Jewish people in the estimation of the non-Jewish community. (The sources for this idea may be found in the Talmud at *BT* Sanhedrin 26b and Bava Batra 10b, in Maimonides' *MT* Hilkhot Matt'not Aniyyim 8:9, and in the *SA* Yoreh Dei·ah 254:1.) Because taking from non-Jewish sources shames the Jewish community and the poor themselves, those who do so become ineligible to serve as witnesses (*BT* Sanhedrin 26b and Rashi *ad locum, s.v. okh'lei davar aḥeir p'sulim le'eidut; MT* Hilkhot Eidut 11:5). If a non-Jewish king gives Jews money for charity, Jews may take it "for the sake of peace," so as not to offend the ruler, but Maimonides' decision (at *MT* Hilkhot M'lakhim U-milḥ'moteihem 10:10; see also *SA* Yoreh Dei·ah 254:2 and 259:4) is that they are discreetly to give such funds to non-Jewish poor people so that the king does not hear of it. Since the king will be able to recognize donated objects, however, those must be retained by the Jewish community (gloss of the Rema to *SA* Yoreh Dei·ah 254:2).

All of this changes in modern times, when Jews are full-fledged citizens of the Western democracies in which they reside rather than tolerated minorities. As citizens, they may, if eligible, avail themselves of government welfare programs such as unemployment benefits and food stamps without worrying about sullying the reputation of the Jewish people. Still, both because the Jewish tradition imposes this burden and because American law presumes the aid of private charities, the Jewish community continues to have the duty to take care of its own needy and, to a lesser extent, needy non-Jews so as to make sure that everyone's basic needs with respect to food, clothing, shelter, and healthcare are met, and that everyone gets needed assistance to qualify for and find a job. Rather than begging or endangering their lives, Jews in need not only may, but must, avail themselves of the assistance offered by both the government and the Jewish community to help them satisfy their immediate needs and ultimately become self-sustaining (*MT* Matt'not Aniyyim 10:19; *SA* Yoreh Dei·ah 255:2).

Establishing a Hierarchy of Need

As a general rule, women were traditionally to be aided before men—assuming that there were not enough funds to assist both men and women—because "it is not unusual for a man to go begging, but it is unusual for a woman to do so" (*BT* K'tubbot 67a; *SA* Yoreh Dei·ah 251:8). This gender-based differentiation presumably was based on fear for the physical safety of women who wander in the streets soliciting funds.

According to traditional sources, family members (and, again, especially women) are to be aided first, then close friends, then the poor of one's own community, then the poor of other Jewish communities, and then the non-Jewish poor (*Sifrei D'varim* §63 on Deuteronomy 15:7, *MT* Hilkhot Mat-t'not Aniyyim 7:13, *AT* Yoreh Dei·ah 251, and *SA* Yoreh Dei·ah 251:3). However, the record of medieval Jewish communities that put themselves out for refugees fleeing persecution and expulsion is truly amazing, with many communities displaying the impressive ratio of four contributors coming together to help one single relief recipient. (For evidence of this, see S. D. Goitein, *A Mediterranean Society,* vol. 2, pp. 139–142; see also p. 128, referring to the Egyptian Jewish community in 1160.) Redeeming captives (called *pidyon sh'vuyim* in the sources and discussed in detail elsewhere in this volume in my chapter on the *halakhah* of caring for the needy), though, takes precedence over helping homeless or destitute Jews, for those in captivity are in greater danger than the poor of sexual violation and, ultimately, of losing their lives. Furthermore, Jews must support synagogues and other communal needs. The *Shulḥan Arukh* thus summarizes the hierarchy of recipients of one's donations as follows: "There are those who say that the commandment to [build and support] a synagogue takes precedence over the commandment to give charity (*tz'dakah*) to the poor, but the commandment to give money to youth to learn Torah or to the sick among the poor takes precedence over the commandment to build and support a synagogue" (*SA* Yoreh Dei·ah 249:16).

Because starvation is taken to be a more direct threat to a person's life than exposure, one must feed the hungry before clothing the naked. If a man and a woman come to ask for food, we help the woman before attending to the man's needs, because the man can beg with less danger to himself. For the same reason, if a man and woman come to ask for clothing, or if a male orphan and a female orphan come to ask for funds to be married, we help the woman before attending to the needs of the man (*SA* Yoreh Dei·ah 251:7–8).

As noted, however, redeeming captives takes precedence over sustaining the poor and clothing them, and there are few commandments depicted in halakhic literature as being more important than redeeming captives. "Therefore, the community may re-allocate the usage of any money it collected for communal needs for the sake of redeeming captives" (*SA* Yoreh Dei·ah 252:1; see also 252:3).

Interestingly, despite the fact that Jews were often persecuted by non-Jews and were almost never supported by them, both the Talmud (at *BT* Gittin 61a) and Maimonides (at *MT* Hilkhot Matt'not Aniyyim 7:7) require us to care for the poor and sick among the gentile nations of the world, and also to bury their dead. The reason for this is given both negatively as *mi-p'nei eivah* ("to avoid stirring up gentile hatred of Jews") and also positively as *mi-p'nei darkhei shalom* ("for the sake of maintaining peaceful relations between gentiles and Jews"). The poor of other nations, though, come at the bottom of the list of eligible recipients.

Tz'dakah Priorities in Our Time

World overpopulation, illness, and poverty are probably more acute now than they have ever been. Even in the United States, poverty is spreading, with many of the "working poor" in unskilled or semi-skilled jobs living below the poverty line. Since the 1960s, many of these people have received government benefits that have enabled them to achieve a minimal standard of living, such as housing subsidies, food stamps, Aid to Families with Dependent Children, and direct cash payments, but during the administration of President George W. Bush, Congress curtailed or severely limited many of these programs. Narrowing the focus further to the Jewish community, the 2000 National Jewish Population Study (available at www.ujc.org/njps) found that a full 19 percent of Jewish households in the United States earn less than $25,000 a year, which sum is under the 2011 Federal Poverty Level for a family of four.

How, then, shall we distribute our funds? The old rabbinic model of concentric circles of recipients would argue that after taking care of oneself and one's family, one should donate first to one's synagogue and educational institutions, for such institutions have no other sources of funds. Then one should donate to other Jewish causes, such as Jewish Family Service, Jewish Federation Council, Israeli charities, and the like. Finally, one should donate to general causes, such as American Jewish World Service and United Way. That category is last not only on the basis of the model of concentric circles of concern, but also because those charities are the most likely to get support from non-Jews and/or the government.

While I know of no rabbinic ruling that sets actual percentages for contemporary giving based on the Jewish tradition, it seems reasonable to suggest that fifty percent of one's gifts should go to synagogues and Jewish educational institutions, forty percent to other Jewish causes, and ten percent to non-Jewish causes. Depending on one's income and stage in life, one might, or might not, include one's synagogue dues as part of this calculation of *tz'dakah,* and one might, or might not, include the tuition for one's children or grandchildren to attend Jewish schools, youth groups, and camps as part of one's *tz'dakah* (*MT* Matt'not Aniyyim 10:16; *SA* Yoreh Dei·ah 251:3).

Synagogues and Jewish educational institutions regularly try to keep what they charge as low as possible so as not to discourage participation, and they provide for dues relief and scholarship aid as well; in doing so they depend on wealthier Jews to contribute beyond the stated dues or tuition amounts to keep these institutions afloat, and so Jews who can afford to help should contribute beyond the stated costs and should support these institutions even when their own family is not using them at present so that the Jewish tradition and community can thrive.

With what should we provide the poor whom we help? Here Jewish values set clear priorities: we must first seek to save life and health by supplying food, clothing, shelter, and medicine. The methods for doing so will surely differ in many respects from those of the past, but even the classical *tamḥui* (soup kitchen) and shelter provided by the synagogue are alive and well as projects of many Jewish communities today. We must also seek to provide the skills and tools needed to enable people to become self-sufficient. Finally, we must help children and adults attain a Jewish education through support of Jewish institutions and of scholarship aid.

Giving Gifts to Individuals

The concerns of meeting the needs of the poor without robbing them of dignity are the governing principles of Maimonides' famous ladder of gifts, graduating from least to most virtuous: (1) to give, but to do so without joy; (2) to give less than is fitting, but to do so in good humor; (3) to give what is fitting, and to do so cheerfully, but only after being asked; (4) to give what is fitting, and to do so cheerfully *and* before being asked; (5) to give what is fitting, and to do so cheerfully and before one is asked, *and* to give one's gift in such a manner that, although the recipient of the gift knows the donor's identity, the donor does not discover who the recipient of the gift is; (6) to give what is fitting, and to do so cheerfully *and* before being asked, *and* to give one's gift in such a manner that, although the donor knows the identity of the recipient, the recipient does not know the identity of the donor; and (7) to give what is fitting, and to do so cheerfully and before one is asked, and to give one's gift in a way so that neither the donor nor the recipient knows each other's identity. Finally, (8) the highest form is not to give recipients anything at all as a handout, but rather to lend them money, take them into a business partnership, or find work for them—for in all these cases, they will be able to support themselves and thus to retain their full measure of self-respect (*MT* Hilkhot Matt'not Aniyyim 10:7–14).

In our own time, individuals often worry that their gifts to individual beggars in the street may be given to people who do not really need their aid, or that the funds they give out may be misused to finance a drug habit or to purchase alcohol. Individuals approached on city streets for gifts of charity may also worry about their personal safety. Furthermore, it is certainly the case that charitable institutions are generally much more able than individual citizens to discern who is truly needy, and such agencies can, in accordance with Maimonides' principles, deliver goods or services without compromising the identity of the donor or receiver.

It is therefore best of all to refer beggars (and maybe even offer to take them) to the offices of organizations established specifically to deal with these needs, including governmental and private facilities, Jewish Free Loan societies, and Jewish Family Service agencies. When that is not possible, one must donate something if one can and, in any case, one must at least treat such people kindly (*BT* Bava Batra 9b, *MT* Hilkhot Matt'not Aniyyim 10:5). When possible, one should try to give gifts that cannot be abused or misused. Certificates for food from supermarkets or restaurants, for example, are better gifts than money.

In the end, then, even though the vast majority of one's charitable giving should be to social service, religious, and educational institutions, Jewish law requires us to respond to a beggar's immediate needs. In that situation, even though Jewish law would prioritize giving to Jews over non-Jews, it does not seem practical or kind to attempt to discover if a beggar is Jewish. Furthermore, one should try to ensure that the gift will be used for food or clothing rather than alcohol or drugs.

Gifts to the Community

As Rabbi Jacob Neusner points out in his *Tz'dakah: Can Jewish Philanthropy Buy Jewish Survival?* (1982; reprint, New York: URJ Press, 1997, pp. 32 and 67ff.), in our own day, the shared work of collecting and distributing charity is a significant mechanism through which individual Jews *become* a Jewish community. Many of the details described in the traditional laws for collection and distribution, though, are out of place in the modern world. Designating two people to collect funds and three people to decide how to distribute them, as Jewish law does (*BT* Bava Batra 8b, *MT* Hilkhot Matt'not Aniyyim 9:5), seems blatantly autocratic to us; even thirty is too small a number for the boards of directors of many of our larger charitable organizations, to say nothing of governmental agencies. And delivery of the aid is much more efficiently and honorably done through the mail or through direct deposits in bank accounts rather than by delegations traveling door-to-door.

If paying taxes fulfills some part of our obligation to provide education, social services, and general culture for the poor, then we have a concomitant religious duty (as well as a civic one) to get involved in government so as to be in a position to ensure that the funds are equitably, honestly, and wisely apportioned. Jews *qua* Jews certainly do not have the right to determine government policy; but we do possess not only the right, but also both a Jewish and a civic duty, to get involved in the discussion of public policy on these issues, and in such discussions we may and should bring to the table our specifically Jewish perceptions and values. (For more on this, see my *To Do the Right and the Good,* ch. 4.)

The Jewish tradition cannot be interpreted to require any particular ideological or political stance in responding to the problem of poverty. Nevertheless, some guidelines clearly emerge from Jewish concepts and law. Specifically, in light of the notion that God's image is embedded in each of us, preserving the dignity and economic viability of all concerned must remain a paramount concern when determining the recipients of aid, the methods of collection and distribution, the programs of prevention, and all other related factors in this area.

Because the best type of aid by far is to prevent poverty in the first place, the clear mandate of the Jewish tradition for both teenagers and adults is to support governmental and private programs of education in general and job training in particular (*BT* Bava Batra 8b; see also Maimonides' comments at *MT* Hilkhot Matt'not Aniyyim 9:5). Tutoring programs to help teenagers finish high school and sex education programs to help them avoid pregnancy are critical to enable young people to become self-sustaining adults. This priority supports the Jewish parental responsibility—and, by extension, the community's duty—to teach children a form of gainful employment (*BT* Kiddushin 29a), and it accords well with Maimonides' hierarchy of charitable obligations.

For those who permanently or temporarily cannot work, immediate sustenance should be available with few, if any, questions asked. Jewish programs like Mazon and Sova do this now on an ongoing basis. The late Mickey Weiss, a Los Angeles produce distributor, began what became a nationwide effort to get produce distributors to donate their leftover fruits and vegetables each day to local soup kitchens, and some restaurants and caterers donate their leftover food to them as well. In addition, synagogues and Jewish Family Service agencies collect money for the needy before Passover in *ma·ot ḥittim* campaigns and/or on Purim as part of the *mitzvah* of *mattanot la-evyonim,* the giving of gifts to the poor that is traditionally one of the components of Purim celebration (Esther 9:22). In the end, Jewish law holds us responsible for ensuring that our combined private and governmental efforts supply food for the hungry, just as Jewish soup kitchens of yore did.

In addition to food, Jewish law requires us to provide clothing and shelter to the destitute. Therefore, housing must be provided to the homeless, preferably on an ongoing basis, but at least on nights with cold or inclement weather. If poor people have housing of their own, they should be permitted to retain it even while getting public assistance. Long before modern bankruptcy law protected one's home and one's means of earning a living, Jewish law stipulated that qualifying for welfare programs should not require that poor people lose their homes or sell their tools for employment (*MT* Matt'not Aniyyim 9:14), for the ultimate goal is to help people become self-sufficient.

Collectors and distributors of charity funds have a responsibility to act honestly, discreetly, and wisely in their sacred tasks. This includes striking a delicate balance between assuring that those who ask for aid are truly in need, while simultaneously preserving their privacy and honor as much as possible.

For their part, the poor also have duties. These include the obligation to manage responsibly whatever resources they do have, and, if at all possible, to seek training and employment that will extricate them from poverty (*MT* Matt'not Aniyyim 10:18). Those who cannot work or find employment must try to contribute to the community in some other way. Communal officials have the right and duty to ensure that people receiving aid are living up to these responsibilities, but they must do so tactfully and respectfully.

Charitable Gifts to Foundations and Institutions

In recent years, some of the wealthiest Jews have chosen to establish their own eleemosynary foundations rather than contribute to existing charity funds. They do this to better control how their money will be used and, at least in some cases, to guarantee some name recognition for their gifts. Although classical Jewish sources speak most often of communal agencies collecting and distributing funds, historically there have always been wealthy individuals like the Rothschild family that distributed funds on their own. One can hardly gainsay the good that these foundations do, and donors certainly have the right to contribute to the causes of their choice. However, wealthy people, like people of lesser means, have the duty to contribute to communal charity funds as well. That is part of the thick sense of community within Judaism that insists that we work together in meeting communal needs. Private giving on one's own terms and in one's own name must come after fulfilling one's obligations to the community's organizations and funds.

When a Service Is Offered

May a charitable institution that offers services give preferential treatment to donors and volunteers? For example, the Ramah camps almost always have a long waiting list. May children or grandchildren of their major donors and of the members of their lay committees jump to the head of the line?

In a legal setting, the Torah establishes crystal-clear guidelines. "You shall not be partial in judgment. Hear out low and high alike. Fear no one, for judgment is God's alone" (Deuteronomy 1:17; see also Exodus 23:2, 6). "You shall not render an unfair decision. Do not favor the poor or show deference to the rich; judge your kinsman fairly" (Leviticus 19:15). "When a stranger resides with you in your land, you shall not wrong him. The stranger who resides with you shall be to you as one of your citizens; you shall love him as yourself, for you were strangers in the land of Egypt: I, the Eternal, am your God" (Leviticus 19:33–34).

The rabbis of the Mishnah and Talmud added many more procedural rules to ensure impartial treatment of all who come before the court. For example, one litigant may not be required to stand while the other is permitted to sit (*BT* Sh'vu·ot 30a); both parties to the case must wear clothing of similar quality (*BT* Sh'vu·ot 31a); judges must understand the languages spoken by all the people appearing before them (*BT* M'naḥot 65a); and witnesses may not be related to each other or to the litigants (*M* Sanhedrin 3:1 and 4). Through rules such as these the Torah and the rabbis of classical antiquity made procedural justice a reality. If these rules are applied directly to our case, they would clearly require that no special privileges apply to major donors or to volunteers.

But are rules devised to ensure fairness in court reasonably applied to nonprofit organizations? In some ways, they are. Like courts, those making decisions on behalf of nonprofit institutions must be concerned with questions of fairness, for that moral (and quintessentially Jewish) duty applies to all people and all groups in every setting. Moreover, nonprofit organizations are well warned to "hear out high and low alike," for otherwise they stand in danger of failing to serve some of the very people they were created to aid.

In other ways, though, nonprofit organizations differ from courts. First, while courts are established and funded by communities, nonprofit institutions depend for their very existence on the voluntary service and donations of people who believe in their cause. The nonprofit setting therefore invariably involves a level of passionate commitment that ideally never exists in court, where judges are supposed to be neutral to all parties. Furthermore, the basic nature of justice requires that judges not have any financial relationship with anyone involved in the trials over which they preside. Nonprofit institutions, on the other hand, are almost always run by paid employees whose salaries are funded by gifts they themselves must solicit from donors committed to the cause—in some cases, because they themselves or members of their family benefit from the service the institution provides. (For instance, in the example given above, the decision about which children will come to camp rests with a camp director whose salary is paid by an organization that depends on donations, some of which come from the parents or grandparents of the children involved.) As a result, the level of dispassionate fairness expected of judges in court can rarely, if ever, be achieved in running nonprofit organizations.

In fact, one could reasonably argue that nonprofit agencies should not treat everyone alike. The money and effort that some people contribute to their favorite cause, after all, do create a kind of debt of gratitude, and there is nothing inherently ignoble about acknowledging and responding to the reality of that debt. Indeed, when someone has been donating to an institution or working for it on a volunteer basis for a long time and only then needs a special favor, there does seem to be a debt of gratitude that the institution bears toward that person. The extent of that debt and what the institution should be prepared to do in response will appropriately vary with the nature of the request, the size of the donated money or service, and the length of time over which the relationship has developed. But Jewish sources do recognize such debts of gratitude: one is supposed to recognize favors not only in words, but also in deeds. This is clearly true with regard to God, as the Mishnah at *M* B'rakhot 9:5 says that "a person must thank God for the bad as well as the good. . . . One must be thankful without measure for whatever God measures out to you." Similarly, one needs to show gratitude to human beings who have helped us. (Volunteer work and donations that are undertaken in the first place for the sake of garnering special treatment, however, undermine the very character of charitable work or philanthropy. As a result, it would be morally less worthy—and possibly even wrong—for someone to donate money to an institution for the sole sake of getting special treatment. That is the kind of situation educational institutions sometimes encounter, when rich donors suggest that they will finance the school's new building but only on condition that their own children are admitted. Many nonprofit institutions are not able to resist such financial pressure, but surely everyone involved understands that such gifts, although a definite contribution to the institution, are not morally pure.)

Along these lines, Rabbi Joseph ibn Migash (1077–1141, writing in his responsum no. 202, ed. Warsaw, 1870, p. 31a) discusses the talmudic saying, "Into the well from which you have once drunk water, do not throw clods of earth" (found at *BT* Bava Kamma 92b). If, says ibn Migash, this applies to inanimate things, how much the more so should one show gratitude to human beings! (For a fuller discussion of the rabbinic concept of appropriate gratitude, see Louis Jacobs, *Theology in the Responsa* [1975; reprint, Oxford and Portland, OR: Littman Library of Jewish Civilization, 2005], p. 41.)

Moreover, as we have seen, Jewish law, as well as general morality, recognizes that duties flow out of relationships. Hence my obligations to my family are greater than my duties to my community, and those, in turn, are greater than my obligations to other human beings. Through donating money and/or time, a person becomes part of an institution's extended family. Viewed this way, special treatment for such people would be justified as part of the general sense that one's obligations to one's own relatives exceed one's obligations toward others.

To avoid even the taint of unfairness, however, nonprofit organizations would be well advised to establish official policies defining these forms of special treatment and who is eligible for them. In doing so, institutions are free to decide for themselves how long a relationship with a donor must go on, and to what extent, before that donor acquires any special claim on the services of the institution. Some organizations have already done this. For example, the Los Angeles Jewish Home, which has a long waiting list of individuals hoping to be admitted, has created a specific policy to govern such matters, thus guaranteeing that everyone can know the rules of the admissions procedure. This does entail the danger that people will give to the institution in order to get the special favors later on, thus sullying at least somewhat the purity of their gifts. The longer the relationship with the institution goes on, however, the less that will be a problem.

The Morals of Fundraising

In raising funds, many moral issues may arise. Three of the most common problems are gambling for charity, the collection of unpaid pledges, and donations of ill-gotten gain.

May bingo and more serious forms of gambling be used to raise funds for synagogues and other Jewish institutions? The United Synagogue of Conservative Judaism has prohibited this for years, based on the sense that gambling, by its very nature, is morally problematic. Because everyone who participates knows perfectly well that not everyone will win, but still, somehow, personally expects to be the winner, one could argue that whoever does win is effectively stealing from all the rest. Moreover, for some, gambling becomes an addiction, sometimes to the point of making such people unable to earn a living or keep enough to sustain themselves and their family. The Mishnah and Talmud already recognize these dangers (*M* Sanhedrin 3:3; cf. *BT* Sanhedrin 24b–25b). Thus Jewish fundraising activities should not "put a stumbling block before the blind" (Leviticus 19:14) by using casino nights and other gambling opportunities to raise funds. On the other hand, one might argue that as long as the money involved is not substantial, such evenings are effectively social evenings that also garner some money for the synagogue, and so some synagogues have allowed bingo nights, stipulating that the amounts of money involved are small. The question of synagogue-sponsored gambling is discussed elsewhere in this volume by Rabbi Craig Scheff in his chapter on the *halakhah* of synagogue life.

What should a Jewish institution do with donors who repeatedly make pledges and then fail to make good on them? When this happens once, every effort should be made to ensure that the donor did not pledge under one set of economic circumstances and then find him or herself with vastly less money than anticipated. In such a situation, the institution should discreetly and reasonably work out an arrangement with the individual involved. (Sometimes, it will even be appropriate for an institution to forgive a pledge entirely.) When an individual fails again and again to make good on his or her pledges, however, institutions guided by halakhic principles should refuse to accept any further pledges from that person. Needless to say, honors awarded to donors in that setting should not be extended to individuals who merely pledge, but do not actually pay.

Finally, nonprofit organizations occasionally accept donations from people who, as it later turns out, obtained their assets illegally. What should happen to the money donated or facilities endowed? How should the donors be treated within the community? These are hard issues, dealt with in my rabbinic ruling for the CJLS, "Donations of Ill-Gotten Gain," which is now available on the website of the Rabbinical Assembly.

Although much regarding the economic and social realities in which Jews have found themselves has changed over the centuries, the perceptions and values of Judaism's traditional sources still have much to say to us in informing our own understanding of poverty and our approach to respond to it. Judaism's keen sense of communal responsibility requires us to go beyond thinking only about ourselves and our families to care for the entire community and, indeed, for other human communities as well. In doing so, Judaism counters a selfish, individualistic strain in Enlightenment thought and thus contributes immensely to making us moral and worthy of existing in an ongoing covenantal relationship with other Jews, with other human beings, and with God.

Repentance

DAVID H. LINCOLN

In his article about repentance in *Contemporary Jewish Religious Thought* (edited by Arthur Cohen and Paul Mendes-Flohr [New York: Free Press, 1988], pp. 785–794), Ehud Luz points out that the numerous biblical references to *t'shuvah* ("repentance") are almost exclusively directed to the community of Israel as a whole rather than to the individual. The sages of post-biblical times, however, were more concerned with *t'shuvah* of the individual. And, in the intervening centuries, both concepts of repentance—*t'shuvah* as a communal challenge and as an individual's personal responsibility—have become indispensible parts of the larger picture. Here, however, I wish to discuss in particular the path of *t'shuvah* for today's Conservative Jewish individual, and specifically to draw my ideas from the masterful exposition of the topic in Maimonides's law code, the section of the *Mishneh Torah* called Hilkhot T'shuvah. (Most of the texts presented in this chapter appear in the translation of Philip Birnbaum, who published his collection of texts from the *Mishneh Torah* under the title *Maimonides' Mishneh Torah* [New York: Hebrew Publishing Company, 1944].)

T'shuvah

The Hebrew word *t'shuvah* is related to the word meaning "to turn" or "to return." Indeed, the expression "to return in *t'shuvah*" is part of the vocabulary of modern Hebrew. But Professor Luz makes a distinction between two different types of "returning" current in our times. One tends to emphasize the restorative aspect of *t'shuvah* as a return to Judaism's traditional teachings and way of life. A person who makes this kind of return typically relinquishes many of the customs and values of the secular world. He or she will at the same time accept the authority of rabbinic leaders and their beliefs. There is, however, another kind of *t'shuvah,* one more in tune with the definition of the philosopher Franz Rosenzweig, who suggested a form of "returning" to Judaism that would integrate the values of Western humanism with the rituals and moral positions of the Jewish faith. Rosenzweig, who died in 1929, serves even today as a model for modern educated Jews seeking a way to return to their religious tradition without abandoning all that is positive in modern culture. As such, Conservative Judaism teaches that returning to God in repentance does not and should not require abandoning or rejecting the secular world.

The Confession of Sin

Maimonides begins his exposition of the traditions of repentance by insisting that the inner urge toward *t'shuvah* be given vocal expression. "How does one confess?" he asks rhetorically, then answers with the simple idea that one must say aloud, "I regret my acts and am ashamed of them" (*MT* Hilkhot T'shuvah 1:1). Mention is made of sacrificial offerings intended as ritual demonstrations of the desire to undo one's own sins, but Maimonides notes that only repentance and the catharsis of Yom Kippur are left to us today as vehicles for self-motivated return to the service of God.

The sincere recitation of liturgical confessions constitutes our method of asking God for forgiveness today. We realize that we may not have committed all the sins enumerated in the standard text, but we join with the congregation in reciting the full litany nevertheless, deriving security from the presence of other worshipers also attempting to approach God in penitential prayer. In any congregation, we know, there are those (such as ourselves) who have transgressed. But we console ourselves by admitting that there must also be a majority of good people with whom we can associate and from whose example we can learn to do better. By confessing our sins as a community, we seek the strength to repent as individuals.

Nor must we suppose that people either do or do not have the inner fortitude to repent for past transgressions and that those who do not are simply out of luck. That kind of inner resolve, our tradition teaches, is itself one of God's gifts and, at that, one for which we pray daily. Indeed, in the daily Amidah, a prayer that tradition dictates be recited three times daily on every weekday of the year, the fifth benediction includes a plea that God "help us fully to repent all our misdeeds" and then concludes by acknowledging God not only as the One to whom one *may* direct one's penitence, but as the One who specifically "desires the repentance of sinners."

Sins against God and Sins against People

It is generally accepted that Yom Kippur effects atonement only for sins against the ritual strictures of Scripture (*MT* Hilkhot T'shuvah 2:9), but that sins committed against a fellow human being must be dealt with in another way. The sinner, for example, must compensate the victim in the case of robbery or injury, but mere payment is not enough. One must also try to appease the wronged party and ask formally and earnestly for that individual's forgiveness.

Approaching the equation from the other direction, Maimonides teaches us that, when approached for forgiveness by someone who has done us wrong, we should forgive wholeheartedly and neither bear a grudge nor show cruelty by a refusal to accept the apology (*MT* Hilkhot T'shuvah 2:10). Indeed, the Torah's commandment at Leviticus 19:18 not to bear a grudge could easily be imagined to apply specifically to situations like this.

The custom has also evolved of approaching those with whom we have had some disagreement and asking for their forgiveness before the Kol Nidrei service, and this practice should be encouraged. It is understood as almost self-evident that we cannot dare approach God for divine pardon before pacifying those fellow human beings whom we have even possibly wronged.

Of particular interest is the case of Jews who stand aloof from the community, as discussed by Maimonides at *MT* Hilkhot T'shuvah 3:11. Such people separate themselves from the Jewish people, take no interest in its distress, and decline to share in its festivals and its fasts. Such people according to Maimonides are an affront to their people and to God, and they have no share in the World to Come. But even they have the potential to return to God in repentance, regardless of how far removed they may be from any sense of personal involvement in the destiny of the Jewish people. What Maimonides would have made of those in our modern communities who neither fast nor participate even marginally in the rituals of Judaism but are nevertheless very involved in communal life is hard to say. Such people feel very strong ties to their own Jewishness by virtue of their commitment to the community and, no doubt, would bristle mightily at the suggestion that ritual observance is the only yardstick by which to measure Jewish commitment. We can respect such people for their efforts and for their emotional involvement in communal life. But we cannot reject Maimonides's teaching that a Jew who lives contrary to the commandments of the Torah is still called upon to repent. Such people, therefore, should not be condemned or dismissed; instead of continuing to live lives informed by a strong sense of Jewish identity yet not engaged with traditional Jewish ritual and observance, they should be encouraged to consider *t'shuvah* in the Rosenzweigian sense.

Inadvertent Offenses

Repentance applies to all sins, even those barely noticed when committed. It is for this reason, in fact, that tradition endorses the concept of a litany of sin and a general Day of Atonement intended to cover all forgotten and overlooked indiscretions. According to Jewish tradition, for example, people who accept as a gift part of a meal that is insufficient to satisfy its owner are guilty of at least a form of robbery, because they are in effect taking for themselves what should rightfully belong to another (*MT* Hilkhot T'shuvah 4:4). Yet which of us would know that at the moment? Similarly, gazing at members of the opposite sex lustfully and speaking highly of ourselves at the expense of others are forms of degradation that are forbidden, but regularly committed by most of us almost inadvertently. In a similar category are certain obnoxious activities like gossip and slander, which are generally committed so automatically as almost never to call attention to themselves. All these and similar misdeeds do not preclude repentance, but simply make it more difficult to attain. If a person is sincerely remorseful and repents wholeheartedly, then such an individual will, to use the traditional formulation, surely have a share in the World to Come.

Free Will

Free will is granted to all people. With their intelligence and reason, humans are always presumed to know what is good and what is evil. Indeed, the Bible recounts the story of Adam and Eve eating from the fruit of the Tree of Knowledge of Good and Evil to teach that this ability is part of the common heritage of all humanity. Adam and Eve could have remained childlike in their innocence, but the consequence of their sin is that all people today are deemed able to know the difference between acceptable and wicked behavior.

Thus, every human being, with no exception, has the capability of becoming a righteous individual or a wicked sinner. In fact, Maimonides regards the doctrine of free will as the great pillar of the Torah upon which the divine commandments all rest. He writes that one should not believe the absurd statements of those fools, Jews and non-Jews alike, who imagine that a child's future character, good or bad, is determined by God as early on as that person's conception (*MT* Hilkhot T'shuvah 5:2). This would be tantamount to saying that the individual is compelled by fate to follow a certain line of conduct, an idea wholly inimical to the lessons of Scripture. According to the Torah, one's conduct is entirely in one's own hands and cannot be influenced by external factors. (At *MT* Hilkhot T'shuvah 6:3, Maimonides even goes so far as to interpret the biblical references to God "hardening" Pharaoh's heart as punishment for past sins rather than as an inexorable decree that Pharaoh be an evil person.)

No one can be forced to be good or bad. Indeed, if one were compelled to act according to the decree of fate, then there would be neither freedom nor choice at all, and the zeal or recalcitrance one shows in obeying the commands of the Torah would thus reflect neither well nor poorly on the individual in question. It would also be useless to study or attempt to acquire a skill, since no one could ever attain anything other than what had been previously ordained; destiny would be unavoidable. Modern Jews should fully embrace the notion that we are in full command over all our actions at all times, that we always have the choice to act morally or immorally, and that this choice is completely unrelated to the extraneous details of someone's education, upbringing, culture, or talents. The meaning of *t'shuvah* for moderns derives directly from this set of ideas: in the freedom to embrace good lies the freedom to desist from embracing evil, and the act of turning away from the path of iniquity and sin is precisely how modern Jews should define repentance.

The Ten Days of Repentance

Blowing the *shofar* on Rosh Hashanah, says Maimonides, awakens us from our slumber and asks that we remember our Creator (*MT* Hilkhot T'shuvah 3:10). Furthermore, all people should regard themselves throughout the year as though they were half innocent and half guilty. If one commits even one additional sin, therefore, the scale of guilt is then tilted toward evil and one has fully to bear the responsibility of those actions. It is a worthy custom to give charity and perform good deeds between Rosh Hashanah and Yom Kippur to a far larger extent than during the rest of the year. The special S'liḥot prayers, described in this volume in the chapter on the festivals, are recited from before Rosh Hashanah until Yom Kippur in order to stimulate the desire to return to God in full repentance. Indeed, the prolonged process called traditionally by the Hebrew name *ḥeshbon ha-nefesh,* literally "an accounting of the soul," that precedes and continues into the High Holiday season is intended to help us own up to the ways in which we have sinned, so as to make us able to address our shortcomings and transgressions directly and specifically during the days leading up to Yom Kippur as well as on Yom Kippur itself.

The Tashlikh ceremony, usually performed on the first day of Rosh Hashanah, involves going to a body of water and, by tossing some crumbs into the water, symbolically casting away one's sins. It is true there was a time when many rabbis derided this ceremony as simplistic and potentially misleading and that the Vilna Gaon himself was of the opinion that the time spent at Tashlikh could be far better spent studying Torah. However, moderns do not need to set it aside: because it is an exercise in symbolism, not magic, the ceremony has the ability to encourage us to see *t'shuvah* as something attainable, as something no more complicated than emptying our pockets of crumbs. The practice of symbolically transferring one's sins to a live chicken which is then slaughtered is favored by some hasidic sects. As mentioned by Alan Lucas in his discussion of the High Holidays, there is also a version of the ceremony that involves the symbolic transfer of one's sins to coins which are then given to charity. Because of the inherent cruelty to the animals involved in the original version of the ceremony, it makes far more sense to opt for the version of the ceremony featuring the giving of *tz'dakah* (for which a liturgical setting is provided in *Maḥzor Lev Shalem*) or on the recitation of S'liḥot and/or participation in Tashlikh to grant physical reality to the desire to repent.

The days between Rosh Hashanah and Yom Kippur are also the traditional time of the year to study those classic works that have been composed over the centuries that are specifically intended to awaken in us the desire to renounce sin and live godly lives. Of these, the best known are probably the *M'sillat Y'sharim* ("The Path of the Just") by Rabbi Moses Ḥayyim Luzzatto (1707–1746) and available now in a new English translation by Rabbi Ira Stone (Philadelphia: The Jewish Publication Society, 2010), the *Sha·arei T'shuvah* ("The Gates of Repentance") by Rabbi Yonah Gerondi (d. 1263) and available in the English translation of Shraga Silverstein (Nanuet, NY, and Jerusalem: Feldheim, 1967), and the *Tomer D'vorah* ("The Palm Tree of Deborah") by Rabbi Moses Cordevero (1522–1570) currently available in several English translations including one by Rabbi Louis Jacobs (London: Valentine, Mitchell, 1960).

Misdeeds for Which There Can Be No Practical Repentance

Writing in the *Mishneh Torah* at Hilkhot T'shuvah 4:3, Maimonides notes that some misdeeds by their nature preclude the possibility of repentance. Generally, these are sins that are committed against another person without it being possible after the fact to identify the wronged party, thus also not to pay compensation or to ask for pardon. In this category, Maimonides mentions one who curses the entire people and not an individual, one who shares stolen property with a thief, one who finds lost property and does not publicize it in order to return it to its rightful owner, one who despoils the poor (including orphans and widows), and one who takes bribes to subvert the course of justice.

Moderns should ponder this list thoughtfully. Maimonides is not contradicting his theory that all people can repent of all sins, but simply noting that the basic requirement for repentance involves making restitution and peace with the wronged party, and that there are instances in which this is so impractical as to be effectively impossible. Thus the belief that the gates of repentance are always open has to be tempered with the sobering reality that there are times when it will not be simple, or perhaps not even possible, to identify the aggrieved party, or all the aggrieved parties, at all. It is through the contemplation of this aspect of reality that the urgency of prayer on Yom Kippur will gain its fullest force for many.

The Power of Repentance

To achieve true repentance, one must not only focus on deeds done, but also on the negative and destructive emotions like anger, hatred, envy, greed, and gluttony that lead people to transgress. When people become addicted to such emotions, they find it hard to get rid of them, and this is so despite the prophet's simple instruction to the wicked and the guilty among us that they simply give up their evil ways and their wicked thoughts (Isaiah 55:7). Still, true and sincere penitents are loved by the Creator as if they had never sinned, a remark that echoes throughout rabbinic literature. ("Did not Reish Lakish once say," the Talmud asks rhetorically at *BT* Yoma 86b, "that the greatness of repentance lies specifically in its ability to take willful acts of disobedience and transform them into merit?") Furthermore, the reward is great for those who have tasted sin and nevertheless suppress the evil impulse: "Where repentant sinners stand," our sages teach, "even the [ever] righteous are unable to stand" (*BT* B'rakhot 34b). This implies that the merit of those who repent is superior to that of those who never sinned, for the former had to exert greater effort in suppressing their impulse to turn away from God's law.

Forgiving and Forgetting

Those who repent should be exceedingly humble in their behavior (*MT* Hilkhot T'shuvah 7:8). If ignorant people insult them by reminding them of their past deeds, they should pay such people no attention. As long as they regret their former lifestyle, their merit is not to be questioned. Modern Jews should take this to heart. We have in our congregations many who have become observant later in life, as well as many who have converted to Judaism. It is of the greatest importance that their decision to turn or return to the ways of Torah be respected by not repeatedly being mentioned aloud. To remind penitents of their past can be very hurtful and we should rather delight in their decision to become observant or to join the Jewish people.

Forgiving the Unforgiveable

Is there such thing as vicarious forgiveness? Simon Wiesenthal spent many months in German death camps and experienced torture and indescribable horror at the hands of the Nazis firsthand. Eventually, a dying SS man begged forgiveness for his crimes from Wiesenthal. Wiesenthal reports that he actually felt a tinge of compassion for the man, but chose instead to say nothing and instead walked quietly out of the room. (The author tells the full story in *The Sunflower,* originally published by Schocken Books in 1976 and then in an expanded edition in 1998.) Did he behave properly? Surely, that is not a question for others to answer, but the bottom line has to be that even if Wiesenthal *had* forgiven the man, he could only have done so for crimes committed against himself. The murdered are not in a position to forgive, and neither is any living person other than the wronged party. Indeed, the only way in which a murderer can reasonably seek forgiveness is through repentance itself, the process whereby the sinner bypasses the world and pleads his or her case directly before God. When we are asked to forgive sins committed by other people against deceased third parties, the fact that those third parties are dead and thus unable to forgive does not grant us the right to speak on their behalf.

Yet granting others forgiveness in a global way is a moral imperative. We can, for example, admire the Truth and Reconciliation proceedings held in South Africa in the mid-1990s, which were planned to create a context for the wronged of a nation to forgive those who were responsible for their misfortune. Archbishop Desmond Tutu's words go straight to the heart of the matter: "Without forgiveness there can be no future and without memory there can be no healing." (Many South African rabbis were critical of his stance at the time, however.) The modern Jewish attitude was succinctly stated by Abraham Joshua Heschel, whom I cite as quoted by Simon Wiesenthal in *The Sunflower,* ed. 1998, pp. 130–131: "No one can forgive crimes committed against other people. It is therefore preposterous to assume that anybody alive can extend forgiveness for the suffering of any one of the six million people who perished."

That should be our attitude as well. Forgiveness can only be extended for wrongs personally suffered. Other instances of sinful behavior, no matter how extreme, can only be dealt with through the medium of intense, introspective repentance founded on faith in a forgiving God and in the ability of even the worst sinner to turn back to the ways of decency and goodness. We may thus make a reasonable distinction between encouraging others to repent of their sins by talking about God's endless capacity to forgive, but without going so far as actually to forgive someone for actions taken against others. In the end, only the aggressed-against party can forgive the aggressor.

Context Is Everything

It may be difficult to ask others to forgive you. Some of the affected parties may be far away or impossible to locate. Others may have died. Rabbi Ovadiah Yosef, spiritual leader of Sephardic Jewry in Israel, offers some suggestions in his *Hilkhot Erev Yom Ha-kippurim* 82:8:9, where he states that although one should always directly contact a person one has wronged and ask for forgiveness, this is not always possible (Ovadiah Yosef, *Sefer Yalkut Yoseif: Piskei Halakhot Be'inyanei Ḥaggei U-mo·adei Ha-shanah* [Jerusalem: Y'shivat Ḥazon Ovadiah, 1984], p. 81). If the offended person is out of town, a letter can be written. For moderns, a telephone call or e-mail will often suffice to get things started. If the offended person has died, tradition dictates that a *minyan* should be assembled at the grave and prayers for forgiveness and even posthumous reconciliation intoned—a powerful, moving ceremony that moderns have abandoned to their own detriment.

In the event that someone refuses to forgive, one should not desist but continue to ask for pardon up to three times. However, if the offended person is one's rabbi, one should try even one thousand times (Maimonides, *MT* Hilkhot T'shuvah 2:9).

The Kol Nidrei prayer, discussed by Rabbi Alan Lucas at length elsewhere in this volume, should also to be mentioned in this context. For observant Jews, the recitation of Kol Nidrei, an Aramaic formula recited at sunset on the eve of the Day of Atonement, becomes the threshold to the holiest day of the year. The prayer says that all vows and oaths that we may swear or pledge, and that we may inadvertently violate, should be annulled and made void and of no effect. For anti-Semites, however, Kol Nidrei was taken merely to constitute evidence that Jews are duplicitous and two-faced. As a stand-alone statement divorced of its historical context, the prayer does seem to suggest that there is no such thing as a promise or oral contract that cannot be broken in Judaism. In fact, however, context is everything and the prayer refers only to personal vows: those made by individuals in relation to their own conscience or to God, not interpersonal ones made by an individual to another person. In fact, if one wishes to free oneself from a vow made to a second party, the process is extremely complicated and involves appearing before a religious court and formally seeking release from one's vow-bound relationship.

In *A Jewish Theology* (London: Darton, Longman & Todd, 1973; p. 259), Rabbi Louis Jacobs makes a summation that should be our guide today:

> . . . it can be seen that the teachings regarding sin and repentance as these appear in the sources strike on the whole a balance between childish irresponsibility for which saying sorry is enough and morbid guilt for which nothing one does to repair the wrong is enough. The need to find peace in one's soul by shedding the guilt load by constructive means, thus making good the harm that has been done, [and effecting the] renewal of one's personal life [and] reconciliation with God and with one's fellows: these, far from being infantile, are tests of a mature personality.
>
> Special emphasis is given to these themes in the Jewish tradition on the Day of Atonement and the days preceding it, the Ten Days of Penitence. It remains to be said that repentance is not a seasonal matter; yet there is point in setting aside a special period in which the Prayers and the ritual can succeed in reminding man [sic] at the beginning of the New Year to lead a new life in the presence of God.

Asot Mishpat

Acting Justly

. . . what does the Eternal require of you if not to love mercy, to do justice, and to walk humbly with your God?

(Micah 6:8)

When the prophet Micah set himself to identifying the three great categories under which all the commandments of the Torah could somehow be subsumed, the second one he mentioned had to do with the pursuit of justice. And so too does the second section of *The Observant Life* treat specifically of commandments related to the different ways in which individuals are to relate to others with equity and fairness. Although many of the topics considered here will strike at least some readers as areas of wholly secular interest, nothing could be further from the truth. Here, for example, are to be found chapters about the halakhic dimension of living in a democratic society and about issues related to being a moral citizen. Chapters in this section also discuss the various ways that individual Jews are called upon to serve within the institutions of society, for instance the criminal justice system or the military, and set forth the halakhic implications of the various roles they may be called upon to accept as members of that society. Other chapters in this section examine the world of business and consider the specific interface that the faithful should seek to establish between the *halakhah* as it has evolved to our day and practices of the workplace that are considered in most places normative and natural. And here too will be considered the relationship between employers and employees, and among co-workers, and also the question of the contracts deemed legally to bind people to each other in business relationships of various sorts. This section also features several chapters specifically devoted to financial matters, including borrowing and lending money, taxation, and inheritance law. The laws that govern gossip and talebearing are considered in a chapter unto itself. Also, this section includes a chapter considering the complex issues relating to intellectual property, applying the specific orientation towards such matters that the *halakhah* has traditionally taken to such matters and applying it to issues new to the so-called Information Age. All together, the chapters in this section constitute a large lesson in how the Torah imagines members of society to have the potential to live together constructively and peacefully, and how the successful functioning of society in all of its various aspects should ideally reflect the way God's own work as the One "who establishes peace in the heavens" inspires the faithful to pray that the world they inhabit too be characterized by peaceful relations between the various segments of society, and also between individuals guided by Jewish values to live at peace with the world.

Citizenship

JANE KANAREK

It has become commonplace in some Jewish circles to state that Judaism and democracy are incompatible and that belief in both requires one to impose Western values on a non-Western tradition, thus altering, and perhaps even deforming, Judaism. This assertion, however, ignores a strong current of Jewish history and thought that flows from the biblical to the talmudic period, through the medieval period and into contemporary times. There *is* a Jewish democratic ideal, though admittedly it is not identical to the one that characterizes most contemporary Western states; indeed, it actually runs counter to the Western democratic tradition in certain key areas. Nevertheless, there is still much in the Jewish tradition that can help citizens of modern states understand the notion of democracy in a Jewish context and to then develop a sense of their place in secular society.

The Pursuit of a Just Society

The famous biblical command at Deuteronomy 16:20, "Justice, justice you shall pursue," implies categorically that a Jew must engage in the continuous pursuit of a just society—a pursuit that will inevitably be connected not only with interpersonal behavior among individuals, but also with the ethical construction of the larger society in which those individuals live. Indeed, the legal principle *dina d'malkhuta dina*—the law of the land is the law—depends on this very idea of a just society. *Dina d'malkhuta dina* acknowledges the legitimacy and applicability of a non-Jewish legal system to Jews, but Jews are obligated to obey the laws of the land only when they apply equally to all. In other words, a non-discrimination principle lies at the heart of our commitment to living as Jews within a democracy. Our responsibility toward this ethical construction of society is in turn tied to the larger Jewish ideal of a covenantal community bound to God, including a firm commitment to the fulfillment of this ideal of justice. The issue, then, is not whether Judaism and democracy are identical, but whether their common goal of establishing a just and decent society is a strong enough link to render unimportant the specific ways in which they differ. Thus, the critical ideas for Jewish citizens of democratic states to ponder are clear. Where do Jewish values and democratic ideals intersect and where do they diverge? What exactly can Judaism teach us about the ethics of living in a democratic society? Can a profound commitment to *halakhah* enhance our ability to thrive in the democratic context, or must those goals—remaining committed to *halakhah* and thriving in a democratic setting—always exist at least slightly at cross-purposes with each other? In this chapter, I isolate several discrete aspects of living in a democratic society, particularly as delineated in the U.S. Constitution's Bill of Rights, and the ways in which our Jewish texts encourage us to help create and participate in such a society.

The Democratic Ideal

One of the defining features of contemporary democracies is the right of all adult citizens to vote. Merely granting this right to its citizens, however, does not make a country into a democracy. Freedom of religion, freedom of speech, freedom of the press, and freedom of assembly are all also essential components of democratic societies. In addition, under the American federalist model, the separation of powers among the legislative, judicial, and executive branches of government is also considered a key component of democracy. On the surface, it would seem that none of this could possibly be further from the Jewish model set forth in our classical sources. A closer look, however, will point to similarities between the two.

The Bible describes an elite ruling class made up of priests, prophets, judges, and kings. It is definitely not a society in which the majority rules through the "one person, one vote" principle. However, the Torah includes a passage governing the behavior of the king of Israel, a political authority whom we first encounter in Deuteronomy 17:14–20. There, God tells the people that *when* they finally enter the Land of Israel, *if* they decide to imitate the other nations and choose a king, they may do so. Like all Jews, however, that king will be subject to the law of God. Even his identity is prescribed by Scripture: the king must be an individual chosen by God and he must not be a foreigner. The king cannot have an unlimited number of horses in his stable or wives in his harem, nor may he have an unlimited amount of gold or silver in his treasury. He must keep a copy of the Torah at hand and follow its laws. The king is most definitely not described as an absolute monarch: he is not above the law and neither can he create laws to his own liking. Furthermore, the king's power is limited precisely because he is bound by an already existing law code, the Torah. In addition, not all powers of governance are concentrated in the king, who clearly is intended to share power with the priests (who are in charge of the sacrificial cult) and at least to be sensitive to the monitory presence of prophets (who purport to provide divine guidance in matters of state). Although Maimonides (at *MT* Hilkhot M'lakhim U-milḥ'moteihem 1:1, basing himself on Deuteronomy 17:15) rules that the appointment of a king upon entrance to the Land of Israel is a commandment, not merely an option, it is hard to read the biblical text as claiming that monarchy is the ideal form of governance. Rather, it is presented as a concession that God makes to the people and, moreover, a concession around which God must place certain important safeguards.

In 1 Samuel 8, when the elders of the community are depicted as assembling and demanding a king from the prophet Samuel, the dangers of kingship are even more strongly articulated. There, the prophet warns the people of the inevitable abuses of power that a king may commit: forced military conscription, the unilateral seizure of private land, and the imposition of slavery on unruly subjects, among others. Once again, we get the picture that kingship itself is a concession to the people's needs—needs that are driven by the people's (slightly ignoble) desire to imitate surrounding societies' methods of governance. Having evaluated the concept of kingship so negatively, the Bible could perhaps have intimated what form of government would be superior. But we seek such references in the pages of Scripture in vain.

Rabbinic literature, however, is different. For example, in the Talmud at *BT* B'rakhot 55a, we begin to see intimations of a different ideal of government, one where communal opinion is a serious factor:

> Said Rabbi Isaac: "One does not appoint a leader for a community without consulting the community, as it is written, 'See, the Eternal has singled out by name Betzalel' (Exodus 35:30). Said the blessed Holy One to Moses,

> 'Moses, is Betzalel worthy in your opinion [to be a leader]?' Moses answered God, 'Ruler of the Universe, if he is worthy before You, how could he possibly not be worthy before me?' God said to him, 'Even so, go and ask them.' He went and asked Israel, 'Is Betzalel worthy before you?' They said to him, 'If he is worthy before you and to the blessed Holy One, how could he possibly not be worthy before us?' "

In this passage, the selection of leadership is not presented as a unilateral decision from on high, but rather as a proposal that requires the people's consent. (In its own way, the story cited above from 1 Samuel 8 makes a similar statement; the will of the people was determinative in the establishment of the monarchy.) Even more interesting in the talmudic text, though, is the detail that God insists on the people's input, despite Moses's clearly enunciated wish to accept God's choice unconditionally. God's choice of Betzalel thus became an opportunity to demonstrate the need for communal participation in the choice of a leader, even though such participation could easily have been sidestepped had Betzalel been chosen by divine fiat alone. Although the people ultimately base their choice of a leader on God's proposal and Moses's authority, the passage cited emphasizes the rabbinic supposition that communal consent should be a prerequisite to the appointment of leaders.

Medieval Jewish sources also demonstrate a clear distaste for the biblical model of kingship in favor of a more democratic model of government. While medieval Jews lived under monarchies, they (unlike their biblical forebears) did not choose to imitate the authoritarian non-Jewish governments under whose secular authority they lived when it came to setting up structures for overseeing their own Jewish communities. Instead, they created the *kahal,* a self-governing institution in which communal decisions were made by an elected leadership. Elijah Mizraḥi, a sixteenth-century rabbi from Constantinople, even wrote the following endorsement of the democratic principle in his fifty-third responsum: "And according to our holy Torah's decree at Exodus 23:2, 'Incline after the majority,' we follow the will of the majority. Indeed, one who disputes with the majority is called a sinner. And it makes no difference whether that majority is made up of rich people or poor, sages or laypeople, since the entire community is called a court for communal matters" (ed. Jerusalem, 1938, p. 146). By understanding the biblical injunction to "incline after the majority" to imply an obligation to "follow the decision of the majority," Mizraḥi gives us a vision of communal authority that is anchored in the concept of majority rule, regardless of wealth or rabbinic learning. His vision is a radically anti-monarchical one. And, eventually, it became the norm in Jewish communal circles.

Therefore, to say that Judaism is inherently undemocratic is not consonant with our tradition as it has developed over the centuries. Perhaps already inherent in the biblical notion of a mandatory division of power between priests and kings, the rabbinic push toward popular consent (as evidenced in the medieval model of the *kahal*) resonates strongly with the ideals of democratic societies as they developed in the Western world.

So too is Judaism's injunction toward the creation of a just society. Democracy, with its ideal of universal suffrage, its protection of free speech, and its many avenues of legitimate, legal protest, comes closest to providing us with the ability to fulfill the Torah's command to create a just society. By providing each citizen with a voice in the governance of the state, democracy enables competing visions to be heard. Change, at least ideally, can ensue from the ground up instead of being imposed from the top down. This does not mean that democracy is a perfect system of government, and neither does it mean that a better one may not eventually be devised. But, at least for now, democracy best enables us to build a just community, and our ethical duty as Jews living in covenant with God is to work to perfect our communities by participating fully in their structures and institutions. In the words of the prophet Zechariah: "With truth, justice, and peace you shall judge within your gates" (Zechariah 8:16).

The Separation of Church and State

The United States Constitution is famous for its First Amendment: "Congress shall make no law respecting an establishment of religion, or prohibiting the free exercise thereof; or abridging the freedom of speech, or of the press; or the right of the people peaceably to assemble, and to petition the government for the redress of grievances." The meaning of these famous words has been the subject of debate for centuries. Sometimes, they are understood simply to prohibit the government from favoring one religion over another and to require that all religions and religious groups be treated equally. At other times, they are understood to prohibit the government from acting to support any religion at all. This latter interpretation is popularly called the doctrine of the separation of church and state.

The distinction between these two views is dramatic. According to the first interpretation, the government can legally give money to religious institutions, as long as it gives equally to all faiths and denominations. According to the second interpretation, however, the government cannot give money to any religious institution at all—because doing so would appear to favor the religious enterprise in general, and thus constitute a violation of the principle of the separation of church and state. Jews in the United States have traditionally favored the second interpretation, viewing absolute non-interference by government in any religious activity as the best way to secure religious freedom for all. Other Western democracies, such as Canada and Germany, also guarantee religious freedom, but permit the state to become involved in religious life much more widely than is accepted in the United States.

How does Judaism view the concept of a secular government wholly restrained from becoming involved in religious affairs? While the Torah describes a governmental system in which politics and religion are intertwined, rabbinic theorizing nevertheless does not imagine a complete merging of these two realms. In fact, rabbinic literature understands the division of roles between priests and kings as reflective of God's will: "Moses requested that priests and kings be descended from him. The blessed Holy One said to him, 'Do not come close' (Exodus 3:5). That is to say, God said to him that his sons were not to offer the sacrifices, because the priesthood had already been designated for his brother Aaron . . . and that the kingship had already been designated for David. Even so, Moses merited both of them . . . priesthood [and] kingship" (*Sh'mot Rabbah* 2:6).

In this striking *midrash,* even Moses, our paradigmatic leader, does not merit that his authority be transmitted through him to his direct descendants. More to the point, the text clearly implies that the various functions of government are permanently to be divided between Aaron's descendants (the priesthood) and David's (the royal house). In other words, kings will not be responsible for Temple sacrifices and priests will not wield political power.

Although the vision of government in the Torah is a religious one, the *midrash* cited above emphasizes the problematic nature of any effort to merge religious functions and governmental ones. While the leadership of Moses himself may have embodied both of these realms, God ultimately does not acquiesce to Moses's demand for his descendants—who will presumably be less worthy than the greatest of all prophets. A formal separation of powers—and, even more specifically, a formal separation of politics and religion—appears to be part of the divine order. This separation of our political identity as citizens of the states in which we live from our religious identity as Jews enables us to remain citizens of modern democratic states while still maintaining our ongoing group identity as Jews. Rabbi Vernon Kurtz writes about many details relative to the separation of church and state elsewhere in this volume in his chapter on civic morality.

The State of Israel provides a special challenge when it comes to the relationship between religion and state. Israel, after all, is a state that defines itself both as Jewish and wholly democratic. But because politics and religion are linked in Israel, the question of how to create a state whose public character is Jewish and yet which does not discriminate against its non-Jewish citizens remains controversial. In addition, the role of the synagogue in such a state, and the corollary issue of the proper governmental voice in what would be considered internal religious matters in most other countries, remain points of contention.

Currently, state and synagogue are intertwined realms in Israel. Only the Orthodox rabbinate is officially recognized by the state, a decision that effectively relegates all non-Orthodox movements to second-class status. However, even this official enfranchisement has not settled the question of what it means to be a Jew in a Jewish democratic state. Whether the separation of synagogue and state is a workable solution for Israel is a key question that will have to be answered in the years to come as Israeli democracy matures.

Freedom of Speech

The frank outspokenness of the prophets demonstrates unequivocally that the freedom to speak out openly rests at the core of the Jewish religious experience. Time after time, the prophets speak out against societal wrongs, calling the people to task for their sins and demanding their repentance. In the *haftarah* for Yom Kippur morning, Isaiah openly and bitterly chastises Jews who place great value in ritual fasts while continuing to oppress laborers (Isaiah 58:3). This cannot have been a popular message, yet nowhere does Scripture imply that the prophet did not have the right to speak out, even forcefully, against injustice where he saw it. Nor do the stories of prophets being punished for speaking out forcefully teach otherwise; they merely attest to the ill ease their words occasioned in the authorities at whom they were aimed.

Like Isaiah, other prophets also did not hesitate to speak their minds. Together, they present us with a model of freedom of speech exercised in the face of great societal wrong and in the face of authority. This freedom is not presented as a right to be taken lightly or as a privilege to be abused. Rather, the prophetic model encourages us to speak out when we deem it necessary to right a wrong—even in the face of a powerful political authority.

In the United States today, the First Amendment's guarantee of freedom of speech protects the right of Americans to such outspokenness. But freedom of speech should be considered not only a right, but also a privilege. Americans, and the citizens of other democratic states, are privileged legally to be permitted to express their beliefs in public, even when they run against societal norms.

Judaism does not guarantee the unlimited right to freedom of speech. Indeed, Jewish law recognizes the power of speech to shape behavior and so tries to set limits to that freedom. Following Deuteronomy 17:12–13, the Mishnah (at *M* Sanhedrin 11:2–4) mandates death by strangulation for the rebellious elder, the *zakein mamrei,* who teaches rulings that contradict those of the Sanhedrin. The rebellious elder receives the death penalty only if he teaches people to act contrary to the court's rulings, however. If the *zakein mamrei* makes it clear that the ideas he is espousing are his personal views but does not encourage students to act in their light, he is exempted from the death penalty. Thus, the Mishnah endorses the concept of freedom of speech, as long as that speech does not carry over into forbidden action. While this is clearly a more limited conception of freedom of speech than the model of prophetic outspokenness, what is significant here is the recognition that constraints on freedom of speech are necessary and do not constitute violations of the civil rights of citizens in and of themselves.

American jurisprudence has also not interpreted the First Amendment guarantee of freedom of speech as an unlimited right. As the Supreme Court justice Oliver Wendell Holmes, Jr., famously wrote (in *Schenck v. the United States,* 1919), the right to free speech does not extend to falsely shouting "Fire!" in a crowded theater. Combining the prophetic tradition with the more cautious mishnaic passage leads us to conclude that individuals should be encouraged to speak out against societal wrongs, recognizing the fact that our words have the power to inspire people to act. Jewish tradition encourages us to speak out, but also warns us to be both careful and cognizant of the ways in which people may turn those words into actions.

Freedom of the Press

The case of the rebellious elder is also illustrative of the concept of freedom of the press. In many ways, freedom of the press is merely a subcategory of the freedom to disseminate information. Similarly, although the Mishnah's teaching about the rebellious elder admittedly does try to stop him from teaching, it does not absolutely forbid him from doing so. People are permitted to hear his opinions. The court may not like his ideas, but it ultimately cannot prevent their dissemination. While this position is not identical with freedom of the press as it is usually construed in Western democracies, the two share the common assumption that the right to proclaim one's views in public—the functional equivalent in ancient times of publishing them in daily newspapers or posting them on-line—is a positive feature of society and not something to be squelched or prevented.

With a different emphasis, the Mishnah takes a positive attitude toward recording and honoring conflicting legal opinions and advocates the preservation of minority views. "Since the law follows the majority, why do we teach minority opinions along with majority ones?" the Mishnah asks rhetorically. And then it responds: "So that another court may come and, viewing the minority opinion [as more correct than the majority one], wish to rely on it [for a new ruling]" (*M* Eiduyyot 1:5). Here, the Mishnah explains that preserving a multiplicity of opinions is not something to which the court reluctantly acquiesces, but is rather a societal good in its own right. Indeed, the future applicability of the law may in fact depend on the preservation of earlier (and even previously rejected!) opinions. Authoritative sanction of one position does not demand the erasure of another. Instead, *M* Eiduyyot 1:5 mandates the preservation of both opinions in a thoughtful, worthy debate.

Our contemporary guarantee of the freedom of the press rests on a similar supposition: that different and competing views should be heard and are necessary for the healthy functioning of society. A free press ensures that these varying opinions and positions will be written down, ensuring their preservation for future generations and therefore, should it prove necessary, their reuse. *M* Eiduyyot 1:5 encourages such a proliferation of opinions. Following its spirit we should encourage the proliferation and dissemination of many opinions, promoted through both a free press and free speech.

A cautionary note, however, must be added to this discussion about freedom of speech and freedom of the press. As mentioned earlier, speech, whether verbal or written, is regarded seriously in Judaism. In exercising these freedoms, we should be careful not to injure others intentionally and wrongfully. Maimonides comments in detail on this aspect of the "freedom" to say what one wishes (at *MT* Hilkhot Dei·ot 7:2):

> There is a sin greater than talebearing . . . and it is [thus rightfully called] *l'shon ha-ra,* evil language. This applies to one who speaks derogatorily of one's fellow even though what one says is actually the truth. Indeed, someone who lies is called a defamer. One who engages in *l'shon ha-ra,* by contrast, is someone who sits and says, "So-and-so did this act and these are his ancestors, and I heard such-and-such about him," and then continues to say derogatory things. About this the Bible says, "May God cut off all smooth-talking lips, the tongue that speaks arrogance" (Psalm 12:4).

While the full legal details of *l'shon ha-ra* are complex (and are discussed in much greater detail elsewhere in this volume by Rabbis Kassel Abelson and Benjamin Kramer), the injunction not to injure others intentionally through the medium of speech remains foundational. Freedom of speech and the press should consequently be viewed as privileges rather than as blanket freedoms to say or publish whatever one wishes. The prophets spoke out in the face of societal injustice. The Mishnah suggests that we preserve minority opinions in order to ensure fair legal rulings in the future. In the Jewish view, the values of free speech and free press (i.e., the right to speak or publish information freely) rest on the fundamental belief that our society is not yet ideal and therefore requires constant recalibration, constant improvement. These two freedoms are part of that balancing mechanism.

Freedom of Assembly

Freedom of assembly is yet another First Amendment right essential to the maintenance of a truly democratic society. The right to assemble both enables the building of communities and also, similar in this respect to freedom of the press, can be understood as a subcategory of the right of free access to information. Central to this right is the concept that groups of people can often effect change more successfully and effectively than individuals.

In the Jewish view, assembly is not merely a right but is actually deemed a necessity. Indeed, certain *mitzvot* may not be fulfilled in the absence of a community, here generally understood to consist of at least ten adults. One of the most striking examples of this is the concept of *minyan,* the quorum of ten adult Jews necessary for communal prayer. In requiring ten worshipers for prayer, Judaism recognizes the primacy of community in our endeavors. Those aspects of the prayer service that are termed liturgical sancta (*d'varim she-bi-k'dushah*) are the sections that require ten people. A group of people helps to create holiness, as the psalmist wrote, "In assemblies bless God, the Eternal, from amidst the wellsprings of Israel" (Psalm 68:27). Judaism recognizes the power of the community to accomplish what the individual cannot. In this spirit, freedom of assembly is both a privilege of which we should avail ourselves and a right we should be prepared to defend. However, it is also a privilege to be treated responsibly, as are freedom of speech and freedom of the press. Ultimately, by requiring the assembly of the community to fulfill the religious obligations of its members, the *halakhah* is promoting the view that the right to assemble may never be casually, arbitrarily, or permanently abrogated by civil authorities.

Equal Protection

The Fourteenth Amendment guarantees certain rights to citizens of the United States as follows: "No state shall make or enforce any law which shall abridge the privileges or immunities of citizens of the United States; nor shall any state deprive any person of life, liberty, or property, without due process of law;

nor deny to any person within its jurisdiction the equal protection of the laws." This guarantee of due process and equal protection has come to be one of the central tenets of American constitutional jurisprudence. Traditional Judaism, however, with its strict delineation of roles, often runs counter to this amendment's vision. Until recently, for example, women have not been counted in a *minyan* or been permitted to be rabbis. (For the most part, this is still the case among Orthodox Jews.) Caste distinctions between priests, Levites, and Israelites remain in place, although the specific way they are applied differs from community to community. While most examples of caste distinction are admittedly benign—reserving the first and second *aliyot* for priests and Levites or only permitting *kohanim* to ascend to the *bimah* to recite the priestly benediction—it is important to acknowledge that Jewish law does codify distinctions between Jews in law.

However, Jewish law not only codifies distinctions between Jews, but also does so between Jews and non-Jews. The Mishnah, for example, at *M* Bava Kamma 4:3, teaches that "if an ox of an Israelite gores an ox of a gentile, [the Israelite owner] is exempt [from paying damages]. If an ox of a gentile gores an ox of an Israelite, however, whether the ox is or is not in the habit of goring, [the gentile owner] pays complete damages." The Mishnah thus applies the law of damages asymmetrically to the Jew and the non-Jew. And, indeed, while the unequal treatment of Jew and non-Jew is certainly part of Jewish tradition, a different perspective is also found, as exemplified in the rabbinic story about the ancient sage Shimon ben Shetaḥ found at *D'varim Rabbah* 3:3 and cited below by Rabbi Jacob Blumenthal in the chapter on commerce. In that striking story, the sage goes beyond the strict letter of the law that permits him to keep lost property of a non-Jew. Instead, he orders his students to return a precious stone that the former owner had apparently forgotten was hanging around the neck of a donkey he had sold; the sage does so despite the fact that the stone would have made him a rich man. This story teaches that it is improper to treat Jews and non-Jews in an unequal manner merely because the law formally sanctions such behavior; such actions should be avoided by decent people eager not to bring disrepute to the laws of the Torah.

The Talmud thus presents us with two very different models of the way others should be treated: as lesser or as equals. Guiding us in our choice between the two should be the biblical injunction, "There shall be one teaching and one law for you and the stranger who resides with you" (Numbers 15:16; cf. Exodus 12:49). The choice is between reinforcing the inequalities that our ancient traditions sanction or turning away from them by embracing Shimon ben Shetaḥ's model of just behavior toward all people. We should choose the path that reinforces the biblical injunction of impartial justice toward all.

Voting and Running for Office

American law does not contain a strict obligation either to vote or to run for office. However, the continued functioning of the democratic system is contingent to a large extent on our voting in elections, and to a lesser extent on our being willing to run for office as well. While Jewish law does not point us toward a strict obligation in either sense, it is incumbent on us as citizens who have a stake in maintaining and shaping our democratic system, at the very least, to vote. It is one of the ways in which we can individually follow the biblical injunction with which we began this discussion, "Justice, justice you shall pursue" (Deuteronomy 16:20).

Jews have lived in many different societies throughout our history, ranging from monarchies to caliphates to dictatorships. While Judaism does not specifically advocate for democracy over other forms of government, it does contain a strong democratic strain. This strain guides us toward how to best live as citizens of a democratic society. We must speak out in speech and in writing while being careful with our words. We must remember that a communal assembly has more power than an individual. We must take responsibility for our tradition and lean it toward equal treatment for all. We should all vote. Democracy provides us with a unique opportunity of citizenship: the privilege of participating in and constructing a more just society and thus to participate in bringing about the realization of the prophet Amos's prayer that the world be a place where justice flows like a river unimpeded and righteousness like a mighty stream (Amos 5:24).

Civic Morality

VERNON H. KURTZ

The topics of authority, citizenship, and morality are so inextricably intertwined within Jewish tradition that it is almost impossible to speak cogently about one without making reference to the others, and this is especially so when all three issues are viewed through the prism of the *halakhah*. At the same time, approaches to these issues are far from monolithic in the Jewish tradition, as they have been heavily influenced by the historical period, geography, culture, and ideological background of various Jewish thinkers.

The Torah understands the covenant between God and the Children of Israel, as encapsulated in the revealed laws and norms Moses transmitted to the people, to be the basis for the political authority of the Israelite community to govern itself, but the matter of leadership was specifically understood to be a function of Moses's prophetic vocation. Later on, as the opening *mishnah* in *Pirkei Avot* (*M* Avot 1:1) implies, Moses was replaced by others, including non-prophets, who assumed his mantle of leadership. The biblical narrative also makes it clear that the priests had a measure of authority in the community, and there are many passages in the Bible that refer either directly or obliquely to the rivalry that must naturally have existed in ancient times among priest, prophet, and king. With the destruction of the Temple and the exile of the Jewish people to Babylonia in 586 B.C.E., Jews began to live under the sovereignty of other governments and were subject to the laws and statutes of those nations. Indeed, by the time of the destruction of the Second Temple by the Romans in 70 C.E., the dispersion of the Jewish community to the lands of a very far-flung Diaspora had become a long-standing reality. Therefore, it became critical for Jewish law and culture to make provisions for accommodating the laws and societal norms of the countries in which Jews resided.

Inevitably, this led to concerns about how Jews of those lands should think about the authorities that ruled over them. In the Mishnah, for example, we read the words of Rabbi Ḥananiah, the Deputy High Priest, at *M* Avot 3:2: "Pray for the welfare of the government, for if people did not fear it, they would swallow each other alive." Rabbi Ḥananiah lived during the time of the Roman occupation of Palestine and may have personally witnessed the destruction of the Temple. For him, the ruling authorities were the glue necessary to hold society together. Much like Machiavelli would later opine in *The Prince,* Rabbi Ḥananiah understood government and authority as necessary to regulate human nature, lest human beings tear one another apart. But, while he clearly appreciated the value of governance in a theoretical sense, this rabbi's opinion of government itself as it played out in political reality is essentially negative.

There were also, however, positive responses to ruling authorities and governmental responsibilities. For example, Rabbi Shimon ben Lakish, who lived in Palestine in the second half of the third century C.E., is quoted in *B'reishit Rabbah* 9:13 as saying that the famous words of the first chapter of Genesis, "Behold it is very good," allude to the kingdom of the Romans. "But *is* the kingdom of the Romans very good?" Rabbi Shimon asks rhetorically. And then he answers his own question by explaining that it is indeed good because "it exacts justice from humanity." And that, apparently, is the best for which people can hope from a government!

The Law of the Land

Perhaps the most famous of the ancient dicta concerning the relationship of Jewish citizens to the countries in which they live, and specifically to the legal and justice systems of those countries, was that formulated by Samuel, a native of Babylonia who returned to his native land after a stint in the Land of Israel as one of the disciples of Rabbi Judah the Patriarch, the editor of the Mishnah. Samuel became instrumental in building the center of Jewish learning in Babylonia, and it was he who formulated the much-cited principle of *dina d'malkhuta dina,* that the law of any country is to be considered legally binding on the Jewish residents of that country. Much more than just an accommodation to ruling authorities, this statement expressed Samuel's conviction that there are times when a non-Jewish legal system functions as an extension of Jewish law. Although none of the four different talmudic passages in which this principle is cited (*BT* N'darim 28a, Gittin 10b, Bava Kamma 113a–b, and Bava Batra 54b–55a) explicitly sets forth a legal foundation for the dictum, Samuel's doctrine eventually became the basis for defining both the responsibility of Jews to the governing authorities in the countries in which they lived and also the specific conditions under which the Jewish legal system can accommodate the laws of the majority culture.

To a large extent, this principle, which is discussed in greater detail in several chapters of this book and particularly in the ones regarding the criminal justice system by Rabbis Laurence Sebert and Abigail Sosland, governed the manner in which the Jewish community related to governing authorities and to their laws in the lands of the Diaspora. Indeed, this principle was invoked many times throughout the medieval period to justify Jewish compliance with a non-Jewish government's method of taxation, with its recording of real estate transactions, with the implementation of its civil laws, and with its practices with respect to the minting of coins and the valuation of money. Because these were seen as being outside the realm of Jewish legal authorities, and also because most of these areas concerned financial matters never totally governed by the Jewish community on its own terms, *dina d'malkhuta dina* was invoked as the operative principle in such matters. However, religious matters such as marriage, divorce, and issues of personal status were still routinely referred to the rabbinical courts.

As Jewish communities became more integrated into the majority gentile culture, especially in Western Europe, applications of the principle of *dina d'malkhuta dina* became more expansive and eventually provided the legal and philosophical framework for Jewish accommodation to modern Western society. But although many religious reformers used the principle to justify their interest in living lives more in consonance with the people of their state, more conservative rabbinic authorities rebelled at the integration of the Jewish community in the wider society. Fearing that such integration would result in a concomitant loss of religious fervor, they balked at applying the principle to matters of purely religious or ritual concern. But even the most conservative authorities never denied the validity of the principle itself, even if they sought to limit its application in practical terms.

For almost two thousand years, Samuel's statement governed Jewish participation in diaspora communities and, for as long as it was not an independent Jewish state, even in the Land of Israel. However, when the State of Israel came into being in 1948, the citizens of Israel were in a position, finally, to create a version of government rooted in the values of *halakhah* and Jewish tradition. It is important to recognize, however, that the State of Israel is a secular state and that Jewish law, while imposed in areas of personal status and life-cycle events, is not the law of the land that governs the lives of its citizens in other arenas. The principle of *dina d'malkhuta dina* thus remains relevant even to the lives of Israelis. Although some scholars (such as the first Ashkenazic chief rabbi of Palestine, Rabbi Abraham Isaac Kook) believed that the birth of the State of Israel would signify the onset of the messianic hopes of the Jewish people and, thus, that religious value could be granted even to secular politics and to its laws, others (such as Professor Yeshayahu Leibowitz [1903–1994], an author and philosopher at the Hebrew University of Jerusalem), believed that the Jewish state meets worldly needs exactly like all states and, thus, its authority is likewise rooted in the ancient concept of *dina d'malkhuta dina*. Nevertheless, most of this essay concerns itself with life in the Diaspora, and especially in the United States.

The Separation of Synagogue and State

As Rabbi Kanarek wrote in her chapter on citizenship matters, one of the cardinal principles governing the life of American Jews is the notion that there should be, to use the traditional phrase, a separation between church and state. Indeed, the Bill of Rights, ratified in 1791, based on amendments that James Madison submitted to the first session of Congress, guarantees freedom of religion for all: "Congress shall make no law respecting an establishment of religion, or prohibiting the free exercise thereof."

This statement has impacted American Jewish life from that time onward, but many issues remain unresolved, and the Jewish community is divided regarding how, or even whether, they should ultimately be resolved. I discuss the more prominent of these issues in the next few sections of this chapter.

Religious Displays

On the American scene, there has been an overall consensus based on the Establishment Clause (that section of the Bill of Rights mandating the separation of church and state) that the public square should be devoid of any religious symbols. Most Jewish civil and religious authorities, for example, feeling that the wall of separation between religion and state should be breached neither for majority nor minority faiths, have traditionally opposed the placing of both Ḥanukkah menorahs and crèches on public property during the period around Ḥanukkah and Christmas. However, there have been some Jewish communities, led by the Lubavitch organization, that have petitioned for (and often received) the legal right to place menorahs on public property. The debate over the Establishment Clause is thus alive and well within the Jewish community, as Jews argue whether it is in the best interests of the Jewish community to understand that clause to imply a total prohibition of religion in the public square (because such displays will inevitably favor one religious tradition over another), or whether it should merely be understood as a blanket requirement that the public square be equally open to displays by members of all religions. Most members of the Conservative movement have generally felt more comfortable with the former opinion, and have worked, therefore, for a general ban on all religious symbols in the public square, lest allowing such displays nudge the country down a slippery slope toward a world in which church and state are increasingly less separated.

While there is no specific halakhic obligation to oppose the use of the public square for religious symbols (and in the case of Ḥanukkah, the impetus for doing so comes from the *mitzvah* to publicize the miracle of the holiday), civic-minded Jews should work to limit these displays. Displays promoting one religion invariably imply something about other religions as well; as a result, they may be seen as implying government sponsorship of specific religious ideas and a concomitant insensitivity to the diverse faiths that are part of the American landscape. There is also the real danger that opening the public square to the religious symbols of mainstream Judaism and Christianity will also, perhaps inevitably, open that square to religious groups that are overtly hostile to Judaism, such as Jews for Jesus or other missionary groups devoted specifically to eradicating Judaism by encouraging Jews to adopt other faiths. Should we pay the price of allowing such groups to claim their space in the public domain, merely to secure the right to set up a Ḥanukkah menorah where it arguably doesn't belong in the first place? It seems to this author that the most prudent approach is to work to limit, perhaps even outright to ban, all religious displays on public ground.

Prayer in Public Schools

The Conservative movement feels that public prayers in schoolrooms, at public sporting events, and at other similar venues should be prohibited by law. This position is not rooted in any sort of hostility to other religions, but rather out of a sense that each person's religious freedom needs to be protected from the coercive influence of the majority.

In 1996 the Rabbinical Assembly passed a resolution declaring organized prayer in public school to infringe on the constitutionally guaranteed separation of church and state in the United States. As a result, the Rabbinical Assembly proceeded to urge its members to "oppose any legislation in the United States that permits organized prayer or moments of silence for the purpose of prayer and meditation in the classrooms, at graduation ceremonies, school sporting events or at any other school-related event, whether led by students or other individuals."

The Rabbinical Assembly, in a social action policy position issued in 1999, took the position that it "must stand up for Constitutional guarantees which protect our children from the imposition of other faith systems." While it might seem exaggerated to see grave danger in a group of third graders reciting a simple prayer together at the beginning of the school day, the reality is that the imposition of prayer, including prayer so wan as to be unattributable to any specific religious tradition, in the public school classroom is a very significant breach in the traditional and legally ordained wall between church and state. That is precisely why prayer in schools is such a hot issue for those who support it, but it is also exactly why Jewish citizens should oppose it categorically.

In 2000, another Rabbinical Assembly resolution dealt specifically with prayer at public school sporting events. It urged its members to "offer strenuous objection to Congress' endorsement of prayers at public school sporting events and to continue to advocate the moral and constitutional obligation to prevent the imposition of religious beliefs and practices within the public sphere."

School Vouchers

The issue of whether governments should provide aid to parochial schools has been a contentious point of debate, no less within the Jewish community than it has been in the national forum in the United States. The Rabbinical Assembly has passed several resolutions at its annual meetings against the use of state aid for parochial schools, fearing that such vouchers will lead the government to become involved in aspects of religious education; but even within the membership of the Assembly, opinions vary widely. Generally speaking, people who oppose the introduction of vouchers usually cite their concern for the separation of church and state. Others, especially within (but not limited to) Orthodox communities, believe that vouchers can be used appropriately to promote Jewish continuity through support of Jewish day schools. In a certain sense, this ongoing discussion is really about the Establishment Clause and its role in American Jewish life.

It is important to note that this issue concerning vouchers is specifically an American one. In Canada, for example, aid is given to Jewish day schools in some provinces but not in others. In Europe and South America, where there is little separation between church and state, the situation is very different. In Israel, of course, schools are supported by the government, but aid to state-sponsored religious schools is directed almost exclusively to Orthodox institutions. The Conservative/Masorti movement has been lobbying to gain more governmental support for its educational services, as has the Reform movement.

As a summary of some of these issues, I wish to quote at length a position paper adopted in 2003 by the Leadership Council of Conservative Judaism, a group composed of the major organizations and institutions of the movement including, among many others, the United Synagogue of Conservative Judaism, the Rabbinical Assembly, and the Jewish Theological Seminary. It is entitled "Separation of Religion and State" and reads, in part, as follows:

> The Leadership Council of Conservative Judaism in the United States affirms its endorsement, both in principle and in practice, of the wall of separation between religion and state. The Conservative movement has long championed the separation of religion and state. We have passed resolutions opposing prayer in public schools and at after-school activities. We have taken the position that our own religious viewpoint and observance must be protected from government interference; by the same token, no one particular religious group should be allowed to impose its values upon the public realm. Our approach involves the realization that we, as religious leaders, ought to raise our voices and let our public officials know that many of us do not endorse state-sponsored religion. Our government representatives need to hear not only from the fundamentalist leaders; they must hear from Conservative Jews as well. We must help them understand that a person of faith can sincerely oppose issues like school prayer out of the desire to protect our children from proselytization.
>
> We intend to let our officials in Washington know that we want to see the wall of separation remain high and that we oppose any legislation, present and future, which would chip away at this wall. We believe, in keeping with the U.S. Constitution, that citizens must be protected from government establishment of religion.
>
> Taxpayer dollars must not be used to fund religious organizations providing social services without necessary constitutional protections, since it is a clear violation of the separation of religion and state. This is true whether the procedure comes via legislation or by act of the Executive branch of our government. We are very concerned that there could be religious coercion or proselytization, however subtle, used against clients in the distribution of social services. The Conservative movement posits that it is the responsibility of government to be the main provider of social services. We further oppose

federal dollars being used to fund salaries of social service providers who may discriminate in hiring practices. While religious groups are constitutionally prohibited from proselytizing, there would be ample opportunity for those groups to promote their religious agenda with government funds.

We join with many religious groups in opposing religious displays on government property or with government funds. Such displays of overtly religious symbols are best kept out of the public sector, such as government and public school buildings.

We would and do oppose injection of religious speech, including prayers and sermons, into public schools. Loss of funding by organizations refusing to allow such speech would severely endanger the wall of separation. Such actions amount to coercion of public schools and the students attending them, who would be forced to listen to religious teachings that may be totally inappropriate and unwanted by them. The Conservative movement in the United States reiterates its stand against such breaches of the division between religion and government functions, precisely because of the inherent compulsion they threaten.

We also strongly oppose changing the tax code which prohibits houses of worship from participating in electioneering. Because the government assumes that the work of places of worship is charitable and not political, this bill would open a dramatic loophole in the campaign finance system.

Finally, we are most concerned about attempts to reintroduce public worship in the United States. Such legislation has repeatedly failed to find majority support in Congress. The Constitution already guarantees all Americans freedom of worship. Any legislation that would promote religion is therefore unnecessary. We fear that it belies a hidden agenda of fostering religion, perhaps even a specific religion or religious view. As such it has no place in this land of freedom. That is why we must let our voices be heard. Religious leadership must be at the forefront of the movement to prevent governmental establishment of religion, as set forth in the Bill of Rights.

Affirmative Action

The same issues that divide members of the Jewish community in the United States with respect to school vouchers also divide them with respect to the issue of affirmative action. There are some within the Jewish community who support the use of affirmative action to enable those communities whose members have been the traditional victims of discrimination to enter the mainstream of American society by granting them special advantages in school and in the workplace.

Jews who support this kind of assistance to minority groups argue that when the Torah commands the Israelites to be kind to and respectful of strangers in their midst (as it does in no fewer than thirty-six different passages), the intention surely is to include the disadvantaged and those who have faced discrimination. Furthermore, the Torah repeatedly reminds the Israelites that they themselves once stood in the place of those minorities: "For you know the feelings of the stranger, having yourselves been strangers in the land of Egypt" (Exodus 23:9).

As a result, some in the Jewish community believe that minority groups in our society, as the modern-day equivalents of the biblical strangers in our midst, must be afforded advantageous, even preferential, treatment in order to help them integrate into society at large. Since Jews have felt the scourge of being outsiders many times throughout the course of their history, they believe that the Jewish community should be at the vanguard of this movement.

Others, however, feel that Jewish communities have in the past been subject to quota systems that acted as impediments to admission and advancement, and that the best way to deal with the issue of discrimination is to support programs that promote equal opportunity for all. The same Torah, they note, that calls for kindness to strangers also states and restates the notion that there must be "one law"—that is, one set of rules and laws—for both citizens and the strangers in our midst (cf., e.g., Leviticus 24:22 or Numbers 15:15–16). This debate spreads across religious denominations as well as political parties.

As these issues are currently being debated in the Supreme Court, it remains to be seen whether the Jewish community will support judicial decisions in these cases and whether, if they do come to support them, they do so enthusiastically or begrudgingly.

Marriage and Divorce

To a large extent Jewish communities in the Diaspora have voluntarily limited their authority to areas of personal status. And indeed, life-cycle events including conversion, marriage, and divorce are almost universally understood to belong well within the realm of religious authority.

When a rabbi performs a wedding in the Diaspora, he or she is almost always acting both as a religious and a civil authority in the creation of the marital bond. The Conservative movement holds, therefore, that if divorce is to take place, then both a civil and a religious divorce must ensue. And because each serves a different function, each is considered indispensable. Under the principle of *dina d'malkhuta dina,* the civil court is enjoined to decide upon areas of property division, child custody and support, and other items pertaining to the separation. However, a Jewish bill of divorce, called a *get* in Hebrew, is required in order for each of the partners to remarry according to Jewish law.

There are a variety of scenarios, but central to all *get* procedures is the *beit din,* a rabbinic court, which gathers to write or commission the document that terminates the religious status of the relationship. It also supervises the delivery of the *get* to the wife. Traditional Jewish law dictates that the husband must initiate and deliver the *get* to his wife. Should this not occur, neither the husband nor the wife will be able to remarry according to Jewish religious ritual. In order to solve this problem even before it may occur, many Conservative rabbis add a prenuptial agreement to the *k'tubbah,* the Jewish marriage document, requiring both husband and wife to agree in advance to seek a *get* from a *beit din,* should they ever seek a civil divorce. (This addition is generally called "the Lieberman clause" after its originator, Professor Saul Lieberman of the Jewish Theological Seminary.) The efficacy of this clause is a matter of debate. There have been cases in which a recalcitrant husband who refused to initiate the *get* proceedings was brought to a civil judge as a means of forcing the issue; although some civil courts have agreed to act in such instances, others have declined. As a result, many Conservative rabbis now use a "Letter of Intent" that has the same effect as the Lieberman clause, but is written in English and witnessed separately, and which is more likely to be enforced by the civil courts. And there are also rabbis who advise congregants in the process of divorce to include within their civil divorce agreement a clause requiring that both parties participate in the *get* procedure. In this way, the power of the civil court is used to strengthen the hand of rabbinic legislation. Most do not see this as a weakening of the separation of the wall between religion and state, but as merely a way of enlisting civil support in the pursuit of justice for women who will otherwise be hampered in future efforts to remarry according to Jewish law.

Conflicts between Civil Law and Halakhah

What happens when civil law and *halakhah* are in conflict? What ought one do when one finds oneself in opposition to a policy of the ruling authorities, on religious grounds? Are there times when the priorities of religious tradition are more important than the concept of *dina d'malkhuta dina*? Should one be able to voice one's personal objection to a civil law on a religious basis, or must one join with others as part of a unified communal stance?

There is a long history of Jews standing up to ruling powers. From Moses to Jeremiah to Isaiah to the Maccabees, Jews have stood up to ruling authorities—whether those authorities have been of their own people or of other nations. Time and time again, the prophets demanded that ruling authorities abide by the highest standards of justice, ethics, and morality and not simply ignore laws they found personally inconvenient. In addition, civil disobedience in the pursuit of a higher moral, ethical, and just law has always been considered wholly appropriate behavior. Indeed, civil disobedience has a long and honorable tradition in the *halakhah*. And while Jewish law believes that value of human life is all-important, it dictates that people must choose to defy the authorities, even at the cost of their own lives, rather than obey a law or decree that would otherwise require them to commit murder, to engage in immoral sexual relations, or to worship idols (*BT* Sanhedrin 74a). The principle is simply that one remains responsible for one's actions at all times. Jewish law does not sanction the excuse that one was simply following orders to justify the performance of immoral or illegal acts. (This concept is discussed as well by Rabbi Michael Graetz in his chapter on the *halakhah* of military service.)

Following these religious dictates, some American Jews were supportive of civil disobedience in defense of civil rights during the 1960s, while others felt justified in participating in similar protests during the Vietnam War. Others, however, felt that there are ways to protest governmental policies without breaking any current laws. These are very complex issues with no simple answers. But Jewish law is clear that morality and justice are the standards by which civil law and human actions are measured. Sometimes it is with respect to the nuances of those definitions that the most interesting and passionate debates take place.

In areas where Jewish law and civil legislation collide, there are also no simple answers. When religious dictates require that an individual follow personal religious laws that oppose civil statutes, decisions can become quite complex. For example, civil laws concerning abortion in some jurisdictions may not be in total consonance with normative Jewish law. Inheritance laws as promulgated by civil authorities may conflict with the laws of the Torah. Military dress codes may require an uncovered head during military service. It would be easy to cite many other issues with the potential to create conflict between the law of the land and Jewish religious dictates. How does one decide which legal system to follow? In some cases, *dina d'malkhuta dina* applies, and in such cases we must follow the law of the civil courts. In other cases, mostly in the realm of personal religious conviction, Jewish law is supreme and we are required to follow it even if it means coming into conflict with civil regulations. Obviously, it is essential when navigating these waters to have a clear understanding of what is actually required by Jewish law and what is mere custom.

Judaism considers the welfare of the community to be an important value for each individual. Thus, being a citizen of a country entails obligations, responsibilities, and adherence to the rule of law. When these laws are in opposition to *halakhah*, rabbinic authorities must decide which law to follow. It is important to realize that instances of civil law being in total conflict with the laws of the Torah are extremely rare and that, therefore, Jews in the Diaspora are generally required to obey the law of the land. Whether in Israel or in the Diaspora, the *halakhah* dictates that Jews be loyal citizens of the country in which they live. Good citizenship is seen as an important value in Jewish life, and working to enhance the welfare of society is deemed not only an appropriate exercise, but a religious requirement as well. The very fact that almost all congregations include a prayer for the welfare of the worshipers' country in their Sabbath prayers should be seen as a liturgical extension of this same principle. These and other issues relating to citizenship are discussed elsewhere in this volume in greater detail by Rabbi Jane Kanarek in her chapter on that specific topic.

In the Talmud, at *BT* Z'vaḥim 102a, Rabbi Yannai is quoted as saying: "Let the awe of kingship always be upon you." He used Moses's behavior in Pharaoh's court as his example, but his advice is clearly applicable to all forms of government, not just ruling royalty. Even though he disagreed with Pharaoh, Moses had to be respectful of Pharaoh's position. And, Rabbi Yannai teaches, so must we all! In that same passage, however, we learn that Rabbi Yoḥanan inferred the same principle from the story of the prophet Elijah and the wicked King Ahab, as told in 1 Kings 18, in which Elijah is depicted as showing Ahab the respect due a king in spite of the strong opposition he always displayed toward Ahab's reprehensible behavior. Thus, Jewish tradition understands that respect for governmental authorities is always appropriate, and that this is the case even when one disagrees strongly with some specific policy. At the same time, the system presumes that these authorities are sufficiently imbued with respect for justice and morality for the Jewish community to feel comfortable following their lead. If not, then opposition may and must be voiced.

In most Western countries in which Jews currently live, differences of opinion are more about nuance and detail than about major legal principles. But debate is healthy and there will always be controversy concerning issues that relate to citizenship and morality. These debates are healthy for all societies, however, and should not be shunned or downplayed. The strength of any society rests in no small part on its willingness to engage in passionate debate about the principles that guide it forward and the rules it establishes as the norms of accepted or desired behavior. To squelch debate, therefore, is to deprive society of one of its most potent sources of creative energy and to open the way to despotism.

The Secular Justice System

LAURENCE A. SEBERT

Most Jewish citizens of modern Western republics take their participation in the justice system of their countries for granted. Yet, from a Jewish perspective, that is a most unusual development, because it was a clearly enunciated goal of rabbis and other Jewish communal leaders for nearly two thousand years to prevent members of the Jewish community from using the non-Jewish court system. Rabbi Tarfon, for example, noted (in a comment recorded at *BT* Gittin 88b) that intra-Jewish disputes should never be taken to the secular justice system, "even should their law be the same as Jewish law [in the matter under consideration]." Rabbinic authorities continued to militate against the use of non-Jewish courts throughout the medieval period and enacted harsh sanctions against those who employed their services. Rabbi Joseph Karo codified this attitude as law (*SA* Ḥoshen Mishpat 26:1), concluding his remarks with these sharp, unambiguous words: "Anyone who goes [willingly] before a gentile court to adjudicate a dispute is a wicked individual and is close to being a blasphemer. It is as though such a one has formally rejected the Torah of Moses."

The possibility of avoiding interaction with the gentile justice system entirely was directly related to the fact that, at least during most of the pre-modern period, civil authorities granted Jewish courts wide-ranging autonomy to handle internal disputes, including minor criminal matters. More serious crimes, such as rape, murder, or crimes against the state, were still brought before the government authorities. For example, King John signed a charter in 1201 reconfirming such rights for Jews in England: "Know that we have granted, and by our present charter confirm to our Jews in England, that the breaches of right which shall occur among them . . . [may] be examined and amended among themselves according to their law, so that they may administer their own justice among themselves" (quoted in Salo Baron, *A Social and Religious History of the Jews,* vol. 2 [New York: Columbia University Press, 1937], p. 92).

Professor Baron indicates that these circumstances prevailed in the Muslim world as well. He points out, for example, that "among the numerous Arabic documents from medieval Toledo, not one is found in which two Jewish parties figure as signatories to a contract before a non-Jewish court" (ibid.). Also, the large number of civil cases discussed by rabbis in their voluminous writings indicates that such civil matters were routinely brought before rabbinical courts for adjudication. For example, Rabbi Asher ben Yeḥiel (c. 1250–1327), one of the leading rabbinic authorities of Spain and Germany in his day, wrote more than one thousand responsa that survive today; over eighty percent of them deal with matters of civil law.

The spirit of emancipation that swept through the Western world in the nineteenth century changed all that. Once Jews could become individual citizens of modern countries, the base of Jewish power began to shift. The Jewish community was no longer a separate, autonomous entity. The authority of internal Jewish courts suffered severe erosion. As a result, Jewish courts of law gradually ceased to be the sole address for resolving civil disputes among Jews. Questions of property and theft once routinely put to rabbis slowly tapered off as Jews increasingly brought their legal disputes—both civil and criminal—to the secular courts of the countries in which they lived, and the spiritual and intellectual descendants of those rabbis were, in time, left solely to consider decisions regarding religious law.

Many of the leading rabbinic authorities of the time lamented this change. Rabbi Ezekiel Landau (1713–1793), one of the greatest halakhic authorities of his day, complained bitterly and openly about the degree to which Jews were turning to gentile courts, a development he felt was so dangerous that "all three pillars of the world, are shaken: the Law, Truth, and Peace" (quoted in *The Principles of Jewish Law,* ed. Menaḥem Elon [1975; reprint, Piscataway, NJ: Transaction Publishers, 2007], p. 34). While some Jewish communities have managed to retain their separate legal apparatuses into modernity, it has not been a widespread or successful effort. As a result, Jewish law relating to civil and criminal matters largely atrophied, and it was not until the founding of the Jewish state that Jewish courts were once again widely responsible for civil and criminal law.

Dina D'malkhuta Dina

Following emancipation, drastically and dramatically changing historical circumstances effectively limited the application of Jewish law in non-ritual matters. However, there had also been gradual internal shifts that made these changes, if not wholly desirable, then at least acceptable to Jewish religious authorities. From a theological perspective, Judaism can recognize the primacy of only one law, the law of the Torah. Still, for centuries, Jewish law managed to accommodate itself to the authority of local governments. As early as the third century C.E., the talmudic sage Samuel ruled that, at least in certain cases, "The law of the land is the law" (*BT* N'darim 28a, Gittin 10b, Bava Kamma 113a–b, and Bava Batra 54b–55a). This principle, *dina d'malkhuta dina* (in Aramaic), is cited, discussed, and analyzed numerous times in this book, but it was originally applied only in a very narrow way to justify taxation, and the related seizure of property, by secular authorities. From the time of Samuel onward, however, there has been a gradual broadening of this principle to include most areas over which civil secular law claims authority.

Even though "the law of the land is the law" means that secular governments have the legitimate right to tax and fine the citizens under their jurisdiction, this principle was not extended, nor could it conceivably ever have been extended, to grant secular courts the right to govern Jewish religious beliefs or activities. Laws of religious observance, therefore, remained strictly off-limits to non-Jewish authorities. No king or legislature could be allowed to rule on Jewish practices such as Shabbat or circumcision. Certainly, any attempt to outlaw such practices was vigorously opposed. (This is a distinction similar to the principle of the separation between church and state discussed elsewhere in this volume by Rabbis Jane Kanarek and Vernon Kurtz.) But to sanction submission to another set of laws, even those that would normally fall under the general rubric of civil or criminal law, it became vitally important to establish their legitimacy from the perspective of Jewish ideology.

Well before Samuel's statement, the prophet Jeremiah had spoken this divine oracle to those Jews exiled to Babylon: "Thus said the Eternal One of Hosts . . . seek the welfare of the city to which I have exiled you and pray to the Eternal on its behalf—for in its prosperity shall you prosper" (Jeremiah 29:4–7). The prophet's oracle provided later rabbinic authorities with a utilitarian approach to accommodation. Pray for the peace of your cities and your countries, and cooperate with their authorities, the prophet explained, because doing so will almost always be in your own best interests. Samuel's principle may have simply been an extension of this practical approach to getting along with the establishment. In the centuries that followed, this principle was extended and legal rationale was applied in order to justify its use.

Some post-talmudic authorities followed Jeremiah's lead and considered it to be God's will that Jews obey the laws of foreign rulers. It was their understanding that God had exiled the Jews from their land. Therefore, they concluded, it must also be the will of God that the Jews live under the rule and authority of their non-Jewish hosts and be subject to the latter's laws.

Rashi (at *BT* Gittin 9b, *s.v. ḥutz mi-gittei nashim*) also suggests divine approval for submission to gentile justice systems, but justifies his position using a different source entirely. The talmudic interpretation (at *BT* Sanhedrin 56a) of the instructions given to Noah after the flood (Genesis 9:1–17) posits that all nations are obligated to follow seven basic laws, usually referred to as the Noahide laws; among these is the requirement to have a system of justice. Since the Torah thus requires that gentile courts exist, they must *ipso facto* exercise legitimate authority for all who live under their rule.

Rashi's grandson, Rabbi Samuel ben Meir, called Rashbam, takes a different, slightly more logical approach. He suggests that Jews are subject to the law of the land based on the notion of a social contract, and contractual agreements between two parties only work because each side agrees to its terms. The same logic can apply to large groups of people. He states: "All taxes on property and income, and the customs of the laws of the kings . . . are legal, since all the inhabitants of the country willingly accept the laws of the king" (Rashbam to *BT* Bava Batra 54b, *s.v. v'ha-amar*).

The Limits to Legitimacy

There were, however, boundaries to the purview of these courts. The rulings of non-Jewish courts had to be objective and fair. Maimonides, for example, makes the following statement in the *Mishneh Torah:* "The general rule is that any law promulgated by the king to apply to everyone, and not to one person alone, is not deemed robbery. But whatever he takes from one particular person only—and not in accordance with a law known to everyone, but by doing violence to this person—is deemed robbery" (*MT* Hilkhot G'zeilah Va-aveidah 5:14). Whether or not the state's law was legitimate was not a matter of its mirroring the strictures of Jewish law. Rather, the laws of the state were held up to a more universal standard of justice and fair play.

The careful balance between religious and civil legal authority began to tilt toward the civil authority at the time of emancipation. As Jews were granted citizenship, they became subject to all civil laws. Napoleon tried to hammer out these differences through the famous "Sanhedrin," an assembly of Jewish lay and religious leaders, convened in 1806. One question he posed to the assembly concerned the conflicting needs of Jewish and civil divorce. The answer he was seeking was that the civil authorities held sway, and such an answer did indeed come from the pen of Rabbi Ishmael of Modena, who, because he was not in attendance, responded in writing. Rabbi Ishmael (as cited in *The Jewish Political Tradition,* ed. Michael Walzer [New Haven: Yale University Press, 2000], vol. 1, p. 451) agreed that "we are obligated to follow the laws of the kingdom just as we do the laws of our holy Torah, for they are both together good. Hence, where Torah law requires a man to divorce his wife, he must first go to the gentile courts and do whatever is necessary to obtain a civil divorce, and then go to the rabbi and give a *get* to his wife in accordance with our holy Torah." Rabbi Ishmael somehow managed to satisfy everyone with his answer. He satisfied Napoleon by agreeing that the state's laws must come first. But he also managed to comply with Jewish law by giving it the last word. The divorce of a Jewish citizen of Napoleon's France was not to be deemed complete until it was formally ratified by a rabbinic divorce.

The final step along this road was taken by the leaders of the Reform movement in Germany, who sought to abolish the primacy of Jewish law whenever it conflicted with civil authority. In the mid-nineteenth century, for example, Rabbi Samuel Holdheim of Germany (1806–1860) was a proponent of the abolition of Jewish autonomy on all counts. His goal in doing so was the full integration of Jews into society. Removing the obstacles to acceptance meant completely relinquishing Jewish authority in such civil matters as marriage and divorce.

As a result of these internal and external changes, *dina d'malkhuta dina* became the law of the Jews in a way that its ancient proponents could not possibly have imagined. So accepted as a bedrock foundation of Jewish legal thinking did this principle become, in fact, that rabbis began to cite it to justify the fact that even religious Jews were turning to non-Jewish courts for legal rulings in essentially civil disputes between themselves and their fellow Jews. That is the situation which prevails today, even in Israel. In the modern State of Israel, the law of the land is an amalgam of the Turkish, Muslim, British, and Jewish legal systems. Yet even in Israel it is only in the area of personal status—which rubric encompasses, among other things, marriage and divorce—that rabbinic courts hold sway openly and freely.

That Jews throughout the world today operate freely within the secular justice system is a given. And that they do so with the blessing of rabbinic authorities merely indicates the degree to which *dina d'malkhuta dina* has prevailed as an overriding legal principle. When facing civil or criminal issues, it is expected that Jews will turn to the secular courts for adjudication. The rules of those courts govern the actions of all citizens, including Jewish ones.

Crime and Punishment

ABIGAIL N. SOSLAND

Even in wholly secular contexts far outside the walls of churches and synagogues, the vocabulary used to describe judicial punishment often derives directly, or at least indirectly, from the spheres of religion and theology. Lawyers, judges, and modern legal scholars, for example, often speak about the need to punish evil in the world, or about the idea that there should be an essential, final reckoning for every individual and his or her deeds. Indeed, in modern Western countries, secular notions of justice seem almost intrinsically linked to themes that derive from biblical tradition. This is not even that hard to explain, in that our most basic theories of good, evil, and justice derive directly from Scripture, and it is for the most part through the contemplation of biblical texts that Western cultures have come to understand the value and reasonableness of punishment for wrongdoing.

Imposing Penalties

Legal scholars offer two main motivations for court-based punishment of the guilty, deterrence and retribution, and both of these can be traced directly back to biblical ideas.

The concept of deterrence underlies the many directives in Scripture to punish the guilty in a public fashion. Consider, for example, the words with which the Torah concludes its injunction publicly to execute one who incites another to idol worship: "And all of Israel will see and be afraid, and they will not continue to do this evil thing in your midst" (Deuteronomy 13:12). Furthermore, many of the punishments described in the Torah were clearly designed to act as deterrents, including the (brief) public display of the corpses of executed criminals so that they could be seen by the community (Deuteronomy 21:23).

The notion of retribution also appears throughout the biblical text. The *lex talionis* justice model of the post-Sinai list of regulations—an eye for an eye, a tooth for a tooth, a life for a life—had actually already appeared in God's commandments to Noah in Genesis 9:8: "Whoever sheds the blood of a human being, by a human being shall that one's blood be shed." But since, as we shall see below, rabbinic lawmakers never took the principle of *lex talionis* literally, it is clear that—at least for the rabbis—this type of scriptural ruling could only be explained as part of the larger philosophical effort to develop a public response to criminal activity.

In addition to deterrence and retribution, however, the Torah also suggests two additional rationales for judicial punishment. First, the concept that pure evil must somehow be obliterated from the community is repeated nine times in Deuteronomy (at Deuteronomy 13:6; 17:7 and 12; 19:19; 21:21; 22:21, 22, and 24; and 24:7), usually with the words *u-vi·arta ha-ra mi-kirbekha,* that is, "you shall eradicate [literally, burn out] evil from your midst." Second, the idea that justice can help to rid the world of evil is carried even further through the biblical notion that justice actually cleanses the land and purifies the connection of its citizens with God. For example, the execution of murderers is specifically described as an act of national purification and expiation: "You shall not pollute the land in which you live, for blood pollutes the Land—and the Land can have no expiation for blood that is shed on it except by the blood of the one who shed it" (Numbers 35:33).

Equally important, however, is the spiritual connection between pursuing justice and remaining holy. When Achan is executed for disobeying God's law and taking unauthorized loot from Jericho, the point is made clear that his sin weakened the people's connection to God, which thus needed to be subsequently strengthened anew. And, indeed, after the people stone him for his sin, the text notes, almost with palpable relief, that "the anger of the Eternal then subsided" (Joshua 7:26). The moral of the story could not be clearer: God on high is appeased through the administration of justice below.

Despite the Torah's clear theoretical directives to establish justice in the land, the actual authority to administer judicial punishment has been limited throughout Jewish history, and that is to say the very least. Since the destruction of the Second Temple and until modern times, in fact, Jews have lacked the ability or the means to adjudicate most criminal cases. It is so, of course, that Jewish courts in different places and at different moments in history have had varying degrees of jurisdiction over internal Jewish affairs, but, even when vested with the greatest authority, they were always accountable to the dominant powers under which they lived. But, as Rabbi Laurence Sebert explains above, things changed dramatically in the post-Enlightenment world. For the first time, diaspora Jews became part and parcel of the judicial system of their own nations. They were no longer solely on the receiving end of the criminal justice system, but, at least eventually, came to sit as members of juries and as judges, even as justices of the supreme courts of certain nations. Jewish politicians have authored criminal legislation, Jewish attorneys have defended and prosecuted criminals, and Jewish corrections workers have served in prisons and other correctional facilities. As Jews have helped to build the modern, secular legal systems of their host countries, they have also had the unique opportunity to integrate aspects of Jewish legal thought into the values of the justice systems of those countries. This, too, has been a significant development of modern times.

The question of how much allegiance exactly Jews should have to civil law systems is an ancient one. As far back as the first generation of talmudic scholars in ancient times, for example, the great teacher Samuel established our obligation to obey the rules of the "kingdom" in which we reside. Samuel's statement has been understood by rabbinic scholars through the centuries as applying to civil cases only. Thus, even today, the concept of *dina d'malkhuta dina,* literally, "the law of the land is law," demands that Jews pay taxes to the countries in which they live, obey traffic laws, and abide by the civil and criminal codes of law that pertain in their jurisdictions.

In criminal law, however, Jewish tradition has long recognized that even secular courts had their own rules by which to abide, specifically the seven Noahide laws given to those outside of the Sinai covenant. Included in these laws were both the prohibition against murder and the obligation to establish courts, both of which imply the need for some sort of Noahide judicial system charged with maintaining peace and order for those under its jurisdiction. Also, the laws instituted for a Jewish king, specifically as set forth in Maimonides' *Mishneh Torah,* allowed the king to go beyond the court's usual procedure in order to establish peace in his kingdom (*MT* Hilkhot M'lakhim U-milḥ'moteihem 3:8). These extralegal privileges were understood to apply to non-Jewish kings as well, and thus Jewish allegiance to that king's laws and the laws of the state in general was required in criminal cases just as in civil law (gloss of the Rema to *SA* Ḥoshen Mishpat 369:8).

Thus, a Jew sitting on a jury in a criminal case may not take Jewish law as a standard in a secular court, but must follow the codes of law as explained by the secular judge. When the secular law seems to conflict with Jewish law, observant Jews must still follow the secular law, with the understanding that Jewish law has given secular governments the responsibility to set up courts and to establish peace. Doing so, therefore, does not constitute breaking with the *halakhah* at all, but rather living up to its requirements in this specific setting. What responsible Jews should do, therefore, is to use the values and the history of Jewish jurisprudence to inform their decision-making. It is these values that may help us to make intelligent, ethical decisions beyond the letter of the secular law.

Jews are permitted to take a witness's oath to affirm that their testimony is truthful when participating in a secular trial. This was not always the case. The early rabbis wanted to believe that no God-fearing Jew would lie in court (the biblical injunction not to bear false witness seemed incentive enough), so the Mishnah does not even require that witnesses take oaths not to lie. Instead, it includes detailed instructions regarding the best way for the court forcefully to adjure a witness to tell the truth (*M* Sanhedrin 4:5) and leaves it at that. Indeed, the Tosafot (commenting on *BT* Kiddushin 43b, *s.v. v'hashta d'takkun rabbanan sh'vu·at heiset*) declare that any witness who takes an oath should not be trusted at all, because anyone who would not fear breaking a biblical injunction would surely take a false oath with impunity. Menaḥem Elon, a respected Israeli jurist who served for decades on the Israeli Supreme Court reports, however, that this law shifted over time, as interactions between Jews and secular courts became more common. By the fifteenth century, for example, the Sephardic authority Rabbi Shimon ben Tzemaḥ Duran (known as the Rashbatz) established that even swearing with one's hand on a Torah scroll should not be considered a vain oath *ipso facto* if the court feels that "the people are not taking seriously the prohibition against giving false testimony" (Menaḥem Elon, *The Principles of Jewish Law* [1975; reprint, Piscataway, NJ: Transaction Publishers, 2007], p. 1701). And Rabbi Moshe Isserles (1520–1572) wrote in his commentary on the *Shulḥan Arukh* that it is permissible to take an oath "if the court sees a temporary need to adjure the witnesses to tell the truth" (gloss of the Rema to *SA* Ḥoshen Mishpat 28:2). In a case where a witness's oath would encourage a trial to be taken more seriously, it is therefore well within the framework of halakhic permissibility to swear to tell the truth, even with one's hand on a Bible. In such a case, however, it goes without saying that a Jewish citizen must place his or her hand on a Jewish Bible.

Capital Punishment

Starting with the narrative of Cain and Abel in Genesis and moving forward to Deuteronomy's injunction always "to choose life" (30:19), the sanctity of human life is woven through the biblical text as one of its most supreme and central values. It is therefore just a bit surprising that the Torah is clear and unambiguous in demanding that certain crimes by their very nature require that their perpetrators be punished by being put to death. As demonstrated by Rabbi Jacob Milgrom, in most cases dealing with sins of religious or personal nature the rabbis saw this kind of punishment as primarily resting in God's hands (see "The Encroacher and the Levite," in his *Studies in Levitical Terminology* [Berkeley: University of California Press, 1970], pp. 5–59). Indeed, in contexts where the Bible establishes death as the just penalty without any further qualification, the rabbis often understood this to mean death "at the hands of heaven." (In such cases, the grammatical difference between the Hebrew *yamut,* "will die," and *yumat,* "will be put to death," serves as a clear sign that some offenders will be punished with death that will come to them without any earthly intervention; cf. in this regard the *midrash* of Rabbi Ishmael presented in the Talmud at *BT* Sanhedrin 84a.)

At the same time, in order to build a just society, the rabbis assumed the responsibility of sentencing the most serious public offenders to death after finding them guilty in human courts. Even in such extreme circumstances, however, they were careful to balance the need for justice with the desire to minimize the pain and humiliation of even the most depraved and unrepentant offender. This ethic is clearly laid out in the biblical sources. Despite the seemingly frequent mention of death as the punishment for crimes such as idolatry, sexual misconduct, or murder, the biblical text also includes many rulings aimed at preventing overly cruel punishment, as well as at protecting the rights of the accused. Thus, a willfully wrong accusation could lead to the accuser being personally punished, as, for example, in the case of a man who makes a false accusation regarding his wife's virtue (Deuteronomy 22:13–19). Justice had to be meted out speedily, as spelled out in Kohelet 8:11, as well as in rabbinic literature (cf., e.g. *BT* Sanhedrin 32a). Even the bodies of executed criminals put on public display for the community to see had to be taken down before nightfall, in recognition of the sacredness of the divine image that even the most reprobate sinner was deemed to bear (Deuteronomy 21:22–23).

The rabbis of the Mishnah and Talmud preserved the tradition of seeking a workable balance between justice and mercy. On the one hand, they developed a judicial system that provided severe penalties for certain types of criminal acts; the rabbinic methods of capital punishment—stoning, burning, decapitation by sword, and strangulation—are described in great detail in the talmudic tractate Sanhedrin, where the relevant texts go far beyond any biblical directives for execution in terms of gory and imaginative detail. On the other hand, the rabbis also introduced into the legal system a number of brakes designed to favor the accused in a capital trial. These factors—including very exact and exacting evidentiary standards, extremely detailed trial regulations, and even the specific rules governing execution—conveyed their serious discomfort with the prospect of actually convicting accused persons when it could lead to their execution. In grappling with these two competing concerns—the desire to rid the community of crime and criminal behavior, and the equally profound desire to protect and defend the sanctity of human life—the rabbis displayed marked ambivalence toward capital punishment itself and their putative role in it.

Perhaps the best-known mishnaic quote on the topic is found at *M* Makkot 1:10. There, in a brief discussion of court executions, we find the statement of Rabbi Eleazar ben Azariah to the effect that a court that kills one person in seventy years is to be labelled *ḥavlanit* ("destructive"). For centuries, this statement has been adduced to "prove" that rabbinic tradition, for all that it supported the concept of capital punishment in theory, actually opposed it in practice. In fact, however, rabbinic tradition was far less monolithic than this explanation suggests. Certainly, the mishnaic regulations governing capital trials support this abolitionist understanding to some degree. For example, evidentiary requirements alone could have kept almost any perpetrator from receiving a capital sentence: only the testimony of two eyewitnesses could be used to convict the accused, and no circumstantial evidence of any kind was accepted (cf., e.g., *MT* Hilkhot Rotzei·aḥ U-sh'mirat Nefesh 5:14, Hilkhot Eidut 4:1, and Hilkhot Sanhedrin 20:1). In addition, witnesses were required to attest that the accused had been duly warned of the potential penalty—death by execution—before committing the crime in question. And the perpetrator must have formally declared his or her intent to commit the crime in question anyway, after first having heard and understood their warning (cf. *MT* Hilkhot Y'sodei Ha-torah 5:4).

In tractates Sanhedrin and Makkot, the Mishnah also describes the extent to which the two witnesses were to be questioned. If, for example, either witness could not pinpoint the time or the day on which the crime had been committed, or if their testimony differed in even the slightest detail, the testimony of both parties was disqualified (*M* Sanhedrin 5:1). The witnesses were also carefully admonished about the potential consequences of their testimony (*M* Sanhedrin 4:5), and lying witnesses could themselves be convicted of perjury and sentenced to the same punishment that the accused would have received, had their lie gone undetected (*M* Makkot 1:1–6). Finally, if the accused was convicted, the witnesses were expected to carry out the execution with their own hands, thereby guaranteeing that they would take their roles with the utmost seriousness (*M* Sanhedrin 6:4, citing Deuteronomy 17:7).

In the opening chapter of tractate Sanhedrin, the Mishnah offers precise details regarding the court authorized to try capital cases. While only three judges were required for civil cases, a capital case required twenty-three judges. The arguments for the defendant's innocence were to be presented, and the judge with the least seniority would offer his opinion first, lest the more senior judges influence his thinking. A verdict of "not guilty" was to be handed down on the same day the trial ended, in order to prevent undue anxiety for the accused. If the accused was found guilty, however, the formal pronouncement of the verdict would be withheld overnight so that any proof or argument for the defendant's innocence that had somehow not been brought forward could be presented in the morning. The judges could reverse the decision from guilty to innocent, but a verdict of not guilty in a capital case could not be reversed (*M* Sanhedrin 4:1). Even as the accused was walked to the place of execution, guards would stand watch at the courthouse in case any new witnesses were to come forward or exonerating evidence be adduced. Until the final moment, the court was directed to seek any possibility to prevent the execution from taking place (*M* Sanhedrin 6:1).

These are just a few of the safeguards established by the rabbinic tradition to ensure that no innocent person would ever be sent to his or her death by the court. On top of these highly restrictive rules, it was also the case that certain people were categorically exempted from the death punishment because they could never be held accountable for their actions: the deaf-mute (although deaf *or* mute defendants were not automatically exempted), minor children, and the mentally ill (*MT* Hilkhot Ḥoveil U-mazzik 4:20). The mentally ill individual was defined by the Talmud as one who "goes out alone at night, sleeps in cemeteries, and rips his clothing" (*BT* Ḥagigah 3b). But even temporary insanity was protected by Jewish law and a person could not be held responsible for something done during a period of madness, even if that same individual subsequently became lucid again.

After surveying these strictures and laws, one could conclude that the rabbis were basically opposed to capital punishment and sought to curtail its application to the greatest extent possible without actually contravening the law of Scripture. Still, to read the rabbinic texts as simply a challenge to capital punishment is to ignore the complexities of the issue. Indeed, even some of the exemptions seemed to come with exceptions. That the accused is not mentally competent to stand trial, for example, needs to be specifically proven in each case, unless the accused meets the exact standard for a standing diagnosis set out by the Talmud. In addition, each court can make its own ruling regarding whether the accused is legally unfit to stand trial. (For a more detailed discussion of this topic, see Jacob Bazak's book, *Aḥrayuto Ha-p'lilit Shel Ha-lakui B'nafsho* [Jerusalem: Kiryat Sefer, 1973].) Maimonides even allows executing a person who is sick or mentally ill if the accused is a danger to others. (This is based on the injunction to kill a *rodeif,* one who is chasing another with the intent to take his or her life. And if the court itself actually witnesses a mentally ill person killing someone, they may execute him or her, as Maimonides explains, so that "evil will be eradicated from Israel" [*MT* Hilkhot Rotzei·aḥ U-sh'mirat Nefesh 2:9]. Thus, protecting the community becomes, in this case, the most important value, one worth pursuing even at the expense of human life.)

If the rabbis intended entirely to eradicate execution as a means of judicial punishment, then why did they preserve traditions describing the exact way a criminal was to be punished in the most explicit detail? Some scholars argue that, since the Sanhedrin lacked the authority to execute by the time of the Mishnah, those passages must have been written for theoretical purposes only, just as the Mishnah comments on many other aspects of Torah law, such as sacrificial law, that had become solely theoretical by the beginning of the third century C.E. In this way, the rabbis may have been trying to simply paint a picture of an ideal and just community. Alternately, as Beth Berkowitz argues in her book *Execution and Invention: Death Penalty Discourse in Early Rabbinic and Christian Cultures* (New York: Oxford University Press, 2006), the whole discussion may have been simply an attempt to project a sense of the rabbis' own authority. By showing the extent to which they could imagine—and, presumably, carry out—executions and the like, the rabbis projected an aura of authority and power that the average citizen would certainly find, if not intimidating, then certainly arresting.

Perhaps the most authentic reading of the sources on capital punishment is as a series of cautionary texts that reflect a strong sense of ambivalence about taking human life. In fact, the "one in seventy years" quote is only a part of a larger passage found at the end of the first chapter of tractate Makkot. From the larger context, it is clear that certain rabbinic factions believed strongly in the deterrent effect of executions and wanted to see them happen with some regularity. When Rabbi Tarfon and Rabbi Akiva announced that if they had been on the Sanhedrin, no one would ever have been killed, we can almost hear the challenge in Rabbi Shimon ben Gamliel's sharp response that such a view, if it held sway, would only serve to "increase bloodshed in Israel" (*M* Makkot 1:10). Rabbi Shimon ben Gamliel, the head of the Sanhedrin at the time, clearly puts forth his view that maintaining capital punishment as a possibility is required for a reason—and that the reason is not merely a function of our abiding wish to remain faithful to scriptural law. If capital punishment were to be abolished, he tells his colleagues, society would be making a huge error of judgment.

Rabbi Shimon ben Gamliel was not alone in his opinion, but, ultimately, the Jewish courts decided that the authority to impose the death penalty was a power they did not want. Decades before the Second Temple was destroyed, in fact, the Jewish courts of Roman Palestine saw that violence had actually increased in their day (despite a spate of recent executions), and they thus chose to put a moratorium on deciding capital cases. Thus, in 30 C.E., the Great Sanhedrin moved out of the Temple precincts specifically in order to limit its own jurisdiction. (According to rabbinic tradition, the Torah only permitted the courts to legislate capital cases while the Great Sanhedrin sat in the shadow of the Temple.) And so, by the time the Romans actually destroyed the Temple in 70 C.E., Jewish courts had already stopped adjudicating capital cases and thus could no longer claim jurisdiction over such issues as were now in the hands of Roman courts (*BT* Sanhedrin 37b).

Had executions thus ceased even before the Temple was destroyed? Unofficially at least, they had not. The Talmud reports a number of instances of formal or informal execution, often with the blessing (and under the watchful aegis) of the Romans and other rulers. Indeed, as late as the medieval period, Jews continued to maintain a kind of derivative authority to impose the death penalty, especially on informers: they would simply turn them over to the secular authorities and allow the state to carry out the execution. Maimonides refers to this as a common custom "in the cities of the west," where it was apparently possible even in Maimonides' day to have informers executed, either by the community itself or through the penal system of the "nations" (*MT* Hilkhot Ḥoveil U-mazzik 8:11). In his responsum to the community of Cordoba, the great talmudist and legal scholar Rabbi Asher ben Yeḥiel (c. 1250–1327) advocated cutting out informers' tongues, but he allowed his community to do as it saw fit in meting out justice (*T'shuvot Ha-rosh,* responsum 17:8 [ed. New York, 1954, p. 20d]). His son, Rabbi Judah ben Asher of Toledo, also among the greatest halakhic authorities, describes the killing of informers as a communal obligation and reports how Rabbi Joseph ibn Migash executed an informer during the last hours of a Yom Kippur that fell on Shabbat (*Zikhron Y'hudah,* responsum 75 [ed. Berlin, 1846, p. 55a]).

One cannot, therefore, derive anything even remotely approaching an unequivocal sense from Jewish codes or Jewish history that executing a criminal is inherently wrong or by its very nature unjust. But the modern world has much to learn from the caution and seriousness with which the rabbis of the

Mishnah and the Talmud handled capital cases. For Americans, in particular, this should be an especially sensitive issue. Given the number of cases in the United States in recent years, for example, in which death row inmates were exonerated after years of incarceration—not to mention instances in which already executed individuals were unequivocally vindicated and posthumously cleared of wrongdoing—the American death penalty system seems to require revamping along the lines of the *halakhah*. In addition, statistics show that there is a strong racial aspect to the death sentence as it is carried out in the United States, insofar as black Americans are far more likely to be sentenced to death for murder than white Americans convicted of the same crimes. (When the victim is white, the likelihood of the death penalty also increases dramatically.) The biblical notions of pursuing justice and judging others without concern for social status demand that Jewish jurists and jurors alike look at the evidence carefully and take into account all the possible loopholes in any capital case. The concept of *dina d'malkhuta dina* cannot be ignored and the requirements to convict or acquit need not—and, in the secular justice system, should not—come directly from the rabbinic sources, but from the secular law of the land. Still, the values of Jewish tradition, the level of deliberation with which the rabbinic courts were to handle death penalty cases, and their sense of grave responsibility should still inform our participation in such matters.

Once a sentence of death has been established, Jewish law also has much to teach about how to carry out executions. The rabbis devoted much of their legislative energy to the formulation of rules designed to guarantee that public executions were carried out in a compassionate way that displayed concern both for the emotional well-being of the convicted before death as well as for the sacred dignity of his or her body after execution. The Talmud develops these core concepts in a number of different contexts, but the clearest summary of general principles is this: "Anywhere that execution is ordained by the Torah, you are not permitted to draw it out or to make it more severe [than it would naturally be]. Rather, you must carry the sentence out as kindly as possible" (*BT* Sanhedrin 52b, 82b, and 89b). Thus, according to the Mishnah, once the verdict was confirmed by the court, execution had to follow immediately and this was considered an act of mercy toward the accused; delaying the punishment, even for one additional night, was forbidden as being unnecessarily cruel (*M* Sanhedrin 6:1). In the United States today, convicts facing the death penalty often remain on death row for years while various avenues of appeal are pursued. Rabbinic tradition does not look at all askance at the concept of appealing a severe verdict, but teaches us that there should never be unnecessary delay in carrying out a sentence that can no longer be appealed.

There are regulations that governed the actual execution as well. Indeed, an entire chapter and a half of Tractate Sanhedrin is devoted to developing methods of execution deemed unlikely to defile a criminal's body. The specific method of execution was ordained by Scripture as a function of the specific crime they committed. For example, criminals whose execution called for burning would be burned internally, so as not to cause unnecessary damage or disfigurement to the outside of their bodies. (The accused would be immobilized by burial in sand up to the knees, whereupon a scarf would be wrapped around the neck and pulled from both sides, and a burning wick forced down the throat.) While to modern ears this may sound particularly gruesome, in the context of the time in which these laws were developed it was the more merciful way of carrying out the prescribed biblical punishment, and it allowed the family of the deceased to bury the executed individual in the normal way with a wholly intact body. While the methods of modern executions may be different, the basic concept should certainly follow similar principles: the method of execution that will least damage the body of the individual being executed should always be preferred. Thus, lethal injection is preferable to older methods that invariably damage the body, such as decapitation by guillotine, immolation at the stake, or death by firing squad or in the electric chair.

Incarceration

The concept of incarceration is not foreign to Jewish tradition. Joseph was incarcerated in Egypt, for example, as were Samson in Gaza, Jeremiah in Jerusalem, and kings Jehoiachin and Zedekiah in Babylon. (Interested readers may profitably consult David Blumenfeld's essay on the topic published in *Conservative Judaism* 60:3 [Spring, 2008], pp. 42–58.) In later times, some of the greatest rabbinic leaders were imprisoned by local authorities, and talmudic tradition (at *BT* B'rakhot 54b) even ordains a benediction to be recited upon release from prison, known as Birkat Ha-gomeil, which acclaims God as the One "who grants kindness to the undeserving." (This blessing is also recited in other contexts as well, such as upon recovering from serious illness or after surviving a serious accident.)

Jews have not only been imprisoned by others, however. That there were Jewish prisons in talmudic times, for example, is evidenced by the question preserved in the Talmud (at *BT* Yoma 70a) about the requirement of affixing a *m'zuzah* to the doorway of the prison building in Meḥoza, a town that had only Jewish residents at the time. And a comment of the talmudic teacher Rav (preserved at *BT* Sanhedrin 17b and *Y* Kiddushin 4:12, 66b) that forbids any Jew from living in a town that has neither a doctor nor a (public) bathhouse, and which fails to maintain a court invested with the power to punish or imprison, merely makes the point that much clearer. Rabbinic courts continued this use of incarceration into the Middle Ages. In the eleventh century, as Rashi explains in his comment to *BT* P'saḥim 91a (*s.v. beit ha-asurin shel yisra·el*), the courts would imprison a man in order to compel him to divorce a woman with whom he had entered into a forbidden marriage. And, indeed, rabbinical courts in modern-day Israel have the same possibility at their disposal. Later, Jewish prisons were common in Jewish communities throughout Europe and Spain. (The concept of what we would call "house arrest" was also developed by the courts in those places.) According to Menaḥem Elon, offenders in Poland and Lithuania as recently as the eighteenth century were placed in a *kuna* (the Polish word for "stocks"), which involved being humiliated publicly by having one's neck and hands tied to a chain attached to the outside of the synagogue (Menaḥem Elon, "Incarceration under Jewish Law [Hebrew]," *Sefer Yoveil L'Pinḥas Rosen* [ed. Haim Kohen; Jerusalem: Histadrat Hastudentim shel Ha-universitah Ha-ivrit, 1962], pp. 171–201). And some Jewish communities used imprisonment to punish errant ideologues, including followers of Shabbetai Zvi and early adherents of Hasidism.

It is surprising, then, how rarely the subject of prison appears in rabbinic discussions. As Columbia Law professor George Fletcher points out, "Jewish law elaborates on refinements in capital punishment, yet it has a tendency to regard the use of imprisonment as something below the level of legal supervision" (as cited in David Gordis's anthology *Crime, Punishment, and Deterrence: An American-Jewish Exploration* [Jersey City, NJ: KTAV, 1991], p. 30).

This reticence makes more sense when we look closely at the role prisons have played in Jewish tradition. First, the notion of punitive imprisonment is a relatively late one for Jews and non-Jews alike. Prison as punishment only became common in secular law in the fourteenth century, and, concomitantly, there is scant mention of this kind of imprisonment in rabbinic texts prior to this period as well. Instead, incarceration was largely seen as a means to an end, a way of guarding the offender until the time of judgment and execution, or as an administrative tool designed to compel prisoners to pay their debts or to comply with some judgment by the ruling authority. The unfortunate man caught gathering sticks on Shabbat (as described in Numbers 15:32–36), for example, is depicted specifically as being held in "the *mishmar,*" apparently a kind of early Iraelite prison, until his fate could be determined. And King Artaxerxes gives Ezra administrative power specifically to imprison anyone who did not obey his orders (Ezra 7:25–26).

Imprisonment was often used as an extralegal measure when the stipulated punishment could not be administered for some reason. When a murderer could not be convicted on the evidence at hand, for example, the court would place the accused in prison. And prison was also recommended for anyone who had committed one of the major religious sins tradition taught would be ultimately punished by death at "the hands of God." By imprisoning such an offender, the community could feel that a sense of justice had been served, even before any heavenly punishment had been meted out.

The severity of the prison sentence could vary. Lighter penalties for those whose guilt had not been proven beyond doubt consisted of incarceration with limited food. Harsher conditions were reserved for repeat offenders; indeed, once a person had repeated the same offense three times and had been duly punished for each instance of wrongdoing, the prisoner would be fed barley until, literally, "his stomach would burst" (*M* Sanhedrin 9:5). The idea that the prisoner might die due to the harsh conditions of prison life was actually part of the plan, according to Elon, reserved for these repeat offenders who had shown they could not be rehabilitated. Although Elon himself wonders if this was carried out in practice, it is noteworthy that the idea was never formally abandoned. Maimonides calls for the same punishment the Mishnah recommends for repeat offenses: a scant ration of bread and water, to be followed if necessary by barley to make the stomach burst (*M* Sanhedrin 9:5, *MT* Hilkhot Rotzei·aḥ U-sh'mirat Nefesh 4:8).

Even in talmudic times, however, incarceration—for any purpose—required certain special precautions. Because imprisonment was a measure outside the official rabbinic legal system, the rabbis had to be particularly cautious about jailing innocent people, even when the imprisonment was to be of limited duration. In the fourth century, for example, Rabbi Yossi demanded that offenders not be incarcerated without some proof: "Do you pick someone up in the market and demean him?" (*Y* Sanhedrin 7:8, 25a). Rabbi Yossi's question makes it clear that the rabbis could be guilty of occasional abuses of their power and authority, and that it was deemed crucial, at least by some, to ensure that no such abuses occurred.

Modern prisons respond to the same need that execution once filled, as Rabbi Elie Spitz argues in Gordis' book cited above (pp. 49ff.). Incarceration today, according to Spitz, in fact accomplishes all three of the main roles that capital punishment once played in Jewish life: retribution, deterrence, and a "realignment of God with creation," or a sense that a certain act has been properly punished (p. 52). Indeed, the modern prison system is designed for retribution and deterrence, as well as rehabilitation and penitence. (This latter function is, at least etymologically, implied by the eighteenth-century term "penitentiary," employed by Quakers and other prison reformers who believed, at least in theory, in the possibility of finding a penalty that is both just and merciful, meted out according to the very balance of values the rabbis thought optimal and desirable.)

In practice, however, modern corrections systems are far from perfect. For example, the U.S. Bureau of Justice Statistics reported in 2010 that the adult prison population was approaching 2,300,000, the highest number in its history. The overcrowding alone has brought numerous calls for reform, as the lack of resources in American prisons has led to poor sanitary conditions and limited opportunities for rehabilitation for the incarcerated. Prisoners also receive little preparation for reentry into the world outside the prison walls.

Perhaps another model of justice might aid an analysis of modern prison systems. In addition to the actual prisons mentioned just a few times in the Mishnah and Talmud, the Bible describes the six *arei miklat,* cities of refuge, to which accidental killers could flee to escape the vengeance of their unintended victims' families (Numbers 35:9–29 and Deuteronomy 19:1–10). The cities of refuge were meant more to protect than to punish, but the forced isolation these cities imposed on their unwilling residents became a topic for much deliberation in rabbinic discussions. As Rabbi Shlomo Lipskar argues in his article "A Torah Perspective on Incarceration as a Modality of Punishment" (published at www.jlaw.com), these cities of refuge can be useful tools in understanding how prisoners are to be treated according to Jewish tradition. These cities, for example, had to be in very specific locations. They had to be located near bodies of water and near markets where there was a sizable population. When a person was brought to a city of refuge, his or her teacher had to be brought along as well—and if that teacher taught others, then the whole school had to move into exile to ensure the continued learning of the detainee (Maimonides, *MT* Hilkhot Rotzei·aḥ U-sh'mirat Nefesh 7:1). As Lipskar writes, "The detriment of limiting the teacher's freedom is balanced against [the] benefit of giving the incarcerated an opportunity for life through rehabilitation." These rules for the biblical cities of refuge could be a useful basis for Jews attempting to determine the ethical constraints of incarceration as punishment: Jewish values demand that such places of confinement be livable and that they be places filled with learning and potential for growth.

While there are not many Jewish laws about prisons *per se,* there are many aspects of rabbinic thinking that could guide modern principles of incarceration. Lipskar, the founder and chairman of the Aleph Institute (a Jewish educational and advocacy agency for imprisoned Jews of all backgrounds and their families), also points to the importance of encouraging *t'shuvah* (repentance) in the prison setting. The rabbis taught that there are three stages through which the would-be penitent must pass before repentance can be deemed complete: they must be able to admit their guilt, they must be able to express remorse, and they must be capable of undertaking a commitment to act differently in the future. Encouraging this kind of mental, emotional, and spiritual readiness to change requires a particular kind of setting for convicted criminals: a place where the incarcerated can reflect on their deeds, as well as a place where they can have the kind of counseling and training courses that will guide them to renounce evil and embrace the path of righteousness and goodness. Religious counseling, as well, Lipskar argues, is needed to guide inmates to paths of spiritual connection and to teach Jewish prisoners the power of Jewish tradition, thus opening up the potential for more meaningful lives both within the prison setting and outside of it.

Corporal Punishment

Perhaps the most common of rabbinic punishments was the administering of corporal punishment for all sorts of offenses, whether ritual or criminal in nature. Indeed, "spare the rod, spoil the child" is not simply an adage; it is a biblical verse found at Proverbs 13:24 that literally reads, "The one who spares the rod hates his child." Inasmuch as the rabbis saw the *beit din* as an earthly stand-in for the heavenly Parent, the idea of physical discipline—lashes, called *makkot* or *malkot*—could only help to inculcate the appropriate values in the community.

The Torah stipulates that a judge may order an offender flogged "according to the level of his wickedness" (Deuteronomy 25:2). Even the worst criminal could not be flogged indefinitely, however: "He may be given up to forty lashes, but not more, lest, by being flogged to excess, your brother be degraded before your eyes" (Deuteronomy 25:3).

The rabbis turned these few words into an entire series of legislated punishments, described in detail in the mishnaic tractate Makkot. Rabbinic discretion allowed the rabbis to make these lashes their penalty of choice in many different cases. For ritual offenses that were biblically punished with death at the hands of heaven, or for *kareit*—a debated term that most believed meant excision from the community in the World to Come—the rabbis added lashes as a penalty from the earthly courts that would, they hoped, exempt the offender from heavenly punishment. Thus, if someone were punished sufficiently in this world, that person could escape death or *kareit* (*M* Makkot 3:15). The *beit din* was permitted to flog someone even when it was not in accordance with Torah law; indeed, if someone disobeyed a court order or publicly broke a rabbinic ruling, the rabbis could inflict punishment because, as Maimonides wrote, "the moment requires it" (*MT* Hilkhot Mamrim 2:4).

The Mishnah and the rabbinic works that followed it offer specific instructions about how and when to administer these lashes. Beyond these rules and strictures, however, the rabbis allowed themselves a substantial amount of liberty in the case-by-case administering of discipline. Throughout both the rabbinic and medieval periods, in fact, the *makkot* were a central component of the judicial punishment system.

In part, the Mishnah limits the potential for rabbinic abuse by fixing the maximum punitive sentence at thirty-nine lashes, in case an accidental extra lash should make the total exceed the biblical limit of forty (*M* Makkot 3:10). Maimonides calls for caution based on the physical condition of the offender, and determined that even those wrongdoers who appear strong and healthy should only receive thirty-nine lashes (*MT* Hilkhot Sanhedrin 17:1). The lashes were to be given in three segments: one-third to the front of the body and two-thirds to the back of each of the prisoner's shoulders. In this way, the rabbis carefully heeded the Torah's clear directive against exacerbating the physical pain or shame of the offender. The lashes were given with a leather strip, carefully measured, folded in half, and then folded again. The representative of the court could flog the offender with all of his strength, but he could only use one hand. While the lashes were being given, admonishing biblical verses from Deuteronomy 28 and 29 would be read aloud: "If you do not carefully observe these commandments . . ." (*M* Makkot 3:12–14, citing Deuteronomy 28:58).

Certain kinds of lashes, however, were not limited to forty. These *makkot mardut,* as they were called, were given to coerce individuals into following rabbinic rulings, and there was no upper limit for such disciplinary measures (Tosafot to *BT* Nazir 20b, *s.v. rabbi y'hudah omeir*). For example, if a person were to eat *matzah* on the day before the *seder* or were to refuse to build a *sukkah* despite a rabbinic demand, lashes could be given until compliance was achieved, even, if necessary "until his soul leaves him" (*BT* K'tubbot 86a–b, *MT* Hilkhot Ḥameitz U-matzah 6:12). If the agreed-upon number of lashes was given, the person administrating the lashes could not be held accountable for his prisoner's death, but if there were even a single extra lash, the court would consider it an act of negligent homicide (*MT* Hilkhot Sanhedrin 16:12).

Today, discussion of the laws of *makkot* has become a moot point. In 1950, judicial corporal punishment was prohibited by Israeli law, and Western democracies generally have not used this sort of discipline in their penal systems for decades. Still, great debate continues to surround the subject of corporal punishment in the classroom and at home, especially among educators and scholars of child behavior. (The issue of parental discipline, corporal and otherwise, is discussed by Rabbi Daniel Nevins in his chapter in this volume on parents and children.)

Excommunication

Maimonides enumerates twenty-four specific offenses which are correctly to be punished not with execution, incarceration, or flogging, but with excommunication (*MT* Hilkhot Talmud Torah 6:14, cf. *SA* Yoreh Dei·ah 334:43 and *BT* B'rakhot 19a). These are the sins of insulting the learned, insulting an officer of the court, insulting others by calling them slaves, refusing to answer a subpoena to appear in court, treating Torah or rabbinic law disrespectfully, refusing to accept the judgment of a duly constituted *beit din,* showing disregard for the safety of others by keeping dangerous animals or utensils unsafely guarded, selling property to a non-Jew without first accepting full responsibility for any injury that may befall a fellow Jew on that property, participating in the proceedings of a gentile court if it is clear that the verdict may oblige a fellow Jew to pay damages that would not be similarly ordered by a *beit din,* a butcher who is also a *kohein* withholding the priestly emoluments from other *kohanim* and instead keeping them for himself, profaning the second day of festivals as they are observed in the Diaspora, performing forbidden labors on the afternoon of Erev Pesaḥ, taking God's name in vain both in the context and not in the context of oaths, leading others to eat sacrificial meat outside Jerusalem, fixing the Jewish calendar outside of the Land of Israel, putting stumbling blocks before the blind, standing in the way of others in their effort to perform one of the commandments of the Torah, selling unkosher meat as kosher, a kosher slaughterer forgetting to have a trained rabbi check the blade of his slaughtering knife for nicks, for men arousing themselves sexually, entering into business relations with an ex-spouse, for sage to behave indecorously, and excommunicating another for no valid reason.

Although modern readers will relate to these specific offenses in very different ways, ranging from sharing the ancients' outrage regarding someone who would willfully mislead the public by selling unkosher meat as kosher to finding excessive the notion of excommunicating ex-spouses who maintain or begin a post-divorce business relationship, the basic idea here is that the court need not feel unable to address abuses in society that do not specifically fall in any pre-determined category of wrongdoing. But regardless of how moderns relate to any specific issue for which the ancients were prepared temporarily to forbid a fellow Jew regular contact with the community, the point is that the courts need to feel responsible for maintaining public order and a basic level of public morality, even when doing so requires acting outside the biblical framework laid down in the Torah itself.

There were different names for excommunication in ancient and medieval times, *ḥeirem, niddui,* and *n'zifah* being the most well known, and each was slightly different from the others in terms of how long it lasted, the specific type of interaction with others it forbade, and the way it might be ended early or cancelled. Nor was this solely a matter for the courts, at least not originally; although eventually excommunication did become restricted to the courts, in older times it was the right of any sage to place someone who was acting in a manner detrimental to the welfare of the public under a ban. Moderns, even if not willing to endorse a return to the use of excommunication as a method of protecting the public from itself, can still admire a justice system that is willing to do what it takes not merely to punish the criminal but also to ensure a proper level of public respect for the law.

It would be simple, but also facile, to dismiss these laws governing the halakhic approach to crime and punishment as irrelevant today merely because they have fallen into desuetude. Indeed, within the warp and woof of these laws are principles that even today can guide modern Jews seeking to interact ethically and in a principled manner with the secular justice systems of the countries in which they live. The laws regarding courtroom procedure, testimony, perjury, corporal and capital punishment, excommunication, and incarceration are founded on legal principles that Jewish tradition regards as divine in origin. Jewish citizens of modern states, even as they willingly submit to the authority of secular governance, should allow these principles to inspire them to seek to perfect the justice systems in their own jurisdiction, thus making them more rooted in eternal principles, more just, and more equitable than they otherwise might be. Moderns seeking to submit to the laws outlined in this chapter will obey them best by allowing them to inspire in their hearts an unquenchable thirst for justice.

Military Service

MICHAEL GRAETZ

Why is there a need for the Jewish nation to have a standing army at all? After all, Abraham went to war when necessary, but the narrative in Genesis 14 makes it clear that this is not a standing army and that Abraham's servants are merely pressed into service to deal with specific cases of aggression (in this case, to undertake the specific mission of saving Lot from captivity). The defensive war against Amalek described in Exodus 17 is much the same story, only on a grander scale. Here too, however, Joshua is commanded to choose men and then to begin the fight. It is clear that this is no standing army, merely an *ad hoc* group formed on the spot for the purpose of national self-defense.

Later in the Torah, though, Israel engages in battle with nations that attack them on their way toward the Land of Israel. And since the openly stated goal of leaving Egypt and wandering through the desert in the first place was to "inherit" the Land of Israel (as stated explicitly at Deuteronomy 4:1 and 11:8), it becomes clear that an army will be required to accomplish that goal. Thus, the Torah contains laws about creating a standing army, laws of conduct for combat, and laws about armies in general, as well as specific instructions relating to the taking of captives, the distribution of booty, the maintenance of army bases, and the specific way the war against the Canaanite peoples is to be fought.

Later biblical books, however, reflect evolving assumptions. The Book of Joshua, for example, assumes the existence of a standing army organized by Joshua and operating according to the laws of combat presented in the Torah. By the time we get to the Book of Judges, on the other hand, we get the impression that any standing army was disbanded once the land was conquered and settled. Instead, a kind of regional or national militia is called into being as needed specifically to defend a specific region or city that is being threatened. Indeed, the Book of Samuel (cf. 1 Samuel 8:10ff.), citing reasons that Israel should not wish to have a king, points out that a king would draft men for a standing army. This warning turned out to be prescient: by the time the kingdoms of Israel and Judah are established political entities, there are standing armies in both countries.

Different Types of War

Rabbinic literature introduces two terms not found in the Bible to distinguish between different kinds of war: *milḥemet r'shut,* a discretionary war, and *milḥemet mitzvah,* an obligatory one. There is some imprecision about the terminology, however. At *M* Sotah 8:7, for example, Rabbi Judah uses the terms *milḥemet mitzvah* and *milḥemet ḥovah* for precisely the same two categories (*mitzvah* is usually translated as "commandment," *ḥovah* as "obligation"). Thus *milḥemet mitzvah* can refer to both kinds of war, which inevitably leads to confusion in the sources. Nevertheless, the concept that some wars are obligatory (because, like the war against the Canaanites or against Amalek, they are commanded by God or because they are in response to aggression from an enemy nation) while others are optional (like David's wars undertaken to expand Israel's borders) remains clear. Maimonides (e.g., at *MT* Hilkhot M'lakhim U-milḥ'moteihem 5:1 ff.) uses the first set of terms exclusively, and does not refer to Rabbi Judah's terminology at all.

Conscription

The census described in the opening chapters of the Book of Numbers is clearly taken in order to prepare an army, and the fact that a similar procedure is recorded in later biblical books suggests that there must have been some sort of compulsory draft in ancient Israel, at least at certain times and in response to specific national needs. In certain instances, such as the war against Midian described in Numbers 31, the number of men to be called up to participate in a war is formally specified.

The impression the biblical texts give is that every male from twenty to fifty years of age was expected to be available for army service. It also appears that different groups of men, perhaps chosen by tribal affiliation, were trained in specific duties and specific weapons (cf., for example, the specific tasks assigned the fighters from each tribe at 1 Chronicles 12). It appears as if the standing army was small in number, but the total number could easily grow quite large, as all men who had been trained as soldiers were understood to constitute reserve units that could be called up at need. For example, we are told at 2 Chronicles 26:13 that King Uzziah had over 300,000 soldiers in reserve.

While the draft is presented as universally applicable to all men in the right age categories, Deuteronomy 20 does isolate four specific categories of individuals who are formally exempted from military service: those who have built new houses, those who have planted new vineyards, engaged men who have not yet married, and the constitutionally timid. The first three categories are all dependent upon specific acts. Thus, one is exempt until one's newly built house is formally dedicated, until the grapes from one's newly planted vineyard have been harvested, and until one's marriage has been consummated. (Deuteronomy 24:5 specifies that the new husband's exemption is for a full year. Later, the *halakhah* extends the other exemptions to a full year as well; cf. *MT* Hilkhot M'lakhim U-milḥ'moteihem 7:10.) The last category of exemption, however, is unlike the others and appears to constitute the grounds for a sweeping policy of exemption: persons faint of heart are not to be drafted, either because they themselves will be useless in combat or because they may influence other soldiers to give up the fight. This lays the groundwork for the general permission to exempt from service individuals deemed unlikely to serve bravely or with distinction.

The rabbis restricted these exemptions to army service during a discretionary war. In an obligatory war, however, the Mishnah rules at *M* Sotah 8:7 that there are no exemptions and that all must join in the battle, even if that means bridegrooms, and even brides, leaving the bridal chamber itself to join the fighting. (Maimonides goes into great detail about these categories in the *Mishneh Torah;* he codifies the notion that even women must serve in an obligatory war at *MT* Hilkhot M'lakhim U-milḥ'moteihem 7:4. In the context of an obligatory war, there is no concept of women being exempt from conscription.)

Although one can make a good scriptural case for always seeking to resolve conflict through peaceful means, the modern notion of conscientious objection to war itself does not exist in Jewish law and, indeed, the notion that one may legitimately be opposed to all wars with no exceptions is contrary to the plain meaning of Scripture and its halakhic elaboration over the ages. In other words, emotional or psychological unsuitability for battle is a valid claim, as outlined above, but formal objection to war in any form is not. Perhaps this is a direct result of the fact that the *milḥ'mot mitzvah,* that is, the obligatory wars described in Scripture, are invariably accompanied by a report of divine approval for the undertaking. In modern Israel, even though the possibility of exemption from the Israel Defense Forces (IDF) on the grounds of conscientious objection exists in theory, this happens only very rarely and Israelis who do claim exemption on those grounds are generally exempted, if they are exempted at all, on grounds of unsuitability for military service. (For more on the question of when to seek peace and when to resort to war, readers may consult my essay in the *Etz Hayim,* pp. 1382–1390.)

In a war of obligation, the sole exemption is for the fainthearted individual who is specifically excluded not as a nod to his unsuitability *per se,* but simply because he might cripple the war effort. Moreover, since the Talmud (at *BT* Sanhedrin 72a) endorses the principle of self-defense—pithily stated as *ha-ba l'horg'kha hashkeim l'horgo* ("if someone is seeking to kill you, you may strike out and kill that person first")—the nation is deemed to possess not merely a right, but a sacred obligation, to attack murderous enemies before they embark on a campaign to destroy the nation. Indeed, in such a situation, declining to participate in a war because one is opposed to all acts of killing in war is the moral equivalent of treason. The question of whether conscientious objection would be permitted in a war of discretion, on the other hand, is a thorny one, but also not one of much relevance in modern Israel: since statehood was proclaimed, the armed forces have been in a constant state of war with enemies whose avowed goal is the destruction of the Jewish state and the decimation of its Jewish citizenry, and so a consensus exists that Israel's state of war is at least a kind of war of obligation. In recent years, however, this consensus has been questioned regarding specific military actions undertaken to defend Israeli settlements in West Bank areas captured during the Six Day War, with some Israelis arguing that those actions are more akin to a war of discretion.

It seems clear that the one specific war of obligation in the Torah, the war undertaken to annihilate the Canaanites and settle the Land, is no longer a standing *mitzvah.* This is because of the general rule that the nations of that time no longer exist (as codified already in the Mishnah at *M* Yadayim 4:4), which prompted Maimonides (at *MT* Hilkhot M'lakhim U-milḥ'moteihem 5:4) to rule that this is one of the commandments that cannot be kept because there is no way to keep it in the specific terms the Torah sets out (cf. also Maimonides' *Sefer Ha-mitzvot,* positive commandment 187).

The question of exemption from army service is one of the major debates in Israeli society. Since the earliest days of the state, men who study full-time in *y'shivot* have been given an exemption from military service on the grounds that Torah study is equivalent to military service. As the number of such exemptions has grown, the public debate over this issue has become more shrill and emotional. Some religious elements have introduced the concept of special religious academies, called *y'shivot hesdeir,* in which soldiers can both pursue Torah studies and fulfill their regular army service at the same time. There is also a blanket exemption from army service for women who declare themselves to be "religious." Again in this context, an alternative "national service" for young women that parallels army service has been developed for young women unwilling to abandon entirely the concept of serving their country in a way analogous to military service.

The Va·ad Halakhah of the Rabbinical Assembly of Israel has published responsa on both of these issues, ruling in both instances that, since modern Israel is constantly engaged in a legitimate war of defense for its own survival, no one capable of military service can legitimately be considered exempt. (These responsa are discussed elsewhere in this volume in the chapter about Israel by Rabbi Martin S. Cohen.)

Jewish Views of War

In many ways, the codes of conduct of the IDF are a direct development of the Jewish view of war and how war should be waged, as both these concepts developed in later biblical tradition and in rabbinic Judaism. As a result, the emphasis is on defense as a reason to justify going to war. Indeed, this value is reflected in the very name of the Israel Defense Forces. Unfortunately, the State of Israel has been under threat of military attack from the very beginning of its existence, and thus has had to keep a standing army ready to defend the lives of its citizens. Indeed, this army has had to operate in open wars and in wars of attrition during the whole period of its existence.

A large number of works on war and army life have been composed over the years since 1948 by many rabbis in modern Israel, a large number of whom themselves have served in the IDF chaplaincy. Some of the most famous works are by Rabbis Shlomo Goren (the first chief chaplain of the IDF), Shmuel Min-Hahar, and Rabbi Mordechai Piron, all of whom served in high positions in the army rabbinate. Unfortunately, most of these works deal almost entirely with problems associated with remaining faithful to Jewish religious law while on duty in the army, and very few of them are devoted to the ethical problems raised here, or to other ethical issues that arise from army life, such as relationships between commanders and subordinates. (Some of these issues will be discussed later in this chapter.)

The Holiness of the Army Camp

The standing orders of the general staff of the IDF (called *p'kuddot matkal*) concerning booty and wanton destruction of property have as their epigraph Deuteronomy 23:15 ("For the Eternal, your God, walks among you in your camp to save you and to bring down your enemies to defeat; therefore, let your camp be a place of holiness"). This is understood as a sacred obligation to ensure that the army conducts itself according to the principles of ethical and just behavior.

In 1994, a special commission established by the IDF and headed by Asa Kasher (an Israeli professor well known for his work in ethics and himself a bereaved father whose son died during his IDF service) published "The Ethical Code of the Israel Defense Forces," also known as "The Spirit of the Israel Defense Forces." The code was meant to give guidance to soldiers in the IDF and also to reflect the values that underlie the uniqueness of the IDF as the Jewish army of a Jewish state. Professor Kasher set forth the basic premise of his report in these words: "The IDF is different from other armies. The basic function of this document is to concretize a common language and standard of evaluation for values and norms. Its very existence creates a motivation to operate by its standards."

Some of the main points of the document are as follows:

1. Soldiers must always be aware of human life, and should be ready to endanger themselves or other persons only to the extent necessary to fulfill the mission.
2. Soldiers should use their weapons to defeat the enemy only to the extent necessary, and must show restraint by preventing harm to human life, honor, or property when force is not necessary.
3. Soldiers must fight and make an effort to succeed in battle to their utter limit. Even though doing so might actually endanger their lives, soldiers must struggle to overcome the enemy and not to surrender.
4. Soldiers must always help comrades in need, no matter the danger, and even if the effort could conceivably cost them their own lives. Soldiers must do all that is necessary, even to the extent of endangering their own lives, not to leave wounded soldiers on the battlefield.
5. Soldiers must act in such a manner that their personal opinions about public, social, or ideological issues will not impact upon their military actions.

6. Soldiers must act fairly and in a restrained manner, and must always be well informed and conduct themselves professionally in all instances of contact with civilians who live or are present in the areas that the IDF controls.

The very publication of this very worthy document earned its authors praise in some quarters and condemnation in others. The official IDF stance was very positive about the effort to create a climate of moral awareness in the army, but others felt that publishing such a document would be counterproductive, because it might confuse soldiers and keep them from feeling wholly bound to fulfill their assigned tasks. It was also noted that reality on the battlefield is often very different from the way things look from a professor's study. And some critics took the stance that war and morality were inherently incompatible, so the whole effort to infuse the former with the standards of the latter was *ipso facto* disingenuous.

It is interesting that many of the questions raised in this document are discussed in detail in halakhic sources. The codes of the IDF stress that there is a sanctity to life that must be respected, even as soldiers are preparing to kill enemy soldiers who themselves are attempting to kill them, and that one must avoid wanton or unnecessary loss of life. To underscore the fact that killing the enemy should be a source of regret even to soldiers who have fought bravely and who are proud of their efforts, the IDF places less of an emphasis on medals and ribbons than other modern armies.

Destruction of Property and the Spoils of War

Another law concerning war has to do with destruction of property before and during battle. At Deuteronomy 20:19–20, the Torah rules that, when setting up a siege against a city, the army should not cut down fruit-bearing trees in order to build a siege ramp; only those trees that are clearly not fruit-bearing may be used for that purpose. For a rule of battle, this law suggests unusual sensitivity to the need to prevent unnecessary destruction, proscribing even behavior by invading armies that would be harmful to future inhabitants of the land on which the battle is taking place. It is permissible, however, to destroy a tree if it is felt that such an act will help win the war by damaging the emotional or psychological state of the enemy (Naḥmanides, *Hassagot L'sefer Hamitzvot La-rambam*) or if those trees may provide cover for enemy soldiers (Rabbi Moses of Coucy, *Sefer Mitzvot Gadol*, negative commandment 229); indeed, only pointless aggression against trees is outlawed.

These rules are also reflected in General Staff Orders of the modern IDF, which contain specific rules prohibiting the wanton destruction of enemy property, except for certain instances in which the property in question could conceivably cause harm to IDF soldiers.

No personal booty can be taken by individual soldiers under any circumstances. Instead, all property seized from the enemy must be turned over to the IDF, which has special units whose job is to handle these objects. Much use was made of these units during the war in Lebanon, when they methodically searched for booty taken from village homes and then arrested the IDF soldiers who had taken such possessions. The thrust of the rules and the administrative procedures is to implement the expansive meaning of "let your camp be a place of holiness" (Deuteronomy 23:15).

Prisoners of War

In considering the issue of prisoners of war taken during the wars leading up to the conquest of the Land of Israel, the Bible takes a stance that moderns almost invariably evaluate as brutally cruel. The story of Israel's war against Midian, recounted in Numbers 31, is a good example. Although the soldiers had slain every male, Moses is enraged that they had brought back all the females and children as captives. He points out that the captive females might conceivably entice Israelites to worship foreign gods, and that the Midianite male children would eventually grow up to be soldiers. Thus, he instructs the Israelites to kill all the male children and all women who have had carnal relations with men, so that only women who have had no sexual experience would be spared. Every soldier then had to undergo ritual purification and bring a sin offering.

Other passages in the Torah present slightly different laws regarding prisoners of war. The law regarding captured women presented at Deuteronomy 21:10–14, for example, is not at all what one would expect after reading the story of the war against Midian: here, a woman may be spared merely because a soldier finds her attractive, and no specific mention is made of her virginity or prior carnal relations. The law does assume, however, that the soldier's ultimate desire is to make the woman his wife. The Torah therefore demands that she be made less beautiful by trimming her hair and paring her fingernails (or perhaps by letting them grow—the text is unclear), and that she be given a month to mourn her slain parents. This woman cannot be enslaved but must be treated as a wife. If the soldier later tires of her, she must be divorced, as would be the case with any rejected wife.

On the face of it, this law of the *y'fat to·ar* ("beautiful woman") seems to be aimed at preventing mass rape and the abuse of vulnerable women. The Torah acknowledges that lust can overpower men who are engaged in battle, and particularly the lust that comes with wielding power over others. At the same time, it seeks to control that passion and to curb the power that makes possible its fulfillment.

In our day, this law is the source of many disturbing rulings, and the halakhic ramifications of those rulings throughout the generations are even more disturbing. For example, to whom does this law actually apply? Some authorities say that, since the Canaanite nations are subject to *ḥeirem* ("total annihilation"), it is clear that the law cannot apply to them and must, therefore, apply only to women captured in other wars. Others disagree and argue that, since this law obviously overrides other rules that normally govern sexual behavior, it may thus be presumed to override the *ḥeirem* rule as well. Then there are those who argue that the law does not apply to Israelite women at all, even those who might have been seized as prisoners of war in one or another of the wars between Israel and Judah. (For a discussion of *ḥeirem* itself, see my article on war and peace issues in the *Etz Hayim,* referenced above.)

Another disturbing aspect of this issue involves the question of why a woman should only be considered protected under the statute once she has already been violated by a soldier. In any case, the substance of this law is problematic for our modern sense of what the rules of war should reasonably and decently be. Paradoxically, if a soldier's desire for some particular woman were merely an outgrowth of his need to indulge himself sexually, then the forceful violation of a female prisoner-of-war would be a clear transgression of the law. The law permits sex with the woman only if the desire is so great that the soldier in question would lose his ability to obey orders, and thus to fight effectively, if it were not permitted. Thus, there emerges from our sources a major (presumably regretful) concession to human weakness in an extreme situation where the greater good—in this case, the survival of the nation—must be considered of paramount importance. The major codification of this set of laws may be found at *MT* Hilkhot M'lakhim U-milḥ'moteihem 8:2ff.

In any event, moderns will abhor any law that suggests that the violation of defenseless women can ever be appropriate and feel that this abhorrence, if anything, should be even more intense in the heat of battle when the normative rule of law is suspended (or at least inoperative) as armies fight each other for terrain temporarily under the jurisdiction of no civil authority at all. Perhaps the best way to relate to the willingness of the *halakhah* to sanction such behavior is to take it as an extreme statement of the principle that nothing, including maintaining the norms of "regular" morality, can override the obligation of the nation to defend itself successfully against foes attempting violently to annihilate its citizenry. That the Torah chooses to express that notion through legislation that sanctions behavior at the very edge of tolerability—and, indeed, even beyond it—should be taken to underscore the supreme importance of freeing the nation's military to act as it must in times of war if the survival of the nation is at stake. That truth notwithstanding, however, it is certainly right and good for modern armies categorically to outlaw the abuse of civilian women who might come under its control, as is the case with the IDF.

Obeying Orders and the Limits of Obedience

The biblical idea of kingship, especially as it is fleshed out in the Bible's historical books and in the books of the prophets, is not that the king's authority is a divine right, but rather that it exists, if it does, as a function of national will. Thus divine law is above royal law and so the prophets are able to criticize the king, even to his face. This view is expressed in rabbinic literature as well (e.g., *BT* Sanhedrin 49a). My colleague, Rabbi Jane Kanarek, discusses this concept in more detail elsewhere in this volume in her chapter on *halakhah* and citizenship.

The king cannot summarily execute a person, even one accused of treason. Rather, all the procedures and customs of a legal trial and evidence must be followed. While some authorities think that the normal procedures may be relaxed somewhat in the case of treason, others do not (cf. the talmudic traditions in this regard cited at *BT* Sanhedrin 36a and cf. also the comment of the Tosafot there, *s.v. rabbah bar bar ḥana*).

Indeed, one of the greatest medieval halakhists, the Meiri (Rabbi Menaḥem Meiri of Provence [1249–1315], in his commentary to *BT* Sanhedrin, ed. Sofer [Jerusalem: Kedem, 1965], pp. 46–47 and 204), says that there is no basis in the Torah for the king's authority to put rebels to death. Instead, the Meiri develops the idea that the special authority of the king derives from a contract between him and the nation: the nation gives up some of its basic rights of property and freedom of movement to the ruler, and in turn the king leads them in war and works for their general welfare.

The narrative that serves as the foundation story for these laws revolves around the summary killing of Abner and Amasa by Joab (as described in 2 Samuel 3 and 20 respectively), events so laden with meaning that King David is actually reported at 1 Kings 2:5 to have mentioned them on his deathbed. In rabbinic tradition, however, Amasa together with Abner refused to be a party to the massacre of the priests of Nob (cf. the rabbinic exegesis of 1 Samuel 22:17 at *Y* Sanhedrin 10:2, 28b), and it was thus Amasa's piety that brought about his death. When challenged by Solomon at the heavenly court, Joab pleaded that he murdered Amasa only because the latter had been tardy in obeying David's order to gather an army (as found at 2 Samuel 20:4–5). According to the rabbis, however, the real reason for the delay was that Amasa was loath to interrupt the studies of those whom he was to summon, believing that supporting their Torah study overrode his duty to obey the royal command (*BT* Sanhedrin 49a).

In trying to understand all the aspects of this case, the rabbis came to the conclusion that soldiers do not fulfill their complete moral obligation if they do not object to what seem to them to be unjust commands. (See *BT* Sanhedrin 20a on the justification for the killing of Abner.) Furthermore, it is not enough simply not to participate in such an order. Instead, one must actively resist unlawful orders, and one must do so even if one thinks that, in the end, the protest will make no difference. The Talmud (at *BT* Shabbat 55a) expands this point of view into a general doctrine regarding the question of what distinguishes evil people from the righteous.

The demand on the soldier to distinguish right from wrong and to act on that distinction (which is formally widened in the sources to include all those who are part of any hierarchy of power even outside the military), might be taken as an extension of another principle in Jewish law: namely, that there is no agency for the performance of evil deeds (cf. *MT* Hilkhot Me'ilah 7:2; *SA* Ḥoshen Mishpat 182:1). Thus, if an officer kills one of his own soldiers unjustly at the king's command, Jewish law holds the officer personally responsible, not the king. This is because each person is viewed as an autonomous moral agent: the fact that the king has commanded a particular deed does not absolve the officer from fulfilling God's prior command, which takes supreme moral precedence over the order of the mortal king. Jewish law does not recognize the subordinate's traditional excuse, "I was only following orders."

Does the case of Uriah the Hittite not contradict this rule? In his stinging indictment recorded at 2 Samuel 12, the prophet Nathan directly and unambiguously indicts David of Uriah's murder (cf. 2 Samuel 12:9, "You have killed Uriah the Hittite with the sword"), apparently ignoring the fact that David neither killed him nor even personally sent him into the thick of battle where he was killed by the enemy. And what of Abiathar's comment to David recorded at 1 Samuel 22:21 to the effect that Saul had "killed the priests of Nob," when it was actually Doeg who did the killing? Both these remarks seem clearly to blame those who gave the orders, and either to absolve—or at least to ignore—the guilt of the individuals who obeyed them. Radak (Rabbi David Kimḥi, the great medieval Provençal commentator), commenting on 2 Samuel 12:9, assumes that the law enjoining soldiers to refuse such orders is an ideal to which men may aspire, but which most will not actually attain. The crushing conformity of the military system and the fear of punishment combine to justify the decisions of the soldiers involved to follow their kings' commands. Therefore, the king is not free from guilt and the verses cited above merely attest to this fact.

The code of the IDF puts the burden on the individual soldier to refuse to obey a command that is "unlawful on the face of it" (*bilti ḥukki be'alil*). On the other hand, this sweeping statement is qualified by many subordinate clauses that specify when and under what circumstances a soldier could be exonerated for refusing to obey a direct order. Such a soldier, for example, would have to be fairly learned in the law and in ethics to be able to discern whether or not a given command falls under the category of "unlawful on the face of it" in the first place, and this comes close to Radak's sense that average soldiers should almost never feel fully empowered to decide for themselves whether or not an order is lawful. (This is similar to the rule in the U.S. Army Field Manual to the effect that the obligation of the soldier to obey is primary.)

Soldiers are not expected scrupulously to weigh the legality of every command they receive. Indeed, the nature of the army structure, which depends entirely on the willingness of each level of the hierarchy to follow the commands of the next level up, makes it difficult to grant full moral autonomy to individual soldiers. On the other hand, the *halakhot* regarding soldierly conduct rest on the supposition that every individual is a fully autonomous moral being and that no one can ever excuse the commission of sin, even one less grievous than murder, with reference to orders received from another.

Abner and Amasa, who refused to fulfill a command that seemed to them "unlawful on the face of it," were celebrated in tradition as extremely sensitive and gifted individuals who were able to discern the unjustness of the king's command. And, indeed, the obligation to rank the commandments of God over those of an earthly king was codified by Maimonides in the *Mishneh Torah* at *MT* Hilkhot M'lakhim U-milḥ'moteihem 3:9. In the end, the *halakhah* considers the obligation of the soldier to act morally as a supreme value, thus leaving the possibility of disobedience far more open than is the case in most modern army codes.

The Ranking System

An army operates based on a hierarchical system of ranking, and the performance of the army in battle as a whole depends upon the internal discipline of each soldier in that hierarchy. To this end, soldiers are taught the supreme value of discipline as part of their army training, and one of the most basic aspects of that concept of discipline is the simple notion that soldiers must, as a matter of course, follow the orders given by their superiors in rank. Thus, armies throughout history have relied upon training that in some sense contradicts the idea of an autonomous individual with free choice. The supreme value of protecting the nation and its citizens from annihilation can be used to justify the training methods and the ranking system of an army. On the other hand, the idea of an army camp being "holy space" places clear boundaries on the extent to which this avenue of justification can be reasonably travelled.

Most armies have codes of conduct that spell out the rights and the responsibilities of soldiers and officers at every level of command. These codes are based in part on civil laws of the countries in question, and also, inevitably, on the moral standards prevalent in those countries. In Israel, the code of conduct that governs the IDF is both comprehensive and strict. There is, as in other armies, a large corps of lawyers and judges whose duty it is to maintain justice and fairness in the command structure. And, although extreme conditions occasionally produce a certain amount of deviation from socially accepted norms in military action, the Adjutant General Corps of the IDF works very hard to address these deviations and to maintain the rule of law and morality in the army.

The Right to Religious Observance in the Military and the Chaplaincy

There is no question that one of the basic human rights is the right to practice one's religion freely, openly, and peacefully. Most armies in the modern world recognize this and go out of their way to allow soldiers a great deal of leeway in the practice of their religion. Clearly the freedom to worship freely will become an important reason behind any soldier's satisfaction or dissatisfaction with army service.

In Israel, the army is committed to creating an ambience conducive even to very strict religious observance. Accordingly, all food on IDF bases is kosher, and specific requests for special stringency in *kashrut* in ways that have been approved by the IDF rabbinate are honored as well. Each year at Passover time, for example, there is an army operation known as Operation Passover (*Mivtza Pesaḥ*) in which thousands of reserve soldiers are called up specifically to assist in the *kashering* of every kitchen and dining area in the Israeli army, including even the small kitchens of remote outposts. In addition, the army officially observes Shabbat. Of course, Jewish law permits the desecration of Shabbat in order to save lives, but, in normal situations, the Shabbat laws are observed on army bases.

In addition, there is a large chaplaincy corps consisting of rabbis and assistants on many different levels. There are synagogues and houses of study throughout the army, and time is set aside for devotional study by soldiers on all levels. On Sukkot most army bases erect a *sukkah,* and on Passover every army base has its own *seder* that soldiers on duty may attend. Indeed, there are even mobile *seder* kits for every soldier, even if they are on active duty and alone with a small patrol. The Israel army rabbinate has even produced a special version of the Haggadah for soldiers on active duty, which presents a shortened version of the text containing only those sections that absolutely must be read for the *seder* to be meaningful. Also, all IDF casualties are handled by the army *ḥevra kaddisha* (burial society), and the bodies of all soldiers who die while on duty are treated according to Jewish law.

In many modern armies outside of Israel, the chaplaincy corps has a Jewish section that oversees the religious needs of Jewish servicemen and women. However, it also occurs regularly that such rabbis are called upon to counsel and help people of other faiths. The same is true in the Israeli army, where the army rabbinate also counsels and assists Druze or Bedouin soldiers.

Allegiance to a Secular State

Jewish law regarding armies is predicated on the existence of a ruling king, a functioning priesthood, and the existence of a government of Torah sages, all of whose authority derives directly from God. Thus, one might suppose that modern Jews would have difficulty in serving in an army created by a secular state, even a Jewish secular state such as Israel. Indeed, this question does arise in rabbinic responsa.

The major halakhic justification for finding it permissible to serve in such secular armies is the rule that the law of the state is equivalent to Torah law in all matters that do not directly contradict Torah law. (This is the principle known by its pithy rabbinic formulation *dina d'malkhuta dina,* which has been cited in many chapters of this book.) Since the Torah does provide for armies, and since much of the way in which modern armies operate is entirely consistent with Jewish law, the principle of *dina d'malkhuta dina* can easily be used to justify the sense of obligation that citizens of secular states feel toward service in the military.

In the State of Israel, some Jewish religious groups deny the validity of the secular state altogether. They contend that until the state is reconstituted according to the principles and strictures of *halakhah,* it has even less claim on their lives than would a non-Jewish secular state in the Diaspora. Even though this group constitutes only a very small minority in Israel, it is very vocal and manages to sow the seeds of conflict and tension over the issue of military service even among Jews who would otherwise have no hesitancy at all about serving in the army. Still, many rabbis have responded to the challenge of this fringe group directly, noting that even those who question the authority of a secular government still have a basic obligation to support the efforts of an army that has as its central mission the defense of property and lives of Jews living in Israel. As such, even the most strictly religious Jew can be part of the army without feeling that such service inevitably implies allegiance to the notion of the validity of a secular Jewish state. The specific question regarding the obligation of Jews living outside of Israel to participate in the defense of the Land of Israel by serving in the IDF is discussed elsewhere in this volume in the chapter on Israel by Rabbi Martin S. Cohen.

Commerce

JACOB BLUMENTHAL

The ethical and moral questions that continually challenge those engaged in business—either as sellers or as consumers—are legion. How far must a merchant go in revealing defects in merchandise to a customer? How aggressive can a salesperson be in marketing a product to consumers? What constitutes a fair price for an item or commodity? How do businesspeople price their goods in a competitive market while still guaranteeing that they can earn a living? What responsibilities do consumers have within this system, and what recourse do they have when they have been wronged? To all these questions, Jewish tradition provides clear answers rooted in strong ethical standards and clear legal principles to guide our behavior.

Honesty

The halakhic foundation of all business-related law in every time and place is the bedrock concept of absolute and scrupulous honesty in all commercial dealings. And behind the system of specific laws and legal precedents codified by halakhic authorities stands the biblical insistence on absolute integrity in commercial affairs, as exemplified in the eighth commandment,

"You shall not steal" (Exodus 20:13 and Deuteronomy 5:17). While some commentators, such as Rashi and Rashbam, actually feel that the eighth commandment prohibits kidnapping and that it is the tenth commandment ("You shall not covet . . . anything that is your neighbor's") that prohibits theft of property, all agree that stealing property is absolutely forbidden by Scripture, and it is this concept that serves as the basis for the *halakhah* of commerce. Indeed, since the prohibition of theft presumes the principle of private property (since, absent private ownership of goods, how could anyone steal anything from anyone else?), the Torah may be understood to see as theft any kind of effort or willful misrepresentation that results in an unfair transfer of ownership. The goal of the laws that govern commerce is to prevent the unjust, unwarranted, or unwilling transfer of property or money from its rightful possessor to another person.

At Leviticus 19:11, the Torah makes this connection explicit, beginning the verse with the language of the eighth commandment ("You shall not steal") and then defining the concept clearly: "And you shall not deal deceitfully or falsely with one another." Moreover, in this context we are reminded that such ethical behavior leads directly to the attainment of holiness, which Scripture presents as one of the great goals of the spiritual endeavor: "You shall be holy, for I, the Eternal, your God, am holy" (Leviticus 19:2). As the *Etz Hayim* notes in its commentary on this passage, we do not create holiness only within the realm of religious ritual; rather, "everything we do has the potential of being holy," including our daily conduct of business affairs. Moreover, the story of the creation of the world that opens the Torah makes it clear that, while we may hold temporary title to possessions, God is the ultimate owner of everything. We are, in this sense, simply stewards of God's property (i.e., the world and everything in it), and our mission is to use it righteously, honestly, justly, and for holy purposes.

The rabbis reinforced and expanded upon these biblical demands. At *BT* Shabbat 31a, for example, the Talmud presents the great teacher Rava's lesson about what happens when a person leaves this world and approaches the heavenly court for judgment: "At the time a person is brought to judgment they ask: 'Did you conduct your business affairs faithfully? Did you set time for study of Torah? Did you look after your obligation to procreate? Did you conduct yourself so as to bring salvation to the world? Did you argue [i.e., respectfully and in an intellectually productive way] about the law? Did you bring logic and common sense to bear in your studies?' And even if all the answers are correct, a favorable evaluation will only be granted to those who consider as a true treasure the fear of heaven that they have [successfully] inculcated in themselves over the course of their lifetimes."

Note that business conduct is at the top of Rava's list! Although the other questions have a far more overtly religious or spiritual feel to them—and even the question about having children is couched, in the original text, in language that resonates with the sense of religious obligation, not merely as a way to produce heirs—it is Rava's opinion that the conduct of mundane trade and transactions will be the first test of one's worth on the ultimate day of judgment. Nor was Rava's view a mere minority opinion. On Yom Kippur itself, which the sages of ancient times understood to constitute the Jewish people's annual rehearsal for their day of final judgment, the liturgical stress is clearly on ethical conduct. Indeed, the same Hebrew phrase used by Rava to denote business affairs, *massa u-mattan,* is mentioned specifically in the long confessional prayer (Al Ḥeit) recited on Yom Kippur, along with a variety of other acts related to everyday commerce. At the core of both Rava's remark and its liturgical amplification is the understanding that behaving dishonorably in commerce is as much a sin against God as it is a sin against other people.

As a result, business affairs are always to be conducted with the sense that there is a Third Party witnessing the transaction. For example, while a sale is not generally considered complete in Jewish law until the purchaser has actively taken possession of the purchased item or commodity, at a certain point in negotiations one is considered morally, if not fully legally, committed to follow through. Indeed, at *M* Bava M'tzi·a 4:2 the Mishnah specifically declares that "the One who punished the generation of the flood [in the time of Noah] and the generation of the dispersion [after the incident concerning the construction of the Tower of Babel] will punish those who do not stand by their word." The theological idea behind this imprecation is the same one that underlies Rava's list of questions: the ever-vigilant God of history demands that every commercial transaction be carried out with the purest of intentions. Integrity is thus not only a savvy way to ensure repeat business, but should, and far more importantly, also be a manifestation of the *yirat shamayim*—the fear of heaven—that characterizes the God-fearing individuals involved.

Judaism, always a religion of realists, recognizes that general exhortations to be honest will not suffice, and thus Jewish texts enjoin scrupulous behavior in many specific settings and under many specific circumstances. For example, the Torah prescribes the honest use of weights and measures at Deuteronomy 25:13–15: "You shall not have in your pouch alternate weights, a larger and a smaller. You shall not have in your house alternate measures, a larger and a smaller. You must have completely honest weights and completely honest measures if you are to endure long on the soil that the Eternal, your God, is giving you." In his commentary to this passage, Samson Raphael Hirsch notes that the reference to one's "house" implies that not only may one not *use* inaccurate measures to trick one's customers, but that even *possessing* such tools is forbidden—lest a person be tempted to use them, or others use them inadvertently. The Torah wishes not only to punish fraud, but to prevent it as well.

Moreover, the Talmud gives specific examples of how this should be practiced in the marketplace. For example, at *BT* Bava Batra 89a, the Talmud describes a system of *agardamin* (inspectors, from the Greek *agoranomos*) to scrutinize the marketplace and ensure that certain types of measures are accurate. While other aspects of honest behavior are left to individual conscience, here the Talmud (and the later codes as well) emphasize society's obligation to ensure honesty in commerce and not merely to hope for the integrity of merchants.

Free Market Competition

In a totally free market, the forces of supply and demand determine the fair price for particular goods or services. In general, it is healthy competition among businesses that keeps prices affordable for the consumer while guaranteeing a fair profit for the merchant.

In the real world, however, various forces conspire to interfere with the "ideal" marketplace, and this creates ethical conundrums that the *halakhah* must attempt to unravel. For example, in the Mishnah (at *M* Bava M'tzi·a 4:12), we read of a situation in which competition exists, but one seller seeks unilaterally to lower prices. Rabbi Judah says a merchant may not set a price lower than the prevailing market price, but his colleagues reply that such a merchant should be "remembered for a blessing." Rabbi Judah's sympathies clearly lie with the merchant whose profit margin will suffer because of a competitor's preemptive move. The sages, on the other hand, side with the consumer who will only be delighted if prices go down. The later codes generally follow the principle set by the talmudic sages (and not Rabbi Judah), and proceed on the basic assumption that the needs of the broader community must outweigh those of the individual merchant.

Later texts reflect differing opinions about the precise extent of permissible competition among merchants. A classic debate is presented in the Talmud at *BT* Bava Batra 21b–22a, where the rabbis consider the permissibility of opening a new business in close proximity to an existing one. Rav Huna argues that the important principle is that businesspeople should be able to protect their livelihoods: "If a person in an alley establishes a mill and another person comes to set one up next to it, the existing owner can prevent him from doing so by claiming, 'You are interfering with my livelihood.'"

Other voices, however, support the idea of a completely open market: "A person may open a shop next to an another person's shop, or a bathhouse next to another person's bathhouse, and the existing owner does not have the power to prevent it, because the new business owner can say, 'You do what you wish on your property, and I will do what I wish on mine.'"

After extended discussion, Rabbi Huna ben Yehoshua (who lived many centuries later than his similarly-named predecessor) is depicted as coming to a conclusion in three parts. A resident of the same alley as someone who owns an existing business may indeed open a competing shop or service. The residents of one town, however, may prevent someone from another town from setting up a shop in their own town if it would compete with existing local businesses. And it remains an open question whether a resident of one alley can prevent the resident of another (local) alley from opening a competing establishment in a street common to both. Thus, the Talmud sets a limited precedent for free competition by balancing the rights of merchants with the interests of consumers. However, there are no similar restrictions on wandering peddlers who appear in a town on market days, or on purveyors of wholesale merchandise, as both of these groups are deemed to require more latitude if they are fairly to compete with each other.

There are several constraints on the free market system that characterize post-talmudic discussion among halakhic authorities. For example, many note the difference between situations where adding competition will merely decrease the profitability of existing businesses, as opposed to situations where competition will utterly destroy the livelihood of such businesses. If a market is too small to support an additional vendor, for example, some authorities limit the amount of competition that may reasonably be introduced. One principle used by these authorities is the scriptural concept of *hassagat g'vul,* the stealthy "moving of one's neighbor's landmark" that derives from Deuteronomy 19:14: "You shall not move those of your countryman's landmarks set up by previous generations on the property that will be allotted to you in the land that the Eternal, your God, is giving to you to possess." In effect, infringing on another's livelihood is a form of stealing that other individual's "sales territory."

Efficiency and scale also affect the ability to limit competition. It is often the case that a potential competitor will pose a threat to an existing business, simply because the rival can manufacture some specific product more cheaply. (This could be due to better organization or a more technologically advanced manufacturing method, or perhaps because the competitor deals in larger volume and so has concomitantly lower unit costs.) In cases where an existing business can solve the issue simply by becoming more efficient and thus able to compete effectively, there is no justification for limiting entry of a competitor. However, if the issues are more complex—such as, for example, if an existing business cannot possibly achieve the economy of scale of a potential competitor—some authorities would constrain competition. There are also precedents in the responsa literature that allow for restraint of competition for a limited period in order to allow existing enterprises enough time to adjust their methods and prices, but then open the market to full competition after that initial period of adjustment and accommodation ends.

Today, it is common for national chains to succeed in new markets by overwhelming local businesses, thus threatening the livelihood of the small business owners. Indeed, local authorities in such municipalities often face the difficult choice of whether to allow large national retailers to compete in their jurisdictions, weighing the benefit of lower prices for consumers against the havoc that the presence of such businesses will wreak in terms of existing local businesses. It is also true that large retailers will generally generate larger tax revenues that will help the communities in which they are located. At the same time, there may be a corresponding loss of vibrancy in neighborhoods where smaller shops, which cannot remain solvent in the face of the competition, are forced to close. Further, these larger businesses may ultimately become monopolies in their markets, eliminating the kind of price constraints that are only really guaranteed by competition in the marketplace.

As evident in the case from Bava Batra cited above, these issues are further complicated by geographical concerns. In talmudic society, things were simpler than they are today: the local market was an alley in a given town where merchants congregated to do business, and the outsider was someone who did not pay the local poll tax. With today's increased mobility, however, a market described as "local" can include businesses situated at great distances from each other, and multiple jurisdictions can reasonably be said to constitute one market. Moreover, computer networks and technology, coupled with efficient warehousing and shipping, can allow certain goods to be traded at the retail level even over thousands of miles at much reduced cost. (For example, buying a book on-line while in one's own home may seem like a local event, even though the actual book one is purchasing might actually be several thousand miles away.)

Even these limited ways in which the rabbis sought to protect businesses from the danger of failure caused by unfair competition may still be ineffective. And, truth be told, there is very little halakhic precedent for thinking about commerce as it has actually evolved in our day—where the difference between local, national, and international markets exists profoundly in some contexts and barely at all in others. Instead, our Jewish response needs to center around innovative ways to ameliorate the "economic dislocation" caused by these developments, to assist local or smaller businesses to gain efficiency through technology by helping them alter their focus to local "niche" markets or more personalized service, and to provide permanent or temporary incentives designed to encourage use of local vendors. We must also find morally acceptable ways to determine when businesses are no longer viable.

Fair Prices

We have already seen how, in the Mishnah (at *M* Bava M'tzi·a 4:12), the sages celebrate competition and applaud merchants who offer lower prices. The sources also discuss what constitutes a fair price. Earlier in that same chapter (at *M* Bava M'tzi·a 4:3), the Mishnah defines an unfair price as one more than one-sixth higher than the regular market price of the product in question at the time of sale. And the Mishnah labels the act of charging an unfair price as *ona·ah* ("fraud"), a concept derived from the verse at Leviticus 25:14: "When you sell property to your neighbor, or buy anything from your neighbor, you shall not defraud [*al tonu,* using the verb related to *ona·ah*] one another."

This rule applies to both the buyer and the seller, so that either may reasonably retract from a proposed sale if the agreed-upon price differs by more than one-sixth from the value of the article at the time the sale actually is to go through. (Even if the differential is exactly one-sixth, the wronged party may demand repayment of the difference.) The assumption behind the principle of *ona·ah* is that both buyer and seller have the same intention, which is an exchange of goods and/or money of more or less equivalent value. It assumes that both parties have as much knowledge as possible of the market conditions that determine the value of the item at the time of the transaction and that both understand that the merchant is in business to make a reasonable profit. Even after the sale is complete, in fact, the possibility of retraction continues to exist in cases where it becomes clear that these assumptions were incorrect. For buyers, however, the ability to determine that overcharging has occurred is limited to the time in which the item can be appraised by an expert. Sellers, on the other hand, have a longer, even unlimited, time to retract the sale if they realize that the price was unfair because, since they no longer have the object in question in their possession, they cannot be constrained to show it to a putative appraiser within a given time limit (*M* Bava M'tzi·a 4:3–4). Thus, despite the fact that we would normally assume that merchants are experts in the value of their own merchandise, the Mishnah applies the principle of *ona·ah* to both the buyer and the seller. However, while merchants are given an extended period to discover mistakes, they still must seek redress of errors as soon as they discover that they undercharged, or else the assumption is always that they have forgiven the difference.

The applicability of the *ona·ah* rule is limited, however. A merchant may, for example, indicate openly to a customer that the price being asked is higher than normally permitted and, if the customer agrees to pay the price anyway, the transaction is deemed valid. In addition, the Mishnah (at *M* Bava M'tzi·a 4:9) specifically excludes transactions such as those involving promissory notes and real estate from this rule. The most common explanation for this is that these involve much more subjective and time-sensitive evaluations, thus making it more difficult to set a benchmark value for them. To subject them to the rules of *ona·ah* would make the validity of these transactions too uncertain. However, some later sources rule that in extreme cases, the principle of *ona·ah* can still apply (see, e.g., the gloss of the Rema to *SA* Ḥoshen Mishpat 227:29).

Furthermore, Maimonides makes an important distinction between essential goods, called *ḥayyei nefesh,* and non-essential goods (at *MT* Hilkhot M'khirah 14:1–2). According to him, a community may set a price for essential goods such as wine, oil, and flour, either by lowering prices that are too high or by raising prices in order to reduce risk to producers and ensure an adequate supply of the commodity in question. The one-sixth margin is then applied to this price and may be enforced through agents of the communal rabbinical court.

Monopolies

We have seen that the free market, with some limitations, can and should be used to encourage competition and to control prices. The community can encourage such competition to avoid monopoly situations.

If the establishment of a monopoly constitutes a clear benefit to society, however, there is clearly support in Jewish tradition for communal authorities permitting, or even encouraging, them to exist—and this is particularly true if they are deemed to provide essential products or services (akin to Maimonides' *ḥayyei nefesh* services discussed above). For example, certain modern industries, such as utilities, are so intensive in terms of the infrastructure investment they require that it may be more expensive for consumers, at least initially, to have more than one company enter the market. However, even sanctioned monopolies must be closely regulated to ensure that the benefit to the public remains real and that such businesses do not accrue excess profits at a cost to consumers.

The rabbis often confronted situations where merchants acted in concert with each other to manipulate prices. They were particularly sensitive to this issue when it came to products used for ritual purposes. For example, the Mishnah at *M* K'ritot 1:7 tells story of Rabbi Shimon ben Gamliel's response when he saw that the vendors of Jerusalem were conspiring to overcharge for birds needed for certain kinds of sin offerings in the Temple. Incensed, he found scriptural support for changing the law to lower the number of birds required, which effectively brought the price back to what he considered reasonable. Similarly, Rabbi Shimon's disciple, Samuel, threatened pottery merchants with a change in the law if they overcharged for new pots in the weeks leading up to Passover. When confronted with this type of blatant price collusion, the rabbis did not hesitate to use their power to control the situation.

The Halakhah of Advertising

Caveat emptor—"let the buyer beware"—is not a Jewish concept. While consumers have responsibilities to be careful in the marketplace, sellers have an equal or even greater responsibility to promote their products fairly and to represent them accurately.

The Mishnah lays the foundations for law in this area of commerce at *M* Bava M'tzi·a 4:11–12. For example, we learn there that, should a person contract to buy produce from a particular field, the seller may not mix in produce from another field; this is so even if the added produce is of equivalent quality. However, in a case where the quality of the product in question is clearly enhanced by the substitution, such as would be the case if a wine merchant were to add stronger wine to a weaker wine, that kind of substitution is permissible. However, later authorities limit this permission, stressing that if such a substitution is not to the satisfaction of the buyer (e.g., the taste of the wine is changed, or it affects other factors important to the buyer), the buyer can refuse the sale.

The case of adding water to wine is more interesting. (In ancient times, wine was produced, shipped, and generally sold in concentrated form. The consumer then diluted it for use later on.) At the retail level, then, a wine merchant must provide disclosure if the wine has already been diluted, but the Mishnah prohibits selling diluted wine at the wholesale level, "since this is only done for the sake of deception" (*M* Bava M'tzi·a 4:11). Obviously, this would not be the case in a locale where doing so was the regular practice of wholesalers.

The rabbis were also aware that the appearance of goods is very important to increasing sales, and were thus concerned that sellers not deceive consumers by presenting their wares in a way that was deceptive. This is termed *g'neivat ayin,* which term refers specifically to the act of illicitly creating an illusory effect for one's own benefit. (The term *g'neivat ayin* literally means "stealing the eye," i.e., of the consumer.) Examples given in the Mishnah at *M* Bava M'tzi·a 4:12 include cosmetically altering the appearance of goods or even animals for the sake of making them appear healthier or younger than they really are. This does not mean that merchants may not enhance their products with decoration to make them more attractive, but only that they may not hide imperfections by doing so.

Earlier in this same passage, the sage Abba Shaul prohibits a merchant from selling pounded beans that have already been sifted. His concern is that the merchant will have two reasons to raise the price: because the beans are now being sold without their husks and stems (resulting in a higher quality product), and also in order to compensate the merchant for his effort. Abba Shaul thought this would make it impossible for the consumer to compare the price of this merchant's beans with the beans of another merchant who simply sells whole beans, taking into account the presence of waste material and not having any extra labor to include in the price. The sages, however, permit this practice as long as the merchant does not "steal the eye" by placing the sifted product on top and the unsifted beans below, thus creating a false impression in the mind of the consumer.

Parallel to the concept of *g'neivat ayin* is *g'neivat da·at*—fooling consumers mentally. (The expression *g'neivat da·at* means literally "stealing the opinion" by creating a false impression in the mind of the consumer.) Maimonides states in the *Mishneh Torah* at Hilkhot M'khirah 18:1: "It is forbidden to deceive a person in business dealings, or to fool them mentally. . . . If one knows that a product has a defect, it must be disclosed to the buyer. Even to deceive a consumer using [mere] words is forbidden." Finding the precise line between presenting one's wares in an attractive and positive light without crossing the line into misrepresentation is a challenge every businessperson must face. The *halakhah,* however, is clear that while merchants may encourage consumers to make a particular purchase, they may in no way endeavor to deceive consumers about the quality of the goods being offered for sale.

Furthermore, Jewish law seriously constrains the ability of vendors to limit liability for defects found later. Contracts containing broad releases from responsibility are thus not enforceable, although clauses referring to specific defects may be deemed licit (*MT* Hilkhot M'khirah 15:6). The rationale for this is clear: at the time of purchase, buyers will normally not be overly concerned about such disclaimers on the part of merchants because consumers do not generally expect the products they purchase to be defective. Furthermore, a seller may also not minimize the importance of a defect while disclosing it, but must allow buyers absolute freedom in determining whether or not they wish to purchase a given item by being totally frank about whatever defects the product might have (*MT* Hilkhot M'khirah 18:1).

Sellers also may not give advice to less-educated consumers that will unfairly influence them to prefer some particular product. This is based on the biblical verse (Leviticus 19:14): "You shall not insult the deaf, or place a stumbling block before the blind. You shall fear your God: I am the Eternal." In today's marketplace, consumers often shop for complex items (for example, electronics) about which they may not have enough expertise to make a fully informed decision; this is certainly a different reality from ancient times, when consumers were generally dealing with simpler items, such as a hammer or a pound of butter. Thus, it is important for vendors to be aware that their special expertise entails a special level of responsibility, and that they must therefore be exceptionally careful not to manipulate a consumer's decision unfairly.

The principles described above can also be applied to certain unethical promotional activities, such as "bait and switch" advertising, in which a product available only in very small quantities is advertised at a very low price merely to lure customers to a store so that a merchant can attempt to sell a far more expensive item in its stead. This is clearly a case of *g'neivat da·at:* an instance in which one's intention is being purposefully, and unjustly, manipulated by an unscrupulous advertiser.

At *M* Bava M'tzi·a 4:12, the Mishnah records an interesting disagreement between Rabbi Judah and the sages. Rabbi Judah states that "a store owner may not distribute parched corn or nuts to children, since this accustoms them to come to that store." The dispute appears to involve the case of children sent on errands to local stores. Given the choice, any child will choose to enter a store with a history of giving out treats for free, and this will certainly be so regardless of the price of the goods on sale in that particular shop. The sages, however, seeking to preserve the sense of free competition they valued in the marketplace, allowed this practice since, as the Talmud explains, other shopkeepers were always free to offer even better treats! The key, of course, is finding the boundary between the valid promotion of wares, on the one hand, and, on the other hand, *g'neivat da·at,* unfair manipulation of the consumer—which is particularly true of modern advertising and promotional techniques directed toward children. And moderns may well wish to favor Rabbi Judah's position, which seems to reflect the idea that, when no parent is present to help direct the child's decision responsibly, the marketplace itself has to be regulated to ensure that children are not artfully manipulated into wasting their parents' money. Surely there is ample halakhic justification for moderns to set standards with respect to the promotion of products that are clearly harmful to children and adolescents, such as alcohol, tobacco, violent movies and video games, and the like.

Finally, it is clearly preferable to promote products based on their own merits rather than by disparaging the products of a competitor. In the Palestinian Talmud (*Y* Ḥagigah 2:1, 77c), Rabbi Yossi ben Ḥanina states, "Extolling one's own virtues by disparaging another person causes one to lose one's share in the World to Come." Translated into the world of commerce, this does not mean that advertisers may not make claims in the marketplace about the worth, or even the superiority, of specific products. However, they must not do so fraudulently or in a purely negative mode (i.e., not by speaking highly of onc's own wares, but solely negatively about those of others). In fact, concealing a competitor's advantages may constitute *g'neivat da·at* no less clearly than concealing the flaws in one's own products, insofar as both procedures leave the consumer misinformed.

Being an Ethical Consumer

Thus far, the material presented has focused mostly on the responsibilities that sellers have in the marketplace. However, Judaism places important demands on the consumer as well.

For example, at *M* Bava M'tzi·a 4:10, the Mishnah defines the concept of *ona·at d'varim,* verbal fraud: "Just as the concept of *ona·ah* ("fraud") can be applied to commercial business transactions, so too can the concept of *ona·ah* be applied to commercial speech. One should not say, 'How much is this item?' without having any real intention of purchasing it." Misrepresenting oneself as a potential purchaser causes salespeople to waste time they might better spend with other customers. It may even constitute a mild form of inflicting mental anguish, in that misrepresenting one's intention to make a purchase will inevitably raise the hopes of a vendor unfairly. This does not mean that price-comparison shopping is not permitted, but rather that one must be upfront about one's intentions when speaking with a salesperson.

As noted above, customers share in the responsibility for ensuring that transactions are fair. Thus, for example, if a person receives too much change back in a transaction, the error must be reported to the vendor and the change returned. Similarly, if an item is clearly mispriced (say, an $80.00 shirt accidentally priced at $8.00) or its value incorrectly identified, one must at least bring the matter to the store's attention, giving the vendor an opportunity to recognize the problem and determine the correct price. Furthermore, sellers have the right, even for an extended period of time, to retract a transaction if they discover their mistake.

The Consumer as Investor

An interesting development in our own era is that so many consumers are also business owners through their participation in equity investments, especially stock ownership. In previous generations, this was true only indirectly in that individuals would place whatever savings they had in a bank account and the bank would invest those funds as it saw fit, or else individuals would participate in defined-benefit pension programs in which paid managers invested the funds and the participants in the plan were not directly involved in those decisions. Today, however, an unprecedented number of individuals own stocks directly (either as part of a savings strategy or through employee stock ownership programs, mutual funds, or retirement investment programs), and are thus much more directly involved in issues pertaining to business ownership. (The current American tax structure actually encourages this trend by allowing pre-tax investment and deferral of taxation on capital gains for funds saved for retirement. Similar programs are now planned or in place to encourage families to save for higher education and to further encourage other forms of saving.) The result of these developments is that the clear distinction that once existed between the owners of a company and its customers no longer applies quite as it did in earlier times. In today's economy, a large percentage of the population, at least on paper, holds both roles simultaneously!

It is therefore an interesting question to consider whether there are special ethical concerns involved in consumer equity investment. A fundamental concern is whether Jewish ethics allows for such capital investment in the first place. In general, the texts presented above indicate a respect for the kind of capital investment that creates a free market system and allows the economy to grow to meet the needs of society. However, as we have seen, such ownership comes with responsibility toward workers, consumers, and society as a whole. It is a legitimate reading of Jewish values to say that as long as owners/investors act in accordance with such concerns, equity ownership by the masses is legitimate—and even desirable.

All the same, two basic issues stand out that differentiate equity (i.e., stock) investment from more traditional forms of consumer investment such as bank deposits. First, the fact that shareholders are considered the "owners" of a company means that they are therefore personally associated with the products and behavior of that company. Second, there is a greater risk of financial loss involved in this type of investment.

Regarding the first issue, the ethical responsibilities for an average investor are likely quite limited. Average shareholders do not have direct responsibility for the actions of a company, since their stake is too small to affect corporate policy, and those who own stock in a company through a mutual fund are even less directly responsible for that company's activities. Professor Aaron Levine, writing in his *Case Studies in Jewish Business Ethics* (Jersey City, NJ: KTAV, 1999, p. 370) notes that those who hold a five percent or higher stake in a public company may have greater ethical responsibility because of the rabbinic principle of *marit ayin* ("appearance") that requires that a Jew strive not only always to behave ethically but also always to avoid even giving the impression of engaging in wrongdoing of any sort. Because such a stake is not held anonymously (since the government requires public disclosure of that kind of investment), the name of the individual in question will inevitably be associated with the practices and policies of the company of which he or she is a significant owner. But even here, the issue is not one of direct responsibility but rather one of secondary association with problematic behavior.

However, given the choices we have as investors, we may find that, as Jews, we want to hold ourselves to a high personal standard when it comes to investment. Levine turns to Rabbi Joseph B. Soloveitchik's "*kibbush* mandate," which "amounts to a charge to self-actualize by realizing one's God-like potential as a creative human being." (The word *kibbush,* literally "conquest," refers in this context to "conquering" one's own baser instincts.) He continues: "Illustrating a perversion of the *kibbush* mandate is the production and sale of cigarettes. This judgment is not predicated on the ability of *halakhah* to establish a clear-cut prohibition against smoking. Suppose, for argument's sake, that a clear-cut prohibition against smoking cannot be established. Nonetheless, the causative links medical science has established between cigarette smoking and various dreadful diseases is undeniable. Far from advancing human dignity, the tobacco industry degrades human existence by causing disease, misery, and pain. Its very existence perverts the *kibbush* mandate" (Levine, *Case Studies,* p. 374).

It would, for example, therefore be morally indefensible to invest directly in certain companies. Furthermore, individuals are encouraged to tailor their investments to avoid companies that specifically violate their own personal ethical sensibilities. For example, if one feels strongly about animal rights, one's investments should display concern for the welfare of animals. Again, this holds true on a direct investment basis, and is somewhat less applicable for small investments or those done through a secondary vehicle such as a mutual fund. Nonetheless, ethically sensitive Jewish investors should shape their investment strategy to match their moral values and not rely on the letter of the law to permit themselves to own even minuscule parts of corporations that engage in activities or produce goods of which they do not approve ethically.

Aside from the ethical considerations surrounding "ownership," equity investment generally involves a far greater risk factor than more traditional consumer savings vehicles such as savings accounts and defined-benefit pension plans. (This is particularly true since many of these more traditional forms have government-backed insurance that greatly reduces the risks involved.) The question from the point of view of the *halakhah* is whether this increased risk turns the investment itself into a form of gambling, and whether gambling is a serious enough ethical problem from a Jewish perspective for people not to engage in even as accepted a practice as high-risk investment for that reason. There is not a simple answer to either question.

Rabbinic attitudes toward gambling are ambiguous. Some sources are not critical of this practice. For example, in his gloss to *SA* Oraḥ Ḥayyim 338:5, the Rema prohibits gambling on Shabbat not because gambling itself is prohibited, but because he considers it enough of a business transaction to constitute a transgression of the Shabbat laws. However, talmudic sources present a more ambivalent attitude. The Mishnah at *M* Sanhedrin 3:3, for example, includes gamblers among those who are ineligible to serve as witnesses. The Talmud, however, cannot decide why exactly they are so prohibited, positing at *BT* Sanhedrin 24b–25a alternately that the reasoning may be that serious gamblers engage in a form of robbery (that is, they engage in actual illegal behavior), or else merely because such people "are not engaged in the general welfare" of the community (that is, they have insufficient moral standing to serve as witnesses whose word will be believed). According to modern responsa of the Committee on Jewish Law and Standards, the latter opinion is the dominant one. (The CJLS opinion also limits the prohibition regarding witnesses to "full-time" gamblers and not to individuals who pursue other professions and who occasionally gamble.) These modern Conservative responsa do, however, express grave concern regarding the practice of gambling and seek to discourage it, seeing it as problematic behavior that lowers the standards and standing of institutions or individuals engaged in it. (See Rabbis Leon Fink and Aaron Blumenthal in *Proceedings of the CJLS 1927–1970,* pp. 1504–1523, and Rabbi Henry Sosland in *CJLS Responsa 1980–1990,* pp. 794–797.) The question of whether synagogues should permit gambling on their premises or utilize games involving gambling to raise funds is discussed elsewhere in this volume by Rabbi Craig Scheff in his chapter on the *halakhah* of synagogue life.

Given these concerns, it is halakhically reasonable to ask whether ordinary investors can succeed in the equity markets through their own skill, or whether the risks of the market that cannot be controlled by the individual investor are so great as to push stock investment into the realm of gambling. In particular, the sources cited seem most concerned about the effect of gambling on the gambler's moral character. Some investors are prone to become giddy with success when their investments flourish and respond by taking ever greater risks, thus becoming closer and closer to the status of true "gamblers." Others, when faced with the downswing of a market and facing tremendous losses (especially if those losses were "on margin" and need to be repaid), are prone to begin cutting corners and begin a downward ethical spiral. While Jewish ethics and law do not constrain consumer investment significantly, high-risk investing should be undertaken with full cognizance of the wide range of moral and ethical pitfalls that face the investor both in times of success and failure.

Given the specialized knowledge that equity investment requires, consumers in our day often turn to advisors and brokers for assistance in such decisions. It has already been noted that "experts" in other fields (such as shopkeepers with specialized knowledge) have a particular set of ethical responsibilities. Concepts such as *ona·at d'varim* ("verbal fraud"), *g'neivat ayin* ("stealing the eye"), and *g'neivat da·at* ("stealing the opinion") are extremely important when it comes to financial advice. For example, these principles require full disclosure of any conflict of interest an investment advisor may have, that all information about an investment choice be explained clearly, and that advisors be certain that investors understand fully the degree of risk involved with a particular investment decision.

The Halakhah of Ethical Commerce

With money at stake, there is constant temptation to cut ethical corners.

Several rabbinic principles are cognizant of this and raise the ethical bar even higher. The first principle of ethical commerce is for businesspeople always, and to the best of their ability, to act *li-f'nim mi-shurat ha-din*—"beyond the letter of the law." A wonderful example is given in an early code of Jewish law, the *She'iltot* (chap. 38, trans. Rabbi David Golinkin):

> It happened that Rav Safra had wine for sale, and a potential buyer came to him while he was reciting the Sh'ma. The customer said, "Sell me this wine for such and such a price." Rav Safra did not answer [so as not to interrupt the Sh'ma]. Assuming that he was unwilling to settle for the price offered, the customer added to his original offer, and said, "Sell me this wine for such and such a price." Rav Safra still did not answer. Upon finishing the Sh'ma, Rav Safra said to him: "From the time you made your first offer, I had resolved in my mind to sell it to you. Therefore I may take no greater amount [than your first bid]."

By refusing to accept the higher sum to which he was entitled by law, Rav Safra was pointing to a higher standard of ethics than the law requires: that one's personal integrity should always outweigh one's potential for profit, even—one could even say, especially—when the law does not require one to do so. (This famous story, referred to in the Talmud at *BT* Makkot 24a and retold by Rashi in his commentary *ad loc., s.v. rav safra,* is discussed elsewhere in this volume by Rabbi Kassel Abelson in his chapter on the *halakhah* of personal integrity.)

The second principle has to do with the twin concepts of *kiddush ha-sheim* (the sanctification of God's name) and *ḥillul ha-sheim* (the profanation of God's name). As Rabbi David Golinkin reminds us in his article "Some Basic Principles of Jewish Business Ethics," published in the *United Synagogue Review* (Spring, 2003), Jews living in a non-Jewish society have a special responsibility to bring honor to Judaism and to God's name by living lives of uncompromised moral integrity. To illustrate that point, Rabbi Golinkin retells a story that appears in rabbinic literature at several locations, most prominently at *D'varim Rabbah* 3:3. There, we read that the ancient sage Rabbi Shimon ben Shetaḥ once bought a donkey from a non-Jewish trader. When his disciples came by to admire his purchase, they were delighted to notice a gem hanging around its neck, which Rabbi Shimon had apparently not noticed when arranging the purchase. They considered the find an auspicious piece of good fortune to be celebrated, but Rabbi Shimon refused to profit from what he presumed logically had to be the seller's oversight and summed up his feelings neatly in a single sentence: "I bought a donkey, not a gemstone." He returned the gem to the man from whom he had bought the donkey, whereupon the latter exclaimed, "Blessed be the God of Shimon ben Shetaḥ."

To have kept the gem would have been permissible—the merchant knew nothing of it and the donkey was apparently purchased with its accouterments—but to return it was more than merely ethical behavior. It was an act of *kiddush ha-sheim,* a means of sanctifying God's name in the world, the practice of those individuals who feel called upon always to act with integrity and to meet, and then exceed, the expectations placed upon them by Jewish tradition.

Judaism is a religion that stresses that moments of holiness are accessible through even the most mundane acts or decisions. Most assuredly, the specific *halakhot* and general principles we have examined in this chapter guide us as we seek to make the best decisions and reach for holiness in each of our commercial transactions each and every day.

Between Employers and Employees

CHERYL PERETZ

There is no doubt that the past century has brought significant changes to the parameters of the employee-employer relationship in all settings. Indeed, as corporations strive to meet their bottom lines and as employees move freely from one company to another, the relationship between employers and employees has changed dramatically from what it was, or was imagined to be, even half a century ago, and it has become concomitantly difficult to establish and maintain a relationship of trust and loyalty between employees and their employers of the kind that was once expected by both parties. Indeed, many companies have undertaken specific programs (where once none would have been deemed necessary) to motivate employees, to inspire their loyalty, and to create positive work environments.

Long before discussions of labor law and corporate ethics emerged as topics for discussion in secular society, the Torah established a model for discussing the concepts of equity and fairness between employees and their employers, introducing employment principles regarding work agreement, fair wages, fair treatment, and the tenor of the overall relationship between employer and employee as topics of public debate. One such principle, for example, is found in Deuteronomy: "You shall not abuse a needy and destitute laborer, whether a fellow countryman or stranger in one of the communities of your land. You must pay him his wages on the same day, before the sun sets, for he is needy and urgently depends on it; else he will cry to the Eternal against you and you will incur guilt" (Deuteronomy 24:14–15). From this text, some fundamental understandings of the relationship between employee and employer emerge.

Employers and Employees

On one level, the Torah treats the relationship between employer and employee as a simple leasing contract so that the worker's time, effort, and expertise are considered as though the employer were leasing them for the period of employment. In return, the worker receives payment for the services provided. This model is taken so seriously, in fact, that the rabbis of ancient times often discuss the relationship between worker and employer in terms and using language usually reserved for the leasing of property, such as fields, animals, or goods. As a result, the rabbinic attitudes regarding the worker and employer emerge from the laws of contract negotiation and cancellation, pricing, and the like. And since the relationship so perceived thus involves the buying and selling of services, employers are therefore not deemed to have any claims over their employees outside of those that might impact the quality or worth of the work to be done. Likewise, the employee's only responsibility is understood to be fulfilling his or her contractual obligations in good faith, without delaying the effort through inappropriate work stoppage or by placing other barriers in the employer's path. Thus, the same principles that govern the enacting and cancellation of contracts also serve as the basis for determining the rights and responsibilities of both parties in the employee-employer relationship.

Nevertheless, anyone familiar with the nature of the workplace will know intuitively that nothing as detached and impersonal as the words of a contract, or even of a less formal agreement, could ever satisfactorily guide employers and employees into a productive and worthy relationship without there also being some kind of personal relationship between the two parties. Using the context of indenture and servitude, the Torah says as much when it ordains that "as for your Israelite kinsmen, no one shall rule ruthlessly over another. . . . For it is to Me that the Israelites are servants; indeed, they are My servants, whom I freed from the land of Egypt: I am the Eternal, your God" (Leviticus 25:46–55). Admonitions of this sort will serve to remind both employer and employee that both equally are servants of God and that both, therefore, must behave accordingly.

The Talmud, at *BT* Bava M'tzi·a 10a (and cf. also *BT* Kiddushin 22b, Bava Kamma 116b, and Bava Batra 10a) expands this concept by adding the observation that we are to consider ourselves bound to serve God alone, and that we are not, therefore, to think of ourselves as simply bound to serve others who themselves are bound to serve God. So, while acknowledging that the social construct of employment inevitably will create some imbalance between a boss and his or her workers, the Torah is equally quick to assert that individual rights and freedoms must be maintained. Because each party enters into the agreement freely and willingly when agreeing on the terms of employment, the moral relationship between the employee and the employer demands reciprocal fairness.

The equity and justice of the Jewish system of law demands that the relationship between employer and employee be understood as a kind of symbiosis in which both parties are free agents possessing specific rights and responsibilities in relation to each other. In this chapter, I will explore the basic approach of Torah law to those rights and responsibilities, focusing specifically on the status of both employee and employer, the roles they may reasonably expect each other to play in the workplace, the payment of wages, the question of eating and resting on the job, matters related to sexual and other kinds of workplace harassment, hiring and dismissal practices, and issues relating to benefits and to severance pay.

It is important to note that, in addition to whatever codified legislation has developed, Jewish employment law, like the laws that cover other kinds of business dealings, relies heavily on the precedent created by local custom, called *minhag ha-makom* in the sources. This was already established in the talmudic era in the context of a discussion about the need to provide food for workers while at work and the acceptable hours one can demand workers to be on the job. In both cases, the Talmud states unequivocally that local *minhag* governs that decision. Going further, the Talmud (at *BT* Bava M'tzi·a 83a and parallels) indulges in a bit of hyperbole to declare unreservedly that "everything [in business dealings] follows accepted custom." The Palestinian Talmud (at *Y* Bava M'tzi·a 7:1, 11b) extends this to mean that, within given parameters, *minhag* can override enacted law, even biblical law. This approach has characterized the business arrangements between workers and their employers for centuries and continues to do so today. As we will see presently, this concept can have profound implications for the employee-employer relationship. By accepting that conventional business practice can be the basis for determining Jewish law in the employment relationship, we open the door to a wide range of issues that the ancients could not have imagined and regarding which, therefore, they cannot be faulted for having failed to enact legislation.

It is also necessary to recall that none of this obviates the obligation both of employers and employees to obey the civil law of the jurisdiction in which they reside; this principle, often referenced with the talmudic dictum *dina d'malkhuta dina* (*BT* Bava Kamma 113a–b, *et al.*) and cited in many other chapters of this volume, remains in full force even when its specifics deviate from the Torah's ideal of how things should be in the workplace.

The Value of Labor

To understand the nature of the employee-employer relationship as the *halakhah* views it, one must first endeavor to understand the value that the Torah places on work itself. The concept of labor is introduced in the earliest narratives of the Torah. In the well-known account of the Garden of Eden, Adam and Eve are given but one mandate: not to eat the fruit from the Tree of Knowledge of Good and Evil. And, indeed, when they do eat from that tree, they are banished from the Garden of Eden. As further punishment for his part in this act of supreme disobedience, Adam is told that the land will—at least as far as humanity is concerned—forever be cursed, and that only by the sweat of their brows would humans ever manage to earn their bread (Genesis 3:17–19). It is easy to see how this might lead one to conclude that human beings were not originally intended to have to labor at all, but that work was inflicted on them only as a punishment for Adam's sin and is thus best to be understood as a kind of lingering curse to be borne in our day by all because of the evil committed by our common forebear. Troubled by this apparently disdainful attitude toward labor, some biblical commentators suggest that, rather than taking this verse to suggest that having to work is a curse from God, one should view Adam and Eve's acceptance of the burden of working in the world as the great transformational moment in their development from their childlike existence in the Garden of Eden to the "real" world of adulthood. Before this moment of growth and transformation, humans are depicted as children who simply assume that God will provide for all their needs. From this moment on in the narrative, however, it is clear that humans are going to have to earn their own livelihoods and produce their own sustenance.

The rabbinic sources, far from viewing work as a horrific curse levied against humankind, view work as a necessary feature of human development and the growth of moral consciousness. A study conducted by Bilha Mannenheim and Avraham Sela, published as "Work Values in the Oral Torah" in the *Journal of Psychology and Judaism* (vol. 15 [1991], pp. 241–259), identified over nine hundred statements about work that appear in the texts of the Babylonian and Palestinian Talmuds and in the early *midrashim*. Of those, the authors categorized eighty-four percent as essentially positive, suggesting a "high esteem of work and craft." Beyond recognizing that work is essential in helping individuals to earn their livelihoods, the rabbis also emphasized how working helps individuals learn to take responsibility for society in general and, more specifically, for the proper maintenance of the social order. In a remark preserved at *BT* N'darim 49b, Rabbi Judah and Rabbi Shimon both declare, "Great is work for it brings honor to the worker."

The importance that the classical rabbis placed on work can be seen in the way they imagined the study of Torah and the pursuit of a livelihood intertwining in the ideal life. Although Torah study was considered to be the most virtuous of all pursuits, the rabbis were also realistic in their understanding that, for the world to exist, the study of the Torah had to be combined with work in the world. One example of this perspective is found in *Pirkei Avot*, the tractate of the Mishnah devoted to the ethical teaching and homilies of the sages, where we read (at *M* Avot 2:2) the teaching of Rabban Gamliel: "Excellent is the study of Torah combined with worldly occupation, for the energy expended in both pursuits [is so great that] sin is forgotten. And, moreover, all Torah study undertaken by one who lacks gainful employment is for naught and even becomes a cause of sin."

Maimonides codifies the obligation to work even when combined with Torah study, at *MT* Hilkhot Talmud Torah 3:10–11:

> Whosoever has the idea that one should immerse oneself in the study of Torah and not work for a living, but rather be sustained by charity, defames God's name, cheapens the Torah, extinguishes the light of faith, causes oneself ill, and removes oneself from the World to Come. For it is forbidden that one benefit from words of Torah in this world . . . [and so] all Torah study that is not accompanied by work will [in the end] be valueless and end in sin. Ultimately, such a person will steal from others. The ideal is for one to be sustained by the efforts of one's own hand, [and this was] a characteristic of the pious of early generations. In this, such a person merits all the honor and good of this world and the World to Come, as it is written: "If you eat by the work of your hands, happy are you, and it will go well for you" [Psalm 128:2]. This verse can be interpreted as follows: "Happy are you" means "in this world," but "it will go well for you" is a reference to the World to Come.

The rabbis also believed that work is essential both to personal development and also to success in achieving religious depth and meaning. It is through work that humans assume their places in the social order as active agents who, like Adam, take from the world only by virtue of their own work. Work is a pathway to personal health, a conduit to greater understanding of Torah and of faith, and a mechanism through which one ultimately comes to leaves a mark on this world. This is no less true for those who did (or do) physical labor as it is for the work of office professionals of today. For a person's work to achieve and maintain this degree of personal and religious meaning and expression, the specific dynamics of the employee-employer relationship must, however, have extremely clear definitions and boundaries.

Wages

The set of rules and standards that the *halakhah* develops from the biblical passages regarding the payment of wages focuses primarily on the elaboration of the requirement that wages must always be paid on time. Speaking of the worker hired on a daily basis, for example, Leviticus 19:13 ordains that wages must be paid out on the same day that they are earned, saying explicitly that "the wages of a laborer shall not remain with you until the morning." At *M* Bava M'tzi·a 9:2, however, the Mishnah explains that while the Torah's pronouncements are designed to create the fairest and most reasonable earning environment for day laborers, the requirements to pay on time may also refer to any previously agreed-upon pay period—be it daily, weekly, monthly, or at some other predetermined interval. This leniency derives from the Torah's own strictness with respect to the treatment of day laborers: in the verse from Deuteronomy 24 cited above, the Torah specifically explains that one should presume that day laborers live hand-to-mouth and are thus totally reliant on the wages they earn daily to cover their most immediate expenses, even the purchase of food for their families. Because we understand that such workers and their families will be unable even to eat without their daily wages, we must exert ourselves maximally to provide them with the money they have already earned. In other situations, where the need for daily compensation does not exist as acutely, the law can be more flexible. Practically speaking, the *halakhah* mandates that, regardless of the specific pay period agreed upon at the time of employment, employers have an obligation to pay the wages of their employees at the appropriate time without undue delay. An employer who purposefully withholds payment, according to Maimonides (at *MT* Hilkhot S'khirut 11:2), is classified as an *osheik* ("an extortionist") and may be considered to be breaking as many as five different biblical commandments concurrently.

Since the reason the Torah gives for on-time payment of wages is that the worker is poor, one might ask about the need for on-time payment of wages in a case where the employee fails to demonstrate financial need or when it is known that the employee has other means of livelihood and is not poor. In other words, if the *halakhah* finds the wherewithal to permit the relaxation of the Torah's daily payment schedule if the employee does not demand it, then why should it be so wrong to delay payment in cases where employees do not urgently need their daily (or weekly, or monthly) wages to buy food for their families? This question is asked in the Talmud at *BT* Bava M'tzi·a 112a: "Why does a worker ascend upon a ladder, suspend himself from a tree, and place himself at risk, if not for his wages? . . . One who withholds the pay of a worker, it is as if he has taken his spirit from him." The timely payment of wages, therefore, is about more than just financial neediness. It is also about the worker's spirit, about his or her sense of self-worth and purpose. Therefore, regardless of financial need, all employees have the right to receive on-time payment of wages. This, and many other aspects of the employer-employee relationship are discussed by Rabbi Jill Jacobs in her responsum, "Work, Workers, and the Jewish Owner," approved by the CJLS in 2008 and available to the public on the website of the Rabbinical Assembly. A concurring opinion paper by Rabbi Elliot Dorff is also available on the Rabbinical Assembly website.

Eating on the Job and Other Non-Financial Benefits

Employers owe their workers more than just their wages, however, and Jewish law addresses one aspect of the non-financial benefits to which employees are entitled in its elaboration of Deuteronomy 23:25–26. There, the Torah states clearly that workers have the right to eat grapes or any other kind of produce while working in the fields, and that this perk comes to them in addition to whatever wages the employer has agreed to pay the employee for his or her work. Maimonides also uses this verse to establish that the employer's obligation to provide this benefit continues throughout the duration of the employee's contract (*MT* Hilkhot S'khirut 12:1). In the fourteenth century, however, Rabbi Jacob ben Asher used earlier comments from Maimonides to limit this benefit only to the worker him or herself and to specify that this right applies only during work hours. Moreover, he prohibits overeating or abusing the employer's largesse:

> The worker in the vineyard may not eat bread or other food together with the grapes in order to be able to eat more grapes . . . and may not crush the grapes on a rock even if this is done by his wife and children, which would not require that he stop working to do it . . . and Maimonides wrote that one who stops working in order to eat during the working hours, or who eats before the completion of the work day, transgresses a negative *mitzvah* [and is guilty of theft] (*AT* Ḥoshen Mishpat 337).

According to Jacob ben Asher, then, it is the worker's responsibility not to abuse this right by overeating, by overstepping the boundaries of benefit eligibility, or by causing work stoppage. In turn, the employer allows the employee to eat, thus to maintain the energy necessary to complete the requirements of the job. If, however, the worker violates the parameters inherent in the right to eat the employer's produce, that worker is no longer to be seen as a hungry individual exercising one of his or her basic employee rights, but is henceforth to be considered a thief whose abuse of the privilege to eat the employer's produce constitutes stealing from the employer and who is therefore in direct violation of Torah law.

Today, this *halakhah* still applies directly to all workers involved in agriculture or in the food industry. It is not uncommon, for example, for a restaurant to allow its employees to eat a meal prepared in that restaurant while on duty. The *halakhah* does not insist that all employers under all circumstances have an obligation to feed their employees. The Talmud, however, does establish this absolute requirement: "Where it is the custom to provide food, the employer must do so" (*BT* Bava M'tzi·a 83a). Also, by doing so, the company establishes its own custom, so this could become an issue if a company had been in the practice of providing food for its employees (or of providing some other benefit) and later considers ending that benefit.

The application of this law for the modern employee and employer, however, is not limited only to the question of the right of employees to eat on the job. To the extent that food is necessary for the employee's continued ability to complete a job, that employee should be granted time to eat at work, provided that the employee recognizes that the time allocated is provided specifically to enable him or her to continue working. Nevertheless, caution must be exercised to avoid abuse by ensuring that this kind of permission to eat on the job does not turn into theft. In most work environments, *minhag ha-makom* and the pertinent labor laws outlining acceptable break assignments guarantee that a fair boundary can be established between workers' rights and employers' needs.

One could certainly ask the question of the application of these ideals in companies that produce other products or goods. Does the same obligation to provide those goods to the employee exist? It seems to me that the above establishes two guiding principles that one would need to consider:

1. Could the goods produced have a direct impact on the person's ability to do their work? Do they provide for a physiological need for the employee that would contribute to his or her ability to get their work done? If so, it does seem that these same principles would apply and an employer would need to make them available. One could argue that there could be a psychological impact which would require a much more lengthy discussion and analysis.
2. What is the custom of the particular industry and/or marketplace?

Employee Obligations

At the core of the Torah's view of the employer-employee relation is the conviction that the workday is for work and that workers during their hours of employment are to focus solely on fulfilling the job responsibilities as outlined by the employer. That being the case, an examination of the obligations of employees is also fitting and necessary.

In most discussions of labor relations, far greater attention is paid to obligations of employers than to the responsibilities of employees. Nonetheless, by virtue of the employment agreement, and as emphasized in the text from Rabbi Jacob ben Asher cited in the preceding discussion, employees have a clear obligation to do what it takes to complete the task or tasks they have been hired to perform. According to rabbinic law, it is not unreasonable for employers to oversee the way employees manage their time, and the same applies to all sorts of possible distractions that could conceivably interfere with the maintenance of a productive work atmosphere, even an employee's secondary employment.

One classic *midrash* speaks bluntly of the impropriety of wasting time or using time on the job for other purposes. There, a story is told of one Abba Joseph who was interrupted at his work and asked to help solve a problem. Willing to help solve the problem, Abba Joseph explained that he could nonetheless not come down off his scaffold, because he had been hired for the day and could not take undue advantage of his employer (*Sh'mot Rabbah* 13:1).

In the same section of the *Arba·ah Turim* cited just above and based on similar statements from Maimonides, the author continues to limit the activities of employees outside their main places of work to the extent that these activities will impinge on their ability to fulfill their job responsibilities, while also reinforcing the obligations of employers to offer some similar kind of consideration in return:

> One [i.e., an employee] may not work [elsewhere] at night, and then hire oneself out in the daytime, nor may one fast or mortify one's flesh, because these practices will weaken one and render one unable to do the work of the employer properly (as Maimonides wrote). In the same way that an employer is not allowed to steal the wage of his employees nor delay their payment, so too the worker is not allowed to idle time away, a little here and a little there, until a whole day is spent fraudulently. After all, the sages freed the worker from the obligation to recite the Grace after Meals in a formal company of worshipers, and also from the obligation to recite the fourth blessing of the Grace. It is in this way that one is obligated to work with all of one's strength.

The employee's first and foremost responsibility, therefore, is to fulfill the requirements of the job he or she was hired to do. It follows that, if a person is freed from *mitzvot* in order to concentrate on his or her job, how much the more so must there be an obligation to fulfill requirements of the job itself in a satisfactory and timely manner. (Otherwise, the exemption from *mitzvot* would be pointless.) In fact, in addition to shortening the Grace after Meals, the Talmud (at *BT* B'rakhot 46a) awards workers the flexibility to pray from the location of their work and, when necessary, to shorten the text of certain fixed prayers.

Unless exceptions are laid out in the terms of employment at the time of the initial agreement, or unless special circumstances are discussed and approved by the employer, any violation of these norms of conduct could reasonably result in an employee's dismissal. The most challenging of these circumstances in today's workforce by far, however, is the issue of secondary employment. To make ends meet, many people find it necessary to hold a second job. While one could try to argue that there is a prevailing custom in today's work environment that permits employees to take secondary work when they are not working for their primary employers, such secondary obligations could still result in an interruption, or at least in a diminution, of those employees' ability to work at full capacity in their primary jobs. Therefore, in the absence of any written policies agreed to formally at the time of employment, it is halakhically advisable for employees who are considering taking on additional work to consider carefully the time commitment that may be involved and/or to consult with their primary employers in advance in order to ensure that any additional employment will not impair their preexisting commitment to their primary places of employment.

In addition, as part of the employment agreement, but also to avoid the possibility of inadvertently stealing from one's employer, an employee should be cautioned against entertaining any distractions that could conceivably compromise the worth of time that belongs to the employer and/or the ability of an employee to focus fully on the work he or she is being paid to perform. This could include such activities as taking personal phone calls while on the job, socializing with co-workers in non-job-related ways, surfing the Internet on an employer's time or using the employer's Internet access for personal ends, or generally devoting time to personal chores or looking after one's own business on company time.

In return for the employee's good faith efforts to fulfill the job requirements, the employee has the right to expect, and the employer has the obligation to provide, fair treatment in addition to fair wages and fair benefits. We have already mentioned the Torah's law found at Deuteronomy 24:14 forbidding an employer from unjustly dominating an employee. The midrashic amplification of this verse (at *Sifra* B'har, *parsh'ta* 6:2) is that one should not ask a servant to heat up an employer's cup unnecessarily—or to perform any unneeded task—simply to keep the servant busy or to assert one's authority. Also, the *midrash* explains that a worker should not be told to carry his employer's clothing to the bathhouse or do other such demeaning work which is not specifically provided for in his or her contract. Consequently, an employee has every right to expect that the work that he or she is asked to do will be meaningful, productive, and dignified.

Sick Leave

Jewish law also addresses the issues of employee illness and its impact on one's ability to work. The Talmud (at *BT* Kiddushin 17a) says that Hebrew slaves were allowed to miss as many as half the days of their indenture due to sickness or injury without being liable for the time lost. (That is to say, laborers were free to leave at the expiration of the term and were not liable to compensate their masters for time lost.) In another passage (at *BT* Bava M'tzi·a 78a), the Talmud speaks about an animal that has been rented to carry a load or to perform a certain task. While engaged in the task or carrying the burden, the animal may become unexpectedly weakened by illness, and its ability to do the task for which it was rented thus diminished. The ruling there is that the animal's illness is the renter's poor fortune, and that full rental fees, regardless of the animal's diminished abilities, are still due. If, however, the animal was incapacitated to the point at which it could not do the job *even* poorly, then the renter need not pay the rental fees. In human terms, this suggests that, should an employee become ill to the degree that his or her ability to complete the job is compromised, even seriously, then the employer must still pay his or her wages. If, on the other hand, the illness renders the employee wholly incapacitated, then the employer is no longer responsible for payment.

Later Jewish legal authorities differ on how this law should actually work. In the *Shulḥan Arukh* (at *SA* Ḥoshen Mishpat 310), the law is stated just as above: in the event of partial incapacitation, the renter (or, in this case, the employer) is still liable to pay the rental fee (or the worker's wages). Two later Ashkenazic authorities, however, Rabbi Betzalel Ashkenazi (author of the sixteenth-century *Shittah M'kubbetzet* commentary on the Talmud), and the Vilna Gaon, Rabbi Elijah Kramer, both read the talmudic law to say that in the case where the illness causes partial incapacitation, the renter or employer need only pay partial rent or a partial wage, and that the amount to be paid should approximate the percentage of work actually accomplished. As a result of this disagreement between halakhic authorities, it feels exaggerated to say that the *halakhah* demands full payment of rent or of wages in the case of illness. Nevertheless, the *minhag ha-makom* in most industries and for most classes of employees (except those contracted to work and be paid by the hour) is to allow for some form of sick leave with pay. In instances of illnesses of longer duration, employees might seek coverage from short-term and/or long-term disability insurance to cover the payment of the wages, though it is not the employer's responsibility to provide and/or pay for such coverage.

Family Leave

Not surprisingly, the classical Jewish texts do not mention or allow for maternity leave or paternity leave. Since women did not generally work outside the home and men did not stay home to care for their children, there was no need for either kind of leave. In our world, however, since we consider a mother's choice to nurture and nurse her infant to be a basic civil right, it seems wrong to deny a similar bonding experience with a newborn to fathers merely because it is not halakhically mandated. Moreover, the accepted business practice, often mandated through legislation, is to allow both women and men the benefits of family leave. There is certainly no obvious reason why modern Jewish jurists should not adopt this entirely salutary innovation merely because of an absence of precedent.

Sexual and Non-Sexual Harassment in the Workplace

The imbalance of power in the employee-employer relationship can often create a climate vulnerable to the appearance (and certainly also to the reality) of harassment. Needless to say, the embarrassment, oppression, and psychological ramifications of harassment make any such misuse of power and authority a violation of *halakhah* and Jewish ethics. This applies to any act of harassment, but sexual harassment, probably the most recognized form of harassment today, also adds sexual immorality to the list of halakhic norms being violated.

As mentioned above, Leviticus 25:55 reminds workers and employers that both are servants of God and none other. No one person is permitted, therefore, to exercise inappropriate power over another, whatever the social imbalance in their relationship.

While this injunction is applicable to any two people in any relationship, the prohibition within the employee-employer relationship is made more vivid through the Torah's mandate in Exodus: "You shall not ill-treat any widow or orphan. If you do mistreat them, I will heed their outcry as soon as they cry out to Me, and My anger shall blaze forth . . ." (Exodus 22:21–23). Like the widows and orphans of scriptural antiquity, employees are often entirely aware of their economic dependence on their employers, deeply fearful of negative repercussions, and, practically speaking, unable to defend themselves against abuse or harassment. Rabbeinu Yonah, a contemporary of Maimonides, interprets this further in his *Sha·arei T'shuvah* ("The Gates of Repentance") 3:60, where he writes that if someone fears someone else and is embarrassed to challenge that other person's authority, then the latter cannot feel free to command the person who fears him or her even to do the most minor task unless it accords with that person's will or unless it is deemed for his or her ultimate benefit. Certainly, we can understand how this speaks to the relationship between employee and employer. Because employees rely on their employers for economic sustenance, but also because of the natural desire to seek validation from those in positions of authority, employees are often fearful of their employers and may choose not to speak up, even when the fear of harassment is real, to avoid embarrassment or to avoid jeopardizing their job security. Employers must, therefore, be careful never to oppress employees, even inadvertently, and must avoid even the appearance of abusing their power over those who work for them, let alone actually exercising such power to dominate them.

Hiring and Firing

As we have already seen, the employment agreement is understood by the *halakhah* to be a kind of leasing contract in which employees sell their services and employers agree to purchase those services for agreed-upon terms. But the *halakhah* also recognizes that employment agreements differ in certain basic ways from lease agreements. Foremost among these are the issues relating to the termination of employment: lease agreements invariably specify the date on which the arrangement will end, while employment agreements are often left open-ended. While most halakhic sources that discuss the boundaries of the employment relationship spend much more time discussing the termination of employment than its initiation, it is important to recognize that both aspects of the employer-employee relationship—when they begin *and* when they might end, and under what circumstances they will begin *or* end—should be discussed at the outset, so that agreement in both regards can be reached in good faith.

In both of these matters, as in all other aspects of business law, rabbinic law places a strong emphasis on the value of words and requires accuracy and honesty in words that are spoken and in agreements made as part of the initial negotiation process. (See, for example, the long discussion in the Talmud at *BT* Bava M'tzi·a 49b–51a.) An employee, therefore, who misrepresents his or her qualifications and/or abilities is guilty of *ona·at d'varim,* a general term used in the sources to denote deceptive language both in its oral and written guises. Likewise, an employer who misrepresents the nature of work the employee will be asked to do, the working conditions under which the employee will labor, or the terms of employment that will govern the employee's position is also guilty of *ona·at d'varim.*

Throughout the past few decades, regular employee separations have become a fact of organizational life in both for-profit corporations and not-for-profit agencies. In the corporate world, poor job performance and insubordination are no longer the only reasons for dismissals. Layoffs, job termination, and corporate shutdowns have contributed to an increase in job dismissals. Employee dismissal can be a result of the employee's behavior, even if the behavior in question is only tangentially related to the job, or it can be driven by the economic needs of the employer or by other influences from the marketplace. But although many states still operate under an implicit provision of employment-at-will, employers are cautious, in particular with firing, to avoid the high cost of labor litigation.

Once an employer and employee agree to terms of employment, there is an implicit understanding that the two have entered into a contractual agreement. In the absence of specific contractual provisions to the contrary, many states today define employment for an indefinite period as terminable at will by either party. This means that where a contract of employment is indefinite in duration, both the employee and the employer have the right to terminate the employment at any time with or without cause, and either with or without due notice.

For moderns accustomed to think of these practices as normative, the halakhic rulings that govern the termination of employment are likely to cause feelings of discomfort. Jewish law regards the termination of an employment agreement as a right, within certain parameters, for either party. Inherent in this right, however, are also responsibilities that may vary depending on matters of timing and circumstance. Maimonides rules that even after an agreement takes place, but before the work actually commences, either the employer or the employee may, in fact, sever the agreement, leaving no legal claims against the other. An exception applies, however, in a case of workers who may possibly have been able to find other employment had the agreement not been made with the employer for whom they expected to work, but who now find themselves unemployed as a consequence of the retraction (*MT* Hilkhot S'khirut 9:4). In such a case, compensation is due to the employees equivalent to the amount they might have earned had they managed to find work for the precise period in which they had expected to work for the employer who is now terminating the agreement. In the case of daily workers, this equaled one day's pay for what would be considered the least amount of work for the least amount of pay that such workers could demand in the marketplace. This does not imply that workers should be paid at their usual level of compensation for the work for which they might be trained; rather, the amount is tied to the work that they could be expected to accept, even out of desperation, in the event that employment in their chosen field of work was not available.

Just as the *mishnah* from Bava M'tzi·a permits the establishment of longer pay periods than the daily one mentioned in Scripture when such an extension suits both employer and employee *and* is formally agreed upon by both, here too the concept of an agreed-upon extension can be applied to override the default position of the *halakhah*. Today, this might mean that an employer should feel obligated to pay the employee until he or she is able to secure other work (or perhaps until unemployment benefits begin—in which case the employee receives, generally, the lowest common wage for work in his or her field). Given the reciprocal nature of the employee-employer relationship, the same obligation not to walk away from a contract at will applies to the employee who wishes to retract an entered-upon agreement. The question of severance pay *per se* is discussed below.

However, the parameters for retracting an agreement change once the work commences. In the case of an employee hired for a finite amount of time, for example, there is no halakhic basis for insisting that employment continue beyond that period. In such a situation, neither the employer nor the employee is obligated to extend the agreement, regardless of what the other party might want. Since this is established in the terms of employment at the outset, the end of the work period signifies the end of both parties' responsibilities toward each other.

The primary difference between the *halakhah* and modern business practice appears in the case of an employee hired for a long-term position whose employment agreement does not mention a termination date. Here, the *halakhah* allows the employee much more flexibility and leniency than it does the employer. The employee operates within a structure of employment at will, and is allowed to terminate the employment at any time. This principle is found in the *Shulḥan Arukh* and is based on an earlier statement of

Maimonides allowing workers to end their work even in the middle of the time period for which they were hired. We read that workers can indeed end their work, and they may do so even if they have already been paid for the period and no longer have the money to return (*SA* Ḥoshen Mishpat 333:3). In such a case, the money already owed becomes a debt owed to the employer, a contingency the employer is deemed to have accepted by contracting with the employee in the first place. The reason cited for this leniency is that workers are not slaves. In other words, by hiring out his or her services, an individual does not enslave himself or herself to another and, more to the point, does not, in so doing, relinquish the basic human freedom to accept or decline other employment as one sees fit. Halakhically speaking, then, the preservation of the individual's commercial freedom remains paramount. Out of this concern, the Rema, in his comment on the statement of the *Shulḥan Arukh* cited just above, established that while employers can offer long-term or even life-long contracts to employees if they wish to do so, a worker may not commit himself for more than three years at a time—three years being the dividing line between the biblical definition of a worker and an indentured servant.

An employer, like an employee, can, of course, terminate a work agreement. However, unless the term of employment agreed upon at the outset has expired, implicit in Jewish law is the need for just cause before the termination of an employee can legitimately take place. Given that the employment agreement in Jewish law is understood as a contract, failure to comply with the terms of the agreement can reasonably result in its early termination. As discussed earlier, employees are required to fulfill their job requirements in good faith and to the best of their abilities. Consequently, employees who do not adequately fulfill the responsibilities of their jobs as agreed upon at the time of employment can, in fact, be discharged. There is no halakhic right not to be fired for just cause.

Being fired, of course, impacts employees in a wide variety of ways, not only in terms of lost income. There is also the issue of social stigma to consider, as well as issues of mental anguish and grief. Nor do these result solely when an employee is fired for cause. Indeed, modern corporate life in recent years has been greatly impacted by the phenomena of retrenchment and job elimination, both of which have resulted in the discharge of large numbers of employees for causes not at all related to job performance and neither of which makes being fired any more palatable or socially easy to bear: despite the circumstances, the cardinal point is always that the employee still suffers from the loss of his or her job. While there is nothing in the *halakhah* that legally mandates that any assistance be provided by an employer who fires an employee, there are certainly forms of assistance that will cushion the impact of the job dismissal dramatically. The same ethical principles that drive the following discussion of severance pay, however, also apply to other forms of assistance: interest-free loans, career counseling, personal counseling, placement assistance, and retraining.

Before turning to the discussion of severance pay, there is one related topic to address. Employee dismissals inevitably stir up questions among those left on the job, and these questions often lead to gossip about the dismissed employee. Even people motivated principally by thoughtfulness and kindness (that is, people who are primarily concerned for the welfare of the person who has been terminated) will inevitably want to know why a person has been dismissed. Since the nature of the workplace has changed so dramatically over the centuries, it is difficult to find traditional halakhic sources that directly address the question of how to discuss an employee's dismissal within a business or organization. However, the laws prohibiting *l'shon ha-ra* ("gossip," derived from Leviticus 19:16, "You shall not go about as a talebearer among your people") and the laws mandating that Jews actively protect the reputations of others both call for discretion in these matters. Thus, it is forbidden to disseminate any information about a discharged employee that might lower that person in the eyes of others, and this would certainly be the case regardless of whether or not the information under discussion was accurate. At *Pirkei Avot* 2:10, Rabbi Eliezer teaches: "Let another's honor be as dear to you as your own." *Avot D'rabbi Natan,* a midrashic amplification of the text of *Pirkei Avot*, expands this idea further: "How is this so? It teaches that just as one has regard for one's own honor, so must one have regard for the honor of others; just as one desires that there should be no shadow cast on one's own good repute, so must one be anxious not to damage the reputation of others" (*Avot D'rabbi Natan*, text A, ch. 15).

When someone is dismissed from a job, open discussion about the circumstances of that person's dismissal will almost certainly lower his or her status in the eyes of the remaining workers. For this reason, Jewish law limits sharing any information about dismissed employees unless it is vital that the person to whom one is speaking have the information. Furthermore, any who engage idly in discussions about an employee's dismissal are clearly engaging in the dissemination of *l'shon ha-ra*. It is also possible to imagine a situation in which the gossip and rumors that swirl around an individual's dismissal could end up causing even more damage to the discharged employee than the discharge itself. *L'shon ha-ra* and the laws relating to gossip and slander are discussed elsewhere in this volume by Rabbis Kassel Abelson and Benjamin Kramer, and with special reference to the workplace by Rabbi Barry Leff.

Severance Pay

Although severance pay has been considered a basic form of compensation for loss of income due to dismissal throughout the Jewish world, it is difficult to say unequivocally that the provision of severance pay for a terminated employee is a halakhic requirement. Rather, it is a complex issue to which Jewish texts take a wide variety of approaches. On the one hand, it is possible to argue that Jewish sources provide a firm basis for the obligation to provide severance pay. Yet there is no universally agreed upon standard and, while some authorities have ruled that there does indeed exist a halakhic mandate to provide severance pay for dismissed workers, others have determined that offering to pay employees for work they do not actually do is merely an example of righteous behavior—that is to say, an act of kindness and decency—but not one of obligation. *Minhag ha-makom,* local custom, is another consideration that must be taken into account in determining whether or not to provide an employee with severance pay, as would be the specific reason for the dismissal.

Some authorities find legal precedent to support the notion of mandatory severance benefits in the biblical concept of *ha·anakah,* a bonus or dismissal gratuity that the Torah ordains be paid out to manumitted Hebrew servants at the conclusion of their six years of indentured service. "If a fellow Hebrew, man or woman, is sold to you," the Torah decrees, "he shall serve you six years; and in the seventh year you shall set him free. When you do set him free, do not send him off empty-handed; furnish [*ha·aneik ta·anik,* the verbal form of *ha·anakah*] him out of the flock, the threshing floor, and the vat [i.e., from the largesse] with which the Eternal, your God, shall have blessed you" (Deuteronomy 15:12–16).

While the Talmud and later rabbinic codes consider this argument compelling, most of the latter did not codify an absolute legal requirement to provide severance pay based on this comparison between the manumitted Hebrew servant and the dismissed employee. *Sefer Ha-ḥinnukh,* the thirteenth-century outline of the commandments of Scripture attributed by tradition to Rabbi Aaron Halevi of Barcelona, does extend the Torah law to the workplace, ruling that an employer, because of the blessings bestowed upon him by God, should feel obliged to extend the concept of *ha·anakah* to anyone who has worked for him and who has then been dismissed, even if such a person only worked for a short time (*Sefer Ha-ḥinnukh,* commandment no. 450). The text does not say precisely why this should be the case, but perhaps it is simply a matter of wishing to grant reality to a beautiful ethic that might otherwise not be observed. In other words, while there are no longer

Hebrew servants of the kind referenced above, the essential kindness that underlies the whole concept of *ha·anakah* can still motivate an employer to grant severance pay to a dismissed employee as an act of compassion and sympathetic caring.

The rationale for severance pay as both an act of charity and also as an act of righteousness was perhaps best expressed in the contemporary ruling of Rabbi Uzziel, the late chief rabbi of Israel, published in his *Mishp'tei Uzzi·el* commentary to *SA* Ḥoshen Mishpat 331 (ed. Tel Aviv, 1940, pp. 212–216), where, based on Proverbs 2:20 ("In order that you should go in good ways and follow the path of the righteous"), he authorized an Israeli court to insist that severance pay be offered to employees whose employment was being terminated.

At the same time, there is also precedent for obligating employers to provide severance pay on the basis of what could be called an extralegal rationale. According to this explanation, offering severance pay is an act of righteousness and, as such, distinct from and unrelated to any separate legal claims terminated employees may have on their former employers. The thirteenth-century scholar of Provence, Rabbi Menaḥem ben Shlomo Meiri, for example, expressed this in his commentary to *M* Bava Kamma 6:4 in the following way: "One who does not pay what is required in order to be clear before heaven cannot be considered to be a valid witness before the rabbinic courts." This was also the opinion of the fourteenth-century Franco-German halakhic authority Rabbi Mordecai ben Hillel, who (in his *Sefer Mord'khai,* Bava M'tzi·a 257 to *BT* Bava M'tzi·a 24b) maintained that a *beit din* has the right to force wealthy people to do righteous deeds, even beyond the precise letter of the law, strictly as an act of righteousness. In the case of discharged employees, however, it is important to note that his ruling is about the ability of the rabbinic court to legislate acts of compassion, not about the rights of the worker to receive severance.

The rabbis were in agreement that *dina d'malkhuta dina,* that the law of one's country serves as the ultimate arbiter of one's legal obligations. (This legal principle, mentioned above but first formulated by the famous Babylonian teacher Samuel, is found in the Talmud at *BT* N'darim 28a, Gittin 10b, Bava Kamma 113a–b, and Bava Batra 54b and 55a and is discussed at length by many authors elsewhere in this volume.) On this basis alone, however, since there are no laws in our country mandating the payment of severance benefits, we would have to conclude that there is no reason to consider such payments mandatory. However, consideration must also be given to the fact that severance pay has been *minhag ha-makom,* local custom, in Jewish communities throughout the generations and has increasingly become the accepted business practice in corporations and companies. Although it is most common in cases of layoffs or position elimination, severance pay is also sometimes provided as a goodwill gesture when an employer dismisses an employee for poor job performance or other for-cause reason. At times, it is also used as an incentive to motivate a discharged employee to sign a separation waiver specifying that no further action will be taken against the company.

Since it is difficult to say that there is any sort of consensus among halakhic authorities regarding severance pay, it is not possible to say that the *halakhah* today requires that Jewish employers pay it. That said, it does seem plausible to say that in situations where it is accepted business practice to do so—or when the employer has been blessed with such financial means that offering severance pay will not have any sort of profound impact on the employer's own wealth—the employer is encouraged to offer severance pay and to act kindly and generously toward the former employee.

How much severance pay should be offered? When considering the question of *ha·anakah,* the Torah simply establishes the obligation to give from the "flocks" and the "threshing floors," but does not establish how much is to be granted the servant leaving his master's service. The Talmud, however, does establish the minimal amount. In a discussion about the going rates for payments of various sorts, the Talmud (at *BT* Kiddushin 17a) debates, without resolution, the amount of appropriate *ha·anakah.* The talmudic debate focuses on establishing the normative sum for the time and place in which one is living, thus making local custom paramount. In instances where severance is offered today, prevailing customs vary based on the circumstances of the job termination. In the case of layoffs or job elimination, for example, companies usually factor in the length of service, the length of time the employee might need to find another position, and the amount of time an employee will have to wait for unemployment benefits to begin in the jurisdiction in which the employee lives. Once a formula is created, it is often assigned uniformly to all those who are being displaced. When severance is offered in cases of for-cause termination, however, practices become far less uniform. There are instances, for example, when severance pay in cases of for-cause dismissal is given through the end of a week, the end of a pay period, or some other allotted time frame. Given that severance also helps ensure that the employee does not become reliant on charity of other sorts, and given that the whole point of severance payments is to help cushion the financial blow of being out of work, it is arguable that the amount of severance in cases of for-cause dismissal ought to cover the time the employee will have to wait before being able to collect unemployment insurance benefits.

The dynamics of the employer-employee relationship are likely to continue changing in this century and beyond. As Jews, we are fortunate to have the opportunity to combine local custom, secular and religious law, Torah values, and the wisdom of our ancestors as a means to understanding the changing expectations for developing workplace relationships, to establishing mutually satisfactory employment agreements and compensation, to determining appropriate working conditions, and to resolving issues related to hiring and firing. Ours is a living Torah that asks employees and employers to remember that each is ultimately a servant of God, and that they are in relationship to one another, need one another, and are deserving both of fair and equitable treatment *and* of a level of recognition of their basic human dignity that ultimately acknowledges that God resides with us in the workplace.

Among Co-Workers

BARRY J. LEFF

Traditional halakhic literature does not recognize co-workers as a distinct category of individuals within the workplace hierarchy. There are principles and laws that guide the relationship between employers and employees, of course, stipulating the rights and responsibilities of both parties. However, the *halakhah* also addresses issues of competition among independent tradespeople and, of course, the traditional literature addresses conduct among people in general in great detail. From all these sources, it is possible to develop a sense of the *halakhah* of being a co-worker, even though the Talmud predates the existence of large corporations and their attendant bureaucracies by over a millennium.

Working Together

Co-workers in the modern corporation, government, or nonprofit enterprise frequently face complex issues in their relationships. What kinds of behavior are permissible when co-workers compete with one another for a promotion only one of them can get? Is a co-worker allowed to report true but derogatory information about a colleague if the dissemination of that information will enhance his or her own chances for promotion? If one co-worker sees another doing something wrong, is the obligation to rebuke the other person affected by the fact that the rebuking party could conceivably profit by lowering the esteem in which their common boss holds the rebuked individual? Are co-workers obligated to report when they see others engaged in activities clearly contrary to the best interests of the corporation, and is it relevant that the superiors to whom such a report will have to be made will almost always be fellow employees of the same parent corporation? What if a co-worker learns that someone is violating a corporate policy, but not one he or she personally considers crucial, or even important? How do the rules prohibiting idle gossip apply when co-workers gather around the water cooler (or the coffee pot, or in an off-site setting) with their colleagues? What should be considered appropriate guidelines for romantic relationships with co-workers? None of these questions is addressed directly in our sources. Yet all are highly relevant to the modern workplace and, in the end, all can have answers that derive directly from Jewish tradition.

On top of all that, it also bears mentioning that the nature of relationships in the modern work environment is complex. Some people are team members who work closely with other individuals. Others are expected to work independently and are rarely called upon to interact much with colleagues. Some people work in matrix organizations, where there is a formal chain of command featuring designated supervisors, yet people in such settings are often assigned to projects under individuals who are not formally their own supervisors. In such an organization, a person might be responsible for getting certain tasks accomplished through the work of others without having any direct authority over those other individuals; is such a person an "employer" in the halakhic sense of the word? In large organizations, many people other than a worker's direct supervisor can have a powerful impact on furthering or hindering that individual's career. Determining who exactly is the "employer" in terms of responsibilities the *halakhah* lays out for the employer-employee relationship is not always a simple task.

To understand the ways in which Judaism calls on us to act toward fellow employees, the principles we need to examine mostly derive either from those intended (in their original settings) to guide behavior among independent tradespeople—I believe that this is reasonable because, in a sense, employees in most modern workplace settings are more like independent contractors competing for promotions and raises—or from those basic principles intended to guide behavior among people in general, such as the prohibition of gossip. An understanding of employees' obligations toward their employers is also relevant, as there inevitably will be situations in which it will appear that a worker's obligations to a fellow employee conflict with that same individual's obligations to his or her employer. Employer-employee relations are discussed in the previous chapter by Rabbi Cheryl Peretz as well as in the next chapter by Rabbi Jane Kanarek on contracts. This chapter briefly describes some of the relevant principles that apply specifically to co-workers, and then presents some fictional case studies to illustrate just how those principles could be applied in practice. What makes determining the proper course of action difficult is the fact that, when dealing with the workplace, we often find two or more legitimate principles in conflict. In such cases we have to weigh the respective worth of the competing values in the context of the situation itself to determine which should take precedence at any given moment. The ethical values we absorb from studying our sacred sources will almost always provide us with ample context to decide between competing values and conflicting principles.

The Halakhah of Being Co-Workers

The following is not an exhaustive list of principles that govern behavior among co-workers. Rather, it is a description of a few of the principles that most commonly arise in co-worker relationships in the modern workplace.

In the original sources, some of these halakhic principles are applied only to relationships among Jews, while others are granted broader application. But although it is widely accepted that ritual commandments are applicable only to and among Jews, ethical and moral commandments regulating behavior among people in secular settings today should apply equally to all people without distinction and thus govern both the relationship of Jews toward other Jews and also toward gentiles. From our traditional literature, we can identify several reasons for extending these principles of behavior to relations between Jews and non-Jews. Chief among them are the concepts of acting *mi-p'nei darkhei shalom* ("for the sake of peace"), lest the practice of treating Jews differently from non-Jews come to build resentment among non-Jews and hinder relations with them, and the concept of acting always to avoid *ḥillul ha-sheim* ("the desecration of God's name"): if we treat non-Jews according to a different ethical standard than other Jews, they will inevitably come to think poorly of Judaism and, by extension, of Jews as well. However, the most compelling reason to apply halakhic standards to relationships in the workplace between Jews and non-Jews is simply to recognize formally that all of God's children are created *b'tzelem elohim* ("in God's image"), and therefore deserve to be treated decently and fairly.

Improper Speech

Other than during playoff season, undoubtedly the favorite coffee break topic of conversation among co-workers is the behavior of other co-workers. Although this talk may take many different forms and cover a wide range of topics, most forms of improper speech (and conversations about those not present are almost always inappropriate in one way or another) are loosely lumped together in Jewish tradition under the general rubric of *l'shon ha-ra* (literally, "the evil tongue"), a general term usually taken to denote gossip. However, as described by Maimonides at *MT* Hilkhot Dei·ot 7:2, there are actually three different forms of improper speech described in our sources. The worst is *hotza·at sheim ra* ("creating a bad name"), which denotes slander at its worst: in Jewish tradition, saying negative things about another person that are untrue is the worst form of gossip. The term *l'shon ha-ra,* strictly speaking, specifically denotes the act of talking about other people with information that, while negative and damaging, is essentially true. (Americans versed in libel law will want to note that, unlike in civil law, the truth of a damaging statement does not affect its status as *l'shon ha-ra.* In Jewish tradition, the important point is solely that the data imparted is not information its subject will likely want shared with others. Therefore, *l'shon ha-ra* can include content ranging from a person's relationships to his or her medical conditions to information relating to job performance.) *R'khilut,* gossip *per se,* is information about a person that might even be positive—but which the speaker does not have the right to share with anyone else. For example, if someone who has been trying to become pregnant for some time finally succeeds, it is clearly good news. Yet the simple fact that the person involved might not want the whole world informed before she personally chooses to tell others is deemed highly relevant. Telling this news without permission, therefore, is forbidden by Jewish law under the general rubric of *r'khilut* even when it involves what most would easily consider to be happy tidings.

Furthermore, the Talmud (at *BT* Arakhin 15b) teaches that three people are damaged by improper speech: the subject of the gossip, the person doing the talking, and the person doing the listening. (The actual talmudic text, in fact, states this lesson more urgently: it actually says the three are *killed* by improper speech!) Idly talking about co-workers, therefore, is to be condemned in the strongest terms. If there is a valid reason to share the information—for example, if a co-worker's wellbeing is at stake for reasons that he or she will never know unless told, and those reasons will reflect poorly on a different co-worker or on a supervisor, or on the owners of the business—then sharing information might actually be required, and this might be so regardless of the consequences one could incur for speaking up. However, this will rarely be the case and, in general—and always in cases of doubt—the default position should always be to keep one's mouth shut, to walk away from others' inappropriate conversations, and perhaps even to ask others to stop their inappropriate conversations in one's presence.

Other matters relating to question of *l'shon ha-ra* are discussed elsewhere in this volume by Rabbis Benjamin Kramer and Kassel Abelson.

The Obligation to Rebuke

It is written in the Torah that "you shall not hate your brother in your heart: you shall surely rebuke your neighbor, and not bear sin on his account" (Leviticus 19:17). In simple terms, this means that when we see people doing wrong, we are obligated to rebuke them so that they can mend their ways in the future. Of course, this could easily be misconstrued as meddling in other people's business and, indeed, the Talmud limits the applicability of this commandment to situations in which we think others will be receptive to the criticism and will change their ways. In fact, we are told that just as it is a commandment to criticize people when we think they will listen, we are commanded *not* to criticize others if we believe they will not listen (cf. Rashi's application of Rabbi Ilaa's comment to that effect found at *BT* Y'vamot 65b to the verse from Leviticus mentioned above). Maimonides adds that, before rebuking someone, one must be certain that one's motives are pure: that the rebuke is strictly for the other party's benefit, not an act of ego gratification on the part of the rebuker. Also, one who embarks on the performance of this *mitzvah* needs to let the other person know that one is acting solely for the benefit of the person one is attempting to rebuke (*MT* Hilkhot Dei·ot 6:7).

In the workplace, the key to rebuking a co-worker productively is understanding the difference between tattling and rebuking: rebuke (in Hebrew, *tokheiḥah*) can only be directed to the party concerned, not ever to a third party. Moreover, before embarking on a workplace *tokheiḥah,* it is critically important to examine one's motives. At work, employees often find themselves acting out of selfish motives, particularly to make themselves look good at the expense of co-workers by criticizing them in public venues, such as meetings. Our tradition teaches that a rebuke should never occur in such a public setting. Rather, it should be done quietly and privately. A good test for co-workers wondering if they are acting selflessly or selfishly is simply to ask if there is any plausible personal benefit to be derived from rebuking the co-worker in question. If there is, then one must determine whether that benefit is the motivating factor in one's decision to issue the rebuke. If one is uncertain how to answer the question, the wise course of action will always be to do nothing.

Stumbling Blocks

The Torah teaches us at Leviticus 19:14 that we may never put a stumbling block before the blind, a prohibition widely understood to constitute doing anything that risks causing another to stumble or fall, either figuratively or literally. Leaving liquor out where an alcoholic can access it, for example, would be putting a stumbling block before the blind. Offering a box of doughnuts to someone on a diet would be another example—not of heinous, horrific behavior, but of behavior intended simply to encourage someone to act in an unhealthy, negative way. Both are forbidden by the scriptural commandment. We have no obligation to test our own willpower or restraint, but we are forbidden to test others. Therefore, while we merely behave sensibly by avoiding situations in which we might be tempted to sin, we are actually prohibited from creating situations in which others might be drawn to act inappropriately. Offering to let a co-worker download a copyrighted software program using a license you purchased for your personal use would be an example of such behavior. You, the purchaser, might feel that the sin is not yours because it is the other person who is doing the illegal act. However, since the person doing the downloading would not be participating in the fraud if you had not suggested it and facilitated it, you are in violation of the commandment not to put a stumbling block before the blind. It is also a violation of secular law to allow someone to download or copy copyrighted software without a license or without specific permission and that means there will also be the halakhic principle of *dina d'malkhuta dina* ("the law of the land is the law") to consider. It is contrary to Jewish law to violate civil law.

Respecting Boundaries

Hassagat g'vul literally means trespassing boundaries and is forbidden formally at Deuteronomy 19:14 with these words: "Do not move the boundary marker of your fellow, one set up by the previous generations, in the property which will be allotted to you in the land that the Eternal, your God, is giving you to possess." Maimonides (in *MT* Hilkhot G'neivah 7:11) understands this to include only boundaries set up by previous generations in the Land of Israel, but he also finds a way to make moving boundary markers outside the Land of Israel forbidden as well: since for Maimonides moving a boundary is an act of theft, the sole difference between doing so in the Land of Israel and in the Diaspora is that the former results in violating two different commandments (theft and *hassagat g'vul*), while the latter is "merely" an act of theft.

The Talmud extends this concept to tradespeople, and this brings us closer to the issue as it relates to co-workers. In the Babylonian Talmud, at *BT* Bava Batra 21b, we find the following teaching: "If a resident of an alley sets up a mill to grind grain for others, and then a fellow resident of the alley comes and sets up a mill in the same street, the law is that the first one can stop the second one, for he can say to him, 'You are cutting off my livelihood!'" A similar example illustrates the same principle by noting that fishermen must respect each other's fishing areas and not put their nets in spots where others already have their nets cast. Both of these instances are considered logical extensions of the concept of *hassagat g'vul.* In terms of the workplace, the *halakhah* can be interpreted to suggest that co-workers must respect each other's space. This way of working and thriving together can take many forms, however. Part of it would certainly involve the concept of honoring other people's privacy. In many modern offices, people work in cubicles that offer only minimal privacy. We need to take care not to listen in on other people's phone conversations or to read things left lying on their desks. This concept can also apply to nonspatial territory—that is, the "space" someone occupies in the staff hierarchy. If someone has certain responsibilities, it could be encroaching on that person's space if a co-worker were to lobby management to have some of that person's responsibilities transferred to him or herself, or if an employee were to take it upon him or herself to do things that others have been previously looking after even without a formal petition to management. That is just as much *hassagat g'vul* as moving a neighbor's fence in the middle of the night and is, as such, forbidden.

Modesty

Modesty is not a much-valorized concept in modern society in general, nor is it much esteemed in the workplace, but Judaism values modesty for its own sake. The Hebrew word for "modesty," *tz'ni·ut,* is usually associated with the strict dress code followed by many Orthodox women, but *tz'ni·ut* is about more than just clothing. *Tz'ni·ut* is about having a modest approach to life: being modest in both dress and behavior. (Elsewhere in this volume, Rabbi Gordon Tucker argues for a more comprehensive treatment of *tz'ni·ut* among contemporary Jews in general.) However, *tz'ni·ut* is also a principle applicable to workplace romances. Even assuming that a relationship between co-workers is not inappropriate and does not constitute a problem for their common employer, workers pursuing a romantic relationship should continue to conduct themselves decorously and professionally in a work setting. The standard of *tz'ni·ut* should be that public displays of affection and other forms of even relatively benign flirting are inappropriate in the workplace. Such behavior should be reserved for private times, and this rule should apply even to married couples.

Workplace Situations

In simple situations involving only one of the principles adduced above, it should be relatively simple to decide how best to proceed. Jewish tradition provides clear guidance that gratuitous gossip about others, no matter how accurate or truthful, has no place in the workplace—or anywhere else. One is obligated to act with integrity, and it is irrelevant if it is difficult, inconvenient, or costly to do so. In simple cases, such as when a group of employees is tempted to cover up a clearly identified safety problem because they want to save the company the expense of fixing it, it does not take a professor of ethics to figure out what is the right course of action. In most of the recent whistle-blowing cases, while it took great courage for the whistle-blower to come forward, there generally was no question that coming forward was the right thing to do.

Not all situations that we encounter in the workplace are so simple, however. The real world is a complicated place. Quite often we encounter situations that pit two values we esteem against one another, thus requiring that we weigh them in a way that is unsettling or even morally awkward. This is never going to be a simple task. This section will provide a few examples of modern situations to see how we would apply Jewish values in the workplace.

In my first situation, the manager of a fast-food restaurant, Joe, has an affair with a married employee of the restaurant, Linda. During the relationship, they leave explicit messages for each other as in-office voice-mail messages. Another employee, Stan, accesses the voice mail inadvertently. What should he do? Should he rebuke the couple? Notify the owner of the restaurant? Notify Linda's husband? Or should he ignore the whole thing, figuring that it isn't really any of his business? There are many values that could come into play in this situation:

- Should Stan rebuke the couple? There is, as noted above, a strong halakhic obligation to rebuke people when one knows they are doing wrong. However, we are cautioned not to rebuke people if we don't think they will listen to the rebuke. Furthermore, rebuke is a very delicate thing, and must be motivated solely by concern for the other person. In this case, Stan could also be putting himself in an awkward position, because he should not have been listening to other people's voice mail conversations in the first place. Even if the voice mail was accessed by accident initially, it was hardly necessary to listen to the whole thing once his error became obvious!

- Should Stan respect his manager's privacy and do nothing at all? Stan, who listened in on the other person's voice mail, certainly should not have done so, and this was clearly a violation of Joe and Linda's privacy. Even couples who engage in inappropriate behavior still maintain their right to privacy, after all. That is why secular law requires a court order before even police, let alone civilians, can do things like listen to other people's voice mail.

- Should Stan report the affair to others? Joe and Linda engaged (or, at least, appears to have engaged) in an adulterous relationship. Under traditional Jewish law, if Linda is Jewish and married, the penalty would theoretically be death for them both. This offense is taken very seriously by halakhic authorities, partially because it is seen not solely as an offense against the betrayed spouse, but also as a crime against God, the divine Author of the law forbidding adultery. As serious as the crime is, however, the standards of evidence in *halakhah* are very high indeed, requiring warning in advance and eyewitnesses to the deed before the ultimate penalty could ever be imposed. A couple certainly would never have been convicted, let alone executed, on the basis of hearsay evidence alone, which is precisely what we have in this case. The person who uncovered the evidence certainly does not get to act as judge, jury, and executioner—which, in a sense, is what would happen if Stan were to report on the affair to others.

- Do Joe and Linda have a right to speak privately to each other? Even if they *were* married to each other, it would be immodest to leave sexually explicit messages on a system that other people could conceivably access.

- Do the laws against gossip forbid Stan from telling anyone about what he heard? There is some question whether or not the laws of *l'shon ha-ra* would apply in this case. Certainly Stan would be barred from telling just anybody about what he heard. On the other hand, one could make a case that it would not be *l'shon ha-ra* to share the information with a presumably unknowing spouse, because it is information that might be directly relevant to whether or not that person would want to stay married to the unfaithful partner. Given the prevalence of serious sexually transmitted diseases, including potentially fatal ones such as AIDS, it could even be a case of *pikku·aḥ nefesh,* of saving a life, to inform the spouse that he or she may have been exposed to a deadly virus.

There are competing values at play here, and different people could weigh the competing values differently. The simplest halakhically defensible course of action would be for the employee to rebuke one or both of the parties involved in the relationship *if* it seems possible to administer the rebuke in the proper spirit, as described above. However explicit the voice mail messages may have been, there is no definitive way to know that it isn't some kind of game the couple is playing, and, of course, the employee, Stan, has no way of knowing whether or not the relationship he heard them discussing was ever actually consummated. Furthermore, the information was acquired wrongly, through ignoring other people's boundaries. If the employee in question actually walked in on the couple engaged in an illicit act on the work premises, a stronger case could be made that others should be informed—both because the evidence is irrefutable and because it was not collected improperly. The employee in question should either say nothing at all or else speak to the parties concerned discreetly, albeit sternly and seriously.

My second situation features the concept of *g'neivat da·at,* literally "stealing another's ability to hold rational opinions," but in this context denoting the creation of false impressions of any sort. (The concept of *g'neivat da·at* is discussed in detail elsewhere in this volume by Rabbi Jacob Blumenthal.) One employee, Dave, is competing against another employee, Mike, for a promotion. Mike is receiving a lot of praise and compliments for a lengthy study he recently turned in to the company's management. Dave discovers, while doing his own research, that Mike actually plagiarized most of the information from the Internet. What should he do?

Should Dave report the information he has uncovered to management, thereby enhancing his own chances for promotion and hurting Mike's? He could, of course, rebuke Mike directly. He could also simply say nothing, figuring that to do otherwise would be to engage in *l'shon ha-ra* and possibly to violate the concept of *hassagat g'vul* as it applies to Mike's "place" in the structure of the company. One thing Dave clearly *cannot* do is to tell other employees about Mike's behavior in the hope that word will get back to management. Such tattling would clearly constitute *l'shon ha-ra.*

The appropriate approach for Dave to take would be to confront Mike directly, giving Mike an opportunity to correct any mistaken impressions that he might have given management. This would also give Mike an opportunity to act with integrity, so that the competition for the promotion could proceed on an honorable basis. Mike is guilty of *g'neivat da·at.* This is a serious matter, and if Mike refuses to issue a clarification or correction to his report, it would *not* be *l'shon ha-ra* for Dave to report his findings to management—

not simply because of his interest in the promotion, but because as an employee of the corporation he has some responsibility to protect the best interests of the business that hired him.

Let's look at a variation on this issue. Instead of discovering that Mike had plagiarized information in a report, suppose that Dave noticed that Mike seems to spend a disproportionate amount of his time recreationally surfing the Internet at work. Is this something permissible to share? In this case, the answer would be no. If Dave is not Mike's supervisor, he doesn't know about Mike's performance or whether this is having an impact on his work. It is also unlikely that Dave could have discovered Mike's Internet surfing without violating Mike's space in some way—watching his computer screen, for example, when he should have been watching his own. In this case, lacking evidence of any harm to the corporation, there is little reason to report the behavior even if it could help Dave's own chances for promotion. To tell management would fall more directly into the category of *l'shon ha-ra* for a selfish purpose than that of protecting the interests of the corporation. Furthermore, *hassagat g'vul* would apply in two senses: Dave should not have been violating Mike's space by being so aware of his activities, and he should not further violate Mike's "space" in the company by hurting his chances for promotion with information that is not necessarily directly related to his job performance or capabilities.

The workplace is an environment full of potential stumbling blocks for someone who takes seriously the commandments that govern relationships among people. The opportunities to engage in gossip, to violate other people's space, and to act selfishly (while feeling self-righteous, even pious, for doing so) are rife. To call someone a "God-fearing" person sounds rather quaint in the twenty-first century. However, being "God-fearing"—being motivated in life by deep feelings of *yirat shamayim,* the fear of heaven—is probably the best way consistently to make the right, or at least the best, choices. When confronted with difficult situations, whether at work or in life in general, acting with courtesy, generosity, and kindness, and remembering that everyone is created in God's image, is the best way to determine how to apply competing values in complex situations, certainly including issues that may come up among co-workers in even the largest corporation.

Contracts

JANE KANAREK

In a famous lesson preserved in the Talmud at *BT* Shabbat 31a and attributed to the great talmudic sage Rava, we are made privy to a list of the various questions an individual can expect to be asked on Judgment Day. The very first one among them is: "Did you pursue your business deals honestly?" Although this famous rabbinic maxim does not mention the written contracts that are so common in today's world, it does emphasize a point that is central in all rabbinic discussions about contractual relationships: the obligation of integrity. Indeed, this teaching serves as an overarching statement about the importance of both parties to a contract treating each other fairly, as well as being a reminder that, ultimately, all workers are servants of the same God. Both these principles function as fundamental assumptions of rabbinic discussions concerning contracts. And although it is surely the case that the original discussions are generally about contracts between two Jewish individuals, moderns contemplating this material can and should derive meaningful lessons about the way contracts in general should work, even in a non-Jewish business environment.

Jewish law differentiates between two types of workers, the day laborer (*s'khir yom*) and the contract laborer (*kabb'lan*). A day laborer is defined as someone who is hired for a specific period of time, whether a day, a week, a month, or a year. The employer is responsible for paying the worker promptly after the period of hire ends. A contract laborer, on the other hand, is defined as someone who is hired to complete a certain amount of work and must be paid once that work is completed and transferred to the employer (see, e.g., the *AT* Ḥoshen Mishpat 339). Details of rabbinic labor law, much like contemporary contract law, are quite intricate. In this chapter, I attempt to extrapolate a halakhic approach to modern contracts from the verbal and written compacts discussed in such great detail in classical rabbinic sources. First, however, I trace out some of the main requirements of Jewish law that apply to modern contractual relationships.

Negotiating a Contract

At the foundational level of contract law lies the following biblical commandment: "You shall neither steal nor deal deceitfully or falsely with one another" (Leviticus 19:11). This verse makes honesty in our dealings with one another, and specifically in our business dealings, a central element in the scriptural approach to daily living. It was precisely this kind of honesty that Rava meant in his lesson about the questions one will face on Judgment Day, and it is one of the key elements—perhaps even *the* key element—that is required of contract negotiations, both by employers and employees.

Explicitness of the terms of hire is an essential aspect of all contract negotiations. This precision is dictated by a passage in the Mishnah found at *M* Bava M'tzi·a 7:1, where the text teaches that a person who hires workers and then later demands that they arrive earlier or stay later than is customary in that locale cannot force them to comply with this new requirement in violation of local custom. The *Shulḥan Arukh* extends this statement further and adds that even if employers increase the employees' wages, they still cannot demand this additional work because it was not stipulated at the time of hiring (*SA* Ḥoshen Mishpat 331:1). Extrapolating from the *Shulḥan Arukh*, then, an employer cannot, at a later date, demand more than is written into the original negotiated contract; one must therefore be very careful to delineate the precise demands of the job during negotiations. For moderns, this list of details to be negotiated in advance could reasonably be expanded to include such items as the amount of vacation time, sick leave, and overtime pay being offered. In turn, the employee must also take care to ensure that a precise specification of duties occurs in negotiations. However, the general custom in a given locale or industry as to working hours and vacation time need not determine contractual limits if both parties mutually agree to a different arrangement. In other words, within certain limits, the parties to an agreement are free to negotiate whatever agreement suits them both. I will return to this idea later in this chapter when I discuss human rights violations in contracts.

Clearly, central to all contract negotiations is the condition that both parties agree freely and willingly to the contract. Both parties should know precisely the conditions to which they are agreeing. In classical Jewish law, employment agreements can be made official in a number of different ways, generally by means of a physical act of some sort undertaken to indicate the acceptance of the contract at a specific moment in time. (Without this act, the contract is not considered binding.) In the case of a day laborer, the simple commencement of work by the employee indicates the contract's acceptance (*AT* Ḥoshen Mishpat 333). With respect to a contract laborer, the employer's act of taking temporary possession of the employee's tool or tools of trade—for example, taking a scribe's stylus from his hand—also indicates contractual acceptance (Tosafot to *BT* Bava M'tzi·a 48a, *s.v. v'ha ba·ei l'mimshakh tis'poret*). Crucial to all of these cases is the concept that the two parties' actions demonstrate their agreement to the contract. In contemporary times, the signatures of employer and employee to the document generally indicate such an agreement.

Living Up to the Terms of a Contract

Jewish law differentiates between a finalized contractual agreement and the verbal agreement that precedes its formal acceptance. While, in both instances, Jewish law expects that the parties will live up to the terms of the contract, there is also a profound difference between the two because in a verbal agreement either party can withdraw without financial penalty. Jewish law, though, disapproves of such an action and indicates its displeasure with those who break a verbal commitment. "One who negotiates verbally does not commit to a finalized agreement [i.e., may renege without penalty], but the sages' spirit is displeased with this person" (*BT* Bava M'tzi·a 48a). Such a statement indicates the sages' realization that while they lacked the power formally to impose sanctions against the reneging party (because, since the contract had never been finalized, it cannot be said technically to have been violated), they did need to find a way to discourage people from reneging on agreements that were all but finalized. Their admonishment, caustic and clearly heartfelt, should caution any party to an agreement—employer and employee alike—against a quick withdrawal from a verbal agreement. The next section will discuss more fully this issue of contractual withdrawal.

Once a contract formally goes into effect, however, Jewish law expects compliance with its conditions by all parties. This is particularly true in the case of contractual labor. The Mishnah at *M* Bava M'tzi·a 6:2 teaches that whichever party changes the conditions in a work agreement, or whichever party reneges, is at a legal disadvantage. In contractual labor, Jewish law places employer and employee under precisely the same obligation to follow the terms of an agreed-upon contract; neither party has more legal rights than the other due to status, station, or rank.

In the case of the day laborer, a different situation arises. Here, instead of maintaining the equality of employer and employee, the *halakhah* is careful specifically to protect the employee against abuse. Both Leviticus 19:13 ("You shall not defraud your fellow nor shall you steal; you shall not let the wages of a worker remain with you until morning") and Deuteronomy 24:15 ("You must pay a worker's wages on the same day") are concerned with protecting workers and ensuring that they receive their due wages from their employers promptly. Maimonides bases himself on these two verses in listing the prompt payment of wages as a positive commandment and in his demand that wages be paid directly after the conclusion of the period of hire (*MT* Hilkhot S'khirut 11:1–2). Today, we usually stipulate regular times for payment as part of an initial agreement between employer and employee. (This is discussed above in more detail by Rabbi Cheryl Peretz in her chapter on employer-employee relations.) In addition, since today's wages are not limited to money but often include valuable benefits such as health insurance and paid vacation leave, these two verses should be understood to command the timely fulfillment of all contractual obligations of employer to employee, not merely the paying of wages. Underlying these verses from Leviticus and Deuteronomy is the concept that workers should never be put in the awkward position of having to argue that their contracts be upheld; the fact that workers labor for their livelihood, working for the very food they and their families eat, makes the prompt payment of wages a moral issue as well as a legal one. Prompt fulfillment of the contract is the employer's obligation, and is specifically intended to prevent undue suffering on the part of the employee.

When May a Contract Be Broken?

The *halakhah* differentiates between the contract laborer and the day laborer with respect to the issue of when, and under what circumstances, a contract may be unilaterally broken: although a contract laborer technically has no formal legal right to break a contract, a day laborer does indeed have such a right. This difference is based on the rabbinic understanding of Leviticus 25:55. If a day laborer begins work in the morning and reneges at midday, such withdrawal is deemed valid. Indeed, even if a laborer has already received payment for work as yet undone and no longer possesses the money to repay his employer, that laborer can still renege and the money will simply become a debt, as it is said, "Because the Israelites are My servants" (Leviticus 25:55), which is to say: "My servants and not the servants of servants!" (The above is a paraphrase of the *SA* Ḥoshen Mishpat 333:3; based on *BT* Bava Kamma 116b and *BT* Bava M'tzi·a 10a.)

Underlying this distinction may be the rabbis' recognition of the potential for abuse in the case of the day laborer, who is more easily replaced than a skilled contract laborer. The rabbis thus protect day laborers by formally recognizing their right to withdraw from a contract.

However, despite the lack of formal legal permission, in practice contract laborers may also renege on an agreement. Indeed, the *Shulḥan Arukh* (at *SA* Ḥoshen Mishpat 333:4) actually goes so far as to set the terms for such withdrawals. A signed contract does not commit a worker irrevocably to its terms. While not to be taken lightly, employees do retain the right to leave their work even if a formal contract is in place. However, this does not free them from their obligations to their employers. If wages have already been received for work not yet completed, the money must be repaid. And, of course, an employee who leaves his or her employment does not receive payment for work left uncompleted.

For example, a day worker will be paid only for time actually worked. In the case of a contract worker, however, one estimates the value of the amount of work yet to be completed, subtracts this from the full hiring cost, and pays the worker the difference. So for example, if a worker is hired to manufacture clothing and completes half the project, but the monetary worth of the unfinished portion is greater than that of the finished portion, the employee will receive the lesser amount (*SA* Ḥoshen Mishpat 333:4).

However, this situation of payment for completed work applies only to the case where an employee breaks a contract for work that is not deemed urgent. In the case of urgent work, the worker does not have the right to break the contract without additional penalties. The *Shulḥan Arukh* brings several examples (*SA* Ḥoshen Mishpat 333:5). In one, workers have been hired to remove flax that has been steeping in a pond—an act that, if not done at the correct time, will cause irremediable economic loss to the pond's owner. In another, a donkey has been leased from its owner to bring flutes to a wedding or to a funeral, both of which are time-bound events that require that deliveries be made at a particular time if they are to be at all useful to the individual leasing the goods. In these instances, if the workers renege and the employer cannot hire replacements at the same rate as the former workers, the employer has two options. The employer may hire new workers at a higher rate, with the difference in wages to be paid by the former, i.e., reneging, workers. Alternatively, the employer may deceive the original workers by telling them they will be paid at a higher rate and then, once the work is completed, pay them at the original rate. (The law makes an exception, however, for a worker who withdraws from an agreement due to an unforeseen accident or tragedy, such as illness or the death of a relative. In such a case, the *Shulḥan Arukh,* at *SA* Ḥoshen Mishpat 333:5, determines that the employer must pay the workers for the work already completed.) Although the recommendation of the *Shulḥan Arukh* that recalcitrant workers be deceived by their employers should not necessarily be implemented, it reflects a desire to protect employers and to safeguard their rights when other methods of redress, such as going to court, will not be expedient enough to prevent significant financial loss. Moderns reading this passage should not take it as *carte blanche* to solve labor disputes with deception, but rather as an indication of the supreme value the sages of ancient times placed on promises, whether related to work or not, freely undertaken by uncoerced individuals.

The above ruling demonstrates that while employees retain the right unilaterally to terminate a contractual agreement, that right is not granted free of consequence; this is particularly so when the worker's decision not to finish work he or she has agreed to complete will cause financial loss to the employer. The law seeks to balance the rights of workers as free agents against the security of employers, who need to know that their work will be completed in a timely and economical manner. In breaking a contract, then, employees should consider the amount of disruption that their decision will cause to the employer. So, for example, canceling a contract to cater a wedding shortly before the event falls under the category of work that needs to be done at a precise time and may not be cancelled without penalty. Therefore, if the work is pressing and needs to be accomplished immediately or quickly, or if the jobs are ones for which it will be difficult for an employer to find replacement workers, employees should provide their employers with sufficient notice to enable them to hire substitute employees.

The sages of ancient times did not, however, focus only on the rights of employees to terminate contracts. Employers also possess certain rights to end contracts, and these rights exist even without the obligation to issue advance warning to employees. A talmudic tale preserved at *BT* Bava M'tzi·a 109a–b illustrates this point well:

> Runya was Ravina's gardener. He ruined Ravina's garden, whereupon Ravina dismissed him. Runya came before Rava and said to him, "See, sir, what was done to me!" He replied, "He did well." Runya said, "But he did not warn me." Rava said, "It is not necessary to warn [in a case such as this]." Rava was acting in accordance with his own principles, for Rava has also said: "A primary teacher, a gardener, a butcher, a surgeon, and a town barber—all these are considered permanently warned." The general rule is that any job that entails the possibility of loss that, were it to occur, would be deemed irrevocable, [the workers in such jobs are considered] as being permanently warned [that poor performance may lead to their immediate dismissal].

According to Rava, employers can expect a high level of professionalism in the work done by their employees. In the case of work where errors can have serious consequences, employers retain the ongoing right to terminate immediately an employee's employment. Again, the deciding point is the issue of irrevocable loss. Moderns can accept the basic principle of the *halakhah* while reserving the right to determine which types of error are to be considered irrevocable in our society and in our time.

While classical law does not enumerate every instance in which a contract may be broken, the general expectation is that employers and employees will adhere to the contract's specific terms. However, should either party break the contract, the guiding principle is always one of maintaining the integrity of both parties. Employers retain the right to expect that work will be competently and economically carried out and they must be compensated for any irrevocable loss. Employees have the right to be paid for services rendered without being subject to abuse.

Contracts That Abrogate Basic Human Rights

In our increasingly global economy, contracts that abrogate human rights have become a more pressing concern. Whether the issue is sweatshop labor or the case of farm workers who labor for barely a subsistence wage, human rights violations touch, directly or indirectly, on the daily existence of all citizens. In approaching a discussion of contracts that abrogate basic human rights, an initial look at some of the laws concerning the institution of slavery will be instructive.

The Torah describes two main classes of slaves, Hebrew slaves and Canaanite slaves. Hebrew slaves are comparable to what moderns would call indentured servants in that they work for their masters for six years with no monetary compensation and then, in the seventh year, they may go free (Exodus 21:2–6 and Deuteronomy 15:12–18). Canaanite slaves, on the other hand, are the perpetual property of their masters and are even passed on as inheritance to their owners' children (as formally specified at Leviticus 25:44–46). I focus here on the category of Hebrew slaves.

In the *Mishneh Torah* (at *MT* Hilkhot Avadim 1:9), Maimonides states that owners must treat their Hebrew slaves identically to the way they treat themselves with respect to the food, drink, clothing, and dwelling they provide. A double standard with respect to the living conditions of owners and slaves is condemned as unworthy behavior and is formally forbidden. This ruling sets a high standard for the relationship between employers and employees. However, it is important to note that this ruling refers to slave labor and not to free labor.

The *Sifra,* the ancient rabbinic *midrash* to Leviticus, contains a passage that illustrates the difference between these two categories: "'You shall not burden him [that is, a Hebrew slave] with the work of a slave' (Leviticus 25:39)—*him,* you shall not burden with the work of a slave, but you may burden a free person with the work of a slave" (*Sifra* B'har, *perek* 7:2). This passage seems to permit an employer to engage a free person (i.e., one who has the right to refuse the job in the first place) in demeaning work, something forbidden in the case of a slave. Underlying this section is the idea that a slave is forced into labor by debt or some other dire situation, while a free person agrees to work out of his or her own volition. The ability of free people to choose the type of work that suits them, or that they wish to undertake, seems to be a key aspect of the distinction between slave and free worker. While slaves may not leave their place of employment until the period of mandated servitude ends, free workers may leave at any time.

As mentioned earlier, the Mishnah at *M* Bava M'tzi·a 7:1 states that an employee may not change the terms of employment to differ from local custom, unless those changes are agreeable to both parties. While the Mishnah cites this principle in a way that is beneficial to workers, this passage also implies a benefit to employers: in an area where wages are low and hours are long, an employer has the right to demand these same conditions from employees without contractual specification. A further implication would be that it is not necessary for a company functioning in a poor economy to pay the same wages to its employees as it might be required to pay in a more robust economic setting.

In addition, as also previously mentioned, the *Shulḥan Arukh* formally stipulates that an employer and an employee may set whatever terms of work they wish before work commences, even if they contravene the local customs (*SA* Ḥoshen Mishpat 331:1). Therefore, in theory, even if the workweek in a given locale is generally along the five-day, forty-hour model, employer and employee can stipulate a six-day, seventy-two-hour week if they both wish to do so. Again, the main condition is that both parties agree to the terms.

The *halakhah* does not suggest, even obliquely, that individuals should not be free to accept even the most arduous conditions of labor if they feel they are being properly and amply compensated for their efforts. A question that will pose itself to moderns in light of that fact, however, is whether one may freely agree temporarily to suspend any of one's basic human rights as part of a work contract. In theory, one should be free to make any contractual arrangements one wishes. When it comes to the suspension of basic human rights, while laborers may technically be free to sign or not to sign the agreement, their life situation often renders them powerless to argue with any conditions that an employer may wish to stipulate. In considering this possibility, we may refer back to the rulings that caution us against the mistreatment of a slave. A person who must work under brutal conditions for what may not *even* be a subsistence wage is closer to the biblical model of a Hebrew slave than a free person. The employer would therefore not be able to claim the "custom of the place" as a sufficient guideline for the treatment of employees.

Equally strong are the words of Deuteronomy 24:14–15: "You shall not defraud a poor and destitute worker, whether a fellow countryman or a stranger, in one of the communities of your land. On the same day you must pay him his wages, before the sun sets, for he is needy and urgently depends on it; otherwise, he will cry to the Eternal against you and you will incur guilt." These verses, as previously noted, mandate the timely payment of wages and promise God's protection of the poor worker; God is ever on the side of the downtrodden. This too would argue against the violation of workers' human rights, even in cases in which the workers have technically agreed to the suspension of their own basic rights.

A talmudic interpretation of this verse preserved at *BT* Bava M'tzi·a 112a undertakes to explain the importance of the words "and urgently depends on it" in Deuteronomy 24:15. Literally, the Hebrew means "for his soul (i.e., his life) depends on it," and the use of this particular turn of phrase was understood to strengthen the ethical demand inherent in the verse by asking about the worker who so urgently needs to be paid:

> It has been taught as follows regarding the words, "and urgently depends upon it." Why would someone ascend an embankment, suspend oneself from a tree, and risk death itself [to accomplish the task one was hired to perform]? Is it not for the wages? And another interpretation of the words "and urgently depends upon it" suggests that one who withholds an employee's wages, it is as though that employer were depriving that employee of life itself.

Though this passage discusses only the payment of wages, it emphasizes the reasons why a worker would risk even life and limb to keep a job. Workers take risks so that they may be paid and earn a livelihood. Indeed, employees are often wholly dependent on their wages to provide the most basic necessities for themselves and their families. Employers should therefore be careful not only to pay promptly, but also to ensure that employees receive, at the very minimum, a living wage. Extreme need can often make individuals desperate. To play on that desperation to extract an agreement from a worker in which he or she "agrees" to work under inhumane conditions or for substandard wages is not to bargain cleverly or astutely, but rather to steal from the poor and to act deceitfully. This and other issues relating to the employer-employee relationship are discussed by Rabbi Jill Jacobs in a detailed responsum, "Work, Workers, and the Jewish Owner," approved by the CJLS in 2008 and available on the website of the Rabbinical Assembly.

In addition, it is important to remember the principle that workers are free to leave their employment at any time because ultimately they are servants not of their employers but of God. This ethical injunction teaches us that employers do not have complete authority over their workers, even when they have the power, if not the right, to withhold a worker's food, shelter, or clothing. Ultimately, the Torah teaches, God will hear the cries of the destitute.

Religious Observance Issues in Contracts

In the United States, federal law requires employers reasonably to accommodate the religious practices and beliefs of employees as long as those practices and beliefs do not cause undue hardship to the employers' business. Both "reasonable accommodation" and "undue hardship" are relative conditions, though, and depend on the specific facts of the employment situation. The burden of fulfilling this law rests on both employer and employee.

During a job interview, it is impermissible for an employer to ask applicants about their religion or religious observance. However, it is important that when a job is accepted or one's Jewish practices change while in an existent job, that one inform one's employer. Employers are mandated to help accommodate employees, though not necessarily with the specific accommodation that an employee demands. In addition, the law maintains that an employer may not simply refuse to accommodate an employee for irrelevant reasons, but must actually prove the negative effect such accommodation would have on his or her business. In turn, it is the employee's responsibility to help resolve these conflicts between religious observance and workplace needs. This may include taking Jewish holidays as vacation days, exchanging work shifts with other employees, or arranging to work late on days that do not conflict with Shabbat and holidays. Employers are not obligated to compensate employees for time taken off because of religious observance. These accommodations need not be specified in the contract, but it is important that they be agreed upon verbally.

The Mishnah at *M* B'rakhot 2:4 provides an early example of the balancing of religious behavior with workplace obligations. "Artisans may recite [the Sh'ma] at the top of a tree or at the top layer of a stone wall, something that they are not allowed to do when reciting the Amidah prayer." When reciting the Sh'ma, a relatively short prayer, workers are not to interrupt their labor for the amount of time it would take them to descend from the tree or building. However, when it comes time to recite the Amidah they may break from their work for the longer time that it would take them to descend, pray, and re-ascend. In this short *mishnah,* one may discern a clear attempt to balance the demands of religious observance with the exigencies of loyal service to an employer. Neither party enjoys a position of absolute privilege over the other, yet workers are granted the ability to fulfill both obligations—those to their employers as well as those to God.

Balance is key to an understanding of the nature of contracts. Both employer and employee retain rights in the negotiation and upholding of contracts, yet neither has absolute primacy over the other. Both the need of employees to preserve their own dignity as well as the parallel need of employers to have their work done competently and promptly are recognized as legitimate and reasonable. Jewish law asks that both parties be specific in their demands of each other in order to ensure a fair and just workplace.

Taxation

DAVID J. FINE

The Mishnah devotes a great deal of space to discussing how best to collect tithes and other taxes imposed on the Israelite laity by the Torah in an accurate and accountable way. At the root of all these discussions, however, lies a single principle: Jewish law and ethics require one to pay one's taxes honestly. One may not commit tax fraud. The process of taxation is one of the oldest social systems on earth, and Judaism requires honesty of taxpayers—whether the taxes be Jewish in nature or imposed from outside the Jewish community by a non-Jewish, secular government. However, Jewish ethics do not require us to pay more in taxes than we are legally required to pay. There is no objection to employing tax shelters and other legal means of reducing one's tax burden. The criteria for acceptability of such actions is that they be fully legal.

Paying Up

One could conceivably account for so many deductible expenses and employ so many other tax benefits that, in the end, one owes no taxes at all. There is nothing unethical about this scenario. One is not a bad person for using the law to minimize, or even eliminate, one's tax burden. The litmus test of acceptability is not whether or not one gave money to the government, but whether or not one was honest in obeying the law. Even if one discovers a loophole that would cost the government great amounts of money, it cannot be the responsibility of the taxpayer to reimburse the government for that lost revenue. The taxpayer is responsible only for obeying the tax code as it stands.

This rather neutral approach to the laws of taxation flows directly from the talmudic concept of *dina d'malkhuta dina,* that the law of the land is the law. This rule, stated by the sage Samuel in the Talmud (at *BT* Gittin 10b, N'darim 28a, and at several other locations), became a legal principle accepted throughout the history of Jewish law. Indeed, although Jewish law is theoretically constructed to govern the Jewish people, for most of its history (including during the nascent period of rabbinic law in the mishnaic and talmudic eras) the Jewish people did not enjoy self-rule. Jewish law, therefore, had to function under a broader legal system in whichever kingdom or empire the Jews resided. Samuel's dictum states that when Jewish law and state law are in conflict, Jewish law bows to the state law by acknowledging the supremacy of its jurisdiction. *Dina d'malkhuta dina* means that Jewish law is not the "supreme law of the land." The application of this principle is chiefly to monetary matters—although its application to participation in the criminal justice system is discussed elsewhere in this volume in the chapters by Rabbis Laurence Sebert and Abigail Sosland—and the rabbis were careful not to apply the principle more broadly lest the relevance, authority, and application of Jewish law be diminished in the process. But in monetary matters, including taxation, the law of the land was supreme. (Below, I address the situation that pertains when the government itself is deemed ethically unworthy of receiving tax monies.)

The application of the principle of *dina d'malkhuta dina* to taxation is simply that Jews have to pay their taxes. Failure to do so violates not only secular law, but Jewish law as well. Evading taxation is unlawful and is considered to be a form of theft. Why theft? If, by law, one owed a certain amount of money to the government, then the government has claim to those funds. If one maintains possession of funds that rightfully belong to the government, one is essentially robbing the government of its money. The medieval commentators warn that one could be endangering one's existence, or at least one's station in society, by unlawfully evading taxation. To put oneself and one's family in such danger is irresponsible and unethical. From today's perspective one can add that it reflects poorly on the Jewish people and feeds anti-Semitic stereotypes when a Jew, especially an outwardly observant one, is convicted of tax fraud. But ultimately, one should pay taxes properly not because of fear of punishment, individually or communally, but simply because it is the honest and right thing to do. Whether or not the government is likely to discover the evasion is immaterial. The fact that it is illegal makes it theft, and thus an act not solely of defrauding the government, but also of stealing from its citizens.

Refusing on Ethical Grounds to Pay a Portion of One's Taxes

One may not refuse to pay a portion of one's taxes, and this is the law even if one finds some aspect of government policy objectionable. The principle of *dina d'malkhuta dina* acknowledges that any legitimate government has the right to levy taxes. As long as the government is accepted by the citizenry as legitimate, then it has the right to govern. The halakhic literature discusses, for example, the question of whether citizens might reasonably refuse to pay their taxes because their king has begun to behave erratically, or has been unfair, or has made the poor, inequitable, and unjust decision to tax one part of his kingdom but not another. In all these cases, the rabbis of the time concluded that the law of the land, at least in monetary matters, is supreme. As long as the king in question remains the rightful king, he may enact whatever legislation he wishes. One may disagree with the king, but that does not reduce one's tax burden. Since the king has the right to make laws, the taxable portion of one's monies belongs to the king once the law is enacted. One steals from the king by failing to remit the monies as taxes.

The only "loophole" that Jewish law offers the citizen anxious not to pay taxes on moral grounds supposes a situation in which someone claims reasonably and justifiably that the taxing government is illegitimate. In a dictatorship in which the power to govern has been seized rather than conceded by the governed, one may evade taxation (if one can) and not worry about acting unethically. However, such an approach would carry other more immediate hazards.

Assuming that the government is legitimate, what does one do if one has an ethical problem with some aspect of the government? One may protest and lobby against that which one finds immoral, but, at the end of the day, the taxes must be paid. As a member of a society, one may disagree with the society's decisions, but one must still comply with its rules. This reflects a basic appreciation of pluralism and the codification of one of its most basic tenets: that, for all one may debate and argue about specific points of the law or of government policy, in the end one is obliged by virtue of one's citizenship to abide by the laws of the land as enacted by legitimate officials.

The Extreme Situation

There are extreme circumstances, however, when it is indeed unethical to support a government engaged in immoral activities, and this applies even when the government was duly elected by a majority of the citizenry. In such circumstances, the ethical thing to do is to remove oneself from the community of those bound by the government's decisions. As an example, many Germans, non-Jews as well as Jews, emigrated from Germany after the Nazis came to power in 1933. The Jews, of course, were fleeing while they still could. But many non-Jewish Germans fled their homeland to avoid participating in activities and undertakings that were clearly and wholly immoral, yet which no citizen had the option not to support through taxation. To separate oneself in that way from a taxing authority is the only practical way to evade or avoid taxation. It is an example of paying an enormous price to live ethically, but it is the nature of the marketplace that things of great value almost always come with concomitantly high price tags.

There are other times when one has a moral objection to a particular policy or policies of the government, but is not so overwhelmingly bothered to consider emigration. How can one support something that one deems immoral? This falls under the rubric of *dina d'malkhuta dina*. Paying taxes is a purely monetary issue: it constitutes the payment of a debt to the government. What the government does with the funds is a different matter, and one does not incur guilt for supporting programs one objects to merely by paying one's taxes. This approach is grounded in the fact that no one earmarks portions of one's tax money to various different government programs. The money goes into the government's general treasury. Therefore, the withholding of taxes is forbidden.

Paying Taxes from Which One Derives No Benefit

One does not pay taxes for oneself. One pays taxes as a member of society to the government that is entrusted with caring for society as a whole. Therefore, for example, choosing to send one's children to private school ought not exempt one from property taxes used to support a public school budget. Jewish tradition teaches that we should be responsible for one another and give of ourselves to help others in their needs. To an extent, taxation fulfills this ideal. By paying taxes one supports all the people who are helped by the government. Nevertheless, the bottom line is that paying legally imposed taxes is a legal obligation and we are expected and required to pay our taxes regardless of whether our children attend public school or, indeed, whether or not we have children at all.

Nobody likes to pay taxes. Yet, by paying taxes, we become a part of the greater community of citizens invested in the betterment of society through the undertaking of projects and programs no individual could ever afford on his or her own.

Loans and Lending

TRACEE L. ROSEN

The idea of people lending money to each other was just as much a feature of the ancient world as it is of modern times. Indeed, the Torah mentions lending in a number of places and contexts. Exodus 22:24, for example, states: "If you lend money to the poor among My people, do not act toward them as creditors. Charge them no interest!" This is reiterated at Leviticus 25:36–37: "If your kinsman, being in [financial] straits, comes under your authority as though he were a resident alien, let him live by your side. Be a God-fearing individual and do not charge him advance or accrued interest. Let such a person live in your midst as a kinsman. Neither lend him your money at advance interest nor give him your food at accrued interest." Deuteronomy 23:20–21 explores the notion in more detail: "You shall not charge interest on loans to your countrymen, whether in money or food or anything else that can be considered interest; but you may charge interest on loans to foreigners. Do not charge interest on loans to your countrymen, so that the Eternal, your God, may bless you in all your undertakings."

The key to understanding these texts from the Torah properly is that they all suppose the act of lending money to fellow Israelites in times of difficult economic straits to be an act of righteousness and kindness. And, indeed, we are commanded multiple times in the Torah to behave righteously toward strangers, poor people, orphans, and widows. Because they are economically powerless, it is deemed an act of great immorality to exploit their distress to our own financial gain. Giving gifts of charity, of course, is one way to help the poor and the powerless. But the Torah seems to recognize, at least tacitly, that almost all people will be capable of lending far greater sums of money than they will be able to give away outright as charitable gifts; therefore, sometimes the greater kindness will be to lend money rather than to give the needy a gift that will be insufficient to meet the demands of the moment.

Interest

The Torah uses two terms for interest: *neshekh* (from the root meaning "to bite") and *tarbit* (from the root meaning "to increase"). The Jewish Publication Society 1985 translation of the Torah translates the two terms as, respectively, "advance interest" (i.e., interest deducted before the loan is disbursed) and "accrued interest" (i.e., interest payable in addition to the principal amount). Other scholars have argued that the two terms refer to the same interest, one from the point of view of the debtor (who sees the interest as taking a bite out of his meager resources), and one from the point of view of the creditor (who perceives the interest payment as a legitimate increase over the original loan amount to be paid out as compensation for his trouble).

By either name, charging interest on loans to the poor—in effect, levying a fee for the help the Torah commands be extended to them—was considered, to say the very least, incongruous with righteousness. The prophet Ezekiel, for instance, describes the deeds of a righteous person as one who "has not lent for *neshekh* or exacted *tarbit* . . . [who] has abstained from wrongdoing and executed true justice between other people—such an individual is [properly called] righteous. Such an individual shall live, declares the Eternal God" (Ezekiel 18:8–9). Similarly, the author of the fifteenth psalm describes the person worthy of dwelling in God's tent—that is to say, one who merits proximity and intimacy with the Almighty—as, among other things, one "who has never lent money on interest" (Psalm 15:5). And Nehemiah's censure of the nobles and prefects of the Jewish community who pressed claims on loans made to fellow Jews is recorded at Nehemiah 5:7. Even a cursory survey of these ancient sources makes it clear that predatory lending was practiced in ancient times, and that it was condemned by the prophets and by the greatest leaders of the Jewish people as being immoral, exploitative, and contrary to the will of God.

In biblical times, of course, Israel was primarily an agrarian society. In such a setting, taking a loan was the last-resort method of survival, often just one step away from selling oneself into (indentured) servitude. This is indicated clearly in the words of Scripture, which notes that in times of blessing Israel's land would provide such abundant produce that the people "will be a creditor to many nations, but a debtor to none" (Deuteronomy 28:12). Conversely, among the curses associated with faithlessness to God's covenant listed later in that same chapter, Israel's fate is described in precisely opposite terms: God's horrific response to Israel's endemic disobedience will be to allow it to become a nation of debtors (28:44).

It is crucial to remember, however, that the biblical view of lending is rooted in the assumption that loans function primarily in society as a means for the wealthy to assist people in dire economic circumstances. The exclusion in Deuteronomy exempting the non-Jew from these restrictions, in fact, is the exception that proves the rule. By suggesting that, when charity is not the motivating factor, interest may be charged as a "normal" expense of doing business, Scripture is also underscoring the fact that the "normal" pattern would be for the wealthy Israelite individual to help his or her destitute co-citizen with a loan of money as a charitable act, as a kindness. Conversely, the permission granted Jews to lend on interest to non-Jews, rather than being discriminatory, merely ensured that an unfair situation did not arise whereby Jews were forced to lend money interest-free to people who were not required to reciprocate.

The Expansion of Interest Prohibitions in Rabbinic Times

The rabbis of talmudic and geonic times expanded the prohibition against taking interest from a fellow Jew beyond the realm of simply collecting additional money on money lent, or, to speak in nonmonetary terms, of returning two barrels of grain for one barrel borrowed. (The prohibition of lending on interest was never understood to refer solely to loans of money.) These expanded prohibitions included, for example, laws against charging extra for allowing installment payments on goods purchased if the total of the payments would end up exceeding the original cash purchase price of the goods in question (*BT* Bava M'tzi·a 65a). The rabbis even went so far as to prohibit borrowing an item and then returning not the item borrowed but something of higher value, and they also forbade exchanging one type of work for work of a higher value, allowing a lender to live on one's premises rent-free (even if he or she had done so previously), or giving certain kinds of gifts to lenders that could be construed as payment for their loans (*BT* Bava M'tzi·a 75a ff.). Indeed, one may not even give a gift to another in anticipation of a future loan. And certain types of speech are prohibited if they could be taken as a kind of "interest" on a loan offered—such as supplying the lender with valuable information, or even greeting him or her in a way that one would not have done previously (*BT* Bava M'tzi·a 75b, *T* Bava M'tzi·a 6:17). These types of transgressions are known as rabbinic interest (called either *ribbit d'rabbanan* or *avak ribbit*—literally, the "rabbinic interest" or "dust of interest"), as opposed to Torah interest (called either *ribbit de'oraita* or *ribbit k'tzutzah,* literally "Torah-based interest" or "fixed-rate interest"). For the average citizen, of course, the difference has no practical importance.

In addition, the rabbis proscribed the practice of one Jew lending money to another through the use of a non-Jewish intermediary. While technically within the letter of the law, the rabbis explained homiletically that such behavior is morally wrong because it transgresses the clear intent of the scriptural prohibition: "Rava said: Why did the divine law mention the exodus from Egypt in connection with interest. . . ? The blessed Holy One declared, 'It is I who distinguished in Egypt between the firstborn and one who was not a firstborn; even so, it is I who will exact vengeance from one who gives money to a gentile to lend it to an Israelite on interest'" (*BT* Bava M'tzi·a 61b).

Moreover, while Torah law seems unequivocal in its permission to charge interest to non-Jews ("but you may deduct interest from loans to foreigners," Deuteronomy 23:21), the rabbis of the Talmud and subsequent generations debated the wisdom and permissibility of charging interest when extending loans to the gentile poor (cf., e.g., the explication of Psalm 15:5 at *BT* Makkot 24a and also the discussion of the question of lending to gentiles on interest at *BT* Bava M'tzi·a 70b). Maimonides, for his part, unequivocally permits charging interest to non-Jews, and even goes so far as to encourage the practice and to describe doing so as the fulfillment of a commandment (*MT* Hilkhot Malveh V'loveh 5:1). Others disagree (cf., for example, the comment *ad locum* of the Ravad) and even Maimonides himself withdraws somewhat from his blanket endorsement of the practice in the remainder of that same chapter of the *Mishneh Torah.* Jews today would do best to make a distinction in their minds between lending as a kind of *tz'dakah* (in which case it would be as wrong to charge interest as it would be under any circumstances to "sell" one's generosity to a person in need) and lending in the commercial context. In no event, however, may one Jew lend money on interest to another without falling back on the *hetteir iska* described below or on some other similar way to remain faithful to the letter of the law while still being able fully to participate in the world of business. The specialized question of whether synagogues may issue interest-bearing bonds was the topic of a responsum written by Rabbi Ben Zion Bergman and adopted by the CJLS in 1988. Rabbi Bergman's responsum is printed in *CJLS Responsa 1980–1990,* pp. 319–323, along with a dessenting opinion by Rabbi Avram Reisner on pp. 324–328.

In our day, there are special societies that exist to facilitate lending money to Jews as an act of charity (these are described in detail below), but the reality in our world is that most loans are sought from banks or other lending institutions as commercial enterprises, rather than as acts of charity. As the *halakhah* of lending developed, it was forced to take economic reality into account and to deal with situations in which lenders were acting in their own commercial interests rather than compassionately, and borrowers were often not destitute at all. In fact, borrowers in our world are often wealthy individuals seeking to make even more money by undertaking new business ventures they lack the capital to fund out of their own pockets! How the *halakhah* copes with this new reality is the subject of the rest of this chapter.

The Hetteir Iska

The prohibition against taking interest from another Jew was taken so seriously that the Talmud actually rules that participating in such a loan represents a transgression not only for the lender and the borrower, but also for the guarantor(s), the witnesses, and even the scribe who writes up the loan agreement (*BT* Bava M'tzi·a 75b). Nonetheless, as the financial realities of the medieval period changed, some sort of device was required whereby merchants and businesspeople could borrow money in order to finance their trading activities.

As it happens, the *Shulḥan Arukh* (*SA* Yoreh Dei·ah 177) describes just such an instrument. Referred to there as *torat iska* ("business law"), the document restructures what we would normally understand as a loan into a kind of business partnership. In such an agreement, the financier (or silent partner) is construed as an employer who hires the borrower (the managing partner) to invest a certain amount of funds in some enterprise in order to make a profit for them both. The silent partner agrees to pay the managing partner a token sum as compensation for the work involved in managing the investment. (Otherwise, the borrower's work could be perceived as a kind of nonmonetary interest payment to the financier.) The money deposited is defined as half loan, half deposit (*ḥatzi milveh, ḥatzi pikkadon*). The borrower is required to repay the loan portion (without interest, of course), but the deposit portion is handled differently: the silent partner is entitled to half the profits from the undertaking up to a specified amount. (Of course, in the event of loss, he also bears half the exposure.) Then, as would be the case in any partnership, the managing partner is considered reasonably entitled to whatever profits remain after the silent partner has been repaid.

The *iska* gradually fell into disuse during the medieval period for two reasons. For one thing, silent partners did not want to subject half their principal to loss in the event the venture was unsuccessful. And, for another, the managing partners did not wish to relinquish fifty percent of their profits to the silent partners who "merely" provided capital, while the managing partners invested all the efforts and labor.

To encourage Jewish investment in Jewish enterprises, however, the medieval rabbis developed modifications to the *iska* arrangement that were designed and intended to give it more of the features of a conventional loan. Rabbi Meir of Rothenberg, one of the greatest halakhic authorities in medieval Germany, for example, ruled that the instrument be structured as an investment with the purpose of earning a profit for the investor. According to this system, once the profit reaches a certain point, the entire sum invested plus the accrued profit automatically becomes an interest-free loan, and the remaining profit belongs solely to the managing partner. Some rabbinic authorities challenged this decree because the borrower is forced to work a long time without pay in order to compensate the financier. Others argued that this amounted to an imputed interest arrangement.

Three centuries later, Rabbi Mendel (Menaḥem) Avigdor of Cracow (d. 1599, also known as Isaiah Menaḥem ben Yitzḥak) amended the form of the *hetteir iska* to make it more attractive to financiers. In his construct, the financier may specify conditions relating to the use of the funds. If the managing partner does not follow these conditions, responsibility for all losses falls upon the managing partner. To protect the silent partner's share of the profits, the *hetteir iska* stipulates that the managing partner's claim to the profits from the *iska* will require the borrower to take a solemn oath, which must be corroborated by two witnesses. If the borrower does not want to take an oath (which Judaism regards as a very serious matter, and which traditional Jews normally seek to avoid if at all possible), the financier states in the document the amount of "compromise money" (*s'khar hitpash'rut*) to be paid to enable the borrower to avoid the oath. In order to increase the likelihood that the compromise money will be paid, the *iska* agreement lays claim to any of the managing partner's profits from all ventures undertaken during the term of the agreement. Assuming that the managing partner will not wish to take the oath *or* to allow his or her records to be audited, the strong incentive is to pay the compromise money, so that it, in effect, becomes the targeted rate of earnings on the loan.

Using a variation of the format proposed by Rabbi Mendel, all Jewish lending and interest-bearing deposits in the Land of Israel are defined as being transacted in accordance with the requirements for a *hetteir iska.*

A sample text for a *hetteir iska,* adapted from Aaron Levine's *Case Studies in Jewish Business Ethics* (Hoboken, NJ: KTAV and New York: Yeshiva University Press, 2000, pp. 109–110) is as follows. (The reference to *Sefer B'rit Y'hudah* is to the book of that name by Rabbi Yaakov Yeshayahu Bloi (Jerusalem: D'fus Akiva Yosef, 1976.)

I, the undersigned, have received the sum of $__________ from __________________ (hereafter referred to as the "Investing Partner"), for investment in an *iska* partnership, subject to the following terms:

In exchange for the aforementioned sum, the investing partner shall acquire a share (in the value of the funds received) in any investment, real estate, or business which I own. In the event that no such investments exist, the investing partner will acquire partnership (in the value of funds received) in any future investment that I shall make. The investing partner hereby appoints me as an agent to execute this investment (or investments) as I deem appropriate on his/her behalf. This investment (or investments) shall be owned jointly by the investing partner and myself. Any profits realized or losses sustained shall be shared equally between the investing partner and myself.

Any claim of loss must be verified through the testimony of two qualified witnesses in, and under conditions acceptable to, a Jewish court of law. Any claim regarding the amount of profit generated by this investment (or investments) shall be verified under solemn oath, before and under conditions acceptable to a Jewish court of law.

It is agreed that if I return the above-mentioned principal to the investing partner, together with an additional $__________ as payment for his/her share of the profits which are generated, then I will not be required to make any further payment, nor will I be required to take an oath. I am obligated to make this payment on or before _______. If payment is not made by this time, the terms of this *iska* shall continue.

I have received one dollar from the investing partner as payment for my services during the term of our partnership.

In the event of any conflict between the terms of this *iska* agreement and the terms of any other agreement signed by the two parties in regard to these funds, the terms of this agreement shall prevail.

This agreement shall follow the guidelines of *hetteir iska* as explained in *Sefer B'rit Y'hudah*.

It is agreed that any dispute which may arise in connection with this agreement shall be submitted before ________________. Judgment rendered by the aforesaid authority may be entered in any court having jurisdiction thereof.

Dated ________________________

Signature of the Recipient ________________________________

Signature of the Investor ________________________________

(Optionally, there may be a section for witnesses' signatures.)

The Sabbatical Year and the Prozbul

Three times in the Torah, the Israelites are commanded to practice a year of release every seven years (Exodus 23:10–11, Leviticus 25:1–7, and Deuteronomy 15:1–3). The major feature of the sabbatical (or *sh'mittah*) year is the requirement to let the land lie fallow; solely produce that grows on its own may be consumed. Only the description in Deuteronomy adds an additional requirement: "Every seventh year, you shall remit debts. This shall be the nature of the remission: every creditor shall remit the due that he claims from his fellow; he shall not dun his fellow or kinsman, for the remission proclaimed is of the Eternal. You may dun the foreigner; but you must remit whatever is due you from your kinsman" (Deuteronomy 15:1–3).

The law at Deuteronomy 15:7–9 goes on to make clear the distinction between Israelite and foreigner in this regard:

> If, however, there is a needy person among you, one of your kinsmen in any of your settlements in the Land that the Eternal, your God, is giving you, do not harden your heart and shut your hand against your needy kinsman. Rather, you must open your hand and lend enough to cover that person's needs. Beware lest you harbor the base thought, "The seventh year, the year of remission, is approaching," so that you are mean to your needy kinsman and give nothing. For that kinsman will cry out to the Eternal against you, and you will incur guilt.

As a general principle, all Torah laws dealing with agriculture only apply within the boundaries of the Land of Israel. (See a more detailed discussion of these laws and their applicability in Rabbi Martin S. Cohen's essay on Israel elsewhere in this volume.) In regard to the sabbatical year, however, the general opinion is that, although the Torah law of release was deemed suspended during a time when the observance of the jubilee year was no longer operative and when the majority of Jews no longer lived in the Land of Israel (as noted at *BT* Gittin 36a–b; cf. Rashi to Gittin 36a, *s.v. ba-sh'vi·it ba-z'man ha-zeh* and Tosafot *ad loc., s.v. ba-z'man she-attah m'shammeit*), the remission of debt should continue to be observed as a matter of rabbinic law (*MT* Hilkhot Sh'mittah V'yoveil 9:3).

As mentioned earlier, the Torah's underlying assumption about loans and debts is that only an impoverished individual would borrow money, not a businessperson seeking funding for potentially profitable commercial or financial activities. The whole concept of providing a regular cycle of release from debt was rooted, therefore, in the desire to provide the poor with regular opportunities for fresh starts, by making it more or less impossible for them to sink under an ever-increasing burden of debt. This concept goes hand in hand with the laws against charging interest. Both are social engineering policies designed to forestall widening the chasm between the haves and the have-nots in society. Helping the poor to become more self-sufficient through these two policies also meant a reduction in the number of Jews who would be required to sell themselves (or their children) into indentured servitude to repay their debts. This is attested to in Deuteronomy 15, where the section following our passage deals specifically, and not at all coincidentally, with the treatment of the Hebrew indentured servant.

At the deepest level, these laws are a powerful translation of the dogmatic notion that everything we own ultimately belongs to God from the realm of pious ideas into the world of real people and their very real needs. Being willing to release a loan, therefore, is a kind of tacit acknowledgment that all wealth is on loan from the Creator anyway! Moreover, the *Sefer Ha-ḥinnukh* argues cogently that the faith in God evidenced (and, ideally, strengthened) by this act of release will help to keep people from coveting their neighbors' possessions and from resorting to theft to obtain them (*Sefer Ha-ḥinnukh,* commandment no. 448. If we are prepared to give up what is rightfully ours, after all, how much the more so should we be prepared to discipline ourselves *not* to take what is *not* rightfully ours!

Nonetheless, the exhortations in the Torah against refraining from lending at the approach of the sabbatical year notwithstanding, it was common practice by the late Second Temple period for lenders to refuse to lend to the poor out of fear that the sabbatical year would cancel the debt before it was paid back. This led the great sage Hillel to devise a legal document known as a *prozbul* as a way to override the release of debt and thus encourage charitable lending.

The text of the *prozbul* is as follows: "I hand over to you, so-and-so, the judges in such-and-such a place, [my loan documents,] so that I may be able to recover any money owed to me from so-and-so at any time I shall desire." The *prozbul* was then signed by the judges or witnesses (*M* Sh'vi·it 10:4, cf. *BT* Gittin 36a and *MT* Hilkhot Sh'mittah V'yoveil 9:18).

The premise of the *prozbul* was the firm rabbinic notion that the sabbatical year only released monies owed by one individual to another. However, debts owed to a court of law were not cancelled by the sabbatical year. Hillel decreed that, in order to maintain a supply of funding for the poor, creditors could bring any loan documents to a court and assign those debts to the court. (Of course, this had to take place before the sabbatical year cancelled those debts.) The understanding was that the original lender would be responsible for collecting the debt for the court, and that the court would automatically return the proceeds to the lender once the monies were duly collected.

By this action, Hillel addressed the very real possibility that people would be unwilling to lend money because the Torah's laws of release opened them up to substantial financial loss. In doing so, however, he created a profound philosophical dilemma. How could a rabbi act directly to abolish (or at least undermine) an explicit law of the Torah? The rabbis of the Talmud solve this by claiming that the *prozbul* only applies in times when the remission of debts is operative as a rabbinic law, and not under circumstances when the complete Torah law applies (*BT* Gittin 36a–b, cf. *MT* Hilkhot Sh'mittah V'yoveil 9:2 and *SA* Ḥoshen Mishpat 67:1). And, although it is certainly true that Hillel lived and worked while the Second Temple was still standing (and thus when the Torah law of sabbatical years appeared to be applicable), later commentators pointed out that once the observance of the jubilee year was no longer in effect, observance of the sabbatical year was actually considered the fulfillment merely of a rabbinic enactment. Since this was the case in Hillel's time, the *prozbul* did not formally abolish a Torah-based law and, since virtually all halakhic authorities agreed (and still agree) that a duly constituted *beit din* may nullify earlier rabbinic enactments, Hillel's innovation was considered justifiable. (Regarding the specific circumstances under which a *beit din* may annul the work of an earlier *beit din,* see *MT* Hilkhot Mamrim 2:1–3.)

Later authorities subsequently argued whether or not the use of a *prozbul* could be enacted verbally, and whether it was mandatory or entirely optional. The Rema, in his gloss on the *SA* Ḥoshen Mishpat 67:20, for example, held that if the lender orally declared the intent to execute a *prozbul,* there was no need actually to write one out. Moreover, Rabbi Yeḥiel Mikhel Epstein, author of the monumental nineteenth-century law code the *Arukh Ha-shulḥan,* holds that there is no longer a need for a *prozbul* at all since Jewish courts of law no longer have the authority to collect debts.

There are also certain kinds of debts that are not cancelled during the *sh'mittah* year even without a *prozbul.* These include debts incurred as legal penalties (e.g., payments relating to a *k'tubbah* settlement or the payment of civil fines to a court of law; cf. *MT* Hilkhot Sh'mittah V'yoveil 9:12), loans secured by physical collateral (*MT* Hilkhot Sh'mittah V'yoveil 9:14), monies owed to workers for work done (*SA* Ḥoshen Mishpat 67:15), monies owed to shopkeepers for products purchased (*SA* Ḥoshen Mishpat 67:14), loans to orphans and pledges to charity (*SA* Ḥoshen Mishpat 67:28, cf. *Arukh Ha-shulḥan,* Ḥoshen Mishpat 67:8), and loans explicitly written for terms longer than seven years (*SA* Ḥoshen Mishpat 67:9–10).

The Halakhah of Bad Debt

Having taken out a loan, what happens when the borrower asserts (or convincingly demonstrates) an inability to repay it? Although we have already discussed the remission of debts every seven years, that is not the same case as individual bankruptcy because the year of release technically applies to all debtors equally and regardless of an ability to repay.

As a general rule, Jewish law provides no mechanism for releasing an individual from an obligation to repay a debt, nor is there any Torah-based or rabbinic parallel to the modern notion of seeking protection from creditors by filing for bankruptcy. Only a creditor may forgive a debt.

Nevertheless, the Torah and rabbinic law do provide two mechanisms to protect borrowers from harassment by creditors. At Deuteronomy 24:10–13, we read: "When you make a loan of any sort to your countryman, you must not enter that person's house to seize the pledge. You must remain outside, while the individual to whom you made the loan brings the pledge out to you. If the borrower is a needy person [and the pledge is a garment], you shall not sleep in it overnight; instead, you must return it to the borrower at sundown, so that the borrower may sleep in his garment and [will thereby come to] bless you; and this will be to your merit before the Eternal, your God."

From this, the rabbis concluded that it was prohibited for a lender to pressure a borrower when it is known that the borrower is unable to repay; they also ruled that a lender should not even walk in front of a debtor's home because it may cause embarrassment or shame (*BT* Bava M'tzi·a 75b). Also, when confiscating items pledged as collateral, one is required to leave the borrower with certain basic necessities, such as a thirty-day supply of food, a year's worth of clothing, and the tools or equipment the borrower needs to pursue his or her trade or business. (More detailed information is available in Rabbi Yitzchok A. Breitowitz's comprehensive essay "Bankruptcy: A Halakhic Perspective," published on-line at www.jlaw.com.)

Even with these two protections in place, however, the debt itself is not discharged until the lender is actually repaid. In our world, therefore, the key questions have to do with the power of secular courts. Is a civil filing to discharge debt in a bankruptcy court valid from a halakhic point of view? Can the *halakhah* endorse the notion that a secular court can dissolve a borrower's debt? Can (or should) the *halakhah* nod to civil bankruptcy?

Two concepts are key here. First, we must consider those practices referred to in the literature as *minhag ha-soḥarim,* the customs of the local merchants. According to the Mishnah at *M* Bava M'tzi·a 7:1, one must follow the local practices in business dealings. Furthermore, the Palestinian Talmud cites the opinion of Rav Hoshea to the effect that this is so even when those local practices appear to violate *halakhah* (*Y* Bava M'tzi·a 7:1, 11b). Second, the well-known talmudic principle of *dina d'malkhuta dina,* the law of the land is the law (*BT* Bava Kamma 113a, *et al.*), is surely applicable here as well, as it specifically applies to civil, and especially to financial, laws.

Therefore, when two parties contract a loan in a place where civil bankruptcy laws exist, even though there are no specifically Jewish provisions for allowing such an arrangement to be discharged by bankruptcy, the applicable civil laws apply under Jewish law as well. This is, however, a matter of legal, not moral, principle. Invariably, the morally correct course of action is for the debtor to repay all incurred debts at whatever future point the funds become available. In other words, one may consider oneself legally quit of debts after being granted bankruptcy in a civil court, but the ethically responsible Jew should never feel free of the moral burden of repaying what he or she has borrowed once such repayment becomes feasible.

Charitable Giving vs. Lending

The larger questions revolving around the *halakhah* of charitable giving are discussed elsewhere in this volume by Rabbi Elliot Dorff, so here I will limit myself to discussing the specific way they relate to the laws regarding lending and the remission of debt. As mentioned, those laws were clearly intended as a social safety net to allow poor people to retain dignity, to keep from sinking into an irrecoverable debt situation, and to avoid having to sell themselves into indentured servitude—a necessary evil the Torah regards with the greatest disdain, since it undermines the effects of God's liberation of Israel from bondage in ancient Egypt.

The primary means utilized by Jewish communities today to fulfill this commandment is the institution of the Jewish Free Loan Society. During the eighteenth and nineteenth centuries, organizations known as *ḥevrot g'milut ḥasadim,* abbreviated as "*g'maḥs*" ("societies for acts of charitable lovingkindness"), became commonplace throughout European Jewish communities and provided loans to the poor to assist them in becoming self-sufficient. In the United States, free loan funds began in individual synagogues. By the nineteenth century, however, separate benevolent societies had been established to assist new immigrants in establishing themselves in their new homeland.

The organizing principle behind these societies was not only the biblical prohibition against charging interest, but also the ideal espoused by Maimonides in the *Mishneh Torah* (at *MT* Hilkhot Matt'not Aniyyim 10:7):

"There are eight degrees of charity, each one higher than the other. The highest degree is to aid a Jew in want by offering a gift or a loan, by entering into partnership with that person, or by providing work so that such a person may become self-supporting and not have to ask other people for anything." And, indeed, these early funds were instrumental in providing the initial capital investment necessary for many of the early Jewish immigrant peddlers, merchants, clothing manufacturers, and entrepreneurs to open businesses.

Free loan societies operate differently than charitable funds. Although they provide interest-free loans, the criteria for qualification are often more stringent than those of for-profit lenders. For example, a borrower may be required to provide a co-signer who will assume the obligation to make monthly payments during periods when the borrower is financially unable to do so. The *mitzvah* of lending interest-free does not obligate the lender to assume the kind of risk that is normally priced into an interest-bearing loan.

Today, loans are often made available to individuals for a number of purposes. In Los Angeles, for example, the Jewish Free Loan Association (JFLA) not only lends to people for emergency situations (such as unexpected medical expenses), but also to assist students to pay for higher education, to assist new immigrants in resettlement, to help underwrite couples seeking infertility treatment or attempting to adopt children, to provide small businesses with the necessary capital to open or to stay in business, and to help women and children who need to escape from domestic violence situations. With nearly five million dollars in outstanding loans, the JFLA has helped over 300,000 families since its inception in 1904, and has experienced a repayment rate of over ninety-nine percent. It is easy to imagine that this kind of sustained, thoughtful philanthropy is precisely what Maimonides had in mind.

In the United States, over forty Jewish communities throughout the country provide community-wide Free Loan Associations. (Interested readers will find most of them listed on the website of the International Association of Hebrew Free Loans.) In addition, many synagogues sponsor such funds. In Israel, there are literally thousands of free loan organizations that provide not only money to lend, but also many of the essentials to families in need, including baby supplies for new families, medical equipment for home health care, and other similar kinds of assistance. Local rabbis will usually be able to put people in need in contact with appropriate agencies.

It is incumbent on Jewish communities everywhere to ensure that funds are always available for free loans to community members in need of assistance to get themselves back onto the road of self-sufficiency with dignity. For more information on establishing a free loan society, readers may contact the International Association of Hebrew Free Loans via its website.

Witnessing a Loan

"Rav Judah said in the name of Rav: One who has money and lends it without witnesses infringes the biblical commandment, 'You shall not place a stumbling block before the blind'" (*BT* Bava M'tzi·a 75b, citing Leviticus 19:14). Rashi offers the rationale behind Rav's lesson: loaning money *not* in the presence of witnesses gives the borrower the opportunity to consider defaulting on the loan. Maimonides, writing in the *Mishneh Torah* (at *MT* Hilkhot Malveh V'loveh 2:7), and Rabbi Joseph Karo, writing in the *Shulḥan Arukh* (at *SA* Ḥoshen Mishpat 70:1), both require that there be witnesses to a loan. The requirement for third-party witnesses and loan documentation is not only protection for the lender, but also for the borrower's own good.

The requirements for being a witness to a loan are essentially the same as the requirements for witnessing other Jewish legal documents. The witnesses must be unrelated to either party and unrelated to each other. They must also be able to identify the parties to the transaction, in case they are called upon to do so in the context of future legal proceedings. For this reason, they may not sign the loan document without having first met the parties involved. Furthermore, a document with only one witness is invalid. (If, however, the borrower swears a solemn oath that the loan has already been paid back, the borrower is believed; cf. *MT* Hilkhot Malveh V'loveh 14:10.) Nonetheless, most halakhic authorities require written and fully witnessed documentation to any loan.

From a modern perspective, loan documentation is standard practice for all loans made by lending institutions to both businesses and individuals. However, such documentation makes even more sense in a loan between two individuals, especially if they are family members. Most communal rabbis today can attest to the high number of instances of family conflict that have their roots in financial transactions, and especially in issues relating to loans.

In general, the Jewish attitude toward individual wealth can be summed up by these words from the first verse of the twenty-fourth psalm: "The earth is the Eternal's and all it contains." And, indeed, from the Jewish perspective, we are merely the conservators and stewards of wealth that ultimately belongs to God. But the situation is more complex than that, because Scripture specifically allows for the enjoyment of private possessions and private property, and endorses the concept that work should be rooted in the wish of the individual to profit from his or her own labor. The Jewish economic ideal, therefore, is a combination of the capitalist ethic (in which each person profits according to his or her talent and industry) and the socialist ideal (in which each member of society offers what he or she can in return for earning the right to whatever one needs to subsist or, in a richer society, to live well). The key concepts that underlie all *halakhot* regarding lending and borrowing, however, are relatively simple. With wealth comes responsibility, and with great wealth, great responsibility. It is indecent to charge the poor for the help extended to them. And, although it is reasonable to derive profit from commercial enterprises involving the lending of money, it is nonetheless the responsibility of the faithful always to conduct their business dealings in a way that honors the core concept that wealth does not belong to the wealthy (or, for that matter, to any mortal beings at all), but solely to its ultimate Creator.

Intellectual Property

MARTIN S. COHEN

By its very nature, there is nothing quite so intangible as an idea. Neither exactly coterminous with nor identical to the words that express it to the world, the idea is the most basic building block of the theories that human beings have developed to explain and organize the world in which we all live. But what is an idea, really? Can one possess an idea in the same way that one possesses other things in the world? Surely they can be shared, but can ideas be sold or given away? Can they be stolen? Moderns tend to think so and have developed the elaborate journalistic, academic, and literary standards that repudiate plagiarism, along with extensive copyright, trademark, and patent laws that govern the ideas behind literary, musical, artistic, scientific, and technical inventions and innovations, and treat them as though they were tangible goods in need of legal protection against inappropriate use. The laws themselves are extensive and complicated, but the basic underlying concept is simply that stealing the ideas in a book from their author is no less dishonest than stealing the book itself from a bookshop. As a result of the intellectual climate created by such legislation, secular society tends to deem the ideas of individuals to be part of their wealth and part of their estates, thus something that belongs to them no less profoundly or legally than their physical assets.

Traditionally, whether legal recourse was possible in cases of misappropriation of intellectual property depended on how the ideas in question were previously registered. This is no longer generally so: neither English nor European law still requires registration of copyright as a prerequisite to legal action and, since becoming a party to the Berne Convention in 1988, neither does the United States. Patents, on the other hand, do have to be registered, as do trademarks. Still, the common conception is clearly that registration via copyright or patent has to do with the question of possible legal recourse, not with the basic question of whether someone does or does not own the novel ideas and concepts of which one conceives. And this is certainly so regardless of whether the individual involved does or does not profit financially (or at all) from the purloined concept in question, just as the concept of theft is deemed to be unrelated to the question of how the thief, prior to being apprehended, had been planning to profit from a stolen object. (Readers interested in a full discussion of the halakhic dimension of copyright law may profitably consult Rabbi Israel Schneider's essay on the topic published in *The Journal of Halakhah and Contemporary Society* 21 [Spring, 1991/Pesaḥ, 5751].)

Stealing Intangible Things

In secular society, the legal distinction between consequentially owned property (i.e., property whose theft provides grounds for legal action) and inconsequentially owned property (i.e., property whose theft is forbidden by law, but which is specifically *not* deemed important enough to warrant that legal action be taken against someone who steals it) has to do with value. For example, the used tissue at the bottom of someone's wastepaper basket belongs to the owner of the basket and taking it without his or her permission would therefore constitute an act of theft, but no court would ever try anyone for such a crime. This is not so, however, for a carton of unopened boxes of tissues in a drugstore's warehouse and thus someone who steals such property may very well face criminal sanctions. The *halakhah* also recognizes this distinction in types of property. Indeed, Maimonides opens the section of the *Mishneh Torah* dealing with the laws of theft with two clear statements to this effect: although the Torah forbids the theft of anything at all, one is only liable to suffer the legal consequences of one's sin if one has stolen property worth more than a single *p'rutah* (*MT* Hilkhot G'neivah 1:1–2, cf. *SA* Ḥoshen Mishpat 348:1–2). A *p'rutah*—the penny of ancient Israel—may or may not have been worth seizing, but the principle behind the law is easy to seize: to be liable for stealing, you have to steal something of consequential value. Of course, it is possible that one individual's inconsequential garbage may well be another person's very consequential treasure—consider, for example, a note consisting of just a few words written by a beloved grandmother on her deathbed or a scrap of newspaper with a celebrity's signature almost illegibly (but not *quite* illegibly) scrawled in the margin—but here too the marketplace sets the price: if someone would purchase the item in question for more than a *p'rutah,* then its theft becomes an actionable offense.

The *halakhah,* however, also has another criterion for the consequentiality of property, one much less in sync with the laws of secular society: in Jewish law, the property in question must have real, physical existence. In the *Mishneh Torah,* for example, Maimonides makes it clear that one may only sell or give away (e.g., as gifts or as posthumous bequests) things that exist in real space (*MT* Hilkhot M'khirah 22:13, cf. *SA* Ḥoshen Mishpat 203:1). As a result, Maimonides further notes than one may neither claim nor transfer ownership of something as intangible as the smell of a particular variety of apple, the taste of some specific kind of honey, or the hue of some special kind of crystal (ibid. 22:14). These things exist, obviously. But they do not exist in a sufficiently concrete way to allow for their ownership, their sale, their purchase, or their formal receipt as a gift. Nor, by logical implication, can they be stolen. (An enterprising merchant may therefore either sell restorative smelling salts to weary travelers in need of an olfactory pick-me-up or else rent them out for travelers' temporary use. But such a merchant cannot sell or rent out the scent alone, and neither can he claim to own it.) The talmudic teacher Rava stated famously, "Words conceived of mentally but otherwise left unspoken have no legal importance" (*BT* Kiddushin 49b; literally, "words of the heart are not words"). Although this dictum was developed in an entirely different context—Rava was speaking of business negotiations in which a seller failed to mention the reason he wished to sell off his estate to the purchaser, but then later wished to act as though he had—his words nevertheless encapsulate the rabbinic attitude toward intellectual property: it exists, obviously, but not consequentially enough to be taken seriously as property in the context of property law.

In a different talmudic passage, the same point was made about the intangible aspects of sacred items. The Talmud records a tradition taught by Rabbi Shimon ben Pazi in the name of Rabbi Joshua ben Levi (who taught it in the name of Bar Kappara) to the effect that neither sound nor appearance nor odor was deemed consequential enough to warrant the prohibition of making unauthorized use of Temple property apply to one who sees, smells, or hears something in the Temple (*BT* K'ritot 6a). The rabbis' line of thinking is the same as Maimonides' would be centuries later: making unauthorized use of Temple property is a sin, but inconsequential things—not things that do not exist at all, but things that do not exist *enough*—do not activate the Torah's formal prohibition against the kind of trespass called *me'ilah* in the classical sources. And these principles about the distinction between consequential and inconsequential property are legally relevant in other contexts as well. For example, the special regulations that pertain to deathbed bequests (discussed below in my chapter on the *halakhah* of bequests and inheritance) only apply to items of consequential existence; the nearly dead may not bequeath the right to live in a certain house or the right to eat certain food to others, "for living and eating and other things in the same category," Maimonides writes, "are as little existent in physical reality as speech or sleep and cannot, therefore, be transferred from one owner to another" (*MT* Hilkhot Z'khiyyah U-mattanah 10:15).

Needless to say, the traditional approach of the *halakhah* is overridden in practical terms by civil legislation that certainly accepts the possibility of owning intangible goods fully, a point already made by Rabbi Yeḥiel Mikhel Epstein (1829–1908) in his *Arukh Ha-shulḥan*, Ḥoshen Mishpat 212:3.

Quoting and Citing the Works of Others

The phrase *ein ba·alut l'ḥokhmah* (the concept of ownership does not apply to wisdom, i.e., to intellectual ideas) captures the halakhic principle that ideas are not sufficiently consequential to be owned. Therefore, from the viewpoint of the *halakhah*, the propriety of citing others' ideas or insights as one's own should be considered not so much in the context of property law but rather as a function of basic ethical behavior.

An anonymous teaching appended to *Pirkei Avot*, one of the earliest collections of Jewish ethical and moral dicta, notes that one of the marks of true Torah scholars is that they invariably cite remarks they have heard in the names of the individuals from whom they heard the remarks in the first place (*M* Avot 6:6). Furthermore, those who do so are said to bring redemption to the world. The Mishnah's example is Queen Esther: when she went to tell King Ahasuerus of the plot against his life, Esther formally noted that she was merely relaying the report of her cousin, Mordecai. (This lesson, quoting Esther 2:22, is cited in the Talmud at *BT* M'gillah 15a in the name of Rabbi Eleazar, who taught it in the name of Rabbi Ḥanina.) The underlying legal principle, however, is often missed by those who quote the passage: the point is not that the *halakhah* forbids one to quote a source without giving the remark its correct attribution, but precisely that no such prohibition exists and that those who scruple to do so anyway are therefore conducting themselves *li-f'nim mi-shurat ha-din*, which is to say that they are acting on principle and with exceptional devotion to the spirit of the law. Such people, *Pirkei Avot* is saying, hasten the dawn of redemption because of their noble and fine behavior, and because of their extralegal devotion to the Torah's ideal of honesty in all matters.

This concept—that it is just and right, but not legally requisite, to cite spoken words in the names of their original speakers—applies to words and lessons of Torah as well. One version of the statement from *Pirkei Avot* cited above refers specifically to citing spoken words that one has heard from one's rabbi or teacher, the implication clearly being that one has heard a lesson on some Torah subject (*Kallah Rabbati,* chapter 2). And the most oft-cited source for the concept, the one in the Tosefta (a parallel work to the Mishnah containing statements made by the same rabbis cited throughout the Mishnah, but which were for some reason excluded from that work), makes the same point. There, at *T* Bava Kamma 7:3, we read that one who slinks around after a rabbi or a teacher, and who subsequently teaches that rabbi's or teacher's lesson without proper attribution, is called a thief. The point here, though, is precisely that such a person is *called* a thief because of his or her outrageous, ignoble behavior even though such an unprincipled individual is not actually subject to punishment under the law forbidding theft. Indeed, the text goes on to note that such a person may even derive some merit from his or her reprehensible efforts, just as thieves can obviously expect to be nourished by eating food that they have stolen. Nevertheless, for all that it may be theoretically licit to repeat lessons learned from others for the sake of studying and teaching others, or even merely to copy them down in writing for oneself to consult later on, decent people will always be distinguished by their custom of citing those lessons in the names of the specific individuals from whom they first learned them.

The obligation to recite lessons in the names of the individuals who originated them is even deemed to yield posthumous benefit to those original teachers. At *BT* Y'vamot 97a, for example, the Talmud cites a lesson based on Song of Songs 7:10 taught by Rabbi Yoḥanan in the name of Rabbi Shimon bar Yoḥai that declares (just a bit fancifully) that, when a lesson they once taught is cited in their names in the world of the living, the lips of the deceased, presumably motivated by feelings of gratitude, pride, joy, and excitement, somehow begin to recite the lesson in silent unison. It is not because they own or owned the ideas being cited that they are pleased, however. Just to the contrary: it is precisely because there is no ownership of intellectual property that they are so delighted to be remembered anyway and to have their lessons properly attributed to them. A similar notion underlies the lesson of Rabbi Ḥiyya bar Neḥemiah preserved at *Kohelet Rabbah* 2:22 to the effect that, were it not for scrupulous students who teach others lessons they have learned in the name of the rabbis from whom they themselves learned them, the *torah* of those rabbis would eventually be completely forgotten. (The point of the lesson is clearly that quoting lessons in the names of those who first taught them is a sacred responsibility and the decent thing to do. Rabbi Ḥiyya even goes so far as to suggest that this concept of enduring posthumous recognition is the factor that motivates many teachers to instruct their pupils diligently and carefully in the first place.)

The notion that intellectual property—ideas and thoughts—cannot be owned is relevant in determining how severely to punish the thief when the book (or, for that matter, any other medium) containing those ideas is stolen. The Rif (Rabbi Isaac Alfasi, 1013–1103), for example, writes about a case involving the theft of a book of new interpretations (*ḥiddushim*) of passages from the Torah (see his collection of published responsa, responsum 133, ed. Leiter [Pittsburg: Makhon Harambam, 1954], pp. 87–88). The thief was apprehended but took an oath (presumably unprompted by the court) that he would be willing to return the book to its owner if he could first copy its text for his own use and edification. The man, the Rif decided, was guilty of transgressing three distinct commandments. First, the theft of the volume itself was forbidden. Second, it is forbidden to take an oath that can only be upheld by breaking a law of the Torah (in this case, by refusing to return the purloined book if permission to copy out its contents were to be denied). Finally, because of the specific circumstances of the theft, the man was deemed guilty of robbery as well. (Robbery, the act of forcibly taking someone else's property, is prohibited by the Torah at Leviticus 19:13. Theft, the purloining of other people's things, is prohibited just two verses earlier. For more on the distinction between these two kinds of criminal activity, see Maimonides' comments at *MT* Hilkhot G'zeilah Va-aveidah 1:3.) Taking an oath that could only be fulfilled by breaking Torah law was deemed criminal and sinful, but this clearly was not the case regarding the thief's interest in copying out of the book's contents for his own edification.

Comparing the Rif's judgment to modern secular law is instructive. Today, simply committing an idea or a spoken word to writing for personal use is not generally deemed an infringement of copyright. (Depending on the circumstances, however, such an action may well be a breach of confidence or misuse of confidential information, either of which may well be deemed actionable offenses.) This is because ideas cannot be copyrighted until they are recorded in material form, e.g., by being written down, drawn, preserved in a sound or video recording, or otherwise saved electronically. Thus, writing down a lesson heard orally would not be deemed a breach of modern copyright law, but copying the same material from a published book could certainly—at least under the right circumstances—be understood to constitute such a breach. The halakhic approach, on the other hand, considers the theft of the book alone to be an actionable offense, whereas copying its contents without proper attribution is simply base behavior that, while not illegal *sensu stricto,* does not reflect the highest ethical standards to which a principled person should naturally aspire.

The halakhic principle is thus that individuals may not claim ownership of thoughts, even their own original ideas. This concept is so central to the halakhic worldview that, even though it is morally wrong to cite ideas without crediting those who first conceived them, doing so anyway does not constitute an act of theft. Nevertheless, people who fail to attribute remarks and concepts to the people from whom they learned or heard them are deferring the eventual redemption of humankind by failing to embody the highest ethical standards. In that sense, the law here is analogous to the law that pertains when one has indicated one's wish to purchase a given item and has already paid for it. Although one may withdraw from the transaction up until the item itself changes hands (and not merely the money being paid for it), the ancient sages pronounced a curse on those who do not stand by their word precisely because, although they are technically not behaving illegally, they are certainly behaving reprehensibly and dishonorably (*M* Bava M'tzi·a 4:2). Here too, it is not illegal to cite ideas that others once conceived without reference to those people; it is merely unworthy behavior in which no principled person should ever engage.

The forthcoming volume, *From Maimonides to Microsoft: Jewish Copyright Law Since the Birth of Print,* edited by Neil W. Netanel and David Nimmer and to be published by Oxford University Press, will be an invaluable resource with respect to all the issues discussed above.

Internet File Sharing, Downloading, and Copying

As noted above, the *halakhah* distinguishes clearly between the information itself and the medium in which that information is presented and preserved. It is, therefore, unequivocally wrong to steal a book, while it is clearly permissible, if ignoble, to cite the information in that book without permission and even without attribution; the former constitutes theft, whereas the latter does not. As we have seen, the noble and principled path lies in attributing information to its proper source. But even if one fails to achieve the highest ethical standard, the resultant act is base, not criminal, behavior.

In other words, even though thoughts and ideas may have some physical existence as electric impulses within the human brain, they are not physically existent enough for their misappropriation to trigger the penalties for theft. But what of computer programs and other electronic files, especially those downloaded from the Internet? When divorced from the medium in which they are preserved and presented to the public, such files too are merely electronic impulses organized into conglomerations of binary code that computers can decipher and translate into discernable, usable data. Does it therefore follow that their misappropriation (for example, through a file-sharing program that allows computer users to download copyrighted material from a site on which they have been made available by people who neither own them nor have the right to distribute them) is not formally an act of theft? After all, the physical medium—such as the hard drive on which the data is originally stored—is not being taken, not even briefly; it is merely the data that is being copied and moved.

This question can and should be addressed both theoretically and practically. From the point of view of the *halakhah,* the act is, strictly speaking, not one of theft because nothing of sufficiently consequential existence is being taken. Practically speaking, however, it is nonetheless forbidden if the act of downloading the file can be expected to have a negative financial impact (or even a potentially negative financial impact) on the owner of its copyrighted material—and this is so whether the material was copied directly from the developer or from a third party who acquired it legally. And it is also important to realize that it is entirely possible that the ancient rabbis would have developed the *halakhah* quite differently if they had had any inkling of how computer technology would transform the very enterprise of knowledge, making it possible to transmit almost incalculable amounts of information electronically without any physical medium at all.

The classical locus for the relevant halakhic discussion is the much-cited text preserved in the Talmud at *BT* Bava Batra 21b, where the decision of Rav Huna is preserved: "If a resident of an alley sets up a mill and another resident of the alley wants to set up one next to him, the first has the right to stop him, because he can say to him, 'You are interfering with my livelihood.'" (This passage is discussed elsewhere in this volume by Rabbi Jacob Blumenthal in his chapter on the *halakhah* of commerce and by Rabbi Barry Leff in his discussion of co-workers.) In other words, the *halakhah* prohibits any act that impacts negatively on someone else's preexistent ability to earn a reasonable living—and this is the case even if the action under question would be considered perfectly legal under other circumstances.

If there will be no discernible negative impact on anybody's ability to conduct business successfully, then it seems clear that there is no halakhic problem in the download. For example, this would be true of music or computer games that are not available for commercial sale, since there is no opportunity for the owners to profit from them financially. The distinction between copying works that cannot bring their copyright owners any further profit (because they are no longer for sale) and those still able to generate revenue for those owners, of course, is generally not taken into consideration in the civil law of most countries.

Of course, this is all theoretical because the principle of *dina d'malkhuta dina,* the dictum obliging Jews to follow the laws of the land (especially in monetary matters), is entirely applicable to the question of file downloads. But it is instructive to see how civil law is far stricter than the *halakhah.* (Whether the classical *halakhah* would have developed in a different direction in the realm of intellectual property had the potential for profit been as vast in the talmudic era as it is in the modern world is an interesting question to ponder. But no such legal fiction was devised, and thus the halakhic principle that ideas *per se* cannot be stolen remains the basis for Jewish thinking about the ownership and use—or misuse—of intellectual property.)

Halakhic literature provides some framework here for thinking about the issue in a more practical way. For example, Maimonides notes that when the Torah (at Exodus 22:8) requires that an apprehended thief pay the owner twice the value of the stolen item, it limits that obligation to thieves who have stolen things that have intrinsic value (*MT* Hilkhot G'neivah 2:2). Therefore, one who steals a promissory note, which has value because it records a debt but which itself has no intrinsic value (because the ink and paper of which the note consists have no worth in terms of their resale value), does not become obliged to make double restitution of the amount specified in the note. It is, of course, nonetheless forbidden to steal promissory notes for the reasons noted above: they exist in physical space and they are worth more than a *p'rutah* to their owners! Thus, even if one could argue that the electronic impulses that were downloaded illegally have no intrinsic value in and of themselves (because they are not sufficiently existent), the fact that the act of taking them will have negative financial impact on the owner of their copyright makes the act forbidden. Whether Maimonides would actually have ruled that such an act of misappropriation requires a double payment is a good question!

Nor is it relevant if the person from whom the file was downloaded had illegally downloaded the file originally: stealing from a thief is also clearly forbidden. Indeed, Maimonides does not stop at noting that "it is forbidden to purchase an article obtained by robbery from the robber," but goes further and forbids one from even deriving any benefit at all from something obtained by robbery (*MT* Hilkhot G'zeilah Va-aveidah 5:1–2; cf. Hilkhot G'neivah 5:1–2). Furthermore, whether or not the purchaser knew for a fact if the item had been stolen is not ultimately relevant because it is forbidden to purchase anything that one feels was probably stolen as well (*MT* Hilkhot G'neivah 6:1). One may not, for example, purchase wool or milk or lambs from a shepherd because, under normal circumstances, those would belong to the owner of the flock and not to the shepherd. On the other hand, one may purchase milk or cheese from a shepherd in a wilderness setting because it was common knowledge in ancient times that the owners of flocks would regularly allow the shepherds in their employ the right to sell off whatever would probably spoil before they could bring the flock back home. It thus follows that the burden of moral responsibility rests with the individual doing the downloading, just as it rested in ancient times with the potential purchaser in the examples cited above. If one is doing something that would normally be considered legal—for example, purchasing a song from an Internet source that is reliably known to purchase the rights to the songs it sells—then one may proceed, even absent specific knowledge about how the Internet provider acquired the rights in question. If, on the other hand, one is making a purchase that might be considered spurious, then one is in precisely the situation of the individual contemplating the purchase of wool from a shepherd who clearly does not own the flock which he tends for a living. In the end, the question of whether computer files are real enough that their (mis)appropriation would be considered theft will almost always be subordinate to the more important question of whether the act of downloading the file in question will have a negative financial impact on the legal owner of the file.

Interested readers will find a fuller discussion of this topic in a 2007 responsum on the topic written by Rabbi Barry Leff, approved by the CJLS, and currently available on the website of the Rabbinical Assembly.

Reproducing Printed Materials

For many years, it was considered normal and entirely acceptable for teachers and university instructors, including those who taught at seminaries and other religious institutions, to create large photocopied anthologies of copyrighted materials ("sourcebooks") and then to sell them to the students in their classes without obtaining permission from the copyright holders. Sometimes this was done directly by the professor, but sometimes the institution itself was directly involved, often selling the sourcebook through its own bookstore. From the narrowest halakhic perspective, this activity is probably not formally an act of theft, since no books were actually stolen. Yet it remains strictly forbidden by *halakhah* to copy materials in this way if the material is also available for purchase in its original published form and the act of copying thus results in diminished profits for the owner of its copyright. Although the act generally remains forbidden by civil law as long as the copyright is in effect (i.e., even if the book in question is out of print), the *halakhah* would not consider there to be any impediment to copying materials that are no longer available for sale and would merely consider it to be fine and decent behavior for the copier to distribute the material in its author's name or its authors' names. Again, the principle is that intellectual property cannot be stolen, but that it is strictly forbidden to restrict or diminish the potential profit of someone attempting to sell his or her own material in the marketplace. In any event, of course, Jews remain obligated to comply with the secular laws regarding copyright infringement.

A Jew trying to live in harmony with the *halakhah* need not feel obliged to avoid borrowing books from public libraries merely because he or she might otherwise be motivated to purchase the volume. However, in the spirit of the rabbinic animus against any activity that denies authors the profits they might otherwise realize from their ideas, it would be entirely reasonable for library patrons to press for the establishment of compensatory programs that would speak directly to the issue of revenue lost to authors because of the legal right of libraries to meddle in the marketplace by providing commercial property free of charge to all. (Such programs already exist, for example, in Canada and the United Kingdom.)

This line of reasoning will also apply to materials copied for personal use. As firmly stated by Rabbi Moshe Feinstein (in his collection of responsa *Igg'rot Moshe,* Oraḥ Ḥayyim 4:40, sect. 19, ed. New York, 1982, pp. 66–67), the *a priori* assumption must always be that someone who stands to profit from the sale of merchandise will not wish anyone to undermine that potential for profit by copying the material in question. Therefore, unless one has the specific permission of the copyright holder to do so, materials, including sermons and lectures on religious topics, may not be copied if they are available for purchase. (For a full survey of halakhic opinion regarding many of the topics covered in this chapter, Hebrew readers may wish to consult the comprehensive *Mishnat Z'khuyyot Ha-yotzeir* [Jerusalem: Heikhal Naḥum, 2002] by Naḥum Menashe Weissfisch.)

Gossip, Slander, and Talebearing

BENJAMIN J. KRAMER

The Torah notes in the first chapter of the Book of Genesis that God created the world through the medium of speech (i.e., by speaking aloud the words "Let there be light!" as related at Genesis 1:1). According to the traditional interpretation, the lesson embedded in the narrative is not solely that words are possessed of a kind of lasting creative power that belies their ephemeral nature, but also that the ability to use words creatively and profoundly is an essential and definitional aspect of God's unique nature. It is thus of surpassing importance that Scripture, when turning to the story of the divine creation of humanity, features God as deciding to create that first, uniquely human, being "in the form of God" (Genesis 1:27) *specifically* by endowing it with that *specifically* unique feature of divinity, the power of speech. This divine decision heralds the later notion that the intended role of humankind is to serve as God's partners in the world. We human beings have thus been given the divine power of speech in order to enable our participation in the ongoing work of sustaining God's creation.

The nature of what we create, of course, depends upon how we use our speech. Speech can be used actually to further the work of creation, as suggested by the narrative in the second chapter of Genesis where Adam gives names to all of the animals. Alternatively, it can be used to undo the work of creation, as in the third chapter of Genesis where the serpent—a beast, to be sure, but one playing an almost human role in this particular story—uses speech to entice Eve to eat the forbidden fruit, which seductive act leads directly to her and Adam's expulsion from the Garden of Eden.

The ability to speak thus carries with it a great responsibility. In the Talmud, Rabbi Joseph ben Zimra is heard to teach that this is precisely why God encased our tongue behind the fortified double wall of our teeth and lips: to serve as a physical reminder both of the divine power of speech and also of the need to wield that power responsibly (*BT* Arakhin 15b). As the Book of Proverbs says, "Death and life are in the power of the tongue" (Proverbs 18:21).

The Biblical Prohibitions Regarding Defamatory Speech

Because of the potentially damaging power of speech, the Torah contains considerable legislation defining the parameters of proper speech. These laws, many of them very well known even in general circles, include the specific prohibitions against cursing a parent (Exodus 21:17), against lying in general (Exodus 23:7), against perjuring oneself by lying in court (Exodus 20:13 and Deuteronomy 5:17), against making false oaths (Leviticus 19:12), and against cursing God (Leviticus 24:15). But the verse that becomes the most generative in terms of the *halakhah* of defamatory speech is the important piece of legislation found at Leviticus 19:16:

> Do not go out as a *rakhil* among your people, nor may you stand upon the blood of another; I am the Eternal.

Clearly, the verse turns on the precise definition of the word *rakhil*, which has traditionally been taken to refer specifically to someone who talks about other people or who freely recounts what other people have done or said. Ibn Ezra, writing in his famous commentary *ad locum*, notes that the word *rakhil* is related to the word *rokheil* ("merchant") and explains that "just as the merchant buys from this one and sells to that one, so too a *rakhil* tells this one what he heard from that one." The fact that the Torah formally and categorically prohibits one from being a *rakhil* obviously implies that such behavior is negative; however, it does not say why exactly this is so. As a result, the second half of the verse, obscurely forbidding one Israelite from "standing upon the blood" of another, has traditionally been taken by some commentators to imply that talebearing is prohibited specifically because of its enormous potential to cause actual (as opposed to theoretical) harm to others. (See in this regard, for example, the commentary of Joseph Bekhor Shor to Leviticus 19:16 and also the early rabbinic minor tractate *Derekh Eretz Rabbah*, ch. 11; cf. also *MT* Hilkhot Dei·ot 7:1. The idea is that the reference to the "blood" of the victim, presumably the gossiped-about party, implies that talebearing risks leading not just to hurt feelings or public embarrassment, but actually to violence, perhaps even to death. Whether this is meant as hyperbole or not is unclear, but certainly the use of this kind of language is meant to highlight the severity of the prohibition.)

In addition to the prohibition found in the Book of Leviticus, there are two narratives in the Book of Numbers which serve to reinforce the notion that talking about other people, or recounting what other people have done or said, carries with it the potential to cause great harm, even death.

The first narrative is found at the beginning of Numbers 12:

> Miriam and Aaron spoke against Moses because of the Cushite woman whom he had married; for he had married a Cushite woman. And they said, "Has the Eternal indeed spoken only through Moses? Has God not spoken also through us?" (Numbers 12:1–2)

As a result of talking about Moses in this way, Miriam is stricken by God with a skin disease so horrible that she appears "as one who is dead."

The second narrative appears in Numbers 13. As the chapter ends, the scouts that Moses had sent to investigate the land of Canaan return and report to the people what they saw:

> They maligned the land which they had explored to the Israelites saying, "It is a land that devours its inhabitants; all the people whom we saw there were men of great size" (Numbers 13:32).

In light of the scouts talking in this negative, defamatory way about the Land and its people, the Israelites become reluctant even to attempt to conquer the land. And then, as a result of their reluctance, God decrees death on that entire generation and delays the conquest of Canaan for forty years, the time deemed necessary for a new generation to come of age.

Interestingly, Rashi, in his commentary to Leviticus 19:16, *s.v. lo teileikh rakhil,* connects the word *rakhil* to the word *m'raggeil* ("spy") because it is the way of gossipmongers to spy on their friends so that they can later share publicly "whatever bad thing they happened to see or hear." Such a description seems to fit well the scouts in the story in Numbers 13, who seem not only willing but actually eager to report on all the negative things they saw in the land, an insight not made any less relevant by the fact that the verb used with respect to the scouts' mission as described in Numbers is not actually *l'raggeil* at all, but a different verb, *la-tur*. (The more relevant point is that the spies are invariably referred to as *m'ragg'lim* in rabbinic literature.)

Both the law of Leviticus 19:16 and the two narratives in Numbers impart the same idea: that when we talk about other people, including when we recount accurately what they do or what they say, there concomitantly comes into existence the possibility for doing harm—either to ourselves or to others, or to both ourselves *and* to others. And the fact that, in all three instances, the harm is equated with death is a crucial point to take to heart regardless of whether the word "death" in this context is understood literally to denote physical demise or metaphorically to reference spiritual ruin. This reflects an understanding of the immense power of speech and its ability to destroy creation. Indeed, if speech is a divine tool of creation that God used to give life to the universe, then it only makes sense to posit that its misuse would result in the destruction of life, the undoing of creation. This understanding was not lost on the rabbis of the Talmud, who taught that, indeed, talking about other people has the potential to kill . . . and not only to kill one person, but three: the person who talks, the person who listens, and the person about whom the gossip is being spread (*BT* Arakhin 15b, and cf. also the minor tractate *Derekh Eretz Rabbah*, ch. 11).

The Limits of Prohibited Speech

Unlike most of the prohibitions in the Torah, especially those which remain applicable to Jewish life after the destruction of the Temple, the prohibition in Leviticus 19:16 has been largely ignored as a subject of in-depth legal analysis. The Talmud, for example, refers to the prohibition only a few times and most of the subsequent codes of Jewish law, including the authoritative *Shulḥan Arukh*, are silent on the topic. This is likely attributable to the broad and vague nature of the prohibition, as well as to the difficulty in legislating the details of something as complex as the manner in which we speak. Nevertheless, there have been rabbis who have addressed the topic over the centuries, including, in more recent times, a comprehensive treatment of the prohibition by Rabbi Israel Meir Kagan (1838–1933) in his *Sefer Ḥafeitz Ḥayyim*. That volume comprises a relatively detailed collection of laws revolving around the prohibition in Leviticus 19:16, even though the author, unlike the authors of other halakhic compendia covering different topics, did not have a huge set of antecedent works on which to draw. Still, drawing on the sources that do exist and reading them in light of the *Sefer Ḥafeitz*

Ḥayyim, a fairly clear picture of the law as it pertains to forbidden speech begins to emerge. (Because of the immense popularity of the book, its author is often referenced simply as "the" Ḥafeitz Ḥayyim, almost invariably pronounced in the Ashkenazic style as "Ḥofetz Ḥayyim.")

It is almost universally agreed upon that the division of the types of speech encompassed by the biblical prohibition fall into three categories of increasing severity.

The basic prohibition is called *r'khilut* (as noted, from the word *rakhil* in Leviticus 19:16; cf. *Y* Pei·ah 1:1 and commentary *ad locum* of Rabbi Shlomo Sirilio; *MT* Hilkhot Dei·ot 7:1; Maimonides' *Sefer Ha-mitzvot,* negative commandment 301; and *Sefer Ha-ḥinnukh,* commandment no. 243). This is defined as the act of saying about another person anything at all that may potentially cause that person physically, emotional, or financial harm. One therefore transgresses the prohibition against *r'khilut* even if it what one says is true, even if it is not negative, and even if the person about whom one is speaking would say the exact same thing (*Sefer Ḥafeitz Ḥayyim,* Hilkhot Issurei R'khilut 1:4–5, ed. Jerusalem, pp. 184–185). A classic example of *r'khilut* is found in 1 Samuel 22, where Doeg the Edomite is heard to tell King Saul that Aḥimelekh, a priest serving in the sanctuary at Nob, had given David food and provisions. Saul, who is in pursuit of David, infers that Aḥimelekh is conspiring against him with David and proceeds to order the murder all of the inhabitants of Nob. The information Doeg tells Saul is neither negative nor false, and since Aḥimelekh was not in fact conspiring against Saul, he would undoubtedly (or almost undoubtedly) have told Saul the same thing had he been asked. (This observation is Rabbi Joseph Karo's, cf. his *Kesef Mishneh* commentary to *MT* Hilkhot Dei·ot 7:1.) Nevertheless, because Doeg's words had the potential to cause harm, he committed *r'khilut*—and this would have been true no matter what his intentions had been and regardless of whether or not any harm actually came from his words.

A more severe form of the prohibition is called *l'shon ha-ra* ("the tongue of the wicked individual") and is defined as the act of saying anything at all about another person that is negative, even if it is true. *L'shon ha-ra* is more severe than *r'khilut* because it entails the clear intention to cause harm. And there is also a subcategory of *l'shon ha-ra* known as *avak l'shon ha-ra* ("the dust of *l'shon ha-ra*") which, while not technically prohibited, is still something the upright will strive to avoid. In this category, among other things, falls speech that entices others to speak *l'shon ha-ra*, such as the act of speaking favorably about someone in the presence of that person's enemies when the likelihood is that doing so will merely provoke the party to whom one is speaking in turn to speak poorly of that same individual (*MT* Hilkhot Dei·ot 7:4).

The most severe form of the prohibition is called *hotza·at sheim ra,* which is defined as the act of saying something about another person that is negative and false. The term comes from Deuteronomy 22:14 (although the prohibition is derived from Leviticus 19:16, as recorded in the name of Rabbi Eleazar in *BT* K'tubbot 46a), which discusses the law of a man who falsely proclaims his bride to have not been a virgin at the time of their marriage. The term is used in the sources more widely to describe the act of speaking lies that are intended not to inform but specifically to defame.

The Danger of Simultaneous Transgression

While all three categories—*r'khilut, l'shon ha-ra,* and *hotza·at sheim ra*—are derived from the prohibition of Leviticus 19:16, one who transgresses them is likely to be simultaneously transgressing other prohibitions as well. In fact, the introduction to *Sefer Ḥafeitz Ḥayyim* (ed. Jerusalem, 1975, pp. 11–24) lists seventeen possible prohibitions that one could simultaneously transgress with a single statement, among them the biblical prohibitions of putting "a stumbling block before the blind" (Leviticus 19:14), of hating one's brethren in one's heart (Leviticus 19:12), and of general wrongdoing toward others (Leviticus 25:17). And making the situation even more complex is the underlying assumption that both the one who utters improper speech *and* the one who listens to it are considered to have transgressed when any of the above-mentioned sins is committed. Obedience to the law as it applies to improper speech thus requires moment-by-moment vigilance in a way that other categories of the law simply do not.

Fortunately, our tradition understands this challenge and makes a distinction between those who transgress only occasionally and those who transgress habitually. (See in this regard, e.g., *Sefer Ḥafeitz Ḥayyim,* Hilkhot Issurei L'shon Ha-ra 1:3, ed. Jerusalem, p. 45.) Still, any transgression should be taken seriously. Indeed, since God created us in the divine image and gave us the power of speech specifically so that humanity might join with God in the ongoing work of creation and the maintenance of creation, any improper use of speech should be viewed as tantamount to a rejection of the notion that humankind, created in the divine image, constitutes the crown of God's creation. (See further in this regard the comment of Rabbi Judah Loew ben Betzalel of Prague, called the Maharal, in his *Ḥiddushei Aggadot* to *BT* Arakhin 15b.)

When the Prohibitions Are Waived

While Leviticus 19:16 establishes a broad prohibition that forbids almost all speech about other people, there are some occasions when it is permissible, or even required, to speak about other people. Such speech is referred to as *l'shon ha-ra l'to·elet* ("*l'shon ha-ra* for a beneficial purpose"). Thus, for example, when a potential employer eager to avoid hiring an incompetent worker seeks to talk about the potential employee with his or her previous employer, it is permissible for the former employer to speak honestly about the competency and suitability of the individual in question. Similarly, if one hears someone mention impending plans to cause harm to another person, one is required to inform the intended victim. Needless to say, these conversations should not take place in public, but rather in a private setting in which none but the intended party hears what one is in this context permitted to say.

The basis for waiving the prohibition in such cases is the second half of Leviticus 19:16, the part of the verse forbidding the act of "standing upon the blood of others." While this phrase is generally understood as providing the basis for the prohibition, as discussed above, it is also regularly understood as implying a limitation on that prohibition as well. As a result, the prohibition of speaking negatively about others is formally understood not to apply when silence will possibly bring harm to an innocent third party (*Sefer Ḥafeitz Ḥayyim,* Hilkhot Issurei L'shon Ha-ra 10, ed. Jerusalem, 1975, pp. 158–180 and Hilkhot Issurei R'khilut 9, ed. cit., pp. 212–238 and the *Be'eir Mayim Ḥayyim* commentary *ad locum*).

There are other instances when some authorities permit speech that may appear to violate Leviticus 19:16, such as repeating statements that were made publicly or relating stories without the use of proper names. However, when there is the possibility of causing harm, even if that possibility is remote, one should not rely on leniencies.

Generally speaking, it is considered a *mitzvah* to give testimony in court regarding the criminal or sinful behavior of others (*MT* Hilkhot Eidut 1:1), and this is obviously the case even when that same report would constitute defamatory, thus forbidden, speech in any other context.

Modern Applications

The prohibition of Leviticus 19:16 is usually presumed to refer primarily to verbal speech. However, the prohibition actually extends to all forms of communication, including non-verbal forms of communication such as letter-writing, the publication of information in books or newspapers, or even communicative but non-verbal gestures like winking (cf. *Sefer Ḥafeitz Ḥayyim,* Hilkhot Issurei L'shon Ha-ra 1:10, ed. cit., p. 188 and also cf. Rashi's comment on Leviticus 19:16, *s.v. lo teileikh rakhil*). Thus, as the ways in which we communicate become incrementally more complicated and sophisticated with each passing decade, so too do the laws governing defamatory speech also become concomitantly more complicated. The advent of the

Internet in particular has brought new challenges to observing this *mitzvah,* as amply demonstrated by Rabbis Elliot Dorff and Elie K. Spitz in their responsum "Computer Privacy and the Modern Workplace," which was approved by the CJLS in 2001 and is available to the public on the website of the Rabbinical Assembly.

From a consumer perspective, the Internet has brought moderns the ability to read, listen, and see in far greater quantity, and with far great diversity, than ever before. In turn, this development exponentially increases the likelihood of engaging in forbidden forms of communication. And this problem is only exacerbated by new and evolving genres, which make it difficult for even savvy Internet users to guess in advance which sites are likely to contain inappropriate language or information. The many ways and opportunities to communicate across the Internet, combined with the Internet's culture of sharing and its built-in cloak of (perceived) anonymity, often lead people to write things on-line they would never say in person. But the possibility of transgressing the laws regarding defamatory speech goes beyond merely writing negatively about someone in a place where others may read what one has written. For example, posting pictures of oneself and others on a social networking site could possibly constitute *r'khilut* if the pictures imply something negative about one of the individuals in the picture. So too could the conspicuous absence of a perceived intimate from one's list of social networking "friends" be considered *avak l'shon ha-ra,* since it might give rise to negative comments about the excluded individual.

Perhaps the most dangerous aspect of the Internet in the context of the prohibition of Leviticus 19:16 is the large number of people with whom one can communicate instantly and the often enduring nature of those communications. An email containing *r'khilut,* for example, can be forwarded to countless people in an instant. A comment containing *l'shon ha-ra* posted on-line can easily be copied and re-posted in any number of on-line forums where it might remain long after the original post has been deleted.

The potential for harm from the improper use of speech has never been greater. Nor has it ever been easier to transgress these prohibitions. Consequently, there has never been a time in which there was a greater need for each of us to develop a nuanced understanding of the myriad ways in which one does and does not transgress the prohibitions of Leviticus 19:16. Until then, we would do well to live by the dictum of Rabbi Yossi, who was so zealous in terms of the words he chose to speak aloud that he could say, "In all my days, I never once had to look behind me after I spoke" (*BT* Arakhin 15b).

Bequests and Inheritance

MARTIN S. COHEN

In our acquisitive and deeply materialistic world, few things are deemed more sacred than the right of citizens to use and control their property as they see fit. This right is, in fact, so basic to the way our culture thinks about wealth that it is imagined actually to trump death itself: the right to distribute one's possessions posthumously is not merely endorsed by law and custom, but widely accepted as a basic human right.

As a result, Western society has developed the notion that one of the basic obligations of wealth consists of composing a will instructing an executor to take hold of one's assets after one's demise and to distribute them according to one's specific wishes. Indeed, most adults reading this will probably have already prepared wills. But although this is entirely rational and probably even as it should be, there is some cultural conditioning afoot here as well: the fear of dying intestate is endlessly stoked in movies and on television shows that dramatize the unanticipated consequences that seem almost inevitably to ensue when people die without first having made clear their wishes regarding the disposition of their estates. As a result, it is considered prudent, thoughtful, and entirely normal in our society for people even of modest means to compose written wills.

It therefore poses a special challenge when the Torah at first blush appears totally unconcerned with the right of individuals to bequeath their estates to whomever they wish (and in whatever way they deem just or reasonable), and instead ordains a specific plan for making one's bequests. To further complicate the matter, the Torah does not appear to view the quality of the relationships that existed in life between legator and heir as a decisive factor in calculating the size or extent of posthumous bequests. Also troubling is that the inheritance laws of the Torah show blatant favoritism to males: daughters only inherit in the absence of sons and only paternal relatives are considered legitimate heirs. And no less inexplicable to moderns will be the overt privileging of the firstborn that Scripture not only permits and endorses, but appears actually to require.

This chapter, which explores the basic approach of Torah law to the question of inheritance, bequests, and wills, encourages readers temporarily to suspend their preconceived notions about posthumous gift-giving. Much of what is written here may strike most moderns as archaic and impractical. But while that may be the case, there are also entirely acceptable ways for moderns to incorporate these laws into their own lives while abandoning neither their own sense of fairness nor their basic allegiance to the *halakhah* as it has come down to us from previous generations. The goal of this chapter is to show exactly how that might work for moderns eager to live lives characterized both by consistency with contemporary values and fidelity to the laws of the Torah.

Obligations to Children

The basic assumption of Torah law is that, in the general course of things, children will inherit the entirety of their parents' estates. The inclusion of daughters in the general category of children—albeit only in the absence of sons—is presented in Scripture, however, not as the original Israelite practice but rather as an innovation undertaken by Moses after consultation with God when he was approached by five women, the daughters of one Tzelofḥad, who did not take kindly to being passed over entirely in favor of their late father's more distant male relations when it came to the disposition of his estate. So even at the most basic scriptural level, the laws of inheritance were deemed eminently subject to revision in the light of fairness and reasonableness.

The story is told in detail in the twenty-seventh chapter of the Book of Numbers:

> The daughters of Tzelofḥad ben Ḥeifer (who was the son of Gilead, who was the son of Makhir, who was the son of Manasseh) of the tribe of Manasseh ben Joseph came forward—the names of his daughters were Maḥlah, Noa, Ḥoglah, Milkah, and Tirtzah—and stood before Moses and before Eleazar the priest, and before all the princes of the people and, indeed, before the entire congregation at the entrance to the Tent of Meeting, and said as follows: "Our father, who was not one of the congregation of Koraḥ who rebelled against the Eternal, died in the desert for his own sins, but he had no sons. Why should our father's name vanish from his clan merely because he did not have a son? Give us a share of land amidst the male relations of our father!" Moses took their case before the Eternal, whereupon the Eternal said to Moses as follows, "The daughters of Tzelofḥad are speaking reasonably. Give them a share of land amidst the male relations of their father. Indeed, transfer their father's estate to them! And tell the Israelites as follows, 'If a man dies without having a son, then his estate should pass to his daughter. If he has no daughter, then his estate should pass to his brothers. If he has no brothers, then his estate should pass to the brothers of his father. If his father had no brothers, then his estate should pass to the closest relations he has within his clan so that that individual inherit his estate.'" This shall be a permanent law for the Israelites, just as the Eternal commanded Moses be the case (Numbers 27:1–11).

The legal principles presented in this passage were debated and analyzed intensively by the rabbis of the talmudic era, and are discussed in the eighth chapter of the talmudic tractate Bava Batra. Nevertheless, the most accessible exposition of the laws governing inheritance is in Maimonides' *Mishneh Torah,* where, in the first chapter devoted to the laws of inheritance (i.e., at *MT* Hilkhot Naḥalot 1:1–13), Maimonides isolates the following halakhic principles for when no binding alternate arrangements have been made. (The special case of oral deathbed bequests is discussed below.)

- If a deceased individual leaves behind sons, the sons inherit the estate in its entirety. If the decedent leaves daughters but no sons, the daughters inherit the estate in its entirety.
- The descendants of a more entitled heir take precedence over those of less qualified one, and thus would the male *or* female great-great-grandchild of a decedent's son take precedence over the decedent's daughter. If the decedent had no son but did have a daughter, that daughter inherits the estate in its entirety. If that daughter is no longer alive, then her direct descendant(s) of either gender inherits the estate.
- If a decedent had no children at all, or if those children died without leaving any descendants at all, the estate passes to the decedent's father.

If a childless decedent has no father at the time of death, then any male descendants of that father (for example, the decedent's brothers or half-brothers) inherit the estate. If no male descendant of the decedent's father is alive—or if the decedent's father had no male descendants—then the father's female offspring (or, if they are not alive, their descendants) inherit the estate.

- If a decedent has no living descendants and his father *also* has no living descendants, then the estate passes to the grandfather of the decedent or, if he is not alive, to his male descendants. In the absence of male descendants, the estate passes to the grandfather's female descendants.
- Estates are to be divided equally among equally qualified heirs or their descendants. Thus if a decedent had two sons who predeceased him (and neither of whom was his father's firstborn), one of whom left behind three sons and the other of whom left behind one daughter, the three grandsons together inherit half the decedent's estate and the granddaughter inherits the other half.
- Because the search for a legitimate heir continues indefinitely until the estate can legitimately be disbursed, Maimonides can write that, no matter how far afield we must search, an estate can always be legitimately disbursed because, in the end, "there is no such thing as a Jewish individual totally and utterly without heirs."

There are some other operative principles in the *halakhah* of inheritance. A firstborn son, for example, inherits a double portion of his father's estate in accordance with Deuteronomy 21:15–17, which deals with the specific case of a man with two wives he loves unequally:

> In the case of a man who has two wives, one of whom is beloved and the other one of whom is scorned, and, although both the beloved and the scorned wives bear him sons, the firstborn son is the child of the scorned wife, [the law is as follows]: when he prepares for the posthumous disbursement of his estate among his sons, he may not treat the son of the beloved wife as though he were the firstborn, thus acting to the detriment of the real firstborn, the son of the scorned wife. Instead, he must recognize the son of the scorned wife as his firstborn son and grant him a double portion of his estate. Because that son was born of his first efforts to reproduce, he is entitled to the advantages that accrue to the firstborn.

Another point of traditional *halakhah* codified by Maimonides is that mothers cannot inherit their sons' estates, nor are wives ever to be considered the heirs of their husbands (*MT* Hilkhot Naḥalot 1:8). According to rabbinic law, however, a wife is to be supported by her deceased husband's estate for the rest of her life unless or until she remarries, at which time her new husband becomes responsible for supporting her and the remainder of her deceased husband's estate passes fully to the latter's children. If her deceased husband's estate runs out while she is still alive and unmarried, her children have the duty of supporting her as part of their obligation under the Torah's command that children honor their fathers and mothers. Husbands, although not considered by scriptural law to be the heirs of their wives, were nonetheless enfranchised and recognized as their wives' heirs by rabbinic edict because they bore the responsibility for supporting their wives during their lifetimes. Thus, husbands inherit their deceased wives' entire estates, regardless of the existence of children or other blood relations.

As noted above, estates are only divided when several individuals bear exactly the same relationship to a decedent. In other words, if a decedent had two daughters, each inherits half of their father's estate. (The rule stated above regarding the firstborn son constitutes the sole exception to this rule.) An only child, on the other hand, does not have to share the estate with any other of his or her parents' relations since none of them is considered as close to the decedent as a son or daughter.

Making a Will

The Torah's laws of inheritance, according to which a distant great-grandchild can displace a decedent's own daughter as rightful heir, seem to fly in the face of what most moderns would consider reasonable and equitable. Moreover, Maimonides' principle that "a mother's relations are not considered family in the context of the laws of inheritance" (*MT* Hilkhot Naḥalot 1:6) seems impossible to square with a more modern sense of the equal standing of mothers and fathers in their children's lives, and our sense of gender equality in general. Additionally, merit would seem to us an important consideration in determining bequests, so that the traditional stance of privileging even an estranged, distant son over a devoted, caring daughter seems beyond inappropriate. Furthermore, the principle that a firstborn son inherits a double portion of his father's estate because he was born of "his [father's] first efforts to reproduce" effectively endorses favoring one child over another, which biblical precedent itself clearly demonstrates over and over to be a very bad idea. I will return below to the status of the firstborn son and to the relationship of that status to the *halakhah* of inheritance.

The laws listed above all apply only when no other arrangements have been previously made. As a result, there are several options available to those who wish to uphold the values of Torah while still asserting their own moral reasoning or ethical sensitivity. The solution simply involves establishing alternate means of disposing of one's estate before or upon one's demise, thus pre-empting the applicability of the Torah's inheritance laws. Such an approach is fully in keeping with *halakhah,* even as understood by the most conservative authorities. Absent formal, legal innovations imposing egalitarian principles on the laws of inheritance and short of declaring the traditional favoring of the firstborn to be inoperative, these principles can be used to allow a modern approach to the issue of inheritance that maintains fidelity both to our own ethical principles and to the traditional *halakhah.*

There is no halakhic requirement for individuals to compose written testaments detailing their wishes concerning the disbursement of their estates after their deaths. This simply reflects the fact that *halakhah* does not allow an individual to bequeath possessions to individuals outside the Torah's hierarchy of potential heirs delineated above. Consider, for example, Maimonides' oft-cited dictum: "One may neither bequeath one's estate to someone outside the scripturally endorsed line of inheritance nor refuse to bequeath one's estate to whomever scriptural law designates as one's rightful heir" (*MT* Hilkhot Naḥalot 6:1).

This, however, does not mean that individuals are completely powerless with respect to the posthumous distribution of their own possessions. The simplest way effectively to override the basic law against assigning a portion of one's wealth to someone outside the halakhic chain of inheritance is to make a gift (of money or other physical possessions) to that person while one is still alive. (Because, however, the *halakhah* presumes that owning private property is a function of an individual's will to possess it, such relationships between people and things terminate with the death of the individual. One cannot, therefore, arrange gifts to living people that will be distributed only after one's death, as stated clearly in the Mishnah at *M* Bava Batra 8:6.) However, if one can afford to divest oneself of a specific asset while still alive, this is by far the optimal method of circumventing the traditional laws governing inheritance.

One may also consider expressing one's desires regarding the disposition of one's estate in a formal letter to one's heirs. Such a document could, for example, instruct one's heirs at the time of one's death to take the parts of the estate they are due to inherit in accordance with Torah law and then to disburse them further according to the decedent's specific wishes. The Talmud already lays the groundwork for this kind of effort. Indeed, a dictum of Rabbi Meir preserved in several places in the Talmud (e.g., at *BT* Ta·anit 21a, K'tubbot 70a, and Gittin 14b–15a and 40a) states that "it is a *mitzvah* to honor the wishes of the dead"—and this would certainly include their wishes concerning the posthumous disposition of their property. Of course, one has no way of knowing with certainty if one's heirs will indeed carry out one's instructions, especially when doing so requires the distribution of funds and items that would otherwise remain their own. Furthermore, the *Shulḥan Arukh,* at *SA* Ḥoshen Mishpat 252:2, specifies that this method of bequeathal—namely, for the heirs first to inherit the estate in accordance with the Torah's laws and then to distribute the estate in accordance with the wishes of the legator—requires that the goods or monies in question be isolated from the rest of the estate before the legator's death and formally entrusted to a third party.

The classical sources even discuss how to transfer the formal title of property to others while still retaining the right to any income generated by that property during one's own lifetime, a procedure that will appeal in particular to individuals of more modest means. Technically, this is accomplished by giving the gift of one's estate (or a portion thereof) to anyone to whom one wishes "from this day and until after my death" (*SA* Ḥoshen Mishpat 257:6). By then failing actually to give over the specific funds or items, one becomes, so to speak, indebted to the future recipient of one's largesse, and one's heirs then have no choice but to honor that debt once they come into control of the estate (just as they must settle any outstanding debts a legator leaves behind at death). In theory, because the gift is formally a debt, one cannot subsequently change one's mind and revoke the gift. Nonetheless, the law also considers the possibility of contracting such a debt on the specific condition that one *may* change one's mind at a later date and subsequently return those items or funds to one's estate (*SA* Ḥoshen Mishpat 257:7). Furthermore, the addition of such a clause to a declaration of indebtedness guarantees that not only the principal, but also whatever added value the goods or monies may have acquired in the meantime, will both revert to one's estate.

These matters are extremely technical and require careful thought and planning. However, if undertaken under the guidance of a rabbi well-versed in halakhic matters, it is certainly possible to disburse one's estate in accordance with one's personal wishes while still acting wholly in accord with the *halakhah*. It will always also be a good idea to consult a lawyer with expertise in estate planning to ensure that the arrangements one has set in place are in accordance with civil law. (It is crucial always to recall that the secular laws in any given jurisdiction that govern the posthumous disbursement of one's estate, including estate tax laws, may never be ignored or sidestepped.) Interested readers may profitably consult Dayan Dr. Isadore Grunfeld's *The*

Jewish Law of Inheritance: Problems and Solutions in Making a Jewish Will (Oak Park, MI: Targum Press and Jerusalem: Feldheim, 1987).

Deathbed Bequests

The laws about bequests by somebody so weakened by disease that he or she is bedridden (called a *sh'khiv mei-ra* in halakhic literature) are set forth by Maimonides in the section of the *Mishneh Torah* devoted to the laws concerning gift-giving. An individual to whom a *sh'khiv mei-ra* makes a bequest, either in writing or orally, acquires the items in question upon the death of the *sh'khiv mei-ra* even if a formal transfer of the property in question was neither executed nor even attempted. This is the case because rabbinic law considers the words of a *sh'khiv mei-ra* to have the force of a duly executed written document even though oral agreements under other circumstances do not normally carry that kind of legal weight (*MT* Hilkhot Z'khiyyah U-mattanah 8:2).

Some authorities suppose that the reason the Torah does not make provisions for wills composed by healthy people is that such bequests (as long as they are made during one's lifetime and are not revoked before one falls deathly ill) will ultimately acquire the force of the deathbed gifts of a *sh'khiv mei-ra* anyway. (This, for example, as the opinion of Rabbi Meir ben Barukh of Rothenberg [c. 1215–1293], whose thoughts on the matter are preserved in the *Sefer Mord'khai* of Rabbi Mordecai ben Hillel [c. 1250–1298], Bava Batra 591 to *BT* Bava Batra 135b.) Indeed, on this view, the only difference between the will composed in writing by a healthy individual and the oral deathbed bequest of a *sh'khiv mei-ra* is that the former has no legal status until the legator becomes deathly ill and acquires the status of a *sh'khiv mei-ra*. At that point, the will becomes merely the *sh'khiv mei-ra*'s advance description of his or her deathbed wishes and thus acquires the same legal status as bequests made orally or in writing at the appropriate time. Because this is not a universally held opinion, however, the suggestions made above regarding the ideal arrangements for the posthumous disposition of one's estate should be followed whenever possible. In the event that no previous arrangements had been made and that a will had been prepared, however, heirs may certainly consult a rabbi regarding the reasonableness of imagining the terms of that will to have acquired the force of the declaration of a *sh'khiv mei-ra* as the life of the legator in question drew to a close.

The law of the *sh'khiv mei-ra* rests on the fundamental concept of Jewish law that there exists no gray area between life and death, no no-man's land between the world of the living and the realm of the dead. The requirements for transferring property are less stringent when an individual is dying than at other times simply because that is how things are when someone is in the last stages of life. But the underlying principle—that lucid patients remain fully in control of their possessions until their final breaths of life are drawn—is the core idea that engenders the laws of the *sh'khiv mei-ra.* These laws, therefore, are not after-the-fact leniencies or unimportant details, but the concretization in law of one of the most basic principles of the traditional Jewish worldview. As such, they deserve the attention and the respect of moderns anxious to live lives of fidelity to Torah and its values.

Leaving Money to Charity

In the absence of prior arrangements, scriptural law does not envision a situation in which an individual's money will be given over to charity rather than to one's heirs. Nevertheless, in modern times many individuals do choose to express their support for various charities by bequeathing gifts to those organizations from their estates. Even though unrecognized in the traditional sources, this is certainly a praiseworthy practice, one that demonstrates the consummate value that the legator placed on the *mitzvah* of *tz'dakah* and allows him or her to continue to effect good in the world even posthumously.

The simplest way to accomplish this is as outlined above: either by directing one's halakhic heirs to pass along a portion of their inheritance to specific charitable organizations (under the general principle that it is a *mitzvah* for them to carry out the wishes of the dead), or else to create a kind of indebtedness to a charitable organization that one's heirs will be obliged both morally and legally to honor. Should neither of these apply to a given situation in which a deceased individual has left money to a charity in a will, a rabbi should be consulted about the reasonableness of considering the will to have acquired the force of a *sh'khiv mei-ra*'s declaration as the decedent entered the throes of death. Under American law, there also exists the possibility of establishing a charitable remainder trust in which the principle is transferred to a charity in one's lifetime, but the interest goes to the donor until he or she dies. The laws governing charitable giving in general are discussed elsewhere in this volume by Rabbi Elliot Dorff.

The Firstborn Son

As noted, the Torah clearly mandates that a firstborn son receive a double share of his father's estate because he is deemed at Deuteronomy 21:17 to represent his father's first attempt to reproduce. (The phrase in question, *reishit ono,* literally means "the beginning of his strength" and is rendered in a wide variety of ways in various translations). The Torah's underlying assumption here seems to be that a man will be more invested in a child (and specifically a male child) that he produces with the full force of his youthful vigor than he will be in the children of his later years. What could be the source of such an odd notion? One approach would be to suppose the law to be rooted in some sort of quasi-scientific belief that the first son a man fathers simply *is* the recipient of his inner essence in some empirical and legally profound way that subsequently born children simply are not. Another would be to take the law as part of Scripture's complex notion that the firstborn sons of Israel were originally destined to be its priests (see, e.g., Numbers 3:11) and so to imagine that the double share of a father's estate given to his firstborn son is meant to serve as partial compensation for the loss of the various emoluments that the firstborn would have received as a priest had the original plan remained in effect. Regardless of how it is explained, however, the whole concept will be one moderns find difficult to justify.

There are, however, halakhic solutions for those who wish to sidestep the scriptural requirement of leaving a double portion to firstborn sons. The simplest is to divide one's estate into twice as many portions as one has children. The second portions for all *but* the firstborn may then be written up as debts to the non-firstborn (or alternatively as gifts to them in accordance with the principles discussed above). When it comes to the formal distribution of the estate, the firstborn will indeed receive twice as much of the remaining estate as any sibling. The siblings in question, however, will end up with precisely the same amount as their eldest brother, once the "debts" to them are paid off. (For example, if a man has three sons, he would divide his estate into six parts, then create a one-sixth debt to each of the two younger sons. When the man dies, the firstborn would receive a double portion of the part of the estate against which there are no outstanding debts or liens—in effect, two-sixths of the original estate—and the others would each inherit a single sixth. After the sixths owed to the younger sons are paid out, however, all of the sons will end up with exactly the same amount.) In arranging one's will in this specific way, the letter of the law is respected without actually giving any of one's children a greater share of one's estate than one wishes. And, of course, one could act analogously to disburse one's estate to others of one's intended heirs as well.

Gender Issues in Inheritance Law

No aspect of traditional inheritance law will seem to moderns as problematic as the absolute disenfranchisement of daughters when a decedent leaves behind a son. (The revision of the law brought about by the complaint of the daughters of Tzelofḥad, sometimes in a slightly exaggerated way cited as an example of the egalitarian principle in Judaism, specifically grants daughters the right to inherit their fathers' estates solely in the absence of sons.) Furthermore, as noted above, even the descendant of a legator's deceased son takes precedence over a daughter. Nor should any of this be supposed to be a matter of theoretical concern only: in 1943, the chief rabbinate of Palestine felt compelled to enact a *takkanah* (that is, a formal legal pronouncement) putting daughters on an equal footing with sons with respect to inheritance law. (And in modern Israel, the Inheritance Law passed by the Knesset in 1965 considers widows to be the legitimate heirs of their husbands and grants daughters and sons equal shares in the estates of their deceased parents.)

The kind of society the Torah's laws appear clearly to presuppose—one in which a woman passes from being her father's daughter to her husband's wife and in which women do not work outside the home—is so radically different from the norm in Western society that the traditional laws themselves may thus seem hopelessly outdated, even to the point of being arbitrary and illogical, and thus impossible even theoretically to justify from the vantage point of the modern world. Nevertheless, it is hard to imagine that the ancient world differed all that dramatically from the modern one in precisely the ways that are the most relevant for this discussion. Surely, for example, parents in ancient times felt equally devoted to their daughters as to their sons. And it must surely have struck ancients as no less meanspirited and wrong than it does moderns to favor a dissolute, alienated son with the entirety of his parents' wealth to the complete exclusion of a devoted, caring daughter. It follows, therefore, that it is not all that reasonable to explain away the inheritance laws of Scripture as vestigial, thus irrelevant, features of a world totally different from our own.

It is possible, however, to imagine that their meaning might lie precisely in their arbitrariness. As mentioned above, the Torah—and Scripture in general—emphasizes the idea that the world and everything in it are God's and that we human beings should see ourselves as no more than the temporary stewards of our possessions. Focusing on our "right" to disburse our wealth however we see fit would thus be inimical to cultivating a sense of the world as truly belonging to God. Still, the urge to define one's worth in terms of the things one owns—and, especially, in terms of the money one controls—is unyielding for most people. And so, perhaps, the Torah proposes a number of ways to loosen this typical human outlook. Obviously, people can make all sorts of plans to distribute their wealth posthumously as they wish. But by setting out inviolable guidelines regarding the disposal of that wealth in the absence of prior arrangements, the Torah suggests that the only possessions that we can ever truly and completely possess and control are our values, our learning, our insights into the ways of the world, and our devotion to God and the *mitzvot.* By insisting that the disbursement of items of value, including money itself, is so unimportant that a few predetermined principles are deemed capable reasonably of governing the entire process, Scripture is expressing itself entirely clearly about the ultimate value of those kinds of assets. Moderns would be well advised to take to heart the admonition that we misplace our values when we focus too much on materialistic concerns. Indeed, by attempting to disburse our estates both in accordance with our wishes but also cognizant of the Torah's values concerning wealth, we can effectively demonstrate our acceptance of Scripture's underlying philosophy about what constitutes true wealth.

In the end, the ultimate value of money is the great chimera of our times. It is so powerful an illusion, in fact, that most people find the general disconnect between happiness and financial wealth to be either amusing or entirely irrelevant to the way they view the world. But it is precisely in this context that modern Jews can evaluate the inheritance laws most meaningfully: by finding the favoritism and sexism inherent in them at least as illuminating as off-putting. Expressing itself through the medium of law, the Torah ordains a preordained, arbitrary, non-merit-based system of disbursement for those who do not scruple to override its requirements in advance precisely to suggest the ultimate folly of considering money to constitute one's real wealth. That lesson will surely be difficult for moderns to swallow, but the same Torah that ordains the laws governing inheritance also provides us with ways around them, thereby allowing us to learn a profound lesson while enabling us ultimately to leave our estates to whomever we deem worthy.

Those who wish to remain faithful to the letter of the law, but who do not wish to disenfranchise their daughters, are, of course, free to work along the lines proposed above with respect to the scriptural requirement that a firstborn son receive double the inheritance of his younger brothers. By recalling that unpaid debts constitute liens against the estate of any deceased individual, one can easily end up distributing one's estate in accordance with one's personal principles and wishes, while formally nodding to the deeper lessons embedded in the *halakhot* of bequests as laid out in Scripture and developed by the rabbis of classical times.

A famous *midrash* preserved at *Kohelet Rabbah* 5:20 observes that when we enter the world, our hands are clenched as though to say, "Everything is mine; I will inherit it all." But when we depart from the world, our hands are open, as though to say, "I have acquired nothing from the world." That is not quite true, of course: we acquire many things in the course of our lifetimes.

But embedded in the *midrash* is a profound truth, for although we do acquire much as the years of our lives pass, what we acquire of true value—what we ought truly to aspire to leave behind to our children and grandchildren—is not anything we can hold in our hands. And it is just that intangible, but fully real, legacy of wisdom, experience, insight, and moral example that we should endeavor successfully to bequeath to our descendants after us.

Ethical Wills

Although nothing is more central to modern secular life than the pursuit of wealth, the inheritance laws are designed to suggest powerfully that people consider leaving their heirs—and especially their children—with more than just their property as their lasting legacy. And so Jews have for many centuries produced ethical wills designed to bequeath not money but values, morals, and wisdom to subsequent generations. The earliest examples of such wills are in the Bible itself. The first seven chapters of the Book of Proverbs, for example, contain passage after passage in which an anonymous father offers his son the distilled wisdom of his life. Although the context there does not specifically mark these wise passages as deathbed bequests, they may be read that way and so may be taken as early examples of just the kind of moral lessons a parent may wish to leave a child.

In 1927, Israel Abrahams published a collection of ethical wills that included the most famous examples of such literary wills in Hebrew and English. (See his *Hebrew Ethical Wills* [Philadelphia: The Jewish Publication Society]; reprinted in 1976 with an introduction by Rabbi Judah Goldin and in 2006 in an expanded edition with a new introduction by Lawrence Fine.) In recent decades, Rabbi Jack Riemer and Nathaniel Stampfer have also produced both an anthology of modern ethical wills entitled *Ethical Wills: A Modern Jewish Treasury* (New York: Schocken, 1986) and a guide to producing one oneself: *So That Your Values Live On: Ethical Wills and How to Prepare Them* (Woodstock, VT: Jewish Lights Publishing, 1994). Although there is no specific halakhic requirement that an individual produce an ethical will, it is a time-honored and deeply meaningful exercise in values clarification that moderns may well wish to adopt and adapt to their own situations. Surely most modern readers will endorse the idea that money and property may indeed be nothing more than vanity and breath, but every individual has a legacy worth bequeathing to subsequent generations. This ethical bequest includes one's sense of ethics, of morality and of right and wrong, and one's code of personal conduct as well as one's philosophy of life and faith; these alone are the true items of lasting value in anyone's estate. Nor is any of this idea in conflict with the Torah's teachings regarding wealth and its posthumous disposition. People will inevitably have strong wishes about the way their money is disbursed posthumously. Indeed, Scripture undoubtedly expects that to be the case. But the law nonetheless organizes itself in such a way as to encourage people to identify the true wealth they possess as their personal moral bearing, their wisdom, and their faith, and to consider finding a way to bequeath these precious gifts successfully to their heirs. An ethical will can also contain a family history, including specifically the kind of personal recollections that will one day serve as a precious legacy to one's children and, especially, to one's grandchildren.

Writing an ethical will does not require special literary skill or talent. Nor, of course does it have to be written at all; an ethical will can be audio- or videotaped and be just as effective as a written document. Rather, it involves identifying carefully what one has learned from life, specifying what one knows now and that one's heirs would be better off knowing sooner rather than later, and distinguishing clearly between those of life's lessons one has come to consider supremely valuable and those that one has finally concluded are merely worthwhile. It involves sifting the experiences of a lifetime, then brushing away the chaff and considering the kernels of wisdom and experience, and passing them along to one's heirs as one's true and permanently enduring legacy. Every individual will go about this sifting process differently. But all who wish their legacies to be not money and jewelry but profundity and wisdom ought to engage in this enterprise seriously either by writing or recording the stories of their lives, or simply by contemplating the days of their years carefully and methodically enough to distill from them their essential lessons. Doing so will bequeath something to their heirs that will be, as Scripture says of the valorous wife at Proverbs 31:10, more precious than rubies. In the end, whether or not one actually composes an ethical will, the Torah wants us to take to heart the core value inherent in the concept of such a will itself: that we cannot live on after death in our heirs' wallets as meaningfully as we can in the chambers of their hearts and in their moral consciousnesses.

Nor is it necessary to suppose that the composition of one's ethical will, any more than one's "regular" will, needs to be pushed off until one is facing the end of one's days. Indeed, composing such a document while one is in good health and then reviewing and discussing it with one's children, certainly including one's adult children, can be a wonderfully meaningful experience for all concerned and an opportunity for the author's sons and daughters to clarify their understanding of their parents' values and moral bearing. In this vein, helping a relative or a friend to create an ethical will can be a great kindness, especially toward people suffering from long-term illness.

Being an Heir

This chapter has so far considered the issue of bequests and inheritance from the vantage point of the pre-deceased legator. But the issue must also be considered from the point of view of the heir, and specifically the heir whose parent's will is not composed according to the strictures and guidelines of the *halakhah.*

Indeed, parents may sometimes communicate to their children wishes for the disposition of their estates that run counter to the laws of the Torah. In such instances, does the commandment to honor one's parents obligate one to violate the letter or the spirit of Torah law? Is the situation different when the law in question is a rabbinic injunction rather than a Torah law? Is it relevant if an heir's parents were not Torah-observant Jews or even if they were not Jewish at all? Does it matter whether the wishes in question were formally written into a will or merely transmitted orally?

On this subject Maimonides writes (at *MT* Hilkhot Mamrim 6:12; cf. *SA* Yoreh Dei·ah 240:15) as follows: "When a parent instructs a child to transgress one of the laws of the Torah, regardless of whether the specific instruction is to do something forbidden by Scripture or to refrain from doing something commanded, that child may not obey those instructions, as it is written, 'One must fear one's mother and father, yet keep My Sabbaths' (Leviticus 19:3), which is to say: all of you are obliged to honor Me."

Clearly, this principle would apply if a parent asks for funeral arrangements to be made that include customs or practices forbidden by Jewish law, but it also applies to the laws of inheritance. Nevertheless, it should almost always be possible to remain faithful to the laws of the Torah while still obeying a parent's wishes. Children whose parents have made halakhically appropriate arrangements regarding the disposition of their estates can simply follow their parents' instructions. Children whose parents die intestate, on the other hand, may rely on the absence of written instructions to act in accordance with the laws of the Torah. And children whose parents have failed to take any of the measures delineated above but who did leave written wills can seek rabbinic counsel regarding the feasibility of assigning the force of the declaration of a *sh'khiv mei-ra* to the codicils of a parent's will. Of course, also operative will be the principle of the talmudic sage Samuel, *dina d'malkhuta dina* ("the law of the land is the law"; *BT* Bava Kamma 113a–b and several other places in the Talmud), according to which the civil law of the country in which one lives must always be scrupulously obeyed.

Indeed, the combination of the Torah commandment to honor one's parents, the laws regarding the *sh'khiv mei-ra,* the rabbinic principle that it is always a *mitzvah* to honor the wishes of the deceased (even when those wishes were not actually expressed by the decedent on his or her deathbed), and the principle of *dina d'malkhuta dina* makes it highly reasonable to obey instructions made in the lifetime of deceased parents regarding the disposition of their estates. It will never be a wise course of action for an individual untrained in *halakhah* to act without consulting first with a rabbi capable of determining the best way to proceed without contravening any of the Torah's laws. In any event, the necessary tools are clearly available to all who are eager to find a way to remain faithful to Torah law without contravening the clearly expressed wishes of a parent with respect to the disbursement of his or her estate.

Ahavat Ḥesed

Deeds of Lovingkindness

. . . what does the Eternal require of you if not to love mercy, to do justice, and to walk humbly with your God?

(MICAH 6:8)

When the prophet Micah suggested that all the obligations of the Jewish people toward their God fall into one of three categories, the first rubric he mentioned was the one he labeled "the love of kindness." The Hebrew term *ḥesed* implies more than mere kindness, however, pointing to a wider category of beneficent qualities in which moderns would likely include compassion, empathy, mercy, consideration, and concern. As such, and although the prophet omitted to mention which commandments exactly he imagined falling into this specific category, we have adopted his words as the title for this third section of the book, the one devoted to fleshing out the halakhic dimension of interpersonal relationships. Considered here are inter-familial relationships, of course, including the relationships between spouses, between siblings, between parents and children, and between grandparents and grandchildren. But also considered here are the halakhic dimension to being unmarried in a mostly married world and the special halakhic situation of gay men and women. (Regular life in both groups features relationships that are generally supposed to fall outside the usual halakhic rubrics, but which our authors show to be no less fertile ground for worshipful obedience to divine law than the more traditional ones.) The halakhic dimension of the relationship between neighbors is the subject of a full chapter, as are the halakhic aspects of the relationships between the Jewish community and other faith communities, and between individual Jewish people and the members of those other communities. Considered as well is the very complex subject of Jewish medical ethics, here understood as a broad topic subsuming the various ways that the *halakhah* dictates that people relate to their own bodies, to those bodies' abilities and inabilities, and to the ideal of good health itself. And, this section also includes a chapter relating to the relationship of society to individuals with permanent disabilities in light of the *halakhah* and one relating specifically to the halakhic dimension of the relationship between human beings and animals. And then, as it only fitting, the section concludes with a long chapter about the relationship of humanity to the world itself. Almost all the chapters in this section are innovative in one way or another. But all have in common the basic assumption that infusing halakhic values into the complex web of relationships we pursue throughout our lives has as its great reward the ability to bring an individual ever more profoundly into God's presence. To find God in relationships that appear not to involve God at all—that is the great gift of the Torah to a people bereft of its Temple and its priesthood, but amply endowed nevertheless with an almost endless arena of settings and opportunities to seek communion with the divine through fidelity to divine law.

Marriage

DAVID J. FINE

Rather hopefully, Jewish tradition teaches us that God is personally involved in the making of marriages and that the altar itself sheds tears at the breakup of a first marriage (*BT* Gittin 90b). Indeed, this image of God as divine matchmaker has survived for so long precisely because finding "the perfect match" is so difficult that its success can only rationally be attributed to God, while it seems that the failure of a marriage must be no less painful to God than to the spouses whose union has irrevocably ruptured. But how exactly does all that work? And how can men and women use that information actually to find the ideal spouse?

In the second chapter of Genesis, the Torah teaches that Eve, the first woman, was created because God saw that it was "not good" for Adam to be alone. And, indeed, when we seek a mate, we are looking for the one who will relieve us of loneliness, who will make our lives more meaningful by sharing them with us. The most important thing to look for, then, when we choose a mate, is the quality of compatibility: the wise among us will always seek someone with whom they enjoy spending time, and with whom they can see themselves living and aging, and in whose company they can imagine themselves growing old. Friendship is the foundation upon which all happy matches rest.

Choosing a Mate

There are also other factors well worth considering when attempting to choose a mate, and many of these will vary from individual to individual, or even from decade to decade in a single individual's life as he or she ages and matures. (Indeed, people can sometimes spend years looking for a mate who meets a particular set of qualifications, only to end up finding happiness with someone entirely different.) Some, for example, will look for people with similar interests, while others are especially drawn to people different from themselves. Some people will place more value on physical appearance, emotional temperament, or intellectual ability than others. And still others will only learn what they were truly seeking in another once they have somehow managed to find that person. While dating can often be a frustrating and draining experience (both in terms of time, money, and emotion), those who keep their minds and hearts open to possibilities will probably find the process of dating enjoyable, exciting, and, eventually, fruitful.

When looking for a mate one should not close doors based on extraneous, unimportant details, and one must avoid the temptation to prejudge. Our Jewish faith teaches us, for example, that individuals seeking love in their lives should be blind to race. Indeed, people of different racial backgrounds—or of different national or socioeconomic backgrounds—can make wonderful partners, even though those differences will, no doubt, eventually need to be addressed. (However, learning to respect those differences could very well strengthen a relationship.)

There is, however, one distinction that traditional Judaism makes that might appear contrary to this blanket endorsement of compatibility regardless of background, and that is the traditional requirement for *intra*marriage. Intermarriage, the marriage of a Jew and a non-Jew, while not at all uncommon among American Jews, is forbidden by Jewish law (see, e.g., *MT* Hilkhot Ishut 4:15), and Conservative Judaism has endorsed this as a reasonable and necessary restriction for several reasons. First, we are a tiny people and, as such, every new Jewish family makes a difference, just as every Jew who does not form a Jewish family makes a difference. (Studies have shown conclusively that intermarried couples overwhelmingly do not raise Jewishly committed children. According to the 2000–2001 National Jewish Population Survey, for example, only one-third of children in households with only one Jewish parent are raised as Jewish children. And even among the third that *are* raised Jewish, the intensity of their commitment is often dramatically lower than that of Jewish children raised by two Jewish parents.) Second, Judaism is not only the religion of the synagogue: it is also the religion of the Jewish home. (Survey after survey has shown that, contrary to what most might think, the most widely observed Jewish tradition is not going to synagogue on Yom Kippur, but going to a *seder* on the eve of Passover. Without the ongoing experience of home rituals, it is dramatically less likely that children growing up in partially Jewish homes will commit to Judaism as adults.) As a result of these two realities, Conservative Judaism endorses the ancient Jewish prohibition of intermarriage and thus does not recognize the marriage of a Jew to a non-Jew as being halakhically existent. This rule applies to all marriages, including those where the couples are beyond their childbearing years. For this reason, Conservative rabbis and cantors are forbidden to officiate at, or even be present at, intermarriage ceremonies. This position does not signify any lack of love or concern for those Jews choosing to marry non-Jews. But a rabbi or cantor cannot condone that which the tradition unequivocally forbids.

While Conservative Judaism does not permit the formation of intermarriages, many Conservative synagogues encourage the involvement of intermarried families in synagogue life. Indeed, while Conservative rabbis will do what they can to discourage an intermarriage before it takes place, common decency demands that a Jewish individual's decision to marry a non-Jew be accepted, and that his or her autonomy to make that decision be respected. The extent of outreach and involvement will vary from synagogue to synagogue, but acknowledging the challenges that intermarried couples face in choosing to make Judaism a part of their lives is not only permitted by tradition, but it is a sensible way to deal with the reality of intermarriage. And it is also so that many rabbis admire and respect intermarried couples who, despite the challenges they face, choose to find a place for themselves and their children among the Jewish people. Nor should this acceptance of reality be limited to the clergy: parents too, even those who have spent decades vigorously encouraging their children to marry Jews, should respond in a practical manner with love and support when a different decision is made and a new reality emerges.

At this time, the rabbis and lay leaders of the Conservative movement are engaged in a serious discussion about the question of same-sex marriage. Traditionally, Judaism has always defined marriage as a union between a man and a woman. Indeed, intimate sexual relations between two men have long been considered strictly forbidden by Jewish law. Nor has the traditional interpretation of the law been more liberal with respect to lesbian couples. (Halakhic opinions on male homosexuality have traditionally been somewhat different from those on lesbianism, regarding which there is no explicit prohibition in the Torah. But the end result of those attitudes in law has not been dramatically different for women than for men.) In 2006, the Conservative movement's Committee on Jewish Law and Standards approved three opinions on the issue of same-sex relationships, two of which maintain the traditional prohibitions and the third maintaining that, while male homosexual intercourse remains forbidden, other expressions of intimacy between same-sex couples are no longer prohibited because of the principle of *k'vod ha-b'riyyot,* the concern for the dignity of human beings. (See Joel Roth, "Homosexuality Revisited"; Leonard Levy, "Same-Sex Attraction and *Halakhah*"; and Elliot Dorff, Daniel S. Nevins, and Avram I. Reisner, "Homosexuality, Human Dignity, and *Halakhah.*" These papers are available on the Rabbinical Assembly website," and will be published in a forthcoming volume of *CJLS Responsa.*) Two consenting opinions were filed. (See Baruch Frydman-Kohl, "You Have Wrestled with God and Human and Prevailed: Homosexuality and *Halakhah,*" and Loel M. Weiss, "A Concurring Opinion to Rabbi Leonard Levy's Teshuvah: Same-Sex Attraction and *Halakhah.*") Dissenting opinions were also filed that disagreed with the decision maintaining the prohibition on male homosexual intercourse. (See Myron Geller, Robert E. Fine, and David J. Fine, "A New Context: The *Halakhah* of Same-Sex Relations," and Gordon Tucker, "Halakhic and Metahalakhic Arguments Concerning Judaism and Homosexuality." All these responsa too are available on the Rabbinical Assembly website.) All these opinions decry civic discrimination against gay men and lesbian women. A 1992 decision of the Committee on Jewish Law and Standards forbade same-sex marriage, a subject not directly addressed by the 2006 approved opinions but which will surely continue to be discussed with respect to the legal, liturgical, and ethical implications of such unions. This matter is discussed in further detail below by Rabbi Elliot Dorff in his chapter on *halakhah* and same-sex relationships.

When Spouses Differ

All couples must work out how exactly they are going to live together. And, indeed, the issues couples face range from the profoundly important to the picayune: when and where to eat, what movie to see, where to go on vacation, how to handle financial matters, how much time each spouse spends alone, and how much he or she is expected to spend with family are among the various issues that all couples address. Since Judaism is a religion that concerns itself with even the most ordinary aspects of daily life, questions of religious observance will often become pivotal issues in a marriage, especially when the two spouses come from different kinds of Jewish backgrounds. In a sense, this is inevitable: part of the wonder and magic of Judaism is that it allows us to bring holiness—and a sense of God's real presence—into every aspect of our daily lives, even the most banal. The pervasive interest of Judaism in every aspect of life is its greatness, but this will invariably also raise challenges for husbands and wives seeking to live together in peace.

What a couple should do when they differ about matters of religious observance depends on the nature of the difference under consideration. When spouses come from different backgrounds, for example, keeping a kosher home can easily become a major issue. The spouse who wishes to keep a kosher home is obviously going to be deeply unhappy living in a non-kosher home, but there is also room for flexibility. The kosher spouse, for example, need not insist that the non-kosher spouse keep kosher out of the home. While one should always be concerned about sending conflicting messages to children, the religious observance of both spouses should ultimately be presented, even to children, as a matter of personal choice and, practically speaking, this is probably a wise policy to pursue even when the more traditional spouse considers his or her level of observance mandatory and requisite. The key concept is to be open, flexible, and generous. And, indeed, sometimes the mere acknowledgment of the issue under dispute can facilitate the discovery of an acceptable common ground. Nor should these decisions be viewed as once-and-for-all resolutions, but rather as things that a couple may very well revisit over the course of the years as they grow individually and together.

Many issues of religious observance will be discussed and explored before marriage, but others will only arise later on. Our religious journeys continue throughout our lives, and will often lead us in unforeseen directions. And sometimes even long-expected events bring unexpected issues in their wake. The arrival of children, for example, may be eagerly anticipated, but will inevitably bring in its wake a whole new set of issues with which spouses will now suddenly have to deal.

In the end, the key to success is learning to be at peace with a bit of inconsistency. A family might determine that its own equilibrium will be best maintained by being stricter about some aspects of observance and more lenient about others. A family might agree on keeping a kosher home, for example, but not on observing Shabbat strictly. A family might agree to attend services together as a family on Yom Kippur, but not on Sukkot. It would be ideal if all issues could be resolved simply and consistently, but that will rarely, if ever, be the case in most families. The solution, therefore, is to live with that aspect of family life, and not to feel bad about adopting a pattern of Jewish observance that is idiosyncratic or that even feels just a bit quirky. In the end, showing respect for one's spouse (in this specific matter as in most others) will always be more important than struggling to be always on precisely the same page.

When observed properly, Jewish practice can only enhance the quality of family relationships, both between spouses and between parents and children. Of course, both spouses must become comfortable with the level of observance that prevails in their common home in order for religion truly to function as a source of comfort and strength in a marriage. When difficult issues arise, the congregational rabbi can always be approached as a mediator. Some avoid asking a rabbi's advice on the assumption that the rabbi will inevitably take the side of the one who wants to be more observant. While any rabbi will, of course, seek to encourage Jewish observance, he or she will also want to help the couple find a solution that will work for both of them. Most thoughtful rabbis are not "either-or" types and as such will not insist on a single approach to Jewish observance once they understand that such an approach will fail for a specific husband and wife. Rather, the practical rabbi will want to work with the couple to find a solution that brings Judaism into their lives in a way that makes both parties comfortable without alienating either.

Resolving Disputes

Turning to one's rabbi for counsel is the traditional way to resolve disputes between spouses. In ancient and medieval times, in fact, rabbis also served as local judges (a function limited in our day mostly to the adjudication of matters of divorce and conversion). However, the rabbi should always be presumed ready to help when there is discord between spouses. Indeed, if the disagreement is based on questions of Jewish observance and commitment, then the rabbi is the ideal person to go to for help. But even when spousal disagreements are more severe or not specifically about matters of Jewish observance, the rabbi can still help, even if only by referring the couple to a competent marriage counselor. Rabbis do not refer couples along because they do not wish to help, but because they wish to help a couple in distress find someone with the training and the expertise to help them effectively. Of course, many rabbis *are* trained counselors.

There is nothing wrong with asking for help. Indeed, it is the proper and right thing to do when the future of a marriage is at stake. Marriage is a sacred covenant between two parties who have agreed to do right by each other, which agreement surely includes the obligation to do all they can to resolve serious problems. To do so is an expression of the commitment inherent in marriage and thus, even in times of stress and tension (or perhaps *especially* at such times), seeking help is an expression of love.

Marriage and Sexuality

Procreation is not the sole, or even the primary, purpose of sexual intimacy. In addition to *p'riyyah u-r'viyyah* ("procreation"), the maintenance of regular marital relations is a *mitzvah* in its own right that has its own name, *onah*, and is one of the three marital obligations of husbands toward their wives mentioned at Exodus 21:10. The *mitzvah* of *onah* exists as an obligation in its own right and thus applies even when procreation is not a possibility. Husbands and wives, therefore, are commanded to pursue regular intimacy with each another for its own sake. Although most couples will choose to establish the sexual rhythm of their own relationships, it is instructive that our classical sources (e.g., Maimonides at *MT* Hilkhot Ishut 14:1) take a decidedly unromantic approach to the issue and ordain that intimacy simply be a function of the health, strength, and fatigue of the parties involved. In our day, it is universally agreed that sexual intimacy is a basic human need that should not be denied and that the satisfaction of that need within marriage will strengthen the trust and friendship between husband and wife. Sexual intimacy is obviously not all there is to marriage, but at least for most couples it will be the foundation stone upon which much else will rest.

In 1996, the Rabbinical Assembly published *"This Is My Beloved, This Is My Friend": A Rabbinic Letter on Intimate Relations*. Written by Elliot Dorff, the document posited that, since people are created in the image of God, sexual intimacy should be understood as a God-given opportunity to infuse holiness into our lives. There will always be issues to consider in determining how best to use this sacred opportunity—issues relating to modesty, mutual respect, honesty, love, fidelity, health, and safety—but these concerns, Conservative Judaism teaches, are best protected within marriage, a relationship that is by its very nature holy. *This Is My Beloved* also addressed the issue of non-marital sexual relations between single people. Somewhat controversially, it suggested that many of the same concerns that ought to characterize sexuality within marriage should also govern pre- or post-marital sexual relations. The frankness of this admission shocked many, who took these passages to constitute a retreat from tradition's unyielding expectation that sexual relations take place solely within the context of marriage. There was and is much disagreement about how to address the issue of sexual relations outside of marriage, but what Conservative rabbis do agree upon is that sexual intimacy, within or outside marriage, may never be used to degrade or unfairly dominate another. Rabbi Jeremy Kalmanofsky discusses this issue in detail in his chapter on the *halakhah* of being single.

The prevalence of sexual activity outside the context of married life has had its impact on issues relating to the establishment of sexual compatibility within marriage for never-before-married spouses. For example, individuals who might once have entered marriage with only vague expectations of what sexual intimacy would entail often enter marriage now with highly developed sexual expectations that can be difficult for even the most willing spouse always to accommodate. This may create problems that used not to exist, and, although they can be overcome, it is hard to think of the absence of premarital innocence as a great step forward in helping people subsequently to live happily as husbands and wives.

There are those who argue that premarital sex is desirable, even essential, for a couple to determine whether they will be sexually compatible. Jewish tradition rejects this argument. As with all other aspects of married life, sexual intimacy is best achieved incrementally by spouses who love each other and who are willing to learn slowly how best to be intimate with each other. Difficulties should be addressed honestly by the couple. When they are unable to resolve basic difficulties, professional advice can and should be sought. Often, problems of intimacy will be rooted in deeper issues that a trained counselor can help the couple recognize and address. Seeking help where help is needed is neither shameful nor counterproductive. Sensitive rabbis will always actively encourage spouses floundering in their attempts to establish a happy intimate life together to seek the guidance of professionals who can help.

What avenues of sexual release should exist, then, for people who are unsatisfied with marital intimacy, who face long periods away from their spouses, or who are still unmarried? Most Conservative rabbis would not endorse the talmudic view that female masturbation is by its nature an example of lewd behavior and that seminal ejaculation outside of heterosexual intercourse is *ipso facto* sinful. But while the Committee on Jewish Law and Standards has not yet formally addressed the question of masturbation, most rabbis consider masturbation permissible as long as it does not become a way for single people to avoid getting married or for married people to avoid having children. The question of erotic imagery in print or on screen can be considered in the same light: if it leads an individual or a couple successfully to fulfill the *mitzvot* of *onah* and *p'riyyah u-r'viyyah*, then it can be seen as benign or even useful; if it leads people away from the fulfillment of their obligations in either regard, its influence must be deemed essentially negative and thus something to avoid.

Jewish tradition has its own ancient remedy to the challenge of maintaining passion within marriage. Once a month, when a woman is menstruating, the Torah (e.g., at Leviticus 18:19) forbids all sexual contact and ordains that contact can only be resumed after a woman immerses herself in the *mikveh*, the ritual bath. At the heart of the concept of *tohorat hamishpaḥah*, "family purity," rests the profound and inspiring lesson that sanctifying sexuality by making it subject to the law of Scripture imbues human life with holiness. The laws of family purity are discussed in detail by Carl N. Astor in his chapter in this volume on the Jewish life cycle.

Dealing with Adultery and Infidelity

Adulterous relations are strictly forbidden by Jewish law. (While the famous "Thou shalt not commit adultery" of the Ten Commandments [Exodus 20:13 and Deuteronomy 5:17] is taken by tradition to refer specifically to the sin of men engaging in sexual relations with married women, the approach of most rabbis today is to extend the concept to prohibit to all relations that violate the trust of the marriage. Nor should this approach be viewed as a radical departure from traditional norms, but merely one reflective of the general sense that it can never be reasonable to permit behavior that erodes the trust between spouses.) Indeed, while all non-marital sexual relations were traditionally forbidden, an adulterous relationship was always considered a greater offense than a non-marital relationship between unmarried adults. Futhermore, a woman who has committed adultery is forbidden in the future not only to her lover, but also subsequently to her husband, who is supposed to divorce her. (The Mishnah's formula at *M* Sotah 5:1 is as pithy as it is clear: *k'sheim she-asurah la-bo·eil, kakh asurah la-ba·al,* "just as the adulteress is forbidden to her lover, so is she forbidden to her husband.") And although most moderns will find even more extreme the notion (codified by Maimonides at *MT* Hilkhot Issurei Bi·ah 1:6) that adulterers should face execution by strangulation, the general willingness of moderns to regard adultery as a peccadillo rather than as one of the gravest of sins is a sign of ethical degeneracy, not moral progress. From the vantage point of Judaism adultery should be considered a denial of the most basic aspect of marriage, its holiness. Insisting on the exclusivity of sexual partners within marriage is an assertion of our humanity, the declaration of the sacred in our lives. From the Jewish perspective, God is truly a partner in all marriages.

Even so, most rabbis will acknowledge the possibility of moving past adultery toward reconciliation. Indeed, it is often the case that a couple, after a period of estrangement in which one or both spouses had outside affairs, may be able to reconcile. Must they divorce anyway? In a situation like this, most rabbis will encourage reconciliation as a reasonable way to move forward and counsel that compassion must direct the application of tradition. Since in this case the severity of the law is intended to protect the dignity of marriage, we are only supporting the law's intention by accepting a decision to forgive.

Becoming Parents

For almost all couples, becoming parents is one of the great defining moments between husband and wife. According to Jewish law, procreation, called in Hebrew *p'riyyah u-r'viyyah,* is a *mitzvah,* a divine commandment. Although the traditional sources limit the actual obligation to procreate to men (cf., e.g., Maimonides' opinion as expressed in the *Mishneh Torah* at Hilkhot Ishut 15:2), most modern rabbis understand that there is something profoundly counterintuitive about considering *p'riyyah u-r'viyyah* solely to be a husband's obligation and that, as a result, women should feel just as called upon as men to produce the next generation of committed, engaged Jews. Indeed, the ideal in Jewish tradition is for a husband and wife to raise children together, as the liturgy has it, to "Torah study, the wedding canopy, and a life of good deeds."

Judaism teaches us that we do not live in the world only for our own sakes. We inherit what was given to us by our parents, and we are obliged to pass that on to the generation to come. When we have children and teach them how to live in the world, part of us lives on in them. And while we are always busy with the hectic details of our busy lives, in the final analysis it is our family relationships that will ultimately be remembered above all. One need only walk through a Jewish cemetery—or any cemetery—and read the inscriptions on the gravestones to see how universally true this is. "Beloved Husband," "Loving Mother," "Adored Grandfather" are what one will find inscribed on the stones, not "Earned a Lot of Money," "Had a Great Job," or "Drove a Fabulous Car." Marriage, children, and grandchildren are what last.

When is the right time to have children? Maimonides thinks seventeen to be the ideal age for a man to become a father, but only sees a real problem of avoiding the *mitzvah* of procreation once a young man turns twenty (see *MT* Hilkhot Ishut 15:2). He makes an exception for young men wholly devoted to the study of Torah, but most moderns will find these ages impossibly young for a successful foray into the world of parenting. In our world, many couples talk about wanting to postpone having children until "the time is right." But when exactly *is* the right time? A couple must feel secure and comfortable in their marriage. They should feel emotionally prepared to have a child, although emotions are often highly unpredictable when it comes to having children. Other factors feel more important than they actually are: it makes things easier if a couple is able to buy all the things that purport to making child rearing simpler, but children can be successfully reared within all economic frameworks and by parents who can afford very few luxuries in their lives. Potential parents should want to be parents, though, and sometimes a couple's anxieties and concerns do make waiting the appropriate thing to do. From the Jewish perspective, couples may delay procreation as long as they do not intend to postpone their obligation to have children beyond a reasonable limit, thus effectively electing consciously *not* to have them. Conservative Judaism permits the use of birth control under these circumstances specifically to avoid conception. (The question of birth control is discussed in much more detail below by Rabbi Avram I. Reisner in his chapter on Jewish medical ethics.) But every couple should feel called upon by tradition and by law to have children if they are physically and emotionally able. While it is completely understandable to worry whether one is capable of being a good parent, one can only become a good parent by becoming a parent—and then by getting good at it. Rabbi Daniel S. Nevins discusses the relationship between parents and children in detail elsewhere in this volume in a chapter specifically devoted to that topic.

Reproductive Issues

As noted above, Jewish tradition places great importance on procreation. As a result, pregnancy, both wanted and unwanted, almost invariably raises various halakhic issues. Many of these are discussed below by Rabbi Avram I. Reisner in great detail. I therefore set forth only some basic principles.

There are times when pregnancy is unwelcome. In a series of papers approved in 1983, the Conservative movement's Committee on Jewish Law and Standards supported the concept of therapeutic abortion (*CJLS Responsa 1980–1990,* pp. 800–832). The reasoning behind this stance is instructive. Although a fetus is definitely a potential life, it is not considered an autonomous person with the same rights as fully viable human beings by Jewish law or tradition. Therefore, when the mother's life is in danger, the Mishnah (at *M* Ohalot 7:6) requires that the pregnancy be terminated and the mother's life saved. (The principle that the fetus is not a human being is learned from a passage of the Torah that requires monetary damages from a man who strikes a pregnant woman and causes a miscarriage [Exodus 21:22–23]. If the fetus were a full human being, the offender would have been guilty of murder, yet the Torah holds him liable only for monetary damages. This was taken to demonstrate adequately that a fetus is not considered fully to be a human being.)

Based on the mishnaic principle stated above, rabbis have always agreed that abortion is not merely permitted, but actually required, when a woman's life is in imminent danger. There is disagreement, however, when a woman's life is not in imminent danger, but her physical health or her mental well-being are threatened or compromised. The questions that arise are the same ones with which society in general has been wrestling for decades. To what degree should a woman's health be at risk, in order for us to consider her situation as being morally akin to a woman who will not physically survive the continuation of her pregnancy? What if the danger is to her psychological state rather than to her physical well-being? What if a woman is emotionally unstable, rather than, strictly speaking, psychologically ill? And other cases must be considered as well. What about cases in which it is clear that a specific fetus is carrying a serious and untreatable disease? Or cases in which the birth of a child and the attendant responsibilities that devolve upon its parent or parents will be ruinous economically? In its 1983 deliberations, the Committee on Jewish Law and Standards ruled that "an abortion is justifiable if a continuation of pregnancy might cause the mother severe physical or psychological harm, or when the fetus is judged by competent medical opinion as severely defective." (To read the full consensus statement by Rabbis Ben Zion Bokser and Kassel Abelson, see *CJLS Responsa 1980–1990,* p. 817.) Although the issue continues to be debated passionately, the introduction of the rubric of psychological harm into the equation provides much leeway to the woman in making her decision. According to the CJLS, while the father (and others, including a woman's family, her physician, and her rabbi) should be consulted, the decision is ultimately the woman's since it is a question of her health or well-being, and since she is the pregnant individual. Many of the halakhic issues involved in abortion are discussed below in the chapter on medical ethics by Rabbi Avram I. Reisner.

There are other times when pregnancy is wanted but elusive. While recognizing that Jewish law does not require that couples seek medical assistance in bearing children, the Committee on Jewish Law and Standards has permitted a wide range of options that may reasonably be explored. Again, more details on these issues may be found in Rabbi Reisner's chapter.

Adoption has always been considered a praiseworthy way to create a family. Indeed, the Jewish attitude has always been that adoptive parents perform an act of great lovingkindness (*g'milut ḥesed*) by providing a home for children in need. If the birth mother of a child is not Jewish, adopted children must be converted to Judaism at the time of adoption or soon after. (Various specific issues relating to the conversion of adopted children were discussed by the Committee on Jewish Law and Standards in 1987 in a paper by Rabbi Avram I. Reisner that appears in *CJLS Responsa 1980–1990,* pp. 391–417. Adoption as a solution to infertility and as an act of lovingkindness toward the child in need of adoption is discussed in a 1994 paper by Elliot Dorff, subsequently published in *CJLS Responsa 1991–2000,* pp. 461–509. If an adopted child is known unequivocally to have an unambiguously Jewish birth mother, then conversion is not required.)

The Committee on Jewish Law and Standards has also endorsed a range of medical approaches to infertility. Artificial insemination was discussed favorably in a 1978 paper by Rabbi Morris Shapiro, which argued that a man who donates sperm to a sperm bank for helping infertile couples should be credited with having assisted them in the performance of the *mitzvah* of procreation and not condemned for having "wasted" his semen. In 1994, the Committee confirmed the permissibility of artificial insemination by adopting a comprehensive paper written by Rabbi Elliot Dorff, which also extended to egg donation (*CJLS Responsa 1991–2000,* pp. 461–509). Then, in 1995, the Committee also approved a paper by Rabbi Aaron Mackler permitting *in vitro* fertilization (*CJLS Responsa 1991–2000,* pp. 510–525). Overall, the Committee has sought to lay the groundwork for permitting a wide range of medical procedures designed to assist couples in their effort to fulfill the commandment of *p'riyyah u-r'viyyah,* of procreation.

Adoption can serve infertile couples as a simpler path toward family life than the use of reproductive technologies. Although adoption has not traditionally been deemed the technical fulfillment of the *mitzvah* of *p'riyyah u-r'viyyah,* it should be wholeheartedly embraced as a valid method of creating vibrant Jewish families by couples willing and able to open their hearts and their homes to adoptive children. While the Committee on Jewish Law and Standards has ruled that artificial insemination does fulfill the *mitzvah* if the husband's sperm is used, "infertile couples are under no obligation to use modern technology to have children" (Elliot Dorff, "Artificial Insemination, Egg Donation, and Adoption" *CJLS Responsa 1991–2000,* p. 469).

Artificial insemination raises some quite complicated questions, however. There are two kinds of artificial insemination: artificial insemination of a woman with her husband's sperm and artificial insemination of a woman with a donor's sperm. Most rabbis do not object to artificial insemination when the sperm is that of a woman's own husband. (It is also true that some Jewish authorities require that the reproductive technicians extract semen that has been deposited by the husband through a "normal" act of intercourse. This method of harvesting sperm, however, is widely considered inefficient and is rarely successful. Rabbi Dorff has argued against insisting on this requirement, since, in a case where the point of the effort is to fulfill the *mitzvah* of procreation, the greater goal may be permitted to take precedence over the specifics of procedure.) Artificial insemination by an outside donor is the more complicated procedure from the vantage point of the *halakhah*. The halakhic issues involved in this procedure are discussed in detail by Rabbi Reisner elsewhere in this volume.

The boundaries of marriage become even more complicated when one considers the possibility of surrogate motherhood. In the Torah, Sarah allowed Abraham to be intimate with her maidservant Hagar in order to have a child, an arrangement that did not work out well in the end for either Sarah or Hagar. On the other hand, Rachel and Leah seemed to have been comfortable with Bilhah and Zilpah, their respective handmaidens, whom they sent to Jacob to become pregnant. Of course, surrogate motherhood today does not require that sexual relations take place between the husband and the surrogate. Nevertheless, the possibility of emotional harm to any of the involved parties, and even of bitter dispute over custody once the child is born, is real. The Committee on Jewish Law and Standards carefully reviewed the many issues relating to surrogate motherhood and approved two papers in 1997, one by Rabbi Elie Kaplan Spitz and the other by Rabbi Aaron Mackler. Both papers agreed that Judaism does not categorically forbid surrogate motherhood. Both agreed on various limitations and protections to the parties, but Rabbi Spitz's approach was far more accepting of surrogacy. (For a more nuanced discussion of the issue, see Rabbi Spitz's and Rabbi Mackler's responsa, published in *CJLS Responsa 1991–2000,* pp. 526–557.)

A corollary issue discussed by the Committee was the Jewish identity of children born to surrogate mothers. Depending on the origin of the original ovum, a surrogate may be the genetic and the gestational mother of a fetus she is carrying, or only its gestational mother. The former case is relatively simple to unravel halakhically: the surrogate is the mother and the baby's status follows her own: if she is Jewish, then so is the child, but if she is not Jewish, then the child must be converted as an infant if it is to be raised by a Jewish couple as their own. But what is the case if the surrogate is solely the gestational mother? In 1997, the Committee on Jewish Law and Standards adopted a paper written by Rabbi Mackler that concluded that the gestational mother, not the genetic mother, is the mother of record in Jewish law (*CJLS Responsa 1991–2000,* pp. 551–557). While many have found this position counterintuitive, it is also possible to find within its details some powerful lessons: that Jewishness is a social construct rather than an inalienable part of anybody's genetic heritage, that converts to Judaism are just as Jewish as born Jews, and that newborn children are not merely fertilized ova, but rather the products of parenting, and of their parents' care and love.

Choosing to Remain Childless

Some couples defer the decision to have children because of a wide range of anxieties about parenting, about money, or about various other circumstances, but there are also couples who intend from the start not to have children. Whatever a couple decides, their decision must be accepted by their family and their community. Judaism sets many ideals, and not everyone will be able to fulfill them all. It should be possible to regret a couple's decision, especially one that contravenes traditional Jewish attitudes, without ostracizing those who make them or making them feel unwelcome in our communities. But it is also always worth remembering that being childless may not be the active choice it appears to outsiders to be and that outsiders should therefore not make assumptions about others' intentions or pry into what may be a private decision, perhaps even a deeply painful one, to which another couple has come only reluctantly.

Those who do not have children, whether they choose not to or cannot become parents, should seek other ways to transmit their values and their wisdom to the next generation. Being an "aunt" or "uncle" to relatives' or friends' children can be very rewarding. Working as an educator or in other helping professions can also be a way of raising up the next generation. The ultimate goal, though, is always to offer of ourselves to others, to give to the world rather than just take from it. The most traveled path toward this great and selfless goal is to become parents, and so to transmit the heritage of our ancestors to a chain of descendants we hope will remain unbroken for long centuries after we personally pass from the scene. But it is not the only way—and a mature community committed to respecting the personal decisions of its members will acknowledge the possibility of alternate methods of transmitting the heritage of Judaism to future generations.

Losing a Spouse

Up to this point, this chapter has focused on learning to live with a spouse, but the time will also come for many to learn how to live without a beloved partner. Losing a spouse is like losing one's anchor in life: no matter what the particular circumstances, the loss will be devastating and traumatic for the surviving wife or husband. Yet people can and do survive the death of their spouses. Humans are tremendously adaptable and resilient creatures. We are capable of making adjustments, even excruciatingly painful ones, even those so difficult and painful that they feel impossible to contemplate in advance. Tradition encourages us to focus on life even in the face of tremendous loss.

As described in general terms by Rabbi Carl Astor above in his chapter on the Jewish life cycle, Judaism provides rituals for dealing with the loss of our loved ones. When a husband or wife dies, the surviving spouse attends to the burial and then mourns formally by sitting *shivah* for a week and saying Kaddish for thirty days. (Some will say Kaddish for eleven months or for a year, however, especially when there are no children willing or able to do so.) The *yahrtzeit* (anniversary of a person's death) is observed every year by lighting a twenty-four-hour candle and by saying Kaddish in a synagogue.

One may also visit the grave—and, indeed, it is traditional to do so on the *yahrtzeit,* as well as during the days before or immediately after Rosh Hashanah—at which time many follow the custom of placing a pebble on the memorial stone as a sign that they were there. And the Yizkor Service, a service of remembrance recited four times a year in synagogue, includes specific prayers widows and widowers may recite in memory of their late spouses. The experience of losing a beloved spouse can also provide the mourner with support, sometimes from unexpected quarters. Friends and family demonstrate the depth of their affection for the new widow or widower by being present throughout the mourning process, thus using the simple fact of physical presence to help her or him through the most difficult of life's tragedies. Going to the synagogue to say Kaddish often helps a bereaved individual make new friends and develop a sense of belonging to a community. Saying Kaddish also affirms faith in God. Even though the bereaved individual may feel indescribably lonely, acknowledging that death is part of life is the first step in accepting one's loss and in finding the strength to move forward in life.

The rituals for losing a spouse through divorce are restricted to the legal procedures connected with the *get,* the Jewish divorce document. The technical requirements of Jewish law emphasize the importance of the bond of marriage, and guarantee that it will never be severed in a cavalier manner. The laws that pertain to Jewish divorce are also discussed by Rabbi Astor in his chapter on the Jewish life cycle.

The Halakhah of Remarriage

Although it will surely be the case that the prospect of remarriage will feel quite different to divorced individuals than to widows or widowers, many laws apply similarly to people in both situations. According to Jewish law, for example, a woman must wait ninety days after her husband dies or after she becomes divorced before she can remarry (cf., e.g., *SA* Even Ha-eizer 13:1). The chief reason for this waiting period is to avoid any dispute of paternity later on. (If a woman were to marry a month or two after her first marriage ended, and became pregnant right away, the father could be conceivably either the first or the second husband. Nor is this a wholly unlikely possibility. As any marriage counselor will verify, it is not at all uncommon for couples to remain sexually intimate even while on the brink of separation.) The theory was that, if three months separate the two marriages, then it will be highly unlikely that such a question of paternity could arise. The ninety-day waiting period did not apply to men, however, because there was no analogous concern: as long as the man's new bride has been unmarried for at least ninety days, he may reasonably assume himself to be the father of any children subsequently born to her. Given that paternity can be determined scientifically today, many rabbis are willing to relax this ninety-day requirement under circumstances that warrant a more lenient approach to tradition. Similarly, one is not supposed to marry within thirty days of experiencing the death of a close relative. The tradition recognizes the difficult psychological demands of being both a mourner and a celebrant at the same time. Losing a spouse can be particularly painful, and for this reason the *halakhah* requires a man to wait until all three pilgrimage festivals have passed before remarrying. But when there are special circumstances, such as a man being the father of young children, he is permitted to remarry as soon as *shivah* is complete (*SA* Yoreh Dei·ah 392:1–2). Today, we would consider it unseemly for a man to remarry less than a month after the loss of his wife even if he does have very young children at home.

Overall, the *halakhah* teaches us that a great deal of time need not pass before either a man or woman can remarry (*SA* Even Ha-eizer 13). While marriage is sacred, it is deemed irrevocably to end with death or divorce, and subsequent remarriage is not deemed at all inappropriate. Indeed, remarriage was common in ancient and medieval times, and medieval records show that even multiple remarriages were not unknown. In this regard, however, widowed people are in their own category. Those who are remarried, for example, carry with them the memories of their deceased first spouses and their new spouses should honor and respect those memories. Although it is customary not to light a *yahrtzeit* candle for a deceased spouse in the home one shares with a new husband or wife, it is not forbidden to do so; nor should a remarried individual feel that it is in poor or even questionable taste to recite Yizkor prayers in memory of a late spouse. Even as we move ahead, one cannot and need not let go of the past.

The Ethics of Divorce and Post-Divorce Spousal Support

In his chapter on the Jewish life cycle, Rabbi Astor provides a detailed survey of the laws and traditions that pertain to Jewish divorce. Here I discuss the ethical issues that divorce often brings to the fore.

Maimonides, who in addition to being one of the greatest Jewish scholars of all time was also a physician, said that it is better to amputate an arm that is beyond healing than to risk allowing it to poison the rest of one's body. This pragmatic approach is typical of Judaism in many different contexts, and it suggests the Jewish approach to divorce as well. Divorce is tragic. In many ways, it is just like cutting off a limb. But, like cutting off a diseased limb, it is not fatal. When it is clear that a marriage is not working, that it is bringing more pain than joy, that the love that once bound two spouses together is atrophying rather than growing stronger, and that counseling has not helped in resolving the problems a couple is facing, then it may be better for the spouses to separate rather than continue to live in misery.

Jewish law has no-fault divorce. The specific procedure for obtaining and delivering a *get* is described in Rabbi Astor's chapter, but the basic position is that one is not required to present evidence of cruelty or infidelity to the court, nor is one obliged to declare a specific reason for wanting to end a marriage. As long as the couple agrees, they can go before the *beit din,* the rabbinic court, and obtain a divorce.

The wife must accept the *get* freely and not under compunction or duress. And the husband must indicate his intentions by authorizing its writing. Once the particulars of a divorce are worked out, it is unethical for either spouse to obstruct the proceeding by refusing either to authorize the *get* or to receive it. Indeed, once a couple formally decides to divorce, it is sinful and morally reprehensible for one spouse to hold the other hostage by failing to cooperate with the religious requirements that a *get* be written, delivered, and accepted. Unfortunately, it still sometimes does happen that a man agrees to a divorce, then refuses to grant his wife a *get* out of spite or in anger. Because no scribe may write a *get* unless formally charged with writing one, and because the traditional *halakhah* requires that the husband formally initiate the divorce proceedings rather than the wife, the result of this kind of meanspirited intransigence is that the wife becomes an *agunah,* a woman "anchored" to her husband, since she cannot remarry as long as he refuses to authorize the writing of a *get.* Traditional solutions have involved bringing all kinds of social pressure to bear on a husband who refuses out of spite to authorize the writing of a *get* for a woman to whom he is married, but with whom he clearly has no interest of maintaining a viable marriage, in order to coerce him to authorize the *get.* This procedure is often successful, but, in the end, the traditional *halakhah* still makes the wife in such a situation ultimately dependent on her husband's decision. The Conservative movement does not allow men to hold women hostage in this way. When a man does not authorize the *get* after repeated attempts by the woman and her rabbi, the movement's central *beit din* (rabbinic court) will declare the marriage null and void, in effect annulling the marriage. As mentioned above by Rabbi Carl N. Astor in his chapter on the Jewish life cycle, this rabbinic procedure, called *hafka·at kiddushin,* is used sparingly and only when there are no other alternatives. It is a bold use of rabbinic authority, one that many Orthodox rabbis endorse in theory but too often decline to invoke.

From an ethical perspective, when one spouse has decided that the marriage must end and there is no hope of reconciliation, the other spouse must respect the decision and cooperate in divorce proceedings. Just as a husband must authorize a *get,* so must a wife cooperate with the *beit din* in receiving a *get.* In circumstances where the wife is unwilling or unable to cooperate, the *beit din* has procedures to grant the *get* themselves and permit the husband to remarry. When one party to a marriage wishes a divorce but the other party wishes to remain married, the applicable laws are extremely complex and couples who find themselves in that situation should consult a rabbi to determine how the law applies to their circumstances.

A Jewish marriage contract is called a *k'tubbah.* In ancient times, the *k'tubbah* was devised to protect the woman's economic security in the event that she outlived her husband or their marriage ended in divorce. Essentially, the *k'tubbah* is a lien on the husband's estate that sets aside a certain significant amount to be paid to a wife upon her husband's death or in the event their marriage ends in divorce. As such, the sum mentioned in the *k'tubbah* was understood as a kind of debt to the wife, thus allowing its payment to take precedence over the disbursement of any inheritance that might posthumously be distributed to a man's heirs. A woman was thus assured a piece of her husband's estate.

The *k'tubbah* is used today in Jewish marriages as a symbolic document passed down by tradition. In contrast with most Reform and Reconstructionist rabbis who do not use *k'tubbot* featuring the traditional text, most Conservative rabbis—notwithstanding the discomfort many feel with the original text's non-egalitarian format—use the traditional phrasing, finding overriding importance in sanctifying marriages with precisely the same words that have been used by the Jewish people for over a thousand years. In practice, all women formally waive the right to their *k'tubbah* payments as a part of the divorce proceedings before the *beit din,* since whatever separation or divorce settlement that the couple has agreed to or that has been imposed by the civil court supersedes the settlement specified in the *k'tubbah.*

The lesson of the *k'tubbah*—that, even if a marriage should dissolve, husbands retain responsibility to provide support for their wives—is still very relevant for moderns. Of course, in our world a wife may well have a greater income or more wealth than her husband. The civil courts take this into account in setting alimony payments and in determining how best to divide a couple's property between them, which is as it should be: Jewish ethics require that a husband and wife behave responsibly toward each other in the event of divorce. The terms and extent of that responsibility are worked out through mutual agreement, by binding arbitration, or by the courts, just as the *k'tubbah* once formally specified the extent of a husband's obligation to provide for his former wife. The details may have changed, but the ethical principle remains the same: while divorce is an acceptable way to end a marriage, one cannot simply walk away from a former spouse. While this is especially true when children are involved, the difference between childless couples that divorce and those with children will have to do with the extent of provision, not with the issue of whether there should be provision at all. Like all *bona fide* contracts, pre-nuptial agreements between parties engaged to be married must be respected in the event of divorce.

Sharing Wealth

In a healthy contemporary marriage, economic responsibility is shared by husband and wife. This constitutes a major difference between marriage in its classical guise and its modern-day version. According to talmudic law, husbands were completely responsible for all the needs of their wives. That reflected a society in which women did not generally function as economically independent individuals. (However, there were exceptions to the rule even in ancient times, and we do read about women who owned property and managed to amass wealth millennia ago.) Still, in the normal course of events, the Talmud provides that a woman who enters a marriage with her own property retains the individual title to her possessions. Her movable property (i.e., her trousseau) was hers to do with as she wished. Things became more complicated, though, if she owned real estate. In such a case, the land remained hers but the husband acquired the right to utilize the yield of the land as he saw fit, and to keep whatever profit he could make from it. Similarly, anything that the wife produced during the marriage—such as clothing, jewelry, or different kinds of handmade crafts—belonged to her husband. (The laws of a wife's property rights are discussed in great detail in the eighth chapter of the talmudic tractate K'tubbot.) Although this arrangement will probably strike moderns as essentially unfair to wives, the underlying principle was, at least in its day, cogent: since it was the husband who had to provide for all the economic needs of the wife, it was deemed reasonable to expect her to contribute whatever she earned to the household income. Were she to leave the household through divorce, however, the earning rights connected to her own land reverted wholly to her.

The lesson from tradition is that spouses have a mutual responsibility for each other's financial well-being. They may have entered into the marriage with separate property. (Indeed, property that clearly belonged to one spouse before the time of marriage ought to return to that individual should the marriage be dissolved.) But while a marriage endures, tradition teaches us that, just as responsibility for expenses must be shared, so too must income, including income from assets. The married couple forms a corporate body while they are married. Wealth and income are shared, as are debts and expenses. While one spouse may work and another spouse may support the family in other ways, both are partners and share in the responsibility and decision-making, in the joys and the sorrows. Just as the Talmud ordains that the property of the woman be merged with that of her husband during the time that she is married, so should property in contemporary marriages be treated as common wealth. The economic union of husband and wife mirrors the strength and sacredness of their union.

Other than by reading the chapters in this volume by Carl N. Astor, Elliot N. Dorff and Avram I. Reisner, readers interested in learning about many of the topics discussed above will do well to consult Rabbi Dorff's *Matters of Life and Death,* as well as his *"This Is My Beloved, This Is My Friend": A Rabbinic Letter on Intimate Relations*. Other important resources are Michael Gold's *Does God Belong in the Bedroom?* (Philadelphia: The Jewish Publication Society, 1992), Aaron L. Mackler's *Life and Death Responsibilities in Jewish Biomedical Ethics* (New York: JTS Press, 2000), and Perry Netter's *Divorce Is a Mitzvah: A Practical Guide to Finding Wholeness and Holiness When Your Marriage Dies* (Woodstock, VT: Jewish Lights Publishing, 2002).

Sex, Relationships, and Single Jews

JEREMY KALMANOFSKY

The Torah promises that Jewish law is not only obligatory, but that it is *good,* impressing the nations with its wisdom and nobility (Deuteronomy 4:6). Those who walk the path of *halakhah* must hope that ancient and medieval norms still retain the capacity to sanctify us, refine us, and help us build a better society. But modern Jews are always at least dimly aware that when we practice Judaism, we live out the values of ancestors who lived twenty, fifty, or one hundred generations ago. Many of the youngest practices in Jewish law are literally medieval, relative newcomers a mere five hundred years old, while the truly ancient ones come to us from a world almost unimaginably different from our own.

Conservative Jews often must undertake an uneasy negotiation between the contemporary values we hold proudly and those ancient mores that produced Jewish norms in the first place. Sometimes classical tradition intersects with modernity in thrilling ways, revealing unexpected profundity. But sometimes, even when we remain faithful to sacred norms, foundational halakhic values are so different from contemporary mores that today's Jews struggle to bring them into conversation with each other.

Few topics illustrate this disjunction more clearly than do the *halakhot* concerning unmarried people and their intimate lives. This body of law comes to us from pre-modern times, when people married early, struggled to produce enough children to maintain tiny, vulnerable societies, and held very different attitudes about sex, the body, and gender relations than those held by people in our own day. How should Jews relate to this body of law today?

Sexuality

Contemporary Jews often assume that normative Judaism encourages us to be sexually fulfilled. In some ways, this is true: Judaism rejects celibacy and considers regular, satisfying sex to be an integral part of marriage. And, indeed, some authorities, especially within the mystical traditions, celebrate erotic intimacy and joy. But, in other ways, the *halakhah* manifests grave suspicion about enjoying sexual pleasure for its own sake, and legislates ways to counter erotic impulses. (For instance, consider the Talmud's ruling that a man "who intentionally arouses himself is to be excommunicated" [*BT* Niddah 13b]. In its original context, this text specifically forbids only masturbation, but later authorities [e.g., *Shulḥan Arukh* at Oraḥ Ḥayyim 240:1 and Even Ha-eizer 23:3] understood it to discourage sexual arousal in general.) Although this tendency is especially linked to ascetic strains in medieval philosophy and mysticism, these values indelibly stamped halakhic decisions as well. For example, Maimonides believed the reason for circumcision was to curtail a man's sex drive by wounding his penis, thus diminishing his capacity for pleasure (*Guide for the Perplexed* III 49). Maimonides treated this ascetic stance not only as a philosophical idea, but as a legal norm as well: "The sages frown on all who have frequent sex, on men who are always approaching their wives like roosters in a henhouse. Such men are terribly perverted, for this is the crude behavior. Whoever minimizes sexual relations is considered praiseworthy" (*MT* Hilkhot Issurei Bi·ah 21:11).

We will discuss specific rules more fully below, but we can say here that classical *halakhah* restricts sexual pleasure to marriage, and even there delimits it to the context of performing at least one—and preferably two—*mitzvot:* procreation and *onah,* the obligation of husbands to maintain regular sexual relations with their wives.

Experiencing sexual pleasure would only distract one from the proper, selfless performance of these *mitzvot,* according to Rabbi Joseph Karo, author of the *Shulḥan Arukh:* "Even when a husband is with his wife," he writes, "he should not be mindful of his own pleasure, but should think of himself as a person paying off a debt—in that he owes her *onah* and must fulfill his Creator's command, and so that he might have children who study Torah and fulfill the commandments" (*SA* Oraḥ Ḥayyim 240:1).

In contrast to their married neighbors, who have at least this unromantic outlet, unmarried men are forbidden from touching unmarried women in any sensual way, or even from looking at them in most cases (*MT* Hilkhot Isurei Bi·ah 21:1–2). Indeed, classical sources even go so far as to forbid men to touch their own bodies below the navel, lest this prompt them to fantasize sexually, let alone actually to masturbate (see, e.g., *SA* Even Ha-eizer 23:4).

Needless to say, contemporary views of sexuality differ greatly from this approach. After Freud, we usually think of the repression of sexual desire as a problem, not a solution! Indeed, moderns generally look with suspicion on sexual abstinence, even among single people, let alone within marriage. Refraining from sex is often seen, perhaps glibly, as a marker of neurosis or confused sexual identity. Most Jews are probably among the sixty percent of Americans who, year after year, tell the Gallup poll that they do not believe sex between unmarried adults is immoral. The attitudinal transformation from pre-modern to modern times can hardly be overestimated, as the historian Haym Soloveitchik wrote in his essay "Rupture and Reconstruction: The Transformation of Contemporary Orthodoxy" (*Tradition* 28 [1994], pp. 64–131). Discussing even very traditional Jewish communities, Soloveitchik described the "major transformation of values that had been in the making for close to a century, namely the gradual disappearance of the ascetic ideal that held sway over Jewish spirituality for close to a millennium. While there was sharp division in traditional Jewish thought over the stronger asceticism of mortification of the flesh, the milder one of distrust of the body was widespread, if not universal. The soul's control over the flesh was held to be, at most, tenuous, and without constant exercises in self-denial, there was little chance of man's soul triumphing over the constant carnal pull. . . . The thousand-year struggle of the soul with the flesh has finally come to a close" (p. 81).

More than just attitudes have changed, however. Contemporary sexual behavior in North America, Israel, and other Western countries would have been inconceivable to Jewish legal authorities of the past. Of course, just from reading law books by rabbis, it is impossible to know how people actually behaved. The fact that *halakhah* mandated a rule does not necessarily mean people followed it. Indeed, we do know that medieval Jews often had far looser sexual standards than their rabbis would have wished (as documented by David Biale in his *Eros and the Jews* [New York: Basic Books, 1992], pp. 60–85).

Today's fault lines, however, are utterly different from historical ones. For instance, while classical halakhic sources forbid unmarried men and women even to be alone together (see, e.g., *BT* Avodah Zarah 36b, and *SA* Even Ha-eizer 22:2), unmarried people today share considerably more intimacy than unchaperoned visits. More than ninety percent of never-married American women have had sexual intercourse before age thirty, and seventy-four percent have done so before age twenty, according to 2002 data from the National Center for Health Statistics. The median age for first intercourse is seventeen for both males and females, according to that same 2002 report. While the rate of sexual abstinence among American teens has risen markedly over the last two decades, still around one in three Americans (both males and females) has had sexual intercourse before age eighteen, and nearly two-thirds have had intercourse before age twenty, according to a 2011 report by that same National Center for Health Statistics. Interestingly, these data instantiate the talmudic sages' view that people should begin having sex in their mid- to late-teenaged years if they do not wish their sexual drives to spin out of control (see *BT* Kiddushin 29b). But, of course, the sages of old assumed that people necessarily would marry to satisfy those hormonal surges. Today, marriage may be years away for people in their early twenties. Should *halakhah* demand that never-married adults simply quash their sex drives entirely? Moreover, many divorced and widowed adults find themselves partnerless, yet desiring the kind of active sex life they had when they were married.

Given the chasm between contemporary sexual standards and classical ones, profound issues emerge for observant, unmarried Conservative Jews. Should Conservative *halakhah* propound the traditional rules about separating the genders and restricting sex to married couples intent on fulfilling the *mitzvot* of procreation and *onah*? Should single Jews treat this as normative guidance? Can Conservative Jews affirm with integrity the classical suspicion of all sexual pleasure and observe the *halakhot* designed to reduce it?

Despite our very great difference from our ancestors, the values expressed in traditional *halakhah* remain relevant today. We should commit ourselves to traditional strictures as an aspirational ideal in which only the *most* loving, *most* committed, and *most* faithful relationships are wholly appropriate for the *most* intense kind of human intercourse. At the same time, we should be honest in admitting that not all sexual contact outside of marriage is wrong, and that even less traditional sexual behavior can still express deep Jewish values and sanctify life. Rabbis and teachers should help Jews prioritize their values, assisting them in mapping out which behaviors are particularly strongly interdicted and which less so. Indeed, the Conservative movement followed just this approach when the Rabbinical Assembly Commission on Human Sexuality published its 1996 pastoral letter, *"This Is My Beloved, This Is My Friend,"* by Rabbi Elliot Dorff. Although that pamphlet's discussion of ethics and norms is richly suffused with reference to Jewish sources, Dorff's aims are more generally ethical and social than narrowly legal, as is the focus of this chapter.

Premarital Sex

A common misconception is that Judaism permits non-marital sex—that is, consensual sex between unmarried adults. True, the *halakhah* does not forbid sexual intercourse between a man and a single woman in the same unequivocal way it bans sex between a man and a close relative or between a man and another man's wife, which the Torah regards as capital crimes. Nor does Jewish law consider it adultery, technically, if a married man has sex with a single woman. (However, this promiscuity is considered a moral breach; and some authorities consider it grounds for divorce, as Rabbi Moshe Isserles, the Rema, reports in his gloss to *SA* Even Ha-eizer 154:1.) Nor is the child born to a single woman considered illegitimate (unless the father were her close relative). Thus, the technical Hebrew term *mamzeir* applies more narrowly than the category of "bastard" in colloquial English, as it refers only to the offspring of forbidden unions and does not include children merely born out of wedlock.

These qualifications notwithstanding, halakhic tradition unambiguously condemns sex outside of marriage as *z'nut,* a pejorative term meaning "harlotry" or "licentiousness." Leviticus 19:29 warns fiercely, "Do not make your daughter into a harlot, lest the land itself fall into harlotry and become filled with depravity." The *midrash* explains: "This refers to a man who surrenders his unmarried daughter except in marriage, or to a woman who surrenders herself except in marriage." (This *midrash* is found at *Sifra* K'doshim, *perek* 7:1–2, and is the source for Rashi's commentary on the verse. *BT* Sanhedrin 76a, as it appeared in manuscripts, matches the *midrash;* today's printed editions of the Talmud lack the clause about a single woman's consent to have sex.) Traditional authorities universally agree that sex between single people—including consenting adults—is forbidden at least by rabbinic enactment, and some consider it banned by Torah law. The words of Rabbi Jacob Emden (1697–1776) attest that the very idea of non-marital sex is incompatible with traditional halakhic sensibilities: "Is there any authority who has ever said that licentious intercourse with a single woman (*derekh z'nut*) should be permitted, regardless of whether by rape or seduction? God forbid even considering such a possibility! It should be self-evident that this is universally held to be completely forbidden, either by Torah edict or rabbinic enactment" (*She'eilat Ya·avetz* part 2, responsum 15 [ed. Lvov, 1884, p. 8b]).

Particularly interesting is that this quotation comes from an (in)famous responsum in which Emden permits a man to keep a concubine (the technical term is *pilegesh,* really a second-class wife more than a prostitute) on the condition that the woman remain faithful to him alone. To Emden, concubinage with commitment is in principle permitted (as will be discussed with additional detail below); but simply choosing to have sex without the intention of marriage and without sexual exclusivity is unthinkable. The very absurdity of such an idea is conveyed by his lumping the rapist and the seducer in the same category: for Emden, both men are to be considered criminals who degrade women. The woman herself, in a case either of violence or seduction, he considers a victim who could not possibly have consented to *z'nut.*

Authorities disagree on the textual basis for the prohibition against non-marital sex. Maimonides stands at the strict end of the spectrum, regarding any sexual intercourse involving an unmarried Jewish woman as a violation of the biblical commandment "Let there be no female prostitute (*k'deishah*) among the daughters of Israel, and no male prostitute among the sons of Israel" (Deuteronomy 23:18). Rambam rules that both male and female partners in illicit intercourse are guilty of this biblical sin: "Anyone who fornicates with a woman licentiously (*z'nut*) outside of marriage is liable to biblically-mandated flogging, for he has fornicated with a prostitute" (*MT* Hilkhot Ishut 1:4; also see Hilkhot Na·arah B'tulah 2:17). Another important codifier, Rabbi Jacob ben Asher (c. 1269–c. 1343), agrees in his *Arba·ah Turim* at *AT* Even Ha-eizer 26.

However, most authorities reject this view, beginning with Maimonides' famous interlocutors, Rabbi Abraham ben David (called Ravad, c. 1125–1198) and Rabbi Moses ben Naḥman (called Naḥmanides or Ramban, 1194–1270). Indeed, the prevailing view is that non-marital sex is forbidden by rabbinic decree (cf., e.g., *SA* Even Ha-eizer 26:1). Some explain the reason for this decree as promoting the *mitzvah* of formal marriage, as prescribed in Deuteronomy 24:1: "When a man takes a woman and marries her. . ." This means, they say, that "when a man wishes to have sex, he must do so through formal marriage" (*Responsa of Rabbi Isaac ben Sheshet,* no. 425 [ed. Vilna, 1879, p. 134b], to which may be compared the responsum printed in the *Responsa of Rabbi Solomon ibn Aderet Attributed to Naḥmanides,* no. 284 [ed. Warsaw, 1883, p. 121]). In our day, when marriage has lost some degree of sanctity in people's eyes, this argument may acquire new power: refraining from intercourse until marriage certainly would help a couple feel an added intensity and seriousness to marriage.

Other writers relate the prohibition on non-marital sex to the rabbinic decree against *yiḥud,* that is, forbidding men from being alone with a single woman and, in some sources, even from looking at an unmarried woman (cf., e.g., *BT* Avodah Zarah 20a or 36b). Given such a stringent restriction, the sages could not have meant to leave open a loophole permitting consensual pre-marital sex, as long the couple were chaperoned or kept their eyes closed.

Finally, it is worth emphasizing Ravad's alternative interpretation of the prohibitions of *k'deishah* in Deuteronomy and *z'nut* in Leviticus, which are the specific concepts Maimonides used as the basis of his ban on all non-marital intercourse. Ravad reads these prohibitions as forbidding Jews from becoming—or hiring—what we would generically call prostitutes: women who "make themselves available and who surrender themselves to any and every man," or women "who sit in a brothel." (These comments appear in Ravad's glosses to *MT* Hilkhot Ishut 1:4 and Hilkhot Na·arah B'tulah 2:17.) Even according to Ravad's relatively lenient ruling on premarital sex, the Torah is still understood clearly to be forbidding Jewish men and women from participating in sex commerce on either the supply- or demand-side. For his part, Naḥmanides concurs in his Torah commentary, explaining Deuteronomy 23:18 as a commandment ordaining that Jewish authorities eradicate the base and exploitative business of prostitution from their locales.

The Laws of Niddah and Single Women

In the responsum mentioned above, Rabbi Isaac ben Sheshet raises another commonly cited reason for banning premarital sex: unmarried sex partners will almost inevitably violate the laws of *niddah,* the prohibitions surrounding men's contact with menstruating women. As is well known, Torah law (at Leviticus 15:19) prohibits men and women from having sex while a woman is menstruating for a minimum of seven days from the expected or actual onset of her period until she immerses herself in the ritual bath called a *mikveh* (as explained by Maimonides at *MT* Hilkhot Issurei Bi·ah 4:3). Without immersion, the prohibition lasts indefinitely and its violation carries the penalty of *kareit,* usually understood to denote a premature death imposed directly by heaven. "Menstruants . . . can only rise from impurity by immersion. Even many years after [bleeding ceases], a man who has sex with such a woman is liable to *kareit* unless she has immersed properly in a proper *mikveh*" (*SA* Yoreh Dei·ah 197:1). The general name for the laws that govern menstrual separation and purification is *tohorat ha-mishpaḥah,* family purity. These are discussed in detail by Rabbi Carl N. Astor in his chapter on the Jewish life cycle elsewhere in this volume.

A rabbinic stringency extends the period of separation for seven "clean" days after a woman's bleeding ceases. Also, Torah law prohibits even non-sexual physical contact during the *niddah* period and the subsequent seven-day waiting period until immersion in the *mikveh,* based on the verse "Do not come near a woman during her menstrual separation to reveal her nakedness" (Leviticus 18:19), which the *halakhah* takes as prohibiting any *kirvat basar* or "physical nearness" (*Sifra* Aḥarei Mot, *perek* 13:2, *MT* Hilkhot Issurei Bi·ah 11:18). This law of *niddah* applies to all Jewish women, single or married, old or young (gloss of the Rema to *SA* Yoreh Dei·ah 183:1). By custom, however, unmarried women do not immerse themselves after their periods. Hence, all unmarried women are presumed to be in a state of *niddah.*

Contemporary mores notwithstanding, *tohorat ha-mishpaḥah* has been central to Jewish observance for centuries and still is indispensable to the religious regimen of all Orthodox Jews. Though the laws of *tohorat ha-mishpaḥah* have been derided by some as stigmatizing the healthy female body, lately, it has inspired loyalty among a growing number of non-Orthodox Jews. For years, Conservative authorities were largely silent about this *mitzvah.* But recent writers have undertaken a sympathetic reevaluation of *niddah,* treating it as a celebration of human reproductive power. In 2006, the CJLS approved three papers, by Rabbis Miriam Berkowitz, Susan Grossman, and Avram Reisner, sympathetically expounding the practices surrounding menstruation. Each of these papers advocated some leniencies from the classical practices; for example, Grossman and Reisner permitted couples to jettison the seven additional, rabbinically legislated, "clean" days after bleeding ceases. These papers are all available on the website of the Rabbinical Assembly.

The argument from *niddah* against non-marital sex is not dispositive, however. The *halakhah* expects women to begin visiting the *mikveh* immediately before their weddings (gloss of the Rema to *SA* Yoreh Dei·ah 192:2). The connection between marriage and immersion is rooted in the reasonable assumption that an unmarried woman using the *mikveh* would effectively advertise that she is sexually active, and therefore would probably be too embarrassed to immerse herself (gloss of the Rema to *SA* Even Ha-eizer 26:1). But nothing prohibits an unmarried woman from immersing, even if she might have to endure suspicious questions from the *mikveh* attendant, as Rabbi Grossman stresses in her responsum. Unmarried couples who seek to infuse additional sanctity to their sexual relationship by observing the laws of *niddah* should abstain from sex and other intimate physical contact at prescribed times, after which (either following seven blood-free days, in accordance with the long-practiced norm and the CJLS responsum by Rabbi Berkowitz, or after the minimum of seven days from the onset of menstruation, as argued in the CJLS responsa by Rabbis Grossman and Reisner), the woman should immerse after sundown. If an unmarried couple has sex following this practice, they would not violate the biblical *niddah* prohibitions.

Accidental Marriage?

According to tradition, one way to contract a marriage is for the couple to have sexual relations (*M* Kiddushin 1:1). This being the case, might Jewish couples have created countless unintended marriages by having non-marital sex, thus making adulterers and *mamzeirim* of countless unwitting people? The question of whether non-marital sex actually contracts marriage has a long history, beginning in geonic times and continuing until today. The issue turns on an optimistic legal presumption that no one would willfully engage in illicit sexual relations. "A person would not intend his own sexual intercourse to be an act of mere harlotry (*be'ilat z'nut*)," says the Talmud, but instead can be presumed to have intended by his act to contract marriage (*BT* Y'vamot 107a). In pre-modern times, when non-marital intercourse was surely much rarer than today, this may have been a reasonable assumption about people's motives. But modern Jews often marry years after they become sexually active and it seems entirely clear that they do not mean to wed when they go to bed. Should we base our presumptions about their state of mind on the talmudic lesson cited above? Are college students who maintain a two-year exclusive sexual relationship to be considered married? What about a couple who live together for four years before splitting up? Are their subsequent relationships reasonably to be considered adulterous?

A minority view with some contemporary adherents does indeed hold that, even without a wedding, when a couple behaves as married people do, cohabiting and maintaining an exclusive sexual relationship, their union is an example of the kind of non-ideal but real marriage that can be dissolved only by formal divorce. In practice, couples who live together without formal *kiddushin* stray close to accidentally contracting a halakhic marriage. Jewish couples who live with a person with whom they are sexually intimate and then marry another should know that a minority of Orthodox authorities may regard their children as *mamzeirim* or refuse to perform their subsequent weddings. (The most prominent advocate of this position was Rabbi Yosef Eliyahu Henkin; see his *Peirushei Ivra* [New York, 1950], pp. 87–117. Although in 2000, the CJLS accepted the view of Rabbi Elie Kaplan Spitz that rabbis should render *mamzeirut* "inoperative" by refusing to hear evidence of such status [*CJLS Responsa 1991–2000,* pp. 558–586], Conservative Jews should also be aware that our Orthodox brothers and sisters take this matter very seriously. Thus, Conservative Jews could still experience heartache if they discover that they or their children are unable to marry those whom they choose.)

Most authorities, however, follow Maimonides, who states that only formal *kiddushin* according to the traditions of Moses and Israel can create a valid marriage that requires a *get* for dissolution (*MT* Hilkhot Geirushin 10:18–19; *SA* Even Ha-eizer 26:1 and 149:6; Rabbi Yeḥiel Mikhel Epstein, *Arukh Hashulḥan,* Even Ha-eizer 149:11–13 and Rabbi Moshe Feinstein, *Igg'rot Moshe,* Even Ha-eizer 4:59, ed. New York, 1985, pp. 116–117). They rule that sex is presumed to indicate marriage only when a couple has explicitly indicated their intention to marry according to Jewish tradition. According to this view, then, non-marital sexual relations cannot lead to inadvertent marriage.

Conservative authorities have taken conflicting stances on this question. The Va·ad Halakhah of the Rabbinical Assembly of Israel unanimously endorsed a 1991 responsum by Rabbi Pesaḥ Schindler, following Maimonides on this question, which denied halakhic standing to any relationship that lacks formal *kiddushin* according to Jewish practice (including those granted legal stature by nonreligious civil marriage ceremonies) and which also affirmed the prohibition on all non-marital intercourse. On the other hand, the Joint Beit Din of the Conservative movement, under the leadership of Rabbi Mayer Rabinowitz and following an opinion of Rabbi Isaac Klein, requires a *get* to dissolve a civil marriage. Individuals who have lived intimately with members of the opposite sex should consult a rabbi to discuss their status and determine whether they should execute a formal divorce before a subsequent marriage.

Contemporary Concubines?

One additional Jewish legal concept should be addressed with respect to sexual relations among single people: the aforementioned status of the concubine, called *pilegesh* in Hebrew. From time to time in the annals of halakhic discourse, concubinage arrangements have been invoked to resolve painful personal problems, such as when common-law couples could not marry under Jewish law. In such cases, rabbis occasionally directed couples to remain together as man and concubine without formal marriage. (For example, Rabbi David Zvi Hoffman took this view in *Responsum M'lammeid L'ho·il,* part 3, responsum 8 [ed. Frankfurt, 1926, pt. 3, pp. 16–17].) In contemporary times, some suggest employing concubinage in place of standard marriages, thus, at least theoretically, preempting *agunah* tragedies. Since most authorities hold that a relationship with a *pilegesh* is not a formal marriage and thus requires no *get* to dissolve, no such woman needs to feel herself "anchored" to her mate. (The status of *agunot* is discussed in more detail above by Rabbi Carl Astor in his chapter on the Jewish life cycle.)

A few years ago, Professor Zvi Zohar of Bar-Ilan University floated the extraordinary suggestion that concubinage offers observant single people a halakhic rubric for non-marital sexual relationships. (This article can be found in the Israeli journal *Akdamut* 17 [Shevat, 5766], pp. 11–31 published alongside three critical responses, pp. 33–82.) Zohar notes that in the Israeli "national-religious" community—which, in this respect, resembles modern Orthodox and observant non-Orthodox Jews in North America—people appropriately delay marriage until they attain emotional and financial maturity, but have sex nonetheless. Should they simply be considered sinners? Zohar sees concubinage as a way for well-intentioned people to remain within Torah norms by committing to exclusive, ethical sexual relationships without marriage, a solution that would also allow them to observe *niddah* laws without embarrassment. Zohar marshals a sound argument that *pilegesh* arrangements should be halakhically valid, although he probably underestimates the weight of medieval and early modern authorities siding with Maimonides to oppose this view.

Conservative Jews should reject this suggestion on moral grounds. An exploitative system like concubinage—applied however loosely or metaphorically—can provide no model for intimate relationships of dignity and mutuality. As Michal Tikuchinski and Rachel Sperber Frankel point out in their rebuttal to Zohar, *pilagshot* through history probably were not self-possessed women in ethical relationships. They were "servants, maids, non-Jews, rape victims, widows, sluts, and orphans. In contrast, the men who held concubines were otherwise married, or were ineligible to marry, or sometimes were financially wealthy and poor in scruples" (*Akdamut* [Shevat, 5766], p. 71). Perhaps modern *pilagshot* would not be exploited so basely, but such arrangements seem more likely to invite abuse than to foster care and responsibility.

Nevertheless, Sex Outside Marriage

Any honest reporting of Jewish tradition on sexuality must affirm marriage as the ideal setting for intercourse. The exclusive fidelity of marriage permits couples to understand sex as an expression of the kind of most intimate love, care, and joy that characterize marriage at its finest. Furthermore, understanding marriage as the exclusive licit venue for sexual relations also highlights the role of sexuality in the performance of one of the most sacred of all *mitzvot:* the commandment to create new life and carry the human community forward into the next generation. In most cases, especially among young people, unmarried couples are unprepared to face that possible outcome of their behavior. Since it is ethically dubious to risk consequences one cannot handle, and since no form of birth control is perfect, people unprepared for parenthood ideally should refrain from sexual intercourse. In the end, Judaism teaches us that the sanctity of sex is inextricably tied to the features of fidelity and procreative capacity within a marriage. Conservative *halakhah* should affirm that marriage with *kiddushin* and a *k'tubbah* constitutes the ideal setting for sexual relations. In the vocabulary of traditional law, sexual intercourse belongs in marriage *l'khat·ḥillah,* that is to say, as its optimal setting.

Promiscuous sex without commitment is a physical pleasure that deliberately avoids both the spirituality of ultimate intimacy and the commandment of procreation. *Z'nut,* therefore, is a degraded version of sexual intercourse (Dorff, *"This Is My Friend,"* p. 31). This is why traditional *halakhah* forbids licentious sex, and why Conservative *halakhah* affirms that prohibition. In the language of traditional law, it is forbidden to have multiple partners in the same time period or to have sex without emotional engagement or meaningful, enduring commitment.

But if marriage is the ideal venue for sex, and if promiscuity is deemed altogether forbidden, might there be some middle ground status to assign to sexual relations that take place within a committed relationship that is not a marriage? Adapting another traditional term, is there a *b'di-avad* condition, a non-optimal but legally defensible sexuality for single people?

One way to begin to address this question in halakhic terms would be to focus on the relative severity of the prohibitions involved. While a rabbinic maxim (at *M* Avot 2:1) holds that one should treat minor commandments as seriously as major ones, Jewish law also demands moral reasoning in prioritizing *mitzvot.* Borrowing an analogy from another area of *halakhah,* in certain situations it is better—or at least less bad—to sip the broth of a forbidden stew than to eat the forbidden meat within (*BT* Yoma 82a). As noted, most authorities regard sex outside of marriage as a rabbinic prohibition. That certainly does not mean we should take it lightly, but it means we should see this prohibition in perspective. Indeed, in some ways the classical sages themselves treated it as a comparatively lighter rule, as two examples illustrate. *Kohanim* may not marry women who have slept with men forbidden to them. But violating the prohibition on non-marital sex is not considered serious enough to disqualify an unmarried woman from later marrying a priest (*BT* Y'vamot 61b, *SA* Even Ha-eizer 6:17). Also, even in mishnaic times, non-marital sex was not entirely unheard of. In Judah, in the south of the Land of Israel (in contrast to the rabbinic heartland in the Galilee), engaged couples were commonly left unchaperoned, and thus had the opportunity to have sex (or, at least, to be tempted to do so). The sages did not necessarily approve of this "loose" behavior, but neither did they change the Judean practice. The strongest action they took was to deny Judean men the power to sue if their brides proved not to be virgins. After all, given their common intimacy, who was most likely responsible for this state of affairs? (*M* K'tubbot 1:5, *BT* K'tubbot 12a).

Another way to develop an approach to non-marital sex might be to focus on the moral qualities such a relationship potentially embodies. For example, while non-marital sex remains forbidden, a relationship that manifests honesty, mutuality, fidelity, respect, and a sense that one's partner too was created in God's image is less troubling Jewishly than one that lacks these virtues. Rabbi Dorff pursues this argument for basing sexual ethics on moral qualities even in unsanctioned, non-marital relationships, in his pamphlet *"This Is My Beloved"* (see especially pp. 30–31). In this view, unmarried couples could fulfill a number of specific laws that would imbue even an unsanctioned relationship with virtue, and manifest the high degree of emotional commitment and affection needed to grant dignity and worth to any sexual relationship. Exclusive fidelity is first on that list of virtues and is presumed in every Judaic discussion on sex and holiness, while infidelity is universally regarded as poison. As the Talmud teaches (at *BT* Sotah 3b), "Promiscuity eats through a home like a worm eats through a plant." The *Shulḥan Arukh* catalogues other prohibitions: "A person must not have sex in front of other people. . . . It is forbidden to have sex in public places, like markets, streets, parks, or forests, but only in a private home. . . . A person must not have sex with his wife when he is angry with her. If he has resolved in his heart to divorce her, even if he does not loathe her, he must not have sex with her (i.e., even while still married). A person must not have sex when either partner is intoxicated. A person must not have sex while fantasizing about someone else" (*SA* Even Ha-eizer 25:2–10). Another important *halakhah* about sexual modesty demands that people not discuss their sex lives with outside parties. Although the Torah repeatedly forbids lying in general (see, e.g., Exodus 23:7), the sages regarded it as honorable to lie about one's sex life to preserve one's privacy and one's partner's modesty (*BT* Bava M'tzi·a 23b).

Unmarried people should uphold these same norms in their sexual relationships. If these are ignored, sex will be cold-hearted when it should be tender, crass when it should be modest, deceptive when it should be sincere, unthinking—or, God forbid, nonconsensual—when it should be the product of mutual feelings of passion and love. Without mutual commitment to these values, a sex partner can become only a warm body to exploit for one's own immediate comfort. (For example, the Talmud, at *BT* M'gillah 13a, reports that King Ahasuerus took Esther to bed to ease the cold of a long winter night.) Such an orientation fundamentally degrades one's partner by turning him or her into an object, potentially risking the eventual violation of the commandment: "Do not hate your fellow human being in your heart" (Leviticus 19:17).

In this vein, we must stress that a single person in a non-marital sexual relationship may never abet another's adultery. A single man who sleeps with a married woman is guilty of formal adultery, a death penalty crime, and a single woman who sleeps with a married man is guilty of the same sin in moral, if not in strictly legal, terms.

Another halakhic approach to non-marital sex might favor sharing sexual intimacy without penetration. In halakhic terminology, intercourse only happens at the moment of *ha·ara·ah,* when the tip of the penis penetrates the vagina. The various other ways people might stimulate each other are called intimacy *derekh eivarim* (literally, "of the limbs") or the intimacy of *n'shikah* (literally, "kissing") in which the penis touches, but does not enter, the vagina. To be sure, all authorities forbid intimacy *derekh eivarim* outside of marriage; but most agree this prohibition is a rabbinic enactment, a "fence around the Torah" designed to forestall more serious violations. Since even intercourse outside of marriage is only a rabbinic prohibition, forbidding sexual contact even *derekh eivarim* could be described as "building a fence around another fence," which the *halakhah* generally regards as excessive and counterproductive (see *BT* Beitzah 3a).

Moreover, rabbinic restrictions are conditioned on the public's ability to meet their stipulations. "A court must not enact a decree unless most of the public can fulfill it," the Talmud decrees at *BT* Bava Kamma 79b. Technically, this principle restrains a court's legislative power to enact new laws, and should not undermine already enacted ones. Still, perhaps the rabbinic rules against sex *derekh eivarim* might be considered beyond most contemporary people's capacity to observe. Those who wish to keep their non-marital sexual acts within halakhic boundaries might consider limiting their sexual activities to this category.

At the same time, the idea that sex *derekh eivarim* is appropriate for non-marital sexual activity needs several halakhic qualifications. First, there are the *niddah* restrictions. As noted above, until a woman immerses in the *mikveh* following menstruation, all affectionate physical contact remains forbidden. Next, one must reckon with Maimonides' view that even nonpenetrative contact between those forbidden to each other is forbidden by the Torah, not merely by rabbinic law: "We are forbidden from drawing near to any sexual prohibition, even without penetration, such as hugging and kissing and similarly promiscuous acts. . . . Figuratively, the Torah at Leviticus 18:6 can be read to say: 'Do not draw near to any intimacy that will bring in its wake the revelation of nakedness'" (*Sefer Ha-mitzvot,* negative commandment no. 353). This view is consistent with Maimonides' claim that all sex outside of marriage is biblically prohibited. Although Maimonides holds a minority position here, it is still a formidable one given his immense halakhic stature. Nevertheless, estimable authorities challenge Maimonides, and we may build a more permissive conclusion upon their objections. In particular, Naḥmanides argues that the prohibition against "nearing" sexual prohibition by "hugging and kissing" and non-penetrative sex is a rabbinic enactment (*Hassagot L'sefer Ha-mitzvot La-rambam, ad loc.*). To be sure, he regards the prohibition as in force, merely of a lower status. As noted, however, Conservative *halakhah* might set such rabbinic restrictions aside on the grounds that most people today are incapable of upholding it.

Finally, there is the prohibition of destroying semen, which the Talmud homiletically compares to murder (at *BT* Niddah 13a). Influenced partly by the mystical ideas that sperm ejaculated other than to produce children produces demons instead, and that wasting sperm is somehow equivalent to killing one's own children (see *Zohar* I 219b), most authorities strongly condemned the ejaculation of semen except in the context of genital intercourse. In turn, this not only prohibits masturbation by men, but also bans the kind of "hugging and kissing" that might lead to climax, including even *coitus interruptus* (*SA* Even Ha-eizer 23). Conservative *halakhah* should follow the alternative line of argument pursued by the Tosafot instead. These medieval talmudists note that since the Talmud permits anal sex, which cannot possibly result in conception, it follows that destroying semen cannot be forbidden absolutely. Rather, they taught, the prohibition against wasting semen applies only to men who systematically avoid procreation altogether; occasional non-procreative ejaculation, on the other hand, is not forbidden *per se* (Tosafot to *BT* Y'vamot 34b, *s.v. v'lo k'ma·aseh*). Rabbi Joseph Karo was aghast at this. "One who cares about his soul will shun such a decision . . . if [he] had seen what the Zohar wrote about the severity of the punishment for wasteful emission of semen—that it is the worst sin in the Torah—he would never have written what he did" (*Beit Yoseif* to *AT* Even Ha-eizer 25, *s.v. umah she-katav*). Rabbi Karo's statement demonstrates how a legal authority's aesthetic and moral values shape his determination of law. Given our society and prevailing views of sexuality and science, Conservative *halakhah* cannot compare the wasting of semen to the murder of children. Nor can this prohibition be maintained as the basis for a ban against masturbation or other forms of non-penetrative sexuality. Nonetheless, this lenient view should not be used as a means of avoiding the *mitzvah* of procreation, which people should strive to fulfill as soon as they are ready and able.

No *halakhah* forbids female masturbation. Some talmudic commentators did ban it, on the grounds that the prohibition on destroying "seed" also applies to women, whom they assumed emit some procreative substance in sexual climax, just like men. Conservative *halakhah* should not base itself on the errors of medieval medicine. Even if one wished to re-affirm the prohibition against male masturbation on the grounds of destroying semen, as Orthodox authorities do, this would have no relevance for women's autoeroticism or orgasm outside of intercourse.

After Divorce

All that has been said about non-marital sex applies to single people regardless of whether they have or have not been married previously. However, divorced people should be aware of some specific *halakhot* that apply to them. First, rabbinic tradition requires that a woman wait at least ninety days before remarrying after a divorce, thus guaranteeing her ability to be perfectly certain that she is not pregnant with her ex-husband's child (*SA* Even Ha-eizer 13:1). Nowadays, when women who suspect they might be pregnant can take tests that yield conclusive results, the length of the waiting period is less critical. Also, the *halakhah* presumes that if a divorced couple were to have sex again together, that act would constitute formal remarriage. Then, should they wish to redissolve their new "marriage," they would have to do so formally, i.e., with a *get* (*M* Gittin 8:9, *BT* Gittin 81a, *SA* Even Ha-eizer 149:1).

Remaining Single

"God did not create the world as a wasteland, but so that people would dwell in it," the prophet says at Isaiah 45:18. The talmudic sages interpreted this to mean that each of us—if we can—should play our indispensable roles in God's providential plan by bringing another generation to life. Each human being bears God's image, so creating more people expands the divine presence in the world, more than merely metaphorically. In contrast, refusing to have children withholds the divine image from the world, and is homiletically compared to murder, which similarly diminishes the presence of God (*BT* Y'vamot 62a–64a). Moreover, Genesis 2:18 asserts that "it is not good for a person to be alone." God's wisdom provided that Adam would find a mate and that their children should seek to do the same. When men and women come together, God's presence dwells between them in a way no single individual can experience on his or her own (*BT* Sotah 17a).

These teachings, among others, add meaning to the Torah's commandments that Jews should marry and have at least two children, as the rabbis understood the famous verse "And God blessed them and said, 'Be fruitful and multiply, fill up the earth and subdue it'" (*SA* Even Ha-eizer 1:1–8). Rashi observes that, when this directive appears in Genesis 9:7, it functions as a commandment to Noah to procreate. But at Genesis 1:28, it is not a true commandment prescribing behavior, but rather a divine blessing (see Rashi's comment to Genesis 9:7, and cf. *BT* K'tubbot 5a). Indeed, an ancient *midrash* understands this phrase "be fruitful and multiply" as the blessing God pronounced at Adam and Eve's wedding (*B'reishit Rabbah* 8:13).

Both blessing and obligation, the compound *mitzvot* of marriage and procreation express three main propositions: that we are obliged to maintain the human community through raising children (*SA* Even Ha-eizer 1:1); that human felicity is best found with a loving partner, even if a couple proves unable to have children (*AT* Even Ha-eizer 1, based on *B'reishit Rabbah* 17:2); and that we should commit ourselves to an exclusive relationship in which our natural sexual impulses can be satisfied and sanctified, without being corrupted (*SA* Even Ha-eizer 25:1, *Arukh Ha-shulḥan,* Even Ha-eizer 1:11–14).

Classical *halakhah* commands men to procreate, while not obligating women (*SA* Even Ha-eizer 1:1 and 1:13; *Arukh Ha-shulḥan,* Even Ha-eizer 1:2). This counterintuitive approach seems to assume that all women would want children, while men would have to be commanded to bear the burdens of fatherhood. Thus, all halakhic authorities regard a man as legally obliged to marry, and see marrying as a necessary step toward fulfilling the *mitzvah* of procreation. Sephardic tradition even favors compulsory marriage (*SA* Even Ha-eizer 1:3) although Ashkenazim held that even when Jewish courts had police power, they should not compel a man to marry (gloss of the Rema, *ad loc.*). In a parallel discussion concerning women, a minority position holds that they too are obliged to procreate (*BT* Y'vamot 65b–66a) and a minority insist that women too must marry (see, e.g., the gloss of Rema to *SA* Even Ha-eizer 1:13). However, the majority view follows Maimonides, who denies the existence of such a halakhic requirement (see *MT* Hilkhot Issurei Bi·ah 21:26). Conservative *halakhah* should note this formal distinction between men's and women's obligations, but should assign it no practical significance. After all, since men and women need each other to raise up new generations, Jewish women should feel ethically obliged to fulfill the *mitzvot* of marriage and procreation. (The question of whether same-sex unions could fulfill the obligation to marry is discussed in the next chapter by Rabbi Elliot Dorff.)

As we outlined with respect to premarital sex, Conservative *halakhah* should distinguish between those laws which constitute aspirations for ideal observance (labeled in Hebrew *l'khat·ḥillah*), those which unambiguously forbid behaviors incompatible with Jewish values, and those that occupy a more elastic middle ground, which are defensible accommodations to the rough reality of our world (i.e., labeled as valid *ex post facto* or, to use the traditional talmudic term, *b'di-avad*). As an ideal, the Jewish legal tradition expects people to marry and to have children. Doubtless, most people want this for themselves as well. At the other end of the spectrum, Jewish law rejects a person simply choosing to remain unwed because of temperament or personal preference. All Jewish authorities agree that God calls us to build relationships with loving partners.

But most unmarried or childless people are not flouting *halakhah* or fleeing from the *mitzvot,* nor are most inveterate loners. Most have simply not had the good fortune to find the right person or have struggled unsuccessfully with infertility issues despite their own best efforts and extensive medical intervention. *Halakhah* should not take a harsh tone toward people who doubtless wish to fulfill these commandments, but find themselves unable to do so for social or personal reasons. Such cases should call forth regret and empathy, not censure.

For single Jews, the *halakhah* offers both encouragement and sensitivity. Practically speaking, the *mitzvot* of marriage and procreation cannot wait indefinitely; single Jews should pursue these commandments as soon as is practicable. Yet the *halakhah* also maintains a well-attested view that no one is expected to accept a bad match, and no one should ever be forced to marry against his or her will (*BT* Kiddushin 41a). Even the most fervently pro-marriage sources in our tradition do not prefer any marriage whatsoever to no marriage at all, as can be illustrated with a talmudic ruling: "One who vows to purchase a house or marry a woman . . . is not compelled to fulfill the vow immediately, but only when he finds one suitable for him" (*BT* Bava Kamma 80a, *SA* Yoreh Dei·ah 219:1). This interesting text proposes that one may even postpone fulfilling a vow—itself a possible biblical transgression—rather than be pressured into an unhappy union. Our legal tradition is even aware that pressuring people into marriage can indirectly promote adultery, since a loveless couple will eventually grow apart and might end up seeking other partners. Thus, the *halakhah* discourages people from marrying across very wide age gaps, assuming the partners will be unable to satisfy each other (*BT* Sanhedrin 76b, *MT* Hilkhot Issurei Bi·ah 21:26, *SA* Even Ha-eizer 2:9). A trenchant talmudic passage observes that a loving couple can sleep on a bed as narrow as a knife's edge, but, for a loveless pair, a bed sixty cubits wide would be too small (*BT* Sanhedrin 7a). Among other considerations that could legitimately delay marriage are the need for financial stability and the need to progress further in Torah study (*BT* Sotah 44a, *MT* Hilkhot Ishut 15:2, *SA* Even Ha-eizer 1:3). To sum up, the *halakhah* does not sanction the personal decision never to marry and directs single Jews to pursue marriage, the ideal venue for the blessings and obligations of love and child rearing. Still, single people have no obligation to marry anyone other than a suitable and loving mate.

Single People and Children

It is a biological fact that every child has both mother and father. But biology is no longer destiny. Increasingly, single people are becoming parents, by design or not, and building nontraditional families. Indeed, more than 40 percent of women who gave birth in the United States in 2008 were unmarried, according to the National Center for Health Statistics. This trend can be traced to the prevalence of non-marital sex (since inevitably there will be unplanned pregnancies), advances in reproductive technologies, economic empowerment (which enables women to bear children outside the traditionally enjoined framework of a committed relationship with a man), and changing social views (such as the common, if not universal, legal permission for single people to adopt children). As a result of these shifts in modern circumstances, unmarried Jews face life-defining choices regarding parenthood that would have seemed far-fetched to generations past. The *halakhah* must offer them normative guidance.

Birth Control

The larger issue of the place of birth control in Jewish law is discussed below by Rabbi Avram I. Reisner in his chapter in this volume on Jewish medical ethics. Here I will discuss only the aspects of the issue relating specifically to single people.

Being a parent is the paramount ethical responsibility. Ideally, people who are not prepared for children should not risk producing them inadvertently. Until the day they are ready to accept the blessing and shoulder the commandment of bringing new life into the world, sexually-active singles must use some method of contraception to guard themselves against assuming responsibilities they are unprepared to fulfill. Over the past centuries, halakhic authorities have generally discouraged contraception. But they were ruling for married couples, whom they encouraged to reproduce without delay. When thinking about the issue as it applies to sexually-active single people, however, a different conclusion will be appropriate.

Admittedly, most contraceptive methods present the halakhically faithful with certain technical legal problems. As noted above, only men are legally commanded to procreate. Therefore, the *halakhah* generally frowns on the use of condoms, since men who use them actively destroy semen, which is taken to nullify the *mitzvah* of procreation. Nevertheless, sexually active bachelors should use condoms, since this both can inhibit conception and—especially in the age of AIDS—can save lives. The Torah obligates us to preserve our own lives with these unambiguous words: "For you must guard yourselves very well" (Deuteronomy 4:15). The Talmud teaches that "whatever poses a danger to life is more strictly forbidden than a ritual prohibition" (*BT* Ḥullin 10a and *SA* Ḥoshen Mishpat 427:9–10, and cf. the Rema's comment to *SA* Yoreh Dei·ah 116:5), and such precautions certainly take precedence over delaying the fulfillment of the *mitzvah* of procreation. Condoms are the only devices that reduce—although without totally eliminating—the risk of AIDS and other sexually transmitted diseases. If either partner may have been exposed to AIDS or another such disease, they must use condoms if they engage in sexual intercourse. If either partner definitely carries HIV, they must refrain from sexual contact that exchanges bodily fluids.

Condoms are effective—about 98 percent of the time when used correctly—but can be used incorrectly, in which case their effectiveness drops to 85 percent, or break, in which case they are of little use. Sexually active single people might also use additional, even more reliable methods of contraception in addition to condoms. Traditionally, the *halakhah* prefers women's contraceptive methods, such as birth control pills, IUDs, or diaphragms, because women who use them do not, in so doing, nullify a *mitzvah* obligation. Sexually-active single Jewish women should obtain and use one or another of these devices. In principle, any of these might be permissible, although authorities generally have preferred the pill (e.g., the *Tzitz Eliezer* vol. 9, responsum 51, part 2, ch. 4, ed. Jerusalem, 1965, pp. 219–223), since it indirectly inhibits conception without actually destroying spermatozoa, and does not interfere with a woman's subsequent ability to have children. This is also the position taken in a responsum by Rabbis Miriam Berkowitz and Mark Popovsky approved by the CJLS in 2010. Interestingly, the talmudic sage Rabbi Yossi proposed that any unmarried woman having non-marital sex may be assumed to use some sort of makeshift diaphragm "to protect herself" (*BT* K'tubbot 37a). The Talmud neither explicitly authorizes nor forbids this practice, but Rabbi Yossi apparently regarded it as prudent. We should behave no less thoughtfully today.

No halakhic authorities regard abortion as a Jewish woman's right to exercise at will. Indeed, Judaism regards aborting a fetus as a very grave move, to be undertaken only as a last resort. Absent extreme circumstances, abortion is usually forbidden. In 1983, the CJLS stated the following by consensus: "An abortion is justifiable if a continuation of pregnancy might cause the mother severe physical or psychological harm, or when the fetus is judged by competent medical opinion as severely defective" (*CJLS Responsa 1980–1990*, p. 817). This issue is discussed in detail in Rabbi Reisner's chapter on medical ethics.

Artificial Insemination

In earlier times, children born outside of marriage were generally conceived accidentally. But in an age of changed mores and dramatic technological advances, women may become pregnant without having sex at all through artificial insemination. Most often, this method is employed by infertile couples, either using the husband's semen (known as AIH, or artificial insemination by husband's semen) or that of another donor (DI). Nowadays, increasing numbers of unmarried women are electing to become pregnant through DI. Various motivations may prompt a single Jewish woman's decision to have a child on her own. Most will choose to have children through DI because they deeply desire to be mothers and to raise a Jewish child with love, but have not had the good fortune to find the right husband. (Also, DI is usually the most reasonable route to pregnancy for lesbian couples.) Can the *halakhah* sanction this practice?

Most halakhic rulings on artificial insemination address only its use by married couples and, at least to date, few halakhic authorities have considered whether single Jewish women may use DI to conceive a child. As of this writing, in spring 2012, Rabbi Susan Grossman is preparing a paper for the CJLS which will permit DI for single women, but that paper has yet to appear. Of those who have written on the topic to date, including Conservative authorities, none has permitted it. Among Orthodox authorities, for example, Rabbi Eliezer Waldenberg, in a responsum published in *Tzitz Eliezer* (vol. 9, responsum 51, part 4, ch. 2, ed. Jerusalem, 1865, pp. 246–248), forbids DI in all cases on two grounds. First, there is a possibility, remote but not negligible, that children born from DI will find themselves inadvertently in an incestuous relationship. Because sperm banks use a single donor for as many as fifty different inseminations, because men can donate repeatedly over time, and because donor records are kept confidential to forestall paternity suits, it is conceivable that two people with the same biological father could marry. Second, Rabbi Waldenberg strongly emphasizes the Talmud's imperative (documented, e.g., at *BT* Y'vamot 42b) to establish biological paternity with certainty. Rashi comments there that "the divine presence only rests on those who know with certainty the parentage of their children." By definition, DI conceals this knowledge.

Among Conservative authorities, Rabbi Elliot Dorff wrote that "the psychological and social implications of creating families in these new ways are far from clear and thus a formal ruling regarding them on behalf of the Jewish tradition is premature" (*Matters of Life and Death,* p. 114). In his writings on medical ethics, including a 1994 responsum unanimously approved by the CJLS, Rabbi Dorff has argued that the question of single mothers becoming pregnant through DI must be evaluated by studying the success of single-parent families psychologically and socially (*CJLS Responsa 1991–2000*, pp. 461–509). Since Jewish tradition favors two-parent families, and since sociological data suggests that children raised in single-parent homes often do less well than those raised in two-parent homes, Rabbi Dorff believes that the burden of proof has not yet been met freely to permit DI for single women.

Rabbi David Golinkin, head of the Va·ad Halakhah of the Rabbinical Assembly of Israel, also rules against DI for single women (*Responsa of the Va·ad Halakhah*, vol. 3, pp. 83ff.). His 1989 responsum, passed by a 4–1 vote, argues similarly to Rabbi Waldenberg in fearing unintentional incest and uncertain paternity. Since women have no formal obligation to procreate, Rabbi Golinkin writes, a man is forbidden to donate sperm to help her, and she is forbidden to suborn a man to waste semen. Furthermore, Rabbi Golinkin views single motherhood as weakening the traditional Jewish family and feels that single women should therefore subordinate their non-obligatory desire for children to the common weal. Instead, they should adopt children, or redouble their efforts to find suitable mates, he writes. Rabbi Golinkin quotes approvingly the statement of former British chief rabbi Immanuel Jakobovits to the effect that DI is human "stud-farming," which "severs the link between the procreation of children and marriage" and leaves procreation "arbitrary and mechanical, robbed of those mystic and intimately human qualities which make man a partner with God in the creative propagation of the race" (ibid.).

Nevertheless, pending Rabbi Grossman's responsum, at least five lenient lines of argument can be advanced in favor of DI for unmarried Jewish women.

First, as a technical point of law, it is all but impossible that a DI child could fall into inadvertent incest. Outside Israel, the sperm donor may be presumed to be a gentile, whose biological parentage has no halakhic standing (*SA* Yoreh Dei·ah 269:3). As Rabbi Moshe Feinstein argues, therefore, even if a child of DI were somehow to marry a biological sibling (i.e., one born from the sperm of the same donor), this would not constitute incest in halakhic terms (*Igg'rot Moshe*, Even Ha-eizer 2:11, ed. New York, 1963, pp. 322–324). In this sense, therefore, an anonymous gentile sperm donor would be halakhically preferable to an anonymous Jewish donor. (Some sperm banks provide information on the religion, race, or ethnicity of the donor, which makes it possible for a woman to choose.)

Second, even when an anonymous Jewish donor is used, there are ways to ensure that no inadvertent incest (even in halakhic terms) occurs when DI children marry. Indelicate though it may be, DI children should ask their prospective in-laws if any possibility exists that the couple share a biological relationship. Then, if necessary, DNA testing can resolve the question. These questions could be embarrassing, but better a few awkward moments—which in all events take place within a relationship of honesty and trust—than possibly transgressing a biblical injunction.

Third, using a known, directed donor (such as, for example, a known friend) obviates virtually every technical problem pertaining to anonymous donations. This method provides the child with knowledge of his or her paternity and his or her father's medical history, and conceivably makes plausible a relationship for the child with his or her biological father. It may also provide a childless Jewish man, heterosexual or gay, with an opportunity to fulfill the *mitzvah* of procreation.

Fourth, it seems ethically flimsy to argue that difficulties pertaining to single parenthood should preclude DI from the outset. This is tantamount to saying that DI children are better off not existing at all, rather than suffering social or economic hardships, which in all events are entirely surmountable in stable single-parent families. Besides, today's single DI mother may marry tomorrow. Should the *halakhah* prevent a Jewish child from entering the world because he or she might suffer particular problems in life? As Rabbi Dorff argues, in light of the demographic crisis facing the Jewish people, our tendency ought to be to maximize, not restrict, the number of Jews in the world (*Matters of Life and Death*, pp. 95–96).

Finally, it is instructive to compare the situation of DI children with another field of *halakhah* that maintains a category for prohibiting or permitting acts based on unintended negative consequences. Shabbat laws, for example, codify that "unintended labor is permitted" (*BT* Shabbat 42a). Thus, for example, one may drag a chair across the yard, even though its legs may dig a furrow in the soil, which would be forbidden if it were an intentional act. However, this law applies only when the negative consequence of the act is not certain to follow. The chair legs might not cut into the soil at all! If the negative consequences are *inevitable,* however, the act would be forbidden. This concept is expressed in halakhic sources with a pithy rhetorical question: "Can you cut off a chicken's head without it dying?" (*BT* Shabbat 75a). Single parenthood is like the former category, not the latter. DI *may* result in social problems for the child and parent. It *may* weaken family structures. But it is not *certain* to do either. It could also result in a happy, healthy Jewish child who lives a life devoted to Torah study, worship, and righteous deeds. When single women are prepared to take the enormous physical, personal, and economic risks to try to raise a Jew, they might rely on this alternative line of reasoning.

Adoption

Adoptive parenthood is not a classical halakhic institution. That is, halakhic sources never consider the modern concept in which a child becomes the "naturalized" child of a couple who are not his or her biological parents. Indeed, there is no classical Hebrew word for adoption; the term *immutz* was coined in modern times. True, the classical sages lavishly praise those who raise children who are not their own biological offspring (as, for example, at *BT* Sanhedrin 19b). But they viewed this as a great act of *tz'dakah* rather than as some sort of virtual parenthood. Thus, as there is no halakhic assumption that adoption is something only a married couple can do, there are no classical obstacles to single people adopting children. There may even be a biblical precedent for single-parent adoption: Mordecai is said to have raised his young cousin Hadassah/Esther, and the Book of Esther makes no reference to him having a wife.

Rabbi Dorff raised the same concerns about single-parent adoption that he discussed regarding DI for single women: "Single parents often do a remarkable job of raising their children, and it is certainly better for a child to have one caring parent than temporary foster parents or no parents at all. Still, if the child could be adopted by two parents, that might well be better for the child's welfare" (*Matters of Life and Death,* p. 114). Rabbi Golinkin concurs that adoption by single parents does pose some of the same problems of DI, including potentially weakening the stability of family as an institution. But on balance, he rules, it is permitted.

The Halakhah of Being Single

For the most part, being single need not affect a Jew's halakhic observance. Being unmarried confers no special duties, nor exempts from any. Certainly, it can be difficult for single people to integrate into communities that often focus on attracting families with young children, educating Hebrew school kids, and celebrating bar and bat mitzvahs. Our communities should generally strive to better serve the unmarried, not only the *kinder* and their parents. At the same time, despite social obstacles, single Jewish adults should pursue their own growth in observance, spiritual depth, and learning, and not wait until marriage. In all areas, these *mitzvah* commitments are no different for the partnered or single. Unmarried Jews should pray and study, give *tz'dakah,* visit the sick, comfort mourners, and keep kosher homes all in exactly the same way their married neighbors do. (True, there is an Ashkenazic tradition that unmarried men do not wear a large outer *tallit* until marriage. But this is a custom, not a rule, and in fact the *Mishnah B'rurah,* one of the major Ashkenazic authorities of the twentieth century, calls this practice "astonishing," since no logic exempts an adult from a *mitzvah* by dint of marital status. [See the *Mishnah B'rurah* to *SA* Oraḥ Ḥayyim 17, note 10.] Presumably those who follow this custom would expect unmarried men to wear the *tallit katan* or four-cornered fringed undergarment to fulfill the *mitzvah* of *tzitzit.*) You don't have to be married to recite Kiddush or light Shabbat candles, or cook celebratory meals, or make Havdalah when sacred times conclude. Although conventional gender and family roles may assign these practices to a father or a mother, in fact *halakhah* considers these *mitzvot* to apply to single men and women equally as to their married counterparts.

When it comes to the rules and ethical standards concerning romantic and sexual relationships, however, Conservative *halakhah* should confront the ways in which single people today face different problems and possibilities than our sages ever imagined. Failing to give guidance in these areas would turn the realms of love and sex, for the vast majority of Jews from their later teens into their twenties and thirties and beyond, into *halakhah*-free zones. It would be to concede that the traditions of Jewish law have nothing to say to the modern situation. That would be faithless. Instead, when we bring even these realms into conversation with our legal traditions, we keep our faith in the renewed the power of *halakhah* to make life meaningful. And we aspire to fulfill "the short verse upon which all the Torah depends," namely: "Know God in all your ways" (Proverbs 3:6, as cited at *BT* B'rakhot 63b).

Same-Sex Relationships

ELLIOT N. DORFF

Classical Jewish tradition, based primarily on Leviticus 18:22 and 20:13, sees same-sex relations between men as forbidden—and, indeed, as an "abomination" (*M* Sanhedrin 7:4, *BT* Sanhedrin 54a, and *MT* Hilkhot Issurei Bi·ah 1:14.) These texts refer to male homosexuality, but rabbinic tradition added a prohibition against sex between women as well (*Sifra* Aḥarei Mot, *parsh'ta* 8:8; *MT* Hilkhot Issurei Bi·ah 21:8, and see *BT* Y'vamot 76a). That view was shared by most Christian and Muslim authors without further discussion until very recently. In fact, the only serious question that ever arose in Jewish literature about homosexuality was whether two men traveling together could share the same bed. While some say no, they could not (following the opinion of Rabbi Judah as cited in the Mishnah at *M* Kiddushin 4:14 and codified by Rabbi Joseph Karo in the *SA* Even Ha-eizer 24), the ultimate halakhic position is that men may share a bed because "Jewish men are not suspected of engaging in same-sex intercourse" (*M* Kiddushin 4:14, *BT* Kiddushin 82a, *MT* Hilkhot Issurei Bi·ah 22:2, and Rabbi Joel Sirkes, *Bayit Ḥadash* to the *AT* Even Ha-eizer 24).

Despite that assertion, contemporary scientists have determined that somewhere between three and ten percent of the human population has always been homosexual in orientation. (The range in estimates stems from differing definitions of homosexuality and from the large numbers of gay individuals who remain closeted.) For centuries, such people either repressed their desires for gay sex, often refusing to admit them even to themselves, or engaged in such sex more or less openly, depending upon the degree to which their society accepted or even lauded it. So, for example, in Plato's *Symposium,* Socrates sees same-sex relations between master and student as a culmination of their intellectual relationship. In modern times, spurred by the new Enlightenment ideas of individual rights, the French Penal Code of 1791 and the Napoleonic Code of 1804 took freedom of contract to its logical conclusion by decriminalizing same-sex relations in private between consenting adults, a precedent followed in the early twentieth century by Belgium, Italy, Luxemburg, Monaco, Portugal, Rumania, Spain, the Netherlands, Mexico, Guatemala, Bolivia, Brazil, Paraguay, Uruguay, and Venezuela. (For a fuller discussion of these developments, see David F. Greenberg, *The Construction of Homosexuality* [Chicago: University of Chicago Press, 1988], p. 352.) In more recent times, the United States (through the U.S. Supreme Court decision *Lawrence v. Texas* 539 U.S. 558 [2003]), as well as Canada, the United Kingdom, and Israel, have also decriminalized gay sex in private by consenting adults.

Rethinking the Matter

New medical knowledge about the etiology of sexuality has led some denominations of Judaism and Christianity to rethink their position regarding gay individuals and even their evaluation of same-sex relationships themselves. For example, since 1973, Reform synagogues whose primary outreach was to gays and lesbians have been accepted as members of the Union of American Hebrew Congregations (now called the Union of Reform Judaism), and in 1990, the Reform seminary, Hebrew Union College-Jewish Institute of Religion, changed its policy to make openly gay or lesbian candidates eligible for admission to rabbinical school. In 2002, the Reform rabbinic organization endorsed the right of rabbis to choose whether or not to perform commitment ceremonies for gays and lesbians, either choice being supported as legitimate by the rabbinic body as a whole. (More material is available at the website of the Central Council of American Rabbis at www.ccarnet.org.)

For their part, most Orthodox spokesmen have made it clear that they think that no change from traditional attitudes is called for. The most liberal among them distinguish between gay sex, which they decry as forbidden, and Jews who engage in such sexual activities, whom they are prepared to accept nevertheless as members of the Jewish community. Even for these Orthodox liberals, such Jews are engaged in a particularly egregious sin, one that Scripture openly labels an "abomination." The 2001 documentary film *Trembling Before G-d,* however, demonstrated beyond any doubt that the Orthodox community, including the "ultra-Orthodox" (*ḥareidi*) segment, includes gay men and women who nevertheless identify as Orthodox and live as Orthodox Jews in every way but their sexual lives. As a result, the wide agreement within Orthodox circles prohibiting same-sex relations will not save the Orthodox community from the difficult question of how to respond to their members who are gay and who choose not to remain celibate.

1990–1996: The First Efforts of the Conservative Movement to Address the Issues Involved in Same-Sex Relationships

It is only in the Conservative movement that the issues involved in same-sex relationships are still being actively discussed on an official level. The fact that Conservative Jews are deeply divided over this issue does not mean, of course, that we cannot see this topic as a potential source of mutual commitment and cooperation. Indeed, the controversy itself underscores a real strength of the movement, for it shows that Conservative Jews are not interested in pretending that the issues involved are simpler than they really are. Moreover, the high degree of mutual respect and civility that have marked the Conservative movement's discussion of this topic illustrate in very clear ways the Conservative movement's commitment to pluralism, and to the conviction that serious, intelligent, and morally sensitive Jews can disagree with each other on important issues and nevertheless continue to live our lives as part of one movement and community.

Not everything about this topic is in dispute. In May 1990, the Rabbinical Assembly, the organization of Conservative rabbis, passed a resolution about some aspects of this issue, and the United Synagogue of Conservative Judaism, the Conservative movement's synagogue arm, adopted an almost identical resolution in November 1991. Unlike a rabbinic ruling approved by the Committee on Jewish Law and Standards, a resolution is not intended to be a legal statement but rather an expression of the consensus of the rabbis or lay leaders as a group. It is thus not legally binding, but it does articulate what the rabbis and lay leaders believe. Jewish law has always been the product of an interaction between legal precedents and the ongoing life of the Jewish community committed to Jewish law (for more on this, see my *For the Love of God and People: A Philosophy of Jewish Law* [Philadelphia: The Jewish Publication Society, 2007], chapters 5–7), and so such statements are important factors in guiding the development of Jewish law even if they are not themselves legal rulings. Here is the slightly fuller, Rabbinical Assembly version (as printed in *RA Proceedings 1990* [New York: The Rabbinical Assembly, 1991], p. 275):

> WHEREAS Judaism affirms that the divine image reflected by every human being must always be cherished and affirmed, and
>
> WHEREAS Jews have always been sensitive to the impact of official and unofficial prejudice and discrimination, wherever directed, and
>
> WHEREAS gay and lesbian Jews have experienced not only the constant threats of physical violence and homophobic rejection, but also the pains of anti-Semitism known to all Jews and, additionally, a sense of painful alienation from our own religious institutions, and
>
> WHEREAS the extended families of gay and lesbian Jews are often members of our congregations who live with concern for the safety, health, and well-being of their children, and
>
> WHEREAS the AIDS crisis has deeply exacerbated the anxiety and suffering of this community of Jews who need in their lives the compassionate concern and support mandated by Jewish tradition,
>
> THEREFORE BE IT RESOLVED that we, the Rabbinical Assembly, while affirming our tradition's prescription for heterosexuality,
>
> 1. Support full civil equality for gays and lesbians in our national life, and
> 2. Deplore the violence against gays and lesbians in our society, and
> 3. Reiterate that, as are all Jews, gay men and lesbians are welcome as members in our congregations, and
> 4. Call upon our synagogues and the arms of our movement to increase our awareness, understanding, and concern for our fellow Jews who are gay and lesbian.

As a movement, then, Conservative Jews stand on record in favor of full civil rights for gays and lesbians and for protection from attack and discrimination. Our support for "full civil equality" clearly precludes discrimination in housing, jobs, and healthcare. Further, even those Conservative Jews who do not condone Jewish religious ceremonies to celebrate the unions of gays or lesbians generally do support such ceremonies in civil law (whether called "domestic partnerships," "civil unions," or "marriages"). We also officially welcome gays and lesbians, as we welcome all Jews, to Conservative congregations, even though some congregations may not be willing formally to extend "family" memberships to gay couples.

In the fall of 1991 and the spring of 1992, the CJLS, charged with interpreting Jewish law and ethics for the Conservative movement, devoted four meetings to matters regarding homosexuality not covered by the resolution cited just above. In March 1992, the CJLS approved four responsa on the issue as valid halakhic ways of responding to the issues that same-sex relationships raise. Three maintained the view that sex within such relationship is forbidden. One, by Rabbi Joel Roth, based that prohibition on the concept that same-sex intercourse between men is a *to·eivah* ("an abomination") that should be considered wholly forbidden (*CJLS Responsa 1991–2000,* pp. 613–675). Another, by Rabbi Reuven Kimmelman, condemned it as something likely to undermine family-centered Judaism (*CJLS Responsa 1991–2000,* pp. 676–685). The third, by Rabbi Mayer Rabinowitz, maintained that legitimizing gay sex would require an impermissible uprooting of a law of the Torah (*CJLS Responsa 1991–2000,* pp. 686–690). Taking a different view, however, I wrote a responsum that maintained that male-male intercourse should not be seen as a *to·eivah* because that presumes that sexual orientation is a matter of choice, and a rebellious one at that, but scientific evidence already available at the time confirmed the ample testimony of gay people themselves that they did not choose their sexual orientation (*CJLS Responsa 1991–2000,* pp. 691–711). In any case, I argued that gay people would rightfully disregard whatever the CJLS said about their intimate lives because it had never told heterosexuals what the tradition requires of them, and so I recommended that a commission be established to study the entire issue of human sexuality as it intersects with Jewish law.

Based on these responsa, the CJLS adopted a resolution at that time declaring that commitment ceremonies should not be performed by Conservative clergy and that sexually active gay people should not be admitted to the movement's rabbinical and cantorial schools. The fourth responsum, the one in which I called for a commission on human sexuality, considered these last provisions to be subject to possible revision after the proposed commission completed its work. It was left to each synagogue rabbi to determine the extent to which gays and lesbians could be teachers or youth leaders within the congregation and the extent to which they would be eligible for positions of synagogue leadership and honors within prayer services. Moreover, according to the rules of the Rabbinical Assembly, individual rabbis were free to perform commitment ceremonies for gays and lesbians on their own authority; they simply could not claim that they were acting with the endorsement of the CJLS in doing so. It is not clear whether Rabbinical Assembly rules apply to cantors, but presumably if individual rabbis were free to perform such ceremonies, cantors were free to do so as well (but again, without the endorsement of the CJLS).

In May 1992, after some debate, the Rabbinical Assembly convention passed a resolution directing its leadership to create a Commission on Human Sexuality to study how the Jewish tradition should be applied to all aspects of sexuality, both heterosexual and homosexual. The Commission's members vigorously debated the various issues implicit in the conflict between tradition and acceptance. Through discussion with committed Conservative Jews who are gay and their families, the Commission learned that many such people live observant Jewish lives within monogamous relationships and, in some instances, are raising Jewish children. In the course of the Commission's research and its interviews with a number of mental health professionals, it also learned that, just as there is no single heterosexual mode of sexual or social expression, so is there a wide spectrum of feelings and behaviors that characterize same-sex relationships. We therefore must be careful to avoid stereotypes and generalities concerning gay men and lesbians.

Ultimately, the Commission, which met between 1992 and 1994, endorsed a document that I wrote, *"This Is My Beloved, This Is My Friend": A Rabbinic Letter on Intimate Relations.* (It was originally published as a pamphlet in 1996 and now appears as the third chapter of my book *Love Your Neighbor and Yourself: A Jewish Approach to Modern Personal Ethics* [Philadelphia: The Jewish Publication Society, 2006].) The letter focused on how the Jewish tradition understands the role of sexuality in life and how it wants heterosexuals to shape their sexual behavior. In the last section, however, to fulfill the stated aim of the Rabbinical Assembly and United Synagogue resolutions to make gays and lesbians welcome in Conservative synagogues, the Commission on Human Sexuality recommended that synagogues consider taking one or more of the following steps:

1. Synagogue groups might meet with gay and lesbian Jews to put a face to this issue and to learn how the synagogue could become more welcoming. The goal would be to sensitize synagogue members to the fact that Jewish gays, lesbians, and their families are not an outside group, but are part of the synagogue community and should be treated as such.
2. In those instances where synagogues have programs for special constituencies within the congregation, such programs might be created for gay and lesbian Jews and their families as well. So, for example, information about support groups, such as Parents and Friends of Lesbians and Gays (PFLAG), might be disseminated through synagogue media, and the synagogue might

host such a group. Gays and lesbians, though, should generally be integrated into the ongoing activities of the congregation.

3. Synagogue and school educators might include, as part of the curriculum, a section on sexuality and, within this, some material on homosexuality, including the responsa that were adopted by the Committee on Jewish Law and Standards and the resolutions of the Rabbinical Assembly and United Synagogue. In such courses, it should be made clear that sexual activity, while an important part of everyone's life, is not the whole of it. One consequence of this is that gay and lesbian Jews, like Jewish heterosexuals, should not be seen narrowly as people who engage in certain kinds of sexual practices, but rather fully as people and as Jews.
4. Conservative synagogues—individually, regionally, and nationally—might organize social action programs to advance the civil protections of gays and lesbians.

2003–2006: The Second Wave of Effort

In December 2003, Judy Yudoff, president of the United Synagogue of Conservative Judaism, and Rabbi Reuven Hammer, president of the Rabbinical Assembly, asked the Committee on Jewish Law and Standards to revisit the issues of commitment ceremonies and ordination, and the Executive Council of the Rabbinical Assembly officially asked the Committee to do the same.

This engendered a three-year process in which members of the Committee discussed their philosophies of Jewish law, heard from mental health professionals about the progress in scientific research on issues related to homosexuality, and wrote and discussed responsa that members had written. Ultimately, the CJLS voted on five responsa on December 6, 2006.

Two of the responsa argued that the traditional bans on same-sex relations should be maintained. One, by Rabbi Joel Roth, specifically incorporated his 1992 responsum into its 2006 version and expanded those arguments by arguing against points that would challenge that stance. Another, by Rabbi Leonard Levy, took the same stance but, on the question of ordaining gay people, maintained that admissions committees should not ask about sexual orientation. Rabbi Levy also advised gays and lesbians to consult with mental health professionals about the possibility of becoming heterosexuals.

On the other end of the spectrum, two responsa using different arguments maintained that all prohibitions against same-sex intimacy should be abrogated and that we should therefore ordain qualified gay people and perform commitment ceremonies or marriages for gays or lesbians. Rabbi Gordon Tucker wrote one of these, and Rabbis David Fine, Robert Fine, and Myron S. Geller wrote the other.

The fifth responsum, which I coauthored with Rabbis Daniel Nevins and Avram Reisner, took a middle position. We pointed out that the verses in Leviticus banning gay sex are unclear, as witnessed by the varying interpretations of those verses by contemporary biblical scholars. But whatever the original meaning of those verses was, the rabbis of ancient times understood it to forbid anal sex between males, and so that is the law as it has come down to us. In our responsum, we uphold that ban, but we also invoked the right to undo all the other prohibitions that rabbis later added to it.

Revoking rabbinic law is not something that any rabbi does easily. Why, then, did we argue for doing that in this case?

We justified this legal move in this case on several grounds. First, considerable scientific research, documented and summarized by Dr. Judith Glassgold in the appendix to the responsum, now makes clear many things: that homosexuality itself is not a mental disease, although gays and lesbians may need help in attaining a wholesome attitude about themselves if they live in families or communities that continuously disparage them or discriminate against them; that both heterosexual and homosexual orientations are rooted in a person from a very early age and that people cannot therefore be "convinced" or influenced to be gay; that, conversely, gay people cannot change into heterosexuals and that attempts to make them so actually add to their rate of depression and suicide; that most gays and lesbians want to establish longstanding, loving, and monogamous relationships, and that many do; that gay parents function at least as well as heterosexual parents in producing children who have a good sense of themselves and function well in society; and that children raised by gay parents are no more likely to be gay themselves than children raised by heterosexuals.

Furthermore, we maintained that some fundamental Jewish values require us to change the traditional stance prohibiting same-sex intimacy. These include *k'vod ha-b'riyyot,* the dignity each and every person deserves. The refusal to allow gays and lesbians to form communally-recognized unions (and to dissolve them if necessary), and the refusal to allow them to serve as rabbis is, in the view of the three authors of this responsum, an affront against that dignity. The Talmud itself declares that considerations of *k'vod ha-b'riyyot* can constitute sufficient grounds to abrogate rabbinic prohibitions. The value expressed in the Torah's verse, "It is not good for a person to be alone" (Genesis 2:18), was another motivating factor. That verse, of course, refers to God's creation of Eve for Adam, but loneliness is a problem for every human being, gay or straight.

Finally, three times a day traditional Jewish liturgy has us utter, "the Eternal is good to all, and divine mercies extend over all God's works" (Psalms 145:9). It is hard to understand how such a God would create some people who have sexual desires but can never fulfill them in a way that accords with Jewish law. That seems downright cruel and not the work of a God who is "good to all" and whose "mercies are over all God's works."

On the basis of these scientific, moral, and theological considerations, Rabbis Nevins and Reisner and I ruled that seminaries within the Conservative movement may admit and ultimately ordain qualified gay people, and rabbis may perform commitment ceremonies (and, if necessary, dissolution ceremonies) for gay men and for lesbians. If a male gay couple asks for guidance as to their sexual activities, the rabbi should inform them of the Torah's ban on anal sex. At the same time, the value of *k'vod ha-b'riyyot* requires that rabbis honor the privacy of such a couple by not inquiring as to their past or future sexual activities. The responsum permits specifically Jewish commitment ceremonies but not Jewish marriages because Jewish marriage and divorce rituals do not fit the occasion and involve considerable legal issues that the responsum specifically does not address. Nevertheless, a subsequent Rabbinical Assembly resolution specifically advocates extending civil marriage to gay men and lesbians and encourages them to enter into civil marriages, domestic partnerships, or civil unions, where they exist, even though the secular nature of these ceremonies precludes rabbis from officiating, just as they may not officiate at a purely civil marriage ceremony for a heterosexual couple. The Jewish marriage ceremony speaks of a "bride" and a "groom," and that does not fit the union of two men or two women. Further, the seven blessings of marriage refer to Adam and Eve as models for the new union, but the couple is not, by definition, heterosexual. Only a man can initiate a divorce in classical Jewish law, and so who would do so in a lesbian union? Moreover, some of us have difficulty with the traditional concept and language that in marriage a man "acquires" a woman, and we certainly do not want to extend that notion to gay and lesbian unions when there is no traditional precedent that requires us to do so. Thus new Jewish ceremonies to celebrate and to dissolve same-sex unions will need to be devised, and, as in heterosexual marriages, Jewish gay couples would presumably need some sort of Jewish document in celebration of their union and, if necessary, its dissolution. (This would, of course, be in addition to whatever civil law requires to create or dissolve their union in civil law.)

On December 6, 2006, a majority of the CJLS approved both the responsum by Rabbi Roth and the one that I wrote together with Rabbis Nevins and Reisner. Each received thirteen votes. Members of the CJLS may vote for more than one responsum, even when they come to differing conclusions; and here, as in the past, the CJLS member who exercised that option did so because he wanted to support multiple approaches within the movement. Rabbi Levy's responsum received six votes, the minimum required to make his responsum a valid option for rabbis and lay people within the movement. The responsum by Rabbi Tucker received seven votes and the responsum by Rabbis David Fine, Robert Fine, and Myron Geller received six votes, which would ordinarily be sufficient to qualify as a valid option within the Conservative movement. A majority of those voting, however, ruled that these responsa constituted *takkanot* (singular: *takkanah*), legislative changes in the law rather than judicial ones, thus requiring thirteen votes to be approved. Lacking that, they are now part of the archives of the CJLS as dissenting opinions to the responsa approved.

All the 1992 and 2006 rulings are available in their entirety on the website of the Rabbinical Assembly at www.rabbinicalassembly.org.

I wish now to turn to some specific questions regarding the way the Conservative movement understands the *halakhah* of same-sex relationships.

Same-Sex Relationships and Jewish Sources

Some within the Conservative movement, as noted, regard all forms of both male and female same-sex intimacy to be prohibited, and thus enjoin gay people to remain celibate. A majority of the CJLS has voted for Rabbi Roth's responsum, which takes this position.

Others argue in a variety of ways that the biblical and rabbinic laws forbidding same-sex intimacy can and should be changed. Some would have them changed outright by a *takkanah,* a rabbinic emendation of the law, but that stance has not been approved by the CJLS. Others would have the traditional stance on the issue changed on moral grounds, arguing that morality can and should trump legal tradition when it becomes clear that ancient laws are immoral. Rabbi Tucker's responsum, discussed but not officially approved by the CJLS, takes this approach. Still others would use moral concerns, theological considerations, and new scientific evidence to motivate our use of legal methods to change the law, but without going so far as to issue a formal *takkanah.* That is the position Rabbi Nevins, Rabbi Reisner, and I took in our responsum, and so have Rabbis Fine, Fine, and Geller, although in a different way and with a different result.

One matter that has not, to my knowledge, been discussed anywhere is the issue of whether lesbian couples should observe *tohorat ha-mishpaḥah,* refraining from sexual activity during the menstrual period of either one of them. Traditional sources do not discuss this, of course, because they did not contemplate a lesbian couple as coming within a halakhic framework. The responsum that Rabbis Nevins, Reisner, and I wrote, which permits celebrations of gay unions, did not deal with this either. There are obviously some special problems involved, especially if the menstrual periods of both women come at different times of the month. Still, the CJLS has approved three responsa—one each by Rabbis Miriam Berkowitz, Susan Grossman, and Avram I. Reisner and all three available on the Rabbinical Assembly website—that describe why these laws can be an important part of Jews' sexual lives, and lesbian couples should surely be part of that discussion.

Commitment Ceremonies for Same-Sex Couples

Based on classical Jewish law and the Roth and Levy responsa, Conservative rabbis may refuse to perform any ceremony that would give official Jewish recognition to same-sex couples. On the other hand, based on the Dorff-Nevins-Reisner responsum, Conservative rabbis may choose to perform commitment ceremonies for same-sex couples. New forms for both celebrating such unions and dissolving them are, as of this writing, being created by the Rabbinical Assembly for those rabbis who wish to use them.

Synagogue Honors

Whether gay people may or may not be called to the Torah or given other synagogue honors depends on the decision of the rabbi of any given congregation. Rabbis make this decision on the basis, first, of their understanding of the status of same-sex relations. Those who see such relationships as permissible would obviously see no bar to honoring gay people in this way. Even those who disapprove of same-sex intimacy may nevertheless be willing to call gay Jews to the Torah or give them other honors, just as we regularly involve people in the synagogue service who violate Jewish law in other ways. In any event, because very few, if any, synagogues within the Conservative movement require strict halakhic observance as a condition for honoring people during worship services, gay and lesbian Jews should be welcomed into Conservative synagogues and honored as any other members are. Even for those who disapprove of Jewish commitment ceremonies, the same considerations would permit gay and lesbian Jews to function as members or officers of the board of a synagogue.

Employing Gay Individuals in Synagogue Schools, Camps, and Youth Groups

The question of employing gay men and women in synagogue schools and youth groups, as well as in day schools and camps, is a matter for each individual rabbi to determine. In doing so, rabbis should realize that, according to a wealth of scientific evidence, homosexuals are no more likely than heterosexuals to abuse the children in their care. The issue for most rabbis who have any question about whether to hire gay people as teachers or youth leaders is instead the fact that people in these positions serve as role models for children and teenagers. For those rabbis who oppose same-sex relations on the grounds of Jewish law, this will clearly be a disqualifying factor for gays and lesbians, but such rabbis then need to be consistent and refuse to hire teachers and youth leaders who fail to fulfill other halakhic obligations as well.

For those not opposed on halakhic grounds but who are worried themselves or who fear that parents would be worried that the presence of gay teachers or youth leaders might convince some of their charges to become gay, all scientific evidence indicates that people cannot be convinced to adopt a new sexual orientation at all. Teenagers do engage in sexual experimentation on their own, and we have good evidence to say that, at early stages, this often involves homosexual as well as heterosexual experiences. This will happen, however, without any encouragement from teachers or youth leaders. Indeed, the presence of gay men and women in such roles will help both gay and straight students to talk about these issues in a productive, respectful Jewish context, thus helping to fulfill the fourth of the planks of the resolution of the Rabbinical Assembly and the United Synagogue of Conservative Judaism that urges Conservative synagogues to educate their members about same-sex relationships. Finally, any remaining concerns will diminish if a policy is established forbidding teachers and youth leaders to talk about their personal sex lives except in specific programs approved by, and perhaps attended by, the rabbi.

The Halakhah of Acceptance

In addition to these last three issues, other concerns will also determine the degree to which Conservative synagogues welcome Jewish gays and lesbians, and their families, in accordance with the third plank of the resolutions of the Rabbinical Assembly and the United Synagogue of Conservative Judaism. As the Commission on Human Sexuality noted, synagogues might also establish groups of Parents and Friends of Lesbians and Gays (PFLAG), create curricular materials on sexuality in general and homosexuality in particular (perhaps in conjunction with visits by gay members of the congregation), schedule special services or sessions in which gays and lesbians speak about the issues involved in integrating their Judaism and their sexual orientation, and, in general, actively seek to involve gay Jews in all the activities and organizational responsibilities of the synagogue. Because Judaism has a history of discriminating against gays and lesbians, and because Conservative Jewish institutions are only gradually changing discriminatory policies, it is a positive duty to make the special effort required to attract our fellow Jews who are gay or lesbian, together with their families, to synagogue life within the Conservative movement.

Gay Synagogues

Synagogues try to attract people with a mix of ages and interests, and people do make friends across lines of age, gender, personal status, and profession. Still, our closest friends are usually people of our own age and personal status, for they can easily share all aspects of life as they go through its stages with us. It is therefore not surprising that gays and lesbians have established synagogues with specific outreach to gay Jews. In such synagogues, presumably everyone (including any heterosexual members) would understand the issues involved in being a Jewishly committed gay Jew. Programming would be focused on the needs and interests of gays and lesbians. Gays and lesbians would be able to find a refuge from the harsh realities of discrimination leveled against them in society just because they are gay. And there they would be able to be themselves without worrying that others may stare at them disapprovingly.

Although all this is understandable, the Conservative movement has not sought to establish synagogues with special outreach to gays and lesbians. The reason for this is our desire to be inclusive, not exclusionary: because the only way that gays and lesbians can find understanding and acceptance within the movement is if they become part of it, it seems counterproductive to establish institutions that will keep gay Jews apart. Heterosexual Jews may never have met a gay Jew—or, more likely, may never have known that they have. Only within synagogues serving all populations will they come to recognize the reasonableness of including gay men and women in Jewish life, thereby changing their image from people who are strange and threateningly different to people who are familiar and even likable. Moreover, synagogues can only benefit from the energy and experience of all their members.

Thus, in the ideal situation, gays and lesbians should join Conservative synagogues and take an active role in shaping the synagogue's programming and in serving on its committees and board. Like other subgroups within the congregation (for example: women, men, children, teenagers, young married couples, young adults with children, and older adults), gays and lesbians might have special activities that would give them the opportunity to be with people who share their needs and interests. Within the larger context of a Conservative congregation, however, gay individuals can benefit from association with others, and they, in turn, can benefit others in a fruitful symbiosis. This structure would enable gays or lesbians who seek their own company to do so while still providing the chance for everyone in the congregation to meet and learn from each other. Although this is the ideal, nothing in Jewish law as construed by the Conservative movement would preclude accepting a synagogue with special outreach to Jewish gays and lesbians as a member of the United Synagogue of Conservative Judaism.

Becoming Parents

From a practical standpoint, lesbians who wish to become parents can undergo artificial insemination, and gay men can beget their own biological offspring through surrogate mothers, who (usually) provide the egg and carry the child to term. And both gay men and lesbians, at least in many jurisdictions, can also adopt children. How does the Conservative movement understand such realities?

Conservative Judaism is rooted in, among other things, historical analysis, and so we should begin by noting one incontrovertible fact of Jewish history: namely, that Jewish tradition supposes a model of heterosexual married couples producing and rearing their children as the basic building block of society. At the same time, it presumes that both adults and children will live in an extended family, with grandparents, uncles, aunts, and cousins all in the immediate neighborhood (if not actually in the same house). Moreover, it knows of children who were orphaned, and the Talmud says that when one takes in a child to raise him or her, it is "as if that individual had personally given birth to that child" (*BT* M'gillah 13a) and that such people "do right at all times" (*BT* K'tubbot 50a). Therefore, we should not think of the traditional nuclear family—mother, father, and children—as the only acceptable form of Jewish family life; the reality has always been much more complex than that.

Moreover, Jewish tradition also knew of infertility, and it approved of a variety of steps designed to overcome it. It is actually amazing that three biblical matriarchs faced problems with infertility. In response, Sarah and Rachel urged their husbands to take concubines and have children by them. This was an early form of ovum surrogacy, where the surrogate mother provides the egg and carries the child to term. I discuss this and other techniques for infertile couples to have children at some length in chapters three and four of my book, *Matters of Life and Death,* which are based on my rulings on that topic that were approved by the Conservative movement's Committee on Jewish Law and Standards. Lesbians and gays could make use of these same methods, including adoption.

We know full well, of course, that men are not just sperm donors, nor are women merely egg donors. Both males and females contribute important elements to the education and identity of both the boys and the girls in their care. Therefore, if gays or lesbians choose to have children through any of these methods, they owe it to their children to arrange for an adult of the opposite gender to play a significant role in the children's lives, and for men and women to play roles akin to roles played by the uncles and aunts in earlier days when a child's father or mother died or was incapacitated (or even when a child did not get along with his or her parents). Some gay and lesbian parents might avail themselves of the services of Jewish Big Brothers and Jewish Big Sisters to accomplish this task, just as some Jewish widows and widowers do. Thus, while it might be ideal that a child grow up with a father and mother at home in order to learn first-hand about both genders, one can hardly argue that all Jewish children in the past grew up that way or that all Jewish children of heterosexual parents do so now. It is also true, of course, that heterosexual parents are not necessarily good parents. So, while it is important to provide adult models of both genders, a loving, supportive home seems to be the most important factor in a child's healthy development.

Heterosexual parents regularly discover that one or more of their children is gay or lesbian. Since they often do not expect this, the discovery itself often poses challenges for them. Parental acceptance is a crucial factor in enabling gay and lesbian children to accept their own sexual orientation and to avoid self-destructive behaviors, and so even if parents are first caught off-guard and respond to the news poorly, they need to reaffirm their love for their child as quickly and as strongly as possible and indicate their willingness to learn about what this means for their child. They then need to make sure that their child learns about the risks of sexually-transmitted diseases that apply to all sexual relations (but, in some cases, especially to anal sex), and they need to help their child combat the discrimination and outright abuse to which gays and lesbians are all too often subjected. They should also help their child imagine a future life that is productive and loving. The parents can gain some insights as to how to accomplish these tasks and some personal support for themselves through organizations like Parents and Friends of Lesbians and Gays (PFLAG).

It also bears saying that the Jewish community is suffering from a major demographic crisis, with a reproductive rate at 1.8 per cent, which is far below replacement levels. One must, of course, exert considerable effort to transform a Jewish baby into a learned and practicing Jew, so numbers alone are not enough; but it is also the case that one cannot educate someone who is not there. Thus Jewish gays and lesbians share with Jewish heterosexuals the crucial duty to create or adopt children—three or four, if possible—and to educate them to be practicing Jews. Indeed, the CJLS has approved a 2007 responsum by Rabbi Kassel Abelson and myself entitled "Mitzvah Children" (available on the website of the Rabbinical Assembly) that declares that Jews who are able to procreate have a halakhic duty to have at least one more child than they were planning on having, or to adopt children, for the sake of the Jewish people—and this duty applies to gay and lesbian Jews as much as heterosexual ones.

A Matter of Attitude

Finally, one should note a matter of attitude that pervades everything above. In accordance with the Conservative movement's resolutions, heterosexuals must treat gay people with respect, working against any disadvantages they have in civil law, taking steps to protect them from abuse, and welcoming them into our synagogues. Part of that respect is recognizing that Jewish gays and lesbians should not be defined by their sexual orientation, any more than Jewish heterosexuals are. For both groups, sex is part of life—an important part, to be sure—but not the whole of it. On the contrary, gay and lesbian Jews, like all Jews, are first and foremost people created in the image of God and members of the covenant between God and the people Israel, and they should be considered as such.

As Conservative synagogues take steps to make gays and lesbians feel welcome within our midst, gays and lesbians, like heterosexuals, have the duty to strive to live by Jewish values in all of their relationships, including their sexual ones. Furthermore, like all other Jews, gays and lesbians have the duties of Jewish study and action, including raising children, affiliating and actively participating in a synagogue and in the Jewish community generally, and participating actively in the great Jewish effort to fix our world.

Between Parents and Children

DANIEL S. NEVINS

If honoring one's parents and raising one's children were simple tasks, then the Torah might well have skipped over the stories of the conflicted families of Genesis. And, indeed, thousands of years later, contemporary Jewish families still contend with the very same challenges described in the Bible—issues such as sibling rivalry, parental favoritism, and tension between generations—as well as with a wide variety of modern developments that only add more stress to those same relationships: geographic separation, cultural and religious assimilation, high divorce rates, and a popular culture that promotes addictive and selfish behavior.

Against this challenging backdrop, Judaism continues to promote an ideal family portrait of committed, loving parents and respectful, devoted children. Although this portrait may not be congruent with the inevitable experience of all modern families, Judaism is very practical in the guidance it offers to strengthen family bonds for the benefit of parents and children alike.

The Commandment to Honor One's Parents

As Moses descended from Mount Sinai bearing the Ten Commandments, rabbinic tradition imagined one tablet to contain five statements intended to govern our relationship with God, while the second recorded five brief laws governing relations between people. Oddly, the fifth commandment, "You shall honor your father and mother," was included on the first tablet. Long ago, the rabbis understood this apparent error of placement to suggest a profound truth: that honoring one's parents is to be understood essentially as an act of worshiping God.

This idea is also expressed in midrashic literature, where God is understood to sacrifice some of the honor of the Divine in order to share it with mothers and fathers: "Rabbi [Judah the Patriarch] teaches that the *mitzvah* of honoring one's father and mother is so beloved to the One who spoke and brought the world into being that Scripture equates honoring them with honoring God, revering them with revering God, and cursing them with cursing God" (*M'khilta D'rabbi Yishma·el*, Ba-ḥodesh 8).

In this *midrash* and also in the classical codes of *halakhah,* honoring parents is equated with honoring God. This equation is based upon biblical metaphors in which the Israelites are regularly called children of God and God is regularly described as a divine Parent. At Deuteronomy 14:1, for example, Moses announces to Israel, "You are the children of the Eternal, our God." Later, the stirring words preserved at Isaiah 46:3–4 beautifully describe God supporting the House of Jacob from birth until old age and offering them constant, ongoing divine love. In the Book of Psalms—and this idea echoes throughout the liturgy—God is said to relate to the pious just as compassionate fathers relate to their children (cf., e.g., Psalm 103:13).

Rabbinic literature develops the concept of God's earthly presence, called the Sh'khinah, which is openly described as a kind of mother figure awash in maternal compassion. Furthermore, God is described in a very famous passage as one of three partners—together with the biological parents—in the creation of every child (*BT* Kiddushin 30b and Niddah 31a). God's role as Creator is thus reaffirmed every time that children honor their parents, whose role as their personal creators reflects the glory of God, the Creator of all that exists.

Honoring one's parents is understood as a way to honor and even—within kabbalistic circles—mystically to unite with God's presence. In his great code of law, Maimonides addresses the *mitzvah* of honoring parents in the section called Hilkhot Mamrim, a section otherwise dedicated wholly to heresy. This implies that, for Maimonides, a person who fails to honor his or her parents properly is to be compared to a heretic who renounces the obligation to honor God.

We can now understand how the rabbis interpreted the placement of this essential commandment among the first five of the Decalogue. Yet how is this mighty *mitzvah* to be fulfilled? Just as honoring God requires a range of symbolic and practical gestures, so too does the honoring of our parents.

In both versions of the Decalogue we read, "*Honor* your father and your mother" (Exodus 20:11 and Deuteronomy 5:16). Yet at Leviticus 19:3, we are taught, "Each person must *revere* his or her mother and father." From these verses the rabbis inferred that both honor and reverence are due to both mothers and fathers by their sons and daughters. These two *mitzvot*—to honor and to revere one's parents—are independent, yet they will almost always be intertwined in practical reality. Sometimes it is easy enough to honor a parent with kindness or compassion, but dramatically less easy to do so with reverence. At other times a child may feel deep reverence toward a parent, but be unable to show him or her much love. These concepts may overlap but they are never fully equated in the traditional literature. The Talmud, for example, asks in a famous passage what exactly constitutes reverence, and how honor is different from reverence. Reverence for parents, the rabbis answer, includes not sitting in a parent's chair and not contradicting what a parent declares to be the truth. Honoring parents, on the other hand, is more than the avoidance of insult and includes the obligations to assure that one's parents are fed, clothed, and accompanied when necessary (*BT* Kiddushin 31b). We can extrapolate from these examples that reverence involves acknowledging the authority of our parents, while honor requires that they be made physically comfortable. It should also be obvious that these obligations devolve upon adults with living parents, not solely on children still being reared at home.

Rabbi Joseph B. Soloveitchik, in a collection of his addresses published as *Family Redeemed: Essays on Family Relationships* (New York: KTAV, 2000, p.130), distinguishes between the external norms and the internal experience of filial piety. The *halakhah*, he observes, does not attempt to regulate the emotional side of the parent-child relationship. It rather establishes norms of conduct to ensure that parents attend to the needs of their children, and that children reciprocate when they reach the proper age. Ideally there will be confluence between external devotion and internal love, but the *halakhah* is realistic in its requirement that children demonstrate reverence and honor for their parents through their behavior, not that they love them. Love can and does flower, however, within the supportive environment of honor and reverence.

This internal/external divide parallels the relationship between God and Israel. We show devotion to God via practical actions known as the *mitzvot*, and we are promised rewards in this world and the next in recompense for our devotion. The talmudic sage Rabbi Judah said in the name of Rav, "A person should always seek to be involved in the Torah and *mitzvot,* for even undertaking them for ulterior purposes will eventually lead to doing them for their own sake" (*BT* P'saḥim 50b). Judaism describes a spiritual progression from ulterior motivation to idealistic observance of the commandments, and this parallels the journey from external, ritualistic obedience of divine instruction to internal transformation and the awakening of love for God. This progression applies to the parent-child relationship as well, a relationship that becomes deepened and enriched through the practice of honoring and revering one's parents.

Honoring parents properly may be as important as honoring God, but it is also often equally challenging, and sometimes even more so. Indeed, an old *midrash* actually identifies honoring one's parents as the single most difficult *mitzvah* (*Midrash Tanḥuma,* Eikev §3). As it is nearly impossible for children to appreciate all that a parent has done for them, so too are we unable to comprehend the constant gifts of love and compassion by means of which God allows us to exist on this fragile planet. As we become parents, we begin to comprehend the sacrifices made by our own parents, and we gain greater perspective on the gift of creation.

Obligations of Parents toward Children

The Mishnah and Talmud explore the responsibilities of parents toward children and of children toward parents in tractate Kiddushin (cf. *M* Kiddushin 1:7 and *BT* Kiddushin 29a–32b). Classical texts often differentiate parental obligations on the basis of the gender of parent and child, but the prevailing view today is that it is best to minimize gender-based differences in this regard. Taken in that light, the sources teach us that parents are obligated to circumcise and redeem their sons, to teach all of their children Torah, to teach them a trade, and to see to their marriage. Some add that parents have an obligation to teach their children to swim as well. (These are in addition to the basic obligation of feeding, housing, and clothing their young children.) In general, we may understand these ancient obligations to stand for giving children the spiritual, intellectual, physical, and social skills necessary to live productive and meaningful lives.

Teaching Children

In his chapter on Torah study above, Rabbi Eliezer Diamond discusses the general definition and application of this *mitzvah,* but here I would like to speak specifically about the obligation of parents with respect to their children's Jewish education. The Torah outlines the educational responsibilities of parents toward their children clearly and unambiguously with statements such as "you shall teach these words [i.e., the words of the Sh'ma describing God's unity and the obligation to love God] diligently to your children" (Deuteronomy 6:7). Still, although parents may be their children's first and most formative teachers, most parents will also need to provide professional instructors to complete their children's education. The commandment to study Torah, and to teach children how to study Torah, requires that parents band together to provide the finest Jewish and general education possible for their offspring. Indeed, a solid general education is essential not only for learning marketable skills, but also for stimulating curiosity about, and comprehension of, our remarkable world. But regardless of whether children study Judaism in a full-day or a supplementary program, it is essential that parents reinforce the educational values of school at home.

Each child responds differently to the intellectual challenges of Jewish religion and culture. Parents should seek to maximize their children's exposure to the ideas and sacred texts of our religion. Whether a child is an academic star or a slow learner, the Jewish worth of each lesson learned is infinite. Education must always be tailored to the specific needs and aptitudes of the people to whom it is being addressed.

Even more important than intellectual attainment is the spiritual growth of each individual child. Are our children learning to become decent, considerate, and altruistic people? Do our children feel loved and, equally importantly, have they acquired the ability to share that love with others? Have we imbued our children with a sense of purpose in life beyond the acquisition of material goods? Are they learning skills that will equip them to flourish and to contribute to the improvement of the world? These questions are the benchmarks—we might call them *mensch*-marks!—by which to measure the education of our children. All are essential elements in the education of children. And none can be ignored or dispensed with casually.

Children rarely appreciate the enormous role that they play in defining their parents' self-image. The Book of Proverbs repeatedly speaks of the joy felt by parents when their children act wisely and of the terrible suffering experienced by parents whose children behave badly. The Yiddish word *naḥes* (pronounced *naḥat* in modern Hebrew) captures the special pleasure that parents derive from their children. Seeing children thrive grants the greatest pleasure to parents; witnessing their suffering is the most terrible torture any parent can experience. Toward the end of the Book of Genesis, Judah captures this dynamic powerfully in attempting to explain why his father Jacob cares so deeply for his youngest son, Benjamin. He loves him as intensely as he does,

Judah explains, "because their souls are each bound up with the other's" (Genesis 44:30).

Nevertheless, parents must learn to see their child's development as an internal process, not primarily as a reflection of their own worth. At Proverbs 22:6 we read, "Teach a child in the way to go, and even in old age that one will not stray from it." The goal of Jewish parenting is to raise children to adulthood by teaching them to sanctify life and serve as God's partners in perfecting the world. No child will advance toward this goal in a straight line, and parents must therefore help their children to discover their own unique interests and to develop those skills that will allow them to contribute most richly to the world around them. The contemporary idea of "multiple intelligences" that recognizes people's diverse skill sets accords well with Jewish insights about different types of students. The Talmud astutely notes that "no one can learn Torah except by one's heart's desire" (*BT* Avodah Zarah 19a).

Recalling the Talmud's statement in Kiddushin about parental obligations, we see that the first responsibility of parents is to provide their children with the physical and material environment that will allow them to grow up properly. But beyond feeding, sheltering, and clothing them, parents must guide their children to develop good character. Indeed, while parental love may be unconditional, it nonetheless comes bundled with many diverse kinds of expectations. In the end, however, parents teach their children by setting a worthy example of commitment to family, community, and to the sacred tradition of Judaism for them to follow in their own lives.

When children reach a milestone of accomplishment, it should be their parents' pleasure to help them celebrate appropriately. The Jewish people—which has suffered innumerable set-backs and tragedies—is always eager to celebrate life! Whether the occasion is a *b'rit milah* or a *simḥat bat* ceremony welcoming a baby girl to the community, a bar or bat mitzvah, a graduation, or a wedding party, it is essential that Jewish values be incorporated into the celebration. Food should always be kosher, and the reception should not be extravagant. The Jewish values of hospitality, kindness, *tz'dakah,* and modesty should be showcased at the times of our greatest joy. This is the proper Jewish way of celebration that parents must teach their children, especially in an age of affluence.

Disciplining Children

In the Bible, God employs persuasion, punishment, and even aloofness in order to motivate stiff-necked Israel to return to the Torah's ideals. Famously, the Book of Isaiah opens (at Isaiah 1:2) with a bitter complaint leveled by God against Israel: "I have raised and exalted children, yet they have rebelled against Me!" Yet the role of the prophet is ultimately to help Israel feel that God is reaching out to them, to reassure them of God's love even at times of estrangement. So too must parents find creative and varied ways to reach their children even when they stray far from the family's values and practices.

When parents discipline a child, it may be difficult for the child to accept that guidance with love. Therefore, it is essential that parents begin positively by modeling the type of conduct that they wish to see in their children. They must also resist the temptation to cover up all of a child's shortcomings. Parents whose children do not respond to verbal discipline should institute a logical, reasonable series of consequences to guide their children back to proper behavior. Each child must learn to live within limits established by his or her parents.

Failure to discipline children is an abdication of parental responsibility and may lead the children to what the rabbis called *tarbut ra·ah,* a vulgar pattern of poor behavior. Rabbi Shimon bar Yoḥai (cited by Rabbi Yoḥanan in the Talmud at *BT* B'rakhot 7b) describes *tarbut ra·ah* in a home as more painful than the apocalyptic battle of Gog and Magog! From the story told in the Talmud (at *BT* Bava M'tzi·a 83b) about his son Rabbi Eleazar—who once assisted the Romans and was thereafter no longer known by his dismayed colleagues as Eleazar ben Shimon (that is, Eleazar, the son of Shimon), but rather as "Ḥometz ben Yayin" (that is, "Vinegar, the son of Wine")—we can glimpse how the great challenge of child rearing can be even for some of the greatest of our sages.

The *halakhah* warns parents not to demand excessive displays of respect from their children, lest the strategy backfire. Indeed, one reason that a parent is warned not to hit an older child is that the child might be tempted to strike back (*BT* Mo·eid Katan 17a; see also *BT* Kiddushin 32a). The codes of law state that one who beats an older child should be warned that such behavior will more than likely be counterproductive and such a parent should even be placed under a ban (*AT* Yoreh Dei·ah 240).

Although corporal punishment has frequently been practiced by parents, and is even justified in the Bible at Proverbs 23:13–14, we now understand that the Talmud's warning against striking older children should be applied more broadly, and not solely because the struck child might strike back. Parents who hit their younger children risk injuring them both physically and emotionally, and injuring a child is forbidden by Jewish law. Doing so also constitutes an offense against common decency. The resentments and long-term impact created by the physical punishment of children may have horrific ramifications. Truly abusive parents may forfeit their right to be honored and attended by their children, as seen in the talmudic story of Rav Asi cited below. Instead, parents must discipline children in a firm but reasonable fashion that reinforces the same positive values the parent is seeking to inculcate.

Wayward Children

The hardest adjustment for parents to make is learning how to love an adult child who has strayed from the core values and practices of the family. Should the parent continue to expect that adult children live up to their parents' expectations? Does the child have other virtues that can form the foundation of a new and more realistic relationship? How can a parent make peace with a child's decisions when the parent continues to feel tormented by the reality? What should be the intensity of response in the broad continuum of alienation? Is there a point when a parent should break off relations with a child? These painful questions do not have simple, cookie-cutter answers. Parents struggling with these issues need the guidance and support of their extended family, their friends, and their rabbi. The following sections deal with some situations in which parents may need to respond to a reality other than what they had hoped to encounter.

Intermarried Children

Because Judaism is best understood as an eternal covenant between God and Israel, and because the home is the central arena for practicing and perpetuating that covenant, raising children to marry within the faith is among the highest priorities of Jewish parents. Studies have repeatedly shown that the Jewish children of interfaith marriages exhibit far lower rates of Jewish affiliation as adults than do their peers raised within fully Jewish homes. This Jewish sense of the vital importance of endogamy is reinforced by the movement-wide ban on Conservative clergy officiating at interfaith wedding ceremonies.

Even children raised in intensive Jewish environments nevertheless may decide to marry non-Jews. The non-Jewish fiancé, fiancée, or spouse may be ideal in all other respects, yet there is no getting around the fact that such individuals' identification with the tenets and practices of another religion will inevitably compromise the ability of the Jewish spouse to practice Judaism. The same could also be said of non-Jewish spouses who express no specific other faith, but who are simply not imbued with a sense of allegiance to Judaism and its practices (and even of families where one parent is technically

Jewish but does not identify with the religion). Children born to non-Jewish mothers are considered to be non-Jewish by *halakhah*. Beyond the question of legal status, however, it is exceptionally difficult to transmit Jewish identity positively and profoundly in an interfaith household.

Should a fiancé, fiancée, or spouse decide to convert to Judaism, the Jewish community should encourage him or her to pursue a serious course of study that will constitute successful preparation for entering the covenant. Jews by choice (as converts to Judaism are regularly known) are a source of great joy and pride for the Jewish community, and such marriages are cause for celebration. Indeed, many of the finest, most accomplished, and most celebrated members of the Jewish community—from biblical times until our day—have been Jews by choice. (Conversion is discussed in more detail above by Rabbi Carl Astor in his chapter on the Jewish life cycle.)

Yet it frequently happens that the non-Jewish partner chooses to retain his or her religious (or non-religious) identity. How should Jewish parents relate to their child and his or her non-Jewish spouse? Obviously, no two cases will be identical. The non-Jewish spouse has no obligation to convert, especially if that would be antithetical to his or her own belief system. On the other hand, it is exceptionally difficult to provide children in an interfaith household with the positive and intense Jewish environment necessary to maintain Jewish identity in a world that esteems cultural assimilation as a societal good. Hoping that one's own intermarried child will be the exception to the general rule is inevitable; pretending that such will be the case without massive, ongoing support from the Jewish spouse's family and friends is, however, pointless.

The temptation to synthesize rituals and to retain Jewish symbols in an interfaith wedding should be resisted. A civil secular ceremony is preferable to a wedding that combines Jewish and Christian symbols and features the services of non-traditional rabbis working alongside liberal Christian clergy. Liberal rabbis outside the Conservative movement often rationalize their decision to perform interfaith weddings with reference to promises extracted from the couple to raise their children as Jews. Yet there is no way to enforce such promises, and the message conveyed—that the mere intent to raise one's children as Jewish is all that matters—is potentially counterproductive. Rather, the integrity of Jewish beliefs and rituals should be preserved at the time of marriage.

While observant Jews may be tempted to disengage from their intermarried children, the better option will almost always be to build bridges rather than to foster hostility or constantly to harp on the topic. It is far better for the parents to provide a living example of the beauty, joy, and meaning of a committed Jewish life than to turn away from children who have intermarried. In time, intermarried Jewish individuals may well be inspired by their parents' forbearance to reclaim their religious identity. At the very least, the non-Jewish spouse will learn to admire his or her partner's Jewish heritage.

Diplomacy, patience, kindness, and firm Jewish conviction are required when a family is struggling to remain whole despite internal religious divisions. Jewish parents should clarify that they appreciate and love their non-Jewish sons- or daughters-in-law, and also that Judaism welcomes their conversion should they be so inclined to pursue that path. Yet they must not pressure the non-Jewish spouse of their child to convert.

Jewish parents should certainly not disparage the religion of a non-Jewish son- or daughter-in-law, yet they may also feel fully justified in refraining from participation in the celebration of non-Jewish ceremonies or holidays in an intermarried son's or daughter's home. This position can be very difficult to maintain, particularly if a child's non-Jewish in-laws seem happy to participate in Jewish rituals. Nevertheless, it is essential for the integrity of Jewish belief and practice that Jewish families avoid participating in non-Jewish religious ceremonies. Interested non-Jews married to Jewish family members, on the other hand, should be invited to enjoy Jewish holidays and celebrations, and to learn about Judaism through positive exposure to Jewish customs and ceremonies.

Rather than reacting negatively, or pretending that their child's interfaith marriage is a non-issue, Jewish parents should continue to study and observe their Judaism, thereby providing a positive Jewish example for the family. When the children of an intermarried couple grow older, the impact of their loving and devout grandparents may well inspire them to identify fully as Jews, and, if necessary, formally to convert to Judaism. As Maimonides teaches, the Torah is God's gift of mercy *to* the world, not a punishment imposed *on* the world (*MT* Hilkhot Shabbat 2:3). Even when a child marries out of the faith, parents should continue to teach their sons and daughters the inestimable value of Jewish tradition. Following the divine example as expressed in Isaiah 54:10, the love of parents for their children and their families should never waver.

Apostate Children

An extremely painful, but fortunately rare, situation for Jewish parents is the one in which a child explicitly rejects his or her Jewish identity. The parents, feeling great sorrow and dismay, may ask what more they could have done to instill love of Judaism in such a child. But while this question may be poignant and will certainly be heartfelt, it is almost always posed far too late for its answer to make much difference in the life of the child in question. In some cases, parents may seek to harmonize the children's alien religious beliefs with their own Jewish traditions. For example, such parents may be moved to experiment with synthesizing holidays such as Ḥanukkah and Christmas, or Passover and Easter. Seasonal proximity aside, these holidays are dramatically different in their religious significance and, in the end, the Jewish festivals celebrating our freedom and fidelity to God will be completely undermined by even well-meaning attempts to merge them with Christian holidays. Moreover, such an approach can compound the parents' problem by validating their child's criticism of Judaism as something so elastic and so malleable as almost not to exist in its own right.

Clearly the best course for parents in such trying circumstances is to demonstrate to their child the depth and diversity of Jewish belief and practice in the hope that he or she will agree to return exclusively to Judaism. Parents should consult with their clergy for specific suggestions. Above all they should recall that, as the *midrash* states at *D'varim Rabbah* 2:12, the gates of repentance are always open. Jews who have embraced different faiths and who then wish to return to Judaism should immerse in a *mikveh* under the supervision of a rabbi as a symbol of their willing repentance and their desire to reestablish themselves as proud members of the Jewish community. Although this does not make the returning Jew into a true convert, immersion in a *mikveh* symbolizes the dramatic decision to re-embrace Jewishness and Judaism. This practice is based upon a story from *Avot D'rabbi Natan* (text A, chapter 3), and is attested to in the medieval code *Or Zaru·a* (§112). If a child persists in rejecting his or her Judaism in favor of a different religion, however, the parents should explicitly acknowledge the disagreement and focus instead on other aspects of their relationship. If a child insists on proselytizing Jewish members of the family, however, his or her parents may need to cut off communication until the child modifies his or her behavior.

When Children Engage in Criminal Behavior

When children violate the laws of society, it is a parent's obligation to teach them the necessity of compliance. In the Talmud (at *BT* Kiddushin 30b), we read that parents who neglect to teach their children a useful trade are in effect teaching them to steal. In addition to its simple meaning, we can understand this remark to mean that parents must try to steer their children onto an honest path, and must help those children break addictive or destructive patterns of behavior that may endanger them or the people around them.

Some of these behaviors and behavior patterns will correctly elicit strongly negative parental responses, but there may also be situations in which parents must contact social services or law enforcement authorities for the protection of their child and of society.

The Torah itself describes the case of a rebellious child whose parents present him to the authorities in utter despair, saying: "This son of ours is willful and disobedient; he does not listen to us. He is a wastrel and a drunkard" (Deuteronomy 21:20). The Torah prescribes capital punishment in such a case, but in the Talmud, the sages debate whether this was ever actually carried out (*BT* Sanhedrin 71a). Rabbi Jeffrey Tigay reasonably argues that the court "would probably order the son's execution only when all else had failed" (*The JPS Torah Commentary, Deuteronomy* [Philadelphia: The Jewish Publication Society, 1996], p. 197). It is even possible that it was never carried out, as is clearly suggested at *T* Sanhedrin 11:2. Today, these words stand as a stark admonishment that parental responsibility may never be abdicated merely because a child is rebellious or difficult to discipline.

In any event, we know that some children in every generation ignore the most earnest attempts of their parents and teachers to reform their behavior. In these cases, society must provide the resources that an individual family lacks in order to address the situation. Parents must not ignore the criminal actions of their children or enable them to continue behaving in ways that are self-destructive and constitute a peril to others. In such desperate circumstances, a parent may in good conscience bring criminal conduct to the attention of authorities if they consider such a step necessary to preserve the safety of their child and of innocent bystanders.

Nevertheless, even in such a case the parent must try to reassure the child of his or her love. It is worth recalling that God manages the world through a balance of justice and mercy. Likewise, a parent must be firm with a rebellious child while, at the same time, continuing to offer him or her love and hope for a better future. Even when children are imprisoned, their families and their community should continue to reach out to them and to encourage them to practice Judaism and return to the path of decency and goodness. Prison chaplains and recovery therapists who work with Jews after release perform a sacred service for these individuals, their families, and the entire community.

Parents' Obligations toward Adult Children

The parent-child relationship is a life-long bond and, as such, the Torah's injunction to teach and watch over one's children is not time-limited. The obligation to help children learn survival skills and marry is likewise not limited to a certain age. Nevertheless, Jewish law does not obligate parents to provide ongoing material support for the education, housing, food, or entertainment of healthy adult children. One important lesson that a parent must teach his or her children is independence. Even when children are disabled, parents should seek to maximize their level of independence while at the same time doing everything possible to guarantee their safety and health.

Parents may be uncomfortable with lifestyle decisions made by their children. Parents may not be satisfied with a child's profession, marriage plans, parenting techniques, religious practices, healthcare decisions, or sexual proclivities. Significantly harder to delineate, however, is the precise boundary between loving concern and counterproductive nagging, between constructive criticism and devastating censure. The Torah itself addresses this tension at Leviticus 19:17 with the words: "Do not hate your neighbor in your heart; instead, rebuke your friend and do not tolerate another's sin." This famous verse was interpreted by the sages in ancient times to mean that one demonstration of loving concern involves warning a relative, friend, or neighbor to improve his or her conduct. In the Talmud (at *BT* Kiddushin 30a), Rava identifies the window of opportunity during which a father may attempt to control his son's decisions regarding marriage as being open until a young man reaches his early twenties. (This limit is explained and justified by Rashi in his comment *ad loc., s.v. a-d'yadakh,* where he explains that children will not accept their parents' criticism after that point. In his comment to *BT* Y'vamot 65b, *s.v. lomar davar ha-nishma,* however, Rashi observes that in any event one should offer criticism only if it has a chance of being accepted.) And although Rava was specifically talking about sons and their fathers, the lesson surely applies just as clearly to daughters and to mothers as well.

Parents must therefore exercise diplomacy when criticizing adult children. To ignore vulgar behavior or tragically misguided decisions is not allowed—we must seek to strengthen and improve the lives of our loved ones. Yet there is a point of diminishing returns at which a parent's criticism may not benefit the child, but will rather deepen the estrangement between the generations. Rashi's comments remind us to consider the impact of our critique before offering even the best intentioned advice. The Torah's path of criticizing lovingly and effectively is perhaps the trickiest challenge of parenting adult children.

For some families, the greatest challenge is not disagreement between parents and children, but arguments between the parents themselves, or between the children. It is particularly painful for children to try to negotiate a truce between their parents, and for parents to do the same between their children. Every family experiences ordinary disagreements, but some families contend with chronic and bitter disputes. All members of the family are responsible for disciplining themselves, minimizing hurtful comments and actions, and seeking to reconcile whenever possible. Even parents who are divorced are obligated to treat one another respectfully and to avoid pitting their children against their other parent. Rabbis can supplement the work of family therapists in helping parents and children develop practices that will encourage healing and harmony in the family.

Adopted Children

What are the obligations of parents to their adopted children? Although the modern practice of adoption differs from customs that prevailed in ancient times, the Bible provides a framework for thinking about the obligations of adoptive parents when it reports on the adoption of Moses by Pharaoh's daughter, and on Esther's adoption by her cousin Mordecai. Adoption itself is deemed intensely praiseworthy. The Talmud states, for example, that "whoever raises an orphan in his home is considered by Scripture as if [the orphan] were his [own] child" (*BT* Sanhedrin 19b, where the text clearly applies to mothers as well as to fathers). If an adopted child's birth mother is not Jewish, then the adoptive parents are obligated formally to convert their child with the rituals of circumcision (for boys) and, for boys and girls, immersion in a kosher *mikveh* under the supervision of a rabbinic court.

The act of adoption places reciprocal obligations upon the child and the adoptive parents (Menaḥem Elon, *Jewish Law* [1994; reprint, Philadelphia: The Jewish Publication Society, 2003], vol. 2, p. 827). Rabbi Isaac Klein rules that adoptive parents are obligated to circumcise their sons, and adopted children must say Kaddish for their adoptive parents (Klein, pp. 437ff.). We may extrapolate from this and other rulings that once an adoption is legal according to civil law, the obligations of parents to their adopted children, and of children to their adoptive parents, are absolute and permanent. Adoptive parents must educate and support their children to maturity; children must respect and honor their adoptive parents until the end of their lives.

Unlike other legal systems, Jewish law does not sever the obligations of an adopted child toward his or her natural parents (Elon, p. 827). This means that if a child identifies his or her biological parent, even later in life, he or she should attempt to honor and respect that parent, even if the establishment of a relationship rooted in love feels unlikely or unrealistic. If the biological parent does not want such a relationship, then the child may simply have to respect him or her from a distance.

Obligations of Children toward Parents

The previous sections of this chapter have looked at many of the tensions inherent in parenting children. Similar tensions are frequently experienced in the opposite direction as well, as children grow from being dependent on their parents, to being independent of them, to eventually also becoming responsible for them, and specifically for their health and the preservation of their dignity at the end of their lives. While these challenges were certainly not unknown in ancient times, it has become even more of an issue in our own times with increased longevity yielding the reality that adult children may have caregiving responsibilities for aging parents that last much, much longer than was generally the case in previous generations.

Aging Parents

Jewish law states that if a parent has material resources but lacks the wherewithal to manage them effectively or adequately, the child must labor to ensure that the parent's funds are used to provide appropriately for his or her needs. If a parent is indigent, however, it is the responsibility of the child to provide for his mother and father's health, comfort, and dignity (*SA* Yoreh Dei·ah 240:5).

At the beginning of this chapter, we discussed the obligations of children to respect and honor their parents. These commandments specifically involve respecting their opinions and ensuring that they are properly cared for. Tragically, these two values can come into conflict as children try to balance their elderly parents' desire for independence with the filial obligation to feed and protect them.

In an ideal world, adult children would live in close proximity to their parents and help them make necessary medical and lifestyle adjustments to preserve their independence and dignity to the maximum degree possible. Unfortunately, this ideal is far from the messy reality experienced by many contemporary families. Children seeking to care for their aging parents may need to overcome serious obstacles involving geography, the pursuit of adequate healthcare, the maintenance of appropriate housing, the organization of strained finances, and their own emotional turmoil in order to care properly for their parents. In cases of estrangement, overcoming a long history of disappointment and tension may be the deepest issue of all. In all cases, however, adult children attempting to look after the needs of aging parents will find themselves uncertain and ill at ease about the role reversal in which children take over as caregivers and parents become those in need of support and succor. Even when parents are still able financially and emotionally to look after their own needs, the obligations of adult children toward their parents will differ dramatically from the analogous obligations of young children toward their parents, however. The following sections address some of the most common complications experienced by adult children trying to fulfill their obligations toward their older parents.

Divorced Parents

Honoring one's parents may be the most challenging of *mitzvot,* but this task becomes even more daunting when those parents are divorced. If the child was young when his or her parents separated, he or she may harbor unresolved disappointment and grief for many years. Even when the children are grown, they may have difficulty accepting their parents' decision to terminate their marriage.

Just as parents must learn to accept their children on their own terms, so must children come to view their parents as individuals with their own needs, and not just as providers of material and emotional support for their offspring. This is hard enough for young children, but the logistical aspect of honoring divorced parents becomes even more complicated when the children themselves are adults, especially if the parents live far from each other, and from their children. If bitterness lingers between the parents, it can be difficult for the children to avoid becoming accomplices in a feud that they did not create and that they certainly cannot control. As the psalmist wrote at Psalm 34:15, one of the ways of living life to the fullest is to seek always to make peace between people. Nevertheless, it will seldom be possible for children to fix their parents' broken relationship. And accepting that reality may well be the first step in coming to terms with the divorce of one's parents.

If one parent becomes emotionally distant or physically or emotionally abusive, or if a parent abandons his or her children, it may be psychologically and physically impossible for the child or children involved to fulfill the obligation to respect and honor that parent. In such cases, the child may need to minimize contact with the parent even as the talmudic master, Rav Asi, did in fleeing Babylonia for the Land of Israel after quarreling with his mother (see *BT* Kiddushin 31b). Nevertheless, the Torah commands us to honor and respect parents without reference to the quality of the relationship and to the greatest extent possible. If it is emotionally or logistically impossible for children to attend to their parents personally, they still must ensure that their parents are physically safe and comfortable.

Flash points of tension with divorced families often emerge at holidays and life-cycle events. Will the divorced parents appear together at a bar or bat mitzvah ceremony? Will the estranged parent be invited to stand under the *ḥuppah?* Is it insulting to exclude a parent's new spouse from the festivities? If each parent is hosting a Passover *seder,* whose should the children attend?

Jewish law does not address each of these situations, but Jewish values can still guide us. The *halakhah* requires us to be even-handed in the respect and honor we show toward both parents. As we have seen, Rabbi Soloveitchik observes that there may be tension between the internal bonds of love and the external duties of the law. Children must provide for their parents' physical needs and dignity; they should try to be fair toward both mother and father, and they should be wary of being used as weapons in ongoing skirmishes between their parents. If they can fulfill the external obligations, but not the internal devotion, they are nevertheless making the best of a difficult situation that is beyond their control.

Honoring Parents with Dementia

At Leviticus 19:32, the Torah commands us to rise in the presence of our elders and to "beautify" the face of the old. These twin injunctions may be seen as amplifications of a single idea, as demonstrations of respect for the aged do indeed give the elderly an aura of dignified beauty. The psalmist promises the righteous productivity and vitality even in old age at Psalm 92:15. The Book of Proverbs teaches that "gray hair is a splendid crown through the pursuit of righteousness" (Proverbs 16:31). When the elderly receive their due respect from the young, life is more beautiful, richer, and fuller for the representatives of both generations. And if these injunctions apply to the elderly in general, then how much more so do they apply to one's own elderly parents!

The Torah states at Exodus 20:12 that the reward for honoring one's parents is long life. Nevertheless, long life is not always good life. In modern times, people can live many years with tremendous physical and or mental impairments. One of the saddest and most challenging afflictions for children to encounter is the physical and/or mental decline, perhaps even to the point of dementia, of a parent who in some instances may not even recognize the child who faithfully tends to her or his needs. In some cases, this descent into oblivion can allow a perennially bitter parent-child relationship to mellow. Far more often, however, severe dementia sorely tests the endurance and love of a child for a parent whose personality seems to have fled, leaving behind a needy and unresponsive body. When a parent needs assistance with his or her physical hygiene, it may cause even more embarrassment to have a son or daughter attend to those needs. The dignity of the parent may require the child to seek outside assistance.

Already in the Talmud, we learn about parents whose erratic or demented behavior frustrated their children's attempts to honor them. Rabbi Eliezer states that even if a parent takes a child's wallet and throws it in the sea, the child must not shame the parent (*BT* Kiddushin 32a). And we have already mentioned the story of Rav Asi, whose elderly mother made such unreasonable demands of him that he finally had to flee from her (ibid. 31b). The Talmud seems to approve of his decision, understanding that, at least in some cases, a child simply cannot fulfill his or her filial obligations in the presence of an unbalanced or demented parent. Yet the obligation remains in place, even if it must be met vicariously or circuitously without involving direct parent-child contact.

These stories also throw light upon the rabbis' views about the financial obligations of children toward their parents. Maimonides concludes that children may use their parents' own resources to honor them, but that, if their parents have no money, children must then pay for their parents' food, clothing, and shelter from their own pocket (*MT* Hilkhot Mamrim 6:3). In our day, when healthcare expenses can quickly exhaust a family's resources, a balance must be found that will provide for the parent's dignified existence without impoverishing the younger generation. Financial considerations aside, however, it is surely the emotional weight of attending to the ongoing daily needs of a physically or mentally disabled parent that is most difficult for many children today. This responsibility is perhaps most challenging in cases of dementia when the parent no longer recognizes the child.

Rabbi David Golinkin describes a debate between Maimonides, who allows a child to place a demented parent in the care of others, and Rabbi Abraham ben David of Posquières (called the Ravad), who protests that a child's obligations toward his or her parents cannot reasonably be made a function of that individual's health, mental or otherwise. This medieval debate occurred in a context quite different from our own, one in which extended families lived in close proximity to each other and in which there were no professional nursing facilities available. Golinkin advocates for a middle ground, allowing the appointment of professional healthcare providers, but preferring to keep the parent in his or her own home environment whenever possible ("Institutionalizing Parents with Alzheimer's Disease," in *Responsa in a Moment* [Jerusalem: Schechter Institute, 2000], pp. 37–41).

A parent's safety, dignity, and physical and emotional health should always be their children's highest priorities. Because balancing these values can be exceptionally difficult, families may need to consult with doctors, social workers, and rabbis in order to settle on the best way to serve and honor the mentally deteriorating parent.

Even if the parent retains intellectual clarity, his or her physical needs and anxieties may prove impossible for the children to satisfy. Indeed, adults will sometimes find themselves torn between their obligations toward their children and their parents. While Rabbi Golinkin has demonstrated the permissibility of paying others to provide the medical and physical services that parents require, it remains preferable for the children of senescent individuals to be involved personally in their parents' care to the greatest extent possible.

When Parents' Burial Wishes Oppose Halakhah

At Leviticus 19:3, we read: "Each person must revere his or her mother and father, and you must observe My Sabbaths." The rabbis considered the odd juxtaposition of ideas in this verse and concluded that there may well be cases in which respecting a parent conflicts with other core Jewish values, such as observing Shabbat. The Torah never releases Jewish people from their obligation to observe Shabbat, and the rabbis taught that a child must feel obliged to disobey a parent in order to keep the laws of the Torah (*Sifra* K'doshim, *parsh'ta* 1:10). Nevertheless, even then a child must remain respectful. Rather than chastising the parent directly, for example, the child should initiate a more impersonal conversation about the importance of behaving in accordance with the law and explain how important that concept has become for him or her.

What if a parent asks a child to violate Jewish law by having his or her body cremated? The child should plead with the parent to reconsider this plan and should reassure the parent that his or her body will be treated respectfully after death, and that his or her grave will be maintained in perpetuity by the family. If the parent insists on being cremated, the children should inform the parent that he or she will have to look after making the arrangements on his or her own. Afterward, however, the child should mourn his or her parent in the traditional manner. The specific issues involved in the disposition of cremated remains are examined in more detail above by Rabbi Carl Astor in his chapter on the Jewish life cycle.

The Hearts of Parents and Children

In this chapter, we have addressed many painful situations, especially those in which people must fulfill their parental or filial duties without the framework of a loving and stable relationship. In an unpublished sermon, Rabbi Roderick Young speaks powerfully about such circumstances: "I think that I will be in fulfillment of the fifth commandment only once I have accepted my mother for who she is, and for the path she took, rather than for whom I would like her to be."

There are many other difficult situations faced by parents trying to raise children, and by children seeking to honor their parents. Jewish law addresses some cases, but Jewish values can guide families even in uncharted territory. Safety, comfort, and dignity are the paramount concerns both of parents toward their children, and also of children toward their parents. When it is impossible for one member of the family to satisfy all the demands of Jewish law, he or she should still try to the best of his or her ability to show respect and kindness.

Judaism sees respect for parents as a form of respect for God. Accepting this truth does not require one to insist that one's parents are infallible or that their wishes must always supersede any other values a child might hold; rather, this teaching implies that God has made the world in such a way so as to share the glory of the divine realm with parents for the benefit of the entire family. Children who respect and honor even imperfect parents develop greater virtue themselves, and model the type of commitment that they later hope to see in their own children. Likewise, parents must seek to influence even very wayward children in the hope that they will grow through their difficulties and eventually realize their infinite potential for good.

Thankfully, many families do not experience the profound challenges described above. Rather, most parents and children navigate the ordinary challenges of living in relationship with those we love, supporting them when necessary and giving them room to grow independently as well. It is the intensity of attachment that sometimes makes these relationships so fraught—difficult parent-child relationships are particularly painful, but loving relationships are among the sweetest gifts of life. Jewish tradition supports us in the challenging times and provides many ways in which to celebrate the bonds between parents and children.

The prophet Malachi predicts the return of Elijah, the messianic precursor, by imagining the ancient prophet coming to "turn the hearts of parents toward their children, and the hearts of children toward their parents" (Malachi 3:23). From this we can understand that harmony and peace within the family are essential to the Jewish vision of redemption. Each positive parent-child relationship is another paving stone on the road to salvation and a source of potentially infinite goodness in the world.

Between Siblings

DAVID M. GREENSTEIN

Sibling relationships occupy a paradoxical position in Jewish tradition. Although the foundational first book of the Bible, Genesis, spends a great deal of time and attention on siblings (as does the first part of Exodus), once the Torah shifts its focus from stories of our ancestors to the demands of the good and holy life as revealed through the encounter with the Divine at Sinai, the subject of sibling relationships is hardly considered. This means that any attempt to construct an ethics of sibling relationships from a Jewish perspective requires paying attention primarily to the extensive narrative portions of the Torah. We might also wonder about the possible meanings of this paradox of imbalance.

Biblical Precedents

The earliest story of siblings in the Torah, the tragedy of Cain and Abel, is one of the first tales in Genesis. After mentioning the birth of these two brothers to the first human couple, Eve and Adam, the Torah skips years ahead and presents the two as responsible working men: Cain, we learn, is a farmer, while Abel has become a shepherd. After they both offer sacrifices to God and God seems to favor Abel's offering, Cain becomes angry and depressed, and he eventually kills his brother. It is then that God calls out to Cain, "Where is Abel, your brother?" (Genesis 4:9). This question is freighted with the heavy echo of the first question God asked of Adam after he had sinned, "Where are you?" (Genesis 3:9), and we are clearly intended to consider these questions in light of each other, and then to conclude that, just as we are fundamentally responsible for ourselves and our personal conduct, so are we fundamentally responsible for our siblings and their welfare. God's question to Cain implies that Cain is expected to be concerned with his brother. But Cain rejects this notion and says, "I wouldn't know. Am I my brother's keeper?" (ibid.). This defensive, defiant response also echoes an earlier verse: God had placed Adam in the Garden to work it and "keep it" (Genesis 2:15). Cain, the farmer, assumes the burden of this command to "keep" a garden, but declines the role God tacitly expects of him, to "keep" his brother as well. From this telling, yet subtle, use of language, we learn a profound lesson: that the responsibilities brothers and sisters bear to their siblings are absolute and cannot be shed through negotiation or with reference to one's other obligations or accomplishments.

As with all the Torah's stories, the story of Cain and Abel is as notable for what it omits as for what it tells. One crucial omission stands out especially when this story is compared with subsequent biblical tales of sibling relationships. Later, we encounter brothers and sisters who compete with each other for the affections or gifts of a parent or spouse. Here, however, Adam and Eve play no explicit role in the drama. Though these brothers are the first humans to have human parents, those parents are not the source of their tragic conflict. Rather, the only explanation offered by the Torah for Cain's fury is his aggrieved, venomous envy of his brother's success in connecting to God. It is as if the Torah were saying that the bitterest forms of sibling rivalry do not require parental malfeasance, real or perceived, and that these terrible conflicts can arise even as human beings engage in their most noble strivings. It is a sobering lesson, made even starker by its appearance among the very first lessons Scripture teaches.

The tendency toward sibling rivalry is inherent in the process of growth and individuation that we must undergo to mature. If we submit to the violent feelings that this rivalry engenders, we court tragedy and death. If we deny that we are subject to these feelings, we condemn ourselves and others to misery and suffering. Only by acknowledging the reality of sibling rivalry and learning to master it can siblings hope to find an emotionally healthy and ethical way to live in harmony with each other.

As the stories of Genesis unfold, the Torah describes the first stages of a people's acceptance of the demands of a holy and ethical life. While these stories feature the emotional, spiritual, and moral vicissitudes of spouses and of parents and children, the theme of sibling rivalry is also deeply enmeshed and entwined in this complex web of family interrelationships. Overall, these dramas are wrenching and problematic. There are no happy families in Genesis.

Since the background of these stories is the patriarchal society of the ancient Near East, more attention is given to fathers than to mothers, and more to brothers than to sisters. Still, stories about sisters, or brothers and sisters, are not absent. These include narratives about Lot's daughters, about Laban and his sister Rebecca, and about Dinah and her brothers.

When it comes to stories of brothers, the salient thread running through the Genesis narratives is their inability to dwell together. Later, the psalmist would famously muse that harmonious sibling relations should be especially noticed and appreciated: "See how good and pleasant it is when brothers dwell together" (Psalm 133:1).

It is only in the Book of Exodus that we find a counter-narrative. Exodus opens by marking the transition of the Israelites from family to people. It tells of their liberation from Egyptian enslavement and their transformation into a holy nation. Instead of troubling stories, we find that the redemption of Israel is effected through the concerted efforts of three siblings, each of whom defies sibling stereotypes. Only through the cooperation of these siblings can Israel be redeemed.

From Story to Law

The lessons of these narratives serve as the implicit basis for the laws the Torah subsequently formulates regarding siblings. Sibling rivalry is recognized as a source of potential pain and catastrophe, whether caused by parental insensitivity, the clash of personalities, or the desires of the siblings themselves. On the other hand, the protective instinct that a sibling can have for a brother or sister can become a force for great good in both their lives. The relationship between siblings is almost inevitably fraught with mixed emotions. The ethical challenge, therefore, is not merely to nod to the inherent complexity of the sibling relationship, but to do justice to that complexity, and its attendant ambiguity, by creating a sacred context in which its intricacies can be worked through to the benefit of all involved parties. What instruction does the Torah offer to accomplish this?

The Torah lacks any explicit statement regarding sibling relationships that parallels the *mitzvah* to honor one's parents, given such pride of place in the Ten Commandments, or the fundamental parental mandate to raise children to the love and service of God. Nevertheless, the Torah assumes a deep and powerful bond between siblings, a bond that can be appealed to effectively as the basis for proper ethical conduct toward perfect strangers. Thus the Torah states, "Should your brother become impoverished and need a helping hand, give him support, whether he be a stranger or a resident, so that he may live along with you" (Leviticus 25:35). In other words, just as you would naturally wish to help your brother, so should you extend support to anyone else in need. Similarly, the Torah uses the terms "brother," "friend," and "neighbor" interchangeably in the following fundamental teaching: "Do not hate your brother in your heart, but admonish your friend so that you will not place a sin upon him. Do not seek revenge or bear a grudge regarding the children of your people. Rather, you shall love your neighbor as yourself" (Leviticus 19:17–18, see Rashbam and Naḥmanides *ad loc.*).

This approach recognizes the tension that exists between our self-understanding as independent moral agents and our sense of ourselves as members of a larger group. The Torah invokes the primitive allegiance we may feel toward blood relations and calls upon us to extend that bond outward, directing our actions toward the holier standard of righteousness. It exploits the emotive weight of the term "brother" in order to universalize that sense of responsibility so that it applies to all our relationships. This is a fundamental step in ethical thinking. By viewing the entire population, citizen and stranger alike, as our brothers and sisters, we are concomitantly moved to treat everyone fairly.

Such universalism must not, however, become a totalitarian denial of the special bonds of family. It is generally agreed that those systems of social engineering that have attempted to efface all recognition of familial bonds have eventually become inhuman and unethical. In universalizing its ethics, the Torah subsumes the bulk of issues involving siblings under the same ethical principles that rule all our interpersonal relationships. Nevertheless, it voices certain concerns that apply specifically to sibling relationships, both addressing issues that arise within the framework of the family of origin and seeking to mandate a sense of positive, useful connection between siblings after they have separated and embarked on their own lives.

Siblings and Parents

In a perfect family, all siblings would grow up sustained equally by their parents' love, resources, and guidance. Indeed, the family ideal pictured by our tradition is a stable hierarchy ruled by the principle of fairness. Parents are enjoined to treat their children without favoritism and all children are commanded to respect their parents and maintain their parents' material and psychological dignity. (These obligations and responsibilities are spelled out in more detail above by Rabbi Daniel Nevins in his chapter on the parent-child relationship.) The cumulative force of the biblical narrative is that siblings are enjoined to support and sustain each other, not merely to acknowledge but truly to accept each other as brother and sister. (See in this regard Isaiah 58:7 and the rabbinic development of its implications; and see also below.) To close the circle, such mutual love and support would be a source of great satisfaction for their parents, as evidenced by the narrative regarding Joseph and his brothers at Genesis 50:16–17.

But such equilibrium is often wanting. When children witness their parents treating one of their siblings differently, even those singled out as their parents' favorite may feel resentment toward those parents. Siblings will find their innate sense of loyalty to each other tested, sometimes severely, under the stress of such a situation. Resentment will be directed toward the more fortunate sibling, even if that child tries hard to remain unspoiled and loving toward the other children in the family. The ramifications of parents' failure to parent justly and well will be felt even into their children's adulthood.

The central theme of Torah law as it applies to siblings is that they must behave responsibly toward each other regardless of their parents' shortcomings or failings. This means that resentment over how one's parents behaved in the past should not determine (at least, not wholly) how one relates to one's parents or to one's siblings in the present. In principle, all adult siblings are equally obligated to honor their parents. All are equally responsible for helping their parents maintain a dignified life to the end of their days. And all siblings must treat each other in a brotherly or sisterly way. Inequitable parenting is not considered an adequate excuse for poor behavior by children later in life.

For example, adult siblings must equally attend to their aging father or mother, even though he or she may have overtly preferred one of them as a child. No sibling may try to place the burden of looking after their parent solely on another, either out of anger over the perceived favoritism or out of resentment. In addition, adults siblings are obligated to affirm each other as equals regardless of whether they recall their childhoods to have been painful or not. (In this regard, see the legal material collected at *BT* K'tubbot 68a–b, which discusses the responsibilities of adult siblings toward each other.) Of course, the favored child must tactfully guard against any attempts by the favoring parent to enlist her in his continuing discrimination against a less favored sibling, a point made clearly in the thirteenth century by Rabbeinu Asher (as quoted about a century later by Rabbi Isaiah of Trani in his *Shiltei*

Ha-gibborim commentary on the section of the *Sefer Ha-halakhot* of Rabbi Isaac Alfasi (1013–1103), called the Rif, covering the talmudic material found at *BT* Kiddushin 13b). Furthermore, when a parent passes away, all surviving children are obligated to take care of their parent's funeral and burial arrangements. This cooperation helps fulfill their obligations to their parent, but it also fulfills their obligations to each other—just as Ishmael and Isaac, and later Esau and Jacob, owed it to each other to come together to bury their fathers.

This principle of equality may be extrapolated from the halakhic system, even where it reflects the kind of patriarchal reality that was the norm in most societies until very recently. Thus, after providing for the preservation of patriarchal estates through laws of primogeniture and male inheritance, the prohibition against favoritism and the injunction to equal distribution of assets is biblically and rabbinically affirmed. In his chapter on inheritance law elsewhere in this volume, Rabbi Martin S. Cohen provides a detailed summary of the *halakhah* of bequests, but here it will suffice to note that, in the patriarchal system endorsed by the traditional *halakhah,* brothers inherit equally—other than the firstborn, who receives a double portion of the estate—but are obliged to see to the needs of their sisters until those sisters are married. If the estate is small, the sisters are provided for first, since the brothers are deemed capable of fending for themselves (*MT* Hilkhot Naḥalot 5:2).

These regulations subvert the gender biases we normally associate with patriarchy, but a similar upending of expectations also occurs in the halakhic concept of the obligations married siblings bear regarding parental care. While one might assume that the care of elderly parents would fall to their daughters, the halakhic assumption was that women who married would be occupied fully with the maintenance of their new households. In recognition of this pressure, the *halakhah* mandates that brothers cannot reasonably expect their married sisters to care for their parents. Since a woman's husband could well object to her spending time, effort, and/or money on her parents that might otherwise be devoted to caring for her new family, the obligation to look after senescent or infirm parents became the sole responsibility of sons! (The talmudic discussion appears at *BT* Kiddushin 30b and its halakhic elaboration is found at *SA* Yoreh Dei·ah 240:17.) The ethical integrity of the *halakhah* is striking here, as is its unexpected conviction that men can be both excellent providers and sensitive caregivers.

Nevertheless, it is common, for various reasons, for these obligations to fall unevenly among siblings. Nor is this always avoidable. Perhaps one sibling is simply too far away to be available to parents in another city. Perhaps the emotional damage sustained by one of the siblings is too severe to ignore even years later. In such cases, siblings' obligations to their parents must be met in other ways. If possible, the sibling who is more involved must try to engage the less-involved sibling in planning and decision-making, so that everything is done (at least formally) on behalf of all the brothers and sisters. If that sense of united purpose can be achieved, it will be easier to work out an equitable way to share the inevitable expenses, tasks, and emotional burden involved in caring for older parents later on. (On the question of financial obligations involved in caring for parents, see Rabbi Nevins' comments in the previous chapter of this book.) In the end, it comes down to the simple truth that a *mitzvah* binding on all children in a family should not be left for one sibling to carry alone—a point made obliquely, yet forcefully, in Numbers 32, where Moses appeals to the tribes of Reuben and Gad not to stand by while their "brothers" shoulder the task of possessing the Promised Land. But, beyond that, the less-involved sibling owes his or her more engaged brother or sister another type of support: frank acknowledgment and regular expression of appreciation for that sibling's efforts.

Sharing and Getting Along

The tradition sought to expand the commandment to honor one's parents to include other family members whenever appropriate and possible. The Talmud, for example, reads the fifth commandment to include the obligation to honor one's older brother or sister. (See *BT* K'tubbot 103a and Rabbi Barukh Halevi Epstein's comments in his *Torah T'mimah* on Exodus 20:12, note 86, for a fuller discussion of this reading of Scripture.) Authorities differ in their understanding of this requirement, however. Does it devolve from the primary obligation to honor one's own parents (i.e., should siblings treat each other well to make their parents happy), or is it a separate, independent requirement? This is not an idle question of textual intent, as it leads to the profoundly important halakhic question of who, if anybody, can free younger siblings from this responsibility: can parents ease this obligation (since it was intended, really, to honor them), or is it only the older siblings themselves who may forego their prerogative to demand tangible signs of a younger brother or sister's respect? (For an interesting discussion of this question, see Naḥmanides' comments to the second principle in Maimonides' introduction to his *Sefer Ha-mitzvot*.) Furthermore, opinion is divided among contemporary rabbis as to whether this strictly choreographed social structure is to be taken as inherently desirable, or whether it should be viewed as merely the tradition's response to prevailing social conditions—and thus something that could or should be modified as social realities themselves change over the years.

Respect for an older sibling is a value still cherished in traditional Jewish communities. As Western ideals of individualism and freedom have become more widely adopted, however, Jewish communities (even very traditional ones) have relaxed certain hierarchical expectations. On the other hand, contemporary reality places ever higher demands on all family members—whether they be younger or older—to learn how to respect each other and to find ways to get along harmoniously. The value of family harmony—*sh'lom bayit*—is another whose imperatives are more strongly expressed in our tradition's narratives than in its legal literature. (But see, e.g., *SA* Oraḥ Ḥayyim 203:3).

By the time siblings reach adulthood, they will have acquired deep reservoirs of feeling and habit regarding their parents and each other. Nor will it always be the case that grown children share the same sense of their childhood together. It is unrealistic and unethical to ask people simply to throw away their memories of the past. (Indeed, the commandment to give honor to the elderly is understood at *BT* Kiddushin 33a to teach that every person's accumulated life experience is of inherent value.) The biblical emphasis on narrative in its teachings about sibling relationships may be interpreted as a tacit recognition that these relationships are subject to the divergent and shared narratives that connect siblings to each other. Whether or not siblings will continue to maintain and develop a sense of connection with each other after they leave their common parental home will follow not so much from ethical directives as from the continuing narratives of each one's life.

Intimacy and Distance

The *halakhah* recognizes that separation, rather than sharing, may be the correct course in some cases. Just as one is counseled to keep a distance from a parent if maintaining contact will be destructive to one's well-being, so should one avoid relationships with a sibling if remaining close would be too painful or hurtful. (See the comments of Isaiah of Trani, *Shiltei Ha-gibborim* commentary on the section of the *Sefer Ha-halakhot* of Rabbi Isaac Alfasi, called the Rif, covering the talmudic material found at *BT* Kiddushin 13b, regarding parents and children, and applied, *a fortiori,* by later authorities to siblings.) Another such circumstance may arise due to strained relations between in-laws. The *halakhah* accepts that a husband or a wife may deny his or her spouse the pleasure of siblings' company, but this only pertains within the walls of the spousal home. That is, either spouse may control who is welcome to enter a shared home, but neither may deny a partner the right to visit his or her siblings, or parents, elsewhere. (This is codified by Maimonides at *MT* Hilkhot Ishut 13:14. The commentaries to Maimonides' code discuss whether such a denial must have a valid reason or can be wholly arbitrary.)

In the context of that ruling, Maimonides counsels the restricted wife to visit her parents or siblings monthly, when a family gathering is held, and on holidays. It is interesting that, although the Torah does not formally mandate that Shabbat or holidays be celebrated with any family beyond one's spouse and children, spending the holiday with extended family seems to be an ancient custom (see, for example, *M* K'tubbot 7:4). Indeed, we read at 1 Samuel 20:28–29 that King Saul's son, Jonathan, tells his father that David had gone home to celebrate Rosh Ḥodesh with his family at the invitation of one of his brothers, which information Saul accepts as constituting perfectly normal behavior.

Whatever their relationship might have been when all siblings were alive, the Torah teaches that it is important for a person to be present at the burial of his or her siblings and also formally to mourn their passing. While *kohanim* are forbidden to come in contact with the dead in most settings, the Torah commands them to attend the burial of their spouses, parents, children, and siblings. (The scriptural source for this is Leviticus 21:2–3, but see Maimonides at *MT* Hilkhot Eivel 2:2 for a discussion of whether or not this permission applies to half-siblings as well. The issue of contact between *kohanim* and the dead in our day is discussed in more detail elsewhere in this volume by Rabbi Carl N. Astor in his chapter on the Jewish life cycle.)

Interestingly, this obligation to attend a sibling's burial does not apply to the High Priest, who is barred from attending to the burial of even his closest kin (ibid., verse 11). This reflects his exclusive designation for divine service, but the *halakhah* also supports the right of individuals to assume a status of analogous holiness. A person who has undertaken the ascetic regimen known as naziriteship (*n'zirut*), for example, is also prohibited from burying a parent, a child, a wife, or a sibling (Numbers 6:6–7). The Torah seems to be teaching that we must accept that sometimes there are overwhelming personal forces that may legitimately take precedence even over such primal family obligations as burying one's family members. Still, the salient detail here is that the final choice to adopt a regimen of such strict asceticism is in the nazirite's hands. (And it is also so that, because the nazirite has undertaken this status voluntarily, it is possible to have the vow nullified in a truly compelling circumstance.) The Torah does not tell us how to evaluate the individual who has decided to remove himself from his family for the sake of a sacred quest. That narrative can only be told by the individuals involved.

The Incest Taboo

At the heart of the Jewish sexual ethic rests an elaborate set of incest taboos. These are listed in chapters 18 and 20 of Leviticus, and constitute part of what scholars have come to call the Holiness Code. (The full Holiness Code is said to stretch from Leviticus 17 to 26.) Sexual relations between various relatives are prohibited in simple and direct language, but the prohibition of sexual relations between a brother and sister mentioned at Leviticus 20:17 bears an unusual characterizing term. It is labeled a *ḥesed,* which in this context denotes a disgraceful act, but which is homonymously related to the word meaning "lovingkindness." The point Scripture seems to be making by using such a loaded term here is the potent lesson that there exists in sibling relations a powerful potential for abuse that may attempt to masquerade as a series of caring and loving acts. The Bible forcefully conveys the moral decay of the House of David, for example, by relating the case of the misconceived passion that Amnon bore for his half-sister Tamar. What begins with feelings called love degenerates into manipulation, rape, and "a great hatred," leading to revenge and fratricide (2 Samuel 13). The prohibition against sibling incest applies equally to full brothers and sisters and to half-siblings. And while tradition regularly considers converts to be "like infants newly born" into the family of the Jewish people, proselytes are still prohibited from engaging in sexual relations with any non-Jewish siblings from their original families (*SA* Yoreh Dei·ah 269:1). In recent times, this prohibition has been extended to include sexual relations between adopted siblings as well (see, e.g., the responsum by Elliot Dorff in *CJLS Responsa 1991–2000,* p. 483).

Levirate Marriage

There is one stunning exception to the stringent prohibitions against sexual relations with relatives. Ordinarily, a brother is forbidden to marry a woman who has previously been his brother's wife (Leviticus 18:16 and *BT* Y'vamot 55a). However, the Torah mandates at Deuteronomy 25:5–10 that, in the case of a man who dies childless, his brother must take the widow as his wife "to preserve a name for his brother in Israel." (In context, this clearly applies even if that brother is already married.) There seems to have been a number of concerns underlying this *mitzvah*, called *yibbum* in Hebrew. Posterity is conceived in this context both in biological and in financial terms: the deceased brother's hereditary line would be perpetuated by his surviving brother's act of *yibbum* and the former's estate, a portion of the extended family's land holdings, would thus remain in the family's possession. In addition, a childless widow ran the risk of abandonment and neglect in a patriarchal society, and the practice of *yibbum* spoke directly to this concern by assuring that a man's widow would remain protected within his family circle (see Jeffrey Tigay's remarks in *The JPS Commentary: Deuteronomy* [Philadelphia: The Jewish Publication Society, 1996], p. 482, citing Josephus).

Still, later authorities seem discomfited by the practice. Indeed, the *halakhah* could almost be said to have developed at cross-purposes with itself, restricting this exception to the incest laws to the greatest extent possible. Thus the levir, as the deceased husband's brother is formally known, was obligated to perform the *mitzvah* of *yibbum* only if the brothers had the same father. Moreover, as long as the deceased had fathered any offspring from any marriage, the obligation was considered void regardless of whether those children were male or female, living or dead. Thus, as Maimonides points out (at *MT* Hilkhot Yibbum Va-ḥalitzah 1:7), this sibling obligation was applied considerably more narrowly than in other areas where sibling kinship is relevant, such as mourning obligations and the disqualification of witnesses who are siblings.

Yet, despite these limitations, it seems clear that the Torah desires that the man fulfill his obligations to his dead brother. This is reinforced in Scripture by the story of Onan told at Genesis 38:1–10, where Onan's refusal to try to have a child for his dead brother's sake angers God so grievously that it costs him his life. In light of stories like that, we would expect this command to be categorical, and that any refusal to obey would be condemned as unacceptable. Yet, surprisingly, the Torah offers the unwilling brother an alternative through a ceremony called *ḥalitzah,* as a result of which the widow is free to marry the man of her choice. (The ceremony's name means "shoe removal" and derives from the part of the ceremony in which the widow signals her contempt for her brother-in-law's unwillingness to preserve his late brother's name by removing his shoe in public.)

Over the centuries various authorities and communities came to feel a distinct sense of ill ease with the requirement of *yibbum* and began to advocate that *ḥalitzah* always be chosen over *yibbum.* Another relevant detail, at least among Ashkenazic Jews, was the adoption a millennium ago of the formal prohibition of polygyny known as the ban of Rabbeinu Gershom. This formal ban made it impossible for a levir who already had a wife to take another, even for the sake of performing the *mitzvah* of *yibbum.* Jewish communities in the Mediterranean region and in Muslim lands, however, continued to prefer that *yibbum* be performed. In 1950, to promote unity among Jewish communities and to prevent abuse, the chief rabbinate of the State of Israel outlawed *yibbum,* mandating the sole practice of *ḥalitzah* where necessary. But even this ritual will feel deeply troublesome for many moderns. Though *ḥalitzah* is clearly meant by Scripture to humiliate the brother who is unwilling to meet his obligation to his late sibling, it is commonly experienced today as a humiliation of the widow, who must perform this rite to be free. Discussion has begun to address this problem. In any case, either practice is extremely rare today. Should this sensitive situation arise, a rabbi should be consulted.

However specialized or problematic, these *mitzvot* may provide certain ethical guidelines that are relevant to all siblings. The law of *yibbum* teaches us that it is worthy and right to exert oneself to perpetuate the memory of a brother or sister, especially when the deceased had no children, and that this effort can be motivated, among other reasons, by a desire to keep a late sibling's name alive in the world. And other lessons emerge from the scenario envisaged by Scripture as well. There is, for example, no obligation for the surviving brother to memorialize his lost brother when the deceased has children. This teaches us that it is important to make sure that any memorial efforts on the part of a sibling be coordinated with the decedent's surviving family, whose wishes should generally be given priority.

The mythic significance of *yibbum* can also be interpreted as an attempt to repair the sin described in the first biblical story about brothers. God chastises Cain with the words, "What have you done? The sound of your brother's blood is screaming out to Me from the earth" (Genesis 4:10), and Rashi explains that this reference to screaming refers to the shrieks of Abel's unborn descendants. Leaving aside the simple way the text can be taken to indict Cain of murder, Rashi's take on God's words imagines that Cain is being accused also of ignoring the voice of his brother as it called out to him from the grave. And that is precisely what the commandment of *yibbum* mandates: that a man must hear his deceased brother's voice crying out from the grave for assistance in perpetuating his memory, a principle that can easily be applied not just to childless brothers but to all siblings.

Helping Out

Siblings are commanded by the Torah to help each other when they are in dire financial straits. The Torah imagines that poor people might be forced to sell their property when they fall on hard times, or even sell themselves as indentured servants to pay off their debts. In these cases, the Torah explicitly charges the family of such individuals to come to their aid. A brother or sister must try to buy back his or her sibling's property, or even to purchase his or her freedom. Significantly, this act is called "redemption" and the helpful sibling is called a "redeemer" at Leviticus 25:25, 48. This teaches us that the first obligation in giving *tz'dakah* ("charitable righteousness") is to help one's own relatives—one's parents, then one's children, then one's siblings (including half-siblings), and then other relatives (*SA* Yoreh Dei·ah 251:3). But others place one's siblings even before one's children (see, for example, the comment of Rabbi Elijah Kramer, the Vilna Gaon, in the *Bi·ur Ha-G'ra, ad loc.*).

The *mitzvah* of *tz'dakah* is an example of a broad-ranging, binding *mitzvah* whose fulfillment, by its nature, cannot be completely discharged by any one act. How and when one performs this *mitzvah* is left open to the individual; this *mitzvah* can be fulfilled through the gift of one's self as well as through the giving of one's resources. Thus, giving blood to someone in need of a transfusion would be an example of *tz'dakah*. And, if, as just mentioned, family relationship creates a prior claim upon one's *tz'dakah* choices, some authorities, such as Rabbi A. Sofer-Abraham and Rabbi S. Z. Auerbach, see it as especially incumbent on close relatives to donate blood on behalf of an ailing family member. (These latter opinions are quoted by Rabbi Joel Roth in his responsum on blood and organ donation published in *CJLS Responsa 1991–2000,* p. 214; Rabbi Roth himself, however, questions the legitimacy of this position.)

Thanks to modern medical advances, siblings are in a unique position to help one another in cases where their genetic and biological affinity is medically significant. Organ transplants are less likely to be rejected when the organs derive from close relatives, especially siblings. However, the donation of bone marrow or a kidney also poses some risk to the donor. Therefore, while such a donation would be a fulfillment of the highest *mitzvah* of saving a life, the ultimate decision of whether or not to donate can be made only by the prospective donor-sibling, who must voluntarily decide whether or not to incur the risk. Therefore, there must never be any coercion or attempt to inflict guilt upon the sibling in such matters. The question of live-donor organ transplantation is discussed at length elsewhere in this volume by Rabbi Avram I. Reisner in his chapter on medical ethics.

Because we assume that siblings will wish to help each other in times of need, it is no surprise that Jewish law forbids siblings from committing illegal acts, or from actively supporting each other while doing so, even when such behavior is motivated by the love siblings feel for one another. Siblings are also disqualified from testifying in court on each other's behalf. (Presumably, it would simply be too tempting to tell a falsehood to benefit a brother or sister.) Interestingly, this disqualification of a sibling's testimony does not apply solely with regard to helpful testimony. Damaging testimony is not accepted either. The author of *Sefer Ha-ḥinnukh,* a much-loved compendium of *mitzvot* from early medieval Spain, explains this rule perceptively: "Because relatives always dwell near one another, rising and sitting down as one, it is impossible for them to avoid quarreling with one another from time to time. Were their testimony about each other to be accepted, it could conceivably happen that they might come before a judge in a fit of rage to denounce each other to the king. But when that anger subsided, the relative would practically choke himself out of worry for his kin and what he may have done to him" (*Sefer Ha-ḥinnukh,* commandment no. 596). *Sefer Ha-ḥinnukh* thus captures the volatile nature of sibling relationships and their power to lead us, out of either intense love or uncontrollable anger, to actions that we would later regret. This situation is predicated on the model common in traditional societies, where the extended family endeavors to maintain geographic as well as biological and emotional cohesion. In many ways, this model is changing, though the emotional dynamic at play between siblings remains powerful and real.

New Families and Kinship

Traditionally, siblings are related because they share one or both biological parents. And it is also true that, as noted above, the *halakhah* makes no distinction between full and half siblings in regard to their obligation to mourn, to offer financial assistance, or their disqualification as witnesses in each other's court cases.

Increasingly, however, families in our world are subject to new forces that challenge and reconfigure the old family structures and require new thinking about the nature of family itself. For example, some families are created or modified through adoption, conversion, and new fertility technologies. These strategies create complex questions regarding family relationships.

Legal adoption is a relatively recent development. Whether the Torah itself views adoption as creating a true family bond (see Rabbi Shlomo Kluger's *Ḥokhmat Sh'lomo* commentary to *SA* Even Ha-eizer 1), or whether such a bond is delineated by rabbinic decree (see the responsum of Rabbi Elliot Dorff cited above), all children in a family should be raised to consider themselves as true siblings. (On the specific issue of the priestly status of adopted children, see Rabbi Avram Reisner's, "On the Conversion of Adopted and Patrilineal Children," *CJLS Responsa 1980–1990,* pp. 391–417.)

Some have seen *yibbum* as a biblical prototype for donor insemination and have seized upon it as a solution to the problem of infertility. However, unlike modern donor insemination, *yibbum* can occur only after a brother's death. In a contemporary reversal of the scriptural scenario that yields the concept of *yibbum* in the first place, Rabbi Elliot Dorff has suggested that a sister may, at least under certain specific circumstances, donate eggs to her living, infertile sister, but that a brother may not donate sperm for his infertile sibling. (Rabbi Dorff's remarks were published in his responsum cited above.)

The phenomenon of blended families has increased the incidence of stepsiblings with whom one shares neither biological nor adoptive kinship. In such cases, the obligations deriving directly from such kinship relationships would not apply. However, as noted above, another source of obligation to our siblings is derivative from our obligation to honor our parents, and by extension their partners and children. In addition, there is the general obligation of ensuring *sh'lom bayit*—family harmony—as mentioned above.

A convert to Judaism, setting out on a new path, has traditionally been considered as starting life anew "as a new-born babe" (*BT* Y'vamot 22a). This new status sometimes entails stress and uncertainty regarding a converted person's parents and siblings. There may be feelings of rejection or alienation. Even as converts must be welcomed as they join their new people and, perhaps, their new families, the tradition recognizes that it would be unethical and a betrayal of the sacred nature of the Jewish way of life to pretend that no real relationships exist between converts and their birth families. Therefore the obligations of respect and assistance (in life) and mourning (in death) are incumbent upon converts for parents and close relatives, including siblings. (See Rabbi Joel E. Rembaum, "Converts Mourning the Death of Close Relatives," *CJLS Responsa 1991–2000,* pp. 431–438.)

Choosing Differently

As adults, we have to respect our siblings' choices regarding their lives and their lifestyles. Indeed, just as we want our own choices to be respected, we must extend the same respect and understanding to family members whose choices differ from our own. Siblings who disagree about Jewish observance and lifestyle issues face occasionally painful choices when life-cycle events require them to make decisions together. Some brothers and sisters will be tempted to use the occasion to take a stand on principle, even to the obvious detriment of sibling relationships, but this is almost always a grave mistake. Some will decline to attend weddings or funerals that do not conform to their own religious principles, feeling that attendance at such events confers a kind of legitimacy on them. This may well be a misplaced concern, however, since family members almost always already know where the sibling making the decision to attend or not to attend stands on the specific issue on which the decision turns. Rather, the need of the hour—as much as possible and as explained below—is to be present.

With conversion and intermarriage no longer uncommon, Jews increasingly find themselves in families with non-Jewish relations. Whether these larger family units function as Jewish families is fundamentally a matter of choice. Of course, we yearn for our loved ones to make affirmative Jewish choices, but we also know that this does not always happen. One must therefore try to maintain a friendly relationship with siblings who marry non-Jews, and also with their spouses, even if they decide to create a non-Jewish home together.

Similar difficulties will also arise when a sibling chooses to marry out of the faith or makes a wedding for a child who is marrying a non-Jew. The Committee on Jewish Law and Standards of the Rabbinical Assembly, mindful of the rabbi's public role, requires that no member of the Conservative rabbinate officiate, co-officiate, or be in attendance at an intermarriage. For lay people not bound by such strictures, however, it may be possible to explain that one's attendance does not constitute approval or celebration of intermarriage *per se,* but is meant to be an act of familial solidarity and caring. Especially when a child's intermarriage is a disappointment to his or her parents' Jewish hopes, siblings should attempt to find a way to be as supportive as possible rather than adding sorrow to an already stressful situation by boycotting the event. It must be stressed, however, that all these relationships must be based on mutual respect. Therefore, a person's decision to attend the marriage of a sibling or a sibling's children cannot entail the assumption that that person will forgo his or her own adherence to Jewish values or practices, such as Shabbat or *kashrut* observance, for the sake of participating in the event. One's supportive and even joyous presence at family occasions must be in consonance with one's own self-respect as a Jew. Each sibling must try to accommodate the other.

Sibling relationships have served the Torah as a basic entry point through which to hear God's challenging and sacred call to each of us to nurture our powers of empathy and love, and to overcome our tendencies to envy and competitiveness, so that we may construct lives of holiness and righteousness. Our personal beginnings and subsequent development along this path correspond to the Torah's beginnings and further development of this topic, as Scripture turned its narratives of sibling strife within a family into a sacred teaching that embraces everyone: neighbor, friend, and stranger.

Between Grandparents and Grandchildren

GERALD C. SKOLNIK

The subject of relationships between grandparents and grandchildren receives scant attention in halakhic literature.

While there is some discussion as to whether the obligation to honor one's grandparents is biblical or rabbinic in origin, there is a general consensus that the obligation exists, although to a lesser degree than it does with respect to one's own parents. (Interested readers can review the discussion in the *Arukh Ha-shulḥan,* Yoreh Dei·ah 240:44.) So, although grandchildren are not required to revere their grandparents in the same way that Scripture obliges them to revere their own parents, they may not leave their grandparents destitute if their parents lack the resources to care for them, and they are obligated to recite Kaddish for them after they die if there is no one else to do so.

The author of the *Sefer Ha-ḥinnukh* traces the obligation to honor one's parents to the fact that a child owes his or her very existence to parents—it is the recognition of that ultimate reality that leads to a greater appreciation of God's beneficent role as Creator and Parent of all humanity (*Sefer Ha-*

ḥinnukh, commandment no. 27). While the same might arguably be said about grandparents (who, after all, brought one's parents into the world), Jewish law does not impose the same obligations on children regarding their grandparents as it does regarding their parents.

This lack of halakhic obligation is a two-way street, however. From a halakhic perspective, grandparents are deemed to have little, if any, formal responsibility toward their grandchildren. To be sure, a grandparent who teaches his or her grandchildren Torah is lauded by tradition. The Talmud even states that one who teaches a grandchild Torah is considered personally to have received the Torah at Sinai (*BT* Kiddushin 30a). But even that remarkable statement describes a voluntary act, not an obligation. However, the absence of formal halakhic requirements should not be taken as a sign that Jewish tradition views this relationship as devoid of importance.

Reverence and Respect

Perhaps the best context in which to discuss the obligations of grandchildren to their grandparents is that of the reverence due to the elderly in general. Working on the assumption that most grandparents are older people (and they will surely appear that way to their grandchildren regardless of what the outside observer might conclude), the entire elaborate category of halakhic obligation to honor the elderly devolves upon the grandchildren. Leviticus 19:32 states very clearly, "Rise up before the hoary head, honor the face of the elderly, and fear your God: I am the Eternal." Paying proper respect to the elderly, Scripture means to imply, is comparable to honoring God. (Almost every public bus in Israel contains a poster that quotes this verse, implying that one should offer one's seat to an elderly person.) Indeed, grandparents may well be among the few elderly people with whom a child has regular and sustained contact, and those moments will therefore constitute a precious opportunity to learn about, and implement, the proper dignity and respect due to elderly people. Surely, the potential of this kind of experiential learning is not to be minimized!

As for the potential of this relationship from the perspective of the grandparent, the Torah provides us with a remarkable glimpse into the power of a grandparent's insight (and the capacity of that insight to shape the very destiny of one's child's children) toward the end of the Book of Genesis.

Genesis 48 tells the story of the last days of Jacob. Before his death, Jacob's beloved son Joseph brings his own two sons, born in Egypt, to their grandfather's bedside for a final, patriarchal blessing. As the firstborn son traditionally received a special blessing, Joseph positions his children carefully, placing the older son, Manasseh, opposite Jacob's right hand, which will dispense the choicest blessing, and the younger boy, Ephraim, near Jacob's left hand. But Jacob crosses his hands intentionally, placing his right hand on Ephraim's head and his left on Manasseh's.

Joseph is troubled by Jacob's action, and assumes that Jacob is simply mistaken. But Jacob is depicted clearly as knowing exactly what he is doing. Indeed, he says as much to Joseph: *yadati, b'ni, yadati,* he says clearly, "I know, my son, I know" (Genesis 48:19). Evidently, Jacob saw something in his grandsons' temperaments that led him to believe that the younger child would reach greater heights than the elder. The moment is, of course, exquisitely rich in irony. In his youth, Jacob himself had conspired with his mother Rebecca in an audacious act of deception against his own father Isaac, a deception that garnered Jacob the blessing that, by virtue of birth order, should have been Esau's. But on another level, this is the last of a chain of narratives in Genesis in which a major character breaks the societal convention of automatically conferring the choicest blessing on the firstborn.

As opposed to Jacob's experience with his blind, passive father, in this moment Jacob is still very much the active and engaged parent to his son Joseph and so must be understood as consciously directing his grandchildren's destiny. Isaac's blessing to his son had been procured through subterfuge and deception; as a grandfather, Jacob's is intentionally bestowed to his own grandchildren. And, indeed, once Jacob explains that his actions are not accidental or mistaken, Joseph defers to his father's decision and Manasseh and Ephraim learn an invaluable lesson: that even the mighty Joseph, second only to the king of Egypt, must honor his parent. And, though one would imagine that Manasseh might have felt disappointed by his grandfather's decision, both he and Ephraim appear to gain a new appreciation of the wisdom and insight that their grandfather had accumulated over the course of his most remarkable life.

In an instance such as this, when the classical Jewish sources have generated relatively few explicit, prescriptive guidelines to govern our behavior, the responsibility falls upon us to apply our own common sense (and our sense of decency and appropriateness) to the situation at hand. This is a relationship that is as rich in potential as its partners allow it to be. It also demands the best of both parties.

May You See Your Children's Children

Those men and women who are fortunate enough to be blessed with the fulfillment of the psalmist's famous prayer *u-r'eih vanim l'vanekha* ("May you [live to] see your children's children" [Psalm 128:6]) are presented with a precious opportunity to be both moral educators and sources of pure, unconditional love. From the earliest days of a child's life when a grandparent might serve as a *kvatter or kvatterin* at a *b'rit milah* or *simḥat bat* celebration, or as a participant in a ceremony of transmission of Torah at a bar or bat mitzvah, to older age, when a grandparent may choose to pass down a treasured family heirloom that was an important part of his or her religious life, grandparents can impact the spiritual lives of their grandchildren profoundly. Having grandparents at a Shabbat or holiday table is the realization of the psalmist's hope. And those children who are wise enough to understand, even at a tender age, how fortunate they are to have living grandparents who will love and care for them in the way that only grandparents can, are truly blessed. And who knows? Maybe *their* children will one day carry those grandparents' names . . .

Perhaps, in its reluctance to over-regulate the relationship between grandparents and children, our sages were teaching us the most important lesson of all: sometimes, the harvesting of life's greatest riches is not predicated on discharging responsibilities or fulfilling requirements. Sometimes, what is required most of all is a giving heart.

Neighbors and Neighborly Relations

NINA BETH CARDIN

If you live near me and I live near you, we make claims on each other. This is so, no matter how we feel about each other. Whether I like you or not, whether I choose to care about you or not—these things are of no consequence. Your presence alone demands things of me and my presence demands things of you. You might ask why: why should the fact that I live near you bind us in any particular way? And why do those who live closer make greater claims on us than those who live further away?

The first answer is rooted in the story of creation. We are told there that we are all made in the image of God (Genesis 1:27, 5:1, and 9:6); we all share a bit of God's reflected divinity. I carry a bit of the Divine in me just as you carry a bit of the Divine in you. And the Divine is something we cannot ignore. Just as God's presence in our lives demands a response from us, so too does our presence in the lives of each other. And while this demand is a claim that emanates from every individual, those who stand directly before us have a greater claim than those who dwell at a greater remove.

In the presence of the other, we cannot argue that we did not know. In my presence, you and your claims are right there before me. I dare not turn away from you, for I am your witness even as you are mine whether we have chosen to be so or not. Emmanuel Levinas, the eminent philosopher and talmudist, speaks of "face" as the symbol of the unique, unknowable, invaluable aspect of each individual: "The epiphany of the face is ethical" and "The face opens the primordial discourse whose first word is obligation." (See his *Totality and Infinity: An Essay on Exteriority* [trans. Alphonso Linqis; Pittsburgh: Duquesne University Press, 1969], pp. 87 and 199.)

The Halakhah of Proximity

In neighborly relations, the reality of proximity meets the ethical imperative to seek traces of the Creator in the presence of others. This truth may also be put more prosaically. What you do in your space affects me directly. Aspects of your behavior leech out of your domain and enter mine in many different ways: physically (such as the way your overgrown yard is growing into mine); aesthetically (such as the way the condition of your home's façade, the boat in your driveway, or the tool shed in the front yard affect the look of my own home); and socially (such as the way your alcohol and drug abuse, or your wild poker parties every Tuesday night, affect the ambience of my neighborhood). Pollute your air, land, and water, and you pollute my air, land, and water. Build a wall or high-rise in front of my windows, and you block my view or my access to sunlight. Siphon off the stream just before it reaches my house, and you deprive me of my water supply. Take illegal drugs, and the quality of community life diminishes. Your right to do whatever you please on your property ends when it intrudes upon my rights, my investments, my space, and my spiritual well-being.

This line of reasoning is shared by almost every society that cherishes and respects the private use of property. It balances the interests and rights of one individual with those of another. The challenge comes in determining the line between my rights and your offendedness. How much noise is too much? Who is responsible for an overhanging branch? How high can I build on my property? How close to my borders, and yours, can I put a structure or a tree? When issues of boundaries are in dispute, law intervenes.

But modernity (or, more precisely, manufacturing and technology) has changed the meaning of "neighborhood" in our world. Traditionally, neighborhoods were defined in terms of physical proximity. That definition continues, but we also measure neighborhoods today not solely in terms of walkable distances, but also in terms of the reach of our actions. If we are talking about noise or light, a neighborhood can be defined by the distance that noise and light travel. If we are talking about smoke emissions, a neighborhood must be defined in terms of the distance smoke travels. If we are talking about airborne pollutants, pesticides, herbicides, fertilizers, hormones, and antibiotics that homes, yards, and farms introduce into the ecosystem, then a neighborhood must be defined by the area that the pollutants affect. And we are just beginning to appreciate the ways in which telecommunications and the ubiquitous access to the Internet through our mobile devices can diminish, expand, or otherwise alter our experience of space and thus redefine "neighborliness."

For the purpose of this chapter, though, we explore neighborhood only in its more limited sense of physical proximity: houses that abut yards, homes that share walls, residences that lie along common streets, structures found within common courtyards, and spaces within apartment buildings.

When Rights Collide

Your property's value and your quality of life are affected not only by what happens inside your home but also by the activities and behavior of your neighbors. Indeed, an overgrown yard, a home overrun with cats, or a lawn strewn with disassembled cars or discarded, rusting appliances can degrade both the value of the neighbors' homes and the beauty of the neighborhood. In cases such as these, Jewish law permits the residents of a neighborhood to bring pressure to bear to oblige offenders to clean up their space. "If a resident in an enclosed neighborhood wants to raise a cow or roosters, or bring in a grindstone [to mill grain], his neighbor can prevent him. And such is the law with every other thing that is not normally found in a residential area" (*SA* Ḥoshen Mishpat 161:5).

Today's civil zoning laws are expansions of older attitudes of neighborhood aesthetics and are rooted in the culture of the place. And the *halakhah* of neighborliness is similarly influenced: what is labeled acceptable for a residential neighborhood is most often determined not by a universal law but by local custom. Such laws and customs may not be overridden by the proclivities or tastes of individual property owners. Indeed, Maimonides rules clearly at *MT* Hilkhot Sh'kheinim 5:1 that when homes are built around a courtyard, any neighbor may legally compel any other to contribute to the construction of a door or of any other kind of structure in that courtyard that "it is customary for people in that place to build." (The law is slightly different if the owner is not a permanent resident, cf. ibid. 5:2.)

The ability of neighbors to restrict one another's behavior is based on three distinct rights: (1) the right to protect one's financial investment, (2) the right to preserve the nature and culture of the neighborhood in which one has settled, and (3) the right to find aesthetic enjoyment in one's own home and on one's own property. This being the case, if a neighbor puts up a fence in a community that prides itself on unbounded lawns that flow easily into one another and which thus serve to create a sense of openness and unity, that neighbor may be forced to take down his or her fence. (The feasibility of putting such principles into practice, of course, depends on many factors, chief among them whether the community requires that new residents formally agree to such terms and whether there is a strong neighborhood council to enforce them. Absent that, the impact of social pressure or the culture of the local courts to limit personal expression without written neighborhood covenants will matter most.) Many neighborhoods now have covenants that determine such issues as setbacks, minimum property size, existence and placement of storage units, use of yards, height of structures, and so on. Even where such covenants do not exist, Jewish law argues that local custom is the final authority, and Maimonides' ruling is as clear in this regard as it is succinct: "Everything depends on local custom" (*MT* Hilkhot Sh'kheinim 2:15).

The rules governing laundry serve as a fine case in point. Once women were allowed (or even required) to wash and hang their laundry in a common courtyard because going to local streams to do the washing was deemed unseemly, unworkable, or dangerous (*MT* Hilkhot Sh'kheinim 5:3). The loss of aesthetics in the neighborhood was deemed a necessary sacrifice for the safety of the women and thus a practical necessity that none could protest. However, when washing machines and dryers became widely available and affordable, doing one's laundry in public could reasonably be banned. Yet here too local custom must always prevail: in some places, drying one's wash in the wind is still much preferred to machine drying, both for the enjoyment of the sunshine and the smell of the outdoors as well as for the environmental benefit of reducing the use of fossil fuels. In such places, drying one's clothes in public (which is to say, visibly) may not be forbidden, and may even serve as a proclamation of one's values. The public washing of one's clothes, however, is likely to continue to be frowned upon.

How does Maimonides' ruling intersect with the personal freedom of property owners to conduct themselves as they please on their own property? May a community outlaw all work performed in public or prevent the establishment of so-called "cottage industries" in the privacy of one's home? Does a community possess the right to outlaw start-up companies in residents' basements, or to forbid garage bands from practicing there, or to forbid enterprising citizens from selling kitchen items from their homes simply because most of their neighbors do not engage in the same kinds of activities? The short answer is that neighborhoods may not pass such restrictive covenants, nor legislators such restrictive regulations, as long as the activity itself is not noxious, does not create excess pollutants (including aesthetic ones such as noise and light), and does not attract undue crowds, create parking problems, attract unwanted media attention, draw strangers into the neighborhood late at night, or attract rodents. If there is no specific reason to forbid the existence of specific cottage industries, they must be deemed acceptable and, as such, tolerated. (For a fuller discussion of these issues cast in traditional terms, see the talmudic text preserved at *BT* Bava Batra 20b and Maimonides' selection of laws at *MT* Hilkhot Sh'kheinim 6:9–12.) Nor should the elaboration of these principles be viewed solely as an academic exercise: halakhically minded Jews may well choose to be governed by these norms, even when living in a larger society that is wholly unaware of them.

Limits to What Neighbors Can Protest

Despite these restrictions, however, there are also specific activities identified within the sources as so valued by traditional Jewish society that neighbors do not have the right to forbid them, even if the activity can be demonstrated to be detrimental to neighbors' property values and to a generally agreed-upon neighborhood aesthetic. Judaism values Jewish learning, for example, and allows neighbors to run small schools for the Jewish education of young children out of their homes—even if the increased traffic and noise is unwelcome by others in the community. Interestingly, our sources do not grant this same leniency to schools that offer secular education, the presumption being that there will always be numerous other venues in which such instruction can take place. Even in a society in which secular law must be obeyed, Jewish citizens can use the *halakhah* as a guide in terms of establishing their own sense of what should be allowed and what not, and then proceeding to work for what they feel justified in obtaining.

In various communities around America, similar dilemmas have arisen in many different settings. When, for instance, a new family in town decides to hold prayer services in its home on a regular basis, either in lieu of regular synagogue services or as an alternative to them, this could be seen as combining home and synagogue into one establishment. Displeased neighbors, including Jewish ones, might well complain, then resort to local secular courts to stop this perceived violation of residential zoning laws.

Who is right in such a case? Should a Jewish community's need to create more opportunities for communal worship trump the local zoning laws or aesthetic sensibilities? Or is it reasonable to tag the newcomers as interlopers and spiritual carpetbaggers who, while purchasing their house on the pretext of making it a home, appear to have had the ulterior motive all along of violating that contract by turning their home into a place of "work," and public worship, thus altering the nature of the community? (Nor would the situation be any different if the people involved were not new arrivals at all, but longtime residents who on their own chose to create a new worship venue in their home.) The answer derives directly from the precedent of creating Jewish schools and therefore rests on how the neighbors value the "work" being done in that space. If what goes on there is valued and seen as essential for the Jewish commonweal, then the *halakhah* would oblige them to tolerate it. If the activity promotes the advancement of Jewish community but can be performed elsewhere, the *halakhah* would permit them to object.

Local zoning laws may have a different take, however. When, for example, does dropping your child off at a neighbor's house turn from a favor—even one in which money changes hands—into a business? And would this be a zoning violation or business license issue—or both? Do we zone for a gas station with a convenience store in a residential area? Do we permit people to set up kennels and veterinary clinics in their backyards? May dentists serving the public freely work out of a room in their homes? Do we allow halfway houses to exist in otherwise residential neighborhoods? All these questions are adjudicated in secular courts with respect to zoning restrictions based on secular cultural trends. Separating suburban residential communities into bedroom communities accessible only by car with no commercial establishments, sidewalks, or public places was a particular expression of post-World War II values. Within the halakhic sphere, however, laws reflect the values the Jewish community professes to hold dear, allowing the "communal good" to trump what otherwise would be a set of personal prerogatives. And, indeed, the right to protest against unpleasant, dangerous, or especially irksome or noisy activities on the part of thoughtless neighbors is a permanent one that can be invoked even years after the fact (*MT* Hilkhot Sh'kheinim 5:5).

In the secular world, one often hears the acronym NIMBY ("not in my backyard") invoked to denote an enterprise socially valued by some but perceived as potentially risky or unaesthetic by those whose homes would be in close proximity to it. This often becomes a contentious issue, as it pits the desires, prejudices, and fears of a neighborhood's residents against the needs of the larger community. In our society, for example, some people live in group homes where they can receive support and services to help them live fuller lives; certainly, this type of home is better suited to a residential setting than an industrial one. Yet the residents of neighborhoods in which such group homes are planned have a right to demand that due diligence be undertaken regarding safety, placement, supervision, transportation, and other factors that might affect the well-being of local residents and their investments. And they certainly have the right to insist that no single neighborhood be unfairly burdened by such projects. But if all these precautions and requirements have been met, and if it is clear that placing such a home in the area will have no real ill effects on the neighborhood—then neighbors seeking to act in accordance with *halakhah,* and perhaps a bit of *ḥesed,* should endorse and not attempt to scuttle the plan. And all the more so if it brings good! Indeed, Maimonides' ruling that all the inhabitants of a given street may compel each other to participate in the installation of the kinds of poles and beams that will allow neighbors to carry goods in the street on Shabbat is merely a specific application of the principle that when a community will benefit from an ordinary improvement, it is the obligation of all residents to share in whatever costs are entailed in providing it (*MT* Hilkhot Sh'kheinim 5:12).

Great Good Places

In accord with their contemporary aesthetics, most twentieth-century city planners limited the degree to which a residential district could (or should) include business establishments. This was meant to improve and protect the quality of life for local residents. But many social engineers today believe this was a mistake. Parks, post offices, local restaurants, hardware stores, beauty parlors, and barber shops can all serve as "great good places" where members of the community gather and interact regularly, casually, and meaningfully. Here, people share news, maintain friendships, and build and secure "infrastructures of human relationships." It is only in such places, with regular and frequent interaction, that social intimacy and, in the words of Ray Oldenburg, "the habit of association" can develop. (Readers interested in learning more about the concept of the "great good place" can consult Claude Fischer *et al., Networks and Places: Social Relations in the Urban Setting* [New York: Free Press, 1977].) Indeed, in his landmark book, *The Great Good Place* (3rd ed., New York: Da Capo Press, 1999), Oldenburg argues forcefully that we should work for the return of such places to reinvigorate our neighborhoods and enrich our lives.

For Jewish citizens, this idea has profound implications. Ever since the destruction of the Temple (our preeminent "great good place"), Jews have created great good places wherever they have landed. Our houses of study, our synagogues, our schools, our camps, our philanthropic meeting places, and, more recently, our Jewish Community Centers all serve as regular gathering spots. Daily *minyanim,* organizational meetings, kosher butcher shops, Shabbat kiddush, learning around a rebbe's table, and the like all afford opportunities for regular, meaningful, yet casual and serendipitous local gathering. These, more than anything else, create a sense of community rooted in feelings of mutual concern, shared destiny, and the common willingness to work on behalf of one another. As a result of such interactions, and the knowledge that similar future social interactions are probable, social pressure builds to create peaceful accommodations with one's neighbors. Neighbors who know each other create safer, healthier, and more valued (and valuable) living spaces. Maimonides' law is succinct and clear: "The residents of a city may compel each other to participate in the construction of a wall [around the city] and the installation of bolted gates [in that wall], in the construction of a synagogue, and in the purchase of a Torah scroll or a scroll containing selections from the Prophets or the Writings" (*MT* Hilkhot Sh'kheinim 6:1). Clearly, participation in the creation of a secure, culturally rich environment in which to live is to be considered the common obligation of all neighbors in a town or a city. And when Rambam legislates that even orphans are obliged to participate in the effort to provide fresh, potable water to a city, he is merely choosing a specific way of saying that even people of exceedingly modest means should feel obligated to participate in the effort to foster the common good (*MT* Hilkhot Sh'kheinim 6:7).

Even more, great good places are locales where friends may casually run into each other and where society itself may be seen as promoting the physical, mental, and spiritual well-being of the individual. In light of such research, Jewish citizens should work on the reintroduction and re-creation of modern great good places (be they physical or even located in cyberspace) to strengthen the modern notion of neighborhood. That too is part of the halakhic obligation to use the values inherent in good neighborliness and societal cooperation to create warm, thriving communities. Rambam even rules that one may not plant certain kinds of trees on unowned no-man's land outside of a city's outer boundary if their presence will spoil the city's aesthetic beauty (*MT* Hilkhot Sh'kheinim 10:1).

Noise, Eyesores, and Everyday Pollutants

The amount of noise you are allowed to produce in your home is directly related to the distance between you and your neighbors, the quality of your insulation material, and your neighbors' health.

Take the case of a noisy air conditioner. Notable halakhists have ruled, for example, that the owner of a noisy air conditioner may be prevented from running it until he or she gets it fixed or replaces it. (See in this regard, Eliezer Simḥah Weiss, *Sefer Mishp'tei Sh'kheinim* [B'nei Brak: E.S. Weiss, 1997], pp. 102–103.) The logic is that the noise will surely disturb those in the immediate vicinity: healthy neighbors will be prevented from sleeping at night, while children and the infirm will be prevented from sleeping during the day. In such a case, the neighbors' health concerns (i.e., need for adequate sleep) overrides the comfort of the homeowner who operates a public nuisance in the confines of his or her own home, and this is especially so when the disturbance is due to poor maintenance and is therefore ultimately resolvable. One could easily argue that the same could be said of those who play a radio, television, music player, or computer too loudly, since these devices have volume controls and are used recreationally, whereas an air conditioner's noise cannot be modulated the same way.

Some situations are not so clear. What if the air conditioner was necessary for the resident's health, preventing allergens from invading the home or heat stroke among the elderly, and yet it still bothered the neighbors? Or what if neighbors complain about the noise from a teen band practicing next door? When does one person's music become another's noise? The situation is too complex to justify forbidding outright the cacophonous sounds of budding musicians. One could counter by saying that there is no practical alternative, since all bands need places to practice and all musicians begin as amateurs. We could also note that the noise in question is not the result of malfunctioning machinery, but the essence of the enterprise. And, unlike the air conditioner, the band does not practice all day and all night. Good neighbors will work to accommodate each other, agreeing upon a certain level of amplification during certain hours for fair and reasonable purposes.

Depending on the quality of the building's construction, some accommodation to neighborhood noise is necessary. The *halakhah* ordains a basic tolerance for what have become ordinary sounds, and we would see refrigerators, dishwashers, vacuum cleaners, lawnmowers, normal traffic, the occasional roar of subways, and the wail of police or ambulance sirens as falling into this category. Sometimes, we even find such sounds reassuring! We might need to extend our tolerance to the occasional unwanted human-made sounds, but when the noise consistently reaches beyond a certain reasonable threshold, the disturbed neighbor has the halakhic right to ask and to expect that the noise be diminished or entirely curtailed.

The Talmud determines that eyesores and everyday pollutants are likewise unacceptable (see, e.g., *BT* Bava Batra 17a–18b). One neighbor may not deposit unsightly trash, leaves, garden refuse, or other disposable items close to another neighbor's yard. If one's neighbor does deposit refuse too close to one's own property, one has the right to demand that it be covered, in order to minimize any offensive sights or smells. Similarly, dumping garbage—even on one's own property—is not allowed because such trash could surely be understood to constitute an eyesore, a health hazard, a magnet for rodents and other animals, and/or a source of noxious odors. Nor may one create a dangerous situation, and then consider oneself blameless for the damages that ensue due to the behavior of the wind (*MT* Hilkhot Sh'kheinim 11:1). However, our sources could certainly be interpreted to suggest that something like composting, a relatively benign process that involves the controlled depositing of organic matter into mounds of earth that are regularly turned and subsequently spread around the garden and yard, should be permitted without the neighbors' permission being requisite.

Sheds, workstations, and additional structures must be attractive, neat, devoid of hazards, and at a reasonable distance from a neighbor's property (*MT* Hilkhot Sh'kheinim 9:1), as well as conform to all local zoning ordinances.

While gardening is not generally considered an eyesore or pollutant, one must still be careful about how one plants a garden. Some plants attract bees, for example, and therefore should not be planted too close to a neighbor's property or to the public thoroughfare. Poor drainage not only risks turning one's backyard into a swamp, but can also create a fertile breeding ground for mosquitoes that can assault and threaten an entire neighborhood. Since some viral diseases can be borne by mosquitoes, this becomes not just a nuisance but a public health hazard. With the growing popularity of community and kitchen gardens, more and more beds that used to be consigned to the backyard are now appearing in the front. As long as the beds are neat and well-tended, this should be a welcome development.

Plants and bushes should not be allowed to overrun their beds and encroach on a neighbor's property. Hedges sometimes grow out of control and invade sidewalks and yards. It also often happens that exotic (i.e., non-native) species are planted by well-meaning gardeners and landscapers, only to have them overwhelm native plants, thus becoming a threat to the diversity of the local flora and fauna. While one cannot control seeds that are wind-borne, one can control both what one plants and the reach that one's plants are allowed to achieve on one's property. If one's bushes encroach on a neighbor's lawn, Jewish law empowers the offended neighbor to cut down or remove the portion that has grown beyond the owner's property line. If a tree's limbs or roots threaten to damage a neighbor's house, basement, or yard, or to uproot a neighbor's sidewalk, or to damage a neighbor's lawnmower blades, then the offended neighbor is permitted to remove the offending part of the tree. Similarly, if a tree overhangs a neighbor's yard and obscures the sun, casting too much shade on the neighbor's side, or causing too many leaves to litter the neighbor's property, or otherwise is found to be disturbing, the neighbor may cut its branches back to the owner's property line. (The preceding discussion is based on the material at *M* Bava Batra 2:12–13.)

In an era when the earth itself is under assault from excessive development, the way we maintain our lawns, yards, and trees counts. In these matters, we should be guided not only by how our decisions affect our neighbors, but also by how our decisions may risk harming the environment. That is, given our understanding of the environmental impact of our actions, visual aesthetics and local attitudes may not be the only determining factors of bad neighborliness; environmental responsibility must also be taken into consideration. Manicured lawns require the greedy use of increasingly diminishing water resources, as well as fertilizers and pesticides that pollute the ground water (and, often, local drinking supplies). Letting one's grass turn brown when rain is scarce should become socially acceptable. Indeed, letting a lawn go unwatered might well be entirely proper in a place where water is scarce, unless brushfires are a threat. Better still is designing a yard that thrives on the rain and temperature patterns of the local climate. (Rabbi Lawrence Troster discusses the halakhic dimension of environmentalism in much more detail elsewhere in this volume.)

Avoiding the use of nutrient-heavy fertilizers may mean that one's lawn is not as lush as a putting green, but it might contribute to a healthier environment. Planting drought-resistant ground cover instead of a blanket of thirsty grass addresses many problems simultaneously. Contemporary lawn care and landscaping fads are not God-given ideals of beauty and homeownership, but are rather functions of ever-changing culture and custom. Sometimes being a good neighbor means bucking the trend and leading your community to greater awareness of a greater good. This, too, is halakhic behavior of the highest order, especially when it addresses issues of paramount ecological or environmental importance

The same applies to the overall consumption of resources. The average size of new homes in the United States, for example, became a full fifty percent larger between 1971 and 2001. And with larger homes come larger utility bills, increased greenhouse gas emissions, the need for more complex landscaping services, and an overall increase in the use of limited natural resources. Modesty in our homes, and specifically in square footage, size of gardens, and the luxuriousness of appointments, speaks to an attitude of modesty in consumption and an abhorrence of waste that benefits everyone. Embracing that kind of modest living is also part of the *halakhah* of being a good neighbor.

Air Space

Our property claims include the vistas around us. When we move into a home, it comes with a preexisting view—whether it be of a distant horizon or the façade of the building next door. We have the right to expect to see roughly the same distance (if not precisely the same view) on future days as we do today (cf. *M* Bava Batra 2:4). If there is no high fence today dividing us from our neighbors, we have the right to expect that no high fence will be constructed tomorrow. If we can enjoy the rays of sunrise today in our backyards, we have a right to expect to enjoy them tomorrow. Still, although every homeowner has the right to construct a fence on his property unless it is the custom not to or unless the fence unduly obscures the neighbor's view, no one may build a tall tower on his property that will impinge on neighbors' privacy over the objection of those neighbors (*MT* Hilkhot Sh'kheinim 8:1).

Privacy

One classic sticking point between neighbors has always been the age-old shortcut. Long ago, when walking was still the primary mode of transportation, neighbors expected each other to take the shortest distance between two points, even if that meant cutting across other people's property. Because everybody walked, all benefitted from the possibility of taking shortcuts, and most people indulged their neighbors in this minor act of trespass. Indeed, this was such an ingrained feature of urban life that the crotchety neighbor, famous for yelling at local children for cutting across her yard, was notorious precisely because she enforced a rule that most everyone agreed was to be observed mostly in the breach.

Even the Mishnah mentions the phenomenon of shortcuts. It speaks disparagingly, for example, of cutting through ruins of destroyed synagogues—thus suggesting that other kinds of shortcuts were widely used and considered acceptable (*M* M'gillah 3:3). It was not out of deference to the right of private ownership that the Mishnah outlawed such shortcuts, however; it was out of a desire to preserve the dignity of once-holy space. And, indeed, Maimonides opens the second chapter of the "Laws Governing Neighbors" section of the *Mishneh Torah* with a long series of laws governing the amount of space to which the entrances to houses of various sorts are naturally entitled (*MT* Hilkhot Sh'kheinim 2:1–8). Clearly, privacy is deemed a natural right of people who live in homes! But so is the habit of walking freely for all. Public easements and private control are contested issues whose resolution often varies from neighborhood to neighborhood.

Similarly motivated is Rambam's ruling that "unwanted visibility is an actionable violation of privacy" (ibid. 2:14) and that the purchaser even of a garden can be compelled by the neighbors to put up a fence between that individual's newly acquired property and any adjacent gardens that belong to others (ibid. 2:17). Even the right of householders to install new windows in their own homes is contingent on their neighbors' willingness to allow themselves to be watched from a previously non-existent vantage point (*MT* Hilkhot Sh'kheinim 5:6). (Later on, at *MT* Hilkhot Sh'kheinim 7:1, however, Rambam notes that this law only applies to newly opened windows that look out onto preexistent courtyards; if one already has a window in one's wall and someone builds a courtyard on adjacent property, the latter does not have the right to protest even though the existence of the window will impact on one's privacy.)

Today, however, things are different and the propriety of cutting through someone's property to save a few steps is a bit more questionable according to modern societal norms. Still, how wonderful it would be, in locations and situations where walking is still commonplace (for example, in settings in which children walk to school or in the growing number of walkable communities), if neighbors could agree to overlook the technicalities of trespassing and grant their neighbors permission to cut across their yards, at least occasionally. In communities that do not walk, however, and in which neighbors hardly know one another, shortcuts may be considered legitimately taboo. Even more so, where this modest trespass is not publicly condoned, and especially where security issues are high, it can be downright dangerous to trespass on a neighbor's property without permission. In our highly litigious society, where even burglars occasionally display the supreme *ḥutzpah* of suing for damages connected with injuries incurred in the act of breaking and entering, property owners might choose to limit public access to their property for fear of being held responsible for any harm that might befall the trespasser, and would-be trespassers should in such cases simply obey the law of the jurisdiction in which they live.

Private Property

Jewish texts (both narrative and legal) do not speak of private ownership of property in absolute terms, but rather of the private *use* of common property. All land is a gift from God given to us in trust. "The heavens belong to the Eternal, but the earth God gave to humanity," the psalmist wrote at Psalm 115:16. Scripture thus teaches that humans are given parcels of this earth to use, to watch over, and to care for on behalf of all humanity. We have the right to privacy, of course, but throughout our stewardship, and throughout the time we possess the land, we would do better to think of ourselves instead as its guardians. As such, we have an obligation to pass the land on to the next generation in either the same or improved condition. Ultimately, we will relinquish our hold on the land and others will inherit the rights to its use. And that land will be expected to support and protect them, just as it did us.

The laws of the sabbatical year, according to which the land must be allowed to lie fallow and replenish itself every seventh year, and the jubilee year, according to which the land is returned to its original tribal owners every fiftieth year (as portioned out when the Jews first entered the land in the days of Joshua), together suggest how the *halakhah* views the whole concept of owning land. We can protect our use of the land. We can preserve our rights to behave in certain ways on the land. But we cannot claim to possess the land absolutely. There is no ultimate sovereignty over the land. And, when all is said and done, acknowledging that simple truth will lead us to become the best kind of neighbors not only to those who live around us, but also to those who will live here after we are gone.

Interfaith Relations

JEREMY KALMANOFSKY

Throughout history, in the many pagan, Christian, Muslim, and other societies where they have lived, Jews have wondered how to regard those other religions and their practitioners. Does the Torah demand that Jews be "a people that dwells alone" (Numbers 23:9), shunning non-Jews, remote from all potentially negative social, intellectual, and spiritual influences? Is social contact with non-Jews nothing but a first step toward assimilation? Does religious interchange necessarily promote syncretism? Such views are indeed found in Jewish literature. For example, the thirteenth century author of the *Sefer Ha-ḥinnukh* writes, "Let us banish the thought that there can be anything beneficial about any idolater, and let such a thought never come out of our mouths. Let them not find favor in our eyes whatsoever" (*Sefer Ha-ḥinnukh,* commandment no. 426).

But is this the only rational approach to living among gentiles? Could encountering other faith communities actually enhance Judaism and Jewish society? After all, the sages of antiquity themselves favored translating the Bible into Greek, so that "the beauty of Yefet [Greece] may dwell in the tents of Shem [among the Jews]" (*BT* M'gillah 9b). Moreover, are all other religions to be considered in the same light? Might we consider some religions contemptible, while viewing others as sister-faiths rooted in similar spiritual values to our own?

To examine the *halakhah* as it applies to interfaith relations, we must examine both the rules of the system, as well as the ideological schemes that organize those rules. To stick to the rules alone would be superficial and not help us respond coherently to our neighbors.

Contemporary Conservative Jews must seek a dialectical balance with the adherents of other religions, becoming partners with them to work for the common weal, while also striving to maintain the boundaries that define our Jewish identity. For Jewish communities to thrive with religious and social integrity in a multicultural world, our borders must be firm, yet not brittle. We must affirm that certain cardinal practices and beliefs constitute the foundation upon which Jewish identity rests. We must also avoid reflexive defensiveness that views every outsider as a threat. We must appreciate what we can learn from every human being. Yet we must also appreciate that we can experience Judaism fully only within a covenantal community of Jews. In these matters, we may be guided by the wise pearl of the ancient sages: "If someone tells you there is wisdom among the nations, believe it. If someone tells you there is Torah among the nations, do not believe it" (*Eikhah Rabbah* 2:13). Those who seek to live guided by tradition should avoid narrow-mindedness whenever possible, yet the *halakhah* also insists we avoid idolatry at all costs.

This chapter will addresses normative religious teachings of several different faiths, as well as the communal interactions between Jewish institutions and those of other faiths. But before turning to those important questions regarding wider communities, we should also begin with some comments about the interpersonal ethics individual Jews should have toward gentiles. Although our covenantal community must maintain appropriate social and religious boundaries between Jews and those of other faiths, this warrants neither economic nor ethical discrimination against non-Jews. It is true that the classical *halakhah* mandates stricter ethical behavior vis-à-vis fellow Jews than toward gentiles; we also must concede that isolated *midrashim* speak negatively, even hatefully, about non-Jews. Nevertheless, the dominant trend for centuries has been to view the unethical treatment of non-Jews as *ḥillul ha-sheim,* as the desecration of God's name, which the Torah forbids (Leviticus 22:32). Though religious and social barriers separate us from non-Jews in some ways, ethical obligations still bind us all together as human beings created in God's image. This duty finds apt expression in the teaching of Rabbi Moses of Coucy, one of the halakhic greats of thirteenth-century

France, who wrote in his magnum opus, the *Sefer Mitzvot Gadol* (negative commandment 2, ed. Venice, p. 7c): "I have preached throughout our Diaspora that those who lie to gentiles and steal from them are guilty of profaning God's name. For they cause gentiles to say, 'There is no Torah among the Jews.' But as the prophet Zephaniah said, 'The remnant of Israel will not do wickedness and will not speak falsely, and deceptive speech will not be found in their mouths'" (Zephaniah 3:13).

Idolatry

Over the centuries, Jews have viewed other religions first and foremost through the prism of opposition to idolatry. If a given religion was idolatrous, both the cult and its adherents were—depending on political circumstances—hated, shunned, or condemned to destruction. If a cult was not overtly idolatrous, Jews could be more amicable neighbors. Given that the Talmud generally presumes gentiles to be idolaters—with only exceptional individuals earning better evaluations (see e.g., *BT* Avodah Zarah 65a)—classical Judaism does not always make it easy to build bridges. Nonetheless, today we must try. In the era of al-Qaeda, when religious extremism has been so lethal, and not least of all to Jews, all modern, well-intentioned people should seek interfaith comity and hesitate to anathematize anyone.

Given our contemporary pluralistic inclinations, one might ask whether Judaism should still condemn idolatry so strongly. In today's world, should we discard this traditional attitude and instead live and let live, criticizing no other faith and asking others for the same generosity?

Yet the *halakhah* demands that our Jewish communities not tolerate *avodah zarah*, or "alien worship." We need not seek out pagans to challenge in polemics, but there is no room in Judaism for idolatrous practices. To understand why, let us begin with the first two of the Ten Commandments (Exodus 20:2–5):

> I am the Eternal your God who brought you out of Egypt, the house of bondage. Have no other gods besides Me. Make yourself neither idol nor image of anything that is in the heavens above or on the earth below or in the water beneath the earth. Do not prostrate yourself to them, nor cause them to be worshiped, for I the Eternal your God am a jealous God. . . .

These theological commandments teach two cardinal principles of Judaism: monotheism and the prohibition regarding the use of icons in worship. These *mitzvot* are inviolable. The Talmud demands that one should die rather than transgress them (*BT* Sanhedrin 74a). Faithful to these commandments, we keep faith with Judaism's central, two-fold religious insight: first, that there is only one God in all realms, including heaven and earth, matter and spirit, and life and death; and second, that God may not be rendered in images carved in wood and stone. Instead, Jews who want to see God should look at the human being, created in the divine image; should study the Torah, a record of God's wisdom and will; and should look to history where God's acts and ours move the world toward redemption. Since God is one, unique and ineffable, Jews must venerate only the infinite God who animates all. In retelling the famous *midrash* in which Abraham destroys his father's idols (found at *B'reishit Rabbah* 38:13), Maimonides writes:

> At age forty, Abraham became aware of his Creator. Once he attained this awareness, he began to argue with the residents of Ur, saying: "Your path is not the true path." He smashed the idols and began to teach people that it is improper to worship any but the eternal God. To God alone it is proper to bow and sacrifice, so that *all subsequent generations will know God.* Thus it is proper to destroy and smash all images, *so that none will err and think that the mere images are God* (*MT* Hilkhot Avodat Kokhavim 1:3; emphasis added).

Maimonides' formulation properly emphasizes the theology behind the law, which teaches that God alone is worthy of worship. In this spirit, a guiding principle in our interfaith contacts is that Conservative Jews must shun any activity that blurs our commitment to image-free monotheism.

What exactly is idolatry in halakhic terms? The Bible's wrath was directed partly against polytheistic belief in foreign deities (as Maimonides explains at *MT* Hilkhot Y'sodei Ha-torah 1:6), but the prophets also fought against the use of icons. These two realms of idolatry—improper belief and improper practice—are not necessarily identical. The Talmud, for example, knows that even rank idolaters can hold monotheistic beliefs: "Beyond Tyre and Carthage, where nations know neither Israel nor their heavenly father," they still recognize a single, ultimate transcendent divinity, a "God of gods" (*BT* M'naḥot 110a). Indeed, the simplest interpretation of the golden calf story in Exodus 32 is not that the Israelites followed a false god, but that they tried to render the true God in molten gold. (See the interpretation of this story by Rabbi Judah Halevi in the *Kuzari* 1 97.) Even a Jew who believes in God alone but who venerates one specific aspect of divine creation above all others strays into idolatry. Thus, the *halakhah* proscribes all tangible representations of the Divine, as Maimonides explains: "The essence of the prohibition against idolatry is that we not worship any of the created beings—neither angel, nor sphere, nor star, nor physical element nor anything fashioned from physical elements—even if one knows that the Eternal is God" (*MT* Hilkhot Avodat Kokhavim 2:1).

Thus, wrong belief alone is not the only thing that makes one an idolater. Wrong worship can be equally decisive. Indeed, until Maimonides' day, classical halakhic sources tended to define idolatry less by its errant theology and more by specific forbidden acts, such as kissing or bowing to an idol. Additionally, the Torah's revulsion at idolatry inspired the sages of the Talmud to legislate numerous other measures to keep Jews far from idols.

An object is considered an idol if it meets any of a number of conditions. Worshipers must ascribe divinity to the object and to the being the image depicts. (Therefore, images of ordinary humans are not idolatrous, but those which represent individuals presumed to be endowed with supernal powers are likely to be.) Furthermore, worshipers must commonly venerate the object in physical ways, such as by bowing down to it or kissing it, and the object itself must have been created for that purpose even if people have not yet worshiped it. Finally, the object in question must be something formally singled out for worship. Thus, a sacred tree might be an idol, since a human could have planted it for religious purpose, but no amount of idolatrous worship, no matter how fervent or intense, could render a sacred river or mountain into an idol.

Once one has identified what constitutes an idol, the sages of talmudic times considered it a biblical violation to enter or even pass through a city with an idolatrous shrine (*MT* Hilkhot Avodat Kokhavim 9:9–10). Indeed, they understood the Torah to forbid even looking at an idol—let alone studying the practices and theology of idolatry. Also, it is forbidden to derive any monetary or personal benefit from idols or even from the accouterments of idol worship. It is forbidden to enter an idolatrous shrine, even to get out of the rain. Certainly one must not make or sell idols, nor even the incense used in idol worship. One must not patronize a store whose profits subsidize idolatry. One may not even mention the name of a god worshiped by means of idols. (These laws derive from *MT* Hilkhot Avodat Kokhavim, chapters 2–5, *passim.*) In addition to these restrictions, which were understood to be legislated by the Torah, the talmudic sages added strictures of their own. For instance, one must keep four cubits away from an idol, lest one be seduced by its appeal. One must not bend before an idol, not even to pick up money or to remove a thorn from one's foot. Nor may one may drink from an idol-shaped fountain, lest fellow Jews see and mistakenly suspect their comrade of apostasy (*SA* Yoreh Dei·ah 150:1–2).

Idolaters

In addition to shunning idols and their rites, Judaism demanded that Jews keep far from idolaters themselves. Deuteronomy 7:2 proscribes making a covenant with the Canaanite residents of the Land, and exhorts *v'lo t'ḥoneim.* This phrase, most simply translated "grant them no quarter," was interpreted as banning Jews from admiring anything about idolaters, from their physical beauty to their culture (*BT* Avodah Zarah 20a). Maimonides explained the principle behind this law: praising an idolater "causes one to be bound to him and to learn from his wicked deeds" (*MT* Hilkhot Avodat Kokhavim 10:4). (Incidentally, this same Bible verse and this passage from Maimonides also served as the basis of the infamous December 2010 ruling by Rabbi Samuel Eliyahu, chief rabbi of Safed, forbidding renting property in Israel to gentiles. Although many nationalist rabbis endorsed this view, an even greater number condemned it, including those from ultra-Orthodox, national religious, and liberal streams.)

Maimonides' formulation neatly epitomizes the ancient talmudic sages' broad tendency to impose maximum distance between Jews and non-Jews. This distancing tendency can be seen through the Talmud's application of the biblical prohibition of mimicking the customs of the gentile nations in general. In all ways—including the way they cut their hair or the way they tie their shoelaces—Jews should be distinct. Discussing this view, Maimonides cites several Torah verses and summarizes: "All these address a single overriding concern, that we not resemble them. Instead, Jews should be distinct and recognizable in dress and in all their deeds, just as they are in their knowledge and attitudes" (*MT* Hilkhot Avodat Kokhavim 11:1; cf. Leviticus 18:3, 20:23, and Deuteronomy 12:30). History attests that we have not always remained as distinct as Maimonides proposes. Today, most Jews rarely dress differently from their neighbors. Moreover, few Jews today share the basic assumption that Jews are best off keeping far away from non-Jews. Indeed, modern Judaism itself is at least partly a result of openness toward the gentile world. Most modern Jews see ethical value in setting aside restrictions in which we ourselves would build our own ghetto walls, and instead seek to integrate into a harmonious multicultural society. Today, the prohibition against imitating *ḥukkot ha-goyim*—the customs of non-Jewish peoples—should not be invoked to prevent or limit interaction with other faiths. However, this prohibition should help us maintain distinctions between Judaism and other faiths by forbidding Jewish participation in some religious or quasi-religious cultural practices. An obvious application of *ḥukkot ha-goyim* for North Americans would be to prohibit Jews from having Christmas trees in their homes, even if their intention is not to celebrate Jesus's birth, but merely to keep up an American custom.

One primary way the ancients sought to isolate Jews from non-Jews was by preventing them from eating together. By keeping Jews and gentiles apart at the table, they hoped to discourage intermarriage and to shelter Jews from the seductions of idolatry (Deuteronomy 7:1–4, as amplified at *BT* Avodah Zarah 35b–36b). For this reason, the sages of late antiquity prohibited drinking wine produced by gentiles, even when unrelated to cultic libation, and eating most food cooked by non-Jews, including bread. As a safeguard against intermarriage, these restrictions apply equally to gentiles who worship idols and to those who do not.

Even in talmudic times, however, the prohibition against eating "gentile bread" was observed at best sporadically. Today, this rule applies at most to a private baker, who shares his or her own family's bread with Jews, thus encouraging a social relationship. But when there is no Jewish baker in town, or when gentile bread is of higher quality, one may buy from a gentile commercial baker whose bread can be eaten without establishing a social relationship (*BT* Avodah Zarah 35b, *SA* Yoreh Dei·ah 112:2 and 112:5). Thus breads manufactured industrially can be certified kosher, even though they are prepared by gentiles.

With respect to other foods, according to classical standards even otherwise kosher food cannot be considered permissible if it was cooked entirely by non-Jews. Hence, in kosher restaurants and in the kitchens of kosher caterers who work with exclusively gentile staff, the *kashrut* supervisor ignites the ovens at the beginning of each day and stirs the pots personally, thus taking a symbolic role in preparing the food (*BT* Avodah Zarah 38a–b). The same is true of many factory-produced foods under *kashrut* supervision, although certain technical leniencies can eliminate the need for a Jewish role in industrial cooking. But in general, absent significant or at least symbolic Jewish participation, the classical *halakhah* forbids most food cooked by gentiles.

With respect to wine, the tradition is even stricter. Wine produced by idolaters (called in Hebrew *yein nesekh*) is traditionally forbidden to a Jew even for commercial benefit; since we assume the idolater intended to pour some of it out as a ritual libation, such wine has effectively become an accouterment to idolatry (*MT* Hilkhot Ma·akhalot Asurot 11:1). The sages later ruled that wine of a non-idolatrous gentile, or wine clearly not intended for ritual use (called in Hebrew *s'tam yeinam*) is permissible for commerce, but forbidden for consumption lest it lead to social, and then to more intimate, intercourse. Among Conservative authorities, Rabbi Elliot Dorff's 1985 CJLS responsum recommends that the social prohibitions against gentile wine should "fall into disuse, without protest." He wrote, "If I thought for one minute that prohibiting wine made by gentiles would have the slightest effect on diminishing the number of mixed marriages, I would drop all other concerns and prohibit it on that basis alone. I frankly doubt, however, that prohibiting [gentile wine] will have any effect whatsoever on eliminating or even mitigating that problem" (*CJLS Responsa 1980–1990,* p. 309). But Rabbi Dorff wrote that it is preferable, especially for ritual purposes, to use only wine with *kashrut* certification, because some wines, especially better quality products, may include substantively non-kosher ingredients (ibid., p. 301).

Conservative Jews should follow Rabbi Dorff's direction, focusing on the substantive *kashrut* of our food and wine, and not on who cooks it or with whom we eat it. Given overwhelming changes in our attitudes toward gentiles, the original social context of this legislation no longer applies. A ban on eating food prepared by gentiles will not reduce intermarriage among Jews who attend school, work, and live with non-Jews. For this reason, a Conservative rabbi supervising the *kashrut* of a restaurant or caterer need not insist that a Jew take part in the cooking. On the other hand, Orthodox authorities disagree that changing social mores can overrule classical prohibitions. Contemporary communities lack the authority to reject what ancient sages prescribed, they say, and they therefore continue to observe the rules against gentile food. Many of these issues are discussed elsewhere in this volume by Rabbi Paul Drazen in his chapter about the *kashrut* laws.

Islam

The *halakhah* does not view all non-Jewish religions as idolatrous. "Righteous gentiles" will also reach the World to Come, the classical sages taught—a claim that would be absurd if all non-Jewish faiths were forms of idolatry (*T* Sanhedrin 13:2.) The rabbis of ancient times further developed the concept of the Noahide laws, seven basic precepts that should be common to all societies, including prohibitions of idolatry and blasphemy as well as precepts of ethics and social justice. These Noahide laws establish the grounds on which other religions may be seen as suitable partners for interfaith relations.

Islam is easy to analyze in these terms. Though its claim to possess the ultimate supersessionist revelation obviously is not our view of God's will, Islam teaches monotheism with great rigor, bans idolatry even more stringently than does Judaism, and seeks a just social order. Since geonic times, the vast majority of halakhic rulings have understood Islam to be a non-idolatrous Noahide faith (Maimonides, *Responsa,* ed. Blau, responsum 448 (Jerusalem: Mekitzei Nirdamim, 1957–1986), vol. 2, pp. 725–728; *MT* Hilkhot Ma·akhalot Asurot 11:7). Indeed, the entire thrust of Maimonides' famous "Epistle on Martyrdom" is to defend Moroccan Jews who at least outwardly adopted Islam during a period of intense persecution. Admitting it would have been pious to choose martyrdom—as the Talmud certainly seems to mandate and as most rabbis counseled—nonetheless Maimonides urges Jews to "not choose death," since there is nothing inherently idolatrous in Islam. Ideally, though, he said, Jews should emigrate to escape martyrdom or practice their Judaism in secret (*Epistles of Maimonides: Crisis and Leadership,* ed. Halkin and Hartman [1985; reprint, Philadelphia: The Jewish Publication Society, 1993], p. 30).

The consensus of authorities is not to shun Islam. It is permitted to enter mosques, to observe Muslims at prayer, to possess Muslim artifacts, and to read Islamic sacred writings. If such an unlikely circumstance arose, Jews could conduct their own prayer service inside a mosque, or share space with a mosque or Islamic school (see the comments of Rabbi Ovadiah Yosef in his responsum *Yabbi·a Omer,* part 7, Yoreh Dei·ah 12, ed. Jerusalem, 1993, pp. 226–228).

Christianity

Evaluating Christianity is more complicated. To begin with, the Talmud explicitly labels Christianity as a form of idolatry and treats Sunday as an idolatrous holiday (in uncensored manuscripts at *BT* Avodah Zarah 6b). Moreover, normative Christian doctrine insists that Jesus was both fully human and fully divine, at once a mortal man and the second "person" in God's triune personality. Most Jews saw this as unambiguous polytheism. Moreover, since most churches were filled with icons depicting a person whom the worshipers regard as divine, the case for shunning Christianity was quite strong. Indeed, rabbis in Islamic lands unanimously condemned Christianity outright as idolatrous. (See, e.g., Maimonides, *MT* Hilkhot Avodat Kokhavim 9:4. Current editions of the *Mishneh Torah* read here that "Canaanites" are considered idolaters, but most manuscripts read "Christians." It seems that the text was emended, most probably from fear of censors.)

However, rabbis in medieval Christendom sought accommodation with the dominant religion, rather than total rejection. Rabbi Jacob ben Meir (better known as Rabbeinu Tam, 1100–1171) proposed a novel interpretation, which had the effect of permitting wider interactions, especially business dealings, with Christians. Rabbeinu Tam argued that the Torah imposes a stricter standard of idolatry on Jews than the Noahide code imposes on gentiles. While Jews must worship God alone with no subsidiary powers, he wrote, gentiles were permitted to take oaths "combining the name of heaven with something else." (This "something else" was taken first to refer the saints and later even to the trinity itself. Adapting a talmudic term, Rabbeinu Tam called this theology *shittuf,* or "associationism." See the comments of Tosafot to

BT Sanhedrin 63b, *s.v. asur.*) In this view, a Jew who practiced Christianity surely was guilty of idolatry, while his French neighbor could swear to Jesus or Mary without breaking Noahide law. Apparently, these medieval rabbis knew enough about Christianity to recognize that Christians combined a basic faith in the God of Israel with practices that depart from aniconic monotheism. Thus, Rabbeinu Tam and other rabbis of medieval Europe generally regarded Christians as "idolaters who do not worship idols" (Tosafot to *BT* Avodah Zarah 2a, *s.v. asur*).

This line of reasoning was the subject of significant disagreement among later sages. Many, like Rabbi Moses Isserles (commenting on *SA* Oraḥ Ḥayyim 156), affirmed the associationist concept and concluded that Christianity was a permissible religion for Noahides. Many others followed Rabbi Ezekiel Landau (in his responsum *Noda Bihudah,* second ed.: Yoreh Dei·ah 148, ed. New York, 1960, pp. 92–93) in rejecting this as a mistaken interpretation of Rabbeinu Tam's own view. These rabbis held that a distinction between Noahides and Jews could permit a Jew to accept a Christian's oaths, but could not sustain the definition of associationism as proper Noahide monotheism. This latter position is generally espoused by most Orthodox authorities. In our day, Rabbi Ovadiah Yosef among Sephardim (in his responsum in the *Y'ḥavveh Da·at* 4:45) and Rabbi Eliezer Waldenberg among Ashkenazim (in a responsum in his *Tzitz Eliezer* vol. 14, responsum 91 [ed. Jerusalem, 1981, pp. 166–168]), explicitly consider Christianity to be *avodah zarah,* idolatry.

Yet some in the tradition laid the seeds of a more pluralistic view. Rabbi Menaḥem Meiri, a giant of thirteenth century Provence, argued that Christianity's monotheism and ethics grant it special status. "They worship God in some sense, though their faith is far from ours," the Meiri wrote in his talmudic commentary *Beit Ha-b'ḥirah* at *BT* Bava Kamma 38a. Furthermore, he believed the strict quarantine the Talmud pronounces on idolaters "applies only to those ancient people who were not bound by the ways of religion. They were perpetually absorbed in the worship of idols, stars, and talismans, which are the very essence of idolatry . . . so that every sin and every foul thing was lovely in their eyes" (*Beit Ha-b'ḥirah* to *BT* Avodah Zarah 26a). Rabbi Joseph Karo and the Rema report this position sympathetically in the *SA* Yoreh Dei·ah 148:12. It also bears mentioning that even Maimonides—who, as we saw, explicitly labels Christianity as idolatry—regards the daughter religion as playing a part in providential history in light of its success in bringing Hebrew scriptures to all corners of the world. (These comments appear in uncensored editions of *MT* Hilkhot M'lakhim U-milḥ'moteihem, ch. 11.)

Meiri's critical innovation was to shift the definition of gentile idolatry from a ritual to an ethical one. Surpassing the pragmatic lenience of Rabbeinu Tam, Meiri evaluated non-Jewish cultures less by how they worship in their shrines and more by how they act in society. While ancient idolaters "were polluted in their deeds and foul in their traits," Meiri wrote, "nations bound by the ways of religion, which are innocent of such foul traits, and indeed which punish such behavior, doubtless are not the subject of such laws at all" (*Beit Ha-b'ḥirah* commentary to *BT* Avodah Zarah 22a). This does not lessen the demand that Jews shun idolatry in their own lives. But Meiri teaches that our openness toward non-Jews should be contingent on their ethical standards, and not on the details of their religious rituals. Conservative Jews should adopt this orientation and carry it forward. Following the opinion of Rabbi Abraham Isaac Hakohen Kook (as expressed in his *Epistles,* no. 89, volume 1 [Jerusalem: Mosad Ha-rav Kook, 1962], p. 99), we reject Christianity for ourselves but we need not reject Christian society as a whole: "The correct view is that of the Meiri, that all nations which are bound by proper interpersonal ethical norms are considered as resident aliens [the biblical *geir toshav*] with respect to all human ethical obligations." The ancient definition of a *geir toshav* is a non-Jew who lives with Jews and aligns him or herself with Israel, but does not fully convert to Judaism. Since none may aspire to the status of *geir toshav* without fully renouncing idolatry, Rabbi Kook clearly must understand Christianity as a kind of Noahide monotheism. For his part, Rabbi Isaac Halevi Herzog, Ashkenazic chief rabbi of Israel from 1937 to 1959, ruled similarly that the State of Israel must tolerate Christian churches in the Holy Land: "Christians regard themselves as monotheists. Although we cannot understand how they dilute their faith in the unity of the Creator with the [concept of the] trinity, one cannot deny that they have a concept, however strange, of there existing a provident Creator of the world" (*T'ḥumin* 2 [1981], pp. 174–175).

May a Jew visit a church? Since Christianity is forbidden to Jews, virtually all Orthodox authorities forbid entering a church, even when services are not being held, and even where actual icons are absent. Indeed, the most lenient Orthodox position of which I am aware is that of Rabbi Judah Herzl Henkin, who permits entering Unitarian or very liberal Protestant churches (those that do not accept the divinity of Jesus) when services are not actually occurring, although he advises against doing so lest observers mistakenly suspect one of entering conventional Christian churches (*She'eilot U-t'shuvot B'nei Vanim* [Jerusalem: J. H. Henkin, 1997] no. 35, p. 117). But the dominant view is that even visiting a church to study its art and architecture is forbidden (so Rabbi H. D. Halevi in his *Aseih L'kha Rav* 1:59 [Tel Aviv: Ha-va·adah L'hotza·at Kitvei Ha-ga·on . . . Halevi, 1978], pp. 178–181), as is entering a church to vote in a secular election at a polling station there (so Rabbi Menashe Klein in his *Mishneh Halakhot,* vol. 6, responsum 139 [New York: M'khon Mishneh Halakhot Gedolot, 2000], p. 168). Rabbi Joseph Soloveitchik is reported to have instructed students not to watch John F.

Kennedy's Catholic funeral on television, asking, "What is the difference between entering a church, which is forbidden, or bringing the church into your own house?" (Rabbi Zvi Schechter relates this anecdote in his book on Rabbi Soloveitchik, *Nefesh Ha-rav* [Jerusalem: Reishit Y'rushalayim, 1994], p. 230.)

Conservative *halakhah* should rule differently. Following Rabbeinu Tam and the Meiri, if Christianity is not idolatrous for gentiles, then there can be no biblical prohibition against observing Christian services or rituals, or even in facilitating Christian worship for Christians. At most, the prohibition against visiting a church should be understood as a rabbinic decree which we should let lapse in our day, as one of the class of rabbinic prohibitions which can be set aside *mi-shum eivah,* "because it would cause hatred" between Jews and gentiles. And it certainly would cause friction if we told our neighbors we would refuse to enter their churches because we regard them as pagans! Since it is often proper, neighborly, and civic-minded to attend the worship services of other faiths—to attend a friend's wedding, for example, or to attend a funeral—in such cases one may enter a church as an invited guest even during worship services. To be sure, Jews are absolutely forbidden from attending Christian services as worshipers or from seeking spiritual fulfillment by doing so, or from imitating Christian ways in general. To serve a larger social purpose, however, visiting church services is permissible. Needless to say, this view permits Jews to enter a church building for wholly secular purposes, like meetings or public events.

When visiting a church service, Jews should not participate in the singing of hymns or the recitation of prayers, and they should certainly not join in any rituals. Without being rude, one should make it clear that one has come as a Jewish visitor to a Christian service, not to explore the possibility of converting. Given Christianity's long history of missionary activity aimed specifically at Jews, concerns of *marit ayin*—the obligation not only not to do wrong, but also not to appear as though one is doing wrong—apply. One should be additionally strict, keeping greater distance from Christians who continue to proselytize among our people. Jews for Jesus and other groups of so-called "messianic Jews" recruit Jews to apostasy and should be completely shunned. That this policy should apply even posthumously was the conclusion of a 1994 responsum by Rabbi Paul Plotkin, which was approved by the CJLS and published in *CJLS Response 1991–2000,* pp. 400–402 (cf. the concurring opinion paper by Rabbi Myron S. Geller published in that same volume, pp. 403–407).

Might a synagogue invite a Christian representative to speak during services or in some other context? If Christianity is not idolatry, such an invitation is conceivable in principle, and a community's choice is left to its taste and best judgment. But the demands of *marit ayin* require that Jews consider inviting only Christians whom they know to respect Judaism, and who are in no way involved with missionary work among Jews.

May a Jew possess or sell Christian artifacts? Although we follow Rabbeinu Tam in regarding Christians as "idol worshipers who do not worship idols," Catholics and Eastern Christians do in fact make images of a man they take to be divine and bow to them in devotion. Thus, Jews must not derive monetary or personal benefit from Christian icons that will be worshiped. But Jewish jewelers or merchants are permitted to sell crosses as jewelry or as decorative pieces, since they are only symbols of Christian belief or piety, but are not themselves worshiped. The Rema developed this distinction: "Images to which people bow are considered as idols and are forbidden unless formally nullified [of their religious character]. But a pendant that merely hangs around the neck is a mere remembrance. It is not considered an idol, and it is permitted for a Jew to derive financial benefit from it by selling or displaying it" (gloss of the Rema to *SA* Yoreh Dei·ah 141:1). This view is carried farthest by Rabbi Joseph Saul Nathanson (1808–1875) who permitted Jews to wear cross-shaped military medals, since such medals are obviously not objects of worship, but simply tokens of the king's gratitude and esteem (*Sho·eil U-meishiv* [1886; reprint, Jerusalem and New York: Hotza·at S'farim Shoneh Halakhot, *s.a.*], vol. 1, sect. 3, no. 71, pp. 28b–29b).

This distinction provides the basis for permitting Jews to possess *objets d'art* that depict even pagan, let alone Christian themes. The Rema's point derives from the Talmud's view that some images are for aesthetic value rather than cultic worship (see, e.g., the clear formulation of this principle at *BT* Avodah Zarah 41a). Thus, a very fortunate art dealer might buy or sell Michelangelo's Pietà, since that statue, while Christian, is not a cultic icon. Pagan sculpture poses different questions, since a statue of a Greek god may well have been worshiped in its time. Nonetheless, since there are no more Venus- or Hermes-worshipers today, one may regard such a statue as nullified of religious character and now logically to be considered an exclusively aesthetic object. However, a Jew should not buy, sell, or possess the actual icons of currently practiced pagan religions.

Can Jews pray in a church? Practically speaking, this question is settled by precedent. Either as new communities or because of building damage, many non-Orthodox congregations in fact do rent space from churches. This practice is grounded in the designation of Christianity as Noahide monotheism, not as idolatrous paganism. Most halakhic authorities permit Jewish prayer in a mosque on just this logic. When using church spaces, however, Jews must remove or conceal all Christian symbols.

Can a synagogue open its building to Christian worship? The Committee on Jewish Law and Standards unanimously endorsed Rabbi Elliot Dorff's

1990 argument that synagogues may rent space to non-proselytizing churches (*CJLS Responsa 1980–1990,* pp. 165–184). Rabbi Dorff suggested it may be preferable to offer the social hall before classroom or sanctuary space; however, if necessary, classrooms or sanctuaries may also be used. In that case, Rabbi Dorff recommended that a physical barrier be used to separate the Holy Ark from the Christian service, but that Christians should be permitted to use their own religious symbols while worshiping in synagogues. The Rema's distinction between decorative crosses and icons that actually are venerated during worship suggests a further stringency: one should permit Christians to bring in only decorative symbols but not statues or icons that actually will be worshiped. Additionally, Rabbi Dorff argues one must distinguish between churches that actively, let alone aggressively, seek Jewish converts and those that do not. Being equitable and neighborly is a great value; but to paraphrase King Ahasuerus (Esther 7:8), God forbid that Jews should be drawn to another religion in their own home!

One of the strict prohibitions regarding ancient idolatry appears to pose a natural question about Christianity. Since it is forbidden to mention the name of alien gods (Exodus 23:13, *BT* Sanhedrin 63b, *MT* Hilkhot Avodat Kokhavim 5:11), is it permissible to mention the name of the man Christians take to be divine? Traditional practice is usually strict, as we find Jesus of Nazareth often referred to in halakhic sources by the epithets *oto ha-ish* (that man) or *ha-talui* ("the crucified one"). However, the *halakhah* actually forbids only saying names that indicate divinity (see *Hagahot Maimoniyyot* commentary to *MT* Hilkhot Avodat Kokhavim 5:10, note 3). Uncensored versions of that commentary expressly note that it is permissible to say Jesus's name, "although he is the greatest of all gentile gods." For his part, Maimonides consistently refers to Jesus by his Hebrew name Yeshua (e.g., at *MT* Hilkhot T'shuvah 3:10, uncensored versions), and others use the shortened form, Yeshu. (This abbreviated version was adopted to avoid suggesting that Jesus "saves," as the semantic meaning of Yeshua would indicate.) However, the epithet "Christ" affirms Jesus as "messiah" and "savior," and has been taken by centuries of Christians to imply Jesus's divinity. Therefore, Jews should not apply this term to that man, and should use neither the name nor the epithet as the common casual profanity they have become.

Eastern Religions

Asian religions present different problems than do Christianity and Islam. Eastern religious concepts often are so different from Western ones that calling them monotheistic or polytheistic clarifies little. Yet, generally, we can say that although Eastern religions may posit a supreme unifying divinity without form, these religions are characterized by profuse polytheism and graphic idol worship. For instance, a Hindu temple is a home to idols of major and minor deities, whose worship may include sacrificial offerings of food, water, flowers, and incense. Idols may be bathed and dressed in fine clothes, erected so they can "see" worshipers, accept their offerings, and grant them blessings. How should Jews address such a religion and its adherents?

On one hand, the ethical power of Eastern religions is well known. Buddhism, Hinduism, and Taoism teach non-violence and admirable ethics. Certainly they do not always agree with Judaism, nor are they always moral models, but they surely meet Meiri's standards of communities "governed by the ways of religion." By this ethical analysis, these religions are non-idolatrous. We should extend neighborly relations to them and join them in dialogues and communal projects.

At the same time, the beliefs and practices at the heart of many Eastern faiths are inimical to Judaism and are completely forbidden to Jews. We should consider such religions as non-idolatrous ethically, but as cultically idolatrous. The *halakhah* demands that Jews not enter a shrine where idols are worshiped, let alone participate in their worship. Nor may Jews lend such worship personal or communal financial support. It is forbidden to own idols associated with these faiths until a practitioner of the religion actively negates the idol's religious character and renders it unfit for worship. And it is inappropriate to provide Jewish communal space for such a group's worship. This judgment does not denigrate the spiritual or moral power of these religions. Hinduism, for example, imparts meaning and comfort to tens of millions of people. But Jews cannot walk that path and remain faithful to Judaism.

Numerous Jews today experiment with Buddhism. Many combine Eastern and Western elements into a new amalgam, calling themselves "Jewish-Buddhists" or "Ju-Bus." In the realm of theology, Buddhism is non-theistic, and so cannot be said to posit false or multiple gods. Buddha himself is not understood to be a god, but rather a person who attained enlightenment. In the realm of practice, Buddhism mandates no necessary violations of Jewish tradition. Therefore, to the extent that such theoretical standards are maintained, a Jew might practice Buddhist meditation, study its scriptures, and learn from its insights. However, practice can be quite different from theory, and Jews following this spiritual path must take this into account. In actual popular practice, especially in Asia but also in the West, Buddha and Bodhisattvas (enlightened sages on their way to Buddhahood) are regarded as divine beings—to the point at which statues of the Buddha are kept in shrines, formally and dramatically venerated during worship, showered with gifts, and verbally thanked for the natural bounty of the world. Whatever elite Buddhist theology may be, we should apply a normative Jewish yardstick to Buddhism as it is actually practiced by its millions of adherents in the Buddhist temples of the world. Thus, Jews are forbidden from participating in any ritual, or from entering any shrine, in which idols are venerated. Jews who wish to study Buddhism should do so only in a setting free from images of the Buddha, and solely among those who maintain a strictly non-theistic approach.

The halakhic status of Eastern religions is discussed from an interesting vantage point by Rabbis Mayer Rabinowitz and Avram Reisner in their 2007 responsum regarding the practice of immersing new and used food utensils in a *mikveh* before use, which was approved by the CJLS and which is available for perusal by the public on the website of the Rabbinical Assembly.

Civil Religion

At Jeremiah 29:7, the prophet exhorts his listeners to "seek the peace of the city to which (God) exiled you; and pray to God on its behalf; for when it has peace, so shall you have peace." From this verse, Jews learn that civic well-being is our religious concern.

Cooperation and amity among religious communities is critical to a tolerant and open society. We should pray together with non-Jews for the polity we share; it would have been inconceivable, for example, for American Conservative Jews not to join interfaith services after the World Trade Center attacks. The *halakhah* encodes a related impulse when it prescribes that we should bless God upon seeing a gentile king ("Praised are You . . . who shares the glory of the Divine with all creatures") and eagerly pursue the opportunity to do so (*BT* B'rakhot 58a; cf. *SA* Oraḥ Ḥayyim 224:9). Indeed, Jews have been reciting prayers for their secular governments since at least the twelfth century, as attested by sources from Germany and Spain (see, e.g., *N'tiv Binah* [Tel Aviv: Sinai, 1968, vol. 2, pp. 233–234] of Rabbi Issachar Jacobson, citing Rabbi David Abudarham and the annals of the Jewish community of Worms). Since we pray for the government in our synagogues, it is equally proper to do so in ecumenical settings. Jews should be proud to give a benediction or religious reflection at a civic or interfaith meeting. And we should be proud of Rabbi Haskel Lookstein, who in January 2009 attended an ecumenical service in the National Cathedral in Washington, on the morning after Barack Obama's inauguration, although he was roundly condemned by his Orthodox colleagues for entering a church. Of course, we remain steadfast in our aniconic monotheism. Joining interfaith services should not include participating in non-Jewish rituals or entering into the seductive realm of communal idol worship. But in shared space, we and adherents of other religions may bring our traditions together to improve our common society.

Studying Together

Classical *halakhah* forbids Jews to study idolatry, lest we come to imitate it. But as noted above, Islam and Christianity are not formally to be labeled as idolatrous religions. Therefore, we may study these faiths and their sacred texts. Indeed, such study may even enhance our Judaism by providing us with interesting, even inspiring, comparisons and alternate views. Historical instances of such ecumenical borrowing and mutual influence fill libraries. And because of the extensive literary overlap in our scriptures, studying the Christian testament can particularly illuminate our understanding of early Judaism. The Talmud itself appears once to quote Christian scripture (*BT* Shabbat 116b, apparently citing Matthew 5:17).

With respect to Eastern religions, the question, again, is more complicated. The letter and spirit of the classical prohibition are clearly aimed at preventing Jews from exploring how idolaters worship and learning what they believe about their gods. On the other hand, to forbid such study would clash with contemporary pluralistic values and inculcate needless intolerance. Furthermore, to understand any one religion, it is helpful to see how other religions function in their own cultures. (An oft-repeated maxim in religious studies posits that if you know only one religion, you know none.) A solution for Conservative Jews might be formally to distinguish between academic study, in which learning conveys facts rather than values, and devotional study oriented toward religious growth. When the Torah forbade studying idolatry, there was no concept of the academic discipline of comparative religions, and it must have been assumed that one would only study other faiths' rituals or myths for spiritual enlightenment and inspiration. But in our day, academic study is quite different from devotional study. Insulated by the scientific method of the academy, it would be permitted for a Jew to study the worship of Kami spirits in Shintoism, for instance, but forbidden to seek to feel the devotion of Shinto adherents. Non-theistic Buddhism may be viewed in its own category. Since Buddhism—at least in theory—does not teach about spiritual powers contrasting with Jewish monotheism, one might turn to Buddhism for spiritual edification even beyond the academic mode in which one might study other religions. In principle, it should be permissible to mine Buddhist teaching of masters like Thich Nhat Hanh or the Dalai Lama for insights into human suffering, mindfulness, compassion, and spiritual liberation. But as the practice of Buddhism often strays into idolatrous rites, observant Jews studying Buddhism must be ready to close their books when they encounter teachings about the alternative spirit world. For example, the well-known Tibetan Book of the Dead is full of accounts of the "deities" one encounters after death. This can be of no more than academic interest, not spiritual edification, for an observant Jew.

Turning to the opposite side of this coin: can one study Torah with non-Jews or teach it to them? The Talmud prohibits teaching Torah to gentiles, claiming that the Torah should be the exclusive patrimony of Israel (*BT* Ḥagigah 13a). But why should teaching others the Torah make it *less* the patrimony of Israel? Some propose that gentiles are excluded from Torah study because they will not practice the *mitzvot* they learn, which might suggest that their worth lies in contemplation alone instead of practice. (Of course, none of this applies to gentiles who are prospective converts to Judaism. They may be taught Torah without any restrictions, since they are on their way to adopting the commandments as their own.) Others say the prohibition applies only to the Oral Torah, but that Christians may study the written text of the Bible with us because they affirm its sanctity. Indeed, medieval rabbis did study Bible with Christians, as we see from Rashbam's comment to Exodus 20:13. Still others assume that non-Jews are excluded from Torah study because they may use what they learn against us in disputations—which was a serious problem for medieval Jews forced publicly to defend their faith in public debate.

Each of these reasons can have meaning for Jews today as we evaluate this restriction. In a religious or devotional setting, we should ask our non-Jewish study partners to approach the material with sympathy, with respect, with the possibility of commitment, and without polemical motive. When we are confident that some or all these conditions are met, it is at least appropriate—and perhaps even desirable—to study with non-Jews. Partly by sharing the Torah's inspiring teachings on ethics, for instance, we will forge links with non-Jews together to build God's dominion on earth. As proposed above, formal academic study should be measured by a different yardstick entirely. In a setting that stresses dispassion instead of commitment, a Jew need not refrain from studying any subject with non-Jews.

Intermarriage

Families transmit culture. Therefore, Judaism views in-marriage as critical to the preservation of the faith and has traditionally seen exogamy as tantamount to abandoning the Jewish people, as in this typical passage: "Do not marry them. Neither give your daughter to his son nor take his son for your daughter, for they will turn your children away from Me, and [bring them to] worship other gods" (Deuteronomy 7:3–4).

This is not anti-gentile bigotry, as an outside observer might suppose, but a strategy for maximizing a family's commitment to its heritage and its religious culture. Ancient and modern evidence confirms that houses divided against themselves do not stand for long. When only some members are Jewish, families are unlikely to share rich Judaic lives. Of course, everybody who works in the Jewish world knows individuals who have managed to defy those trends, and who have maintained a strong commitment to Judaism despite being married to non-Jews. We must lovingly invite such families into our communities and not ignore them, but their example does not negate the overwhelming evidence that intermarriage correlates with weak Jewish commitment.

That is why classical *halakhah* forbids Jews from marrying non-Jews, and why we affirm this prohibition as integral to the future of the Jewish people. Some authorities regard this as a biblical prohibition and others see it as rabbinic legislation; all, however, affirm its validity. Rabbinical Assembly members will not officiate at intermarriages, nor may they even be present at the weddings of Jews and non-Jews. Furthermore, the sages of ancient times enacted a ban on sex with non-Jews (Maimonides, *MT* Hilkhot Issurei Bi·ah 12:1; *SA* Even Ha-eizer 16), a prohibition contemporary Jews should likewise affirm.

If a mixed couple marries by non-halakhic means, the marriage has no status in Jewish law. Children of their union take the status of the mother, however, so if she is Jewish then so are her babies. Most Reform and Reconstructionist rabbis accept the children of Jewish fathers and non-Jewish mothers as "patrilineal" Jews. The Conservative movement rejects this departure from the traditional laws of personal status that help the Jewish people define sacred membership and maintain its boundaries. Children of intermarriages are not illegitimate (i.e., they are not in the halakhic category of *mamzeirim*), since that status applies only to children born of a union subject to punishments of excision (called *kareit* in Hebrew) or death (*BT* Y'vamot 49a). Therefore, the offspring of Jewish fathers and non-Jewish mothers are eligible to convert to Judaism. The Jewish parents of non-Jewish children are encouraged to convert them while young and fully raise and educate them as Jews.

The Conservative response to intermarriage derives as much from public policy as from the traditional "four cubits" of the *halakhah*. How precisely communities should relate to those have intermarried, how warmly they should welcome intermarried families, what roles are proper for non-Jewish parents at life-cycle celebrations—these are policy questions without unambiguous halakhic answers. Over the years, the Committee on Jewish Law and

Standards has considered various approaches, ranging from those their authors themselves label as being "harsh" to those their authors prefer to call "welcoming." Rabbi Seymour Siegel wisely counseled each rabbi and community to employ policies that will encourage conversion. His 1982 statement remains illuminating: "In light of individual differences and circumstances, we should leave it to the *mara de'atra* [the rabbi of a specific community] to decide what kind of action will likely lead to conversion of spouses and/or children. This should be the *halakhah* in this very difficult situation" (*CJLS Responsa 1980–1990,* p. 676).

The question of intermarriage is discussed elsewhere in this volume by Rabbi David Fine in his chapter on the *halakhah* of marriage and by Rabbis Daniel Nevins and David Greenstein in their chapters on the halakhic dimension of the relationship between parents and children and the *halakhah* of siblinghood, respectively.

When a Child Converts

Sometimes, sadly, interfaith relations must be negotiated within our own families. How should we react when a family member adopts another faith? Apostates may be bad Jews, but they can never be non-Jews. Jewishness is inalienable, for no one may quit the covenant between God and Israel. Rashi himself gave new halakhic meaning to an old aggadic expression when he said, "A sinning Israelite remains an Israelite" (see his comment in his collected responsa, ed. Israel Elfenbein [New York: Shulsinger, 1943], no. 173, pp. 193–194, and also cf. *BT* Sanhedrin 44a). Thus, even one who abandons Judaism—called in the traditional sources either a *m'shummad* (apostate) or a *mumar* (renegade)—remains halakhically Jewish in important ways. If, for example, a *mumar* were to contract a marriage with another Jew, for instance, that marriage would be valid (*SA* Even Ha-eizer 44:9). Indeed, the persistence of Jewish identity is intended to remind apostates that the door is ever open for their return. If apostates do rejoin the Jewish people, immersion in a *mikveh* is not strictly required, since their Jewishness has never fully lapsed. Most authorities, however, agree immersion would be an appropriate gesture of renewed commitment (see the gloss of the Rema to *SA* Yoreh Dei·ah 268:12).

What about the children of apostates who come from Jewish ancestry but were raised outside of Judaism, and now wish to return to the religion of their ancestors? The CJLS holds that we should base our response toward these "second-generation apostates" to the level of their earlier non-Jewish commitment. Rabbi Gerald Zelizer's 1995 responsum on this theme argues that individuals of halakhically Jewish descent who were actually raised in another religion should be required to undergo formal immersion and be interviewed by a *beit din* (*CJLS Responsa 1991–2000,* pp. 146–150). If such a male individual were uncircumcised, that too would be required, as would the symbolic act of *hattafat dam b'rit* (drawing a drop of blood from the penis) if he had been medically but not ritually circumcised as an infant. For the child of apostate Jewish parents who was not formally a church member, however, rabbis should be "creative and flexible" to devise a proper method for that person to renounce any other religious affiliation and to embrace Judaism. Such acts might include immersion, but could also include a verbal declaration. Furthermore, he wrote, such leniency would be effective in enticing them to return to Judaism.

On the other hand, tradition calls for distinct social and ritual sanctions against apostates. For example, in ancient times, an apostate was not permitted to offer a Temple sacrifice, even though a gentile actually had this right (*BT* Ḥullin 5a). Nor may a *mumar* write a Torah scroll or circumcise a baby. The idea behind such restrictions is that, although apostates may still be Jews in a technical sense, still commanding some loyalty from the community, they cannot join us in practicing Judaism until they renounce alien faiths. Applying this approach to contemporary life, Jews professing other faiths—including those affiliated with Christian groups like "Jews for Jesus" who insist that they are still practicing Judaism—should be excluded from Jewish religious life. They should not be counted in a *minyan,* nor may they be offered public ritual honors or roles, or serve as agents for other Jews doing *mitzvot.* Should they repent and rejoin our people, however, they may resume these roles. Authorities differed on whether or how to readmit the returning apostate, as is evident from the ruling of Rabbi Joseph Karo (in the *Shulḥan Arukh* at *SA* Oraḥ Ḥayyim 128:37) that "an apostate must not raise his hands [to pronounce the priestly blessing], but some say that if he repents he may." The Rema resolved this uncertainty, commenting on the latter clause, "And this is the correct view." This ruling should guide us today.

There is a folk practice of observing mourning rites for a child who abandons Judaism for another faith. This may be based on a misinterpretation of a report about the medieval Rabbi Gershom of Mainz, called the Light of the Exile, who observed two weeks of mourning when his apostate son died, grieving both for the loss of his life in this world and for his forfeit of eternal life as well (see the tale as told in the *Hagahot Asheiri* to *BT* Mo·eid Katan 3:59, 38c in the standard pagination). But in this story, Rabbi Gershom's son had actually died; therefore, the report cannot imply that one should mourn for a living person. One should not follow this perverse custom, which gives up on a person by denying that repentance could change his or her future.

The question of how parents might deal with children who abandon Judaism is also discussed above by Rabbi Daniel S. Nevins.

Speaking to the Dead

The Bible and the sages explicitly forbid witchcraft and necromancy, and condemn many other occult traditions as "Amorite [pagan] ways." For instance, the biblical King Saul's downfall and death are ensured when he consults a medium, the "*ba·alat ov* of En-Dor," to summon the spirit of the deceased prophet Samuel (1 Samuel 28). Imitating King Saul by employing a contemporary medium remains tantamount to *avodah zarah*. Although the Talmud and Jewish lore record numerous cases where people communicated with the dead, the *halakhah* today generally forbids such practices. Maimonides, ruling particularly strictly, forbids any attempt to raise the dead to learn some piece of information from them (*MT* Hilkhot Avodat Kokhavim 11:13). Mediums in our day might use different methods than ancient ones did, but the intent is the same. The *halakhah* forbids seeking occult knowledge through the use of spirit mediums.

Astrology poses interesting challenges. Both talmudic authorities (those cited at *BT* Bava Batra 16b) and medieval ones (most prominently Ibn Ezra, in his "long commentary" to Exodus 23:25) assumed the pattern of stars in the sky affected the governance of the world. Dissenting, Maimonides regarded astrology as *avodah zarah* and forbade any attempt to read the future, by whatever means (*MT* Hilkhot Avodat Kokhavim 11:6–9). Even listening to such "fraudulent tales and lies" is forbidden, and acting on a seer's advice would be worse. All this magic is for "witless fools," Maimonides says (ibid., 11:16). For philosophical and scientific reasons contemporary Jews should follow his judgment. Astrology enshrines superstition over rationality and derides the power of human free will, a basic premise of Judaism. Modern Conservative Jews should not practice astrology.

Interfaith and Faith

"A people that dwells alone, not reckoned among the nations" (Numbers 23:9). So said the gentile prophet Balaam, watching our ancestors camped in the wilderness. But contemporary Conservative Jews know that this is no longer true, if it ever was. As this chapter has explained, modern Jews must negotiate encounters with other mono-, poly- and non-theistic religions, figuring out what we can and cannot share with our neighbors. To do this successfully, we should do so within the *halakhot* that impart Jewish integrity to our actions.

In contrast to this approach, however, the leading twentieth-century modern Orthodox thinker, Rabbi Joseph B. Soloveitchik, believed cooperation over matters of faith and religious teaching was impossible. Jews should cooperate with gentiles only on civic and secular matters, Rabbi Soloveitchik believed, but he forbade interreligious dialogue, as he wrote in one of his major English essays, "Confrontation" (*Tradition* 6:2 [1964], pp. 55–80). Nearly fifty years later, this position prevails among American Orthodox rabbis. Genuine encounter would imply openness to others' truth claims, Rabbi Soloveitchik said, but religious believers must be resolute about their own faith and impervious to counter-claims. Discussing theology with adherents of other faiths, he said, would signal that we Jews would be willing to modify our religious views for the sake of winning friends and making peace.

I ultimately reject Rabbi Soloveitchik's objections, but I hope I do not dismiss them lightly. I hope Jews participate in interreligious encounters that refine, advance, and deepen our faith, not undermine it. Our most central commitments are not on the table. And as we do not enter religious dialogue to win converts, neither can we homogenize our faith commitments in the name of a Judeo-Christian "common ground."

Conservative Jews should draw inspiration from the many others who reject Soloveitchik's model of interreligious encounter as necessarily ending in disputation. Notably, Rabbi Abraham Joshua Heschel was Soloveitchik's disputant in those days, taking part in discussions of the Second Vatican Council in the 1960s. Indeed, "Confrontation" was originally given as a speech at the 1964 Rabbinical Council of America convention, largely in response to the ecumenical overtures of Vatican II.

We should follow Heschel and others, like the philosophers and halakhists Rabbi Elliot N. Dorff of our Conservative movement and Rabbi David Novak (trained Conservative, now neo-Orthodox), who do not regard interreligious encounter as a trap of inevitable syncretism. We need not narrow ourselves hastily, nor poison ourselves by demonizing others. And interreligious dialogue need not consist of one side seducing the other away from its faith. There are powerful social benefits, according to Novak, when religious Jews become partners with religious Christians to propound common religious values in an increasingly secular world. (See Novak's *Jewish-Christian Dialogue: A Jewish Justification* [New York: Oxford University Press, 1989].) For Dorff, there are epistemological and theological reasons for dialogue with others who may have worked out different parts of the puzzle of living in God's world. (See Dorff's *To Do the Right and the Good* [Philadelphia: The Jewish Publication Society, 2002], ch. 3.) Since no mortal human being can possess ultimate truth, and since the Eternal is God of all people and cultures, it may be that God desires religious diversity. Judaism is the best religion *for us,* Dorff holds, but perhaps God brought us all together in a rich, textured world so that we would learn from each other.

As Heschel wrote, deep interfaith encounters seek "neither to flatter nor to refute one another, but to help one another; to share insight and learning . . . to search in the wilderness for the well-springs of devotion, for the power of love and care for man" ("No Religion Is an Island," *Jewish Perspectives on Christianity,* ed. Fritz Rothschild [New York: Crossroad, 1990], pp. 309–324). May we be fortunate to experience interfaith encounters that nurture our religious lives as Jews. May we greet others with openness and respect, but also with faith, unshakably loyal to our sacred tradition, loving God and loving all God's children.

Medical Ethics

AVRAM ISRAEL REISNER

Medicine was hardly humankind's first attempt to challenge God's mastery of the world. Long before Judaism emerged, humanity had managed to tame fire, domesticate animals, develop agriculture to yield more reliable and abundant harvests than nature would otherwise have provided, weave threads together to create fabric for clothing, build shelters against the elements, and communities for companionship and protection. Each of these might have been termed an encroachment on God's domain by philosophers of those times, but when Abraham surveyed the landscape to assess reality, as the *midrash* imagines that he did, he found all those to be clear, and not necessarily negative, features of the Mesopotamian culture that surrounded him. (One version of this *midrash* appears at *B'reishit Rabbah* 38, but it also appears much earlier in the *Apocalypse of Abraham,* a work dated to the second century C.E., and in other sources as well. See Louis Ginzberg, *The Legends of the Jews* [1909–1938; reprint, Philadelphia: The Jewish Publication Society, 2003], vol. 1, p. 189, and particularly vol. 5, p. 210, note 16.)

Of course, idolatry was also part of that world—an undeniable and, to Abraham's mind, wholly undesirable feature of that culture that he felt called to combat as best he could. But as far as the other features of his world were concerned, the *midrash* presents Abraham—standing in for Judaism itself—as affirming and accepting them as a part of the normative divine structure of the universe.

This is a relevant point with which to begin this chapter, because the medical enterprise was one of the fundamental features of human culture in antiquity. Then as now, it was both instinctive and natural to tend to our wounds. The Code of Hammurabi, which comes from Mesopotamia around the time of Abraham, for example, has provisions concerning the responsibilities and the fees of physicians. The Torah, too, relies on this assumption when it makes an assailant responsible for any wounds that he causes. It rules that the assailant must pay for his victim's period of recuperation and for the costs of his cure (Exodus 21:19). It is on this scriptural basis that the Talmud understands that the Torah has granted humanity in general, and physicians in particular, "permission to heal" (*BT* B'rakhot 60a and Bava Kamma 85a).

Permission, though, is not the same as mandate. The mandate applies, of course, with regard to the specific demand of the verse that one who injures another must see to the healing of that person's wounds. This law was further developed in the Talmud (at *BT* Sanhedrin 73a) to require that one attempt to save another's life from attack or some external danger with reference to the verse "Do not stand idly by the blood of your neighbor" (Leviticus 19:16). But what of the desire to seek a cure—for others or for oneself—from illnesses that occur in the normal course of things, neither through accident nor attack? Here the ancients were not so sure that such an event was not God's doing and that attempting to undo it might not be tantamount to rejecting God's right to rule the world, thus a form of blasphemy. May human beings meddle in such things? Clearly, that is where any discussion of Jewish medical ethics must begin.

The Medical Enterprise

The Right to Seek Healing

The first inkling of an answer is found in the Second Book of Chronicles (16:12), where King Asa is described as unfaithful because "ill as he was, he still did not turn to God but rather to physicians." Thus, in commenting on Exodus 21:19, which serves as the primary source for permission to heal, Abraham ibn Ezra (1089–1164, Spain) notes that such permission is not necessarily the same as a command to heal: "I am of the opinion," ibn Ezra writes, "that one should rely directly on the Creator, and not on one's own wisdom, whether through astrology or medicine, for the Torah says [elsewhere], 'I, the Eternal, am your Healer' (Exodus 15:26). There is no need of appointing any other doctor. . . . When the wound is man-made, a human can heal it; but who can heal one whom God afflicts?" (This citation comes from the earlier version of ibn Ezra's commentary, called the "short commentary" by scholars.)

Naḥmanides agrees in theory that it would be improper to seek medical intervention for physical ills, but seems resigned to the fact that medicine is the way of the world. Commenting on Leviticus 26:11, he writes: "In general, when Israel is perfect . . . their affairs are not governed at all by the natural order . . . so that they have need neither of physicians nor of observing any medical regimen. . . . What part have doctors in the realm of those who do God's will? . . . That is the meaning of the rabbinic dictum: 'Medications are not [truly] appropriate for people, but they have grown accustomed to them' (*BT* B'rakhot 60a). If people did not rely on medication, then one would grow sick in punishment of one's sins and be healed at God's behest. But people have grown accustomed to medications and God has left them to the natural results."

Maimonides, however, wrote strongly to the contrary in his commentary to *M* N'darim 4:4. Himself a physician, he embraced the therapeutic arts and, in so doing, insisted that there is an absolute mandate to heal, not solely the half-hearted permission to do so. Furthermore, in his commentary to *M* P'saḥim 4:9, reflecting on the theory that healing should be left to God, Maimonides was anything but gentle in his riposte: "Was it their perverted thought that when a person is hungry and seeks out bread and eats—and, without a doubt, is healed from the weakness that accompanies hunger—that such a person has despaired and does not depend on God? We must label as fools any who think that is so. Just as I thank God at the time of eating for providing that which will satisfy me and assuage my hunger so that I may live and be strong, so I thank God for providing medicine which cures my illness when I am healed. I would not need to refute this ridiculous interpretation were it not common."

Happily, to my mind, Maimonides' thinking carried the day. No serious Jewish thinker in our day questions the mandate to seek healing when we are injured or sick. Rabbi Immanuel Jakobovits (1921–1999), a leading modern authority in the field, cited Rabbi Ḥayyim Joseph David Azulai (1724–1806) in this regard in his *Jewish Medical Ethics* (New York: Bloch Publishers, 1959, p. 6): "The sick individual is duty-bound to conduct himself in accordance with the natural order by calling on a physician to heal him. In fact, to depart from the general practice by claiming greater merit [for oneself] than one ascribes to the many saints [in previous] generations who were cured by physicians, is almost sinful on account both of the implied arrogance [of such a stance] and [on account of] the reliance on miracles when there is danger to life. . . . Hence, one should adopt the ways of all people and be healed by physicians." (Rabbi Azulai's comments may be found in their original setting in his *Birkei Yoseif* commentary to *SA* Yoreh Dei·ah 336:2, ed. Vienna, 1860. This citation is not found, however, in the abridged *Birkei Yoseif* that appears in many editions of the *Shulḥan Arukh.*)

Or, as Rav Ashi put it plainly in a remark preserved at *BT* Bava Kamma 46b: "It is elementary logic: when one has a pain, one goes to the doctor."

But one need not wait to feel pain in order to concern oneself with one's health. Adherents of holistic medicine will insist that one of the greatest errors of modern medicine is that doctors wait for diseases to present themselves before undertaking intervention. According to this school of thought, the time to attend to one's health is when it needs only to be maintained, and not revived or reinstated. Our tradition has never disagreed. While Rav Ashi's comment does sound as though he meant to say that one should turn to a physician when one becomes ill, the Torah had already made it clear that we should conduct ourselves in such a way as to avoid such circumstances, with injunctions such as this from the Book of Exodus (23:25): "Serve the Eternal, your God, and God will bless your bread and your water and . . . remove sickness from your midst." Nor was this a minority opinion. In another context, for example, the ancient sages were only too happy to bend the original scriptural context a bit to understand the words of Deuteronomy 4:9, "Take the utmost care and watch yourself scrupulously," to indicate that one should avoid danger in every way and not bring harm upon one's head. (This was clearly a common interpretation. See *BT* B'rakhot 32b and Shavuot 36a for early uses of the verse in this non-literal sense, and see *Ḥiddushei Ritba* to Shavuot 36a, *s.v. amar R. Yannai,* for a clear medieval statement of this principle.)

And so it was that the proper ways to eat and sleep, to urinate and evacuate, and even the proper way to engage in sexual intercourse, became the stuff of talmudic discussion. (Such practical advice is found scattered throughout the Talmud, e.g., at *BT* B'rakhot 13b and 40a, Shabbat 82a, Makkot 16b, and K'tubbot 48a, among many other talmudic texts.)

Perhaps the words of Maimonides, who had extraordinary erudition both in Jewish law and in secular medicine, summarize the Jewish viewpoint best of all. At *MT* Hilkhot Dei·ot 4:1, 20–21, he wrote: "Since maintaining a whole and healthy body is part of a divine path, for it is impossible that one should understand or discern anything of God when sick, one must therefore distance oneself from those things that risk harming the body, and one must practice those things that are healthful and salutary. . . Whoever practices these things that we have discussed here, I promise that he will not suffer illness all his days until he ages and dies. He will not need a doctor, but his body will remain whole and intact all his days unless his body was flawed from its inception. . . . But all these good practices of which we have spoken are appropriate only for healthy people. One who is sick . . . will have other paths and practices to follow that will be dictated by [the nature of] his illness, as is explained in medical textbooks."

Pharmacology, Surgery, and Legitimate Risk

Not all therapy is benign. Sometimes medicine must make patients sick on the way to making them well. Other times, however, it will just make them sick. Many times harm is immediate and inevitable, be it from the nauseating effect of a drug or the cut of the scalpel, while the desired healing is far from guaranteed. This concept, that physicians must sometimes make people suffer as part of the healing process, was the next theological hurdle for halakhic thinkers to clear: if healing is required and harming is forbidden, then guaranteed cures are to be desired and harmful drugs—especially those that risk harming the patient grievously or permanently—are to be shunned. The sages of classical antiquity repeatedly ruled that harming anyone, even oneself, was forbidden (see, for example, Maimonides' remarks at *MT* Hilkhot Ḥoveil U-mazzik 5:1). But what of cures that involve *preliminary* injury only? And what of uncertain treatments that, for all they may cause harm, constitute the only available therapy in a given patient's situation? In the real world, all treatments are uncertain but some carry significant risk. Are they acceptable or not? This situation, too, has existed since the dawn of time. Surely Naḥmanides was right when he noted (in the *Sha·ar Ha-sakkanah* section of his *Torat Ha-adam*) that it is in the nature of medicine that "there is nothing but risk. What heals one harms another."

On these questions, the classical sages took their cue from an odd biblical tale of four lepers who risked summary execution by entering the enemy's camp in search of food and who justified their risk with these words: "Why should we sit here waiting for death? . . . If they let us live, we shall live. If they put us to death, we shall then die" (2 Kings 7:3–4). Basing themselves on the lepers' reasoning, the rabbis concluded that it is indeed permissible to risk one's life in order to save oneself. But the Tosafot (the French and German interpreters of the Talmud who lived in the twelfth and thirteenth centuries), in commenting on that passage of the Talmud, warned not to throw caution to the winds. "In every case," they argued, "we must do only that which is beneficial." (The comments of the sages are preserved at *BT* Avodah Zarah 27b.

The comments of the Tosafot are found on that same page, *s.v. l'ḥayyei sha·ah la ḥaishinan.*)

What are the halakhic standards for weighing the risk of potential harm against the likelihood of potential benefit so as to make a reasonable determination regarding how to proceed? There has never been a clear, fully unequivocal answer to that question, nor do I imagine that there ever will be. Rather, each case must be evaluated according to its own specifics. Several factors will inevitably weigh into the equation, but none can be declared *the* determinative one in advance and, in any case, each must be weighed against the others on a kind of sliding scale of moral and halakhic value. In the end, the most important issues are, of course, the precise situation, and the specific beliefs of the attending physician, the patient, and, practically speaking, the family and friends who are involved in the patient's care.

The first factor to consider is always the severity of the illness. Immediate fear for the life of the patient justifies more drastic responses than long-range concern, and non-terminal illness justifies less rigorous response than potentially fatal illness. Jewish law ratifies these gradients in principle through its relaxation of otherwise central legal obligations in the emergency situation (termed *bi-she'at ha-d'ḥak,* the hour of pressing need, in rabbinic literature) and through a famous leniency in the laws relating to Shabbat and festival observance that not only permits, but actually requires, that the regular restrictions be set aside on behalf of a mortally endangered patient. This leniency, however, is not invoked on behalf of patients whose lives are not endangered.

Much of what would naturally follow from this legal wrinkle is blurred by the insistence that the mere possibility that a life *might* be lost is sufficient to permit the same level of legal transgression that is mandated when someone's life is unequivocally on the line. (See, e.g., *M* Yoma 8:6, the precedent by means of which the law permits one to drive women in labor to the hospital on Shabbat.) And it is also worth noting the insistence of at least some authorities that "all those who are ill may be presumed to be at risk" (*Y* B'rakhot 4:4, 8b). Still, some illnesses are clearly less acute than others and would thus justify only less intrusive, less dangerous, therapies.

Another factor that must be considered is the likelihood of possible harm coming to the patient in the course of the medical intervention. Some harm and some risk are surely allowed; this much is implied by the very permission granted to the healer to heal because, as Naḥmanides noted in the passage cited above, "there is nothing but risk" in medicine. Nor does a physician have to feel certain about the outcome of a procedure before undertaking it on a patient's behalf and, indeed, a physician should not refrain from treatment out of concern about a possible negative outcome. "Since permission was granted to the healer to heal," Naḥmanides writes further in the *Torat Ha-adam,* "and since it is even a *mitzvah* to do so, [physicians] should not be at all concerned [about possible negative outcomes]. If they behave appropriately, as per their understanding, all treatments are solely judged a *mitzvah* since the Merciful One commanded them to heal." But how much risk of how severely negative an effect is reasonable? These calculations are subject to differing views among halakhic authorities.

A central factor is the proven efficacy of the proposed treatment. Here, later halakhic sources distinguish between a *r'fu·ah b'dukah* ("an established treatment") and one whose therapeutic value is uncertain. But the halakhic concept of an "established" treatment is much narrower than the current concept of an approved medication, and an uncertain remedy is not identical with the category of "experimental treatment" so widely cited by modern-day medical insurers. From the vantage point of *halakhah,* an established treatment must be known to be generally effective. To refuse such a treatment would be considered imprudent, if not sinful, and it should, as a matter of law, be pressed upon an unwilling patient. But other treatments, including those that may be part of the standard repertoire of the physician but that are judged only possibly effective for a given condition in a given situation (which thus includes most treatments), are not to be pushed on the patient, but should be left to the patient's personal discretion. Experimental treatments occupy a still lower tier, so low in fact that it is considered immoral to risk a patient's life by subjecting him or her to such forms of medical therapy, except where the patient's death is deemed otherwise inevitable (and, even then, some halakhic authorities persist in forbidding such treatments).

The physician's skill is also a key factor. Much has been done in modern medicine to make data available to patients regarding the efficacy of treatments offered by various hospitals and physicians. Some treatments may prove more effective in the hands of some physicians than others, and this must be seen as a function of different doctors using different techniques, different equipment, and countless other compounding factors. All things being equal, though, Jewish law has been content to presume that one should follow the recommendations of physicians, and that one should prefer the advice of a great physician over the counsel of a lesser one. But all things are never equal. Almost by definition, these will always be at least somewhat subjective judgments.

Practically speaking, the patient's own judgment will almost always override all these factors. It is true, of course, that Jewish authorities have traditionally deemphasized the concept of ultimate personal autonomy in favor of the concept that patients are not masters over their own lives and, as a result, may neither make any decisions that will shorten their lives—including by suicide or euthanasia—nor choose to harm themselves except for good cause. However, as few forms of medical treatment can measure up to the exacting standards of a *r'fu·ah b'dukah,* it will almost always be a patient's decision whether to proceed with a proposed method of therapy. Happily, most illnesses are not imminently life-threatening, and patients are thus free to accept the limitations of their condition and not subject themselves to additional risk by seeking treatment. It is quite common, and perfectly reasonable, for example, to put off hip-replacement surgery until the pain becomes unbearable, and then to choose to do it with one surgeon and not another, in this hospital and not in that. All these decisions, it turns out, are recognized by Jewish law as properly in the hands of the patient. Indeed, the *halakhah* goes even further: our ancient sages recognized the inner logic of one's own fears and the internal cogency of one's own assessment in matters of one's health, preferring to legitimize such personal feelings even over the assessment of the experts, as long as the course of action chosen is not tantamount to suicide. The Talmud reports this in the name of Rabbi Yannai: "Rabbi Yannai says: if the ill patient says: 'I require this' but the doctor says: 'It is not required'—one listens to the patient. Why is this the case? Because it says in Scripture: 'The heart knows its own bitterness'" (*BT* Yoma 83a, citing Proverbs 14:10).

If a doctor pushes a treatment, even a fully established treatment (i.e., a *r'fu·ah b'dukah*) upon an unwilling patient, the Talmud appears to rule that the patient might be forced to cooperate. Nevertheless, Rabbi Jacob Emden (1697–1776) ruled that even in that case the patient's autonomy is paramount: "If [patients] refrain [from a given treatment] because they do not hold it to be an established one [i.e., a *r'fu·ah b'dukah*], even on the basis of their own opinion alone, they are not to be forced. . . . And they may certainly not be forced [to accept the treatment ordered by a physician] if they fear they will be harmed by it. . . . One may not force them in such a case" (*Mor U-k'tziyyah* to *AT* Oraḥ Ḥayyim 328).

The ways in which these different factors will play out is open to great variation in individual assessment. Cosmetic surgery, prohibited by many as causing harm for no significant benefit, is at one end of the spectrum. Yet others argue that the psychological harm of a bad self-image and possible social fallout is sufficient to justify the small risk and temporary wound that is involved. Treatments for terminal illnesses are at the other end of the spectrum. In a recent case in Israel, an aged patient with gangrene, who was also suffering from other health problems, was resisting the amputation insisted upon by physicians. She was cajoled to consent to the amputation by the Sephardic chief rabbi Mordechai Eliyahu, who argued that the obligation to act to save her life was paramount. Yet, when asked a similar question, the late Rabbi Solomon Zalman Auerbach, himself a very well-known and widely respected Israeli halakhic authority, answered that, given the inherent risks of surgery and the fact that the surgery did not seem likely to address the patient's underlying problems or even to extend the patient's life except very briefly, one should contemplate neither overriding the patient's reservations about the procedure nor even attempting to persuade her to agree to the amputation. (The efforts of Rabbi Eliyahu to urge the patient to agree to the amputation were reported in the Israeli press in early 1990. Unfortunately, she did not survive the surgery. Rabbi Auerbach's ruling is reported by Dr. Abraham S. Abraham in his compendium on medical *halakhah, Nishmat Avraham* [Brooklyn: Mesorah, 2004], vol. 2, p. 321, commenting on *SA* Yoreh Dei·ah 399:1.)

The Relationship of Putative Benefit and Possible Risk

The question of accepting risk for the sake of benefit is at the heart of many issues in Jewish medical ethics. Immunization, which in some cases (as, for example, in the case of the smallpox vaccine) bears some statistically recognizable risk, is a good example. The patient considering inoculation is not ill in any sense; indeed, if the patient actually is ill, the inoculation is better deferred. May healthy patients put themselves at risk against a mere possibility of later infection? Rabbi Israel Lipschutz (known as the *Tiferet Yisra·el,* 1782–1860) wrote in the "Boaz" section of his *Tiferet Yisra·el* commentary to *M* Yoma 8:3 that the infinitesimal risk, which he described as "one in a thousand" (though, in reality, it is much less), is appropriate against the much greater risk of contracting the illness. Would that apply when the risk of illness is smaller and harder to assess? That was part of the public policy debate in the United States in 2003 over whether to vaccinate the population against smallpox. Given that smallpox had been eradicated and that the fear of illness rested solely on the possibility of infection by terrorists who might possibly have procured illegal stores of the virus, was the inherent risk of vaccination with live virus justifiable? I have not yet seen halakhic opinions rendered in this case, but I am certain they will vary. (The topic of vaccination against possible disease was discussed in detail by Rabbi Joseph H. Prouser in a responsum approved by the CJLS in 2005 and now available on the website of the Rabbinical Assembly.)

It is also true that estimates of danger and risk change over time. To the extent that halakhic opinion depends upon those estimates, it too must be flexible. A perfect example is the still much debated position of halakhic authorities on the matter of heart transplants. In a responsum dated July 14–15,

1968, Rabbi Moshe Feinstein ruled that such procedures are forbidden, "for all recipients have died in short order." (This responsum was subsequently published in *Igg'rot Moshe,* Yoreh Dei·ah 2:174, ed. New York, 1973, pp. 286–294.) But in a letter of July 5, 1986, that was published in the journal *T'ḥumin,* vol. 7, Rabbi Moshe D. Tendler, Rabbi Feinstein's son-in-law, wrote that "heart transplants today have converted from the experimental to the therapeutic category. . . . My late father-in-law, Rabbi Moshe Feinstein, was well aware of these developments and permitted heart transplants in his later years." Not all have followed him in this change of heart, however. (For more about Rabbi Feinstein's and Rabbi Tendler's opinions, see Yoel Jakobovits' essay, "Brain Death and Heart Transplants: The Israeli Chief Rabbinate's Directives," *Tradition* 24:4 [Summer 1989], pp. 1–14.)

Immunization is an example of weighing a small risk against a potentially great benefit. But what if the reverse was true and one was considering undertaking an action with no specific benefit, but with great, but not inevitable, risk? The case of smoking, both in law and in society, illustrates this point well. Early medical opinion thought smoking to be healthful, and, given that early halakhic works took that as a fact, it is not at all surprising that the habit of smoking spread actively among religious Jews. But new data collected over the last half century has established definitively the harm caused by tobacco use. Following the report of an advisory committee, the surgeon general issued a warning in 1964, familiar to all in the United States, that "smoking may be hazardous to your health." The early halakhic response was typically defensive. Rabbi Moshe Feinstein responded immediately, in 1964, that since it is common to smoke and since it was a habit of many great sages in the past, it would be improper to forbid it. Yet there were calls in the late 1960s and throughout the 1970s for a rabbinic ruling banning smoking. In the late 1970s, some fifteen years after the report of the surgeon general's committee, non-Orthodox authorities finally weighed in, but tepidly and without much conviction. For example, Conservative scholar Rabbi Seymour Siegel wrote: "It would . . . follow that Jewish ethics and Jewish law would prohibit the use of cigarettes. Smoking should, at least, be banned in synagogues, Jewish schools, and in Jewish gathering places." (Rabbi Siegel's essay, entitled "Smoking—A Jewish Perspective," has been published in *Life and Death Responsibilities in Jewish Biomedical Ethics,* ed. Aaron Mackler [New York: JTS Press, 2000].) A noted Reform scholar, Solomon Freehof, wrote in his book *Reform Responsa for Our Time* (Cincinnati: Hebrew Union College Press, 1977): "Whether Jewish law would have [smokers] give up the habit would depend upon the degree of conviction that the medical profession has come to with regard to it" (p. 56).

But the environment had clearly begun to change. Rabbi David Halevy, then the chief rabbi of Tel Aviv, promulgated a formal decree in 1976 declaring cigarette smoking to be a violation of Jewish law. Yet in an essay published in *Tradition* 16:4 (Summer, 1977, pp. 121–122), Rabbi J. David Bleich retorted that smoking could not be banned. Adding substance to the rather weak case made by Rabbi Feinstein, he argued that, like pregnancy, which carries certain prospective risk to the birthing mother but is allowed and even encouraged, smoking involves no current danger to the smoker and not everyone who smokes is destined to become ill. On its face, that analogy was problematic. Pregnancy, like medical treatment, serves an important purpose that clearly outweighs the risks involved, but smoking serves no such purpose and the risk is more substantial. Maimonides, at any rate, had long since expressed himself clearly about the right to take gratuitous risks: "There are many things that the sages said [to avoid] because they are dangerous to life. Whoever transgresses these, saying 'I am endangering myself, so it is no one else's business' or 'I am not worried about this,' is subject to rabbinic lashes for rebelliousness" (*MT* Hilkhot Rotzei·aḥ U-sh'mirat Nefesh 11:5).

Increasingly, other authorities have found the level of risk to constitute a compelling argument against smoking. Rabbi Eliezer Waldenberg, for example, published a responsum prohibiting smoking in the ultra-Orthodox press in 1982. (The text of the responsum appears in *Assia* 5 [1986]. The responsum was subsequently reprinted, but without the precipitating letter, in *Tzitz Eliezer,* vol. 15, no. 39 [ed. Jerusalem, 1983, pp. 101–103].) Rabbi Mordecai Halperin weighed in on the side of such a prohibition in an article published in that same issue of *Assia,* as did Abraham S. Abraham in *Nishmat Avraham* (vol. 3, p. 321, commenting on *SA* Oraḥ Ḥayyim 427:8). Weighing risk, prognosis, purpose, and personal predilections, it is little wonder that the adage applies, "Judges may only rule as they see fit" (*BT* Bava Batra 131a, Sanhedrin 6b, and Niddah 20b).

One last word is in order about autonomy in medical decision-making. I mentioned above that the patient's autonomy is limited by the prohibition of knowingly shortening one's life, or even knowingly causing oneself damage. Another such limitation on the autonomy of a dying patient specifically stems from concern for the best interests of that patient, when the medical ethic of beneficence (represented by the Hippocratic oath "to do no harm") and the more modern liberal ethic of personal autonomy collide. A medical tendency toward paternalism, which seeks to substitute the doctor's judgment for the patient's, can be particularly antithetical to a patient's autonomy. Therefore, many have sought aggressively to end medical paternalism. But Judaism has always left room for case-specific determinations. Should a physician, for instance, frighten a patient with every last detail of risk, or is it better to hold that information close to the vest? In general, Judaism lauds, and almost invariably requires, truthfulness (cf., for example, the unequivocal commandment not to lie at Exodus 23:7), but the *halakhah* nevertheless cautions that untruth is preferable to causing harm if a person might be harmed by hearing the unadulterated truth about his or her condition (*BT* K'tubbot 17a). Thus, in the clearest case, where it is feared that news of a poor prognosis may yield despair and, by destroying hope, actually hasten the patient's death, it is generally considered forbidden to give that news to the patient. Similarly, where a patient's prognosis is poor, yet medical treatment decisions need to be made, halakhic authorities have tended to take an approach akin to medical paternalism, shielding the patient from disheartening details and letting the physician and family act in the patient's best interests. Under the newer concept of supreme patient autonomy, however, that practice is often condemned as an act of disrespect for the autonomy of the patient, who, it is assumed, would want to hear the full details in order to be able to choose a course of action intelligently. Yet many physicians have protested that patients are often confused and want decisions of such paramount importance taken out of their hands. Such patients now often find, however, that their physicians cannot make decisions for them, due to newer hospital regulations that require the patient's consent and to the ever-present fear on the part of the doctor of accusations of malpractice.

Halakhic authorities to this day largely hold by the older precedents that support the belief that bad news is harmful and should be avoided. Minority voices, however, have begun to query whether truth ought not to be told when a patient demands or even merely requests it, or when the physician's assessment is that doing so will not be harmful. Yet even physicians will often err on the side of secrecy, depending more on the family to determine where the best interests of the patient lie, both with regard to competent patients (whose autonomy is compromised by keeping them in the dark) and with regard to incompetent patients—be they children, mentally challenged individuals, or those newly incompetent at the end of life due to the effects of illness and/or disorienting medications. Judaism maintains a basic level of comfort with the idea that family and community bear the obligation to care for their own, at the same time maintaining a cautious distance from the contemporary liberal insistence on the radically autonomous self. But it must be emphasized that this is basically a factual debate about whether patients are more harmed or helped by knowing the truth, no matter how bitter. Dr. Avraham Steinberg, in his *Encyclopedia of Jewish Medical Ethics* (Nanuet, NY: Feldheim, 2003, vol. 1, pp. 322–325), for example, maintains that newer studies indicate the greater healthfulness for patients to grapple with the truth. If this is so, (though I personally remain skeptical), halakhic opinion will have to change. Rabbi Elliot Dorff, the most prominent voice in the Conservative movement addressing issues of bioethics today, opts for a general policy of being truthful with patients. Whether this is the direction in which future *halakhah* will develop, only time and further empirical data will tell. (Readers interested in the larger issues involved in the debate over medical paternalism will find a very thorough argument in favor of restoring the empathic, caring role of the physician in Edmund D. Pellegrino and David C. Thomasma's *For the Patient's Good: The Restoration of Beneficence in Health Care* [Oxford: Oxford University Press, 1988].)

Organ Transplants

When organ transplantation first began, it was rightly considered to be experimental in the extreme, and Jewish law is not at all hospitable to experimental treatments with substantial, let alone life-threatening, risks. Prior to the development of drugs that combat rejection, a transplanted organ would invariably fail after a short while. It is no surprise, then, that the early rabbinic responses to organ transplantation were all negative. Like Rabbi Feinstein's first responsum regarding heart transplantation, authorities concurred that these were simply not therapeutic procedures. It was considered unnecessary to make the secondary arguments that, even by a Maimonidean stance supportive of medical intervention in general, these procedures seemed beyond the pale of God-given natural remedies and, because early transplants all involved cadaver organs, involved desecration of a corpse, whereas Jewish law demands respect for the body and its timely interment.

Credit for changing the halakhic attitude goes to advances in medicine itself, including the development of appropriate anti-rejection drugs and the improvement of transplant procedures. But credit for overcoming the secondary halakhic objection to the use of organs taken from cadavers belongs squarely to Rabbi Isser Yehuda Unterman, the second chief rabbi of Israel. In 1952, quite early in the transplantation era and a decade before he became chief rabbi, Rabbi Unterman faced the question of whether a cornea taken from the eye of a deceased individual could be transplanted into a living person to restore the latter's sight. In the responsum that laid the foundation for all future responsa permitting organ transplantation, later published in his book *Sheivet Mihudah* (ed. Jerusalem, 1955, pp. 313–322), he permitted the procedure—arguing that the rules of safeguarding human life (*pikku·aḥ nefesh*) applied, according to which the needs of the living override the general rules requiring absolute respect for the dead, and that "it is an instance of great merit to the deceased, and it is gratifying to one's soul, that so great a *mitzvah* is fulfilled with one's body." In truth, that position had precedents in rulings by Rabbi Ezekiel Landau (1713–1793) and Rabbi Ephraim Oshry (1914–2003). Rabbi Landau's ruling forbade an autopsy from being performed solely for educational purposes, but permitted it where the sought-after information would be of immediate value in treating other patients (*Noda Bihudah,* second ed.: Yoreh Dei·ah 210, ed. New York, 1960, pp. 126–127, based on a discussion on *BT* Ḥullin 11b). Rabbi Oshry's responsum (published in the collection *She'eilot U-t'shuvot Mi-ma·amakim* 2:10 (ed. New York, 1963, pp. 53–58) and penned under the most ghoulish circumstances) permitted a Caesarean section to be performed on a woman murdered by the Nazis in an attempt to save her baby. But by placing transplantation firmly under the rubric of life-saving procedures and terming it a *mitzvah,* Rabbi Unterman gave the seal of approval to all subsequent considerations of transplantation. In a highly creative turn, he argued that a transplanted organ, far from needing immediate interment with its body of origin, is not to be considered dead at all, but rather is revived through the transplantation procedure and is "hereafter tied up organically as part of a living organism." (It will have been noted by the discerning reader that all this was based on the notion that organ transplantation is permissible as a life-saving technique, whereas the specific case Rabbi Unterman was considering dealt with saving sight, and could not properly be described as life-saving at all. This, too, was an area of creative assertion by Rabbi Unterman, who argued that even saving sight might be considered "life-saving" insofar as sight might save the life of the individual with newly restored vision in some future eventuality.)

Thus halakhic writers today are almost unanimous in approving of organ transplantation from the deceased. Less than unanimous, however, is their assessment of whether organ donation can be termed obligatory. Here, concepts of personal autonomy intervene. Rabbi Joseph H. Prouser, for example, has written unambiguously that respect for the deceased cannot stand up, in any sense, to the requirement to save life. In a responsum approved by the CJLS in 1995, the author writes: "The preservation of human life is obligatory, not optional. Since all conflicting halakhic duties are suspended . . . withholding consent for post-mortem organ and tissue donation when needed for lifesaving transplant procedures is prohibited by Jewish law" (*CJLS Responsa 1991–2000,* p. 190).

Other writers, however, are more cautious, apparently moved by the intuitive reasoning of Rabbi David ibn Abi Zimra (called Radbaz, 1479–1573) that, even where no risk is incurred, it is still a person's prerogative to maintain his or her own bodily integrity. Thus they speak of the *mitzvah* of donation, of its laudable and pious nature, but cannot bring themselves to prohibit the withholding of consent by the next of kin even though respect for the deceased is clearly secondary to the call to save a life. (Radbaz's responsum is published in his *She'eilot U-t'shuvot Ha-radbaz,* vol. 3, responsum 627 in the standard editions, elsewhere printed as responsum 1052.) Representing this more cautious view, see Rabbi Isaac Jacob Weiss, *Minḥat Yitzḥak,* vol. 5, responsum 7, section 22 (ed. Jerusalem, 1966, p. 30), and Rabbi Eliezer Waldenberg, *Tzitz Eliezer,* vol. 13, responsum 91 [ed. Jerusalem, 1978, pp. 182–184]. Among Conservative writers this seems to be the position of Rabbi David Golinkin, as stated in the *Responsa of the Va·ad Halakhah,* vol. 5, pp. 119–124, and others.

Clearly, if organ donation is an obligation, or even if it is only a non-obligatory good deed, then indicating one's willingness to be an organ donor is desirable. This suggests an affirmative halakhic mandate for organ donor cards, which are often associated with driver's licenses. A word must be said, however, about such organ donor cards and the matter of tissue banking and research use of the cadaver. (Whole organs typically cannot be preserved, and thus are fit only for immediate transplant. Tissues such as skin and corneas, however, can be preserved and may therefore be banked for future use and research.) The permissibility of organ transplantation is predicated on the assumption that doing so can save a life. Where other uses of the donated tissue are contemplated, however, such as for research or tissue banking, permission is not so clear. Again, the ruling precedent in this regard comes from that same responsum by Rabbi Ezekiel Landau, in which he wrote that *pikku·aḥ nefesh* can only be invoked when the patient to be saved is "before us." Much debate revolves around tissue banking and whether such "deferred use" can be permitted, given our growing abilities to preserve tissue. Is a prospective patient considered "before us" or not? While some would reject all such banking, others insist that where an eventual recipient is virtually assured, such preservation to benefit an anticipated patient is acceptable. A proper assessment, then, needs to be specific to the preservation techniques available and the likelihood that each individual type of tissue will, in fact, be used. Research use, however, is generally not permitted. Potential donors, therefore, must indicate on organ donor cards their approval only of specified uses of any potentially harvested organs.

Though the concept itself of organ transplantation from the deceased is widely accepted today, there is still much halakhic dispute around the issue of transplants from living donors. Here, the issue of risk to the donor is the primary consideration, and the donation of renewable resources, such as blood and bone marrow, are usually discussed separately. Generally, it is agreed that blood donation is of negligible risk to the donor and is therefore required, or should at least be encouraged. The same would seem to be true of blood marrow donation, but here the risk of anesthesia, the pain the procedure entails, and the requirement of hospitalization must also be taken into account, as must the acknowledgment that this procedure reaches more deeply into the core of the body. These aspects of bone marrow transplantation have led some authorities, including those prepared to require blood donation, to hesitate to require marrow donation in accordance with the stipulation of Radbaz. (An interesting question for those who find blood donation to be obligatory is whether there are any conceivable circumstances under which they would coerce people to donate blood against their will. Opinions will almost certainly vary.) Skin donation would appear to be in the same category, more similar to the case of bone marrow than to blood donation in terms of risks and procedures. The new liver-lobe transplant procedure also involves a renewable tissue, but as the procedure entails some surgical risk, few are likely to term it obligatory by any calculation and some may reject the possibility entirely. By contrast, kidney transplants and lung-lobe transplants are currently practiced examples of transplants from a living donor that involve nonrenewable organs, and they both involve significant risk to the donor. No authority would require such transplants. Are they even to be considered permissible? Two responsa by Rabbi David ibn Abi Zimra (*She'eilot U-t'shuvot Ha-radbaz,* vol. 3, responsum 627, also known as responsum 1052; and vol. 5, responsum 218, elsewhere published as responsum 1582) set out the parameters of almost all subsequent considerations of this issue.

The first responsum by Abi Zimra is the one referred to above. He argues that the voluntary loss of a limb to save another's life is beyond reasonable expectation. Where there is not a significant danger to the donor, it would be a pious act. Otherwise, though, it should be prohibited. In the second responsum, he stresses that, while one is obligated to accept some degree of personal risk to save another, one is not obliged to risk one's own well-being when the likelihood of harm is "balanced," let alone when harm to the rescuer is the more likely eventuality.

Two schools of thought have developed among contemporary authorities around how to reconcile these two responsa.

One argues that the two are grappling with entirely separate issues. The first deals with the loss of major bodily organs that do not regenerate. In such a case there can never be an obligation to give up a part of one's body, even to save another's life. It may be pious behavior, but such piety is excessive where there might be danger involved. The second approach, on the other hand, deals with standard risk of one's life, where no limb is endangered. In that case, the probability factor is invoked: if the risk is greater than fifty percent (in Radbaz's own terms, when the odds "lean toward certain harm"), engaging in such risk is not required, whereas if it is less than fifty percent, undertaking such an activity is required.

The other school of thought attempts to unite the two responsa into one common theory of risk. There are three categories of risk, according to this reading: leaning toward no harm, balanced, and leaning toward harm. Where the situation leans toward harm to the rescuer, the act is forbidden; where it is balanced, action is optional; where it leans toward no risk, action is required. "Balanced," then, need not be precisely fifty-fifty, but may represent a wide swath in the middle. In the case of even the most benign loss of limb, however, Radbaz feels that there is, in fact, at least some life-risk, despite any claims to the contrary; therefore it is properly in the "balanced" category, and giving up a limb must be viewed as optional. Were the danger greater, giving up a limb to save another should be prohibited. According to this reading, if the assessment of the facts should change, the determination would also change, for risking the loss of a limb is no different than any other risk. (Readers interested in seeing these views set forth formally can consult Rabbi Moshe Hershler's *Halakhah U-r'fu·ah* vol. 2 [Jerusalem and Chicago: Makhon Regenshberg, 1981], pp. 123–124, and Rabbi Eliezer Waldenberg's responsum published in his *Tzitz Eliezer,* vol. 10, responsum 25, ch. 28 [ed. Jerusalem, 1970, pp. 171–172]. Both of these sources are in Hebrew. For an English language consideration of these two schools of interpretation along with much other material, see Part IV of Rabbi Joel Roth's responsum "Organ Donation," approved by the CJLS in 1999 and now published in *CJLS Responsa 1991–2000,* pp. 256–318.)

With regard to live-donor kidney transplants, this distinction between the two schools yields differing rulings, for although it is true that such transplants do involve a non-regenerating major organ, it is also the case that the risk has become quite low. Therefore, according to the first approach, they are *ipso facto* not obligatory, whereas according to the second (which does not recognize a special exception for major organs), agreeing to donate a kidney to save another's life would actually be required—according to those who assess the risk to be insignificant.

This is not a venue in which to make final rulings of any sort, but there is some wisdom in the tendency of the law to seek to compromise in such situations. Kidney donation cannot be said to be required today because significant voices in *halakhah* find that unreasonable, and that is the position taken by the CJLS. The concept of a tripartite analysis of risk inherent in the second school's approach, however, is much more appealing than the bipartite division of the first, because medical reality does not allow real, substantive determinations of fifty-one percent risk as opposed to forty-nine percent. Similarly, lung-lobe transplants cannot currently be required, and their permissibility as voluntary procedures must be determined by weighing the risk to the donor on a case-by-case basis.

I close this section with a final word about tissue and organ banking. Where the tissue to be banked is renewable tissue taken from a live donor, as is the case with blood and bone marrow donation, there appears to be no substantive halakhic question relating to the dignity of the donor (as there is with respect to cadaver tissue banking) because it is done with the donor's full consent. Furthermore, if it is possible to determine that banked blood is likely to be used, then one could argue that it is sufficient that there be some prospective patient in order to allow a blood bank to operate under the general affirmative halakhic obligation to save life. However, this is not usually the case. Banked blood is generally used as "insurance" against unnamed catastrophes that might occur and, absent a need for its use, much of the donated blood will be discarded when no longer fresh. That being the case, one might wonder if blood donation should be allowed. Indeed, Rabbi Menashe Klein (in his *Mishneh Halakhot,* vol. 4, responsum 245 [New York: M'khon Mishneh Halakhot Gedolot, 2000], p. 378–382) concluded that blood-letting is self-injury and must be prohibited, and blood donation can only be permitted to save a life actually "before us."

Many others, however, permit blood banking, arguing variously that the donor's intent to save a life should override the prohibition of self-injury even if this intention might not be fulfilled, or that the permission granted by the donor should suffice to permit self-injury when the substance donated is self-replenishing, as supported by the talmudic precedent of Abba Ḥilkiah mentioned at *BT* Ta·anit 23b. (There, it is told how the ancient sage raised his cloak when passing through a field of thorns, preferring the lacerations to his feet over tears in his garment. When asked by his students why he did so, Abba Ḥilkiah replied, "The skin will heal, but the cloak will not.") Yet others state plainly—and most persuasively of all—that blood donation as it is practiced today is simply not considered an injury at all. Moreover, the newer reality is that blood is likely to be broken up into its components for use, and thus will rarely be stored as whole blood at all. In turn, this dramatically enhances the likelihood that at least some part of the blood will be used. These arguments account for the general acceptability of blood donation and banking among observant Jews today.

Animal and Human Experimentation

In the third volume of his *Contemporary Halakhic Problems* (Jersey City, NJ: KTAV, 1983), Rabbi J. David Bleich begins his chapter on animal experimentation with the story from *Sh'mot Rabbah* 2:2 in which the fact that Moses runs after an errant sheep and cares for it, thus showing boundless compassion for his flock, is God's evidence that Moses is fit to lead the people of Israel. Likewise, biblical law, story, and rhetoric are marshaled in support of the principle of compassion for living things, known under the general rubric of *tza·ar ba·alei ḥayyim* laws (laws intended to prevent the suffering of animals), even though this principle is never explicitly enunciated in the Bible.

Whether claiming to find this principle implied in the injunction to aid in righting a fallen animal (Exodus 23:5 and Deuteronomy 22:4), to allow a threshing animal to eat while unmuzzled (Deuteronomy 25:4), or to allow one's animals to share in one's Shabbat rest (Exodus 20:10 and Deuteronomy 5:14); or whether deriving support from the comeuppance Balaam received for cruelly striking his mount (Numbers 22:32) or from the ancient proverb, "A righteous person will be aware of the needs of his beast" (Proverbs 12:10); or whether merely assuming that human beings should do their best to follow God's own example, for "divine mercy is upon all God's works" (Psalm 145:9)—all agree that this principle is fundamental to the Jewish sense of how animals are to be treated. While it remains a matter of debate whether this principle is properly understood to be a biblical commandment (as most commentators believe) or whether a commandment of solely rabbinic authority, the concept of avoiding pain or injury to animals has had profound legal impact on the development of the *halakhah*. Thus, for instance, one who arrives at a destination after Shabbat has begun is to unload pack animals, despite the general Shabbat restrictions that would prohibit doing so, "out of concern for *tza·ar ba·alei ḥayyim,*" that is, for the suffering of the animal involved (*SA* Oraḥ Ḥayyim 266:9).

That said, the Torah is also entirely clear about the mandate of humankind to exercise mastery over the animals of the world (as set forth in the story of creation itself at Genesis 1:28), and the narrative of Genesis 9 quite explicitly permits the slaughter of animals for food after the flood in Noah's time. Judaism thus understands that animals are to serve humankind, and rejects the arguments of some philosophers that sentience is indivisible and that, as a result, the very same level of respect owed to humans must also be accorded to animals. Indeed, the case of kosher slaughtering exemplifies the complex balancing act between attending to human needs and caring for animal welfare. While animals may be killed for the benefit of human consumption, they must be treated with respect and concern (*ergo* the prohibitions of forced feeding or untoward restraints) and slaughtered with a sharp knife and in one swift motion in order to eliminate, or at least minimize, pain. Furthermore, their blood must be covered up, which some see as a mark of the shame of the slaughterer and others interpret as a form of burial. (What this implies regarding the wearing of leather and furs is subject to differing constructs.)

The specific permission to use animals for medical experimentation, despite their potential suffering, was made explicit by the Rema in his gloss to *SA* Even Ha-eizer 5:14: "Whatever is needed for medicinal purposes or for other things does not entail a violation of the prohibition of *tza·ar ba·alei ḥayyim.*"

The Rema's ruling is exceedingly broad, no doubt in order to allow for future needs that he realized he could not even begin to contemplate. Later commentators, however, did attempt to define this area more closely. Some proposed, for example, that substantial need, not just passing fancy or scientific whimsy, was necessary to justify causing suffering to animals. Rabbi Joseph Teomim (1727–1792) stands out in this regard, insisting that only "great need" can suffice to allow overriding our concern for the suffering of animals (*Mishb'tzot Zahav* to *SA* Oraḥ Ḥayyim 468:2). Thus, for the most part, hunting and bullfighting were understood to be prohibited activities for observant Jews. Furthermore, some proposed distinguishing public need (which could warrant setting aside the general prohibition of causing *tza·ar ba·alei ḥayyim*) from private need (which clearly does not). Still others debated whether profit or the prevention of financial loss might fall under the rubric of "need" in this sense, with some arguing that it should, some insisting that it should not, and yet others establishing a sliding scale in which very great need might justify inflicting increasingly greater pain, whereas lesser need should not (although it might itself justify small or transient suffering). The specific provisions of these dual considerations—that is, what exactly constitutes need and what specifically causes substantial pain—have been subject to the varied views of commentators for centuries.

Ultimately, then, there is no clearly defined Jewish view of medical experimentation on animals. Some have wondered whether experimentation, by its nature, is too speculative to claim the kind of human benefit that would override our concern for animals and their welfare. But, in the end, the pragmatic argument that no progress is possible without experimentation has carried the day. In his *Encyclopedia of Jewish Medical Ethics* (New York and Jerusalem: Feldheim, 2003, vol. 1, p. 264), Dr. Avraham Steinberg attempts to catalogue all the preferred practices that have been proposed: there must be *bona fide* need, one must engage in the least possible number of experiments, all efforts to lessen the animals' suffering must be undertaken, lower life forms are always to be preferred for experimentation due to their less developed sense of pain, and, when the experiment is finished, any animal lingering in pain should be put down mercifully. Other *tza·ar ba·alei ḥayyim* issues are discussed elsewhere in this volume by Rabbi Edward M. Friedman.

What, then, of human experimentation? If the discoveries that such experimentation might yield are deemed potentially important enough, then might not this attitude of reserved permissiveness with respect to animal experimentation have some sort of parallel with regard to experimentation involving human subjects? The answer to this question must begin by acknowledging that the philosophical assumptions governing our relationship to animals are vastly different from those that govern our relationships with other humans. The concept of "putting a creature out of its misery," for example, is one we readily apply to animals, but find unthinkable to apply to a fellow human being. One may slaughter an animal for certain purposes, but ought not to cause it pain. Not so another person. The life of a person is sacrosanct, independent of concern for sentient suffering—and this is the bedrock assumption not only of Western morality, but of the *halakhah* as well—in a way that is not the case with respect to animals. The philosopher Immanuel Kant spoke of the quality of human dignity, by which we are called to treat every person "as an end and not as a means." Judaism developed a similar awareness, using as its model the verse, "You shall love your neighbor as yourself" (Leviticus 19:18). It is that difference that can, and does, lead many halakhic authorities to consider animal experimentation permissible in many cases, while expressing dire concern about any experimentation involving humans.

The way the Western world valorizes the drive toward discovery naturally encourages experimentation. Historically, that experimentation proceeded for the most part without regulation. Therefore, it is not at all surprising that the development of concern for ethical norms with regard to human experimentation arose only later as a response to particularly blatant lapses. Cruel Nazi experiments upon people they viewed as expendable taught the world that medical experimentation needs to be regulated. But even on American soil, the drive to expand knowledge has, at times, led all too easily to harming the weak and unprotected. The researchers of the infamous Tuskeegee syphilis study in Mississippi, which took place over the four decades between 1932 and 1972, knowingly withheld treatment and allowed black men to suffer and die in order to learn more about the natural progression of the then-dreaded venereal disease. In the scandal surrounding the Willowbrook State School in Staten Island, New York, that led to its being closed permanently in 1987, researchers intentionally infected mentally incompetent minors with hepatitis in order to learn more about that disease. These scandals etched the need for fully informed consent by patients and for watchful supervision of all medical experimentation involving human subjects into the consciousness of the American legal and scientific communities. More recently, the deaths of healthy subjects during ostensibly monitored research experiments at the University of Pennsylvania in 1999 and at Johns Hopkins University in 2001 reminded the medical community of the tendency of monitors to grow lazy in their oversight, and of the consequent need that monitors themselves be vigilantly monitored.

At least until our day, very little has been written by halakhic authorities directly about these issues, and much of what has been written has already been mentioned. The preeminent concern of Judaism with the well-being of human beings guaranteed that self-endangerment would be discouraged, although as we have seen, moderate risk in the name of one's own greater good, or that of another, might be undertaken. Only when a patient faces imminent and certain death does it make sense to try unapproved or even untested experimental treatments, since there would be in such a case so little to lose and so much, at least potentially, to gain.

But what of preliminary tests that are only intended to gain new knowledge about the biological activity of a substance, but which hold out no real promise of healing any actual people? Indeed, most of these tests, called Phase I trials, involve healthy volunteers! The most that can be said of such tests, in a most attenuated fashion (since most Phase I trials fail), is that they represent the hope that, in some eventual future, they might lead to the cure of some not yet identified and probably not yet living patient. If there is risk involved—and there is always some infinitesimal risk involved in human experimentation, no matter how rigorous the preceding battery of animal testing may have been—then, given that there is no actual patient before us (as was Rabbi Landau's litmus test), the reluctance of many authorities to permit such experimentation is altogether understandable.

Although still championed by many, this approach leaves much to be desired. The Talmud (at *BT* M'gillah 13b) teaches that God always prepares the antidote before countenancing a wound. While our wisdom will never equal that of heaven, waiting until death is imminent to seek out new therapies and medications seems, to say the least, an ineffective approach to healing. Nor does such an approach speak to our (admittedly limited) abilities to emulate God productively by preparing cures in advance of the needs of specific stricken individuals. Indeed, just the opposite is true: if we wish to anticipate human needs and to prepare cures in advance of needing them, then experimentation—including even human experimentation—will be necessary, for only that type of scientific study will ever provide a true test of how human beings will respond to a particular treatment.

Taking the longer view, then, some modern authorities have ruled that participation in such studies is permissible and even laudable, since there is typically only insignificant risk in such testing. (Otherwise, in theory, it would not be allowed. That was the error in oversight of the University of Pennsylvania and Johns Hopkins cases: they are the exceptions that prove the rule precisely because the deaths in both cases *could* and *should* have been prevented, due to what in retrospect were clearly excessive, yet foreseeable, risks to the subjects involved.) Moreover, given the long development time required for new cures, modern authorities would either waive the Landau requirement that the patient be "before us" entirely, or else understand the concept to refer not only to a particular patient in a hospital bed, but even to a theoretical patient whose ailment we can clearly foresee and for whose sake we wish to prepare a therapeutic regimen in advance. Others would go further still and permit significant risk on a voluntary basis, arguing that a person may voluntarily undertake moderate risk (less than fifty percent, or balanced risk, as suggested by our discussion of Abi Zimra) for a good and sufficient cause. It is hard to judge which approach will eventually carry the day, but my own feeling is that the conservative approach, which relies heavily on Rabbi Landau's test, feels too rooted in the old pietist supposition that it is noble to look solely or mostly to God to heal our illnesses. To me, Maimonides' proactive model is the more cogent: when hungry, seek food and eat. Adam, after all, was placed on this earth both "to till it" as well as "to tend it" (Genesis 2:15). In the end, the bread we eat is said liturgically to come from the earth (cf. the Ha-motzi blessing, which specifically thanks God for bringing forth bread from the earth) but, of course, bread doesn't *really* grow in the earth. Quite the contrary: bread is made possible by God's grace, but it is made real only by the sweat of the human brow that toils to grow the wheat, then to make the flour, then to bake the bread. If we are to treat our illnesses, we shall have to set our efforts in motion well in advance of needing the therapies that will result from those efforts. One can well understand where bread comes from yet still recite the Ha-motzi blessing with feeling. The efforts we expend in seeking out therapies long in advance of need will enhance our success in developing treatments, and in so doing, will fully realize God's grace.

The Communal Obligation of Health Care

Little has been written about a community's obligation to provide health care for its members, because this has traditionally been understood as a personal issue that fell to the individual or his or her family. Indeed, the sources turn to the question of communal responsibility only in cases where no family is present to shoulder the obligation of providing for the needs of an individual. Thus the Rema, discussing charitable obligations in his gloss to *SA* Yoreh Dei·ah 251:3, notes that "one's own sustenance takes precedence over that of any other person. . . . After that, one should give preference to the support of one's parents . . . then of one's children, then of one's siblings, then of other relatives, then of one's neighbors, then of other residents of one's town, and then, finally, of [the needy of] other towns."

The obligation of caring thus spreads out in concentric circles from self-preservation, which concept was discussed earlier, to the obligation of caring for those closest to us, and, finally, to the obligation to look after all who come within our orbit. While the Rema discusses a general obligation of support, this surely includes health care. (*M* K'tubbot 4:9 specifically implies that health care is included in the broader category of obligations to support others. See the commentaries of Rabbi Ovadiah of Bertinoro or Ḥanokh Albeck.) In a recent Conservative responsum on the provision of health care ("Responsibilities for the Provision of Health Care," in *CJLS Responsa 1991–2000,* pp. 319–336), Rabbis Elliot N. Dorff and Aaron L. Mackler present a theological understanding of this mandate. In numerous sources, as they note, we are told to emulate the qualities of the Divine. In *BT* Sotah 14a, for example, we read that just as "God clothed the naked, you should clothe the naked. As the blessed Holy One visited the sick, you should visit the sick. As the blessed Holy One comforted mourners, so should you too comfort mourners. As the blessed Holy One buried the dead, you too should bury the dead." Rabbi Dorff discusses these issues elsewhere in this volume in his chapter on caring for the needy, and the entire issue of who should get scarce healthcare resources (and who should pay for them) in the twelfth chapter of his book, *Matters of Life and Death.*

In a similar vein, *Sifrei D'varim* (Eikev §49) says that just as "the Omnipresent is called merciful, so should you be merciful. . . . Just as the Omnipresent is called compassionate, so should you be compassionate. . . . Just as the Omnipresent is called righteous, so should you be righteous. . . . Just as the Omnipresent is called caring . . . so should you be caring."

To these passages of classic *midrash,* Rabbis Dorff and Mackler add these words: "We praise God in the Amidah: 'You support the falling, heal the ailing, free the fettered, etc.' Accordingly, we are called upon to help others and provide health care to those in need."

Rabbis Dorff and Mackler concur that this obligation traditionally rested upon the family of an individual first, and only then fell to the larger Jewish community. (The community was understood as a kind of "family of last resort" in this context.) However, with the demise of the taxing authority of medieval Jewish communities, halakhic authorities came to understand that the ultimate responsibility for meeting the healthcare needs of its citizens must fall to the duly constituted government. In the United States, of course, such a halakhic determination of government responsibility has no teeth at all. But in Israel, while Jewish law is not sovereign, the claim of Jewish law upon the government is dramatically greater. Indeed, in his "Autonomy and Paternalism in Communitarian Society: Patient Rights in Israel" (published in the *Hastings Center Report* 29:4 [1999], pp. 13–20), Michael Gross takes Israel as an exemplar of such a "communitarian society" in reviewing the impact of such a stance in forming its healthcare system.

Why was this communal obligation so little mentioned in classical sources of Jewish law? In large part, it is because ancient and medieval culture was so dominated by the assumption that individuals would act on their family's behalf that little was left to fall to the general polity. To seize upon an extreme example, that is why the Bible speaks of an individual "blood avenger" (as in Numbers 35) who seeks retribution for wrongs done to the family, rather than imagining a fixed communal justice system. And it is also worth adding that, at least in part, the *halakhah* stressed individual responsibility because the rabbinic system of piety itself addressed the individual, preferring to leave corporate responsibilities to be addressed only should the individual fail in his or her responsibilities and necessitate that broader action be taken. Nevertheless, when imagining the ordered society, the sages of old presumed that such a civilization would include proper public sanitation and available health care. In the only talmudic context in which it is cited (at *BT* Sanhedrin 17b), the following is offered digressively as a rabbinic definition of the good life: "A scholar may not reside in a city that does not have the following ten things: (1) a court of justice . . . (2) a charitable fund . . . (3) a synagogue, (4) a bathhouse, (5) a [public] privy, (6) a physician, (7) a trained surgeon, (8) a scribe, (9) a butcher, and (10) a school teacher." (The meaning of the word translated here as "surgeon" is a bit uncertain. Most commentaries associate it with cutting. Some assume it to be a *moheil,* one skilled in ritual circumcision, while others understand it as "one skilled in bloodletting.")

While the Bible teaches that perfect fulfillment of God's commands could obviate illness, and while good public sanitation and preventive attention can certainly help create a healthy, disease-free society, it is only reasonable to expect that everyone will eventually have need of a physician. The obligation of the individual, therefore, was to take up residence in a community that offered fulfillment of all needs that might be anticipated. It is to some of those rationally anticipated medical needs that we now turn.

The Beginning of Life

Childbearing and Contraception

A Darwinian will unhesitatingly say that one of the keys to the development of all life is an overriding drive for reproductive success and, given that reproduction is clearly necessary for the continuation and success of any species or group, there is little reason to object to that assessment. As a Jew one might put forward the (somewhat parochial) arguments that we Jews are a tiny minority among the peoples of the world and must seek to assure our survival, or that we need to replenish the nation's losses in the Holocaust. From the vantage point of traditional Judaism, however, procreation is sacred simply because God has chosen to be concerned with it from the start. The very first commandment to human beings recorded in the Torah is *p'ru u-r'vu*, "Be fruitful and multiply!" (Genesis 1:28). Furthermore, Scripture records with great interest and in great detail the story of how the first of the matriarchs of Israel reached an advanced age without children, thereby necessitating God's direct intervention to aid her to have children, a detail proclaimed in the first line of the Torah portion read on the first day of Rosh Hashanah. And it is God's response to a similar prayer in the case of Hannah, the future mother of the prophet Samuel, that serves as the *haftarah* for that day. Indeed, our belief in God's willingness to respond to human events and to specific prayers derives in part from the stories of fertility issues that plagued the matriarchs of Israel. Thus, in reaching out to aid the infertile couple, the infertility specialist is merely following God's lead. In the words of an early *midrash* cited at *M* Eiduyyot 1:13: "May one refrain [from procreation]? Is it not apparent that the world was created with an eye to reproduction, as it says: 'God did not create [the world] as a wasteland, but formed it for habitation' (Isaiah 45:18)?"

How, then, is one to fulfill this commandment? It traditionally went without saying that one may do so only within marriage. Indeed, Rabbi Joseph Karo begins his compendium of laws relating to marriage, the Even Ha-eizer section of his *Shulḥan Arukh*, with the following affirmation: "A man is required to marry a woman in order to be fruitful and multiply." But he goes much further, developing the same thought as the kind of negative formulation that can serve as a powerful source for classifying the treatment of infertility as a noble medical art. "Whoever does not seek to reproduce," he writes, "is, as it were, guilty of murder and of reducing God's image [in the world], and drives God's spirit from Israel." (The relationship of unmarried people, gay and straight, to the commandment to procreate is discussed above by Rabbi Jeremy Kalmanofsky in his chapter on the halakhic implications of being single and by Rabbi Elliot Dorff in his chapter on the *halakhah* of same-sex relationships.)

The requirement to bear children is capped by tradition at two live children. However, in the dominant opinion of the followers of Hillel (recorded at *M* Y'vamot 6:6), these two children must be a son and a daughter (*MT* Hilkhot Ishut 15:4). That one must bear children immediately, however, and continue to do so well beyond the minimum until one's health fails (or one's resources do), is not demanded, though it is certainly standard to advise that the performance of a *mitzvah* not be put off.

The rigorously pious cite the aforementioned verse in Isaiah, intimating that there is an obligation to people the earth, as well as Kohelet 11:6, "Sow your seed in the morning and do not hold back your hand in the evening," as establishing the open-endedness of this requirement of procreation. Yet these sources do not constitute legal requirements, but are only hortatory in nature; they are from non-pentateuchal sources that are not generally taken as guides for halakhic practice. Still, the combined weight of these verses and the general emphasis given by the tradition on procreation has, in traditional circles, generally led to shunning any contraceptives.

This raises some issues regarding family planning that deserve mention. There is a well-known tendency among the ultra-Orthodox toward very large families, known officially in Israel as "families blessed with children," with family size decreasing as religious interpretations grow more liberal. In such communities, contraception is likely to be permitted only when a woman's health demands it. Speaking for a more worldly faction of Orthodoxy (who prefer the term "centrist"), Rabbi Getsel Gerald Ellinson points out in *Women and the Mitzvot,* vol. 3, pp. 87ff. (trans. R. Blumberg, ed. A. Tomaschoff; Jerusalem: Department for Torah Education and Culture in the Diaspora of the World Zionist Organization, 1998), pp. 87ff., that the age of majority is thirteen, but the age of marriage and childbearing was traditionally held to be eighteen—as specifically noted in *M* Avot 5:21—and today it is often later. Furthermore, it is normative that all positive *mitzvot* that are not time-bound should ideally be performed as soon as is possible, but they may nonetheless be scheduled in such a way as is convenient. (This was pointed out by Rabbi Abraham Karelitz, popularly called the *Ḥazon Ish,* in his comments to *SA* Yoreh Dei·ah 153:5.) Thus, even in parts of the Orthodox world, it is common consciously to time the intervals between children and to take one's economic situation into account when determining ideal family size, and this may justify some contraceptive use. Within the Conservative community, this more liberal understanding is mostly assumed and limiting family size is normative. Nevertheless, in light of contemporary concerns about the eroding numbers of the Jewish population, Conservative rabbis, too, often urge Jewish couples to think beyond the minimum number of children that the law requires. (In this regard, readers may profitably consult the responsum written by Kassel Abelson and Elliot Dorff entitled "Mitzvah Children" that was approved by the CJLS in 2007 and which is posted on the website of the Rabbinical Assembly.)

The specific form of contraception is also a matter of halakhic concern. Above all else, in determining contraceptive use, is always the safety and efficacy of the method. Where all else is equal, the following hierarchy can be derived from halakhic sources. Most preferable are the birth control pill (and its descendants, the various hormonal contraceptives) and the IUD. This is because there is a strong objection in Jewish law to the unnecessary emission of sperm, and these methods allow the sperm to reach the egg unimpeded. Furthermore, it is generally understood that the prohibition of "wasting seed" is specifically applicable only to men, and these contraceptive technologies are deployed solely by the woman and affect solely her own body.

Next in the hierarchy of halakhic acceptability would be the diaphragm, the cervical cap, and the contraceptive sponge, each of which frustrate conception without requiring any overt complicity on the part of the male. Though barrier methods at heart, each comes with the recommendation of use with a spermicide as additional protection. Some halakhic authorities reject spermicide use outright, though they would still permit the barrier methods without that added protection, precisely because they act directly on the sperm. But others permit them, arguing that the party employing them is not the male, and yet others argue for their permissibility based on the assumption that their efficiency is so limited that some of the sperm can reasonably be expected to proceed unimpeded. In a responsum on contraception approved by the Committee on Jewish Law and Standards approved in December 2010, Rabbis Miriam Berkowitz and Mark Popovsky found grounds to permit the use of spermicide, though they find in the need for its use sufficient reason to place these methods in a secondary category when compared to the hormonal contraceptives and IUD (which do not require such use).

Next along the spectrum would be the condom, since it is specifically intended to frustrate the natural goal of the sperm, and is clearly used by men. Traditionally, this method of birth control has been allowed only where other measures are for some reason not possible. Rabbis Berkowitz and Popovsky maintain it in this place in the hierarchy, though noting advantages to the condom in terms of the absence of side effects, its inexpensiveness and widespread availability, and the potential benefit of reducing the spread of sexually transmitted diseases. They concede that where sexual activity carries more than a hypothetical risk of disease, condom use might be preferred or even required, but insist that "for monogamous relationships in which both partners . . . are found to be disease-free . . . this benefit of the condom is less relevant."

Post-coital hormonal contraceptives, such as the protocols known as Plan B and RU-486, have been subject to much controversy in halakhic discussions, in part because it has not been sufficiently clear if they function by preventing conception, by preventing implantation after conception, or by aborting an early implanted embryo. Judaism, however, does not hold that life begins at conception. Consequently, Rabbis Berkowitz and Popovsky rely on "the broad consensus throughout the medical community" to determine that pregnancy only begins at implantation, and find that Plan B (as opposed to RU-486) prevents implantation and, as such, is functionally equivalent to other hormonal contraceptives. This might seem to move post-coital contraception that does not act to cause abortion of an already implanted embryo into the primary category of acceptability, save that the risk and discomfort of post-coital contraception and its more limited efficacy suggest that it should be permitted only when absolutely necessary.

In their responsum, Rabbis Berkowitz and Popovsky left the use of RU-486, which they found to cause abortion of an implanted embryo, to be considered with abortion. This author does not agree. The ancient sages considered the nascent human stage of the fetus to begin at forty days of gestation (forty days after conception), relying on the visual study of miscarried fetuses in order to determine that the formation of a recognizable fetus does not occur prior to that time. In several mishnaic and talmudic rulings (e.g., *M* Niddah 3:7, *BT* Niddah 30b, and Y'vamot 69b), the sages ruled that the product of conception "prior to forty days is considered as if it were mere water." Thus there seem to be ample grounds for considering RU-486 permissible as a contraceptive under *halakhah,* save that, even more than other post-coital hormonal contraceptives, the significant discomfort it entails should probably consign it to emergency use.

Lastly, tubal ligation and vasectomies, where irreversible, are prohibited to Jewish patients under the general biblical prohibition of castration and its rabbinic extensions. Also, *coitus interruptus* is understood to be forbidden by the Torah, as indicated by the story of Er and Onan in Genesis 38:6–10. Unlike leaders of the Catholic Church, Jewish authorities have never seriously considered the rhythm method because it calls for additional days of abstinence beyond the heavy demands already carved out by the *niddah* laws. Furthermore, because birth control is generally permitted only where sufficient need is determined to exist, more reliable forms of contraception are required. Fetal abortion (the status of "fetus" is granted as of eight weeks from a woman's last menstrual period, which is approximately six weeks after conception), while permitted for cause, should never be used intentionally as a method of birth control. Abortion itself is discussed in more detail below in a subsection of this chapter devoted solely to that topic.

Infertility

One could write a lengthy scientific discourse on the varying forms of infertility and their treatment, the next area of interest when discussing the entanglement of medicine, life, and Jewish law. Here, for the purpose of this chapter, then, it will suffice merely to note that there are two major branches of infertility treatment: *in vivo* and *in vitro*. *In vivo* refers to treatments in which the woman conceives within her womb, as in natural fertilization. *In vitro,* which will be discussed in detail below, refers to the process of fertilizing an ovum outside the womb. Needless to say, where medications or surgery to remove obstructions to the normal development of a fetus are involved, this is analytically no different from any other medical treatment for any other condition. Where the failure lies with the quality of the male sperm, various techniques to sort and transport fecund sperm to the woman's reproductive tract may be employed. These, while not strictly analogous to natural fertilization, have given rise to no principled objection among halakhic authorities, who labor under a strong presumption in favor of whatever facilitates the birth of children to parents who might otherwise not have children at all. (Some of these topics were introduced above by Rabbi David J. Fine in his chapter on the *halakhah* of marriage.)

A technical objection has been voiced by many, however, which does warrant halakhic attention: the question of collecting semen. A prohibition against wasting semen, understood by the ancient sages as one of the principal lessons of the aforementioned biblical tale of Er and Onan (cf. *BT* Y'vamot 34b), is broadly interpreted as prohibiting any emission outside of normal sexual activity within a legitimate union. Most liberal authorities would concur that since semen in this context is being intentionally collected for the purpose of impregnating one's own wife, the procedure should not be seen as an example of wasting seed at all. Indeed, many of those who are not particularly liberal regarding the general prohibition of wasting seed consider this use of semen highly appropriate, and this is the stance of the Conservative rabbinate as well. Others have devised various ways to make the collection of sperm halakhically tolerable. Thus, *in vivo* fertilization techniques between husband and wife, with or without strictures governing the precise method of sperm collection, have found a firm place throughout the Jewish world.

Indeed, only when the germ cells of a donor are introduced into the equation are halakhic concerns raised, whether involving the quite common use of donor sperm or the less common use of a donor egg. I discuss such donations below.

The alternative to *in vivo* treatment is called *in vitro* fertilization: the misnamed but well-known "test-tube baby" procedure first successfully employed in 1978 and often referred to by its acronym, IVF. *In vitro* means "in glass" and refers to fertilization in a petri dish of an ovum that has been surgically removed from a woman, with the intention of implanting the embryo in the womb once successful fertilization has been achieved. The advantage of such a procedure should be obvious given the hurdles to successful infertility treatment within the womb, where conditions cannot be well visualized or easily monitored. Indeed, it is precisely because all factors can be more tightly controlled in the laboratory that this method of fertilization has an optimal chance of success. The disadvantage, of course, is that fertilization "in glass" feels far from the natural fulfillment of the divine command. (By way of comparison, the Catholic Church specifically weds its doctrine in this regard to its understanding of the "natural" character of marital intimacy, thus prohibiting any of these techniques for treating infertility as intrusive corruptions of the sexual ideal.)

Whereas no major Jewish voices bristle at the unnaturalness of *in vivo* techniques (despite the obvious need to transport the sperm), in regard to *in vitro* fertilization, there are some modern authorities who do object. Rabbi Eliezer Waldenberg, a leading Orthodox authority, has categorically prohibited such *in vitro* techniques, and he is not alone. Beside the argument based on the innate unnaturalness of this process, he argues specifically that any use of semen outside the woman's body is to be considered an improper waste of seed. These objections have been met, however, by a clear majority of halakhic authorities who justify this procedure (always between husband and wife, of course) based on the argument that it does not change the fundamental divine structure of the generation of life through the merging of husband's sperm and wife's egg in fertilization, and their subsequent nurturance *in utero*. Not surprisingly, this is also the position of the CJLS. Rabbi Aaron Mackler writes: "The use of IVF . . . accords with our responsibility to be both reverent and active in our partnership with God" (*CJLS Responsa 1991–2000*, p. 514). While it is true that there is some risk to the woman who is medically stimulated to produce multiple eggs in the same cycle (whereas naturally a woman generally produces only one mature egg each month) and that further risk to her exists when these eggs are surgically removed, these risks appear to be exceedingly low and the desirability of conceiving one's own child suffices to permit it.

The larger halakhic problem with the stimulated production of multiple eggs and multiple embryos is to be found in the consequent increase in multiple births. Whether simply stimulating the ovaries to produce multiple eggs for *in vivo* fertilization, or harvesting multiple eggs for *in vitro* fertilization of multiple embryos, often several embryos may implant at the same time. Consequently, physicians suddenly found themselves with patients facing high-order multiple pregnancies—some carrying as many as six, seven, or eight embryos at a time. Because high-order multiple pregnancies are much more dangerous to the mother and to the general health of all the fetuses involved, this was deemed highly undesirable. Thus, where there were not religious objections to abortion on the part of the mother, doctors have often taken to performing selective abortions of some of the embryos, a procedure known medically as "selective reduction." Looking at the matter in 1994, the CJLS ruled, following a responsum by Rabbi Elliot N. Dorff ("Artificial Insemination, Egg Donation, and Adoption," published in *CJLS Responsa 1991–2000,* pp. 461–509, and in the third chapter of Rabbi Dorff's book, *Matters of Life and Death*), that selective reduction, when necessary, was permissible, given the general approach of the Conservative movement that abortion should be permitted upon a finding of need. Yet they considered that the foreseeable need of selective reduction in *in vitro* procedures could and should be avoided by limiting implantations to two (or at most three) embryos at a time, even at the price of a concomitant statistical drop in success rates. At the time, fertility specialists were loath to accept such limits, but success rates have risen such that the practice of limiting implantation has become more nearly the norm, and today the majority of multiple pregnancies actually arise from *in vivo* (and not *in vitro*) procedures.

A second problem lies in the cryopreservation of fertilized embryos. Often, in stimulated egg production for *in vitro* fertilization, more eggs (and subsequently more embryos) are produced than are needed for immediate treatment. Since there is hardship and risk in the process of harvesting eggs, it is deemed advisable to freeze excess embryos for use in a later cycle, if success is not achieved initially (or, down the road, if another child should be desired). But when the couple wishes to bear no more children, fertility clinics have often found themselves in the undesirable position of warehousing excess embryos, with no one willing to foot the continuing cost of their cryopreservation. It is estimated that in early 2003 some 400,000 embryos were in storage in this nation's fertility clinics (see D. I. Hoffman *et al.,* "Cryopreserved Embryos in the United States and Their Availability for Research," *Fertility and Sterility* 79 [2003], pp. 1063–1069).

In some cases, these unwanted embryos have been successfully donated to other infertile couples. But in other cases, the question was whether they might be donated to research (and thus ultimately sacrificed) or simply destroyed. Reviewing the situation, most halakhic authorities determined that, indeed, such embryos could be destroyed since they are well within the forty-day limit at the moment of cryopreservation (which process halts further development), and may therefore be treated as simple tissue; and also because they have no opportunity to develop naturally in their current location outside the womb. Thus, concerning the question of the moment in the United States, Judaism does not have any objection to research on stem cells that are cultured from week-old embryos, even at the price of their destruction. Indeed, the CJLS was moved to approve and encourage research on both embryonic and adult stem cells by the therapeutic potential that such research and such cells might have (Rabbi Elliot Dorff, "Stem Cell Research," accepted by the CJLS in 2002 and available on the website of the Rabbinical Assembly).

A new technique, pre-implantation genetic diagnosis (PGD), has recently come onto the scene and dramatically expanded the advantages offered by IVF. In this procedure, one or two cells are removed from the earliest embryo when it is only some eight cells in size, and the cells are tested for any anomalies in their genetic structure. While this would appear to threaten the developing embryo, in fact this procedure—when used in conjunction with standard IVF techniques of fertilizing several embryos at once—allows the physician to choose which embryo to implant, based on genetic factors. For couples who are carriers of debilitating genetic diseases, such as Tay-Sachs disease or cystic fibrosis, the chance to test embryos before implantation and implant only unaffected embryos saves them the anguish of uncertainty throughout pregnancy and the further pain of abortion should such genetic conditions be discovered later in the pregnancy, as well as the halakhic discomfort attendant upon making such a decision.

The technique of PGD also includes the possibility of selecting the sex of a child as well as other genetic traits. The question on the horizon, then, is whether society as a whole—and Judaism in particular—can tolerate such use of PGD. The matter of the admittedly small risk to the health of the woman in engaging in any form of IVF becomes a deciding factor in this halakhic analysis. The use of IVF to overcome infertility, or IVF teamed with PGD to assure a healthy child in a family prone to inherited disease, is clearly permissible, since its use is predicated upon a need that justifies the minimal risk of IVF. The desire to choose gender or other traits, however, does not appear to provide such a reason and so in these cases it must be considered prohibited. (These determinations were codified in a responsum about PGD by Rabbi Mark Popovsky approved by the CJLS in 2008 and now available on the website of the Rabbinical Assembly.) Nevertheless, in his responsum on IVF, Rabbi Mackler suggests that he might allow such a choice when doing IVF for valid reasons, a point this author reiterated in his response to Rabbi Popovsky's responsum.

In this regard it is appropriate to mention genetic engineering quite briefly, although not much is yet possible nor has the topic been addressed extensively by halakhic writers. It is clear that when the ability to manipulate genetic material safely develops, IVF together with PGD will offer one appealing route through which one might diagnose and "fix" the embryo chosen for implantation. That genetic "fix" might be therapeutic, reversing a known genetic abnormality, in which case I cannot identify any Jewish thinker who would have any hesitation permitting it. On the other hand, it might be intended for the enhancement of some selected trait, and many have already expressed their misgivings about such procedures. Does this portend prohibition, or is it just momentary discomfort? We do permit vaccination, after all, which is merely a low-tech form of enhancement. The final word has not yet been written on whether genetic engineering used for enhancement will be approved or rejected by halakhic authorities, or whether some middle ground will be crafted, permitting some genetic enhancements while forbidding others.

I return now to the matter of gamete donation, the donation of sperm and egg cells. Some conditions causing infertility are easily addressed with one or another of the fertility techniques described above, circumventing problems and allowing the couple to give birth using their own genetic material. But other issues are more intractable, which then raises the question of the acceptability of donation. Some men produce no viable sperm, so that even the new technique known as nonsurgical sperm aspiration, by which sperm may be recovered from the testes of even aspermatic males (those without sperm in their seminal fluid), is to no avail. Some women produce no viable ova or are incapable of sustaining gestation, suggesting donation or surrogacy as the only available options.

Opinion in the Jewish world ranges widely on these topics. On one extreme are those who consider the transfer of donor sperm into a married woman to be tantamount to adultery, for which reason it is always prohibited. (This is, however, an asymmetrical concern: as it is only a late rabbinic enactment that prohibits men from marrying multiple wives, egg donation might well be treated more leniently in this view than is sperm donation.) Others worry about secondary damage to orderly family relations and inheritance. A world populated by donor-conceived children may see a rise in cases of inadvertent incest. Those who would permit the use of donor gametes respond that adultery requires carnal contact, which is not present in these techniques, and thus the concern about incest and confused pedigree is misplaced and entirely insufficient to stand against a couple's desire to bear children. Some prefer, or even require, that a gentile be the donor if the recipient is Jewish, so that the product of conception can be wholly unencumbered by family connections to the donor—since the possible gentile fatherhood of a child by a Jewish mother is halakhically irrelevant and the status of parenthood is halakhically accorded to the gestational, rather than genetic, mother. This understanding of mother-status has clearly been the normative ruling, and remains that of the Conservative movement, although a minority of writers have pushed the theory that Judaism might accord dual motherhood to both the gestational and the genetic mothers, and recently halakhists in Israel have begun shifting to the view that motherhood resides in the genetic mother. (For a normative statement, see the responsum of Rabbi Aaron Mackler submitted to the CJLS in September 1997, "Maternal Identity and the Religious Status of Children Born to a Surrogate Mother," in *CJLS Responsa 1991–2000,* pp. 137–145. For an explication of the minority position, see Rabbi J. David Bleich, *Contemporary Halakhic Problems,* vol. 4, pp. 237ff. Of the changing position of the Israeli rabbinate, see the article "Fertility Treatment Gets More Complicated," that ran in *The Wall Street Journal* of May 14, 2010. The complications inherent in such a ruling are forbidding, however.)

Another reason to prohibit Jewish gamete donation might be that both male and female Jews are under specific halakhic restrictions that limit their right to donate. A woman must undergo risk in egg donation, a risk that is easily overridden by her desire to have children, but which is less easily overcome in the case of donation to another, particularly in the case of anonymous donation. For their part, men are constrained not to waste seed. This prohibition can easily be waived in the case of a man attempting to father his own child, but is less easily overcome for the sake of donation.

That being said, the Conservative responsa on these issues have been supportive of gamete donation. Rabbi Elliot Dorff, writing in 1994 (*CJLS Responsa 1991–2000,* pp. 461–509, also available in the fourth chapter of Rabbi Dorff's book, *Matters of Life and Death: A Jewish Approach to Modern Medical Ethics*), concludes that even the donation of sperm and egg in order to help other infertile couples is sufficient justification for emission not to be considered an act of wasting one's seed and for a woman to undertake the minimal risk involved in egg donation. His responsum was overwhelmingly approved. Rabbi Mackler, writing the next year, concurs. Both take seriously, however, the concern about the biological ties of future generations. Their proposed solution is openness. Optimally, they recommend that children born of donor gametes should know their genetic heritage, both out of traditional concerns regarding incest and the maintenance of familial heritage, as well as the understanding that knowing one's genetic background is psychologically beneficial and often diagnostically and therapeutically necessary. Acknowledging that there may be many reasons why a donor insists on maintaining anonymity, they insist nonetheless that a genetic record of the donor's heritage be maintained and that the child be made aware of its existence, should it become necessary when preparing a medical history that might reveal any relevant hereditary conditions.

This leads to a consideration of the matter of sibling donation. If donation of gametes is permissible, as Conservative thinkers tend to rule, may the sibling of one of the parties in an infertile couple provide the donation, thus maximizing the genetic match of the infertile parent's own gametes? Where there is no fear of an inherited disease, there are two major advantages to such a procedure. First, as already noted, a sibling is most likely to match the genetic signature of the infertile parent, so the child will more closely resemble both of his or her future parents. This trait is employed unapologetically for therapeutic reasons when seeking a matched organ donor. Why should it not be applied to the situation of a gamete donor as well? Second, whereas sperm donation is simple, egg donation is medically and personally difficult, and willing donors are in short supply. Many egg donations are secured only from those who have a personal connection to the infertile couple and are willing to undergo the risk and discomfort specifically to help them, and the typical individual in that situation is often a sister of the infertile woman. The potential psychological complications in family dynamics, however, are huge. Consider an egg donor who comes to see her sister as an unfit and domineering mother, and moves to reclaim her genetic progeny. Or imagine a rebellious teen who knows that he is the product of an uncle's sperm and rejects his father, jeering, "I think I'll just move in with my uncle. He's my real father, anyway." If the laws of incest are in any sense founded upon the vexed family dynamics that arise when boundaries of consanguinity are crossed, then one might question the propriety of such gamete donations between close relatives.

Amazingly, however, the Bible presents precedents that suggest that we should indeed permit this, despite fears of psychological fallout and the aura of incest. Faced with infertility and the prospect that there will be no legacy and no inheritance, the Torah, in Deuteronomy 25:5ff., specifically requires the brother of a childless man to marry his deceased brother's wife, a relationship otherwise forbidden under the incest provisions, so as to bear a son, who "shall be accounted to the dead brother, so that his name may not be blotted out," a biblical institution known as levirate marriage. (*Levir,* the Latin word for brother-in-law, is occasionally used in English with the same meaning in this specific context. This topic is discussed in great detail elsewhere in this volume by Rabbi David M. Greenstein in his chapter on the *halakhah* of siblinghood.)

Similarly, though egg donation was not possible in biblical times, surrogacy was, and it was employed by some of the matriarchs in order to have a son through another woman's agency (see, e.g., Genesis 16:2). In the biblical cases even carnal contact was permitted, so great was the desire to escape the consequences of infertility. In our day, when physical contact is removed from the equation, a strong case can be made that the Torah has sanctioned a permissive stance.

This is not, however, the position taken by Rabbi Dorff, and his stance has been endorsed by the Committee on Jewish Law and Standards. Rabbi Dorff credits the psychological case against sibling donation sufficiently to prohibit sperm donation by a sibling, for while he grants that this is not technically incest (in that there is no physical contact involved), "it *feels* very close" to incest and raises "all kinds of boundary problems for the brothers and the child later on." And he explicitly rejects the analogy to levirate marriage, arguing that that was permitted only since the deceased brother was no longer on the scene. "In that case," Rabbi Dorff wrote, "it would actually be in the child's best interest if the uncle acted as a substitute father."*

However, he does permit sibling egg donation, due to the overriding factor of "the paucity of egg donors." This accords well, in fact, with general practice, in which sibling egg donation is reported to be fairly common, while sibling

*It is interesting and relevant to understanding halakhic precedent that there was a major back-and-forth debate in ancient and medieval rabbinic circles as to whether levirate marriage (*yibbum*) or the release therefrom (*ḥalitzah*) is preferable. The Mishnah (*M* B'khorot 1:7) already reports that whereas it had once been the policy that *yibbum* is preferable to *ḥalitzah,* since men could be trusted to honorably seek to fulfill their obligation to their brother's memory, by the mishnaic period itself (which concluded around the year 200 C.E.), men no longer had such honorable intentions in marrying their sisters-in-law, and, as a result, *ḥalitzah* was to be preferred to *yibbum.* Later (i.e., at *BT* Y'vamot 39b) it is reported that practice again changed to prefer *yibbum,* under the argument that fulfilling the biblical command is more significant than any defect in people's behavior. That, in turn, became a major point of disagreement among halakhic authorities, with Sephardic authorities generally ruling that the practice of levirate marriage should continue, and Ashkenazic authorities always preferring release. (This case is reviewed in detail in Rabbi Yeḥiel Mikhel Epstein's *Arukh Hashulḥan,* Even Ha-eizer 165; in particular, see paragraphs 1–2 and 15). What is significant is that all sources seem to agree that *yibbum* would be preferable, but for the unfortunate personal and sexual involvement of the levir (that is, the living brother), which it is unrealistic to avoid. If so, the altruistic donation of sperm in order to ensure progeny to an infertile brother without any physical entanglement would seem to be preferable even to classic levirate marriage.

sperm donation is exceedingly rare. (This statistic is reported in Richard V. Grazi, *Be Fruitful and Multiply* [Nanuet, NY: Feldheim, 1994], p. 203, citing M. V. Sauer et al., "Survey of Attitudes Regarding the Use of Siblings for Gamete Donation," *Fertility and Sterility* 49:4 [1988], pp. 721–722. Grazi speculates that the difference might lie in the fact that sperm donation requires sexual arousal, rather than Dorff's assertion that this is simply a function of supply.)

In his later responsum, Rabbi Mackler affirms this permission concerning sibling egg donation, but does not express an opinion on sperm donation. While it is not the intention of this chapter to break new ground, it is the opinion of this author that a different position might better accord with halakhic precedent. Indeed, halakhic precedent seems to support permitting donation in both directions, but prudence, in the guise of the psychological arguments marshaled above, suggests that one should avail oneself of the option of sibling donation in either direction only for manifest reasons and with extreme caution.

Finally, a word is in order about surrogacy. As noted, because a biblical model of surrogacy exists, it is difficult to reject it absolutely. However, there has been much concern over the apparent exploitation of poorer women, typically not Jews, as paid surrogates, and Conservative responsa by Rabbis Aaron Mackler and Elie Spitz ("On the Use of Birth Surrogates" and "Surrogate Parenting," both approved by CJLS in June 1997 in a split decision, and published in *CJLS Responsa 1991–2000,* pp. 526–557) try to establish some parameters for the ethical treatment of surrogates. The biblical model assumed that the surrogate would remain in the household with the children whom she birthed, whereas modern surrogacy seeks to alienate the birthing surrogate mother from her biological child, which is much more problematic, at least for the surrogate's emotional state. As was found in the well-known Baby M case of 1986, this can lead to traumatic separation issues. Fortunately, with the rise of *in vitro* fertilization techniques, traditional surrogacy (where the surrogate serves as the egg donor and artificial insemination is performed in her womb) has mostly been replaced by gestational surrogacy (where fertilization is accomplished *in vitro,* either with the egg of the intended mother or with a donated egg—but not that of the surrogate—and then the fertilized embryo is implanted in the womb of the surrogate). Experience has shown that this situation arouses less separation anxiety in the surrogate mothers, since the child does not carry their genetic heritage, and this has proven much to be the preferred method.

In gestational surrogacy, the primary halakhic issue is the religion of the child. Standardly, as we have said, the gestational mother is considered to determine the religious identity of a child at birth. Thus the child of the gametes of two Jewish parents, if born to a gentile surrogate, would require conversion. Since it is clear that such a child is to be raised in a Jewish home, and given that the rabbis of the Conservative movement routinely perform infant conversions, such a case would simply be treated the same as that of the adoption of a child from a non-Jewish background. However, in such a case, the biological child of a male *kohein* or a Levite would not have that status, since such child was not born Jewish and priestly or levitical status cannot be acquired other than through the circumstances of birth. Yet another ramification of this is the fact that it would thus be prohibited for a Jewish woman to serve as a surrogate for a gentile couple, for this would involve her agreement to give up a child who is Jewish at birth (in that a Jewish woman is the birthing mother) to be raised as a gentile.

Whereas in his responsum, Rabbi Spitz embraces the permission granted to Jews to use surrogacy for the sake of bearing their own genetic progeny, Rabbi Mackler writes:

> Minimally, [the] *halakhah* would share the "serious reservations" expressed by the American Fertility Society. . . . Surrogacy cannot be recommended by *halakhah,* and would be ill-advised in most cases. . . . I do not see how *halakhah* can authorize Jewish women to serve as surrogates . . . [and] this provides an additional consideration against halakhically supporting surrogacy. To authorize Jews to use others as surrogates but not serve as surrogates would itself be problematic. . . . Surrogacy cannot be halakhically recommended. . . . Any exceptional cases in which surrogacy is accepted would need to meet specific requirements.

Thus, how readily to use surrogacy remains an area without clear consensus within the Conservative movement.

Abortion

There is a well-known rabbinic expression, *yeish koneh olamo b'sha·ah aḥat* (*BT* Avodah Zarah 10b), which, loosely translated, means that in one single act may be vested a full lifetime's worth of merit. One such act was Rabbi David M. Feldman's publication of *Birth Control in Jewish Law* in 1968 (republished under the title *Marital Relations, Abortion, and Birth Control in Jewish Law* [New York: Schocken, 1987]), which, more than any other modern book I know, has acquired an iconic place in defining the Jewish approach to abortion.

As Rabbi Feldman presents it, all agree that abortion for sufficient cause is permissible; the issue is the sufficiency of the cause. This position has, as its basis, the biblical text of Exodus 21:22–23: "When men come to blows and strike a pregnant woman so that her children come forth, but a tragedy does not occur, [the guilty party] is to be fined. . . . But if a tragedy should occur, you are to take a life for a life."

The sages understood this passage as follows: "'A tragedy'—this concerns the woman; 'he is fined'—this concerns the fetuses" (*M'khilta D'rabbi Ishma·el,* N'zikin 8). From this, we see that the sages of classical times understood that the Torah itself did not consider a fetus to be a human life possessed of infinite value. And they drew operative conclusions from this determination as well, ruling (at *M* Ohalot 7:6) to permit abortion to save the life of the mother: "If a woman should experience trouble giving birth, one may dismember the fetus within her womb and remove it limb by limb, for her life takes precedence over its life. If, however, the majority [of the fetus] has already emerged, then one may not harm it, for one does not set aside one life on account of another." When, then, does human life attain its infinite value? The Mishnah's answer is clear: when the baby is delivered, as defined by the emergence of the majority of its body. (Other versions of the *mishnah* just cited mention the emergence not of the majority of the baby's body, but specifically of its head.)

The conclusion reached by CJLS, penned by Ben Zion Bokser and Kassel Abelson in 1983, is simply this: "The Rabbinical Assembly Committee on Jewish Law and Standards takes the view that an abortion is justifiable if a continuation of pregnancy might cause the mother severe physical or psychological harm, or when the fetus is judged by competent medical opinion as severely defective" (*CJLS Responsa 1980–1990,* p. 817).

Rabbi Feldman went on to note that there have historically been two schools of thought in interpreting the less-than-human status of the fetus. There were those who felt that feticide, while not quite murder, must be viewed as something akin to homicide, and therefore demanded that a need be established that is close to the life-saving standard of the Mishnah. Others argued that the fetus is plainly not a human being and that abortion should therefore not be prohibited at all. Inclined to be more liberal about the grounds for abortion, they nonetheless learned from the Mishnah a hesitancy with regard to the procedure and a respect for the potential that a fetus manifestly holds, thus leading them to prohibit abortion unless there is sufficient cause.

In the CJLS statement cited above, the Conservative movement allied itself with the more liberal understanding, signaling a wider openness to accepting maternal suffering as a reasonable cause for abortion and accepting the loss of a fetus's potential due to its anticipated disability as reason enough to allow abortion. In contrast to the American political faction that labels itself "pro-choice," however, neither Jewish view tolerates the right to abortion on demand as a function of a woman's right to control her own body.

In setting the demarcation of human life at the moment that "the majority [of the fetus] has emerged," the Mishnah seemed to be setting a bright line by which to distinguish that moment. Unfortunately, the meandering path of commentary did not leave the determination alone. And, just as two schools have developed regarding the type of cause that would justify abortion itself, so too has a debate arisen about the meaning of the word "emerged" in the mishnaic text: some claim that it means emergence from the womb into the birth canal, while others believe that it means emergence from the birth canal into the open air. This appeared, for quite some time, to be a debate of purely academic interest. After all, when a child is born, it emerges from both places in fairly rapid succession, and no one, it seemed, would consider an abortion at that point. Therefore, not having any specific relevance to real-life situations, this issue was never resolved.

Enter the procedure known to its opponents as "partial-birth abortion" or, to those unwilling to communicate a bias, as "dilation and extraction" (or, popularly, as D&X). In this procedure, utilized mainly late in a pregnancy, the infant to be aborted is brought out of the womb into the birth canal, while its head, typically too large to be delivered through a not-yet-fully-dilated cervix, is trapped in the womb. A perforation, therefore, is made at the base of the skull and the brain matter removed, effecting the abortion, after which the skull can be collapsed for removal through the cervix. Whether or not to ban this procedure is, today, a public policy matter of huge import. Searching for a Jewish response, the old unresolved debate about "emergence" suddenly became highly relevant, for this abortion procedure occurs precisely after the majority of the fetus has emerged from the womb, but before it emerges into the open air. Is such a fetus "not to be touched," or does the law countenance that it be "dismembered limb from limb"?

Writing a responsum for the CJLS in December 2001, this author argued that, while Jews generally should not participate in or avail themselves of such procedures, the matter being so clearly a subject of current and ongoing debate, in an emergency—if a woman's life were to be at risk—it is appropriate to rely on the definition that provides protection for her and thus to sanction the abortion to save her life. That responsum (written in English, but entitled *Ein Doḥin Nefesh Mi-p'nei Nefesh*) was approved. Rabbi Susan Grossman then presented a countervailing responsum ("'Partial Birth Abortion' and the Question of When Life Begins," CJLS, September 2003) affirming the more lenient position in all cases and permitting the procedure for Jewish patients and doctors. As is the case in many areas where the Conservative movement is not wedded to one policy but embraces a range of ideas, this too has been approved. Both responsa are available on the website of the Rabbinical Assembly.

The Final Path: Treatment of the Terminally Ill

In discussing therapeutic treatments above, what was left untouched was the matter of medical treatment in cases where patients would benefit from medical ministrations even though there exists no rational hope that they might actually be cured or their lives saved. If saving of life is the sole concern of Jewish medicine, it might be argued that simple pain relief unrelated to therapeutic attempts to save lives has no justification, especially in light of rabbinic doctrine that recognized suffering, in some cases, as a sign of divine love or a tool of moral education. Still, no such argument is made in the extensive Jewish medical literature. On the contrary, pain management is deemed to be part of the natural province of the caring physician. Recall Rav Ashi's dictum (preserved in the Talmud at *BT* Bava Kamma 46b as cited above): "It is elementary logic: when one has a pain, one goes to the doctor."

Palliative Care

One reason offered to support the notion of palliative care has been that pain, in some small measure, weakens the patient and contributes to morbidity. But another, more fundamental reason is simply that severe pain is unbearable and, as the ancient sages put it in the Talmud (at *BT* Beitzah 32b), when one's pain is truly overwhelming, "even one's actual life is no life."

When faced with the prospect of suffering, both Rabbi Ḥiyya bar Abba and Rabbi Yoḥanan were asked whether they would welcome such agonies, which could be viewed as a sign of divine love, bringing with them compensation in the World to Come (*BT* B'rakhot 5b). Despite this enticement, both answered identically, saying they would welcome "neither them [the pains] nor their reward." Thus the third justification offered to permit physicians to engage in pain relief is the preference of the patient. Recognizing the importance of that concern, we are told that the sages of classical antiquity refrained from enacting their own stringent rulings where they caused or exacerbated a person's pain. (See, e.g., *SA* Oraḥ Ḥayyim 328:33 and the Rema's gloss to Oraḥ Ḥayyim 317:1.) This has been interpreted as relating only to severe pain, with the regular rules applying for small and common aches. Severe pain, however, even brings in its wake permission to transgress Shabbat. (See *SA* Oraḥ Ḥayyim 328 for elaborate rules to distinguish these cases one from another.)

As we see from the above, a patient's desires certainly do matter. Although we are encouraged to seek the care of physicians and are required to follow their medical judgment when it is unchallenged, the fact is that medical judgments are rarely unchallenged. There are second opinions to be sought and often alternative treatments to consider. It is reported (at *BT* Bava M'tzi·a 85b) that when Rabbi Judah the Patriarch contracted an eye disease, his physician recommended an injection, but the sage declined the treatment, saying, "I cannot endure it." Next the doctor recommended a salve, which was likewise rejected. Only on the third try did the physician craft a treatment regimen that the rabbi found acceptable. Indeed, it is not at all unheard of for a patient to reject a treatment outright, preferring to suffer rather than undergo a particularly uncomfortable treatment regimen. Were the treatment assuredly a solution, the patient would, according to most opinions, be duty-bound to listen. But the nature of medicine is that the outcome of a treatment is never certain. Every patient and every situation is different, and diagnoses are fallible, expressing only probabilities and focusing solely on those factors that the doctors have identified, though there may well be others. Mar bar Rav Ashi, a late talmudic sage, goes so far as to claim (at *BT* Yoma 83a) that there is even a scriptural basis for according patients their autonomy, citing Proverbs 14:10, "The heart knows its own bitterness." This broad understanding of a patient's right to choose what is best for him or herself antedates by far the modern bioethical principle of autonomy, which has become one of the four major principles of bioethics as set out by Tom L. Beauchamp and James F. Childress in the fifth edition of *Principles of Biomedical Ethics* (Oxford: Oxford University Press, 2001).

It is this sense of one's right to choose how to live (rather than the right to decide how and when one will die, to which I turn in a moment) that supports the concept of hospice care. Patients who choose hospice care have despaired of any further positive effect of therapeutic medicine and wish, above all, to be comfortable in their final months, weeks, or days. Whether hospice is offered at home or in an institutional setting, it should offer continuing palliative care and respond to all life-threatening crises. The choice of hospice against unrelenting illness is not a choice of death at the soonest possible moment, but rather a choice of life as best it can be lived until its eventual, God-directed end.

In this regard, much has been written about the matter of pain relief in an impaired patient and the fear that painkillers will hasten that patient's death. Rabbi Elliot Dorff has written that the intention to relieve pain trumps whatever risk there may be of hastening the patient's death (*CJLS Responsa 1980–1990,* pp. 519–580, also available in the eighth chapter of Rabbi Dorff's book

Matters of Life and Death). In my responsum, "A Halakhic Ethic of Care for the Terminally Ill" (ibid., pp. 467–518), I expressed my reservations with that position, writing that I felt that the decision should be driven by expectations, and not by intentions. In other words, if one expects that the patient will die of a specific medication, even if one's desire is simply to relieve pain, it seems to me that this is sufficient reason to prohibit it. The best experts in pain relief insist that this situation should never come to be. (Of course, one cannot rely on having the service of experts in pain relief available at every moment and in every situation.) In any event, all agree that the maximum must be done to keep the patient comfortable.

Euthanasia and the Right to Die

All this skirts the edge of two of the primary issues of modern management of the terminally ill. One has been labeled the issue of the "right to die," and the other is the related matter of euthanasia. In a series of U.S. court decisions over the past quarter century, the American judiciary has determined that "a patient has the right to refuse any medical treatment" and that, in the language of the California Court of Appeal, Second District, 1986, writing in *Bouvia v. Superior Court,* "this right exists even if its exercise creates a life-threatening condition." (This approach was affirmed by the U.S. Supreme Court in 1990. The language of Chief Justice William Rehnquist, writing for the court in *Cruzan v. Director, Missouri Department of Health,* is somewhat less boldly stated: "This is the first case in which we have been squarely presented with the issue of whether the United States Constitution grants what is in common parlance referred to as a 'right to die.' . . . The principle that a competent person has a constitutionally protected liberty interest in refusing unwanted medical treatment may be inferred from our prior decisions.")

No such statement can be made under Jewish law. Patients' autonomy ends where their lives are at stake and the means to preserve life is deemed meaningfully to exist. At the same moment that God offers us the promise of free will, in Deuteronomy 30:19, Scripture enjoins us to "choose life." The martyr Ḥanina ben Teradiyon, in choosing to die at the hands of the Romans rather than at his own hand, expressed it thus: "It is well that the same God that gave life should take it. One should not injure oneself" (*BT* Avodah Zarah 18a). Life is seen as a divine gift, first given by God when God breathed it into Adam (as noted at Genesis 2:7) and then returned to God upon our deaths (as stated at Kohelet 12:7).

It is the wife of Rabbi Meir (known to us as Beruriah, but unnamed in this text from *Midrash Mishlei,* chapter 31) who may have formulated this concept of life as a gift from God the most memorably. When two of Rabbi

Meir's sons died suddenly, she sought to break the news to him by spinning a parable:

> "A man came to me before and left a deposit with me," she said. "Now he has come to take it. Shall I return it to him or not?" [He] responded, "My love, is one who holds a deposit in trust not required to return it?" Said she, "Had you not said so, I would not have given it back." She then took his hand and led him to their sons' room [in which their bodies lay]. . . . At that point she said, "Rabbi, is this not as you said to me, that we must return a deposit to its owner? Scripture says: 'The Eternal has given and the Eternal has taken. May the Eternal's name be blessed'" (Job 1:21).

As one may not harm a deposit with which one is entrusted, so one may not tamper with (or complain about) the natural course of the lives entrusted to our care. These are, admittedly, aggadic statements that have limited force of law. But there is ample legal valence to the idea embedded in Beruriah's lesson to her husband that life is a gift of God, and this outlook leads to the rejection of suicide (Tractate S'maḥot 2:1, *SA* Yoreh Dei·ah 345:1; cf. Rabbi Shabbetai Kohen's commentary, *Siftei Kohein, ad loc.*) and the notion that it is prohibited to do damage to oneself (e.g., Maimonides, *MT* Hilkhot Ḥoveil U-mazzik 5:1). In both cases, the basic explanation of these laws is couched in terms of God's ownership of our lives (cf. Maimonides' comment at *MT* Hilkhot Rotzei·aḥ U-sh'mirat Nefesh 1:4: ". . . for the life of the murdered person is . . . the property of God"). In the end, the principle is simple: because life is a temporary gift granted by God and then taken back by God, Judaism recognizes no basic, inherent, or inalienable right to die.

The matter of euthanasia is a bit confused by the example of the suicide of King Saul depicted in the Bible at 1 Samuel 31. King Saul was neither, it should be noted, a model of religious rectitude nor was he mentally stable, thus hardly making the example of his suicide and that of his squire the stuff of halakhic determination. But several medieval commentators felt the need to justify his actions, particularly in light of the martyrdoms they witnessed personally, some of which did include suicides.

The primary justification for such an act was in light of the well-known provision that one should allow oneself to be killed rather than defame God. Perhaps, it was argued, knowing that one would be tortured and possibly forced to defame God, it would be better to do as Saul did by committing suicide rather than risk defaming God. (This is the opinion of Rabbeinu Tam, as cited in the Tosafot to *BT* Avodah Zarah 18a, *s.v. ve'al y'ḥabbeil atzmo.*) On the other hand, Naḥmanides, writing in *Torat Ha-adam* (*Inyan Ha-hespeid*), wrote simply that "King Saul . . . who was doomed, was permitted." (Some have sought to apply this approach to euthanasia and physician-assisted suicide, arguing that terminally ill patients, knowing that they are doomed, should likewise be permitted these avenues of escape from the ravages of their diseases. This position has not attained any broad support, however, and I would note that Naḥmanides' comments appear in the context of the laws governing eulogies. In these cases of suicide, in order to avoid the indignity of burial without a eulogy, we should entertain any mitigating factor, however slight, to rule the suicide as having been "not of right mind"—and, thus excusing the deceased's suicide, to permit a eulogy. Readers interested in perusing an early collection of texts governing suicide may consult the second chapter of the extra-talmudic Tractate S'maḥot.)

Speaking for the Conservative movement, then, Rabbi Elliot N. Dorff wrote a responsum ("Assisted Suicide," *CJLS Responsa 1991–2000,* pp. 379–393, cf. Rabbi Dorff's book, *Matters of Life and Death,* pp. 176–198) and a summary *Statement on Assisted Suicide* that was approved by the CJLS in 1997 and that was subsequently affirmed by the full Rabbinical Assembly convention in 1998: "Since God infuses each human life with inherent meaning by creating each of us in the divine image . . . and since Judaism views life as sacred and understands human beings to have life on trust from God . . . and since God's creation and ownership of our bodies puts the decision of when life is to end in God's hands . . . [we hold that] suicide is a violation of Jewish law and of the sacred trust of our lives given us by God. Furthermore, [we hold that] assisting suicide is also a violation of Jewish law. . . . No human being may take his or her own life, ask others to help them to do so, or assist in such an effort. . . . Jewish tradition bids us to express our compassion in ways that effectively respond to the patient's suffering while adhering to our mandate to respect the divine trust of life" (*CJLS Responsa 1991–2000,* pp. 398–399).

For most people, it is grappling with the middle ground between euthanasia and pain relief that is the hardest. While we cannot approve of taking a person's life, neither can we look away from the pain and suffering he or she may have to endure in their final stages of life. Effective pain relief is our primary obligation. Nonetheless, lingering, even when not suffering unbearable pain, is often a psychological torture. Thus much thought has gone into the question of whether life-support equipment—and even medication, nutrition, and hydration—might be withheld or withdrawn, in the attempt to hasten death. Here Jewish thinkers have sought very different paths in the attempt to show compassion while not crossing the threshold into God's domain, the taking of life.

The most fundamentalist in their views have argued that we must do nothing that might hasten the patient's death, even out of compassion. That is the sentiment expressed by the extra-talmudic work called Tractate S'maḥot (at 1:1–4), among our earliest sources on the topic, which warns against undertaking any activities in preparation for the patient's death that might affect the patient while that patient is still alive:

> The patient at death's door [Hebrew: *goseis*] is considered living in every regard . . . until the moment of death. . . . One may not move nor wash such a patient nor place the patient on sand or salt until the moment of death. One may not close the eyes. [Indeed,] one who touches or moves such a patient is guilty of murder. Rabbi Meir would liken [such a dying individual] to a flickering candle: when anyone touches it, it goes out immediately.

This was also the view of the nineteenth-century halakhic giant Rabbi Yeḥiel Mikhel Epstein, writing in his magnum opus, the *Arukh Ha-shulḥan,* Yoreh Dei·ah 339:1: "Even though we see that someone is suffering greatly in dying and that death would be better for such a patient, nevertheless, we are forbidden to do anything to hasten death, for the world and all it contains is God's, and such is clearly divine will, may God be praised."

Today that position is most prominently represented in the United States by the Orthodox scholar Rabbi J. David Bleich. He concedes that there is no obligation to heal once the death process has begun, but he reduces that category to a null set by insisting that this leniency applies only to a patient "who cannot, under any circumstances, be maintained alive for a period of seventy-two hours," a determination of fact that no physician can ever make. (Rabbi Bleich set forth this view in his essay "The Obligation to Heal in the Jewish Tradition," in *Jewish Bioethics,* ed. Fred Rosner and J. David Bleich [Jersey City, NJ: KTAV, 1999], pp. 33–35. While he does not precisely say that this situation can never arise, he implies that such is the case. He maintains that in light of current medical techniques, the category of *goseis*—what he calls "the moribund patient"—no longer exists, and that the laws relating to the *goseis* are consequently moot.) Physicians must therefore always seek to postpone death as long as is possible including by the use of extraordinary medical treatment.

Other Orthodox thinkers, however, have managed to carve out some room for compassion beyond pain relief. They rely, in the first instance, upon talmudic precedents that seem to establish the propriety of aiding those in need of death, such as this story from the Talmud: "When Rabbi Shimon ben Lakish died, Rabbi Yoḥanan was extremely distraught. . . . He tore his clothes and cried out . . . wailing on and on until he lost his mind. The sages prayed for compassion for him and he died" (*BT* Bava M'tzi·a 84a).

Others point to the tale of Rabbi Judah's maidservant, told in the Talmud at *BT* K'tubbot 104a. The maid, having decided that Rabbi Judah was suffering too greatly in his final illness, but judging that the prayers of his disciples were keeping him alive, created a diversion so that they would stop their prayers for a moment and thus allow her master's spirit to slip away. The Talmud reports no censure by the rabbis, and later interpreters understood their silence to constitute tacit approval. The medieval formulation of Rabbi Nissim Gerondi (called the Ran, c. 1310–1375), writing in his commentary to *BT* N'darim 40a, came to be the anthem of this school of thought: "It seems to me . . . that there are times when one must pray for compassion, that a person might die—for example, when the patient is suffering very much due to the illness and cannot live."

These texts are all about prayer to God, however, and either about people seeking God's compassionate intervention in bringing about death or about the silencing of prayers that are understood to be keeping a person alive. It is, after all, God's domain of which we speak, and it is hubris to imagine that we may take effective human steps with equal assurance. Thus, it was concluded by early medieval commentators that the proper expression of compassion for the dying lay in restraint, i.e., omitting actions that might delay a patient's death or removing any impediments to that death, while not hastening the death in any active way. Refraining from acting would thus cast the patient before God for divine determination. This approach is first reported by the sixteenth-century Italian scholar Rabbi Joshua Boaz, citing the early thirteenth-century work *Sefer Ḥasidim* by Judah He-ḥasid and his followers (see the *Shiltei Ha-gibborim* commentary to the *Sefer Ha-halakhot* of Rabbi Isaac Alfasi to *BT* Mo·eid Katan §1237):

> One could say that to do something that prevents the immediate death of a patient at death's door [*goseis*], such as chopping wood in the patient's proximity in order to delay the soul's departure or putting salt on the patient's tongue to prevent death, is certainly prohibited. . . . And any similar thing may be removed. But to do something that will hasten death and the departure of the soul is prohibited.

Rabbi Bleich dismisses this as a matter of superstition, moot in light of current technology, and his co-editor, Dr. Fred Rosner, despairs of the task of distinguishing between "prolonging life and prolonging the act of dying." (See his essay "The Jewish Attitude toward Euthanasia," in the volume *Jewish Bioethics* referenced above). But other authoritative Orthodox thinkers have concluded that this precedent should indeed be our guide, expanding the notion of *goseis* to include all who are terminally ill, rather than limiting it as Rabbi Bleich does, and offering differing assessments of what constitutes "hastening death" and what can be classed, instead, as the licit removal of an "impediment to death."

Rabbi Immanuel Jakobovits, a knighted chief rabbi of England and the author of *Jewish Medical Ethics* (New York: Philosophical Library, 1959), the first study of its kind in this field, sought to tease out the various threads in a 1956 Hebrew-language essay published in *Ha-pardeis* (31:1 [1956], pp. 28ff. and 31:3 [1956], pp. 16ff.):

> The law ... teaches definitively that even concerning a person on his deathbed, with only days to live, whoever hastens his death is considered a murderer. . . . The laws are altogether different concerning causing death by omission or by removing an impediment to death. . . . It is even forbidden to prevent the flight of the soul with medications. . . . It appears that the spirit of the Torah is not fundamentally opposed to the request of those that are suffering to be released from their pain. . . . There is no requirement for us to lengthen the life of a person who has despaired [of life], nor to prolong his suffering unnaturally. . . . If the impediment to death is food or drink, without which he could not live, it is clearly prohibited to remove it, for our precedents include only things that are not necessary for life, *per se*. . . . But what is the rule with regard to a patient who is likely to die if he does not receive medication? . . . It seems to me that . . . a treatment that only defers his death cannot be said to fulfill the requirement of returning him to health. . . . Therefore, with regard to a patient of whom it is obvious to us that he cannot be healed, even though one may treat with all sorts of medications, nevertheless, we are not commanded to [do so]. . . . Where the demands of the value of life and the dignity of the patient clash, we have no other option but to avoid a decision by doing nothing, leaving the choice to the One who holds the souls of all life.

This has become the dominant position of the Orthodox world, argued in similar terms by Rabbi Moshe Feinstein (*Igg'rot Moshe,* Ḥoshen Mishpat 2, 73:1, ed. New York, 1985, p. 304):

> When the physicians recognize that it is impossible to restore health and life, and the patient cannot live as he is without suffering, but it would be possible to administer drugs to extend his life as is, with the suffering, they should not administer those medications, but leave him as he is. . . . They should do nothing (Hebrew: *sheiv ve'al ta·aseh*).

Although Rabbi Feinstein rejected the notion of declaring a patient brain-dead, considering all respirator-dependent patients to be alive, he was prepared to rely on the principle of inaction, thereby devising a method to permit withdrawing a ventilator from a brain-dead patient:

> Where the terminal patient cannot breathe, he must be given oxygen. One should administer the oxygen in small doses, for an hour or two, so that when it runs out they can determine if he is yet alive. If so, they should give another dose of oxygen, and so on, until it is determined that he has died. In this way there will not be any concern of causing his death.

Nearly all who have written in this area agree with these authorities that nutrition and hydration—that is, the continued provision of food and water—are necessary. However, with regard to the withholding of life-prolonging medications, not everyone is satisfied that they may be withheld when a patient is suffering. We noted Maimonides' equating of medication and food above, and many voices have insisted that medications, insofar as they are expected not to be futile, but to have a life-prolonging effect, must be continued.

An alternative synthesis suggests itself. In a 1990 CJLS responsum entitled "A Halakhic Ethic of Care for the Terminally Ill," I formulated this synthesis as follows:

> We try, in all our dealings, including healing and including death, to act in that way which corresponds to God's will. The diagnostic problem remains. How do we determine that a particular death is "natural" and timely, according to God's will and plan? . . . By doing everything possible medically, biologically, to treat the life systems of the critical patient, while removing impediments to death—items or procedures that interfere with the natural shut-down of the body's major systems in death—we allow ourselves to see if, indeed, God has ordained the closure of this life. . . . Some of our more recent technologies are mechanical, rather than biological, however, and do not parallel life functions. Thus, for instance, a heart-lung machine . . . does not operate as a biological system, but rather circumvents one. Its function is mechanical, a holding mechanism . . . against the deterioration and death that would follow on cessation of heart and lung function. . . . Taken alone, however, it offers no curative potential. . . . It is thus a candidate for the category of "impediments to death." (*CJLS Responsa 1980–1990*, pp. 475–476)

This distinction is offered by a number of Orthodox authorities as well. It is more restrictive than the former view with regard to medications, not accepting the common view that "pneumonia," though it is treatable "is the old man's best friend" because it will quickly bring an end to his misery, but allowing the withdrawal or nonrecourse to medication only where it is futile or of uncertain effect (see the previous discussion of patient autonomy in the face of medical uncertainty). But it is clearer on the nature of impediments to death, and does not require the subterfuge of intentionally structuring healthcare so that one can exercise the option of omission to attain results that one could not obtain by commission. A ventilator, under this view, is clearly an impediment to death, and may be withdrawn when it is found no longer to be in the patient's benefit. Importantly, this allows the trial of therapy without the concern that, once started, it will be impossible to withdraw it.

Yet another approach to halakhically reconciling compassion for the suffering of the terminally ill and the desire to be aggressive in the maintenance of life has been offered in the Conservative movement by Rabbi Elliot Dorff in his responsum "A Jewish Approach to End-Stage Medical Care" (*CJLS Responsa 1980–1990,* pp. 519–580, cf. Rabbi Dorff's book, *Matters of Life and Death: a Jewish Approach to Modern Medical Ethics,* chapter eight). In each of the former views, the halakhic demand to maintain life trumped other concerns, so that compassion for the patient's suffering could find expression, at best, through acts of omission and the removal of external impediments. Rabbi Dorff suggests that, in fact, the demand to maintain the life of a terminally ill patient might be attenuated in some sense, and our concern for the suffering of that patient might simply override the demands of aggressive care in some cases.

The halakhic case for these conclusions is built on two textual foundations. First, while Rabbi Dorff accepts the expanded range of the rules of *goseis* proposed above, he argues that it was even more appropriate to apply another halakhic category to the case of the terminally ill patient: that of the *t'reifah,* a person who is mortally wounded. And, indeed, Rashi's comments to *BT* Sanhedrin 78a (*s.v. she-hu patur*) suggests that such a life is compromised in morally significant ways. There, Rava is heard to say, "Everyone agrees that one who murders a person who is mortally wounded [*t'reifah*] is not liable." To this, Rashi comments, "Is not liable—since it is recognized that he is mortally wounded, he is considered a dead man."

What should our medical approach to such a patient be? On the one hand, there is a clear instruction in the Talmud at *BT* Yoma 85a that one rescues a mortally wounded party "even though he will only live for a few moments." On the other hand, when high-risk surgery presents the sole possibility of saving a life, those last few moments may be risked in an effort to save that life, as noted above in the discussion about permissible risk. Are those last moments of life to be cherished and protected, or is that not necessary? The Tosafot, the school of thirteenth-century French talmudic commentators, address this question in their comment to *BT* Avodah Zarah 27b, *s.v. l'ḥayyei sha·ah la ḥaishinan,* as follows: "It is possible to resolve the conflict [between the two approaches] by saying that in both cases we act for [the patient's] benefit."

The benefit discussed in both these cases is an extension of the patient's life. However, where the patient's benefit is secured by suffering less (even though the patient may as a result die sooner), it is appropriate according to Rabbi Dorff to conclude that we should recognize the attenuated status of a life of mere moments and relax our general tendency toward aggressive care in order to pursue the patient's benefit: "*In these two cases* acting for the victims' good amounts to trying to preserve their lives . . . that, however, does not mean that in *every* case such a goal would be appropriate . . . Tosafot articulated a *general principle* on the basis of this case— namely, that the proper objective of the medical care of a patient is to act *for his or her benefit*" [emphasis in original].

As with the withdrawal of life-support systems, Rabbi Dorff permits the withdrawal of nutrition and hydration under the general rubric of acting for the patient's greater benefit, judging those too to be mechanically supplied and extrinsic, and therefore properly classed as impediments even under the more restrictive interpretation.

Thus do four different threads emerge in halakhic grappling with the proper limits of medical treatment and compassion. The latter two represent differing positions that have secured CJLS approval. While substantially different in principle, they yield agreement on most practical steps. In order to clarify the practical differences that remain, along with the competing decisions reached in December 1990, the CJLS issued a short paper entitled *Mai Beinaihu?* (What divides them?), the standard talmudic phrase used in teasing out the distinction between closely matched theories. The text reads as follows:

> The points on which they differ are few, but significant. . . . With regard to medication . . . and . . . artificial nutrition [and/or] hydration: Rabbi Dorff would permit withholding or withdrawing such. . . . Rabbi Reisner would prohibit withholding [them] as long as they are believed to be beneficial. . . . With regard to pain relief . . . Rabbi Dorff argues that the intent to alleviate pain controls, Rabbi Reisner that the probable result controls.
>
> Rabbi Dorff might center his objection to Rabbi Reisner's paper in the comment that it is . . . not sufficiently alert to the real emotional needs of patients and their families. Rabbi Reisner might frame his objection to Rabbi Dorff's paper in the comment that it arrives at its sensitivity to patients by degrading the status of their God-given lives, which we are constrained not to do. (*CJLS Responsa 1980–1990*, pp. 581–583)

What none of these four positions denies is that the decisions that guide us in the final days of life are complex and, ultimately, must be a reflection of the patient's own thinking, for "the heart knows its own bitterness" (Proverbs

14:10). To that end, and recognizing that a patient may be unable to make decisions at that point, the Conservative movement has joined those who encourage the preparation of a medical directive appointing a proxy to make healthcare decisions for a patient, in case of his or her incapacitation. Such a document specifically instructs a representative of the patient's determinations in these areas so that the representative might accurately fulfill the patient's wishes. A document to that end is available through the United Synagogue of Conservative Judaism.

The Brave New World: Cloning and Stem Cells

Not two decades ago—on February 22, 1997, to be exact—news of the cloning of Dolly the sheep began the worldwide excitement over the prospect that humans too might be cloned. Some of that excitement was just a bit premature, however. Cloning, as envisioned in light of the birth of Dolly, utilized the exceptional nature of the egg cell to grow to adulthood, replacing its nucleus with the nucleus of an extant adult. Thus the replication of an adult through this process requires growing it from scratch. In effect, this produces an identical twin many years younger than the original. But just as twins vary in their personal traits, so would these cloned twins. Since they would be raised in radically different environments, they would surely be even more unlike. There is no certainty at this point that human cloning will ever be possible, at least not without substantial risk, so consideration of the issue is speculative in the extreme.

Nevertheless, what does Judaism have to say about such a possibility? Obviously, it has not been the subject of any classical text, and in this case, quite unusually, no one to my knowledge has found a case whose principles or extensions seem to apply. We have seen that the *halakhah* has been receptive to the concept of human manipulation of what once would have been considered biological destiny. And so Dr. Avraham Steinberg, in an unpublished paper entitled "Human Cloning: Scientific, Moral, and Jewish Perspectives," prepared for the Institute of Jewish Medical Ethics of the Hebrew Academy of San Francisco and available on-line on the institute's website (www.medethics.org.il), concluded: "From a halakhic perspective, it can be said that there is no substantial, defined prohibition inherent to the activity of cloning humans." Dr. Steinberg went further as well, citing the advice of Rabbi Israel Lipschutz (1782–1860), who wrote in the "Yakhin" section of his *Tiferet Yisra·el* commentary to *M* Yadayim 4:3 (§27) that "anything for which there is no reason to forbid, is permissible . . . for the Torah has not enumerated all permissible things, but rather those that are forbidden." Indeed, in his testimony before the National Bioethics Advisory Commission in March 1997, Rabbi Moshe Tendler spoke of cloning as a valid fertility technique for cases of special need: "Show me a young man who is sterile, whose family was wiped out in the Holocaust, and who is the last of a genetic line—I would certainly clone him. . . . Sterility in biblical terms is an illness. Our duty is to respond to that. Cloning may be a methodology to do so."

Yet one might wonder if it would ever be a method of choice. Rabbi Dorff, speaking personally before that same committee (i.e., not as an official representative of the Conservative movement), raised concerns about the unreasonable psychological burden placed on a clone to represent another person, the dangers of growing commodification of people if cloning is permitted, and, generally, about a loss of the sense of uniqueness we see in each individual if cloning takes root and becomes a normal reproductive technique. And that position quickly came to dominate, not only in the halakhic debate but in the general society as well. In March 2002 both the CJLS, in a responsum on stem cell research by Rabbi Elliot Dorff (published in *Conservative Judaism* 55:3 [Spring, 2003], pp. 3–29 and available on the Rabbinical Assembly website), and the Orthodox Union and the Rabbinical Council of America in a joint statement, stated their opposition to reproductive cloning of the sort discussed here, but their support for therapeutic cloning.

For that was the other dream that the advent of cloning inspired. Would it be possible to replace an egg cell's nucleus with the nucleus of a cell from the skin or fat of a patient in need of transplant, and grow the needed tissue or organ? Such tissue, created with the patient's own DNA, would be immune-compatible, it is hoped, thus unlikely to cause rejection, and would dramatically act to resolve the present shortage of organs for transplant. Representing the potential to heal multiple illnesses and conditions that are not currently under our control, there is little surprise that therapeutic cloning was embraced across the spectrum of Jewish legal opinion.

But, again, a fast-moving development shifted the arena of debate. Scientists in 1998 had isolated the cells of the very early embryo, which give rise to all subsequent tissues of the human body. It is the potential to manipulate these that gave rise to the notion of therapeutic cloning. But in August of 2001 President George Bush banned federal funding for the derivation of such embryonic stem cells, arguing that life begins at conception, and that the harvesting of embryonic stem cells necessarily entailed destroying a living embryo. The Jewish halakhic response was fast and clear: Judaism does not consider life to begin at conception but at a later stage—either at implantation (fourteen days) or the Talmud's classic forty days (cf. the earlier discussion of contraception). Moreover, with regard to embryos left unneeded after fertility treatment, it had already been determined that they could be disposed of, since they were unable to develop naturally outside the womb. Thus the ruling in the spring of 2002 by the CJLS permitting and encouraging stem cell research and therapeutic cloning may be seen as a direct response to President Bush's position.

As I write, scientists are daily making progress toward harvesting stem cells from embryos that begin to develop *in vitro* (called embryonic stem cells) or creating them from adult non-germ cells (called induced pluripotent stem cells), then deriving from them various forms of tissue. The first human experiments of stem cell therapies have begun. The enormous therapeutic potential of this foray into the very basic processes of life, far from being anathema to halakhic thought, is affirmative cause to proceed along that road.

Throughout this odyssey the key words have been life and healing—*v'ḥai bahem,* "you shall live through them" (Leviticus 18:5), a requirement of all the *mitzvot*, and *v'rappo y'rappei,* "you shall surely heal" (Exodus 21:19). Action taken to assure life and health is almost always Jewishly correct; action taken to their detriment, almost always Jewishly discouraged. In the future, there will be countless new twists on medicine's potential to affect our health and heal our wounds and our illnesses. Inevitably, there will also be numerous halakhic opinions voiced about those new techniques, but one simple concept will underlie them all, for Jews have always insisted upon God's concern for our benefit. As Rabbi Jacob ben Asher asserts, in beginning the fourth pillar of his four-part law code, the *Arba·ah Turim* (*AT* Even Ha-eizer 1:1): "May the Holy One's name be praised, for God desires the wellbeing of all creatures."

Caring for the Needy

ELLIOT N. DORFF

Why should I take care of someone in need at all? This question is presented at the center of a story told at the very beginning of the Bible to indicate the pervasive quality of this Jewish value: God asks Cain, "Where is your brother, Abel?" Cain, to his enduring discredit, answers, "I do not know. Am I my brother's keeper?" (Genesis 4:9). Because we are indeed guardians for other human beings, the Torah demands not only that we refrain from harming others, including non-Israelites (see, e.g., Exodus 22:20 or 23:9), but also that we exert ourselves to protect and aid them. This requirement to help others even includes animals, including those belonging to one's enemy: "When you encounter your enemy's ox or donkey wandering, you must take it back to him. When you see the donkey of your enemy collapsing under its burden and might otherwise refrain from helping it up, you must nevertheless help it up with him" (Exodus 23:4–5). More broadly, the Torah demands, "Do not stand over the blood of another" (Leviticus 19:16), which the Talmud (at *BT* Sanhedrin 73a) understands to mean "Do not stand idly by the blood of your fellow." The Talmud thus understands Scripture to be ruling that we have a duty to help someone in distress, whether it be a drowning individual, one attacked by robbers, or one beset by less violent (but no less terrible) misfortunes.

Rabbi Akiva maintains that the Torah's broadest demand to help others derives from its command to "Love your neighbor as yourself" (Leviticus 19:18, as cited at *B'reishit Rabbah* 24:7). Ben Azai, however, contends that the duty to help others in need applies not just to one's neighbor or other Jews but to all other human beings, and he finds this concept embedded in the Torah's assertion at Genesis 5:1–2 that "when God created the human being, God made that being in the likeness of God, male and female God created them." (Ben Azai's interpretation of this verse is found at *B'reishit Rabbah* 24:7 and at *Y* N'darim 9:4, 41c.) These principles establish the framework for how Judaism would have us treat all needy people.

Because the subject of the previous chapter on Jewish medical ethics has direct implications for some classes of needy people—namely, the sick and the medically uninsured—this chapter deals with those issues first. Captives, the imprisoned, and refugees are also at increased peril for their lives, and so their issues come next. Jewish medical ethics has a more indirect relationship, but still a real one, with the next set of the needy treated in this chapter—namely, children given up for adoption, the elderly, and the hungry. Finally, this chapter considers those who can neither acknowledge nor repay the help they get—namely, those who need burial. This list by no means exhausts the classes of the needy—one need only think, for example, of the lonely and the depressed among us—but the fundamental ideas of Jewish law and theology that emerge in analyzing this list can be easily applied to other categories of the needy as well.

Bikkur Ḥolim

The Mitzvah of Visiting the Sick

The commandment to visit the sick (*bikkur ḥolim*) is a requirement of every Jew, not just rabbis, doctors, or nurses, regardless of the relative social station of the patient and the potential visitor. (This point is made repeatedly in the Talmud, e.g., at *BT* Shabbat 127a, Sotah 14a, N'darim 39b–41b, and Bava Kamma 100a, and was formally codified as law by Maimonides at *MT* Hilkhot Eivel 14:4.) In addition, Jews are obligated to visit sick non-Jews as part of the general duty to promote peace between Jews and non-Jews. (See *BT* Gittin 61a, *MT* Hilkhot Eivel 14:12 and Hilkhot M'lakhim U-milḥ'moteihem 10:12, and also *SA* Yoreh Dei·ah 335:9.) As early as the fourteenth century and continuing into the modern era, many synagogues have established Bikkur Ḥolim societies charged with ensuring that sick people receive visitors. (Rabbi Nissim Gerondi, c. 1310–1375, is the first to mention the existence of such societies; see *The Sephardi Legacy,* ed. Haim Beinart [Jerusalem: Magnes Press, 1992], p. 51.)

Why Visiting the Sick Is Important

Sick people are not simply machines that need to be fixed, but rather human beings in need of healing, succor, and encouragement. Thus, whether medicine can cure a person or not, we collectively have the duty to attend to the patient's emotional, psychological, social, and religious well-being. As the Zohar, the classic work of Jewish mysticism, says, "If a physician cannot give his patient medicine for the body, he should [at least] make sure that one gets medicine for one's soul" (I 229b).

The Talmud makes the same point in its own way: "Rabbi Abba, son of Rabbi Ḥanina, said, 'One who visits an invalid takes away one-sixtieth of the pain'" (*BT* N'darim 39b–40a). Another version of the text speaks instead of taking away one-sixtieth of the illness; but whichever is the correct original reading, the Talmud is making a clear statement about the importance of the connection between patient and visitor for the patient's well-being.

There is, first of all, the social aspect of visiting the sick. Because illness often confines a person to one's home or even to one's bed, it is isolating. (And, indeed, except for execution or torture, solitary confinement is the harshest penalty that can be meted out to incarcerated individuals.) While the Talmud's claim that visitors take away a quantifiable amount of the sick person's pain strays into the realm of hyperbole, that claim arises from this understanding of the need for human contact. This social interaction may well affect the patient's physical recovery as well. By confirming that family and friends are keenly interested in the patient's recovery, and also by reminding the patient that there is life outside the sick room for him or her to rejoin, visitors reinforce the patient's determination to become well and to rejoin society, and can also motivate the patient to follow the prescribed regimen of healing, however tedious or painful it may be. In this roundabout way, sympathetic, caring visitors may indeed be said to take away one-sixtieth of patients' illnesses when they leave their bedsides.

Visitors affect the patient on a more religious plane as well. By praying for the patient, and by indicating that prayers are being offered in the synagogue on his or her behalf, visitors invoke the aid of God in the divine guise of ultimate Healer. Jewish prayer is traditionally offered communally, in part because Jewish sources maintain that communal prayer convinces God to grant a request more effectively than private prayer ever can (see, e.g., *BT* B'rakhot 6a and 7b–8a, *Y* B'rakhot 5:1, 8d–9a, and at *MT* Hilkhot T'fillah U-n'si·at Kappayim 8:1). Visitors' prayers and those recited in the synagogue on behalf of the patient thus throw the weight of the entire community behind the patient's own plea to God for recovery.

Why People Are Reluctant to Visit the Sick

Given its importance, why do so few people fulfill the commandment to visit the sick?

Part of the reason is nothing more complex than the inconvenience involved. People must make time in their schedules to visit someone in the hospital or in a recovery facility or nursing home. Then, when they actually manage to find the right building, pay for parking, and locate the right room in the right wing, the patient is likely to be sleeping or out for some procedure, making the whole trip seem as if it were for naught. No wonder so few come back, or even bother to go in the first place.

Those who do find the patient awake must then interact with him or her in strange circumstances that are, by their very nature, going to be uncomfortable for both parties. The ill are often in pain and feel embarrassed by their diminished capacity, symbolized and exacerbated by the unflattering (and often immodest) hospital gowns they are obliged to wear and perhaps also by their altered appearance and disheveled looks. Moreover, patients often worry that they are imposing on their friends who would much rather spend their time elsewhere, thereby adding guilt to the mix of unpleasant emotions that need to be overcome. Visitors, for their part, are put off by the strange (and often frightening) sights, sounds, and smells of hospitals, which starkly remind them of their own vulnerability and mortality. Unless medically trained, visitors may also feel helpless, not knowing what they could possibly say or do to make the patient feel better.

Jewish Advice for Visitors

In spelling out how one should fulfill the commandment of visiting the sick, the classical rabbis provide some practical advice for making such visits more pleasant and effective:

1. *Ensure that your visit will be welcome.* This can often be accomplished simply through consultation in advance of the visit with the patient's family or friends and possibly with the patient him or herself (*BT* N'darim 41a and *MT* Hilkhot Eivel 14:5).
2. *Consider the day of your visit carefully.* "As a matter of good manners," according to the Yerushalmi (in a text preserved at *Y* Pei·ah 3:9, 17d, to which may be compared the parallel lessons at *BT* N'darim 40a; *MT* Hilkhot Eivel

14:5; *SA* Yoreh Dei·ah 335:1 and the *Turei Zahav* commentary *ad loc.*), only family and close friends should visit during the first two days of an illness, and others should wait until the third day. That restriction does not apply, however, to patients with acute, life-threatening illnesses, in which case one should visit immediately.

3. *Time the hours of your visit.* The hours of visitation should not interfere with the patient's medical treatment (*MT* Hilkhot Eivel 14:5). Also, as patients are often at their best in the morning hours (making visits or prayer on their behalf seem unnecessary) and weakest in the evening (making prayers and visits appear hopeless), visitors are encouraged to call in the middle hours of the day. (The sources for this advice may be found at *BT* N'darim 40a and *SA* Yoreh Dei·ah 335:4.) If the patient is helped by visits, however, they need not be limited to one per day (*MT* Hilkhot Eivel 14:4).
4. *Position yourself to make the patient feel comfortable.* Body language counts! Standing over bedridden patients forces them to look up at visitors, emphasizing the visitors' strength and the patients' weakness, truly the last thing one would wish to communicate to patients who already feel debilitated. Furthermore, those who stand convey the impression—often no less accurate than inadvertently communicated—that they do not intend to stay long, that they only want to be acknowledged as having done their duty, and that they surely do not want to get involved in long, drawn-out conversations. To avoid subtly conveying any of these negative messages, visitors should sit at the same level as the patient's head so that their relative heights communicate equality and support (*MT* Hilkhot Eivel 14:6, Tosafot on *BT* Shabbat 12b, *s.v. lo yeisheiv al gabbei mittah v'lo al safsal,* and the gloss of the Rema to *SA* Yoreh Dei·ah 335:3). The Talmud actually suggests that visitors sit on the ground "because the divine presence rests above an invalid's bed" (*BT* N'darim 40a). For the same reasons, physicians should also sit down when checking in on a patient.
5. *Attend to the patient's needs.* Since patients and their immediate families are often reticent to ask for help, visitors should offer to do one or two specific things. Then the patient or family members will understand both the sincerity of the offer to help and the scope of what the visitor is willing to do. As an example, the Talmud (at *BT* N'darim 39b–40a) tells a story in which Rabbi Akiva, while visiting the sick Rabbi Ḥelbo, cleans his house and puts it in order. Other forms of physical care include taking the patient for a ride in a wheelchair (if medically permitted), feeding the patient (if necessary), and less direct, but equally necessary tasks like shopping for groceries, doing laundry, taking over carpool duties, and seeing to the other needs of the patient's spouse and children.

6. *Pray for and with the patient.* According to Jewish law (gloss of the Rema to *SA* Yoreh Dei·ah 335:4), one fulfills the commandment of visiting the sick only if one prays for healing with and for the patient. One may use the short, standard formula stated in the Talmud and the codes (at *BT* Shabbat 12b and *SA* Yoreh Dei·ah 335:6, respectively)—to wit, "May the All-Present have mercy on you among the sick of Israel," and then add whatever one thinks appropriate and meaningful, whether in Hebrew or in English (*SA* Yoreh Dei·ah 335:5).
7. *Speak with the patient.* Aside from prayer, what should a visitor talk about with a hospitalized patient? Some topics that should be raised are practical in nature. Specifically, if patients have not previously filled out a will or an advance directive for health care, they should be encouraged to specify their wishes about the disposition of their property and the course of their medical treatment. The Conservative movement has created a model advance directive in accordance with our understanding of Jewish law on end-of-life issues; it is available through the United Synagogue Book Service and on-line on the website of the Rabbinical Assembly. Patients can thus indicate in advance their wishes about the kind of medical treatment they will want when they can no longer answer such questions directly. More important, an advance directive will help to lift the burden of potential guilt from the person whom the patient has chosen to decide which regimen to follow, and it can prevent stressful acrimony on the part of family members who would have decided otherwise.

Beyond these practical matters, though, how should visitors fill the time during their visit? Jewish legal sources are silent about this, but Jewish theological concepts provide important clues. Every human being, according to the Torah, bears the dignity of having been created in the image of God. The key to speaking with sick people, then, is to bolster their sense of worth.

Illness is inherently degrading. It prevents the person from doing what people of the patient's age normally do. Visitors must be especially on guard, therefore, to avoid infantilizing the patient, because talking down to the patient, even when motivated by kindness, reinforces his or her loss of power and dignity. Instead, visitors should engage the patient in conversation about the patient's normal interests—for example, current events, sports, movies, books, or mutual friends. Doing so makes patients feel that they are still respected as people, that their opinions still matter, and that they are still members of their community.

One of the most enlightening experiences of my early rabbinic career was teaching a series of sessions on Jewish theology to residents of a Jewish nursing home. They had specifically asked for these classes because, as the social worker told me, they were sick of playing Bingo! Visitors will not normally come to a hospital room to discuss Jewish theology, but conversations with patients can and should be challenging and interesting, and they can cover a wide variety of topics. The very normalcy of such discussions communicates that the illness has not diminished the visitor's respect for the patient's intelligence and humanity.

Ethical Wills

Especially for people suffering from long-term illnesses, another set of discussions might surround the creation of an ethical will. Addressed to children, grandchildren, other family members, or friends, such wills are documents in which the author articulates his or her most important experiences, values, thoughts, feelings, dreams, and hopes. Ethical wills may be written, or even recorded in audio or videotape format. There are no requirements in Jewish law governing such documents; most take the form of an extended, personal letter or conversation. They may be addressed to the entire family, specific individuals, or both.

Some of the topics commonly included in ethical wills include the following:

1. The experiences most important to the author in her or his relationship to the recipient or recipients.
2. The values the author considers most critical to living a worthy life, perhaps with some examples to make the points clear and memorable.
3. Reflections on the relationships of the recipients to each other, together with expressions of joy, concern, or hope for their future wellbeing.
4. Specific desires the author has, such as that the children marry Jews, that they care for each other, or that a surviving spouse remarry.
5. An expression of Jewish commitment, together with illustrative examples of what Judaism has meant in the author's life.
6. An account of the family history, including the author's own life story. This often takes up most of the will, and it is most worthwhile in giving children and grandchildren a sense of their roots and heritage. Should negative or embarrassing experiences be recounted in this context? The decision will obviously have to rest with the author of each individual document, but the guiding principle will always be, simply, the issue of whether the story in question provides a valuable enough life lesson to outweigh the chagrin one might feel in telling it.

7. Some proverb or saying the author finds especially meaningful, or perhaps emblematic of his or her philosophy of life.
8. An expression of concern and love for the people receiving the ethical will.

For some examples of ethical wills, including many modern ones, see Jack Riemer and Nathaniel Stampfer, eds., *Ethical Wills: A Modern Jewish Treasury* (New York: Schocken, 1983). For some suggestions for preparing an ethical will, see Jack Riemer and Nathaniel Stampfer, eds., *So That Your Values Live On: Ethical Wills and How to Prepare Them* (Woodstock, VT: Jewish Lights Publishing, 1991).

Talking with a patient about an ethical will and about other timely and important subjects, along with the other steps outlined above, makes visits to the sick a critical part of the person's ability to cope with the illness by providing a sense of community, worthiness, and care. No wonder, then, that the ancient rabbis (cf., for example, *BT* Sotah 14a) understood visiting the sick as an activity we do in direct imitation of God, who visited Abraham when the latter was recovering from his circumcision (Genesis 18:1). Moreover, visiting the sick, both as an act of loyalty and as one of kindness, is, according to the ancient rabbis, one of a small list of commandments that have no limit (*M* Pei·ah 1:1) and that "yield immediate interest [to both the visitor and the patient] while the principal itself redounds to the benefit of those who do them in God's ultimate judgment in the World to Come" (*BT* Shabbat 127a). So important is this concept that these passages are included in the early Morning Service as paragraphs for daily mention and study (*Sim Shalom* I, pp. 8–9).

The topic of ethical wills is covered from a slightly different perspective in the chapter on inheritance law by Rabbi Martin S. Cohen elsewhere in this volume.

Caring for the Medically Uninsured or Underinsured

When physicians could not do much to heal a sick patient, their services were easily attainable, relatively cheap, and, frankly, not much sought after. "The best physician goes to hell," the Mishnah rather pointedly says at *M* Kiddushin 4:14, reflecting people's frustration with doctors' inability to cure.

With the advent of antibiotics in 1938, however, and with the introduction of other new drug therapies and ever-evolving diagnostic and surgical techniques, there has been a great increase in the demand for medical care for precisely the same reason that it has become much more expensive. This raises not only the "micro" questions of how physicians, patients, and their families should treat a given person's disease, but also the "macro" questions of how we, as a society, should arrange for medical care to be distributed. This invokes two basic Jewish concerns: the equitable distribution of healthcare resources, and who will pay for them.

First, the issue of equitable distribution. The rabbinic passages that might give us some guidance about triage—that is, about deciding equitably and reasonably who should get which treatments when resources are scarce—set priorities in five different ways: granting precedence based on priestly status (which is, however, superseded by knowledge of the Torah), prioritizing based on the close relationships of family or the place of an individual in his or her local community, giving special consideration to those who fulfill crucial social needs, favoring those who need the medical care the most, or making triage decisions in the context of total equality—that is, on a first come, first served, basis. For a description of each of these approaches with their attendant sources and my own attempt to formulate an integrated, Jewish approach to this matter, see the twelfth chapter of my book, *Matters of Life and Death: A Jewish Approach to Modern Medical Ethics*.

Next, we must consider the cost of medical care by asking who, specifically, is responsible for paying for the medical care of individual patients. Jewish tradition divides that responsibility among the physician, the patient, the patient's family, and the members of his or her community.

While historically doctors treated the indigent without payment, doctors (like other people) have a right to earn a living. Furthermore, Jewish law imposes the same limit on the percent of income they may donate to charity as it does on other Jews—namely, up to a fifth of their income (*MT* Hilkhot Matt'not Aniyyim 7:5 and *SA* Yoreh Dei·ah 248:1–2). Thus, while physicians should certainly contribute some of their time and effort to provide free medical care for those who cannot afford it, such efforts alone cannot possibly provide access to health care for all who need it.

Individuals must pay for as much of their own medical care as they can, just as they are primarily responsible for their own ransom: "If someone is taken captive," the text in the *Shulḥan Arukh* reads, "and he has property, but does not want to redeem himself, we redeem him [by selling his property and using the funds to do so even] against his will" (*SA* Yoreh Dei·ah 252:11).

Moreover, one must pay for one's own health care before one pays for anyone else's, for, as the Talmud teaches (at *BT* Bava M'tzi·a 62a in a passage based on Leviticus 25:36), saving one's own life takes precedence over saving anyone else's. And in addition to paying for his own health care, a man assumes an explicit obligation in marriage, according to Jewish law (as noted as early as *M* K'tubbot 4:9), to pay for the medical care of his wife—and in keeping with our modern, egalitarian principles, a woman would have a similar duty toward her husband. Similarly, both parents have a duty to provide for the care of their minor children, and even for the care of other relatives, as they do to redeem them from captivity (*SA* Yoreh Dei·ah 252:12). Conversely, as part of the duty to honor parents, Jewish law mandates that adult children provide for the health care of their elderly parents (see my comments below in this regard). True, they may use the parents' resources first (*BT* Kiddushin 31b–32a, *MT* Hilkhot Mamrim 6:7, and *SA* Yoreh Dei·ah 240:5), but when those funds run out, the children have to draw on their own resources to care for their parents, which approach, in any case, Jewish law prefers (see the *Kesef Mishneh* commentary to the *Mishneh Torah* passage cited just above). For further reading on this topic, see Gerald Blidstein, *Honor Thy Father and Mother* (New York: KTAV, 1975), pp. 60–75; and the fourth chapter, entitled "Parents and Children" of my book, *Love Your Neighbor and Yourself: A Jewish Approach to Modern Personal Ethics* (Philadelphia: The Jewish Publication Society, 2003).

The immediate implication of these teachings is that one may not preserve the family fortune and make the Jewish community or government pay for one's own health care or the health care of one's close relations. The exception to this rule occurs when the government itself makes provision for all sick people, regardless of their assets, through a program of socialized medicine, or for the care of clearly specified groups of citizens through programs like Medicare. Absent such provisions in the law, one must provide for one's own health care and for that of one's relatives with one's own assets or through the acquisition of an adequate health insurance policy, either privately or through one's employer.

If one cannot afford health care, then one not only may, but must, utilize public monies for this purpose through programs like Medicaid, and this obligation is taken so seriously that failing to do so is considered in some halakhic texts to be the equivalent of committing suicide. Still, the *Shulḥan Arukh* strongly condemns those who use public funds for their health care when they do not need to do so (at *SA* Yoreh Dei·ah 255:2), and that should surely be our approach today as well.

While the community has an ultimate duty to provide health care, it must be sure to use its resources wisely, for it must balance its commitment to offer health care with the obligation to provide other essential services. The Talmud (*BT* Sanhedrin 17b) lists ten such services:

> It has been taught: a scholar should not reside in a city where the following ten things are lacking: (1) a court of justice that can impose flagellation and

> monetary penalties, (2) a charity fund, collected by two people and distributed by three [to ensure honesty and that wise policies of distribution will be followed], (3) a synagogue, (4) a bath house, (5) a [public] privy, (6) a physician, (7) a surgeon, (8) a scribe [for writing official documents], (9) a butcher, and (10) a school teacher. Rabbi Akiva is quoted [as including] also several kinds of fruit [in the list] because eating them is deemed beneficial for one's eyesight.

The Talmud's list includes several items relevant to health care, including: public baths and toilet facilities, a "surgeon" to perform the most important form of curative care known at the time (namely, bloodletting), and, according to Rabbi Akiva, healthy foods—a recognition that our choice of food is an important way to sustain and protect health. In addition, other necessary services were provided at the time by the Roman government throughout the known world—such as the maintenance of a militia and a police force, and the construction of roads and bridges—and those too would undoubtedly be on the Talmud's list if that had not been so. Because no community's resources are limitless, the community must ensure that all public monies are spent wisely. (Readers may consult Rabbi Avram Reisner's translation and analysis of this same passage above in his chapter in this volume on medical ethics.)

Thus, if a person repeatedly endangers his or her health through practices known to constitute major risks, such as smoking, drug or alcohol abuse, or overeating, the community may decide to impose a limit on the public resources that such a person can call upon for curative or therapeutic procedures. This is akin to the limits set on the ransoming of individuals who constantly sell themselves into captivity (see the relevant texts at *SA* Yoreh Dei·ah 252:6). Individuals must take responsibility for the consequences of their unhealthful behavior, especially after being duly warned through educational programs or by the onset of early forms of potentially much more serious diseases.

Conversely, unless a given drug or medical procedure is so scarce that the government has put limits on who may obtain it, individual patients who have the money to afford something that the government or their private plan does not provide may decide to pay for the drug or procedure privately. Thus, while the *Shulḥan Arukh,* following earlier formulations of Jewish law, limits the amount of money a community may spend on redeeming any given captive in order to deter kidnapping altogether, individuals are nevertheless free to spend as much of their own funds as they wish to redeem themselves or their relatives: "We do not redeem captives for more than their worth out of considerations of fixing the world, so that the enemies will not dedicate themselves to take them captive. An individual, however, may redeem himself for as much as he would like" (*SA* Yoreh Dei·ah 252:4).

This is unfair in one sense, but it is only the unfairness built into any capitalistic system. It is certainly the case that Jewish sources do not require socialism as the basis of government or distributing goods. It is nevertheless an intolerable dereliction of society's moral duty for health care to be provided only to those well enough off to pay for it or to purchase insurance that will pay for it. Furthermore, leaving huge swaths of the population uninsured invariably means that at least some of those people will ultimately get health care in the most expensive way possible—namely, in the emergency rooms of hospitals, usually when they are sickest. Maintaining a system that provides health care begrudgingly and inadequately at the highest possible price is a dereliction of a nation's fiduciary responsibility to spend its communal resources wisely.

Redeeming Captives and the Hierarchy of Need

According to our classical sources, redeeming captives takes precedence over helping any other Jew in need, even the homeless and destitute, because those in captivity are deemed *ipso facto* to be in danger of sexual violation and, ultimately, of losing their lives:

> Redeeming captives takes precedence over sustaining the poor and clothing them, and there is no commandment more important than redeeming captives. Therefore, the community may change the usage of any money it has collected for communal needs for the sake of redeeming captives. . . . Every moment that one delays redeeming captives where it is possible to do so quickly is like shedding that person's blood (*SA* Yoreh Dei·ah 252:1, 3).

Unfortunately, because Jews regularly redeemed their captives, kidnappers saw them as a prime target. To deter future kidnapping, Jewish communities established limits on redemption prices. They nevertheless routinely went beyond those limits, if necessary, to redeem current captives despite the implications of such behavior for the future. The modern State of Israel has several times followed suit, freeing thousands of Palestinian prisoners over the years to redeem just a few Israeli captives.

If the community or family did not have enough money to redeem all of their members taken captive, Jewish law sets the following priorities: "We redeem a woman before a man. If, however, the captors are used to engaging in sodomy, we redeem a man before a woman" (*SA* Yoreh Dei·ah 252:8).

Whether or not one agrees with this assessment that sodomizing a man is worse than raping a woman, it is clear that this ruling constitutes an attempt to prioritize aid based on who is most threatened—and that, surely, is a principle we can accept as cogent and worthy of emulation. Furthermore, this hierarchy of need takes precedence over the hierarchy of social position and personal duty, as the *Shulḥan Arukh* makes clear: "If a man, his father, and his teacher are in captivity, the man takes precedence over his teacher (because saving one's own life comes first), and his teacher takes precedence over his father (because his father brought him into this world, but his teacher prepares him for the World to Come), but his mother takes precedence over all of them" (*SA* Yoreh Dei·ah 252:9).

Halakhic Obligations toward Incarcerated Individuals

Jewish sources from the Torah onward discuss imprisonment for the following reasons: (1) to ensure that a person suspected of a crime will appear for trial and will not interfere with the investigation in the meantime (e.g., at Leviticus 24:12 or Numbers 15:34, and in rabbinic sources at *M'khilta D'rabbi Ishma·el,* N'zikin 6, and *BT* K'tubbot 33b), but only if there was evidence that the suspect committed the offense (*Y* Sanhedrin 7:10, 25a); (2) to ensure that a person convicted of an offense that merits the death penalty or banishment cannot escape before the penalty is carried out; (3) to detain a person for political reasons (e.g., as at 1 Kings 22:27, 2 Chronicles 16:10, and Jeremiah 37:15–16 and 38:4–14); (4) to compel a person to obey an order of the court (as at Ezra 7:25–26); and (5) to punish an individual convicted of a crime (as at *M* Sanhedrin 9:5 and *T* Sanhedrin 12:7–8).

The last of these purposes, the use of imprisonment with which moderns are most familiar, was used in mishnaic times only when a person had three times committed an offense for which the Torah prescribes *kareit* (divine punishment) or when the court was convinced that a person had committed murder but was unable to convict him or her for some procedural reason. It was only later that prison was gradually introduced as a punishment for many more offenses, especially from the fourteenth century on. During the Middle Ages, some Jewish communities even had prisons of their own.

Although the Jews imitated non-Jews in their use of imprisonment as a common form of punishment, and although prison conditions for convicted criminals were worse than for those detained for other reasons (cf. *BT* Sanhedrin 81b), Jewish law required that even convicts be provided with food, clean quarters, and—wholly separate therefrom—sanitary facilities, and that they not be subjected to the kinds of cruelty common in prisons run by non-Jewish governments. Furthermore, since the medieval period, those unjustly imprisoned by the government were seen as captives, thus requiring that the Jewish community redeem them as quickly as possible. (For more detailed information on this topic, see Menaḥem Elon's essay, "Imprisonment," *Encyclopedia Judaica* 8:1299–1303.)

This implies that we, living in modern times, have the duty to do everything we can to ensure that trials are fair and that those justly imprisoned are treated reasonably. Moreover, especially because of the rampant Christian missionary work in America's prisons, we Jews must support Jewish chaplaincy services in the prisons. This is not only a task for rabbis, however; many imprisoned Jews are able to keep their spirits up, retain their Jewish identity, and find ways to avoid illegal activity once released as a result of the efforts of other Jews who take the time to write to them and visit them in prison.

One model for us all in this regard is the program initiated by Gateways Hospital in the 1950s in Los Angeles that culminated in the establishment of Beit T'shuvah, the first Jewish halfway house in the nation. There, Jews coming out of prison (or assigned to live there in lieu of going to prison) learn how to cope with their addictions and acquire the skills necessary for them successfully to avoid illegal activity in the future. Furthermore, they study Jewish texts and engage in Jewish prayer and holiday activities, so that they can see how Judaism and the Jewish community can be a source of support and meaning for them.

In enabling people to put their lives together so that they avoid recidivism, we are following the model of God. In the morning blessings and in the Amidah, God is described as *mattir asurim,* the divine source of freedom for the imprisoned. Furthermore, as Isaiah and the psalmist proclaimed, God is to be known as One who rescues people from prison, whether that be a physical prison or the metaphoric prison of their prejudices, emotions, addictions, or misconceptions. No words could possibly instill hope in the hearts of the incarcerated more than this oracle vouchsafed to the prophet Isaiah: "I, the Eternal, in My grace, have summoned you, and I have grasped you by the hand. I created you, and appointed you, a covenant people, a light of nations opening eyes deprived of light, rescuing prisoners from confinement, from the dungeon those who sit in darkness" (Isaiah 42:6–7; see also Psalms 68:7, 79:11, and 102:20–21).

Halakhic Obligations toward Jewish Refugees

Because Jews have historically been subjected to frequent expulsions, we are all too familiar with the need for help getting settled in a new community and with the reciprocal imperative to provide aid to others. Furthermore, as a corollary of the duty to redeem captives, Jews have a responsibility to rescue Jews from countries in which they are harshly treated. Both of these obligations were at work in the sustained efforts of the American and Israeli Jewish communities to rescue Soviet Jewry in the 1970s and 1980s and Ethiopian Jewry in the 1990s. In fact, the State of Israel, with its Law of Return, has been a refuge for millions of Jews.

In the late nineteenth and early twentieth centuries, when masses of Jews emigrated to North America to escape pogroms in Russia and Eastern Europe, extended family members and unrelated people who had lived in the same community in Europe often organized themselves into benevolent associations, called *landsmanshaften* in Yiddish, which provided the first helping hand to recently arrived immigrants—and sometimes long beyond that. My own grandparents, for example, let another family from their town in Russia live for free in their upstairs apartment in Milwaukee for years.

This historical experience goes back to the very beginnings of our people's history. The Torah commands that Israelites extend hospitality to the stranger, "for you yourselves were strangers in Egypt" (Leviticus 19:34). Travelers from foreign lands, though not protected by law (see Deuteronomy 15:3 and 23:21), could nevertheless count on the moral conscience of other Jews and the feeling of being part of the same people to guarantee their hospitality. Indeed, the Bible is replete with examples of hospitality (e.g., Genesis 18:1–8; 24:28–32; Judges 13:15; 2 Kings 4:8–11; and Job 31:32). Sometimes acts of hospitality were rewarded (as in Joshua 2, 2 Samuel 17:27–29, and 2 Samuel 19:32–40), and, conversely, failure to extend hospitality was often castigated (as at Judges 8:5–9) and even punished (as at Judges 19:22 and 20:17, and at 1 Samuel 25:2–38).

The rabbis extended this duty further, calling it *hakhnasat or'ḥim,* "bringing in guests." It was considered a great *mitzvah,* more important than prayer, an expression of *g'milut ḥasadim* (the bestowing of kindness), and the equivalent of receiving the divine presence into one's midst, thus affording a person benefit in this world and guaranteeing further rewards in the World to Come (see, e.g., *BT* Shabbat 127a–b). On the other hand, the rabbis of classical times condemned those who abused others' hospitality by becoming parasites (see, e.g., *BT* P'saḥim 86b and *Derekh Eretz Zuta* 8:9 [59a]), as did even earlier authors (cf., from a far earlier time, Ben Sira, also called Ecclesiasticus, 29:23–28 and 40:28–30). Starting in the Middle Ages and continuing into modern times, though, it was considered a special honor to house and support a rabbinical student (often by providing meals on days called colloquially *essen-teg* [eating days] by the Jews of Eastern Europe). For more information, see the article "Hospitality," *Encyclopedia Judaica* 8:1030–1033.

These historical and legal precedents indicate the scope of our obligations to Jewish refugees: we must seek to rescue Jews from places and conditions that threaten their lives and, once they arrive in a safe place, we must help them establish themselves with housing and training in language and job skills. This is both an individual and communal duty, for *kol yisra·el areivim zeh ba-zeh,* "all Jews are responsible for each other" (*BT* Shavuot 39a and *B'midbar Rabbah* 10:5). Therefore, Jewish communities must participate in funding the Hebrew Immigrant Aid Society (HIAS), as most Jewish federations do. They must also establish mechanisms to help Jewish refugees who come to their community to learn the local language, gain citizenship, and find food, clothing, housing, schools, and jobs, just as Jewish communities throughout the world cooperated in rescuing and relocating Soviet Jewry. In North America, this is often done through the local Jewish Family Service agency or Federation, to which Jews should also contribute time and/or money. Additionally, individuals should consider ways in which they personally can help Jewish refugees find safety, housing, and the means to earn a livelihood.

The Halakhah of Immigration and Emigration

Ample precedents in the Jewish tradition and in our historical experience make most American and Canadian Jews feel sympathetic to those who wish to become American or Canadian citizens now. After all, many grandparents or great-grandparents of American readers benefited from open immigration laws before 1923; conversely, many of our people died in the Holocaust because the United States and Canada closed their doors afterward. How can the citizens of Western democracies, then, advocate anything other than unlimited immigration? Our hearts still stir when we read or sing Emma Lazarus' poem affixed to the base of the Statue of Liberty, "Give me your tired, your poor, / Your huddled masses yearning to breathe free, / The wretched refuse of your teeming shore. / Send these, the homeless, tempest-tossed to me, / I lift my lamp beside the golden door!" For Americans, this sentiment in favor of immigration also grows from the undeniable fact that the United States, the greatest experiment in pluralism in history, has gained tremendously and continues to benefit from the economic and cultural contributions of immigrants from all over the world.

And yet the harsh reality is that if any Western country were to adopt a policy of open immigration, it would soon become overwhelmed with people seeking to flee conditions of hunger and illness. For all its riches, there is a limit to the number of people the United States can accommodate—and this would still be the case even if Americans were to stretch themselves to the extent that Israel has done. Furthermore, although the bombing of the federal building in Oklahoma City in April 1995 was perpetrated by Americans, the attacks by al-Qaeda terrorists on the World Trade Center and the Pentagon on September 11, 2001, and the subsequent concerns about other acts of terrorism in the United States, have raised real concerns about admitting immigrants who might attack the country from within. Jewish law shares these concerns, for it mandates that we defend ourselves (*BT* Sanhedrin 72a) and that, in conditions of scarce resources, "your own life comes first" (*BT* Bava M'tzi·a 62a).

Therefore, Jewish historical experience and legal principles would dictate that we support a policy very much like the ones the United States and Canada currently have, permitting limited, screened immigration for most people and emergency immigration for refugees from political oppression. Once here, Jewish law would also mandate that we work to help new immigrants learn the local language and find housing and jobs, for the Talmud requires that we help the non-Jewish poor or disadvantaged as well as the Jewish poor (*BT* Gittin 61a).

Orphans and the Ethics of Adoption

When a couple cannot have biological children, adoption is an available option. In Jewish law, one's personal status is a function of one's biological parents, and there is no institution of adoption that would change that. Jewish law does, however, provide for guardianship of minors whose parents cannot take care of them, and the duties of the guardian are very much like those of modern-day adoptive parents. As in most modern legal systems, the welfare of the child is the chief concern in Jewish law, and the court, "the father of all orphans" (*BT* Bava Kamma 37a and Gittin 37a), is responsible for seeing that children are treated well—even to the point of removing a child from the home of his or her natural parents. Moreover, the Jewish tradition highly praises adults who raise minors who are not their biological children, for they "do right at all times." One midrashic text finds the root of this notion in a verse from the Psalms:

> "Happy are they who act justly, who do right at all times" (Psalm 106:3). Is it possible to do right at all times? . . . Rabbi Samuel bar Naḥmani said, "This refers to a person who brings up an orphan boy or girl in his or her house and who [ultimately] enables that orphan to marry" (*Esther Rabbah* 6:1).

Furthermore, along with all others who teach children Torah, adoptive parents are to be seen as if they had given birth to them (*BT* M'gillah 13a and Sanhedrin 19b). It is for this reason that such children may be called by their adoptive parents' names in legal documents and may be called to the Torah as "son (or daughter) of the adoptive parents" (*BT* Sanhedrin 19b, based on 2 Samuel 21:8).

While Roman and American law sever all previous relationships between the biological parent and the adopted child (to the point that, until recent changes, the parties to the adoption were to remain anonymous to each other forever), and while English common law, on the other end of the spectrum, makes the adopting parent no more than a temporary guardian, Jewish law takes an intermediate position. The personal status of the child in matters of Jewish identity, priestly status, and the definition of incest, on the one hand, depends solely upon the status of the child's biological parents. On the other hand, however, Jewish law takes seriously the guardianship of adoptive parents, imposing upon the children involved the filial duties of honor and respect and permitting those children to be known as the children of the adoptive parents. Furthermore, the adopting guardians have the same obligations toward their children as do biological parents. They must be responsible for their children's upbringing, education, and physical accommodations, and they must administer their children's property. If the guardian dies, his or her estate is responsible to provide for their children's care. The demands of guardianship in Jewish law are so strong that they were once invoked in a New York case to extend the obligations of the adoptive father beyond the demands of civil law. (Interested readers may consult *Wener v. Wener* 59 Misc. 2d 959, 301 N.Y. Supp. 2d 237 [Sup. Ct. 1969]; and cf. the appeal, 35 App. Div. 2d 50, 312 N.Y. Supp. 2d 815 [2d Dept. 1970], where the judgment was affirmed but not on its religious grounds.) Similarly, according to Rabbi Moses Sofer (*Responsa,* vol. 1, Oraḥ Ḥayyim 164, ed. Bratislava, 1912, pp. 63a–b), adopted children do not incur the obligations of mourning upon the death of their biological parents, but they do have such obligations when their adoptive parents die. (For a concise compendium of these and other rules concerning adoption, together with the sources for some of the laws mentioned above, see the following articles in the *Encyclopedia Judaica:* "Adoption," 2:298–303; "Apotropos," 3:218–222; and "Orphan," 12:1478–1480.)

In appreciation of the immensely significant role that adoptive parents have in their children's upbringing, and in recognition of the close bonds that adopted siblings create with each other, the Conservative rabbinate, based on my responsum that was approved by the CJLS in March 1994, considers adopted children to have the status of relatives of the second degree (*sh'niyyot*), and therefore sex or marriage between them is prohibited. (See "Artificial Insemination, Egg Donation, and Adoption," in *CJLS Responsa 1991–2000,* pp. 461–509, and reprinted in a slightly different form in my book *Matters of Life and Death,* pp. 37–107.)

Many infertile Jewish couples cannot find Jewish children to adopt because of the high rate of abortion among Jews. This argues for two things. First, Jews should understand that although Jewish law requires abortion when the life or physical or mental health of the mother is at stake and permits it when there is a risk to the mother's life or health above that of normal pregnancy, by and large Jewish tradition prohibits abortion in most situations. Parents should know that even if they cannot or will not care for a child, an abundance of infertile Jewish couples would do so willingly and lovingly, and that makes non-therapeutic abortions even less justifiable. (The topic of abortion itself is discussed above by Rabbi Avram Reisner in his chapter on medical ethics.)

Second, Jewish couples contemplating adoption should consider non-Jewish children, including those of any race. If the birth mother was not Jewish, conversion will be necessary, but in the case of children that is an easy process. Couples might also consider children older than infancy or those with some disability; they, after all, are also God's children, and many more of them are available for adoption. Indeed, Jews with biological children of their own should also consider adopting children into their families as an act of lovingkindness, *ḥesed,* of the first order.

At the same time, couples need to be aware of some of the special legal and psychological issues that may arise in adoption. I discuss them at some length in *Matters of Life and Death* (pp. 107–111, and see also pp. 81–97). None of these concerns, however, should prevent people from adopting children. Moreover, Jews should seriously consider serving as a Jewish Big Brother or Big Sister to children who have only one parent or finding other ways to become involved in the lives of children who need additional adult role models.

Matters relating to the adoption of children are discussed elsewhere in this volume by Rabbi David J. Fine in his chapter on husbands and wives.

Caring for Our Parents and the Elderly

The Torah's command, "Rise before the aged, and show deference to the old" (Leviticus 19:32), bespeaks the Torah's insistence that we treat the elderly with respect. Even though the rabbis of classical times later interpreted "old" in that verse to refer to those who are wise and learned, not simply those who are chronologically old, they interpreted "aged" in that same verse to require standing before anyone (save the truly wicked) who is seventy years old or older (*SA* Yoreh Dei·ah 244:1).

Naturally enough, special duties apply to the elderly who are closest to us—namely, our parents. Jews and others often construe the command to honor parents, the fifth of the Ten Commandments, as chiefly addressed to young children, but this is only part of the story. Indeed, while young children should certainly be taught to honor their parents, they are not really legally responsible to do so until reaching the age of bar or bat mitzvah. Thus the rabbis understood the commandment primarily as governing the interactions between adult children and their elderly parents. That makes the commandment even more critical for modern Jews than it was for our ancestors since, with many people living into their eighties, nineties, and even past one hundred, and with families commonly scattered throughout the country or even the world, adult Jews need clear and wise guidance about what they need to do for their aging parents and how to fulfill these obligations. This becomes especially urgent for couples who find themselves balancing these duties with parallel sets of obligations to their children, to each other as spouses, to their jobs, and to their own welfare.

In addition to the Torah's command to *honor* our parents found at Exodus 20:12 and again at Deuteronomy 5:16, we are also commanded to *revere* them at Leviticus 19:3. While both demands require that we take deferential attitudes toward our parents, the Talmud, as is its common practice, translates the general concept into a specific set of requisite actions: "Our rabbis taught: What is reverence (*mora*) and what is honor (*kavod*)? 'Reverence' means that a son must neither stand in his father's place, nor sit in his place, nor contradict his words, nor tip the scales against him [i.e., in an argument with others]. 'Honor' means that he must give him food and drink, clothe and cover him, and lead him in and out" (*BT* Kiddushin 31b, and see *MT* Hilkhot Mamrim 6:3 and *SA* Yoreh Dei·ah 240:2 and 240:4, and 228:11). Surely in our day, the gendered language of the original source should not be imagined to suggest that the honor and reverence due mothers should be any less; indeed, the Torah itself includes mothers in the original verses requiring honor and reverence toward parents.

Another rabbinic passage on the same page of Talmud requires that, as an act of reverence, one ought not address parents by their first names but rather call them "My father [or: my mother], my teacher." In these talmudic specifications of the biblical commands, reverence involves refraining from certain activities, while honor is paid by fulfilling certain positive obligations. Both apply throughout one's life. Jewish law requires both reverence and honor by daughters and sons for both their mothers and their fathers. (The key rabbinic texts are *M* Kiddushin 1:7, *BT* Kiddushin 29a, 30b, and 31a, *MT* Hilkhot Mamrim 6:6 and 6:14, and *SA* Yoreh Dei·ah 240:14 and 240:17.)

Why should we honor and respect our parents? And should we suppose this must necessarily extend to the parallel obligation to honor elderly people in general? Honor of parents is warranted, of course, as an act of gratitude for their role in our creation and upbringing, as the Talmud teaches at *BT* Niddah 31a. But the rabbis of ancient times understood the point of honoring parents and other elderly people in a more theological way as well: honoring such people prepares the child's psyche for the experience of honoring God. Thus the verse requiring us to stand before the elderly (Leviticus 19:32) ends with "And you shall fear [respect] your God; I am the Eternal," indicating that God is especially involved in this commandment. By respecting and honoring our parents, we also honor God.

A key midrashic text reads as follows: "Rabbi [Judah the Patriarch] says that showing honor to one's father and one's mother is very dear in the sight of the One by whose word the world came into being, for God declared honoring them to be equal to honoring God, revering them to revering God, and cursing them to cursing God" (*M'khilta D'rabbi Ishma·el,* Ba-ḥodesh 8, on Exodus 20:12 and *BT* Kiddushin 30b). Indeed, according to one ancient source, God insists on showing honor to one's parents even more than on showing honor to God (*Y* Pei·ah 1:1, 15d).

Talmudic and medieval literature maintain that the requirements to honor and respect parents also apply (albeit to a lesser degree) to mothers-in-law and fathers-in-law, one's grandparents, and even to one's older brothers, as codified at *MT* Hilkhot Mamrim 6:15 and at *SA* Yoreh Dei·ah 240:22–24 (with the glosses of the Rema taken into account) and 374:6. Presumably, then, they would apply even less to unrelated elderly people. Still, the duties and attitudes that the Talmud requires toward parents shape the ways we are expected to relate to all aged people, as the Torah's command to stand in respect of them makes clear. Laws governing the parent-child relationship are treated in detail elsewhere in this volume in a chapter by Rabbi Daniel S. Nevins, as are those regarding the halakhic dimension of the relationship of grandparents and grandchildren by Rabbi Gerald C. Skolnik.

Abusing Elderly Parents

Physical or verbal abuse of elderly or infirm parents is, unfortunately, a growing phenomenon in our society, especially as people live longer and suffer from the mental and physical disabilities of old age. Jewish tradition has no tolerance for abuse of parents. Minimal respect of parents requires that we do not demean them, and it goes without saying that the Torah forbids harming them outright.

Parents, of course, are protected under the general provisions of Jewish law prohibiting assault and requiring monetary restitution from those who injure others (*M* Bava Kamma 8:1). But parents are in a special category, and the penalty for assaulting them is much harsher: "One who strikes a father or mother shall surely be put to death," the Torah says at Exodus 21:15. The Torah goes further still when it declares that "one who curses his father or mother shall surely be put to death" (Exodus 21:17), and, more generally, that one "who dishonors his father or his mother" be cursed (Deuteronomy 27:16).

Not all parents, of course, are model human beings or paradigms of caring parenting. Some are neglectful, others are nasty, and some are even abusive. According to some Jewish sources (e.g., Rashi on *BT* Kiddushin 32a; cf. Rabbi Abraham Danzig's *Ḥayyei Adam* 67:1), one is required to love them nevertheless, either as a corollary of honoring them or as an instantiation of the command to "love your neighbor as yourself" at Leviticus 19:18. Maimonides (in a letter printed in the edition of his responsa edited by J. Blau as responsum no. 448 (Jerusalem: Mekitzei: Nirdamim, 1957–1961, vol. 2, p. 728), however, does not require love toward one's parents, for "it is possible for a person to honor and revere and obey those whom one does not love." Moreover, one may certainly disagree with one's parents, although not in a way that publicly shames them, as per the rabbinic definition of "respect" cited above.

When parents have abused their children or violated the law, a number of Ashkenazic sources assert that the Torah's commands to honor them and to respect them no longer apply. These include Rashi (in his comment to *BT* Sanhedrin 47a, *s.v. al,* and *BT* B'rakhot 10b, *s.v. gireir atzmot aviv*), the Tosafot (in their comment to *BT* Y'vamot 22b, *s.v. k'she-asah*), Rabbeinu Tam (as cited in the *Sefer Mord'khai* to *BT* Y'vamot, sect. 13), and the Rema (in his gloss to *SA* Yoreh Dei·ah 240:18). Sephardic sources, however, generally assert that the commands to honor and respect parents continue even in the face of abuse or other illegality. This is true for Rabbi Isaac Alfasi (in his redaction of *BT* Y'vamot 22b), Maimonides (at *MT* Hilkhot Mamrim 5:12, but also see 6:11), and Rabbi Joseph Karo (at *SA* Yoreh Dei·ah 240:18). As I have written in a responsum for the Committee on Jewish Law and Standards, the filial duties of honor and respect for parents do not give parents a right to abuse their children, and adults witnessing such abuse must help children extricate themselves from it, for saving a life takes precedence over honor and respect for parents. (See Elliot N. Dorff, "Family Violence," in *CJLS Responsa 1991–2000,* pp. 773–816 and reprinted in slightly different form as the fifth chapter of my book, *Love Your Neighbor and Yourself*). Although I did not include this conclusion in that responsum, it seems to me that parents lose their right to honor and respect if they abuse their children—that is, I side with the Ashkenazic authorities on this issue.

This dispute affects not only the question of whether one must provide for formerly abusive parents, but also, if one must, how precisely one should do so. Ideally, the children should tend to their parents' needs themselves, for, as the rabbis of old note (at *Sh'mot Rabbah* 34:3; see also *BT* K'tubbot 103a), part of the honor of parents comes from their child's personal willingness to care for them. When the relationship between parents and children makes that emotionally impossible, however, children may use the services of others to fulfill their filial obligations (see sources cited in Gerald Blidstein, *Honor Thy Father and Thy Mother,* p. 115). For that matter, even when the relationships between parents and children are good, people may choose to use nursing homes and similar facilities when that arrangement proves to be best for all concerned. In those cases, however, children must still visit their parents as often as possible, at the very least staying in telephone contact if face-to-face visits are not feasible due to distance or other factors. The need we all have for family ties does not diminish in old age; if anything, it may grow even stronger as we cope with illness and the prospect of our ultimate demise. The sages' insistence on providing personal care is thus as important today as it was in the past.

Although some authorities suspend the commandments to honor and respect parents when they have been abusive and although others would permit delegating care of one's parents to others, beating parents and other elderly people is another matter entirely. The former approach is either an exemption from normal duties or permission to perform them in less than the optimal way, whereas behaving violently violates a host of explicit interdictions. One may not assault the elderly just as one may not assault anyone; indeed, the duties to honor the aged would make assaulting them all the more heinous. As for one's parents, the specific prohibitions of the Torah against parental abuse—carrying, as they do, the ultimate penalty of execution—constitute Judaism's unequivocal condemnation of violence directed against one's parents. Other issues relating to difficult parents are discussed elsewhere in this volume by Rabbi Daniel Nevins.

The Burial of Indigents

It is of paramount importance in Jewish law that everyone receive a proper burial. The duty of burial first devolves upon relatives of the deceased (e.g., at Genesis 23 and 25:9; cf. *BT* K'tubbot 48a), but if no relatives can be found, or if they are unable to afford the burial costs, then the community itself must assume the duty. Furthermore, the Talmud (at *BT* Mo·eid Katan 27b) records that, already in its time, there were communal burial societies to carry out that responsibility, a custom that has persisted to this day. (The talmudic text refers simply to a *ḥavurta*, a "society," and the modern name, *ḥevra kaddisha*, literally "a holy society," is merely a refinement of that usage.) Many Conservative synagogues have established such groups, and some communal institutions have as well. (Readers interested in learning how such a project was accomplished with great success in a Conservative synagogue may consult Arnold Goodman's *A Plain Pine Box: A Return to Simple Jewish Funerals and Eternal Traditions* [New York: KTAV, 1981].) The Hebrew Free Burial Society in New York has buried over 60,000 indigent Jewish individuals since it was founded in 1888. On the West Coast, the Jewish Family Service of Los Angeles (JFS-LA), founded in 1854, seven years before the city of Los Angeles was incorporated, began as a communal fund to bury the indigent, and to this day some fifty people are buried each year through its free burial program. The Talmud even requires that, for purposes of maintaining good relations with non-Jews, we bury non-Jews in need of burial as well as Jews (*BT* Gittin 61a, where the text is speaking explicitly about the poor), but only when non-Jews have not fulfilled that duty and only in non-Jewish cemeteries.

One important feature of the JFS-LA program should be noted. Each year, three or four people ask JFS-LA for funds to be cremated instead of buried. Jewish law, however, states that Jews must be buried and not cremated, and that even the expressed will of the deceased to be cremated must be overruled by the scriptural injunction requiring burial (see, e.g., *MT* Hilkhot Eivel 12:1). Thus the Board of Directors of JFS-LA has determined that it will support only burials of Jews in Jewish cemeteries and that no other means of disposing of bodies will be funded. This too is in keeping with the Jewish tradition that forbids us to help others to violate Jewish law, for assisting people to break with tradition would be a clear example of what Scripture calls "putting a stumbling block before the blind" (Leviticus 19:14; see *BT* P'saḥim 22b, Mo·eid Katan 17a, Kiddushin 32a, and Bava M'tzi·a 75b). Furthermore, our sages were clear that "it is forbidden to aid those who commit a sin" (*she-asur l'sayyei·a y'dei ov'rei aveirah*, *BT* Avodah Zarah 55b).

Aspiring to Be Like God in Caring for Others

There are many reasons to care for others: to create a *quid pro quo* reason for others to care for us when we need help, to express our own humanitarian feelings by helping fellow human beings, to contribute to establishing a society in which people care for each other, to live by the commandments of God, to do for others what we expect and hope others would do for us, etc. All of these have echoes in various Jewish texts. (For a more thorough discussion of these motivations to care for others, see my books *To Do the Right and the Good: A Jewish Approach to Modern Social Ethics,* ch. 6, and *The Way into Tikkun Olam (Fixing the World)* [Woodstock, VT: Jewish Lights Publishing, 2005], ch. 2.) Perhaps the ultimate reason to care for others, however, is that we aspire to be like God to the greatest extent that human beings can be godly. Thus it is fitting that I end this essay with the following text taken from *BT* Sotah 14a:

> "Follow the Eternal your God" (Deuteronomy 13:5). What does this mean? Is it possible for a mortal [physically] to follow God's presence? The verse means to teach us that we should follow the *attributes* of the blessed Holy One. As God clothed the naked, you should clothe the naked. As the blessed Holy One visited the sick, you should visit the sick. As the blessed Holy One comforted mourners, so should you too comfort mourners. As the blessed Holy One buried the dead, you too should bury the dead.
>
> Rabbi Simlai taught: the Torah begins with deeds of lovingkindness and ends with deeds of lovingkindness. It begins with deeds of lovingkindness, as it is written, "And so did the Eternal God make garments of skins for Adam and for his wife and clothed them" (Genesis 3:21). It ends with deeds of lovingkindness, as it is written, "And God buried him [Moses] in the valley in the land of Moab" (Deuteronomy 34:6).

Individuals with Disabilities

EDWARD M. FRIEDMAN*

If we live long enough, most of us will eventually acquire some sort of physical or mental disability. Some of us will already have acquired these disabilities at birth or early in life and others will only acquire them much later, but it is the rare individual who will go through life without any disability at all. That being the case, it becomes essential to bear in mind that people with disabilities are not some group of "others" out there waiting for us to consider their plight. Indeed, we need to approach the topic with the understanding that each of us has the potential to become part of this group at any point in our lives, and that we therefore need to learn how to treat people with disabilities as we would wish to be treated ourselves if and when we develop a

*The author wishes to thank his wife, Janice Wald Friedman, and friends, Catherine Ludlum and Stephen Mendelsohn, all disability rights advocates, for making many important suggestions regarding this chapter.

disability. This is part of the *mitzvah* of *ve'ahavta l'rei·akha kamokha,* loving your neighbor as yourself (Leviticus 19:18).

Increasingly, we are coming to understand that people with disabilities are not looking for sympathy or special treatment, but simply seek to live their lives fully and with dignity, without artificial or unnecessary barriers or obstacles to their full participation in society. Modern technology and new ways of providing support to those with disabilities have allowed more people, even those with relatively severe disabilities, to live independently, to earn college degrees, to enter professions, to run their own businesses, to raise children, to care for their elderly parents, to manage their own support systems, to travel freely, and to participate in sports activities, cultural events, and religious services.

As the physical barriers to full participation in modern life gradually come down, attitudinal resistance unfortunately often remains in place. We are frequently afraid of people with disabilities or uncertain about how to relate to them. We tend to treat them as if they were not present or to relate to them either as if they were children or, when they demonstrate their abilities to function capably in the world, as super-achievers worthy only of awe. Neither of these approaches is reasonable. People with disabilities are people first and foremost and possess the same strengths and weaknesses, the same wisdom and foolishness, and the same good and bad qualities as the rest of us. Indeed, they *are* the rest of us. Learning how to treat those with disabilities as people without glossing over those disabilities is not always simple, but it is eminently doable. When we relate to people with disabilities as people first we come to know more about their capabilities, we learn what we may expect of them, and we discover how they may play a more active role in society. While past generations tended to exempt people with disabilities from many halakhic responsibilities, we are realizing that many of these individuals are actually seeking greater, not lesser, involvement in Jewish life. Wherever we can remove attitudinal and physical barriers, we should do so, of course. But we may not stop there and, in the end, it is incumbent upon us to find ways to remove halakhic obstacles to full participation in Jewish ritual life as well.

Beyond this, it is important that we strive to break down the physical and social barriers that often exclude people with disabilities from participating in Shabbat and festival celebrations, and in social events that take place in the synagogue and in the community. At Deuteronomy 16:11, the Torah teaches us to include the Levite, the stranger, the orphan, and the widow in our festival celebrations. As regards the stranger (or the estranged, as the text could also be translated), the teachings of Torah ordain that we not forget people with disabilities when making up our guest lists for the Passover *seder* or for other festival meals. It is contrary to the spirit of the *halakhah* to build a *sukkah,* particularly a communal one, that is not accessible to people with disabilities. It is important to remember people with disabilities on Shabbat and holidays and to include them among our guests at the table. Simple acts of *g'milut ḥesed,* lovingkindness, are appreciated by all people, most certainly including people with disabilities. It is important to greet people, to speak to them, to include them in conversations, and to solicit their opinions. In short, it is essential to make persons with disabilities feel wholly welcome in our communities.

The Halakhah of Access

Our sages were uncertain whether the first biblical verse that comes to mind in relation to people with disabilities, "You shall neither insult the deaf nor place a stumbling block before the blind" (Leviticus 19:14), should only be understood metaphorically or whether it should also be applied literally. The traditional commentaries take the prohibition of insulting the deaf to mean that one may not insult any person, *even* a deaf person who will obviously not hear the insult. (Some rely on the etymology of the Hebrew *t'kalleil,* translated here as "insult," to assert that what is being forbidden is not solely insulting or cursing, but even treating another lightly or inconsequentially.) Likewise, the prohibition on placing a stumbling block before the blind is taken figuratively to mean not performing any act that could cause someone who is "blind" to that matter to transgress. For example, one may not place non-kosher food before Jewish people and then feel blameless should they choose to eat it merely because one did not actually force them to eat anything at all; merely providing the opportunity for wrong-doing is improper.

Even though the law codes seem to ignore the obvious in discussing this passage, the Talmud reminds us that the basic meaning of a verse is never legitimately ignored (*BT* Shabbat 63a). Indeed, the metaphorical interpretations of this verse are reasonable only because the fundamental laws requiring removing barriers from people's paths and treating others with compassion are already taught elsewhere. Their reiteration in connection to this passage in Leviticus regarding people with disabilities should, therefore, remind us of the specific obligation we all have to treat people with disabilities as we would others, and to be concerned for the removal of both physical and metaphorical barriers from their paths.

Whether or not mandated by law (in the United States, for example, the federal government specifically exempts religious institutions from having to comply with the section of the Americans with Disabilities Act that mandates that public buildings be accessible to people with disabilities), Jewish congregations should feel obligated, both legally and morally, to go beyond the requirements of civil law. We should work toward removing all physical barriers that prevent people from entering our buildings and sanctuaries, or from using our classrooms, restrooms, social halls, or *mikva·ot,* or from ascending to the *bimah.* We should seek ways as well to allow blind or deaf people to participate fully in synagogue activities. Listening devices for people with hearing impairment should be provided as a matter of course, as should interpretation in American Sign Language for people who are deaf; large-print books should be provided for those with visual impairment, and Braille volumes for blind people. Nor should we wait to be asked to provide such services or aids. Indeed, making people who may have disabilities feel truly welcome requires making such services available even before they are needed.

So far, I have discussed issues relating mainly to individuals who have physical disabilities. As we move toward a world with no physical barriers, however, we need to work to educate members of our communities to change their attitudes toward people with emotional and mental disabilities also. To facilitate the changing of attitudes, it may be helpful to introduce appropriate educational programming in our religious schools and in our adult education courses, and to utilize the services of a diversity training specialist or a disability rights advocate to assist us in implementing appropriate programming for those with mental or emotional disabilities among us.

Providing access, however, is only a first step. Jewish law speaks of the importance of *k'vod ha-b'riyyot,* the dignity of all God's creatures. Therefore, when we provide access, it should be in ways that preserve the dignity of the individuals gaining access to our institutions. This cannot be done if such people are relegated to service entrances and back alleys to enter our buildings, or are obliged to call attention to their disabilities in a dramatic, public manner, or to make special arrangements in advance to gain access to our facilities. The great goal of imbuing our institutions with *k'vod ha-b'riyyot* requires that we avoid labeling people with psychiatric disabilities in derisive, negative ways, or imposing unwanted medical treatment upon them unless they have been found incompetent or unless they pose a real danger to themselves or to others. Regardless of a person's disability, we should approach all people with compassion and respect for the divine image within them, and we must act toward them as we would wish others to act toward us.

The Traditional Exemption of Blind or Deaf People from Certain Commandments

It seems obvious that blind people should be exempt from *mitzvot* that require that something be seen and that deaf people should be exempt from those *mitzvot* that require that something be heard. Indeed, the traditional *halakhah* provides just such exemptions by decreeing that one should never be penalized for one's disability. However, some early authorities go beyond the obvious exemptions and suggest that blind people should be exempt from virtually all *mitzvot* and that deaf people should be totally exempt. (Regarding blind people, see the remark attributed to Rabbi Judah that the "blind are exempt from the commandments," preserved at *BT* Kiddushin 31a. Regarding the deaf, see *M* Rosh Ha-shanah 3:8.) Most of these sages meant to exempt blind and deaf people from the positive commandments of the Torah only, but still required them to observe the negative commandments. However, there are a few authorities who extend the exemption to negative commandments as well. While these exemptions may be imagined to have at their core the noble desire to remove the burden of guilt from those unable to perform one or another commandment due to disability, not every person with a disability would wish to be let off the hook so easily. Some people with disabilities would like to take on the full obligations of Torah observance, even if they must find alternative ways of fulfilling some commandments. The question, therefore, is not whether the legal mechanism exists to exempt deaf and blind people from the commandments, but whether the moral will exists to find ways *not* to have to exempt them from the norms of regular Jewish observance.

Already in talmudic times, we find the blind sage Rabbi Joseph anxious to participate fully in Jewish life regardless of the fact that blind people, even in his day, were theoretically exempt from certain *mitzvot* (*BT* Kiddushin 31a). Indeed, he expresses the hope that, even though exempt, he receive an even greater reward for following these precepts than those who were actually obligated. Most authorities now consider blind people to be fully obligated by most *mitzvot,* including some that one would normally associate with vision, such as lighting candles at the beginning of Shabbat or festivals and at Havdalah, or wearing *tzitzit* on the corners of one's garment (a commandment Scripture specifically anchors in the subsequent experience of "seeing the fringes" dangling from one's clothing). Unfortunately, these authorities, even when they obligate blind people to perform *mitzvot,* do not generally recognize that blind people may "see" with their hands and thus fully experience the *mitzvah*. Rather, they justify requiring the blind person's performance of the *mitzvah* of *tzitzit,* for example, by explaining that, even if the blind person does not see the fringes, others will see it. Likewise, we are told that blind people may say the blessing for the creation of light, *yotzeir or,* that precedes the morning recitation of the Sh'ma not because they personally benefit from the existence of light, but because others use light to guide the blind or to avoid running into them. We should acknowledge that the blind person, albeit in a different way from the sighted person, personally benefits from the performance of these *mitzvot.*

Generally speaking, deaf people who are able to speak are obliged to observe all the *mitzvot,* as are people who can hear but not speak. The halakhic status of the deaf person who cannot communicate orally has gradually been elevated as methods of communication with deaf people, and the education of deaf people in general, have improved. Initially, because people who were deaf almost never acquired any verbal communication skills, they were assumed to be mentally incompetent. In our day, however, many authorities, such as Rabbi Shalom Mordecai Schwadron in his responsa (New York: E. Grossman, 1967; part II, sect. 140, p. 107) and Rabbi Gedaliah Felder in his book *Naḥalat Tzvi* (Toronto: Felder, 1978; part I, p. 61), now agree that a deaf person with whom communication has been established and who is educable takes on the same obligations as those without such disabilities with respect to all commandments that do not actually require hearing. Some authorities, however, including such relatively recent figures as Rabbi Ḥayyim Medini, the author of *S'deih Ḥemed,* and Rabbi Ezekiel Ḥafeitz, who wrote *M'lekhet Ḥarash,* insist on taking a strict constructionist position and exempt all deaf people who cannot communicate orally, rather than by taking their actual abilities into account. And there are also some like Rabbi Joseph Teomim (1727–1792), the author of *P'ri M'gadim,* who hold this latter view, but only for a person born without hearing or speech, and not for those who lose hearing or speech later in life. Since losing hearing and speech obviously do not render a previously competent person mentally incompetent, such people would then be expected to continue to perform all the *mitzvot* to the extent to which they are capable.

Deaf people are, however, exempt from *mitzvot* that require an individual to hear a particular sound, such as hearing the sound of the *shofar.* The rule that one who is not obligated to perform a *mitzvah* may not fulfill it for another would seem to prevent a deaf person from coming forward to blow the *shofar,* though this would be an obstacle neither for a person who is hearing impaired and still has some residual hearing nor for a person who can hear but not speak. One might ask: may deaf people who can feel the vibrations of the *shofar* blasts fulfill the obligation of "hearing" in that way, or can hearing only be accomplished through one's ears? Can a deaf composer write music and perform it for others? Beethoven could! If someone can experience the sounding of the *shofar,* one might reasonably argue that he or she should be permitted to convey that experience to others in the congregation as well.

The Enfranchisement and Disenfranchisement of People with Disabilities in the Synagogue

According to Rabbi Joseph Karo (*SA* Oraḥ Ḥayyim 55:8), deaf people who can speak, and those who can hear but not speak, are both presupposed to have all their faculties and thus may be counted in a *minyan,* the quorum for prayer—although this inclusive policy does not extend to those who can neither hear nor speak. However, Rabbi David Halevi, the author of the *Turei Zahav* commentary to the *Shulḥan Arukh,* rules that one may not count a deaf person in the *minyan* because such a person would not know when to offer the traditional "amen" to blessings during the service. Many other commentators agree with the law as stated in the *Shulḥan Arukh,* however, and simply suppose that a deaf person can know when to say "amen" by observing others. Rabbi Shneur Zalman of Liadi (1745–1812), writing in the *Shulḥan Arukh Ha-rav* (Oraḥ Ḥayyim 55:11), for example, rules that as long as the majority of the people in a *minyan* can hear and only a minority are deaf, we may count the deaf people as part of the *minyan* even if they do not know when to say "amen." However, he adds that if there are not nine hearing people, the reader should not repeat the Amidah aloud. Rabbi Yosef Ḥayyim of Baghdad (in his *Ben Ish Ḥai,* first year, Va-y'ḥi 6) and Rabbi Yeḥiel Mikhel Epstein (in the *Arukh Ha-shulḥan,* Oraḥ Ḥayyim 124:9), concur with this decision.

As noted, people who can neither hear nor speak have traditionally been supposed to be mentally incompetent, and it has followed logically from that supposition that such people should not be counted in a *minyan.* In more recent times, as the initial supposition has been proven categorically untrue, authorities such as Rabbi Ovadiah Yosef (in his *Y'ḥavveh Da·at,* vol. 2, responsum 6, ed. Jerusalem, 1978, pp. 29–31) have ruled that one may reasonably include people who can neither hear nor speak in a *minyan.* And they surely may thus also receive non-speaking synagogue honors like opening the Ark, or raising or wrapping the Torah scroll.

The status of people with psychiatric disabilities must be determined on an individual basis and may fluctuate over time, according to the condition of the individual's mental health. Earlier attempts halakhically to define such individuals as a class were inconclusive. The Talmud (at *BT* Ḥagigah 3b), for example, gives a list of various signs of a *shoteh,* a mentally disabled person, such as spending the night in cemeteries or compulsively ripping one's clothing. Even there, however, there is some question as to whether one must exhibit all the bizarre behaviors listed to be considered a *shoteh,* or if any one of these is sufficient evidence of mental disability. Maimonides indicates that the list in the Talmud is simply to provide us with a few examples, not a complete list of requirements. And, to prove his point, he notes other types of behavior, not listed in the talmudic passage, that he feels are equally indicative of psychiatric disability (*MT* Hilkhot Eidut 9:9). Rabbi Karo adds that people whose intelligence is limited to the point that they neither understand what is said to them nor comprehend the difference between two conflicting ideas are also to be classified in the *shoteh* category. In modern times, however, halakhic authorities have come to terms with the difficulties of diagnosing mental illness. Rabbi Abraham Isaac Kook, for instance, wrote more than seventy years ago (*Ezrat Kohein,* responsum 68, ed. Jerusalem, 1969, pp. 278–282) that expert professional advice is needed before anyone may be absolved from the obligation to perform the *mitzvot* on the basis of mental disability. Today, the assumption should always be that a person is competent and responsible, unless it is plainly obvious that the case is otherwise. Also, people without psychiatric training should always avoid applying psychiatric labels to others; we should always make every effort to include all Jews in the performance of *mitzvot.* Exemptions from obligation based on mental disability should be granted only when absolutely necessary.

The Impact of Disability on the Halakhah of Prayer

Rabbi Joseph Karo, writing at *SA* Oraḥ Ḥayyim 46:8, implies that people who cannot see or hear are not obligated to recite blessings that refer to these senses and thus should omit God's name from such a blessing if they choose to recite them anyway. The Rema, in his gloss, disagrees; he argues that since these blessings do not necessarily relate to the specific person reciting them, but are a broader recognition that God has created all the varieties of human capability, there is no reason for a person with a disability to omit them from his or her prayers. The accepted custom, the Rema states, is for people with disabilities to recite these blessings as written and they need not omit prayers from the daily worship that thank God for abilities they lack. Blind people may therefore praise God for "opening the eyes of the blind" even though they are unable to see, and deaf people may praise God for the rooster's crowing (the first of the standard morning benedictions), even though they cannot hear it. Likewise, individuals who are themselves unable to stand or walk may still praise God "who straightens up those who are bent over" and "who directs the steps of each person."

Anyone who sees a person or an animal whose appearance is different from what they are accustomed to seeing—and this includes people with certain unusual physical characteristics and disabilities—is instructed by the Talmud at *BT* B'rakhot 58b to recite the blessing ending with the words *m'shanneh ha-b'riyyot,* which acknowledges God for creating variations in humankind. This might sound slightly pejorative, but can also be interpreted as an acknowledgment that what appears at first as disability can also be seen as a sort of blessing, as it may provide those who have a nominal disability with insight and skill levels that they might otherwise never have attained. According to the *midrash* preserved in *Midrash T'hillim* 34:1, for example, David, who initially questioned the purpose of madness in the world, ultimately prays to God to grant him at least the appearance of madness in order to save his life from a hostile Philistine king. Thus we are taught that all sorts of disabilities exist in the world, physical and psychological, and they all provide us with opportunities to look for God and experience divine reality in unexpected ways.

Blind people are permitted to lead the prayers in the synagogue by heart (*SA* Oraḥ Ḥayyim 53:14), which permission would certainly apply as well to a blind individual using a Braille prayerbook. Rabbi Israel Kagan, writing *ad loc.* in the *Mishnah B'rurah* (note 41), cites Rabbi Yair Bacharach who, in his collection of responsa called *Ḥavvot Ya·ir* (no. 176, ed. Lvov, 1896, p. 93b), prohibited a blind person from leading worship on the High Holidays. (During the High Holiday season, when life and death hang in the balance as God judges the world, there was apparently a sense that the leader of the prayer service should meet even more exacting criteria of suitability than during the rest of the year.) Kagan mentions that Rabbi Eliyahu Shapiro, writing in his own halakhic work, *Eliyahu Rabbah,* differs with Bacharach. Rabbi Kagan, however, believes that even according to Rabbi Bacharach the prohibition applies only in the case of the initial appointment, but does not apply to established prayer leaders who later lose their sight.

A person who has a hearing impairment may serve as a prayer leader, but Rabbi Akiva Eiger (as cited by Abraham S. Abraham in his *Nishmat Avraham,* [Brooklyn: Mesorah, 2004], vol. 1, p. 25, in his comment to *SA* Oraḥ Ḥayyim 53:14) rules that a person who cannot hear at all should not lead the prayers if there is someone else available to do so. (This is based on the requirement of the law that one must hear the words one is reciting; furthermore, those who cannot hear their own words may only be deemed to have fulfilled the obligation to pray *ex post facto.*) The question remains, however, whether one who cannot hear at all may fulfill the obligation for others when serving as a prayer leader. Authorities such as Rabbi Shimon Duran (in the *Sefer Tashbeitz* 3:113, ed. Lvov, 1896, pt. 3, p. 20b) and Rabbi Ḥayyim Joseph

David Azulai (in his *Birkei Yoseif* commentary to *SA* Oraḥ Ḥayyim 53:14, paragraph 8) allow a deaf person to lead services throughout the year, but not on the High Holidays. In 2011, the CJLS approved a responsum by Rabbi Pamela Barmash, now available on the website of the Rabbinical Assembly, that formally permitted a prayer leader to conduct the service through sign language for a congregation composed of individuals who understand it.

Priests with various visible physical disfigurements (*ba·alei mum*) were traditionally excluded from serving in the ancient Temple, but it is not entirely clear from the Torah why this should be the case. The commentary in the *Etz Hayim* suggests that maybe their disfigurements would distract worshipers from concentrating on the ritual, or perhaps their physical imperfection would compromise the sanctuary's image as a place intended to reflect God's perfection. Other rabbis have implied that a disability or disfigurement might be viewed as a sign of divine punishment and disfavor and thus suggest to the worshipers that the priest in question might not be an appropriate intermediary between God and the people. All three of these interpretations are somewhat troubling to modern readers. Do we really believe that disabilities are punishment for sin or lack of faith? Should a physically impaired individual be seen as less than perfect because of that disability? Should not character defects, often wholly invisible, be of far greater concern in establishing the personal worth of a putative priest? Are physical disabilities really so distracting that people cannot reasonably be expected to concentrate on their prayers when a leader with such a disability stands before them? And even if these were reasonable concerns in ancient times, is it reasonable or just to impose them on moderns, whose understanding of disability is wholly different?

The question, really, is whether the biblical laws excluding *ba·alei mum* from serving as priests should be translated into strictures concerning the contemporary role of prayer leaders. A number of authorities, including Rabbi Isaiah Horowitz (1565–1630, called the Sh'lah, or the Sh'lah Ha-kadosh, after the acronym of his most famous work, the *Sh'nei Luḥot Ha-b'rit*), believe that a *ba·al mum,* such as a person without arms or one who is unable to walk, would actually be preferable as a prayer leader to one without an obvious physical disability, since God "uses broken vessels" (*Sh'nei Luḥot Ha-b'rit,* Vavei Ha-ammudim, chapter 7). Rabbi Horowitz is referring to the verses in Psalms (34:19 and 51:19) that speak of God being close to the broken-hearted and being especially moved by people who approach worship with broken hearts—that is to say, imbued with a sense of their own inadequacy and wholly divested of arrogance or unearned pride. Referring to people with disabilities as "broken vessels" will strike moderns as odd, perhaps even offensive; but it is still interesting to note how many of our early biblical figures had disabilities of one kind or another, and how these disabilities, on the whole, did not disqualify them in any way from serving as leaders of the people. Moses's speech impediment comes to mind. And some would surely add Jacob's limp and Isaac's blindness to the list.

According to Rabbi Jacob Ḥayyim Sofer (writing in the *Kaf Ha-ḥayyim* commentary to *SA* Oraḥ Ḥayyim 53:64), Judaism's central mystical text, the Zohar (at III 90b) forbids calling upon a person with a disability to serve as a prayer leader, taking the expression "broken vessels" to refer to an exceedingly humble person rather than one with a disability. The Zohar claims that a *ba·al mum* is, almost by definition, someone lacking in faith and his disfigurement or disability testifies precisely to that fact. Therefore, such a person should not represent Israel before God. In time to come, however, the Zohar says that God will raise the dead and that all Israel will be perfected in body and soul. That all physical defects will vanish in the messianic era is a pleasant thing to contemplate, but moderns will want to consider very carefully before allowing this vein of theorizing about the origin of disability to influence their halakhic understanding of who is and is not suitable to lead a community in prayer. The first view, after all (namely, the position of the Sh'lah Ha-kadosh), suggests not only that it would be permitted, but that it would be more desirable, to choose a prayer leader with a disability on the High Holidays than one without any physical blemish. (In this regard, one may recall the legend of Rabbi Amnon of Mainz, reciting his final composition, U-n'tanneh Tokef—the most famous liturgical poem of the High Holidays—before the congregation after the amputation of his arms and legs.) Obviously, the view of the Zohar would be the opposite. Some modern authorities (such as Rabbi Benayahu Dayan, *Divrei B'nayahu*, part 3, Oraḥ Ḥayyim 15, ed. Jerusalem, 1999, pp. 107–114) have ruled in accordance with the rulings of the halakhic authorities previously cited that we should not determine the *halakhah* on the basis of mystical teachings, and that therefore it is permissible for an individual who has a disability or a disfigurement to lead the prayer service.

It is not enough, however, to rule that people with disabilities are permitted to lead our worship services. We must make proactive efforts to see that people who are blind or deaf, particularly children, receive a Jewish education and are provided with appropriate materials to learn Hebrew and to understand the prayers. We must provide Braille texts and prayerbooks and make greater efforts to educate deaf students. Some congregations in recent years have begun to work with children with cognitive impairment, different forms of autism, and other disabilities to prepare them for meaningful bar or bat mitzvah ceremonies in which the whole congregation shares in the joy of the celebration. Such efforts should be encouraged in more of our synagogues. Regardless of the specific disability in question, every effort should be made to help all Jewish children feel connected to their heritage. This will happen, however, only when all children are able to celebrate their Jewishness in the congregational setting without reference to their level of physical or psychological ability.

Rulings that permit people with disabilities to lead services or read from the Torah ring hollow, however, when our sanctuaries are inaccessible to those same people—for example, when people can get through the front door of the building but cannot use the restroom, or when there is no way for an individual in a wheelchair to come forward for an *aliyah,* or when the Torah reading table is too high to permit someone in a wheelchair to read from the scroll. Too many deaf people feel excluded from our synagogues, and from Judaism itself, because we fail to make provisions for interpreting the service for them. Were we to make it known in our communities that we welcome deaf people, and then show that we mean it by providing interpreters or amplification devices, we might be surprised by the response. More rabbis and cantors should be trained in communication with deaf people. Every synagogue should have an accessibility committee that surveys the synagogue's facilities and programming regularly and makes ongoing suggestions about ways to open the synagogue more effectively to all Jews in our community. Once we make our congregations more welcoming to people who have sensory, physical, or psychiatric disabilities, we might then proceed to involve those who join us in leading services or reading Torah.

Calling People Who Are Blind or Deaf to Read from the Torah

The public reading of the Torah on Shabbat, festivals, and other occasions is an opportunity for the community to reaffirm its commitment to the revelation at Sinai. Can a blind person, who obviously cannot read the words directly from the scroll, be called to the Torah and permitted (or even required) to say the blessings? May such a person chant a passage from the Torah to the congregation if the passage in question has been adequately and accurately memorized? Can a deaf person, who can obviously not hear the words of Torah, still be called forward for an *aliyah?* May such a person read to the congregation if he or she cannot hear the passage as it is read aloud?

Rabbi Karo rules at *SA* Oraḥ Ḥayyim 139:3 that a blind person may not be called to the Torah, for it is forbidden to recite even a single letter not actually read from the written text. His assumption, based on traditional practice in talmudic times, is that the person called to the Torah is expected not only to recite the blessings, but also to read the verses from the Torah as well. Even if this is not actually the practice in a given congregation (where a designated reader prepares the reading in advance), he maintains his position, holding that even one who does not actually read from the scroll must nevertheless be capable of doing so in order to receive an *aliyah*. The Rema, in his gloss to this paragraph, notes that Rabbi Jacob Moelin (c. 1365–1427), popularly called the Maharil, long ago permitted a blind person to be called to the Torah and that the community reader, assuming there is such a person in a given congregation, can simply read for him in the same way that he reads for illiterate people. With that comment, the Rema rules that one need not be capable actually of reading the Torah (which may never be read from memory) in order to be called forward to recite the blessings (which often are recited from memory).

Rabbi Israel Kagan writes in the *Mishnah B'rurah* (*ad loc.*, note 13), that the later authorities accepted the opinion of Rabbi Moelin. It is also permissible for a blind person to chant the *haftarah,* the weekly selection from the Prophets, which is generally read from a printed book and which, in any case, may be read by heart or from a Braille text just as acceptably as from printed type. This would surely also be the case with the reading of four of the five special scrolls, the *m'gillot,* which are read in the course of the liturgical year: the Song of Songs on Passover, Ruth on Shavuot, Lamentations on the Fast of the Ninth of Av, and Kohelet on Sukkot. (All of these may be read from parchment scrolls, but usually are read from printed volumes.) However, the fifth scroll, Esther, which actually must be read from a parchment scroll on Purim, falls in the same category as the reading of the Torah. Still, most authorities agree that a blind person is obligated to hear the reading of Esther because of the principle of publicizing the miracle of Purim.

In a responsum adopted by the Committee on Jewish Law and Standards in 2003 and now available on the website of the Rabbinical Assembly, Rabbi Daniel Nevins considers the issue of a blind person reading the Torah publicly for the congregation. The author demonstrates that the reading of the Torah is an obligation upon the congregation, not the individual, and that a Jew who is blind is therefore sufficiently obligated according to all opinions to fulfill this obligation on behalf of others. That much seems clear, but the issue then turns on how exactly it could be done and whether the congregation's obligation can be satisfied with any kind of public recitation other than a direct reading of the Torah from a kosher scroll.

Rabbi Nevins mentions the twelfth-century work by Rabbi Abraham ben Yitzḥak of Narbonne, *Sefer Ha-eshkol,* in this regard. This book has survived in two versions, however, and its ruling on this matter is somewhat unclear. At least one possible interpretation would imply that the blind person could recite the Torah reading from memory so long as a sighted reader followed along from the scroll to correct any errors that the reader might inadvertently make. It is also unclear whether the sighted reader would need to follow along audibly or if it would be sufficient to follow along quietly. Even if this reading of *Sefer Ha-eshkol* could be established as valid, though, it seems to be a unique opinion. Virtually all other authorities state that the Torah may not be "read" by heart.

May a blind person read the Torah portion aloud from a Braille Bible? In such a case, the objection to reading by heart would be removed, but the problem remains that the congregation is obligated to hear the Torah read from a kosher Torah scroll, not from a printed book. Surely a Braille Bible is more like a regular printed Pentateuch than it is like a kosher *sefer torah!* (This rule exists independent of its application to blind individuals—in a synagogue where there is no Torah scroll, or no one capable of reading from it, and where, therefore, the weekly reading is read from a printed volume, no one is called forward in the traditional way for *aliyot.*)

Modern technology, however, may provide a way around this requirement, as it might well be permissible to read from a scroll using a scanning device that allows the blind person to feel the shape of the letters on the scroll. That would obviate the second difficulty insofar as the reader would neither be "reading" by heart nor from something other than a scroll. However, at this point, the devices available are impractical for one who wishes to obtain a wholly coherent reading of the text. Nevins suggests that when such devices are improved, however, we may be able to allow a blind person to read from the Torah for the congregation using such a scanner. In the meantime, he suggests three less satisfying ways in which blind people may be called to the Torah: they may come forward for an *aliyah* and then chant softly after the reader as the text is read aloud, they could serve as *m'turg'manim* (the kind of verse-by-verse translators that no modern synagogues currently use but that were once a ubiquitous feature of ancient synagogues), or they could be honored by being permitted to read a section such as the *maftir* (the verses read from the Torah as part of a special *aliyah* for the person who will read the *haftarah*) from a Braille text, although he implies that this would not be the case when the *maftir* passage is read from a second scroll. (In other words, when the *maftir* simply repeats the last three or more verses of the weekly portion, we need not be so strict about it being read from a printed text. In fact, there is the precedent of the High Priest reciting the Yom Kippur *maftir,* which is *not* part of the day's principal reading, by heart precisely so as to avoid making the congregation wait while he rolled the scroll from the first readings of the day.)

While this last suggestion breaks new ground, the blind person is still excluded from the honor of representing the community through public recitation of verses that have not already been read aloud. A more daring approach would be to build on the foundation of the *Sefer Ha-eshkol* (shaky though it may be) and allow the blind person to read any portion from a Braille Bible, while another follows in the Torah scroll in an undertone to guarantee the accuracy of the reading. As for the reading of Esther, since, after the fact, the reading of the scroll is considered valid even if up to half of the scroll is read by heart, perhaps there are grounds for allowing a blind person to read up to half of the *m'gillah* from a Braille text. These suggestions are in line with the often-expressed wish within Conservative circles to include fully all Jews in our religious practices.

There seems to be little, if anything, written on whether a deaf person may read the Torah for the congregation. Rabbi Jacob Emden in his *siddur* (*Hilkhot K'ria·t Ha-torah,* 20) permits calling a deaf person who can speak to the Torah. He also notes that with more recent therapies, doctors have helped people who could not hear or speak to communicate in writing and in signs and it is clear that they have understanding, can respond to questions, and know to whom we offer prayer. Therefore he would permit such people to be called to the Torah as well.

We have a general rule that a deaf person who can speak—and even one who cannot, but has been educated in a school for the deaf—is obligated by all the laws of the Torah, at least according to some authorities (Schwadron, *Responsa* and Felder, *Naḥalat Tzvi,* both cited above). However there is some question as to what extent, if at all, these authorities would apply this principle to those laws that require hearing. We do have some guidance in this matter with regard to a deaf person reading the *m'gillah* either for his or her own benefit or even for others. Some argue that a deaf person who can speak but not hear may not read the *m'gillah* for others, since one is required to hear what one reads with one's own ears. If someone has some residual hearing there is room to be lenient, particularly if that hearing has been enhanced by amplification devices. However, Avraham S. Avraham in his work *Nishmat Avraham* (vol. 1, p. 337, commenting upon *SA* Oraḥ Ḥayyim 689:2) cites several later authorities who hold that even if one is completely deaf, others who hear that person read can fulfill their obligation in this way. This contemporary work concludes that such a person should not be appointed as a *m'gillah* reader *ab initio*. In the *Encyclopedia Talmudit*'s article on *ḥeireish,* though, we find that there are authorities who permit a deaf person to read the *m'gillah* in the first instance (*Encyclopedia Talmudit,* vol. 17, p. 498). Can we apply this leniency to the reading of the Torah? It seems that it may be possible to do so. If so, then why not allow the deaf person to be called to the Torah simply to recite the blessings without reading from the scroll? He or she could then follow the reading in the Torah while someone else reads.

The other relevant question that is discussed is regarding the recital of blessings where there is a general rule that one should pronounce a blessing loudly enough to be heard by one's own ears. Here too the authorities are divided over the situation with reference to a deaf person. While some authorities (e.g., Rabbi Moshe Schick [1802–1879], called Maharam Schick, as cited in the *Encyclopedia Talmudit,* vol. 17, p. 495, n. 41) do not accept a blessing recited by a deaf person as valid, others (e.g., Rabbi Shimon ben Tzemaḥ Duran [1361–1444] in his *Sefer Tashbeitz* 3:113, [ed. Lvov, 1891, pt. 3, p. 20b] and Rabbi Solomon ben Shimon Duran [c. 1400–1467] in his responsum no. 404, [ed. Livorno, 1742, p. 79a]) argue that since one is obligated by the *mitzvah* itself and the recital of the blessing is valid even if one does not hear the words, a deaf person can recite the blessing for him or herself and fulfill the obligation for others as well. Thus again we have justification for calling a deaf person to the Torah, particularly if he or she is able to follow the reading along with the reader. These same authorities would extend this ruling to allow a deaf person to lead the congregation in worship as well and to count in the quorum for prayer.

If a deaf person is capable of speech but finds it difficult, there is the possibility that the blessings be signed instead of spoken. It would be wonderful if the congregation could learn to respond to the blessing in sign language, particularly when there is a deaf congregant who is frequently called to the Torah.

Might an individual who is both deaf and blind be called to the Torah? The halakhic problems connected with such an honor would be immense, but, even there, a way might be found to apprise such a person of the progress in the reading, thus making it at least theoretically possible to include him or her in the public reading of Scripture.

Deaf people may read the Torah aloud even though they cannot hear what they are reading, but what of deaf congregants in the pews? Again, tradition points the way to innovation with the suggestion that the ancient office of the *m'turg'man,* the simultaneous translator of the Torah reading into Aramaic, be re-introduced as a way of providing interpreters for the deaf who could sign the text as it is read, so that people who are deaf can either read the interpreter's lips or follow the sign language, thereby fulfilling their obligation to "hear" the reading of the Torah.

Could a deaf reader soundlessly read the Torah, then sign it to a deaf congregation without reading it aloud at all? And what of hearing worshipers in a mostly deaf congregation—could a vocal translator "translate" the signed text to them simply by declaiming it aloud for them to hear? All these areas are mostly unexplored in the standard halakhic sources. Part of what the future must bring, therefore, is a continued demand that we find ways to include individuals who have traditionally been excluded from the public reading of the Torah.

The 2011 responsum by Rabbi Pamela Barmash regarding the status of the deaf individual in our day, referenced above with respect to the issue of deaf prayer leaders and available to the public on the Rabbinical Assembly website, suggests unequivocally that Jews who are deaf are responsible for the *mitzvot.* As a result, the CJLS now urges that synagogues, schools, and camps strive to be fully welcoming, accessible, and inclusive to deaf people. In addition, the CJLS ruled that sign language may be used in many instances to fulfill religious requirements. Specifically, they allowed sign language for life-cycle rituals such as weddings and divorces—this was already permitted by the ancient sages—as well as at *b'rit milah* and *pidyon ha-bein* ceremonies. In addition, the CJLS now allows sign language in liturgical contexts: calling a deaf person to the Torah and, if the person does not speak, allowing him or her to "speak" using sign language instead; assigning a deaf person to serve as *sh'li·aḥ tzibbur* by signing the prayers, at least for a congregation that understands sign language; and reading the Torah using sign language for a similar gathering. Besides this, they ruled that sign language may be used to recite prayers that must be articulated and, as suggested earlier, a deaf person might fulfill the *mitzvah* of shofar by sensing the vibrations of the shofar sounds. This will go a long way toward normalizing the relationship of deaf people to the Jewish community.

The Ordination of People with Disabilities

There is a long history mentioned in the Talmud and in later literature of blind individuals who served as rabbis and teachers. Although it is not always clear if these individuals were blind before ordination or were ordained and then subsequently lost their vision, we know today that people with both visual and hearing impairments are able to meet the academic and spiritual requirements of rabbinical schools and thus from that standpoint can be ordained as rabbis. Conservative rabbinical schools, for example, do accept students with disabilities and some graduates are currently serving the Conservative movement. Maimonides states (at *MT* Hilkhot Talmud Torah 1:8–9) that "all Jews are obligated to study Torah whether they are rich or poor, in sound health or ailing, in the vigor of youth or very old and feeble." He goes on to note that "among the sages of Israel were hewers of wood, drawers of water, and others who were blind. Nevertheless they devoted themselves day and night to the study of Torah. They are included among the transmitters of the tradition in the direct line from Moses."

One could, however, raise an objection regarding a person serving as a judge, one of the traditional roles of the rabbi, if that individual has a physical or mental disability, and this would be so even if that disability did not actually interfere with the performance of the duties of a judge. This disqualification seems akin to the disqualification of priests with certain physical characteristics from officiating in the Temple, even though these characteristics did not impair their ability to perform their duties. Maimonides states (at *MT* Hilkhot Sanhedrin 2:6) that a person with a disability may not serve on the court of twenty-three or seventy-one judges required in capital and other important cases, but he adds that in the case of a court of three, we do not insist upon the same strict requirements imposed on judges who sit on a larger court (ibid. 2:7). That is not to say that all restrictions are waived, however, and he specifically goes on to state that, although judges who are blind in one eye may serve, no judge may serve on any court who is blind in both eyes (2:9). When Maimonides rules that one may not ordain even an outstanding scholar who is blind in one eye (ibid. 4:10), however, he is speaking of the ordination of rabbis who will serve as judges, and this standard does not and should not apply to the ordination of rabbis in our own day.

There is also a general rule that one who may not serve as a witness may also not serve as a judge and, indeed, in a criminal justice system that turns solely on eyewitness testimony it seems odd to imagine permitting someone unable personally to see acting as judge. Of course, even a sighted judge only hears what the eyewitnesses come to court to say! And, indeed, Rabbi Menaḥem Meiri, commenting on *BT* Sanhedrin 34b, notes that the early *ge'onim* did permit, or at least seemed to permit, blind judges to serve. (The *ge'onim* were the rabbinic authorities in the centuries following the talmudic era.) An individual may therefore choose a blind person to adjudicate a case, and a community may also choose such a judge and then oblige people to accept that choice. A judge who becomes blind may also continue to serve in the capacity of a judge. Thus, later authorities such as Rabbi Ben-Zion Alcalay, noting the history of blind sages, permit blind people to serve as judges if they are otherwise qualified. (Such judges would obviously recuse themselves from cases that depend on sight for a particular matter.)

Even if we say that a blind person may *not* serve as a judge or may *only* serve under certain conditions, these disqualifications will not prevent the individual in question from performing most other duties as a rabbi, however. This being the case, we should feel free to ordain blind persons who are otherwise qualified to serve as rabbis, and this should certainly apply to deaf persons as well. In so doing, we recognize that rabbinic ordination today is not the same as the ancient ordination of rabbinic judges to serve on a *sanhedrin*. Indeed, speaking realistically and practically, the duties and activities of the modern rabbi could easily be performed by persons with sensory or physical disabilities if they were given the proper assistance. The blanket disqualification of people with disabilities is therefore unacceptable in our day, as it fails to correspond to the tasks we actually assign our clergy or to the responsibilities they accept when they agree to serve as the spiritual leaders of our communities.

The Testimony of People with Disabilities in a Beit Din

Traditionally, blind or deaf people were excluded from giving testimony in a Jewish court of law. Maimonides states (*MT* Hilkhot Eidut 9:12): "The blind, though they recognize voices and thus identify persons, are ineligible [to give testimony] by biblical law, as it is said, 'He being a witness, in that he has seen' (Leviticus 5:1). Only one who can see may give testimony." This is known as *g'zeirat ha-katuv,* a decree derived directly from the wording of a verse, and therefore one not subject to rational argument. As such, this ruling is upheld in both the *Arba·ah Turim* of Rabbi Jacob ben Asher (at *AT* Ḥoshen Mishpat 35) and in the *Shulḥan Arukh* (at Ḥoshen Mishpat 35:12). The Talmud makes it clear that this ruling applies even to blind individuals who wish to testify about things that they saw prior to losing their sight. However, if they later regain their sight, they may then testify to things they saw prior to losing their sight in the first place (*BT* Bava Batra 128a). Nor may blind individuals testify about things they heard or learned through other senses while they were blind. (This is similar to the exclusion of hearsay evidence in U.S. civil courts.) Always, the *halakhah* is willing to risk failing to convict the guilty rather than risk mistakenly convicting the innocent.

Regarding deaf people, Maimonides rules at *MT* Hilkhot Eidut 9:11 that "the status of the *ḥeireish* (deaf-mute) is that of the mentally deficient individual, because he is not of sound mind and is not bound to observe the commandments. This applies also to the deaf individual who can speak and to the mute individual who can hear—although the testimony of either of the last two may be convincing and the mind of the witness sound, it is required that he give oral testimony, and that he be able to hear the judge and the charge addressed to him." Maimonides thus rules that one who cannot speak, even though found totally competent, may not present evidence in writing. Once again, the *halakhah* is supremely concerned with avoiding the wrongful conviction of the innocent, and is willing to avoid wrongful conviction even at the expense of the dignity of a competent person who has a disability. The issue of whether the *ḥeireish* may give testimony in a *beit din* is discussed at length in Rabbi Pamela Barmash's 2011 responsum regarding the halakhic status of hearing-impaired individuals referenced above and available on the website of the Rabbinical Assembly.

Written testimony is generally invalid in Jewish law, except in the case of the *agunah* whose husband is missing but not proven dead. (In such cases, the rabbis were inclined to be as lenient as possible.) Those who cannot speak, therefore, may testify in writing that they know a woman's husband is dead. Likewise there is a leniency for blind people in the case of an *agunah,* so a blind person who has heard from someone else that the woman's husband is dead may testify to that fact (Rabbi Yaakov Reischer [1661–1733], *Sh'vut Ya·akov* part 1, responsum 100 [ed. Offenbach, 1719, pp. 38d–39b]). In our society, we have come to understand that blindness or deafness do not impact mental competence. Halakhic authorities, therefore, should feel challenged by that aspect of empirical reality to seek ways to ensure that the safeguards against wrongful conviction are kept strong and inviolate without denigrating the testimony of competent people who just happen to have disabilities.

Rabbi Menaḥem Meiri (writing in his *Beit Ha-b'ḥirah* to *BT* Bava Batra 128a) is almost alone among the medievals in finding ways to permit people who have lost their vision to testify about things they saw before becoming blind. Examples the Meiri gives include the case of someone who lent money to another person in the presence of a sighted individual who later becomes blind, or a case where someone injured another person in the presence of this once-sighted individual. At the base of the Meiri's ruling is the fundamental recognition that blind people are as mentally competent to testify to things seen before becoming blind as any sighted individual. Although the Meiri's approach was unique in its day, the *halakhah* today can build on it as we seek ways to enfranchise capable witnesses without compromising the way in which the system is weighted to favor acquittal. Indeed, now that the Committee on Jewish Law and Standards has ruled that women may serve as witnesses, it seems inevitable that the exclusion of the testimony of blind or deaf individuals, or of people with certain specific psychiatric disabilities, will be revisited as well. (Responsa by Rabbis Myron Geller and Susan Grossman permitting women to serve as witnesses were approved by the CJLS in 2001. Both are available on the Rabbinical Assembly website.)

It also bears saying that other kinds of physical disabilities—paraplegia or quadriplegia, for example—are not deemed halakhically relevant and do not preclude people disabled in those particular ways from testifying. Mentally ill individuals are traditionally excluded from serving as witnesses even if their particular disability is relatively circumscribed (*MT* Hilkhot Eidut 9:9). The term *shoteh* used in halakhic literature to denote individuals with psychological disabilities is discussed in detail earlier in this chapter.

The Use of Service Animals and Electronic Devices on Shabbat and Festivals

Shabbat provides unique challenges to people with disabilities. In the past, rabbinic authorities had to rule about the permissibility of using canes, glasses, primitive prostheses, and ear trumpets on Shabbat, and particularly about the possibility of transporting them from one's private home into the public street and then into the synagogue. In modern times, the questions have expanded to include queries about electronic devices designed to assist deaf people, motorized wheelchairs and scooters, and elevators and chairlifts for people with mobility impairments. The Torah also explicitly commands us not to make our animals work for us on Shabbat. What impact would this have on the use of service animals such as guide dogs for people who are blind or deaf, or assistance animals for people with mobility impairments?

Early concerns about wearing glasses and prosthetic devices on Shabbat centered on the likelihood of the wearers removing them in the public domain (because of discomfort) and then carrying them, since one of the major prohibitions of Shabbat involves carrying or transporting objects in a public domain, or from a public domain to a private one or *vice versa* (see the chapter by Rabbi Michael Katz and the late Rabbi Gershon Schwartz regarding the laws of Shabbat and specifically the section "Carrying on the Shabbat"). Nowadays, glasses do not rest on the nose alone, but are securely worn around the ears; modern prostheses likewise fit securely. There is, therefore, no likelihood of anyone wanting or needing to remove them in public and, as a result, it is not considered forbidden to wear eyeglasses or other prosthetic devices on Shabbat. Modern authorities have gone back and forth over whether one may include a hearing aid among the items that one may "wear" in public on Shabbat. Part of the indecision stems from the various designs of such devices and the location of their controls, which are sometimes carried in the user's pocket. The hearing aid is compared at different times to an article of clothing, an ornament, or even to an amulet. Rabbi Ovadiah Yosef rules that a deaf person may wear a hearing aid even in a public domain, since it is firmly fixed in the ear and is considered like an article of clothing (*Sefer L'vi·at Ḥein* on the laws of Shabbat, no. 30). As for the use of the hearing aid itself, this too is permitted, provided that it is turned on before Shabbat. Furthermore, its volume may be adjusted on Shabbat (Rabbi Joshua Neuwirth, *Sh'mirat Shabbat K'hilkhatah* [Jerusalem: Beit Midrash Halakhah-Moriyah, 1979] 26:7, p. 227).

Also with regard to the stricture against carrying in a public domain on Shabbat, the *Shulḥan Arukh* (Oraḥ Ḥayyim 301:17) rules that "a person who is lame and cannot walk without a walking stick may go out with it on Shabbat even if it is not tied to that person's body. However, if the person can walk without it and only uses it for extra support, then it is forbidden." Later commentators qualify the last portion to permit a person who *can* walk without a cane, but who may be in danger of falling without it, to use one as well. Crutches, leg-braces, and walkers are in the same category of items that may be taken out if they are needed and used, but may not be carried along simply as a precautionary measure. There is a similar discussion about the blind person's white cane (ibid. 301:18). Some authorities, noting that the blind person can walk without it, are reluctant to allow its use, while others point out how important a cane can be, particularly in unfamiliar territory, in preventing the blind person from tripping or falling over obstacles (*Arukh Hashulḥan,* Oraḥ Ḥayyim 301:72). This is an especially important consideration given that Leviticus 19:14 explicitly prohibits placing a stumbling block before the blind and common sense surely dictates that that law should treat similarly all categories of persons who have difficulty walking safely.

These laws regarding public domains and carrying impact individuals with disabilities in other ways as well. For example, Rabbi Dov Aryeh Klig (writing in his *Sefer Leiv Aryeh* 2:2 [as cited in the *Nishmat Avraham,* vol. 1, p. 149]) permits a blind person to go out into a public domain with a guide dog. Here the concerns are whether the person is (in part) carrying the dog's harness and whether this might be considered working an animal by making it carry (in part) what might be construed as a burden. In both cases, Rabbi Klig rules that there is no problem, since the connected harness is carried by human and dog together, and jointly performed acts are not prohibited as labor.

The question of guide dogs involves other halakhic issues as well. Rabbi Moshe Feinstein (*Igg'rot Moshe,* Oraḥ Ḥayyim 1:45, ed. New York, 1959, pp. 104–105) permits a blind person to enter a synagogue with a guide dog, though there are other authorities who disagree on the grounds that it might be disruptive to worship or cause a desecration of God's name. These latter concerns are not likely nowadays since people are used to seeing guide dogs in public places, including restaurants, banks, and post offices (where other kinds of pets are not permitted), and since the dogs are trained to be inconspicuous during periods of rest. Indeed, most moderns would agree that the greater desecration of God's name would lie in preventing blind people from participating in worship services in a dignified way.

Already in the sixteenth century, Rabbi Joseph Karo wrote (at *SA* Oraḥ Ḥayyim 301:16) of a device akin to a wheelchair that people with amputated legs may use on Shabbat to propel themselves through the streets. Karo permits the use of this device, but is concerned that protective pads on the chair may fall off in the street, and thus he forbids taking them along. In our day, a person with a disability who can get around only in a wheelchair may thus be taken out by a non-Jew into a public domain in order to perform a *mitzvah,* even if there is no *eiruv* (which permits carrying where it would otherwise be forbidden on Shabbat). If the person is capable of moving the chair without assistance, then together with a non-Jewish attendant the person could go even into a public domain as defined by the Torah, the theory being that such would constitute a permissible act because they are both moving the chair together and because one is not Jewish. A Jewish attendant, on the other hand, is not permitted to take the person out into a public domain, even if the wheelchair user can actively help (Neuwirth, *Sh'mirat Shabbat K'hilkhatah* 34:27, as cited in *Nishmat Avraham,* vol. 1, p. 147).

Traditional sources like Rabbi Neuwirth's book do not mention the possibility of a Jewish wheelchair user using a motorized chair on Shabbat or festivals. Indeed, many traditional rabbis appear to be working under the assumption that wheelchair users mostly depend on personal assistants to move from place to place. While this may indeed be the case for someone temporarily incapacitated due to an injury, people who live with a mobility impairment all or most of their lives see the wheelchair, especially a motorized one, as an extension of their bodies that allows them to achieve some measure of independence. To prohibit the use of such devices on Shabbat, or to limit their operation to non-Jewish attendants, is to fail to recognize the distinction between devices that, not unlike hearing aids, magnify the capacities of the person with the disability, and devices that are conveniences used during the week that can meaningfully and reasonably be put aside on Shabbat.

For those who do not follow the Committee on Jewish Law and Standards 1950 ruling permitting driving to synagogue on Shabbat, it may seem contradictory to suggest that one may use a motorized wheelchair to get to a synagogue from one's nearby home while not allowing driving or riding in a vehicle. Yet there is a certain logic when one distinguishes between the car, as a convenience, and the wheelchair, as a necessary extension of the body. As with the hearing aid, one should do what one can to minimize the potential violation of Shabbat. If there is an on/off switch, it should be turned on prior to Shabbat. (And it is also worth noting that the kind of battery pack that powers a motorized wheelchair is clearly different from the internal combustion engines in automobiles, and that those who see the latter as clearly forbidden may yet see the former as permitted.) Of course, for those who accept the 1950 ruling and drive to synagogue and back on Shabbat, one should add as well permission to use a wheelchair lift to allow the wheelchair user to enter the vehicle on Shabbat. People with disabilities who cannot manage stairs should be allowed to take advantage of elevators or chairlifts, though it is preferable to arrange for a non-Jewish attendant to run the machinery or to have the elevator run automatically. From a halakhic standpoint, if the Jewish person has no choice but to run the elevator personally, then he or she should do so in a different manner than on a weekday, thereby implicitly acknowledging that it is Shabbat. (One could, perhaps, push the button with one's elbow instead of one's finger.)

Ritual Innovation as a Response to Physical Disability

Some of our previous discussion raises issues about the purpose of the commandments. Are ritual acts intended to be performed only by the able-bodied in a precise manner as a divine decree, or may one create alternative ways of fulfilling a *mitzvah* for those whose bodies are not able to fulfill the commandment in its normative fashion? Is feeling the vibrations of the *shofar* blast halakhically equivalent to hearing its sound if one is deaf? Is reading the Torah in Braille with one's fingers halakhically equivalent to seeing the text with one's eyes if one is blind? May people without arms put the *t'fillah shel yad,* which normally is worn on the arm, on a leg instead, since their leg serves them as an arm, and thus don two *t'fillin* as is the norm, or must they wear only the *t'fillah shel rosh* on their heads? May people who cannot move their arms wave the *lulav* by moving it on the tray of their wheelchair, or may they carry it around the sanctuary for *hoshanot* in a similar manner? Do we say that such innovative responses to the *mitzvot* are worthy efforts toward inclusivity, or do we brush them off as insignificant, or even perhaps as foolish attempts to create context where none actually exists or should exist? We need to be aware of the spiritual needs of people with disabilities and to be open to whatever suggestions for innovation might allow them to perform the *mitzvot* in some fashion, thus personally to associate more closely with their people and their faith. Even the most unexpected of these suggestions might become normative and unexceptional in time. It is interesting to note that in the latest revised edition of *Sefer Leiv Avraham* (2009), the author, Professor Avraham S. Avraham, suggests that a wheelchair user might fulfill the tradition of stepping back three paces following the Amidah through the use of the wheelchair (p. 55, par. 20).

The words of Maimonides found in the *Mishneh Torah* at *MT* Hilkhot Sanhedrin 24:10 should be our guide in these matters: "Let not human dignity be light in [your] eyes," the greatest halakhist wrote, "for the respect due a person supersedes a negative rabbinic commandment. . . . A judge must be careful not to do anything calculated to destroy someone's self-respect. The sole concern [in the administration of justice] should be the enhancement of the glory of God, for whosoever dishonors the Torah will be dishonored by other people, and whosoever honors the Torah will honored by others. To honor the Torah means to follow its statutes and laws."

Animals

EDWARD M. FRIEDMAN

In the first chapter of the Bible, God tells the first humans, "Be fertile and increase, fill the earth and master it; and rule over the fish of the sea, the birds of the sky, and all the living things that creep on the earth" (Genesis 1:28). The language may be a bit ambiguous, but the implication of the verse is entirely clear: there is a huge variety of fauna in God's world, but humans are to be in charge of all the other creatures.

In the second chapter of Genesis, we get a different picture. Here, Adam is the first being created, not the last, and the animals are created by God from the earth only subsequently, *after* God determines that "it is not good for the man to be alone" (Genesis 2:18). And then, having identified the problem, God announces its solution: "I will create a fitting helper for him" (ibid.). The creatures are then brought to Adam "to see what he would call them." Thus Adam is depicted in the role of sublime taxonomist, charged with the great task of categorizing and defining these other creatures' roles in the world. The Bible reports that, alas, "no fitting helper was found" for Adam among the animals—that was to be Eve's role—but the more crucial point for us to ponder in considering these two accounts is that there are apparently two different ways to consider the animal kingdom: as a host of nonhuman creatures to be ruled over, or as potential "fitting helpers" or partners.

The *halakhah* seeks a compromise between these two extreme positions. We are thus called upon to be compassionate to other creatures, even though we are allowed the use of their labor—and even the bodies of some of these same creatures—to fulfill various needs or desires in our lives. We are allowed to put the animals to work. As of the time of Noah, we are permitted to eat their flesh. We may utilize their skins, bones, and other body parts for clothing, shelter, and other legitimate needs. Yet the Torah puts limits on the degree to which the animal kingdom can be legitimately used by human beings, putting guidelines into place to ensure that animals not be exploited by their human masters.

Cruelty to Animals

The term *tza·ar ba·alei ḥayyim* is used to refer to any act that causes pain to an animal. But although rabbinic authorities debate whether the concept is biblical or rabbinic in origin, all authorities agree that harming animals or causing them undue pain is halakhically prohibited. Most authorities, including such major figures as Rabbi Isaac Alfasi (1013–1103), Rabbeinu Asher ben Yeḥiel (c. 1250–1327), and Rabbi Solomon ben Aderet (1235–1310), rule that *tza·ar ba·alei ḥayyim* is a biblical principle. Others, such as Rabbi Menaḥem Meiri (1249–1315) and Rabbi Mordecai ben Hillel (c. 1240–1298), believe it to be rabbinically derived. Though this debate has some technical ramifications in halakhic discourse, it will be sufficient for most merely to be aware that cruelty to animals violates the teachings of Judaism.

Even among the majority of rabbis who believe that the prohibition derives from the Torah, however, there is no unanimity as to its precise scriptural source. Some, like Rashi, find it embedded at Exodus 23:5 in the commandment to relieve the burden from a fallen beast, even if it belongs to one's personal enemy, and to help raise such an animal to its feet. Other medieval teachers such as Rabbeinu Peretz (in his comments to *BT* Bava M'tzi·a 32b) consider the law to be in the category of *halakhah l'mosheh mi-sinai,* an ancient law without a specific biblical source that is nonetheless universally accepted. Still others, including Maimonides (writing in his *Guide for the Perplexed* III 17), derive the law from the story of Balaam and his talking ass, in which an angel demands to know why the prophet is beating his poor beast (Numbers 22:32). Finally, there are those like Rabbi Moses Sofer, who see the prohibition as a matter of imitating the attributes of God, who is specifically described in Scripture (e.g., at Psalm 145:9) as being merciful and kind. Each of these proposed sources has something to recommend it. Taken together, they make a strong case for arguing that concern for the welfare of animals is reasonably to be considered a sacred charge rooted in our most sacred literature.

Under the rubric of *tza·ar ba·alei ḥayyim,* most authorities forbid only the infliction of gratuitous or excessive pain to an animal. However, when an animal is needed for some legitimate human purpose, one may use the animal even if it suffers some pain, for the rabbis believed that animals were created for our benefit and to serve our needs in the world. One is, therefore, permitted to use an animal to turn a grindstone and one may place a burden on an animal's back, or harness an animal to a wagon, or prod it with a stick to lead it along the way. Thus Maimonides, writing in the *Guide for the Perplexed* (ibid.), states that "the object of this rule regarding *tza·ar ba·alei ḥayyim* is to lead us toward perfection so that we should not assume cruel habits—and that we should not *uselessly* cause pain to others and that, on the contrary, we should be prepared to show pity and mercy to all living creatures except when necessity demands the contrary, [for example,] 'when your soul longs to eat meat' (Deuteronomy 12:20), etc. We should not kill animals for the purpose of practicing cruelty or for sport."

The law also permits killing animals that pose a danger to human beings or to other animals, or that are considered pests, such as rodents and some insects. Rabbi Isaac N. Eshkoli in his book *Tza·ar Ba·alei Ḥayyim Ba-halakhah Ve'aggadah,* (Ofakim [Israel]: I. N. Eshkoli, 2001–2002), p. 157, sees this as a logical extension of the permission given for humans to benefit from animals. All the more so, he would argue, may one kill an animal that is doing damage, as we find in the Mishnah (*M* Mo·eid Katan 1:4). There one is permitted to trap moles and mice in one's field or orchard in the usual fashion in order to prevent damage to one's crops *even* during the intermediate days of a festival or during the sabbatical year, times when one ordinarily would avoid such kinds of labor. Even so, pious individuals over the ages have always tried to avoid inflicting any injury on any creature, whether on purpose or by accident.

Though some authorities question whether it falls under the general heading of *tza·ar ba·alei ḥayyim,* all agree that, in addition to prohibiting the infliction of pain on an animal, Jewish law also requires us, wherever possible, to relieve an animal's suffering, and this is so regardless of whether the pain is a function of natural or artificial causes. Therefore, it is a *mitzvah* to save an animal's life or to relieve its suffering. And thus, although there are restrictions on the ways a Jew may handle an animal on Shabbat—and I return to this concept below—it is nevertheless permitted for a Jew to milk a cow on Shabbat (as long as it is done in an unusual manner) or to instruct a non-Jew to milk it, in order to provide relief to the animal (see Rabbeinu Asher on *M* Shabbat 18:3). Likewise, one may throw pillows and cushions into a pit where an animal has fallen on Shabbat to help it climb out (*BT* Shabbat 128b). Some also permit providing veterinary care to sick animals, whether one's own or another's, on Shabbat among the acts that would otherwise be forbidden, but which are regarded as licit because of the principle of *tza·ar ba·alei ḥayyim.*

It is forbidden to inflict pain wantonly upon any creature simply for the perverse pleasure of seeing it suffer, or to vent our anger or our frustration. Therefore, whenever we utilize the labor of an animal, we must minimize the animal's discomfort. Even the act of slaughtering an animal for food or for some other legitimate purpose must be carried out as humanely as possible to avoid unnecessary suffering.

One specifically modern aspect of the *tza·ar ba·alei ḥayyim* laws has to do with the use of animals in scientific experimentation. Animal rights advocates claim that, contrary to popular opinion, experimentation on animals is rarely necessary and is of limited value to understanding human biological processes. Others reject this argument as naïve, misleading, and specious. The *halakhah* takes a middle path, permitting the use of animals in medical experimentation despite the possibility of causing them suffering. In so doing, however, every precaution must be taken to limit their suffering to the greatest extent possible and it must be the case that some clear benefit to human beings is likely to come from the testing. Certainly, testing cosmetics on animals in a way that causes pain or suffering cannot be justified. However, there are many scientists who believe ardently that much benefit to human beings will come from testing different products or procedures first on animals. To the extent that this is true, Judaism very clearly permits it. However, in light of Judaism's emphasis on *tza·ar ba·alei ḥayyim* as something always to be avoided, we must insist that animals be used in experimentation as rarely, and as kindly and humanely, as possible. The issue of using animals in medical research is also discussed elsewhere in this volume by Rabbi Avram Reisner in his chapter on medical ethics.

Aside from the law of relieving the burden from a fallen animal, the Torah includes many other laws that take the welfare of animals into account. One may not plow with an ox and an ass yoked together, presumably so that the weaker animal is not over-exerted by needing to keep up with the stronger one (Deuteronomy 22:10). One may not muzzle an ox while it is threshing grain and thereby cruelly prevent it from eating while it works (Deuteronomy 25:4). One must chase away a mother bird before taking its eggs or its young from the nest, probably to spare the mother the anguish of seeing her chicks taken away, never to return (Deuteronomy 22:6–7). One may not slaughter an animal and its young on the same day, presumably also to avoid anguish to the animal (Leviticus 22:28).

The rabbis also require us to feed our animals before we partake of food ourselves. (The Talmud presents this lesson at *BT* Gittin 62a, deriving it from the passage in Deuteronomy 11 in which God promises to make it rain if we perform the commandments. The rain will then cause the grass to grow, and the grass, in turn, will provide food for animals. Then, and only then, may we eat and be satisfied.) All these laws help create an attitude of respect for animal life and concern for the welfare of other creatures.

Pets

Until fairly modern times, our rabbis assumed that any domesticated animal found in a home or a barn was there to perform some service for the household. The idea of a household pet whose primary purpose was to please its owners by its presence was unheard of among Jews, and was considered an indulgence that characterized the lives of wealthy gentiles.

Some traditional halakhic sources actually go so far as to consider time spent caring for a pet that has no actual duties to perform in the household to be an act of *bittul torah,* a waste of time that could be better spent on the study of Torah. At Kohelet 6:11, the author says, "Many things increase futility. And what does any of them actually provide for people?" Rashi interprets this verse to refer to the playthings of kings such as monkeys, elephants, and lions, which he considers mere wastes of time that bring no discernible benefit to anybody. The ancient midrashic compendium *Kohelet Rabbah,* commenting upon that same verse, makes a similar comment and includes other animals such as cats, weasels, and squirrels. The conclusion seems clear: it is permitted to keep animals at home if they serve us by performing some useful function, but it is at best a waste of time (and possibly a violation of the laws forbidding cruelty to animals) to keep animals that serve merely to entertain or amuse.

Today, of course, we have an entirely different attitude toward pets. Animals kept as pets can be a source of companionship and joy, and have been shown to have particular value for lonely people, the elderly, or people with infirmities confined to hospitals, nursing facilities, and assisted living residences. Furthermore, learning to care for pets can introduce children (and adults as well) to the value of caring for others and of taking on responsibility for the welfare of other creatures. Also, living together with, and caring for, household pets can inspire us with a sense of symbiotic responsibility for the animal kingdom as a whole, and that sense of responsible interconnectedness with the world's fauna is surely a worthy sentiment to cultivate in its own right.

Nevertheless, one may not feel free to assume that all household pets that are for sale to the general public are raised under conditions that a morally- and halakhically-sensitive consumer should support or endorse. On their website at www.aspca.org, the American Society for the Prevention of Cruelty to Animals describes the practices in place at so-called puppy mills as follows: "Puppy mills usually house dogs in overcrowded and unsanitary conditions, without adequate veterinary care, food, water, and socialization. Puppy mill dogs do not get to experience treats, toys, exercise, or basic grooming. To minimize waste cleanup, dogs are often kept in cages with wire flooring that injures their paws and legs—and it is not unusual for cages to be stacked up in columns. Breeder dogs at mills might spend their entire lives outdoors, exposed to the elements—or crammed inside filthy structures where they never get the chance to feel the sun or a gust of fresh air on their faces." Complaints about such businesses continue to the present time. Though legislation against such practices has been introduced in some U.S. states in recent years, breeders have fought back and, in some cases, been successful in removing legal limitations placed on their operations. Jews should consider themselves forbidden to buy dogs or other pets from businesses that treat animals in the ways listed above; one must therefore investigate commercial sources for pets thoroughly before patronizing them. Many breeders run legitimate businesses that treat animals kindly, of course, and there is no reason not to patronize such establishments. Of course, dogs, cats, and other animals are also always available from public shelters and pounds. And retired racing greyhounds can occasionally be saved from destruction by families that offer to adopt them from rescue agencies.

Purchasing exotic birds and pets is also of halakhic concern on at least two counts. First, one may be threatening endangered populations by acquiring certain kinds of rare birds. Second, and more commonly, it is rarely possible to provide truly suitable conditions for such creatures in our homes. It is clearly a violation of the principle of *tza·ar ba·alei ḥayyim* to acquire a pet if one knows in advance that one will be unable to care for it properly.

We must guard against transgressing the *tza·ar ba·alei ḥayyim* laws, however, even when we have more ordinary pets in our care. Taking animals into our homes obligates us to ensure that they are properly fed and watered. Indeed, as stated above, there is an absolute halakhic requirement to make sure the animals in our care are properly attended to before we ourselves partake of food. We need to see that our animals are housed in places that protect them from adverse weather conditions, and that they have space and opportunity for regular exercise. Keeping an animal in a small kennel or confined to a tiny apartment may be in violation of the principle of *tza·ar ba·alei ḥayyim.* Additionally, we must protect our pets from being abused by young children or other visitors, keep them safe from other animals and from vehicular traffic, and care for their medical needs by arranging for regular visits to the veterinarian.

We also have a responsibility to be good neighbors and see that our animals do not cause damage or injury to the property of others, to other animals, or to people. The Talmud in several places (e.g., *BT* Shabbat 63a, K'tubbot 41b, and Bava Kamma 15b) prohibits keeping vicious animals, particularly vicious dogs, in our homes. And it is our obligation, whether or not local ordinances require it, to clean up after our pets and not leave their waste in our neighbors' yards or in public places. Pet ownership may be a great joy, but it comes with responsibilities as well.

It is easy to become attached to a pet, particularly one that has become a family member of long standing. If such a beloved pet develops a debilitating condition, is euthanasia a halakhic option? Killing an animal in a humane way is not considered a violation of the law prohibiting *tza·ar ba·alei ḥayyim.* Indeed, when an animal is suffering from illness, constant pain, or unremitting disorientation, euthanasia may be the kindest way of dealing with the situation. Here, the observant Jew must seek guidance from the combined counsel of a veterinarian and a rabbi to help determine whether and when it would be a violation of the *tza·ar ba·alei ḥayyim* laws to allow an animal, literally, to suffer to death.

When a beloved pet dies, the loss is often very keenly felt and it is appropriate to acknowledge that grief and to find a means of expressing it formally. Observing the forms of mourning that the *halakhah* developed for human losses—such as sitting *shivah* or saying the Kaddish—are inappropriate, but it can be still helpful to sit with family and friends, even if only for a brief time, and remember the time spent with the pet. Reciting poetry or even biblical passages about the worth of animals would also be appropriate at such a time. There is no specific prohibition against cremating an animal's remains, but since Judaism prohibits cremation of people, some may wish to arrange for the burial of a deceased pet instead. An animal funeral can not only provide an outlet for one's grief and some measure of closure, but can also be an educational experience for children whose first encounter with loss may well be the death of a household pet.

In the end, the experience of owning and loving a pet can provide deep spiritual lessons as well. One of the sages of the great Musar movement of the nineteenth and early twentieth centuries, Rabbi Elyah Lopian, is said, in fact, to have kept a cat and to have insisted on feeding it personally as a means of emulating God's enduring concern for all creatures. (The Musar movement was devoted to the propagation of Jewish ethics. The story of Rabbi Lopian and his cat is retold by Dovid Sears in his *The Vision of Eden: Animal Welfare and Vegetarianism in Jewish Law and Mysticism* [Spring Valley, NY: Orot, 2003], p. 84.)

Animal Labor

As we have seen, the Torah assumes that people will use animals for various tasks and, for their part, the ancient sages affirmed the right of humans to use animals to assist us in our labor. One is permitted to ride on an animal's back, to use an animal to pull a plow or a carriage, to turn a grindstone, or to perform other similar tasks. Some rabbinic authorities did not believe that these common tasks cause particular pain or suffering to an animal and thus do not even raise the issue of *tza·ar ba·alei ḥayyim* in this context. Some rabbis even suggest that animals that are not worked become weakened and bored, so that such activities are actually beneficial to them. (This was the view, for example, of Rabbi Mordecai Jacob Breisch, as expressed in his *Ḥelkat Ya·akov,* Ḥoshen Mishpat, responsum 34 [ed. Tel Aviv, 1992, vol. 1, pp. 316–318] and cf. responsum 35, ed. cit., pp. 318–320.) Others, however, believe that, while animals do suffer while working, this suffering is nevertheless permitted since it benefits humans (cf. the *Da·at K'doshim* of Rabbi Abraham David Wahrman (1770–1840) to Yoreh Dei·ah 24:12, as cited by Rabbi Eshkoli in *Tza·ar Ba·alei Ḥayyim B'halakhah Ve'aggadah,* p. 323, n. 738). The familiar words of the Psalm 126, "he walks along while weeping," are interpreted by Rabbi Judah (*BT* Ta·anit 5a) as a reference to the weeping of the ox as it walks along the furrows it is plowing.

Today, most of the tasks animals have traditionally performed have been taken over by machines, and the riding of animals is primarily undertaken for recreational purposes. Even animals who pull carriages today do so primarily for the tourist trade in some locations. The motive, however, is unimportant: whether animals are used by the tourism industry or actually to labor on farms, the laws governing *tza·ar ba·alei ḥayyim* are still fully applicable. And, as with our pets, working animals also require proper feeding and housing.

The rabbis strictly forbid any participation in spectacles in which animals are pitted against humans or against other animals. The gladiatorial battles of Roman times, including those that pitted human warriors against animals, were totally repulsive to our ancient sages, who considered attendance at such events to contravene the exhortation of the first psalm that the pious should never willingly enter a *moshav leitzim,* an "assembly of depraved individuals." In our own time, bullfights, cockfights, dogfights, and other similar activities are strictly forbidden as violations of the laws that govern *tza·ar ba·alei ḥayyim.* We may not participate in them, we may not watch them, and we may not benefit from them in any way. Even wagering on their outcomes should be considered a form of abetting their existence and thus a forbidden activity.

Do these prohibitions apply to horse races as well? There are sages who permit watching horse races in order to learn the proper art of riding and to learn how to judge the quality of a horse one might purchase. But what of enjoying them without intending to learn any specific lessons about horses or their care? To the extent that these competitions are tests of skill, the *halakhah* can be understood to permit Jews to race their own animals or to watch other horses run. If, however, these contests lead to intentional injury of animals or people, they must be considered forbidden. In our time, strict regulation of these races guarantee, or are supposed to guarantee, that both the jockey and the horse are protected from abuse and injury to the greatest extent possible.

Racing dogs might also be permissible, were it not for the widespread practice of destroying dogs that are no longer able to perform. As long as the current policies are in effect, it is not appropriate for us to support such activities by our patronage.

Betting on such races, like other types of gambling, was prohibited by the rabbis when it took the place of gainful employment or was compulsive in nature. Some authorities are more lenient and allow occasional gambling, however, particularly when part or all of the winnings will be given to charity. The specific question of synagogues sponsoring games of chance as a way of raising funds is discussed elsewhere in this volume by Rabbi Craig Scheff.

It seems clear, according to Rabbi Isaac Eshkoli (*op. cit.*, p. 211) that it is permissible to visit zoos and aquariums in order to look at God's creatures and marvel at the wonders of the Almighty. Rabbi Joseph ben Moshe in his book *Leket Yosher* (Berlin: Tz. H. Itzkowski, 1904), p. 66, tells of his teacher, Rabbi Israel Isserlein (1390–1460) visiting something like a zoo on Shabbat. The master had never seen a lion in his life, so when he heard that two lions had been brought to his city, he decided to see them. Rabbi Ḥayyim Joseph David Azulai (1724–1806) in his *Midbar Kadmut* 2:22 (Jerusalem: Ma·ayan Ha-ḥokhmah, 1957, p. 25) tells of his visit to the London Zoo where he saw different and unusual animals including a very beautiful hundred-year-old eagle. Eshkoli notes that many other rabbis and pious individuals were known to visit zoos in the past. In fact, such visits might well be encouraged as opportunities for pronouncing the blessing thanking God who varies the world's creatures (i.e., by reciting the blessing that ends with the words *m'shanneh ha-b'riyyot*). Eshkoli rejects the notion that visiting zoos and paying admission to see the animals makes one an accomplice in causing suffering to the animals confined in their cages. He notes that, on the contrary, many zoos help to preserve rare and endangered species. At the same time, they allow the visitors to learn more about these creatures and, for the Jewish patron, there is the additional possibility of obtaining important information that may be relevant in one's Torah studies. Rabbi Natan Slifkin, a contemporary Orthodox rabbi, tries to accomplish both of these goals through his books and his website (www.zootorah.com). We can conclude that modern zoos, which take great pains to provide a familiar and comfortable environment for their residents, are not by virtue of their very existence to be considered in violation of the *tza·ar ba·alei ḥayyim* laws.

Shabbat Laws

Do the laws of Shabbat rest include animals? The answer is clear: the fourth commandment of the Decalogue (Exodus 20:10 and Deuteronomy 5:14) specifically instructs us to allow our animals to rest on Shabbat, and the *halakhah* understands this to include not allowing them to labor for our benefit on Shabbat (see, e.g., Maimonides, *MT* Hilkhot Shabbat 6:16).

It is, therefore, forbidden to place any kind of burden on an animal on Shabbat. It is permitted, however, to put a harness or bridle on a horse or any large animal that normally wears one, in order to lead it in and out. Also, small animals, such as dogs, may wear a collar and/or a leash. Even handling animals on Shabbat was traditionally prohibited, for they are in the category of *muktzeh* items, i.e., things which one may not handle because such activity serves no obvious purpose on Shabbat. There is a minority opinion of one Rabbeinu Yosef cited in Tosafot (*BT* Shabbat 45b, *s.v. hakha b'mai askinan*), however, that does not apply this prohibition to a baby chick used to entertain children on Shabbat, and we might reasonably extend this leniency to all household pets nowadays. Indeed, we now understand that household animals themselves benefit from interaction with their human owners. Of course, one is permitted to take an animal for a walk on Shabbat in order to prevent or alleviate suffering.

As mentioned earlier, farmers are permitted to engage in some normally forbidden acts on Shabbat if those actions are deemed necessary to alleviate the suffering of animals. It is considered preferable, however, to engage non-Jewish workers to perform these labors if at all possible. Thus one may engage non-Jews to milk one's cows on Shabbat because it is painful for an animal not to be milked regularly. If necessary, one may milk the cow oneself, although one must do it in an unconventional way, e.g., by emptying the milk into a container of food. Since the prohibition of *tza·ar ba·alei ḥayyim* is generally viewed as Torah law and the rules governing *muktzeh* are rabbinic, the former take precedence over the latter. One may, therefore, assist an animal out of a pond or a pit on Shabbat if it is in distress and cannot extricate itself on its own. Wherever the rabbis permit us to aid animals on Shabbat by performing actions that would otherwise be forbidden, we must exert ourselves to perform them in an unusual or indirect way to signal our awareness of the fact that it is Shabbat.

Slaughtering Animals

The laws governing kosher slaughter are discussed elsewhere in this volume by Rabbi Paul Drazen in his chapter about the dietary laws, so I will discuss them here from the specific vantage point of the principle of *tza·ar ba·alei ḥayyim.*

From the Torah, we learn that Adam and Eve were vegetarians and that it was not until the time of Noah that people were permitted to eat meat. But even then, the rabbis understood Scripture to be placing some restrictions upon them, most notably that they were forbidden from eating any limb of an animal that had been cut off while the beast was still living. (The technical term for such a limb is *eiver min ha-ḥai,* cf. *MT* Hilkhot Ma·akhalot Asurot 5:1).

Scripture endorses the slaughter of animals not only for food, but also as sacrifices. Initially, the Israelites were even told that they must bring animals intended for domestic slaughter to the altar first, where some of their fat would be offered up and then their flesh would be permitted to be eaten. (This legislation is preserved at Leviticus 17:1–7.) Subsequently, however, the legislation at Deuteronomy 12:20–25 was understood to permit profane slaughter even outside the Temple or, in our day, in the absence of Temple and priesthood entirely.

The clear implication of the scriptural narrative, however, is that the ideal state that prevailed in the Garden of Eden was one in which animals and humans lived in harmony and neither ate the flesh of the other. Should Jews strive to imitate that primeval perfection by becoming vegetarians? Or should they at least limit their intake of meat to the greatest extent possible? There are those who take this latter position, arguing that, if slaughter is a concession to human appetite, we should still do what we can to control those carnivorous urges and, at least, to save the ingestion of meat for special occasions. But the *halakhah* clearly permits the slaughter of animals for food and no law requires a Jew refrain from eating meat out of ethical concerns.

There is a well-known story about the great sage Rabbi Judah the Patriarch, preserved in the Talmud at *BT* Bava M'tzi·a 85a, in which a calf, escaping the slaughterer, runs away to seek shelter with the rabbi. The rabbi, however, fails utterly to show compassion to the animal, telling it, "Go back, for this is the purpose for which you were created." As punishment for his lack of sensitivity, Rabbi Judah suffered a painful illness that lasted many years, until he finally showed compassion to a litter of young weasels, which he did while quoting Psalm 145:9: "God's compassion extends to all creatures." The story is not intended to prohibit slaughtering animals, but simply to remind us of the importance of being compassionate to all creatures, even those whose flesh we eat.

Though no specific method of slaughter is specified in the Torah itself, the *halakhah* requires that animals be slaughtered in such a way that will allow the majority of their blood quickly to drain out of the carcass, since it is forbidden to eat blood (cf., among many sources, Genesis 9:4, Leviticus 17:12, and Deuteronomy 12:23). The rabbis require the *shoḥeit,* the ritual slaughterer, to be carefully trained in the laws of slaughtering. For larger quadrupeds, the *shoḥeit* must use a very sharp, long knife to slit the animal's throat in a prescribed manner. (A smaller knife is used for chickens and other fowl.) No undue pressure may be exerted. In fact, the ideal is for the animal not even to feel the cut while it is being made. The quick draining of blood from the severed arteries of the neck leads to rapid unconsciousness and limits any suffering from the act of slaughter itself. Any imperfection, such as a nick, in the knife—or any hesitation by the *shoḥeit*—invalidates the slaughter. The overriding (and underlying) principle is clearly that the animal's life be taken in an atmosphere of respect and dignity.

Over the last century, it became the practice to raise the animal off the ground by its hind legs in order to place it on its back in a frame for slaughter. This shackling and hoisting of large animals can be very cruel and painful for the animal—how could it not be uncomfortable for a cow that weighs, say, a thousand pounds to be suspended by its hind legs as it awaits the slaughterer's knife? Additionally, many injuries to slaughterhouse personnel have occurred over the years due to this procedure. In the interim, various more humane methods of positioning the animals for slaughter without hoisting and shackling have been invented. In the method developed by Dr. Temple Grandin, associate professor of animal science at Colorado State University, the animal is placed in a container that gently turns the beast on its side, then onto its back, until it is the correct position for slaughter. Many kosher slaughterhouses now utilize this more humane and safer procedure for their operations. Others however, have been reluctant to spend large sums of money to change what they have been doing for many years. In the fall of 2000, the CJLS voted unanimously to accept a responsum written by Rabbis Elliot Dorff and Joel Roth that determined categorically that the shackling and hoisting of animals is a violation of the laws of *tza·ar ba·alei ḥayyim* (*CJLS Responsa 1991–2001,* pp. 93–97). Nor should Jews feel content merely not to buy meat that originates in slaughterhouses that shackle and hoist their animals. It is entirely in keeping with the spirit of the *halakhah* to work vigorously for the closure of such inhumane packing houses, not merely to patronize only those that employ more humane methods. (The question of shackling and hoisting is discussed elsewhere in this volume by Rabbi Paul Drazen in his chapter on the dietary laws.) It is precisely the wish to provide consumers with this kind of information, which is currently otherwise unavailable, that justifies the existence of the kind of additional *kashrut* supervision exemplified by the Conservative movement's Magen Tzedek initiative, discussed in more detail below.

Another issue of great concern to many people in recent years has been the inhumane processes used in some segments of the food industry to raise animals for food. While many of these processes deserve public attention, perhaps the best known is that of raising of milk-fed calves for veal. Rabbi Bradley S. Artson, for example, describes the way calves are raised for veal today: "Taken from its mother less than a day after birth, the calf is raised in a crate so small that the animal cannot turn, lie down, or stretch. It is never given water to drink, nor any solids to eat. Instead, it is kept anemic, with a diet exclusively of milk replacers, which is deliberately deficient in iron. This diet causes chronic diarrhea. The animal lives in darkness twenty-three hours a day, in barns storing up to four hundred other crated calves. Fed a steady stream of antibiotics, one in every thirty calves has been found to contain illegal residues of tetracycline, neomycin, and gentamycin. Most are slaughtered after only sixteen weeks" (*It's a Mitzvah: Step by Step to Jewish Living* [West Orange, NJ: Behrman House, 1995], p. 213). Rabbi Artson thus joins a large chorus of modern rabbis who urge that Jews refuse to purchase veal both out of concern for *tza·ar ba·alei ḥayyim* and the possible threat to human health. Indeed, in a long responsum by Rabbi Pamela Barmash that was approved by the Committee on Jewish Law and Standards of the Rabbinical Assembly in December 2007, the author concludes: "We rule that only veal from animals raised under humane standards can be sold, purchased, or consumed. Humane standards for the raising of veal calves include sufficient space for calves to lie down, stand up, turn around, and groom themselves, proper nutrition in a mixed diet appropriate for young calves with sufficient iron, dry, clean bedding, and limited isolation of calves." (The full text of Rabbi Barmash's responsum is available to the public on the website of the Rabbinical Assembly.)

Nor is this specifically a Conservative issue. Rabbi Moshe Feinstein ruled that, while it is permitted to fatten calves for slaughter and to feed them different kinds of food intended to improve the quality and taste of their meat, it is not permitted to cause suffering to the animals by feeding them poor quality food that does not really improve the meat, but simply makes it look more appealing. Rabbi Feinstein sees this process as a deceptive business practice and urges people not to eat such animals, even if they are certified kosher in terms of their actual slaughter procedure (*Igg'rot Moshe,* Even Haeizer, 4:92:3, ed. New York: 1985, pp. 164–165).

Calves are not the only animals mistreated to provide food for people, however. Rabbi Noach Valley writes that some poultry farms "crowd chickens into narrow sheds without windows. They are unable to stretch both wings at the same time. They never breathe fresh air, get exercise, or see sunlight. To avoid feather-pecking and cannibalism, which would naturally result in such inhumane conditions, the birds are cruelly and painfully debeaked, while their heads are held in a machine that is reminiscent of a guillotine" (*Judaism and Animal Rights,* ed. Roberta Kalechofsky [Marblehead, MA: Micah Publications, 1992], p. 209). Laying hens are also regularly subjected to processes that cause needless suffering.

To make the delicacy of *pâté de foie gras,* fatted goose liver paste, it is necessary to fatten geese. This, in and of itself, might not be forbidden, but this has generally been accomplished by force-feeding the animals in a very painful process so that the animals' livers become enormously oversized. The process has been changed in recent years to make it somewhat more humane and to avoid injury to the animal through the feeding. Even so, the abnormal growth of the liver causes undue pressure on the goose's lungs and suffocates about twelve percent of the geese treated this way prior to slaughter. Though this clearly violates the laws governing *tza·ar ba·alei ḥayyim,* some authorities still permit this "improved" process since it provides benefit to human consumers. Other rabbis oppose it, however, and it certainly seems that the weight of halakhic concern for the welfare of animals is on their side.

The Magen Tzedek initiative recently undertaken by Rabbi Morris Allen and other members of the Rabbinical Assembly, mentioned above and discussed elsewhere in this volume by Rabbi Paul Drazen in his chapter on the laws of *kashrut,* addresses many of the issues mentioned here. Founded on the principle that we are what we eat, Magen Tzedek is an ethical seal signifying that kosher food has been prepared with care and integrity. Products carrying the Magen Tzedek seal reflect the highest standard on a variety of important issues: employee wages and benefits, health and safety, animal welfare, corporate transparency, and environmental impact. Readers will find more information at the Magen Tzedek website, www.magentzedek.org.

Wearing Fur and Leather

If animal flesh may be used for food, there should be no question that animal skins, fur, and feathers may also be used for clothing or other legitimate purposes. Indeed, God is depicted at Genesis 3:21 as personally providing leather clothing for Adam and Eve once they are expelled from Eden. Therefore, one may kill an animal to obtain its skin or fur to make clothing or other articles for human use.

As with raising animals for food, the issue of proper living conditions must be addressed no less seriously when the animals in question are being raised for their fur or their leather. And we must also be concerned about not further endangering rare species. Animals in the wild must be captured and slaughtered using humane means. The fact that there is no halakhic concept of leather or fur being "kosher" for wearing (in the same sense that flesh must be kosher for consumption) does not free us from concerns regarding *tza·ar ba·alei ḥayyim*. The image of baby seals being clubbed to death for their skins, for example, is completely contrary to Jewish ethical values. Bone-crushing leg-hold traps, still used in some places, are likewise in violation of the laws of *tza·ar ba·alei ḥayyim*. There are even those who openly question whether animals should be slaughtered for their fur at all, given that synthetic fur is available in our day. While the preponderance of halakhic opinion permits the wearing of fur, it is as essential to uphold the law forbidding *tza·ar ba·alei ḥayyim* in the preparation of clothing, upholstery, or other products made of animal skins or fur, as it is in the preparation of food.

This notion that one may use the pelts of animals as clothing, but must respect the loss of life this entails, also influences other Jewish practices. On the fast days of Yom Kippur and Tishah Be'av, and during the *shivah* week of mourning, for example, it is forbidden to wear leather shoes (*MT* Hilkhot Sh'vitat Asor 1:5, Hilkhot Ta·aniyyot 5:10, and Hilkhot Eivel 5:1). Some people suggest that one reason for the prohibition is that particularly at a time when one seeks compassion and solace for oneself, one needs to show compassion to other creatures as well. Wearing cloth shoes instead of leather is one way to remember that the lives of animals are sacrificed for many of the shoes we purchase.

When a person puts on a new garment, it is customary to say to him or her, "Wear it out and renew it—*t'valleh u-t'ḥaddeish!*" (When addressing a female, the expression would be *t'valli u-t'ḥadd'shi.*) However, the Rema (in his gloss to *SA* Oraḥ Ḥayyim 223:6) notes that "there is an authority [he is referring to Rabbi Jacob Weil] who states that one should not say this in the case of new shoes or other garments that are made from animal hides. The reason is that this implies a necessity eventually to kill another animal from which to acquire the pelt with which to renew the garment in question, whereas it is written in Scripture, 'and divine mercy is over all God's works.' . . . Now, although this reasoning is very feeble and does not seem convincing, many people are nevertheless particular about this and refrain from saying 'Wear it out and renew it' where leather clothing is involved." The

Rema's demurral notwithstanding, one should not recite the She-heḥeyyanu blessing (that is normally recited when one wears a garment or a pair of shoes for the first time) on wearing a new pair of leather shoes or a garment made from animal skins. In a sense, this mirrors the custom of also not reciting this blessing over a new Torah scroll, which, of course, is written on animal skin.

Hunting and Fishing

Hunting has never been a traditional Jewish occupation. The great hunters in the Bible are Nimrod (Genesis 10:9) and Esau (Genesis 25:27), neither of whom was celebrated by our sages as a righteous person. Since it rarely happens that hunters go out to capture animals for kosher slaughter, the Jewish custom is to hunt solely for animals that could serve some other purpose, or to remove an animal that is posing a danger to the community. Seeking out a dangerous animal that is living in the forest but not posing a threat to human life, however, is prohibited unless one has some use planned for its flesh or skin (Rabbi Ezekiel Landau, writing in his collection of responsa entitled *Noda Bihudah,* second ed.: Yoreh Dei·ah 10, ed. New York, 1960, pp. 5–6). Simply killing an animal for sport is not allowed. There is also a concern that, in hunting, one may injure an animal but not kill it, thereby inflicting suffering upon a creature in violation of the injunction forbidding *tza·ar ba·alei ḥayyim.* Rabbi Landau admits that from the standpoint of the law, as long as one is using the animal for some purpose, hunting is permitted. However, he adds that hunting is not something that Jews do. "How can a Jewish person kill an animal with one's own hands without any need, simply to fill a momentary desire?" he asks. In addition to violating the prohibition of wantonly destroying God's creation, hunters often put themselves in danger and thereby violate the law requiring us to guard our lives exceedingly (Deuteronomy 4:9). Perhaps even more to the point, hunters risk becoming hardened and cruel through the act of destroying animal life.

Yet another halakhic concern has to do with fishing. Generally, Jews have engaged in fishing because many sea creatures are permitted as food and there is no concept of ritual slaughter for fish. In recent years, however, we have become increasingly aware of specific problems in the fishing industry. Dolphins, for example, are non-kosher aquatic mammals that often swim above schools of tuna. When fishermen cast their nets for tuna, dolphins are frequently caught in the nets and can be killed in the process. Certainly, if dolphins are mixed with the tuna in the catch and not removed, the mixture is not kosher. But should our concern here be solely with *kashrut,* or also with the needless killing of the dolphins themselves? Given the fact that one can easily find dolphin-safe tuna for sale, Jewish consumers sensitive to the spirit of Rabbi Landau's responsum should prefer to purchase it for both these reasons. Furthermore, in the recreational context, non-kosher fish or other sea creatures should always be returned to the water as soon as possible after catching them so that fishermen may avoid the needless destruction of life.

Genetically Altered Animals

Modern science has been able in recent years genetically to alter animal and plant life by manipulating the DNA found in the cells of living organisms. Generally, this is done to make certain specific species heartier, more resistant to disease, or more fertile. Theoretically, it may eventually even be possible to create new varieties of animal life totally unlike any creature that exists now. Rabbinic authorities are only beginning to grapple with the ramifications of such genetic engineering.

A responsum by Rabbi Avram I. Reisner, approved unanimously by the Committee on Jewish Law and Standards of the Rabbinical Assembly in 1997, deals with one aspect of this issue, while raising a number of subsidiary issues as well (*CJLS Responsa 1991–2000,* pp. 101–111). Rabbi Reisner rules that adding genetic material from a non-kosher animal to a kosher animal does not change the status of the kosher animal to make it non-kosher. This is because the material being transferred is sub-microscopic and the laws of forbidden mixtures tolerate minute amounts of forbidden substances.

Another issue that Rabbi Reisner raises is the prohibition of *kilayim,* the biblical term for mixed species. The Torah prohibits a number of kinds of *kilayim,* most definitely including the crossbreeding of animals or the grafting of plants (Leviticus 19:19 and Deuteronomy 22:9). We do not know the reason behind these prohibitions, but Naḥmanides suggested that these laws were intended to honor the Creator by maintaining the integrity of the species that God initially created. Rabbi Reisner argues that, despite the laws of *kilayim,* genetic engineering is permissible because *kilayim* is a decree of the Torah that is limited to the cases listed in the Torah and which thus need not be extended to other situations. In addition—and, in some ways, more to the point—the rabbis ruled that the products of such forbidden mixtures are permitted, even if the act itself that creates them is prohibited. Rabbi Reisner mentions many other leniencies connected with *kilayim,* concluding that "the transfer of a few genes by genetic engineering techniques [is] far removed from natural sexual contact [and therefore] cannot be seen as prohibited." He adds that, while we must consider the potential risks to human health and establish appropriate regulations as a matter of public policy, it is important to recognize the potential for great benefit to humanity from genetic engineering.

Castrating, Spaying, and Neutering Animals

The Torah, in speaking of animals fit to be offered on the altar, excludes a number of "blemished" animals from being sacrificed. Among these are "anything [with its testes] bruised or crushed or torn or cut" (Leviticus 22:24). The verse, however, continues, "You shall have no such practices in your own land," which was interpreted in the Talmud (at *BT* Shabbat 110b) as a prohibition of castration or sterilization of any male, animal or human. (Women are not subject to punishment for sterilizing themselves, since they are not obligated by the commandment to be fruitful and multiply. And, by extension, female animals are not included in the prohibition, although Maimonides, writing in the *Mishneh Torah* at *MT* Issurei Bi·ah 16:11, believes that there is nevertheless a prohibition for females, merely one that the Torah does not punish them for violating. The *Shulḥan Arukh* follows that ruling at *SA* Even Ha-eizer 5:11.) And, although it is generally accepted that non-Jews are not obligated to observe this prohibition, one may still not ask a non-Jew, even obliquely, to castrate an animal on one's behalf.

One is permitted to sterilize an animal if there is medical need and castration will save the animal's life or heal it from its illness. Nor is there a problem with sterilizing an animal to inhibit reproduction. Indeed, modern veterinarians routinely urge pet owners, unless they are specifically planning to breed their animals, to get all pets sterilized, and some rabbinic authorities concur. They justify this as a matter of preventing *tza·ar ba·alei ḥayyim*—unspayed cats and dogs are at increased risk for pyometra, a potentially fatal uterine infection, as well as various forms of cancer. Far more to the point, the number of unwanted cats and dogs in the United States is immense and growing ever larger. To allow the dog and cat population to increase, only to turn unwanted animals over to shelters that routinely euthanize animals they cannot place, seems peculiar and cruel. Spayed and neutered animals also tend to live healthier and longer lives. Thus, it would seem that these procedures should be considered to be in the best interests of the animal and should therefore be permitted and encouraged by *halakhah*.

From a veterinary point of view, larger male farm animals also are generally better off if they are castrated. (It can also be dangerous to people and to the animals themselves for a group of stallions or bulls to be kept together in the same barn without being sterilized.) The situation regarding female animals is halakhically simpler—since the prohibition is only rabbinic and the concerns for animal welfare are from the Torah, we can easily justify overruling the rabbinic prohibition to uphold the Torah's standard of kindness toward animals. The castration of male animals is more troublesome. However, since it could easily be argued that the law is tied specifically to the issue of reproduction, one could make a strong argument in favor of neutering the animals of any species that is vastly overrepresented in populated areas, the offspring of which will likely be destroyed. Even under such conditions, however, it is preferable that the castration or spaying be undertaken by a gentile veterinarian. The cardinal concept is always the principle of preventing *tza·ar ba·alei ḥayyim,* and as such we must relate to the animal kingdom in a way that is consonant with our role as stewards of God's world, living harmoniously, productively, and kindly with our fellow creatures.

Our sages remind us that, while we human beings like to think of ourselves collectively as the very pinnacle of creation because we were the last creatures produced on the sixth day of creation, we would do better to allow that fact to stimulate humility rather than pride by focusing instead on the fact that the creation of even the smallest insects preceded the creation of all humankind. This recognition that we are all fellow creatures brought forth from the earth by the hand of the Creator should inspire us to have compassion upon our fellow creatures and concern for their well-being, and ultimately to lead us to work together with them in this world to create holiness in a world shared by all living creatures.

The Environment

LAWRENCE TROSTER

The environmental crisis the world faces has no real parallels in human history. Environmentalism, the general name for the response of humankind to this crisis, has, therefore, no true antecedents: it arose as a novel way of thinking about the natural world and humanity's relationship to it, shaped by issues that were not so much unresolved as they were wholly unconsidered by previous generations. As part of the process that has called environmentalism itself into being, however, a distinctly Jewish approach to environmentalism has also evolved.

Before the twentieth century, no religious tradition had to deal fully with the issues and concerns that the environmental movement has raised. And even if some religious traditions did deal in the past, to some extent, with questions related to resource management, water shortages, loss of arable land, pollution control, and even species extinction, these issues now exist on a completely different scale. And other issues are totally novel, without even scant antecedent literature to consult: overpopulation, climate change, toxic waste, and biodiversity are issues that our ancestors could never have imagined.

Why must Jews care about the environment? First, because we are human beings and the environmental crisis affects all humanity. Climate change knows no borders, nor do toxic chemicals in our earth, air, and water. Second, Jews live mostly in developed countries, which proportionally use a greater amount of resources than the rest of the world. Therefore, we should be working toward environmental justice as a means of responding to the commandment of Scripture at Deuteronomy 16:20 that we seek justice in the world. Lastly, as ardent supporters of the State of Israel, it is in our best interest to see the world wean itself from oil-based energy sources and thus to lessen its dependence on many countries hostile to the Jewish state.

Given that environmental ethics is a new area of Jewish concern, there is virtually no traditional Jewish environmental *halakhah*. It is true that, in the last ten years, a body of Jewish scholarship and theology on the environment has come into existence, but the translation of this material into the halakhic sphere has yet fully to be realized. Therefore, this chapter does not have much traditional *halakhah* on the environment to cite. Still, Jewish environmentalists and scholars have begun to draw on sources and ideas from our tradition, which can be used to create the seeds of a halakhic response to Jewish environmental theology and ethics. To the outsider, this process will sound far simpler, and easier, than it actually has been. There are times when traditional Jewish attitudes and values come into clear conflict with some of the most basic assumptions of the environmentalist movement. (This is also a matter of basic orientation: while traditional ethical theory has mostly been concerned with rights, Jewish ethics tends to emphasize duties and obligations.) Also, most classical Jewish sources are based on a premodern cosmology, which conceives of a static universe and a fixed number of species. The modern scientific disciplines of biology and ecology are essential to environmentalism and must be incorporated into Jewish environmental ethics, if the latter is to gain a place at the table in some of the most important discussions that will take place over the course of the next few decades—discussions about nothing less important than the future of our planet and our place on it.

I begin by suggesting theological and ethical concepts that might be applied to environmental issues, which are then considered in light of these concepts. From this unfolds the outline of a proposed *halakhah* of the environment.

Jewish Environmentalism

The fundamental theological concept that underlies all of Jewish environmentalism is that God created the universe and therefore has absolute ownership over all creation. (Among the many scriptural sources for this idea, readers may consult Genesis 1–2, Psalm 24:1, 1 Chronicles 29:10–16, and Leviticus 25:23.) Furthermore, Scripture teaches us that God is the source of life (Genesis 2:7) and the Sustainer of life (Psalm 104:27–28), and that God's creation is inherently and innately good, structured, and ordered in a harmonious way to serve as a reflection of its Creator's glory. (This idea is elaborated forcefully and effectively in Psalm 148, for example.) Jewish tradition uses the term *seider b'reishit* (the order of creation) to describe this grand and purposeful design. This order reflects God's wisdom (see Psalm 104:24), which is beyond human understanding (see Psalm 92:6–7 or Job 38–39).

Central to this cosmology is the understanding that no part of existence lies outside the order of creation. Humans are an integral part of this order: it is humankind that forms, first, a community of worshipers, and then a choir that exists to sing the glory of God's created universe as part of the chorale that is comprised of all of creation. Nor is this specifically a modern idea developed against the background of heightened ecological consciousness; the 148th psalm is essentially an extended poetic elaboration of this very idea.

The eighth psalm nods to the special place that humans occupy in creation. This special place of humanity finds expression in the concept of *tzelem elohim,* the idea that human beings are created in the image of God (Genesis 1:26–27 and 9:6). In turn, this concept implies that humans were put on the earth to act as God's agents for the express purpose of actualizing God's presence in creation. (See my "Created in the Image of God: Humanity and Divinity in an Age of Environmentalism," in *Judaism and Environmental Ethics: A Reader,* ed. M.D. Yaffe [Lanham, MD: Lexington Books, 2001], pp. 172–182.) In the ideal world, humans would serve as the wise and kind stewards of creation. They would help to maintain the balance basic to the order of creation, even while using the resources of the planet for their own benefit within the limits established by God. This balance would be applied within the structures of human society, as well as to the relationships between humanity and the natural world. In the end, humanity has a special responsibility for the created world because of the latter's inherent vulnerability to human exploitation and exploitative technology. And this responsibility extends to future generations as well (cf. Genesis 9:12 and Deuteronomy 29:13–14).

Moderns might find it just a bit difficult to grasp the ramifications of their importance in this cosmology. The earth, never depicted as merely inert matter, is actually imagined to be morally sensitive to human actions (see, e.g., Genesis 4 or Leviticus 18:27–30). And the corollary of this thought has its own chilling implications: there is clear and profound danger for humanity when the order of creation becomes disrupted by violence against its divinely set boundaries.

We affect and are affected in turn. The story of the flood in Genesis is an example of what can happen when the order of creation is disrupted by human evil. Indeed, the specific danger inherent in the sin of creating forbidden mixtures (the *kilayim* prohibitions) results precisely because the boundaries of creation have been blurred (see, e.g., Leviticus 19:19 or Deuteronomy 22:9–11).

The Jewish concept of a perfect world is one characterized by harmony among all creatures. This is set forth most famously at Isaiah 11:1–10, which describes a utopian vision of a world in which no creature kills for sustenance and there is neither war nor injustice in human society. This quest for balance between humanity and the rest of creation is nothing less than an effort to recreate the Garden of Eden, and is among the great goals of Jewish spirituality. Indeed, many thinkers have proposed that the observance of the Shabbat is best understood as the here-and-now symbol of that harmony. In his essay, "Tending to Our Cosmic Oasis," Rabbi Ismar Schorsch, for example, has written, "Shabbat reminds us of our earthly status as tenant and not overlord." (Rabbi Schorsch's essay originally appeared in *The Melton Journal* 24 [1991], and was subsequently reprinted in *To Till and To Tend: A Guide to Jewish Environmental Study and Action* [New York: Coalition on the Environment and Jewish Life, 1994], where this quote appears on page 20). The challenge, of course, is not merely to be reminded of that aspect of reality, but to be inspired by it to act responsibly and intelligently so as to preserve the great planet that has been placed in our stewardship.

Environmental Awareness

In his book *Ecological Identity* (Cambridge, MA: The MIT Press, 1995), Mitchell Thomoshow attempts to describe the type of mindset cultivated by those with a heightened environmental awareness. For one thing, he says, such people will "perceive themselves in reference to nature, as living breathing beings connected to the rhythms of the earth, the biogeochemical cycles, the grand and complex diversity of ecological systems" (p. xiii). But merely seeing oneself as part of the natural world will not suffice—one must also see the natural world as part of oneself. "Intrinsic to an ecological worldview," he writes further, "is the ability to see an ecosystem as part of oneself. This knowledge is gained both through an understanding of scientific ecology and the ability to observe and internalize the interconnections and interdependence of all living things" (ibid., pp. 12–13).

Thus, even a rational scientist sees that there is an aspect to the enterprise that surpasses mere intellectual achievement and approaches the level of philosophy or spirituality. From a Jewish point of view, this is a very resonant concept. Indeed, Maimonides understood the commandments to love and to fear God, found at Deuteronomy 6:5 and 13, in a roughly analogous way:

> When people observe God's works and God's great and marvelous creatures, and when they see in them an aspect of God's wisdom that is without estimate or end, immediately such people will love God, praise God, and long with a great desire to know God's great name . . . [because] when people think about these things, they respond [i.e., naturally] by drawing back and by becoming afraid, and by realizing that they are small, lowly, and fragile, endowed with slight and meager intelligence, standing in the presence of a God who is perfect in knowledge. (*MT* Hilkhot Y'sodei Ha-torah 2:2)

The alleged oppositional nature of religion and science thus vanishes in Maimonides' view that contemplating creation will naturally fill us with the desire to love God and a sense of connection to a greater order of things—and that our awe will be all the more profound when we allow ourselves to be filled with the kind of wonder particularly inspired by science. Perceiving how small a part of the universe our planet is, and considering how brief the history of the evolution of our species has been in the context of the history of the universe, will inevitably fill moderns with a sense of wonder, awe, and humility. This humility can then inspire a sense of reverence for creation and its Creator in us, and can moderate our sense that the world is ours to use and abuse as we see fit.

"Bal Tash·ḥit" and Environmentalism

In the last few decades it has become increasingly recognized just how much waste human beings, especially in the developed world, produce. (In their book *State of the World 1999* [New York: W.W. Norton, 1999], Lester R. Brown, Christopher Flaven, and Hilary French point out that the average person in the developed world consumes thirty-seven tons of resources each year, *excluding* food and energy [p. 41].) In response, the environmental movement created their "three R's" slogan: "Reduce, Reuse, and Recycle." While recycling has become commonplace for many people, most forget that the first R is actually "Reduce"; without reducing our consumption, we take a heavy toll on the environment—no matter how much we try to offset this by recycling. This continuing waste of resources causes great harm to the environment and, in the long run, an economy based on this kind of waste is not sustainable. (A sustainable economy is one where future generations will enjoy the same standard of living as do those alive today.) Wasteful consumption is leading to the degradation of the biosphere.

In the Jewish tradition, the *halakhah* actually deals explicitly with the concept of wasteful consumption. When we waste resources, we are violating the *mitzvah* not to destroy the world, usually known by its Hebrew name, *bal tash·ḥit,* literally, "do not destroy." The classical source is Deuteronomy 20:19–20:

> When you wage war against a city and have to besiege it for a long time in order to capture it, you must not destroy (Hebrew: *lo tash·ḥit*) its trees by wielding the ax against them. You may eat of them, but you must not cut them down. Are trees of the field human then, that they might withdraw before you into the besieged city? Only trees that you know do not yield food may be destroyed; them you may cut down for constructing siege works against the city that is at war with you, until it has been defeated.

This law is the basis of all subsequent *bal tash·ḥit* legislation, which later halakhic sources expanded to include the prohibition of the wanton destruction of household goods, clothes, buildings, springs, or food, or the wasteful consumption of anything at all (see *MT* Hilkhot M'lakhim U-milḥ'moteihem 6:8 and 10). The underlying idea is the recognition that everything we own ultimately belongs to God. Therefore, when we consume in a wasteful manner, we violate our mandate to use creation only for legitimate benefit. Modesty in consumption is a value that Jews have held for centuries, whether on the societal or individual level. For example, one is not supposed to be excessive in eating and drinking, or in wearing the kind of clothes that are more ostentatious than utilitarian (*MT* Hilkhot Dei·ot 5:1–3).

The over-consumption of resources is at the heart of the environmental crisis. As Jews, we are obligated to consider our real needs carefully whenever we purchase anything. When we have a *simḥah,* we are obligated to consider the extravagance of our celebrations. Are the meals overly elaborate? Are there wasteful decorations on every table? We are obligated to consider our celebrations from the vantage point of energy use as well, and to tailor them not merely to our tastes, but to our desire to behave responsibly and nobly with respect to the world in which we live.

Shabbat observance is one way for Jews to embrace the concept of living a sustainable life. For one day out of seven, Shabbat observers limit their use of the earth's resources dramatically. We walk to attend synagogue and drive only when walking is not possible. We do not cook or shop. Shabbat observers use the Shabbat day for relaxation and to contemplate certain key questions. What is the real purpose of human life? Are we here on earth only to get and to spend? Are we living responsibly? As Rabbi Schorsch has written, "To rest [on Shabbat] is to acknowledge our limitations. Willful inactivity is a statement of subservience to a power greater than our own" (*To Till and to Tend,* p. 20).

Pikku·aḥ Nefesh

In the last century, public health measures of various sorts have helped to wipe out many infectious diseases, adding an average of twenty-five years to the life expectancy of American adults. Despite many advances in medicine, however, there are many chronic diseases that are still on the rise, cancer among them, and there is solid evidence that environmental conditions created by the industrial use of toxic chemicals and materials may be a contributing factor in at least some occurrences of these diseases. In May 2001, an international convention was signed banning the use of ten persistent organic pollutants (POPs) and reducing the emission of other industrial toxic waste. This was the beginning of a significant effort to change how toxic chemicals are dealt with, from the perspective of public policy.

There are two contemporary environmental principles that are relevant. First is the "Precautionary Principle," which states that the onus of proving a technological advance to be safe should rest on the shoulders of its creators—and that this proof should be forthcoming *before* the alleged advance is implemented. Thus, in assessing the value to humanity of possibly harmful chemicals, it should be necessary for their developers to detail their possible detrimental effects in advance, rather than moving forward and only then, after the damage is done, to figure out how best to deal with it. This is connected to a second concept, the "Principle of Unintended Consequences," which holds that major technological innovations inevitably come with benign or malign side-effects, and that society should endeavor to identify these in advance and determine whether they warrant introducing the innovations in the first place.

In Jewish tradition, we have an obligation to save and preserve life. This obligation, called in Hebrew *pikku·aḥ nefesh,* is derived in the Talmud at *BT* Sanhedrin 74a from Leviticus 18:5, "You shall keep My laws and My rules, by the pursuit of which humankind shall live. . . ." Similarly, the law at Leviticus 19:28 formally forbids us from harming ourselves knowingly. And there are also numerous texts about the sacred task of protecting public hygiene, texts that range from ones regarding the need to keep noxious materials (which in our own day would surely include industrial by-products) far from human habitation, to others that encourage the proper disposal of human waste (see, e.g., Deuteronomy 23:13–15 or *M* Bava Batra 2:9). In Jewish tradition, the public good overrides the individual's desire for convenience or self-advancement.

While there are many useful and even lifesaving technologies that come from modern chemicals and materials, we have an obligation to be cautious in their use. The sacred value of *pikku·aḥ nefesh* demands that we consider the impact of our use of chemicals and other materials, both in the short term and in the long term. Nor is it solely human life with which we should be concerned, because the use of noxious chemicals impacts on animal and plant life as well. We might also see the Precautionary Principle as a modern form of the warning not to tamper too much with the boundaries of creation.

Energy Consumption and Nuclear Power

The largest sources of air pollution and greenhouse gases come from the production of energy and from transportation-related uses. Electricity is mostly produced by nonrenewable resources such as oil, coal, natural gas, and nuclear power. Only a small percentage comes from such sustainable sources as hydro-electrical, biomass, solar, or wind energy. Transportation-related pollution comes from the use of the internal combustion engine in cars, buses, trucks, airplanes, and trains. The pollution that comes from energy production and transportation is not only responsible for global warming (see below), but has also had a significant impact on human health and has been proven to cause the increase of asthma in children and the elderly. Air pollution also causes acid rain, damaging many ecosystems. While generating nuclear power does not produce air pollution *per se*, the waste products of this process remain toxic for thousands of years and no adequate way of safely storing this material has yet been found. And there is always the fear of a catastrophic accident at a nuclear power plant, which could result not only from malfunction, but also a terrorist attack. None of this is good news.

Given all these factors, there is a clear moral mandate in the Jewish tradition to limit our consumption of electricity, to drive high mileage or hybrid vehicles (and, when possible, meaningfully to limit our use of motor vehicles), and to support the growth of sustainable energy production. Since developed countries are responsible for the majority of global greenhouse gas emissions, consumers in those countries should purchase vehicles that have the highest fuel economy and use public transit, drive slower, carpool, walk, or bike whenever possible. The Jewish community should also support national energy policies that reduce the use of carbon-based energy sources and that encourage the further development and use of sustainable energy.

This moral mandate can be based not only on the principle of *bal tash·ḥit* discussed above, but also on Deuteronomy 29:13–14: "I make this covenant, with its sanctions, not with you alone, but both with those who are standing here with us this day before the Eternal, our God, and with those who are not with us here this day." The sages of classical antiquity interpreted this text (e.g., in the *Midrash Tanḥuma,* Yitro §11) to mean that the souls of all Jews ever to be born stood at Sinai to receive the Torah. Thus the covenant of Torah, with its clearly enunciated concept of humankind as the stewards of the earth, did not merely bind our ancestors who stood at Sinai, but also commits us to the care of creation for the sake of future generations.

Environmental Justice

"Environmental justice" is a term used to describe both the connection between the degradation of the environment and its impact on the poor and on people of color, and also the unequal distribution of resources between the developed and underdeveloped world. Poor people are disproportionately affected by environmental damage. (A large percentage of those who live in poor urban areas, for example, have health problems associated with pollution.) Landfill sites, garbage incinerators, and toxic waste dumps are often found in minority and low-income communities and neighborhoods. Many underdeveloped countries have also been forced by high debt loads to cede control of their natural resources to transnational corporations. While one-fifth of the world's population is living better than any human beings in the history of the world ever have, they are using eighty percent of the world's resources to maintain that august standard of living. Another fifth is struggling just to survive: hundreds of millions of people in our world are malnourished and over a billion people do not have access to clean water. The nations that will suffer the greatest effects of climate change produce the least amount of greenhouse gases, and are therefore the ones least responsible for the creation of these problems.

The Bible suggests that creation itself has been out of balance because of humanity's unchecked egotism and greed since the expulsion from the Garden of Eden. Unlike other creatures, which by their nature live in proper balance within creation, humans have, by virtue of their free will, the ability to upset God's work. This too is bad news for those who take seriously the stewardship of the earth that the Torah grants us.

How, then, should we respond to these inequities? The concept of *tzedek,* usually translated as "righteousness" or "justice," can also mean "equity," and so in the idea of *tzedek* rests the beginning of a practical Jewish attempt to return the world to a more equitable balance of power. In the Bible, *tzedek* is used to describe the proper order of society put in place by God. In Leviticus 19:35–36, for example, the Torah uses the word *tzedek* four times to stress the importance of probity in commerce: "You shall not falsify measures of length, weight, or capacity. You shall have an honest balance, honest weights, an honest *eifah*-measure, and an honest *hin*-measure. I am the Eternal, your God, who brought you out of the land of Egypt!"

To falsify weights and measures can be understood symbolically as a reference to violating the balance of creation and society. Maintaining honest or equitable weights and measures—in other words, insisting that things weigh out justly and fairly in the marketplace—can be seen as a challenge to redress the imbalances in governance and business in the global arena as well.

The Torah has a whole program of *tzedek*-based laws, all of which try to preserve a just distribution of resources across the community. The laws found at Exodus 23:11, Leviticus 25:2–5, and Deuteronomy 15:1–4, which require all fields to lie fallow every seven years and for debts concomitantly to be forgiven, are all examples of this concept of fair-balance *tzedek*. (The sabbatical-year remission of debts is discussed elsewhere in this volume by Rabbis Elliot Dorff and Tracee L. Rosen in their chapters regarding the *halakhah* of charitable giving, and loans and lending, respectively.) So too is the law at Leviticus 25:8–24 that ordains a kind of super-sabbatical every fiftieth year, the so-called jubilee year, in which all land sales are cancelled, properties return to their original owners (with some few exceptions), and slaves are granted their freedom. (The laws regarding the jubilee year are elsewhere discussed in this volume by Rabbi Martin S. Cohen in his chapter on Israel.) *Tzedek* should therefore be at the heart of the Jewish perspective on environmental justice. If we do not live according to *tzedek,* we will continue to see a degraded biosphere. Without *tzedek,* there will be increased competition for ever-diminishing resources, and this will intensify the level of violence and warfare that has been endemic over the last hundred years. According to Thomas Homer-Dixon, writing in his *Environment, Scarcity, and Violence* (Princeton: Princeton University Press, 1999), there is a direct connection between environmental degradation and human conflict. Although there are those who dispute this, I—and I write here both as a rabbi and a Jew—find Homer-Dixon's argument compelling, challenging, inspiring, and terrifying all at the same time. In the twentieth century alone there were more than 100 million war-related deaths, and many millions more died from artificially-created famines, expulsions, and genocide. Since 1945, there have been more than 15 million war deaths, with the largest percentage of victims being civilians. Many of these conflicts can be traced to struggles over dwindling resources resulting from misuse and abuse of the environment.

None of this is good news for anyone who cares about the world. For Jews, who take *tikkun olam* as their sacred mandate, it should sound a call to arms that could conceivably change everything. Environmental justice is a necessity for any kind of human civilization in the long term. Therefore, *tzedek* requires Jews to support the establishment of international treaties designed to help assure the proper distribution of resources.

Biodiversity

Every morning at sunrise, the birds begin to sing in what ornithologists call "the dawn chorus" to signal that they are still alive and can still hold on to their territory. But many won't be singing for too much longer. In North America, for example, twenty-eight percent of the most carefully monitored species of birds are in serious decline. (Interested readers may consult *State of the World 2003,* eds. Lester R. Brown, Christopher Flaking, and Hilary French [New York: W. W. Norton, 2003], pp. 16ff.) Almost all of this decline is a direct result of human activity that has led to habitat loss, introducing non-native predators or diseases into ecosystems that cannot sustain their presence; hunting; constructing power lines and skyscrapers; and human-induced climate change. It is not only the birds who are in trouble, however. There are actually 1.8 million known species of animals, plants, fungi, bacteria, and other kinds of life in our world. (The actual total number of species is not known. Scientists estimate that there could be anywhere from four to forty million species yet to be discovered.) While it is estimated that the natural extinction rate resulted in the loss of between one and three species per year for almost all of history, the current annual extinction rate is at least three hundred to a thousand times the previous historical level—almost all of it the direct or indirect result of human activity. The earth is experiencing a loss of biodiversity unparalleled since the disappearance of the dinosaurs sixty-five million years ago. This too is very bad news.

Our ancestors could not have anticipated the loss of biodiversity that the modern world has produced and, therefore, we look in vain for specific guidelines from the ancients suggesting how to deal with it. From their perspective, after all, there was no natural extinction rate of species at all. God, they believed, created all species at one time. Therefore, there could be no new creatures, and neither could any disappear, save because God willed it. But we know that this is not the case and that humans *are* entirely capable of causing extinction—thus silencing whole sections of the creation choir. It is to this truth that modern Jews must respond.

The Torah's law at Deuteronomy 22:6–7 says that if, while walking along a road, "you chance upon a bird's nest, in any tree or on the ground, with fledglings or eggs, and the mother is sitting over the fledglings or on the eggs, do not take the mother with her young. Let the mother go, and take only the young, in order that you may fare well and have a long life." Commenting on this passage in his commentary to the Torah, Rabbi Moses ben Naḥman (called Naḥmanides or Ramban, 1194–1270) wrote the following words:

> This commandment is a derivative of the prohibition of killing an animal and its young both in one day [stated at Leviticus 22:28], the reason for both being that we should not have cruel hearts and that we should be compassionate. Alternately, it may be that Scripture does not permit us to destroy a species altogether, although it permits slaughter [for food] within that group. The person who kills a mother and its young in one day, or who takes them when they are free to fly, [is regarded] as having destroyed that [entire] species.

It is evident from the first chapter of Genesis and from many other biblical texts (e.g., Psalms 104 and 148; Job 38–41) that God takes care of, and takes great pleasure in, the variety of life that makes up creation. And, although we ourselves might regard a species as unimportant or bothersome, God does not regard them so. The rabbis maintained that we do not know God's purpose for every creature and therefore we should not regard any of them as superfluous. "Our rabbis said: even those things that humans tend to regard as completely superfluous to creation—[pests] such as fleas, gnats, and flies—even they were included in creation. [Therefore, our basic assumption should always be that] God's purpose is carried through everything—even through snakes, scorpions, gnats, or frogs" (*B'reishit Rabbah* 10:7). In environmental terms, too, it is axiomatic that every species has an inherent value beyond its utility to human beings. In this matter, Jewish tradition and modern environmental philosophy are in complete accord. Therefore, we have an obligation to protect the choir of creation by preserving the natural habitats of its members and by making sure that we are not responsible for the extinction of species. We must never pit the preservation of a species against human needs—which we unfortunately do, and all too often, by mistaking our wants for our needs. To do so, speaking in rabbinic terms, would be to deny the wisdom of God the Creator or, even worse, to imagine that we are free to supersede God's plan for the world merely to service our own needs or desires.

Environmentalism and Food Issues

Rabbi Paul Drazen discusses the dietary laws of the Torah at great length elsewhere in this volume, but here I would like specifically to focus on the way that those laws intersect with the issues that I have been writing about in this chapter.

In recent years, the issue of Genetically Modified Organisms (GMOs) has become one of the major concerns both of the environmental movement and also of consumer groups concerned with food safety. In traditional farming, new or improved species are regularly created through cross-breeding with similar species. Indeed, many of the world's food crops were created through such breeding thousands of years ago. More recently, as scientists' ability to manipulate genetic factors has become more sophisticated, the crossbreeding of species for many valuable traits has become a major factor in human agricultural production. With the discovery of DNA, however, an even more powerful tool was created. By splicing genes from one organism into another, crossbreeding could be done in a much shorter time and with much less trial and error. Moreover, gene splicing has also allowed the crossbreeding of organisms that would never crossbreed in the wild and that would not previously have been possible using traditional techniques. These newer techniques have been used in the pharmaceutical industry for several decades to produce hormones, insulin, and other drugs, but some of the recent advances in agriculture have been even more amazing. For example, a gene from an insect has been spliced into corn, thus creating a corn plant that produces its own pesticide. When applied to agricultural products that are used for human and animal consumption, these new organisms are called Genetically Modified Organisms (GMOs).

In formulating a Jewish response to GMOs, there are three issues to consider. Are GMOs safe for consumption? If they are safe, are they kosher? And, even if they are kosher, are they environmentally acceptable for Jews concerned with preserving the world and its fragile environment?

If GMOs are not safe, then Jewish law would prohibit them categorically because we are not permitted to harm ourselves. At this time, there is no categorical scientific evidence that GMOs are unsafe. However, many consumer and environmental groups feel that not enough research has been done to settle this issue. (See, for example, *Made Not Born: The Troubling World of Biotechnology,* ed. Casey Walker [San Francisco: Sierra Club Books, 2000], for a detailed discussion of these issues.)

Second, might GMOs actually be unkosher, since many of them have genes transplanted from non-kosher animals? In 1997, the Committee on Jewish Law and Standards of the Rabbinical Assembly approved a responsum written by Avram Reisner which determined that GMOs are not unkosher, regardless of the origin of their genetic material, because the laws of prohibited mixtures simply do not apply to the submicroscopic manipulation of genetic material (*CJLS Responsa 1991–2000,* pp. 101–111). Others believe that, since a spliced-in gene is present in every cell in the entire organism, it may well constitute a significant enough portion of the total mass of the product to render it unkosher. Rabbi Reisner's responsum also touches on the issue of *kilayim* (forbidden mixtures of animals, plants, grain, and cloth; see Leviticus 19:19) that might conceivably be applied to GMOs to render them forbidden. The *halakhah,* however, has traditionally been very lenient in allowing the consumption of products made of or containing *kilayim,* and that, Rabbi Reisner says, should be sufficient for us to permit them. He also says that, if GMOs can help feed the world's starving population, then they should be permitted under the general category of *pikku·aḥ nefesh* legislation (new laws enacted or existing laws set aside specifically to save human lives). However, many environmentalists question whether GMOs actually will produce the benefits that are claimed for them. Many are also concerned that widespread use of GMOs will lead to greater corporate control of the world's food supply (see, e.g., *Made Not Born,* pp. 1–6). As the years pass, halakhic discourse regarding GMOs will become more focused and more detailed. For the moment, however, we may certainly rely on Rabbi Reisner's responsum, which considers the halakhic issues connected with GMOs not to be a problem.

The third objection is that GMOs can be harmful to the environment by unintentionally spreading bioengineered organisms to natural habitats. These organisms then compete with wild species and may possibly cause the wild species to become extinct, or else may create new hybrids that could severely damage the ecosystem. (This has actually now been observed in areas where fields of GMO crops border fields of non-GMO crops.) While Judaism certainly permits the manipulation of creation for human benefit, especially when it comes to health and healing, we are not permitted by the Torah to alter the boundaries of creation radically. How we balance these two ideas is the central issue in the Jewish discussion about the use of GMOs.

While we now understand, based on the theory of evolution, that species are not static by nature, we can nonetheless make a distinction between the way creation naturally evolves and humans' radical intervention in that process. Genetic engineering crosses species that would never be crossed in the natural world, and does so in a time frame that collapses thousands of years of evolution into a single generation. If we apply the Precautionary Principle and the Principle of Unintended Consequences to consideration of this issue, then this process could well be considered a modern violation of the boundaries of creation and thus an instance of humankind going far beyond the permissible manipulation of creation for its own benefit, without fully considering, or even fully apprehending, the consequences.

For these reasons, Jews should be cautious indeed when it comes to the issue of genetically modified foods. Many of these have been rushed onto the market without much consideration of their environmental impact on other species, or of the long-term effects their introduction might conceivably have on the health of those who consume them. Also, the supposed benefits of GMOs are more difficult to assess than those of new pharmaceuticals created through advances in biotechnology, and will probably not offset the problems they may bring. At the very least, we should be demanding that the regulatory system governing GMOs be strengthened so that risks and benefits connected with these foods can be more carefully assessed before they are brought to market. We should also demand that GMOs be clearly labeled so that those who wish to avoid them are able to do so. Currently in the United States, only food labeled "organic" is required by government regulation to be GMO-free. In Europe, all food products must be clearly labeled if they contain GMOs.

Another environmental issue related to food involves the issue of organic food. Should Jews consume solely organic food? While GMOs may be technically kosher, there are those who believe that Jews should follow a kind of eco-*kashrut,* in which *kashrut* is determined based not only on how select animals are slaughtered or what ingredients are used but also on the way animals and crops are raised. Organic foods are grown by farmers who follow sustainable agricultural practices, which the U.S. Department of Agriculture (USDA) defines as those which "emphasize the use of renewable resources and the conservation of soil and water to enhance environmental quality for future generations." (This definition and much other related information can be found on the website of the USDA-sponsored National Agricultural Library at www.nal.usda.gov.)

The USDA standards for organic animal or dairy products labeled as such require that they come from animals to which no antibiotics or growth hormones have been given, that they be produced without the use of conventional pesticides, and that only fertilizers with synthetic ingredients or sewage sludge be used. Food labeled "organic" must also be neither bioengineered nor radiated.

The nutritional superiority of organic foods over conventional foods is still a matter of scientific debate. However, since organic farming is sustainable farming, eco-*kashrut* suggests that we should support organic farming to the greatest extent possible. There has grown up in the last decade a major Jewish food movement which supports the values of eco-*kashrut* and sustainable agriculture, and much information about this movement and its history can be found on the Hazon website at www.hazon.org. Therefore, Jews should, where possible, follow the values of eco-*kashrut* and prioritize buying local and organic foods in order to avoid GMOs and support local sustainable agriculture.

Population and Consumption

The world population is now more than seven billion people. Although the United Nations has estimated that the world's population will level off and begin to decline in 2050, there will already be anywhere from 7.8 billion to 12.5 billion people on earth at that time. And while many countries have falling birth rates, others do not.

The population issue is not only about the actual number of people on earth, but also about how much those people consume. No one actually knows how many people the earth can support, because such a calculation would have to depend on the per capita level of consumption of each individual. If we use the consumption rates of the developed countries, for example, then what is called the carrying capacity of the earth will be much lower than if we use the consumption rates of citizens of the world's underdeveloped countries. By way of example, every year the average American consumes about forty times as much as the average Mexican or Indian. More to the point is the simple fact that current levels of consumption are not sustainable and have already caused widespread environmental damage.

Is this a specifically Jewish issue? When the Jewish community first debated the concept of Zero Population Growth (ZPG) over twenty years ago, there was a consensus that Jewish losses in the Holocaust and attrition due to intermarriage grant a morally justifiable exemption from promoting ZPG within our own community, even while we could (and perhaps should) advocate it for others. This is still the moral stance of most of the Jewish community and it is the perspective put forward by Rabbi Carl Astor elsewhere in this volume. This issue is discussed at length by Rabbis Kassel Abelson and Elliot Dorff in a 2007 responsum on the topic approved by the CJLS and available on the website of the Rabbinical Assembly.

However, there are other aspects of the issue to consider. Most of the world's Jews live in developed countries and are concentrated in the middle and upper middle classes, where resource consumption is at the highest levels. Given its rates of consumption, the Jewish community can no longer claim a moral exemption from limiting our own population growth. We also do not have the moral right to call for other nations to limit their populations unless we first deal with our own personal and communal consumption. The conspicuous consumption of our celebrations—our bar and bat mitzvah celebrations, our weddings, and the like—is just one example of how we are part of the problem and why, therefore, we must also be part of the solution.

Moderation is at the core of Jewish ethics. Indeed, in the medieval period, Jewish communities often enacted sumptuary laws that regulated dress, celebrations, and food consumption to prevent ostentation and waste. We should follow our ancestors' model and revive such communal standards to demonstrate our fundamental understanding that mindless consumption is antithetical to Judaism.

Climate Change

Since the Earth Summit in Rio de Janeiro in 1992, there has developed a scientific consensus that the increase of carbon dioxide in the atmosphere (an increase caused primarily by the burning of fossil fuels) is causing the warming of the earth and the changing of the climate. This climate change is occurring at an increasingly accelerated rate, and the effects of human-created climate change will become more and more evident as this century wears on. Indeed, one could argue that human-induced climate change poses the greatest challenge of all to human survival, as it will radically alter climate patterns that have been relatively stable for more than 10,000 years and it will produce devastating changes throughout the world. Readers should understand that this concern is primarily related to scale: while humans have always altered their environments for specific reasons on the local level, the kind of change now occurring is taking place on a wholly unprecedented global scale. Of course, the people who will be most affected by climate change will be the ones who contributed the least to the problem—and who will be the least able to survive it. For example, it is projected that crop yields in most tropical and subtropical regions will be reduced, and that fresh water will become even more scarce in the subtropics, where there is already a water shortage. These kinds of changes have already begun to take place and it is countries in the Middle East (including Israel) that will be the most affected by these changes. There will also be increased flood risk for tens of millions of people because of a rise in the sea level, which will also render many river deltas unfit for agriculture because of salinization. It has been conservatively estimated that by 2050 there will be 250 million "climate refugees" from affected areas. (See, for example, the paper by Koko Warner, Charles Ehrhart, Alex de Sherbinin, Susana Adamo, and Tricia Chai-Onn, available on-line at the website of the Center for International Earth Science Information Network, a center within the Earth Institute at Columbia University.) The Intergovernmental Panel on Climate Change (IPCC), a group of hundreds of experts on climate change from around the world convened by the United Nations in 1988, determined that "the effects of climate change are expected to be greatest in developing countries in terms of loss of life and relative effects on investment and the economy" (*State of the World 2002,* eds. Christopher Flavin, Hillary French, and Gary Gardner [New York: W. W.

Norton, 2002], p. 29). Their most recent report (available on-line at the website of the Intergovernmental Panel on Climate Change [www.ipcc.ch]) details the scientific basis for the human causes of climate change, its impacts, and what governments should be doing to mitigate its effects.

To prevent unspeakable disaster, it will be necessary for the world to switch over from a carbon-based energy economy to one based on sustainable resources. By 2050, humanity must reduce its greenhouse gas output by eighty to ninety per cent of present levels. This is the only way to slow climate change and to reduce its effects, and this change will have to come from a combination of new technologies and changes in human behavior. Human beings must think beyond their immediate needs to consider the fate of the whole biosphere.

Our tradition is a rich resource for theological ideas and values that demand we look beyond our individual desires and see ourselves not as masters of the universe, but as servants of God and as stewards of God's world. Climate change is the single greatest example of how we are disrupting the order of creation without any real idea where the changes we have wrought will lead us. Therefore, as Jews, we must make a moral commitment to developing a sustainable economy, and we must adopt personal practices and communal policies that reflect that ideal. We must also urge our governments to become part of an international process to lower carbon emissions. The future of the Jewish community is bound up with the environmental fate of the world.

Globalization

Instantaneous communication and international trade and investment have shrunk the world and broken down countless barriers among people. This process is called globalization. While this process refers to the free movement of people, information, money, goods, and services, globalization can also create major disruptions in local cultures and environments. While globalization has created great wealth for millions of people, many millions more have been bypassed by its benefits. In some cases, it has also had a negative impact upon the environment and human rights, as transnational corporations have transferred industrial production to, and dumped toxic industrial waste in, countries with little ability to maintain environmental or labor standards.

While there are those who seek to reverse the trend toward ever-increasing globalization, it is evident that the real issue is not whether we will have a globalized world, but rather what kind of globalization we will support. Can we create a worldwide economy that is sustainable and that is equitable in the distribution of wealth? Or will globalization turn out merely to be a different version of the age-old struggle between the rich and the poor for jobs and resources? The answer is that there is no answer: the fate of the world truly is in our hands. In this regard, consider the following *midrash* that Jewish environmentalists are fond of quoting: "When God created the first human beings, God led them around the Garden of Eden and said: 'Look at My works! See how beautiful they are and how excellent! For your sake, I created them all. See to it that you do not spoil and destroy My world; for if you do, there will be no one else to repair it'" (*Kohelet Rabbah* 7:20).

In the Aleinu prayer, we ask that the world soon be perfected under the sovereignty of God. And, indeed, the phrase *tikkun olam,* meaning the perfecting or the repairing of the world, has become a major theme in modern Jewish social justice theology, which should certainly be taken to include environmental issues. It is usually used to denote a category of activities to be undertaken by humans in partnership with God, and it is an apt metaphor in light of the task ahead in Jewish environmentalism. Out of ignorance, greed, and egotism, we have damaged the world and silenced many of the voices of the choir of creation. Now we must fix it as best we can, for, as the *midrash* said so long ago, there is no one but us to do the job.

Afterword

MARTIN S. COHEN

There is something to be learned from the fact that the Torah tells the story of Israel's long march away from Sinai in far more detail, and with far more enthusiasm, than it tells the story of the Israelites' journey to the mountain on which they would receive the Torah. True, the time frames are entirely different: seven short weeks from leaving Egypt until arriving at Sinai, which Scripture calls the Mountain of God, and thirty-nine years less a month between leaving Sinai and arriving at the border of the Promised Land. But there is more here than meets the eye at first, more than a mere apportioning out of appropriate space to accommodate the details of a longer story and a shorter one. The journey to Sinai was the flight of slaves, thus a journey to freedom from oppression. But the journey away from Sinai was undertaken by free men and women possessed of the revealed rudiments of divine law, thus a redemptive journey toward freedom not from bondage but from irrelevance and pointlessness, toward lives in and of God, toward the ability finally to accept the great and holy task to define the mission of Israel as the quest to become a nation of priests and a people suffused with ineffable holiness.

The Hebrew word *halakhah,* whatever its historical etymology, has been connected by countless generations with the concept of the journey through life to God. The *halakhah* is thus the stuff of the redemptive journey from a world anchored in time and space to the world behind the world, to the world beyond the world, to the world outside the world that is the sovereign realm of heaven. To walk on this sacred path requires neither impossibly intense preparation nor great wisdom, neither complex training nor innate intelligence nor athletic prowess. Instead, it requires a guileless heart and an open mind, a spirit suffused with the love of God and a soul unsullied by the boastful certainty of the boor or the secret hope for self-aggrandizement that is the hallmark of the willfully arrogant. It requires a certain amount of information, of course, because the *halakhah* is a path of ritual exactitude that none but the well-trained can follow without erring either grievously or at least slightly. But far more important to note is that the pursuit of this specific path toward a life in God requires the kind of profound humility that most have to work at cultivating consciously, and which is a natural feature of the personalities of almost none. The *halakhah* will never beckon successfully, or perhaps even at all, to the self-absorbed.

This *halakhah* of which we speak is not Jerusalem, but it is the path toward Jerusalem that the faithful may follow if they are prepared to set down their burdens and follow their finer selves to the redemptive moment that is the great goal of all religious endeavor undertaken without the hope of tangible reward. It is, therefore, partially a road and partially a door, partially a gate and partially the path that leads up to that gate, but it is also the unseen and unknown journey that lies beyond the gate. To know the *halakhah* is thus to embrace the paradox of a journey that is somehow its own destination, of a journey to heaven any may undertake that is somehow also a journey to the center of the human heart. And why should the path to heaven lie through the secret chambers of the beating heart? The question is key . . . and its answer, sublime: we seek God through the context of our own lives, and through the endless refinement of the law in the context of life as we know it, because, in a day in which the Jewish people is obliged to exist divested by circumstance of Temple and altar, the indwelling of God's holy presence, the Sh'khinah, exists accessibly only within the warp and woof of our daily lives. And there, in the nooks and crannies of the relationships we sustain and the roles we play and the jobs we do, redemption awaits the intrepid pilgrim possessed of the kind of focused will necessary to seek the holy through the sanctification of the mundane, thus to begin to know—or at least to know of—the Creator through the contemplation of creation. In a very real sense, that is the whole Torah. And therefore do I end this very long book with some ancient words: *zil g'mor, go* now that you have been presented with the principles that guide our Jewish lives . . . *and learn* the details as best you can so that you can successfully and productively meditate upon them by day and by night, when you rise up in the morning and when you lie down at night, when you are at home and, most courageously of all, when you must travel down the road that leads far away from home.

MSC
Roslyn, New York
JUNE 1, 2011
יום ירושלים תשע"א

Glossary

(Except where otherwise indicated, the terms listed below are Hebrew words or Aramaic words used in Hebrew.)

afikomen: the piece of *matzah* with which one concludes the *seder* meal on the first evenings of Passover

aggadah: the part of ancient rabbinic works deemed essentially homiletical in nature, as opposed to those parts of those same works concerned mostly with *halakhah*

agunah: a woman unable to remarry because she is not in possession of a formal divorce document

Aleinu: an ancient hymn recited as part of the Musaf Service on the High Holidays and also at the conclusion of every weekday, Sabbath, and festival service of the liturgical year

Al Ḥeit: the longer confessional recited on Yom Kippur

aliyah (plural: *aliyot*): the name given to the honor of being called forward to the Torah to recite the blessings before and after its public recitation, and also the general term for the immigration of Jewish people to the Land of Israel

Amidah: the prayer that serves as the centerpiece of the worship service

amora (plural: *amora·im*): a rabbi of the talmudic period

aninut: the name for the period of time between the death of a relation for whom one must mourn formally and the burial of that person *arba·ah minim:* the "four species" used during the festival of Sukkot consisting of sprigs of willow and myrtle, a palm frond, and a citron

arba kanfot: a kind of four-cornered undershirt to which ritual *tzitzit* (*q.v.*) have been attached

Areshet S'fateinu: a prayer from the Rosh Hashanah liturgy sung directly after the sounding of the *shofar* (*q.v.*).

Ashamnu: the shorter confessional recited on Yom Kippur

Ashrei: the 145th psalm, preceded in its liturgical setting by Psalm 84:5 and Psalm 144:15

aufruf (Yiddish, literally "a calling forward"): the occasion of offering an *aliyah* (*q.v.*) to a bridegroom and/or a bride prior to their wedding

Avodah: the section of the Musaf Service on Yom Kippur in which the ancient Temple ritual for that day is retold.

ba·al t'fillah (feminine: *ba·alat t'fillah*): the individual who leads a prayer service

badeken (Yiddish): the ceremony at which a bride's veil is formally lowered before a wedding

Bar'khu: the formal call to worship in the Morning and Evening Services

bateil b'shishim: the principle according to which the inclusion of a non-kosher substance constituting less than a sixtieth part of the whole is not considered meaningful enough to render the entire mixture unkosher

b'di-avad (or, colloquially, *b'di-eved*): *ex post facto*

b'dikat ḥameitz: the formal search for remaining *ḥameitz* (*q.v.*) that takes place on the evening before the first night of Passover

bein adam la-ḥaveiro: the term designating the commandments that govern relationships between people

bein adam la-makom: the term designating the commandments that govern the relationship between humanity and God

beit din: a rabbinic court

bikkur ḥolim: the act of visiting the sick

bimah: the raised platform in the front of a synagogue

Birkat Ha-ḥodesh: the blessing recited in synagogue on the Sabbath preceding Rosh Ḥodesh (*q.v.*)

b'rit or *b'rit milah:* circumcision itself or the ceremony at which a boy is circumcised *davar ḥarif:* the term for sharp-tasting food deemed especially susceptible to contamination by non-kosher utensils or, according to some authorities, deemed able to transfer traces of dairy or meat foodstuffs from one utensil to another

dreidel (Yiddish): a top with which children traditionally play at Ḥanukkah

Eilleh Ezk'rah: a martyrology recited during the Musaf Service on Yom Kippur

eiruv: either a dish cooked on the eve of a festival as a means of permitting cooking for Shabbat on the days of the ensuing festival *or* a means of enabling carrying on Shabbat by creating a kind of artificial fence around the area in question *or* a means of enabling the residents of homes surrounding a courtyard to carry items from their homes into the courtyard or *vice versa* or from one home to another

eiruv tavshilin: the technical name for the first *eiruv* definition referenced above

Eishet Ḥayil: Proverbs 31:10–31, recited at the Shabbat table by a husband in praise of his wife

Erev Pesaḥ: either the day preceding Passover or, more loosely, the first evening of the festival

etrog: a citron, used as one of the *arba·ah minim* (*q.v.*) on Sukkot

farfel (Yiddish): crushed or crumbled *matzah* (*q.v.*), used in Passover cooking

fleishig (Yiddish): made of meat or containing meat or meat products or by-products, also used to denote the utensils in a kosher home used for meat or foods containing meat

gabbai (feminine: *gabba·it*): one of the individuals who supervise the reading of the Torah during the synagogue service

gelt (Yiddish): gifts of coins or money distributed to children at Ḥanukkah

get: a bill of divorce

gid ha-nasheh: the sciatic nerve

glatt (Yiddish): literally "smooth," used to describe the lesion-free lungs of a kosher-slaughtered animal

g'matriyyah: the use of the numerological values of Hebrew letters to derive hidden meaning from the words they spell

grogger (Yiddish): a Purim noisemaker

haftarah: a lesson from the Prophets read in synagogue on Shabbat and festivals following the Torah reading

Haggadah: the book containing the home liturgy for the eve of Passover *halakhah* (plural: *halakhot*): Jewish law

ḥalav yisra·el: milk produced under Jewish auspices

ḥalitzah: the ceremony whereby a childless widow and her late husband's brother are relieved of their theoretical obligation to wed

ḥallah: the dough tax owed in ancient times to the priests of Israel

ḥallah: the traditional egg bread eaten at Shabbat and festival meals

Hallel: Psalms 113–118, when read liturgically in honor of most festivals of the Jewish year

hamantaschen (Yiddish): a triangular Purim pastry

ḥameitz: leavened foodstuffs

ḥanukkiyyah: the Ḥanukkah candelabrum popularly called a *m'norah* (*q.v.*), especially by English-speaking Jews

Hashkiveinu: the popular name of the second blessing following the Sh'ma in the Evening Service

hattafat dam b'rit: the act of drawing a drop of blood at the site of circumcision undertaken for male converts to Judaism who are already circumcised

Ha-yom Harat Olam: one of the prayers that follow the sounding of the *shofar* (*q.v.*) on Rosh Hashanah

ḥazzan: cantor

heiter iska: a document designed to alter the relationship between lender and borrower into a kind of business partnership

hekhsheir: the symbol of a *kashrut* (*q.v.*) supervisory agency or individual

ḥevra kaddisha: the traditional name for a burial society

ḥevruta (plural: *ḥevrutot*): a study group

ḥillul ha-sheim: an act deemed by its nature to disgrace the divine name

ḥokhmah: wisdom

ḥol ha-mo·eid: one of the intermediary days of Passover or Sukkot

hoshanot: the name of a liturgical sequence recited in synagogue on the mornings of Sukkot *or*, loosely, the willow branches used as part of the *arba·ah minim* (*q.v.*) on that festival

ḥumash: the text of the Torah printed out in book form

ḥuppah: the wedding canopy

Kabbalat Shabbat: the opening liturgical sequence recited in synagogue on Friday evening consisting of Psalms 95–99, the hymn L'khah Dodi (*q.v.*), and Psalms 92 and 93

Kaddish: either the prayer recited by mourners in synagogue *or* one of several versions of that same prayer used as a doxology during the synagogue service *or* a version of that prayer recited after study *or* a longer version of that prayer recited at burials

kapparah: an act that effects atonement or leads to atonement

karm'lit: in the context of the laws delimiting the right to carry things around on Shabbat, an area judged to be similar in some ways to a public thoroughfare and in others to a private domain

kashering or *koshering:* either the act of rendering edible kosher-slaughtered meat by removing the remaining blood *or* the act of making a utensil kosher for use

kashrut: the general name for the Jewish dietary laws

kavush ki-m'vushal: the legal principle according to which prolonged soaking in liquid is considered the equivalent of cooking

kavvanah: intent, especially during prayer

K'dushah ("holiness"): the version of the third blessing of the Amidah (*q.v.*) in which the congregation participates when the prayer is repeated aloud by the prayer leader

keva: fixity, particularly with respect to prayer

kiddush ha-sheim: "the sanctification of God's name," usually used to denote martyrdom

kiddushin: betrothal

kippah: a skullcap, also called a *yarmulke* (*q.v.*)

kittel (Yiddish): a white robe worn by some at certain times of the year during prayer and by bridegrooms

kohein (plural: *kohanim*): a priest

Kol Nidrei: a prayer recited just before the onset of Yom Kippur regarding the annulment of vows

k'ri·ah: the act of tearing a garment as a sign of mourning

k'tubbah (plural: *k'tubbot*): the Jewish marriage document

kvatter (Yiddish; feminine: *kvatterin*): the name given to the person or persons who carry a baby boy into the room in which his circumcision will take place

k'vod ha-b'riyyot ("the honor due all living things"): the concept of innate human dignity

Lag Ba-omer: the thirty-third day of the *s'firah* (*q.v.*)

leivi (plural: *l'viyyim*): Levite

levirate marriage: the marriage of the widow of a childless man with her late husband's brother

L'khah Dodi: a hymn by Rabbi Shlomo Halevi Alkabetz (c. 1500–1580) sung during Kabbalat Shabbat (*q.v.*)

l'khat·ḥilah: a priori

l'shon ha-ra: a general term for gossip or slander

lulav: the palm frond used on Sukkot as one of the *arba·ah minim* (*q.v.*)

Ma·ariv: the Evening Service

maftir (feminine: *maftirah*): the individual called forward to recite the *haftarah* (*q.v.*) and, by extension, the *aliyah* (*q.v.*) offered in synagogue to such a person prior to the recitation of the *haftarah*

Magein Avot: a prayer from the Friday Evening liturgy

maḥzor: a festival prayerbook, especially the one in use on the High Holidays

Malkhuyyot: a passage featuring biblical verses asserting divine sovereignty over the world included in the Musaf Service on Rosh Hashanah

mamzeir: an individual born to Jewish parents who may not legally marry

mara de'atra: the rabbi who serves as halakhic decisor in a Jewish community

marit ayin: appearance, specifically used to denote the appearance of incorrect or immoral behavior when the activity in question is technically within legal bounds

matzah sh'murah: a special kind of *matzah* (*q.v.*) eaten by the very punctilious on Passover or at the *seder* meals, also colloquially called *sh'murah-matzah*

mensch (Yiddish): an upstanding individual

m'gillah: scroll, usually referenced as "the *m'gillah*" to denote the Book of Esther

midrash: a homiletical or hermeneutic text based on a biblical passage

mikveh: a ritual bath

milchig (Yiddish): dairy or containing dairy products, also used to denote the utensils used for dairy foods in a kosher home

Minḥah: the Afternoon Service

minyan (plural: *minyanim*): a prayer quorum

mishlo·aḥ manot: the *mitzvah* (*q.v.*) of sending gifts of food to others on Purim *mishnah* (plural: *mishnayyot*): a paragraph within the larger work of rabbinic law also called the Mishnah

mitzvah (plural: *mitzvot*): commandment

m'lakhah: work, usually in the context of the kinds of work forbidden on Shabbat

m'norah: the popular term in use among English-speaking Jews to denote the Ḥanukkah candelabrum

moheil (feminine: *mohelet*): a person trained to perform ritual circumcision

m'saddeir gittin (feminine: *m'sadderet gittin*): the formal designation of a rabbi trained to write Jewish divorce documents

muktzeh: a term colloquially used to denote materials that it is forbidden even to touch on Shabbat

Musaf: the Additional Service recited on Shabbat and festivals

m'zuzah: a box containing a small parchment scroll affixed to the doorposts of Jewish homes

naḥes (Yiddish): pleasure or satisfaction, especially parental pride in the accomplishments of one's children

Ne'ilah: the closing service on Yom Kippur

niddah: a menstruant, also used loosely to denote menstruation

nissu·in: marriage

notein ta·am: the term used to denote the ability of foodstuffs to alter the flavor of foods with which they are mixed

nusaḥ: the traditional melodies used during the prayer service *or* a term used to denote a version of a liturgical text

n'veilah: a term denoting meat that comes from an animal that died naturally

omer: a sheaf, in the biblical context a sheaf of barley, used in the expression "to count the *omer*" to denote the *mitzvah* (*q.v.*) to count aloud the days between Passover and Shavuot

onein (feminine: *onenet*): an individual obliged to mourn for someone who has died but who has yet to be buried

pareve: containing neither dairy nor meat products

pat yisra·el: bread baked by Jews

Pesaḥ: the Hebrew name for Passover

pidyon ha-bein: the redemption of the firstborn

pidyon sh'vuyim: the redemption of captives

pikku·aḥ nefesh: the doctrine according to which almost all the commandments may be set aside for the sake of saving a human life

piyyut (plural: *piyyutim*): a liturgical poem

prozbul: a document designed to override the remission of debt occasioned by the sabbatical year

P'sukei D'zimra: a series of psalms recited at the opening of the Morning Service

ra·ashan: a noisemaker, generally one used during the reading of the *m'gillah* (*q.v.*) on Purim

ribbit: interest received or paid on a loan

Rosh Ḥodesh: the first day in a Jewish month and occasionally the one preceding it

seder (plural: *s'darim*): the ritual meal eaten on the first nights of Passover *or* a term denoting one of the six larger sections of the Mishnah

se'udah mafseket: the meal eaten before the onset of a fast, particularly before Yom Kippur or Tishah Be'av

se'udah sh'lishit: the "third meal" eaten on Shabbat

s'firah: a term denoting the forty-nine days between Passover and Shavuot

Shabbat: the Hebrew name for the Sabbath

Shabbos: the Yiddish pronunciation of Shabbat, in common colloquial use among English-speaking Jews of Ashkenazic descent

Shaḥarit: the Morning Service

Shalom Aleikhem: a hymn generally sung at home on Friday evening before Shabbat dinner

shalosh r'galim: a term denoting the three pilgrimage festivals of Passover, Shavuot, and Sukkot

shammash: the extra candle used to light the other candles in a Ḥanukkah *m'norah* (*q.v.*) or the longer string used to wrap the other *tzitziyyot* on a *tallit* (*q.v.*); also, a synagogue sexton

shatz: an acronym for the Hebrew words *sh'li·ah* or *sh'liḥat tzibbur* (*q.v.*)

She-heḥeyyanu: the colloquial name for the benediction acknowledging gratitude to God for having reached a specific moment or milestone in one's life

sheimot: a term denoting documents that, because they contain the divine name, may not be disposed of as trash *sheva b'rakhot:* the seven benedictions recited at the close of a Jewish wedding and as part of the Grace after Meals at the wedding feast and during the subsequent wedding week, and by extension the celebratory meals themselves that ensue in the week following a wedding

sh'ḥitah: kosher slaughter

shivah: the Hebrew number seven, used colloquially to denote the mourning week

Sh'khinah: the manifest divine presence

sh'li·aḥ tzibbur (fem.: *sh'liḥat tzibbur*): the individual who leads a congregation in prayer

sh'loshim: the secondary mourning period of thirty days

Sh'ma: the confession of faith recited as part of the Morning and Evening Service

shofar: a horn, today invariably a ram's horn, sounded on Rosh Hashanah and at the end of Yom Kippur

Shofarot: a section of the Musaf Service on Rosh Hashanah featuring biblical verses referencing the sounding of the *shofar* (*q.v.*)

shoḥeit (feminine: *shoḥetet*): a ritual slaughterer

sh'varim: one of the specific notes used when the *shofar* (*q.v.*) is sounded

siddur (plural: *siddurim*): the prayerbook

siyyum: a celebration marking the conclusion of the study of a tractate of Talmud

S'liḥot: a loosely defined set of penitential prayers recited during the High Holiday season

s'tam yeinam: wine that has been produced by non-Jews not specifically intended to serve as an idolatrous libation

sufganiyyot: jelly doughnuts eaten as Ḥanukkah treats

sukkah: a kind of hut used as an outdoors dwelling and/or dining place during Sukkot

s'vivon: the Hebrew term for the *dreidel* (*q.v.*) top used by children on Ḥanukkah

ta·amei ha-mitzvot: the literary genre devoted to exploring the reasons for specific commandments

ta·am ke'ikkar: the concept within the *kashrut* laws that denotes that the law regarding the admixture of non-kosher foodstuffs in a larger amount of kosher food remains in effect even if the non-kosher food is removed as long as its flavor lingers

ta·anit: a fast day

Taḥanun: a series of supplicatory prayers recited on most weekday mornings and afternoons of the year

takhrikhim: burial shrouds

tallit: a prayer shawl

talmud torah: the general term for Torah study and, by extension, a school in which Torah is studied

tanna (plural: *tanna·im*): a rabbi of the mishnaic period

Tashlikh: the name for the custom of throwing crumbs into a body of flowing water on the afternoon of the first or second Rosh Hashanah to symbolize the thrower's willingness to abandon sin

t'fillah: prayer

t'fillah b'tzibbur: public prayer

t'fillin: the leather boxes, sometimes called phylacteries, generally worn during weekday morning prayers

tikkun olam: the "repair of the world"

Tishah Be'av: the Hebrew name for the Fast of the Ninth of Av

t'ki·ah: one of the specific notes used when the *shofar* (*q.v.*) is sounded

t'nayim: a preliminary agreement between the families of a bride and a groom

tohorat ha-mishpaḥah: the general term for the laws of family purity

torah li-sh'mah: the act of Torah study undertaken for its own sake

Tosafot: the name for a specific group of talmudic commentators in France, Germany, and Italy in the early Middle Ages

t'reifah: a term colloquially used to denote non-kosher meat

trope: the system of cantillation used when biblical texts are chanted aloud as part of the synagogue service

t'ru·ah: one of the specific notes used when the *shofar* (*q.v.*) is sounded

t'shuvah: repentance

tz'dakah: charity or, by extension, charitable deeds

tzitzit: the kinds of knotted fringes that hang from the *tallit* (*q.v.*)

tz'ni·ut: modesty, generally in matters of dress and demeanor

Tzur Yisra·el: the divine epithet referencing God as the "Rock of Israel" *ushpizin:* the spectral presence of some biblical personalities imagined to visit the *sukkah* (*q.v.*) during Sukkot

Va-y'khullu: Genesis 2:1–3, sung aloud as part of the liturgy on Friday evening

viddui: confession, often specifically as part of a final liturgical declaration before death

yahrtzeit (Yiddish): the annual anniversary of the death of a loved one

yamim nora·im: the Hebrew term for the High Holidays

yarmulke (Yiddish): a skullcap or *kippah* (*q.v.*)

yibbum: the Hebrew term for levirate marriage (*q.v.*)

yiḥud: the seclusion of a bride and groom immediately following their wedding

Yizkor: the memorial service recited four times annually

Yom Ha-atzma·ut: Israel Independence Day

Yom Ha-sho·ah: Holocaust Memorial Day

Yom Ha-zikkaron: Israeli Memorial Day

Zikhronot: a passage featuring biblical verses asserting the divine willingness always to remember Israel included in the Musaf Service on Rosh Hashanah

Index

BENJAMIN J. KRAMER

Dietary laws *(continued)*
- *See also* Dietary laws, halakhic principles governing; Dietary laws, preparation of meat; Dietary laws, rules regarding animals and animal products; Dietary laws, rules regarding dishes and appliances

Dietary laws, halakhic principles governing
- *bateil b'shishim*, 310, 333, 900
- *b'di-avad*, 331
- *davar ḥadash*, 322
- *davar ḥarif*, 325, 900
- *ḥalav yisra·el*, 323
- *ḥatikhah ha-re'uyah l'hitkabbeid*, 334
- *irui mi-k'li rishon*, 328
- *kavush ki-m'vushal*, 334
- *min b'mino*, 332
- *min b'she-eino mino*, 332
- *notein ta·am*, 321
- *notein ta·am bar notein ta·am*, 321
- *notein ta·am li-f'gam*, 334
- *pat yisra·el*, 323
- *s'tam yeinam*, 322
- *ta·am ke'ikkar*, 334
- *tata·a g'var*, 332
- *See also* Dietary laws

Dietary laws, preparation of meat, 311–317, 866–869
- animal cruelty, 313
- blood, 311–312
- *gid ha-nasheh*, 315
- glatt, 314
- inspection, 314
- *kashering*, 315–317
- liver, 316
- restricted portions, 314–315
- slaughter, 312–314
- soaking and salting, 315–317
- *See also* Dietary laws

Dietary laws, rules regarding animals and animal products
- birds, 309–310
- eggs, 311–312
- fish, 308–309
- insects, 310–311
- land animals, 307–318
- milk, 323
- *See also* Dietary laws

Dietary laws, rules regarding dishes and appliances, 324–334
- dishwashers, 329
- *kashering*, 208–211, 326–331
- knives, 327, 331
- towels, 325
- two sets of dishes, 324
- *See also* Dietary laws

Dina d'malkhuta dina, 361, 428, 440–442, 454–455, 457, 460, 467, 489, 511, 526, 534, 552–554, 567, 579, 604–605

Disabilities, individuals with, 831–855
- and prayer, 838–842
- and ritual innovation, 854–855
- exemption from commandments for blind and deaf, 835–837
- participation in public Torah reading by blind and deaf, 842–847
- providing physical access to participation in synagogue, 834
- psychiatric disabilities, 837–838
- rabbinic ordination of, 847–849
- sensitivity to, 834
- testimony in court by, 849–850
- use of service animals and electronic devices on Shabbat and holidays, 851–854

Disinterment, 294

Divorce, 275–279, 627–630
- after *kiddushin*, 268
- *agunah, see Agunah*
- *al y'dei zikkui*, 278
- and parents, 688–689
- civil divorce, 448
- *hafka·at kiddushin*, 277
- *hetteir mei·ah rabbanim*, 278
- letter of intent, 448
- Lieberman clause, 271, 448
- refusal to grant, 275, 278
- remarriage, 626–627

Divorce, bill of, 275–277, 901
- delivery of, 277, 628
- *m'saddeir/m'sadderet gittin*, 276, 905
- text of, 277

D'varim she-bi-k'dushah, 13, 272, 436

Dying, 282–284
- confession, 282–283, 367–368
- deathbed bequests, 597–598
- euthanasia, 279–280, 757–758, 794–803, 862
- *goseis, goseset, g'sisah*, 797–801
- lying to the, 367–368
- palliative care, 792–794
- recitation of Sh'ma, 283

Ecclesiastes, Book of 180, 290, 843

Egalitarianism, 66–68
- *aliyot* for women, 67
- and *tallit*, 25, 45
- in wedding ceremony, 270, 629
- issues in inheritance law, 599–602
- lighting Shabbat candles, 101
- mixed-gender seating, 67
- ordination of women rabbis, 67
- public recitation of verses regarding Esther in *m'gillah*, 197–198
- rabbinic opinions regarding, 66
- Shabbat morning bat mitzvahs, 67
- women and quorum, 12
- women reading Torah, 67
- women reciting Kiddush, 109
- women reciting Priestly Blessing, 68

Eikhah, 232, 843

Interfaith relations *(continued)*
Jews for Jesus, 78–79, 738
messianic Jews, 78–79, 738
Noahide laws, *see* Noahide laws
renting space to church groups, 75–76
shittuf, 735–736
studying together, 743–744
See also Intermarriage
Intermarriage, 612–613, 744–746
acknowledging in synagogue, 70–71
Conservative rabbi officiating or attending, 63, 613, 745
See also Intermarried couples; Intermarried Jews
Intermarried couples
marriage following conversion of non-Jewish spouse, 259–260
participation of non-Jewish spouses in synagogue life, 70
outreach to, 64, 263, 613
synagogue membership, 64
See also Intermarriage; Intermarried couples, children of; Intermarried Jews
Intermarried couples, children of
acknowledging birth of, 70–71
membership in youth groups, 65
religious school, 65
status of, 64–65
See also Intermarriage
Intermarried Jews
being employed by synagogue, 75
holding synagogue office, 69
intermarried children, 680–682
receiving honors, 69–70
See also Intermarriage; Intermarried couples
Intermediate Days of Holidays, *see under* Holidays
Islam, 734–735
Israel, 339–359
aliyah to, 340–343
as holiest land, 339
burial in, 287, 289, 294
exemption from military service, 478–480
Jerusalem, *see* Jerusalem
Law of Return, 259
leaving, 341, 358–359
obligation to serve in military in, 356–358
pilgrimage to, 343–345
prayer for rain and dew, 184
relationship of Diaspora to, 340, 342
separation of religion and state, 432–433
Tu Bi-sh'vat, 193–194
Western Wall, 345
yishuv ha-aretz, 340–343
Israel, agricultural commandments connected to, 353–356
bikkurim, 355
ḥadash, 348
ḥallah, 354–355
jubilee year, 351–352
kilayim, 348, 354, 872–873
leket, 355
orlah, 348, 353–354
pei·ah, 355
sabbatical year, 351–352
shikh·ḥah, 355
tithing produce, 348–350
Israel Defense Forces
allegiance to a secular state, 489–490
code of ethics, 481–482
exemption from, 478–480
obeying orders, 485–487
obligation to serve in, 356–358
ranking, 487–488
right to religious observance, 488–489

Jerusalem
date of Purim in, 199
destruction of, 230–231
facing during prayer, 16
holiness of, 340, 343–344
pilgrimage to, 343–345
symbolism of in liturgy, 104, 114, 116
Temple Mount, 346–348
Yom Y'rushalayim, 224
Jubilee year, 351–352, 393, 563, 565, 726, 884
Justice, *see* Law

Kabbalat Shabbat, 103–105, 117, 121, 231, 902
Kabb'lan, see Employment, contract laborer
Kaddish, 13, 58–59
Burial Kaddish, 59, 290–291
Full Kaddish, 29, 40, 59, 114, 154, 166
Half Kaddish, 40,46, 48, 59, 112
Kaddish D'rabbanan, 30, 59, 105, 114
Mourner's Kaddish, *see* Mourner's Kaddish
variations during High Holidays, 150
Kashrut, *see* Dietary laws
Kavvanah, 9, 903
K'dushah, 13, 14, 15–16, 19, 28, 29, 35, 40, 41, 112, 114, 118
physical movements during, 14, 15–16
quorum required for, 13
K'dushah D'sidra, *see* Prayers, names of, U-va L'tziyyon
Keiruv, see Outreach
Keva, 9, 92, 903
Kiddush, 149, 151, 170, 174, 175, 178, 183, 214
in synagogue, 106–107
obligation of men and women, 101
on holidays, 52; *see also under* names of holidays
on Shabbat, 109, 114, 115
over beverages other than wine or grape juice, 115
Kiddush ha-sheim, 507, 903; *see also Ḥillul ha-sheim*
Kiddush L'vanah, 237
Kippah, 22–23, 378–380, 903; *see also* Head covering

Contributors

Kassel Abelson, a former president of the Rabbinical Assembly and chairperson of the Committee on Jewish Law and Standards, is the rabbi emeritus of Beth El Synagogue of Minneapolis.

Carl N. Astor, the rabbi of Congregation Beth El in New London, Connecticut, since 1981, received his Ph.D. from the Jewish Theological Seminary in 1996 and is an active *moheil.* He is also the author of the USY sourcebook, *Who Makes People Different: Jewish Perspectives on the Disabled.*

Jacob Blumenthal serves as rabbi of the Shaare Torah congregation in Gaithersburg, Maryland.

Nina Beth Cardin, an author and community rabbi, is active in the Jewish environmental movement, having served as General Consultant to COEJL (the Coalition on the Environment and Jewish Life), and founded the Baltimore Jewish Environmental Network and the interfaith Chesapeake Covenant Community. She also served as the Secretary to the Committee on Jewish Law and Standards of the Rabbinical Assembly and edited its first compendium of responsa.

Martin S. Cohen, the senior editor of this volume, is the rabbi of the Shelter Rock Jewish Center in Roslyn, New York, and the chairman of the editorial board of *Conservative Judaism,* a quarterly journal published jointly by the Rabbinical Assembly and the Jewish Theological Seminary. His latest book, *The Boy on the Door on the Ox,* was published by Aviv Books in 2008.

Eliezer Diamond is the Rabbi Judah Nadich Associate Professor of Talmud and Rabbinics at the Jewish Theological Seminary. He is the author of *Holy Men and Hunger Artists: Fasting and Asceticism in Rabbinic Culture* and related articles delineating the role of asceticism in rabbinic Judaism, and lectures and writes about Jewish liturgy and prayer.

Elliot N. Dorff is Rector and Distinguished Professor of Philosophy at the American Jewish University in Los Angeles and Chair of the Committee on Jewish Law and Standards of the Rabbinical Assembly. Among his twenty-four books on Jewish thought, law, and ethics are four on Jewish medical, personal, and social ethics, including *To Do the Right and the Good, Matters of Life and Death: A Jewish Approach to Modern Medical Ethics,* and *The Way into Tikkun Olam (Repairing the World),* all of which further explore the subjects of his essays in this volume and related topics.

Paul S. Drazen serves on the staff of the United Synagogue of Conservative Judaism. In addition to having served on the Committee on Jewish Law and Standards, he has provided *kashrut* and operational supervision for commercial kosher kitchens.

Arnold M. Eisen is the seventh chancellor of the Jewish Theological Seminary and the author of *Taking Hold of Torah: Jewish Commitment and Community in America* (1996), *Rethinking Modern Judaism: Ritual, Commandment, Community* (1998), and other studies in American Judaism.

David J. Fine is rabbi of Temple Israel and Jewish Community Center in Ridgewood, New Jersey, and an adjunct professor at the Abraham Geiger College at the University of Potsdam in Germany.

Edward M. Friedman is rabbi of Congregation Beth Israel in Andover, Massachusetts. Active in interfaith activities, he has co-chaired the Greater Carolinas Wildacres Interfaith Institute for over a decade.

Michael Graetz is one of the founders of the Masorti movement in Israel and was its first Executive Director. He served as rabbi of the Magen Avraham congregation in Omer, Israel, until his retirement in 2005, during which years he also taught at Kaye College in Beer Sheva and served as Spiritual Director of the Mercaz Shiluv Educational Institute in the Negev, an institute dedicated to communicating Jewish values to the Israeli public. Rabbi Graetz served in the IDF for 18 years.

David M. Greenstein serves as rabbi of Congregation Shomrei Emunah, Montclair, New Jersey.

Jeremy Kalmanofsky serves as rabbi of Congregation Ansche Chesed in Manhattan.

Jane Kanarek is Assistant Professor of Rabbinics at Hebrew College in Newton Centre, Massachusetts, and a member of the Committee on Jewish Law and Standards of the Rabbinical Assembly.

Michael Katz, the associate editor of this volume, has served as the rabbi of Temple Beth Torah in Westbury, New York, since 1979. He is the co-author with the late Gershon Schwartz of *Swimming in the Sea of Talmud* (Philadelphia, 1997) and *Searching for Meaning in Midrash* (Philadelphia, 2002).

Benjamin J. Kramer serves as the rabbi of Congregation Beth Israel in Munster, Indiana, just outside of Chicago. He has an MA in Talmud and Rabbinics from JTS and is a member of the editorial board of the quarterly journal *Conservative Judaism.*

Vernon H. Kurtz, a past president of the Rabbinical Assembly and for many years a member of its Committee on Jewish Law and Standards, serves as the rabbi of North Suburban Synagogue Beth El in Highland Park, Illinois. In addition, he is Adjunct Professor of Rabbinics at Spertus Institute of Jewish Studies in Chicago.

Barry J. Leff is a business executive and chairman of Rabbis for Human Rights in Israel. He has a doctorate in business administration and has authored several responsa on business ethics that have been approved by the Committee on Jewish Law and Standards of the Rabbinical Assembly.

David H. Lincoln is rabbi emeritus of the Park Avenue Synagogue New York City and served for many years as a member of the Committee on Jewish Law and Standards of the Rabbinical Assembly.

Alan B. Lucas is rabbi of Temple Beth Sholom in Roslyn Heights, New York. For many years, he was a member of the Committee on Jewish Law and Standards of the Rabbinical Assembly and authored the responsum on body piercing and tattooing that has become a model for teaching about the halakhic process. He is a Rabbinic Fellow of the Hartman Institute in Jerusalem.

Daniel S. Nevins, the Pearl Resnick Dean of the Rabbinical School and of the Division of Religious Leadership of the Jewish Theological Seminary, serves on the Committee on Jewish Law and Standards of the Rabbinical Assembly, chairing its subcommittee on disabilities and Jewish law. He was formerly the rabbi of the Adat Shalom Synagogue in Farmington Hills, Michigan.

Cheryl Peretz is the Associate Dean of the Ziegler School of Rabbinic Studies at the American Jewish University in Los Angeles. Prior to completing her rabbinic studies, Cheryl earned her MBA from Baruch College of the City University of New York, and spent ten years working in strategic marketing.

Avram Israel Reisner is rabbi of Chevrei Tzedek Congregation in Baltimore, Maryland. He is a longtime member of the Committee on Jewish Law and Standards of the Rabbinical Assembly and a founding member of its bioethics subcommittee. He has a Ph.D. in rabbinics from the Jewish Theological Seminary and an M.A. in bioethics from the University of Pennsylvania. He serves as a governor's appointee on the Maryland Stem Cell Research Fund.

Karen G Reiss Medwed is Assistant Professor of Jewish Education at the Shoolman Graduate School of Education of Hebrew College in Boston and is on the faculty of the College of Professional Studies of Northeastern University. She also serves as a certified *m'sadderet gittin* for the Joint Beit Din of the Rabbinical Assembly.

Tracee L. Rosen serves as the rabbi of Temple Gan Elohim in Glendale, Arizona, a suburb of Phoenix. In addition to rabbinic ordination, she holds an MBA and spent thirteen years in the banking industry.

Craig T. Scheff serves as rabbi at the Orangetown Jewish Center in Orangeburg, New York, and is an adjunct lecturer in Professional and Pastoral Skills at the Jewish Theological Seminary. In 2011, he was appointed president of Israel Bonds' National Rabbinic Cabinet.

Julie Schonfeld served as rabbi of the Society for the Advancement of Judaism, a historic New York congregation. Prior to becoming the Executive Vice President of the Rabbinical Assembly, the international community of Conservative/Masorti rabbis, in 2009, she served that organization as its Director of Rabbinic Development, spearheading numerous projects to strengthen the rabbinate.

Gershon Schwartz ז"ל (1952–2004) served as spiritual leader of the Bay Shore Jewish Center in Bay Shore, New York, the South Baldwin Jewish Center in South Baldwin, New York, and Congregation Beth Sholom in Elkins Park, Pennsylvania. An expert in the laws of Jewish divorce and a member of the Joint Bet Din of the Conservative movement, he was the co-author of *Swimming in the Sea of the Talmud* (Philadelphia, 1997) and *Searching for Meaning in Midrash* (Philadelphia, 2002).

Laurence A. Sebert has been the rabbi of Town and Village Synagogue since 1991. He has served on the Rabbinical Assembly Publications Committee and on the committee that produced *Maḥzor Lev Shalem*.

Gerald C. Skolnik serves as rabbi of the Forest Hills Jewish Center in Forest Hills, New York, and is the vice-president of the Rabbinical Assembly. He writes a weekly on-line column for *The Jewish Week* entitled "A Rabbi's World."

Abigail N. Sosland is on the faculty at the Solomon Schechter School of Westchester in Hartsdale, New York, where she teaches Bible, Talmud, and philosophy. She also serves as the school's Morah Ruḥanit (Spiritual Advisor).

Lawrence Troster is the Rabbinic Director of J Street. He is also an eco-theologian and a religious environmental activist, and has published numerous articles and lectured widely on Jewish environmentalism and bio-ethics, and on the relationship of Judaism and modern science.

Gordon Tucker is the senior rabbi at Temple Israel Center in White Plains, New York. An adjunct member of the faculty at Jewish Theological Seminary and a former member of the Committee on Jewish Law and Standards of the Rabbinical Assembly, he is the translator and the author of the commentary on Abraham Joshua Heschel's *Heavenly Torah*, published by Continuum in 2005.